Dictionary of Literary Biography

1 *The American Renaissance in New England*, edited by Joel Myerson (1978)

2 *American Novelists Since World War II*, edited by Jeffrey Helterman and Richard Layman (1978)

3 *Antebellum Writers in New York and the South*, edited by Joel Myerson (1979)

4 *American Writers in Paris, 1920-1939*, edited by Karen Lane Rood (1980)

5 *American Poets Since World War II*, 2 parts, edited by Donald J. Greiner (1980)

6 *American Novelists Since World War II, Second Series*, edited by James E. Kibler Jr. (1980)

7 *Twentieth-Century American Dramatists*, 2 parts, edited by John MacNicholas (1981)

8 *Twentieth-Century American Science-Fiction Writers*, 2 parts, edited by David Cowart and Thomas L. Wymer (1981)

9 *American Novelists, 1910-1945*, 3 parts, edited by James J. Martine (1981)

10 *Modern British Dramatists, 1900-1945*, 2 parts, edited by Stanley Weintraub (1982)

11 *American Humorists, 1800-1950*, 2 parts, edited by Stanley Trachtenberg (1982)

12 *American Realists and Naturalists*, edited by Donald Pizer and Earl N. Harbert (1982)

13 *British Dramatists Since World War II*, 2 parts, edited by Stanley Weintraub (1982)

14 *British Novelists Since 1960*, 2 parts, edited by Jay L. Halio (1983)

15 *British Novelists, 1930-1959*, 2 parts, edited by Bernard Oldsey (1983)

16 *The Beats: Literary Bohemians in Postwar America*, 2 parts, edited by Ann Charters (1983)

17 *Twentieth-Century American Historians*, edited by Clyde N. Wilson (1983)

18 *Victorian Novelists After 1885*, edited by Ira B. Nadel and William E. Fredeman (1983)

19 *British Poets, 1880-1914*, edited by Donald E. Stanford (1983)

20 *British Poets, 1914-1945*, edited by Donald E. Stanford (1983)

21 *Victorian Novelists Before 1885*, edited by Ira B. Nadel and William E. Fredeman (1983)

22 *American Writers for Children, 1900-1960*, edited by John Cech (1983)

23 *American Newspaper Journalists, 1873-1900*, edited by Perry J. Ashley (1983)

24 *American Colonial Writers, 1606-1734*, edited by Emory Elliott (1984)

25 *American Newspaper Journalists, 1901-1925*, edited by Perry J. Ashley (1984)

26 *American Screenwriters*, edited by Robert E. Morsberger, Stephen O. Lesser, and Randall Clark (1984)

27 *Poets of Great Britain and Ireland, 1945-1960*, edited by Vincent B. Sherry Jr. (1984)

28 *Twentieth-Century American-Jewish Fiction Writers*, edited by Daniel Walden (1984)

29 *American Newspaper Journalists, 1926-1950*, edited by Perry J. Ashley (1984)

30 *American Historians, 1607-1865*, edited by Clyde N. Wilson (1984)

31 *American Colonial Writers, 1735-1781*, edited by Emory Elliott (1984)

32 *Victorian Poets Before 1850*, edited by William E. Fredeman and Ira B. Nadel (1984)

33 *Afro-American Fiction Writers After 1955*, edited by Thadious M. Davis and Trudier Harris (1984)

34 *British Novelists, 1890-1929: Traditionalists*, edited by Thomas F. Staley (1985)

35 *Victorian Poets After 1850*, edited by William E. Fredeman and Ira B. Nadel (1985)

36 *British Novelists, 1890-1929: Modernists*, edited by Thomas F. Staley (1985)

37 *American Writers of the Early Republic*, edited by Emory Elliott (1985)

38 *Afro-American Writers After 1955: Dramatists and Prose Writers*, edited by Thadious M. Davis and Trudier Harris (1985)

39 *British Novelists, 1660-1800*, 2 parts, edited by Martin C. Battestin (1985)

40 *Poets of Great Britain and Ireland Since 1960*, 2 parts, edited by Vincent B. Sherry Jr. (1985)

41 *Afro-American Poets Since 1955*, edited by Trudier Harris and Thadious M. Davis (1985)

42 *American Writers for Children Before 1900*, edited by Glenn E. Estes (1985)

43 *American Newspaper Journalists, 1690-1872*, edited by Perry J. Ashley (1986)

44 *American Screenwriters, Second Series*, edited by Randall Clark, Robert E. Morsberger, and Stephen O. Lesser (1986)

45 *American Poets, 1880-1945, First Series*, edited by Peter Quartermain (1986)

46 *American Literary Publishing Houses, 1900-1980: Trade and Paperback*, edited by Peter Dzwonkoski (1986)

47 *American Historians, 1866-1912*, edited by Clyde N. Wilson (1986)

48 *American Poets, 1880-1945, Second Series*, edited by Peter Quartermain (1986)

49 *American Literary Publishing Houses, 1638-1899*, 2 parts, edited by Peter Dzwonkoski (1986)

50 *Afro-American Writers Before the Harlem Renaissance*, edited by Trudier Harris (1986)

51 *Afro-American Writers from the Harlem Renaissance to 1940*, edited by Trudier Harris (1987)

52 *American Writers for Children Since 1960: Fiction*, edited by Glenn E. Estes (1986)

53 *Canadian Writers Since 1960, First Series*, edited by W. H. New (1986)

54 *American Poets, 1880-1945, Third Series*, 2 parts, edited by Peter Quartermain (1987)

55 *Victorian Prose Writers Before 1867*, edited by William B. Thesing (1987)

56 *German Fiction Writers, 1914-1945*, edited by James Hardin (1987)

57 *Victorian Prose Writers After 1867*, edited by William B. Thesing (1987)

58 *Jacobean and Caroline Dramatists*, edited by Fredson Bowers (1987)

59 *American Literary Critics and Scholars, 1800-1850*, edited by John W. Rathbun and Monica M. Grecu (1987)

60 *Canadian Writers Since 1960, Second Series*, edited by W. H. New (1987)

61 *American Writers for Children Since 1960: Poets, Illustrators, and Nonfiction Authors*, edited by Glenn E. Estes (1987)

62 *Elizabethan Dramatists*, edited by Fredson Bowers (1987)

63 *Modern American Critics, 1920-1955*, edited by Gregory S. Jay (1988)

64 *American Literary Critics and Scholars, 1850-1880*, edited by John W. Rathbun and Monica M. Grecu (1988)

65 *French Novelists, 1900-1930*, edited by Catharine Savage Brosman (1988)

66 *German Fiction Writers, 1885-1913*, 2 parts, edited by James Hardin (1988)

67 *Modern American Critics Since 1955*, edited by Gregory S. Jay (1988)

68 *Canadian Writers, 1920-1959, First Series*, edited by W. H. New (1988)

69 *Contemporary German Fiction Writers, First Series*, edited by Wolfgang D. Elfe and James Hardin (1988)

70 *British Mystery Writers, 1860-1919*, edited by Bernard Benstock and Thomas F. Staley (1988)

71 *American Literary Critics and Scholars, 1880-1900*, edited by John W. Rathbun and Monica M. Grecu (1988)

72 *French Novelists, 1930-1960*, edited by Catharine Savage Brosman (1988)

73 *American Magazine Journalists, 1741-1850*, edited by Sam G. Riley (1988)

74 *American Short-Story Writers Before 1880*, edited by Bobby Ellen Kimbel, with the assistance of William E. Grant (1988)

75 *Contemporary German Fiction Writers, Second Series*, edited by Wolfgang D. Elfe and James Hardin (1988)

76 *Afro-American Writers, 1940-1955*, edited by Trudier Harris (1988)

77 *British Mystery Writers, 1920-1939*, edited by Bernard Benstock and Thomas F. Staley (1988)

78 *American Short-Story Writers, 1880–1910*, edited by Bobby Ellen Kimbel, with the assistance of William E. Grant (1988)

79 *American Magazine Journalists, 1850–1900*, edited by Sam G. Riley (1988)

80 *Restoration and Eighteenth-Century Dramatists, First Series*, edited by Paula R. Backscheider (1989)

81 *Austrian Fiction Writers, 1875–1913*, edited by James Hardin and Donald G. Daviau (1989)

82 *Chicano Writers, First Series*, edited by Francisco A. Lomelí and Carl R. Shirley (1989)

83 *French Novelists Since 1960*, edited by Catharine Savage Brosman (1989)

84 *Restoration and Eighteenth-Century Dramatists, Second Series*, edited by Paula R. Backscheider (1989)

85 *Austrian Fiction Writers After 1914*, edited by James Hardin and Donald G. Daviau (1989)

86 *American Short-Story Writers, 1910–1945, First Series*, edited by Bobby Ellen Kimbel (1989)

87 *British Mystery and Thriller Writers Since 1940, First Series*, edited by Bernard Benstock and Thomas F. Staley (1989)

88 *Canadian Writers, 1920–1959, Second Series*, edited by W. H. New (1989)

89 *Restoration and Eighteenth-Century Dramatists, Third Series*, edited by Paula R. Backscheider (1989)

90 *German Writers in the Age of Goethe, 1789–1832*, edited by James Hardin and Christoph E. Schweitzer (1989)

91 *American Magazine Journalists, 1900–1960, First Series*, edited by Sam G. Riley (1990)

92 *Canadian Writers, 1890–1920*, edited by W. H. New (1990)

93 *British Romantic Poets, 1789–1832, First Series*, edited by John R. Greenfield (1990)

94 *German Writers in the Age of Goethe: Sturm und Drang to Classicism*, edited by James Hardin and Christoph E. Schweitzer (1990)

95 *Eighteenth-Century British Poets, First Series*, edited by John Sitter (1990)

96 *British Romantic Poets, 1789–1832, Second Series*, edited by John R. Greenfield (1990)

97 *German Writers from the Enlightenment to Sturm und Drang, 1720–1764*, edited by James Hardin and Christoph E. Schweitzer (1990)

98 *Modern British Essayists, First Series*, edited by Robert Beum (1990)

99 *Canadian Writers Before 1890*, edited by W. H. New (1990)

100 *Modern British Essayists, Second Series*, edited by Robert Beum (1990)

101 *British Prose Writers, 1660–1800, First Series*, edited by Donald T. Siebert (1991)

102 *American Short-Story Writers, 1910–1945, Second Series*, edited by Bobby Ellen Kimbel (1991)

103 *American Literary Biographers, First Series*, edited by Steven Serafin (1991)

104 *British Prose Writers, 1660–1800, Second Series*, edited by Donald T. Siebert (1991)

105 *American Poets Since World War II, Second Series*, edited by R. S. Gwynn (1991)

106 *British Literary Publishing Houses, 1820–1880*, edited by Patricia J. Anderson and Jonathan Rose (1991)

107 *British Romantic Prose Writers, 1789–1832, First Series*, edited by John R. Greenfield (1991)

108 *Twentieth-Century Spanish Poets, First Series*, edited by Michael L. Perna (1991)

109 *Eighteenth-Century British Poets, Second Series*, edited by John Sitter (1991)

110 *British Romantic Prose Writers, 1789–1832, Second Series*, edited by John R. Greenfield (1991)

111 *American Literary Biographers, Second Series*, edited by Steven Serafin (1991)

112 *British Literary Publishing Houses, 1881–1965*, edited by Jonathan Rose and Patricia J. Anderson (1991)

113 *Modern Latin-American Fiction Writers, First Series*, edited by William Luis (1992)

114 *Twentieth-Century Italian Poets, First Series*, edited by Giovanna Wedel De Stasio, Glauco Cambon, and Antonio Illiano (1992)

115 *Medieval Philosophers*, edited by Jeremiah Hackett (1992)

116 *British Romantic Novelists, 1789–1832*, edited by Bradford K. Mudge (1992)

117 *Twentieth-Century Caribbean and Black African Writers, First Series*, edited by Bernth Lindfors and Reinhard Sander (1992)

118 *Twentieth-Century German Dramatists, 1889–1918*, edited by Wolfgang D. Elfe and James Hardin (1992)

119 *Nineteenth-Century French Fiction Writers: Romanticism and Realism, 1800–1860*, edited by Catharine Savage Brosman (1992)

120 *American Poets Since World War II, Third Series*, edited by R. S. Gwynn (1992)

121 *Seventeenth-Century British Nondramatic Poets, First Series*, edited by M. Thomas Hester (1992)

122 *Chicano Writers, Second Series*, edited by Francisco A. Lomelí and Carl R. Shirley (1992)

123 *Nineteenth-Century French Fiction Writers: Naturalism and Beyond, 1860–1900*, edited by Catharine Savage Brosman (1992)

124 *Twentieth-Century German Dramatists, 1919–1992*, edited by Wolfgang D. Elfe and James Hardin (1992)

125 *Twentieth-Century Caribbean and Black African Writers, Second Series*, edited by Bernth Lindfors and Reinhard Sander (1993)

126 *Seventeenth-Century British Nondramatic Poets, Second Series*, edited by M. Thomas Hester (1993)

127 *American Newspaper Publishers, 1950–1990*, edited by Perry J. Ashley (1993)

128 *Twentieth-Century Italian Poets, Second Series*, edited by Giovanna Wedel De Stasio, Glauco Cambon, and Antonio Illiano (1993)

129 *Nineteenth-Century German Writers, 1841–1900*, edited by James Hardin and Siegfried Mews (1993)

130 *American Short-Story Writers Since World War II*, edited by Patrick Meanor (1993)

131 *Seventeenth-Century British Nondramatic Poets, Third Series*, edited by M. Thomas Hester (1993)

132 *Sixteenth-Century British Nondramatic Writers, First Series*, edited by David A. Richardson (1993)

133 *Nineteenth-Century German Writers to 1840*, edited by James Hardin and Siegfried Mews (1993)

134 *Twentieth-Century Spanish Poets, Second Series*, edited by Jerry Phillips Winfield (1994)

135 *British Short-Fiction Writers, 1880–1914: The Realist Tradition*, edited by William B. Thesing (1994)

136 *Sixteenth-Century British Nondramatic Writers, Second Series*, edited by David A. Richardson (1994)

137 *American Magazine Journalists, 1900–1960, Second Series*, edited by Sam G. Riley (1994)

138 *German Writers and Works of the High Middle Ages: 1170–1280*, edited by James Hardin and Will Hasty (1994)

139 *British Short-Fiction Writers, 1945–1980*, edited by Dean Baldwin (1994)

140 *American Book-Collectors and Bibliographers, First Series*, edited by Joseph Rosenblum (1994)

141 *British Children's Writers, 1880–1914*, edited by Laura M. Zaidman (1994)

142 *Eighteenth-Century British Literary Biographers*, edited by Steven Serafin (1994)

143 *American Novelists Since World War II, Third Series*, edited by James R. Giles and Wanda H. Giles (1994)

144 *Nineteenth-Century British Literary Biographers*, edited by Steven Serafin (1994)

145 *Modern Latin-American Fiction Writers, Second Series*, edited by William Luis and Ann González (1994)

146 *Old and Middle English Literature*, edited by Jeffrey Helterman and Jerome Mitchell (1994)

147 *South Slavic Writers Before World War II*, edited by Vasa D. Mihailovich (1994)

148 *German Writers and Works of the Early Middle Ages: 800–1170*, edited by Will Hasty and James Hardin (1994)

149 *Late Nineteenth- and Early Twentieth-Century British Literary Biographers*, edited by Steven Serafin (1995)

150 *Early Modern Russian Writers, Late Seventeenth and Eighteenth Centuries*, edited by Marcus C. Levitt (1995)

151 *British Prose Writers of the Early Seventeenth Century*, edited by Clayton D. Lein (1995)

152 *American Novelists Since World War II, Fourth Series*, edited by James R. Giles and Wanda H. Giles (1995)

153 *Late-Victorian and Edwardian British Novelists, First Series*, edited by George M. Johnson (1995)

154 *The British Literary Book Trade, 1700–1820*, edited by James K. Bracken and Joel Silver (1995)

155 *Twentieth-Century British Literary Biographers*, edited by Steven Serafin (1995)

156 *British Short-Fiction Writers, 1880–1914: The Romantic Tradition*, edited by William F. Naufftus (1995)

157 *Twentieth-Century Caribbean and Black African Writers, Third Series*, edited by Bernth Lindfors and Reinhard Sander (1995)

158 *British Reform Writers, 1789–1832*, edited by Gary Kelly and Edd Applegate (1995)

159 *British Short-Fiction Writers, 1800–1880*, edited by John R. Greenfield (1996)

160 *British Children's Writers, 1914–1960*, edited by Donald R. Hettinga and Gary D. Schmidt (1996)

161 *British Children's Writers Since 1960, First Series*, edited by Caroline Hunt (1996)

162 *British Short-Fiction Writers, 1915–1945*, edited by John H. Rogers (1996)

163 *British Children's Writers, 1800–1880*, edited by Meena Khorana (1996)

164 *German Baroque Writers, 1580–1660*, edited by James Hardin (1996)

165 *American Poets Since World War II, Fourth Series*, edited by Joseph Conte (1996)

166 *British Travel Writers, 1837–1875*, edited by Barbara Brothers and Julia Gergits (1996)

167 *Sixteenth-Century British Nondramatic Writers, Third Series*, edited by David A. Richardson (1996)

168 *German Baroque Writers, 1661–1730*, edited by James Hardin (1996)

169 *American Poets Since World War II, Fifth Series*, edited by Joseph Conte (1996)

170 *The British Literary Book Trade, 1475–1700*, edited by James K. Bracken and Joel Silver (1996)

171 *Twentieth-Century American Sportswriters*, edited by Richard Orodenker (1996)

172 *Sixteenth-Century British Nondramatic Writers, Fourth Series*, edited by David A. Richardson (1996)

173 *American Novelists Since World War II, Fifth Series*, edited by James R. Giles and Wanda H. Giles (1996)

174 *British Travel Writers, 1876–1909*, edited by Barbara Brothers and Julia Gergits (1997)

175 *Native American Writers of the United States*, edited by Kenneth M. Roemer (1997)

176 *Ancient Greek Authors*, edited by Ward W. Briggs (1997)

177 *Italian Novelists Since World War II, 1945–1965*, edited by Augustus Pallotta (1997)

178 *British Fantasy and Science-Fiction Writers Before World War I*, edited by Darren Harris-Fain (1997)

179 *German Writers of the Renaissance and Reformation, 1280–1580*, edited by James Hardin and Max Reinhart (1997)

180 *Japanese Fiction Writers, 1868–1945*, edited by Van C. Gessel (1997)

181 *South Slavic Writers Since World War II*, edited by Vasa D. Mihailovich (1997)

182 *Japanese Fiction Writers Since World War II*, edited by Van C. Gessel (1997)

183 *American Travel Writers, 1776–1864*, edited by James J. Schramer and Donald Ross (1997)

184 *Nineteenth-Century British Book-Collectors and Bibliographers*, edited by William Baker and Kenneth Womack (1997)

185 *American Literary Journalists, 1945–1995, First Series*, edited by Arthur J. Kaul (1998)

186 *Nineteenth-Century American Western Writers*, edited by Robert L. Gale (1998)

187 *American Book Collectors and Bibliographers, Second Series*, edited by Joseph Rosenblum (1998)

188 *American Book and Magazine Illustrators to 1920*, edited by Steven E. Smith, Catherine A. Hastedt, and Donald H. Dyal (1998)

189 *American Travel Writers, 1850–1915*, edited by Donald Ross and James J. Schramer (1998)

190 *British Reform Writers, 1832–1914*, edited by Gary Kelly and Edd Applegate (1998)

191 *British Novelists Between the Wars*, edited by George M. Johnson (1998)

192 *French Dramatists, 1789–1914*, edited by Barbara T. Cooper (1998)

193 *American Poets Since World War II, Sixth Series*, edited by Joseph Conte (1998)

194 *British Novelists Since 1960, Second Series*, edited by Merritt Moseley (1998)

195 *British Travel Writers, 1910–1939*, edited by Barbara Brothers and Julia Gergits (1998)

196 *Italian Novelists Since World War II, 1965–1995*, edited by Augustus Pallotta (1999)

197 *Late-Victorian and Edwardian British Novelists, Second Series*, edited by George M. Johnson (1999)

198 *Russian Literature in the Age of Pushkin and Gogol: Prose*, edited by Christine A. Rydel (1999)

199 *Victorian Women Poets*, edited by William B. Thesing (1999)

200 *American Women Prose Writers to 1820*, edited by Carla J. Mulford, with Angela Vietto and Amy E. Winans (1999)

201 *Twentieth-Century British Book Collectors and Bibliographers*, edited by William Baker and Kenneth Womack (1999)

202 *Nineteenth-Century American Fiction Writers*, edited by Kent P. Ljungquist (1999)

203 *Medieval Japanese Writers*, edited by Steven D. Carter (1999)

204 *British Travel Writers, 1940–1997*, edited by Barbara Brothers and Julia M. Gergits (1999)

205 *Russian Literature in the Age of Pushkin and Gogol: Poetry and Drama*, edited by Christine A. Rydel (1999)

206 *Twentieth-Century American Western Writers, First Series*, edited by Richard H. Cracroft (1999)

207 *British Novelists Since 1960, Third Series*, edited by Merritt Moseley (1999)

208 *Literature of the French and Occitan Middle Ages: Eleventh to Fifteenth Centuries*, edited by Deborah Sinnreich-Levi and Ian S. Laurie (1999)

209 *Chicano Writers, Third Series*, edited by Francisco A. Lomelí and Carl R. Shirley (1999)

210 *Ernest Hemingway: A Documentary Volume*, edited by Robert W. Trogdon (1999)

211 *Ancient Roman Writers*, edited by Ward W. Briggs (1999)

212 *Twentieth-Century American Western Writers, Second Series*, edited by Richard H. Cracroft (1999)

213 *Pre-Nineteenth-Century British Book Collectors and Bibliographers*, edited by William Baker and Kenneth Womack (1999)

214 *Twentieth-Century Danish Writers*, edited by Marianne Stecher-Hansen (1999)

215 *Twentieth-Century Eastern European Writers, First Series*, edited by Steven Serafin (1999)

216 *British Poets of the Great War: Brooke, Rosenberg, Thomas. A Documentary Volume*, edited by Patrick Quinn (2000)

217 *Nineteenth-Century French Poets*, edited by Robert Beum (2000)

218 *American Short-Story Writers Since World War II, Second Series*, edited by Patrick Meanor and Gwen Crane (2000)

219 *F. Scott Fitzgerald's* The Great Gatsby: *A Documentary Volume*, edited by Matthew J. Bruccoli (2000)

220 *Twentieth-Century Eastern European Writers, Second Series*, edited by Steven Serafin (2000)

221 *American Women Prose Writers, 1870–1920*, edited by Sharon M. Harris, with the assistance of Heidi L. M. Jacobs and Jennifer Putzi (2000)

222 *H. L. Mencken: A Documentary Volume*, edited by Richard J. Schrader (2000)

223 *The American Renaissance in New England, Second Series*, edited by Wesley T. Mott (2000)

224 *Walt Whitman: A Documentary Volume*, edited by Joel Myerson (2000)

225 *South African Writers*, edited by Paul A. Scanlon (2000)

226 *American Hard-Boiled Crime Writers*, edited by George Parker Anderson and Julie B. Anderson (2000)

227 *American Novelists Since World War II, Sixth Series*, edited by James R. Giles and Wanda H. Giles (2000)

228 *Twentieth-Century American Dramatists, Second Series*, edited by Christopher J. Wheatley (2000)

229 *Thomas Wolfe: A Documentary Volume*, edited by Ted Mitchell (2001)

230 *Australian Literature, 1788–1914*, edited by Selina Samuels (2001)

231 *British Novelists Since 1960, Fourth Series*, edited by Merritt Moseley (2001)

232 *Twentieth-Century Eastern European Writers, Third Series*, edited by Steven Serafin (2001)

233 *British and Irish Dramatists Since World War II, Second Series*, edited by John Bull (2001)

234 *American Short-Story Writers Since World War II, Third Series*, edited by Patrick Meanor and Richard E. Lee (2001)

235 *The American Renaissance in New England, Third Series*, edited by Wesley T. Mott (2001)

236 *British Rhetoricians and Logicians, 1500–1660,* edited by Edward A. Malone (2001)

237 *The Beats: A Documentary Volume,* edited by Matt Theado (2001)

238 *Russian Novelists in the Age of Tolstoy and Dostoevsky,* edited by J. Alexander Ogden and Judith E. Kalb (2001)

239 *American Women Prose Writers: 1820–1870,* edited by Amy E. Hudock and Katharine Rodier (2001)

240 *Late Nineteenth- and Early Twentieth-Century British Women Poets,* edited by William B. Thesing (2001)

241 *American Sportswriters and Writers on Sport,* edited by Richard Orodenker (2001)

242 *Twentieth-Century European Cultural Theorists, First Series,* edited by Paul Hansom (2001)

243 *The American Renaissance in New England, Fourth Series,* edited by Wesley T. Mott (2001)

244 *American Short-Story Writers Since World War II, Fourth Series,* edited by Patrick Meanor and Joseph McNicholas (2001)

245 *British and Irish Dramatists Since World War II, Third Series,* edited by John Bull (2001)

246 *Twentieth-Century American Cultural Theorists,* edited by Paul Hansom (2001)

247 *James Joyce: A Documentary Volume,* edited by A. Nicholas Fargnoli (2001)

248 *Antebellum Writers in the South, Second Series,* edited by Kent Ljungquist (2001)

249 *Twentieth-Century American Dramatists, Third Series,* edited by Christopher Wheatley (2002)

250 *Antebellum Writers in New York, Second Series,* edited by Kent Ljungquist (2002)

251 *Canadian Fantasy and Science-Fiction Writers,* edited by Douglas Ivison (2002)

252 *British Philosophers, 1500–1799,* edited by Philip B. Dematteis and Peter S. Fosl (2002)

253 *Raymond Chandler: A Documentary Volume,* edited by Robert Moss (2002)

254 *The House of Putnam, 1837–1872: A Documentary Volume,* edited by Ezra Greenspan (2002)

255 *British Fantasy and Science-Fiction Writers, 1918–1960,* edited by Darren Harris-Fain (2002)

256 *Twentieth-Century American Western Writers, Third Series,* edited by Richard H. Cracroft (2002)

257 *Twentieth-Century Swedish Writers After World War II,* edited by Ann-Charlotte Gavel Adams (2002)

258 *Modern French Poets,* edited by Jean-François Leroux (2002)

259 *Twentieth-Century Swedish Writers Before World War II,* edited by Ann-Charlotte Gavel Adams (2002)

260 *Australian Writers, 1915–1950,* edited by Selina Samuels (2002)

261 *British Fantasy and Science-Fiction Writers Since 1960,* edited by Darren Harris-Fain (2002)

262 *British Philosophers, 1800–2000,* edited by Peter S. Fosl and Leemon B. McHenry (2002)

263 *William Shakespeare: A Documentary Volume,* edited by Catherine Loomis (2002)

264 *Italian Prose Writers, 1900–1945,* edited by Luca Somigli and Rocco Capozzi (2002)

265 *American Song Lyricists, 1920–1960,* edited by Philip Furia (2002)

266 *Twentieth-Century American Dramatists, Fourth Series,* edited by Christopher J. Wheatley (2002)

267 *Twenty-First-Century British and Irish Novelists,* edited by Michael R. Molino (2002)

268 *Seventeenth-Century French Writers,* edited by Françoise Jaouën (2002)

269 *Nathaniel Hawthorne: A Documentary Volume,* edited by Benjamin Franklin V (2002)

270 *American Philosophers Before 1950,* edited by Philip B. Dematteis and Leemon B. McHenry (2002)

271 *British and Irish Novelists Since 1960,* edited by Merritt Moseley (2002)

272 *Russian Prose Writers Between the World Wars,* edited by Christine Rydel (2003)

273 *F. Scott Fitzgerald's* Tender Is the Night: *A Documentary Volume,* edited by Matthew J. Bruccoli and George Parker Anderson (2003)

274 *John Dos Passos's* U.S.A.: *A Documentary Volume,* edited by Donald Pizer (2003)

275 *Twentieth-Century American Nature Writers: Prose,* edited by Roger Thompson and J. Scott Bryson (2003)

276 *British Mystery and Thriller Writers Since 1960,* edited by Gina Macdonald (2003)

277 *Russian Literature in the Age of Realism,* edited by Alyssa Dinega Gillespie (2003)

278 *American Novelists Since World War II, Seventh Series,* edited by James R. Giles and Wanda H. Giles (2003)

279 *American Philosophers, 1950–2000,* edited by Philip B. Dematteis and Leemon B. McHenry (2003)

280 *Dashiell Hammett's* The Maltese Falcon: *A Documentary Volume,* edited by Richard Layman (2003)

281 *British Rhetoricians and Logicians, 1500–1660, Second Series,* edited by Edward A. Malone (2003)

282 *New Formalist Poets,* edited by Jonathan N. Barron and Bruce Meyer (2003)

283 *Modern Spanish American Poets, First Series,* edited by María A. Salgado (2003)

284 *The House of Holt, 1866–1946: A Documentary Volume,* edited by Ellen D. Gilbert (2003)

285 *Russian Writers Since 1980,* edited by Marina Balina and Mark Lipovetsky (2004)

286 *Castilian Writers, 1400–1500,* edited by Frank A. Domínguez and George D. Greenia (2004)

287 *Portuguese Writers,* edited by Monica Rector and Fred M. Clark (2004)

288 *The House of Boni & Liveright, 1917–1933: A Documentary Volume,* edited by Charles Egleston (2004)

289 *Australian Writers, 1950–1975,* edited by Selina Samuels (2004)

290 *Modern Spanish American Poets, Second Series,* edited by María A. Salgado (2004)

291 *The Hoosier House: Bobbs-Merrill and Its Predecessors, 1850–1985: A Documentary Volume,* edited by Richard J. Schrader (2004)

292 *Twenty-First-Century American Novelists,* edited by Lisa Abney and Suzanne Disheroon-Green (2004)

293 *Icelandic Writers,* edited by Patrick J. Stevens (2004)

294 *James Gould Cozzens: A Documentary Volume,* edited by Matthew J. Bruccoli (2004)

295 *Russian Writers of the Silver Age, 1890–1925,* edited by Judith E. Kalb and J. Alexander Ogden with the collaboration of I. G. Vishnevetsky (2004)

296 *Twentieth-Century European Cultural Theorists, Second Series,* edited by Paul Hansom (2004)

297 *Twentieth-Century Norwegian Writers,* edited by Tanya Thresher (2004)

298 *Henry David Thoreau: A Documentary Volume,* edited by Richard J. Schneider (2004)

299 *Holocaust Novelists,* edited by Efraim Sicher (2004)

300 *Danish Writers from the Reformation to Decadence, 1550–1900,* edited by Marianne Stecher-Hansen (2004)

301 *Gustave Flaubert: A Documentary Volume,* edited by Éric Le Calvez (2004)

302 *Russian Prose Writers After World War II,* edited by Christine Rydel (2004)

303 *American Radical and Reform Writers, First Series,* edited by Steven Rosendale (2005)

304 *Bram Stoker's* Dracula: *A Documentary Volume,* edited by Elizabeth Miller (2005)

305 *Latin American Dramatists, First Series,* edited by Adam Versényi (2005)

Dictionary of Literary Biography Documentary Series

1 *Sherwood Anderson, Willa Cather, John Dos Passos, Theodore Dreiser, F. Scott Fitzgerald, Ernest Hemingway, Sinclair Lewis,* edited by Margaret A. Van Antwerp (1982)

2 *James Gould Cozzens, James T. Farrell, William Faulkner, John O'Hara, John Steinbeck, Thomas Wolfe, Richard Wright,* edited by Margaret A. Van Antwerp (1982)

3 *Saul Bellow, Jack Kerouac, Norman Mailer, Vladimir Nabokov, John Updike, Kurt Vonnegut,* edited by Mary Bruccoli (1983)

4 *Tennessee Williams,* edited by Margaret A. Van Antwerp and Sally Johns (1984)

5 *American Transcendentalists,* edited by Joel Myerson (1988)

6 *Hardboiled Mystery Writers: Raymond Chandler, Dashiell Hammett, Ross Macdonald,* edited by Matthew J. Bruccoli and Richard Layman (1989)

7 *Modern American Poets: James Dickey, Robert Frost, Marianne Moore,* edited by Karen L. Rood (1989)

8 *The Black Aesthetic Movement,* edited by Jeffrey Louis Decker (1991)

9 *American Writers of the Vietnam War: W. D. Ehrhart, Larry Heinemann, Tim O'Brien, Walter McDonald, John M. Del Vecchio,* edited by Ronald Baughman (1991)

10 *The Bloomsbury Group,* edited by Edward L. Bishop (1992)

11 *American Proletarian Culture: The Twenties and The Thirties,* edited by Jon Christian Suggs (1993)

12 *Southern Women Writers: Flannery O'Connor, Katherine Anne Porter, Eudora Welty,* edited by Mary Ann Wimsatt and Karen L. Rood (1994)

13 *The House of Scribner, 1846–1904,* edited by John Delaney (1996)

14 *Four Women Writers for Children, 1868–1918,* edited by Caroline C. Hunt (1996)

15 *American Expatriate Writers: Paris in the Twenties,* edited by Matthew J. Bruccoli and Robert W. Trogdon (1997)

16 *The House of Scribner, 1905–1930,* edited by John Delaney (1997)

17 *The House of Scribner, 1931–1984,* edited by John Delaney (1998)

18 *British Poets of The Great War: Sassoon, Graves, Owen,* edited by Patrick Quinn (1999)

19 *James Dickey,* edited by Judith S. Baughman (1999)

See also DLB 210, 216, 219, 222, 224, 229, 237, 247, 253, 254, 263, 269, 273, 274, 280, 284, 288, 291, 294, 298, 301, 304

Dictionary of Literary Biography Yearbooks

1980 edited by Karen L. Rood, Jean W. Ross, and Richard Ziegfeld (1981)

1981 edited by Karen L. Rood, Jean W. Ross, and Richard Ziegfeld (1982)

1982 edited by Richard Ziegfeld; associate editors: Jean W. Ross and Lynne C. Zeigler (1983)

1983 edited by Mary Bruccoli and Jean W. Ross; associate editor Richard Ziegfeld (1984)

1984 edited by Jean W. Ross (1985)

1985 edited by Jean W. Ross (1986)

1986 edited by J. M. Brook (1987)

1987 edited by J. M. Brook (1988)

1988 edited by J. M. Brook (1989)

1989 edited by J. M. Brook (1990)

1990 edited by James W. Hipp (1991)

1991 edited by James W. Hipp (1992)

1992 edited by James W. Hipp (1993)

1993 edited by James W. Hipp, contributing editor George Garrett (1994)

1994 edited by James W. Hipp, contributing editor George Garrett (1995)

1995 edited by James W. Hipp, contributing editor George Garrett (1996)

1996 edited by Samuel W. Bruce and L. Kay Webster, contributing editor George Garrett (1997)

1997 edited by Matthew J. Bruccoli and George Garrett, with the assistance of L. Kay Webster (1998)

1998 edited by Matthew J. Bruccoli, contributing editor George Garrett, with the assistance of D. W. Thomas (1999)

1999 edited by Matthew J. Bruccoli, contributing editor George Garrett, with the assistance of D. W. Thomas (2000)

2000 edited by Matthew J. Bruccoli, contributing editor George Garrett, with the assistance of George Parker Anderson (2001)

2001 edited by Matthew J. Bruccoli, contributing editor George Garrett, with the assistance of George Parker Anderson (2002)

2002 edited by Matthew J. Bruccoli and George Garrett; George Parker Anderson, Assistant Editor (2003)

Concise Series

Concise Dictionary of American Literary Biography, 7 volumes (1988–1999): *The New Consciousness, 1941–1968; Colonization to the American Renaissance, 1640–1865; Realism, Naturalism, and Local Color, 1865–1917; The Twenties, 1917–1929; The Age of Maturity, 1929–1941; Broadening Views, 1968–1988; Supplement: Modern Writers, 1900–1998.*

Concise Dictionary of British Literary Biography, 8 volumes (1991–1992): *Writers of the Middle Ages and Renaissance Before 1660; Writers of the Restoration and Eighteenth Century, 1660–1789; Writers of the Romantic Period, 1789–1832; Victorian Writers, 1832–1890; Late-Victorian and Edwardian Writers, 1890–1914; Modern Writers, 1914–1945; Writers After World War II, 1945–1960; Contemporary Writers, 1960 to Present.*

Concise Dictionary of World Literary Biography, 4 volumes (1999–2000): *Ancient Greek and Roman Writers; German Writers; African, Caribbean, and Latin American Writers; South Slavic and Eastern European Writers.*

Dictionary of Literary Biography® • Volume Three Hundred Five

Latin American Dramatists
First Series

Dictionary of Literary Biography® • Volume Three Hundred Five

Latin American Dramatists
First Series

Edited by
Adam Versényi
University of North Carolina at Chapel Hill

A Bruccoli Clark Layman Book

Detroit • New York • San Francisco • San Diego • New Haven, Conn. • Waterville, Maine • London • Munich

Dictionary of Literary Biography
Volume 305: Latin American Dramatists
First Series

Adam Versényi

Advisory Board
John Baker
William Cagle
Patrick O'Connor
George Garrett
Trudier Harris
Alvin Kernan

Editorial Directors
Matthew J. Bruccoli and Richard Layman

© 2005 Thomson Gale, a part of The Thomson Corporation.

Thomson and Star Logo are trademarks and Gale is a registered trademark used herein under license.

For more information, contact
Thomson Gale
27500 Drake Rd.
Farmington Hills, MI 48331-3535
Or you can visit our Internet site at
http://www.gale.com

ALL RIGHTS RESERVED
No part of this work covered by the copyright hereon may be reproduced or used in any form or by any means—graphic, electronic, or mechanical, including photocopying, recording, taping, Web distribution, or information storage retrieval systems—without the written permission of the publisher.

For permission to use material from this product, submit your request via Web at http://www.gale-edit.com/permissions, or you may download our Permissions Request form and submit your request by fax or mail to:

Permissions Department
Thomson Gale
27500 Drake Rd.
Farmington Hills, MI 48331-3535
Permissions Hotline:
248-699-8006 or 800-877-4253, ext. 8006
Fax: 248-699-8074 or 800-762-4058

While every effort has been made to ensure the reliability of the information presented in this publication, Thomson Gale does not guarantee the accuracy of the data contained herein. Thomson Gale accepts no payment for listing; and inclusion in the publication of any organization, agency, institution, publication, service, or individual does not imply endorsement of the editors or publisher. Errors brought to the attention of the publisher and verified to the satisfaction of the publisher will be corrected in future editions.

LIBRARY OF CONGRESS CATALOGING-IN-PUBLICATION DATA

Latin American dramatists. First series / edited by Adam Versényi.
 p. cm. — (Dictionary of literary biography ; v. 305)
"A Bruccoli Clark Layman Book."
Includes bibliographical references and index.
  ISBN 0-7876-6842-7 (hardcover : alk. paper)
  1. Spanish American drama—20th century—Bio-bibliography—Dictionaries. 2. Spanish American drama—20th century—History and criticism—Dictionaries. 3. Dramatists, Spanish American—20th century—Biography—Dictionaries. I. Versényi, Adam. II. Series.

PQ7082.D7L373 2004
862'.609'03—dc22
                                            2004017988

Printed in the United States of America
10 9 8 7 6 5 4 3 2 1

For Sue, whose energy always inspires

Contents

Plan of the Series xv
Introduction xvii

Isidora Aguirre (1919–) .3
   Alicia del Campo

Hugo Argüelles (1932–2003) 18
   Fabiola Fernández Salek

Roberto Arlt (1900–1942) 27
   Ricardo Szmetan

Antón Arrufat (1935–) .36
   Laurietz Seda

Sabina Berman (1955–) 44
   Francine A'ness

Enrique Buenaventura (1925–2003) 60
   Beatriz J. Rizk

José Ignacio Cabrujas (1937–1995) 77
   Luis Chesney Lawrence

Emilio Carballido (1925–) 87
   Jacqueline E. Bixler

Roberto Cossa (1934–) 106
   Melissa A. Fitch

Sor Juana Inés de la Cruz (1651–1695) 116
   Julie Greer Johnson

Osvaldo Dragún (1929–1999) 125
   Amalia Gladhart

Cristina Escofet (1945–) 138
   Lola Proaño-Gómez

Carlos Felipe (1911–1975) 143
   José A. Escarpanter and Charles E. Workman

Griselda Gambaro (1928–) 153
   Sandra Messinger Cypess

Santiago García (1928–) 167
   Lucía Garavito

Vicente Leñero (1933–) 184
   Stuart A. Day

Germán Luco Cruchaga (1894–1936) 199
   Elsa M. Gilmore

René Marqués (1919–1979) 206
   Lowell Fiet

Ricardo Monti (1944–) 220
   Jean Graham-Jones

Eduardo Pavlovsky (1933–) 236
   Gustavo Geirola

José J. Podestá (1858–1937) 253
   Beatriz Seibel

Juan Radrigán (1937–) 261
   Carolyn D. Roark

Víctor Hugo Rascón Banda (1948–) 271
   José F. Blanco

Carlos José Reyes (1941–) 281
   Christina Marín

Hugo Salcedo (1964–) 288
   Iani del Rosario Moreno

Florencio Sánchez (1875–1910) 297
   Ricardo Szmetan

Luis Rafael Sánchez (1936–) 307
   Gloria F. Waldman

Carlos Solórzano (1922–) 316
   Wilma Feliciano

José Triana (1931–) .330
   Kirsten F. Nigro

Rodolfo Usigli (1905–1979) 341
   Ramón Layera

Egon Wolff (1926–) .355
   José L. Urbina

Books for Further Reading 371
Contributors 375
Cumulative Index 379

Plan of the Series

...Almost the most prodigious asset of a country, and perhaps its most precious possession, is its native literary product—when that product is fine and noble and enduring.

Mark Twain*

The advisory board, the editors, and the publisher of the *Dictionary of Literary Biography* are joined in endorsing Mark Twain's declaration. The literature of a nation provides an inexhaustible resource of permanent worth. Our purpose is to make literature and its creators better understood and more accessible to students and the reading public, while satisfying the needs of teachers and researchers.

To meet these requirements, *literary biography* has been construed in terms of the author's achievement. The most important thing about a writer is his writing. Accordingly, the entries in *DLB* are career biographies, tracing the development of the author's canon and the evolution of his reputation.

The purpose of *DLB* is not only to provide reliable information in a usable format but also to place the figures in the larger perspective of literary history and to offer appraisals of their accomplishments by qualified scholars.

The publication plan for *DLB* resulted from two years of preparation. The project was proposed to Bruccoli Clark by Frederick G. Ruffner, president of the Gale Research Company, in November 1975. After specimen entries were prepared and typeset, an advisory board was formed to refine the entry format and develop the series rationale. In meetings held during 1976, the publisher, series editors, and advisory board approved the scheme for a comprehensive biographical dictionary of persons who contributed to literature. Editorial work on the first volume began in January 1977, and it was published in 1978. In order to make *DLB* more than a dictionary and to compile volumes that individually have claim to status as literary history, it was decided to organize volumes by topic, period, or genre. Each of these freestanding volumes provides a biographical-bibliographical guide and overview for a particular area of literature. We are convinced that this organization—as opposed to a single alphabet method—constitutes a valuable innovation in the presentation of reference material. The volume plan necessarily requires many decisions for the placement and treatment of authors. Certain figures will be included in separate volumes, but with different entries emphasizing the aspect of his career appropriate to each volume. Ernest Hemingway, for example, is represented in *American Writers in Paris, 1920–1939* by an entry focusing on his expatriate apprenticeship; he is also in *American Novelists, 1910–1945* with an entry surveying his entire career, as well as in *American Short-Story Writers, 1910–1945, Second Series* with an entry concentrating on his short fiction. Each volume includes a cumulative index of the subject authors and articles.

Between 1981 and 2002 the series was augmented and updated by the *DLB Yearbooks*. There have also been nineteen *DLB Documentary Series* volumes, which provide illustrations, facsimiles, and biographical and critical source materials for figures, works, or groups judged to have particular interest for students. In 1999 the *Documentary Series* was incorporated into the *DLB* volume numbering system beginning with *DLB 210: Ernest Hemingway*.

We define literature as the *intellectual commerce of a nation:* not merely as belles lettres but as that ample and complex process by which ideas are generated, shaped, and transmitted. *DLB* entries are not limited to "creative writers" but extend to other figures who in their time and in their way influenced the mind of a people. Thus the series encompasses historians, journalists, publishers, book collectors, and screenwriters. By this means readers of *DLB* may be aided to perceive literature not as cult scripture in the keeping of intellectual high priests but firmly positioned at the center of a nation's life.

DLB includes the major writers appropriate to each volume and those standing in the ranks behind them. Scholarly and critical counsel has been sought in deciding which minor figures to include and how full their entries should be. Wherever possible, useful refer-

---

*From an unpublished section of Mark Twain's autobiography, copyright by the Mark Twain Company

ences are made to figures who do not warrant separate entries.

Each *DLB* volume has an expert volume editor responsible for planning the volume, selecting the figures for inclusion, and assigning the entries. Volume editors are also responsible for preparing, where appropriate, appendices surveying the major periodicals and literary and intellectual movements for their volumes, as well as lists of further readings. Work on the series as a whole is coordinated at the Bruccoli Clark Layman editorial center in Columbia, South Carolina, where the editorial staff is responsible for accuracy and utility of the published volumes.

One feature that distinguishes *DLB* is the illustration policy–its concern with the iconography of literature. Just as an author is influenced by his surroundings, so is the reader's understanding of the author enhanced by a knowledge of his environment. Therefore *DLB* volumes include not only drawings, paintings, and photographs of authors, often depicting them at various stages in their careers, but also illustrations of their families and places where they lived. Title pages are regularly reproduced in facsimile along with dust jackets for modern authors. The dust jackets are a special feature of *DLB* because they often document better than anything else the way in which an author's work was perceived in its own time. Specimens of the writers' manuscripts and letters are included when feasible.

Samuel Johnson rightly decreed that "The chief glory of every people arises from its authors." The purpose of the *Dictionary of Literary Biography* is to compile literary history in the surest way available to us–by accurate and comprehensive treatment of the lives and work of those who contributed to it.

The *DLB* Advisory Board

Introduction

Until relatively recently, North Americans have been ignorant of Latin American arts and letters. When Latin American art was considered at all, the most likely reference point was an Aztec or Mayan ruin. This lack of awareness changed with the so-called boom of Latin American literature in the 1960s. Novels such as Carlos Fuentes's *La muerte de Artemio Cruz* (1962; translated as *The Death of Artemio Cruz*, 1964), Julio Cortázar's *Rayuela* (1963; translated as *Hopscotch*, 1966), Mario Vargas Llosa's *La casa verde* (1966; translated as *The Green House*, 1968), Guillermo Cabrera Infante's *Tres tristes tigres* (1967; translated as *Three Trapped Tigers*, 1971), and Gabriel García Márquez's *Cien años de soledad* (1967; translated as *One Hundred Years of Solitude*, 1970) raised consciousness of Latin American literature around the world. These challenging and innovative works suggested creative and imaginative methods of both viewing and writing about the world. Provocatively questioning the established boundaries between reality and fiction, dreams and life, knowledge and interpretation, the literary and commercial success of Latin American literature has influenced the subsequent development of literary forms worldwide.

While Latin American fiction received this attention, other forms did not. Although investigated by a specialized audience starting in the 1950s, Latin American dramatic literature and theatrical performance genres did not begin to receive broad recognition until the 1980s. The pioneering work of José Juan Arrom, *El teatro de hispanoamérica en la época colonial* (1956, Hispanic-American Theatre in the Colonial Era), William I. Oliver's *Voices of Change in the Spanish American Theater* (1971), Leon F. Lyday and George Woodyard's *Dramatists in Revolt: The New Latin American Theatre* (1976), and Gerardo Luzuriaga's *Popular Theater for Social Change in Latin America* (1978), as well as the invaluable *Latin American Theatre Review*, forcefully established the Latin American theater as possessing a level of quality comparable to that of the so-called boom period of Latin American fiction.

As with the Latin American novel, Latin American dramatic literature is the result of a profusion of theatrical forms, dating back to before the European conquest, that are as diverse as the countries that compose the region. Prior to the arrival of the Europeans, the great indigenous civilizations such as the Aztec, the Maya, and the Quechua engaged in ritual warfare and sacrificial offerings that were inherently performative in nature. The only extant indigenous piece of dramatic literature, the *Rabinal Achí* (Rabinal Warrior) first discovered in the nineteenth century, is an example of this kind of spectacle. Told by means of a long series of formal challenges interspersed with dance and music, the play provides an anthropological understanding of Mayan customs such as warfare, ritual, and prisoner exchange. In its use of song and dance as well as masks so heavy that they required multiple actors during performance to enact a single role, the play also reveals a great deal about Mayan theatrical technique.

The paratheatrical elements of indigenous spectacle were skillfully utilized by the mendicant orders, particularly the Franciscans, who followed Hernán Cortés's conquest of Mexico in 1522. Arriving in 1524, the Franciscan friars employed the indigenous population's familiarity with ritual performance to convert that population to Christianity. Wedding Christian theological and political concerns to the spectacular and transformational aspects of ritual performance, the mendicants created a series of anonymously written evangelical plays such as *El juicio final* (circa 1531–1534, The Last Judgment), *El sacrificio de Isaac* (circa 1536–1539, The Sacrifice of Isaac), or *La adoración de los reyes* (circa 1540–1550, The Adoration of the Magi). Once the native people's attention had been captured (so the friars believed), the stories told by the plays would cause them to reform their pagan ways.

By the end of the sixteenth century the Indohispanic Christian society that had spawned a great variety of theatrical spectacles had died. Administration of the colonies had shifted from the hands of the original conquerors and the mendicant orders to those of the Crown and the ecclesiastical authorities, exercised through a complex system of viceroyalties spanning the region. Theatrical activity during this period was largely ceremonial. The plays performed were those of the great Spanish baroque dramatists Ruiz de Alarcón, Lope de Vega, Pedro Calderón de la Barca, and Tirso de Molina, or their Iberian and colonial imitators. Latin American playwrights who incorporated indigenous forms into their own work were few and far between. *El hijo pródigo* (The Prodigal Son) by Juan Espinosa Medrano, an Indian raised by a Spanish priest in the seventeenth century, and the *Loa* (Prologue) to *El divino Narciso* (1690, The Divine Narcissus) by the Mexican nun Sor Juana Inés de la Cruz, with its incipient nationalism, are exceptions.

Where the mendicant orders had focused on mass conversion by any means possible, the Jesuit order focused upon Scholastic education in Latin America, founding a network of schools and universities whose graduates began to assume positions of authority in both secular and religious governance. The Jesuits' emphases on humanistic teaching, on pride in Latin American culture, and on the conviction that the king's authority was not divinely rendered but the result of the will of the people, led to their expulsion from all regions of New Spain in 1769 by Charles III. Charles III's administrative reforms enacted to strengthen industry and commerce greatly increased traffic between the Old and New Worlds, bringing with it an influx of European ideas by writers such as Jean Le Rond d'Alembert, Jean-Jacques Rousseau, Denis Diderot, Adam Smith, Gottfried Wilhelm Leibniz, and Charles-Louis de Secondat, baron de La Brède et de Montesquieu. The increased intellectual and economic ferment, when coupled with Jesuit-inspired pride in Latin American culture and humanistic teachings, created growing resentment against the Church and the colonial authorities, leading to a series of unsuccessful rebellions throughout the region. Nationalistic pride engendered by the wealth resulting from increased economic activity led to the construction of huge, lavish theaters from Mexico City to Santiago de Chile between 1752 and 1802. The 1799 Spanish edition of Rousseau's *Social Contract* (1762) greatly contributed to Simón Bolívar's formation of his lifelong goal of Spanish American independence. Rousseau's musical play, *Pygmalion* (1770), published in Spanish in 1788, greatly influenced a series of neoclassically trained and journalistically formed writers such as the Mexican José Joaquín Fernández Lizardi, the Cuban José-María de Heredia, the Chilean Fray Camilo Henríquez, the Argentine Luis Ambrosio Morante, and the Colombians José Fernández Madrid and Luis Vargas Tejada, who saw the theater as a political and educational forum in which to press for freedom from colonial rule. Their plays and other writings were factors leading to the Wars of Independence that swept the region starting in 1820. Typical of such plays was the Cuban José Martí's dramatic poem *Abdala* (1869).

Alongside the neoclassical theater performed for the Creole elite (those born in Latin America but of European descent) emerged a series of popular theater forms that turned venues such as inns, squares, and circuses into theatrical spaces. Representative of this type of playwriting are José J. Podestá's adaptation of *Juan Moreira* (1886), based on Eduardo Gutiérrez's novel that first appeared as a newspaper serial in 1879 and 1880, and Florencio Sánchez's rural drama *Barranco abajo* (1905, Down the Cliffs). These new forms reflected the bifurcation of Latin American society between the rich Creole elite in power and the masses who remained as politically and financially disenfranchised as they had been under colonial rule. A huge migration of immigrants into Latin America from all over the world at the start of the twentieth century added to the existing gap between rich and poor in the region. New cultural forms, customs, and political ideas brought by these immigrants created significant social and political unrest. This influx can be seen theatrically in the emergence of such forms as the *grotesco criollo* (Creole grotesque, a form of black comedy about characters who try to incorporate themselves into a social system that deforms and destroys them) in Argentina and in works such as *María la tonta* (1927, María the Fool) or *He visto a Dios* (1930, I Have Seen God) by Defillipis Novoa or *Mateo* (1923) and *Stéfano* (1928) by Armando Discépolo.

While political independence from colonial rule was achieved in the late nineteenth century, cultural dependence upon colonial mentality (in which one still perceives oneself as inferior to one's former colonial masters) lasted a great deal longer. In the theater, the effort to break such cultural dependence began in 1925 when a series of university-affiliated and independent theater groups sprang up throughout the region. The organizational structures of these groups and the production styles they adopted varied greatly, but they were primarily concerned with creating a specifically Latin American consciousness capable of speaking to and for the various countries of the region, as can be seen in the work of playwrights as varied as the Mexican Rodolfo Usigli and the Chilean Germán Luco Cruchaga. The dramatists who emerged from the university-affiliated and independent groups spanning the region from Argentina to Puerto Rico included such writers as Isidora Aguirre, Egon Wolff, Emilio Carballido, Osvaldo Dragún, Virgilio Piñero, and René Marqués. These playwrights radically restructure history, ritual, and mythology to treat Latin American political and sociological themes.

In the latter half of the twentieth century, Latin America entered a period of political upheaval. From the CIA-sponsored overthrow of Jacobo Arbenz in Guatemala in 1954 to the Cuban Revolution in 1958, from a series of brutal civil wars in Central America during the 1970s and 1980s to a series of military coup d'états in South America during the same period, several events combined to alter the relationship between theater and society. Latin American theater took on an increasingly political character, with direct repercussions for the artists involved. Figures such as the Uruguayan playwright and guerrilla leader Mauricio Rosencof were imprisoned and tortured. Others, such as the Argentine playwrights Griselda Gambaro and Eduardo Pavlovsky, were forced into exile. Simultaneously, the critique of the political and social context of the 1960s and 1970s led to the creation of new forms of theater throughout the region, frequently based upon the consciousness-raising techniques of the Brazilian educator Paulo Freire. This type of theater sought to enable the audience to speak for itself rather than speaking to the audience in a patronizing attitude that mirrors centuries of colonial oppression. Two of the best practitioners of this approach are the Colombians Enrique Buenaventura and Santiago García.

With the demise of dictatorship throughout the region in the 1980s and 1990s the themes, forms, and theatrical techniques that filled the stage under dictatorship began to shift. Moving beyond its role as an essential site of resistance to dictatorship, Latin American theater in general produced a profusion of forms and performance styles reflecting an initial disorientation on the part of theater practitioners themselves. While the politically and socially engaged theater of the 1960s and 1970s was by no means abandoned, it became less dogmatic, admitting the possibility of magic, sacrament, and a sense of diversion in the theater. Confident of its own identity, the Latin American theater at the end of the twentieth century borrowed from global theatrical forms in order to enhance its own practice. By the early twenty-first century there is a greater anthropological awareness of Latin America itself reflected in the theater, as can be seen in the work of playwrights spanning generations and countries such as the Mexicans Carballido, Sabina Berman, and Victor Hugo Rascón Banda; the Argentines Ricardo Monti, Dragún, Susanna Torres Molina, and Cristina Escofet; the Chileans Marco Antonio de la Parra and Ramón Griffero; or the Colombians Carlos José Reyes and Victor Vivisecas.

A volume on Latin American dramatists should reflect the region as a whole, drawing together playwrights and works that come from all of the various linguistic and geographic areas of the region. Such an ideal collection would include the Francophone and Anglophone Caribbean, the Netherlands Antilles, all of the various Creole areas, and Portuguese-speaking Brazil (see also *DLB 113: Modern Latin-American Fiction Writers, First Series; DLB 117: Twentieth-Century Caribbean and Black African Writers, First Series; DLB 125: Twentieth-Century Caribbean and Black African Writers, Second Series; DLB 145: Modern Latin-American Fiction Writers, Second Series; DLB 157: Twentieth-Century Caribbean and Black African Writers, Third Series;* and *DLB 307: Brazilian Writers*). Such a volume, however, would founder under the sheer weight of the material it would need to collect. This volume on Latin American Dramatists, therefore, has been limited to the Spanish-speaking Caribbean and Central and South America. Even such a demarcation involves a vast geographic and cultural area stretching from the southern tip of Tierra del Fuego to the northernmost reaches of Mexico. While the intention here has been to gather a representative collection of playwrights from the sixteenth century to the present, serving as a summary introduction to the range of work carried out in Latin American drama, there are inevitable gaps and lacunae that will be filled by future volumes. A biographical and bibliographical study of Latin American dramatists is vastly complicated by several factors, including the lack of an archival tradition in Latin America, extremely brief runs of plays frequently lasting only a few days, the scarcity of theatrical criticism, and texts of plays published only in small quantities that immediately go out of print. Consequently, the reader of this volume may be frustrated by incomplete bibliographical or biographical information. In each case the contributors have made their best-faith effort to provide the most comprehensive information available. Above all, this volume should demonstrate the historical richness and contemporary vitality of Latin American playwriting and indicate a promising future for the wealth and strength of the Latin American theater.

—*Adam Versényi*

Acknowledgments

This book was produced by Bruccoli Clark Layman, Inc. Tracy Simmons Bitonti was the in-house editor.

Production manager is Philip B. Dematteis.

Administrative support was provided by Carol A. Cheschi.

Accountant is Ann-Marie Holland.

Copyediting supervisor is Sally R. Evans. The copyediting staff includes Phyllis A. Avant, Caryl

Brown, Melissa D. Hinton, Philip I. Jones, Rebecca Mayo, Nadirah Rahimah Shabazz, Joshua Shaw, and Nancy E. Smith.

Pipeline manager is James F. Tidd Jr.

Editorial associate is Jessica R. Goudeau.

In-house prevetter is Catherine M. Polit.

Permissions editor is Amber L. Coker.

Layout and graphics supervisor is Janet E. Hill. The graphics staff includes Zoe R. Cook and Sydney E. Hammock.

Office manager is Kathy Lawler Merlette.

Photography editors are Mark J. McEwan and Walter W. Ross.

Digital photographic copy work was performed by Joseph M. Bruccoli.

Systems manager is Donald Kevin Starling.

Typesetting supervisor is Kathleen M. Flanagan. The typesetting staff includes Patricia Marie Flanagan and Pamela D. Norton.

Walter W. Ross is library researcher. He was assisted by the following librarians at the Thomas Cooper Library of the University of South Carolina: Jo Cottingham, interlibrary loan department; circulation department head Tucker Taylor; reference department head Virginia W. Weathers; reference department staff Laurel Baker, Marilee Birchfield, Kate Boyd, Paul Cammarata, Joshua Garris, Gary Geer, Tom Marcil, Rose Marshall, and Sharon Verba; interlibrary loan department head Marna Hostetler; and interlibrary loan staff Bill Fetty, Nelson Rivera, and Cedric Rose.

Dictionary of Literary Biography® • Volume Three Hundred Five

Latin American Dramatists
First Series

Dictionary of Literary Biography

Isidora Aguirre
(22 March 1919 -)

Alicia del Campo
California State University, Long Beach

PLAY PRODUCTIONS: *Entre dos trenes,* staged reading, Chilean-North American Cultural Institute, 1952; full production, Santiago, Teatro Talía, 1957;

Pacto de medianoche, Santiago, Teatro Talía, 1954; Mexico City, Teatro del Bosque de Bellas Artes, 1958;

Carolina, Santiago, Teatro Antonio Varas (First Festival of Regional Theater), December 1955;

La micro, Santiago, Escuela de Teatro de la Universidad de Chile, 1956;

Judas Macabeo, based on Howard Fast's *My Glorious Brothers,* Santiago, Sala Maccabi, 1957;

Las Pascualas, Santiago, Sala Talía, Teatro Experimental de la Universidad de Chile, 1957; revised, Antofagasta, Teatro Universitario de Antofagasta, 1976;

Dos más dos son cinco, Concepción, Teatro Universitario de Concepción, 1957;

Población esperanza, by Aguirre and Manuel Rojas, Concepción, Teatro de la Universidad de Concepción, 1959;

La pérgola de las flores, Teatro de la Universidad Católica de Chile, 1960;

Los papeleros, Santiago, Sindicato de Actores, Teatro Carpa, 1963;

Anacleto avaro, Santiago, Compañía Nacional de Teatro, 1964;

La dama del canasto, Santiago, Teatro Silvia Piñeiro, 1965;

Magy ante el espejo, Mexico City, Teatro Juan José Gurrola, 1968;

Los que van quedando en el camino, Santiago, Teatro de la Universidad de Chile, 1969;

Obras breves de Teatro Popular Didáctico-formativo, shantytown presentations, 1969–1973;

Isidora Aguirre (*from Irma Césped,* Teatro chileno contemporáneo: Luis Alberto Heiremans, Isidora Aguirre, *1998; J. Willard Marriott Library, University of Utah*)

Quién tuvo la culpa de la muerte de la María González, Valparaíso, Instituto Chileno-Francés, 1970;

Historia de las Juventudes Comunistas, by Aguirre, Víctor Jara, and Patricio Bunster, Santiago, National Stadium, 1972;

La Desideria en el cielo, Santiago, Sala del Teatro del Angel, 1974;

En aquellos locos años 20, adapted from Armando Moock's *La señorita del Charleston,* Antofagasta, Teatro de la Universidad de Chile, 1974;

La mandragora, adapted from Niccolò Machiavelli's *Mandragora,* Santiago, Sala Petropol, 1977;

Fuente Ovejuna, adapted from Lope de Vega's play, Santiago, Sala del Estadio Español, 1978; revised, Santiago, Teatro Galpón de Los Leones, 1981;

El médico a palos, adapted from Molière's *Le Médecin malgré luy,* Santiago, Compañía Taller Histrión, 1979;

Lazarillo de Tormes, adapted from the anonymous Spanish novel, Santiago, Compañía de Teatro Educacional de Patricia Cuadros, 1980;

Lautaro: Epopeya del pueblo mapuche, Santiago, Sala Caja de Compensación Los Andes, 7 April 1982;

Ricardo III, adapted from William Shakespeare's *Richard III,* Santiago, Sala Andes, 1983;

Edipo rey, adapted from Sophocles' *Oedipus Rex,* Santiago, Compañía de Teatro Educacional de Patricia Cuadros, 1984; revised, Antofagasta, Teatro Universitario Pedro de la Barra de Antofagasta, 1985;

Retablo de Yumbel, Concepción, Teatro Compañía El Rostro, 1986; revised, Montreal, Theater of the University of Quebec, 1987; translated as *The Altarpiece of Yumbel,* Hayward, California State University Theatre, 12 November 1999;

El amor a la africana, Santiago, Sala Café Concert, 1986;

Federico hermano, Santiago, Teatro El Conventillo, 6 December 1986;

Tía Irene yo te amaba, Santiago, Teatro del Angel, 1988;

Diálogos de fin de siglo, by Aguirre and the Teatro Ictus group, Teatro La Comedia, 1988;

Naira Yawiña (Manantial Secreto), by Aguirre and the Teatro Ojo group, Santiago, Museo de Arte Precolombino, 1991;

Mi primo Federico, Madrid, Sala Nuval, 1997;

Manuel Rodríguez, Santiago, Teatro Círculo, 1999.

BOOKS: *Ocho cuentos* (Santiago: Zig-Zag, 1938);

Títeres (Santiago: Zig-Zag, 1945);

Wai-Kii (Santiago: Rapa-Nui, 1948);

Los que van quedando en el camino (N.p.: Privately printed, 1969);

Lautaro: Epopeya del pueblo mapuche (Santiago: Nascimiento, 1982);

La pérgola de las flores: Comedia musical (Santiago: Andrés Bello, 1986);

Retablo de Yumbel (Concepción: Literatura Americana Reunida, 1987; Havana: Casa de las Américas, 1987); translated by Teresa Cajiao Salas and Margarita Vargas as *Altarpiece of Yumbel: A Play* (Santiago: Privately printed, 1991);

Doy por vivido todo lo soñado (Barcelona: Plaza y Janés, 1987);

Los papeleros (Santiago: Torsegel, 1989);

Diálogos de fin de siglo (Santiago: Torsegel, 1989);

Carta a Roque Dalton (Barcelona: Plaza y Janés, 1990);

Los libertadores: Bolívar y Miranda (Santiago: LAR, 1993);

Anacleto avaro (Santiago: Arrayán, 1996);

Santiago de diciembre a diciembre (Santiago: LOM, 1998; Euskal Eria: Txalaparta, 2001);

Manuel Rodríguez: Epopeya popular con música: Centrada en la vida del guerrillero: Teatro (Santiago: CLAN, 1999).

PRODUCED SCRIPTS: *La supresión de Amanda,* radio, Santiago, 1956;

Las poblaciones en Chile, motion picture, Corporarión de la Vivienda, 1972;

El movimiento de la Unidad Popular, motion picture, 1973;

Alsino y el cóndor, by Aguirre and Miguel Littin, motion picture, Nicaraguan Film Institute Productions, 1982.

OTHER: *Carolina,* in *Teatro chileno actual: Antología* (Santiago: Zig-Zag, 1959);

Express for Santiago [translation of *Carolina*], in *The Best Short Plays, 1959–1960,* edited by Margaret Mayorga (Boston: Beacon, 1960);

The Pascualas, translated by Willis Knapp Jones, in *Poet Lore* (Boston: Poet Lore, 1965);

Los papeleros, in *El teatro actual latinoamericano (Antología),* edited by Carlos Solórzano (Mexico: Ediciones de Andrea, 1972);

Anacleto avaro, in *Anthologies,* edited by Rubén Sotoconil (Santiago: Cuadernos del Ministerio de Educación, N.6, 1982);

Lautaro, in *Teatro chileno contemporáneo: Antología,* edited by Juan Andrés Piña (Madrid: Quinto Centenario/Fondo de Cultura Económica, 1992);

Pablo Neruda, *Antología de Pablo Neruda,* edited by Aguirre (Santiago: Editorial Bibliográfica Internacional, 1995);

Retablo de Yumbel, in *Antología* (Madrid & New York: Verbum, 1997);

Altarpiece of Yumbel, translated by Teresa Cajiao Salas and Margarita Vargas, in *Women Writing Women: An Anthology of Spanish-American Theater of the 1980s,* edited by Salas and Vargas (Albany: State University of New York Press, 1997).

SELECTED PERIODICAL PUBLICATIONS–
UNCOLLECTED: *Magy ante el espejo, Revista Universidad de Veracruz* (Mexico) (1992);
Mi primo Federico, Revista Tramoya (Mexico) (1997);
Tía Irene yo te amaba, Revista Tramoya (Mexico) (1998).

Isidora Aguirre, the most recognized and prolific woman playwright in Chile to date, forms part of a generation who, in the 1950s, produced a total renovation in Chilean drama. Aguirre has written more than thirty plays exploring comedy, drama, musical, testimonial, and children's theater; she has also adapted plays of such writers as Sophocles, Niccolò Machiavelli, and Lope de Vega, drawing upon her experience in social work, folklore, dance, art, movies, and music to find her particular voice. In addition, she has explored many other artistic forms. Her novels develop a more introspective and subjective view of history, and she has also devoted work to children, including short stories, a novel, and puppetry scripts. In movies she has worked on two documentaries–about the shantytowns in Chile and the Unidad Popular (a socialist movement)–and collaborated with director Miguel Littin on the script for the movie *Alsino y el cóndor* (1982, Alsino and the Condor) as well as writing the movie version of her novel *Doy por vivido todo lo soñado* (1989). She has received many prestigious awards such as the Premio de la Crítica y Laurel de Oro (1959), the Premio de la Crítica (1960), the Premio Eugenio Dittborn (1981), the Premio del Consejo del Libro y la Lectura (1994), and the Medalla de Santiago (1999) as a recognition for lifetime achievement in the advancement of literature and art. She has received international recognition as her plays have been performed throughout Latin America, the United States, and Europe. Translations of her plays have been published in Germany, the United States, and Brazil, and in 1987 she was awarded the prestigious Casa de las Américas Prize for her 1986 play *Retablo de Yumbel* (Altarpiece of Yumbel).

Isidora Aguirre was born on 22 March 1919, the daughter of an upper-class family in Santiago, Chile. She is the great-great-granddaughter of the Spaniard Isidora Zegers (a composer and founder of the Sociedad Filarmónica de Santiago in 1826) and grew up in what she calls a "tribal family," where all forms of art, music, painting, dance, and literature were stimulated by her parents and the many artists from diverse national backgrounds who visited their home. As a child, she studied dance and music, played piano and guitar, and even composed some songs.

Aguirre's mother, María Tupper Hunneus, was an open-minded artist who was always breaking boundaries but who also worked to maintain a clear sense of her refined social class at a time when her own mother was uncomfortable with the idea of her painting nudes in the School of Fine Arts in Santiago. Throughout her childhood Aguirre was surrounded by art, as she stated in an interview with Patricia Corona: "En vez de leer revistas de niños, sabía de Botticelli, de Leonardo da Vinci" (instead of reading children's books we knew of Botticelli, Leonardo da Vinci). Aguirre also credits her mother's influence for the easy transitions and parallels between life and death in her plays, because her mother used to talk to the dead in a natural manner. Aguirre was also influenced by her mother's best friend, novelist Isabel Allende's grandmother, who instilled in Aguirre the belief in the power of mental energies and spiritual forces.

Her father, Fernando Aguirre Errázuriz, was an engineer and classical music lover who installed small speakers in his children's bedrooms to wake them up for school with music by Johann Sebastian Bach. Her grandparents' home was the center of frequent *tertulias* (literary gatherings) that gave Isidora the opportunity to meet many distinguished artists. She used to hear children's stories from Chilean writer Marta Brunet and was introduced to the muralist David Alfaro Siqueiros.

The cultural context of Aguirre's childhood was marked by a profound admiration for European culture that was exemplified in the habits of the Chilean aristocracy, who sent their children to study in France. Aguirre received her education from a private French nuns' school, Jeanne D'Arc, in Santiago. As the young Aguirre began translating and illustrating French stories for Brunet, she began writing her own works, thus leaving behind her childhood dream of being a dancer as she became aware of two factors: her strong intellect and her not-so-slim legs. When she graduated from school, her father published her first book, the illustrated *Ocho cuentos* (1838, Eight Tales), with the publishing house Zig-Zag.

After completing high school, Aguirre decided to study social work, and from 1938 to 1939 she attended the School of Social Work in Santiago eager to know "por qué habían tantos niños pobres en las calles" (why there were so many hungry children begging in the streets). This concern led her to become familiar with the reality of the shantytowns, where she discovered "women fiercely fighting to feed their children, the injustice of those children condemned to that sort of poverty, and the nobility of many who are born and die in poverty." She also witnessed the unemployment of the nitrate miners after the crisis of 1929, when the critical decline in nitrate exports was worsened by the world's market fall. She realized that with her plays she would be able to speak for those people marginalized by the economic system, and their experiences served to create many of the key characters of her plays. For Aguirre, these contacts allowed her to understand better the conditions and culture of the poor but also to appreciate their dark sense of humor, an element that she has used productively in her dramatic portraits, as she acknowledged in an interview with Loreto Daza.

In 1940 Aguirre married Gerardo Carmona, a Spanish captain who had served in the Spanish Civil War. In 1942 she studied music composition with Juan Orrego Salas but was also living a traditional life: raising children, sewing, embroidering, and working on their small farm, where they suffered economic hardships. Five years after her marriage she returned to Santiago, where she worked in accounting, taught French, English, and music, and wrote puppetry scripts. In 1948, in the midst of financial difficulties, she learned of her husband's infidelity. They did not separate, however, until 1958, when he asked her to annul their marriage so that he could marry his secretary. By then she was dating Peter Sinclair, a British painter ten years her junior, who became her second husband. Between 1948 and 1949 she studied film at the Ecole de Haute Etudes Cinématographique in Paris and met key members of the French intellectual and artistic elite.

As Aguirre attempted to deal with the many aspects of her life–writing, working, and being a mother of five–the Chilean theater scene was also evolving in a new direction. With the emergence in the early 1940s of the Teatro Experimental de la Universidad de Chile (TEUC, Experimental Theater of the University of Chile), the Teatro de Ensayo de la Universidad Católica (Catholic University Rehearsal Theater), and the Teatro de la Universidad de Concepción (Theater of the University of Concepción), there began a process of professionalism of Chilean theater. This movement was devoted to academic training in theater production, the mastering of world and Spanish classics, and the creation of a theater dedicated to Chilean themes from an aesthetic that looked beyond the traditional *costumbrismo* (literature devoted to describing the manners or customs of a particular region) and the touring zarzuela companies from Spain and France that characterized the Chilean stage. Ten years later, the first generation of university-trained Chilean playwrights began exploring Chilean middle- and working-class issues, mostly through psychological realism. Aguirre was part of this prolific generation of writers, including Luis Alberto Heiremans, María Asunción Requena, Egon Wolff, Jorge Díaz, Gabriela Roepke, and Sergio Vodanovic, who worked rigorously to develop a middle- and working-class audience and to unveil the complexities of Chilean identity.

The university theater movement generated a great difference between writers and theater producers. While directors and actors had formal academic training, writers, mostly self-taught, had to put much effort and rigor into their work, as was the case with Aguirre when she began writing drama. Between 1951 and 1953 Aguirre studied playwriting and acting at the Theater School of the Ministry of Education, and from 1955 to 1957 she studied Chilean theater and dramatic techniques at the University of Chile. In order to write the theater of social critique that she was searching for, Aguirre continued her educational process by enrolling in sociology and history courses at the University of Chile.

Aguirre's first attempt at drama writing was a series of light comedies that served as an introduction to the craft based on characters and themes she knew well and felt comfortable writing about–the concerns of the middle class. The dialogue is dynamic, and the characters are well developed, though the premises are simple. A staged reading of her first comedy, *Entre dos trenes* (Between Two Trains), was directed by Hugo Miller at the Chilean-North American Cultural Institute in 1952.

Two years later, her first actual premiere, *Pacto de medianoche* (1954, Midnight Pact), was presented by actor Raúl Montenegro in Teatro Talía and became her first adventure in theater production. *Pacto de medianoche*, a short monologue, was staged along with a translation of Anton Chekhov's (1912, *The Swan Song*) but neither had been given much publicity, so they had little attendance and lacked critical reviews. These stagings were mostly a result of the enthusiasm of the relatively unknown Montenegro, who had arranged to book the theater and rehearsed the play without money or sponsorship. In this first experience, Aguirre did everything from costume designing to making props to arranging the lighting. During intermission, she even prepared the actor for the next play by sewing a sheet to his body in a Greek fashion so he could play a Chekhov character. She also prompted Montenegro's lines from behind a curtain, since he had devoted more time to learning the lines for *Pacto de medianoche*. Montenegro's treatment of her text, and that fluid energy created among the audience, actor, and writer, inspired her passion for theater. This production was also the beginning of Aguirre's long tradition of involvement in the staging of her plays, a practice that she finds adventurous and insightful for her. Although she enjoyed the experience, Aguirre felt the lack of a director in *Pacto de medianoche* created a play that needed more work, and consequently she took it out of production.

As she was presenting *Pacto de medianoche* her next play, the comedy *Carolina* (1955), was selected to be premiered by the TEUC, under the direction of Eugenio Guzmán. It was presented in the framework of the First Festival of Theater from the Provinces, sponsored by the TEUC. *Carolina* is part of a trilogy of one-act plays that mark the beginning of Aguirre's comedies and was also the beginning of a long and fruitful relationship with Guzmán, a young director returning from his studies at Yale with new staging techniques and a fervor for renovation.

In *Carolina,* Aguirre explores a reality she knows well as she pokes fun at the absurdity of a middle-class couple's concerns. The play portrays the relationship between Carlos and his absentminded wife, Carolina. As they await their connection at a train station, Carolina, afraid of the consequences but also of telling her husband, confesses to another traveler that she might have left the stove on before leaving the house. The new acquaintance offers his help and goes back to Santiago with her key to solve the problem. Carolina's peace of mind does not last long, however, as her husband tells her that he has prepared a dangerous trap to catch any possible intruders in their absence. Aguirre portrays the most crucial concerns of the middle class: their homes, their appliances, their clothing, and the happiness of small vacations in the countryside. Carolina is similar to a Lucille Ball character, characteristic of the 1950s middle-class housewife dependent on her husband's rational control of her life. The woman represents nature, intuition, and chaos, while the man appears as the epitome of order in his paternalistic and condescending treatment of his wife.

In 1956 Aguirre's comic monologue *La micro* (The Bus) was staged by the group Los Feriantes from the School of Theater of the University of Chile, directed by Enrique Gajardo and presented at the Teatro Talía. *La supresión de Amanda* (The Suppression of Amanda), a tragicomic monologue, premiered through a radio broadcast in 1956, and a year later *Judas Macabeo,* a drama based on Howard Fast's novel *My Glorious Brothers* (1948), was presented by the Maccabi Group and directed by Hugo Miller. In 1957 Aguirre also began to explore national themes through folklore in *Las Pascualas* (The Pascualas). The play is based on a traditional legend that deals with a mother, a sister, and a daughter as they are seduced by and fight for the same man, who is a reincarnation of the devil. Aguirre, collaborating with the composer Gustavo Becerra and the director Guzmán, incorporates popular religious folkloric traditions and songs into the play. The comedy *Dos más dos son cinco* (Two and Two Is Five) first premiered at the Teatro Universitario de Concepción (Concepción University Theater) in 1957, directed by Gustavo Meza, and the following year in Santiago directed by Charlie Elssesar in Teatro Maru.

Aguirre also began teaching Chilean theater, dramaturgy, dramatic literary techniques, and workshops in playwriting at the University of Chile, the Technical University of the State, and later in a variety of small theater schools. Most of her academic work was done between 1956 and 1973, at which time the military regime of Augusto Pinochet stripped Aguirre of her position as permanent faculty at the University of Chile, along with her rights to a legitimate retirement pension.

Aguirre's interest in writing about the conditions of poverty and marginalization was at first tempered by her own insecurities about portraying a reality so distant from her own comfortable bourgeois environment and upbringing. She found the perfect opportunity, however, in her collaborative work with 1957 Premio Nacional de Literature winner Manuel Rojas. A politically committed man, Rojas gave Aguirre the confidence she needed as they collaborated on *Población esperanza* (1959, Shantytown Hope). Rojas proposed the idea to her when working at a literary workshop together. The production, directed by Pedro de la Barra, premiered at the Teatro de la Universidad de Concepción and met with such success that, along with Los Perlas, a popular picaresque folk duo, it was taken on tour to the surrounding towns and working-class centers (such as the coal mines of Lota, where workers filled the eight-hundred-seat theater). For de la Barra, the guest director, the great success of the tour was evidence of the need to decentralize Chilean theater. Later, the play received acclaim in Santiago at the Teatro Camilo Henríquez, in Montevideo, and in Buenos Aires. Even decades later, in 1986, the Asociación Cristiana de Jóvenes (Christian Youth Association) produced it in Uruguay.

Drawing from her experience as a social worker, Aguirre presents a clear portrait of the conditions of poverty and misery of the inhabitants of a shantytown in *Población esperanza*. Malnourishment, lack of education, and minimal living conditions condemn them to the inability to develop normal human relations. In the end the only possibilities for survival appear to be to unite, to work in solidarity, and to keep hope alive. Aguirre and Rojas succeeded in bringing working-class characters to a milieu mostly devoted to middle-class characters and concerns, reconnecting with the theater of social critique utilized by Antonio Acevedo Hernández during the 1920s and 1930s from a more anarchist position. Although not confrontational, the play is a call for solidarity to the concerned middle class and a call to action for the popular sectors.

The play centers around a social worker who falls in love with a young *poblador* (shantytown dweller) and tries to save him from his involvement in the Mafia; but in spite of her efforts and the hopes for his salvation, she fails in her aim, as he is murdered by the Mafia he was trying to escape. This ending puts into question the possibility of hope and reaffirms the cycle of poverty. Although the play draws upon psychological realism, it

Scene from the premiere of Aguirre's 1960 musical comedy, La pérgola de las flores *(The Flower Marketplace), at the Teatro de la Universidad Católica de Chile (Archivo Escuela de Teatro Universidad Católica; from Claudia Navarro,* Dramaturgia y género en el Chile de los sesenta, *2001; Thomas Cooper Library, University of South Carolina)*

also includes a fragmentary quality that seems to prefigure Aguirre's later Brechtian aesthetics. She develops "type characters" who present a view of their world that tends to break the dramatic center of the piece, as María de la Luz Hurtado has commented.

Many of the critical reviews at the time praised the play for its tender, human, and precise portrayal of the poor, the popular flavor of the language, its vigorous dialogue, and the fact that in spite of their misery, the characters still appear to maintain a sense of humor. Aguirre provides a representation of the poor that manages to generate empathy from the middle-class audience because the play does not present the bases for a class conflict but rather blames the violence, delinquency, and dysfunctional qualities on the material conditions of existence. This representation becomes a clear message for the Christian middle class and their commitment to save the poor from their extreme conditions. In Buenos Aires, a critic writing for *La razón* (1960) highlighted the play as a testimonial of social reality, a denunciation that forces the spectator to analyze and to reflect upon this universal conflict. This first play of social critique with Rojas gave Aguirre the confidence to approach these themes on her own. During this new stage of her writing, Bertolt Brecht's work became a fundamental source of inspiration to create a socially conscious theater and to awaken rather than appease and entertain the spectator.

By 1960 Aguirre's plays had become quite popular and were produced in Santiago's theaters as well as in barrios, unions, and schools, by amateur groups from the provinces of northern Antofagasta, in the nitrate mines in the desert, and in the extreme south in Magallanes. The critic Enrique Bello, writing for *Pro Arte Magazine* in 1960, praised Aguirre as the first "woman of theater" to entertain with dramatic presence and to create real characters within an unreal comedy.

That same year, while pregnant with her last child, Aguirre began writing her most famous play: *La pérgola de las flores* (1960, The Flower Marketplace), a musical comedy that has become a major national icon representing the conflicting relations between popular sectors and the Chilean aristocracy with a profound folkloric and *costumbrista* flavor that presents an image pleasing to both political sectors, and especially to the middle class. With songs by Francisco Flores del Campo, *La pérgola de las flores* was directed by Guzmán and premiered at the Teatro de la Universidad Católica de Chile. It has been staged several times since its first premiere, including performances directed by Andrés Pérez at the Mapocho Station in 2000 and by Carmen Barros, who originally played the protagonist, in 2002. *La pérgola de las flores* also has been produced abroad in Buenos Aires, Havana, Madrid, and Mexico. Outside the commercial circuit, *La pérgola de las flores* has been performed many times in schools and institutions in Chile as well as in American, Canadian, and Australian universities. In Chile it holds the record for the most seen play of all time, along with Don Roberto Parra Sandoval and Andrés Pérez Araya's *La Negra Ester* (1988, Dark Esther); Barros's production was seen by twenty-five thousand spectators in free performances offered by the City of Santiago in the monumental National Stadium.

A *sainete* (one-act intermezzo) in its dramatic structure, *La pérgola de las flores* is based on an historical event during the 1920s and tells the story of Carmela, a young peasant woman who emigrates from a small town in search of a more exciting urban life. Through its songs *La pérgola de las flores* conveys Carmela's naiveté and enthusiasm as her journey entails getting used to the new reality and culture of the city: language, dressing, habits, behavior. It is also a love story: an aristocrat courts Carmela, and she attempts to become more refined to fit into his world, only to realize that her true love is another young peasant with whom she will be able to be herself, devoid of the masks of modernity and upper class, and sharing their common background and values. On a wider level, the play is also the struggle of the *pergoleras* (flower vendors) to oppose the Major's plans to displace the flower marketplace from its central location on the city's main avenue as part of an urban modernization plan. Their strategy is to use Carmela's seduction of the aristocrat to influence the decision making of the powerful sectors.

Beyond its *costumbrismo* and humorous portrait, the play not only stages the *pergoleras'* will to unite but also deals with crucial problems of the time: the migration from rural areas into the urban centers in search of better living conditions; the class inequalities; and the frivolous and superfluous Francophile aristocracy. The play is also a comment on the project of modernization that characterized the cultural ethos of the 1950s and the strong opposition between an aristocracy devoid of its roots, not working for the real betterment of the nation, and a peasantry that appears as a symbol of the grounding traditional values, honesty, and hard-work ethics. The play critiques an unproductive oligarchy and its allies and reaffirms the middle and working class as agents for social change.

The play was a major challenge for Aguirre, as she had not mastered the genre of musical comedy, and the request came to her at a time in her life when she only wanted to devote herself to domesticity; but she wrote in response to the pressures and encouragement of the group and the director. For Chileans this play has become the most recognized of Aguirre's works, as the songs are seen as icons of Chilean identity and the work is seen as having the value of national patrimony. In a personal interview, Aguirre said *La pérgola de las flores* became her most valuable international passport and an extremely useful safeguard during the harsh years of Pinochet's military regime beginning in the 1970s, when she often escaped repression (and was able to help friends being prosecuted) because of the recognition of her name as the writer of the famous *Pérgola*. Nevertheless, the success and attention given to her became a source of jealousy for her husband, who had a difficult time feeling second to Aguirre's devotion to theater and ultimately ended the marriage.

The influence of Brecht on Aguirre's progressive search for an adequate and effective way to use theater as a tool for social awareness and change became evident in *Los papeleros* (1963, The Paper-Gatherers), her first epic drama. It was produced by the Sindicato de Actores (Actors' Union) under the direction of Guzmán and with the music of Becerra in the Teatro Carpa (Tent Theater) of Santiago, later that year by Fray Mocho in Buenos Aires, and by CLETA in Mexico, which took the play on an international tour to Panama and other Central American countries.

Los papeleros is a warm portrayal of the extremely poor presented within a clearly Brechtian form. Aguirre creates a narrator, Julio Galdamez, who opens the play with an explanation of its goal and logic and also intervenes at different moments to address the audience directly, connecting different scenes and episodes and explaining their significance. Julio tells the audience that the comedy is called *Los papeleros* and that it will tell viewers about the lives of the most marginalized urban poor sector–the people who collect paper in dumpsters: "¿Los conocen? Seguramente ustedes nos han visto en la calle, con el saco o con el carrito, recogiendo en los tachos" (Do you know them? You have probably seen us in the street, with the bag, or the cart, searching in garbage cans). He reveals that he lives in a garbage dump.

The introductory verses announce that the play is "la historia de la escoria del hombre y del hombre en la escoria" (the story of man's garbage and of man on garbage) and that theater is the voice of the voiceless: "el teatro con sus licencias nos la viene a relatar, en nombre del papelero que no la sabe contar" (theater with its freedom comes to tell us [the story] on behalf of the paper-gatherers who cannot do that). The introduction points at the same time to the conditions that determine this situation and the absurdity of the social law that dictates "que haya quienes mal vivan, para que otros vivan bien" (that there should be those who live badly, so others can live well).

The *papeleros* in the play work for a dumpster owner who takes a part of their minimal profits and, in turn, allows them to build their dwellings out of garbage materials right next to the garbage or on top of it. The play shows how these conditions of submission and exploitation are a consequence of the poor's lack of awareness, social consciousness, and faith in their ability to change the conditions of their own oppression. In contrast with *Población esperanza* and *La pérgola de las flores,* the conflict of interests between oppressor and oppressed in this play is more clearly and dramatically expressed, as the character of the Capo of the dumpster appears as an unscrupulous, abusive, and lazy man who profits from the work of people in the extreme pole of marginality and dispossession.

Tigre, the son of Romilia, one of the strong women in the dump, arrives in the city in search of his mother and a new life. By living in the countryside with his grandparents Tigre was spared the painful and undignified ways of urban marginality. When Tigre finds his mother in the dump, the encounter forces Romilia to recognize her situation and allows her to express her concerns and desires to keep Tigre away from degradation and oppression. Romilia hopes Tigre will get an education that will enable him to have a better life and avoid being contaminated by the dirtiness, hopelessness, and apathy of the *papelero*'s life. Romilia quickly realizes, however, that Tigre has already learned how to survive as a thief, and she becomes more determined to fight for her dignity and to keep him away from the situation as she struggles to obtain what her boss and the state have promised them: a piece of land away from the dump and construction materials to build decent housing.

Aguirre shows the different aspects of the daily lives of the *papeleros,* developing her characters with human desires, hopes, frustrations, and love. Alcoholism appears as one of the important factors in their degradation, as men gather to drink as a way of forgetting and to express their awareness of their inhuman conditions. They painfully talk of their hands blackened by their jobs, their legs injured from the extensive walking; the years of picking garbage have left indelible marks on their bodies and their psyches. As the *papeleros* sing "Escarbando" (Picking Through) they describe how "one feels a bit of a dog, by picking, and feel and think just like a dog." Their dialogue also reveals the violence and degradation of gender relations as they blame their problems on the lack of hope and energy to fight back as well as their own passivity and conformism. In the neighborhood where Julio searches the cans of a middle-class family, their maid calls him lazy, dirty, and flea-infected, thereby reflecting the distortion of the mentality of those "classless" sectors who ally with the dominant sector's ideology, functioning as mere extensions of an oppressive system.

There is a clear accent on Marianism as the lives of central females characters Mocha and Romilia are redeemed through their maternal instincts and their love for the weak, and for the other. Romilia and Mocha sacrifice themselves for the sake of their loved ones, their community, and their society. Romilia's motherly instinct drives her to fight back as she attempts (albeit unsuccessfully) to mobilize the *papeleros*. She handpicks a delegation of men and women to go to the Capo and request the fulfillment of his promise. Their encounter becomes a grotesque parody of the most evident forms of coercion and manipulation when the Capo, refusing to see them in person and addressing them through loudspeakers, accuses them of disloyalty as he reminds them of the little help he has given them. The *papeleros* never say a word and ultimately leave in silence and resignation.

As Romilia realizes that their passivity is grounded in their fear of losing the little they have, she sets fire to the dump to solve that problem. In the middle of the chaos, the loudspeakers carry the voice of the Capo, who calls them to return to work, while Rucio exhorts them to demand justice and the administrator attempts to arrest Romilia, labeling her mad. The play leaves the audience with an open ending as Julio calls for silence and introduces the last song, which points to the paralyzing multiple options offered to the *papeleros* and reaffirms the theater as a tool for presenting problems for the audience so they find the solutions.

Los papeleros diverged from the bourgeois escapism, psychological games, and introspection that mostly characterized the Chilean theater scene of the early 1960s. Instead, it directly confronted the reality of the dispossessed in an effective and renovated form, forcing the middle-class audience to reflect upon their role in the perpetuation of these conditions.

In 1964 Aguirre explored writing for children with the play *Anacleto avaro,* produced by the Compañía Nacional de Teatro under the direction of Mariano González; this play has been staged many times in Chile and also in Costa Rica and Germany. In 1965 she returned to comedy with *La dama del canasto* (The Lady of the Basket), with songs by Sergio Ortega, directed by Guzmán and presented in the Teatro Silvia Piñeiro. *Magy ante el espejo* (1968, Magy Before the Mirror) premiered in Mexico City under the direction of Juan José Gurrola.

Aguirre's meetings with important intellectual European figures are described in her journal and her interviews as important steps in her intellectual growth. She met André Breton and Eugène Ionesco during her residence in Paris and described Ionesco as a charming and low-key man who was also "Ionescan" in his own reactions. In Cuba she met Che Guevara when he was the head of the Ministry of Industry while she was accompanying future Nobel laureate Dario Fo. Her admiration for Guevara and the strong impression he made on her entered into her theatrical production as she used one of Guevara's phrases from his *Pasajes de la guerra revolucionaria* (1963, Episodes of the Revolutionary War) as the title and the central idea of a play: *Los que van quedando en el camino* (1969, Those Left at the Side of the Road).

At a dinner to celebrate the opening of *Los papeleros*, Aguirre asked Chilean Nobel poet Pablo Neruda for information about the peasants' conditions, and Neruda referred her to Chacón Corona, who was knowledgeable about Ranquil–the site of a peasant massacre in 1934–as he had participated in a strike in support of those peasants. This contact gave Aguirre access to many documents and the opportunity to meet with all of the survivors of the massacre, including Melina Sagredo, the key informant of the events that transpired in Ranquil. This research ultimately resulted in *Los que van quedando en el camino*.

The play was directed by Guzmán, with music by Luis Advis, and premiered in the Teatro de la Universidad de Chile; it was also published in Germany and both staged in theater and presented on radio in Germany, Holland, and Czechoslovakia, and in Mexico by the CLETA collective. The play was written explicitly as an homage to the victims of the Ranquil massacre and also had a key role within the political context of its creation: when it was written in 1969, the government by the Christian Democrat Eduardo Frei was approaching its end, and Salvador Allende was emerging as the Socialist candidate. The Unidad Popular political coalition found a way to capitalize on the shortcomings of Frei's reforms, particularly in the countryside, where he had initiated a long-awaited agrarian reform that had left peasants frustrated with the slow pace and limitations of the process.

The play draws a direct parallel between Frei's agrarian reform and the reforms promised by the government of the 1920s and 1930s. The attempt to establish reforms in the distribution of land caused a strong reaction from the affected oligarchy that ultimately translated into the massacre at Ranquil, a rural community where seventy peasants were executed, while many others suffered prosecution and incarceration. Political repression buried the memory of the event.

The prologue explicitly juxtaposes these two distinct but parallel realities. As the actors summarize the Ranquil story in short statements, a Chorus consistently replies: "Igual que hoy" (The same as today). The Chorus encourages the peasants and the audience to break out of the slavery imposed by the landowners and to defend their land and interests, but also tells how the peasants defended their rights and how the government suppressed the uprising with violence. The message is clearly stated: "las leyes que dicta la clase dominante no le sirven a la clase dominada" (the laws of the dominant class are not good for the dominated class). The revolt of the peasants entered the margins of illegality within the frame of a legal system that only favors those in power. Consequently, *Los que van quedando en el camino* establishes that improvement can only occur through a radical change of the system of privileges. The play criticizes the shortcomings of reformism–implicitly of Frei–and of the false illusion of affecting change without a total transformation of the bases of the socio-economic system.

In the play, Lorenza, a woman who survived the Ranquil massacre, remembers the struggle as she refuses to participate in a present-day march to Santiago organized by the new peasant movement; she is fearful of reliving the trauma she experienced when she lost her mother, daughter, husband (Rogelio), and three brothers. Lorenza relives the story as she narrates the events to Juanucho, her sister's grandchild. As Lorenza struggles to suppress her memories, her three brothers appear before her to ask her to remember the struggle as a good memory. Her dead loved ones convince Lorenza that the only way to honor their memory is for the fight to continue with renewed vigor.

Women once again play a critical role in the play and in the struggle. Lorenza is the vessel of historic memory as she transmits the legacy of struggle to the new generation personified in Juanucho. Aguirre directly asserts the need to put the collective above the individual as the only hope for change, through the sacrifice of Rogelio and Lorenza's love: "usted y yo estamos casados en esta pelea por la tierra y ni con l'acha nos separan" (you and I are married to this fight for the land and no axe will ever be able to separate us). In the end, the peasants are betrayed by the government, which allies with the landowners and ultimately carries out the massacre. The reflection upon this event serves as a catalyst for Lorenza's decision to join the new fight in lieu of "los que van quedando en el camino."

The epigraph of the play is from Guevara: "de los que no entendieron bien, de los que murieron sin ver la aurora, de sacrificios ciegos y no retribuídos, de los que van quedando en el camino, también se hizo la revolución" (of those who did not understand well, of those who died before seeing the dawn, of blind and unreturned sacrifices, of those left at the side of the road, is also made the revolution). This quotation emphasizes the central theme of the drama: the need to recognize the validity of the struggle of those who fell victim to the process.

This play, like so many of Aguirre's works, is written to be performed as street theater and requires a minimum of stage props. The changes in historical times and spaces are designated through a few lighting changes and by some colored panels that constitute the most important element of the staging. There are simple but evocative metaphoric transitions between the present to the past, as when Lorenza, in the present, grabs a handful of wheat that—as she drops it from her hand—metaphorically signifies the hope in their land and the fragility of it, marking the transition to young Lorenza as she prepares to fight for the land. The episodic structure and the use of music and a Chorus create the necessary distance from the audience, and in the end the Chorus calls for active participation from the audience.

During the 1960s Aguirre became actively involved in the political struggle of the Chilean Left and transformed her theater into an important political instrument. As *Los que van quedando en el camino* was instrumental in Allende's political campaign, after he was elected she devoted herself to popular theater, writing short didactic plays to be presented in shantytowns, streets, and parks in Santiago as well as in the regions. This effort was part of the cultural policy of the time of bringing "culture to the people."

In 1970 Aguirre wrote *Quién tuvo la culpa de la muerte de la María González* (Who Is Responsible for María González's Death) with a group from the Chilean-French Institute in Valparaíso. The premiere was directed by Luis Sepúlveda. More importantly, she worked with Cabezones de la Feria, a street-theater performance group devoted to creating educational theater related to current themes, following the style of the Bread and Puppet Theater. Produced by the TEPA group (Amateur Popular Experimental Theater), Cabezones de la Feria presented six scripts during 1972 in Santiago and other cities with Aguirre's texts and music by Alberto Senda.

The need to organize mass spectacles inspired a collaboration with director Víctor Jara and choreographer Patricio Bunster in the preparation of a celebratory event devoted to the history of the Communist Youth, staged in 1972. *Historia de las Juventudes Comunistas* was a massive event in the National Stadium that incorporated the participation of several theatrical groups as well as members of the Communist Youth from various social sectors. In 1974 Aguirre also produced two musical comedies, *La Desideria en el cielo* (Desideria in Heaven) and *En aquellos locos años 20* (In Those Crazy '20s), a play based on Armando Moock's *La señorita del Charleston* that premiered at the Theater of the University of Chile, Antofagasta. In 1976, continuing with the musical genre but in a more folkloric vein, she also wrote two new musical versions for her original *Las Pascualas* from 1957: *Las tres Pascualas* (The Three Pascualas) and *La leyenda de las tres Pascualas* (The Legend of the Three Pascualas).

During the period of the military dictatorship, which began in 1973 when Pinochet and his forces overthrew Allende and initiated mass arrests, tortures, and murders of liberal dissidents, Aguirre devoted herself to writing adaptations of world and Spanish classics such as Machiavelli's *Mandragora* (1518) in 1977, Molière's *Le Médecin malgré luy* (1667, The Doctor in Spite of Himself) in 1979, the anonymous Spanish novel *Lazarillo de Tormes* (1554) in 1980, and Lope de Vega's *Fuente Ovejuna* (1614) in 1978 and 1981. In 1982 a friend of the Painemal Family asked Aguirre to write a play to support the struggle of the Mapuche Indians during the military regime. The dictatorship had enacted a law passed during Allende's government that consequently forced Mapuches to pay for their own land. Aguirre's response was *Lautaro: Epopeya del pueblo mapuche* (1982, Lautaro: An Historical Epic of the Mapuche People). It was directed by Abel Carrizo, with songs by Chilean pop-folk group Los Jaivas, and it premiered in Santiago at the Sala Caja de Compensación Los Andes.

In her introduction, Aguirre expresses her desire to counteract the lack of historicity in the general portrayal of the Mapuche Indians as warriors and brave people who kept the Spaniards at bay from their land in the sixteenth century. Although the Mapuches were considered icons for the discourses of national identity, most modern Chileans were completely unaware of their current struggle to maintain their way of life, their language, their music, and their culture. Aguirre quotes the Mapuches' words "luchamos por conservar nuestra identidad, por integrarnos a la sociedad sin chilena sin ser absorbidos por ella" (we struggle to maintain our identity and to integrate into the Chilean society without being absorbed by it).

The desire to celebrate Mapuche culture and to humanize these historical icons led Aguirre to develop this play around two historical figures: the Spanish conquistador Pedro de Valdivia, who founded the city of Santiago; and Lautaro, a Mapuche Indian who, as a child, was captured to serve Valdivia as a personal aide and who was brought up by him as a disciple but who

Scene from Diálogos de fin de siglo *(Dialogues at the End of the Century), a collaboration between Aguirre and the Teatro Ictus group, which premiered at Teatro La Comedia in 1988 (from María Teresa Zegers Nachbauer,* 25 años de teatro en Chile, *1999; W. E. B. Du Bois Library, University of Massachusetts, Amherst)*

later took advantage of his hybrid status. Lautaro's knowledge of Spanish strategies helped his people confront the Spaniards more successfully and ultimately helped defeat Valdivia, whom he executed in 1554.

When writing the play, Aguirre based her characterization of Valdivia on a letter he sent to the king of Spain. For Lautaro, Aguirre chose an anthropological approach and spent months of observing and living with a Mapuche family, where she was received as "como una pariente, como una mapuche más" (one more relative, one more Mapuche). Aguirre used anthropology and history to construct both the character and the dramatic tension surrounding him while looking to select the most appropriate elements to illustrate the central conflict.

The choreography, songs, music, costumes, sound, and lighting were all products of teamwork in the staging of the play. The director selected some songs by Los Jaivas, whose lyrics fit perfectly into the themes of the play. Aguirre's explicit intention is to provide the audience with a sense of national patrimony so that they can recover and welcome "Los valores y la vitalidad de las dos razas que lo formaron" (The value and vitality of the races that formed them).

Lautaro once again examines the narratives of national identity that had served the official history so well since the colonial times. The Mapuche Indians inhabited the southern region and resisted the advances of the Spanish conquistadors from 1536 until 1655, when the Spanish decided to abandon the battle and established a territorial order that allowed Mapuche communities to live independently for the next two hundred years.

The play opens with a long poem that narrates the individual memory intertwined with the collective memory in a discourse that establishes the Mapuches' cosmogony in clear contrast with that of the Spanish invaders. The Mapuche world is an arcadia where men have been living in freedom and peace, stressing the connection between themselves and nature, and their collective use of land contrasts the notion of private property that guided the greedy behavior of the Spaniards. As the last verse of the prologue states, this war had a beginning but no end, pointing out the fact that the Mapuche people are still struggling for their rights to their land and their culture.

In the first part of the play, Valdivia takes Lautaro away to be his servant, and Guacolda, a Mapuche girl, is declared by the leader Curiñacu to be Lautaro's future wife. As Lautaro grows up alongside Valdivia, his attitude is always dignified and distant, thankful but independent. As Lautaro acquires many skills, Valdivia attempts to assure his loyalty by giving him a Christian name; but Lautaro refuses to accept the name or to eat with Valdivia, to avoid the obligations of his own culture: "The Mapuche must not turn against he who ate from the same plate." Valdivia tries to require Lautaro to see him as a father, but the Indian establishes a clear distance: "But my people's blood is in your hands."

Aguirre humanizes Valdivia by presenting his utopian vision of Chile to accent the contradictions in a more dialectical fashion. As Lautaro decides to take an active role in defending his people against the Spanish, he finds himself torn between two loyalties, feeling as if he were the son of two opposing fathers: Valdivia and Curiñacu, his real father. In the end, the dialogue with Curiñacu's ghost clarifies the terms of Lautaro's necessary parricide to protect his people. The final confrontation of Valdivia and Lautaro is narrated by two women, a Spaniard and a Mapuche. Later, a dying Valdivia confesses to his priest that he does not forgive Lautaro, but legitimizes his actions: "Why pardon if there was no fault. He obeys as I obeyed in this battle, he would be a traitor if he would have been among my troops." Lautaro's decision to expand the struggle gradually brings his destruction by the betrayal of the Picunche Indians who want to end the war. In dying, he asks his people to remember him and keep the struggle, and Guacolda makes a key statement that will have multiple layers of meaning for the audience: "No hay muerte si no hay olvido" (There is no death if there is no oblivion). The sudden transformation of the characters from the past into social subjects of the present carries a powerful message. The final song by Los Jaivas, "Indio hermano" (Brother Indian), once again reaffirms the notion of a pluralistic national identity in which the citizens are a family of brothers and sisters and the idea that the betrayals of the past are the seeds of the present.

Between 1983 and 1985 Aguirre adapted other classics to the Chilean stage: *Richard III* and two versions of *Oedipus Rex*. In 1985 she was requested by the group El Rostro in Concepción to write a play on behalf of "the disappeared"–those who opposed the Pinochet regime and subsequently vanished–that resulted in *Retablo de Yumbel,* the first of Aguirre's plays to be published in the United States (as part of a 1997 critical anthology on Latin American women writers, edited by Teresa Cajiao Salas and Margarita Vargas). At the beginning, the research of the documents and the testimonies gathered by Aguirre was so painful that it took her months before she was able to write. In 1985 the news that three Communist Party members had been murdered compelled her to begin her task. She dedicated the play to them, particularly to social worker José Manuel Parada. While writing the play, Aguirre heard Parada's mother reciting a poem Parada had written in memory of his father–one of the disappeared–and she made it part of the monologue of one of the mothers. *Retablo de Yumbel* was premiered by El Rostro in 1986 and later staged in Montreal, Sweden, and California.

Retablo de Yumbel was based on the case of nineteen peasant leaders who were executed in Yumbel on 14 September 1973 as they were being transported from one detention camp to another. Their remains were found in a clandestine burial site in 1979, but although the trial determined the names of the victimizers, they were freed by the amnesty law provided by the military regime to protect the armed police forces from responsibility for their repressive tactics and violations of human rights. The play begins at the plaza of Yumbel in the midst of the preparations for the celebration of San Sebastian de Yumbel, patron of the town. In honor of this occasion, a theater troupe is rehearsing a play that deals with the prosecution of the saint during the rule of the Roman emperor Diocleciano (Diocletian). In this manner, Aguirre situates the scenes of tyranny, torture, and violence in the times of the prosecution of Christians by the Roman Empire while establishing a clear parallel with the repressive and abusive conditions of the military regime of Pinochet.

This play is consistent with Aguirre's treatment of historical events in which she highlights the need to learn from the sacrifices of the past and to incorporate that knowledge into an active role toward the present. Likewise, the plays are always performed within a Brechtian aesthetics that leaves the audiences with a question or problem to be solved rather than with clear recipes for actions. The recurrent idea is the need to recognize the dead, mourn them, and keep them alive by dignifying their memory through a continuation of their struggle.

Aguirre clearly establishes the time of the action of the play, January 1980, not long after the bodies were discovered. The dramatization of an historical event within the repressive context of the military dictatorship is what allows Arturo Flores to call *Retablo de Yumbel* a piece of testimonial theater because "lleva en forma artística una verdad a un público dominado por el miedo" (it brings in an artistic form a truth to a people dominated by fear).

The parallel between the atrocities of Emperor Diocleciano and Pinochet allows San Sebastian's martyrdom to be equated with that of the disappeared peasants of Yumbel. In the context of the dictatorship, whose discourse labeled the victims as terrorists, and a society paralyzed by fear, this equation gives the victims an extraordinary value. Fear is then circumvented by the strong use of folkloric tradition and of popular religiosity, a clever dramatic strategy to circumvent fear and to transform the massacre into martyrdom. This testimonial value won *Retablo de Yumbel* the prestigious Casa de las Américas Prize.

In 1988 Aguirre wrote another comedy, *Tía Irene yo te amaba* (Aunt Irene, I Loved You), which premiered at the Teatro del Angel in Santiago with the music of P. Solovera and under the direction of Claudio Pueller. That same year she collaborated with Teatro Ictus in a collective creation based on her drama *Diálogos de fin de siglo* (Dialogues at the End of the Century), which premiered at the Teatro La Comedia.

In 1991 Aguirre embarked on yet another collaboration, this time with the Teatro Ojo group, which resulted in *Naira Yawiña (Manantial Secreto)* (Naira Yawiña [Secret Waterfall]), performed at the Museo de Arte Precolombino in Santiago. Six years later, in 1997, her play *Mi primo Federico* (My Cousin Federico) was produced in the Sala Nuval in Madrid directed by José Ramón Pérez and in Valencia in 1998.

Within the context of the redemocratization process that began after Pinochet's regime ended in 1990, Aguirre returned to a theater devoted to historical revisionism, focusing on key figures of the colonial period and the independence movement in Chile and Latin America. At issue in these works are the foundational bases of the contemporary economic and power structures.

Her first play of this type is *Manuel Rodríguez* (1999), a popular epic with music by Manuel López, produced by Carlos Cardoen's foundation and performed in Santa Cruz and Santiago by the Teatro Círculo, directed by Ana María Vallejo. Aguirre uses the story of the revolutionary icon Manuel Rodríguez to explore the bases of the independence process. The play can be read, at many different levels, as a retelling of the story of Rodríguez from a more intimate perspective, making the hero a more human person and putting into question the form in which history has narrated his involvement in the independence process. In the official history, Rodríguez is portrayed as a legendary figure characterized by his relentless rebelliousness and ingenuity, with picaresque overtones of humor and a seductive nature as he used many tricks in order to circumvent the colonial authorities and support the independence movement and the resistance during the period of the Chilean Reconquista (reconquest). Many songs and poems have been written about Rodríguez that elaborate on this icon of freedom and rebellion who was ultimately betrayed by Bernardo O'Higgins, the first governor of the independent Chile, and killed on 28 May 1818 as he allegedly tried to escape while being transported to a southern prison.

The play is written in a Brechtian episodic form and structured in two parts: the first narrates the independence, resistance, and Rodríguez's collaboration with the process. The second part tells about the aftermath of independence, O'Higgins's ascension to power, and Rodríguez's gradual alienation from the power sphere. O'Higgins characterizes Rodríguez as a threat to the consolidation of independence and the political and economic stability required to establish the new nation. Aguirre shows in a Brechtian fashion the world of possibilities that were at hand at the foundation of the country. The first part includes eighteen episodic scenes and the second part thirteen, and the play uses slide projectors, live music, and a minimal number of stage props, allowing for the staging of the play in a variety of spaces and without needing a wealth of resources. The stage is a simple ramp that allows different levels and scenic elements such as trunks, tables, and stools that can also become platforms.

The initial scene establishes the historical facts, the complexities of which are unveiled throughout the play. A lieutenant, uncomfortable with the role O'Higgins has assigned him, chides Rodríguez for not having escaped given the opportunities he has afforded him. As the lieutenant utters the question that will guide the rest of the play–"¿Sabe al menos por qué quieren su muerte?" (Do you know why they want your death?)– he decides to accomplish his mandate and kills Rodríguez, triggering the reflective gaze into the historical past that follows. The next scene, of exiles in Mendoza, goes back to 1816 and becomes the beginning of the historical revisionism. Rodríguez seems to live in the present from the perspective of what has already occurred: "Estaba dormido y soñaba con mi muerte. (Sonríe) O quizás esté muerto y sueñe que vivo! (Pausa) Me ajusticiaba un oficial de nuestro ejército" (I was asleep and dreaming my death. [He smiles] Or perhaps I'm dead and dreaming that I'm alive! [Pause] An officer of our own army was executing me). In chronological order, the play revisits the events that could explain Rodríguez's death, beginning with the encounter between military leader José de San Martín and Rodríguez in Argentina during the period of the Reconquista as he prepares for the organization of the liberation army that will consolidate independence. The cruelty of the captain of the royal forces, General San Bruno, and the incompetence of the new Spanish governor, Marco del Pont, have undermined the image of the Spanish crown, making this moment the perfect time to initiate the resistance.

Aguirre uses comedic elements to ridicule and parody the Spanish rule in the grotesque figure of an inefficient and effeminate Marco and in the exaggerated cruelty of San Bruno. In his language, Marco seems to jump from colonial to modern times as he frequently expresses his frustration by using the contemporary exclamation "Hostias!" Aguirre uses Marco to comment on the theatricality inherent in power as he requests San Bruno to accompany him to visit an orphanage in order to save his deteriorated image and proposes to give the Creoles more ceremonies and nobility titles to appease them for another hundred years.

Aguirre shows how Rodríguez, undeniably a key military factor in the defeat of the Spanish regime, was considered a clear threat to O'Higgins. His persecution is driven by the multiple rivalries and different interests of the protagonists of the revolutionary process and of those who begin consolidating the process from their own bureaucratic, authoritarian positions. The strategic betrayal of Rodríguez is presented through an epistolary dialogue between O'Higgins and San Martín that shows the latter finally accepting the terms of Rodríguez's elimination and consolidating the idea of treason as an historical necessity.

Rodríguez's arrest is announced just as he finally finds the answer to his initial question: "no importa saber 'por qué mueres' lo que importa es saber . . . (Alegre por descubrirlo) ¡Para qué vives!" (It doesn't matter to know why you die, what's important is to know . . . [Joyful in the discovery] What you live for!). With his image fading in the background, he joins the Chorus to reaffirm his eternal presence: "aunque mil veces te maten tu huella queda encendida . . . tu luz ya nunca se apaga" (even if you get killed a thousand times your trace is illuminated . . . your light will never die) with the collective voice of the people.

Los libertadores: Bolívar y Miranda was not staged but was published in 1993 and takes place in 1830, the year of Simón Bolívar's death. Bolívar and his assistant José are the only real characters of the play. Bolívar, in his bedroom, ill and exhausted, encounters in his delirious imagination the various figures who influenced him: Manuela Saenz; his mentor, Simón Rodríguez; the black woman who raised him, Hipólita; his priest, Andujar; his mentor, Francisco de Miranda; and himself as a young man. José is, in Bolívar's eyes, Miranda, and he goes from one character to another, portraying the different figures as they are unveiled in Bolívar's dreams. The stage is divided into several areas marked by simple elements: the park, a prison, his bedroom, and a platform of memories from which a rope-ladder hangs. Throughout the play, Bolívar's encounters with people from his past serve as a forum to narrate important aspects of his life.

The play ends with Bolívar, in his bed, recounting the utopia established in his *Carta de Jamaica* (1815, Letter from Jamaica) as the original moment at which everything was open to realization, when "la historia de América era una página en blanco" (the history of America was like a blank page waiting to be written). Bolívar recites key sentences of his *Carta de Jamaica* in past tense, as a young Simón repeats them in present tense. As Bolívar appears to be correcting the naive optimism of young Simón, the statements of the latter appear as a correction of Bolívar's pessimism, as if reaffirming the utopia of a unified America.

Aguirre's theater has been recognized for its dedication to two major issues: exposing the conditions of the Chilean poor and their marginal sectors, and searching Latin American and Chilean history for the roots of inequality established since the colonial times. Her theater, drawing on Brecht but also on Chilean popular culture, has become a tool for struggle, awareness, and a call for action and social change that is deeply rooted in a profound understanding of the foundational elements of the Chilean and Latin American cultural and economic structures.

Aguirre lives in Santiago, where she contributes to the raising of her grandchildren and continues working on her writing, conducting workshops, and giving lectures at colleges and universities not only in Chile but throughout Latin America and the United States. She was invited to the Women Playwrights Encounter "A Stage of One's Own" at the University of Cincinnati, Ohio, in 1994, and California State University, Hayward, invited her to the American premiere of *Altarpiece of Yumbel* in 1999. She would like her plays to be staged more in Chile, particularly her later historical plays that do not seem to attract the interests of the younger and more postmodern generation of theater artists in Chile. For her, there is a clear need to pass on the legacy of her theater of social criticism in order to maintain the hope for social justice, particularly in the neoliberal, globalized era of the twenty-first century.

Interviews:

Patricia Corona, "Juego con los tiempos, con los vivos y los muertos," *El Sábado de El Mercurio* (January 1999–2000);

Loreto Daza, "Detrás del escenario," *Qué Pasa* <www.quepasa.cl/revista/1506/31.html>;

Eduardo Guerrero del Río, "Isidora Aguirre," in his *Acto único: Dramaturgos en escena* (Santiago: RiL Editores, 2001), pp. 7–18;

María de la Luz Hurtado, "El teatro como tribuna: Isidora Aguirre, Dramaturga," *Revista Apuntes* (2001): 32–40.

References:

Miriam Balboa Echeverría, "Historia y representación en Chile: La voz de Isidora Aguirre," in *Actas del X Congreso de la Asociación de Hispanistas,* edited by Antonio Vilanova, Josep María Bricall, and Elías L. Rivers (Barcelona: Promociones y Publicaciones Universitarias, 1992);

Balboa Echeverría, "Memoria histórica y deseo: Espacio virtual del teatro de Asunción Requena e Isidora Aguirre," *Revista de Estudios Hispánicos* (Río Piedras, Puerto Rico), 20 (1993): 323–326;

Judith Ishmael Bissett, "Delivering the Message: Gestus and Aguirre's *Los papeleros,*" *Latin American Theatre Review,* 17 (Spring 1984): 31–37;

Inés Dölz Blackburn, "La historia en dos obras de teatro chileno contemporáneo," *Confluencia: Revista Hispánica de Cultura y Literatura,* 6 (Spring 1991): 17–24;

Irma Césped, *Teatro chileno contemporáneo: Luis Alberto Heiremans, Isidora Aguirre* (Santiago: Santillana, 1998);

"Chilean Theater 1973–1993: The Playwrights Speak," *Review: Latin American Literatures and Arts,* 49 (Fall 1994): 84–89;

Arturo Flores, "Teatro testimonial: Retablo de Yumbel de Isidora Aguirre," *Hispanic Journal,* 12 (Spring 1991): 123–132;

Patricia González, "Isidora Aguirre y la reconstrucción de la historia en *Lautaro*," *Latin American Theatre Review,* 19, no. 1 (1985): 13–18;

Willy Muñoz, "Isidora Aguirre: La historia incógnita en *Doy por vivido todo lo soñado*," *RLA: Romance Languages Annual,* 8 (1996): 603–607;

Claudia Navarro, *Dramaturgia y género en el Chile de los sesenta* (Santiago: Dirección de Bibliotecas, Archivos y Museos, 2001);

Enrique Sandoval, "Teatro latinoamericano: Cuatro dramaturgas y una escenógrafa," *Literatura Chilena: Creación y Crítica,* 13 (1989): 171–187;

Eduardo Thomas, "Metáforas de la identidad en el teatro hispanoamericano contemporáneo," *Revista Chilena de Literatura,* 50 (April 1997): 39–50;

Adam Versényi, "Social Critique and Theatrical Power in the Plays of Isidora Aguirre," in *Latin American Women Dramatists: Theater, Texts and Theories,* edited by Catherine Larson and Margarita Vargas (Bloomington: Indiana University Press, 1998), pp. 159–177;

María Teresa Zegers Nachbauer, *25 años de teatro en Chile* (Santiago: Ministerio de Educación, 1999).

Hugo Argüelles
(2 January 1932 – 24 December 2003)

Fabiola Fernández Salek
Chicago State University

SELECTED PLAY PRODUCTIONS: *Los cuervos están de luto,* Mexico, Teatro Jorge Negrete, 22 April 1960;

Los prodigiosos, Mexico, Teatro del Músico, 22 March 1961;

El tejedor de milagros, Mexico, Teatro Celestino Gorostiza, 22 May 1963;

La galería del silencio o las fantasías del mono doméstico, Mexico, Teatro El Granero, 28 March 1967;

La ronda de la hechizada, Mexico, Teatro Xola, 9 November 1967;

Medea y las visitantes del sueño, Havana, Teatro Federico García Lorca, 2 January 1968;

La dama de la luna roja, Mexico, Teatro Xola, 18 June 1969;

El gran inquisidor, Templo de Tepozotlán, 5 October 1973;

Valerio Rostro, traficante en sombras, Mexico, 18 April 1978;

El ritual de la salamandra, Mexico City, Teatro Arcos Caracol, 18 October 1981;

El cocodrilo solitario del panteón rococó, Mexico, Teatro Jiménez Rueda, 17 January 1982;

El retablo del gran relajo, Jalapa, Teatro Universidad Veracruzana, 15 February 1982;

Concierto para guillotina y cuarenta cabezas, Mexico, 23 March 1982;

Los amores criminales de las vampiras Morales, Mexico, Teatro El Granero, 3 May 1983;

Los gallos salvajes, Mexico City, Wilberto Cantón, 22 April 1986;

Los caracoles amorosos, Mexico, Teatro Benito Juaréz, 10 August 1988;

Doña Macabra, Mexico, Teatro Hidalgo, 1989;

Escarabajos, Mexico City, Foro de la Conchita, 10 October 1991;

La boda negra de las alacranas, Guanajuato, Teatro Juárez, 1992;

Águila real, Mexico City, Teatro Diego Rivera, 15 August 1992;

La noche de las aves cabalísticas, Mexico, Teatro del Centro Deportivo Israelita, 25 November 1993;

El cerco de la cabra dorada, Mexico City, Foro Sor Juana Inés de la Cruz UNAM, 26 May 1994;

La tarántula art nouveau de la calle de El Oro, Coyoacán, Teatro de Coyoacán, 29 September 1994;

El vals de los buitres, Mexico City, Teatro El Granero, 27 March 1996.

BOOKS: *Los prodigiosos: Pieza en tres actos, prólogo y epílogo (el segundo acto dividido en dos cuadros)* (Mexico City: Edición "Estaciones," 1957);

Teatro de Hugo Argüelles (Mexico City: Oasis, 1961)—comprises *Los prodigiosos, Los cuervos están de luto,* and *El tejedor de milagros;*

Teatro de Hugo Argüelles (Coyoacán: Federación Editorial Mexicana, 1971)—comprises *Concierto para guillotina y cuarenta cabezas, Alfa del alba,* and *Valerio Rostro, traficante en sombras;*

Los cuervos están de luto y El tejedor de milagros (Mexico City: Novaro, 1973);

La primavera de los escorpiones (Mexico City: Novaro, 1973);

Teatro de Hugo Argüelles (Mexico City: Katún, 1983);

Los cuervos están de luto; La ronda de la hechizada; El ritual de la salamandra (Mexico City: Editores Mexicanos Unidos, 1985);

Los gallos salvajes; Los amores criminales de las vampiras Morales (Mexico City: Editores Mexicanos Unidos, 1986);

La tarántula art noveau de la calle de oro y El cerco de la cabra dorada (Mexico City: Universidad Autónoma Metropolitana/Unidad Iztapalapa, 1991);

Los huesos del amor y de la muerte (Mexico City: UNAM, 1991);

El cocodrilo solitario del panteón rococó; Los caracoles amorosos (Mexico City: Universidad Autónoma Metropolitana/Unidad Iztapalapa, 1991);

Escarabajos (Guadalajara: Agata, 1992);

La boda negra de las alacranas: Farsa mágica en un acto (Guanajuato: Sección Editorial de Difusión Cultural, Universidad de Guanajuato, 1992);

Las pirañas aman en cuaresma (Guadalajara: Agata, 1993);

Hugo Argüelles in front of the theater in the Coyocán district of Mexico City that was renamed in his honor in 1995 (from Juan Meyer, La travesía mágica de Hugo Argüelles, *1997; Howard-Tilton Memorial Library, Tulane University)*

Nuestra señora del hueso (Calaca); El ritual de la salamandra; Los gallos salvajes (Mexico City: Gaceta, 1994);

Los amores criminales de las vampiras Morales; Águila real; El cerco de la cabra dorada (Mexico City: Gaceta, 1994);

La noche de las aves cabalísticas: Pieza mágica en dos actos (Mexico City: Centro Deportivo Israelita, 1994).

Editions and Collections: *Teatro de Hugo Argüelles: Antología de comedias, farsas y tragicomedias,* 2 volumes (Veracruz: Gobierno del Estado de Veracruz, 1992);

Trilogía colonial (Mexico City: Plaza y Valdés, 1992)–comprises *Aguila real, La ronda de la hechizada,* and *La dama de la luna roja;*

Las protagonistas veracruzanas, 2 volumes (Veracruz: Gobierno del Estado de Veracruz, 1994);

Obras, 10 volumes (Mexico City: Gaceta, 1994);

Trilogía mestiza (Mexico City: Plaza y Valdés, 1994)–comprises *El cocodrilo solitario del panteón rococó, Los caracoles amorosos,* and *Los gallos salvajes;*

Trilogía musical (Toluca: Universidad Autónoma del Estado de México / Mexico City: Gaceta, 1994)–comprises *Nuestra señora del hueso, El retablo del gran relajo,* and *Las hienas se mueren de risa;*

Trilogía rural (Mexico City: Plaza y Valdés, 1994)–comprises *Los prodigiosos, Los cuervos están de luto,* and *El tejedor de milagros;*

Trilogía de los ritos (Mexico City: Plaza y Valdés, 1997)–comprises *La galería del silencio, El ritual de la salamandra,* and *Escarabajos.*

PRODUCED SCRIPTS: *Las momias de Guanajuato,* by Argüelles and others, television, 1962;

Doña Macabra, television, 1963;

Leyendas de México, by Argüelles and others, television, 1968;

La amante perfecta, motion picture, Interfilms, 1970;

Las cadenas del mal, motion picture, Interfilms, 1970;

Las figuras de arena, by Argüelles and Roberto Gavaldón, motion picture, Cinematográfica Filmex, 1970;

Elena y Raquel, motion picture, Cima Films, 1971;

La primavera de los escorpiones, by Argüelles and Francisco del Villar, motion picture, Del Villar Films, 1971;

Una mujer honesta, by Argüelles and Rafael García Travesi, motion picture, Productora Cinematográfica Trío, 1972;

Hoy he soñado con Dios, motion picture, Cima Films, 1972;

Doña Macabra, by Argüelles and Gavaldón, motion picture, Estudios Churubusco Azteca SA, 1972;
Los perturbados, motion picture, Interfilms, 1972;
Los ángeles de la tarde, motion picture, Interfilms, 1972;
Los amantes fríos, motion picture, Conacite Uno, 1978;
Albur de amor, by Argüelles and Antonio Aguilar, motion picture, Producciones Talileo, 1980;
Nezahualcóyotl, television, 1985;
Los amores criminales de las vampiras Morales, television, XE IPN TV (Canal 11), 1986.

Hugo Argüelles is well known for having brought black humor into Mexican theater. The circumstances he depicts are often tragic, and people are usually portrayed as taking advantage of others in the most selfish sense; yet, he presents the situations in such a way that audiences cannot help but laugh. Animals (and humans who display animalistic behavior) are ubiquitous in Argüelles' plays; there are mourning crows, loving piranhas, laughing hyenas, and dancing vultures. Two fixations in his theater are his oppositions to social conventions and to clerical and political power, which he ferociously chronicled until his death in 2003.

Hugo Argüelles Cano was born on 2 January 1932 in Veracruz, Mexico, the son of Avelino Argüelles, a Spanish peasant who came to Mexico to participate with Emiliano Zapata in the Mexican Revolution, and Virginia Cano, a middle-class Mexican woman and an avid theater lover. At Argüelles's birth the nurse dropped him to the floor, and he suffered a head injury. Though this injury had no lasting physical effects, from then on his mother paid special attention to him, though his father was distant. Argüelles had two younger brothers, Gilberto and Guillermo. Although his parents separated while he was still a child, leading to financial strain for the family, Argüelles stayed with his mother, to whom he was close. As a child he loved to read and write, and by age eleven he was writing and illustrating comics that he later developed into small plays. During his frequent visits to the library and the record store he met the great Chilean poet Gabriela Mistral, who crucially influenced his interest in literature. Together with three other children he created "Fígaro," a puppet theater, for which he adapted fairy tales from Hans Christian Andersen and the Brothers Grimm and even wrote some original plays. The shows lasted for two years and were a neighborhood success, with presentations that sometimes attracted more than two hundred children.

Argüelles was a good student at the Secundaria Colón, a private school he attended. However, he orchestrated his own expulsion in order to attend a public high school with his closest friends. He started studying medicine at the Universidad Nacional Autónoma de México (UNAM) but quit after five years to follow his true vocation: theater. In 1956 he entered the School of Dramatic Art of the Instituto Nacional de Bellas Artes (INBA), where he remained for three years and was taught by two important Mexican writers, Emilio Carballido and Josefina Hernández. Argüelles never married or had children; he was openly gay, though his personal relationships remained private.

In 1957 Argüelles's play *Velorio en turno* (The Wake in Shifts) was awarded the first prize for one-act plays in the INBA. Later he extended it to a three-act play, retitling it *Los cuervos están de luto* (The Crows are Mourning), which later also formed part of his "Rural Trilogy." It won the Premio Nacional de Teatro (National Theater Prize) in 1958 and the Premio de Bellas Artes (Fine Arts Award) from the Consejo Nacional para la Cultura y las Artes (National Council for Culture and Arts) in 1960, and in 1964 the movie adaptation obtained the Periodistas Cinematográficos de México (Cinematagraphical Mexican Press or PECIME) Award.

In *Los cuervos están de luto* patriarch Don Lacho is dying, and in order to bury him quickly when he dies, the family decides to mourn him alive. While being mourned, the dying man confesses that one of his sons is the product of an affair that his wife had, and consequently will have no right to inherit any money. He prefers, however, to leave the son's identity unknown. His daughters-in-law are eager to know whether the youngest son, Enrique, is the bastard. Yet, Enrique is the only noble character in the play. He organizes his father's funeral and is the only one whose motive goes beyond money. In this play Argüelles clearly denounces a world organized around economic gain. The rest of the family sacrifices the youngest son only to increase the size of the inheritance. Argüelles uses the comparison with the crow to show the selfishness of the alleged family.

Los prodigiosos (1957, The Prodigious) was presented for the first time in 1961 and won the Juan Ruiz de Alarcón Prize from the Critics Association. This play, which forms part of the Rural Trilogy, is set in a small town and presents the duel between Consuelo, a psychic, and Santón, a charlatan preacher. Both take advantage of the ignorance of the people and of their human need to believe in something. They are apparently trying to solve a mystery, in which a *nahual* (Mayan animal soul) is raping the women of the town. Santón forces an alliance with Consuelo, but she discovers that he is the *nahual,* and she and her servants plan to trap him. The servants, representing future hope, reveal the truth to the townspeople. The authorities apprehend Santón, but Consuelo is robbed and

Carlos Camara in Argüelles's 1981 play, El ritual de la salamandra *(The Ritual of the Salamander), about a family whose wishes are granted by means of a urinal once used by the Pope (from Edgar Ceballos, ed.,* Hugo Argüelles: Estilo y dramaturgia, *1994; John C. Hodges Library, University of Tennessee)*

killed by a mute named Tacho. In the end, nothing changes. Although the townspeople now know the truth, they continue to visit Santón's sanctuary, demonstrating their ignorance. The play ends with one of the servants screaming to the townspeople and the audiences, "¡Despierten idiotas! ¡Despierten! ¿Hasta cuándo?" (Wake up idiots! Wake up! Until when?).

El tejedor de milagros (The Miracle Weaver, performed in 1963, published in 1961) was adapted for the movies by Carballido and Julio Alejandro in 1962 and earned the PECIME Award. In this play Teófilo and his lover, Remedios, exploit a peasant couple. The peasant woman is about to give birth on Christmas Eve, and powerful people in the town lead the rest of the citizens to believe that this birth is a religious miracle that they have been awaiting. When the "miraculous" child is born, the eager crowd kills him. Juan Meyer reports in *La travesía mágica de Hugo Argüelles: Cuarenta años de dramaturgo* (1997, Hugo Argüelles' Magical Journey: Forty Years as a Dramaturge) that at the Berlin International Film Festival in 1962, Ingmar Bergman told Argüelles, "Es un magnífico filme, pero sobre todo es una espléndida historia. A mí me hubiera gustado dirigirla" (It is a magnificent film, but especially a splendid story. I would have liked to direct it).

The following year Argüelles founded the School of Fine Arts in Puebla. *Doña Macabra* (1963, Madame Macabre), written as a television script, won several awards the same year. In 1972 Argüelles wrote a movie adaptation of it with Roberto Gavaldón, and in 1986 he wrote a stage version that debuted three years later. From 1967 to 1973 Argüelles taught in the School of Dramatic Art at INBA, where he previously studied, and also at the Centro Universitario de Teatro from 1970 until 1973.

In 1967 *La ronda de la hechizada* (The Serenade of the Bewitched) was selected to inaugurate the Cultural Olympics in Mexico City. This play, which forms part of Argüelles's "Colonial Trilogy," has as its protagonist Dominga Parián, a Spanish actress who comes to Mexico in the middle of the sixteenth century to evangelize the Indians. She is in search of herself and fleeing from the rigid rules imposed in Europe by the church. Dominga exemplifies the role that artists play in revealing the truth. In Mexico she confronts Fray Lupercio de Cáncer, who represents the evil, intolerance, and corruption of the Inquisition. At the same time she meets Tecatzin, who becomes her mentor and teaches her about the native oral literature that she promises to propagate. After Cáncer burns Tecatzin, the latter reincarnates and continues encouraging Dominga to sing the indigenous songs and poetry. The inquisitor accuses her of idolatrousness for proclaiming that they do not differ from the Spanish versions. The king sends a letter assuring that Dominga's statements are harmless, and she remains in Mexico repeating the traditional oral literature. She becomes a synthesis of Spanish and Mexican culture. In the 1992 edition of *Trilogía colonial* (Colonial Trilogy) Argüelles stated his point that through hybridization the principles of a new identity are created.

Throughout the 1970s Argüelles occupied several important administrative jobs. In 1975 he was the vice president of the Taller de Escritores Cinematográficos (Cinematography Writers Workshop) and a cultural advisor in the theater programs "Teatro en México" (Theater in Mexico) and "Teatro de las Américas" (Theater of the Americas). From 1976 to 1978 he was secretary of the interior at the Sindicato de Cinematografistas (Cinematographers Union). In 1979 he was elected president of the award committee of the Academia de Ciencias Cinematográficas (Academy of Cinematography Sciences). That same year he was an invited author at the Congress of Latin American Theater in New York. He was also in charge of the theater seminars at the Tecnológico de Monterrey in Monterrey and Mexico City. Additionally, Argüelles mentored students who attended his creative-writing workshops, some of whom became prominent figures in Mexican theater such as Sabina Berman, Jesús González Dávila, Gerardo Luna, Víctor Hugo Rascón Banda, Luis Eduardo Reyes, and Tomás Urtusástegui.

In 1980 the INBA invited Argüelles to write a play for the Compañía Nacional de Teatro (National Theater Company). The result was *El cocodrilo solitario del panteón rococó* (The Solitary Crocodile of the Rococo Cemetery), which debuted in 1982. The main character of this play is Librado Técpan, a frustrated musician who works as the doorkeeper of a cemetery. He has a crocodile instead of a watch dog, and the creature comes to represent his alter ego. Librado lives with three women and wants to remain childless. His biggest failure in life was not being able to succeed as a cellist. He hides this frustration from people in the small town, proclaiming that his true vocation is to teach music to kids. Librado believes he and the crocodile share a similar fate: the crocodile is also a failure, since instead of working in the circus, he works in the cemetery as a guard dog. Librado's most meaningful relationship is the one he has with the crocodile; he sustains long monologues and reflections with the animal. In this play the macho behavior of the protagonist is nothing more than a sad facade to hide his dependency on his mother as well as his failure in life.

In 1981 the Unión de Cronistas y Críticos de Teatro (Union of Theater Chroniclers and Critics) gave Argüelles the Sor Juana Inés de la Cruz Award for best play of the year. The winning play was *El ritual de la salamandra* (The Ritual of the Salamander). The play presents an upper-middle-class family whose wishes are granted by means of a urinal that was probably used by the Pope when he visited Mexico. The urinal apparently has two unusual functions: to grant wishes when rubbed and to reveal true human instincts. In reality it unleashes bestial behavior and the incestuous desires of father and daughter as well as mother and son. The Oedipus and Electra complexes are freely expressed, and the situation becomes almost animalistic in nature. However, the father continues hypocritically denying the situation, justifying his actions through the alleged sacredness of the urinal and the guidance of God. Mother and son are unable to consummate a physical relationship because the son is a closet homosexual.

In the end the father is promoted to a higher position, and the mother, a free spirit, decides to live a nonconventional life. The title refers to the mother's statement: "La salamandra, dice esa leyenda, vive adormilada casi toda su vida, incluso así tiene su cría . . . pero ya cercano su climaterio comienza a apetecer el fuego. Despierta con esa avidez, lo busca y entonces ya sólo vive próxima a él . . . como en una especie de delirio sexual" (The salamander, says the legend, lives asleep almost all her life, she even has her litter in the same state . . . but near her climacteric she starts to long for fire. She wakes up avidly, and searches for it, and then she only lives near it . . . as in a kind of sexual delirium). As she proclaims that she is going in search of men, the father kills her and asks the daughter to take the blame, since he has enough influence to quickly mitigate the consequences of the crime. The father justifies his actions in front of his children by saying that the mother was behaving indecently. In the play false family values prevail in order to maintain social appearances, and the truth is completely put aside. The urinal represents the power of the institutions, civil and religious, that corrupt the individual. The message is that there is no salvation for the middle class, that hypocrisy and social climbing have eroded the whole system.

In 1981 Argüelles taught at Foro Eón and also at the Instituto Mexicano del Seguro Social (Mexican Social Security Institute) or IMSS. That same year the Universidad Veracruzana commissioned him to write a play for the university theater company. The result was *El retablo del gran relajo* (The Altar Piece of the Great Immorality), which premiered the next year. Through this farce Argüelles denounced government corruption and the abuse of power. The satire threatened the polit-

Angel Casarín in the Teatro Jiménez Rueda premiere of Argüelles's 1982 play El cocodrilo solitario del panteón rococó
*(The Solitary Crocodile of the Rococo Cemetery), in which a failed musician talks to a crocodile that he considers an alter ego
(from Edgar Ceballos, ed.,* Hugo Argüelles: Estilo y dramaturgia, *1994;
John C. Hodges Library, University of Tennessee)*

ical establishment, and consequently this theater production was shut down by the university authorities after opening night.

Billed as a two-act musical farce allegory, *El retablo del gran relajo* is quite provocative, with a complicated plot. Emulating the popular theater revue, it is full of songs and music. One of the main characters, Erasmo, wants to be elected city mayor. He is married to Maruca Machuca, who is believed to be crazy. Sidonio is Erasmo's right-hand man and at the same time is conspiring against him with Erasmo's "official lover," Acacia. Erasmo's spiritual adviser suggests buying Napoleon Bonaparte's penis (which is being offered by a seller of physical curiosities and relics) as a means of obtaining power, although he also warns against the abuse of power. Erasmo travels to Europe and meets the seller, and they return together to Mexico for business. Erasmo kills Acacia and some peasants when he finds out that she stole the penis for Sidonio. Later, Maruca witnesses the roasting and eating of Erasmo, now transformed into a drag queen, perpetuated by Sidonio and other conspirators. Sidonio has been blackmailing the curiosities seller (in order to obtain the real penis) by holding his curiosities at customs. There is an accident, and the curiosities are dispersed; the people end up eating the famous organs and body parts. One of the advisors has put together a collage with some of the parts and comments, "¡Sepa usted que en México reinventamos la historia cada día y mezclamos las cosas de tal suerte que lo que ayer fue de un modo, hoy es de otro!" (You should know that in Mexico we reinvent history every day, and we mix things so that what today was one way, tomorrow is another!). Ultimately the townspeople, led by Maruca and some ghosts, rebel against the authorities and kill all the officials.

The abusive power exercised by the authorities is represented through the fixation on the phallic symbol. Another recurrent theme is the reinvention of history; all facts are newly created to fit into the authorities' scheme. The anthropophagy represents how power is abused by politicians and that they have no respect for fellow human beings, including their own kind.

In 1982 the Ateneo Español (Spanish Athenaeum) paid homage to Argüelles as the best author of

1981. He presented his first cycle of staged readings with his students, debuting a group of authors, directors, and actors. *Los amores criminales de las vampiras Morales* (1983, The Criminal Loves of the Morales Vampires) debuted the same year it was written. In this play the two protagonists, Adelfa and Fulvia, have a tragic secret from their childhood. Thirty years earlier, they accidentally killed their father, putting three small human heads impregnated in curare in his soup to enhance the flavor. The women, now in their forties, express happiness over the recent death of their mother, whom they tried to kill deliberately but failed, while they still mourn the father's death. The Electra complex is evident, especially because they describe having erotic dreams about the father, who is their only true love. They even have the father's body, which shrunk as a result of the poison and resembles a little boy doll. The sisters have a suitor who is interested in marrying one of them to inherit their money; after ten years of wooing, he tries to get more intimate with Fulvia and is killed by Adelfa. Later they kill two more suitors, giving them all the shrinking procedure. Men are like puppets for them; the only man they will ever love is their own father. Finally, Adelfa decides to use the curare in their own food, and both women die thinking they will be reunited with their beloved father.

Adelfa summarizes their ill-fated destiny: "¿Acaso la vida nos ha tratado como seres humanos? ¿Acaso no fue ella o el destino quien nos convirtió desde niñas en una especie de muñecas siniestras, moviéndonos los hilos a su antojo? Y siendo, así, mejor . . . mejor necesitamos ver todo esto como un juego o . . ." (Did life treat us as human beings? Wasn't it life or destiny that transformed us since childhood into a sort of sinister dolls, pulling our strings at will? And, that being so, better . . . we better see all this as a game or . . .). This play shows the loneliness and isolation in which these women live.

For *Los amores criminales de las vampiras Morales* Argüelles received the Sor Juana Inés de la Cruz Award for best play of the year in 1985. The same organization honored him for his contribution as professor and author of national drama. In 1986 he adapted the play for a television series. He also presented his second and third cycles of staged readings in which he presented his new breed of authors, directors, and actors. The Secretaría de Educación Publica (Secretary of Public Education) or SEP commissioned him to teach in Michoacán, Jalisco, and Sinaloa. He gave classes in the Compañia Shakespeare, Escuela de Teatro de Abraham Oceransky, and Teatro Manolo Fábregas.

As a tribute to the Mexican theater, in 1984 the Universid Autónoma Metropolitana (UAM) invited him for a reading of *Los caracoles amorosos* (The Loving Snails). It debuted in 1988, earning Argüelles another Sor Juana Inés de la Cruz Award for best play of the year. The subtitle of the play, *Romance, bronca y misterio de los caracoles amorosos y los muertos lujuriosos del burdel del cementerio* (Romance, Row and Mystery of the Loving Snails and the Lusty Dead in the Cemetery Brothel), summarizes the plot.

This play is less pessimistic than other Argüelles plays, because love triumphs in the end. At the center of the play is a small-town love story between Aurelio, a lonely widower whose only child, a prostitute, died, and Arminda, a repressed religion teacher whose fiancé also died. They meet in the cemetery, where they are visiting their loved ones. Aurelio observes Arminda masturbating by her fiancé's grave, and she is perturbed, because she has a virginal image to preserve. They feel an immediate attraction and have an intimate conversation. After some time, when Arminda returns to the cemetery, she tries to bury her sister-in-law at the same place Aurelio's daughter is buried, the only space available (because a prostitute is not considered worthy of a place in holy ground). The unmarked graves, demonstrating their lack of resources, cause a fight between Arminda and Aurelio. In the end, the problem is solved when they open the grave and find two skeletons that are hugging each other. Bruna, the owner of the brothel that is right beside the cemetery, uses this opportunity to save her establishment, which was about to be closed for moral reasons. She blackmails most of the people attending the ceremony. The compromising pictures she possesses represent the hypocrisy of the people; all have their dirty laundry, but keep it hidden. The husbands of the decent women come to the brothel all the time; Arminda is a repressed necrophiliac; and the priest is a pedophile. In the end the attraction triumphs, and Arminda overcomes the social prejudices associated with Aurelio (his prostitute daughter, his inferior social status, and his reputation as a womanizer).

In 1985 Argüelles wrote the epic television series *Nezahualcóyotl* (the poet-king of Texcoco in the fifteenth century); he also directed and hosted the television program *Ensayo sobre teatro contemporáneo* (Essay on Contemporary Theater). He also introduced the fourth and fifth cycles of staged readings from his students' short plays and was appointed professor of theatrical theory at UNAM. He participated as specialized critic in the television program *Aproximaciones* (Approximations). The town of Puerto Veracruz recognized his hard work in Mexican theater and in 1990 named him "favorite son" of the State in homage. The following year *Escarabajos* (Beetles) debuted in Mexico City. It is a revised version of a play titled "La casa paterna" (The Father's House), which takes place and was originally written in 1959; the additional monologues were written and take place in 1991. It also won the Sor Juana Inés de la Cruz

Antonio Miguel and Lilia Aragon in the 1988 premiere at Teatro Benito Juaréz of Argüelles's play Los caracoles amorosos
(The Loving Snails), about a widower and a repressed teacher who meet in a cemetery (from Edgar Ceballos, ed.,
Hugo Argüelles: Estilo y dramaturgia, 1994; John C. Hodges Library, University of Tennessee)

Award for best play of the year. This play has strong resemblances to the work of Tennessee Williams and Eugene O'Neill. The protagonist, Jaime, is a frustrated actor and a homosexual who is preparing for his dragqueen interpretation of Medea, using his mother's ashes as makeup. He retells the past, how his father had abandoned them for a rich woman twenty years earlier but had returned after that wife died. Jaime and his sister have great resentment toward their father, but their mother, like Medea, had been willing to sacrifice everything for her former husband's love. Through Jaime the audience finds out that the happy-family experiment has failed: the mother committed suicide; the father died alone; the sister had a chain of unhappy marriages; and Jaime is a failed actor and a drug abuser.

Once again, Argüelles shows the family as the rotten cell of society. Family life is just the place where people hide their insecurities, weaknesses, and hypocrisy. The title of the play is explained by Jaime's sister, who says, "A veces, fantaseo con una ideas: pienso en ellos como si fueran una familia de escarabajos, si, esos insectos que tenazmente van formando una gran bola de mierda que trasladan de aquí para allá . . . para luego comérsela. . . . Y también para cerrar la entrada de sus nidos. Muchos se quedan detenidos ante la inmundicia que formaron, a veces para siempre" (Sometimes I fantasize: I think of them as if they were a bunch of beetles, yes, those insects that tenaciously form a huge ball of shit that they transport from here to there . . . and later eat it. . . . And also to close the exit to their nests. The filth they formed, sometimes many of them are locked in forever).

In 1992 La boda negra de las alacranas (The Black Wedding of the Female Scorpions) debuted, inaugurating the Festival Internacional Cervantino, and won the Estrella de Plata (Silver Star) Award. The play takes place in Guanajuato in 1973. A woman named Ariela has stolen a mummy named Rogelio Andrade, who apparently asked to be rescued. She finds out through a former servant that Rogelio was the lover of a woman named Aralia in Marfil in 1875. Aralia was a psychic and knew their love was ill fated until somebody from the future brought them together again. Rogelio was buried in a mine, where he became comatose and died, as did Aralia. Ariela is not willing to help and decides to keep Rogelio for herself, bringing him back to life. As he revives, Aralia reappears and both reunite; they have used Ariela to bring them back together, and as a consequence she is dying. The title refers to the ritual carried out by mating scorpions: the female kills and eats the male. Through the whole play, two neighbors spy on Ariela; they constantly make comments about her indecency and are eager to know every step she is taking. They represent the hypocritical and repressed social morality: one of them has an inflatable doll and the other an incestuous relationship with her son, but they are eager to judge and condemn Ariela.

In the 1990s Argüelles was recognized with the publication of several special collections of his work. Additionally, in 1995, the Foro Coyoacanense was renamed Teatro Hugo Argüelles in his honor. Argüelles died of prostate cancer on 24 December 2003 in Mexico City and was cremated.

In an interview included in *Hugo Argüelles: Estilo y dramaturgia* (1994–1997, Hugo Argüelles: Style and Dramaturgy), Argüelles listed five predominant characteristics of his work: "el sentido del 'humor negro'–constante en casi toda mi producción; el realismo mágico–como una forma también predominante a lo largo de toda mi obra; el estudio de caracteres; la crítica social; y el sexo–entendido como reto y afirmación cruel" (the sense of "black humor"–constant in almost all my productions; magical realism–as a predominant form throughout all my work; the study of characters; social critique; and sex–understood as a challenge and cruel affirmation). Another mythical and distinctive feature of his theater is the comparison of human behavior to animal rituals. The animalistic nature often shares space with human nature and obliges the individual to act in an instinctual way. In the end, love, a human rather than animal trait, is the only one that can save some of the characters.

Hugo Argüelles was always strongly critical of social conventions, which he believed hinder the real feelings of human beings. He showed people at their most primitive, exhibiting no compassion toward fellow human beings, who are motivated by their own instincts. Taboo themes such as incest and homosexuality are recurrent in his work, and where others only hint at these issues, he spells them out. Though his excesses may sometimes shock the reader, the master of Mexican "black humor" theater was not afraid of showing people without their social veneer.

References:

Edgar Ceballos, ed., *Hugo Argüelles: Estilo y dramaturgia,* 2 volumes (Mexico City: Instituto Nacional de Bellas Artes/Gaceta, 1994, 1997);

Juan Meyer, *La travesía mágica de Hugo Argüelles: Cuarenta años de dramaturgo* (Mexico City: Escenología, 1997);

Manuel Sanchez Espinosa, "Teatro de Hugo Argüelles," dissertation, University of California, 1985;

Maria Sten, "Orestes murió en Veracruz," *Neue Romania,* 16 (1995): 241–246.

Roberto Arlt

(26 April 1900 - 26 July 1942)

Ricardo Szmetan
University of West Indies–Barbados

SELECTED PLAY PRODUCTIONS: *Trescientos millones,* Buenos Aires, Teatro del Pueblo, 17 June 1932;

Prueba de amor, Buenos Aires, Casa del Teatro, 20 October 1932;

Saverio el cruel and *El fabricante de fantasmas,* Buenos Aires, Teatro del Pueblo, 4 September 1936;

La isla desierta, Buenos Aires, Teatro del Pueblo, 5 January 1938;

Africa, Buenos Aires, Teatro del Pueblo, 17 March 1938;

La fiesta del hierro, Buenos Aires, Teatro del Pueblo, 18 July 1940;

El desierto entra a la ciudad, Buenos Aires, Teatro El Duende, 5 November 1953;

La cabeza separada del tronco, by Arlt and Leónidas Barletta, Buenos Aires, Teatro del Pueblo, 15 May 1963.

BOOKS: *El juguete rabioso* (Buenos Aires: Latina, 1926); translated by Michele McKay Aynesworth as *Mad Toy* (Durham, N.C.: Duke University Press, 2002);

Los siete locos (Buenos Aires: Latina, 1929); translated by Naomi Lindstrom as *The Seven Madmen* (Boston: Godine, 1984);

Los lanzallamas (Buenos Aires: Claridad, 1931);

El amor brujo (Buenos Aires: Rañó, 1932);

Trescientos millones; Prueba de amor: Boceto teatral (Buenos Aires: Rañó, 1932);

Aguafuertes porteñas (Buenos Aires: Victoria, 1933);

El jorobadito (Buenos Aires: Anaconda, 1933);

Aguafuertes españolas (Buenos Aires: L. J. Rosso, 1936);

Viaje terrible: Relato inédito (San Martín: Nuestra Novela, 1941);

Regreso: Un cuento, dos burlerías y un esbozo autobiográfico (Buenos Aires: Corregidor, 1942);

Saverio el cruel (Buenos Aires: Futuro, 1950)–includes *El fabricante de fantasmas, La isla desierta, Trescientos millones,* and *Prueba de amor;*

El criador de gorilas (Buenos Aires: Futuro, 1951);

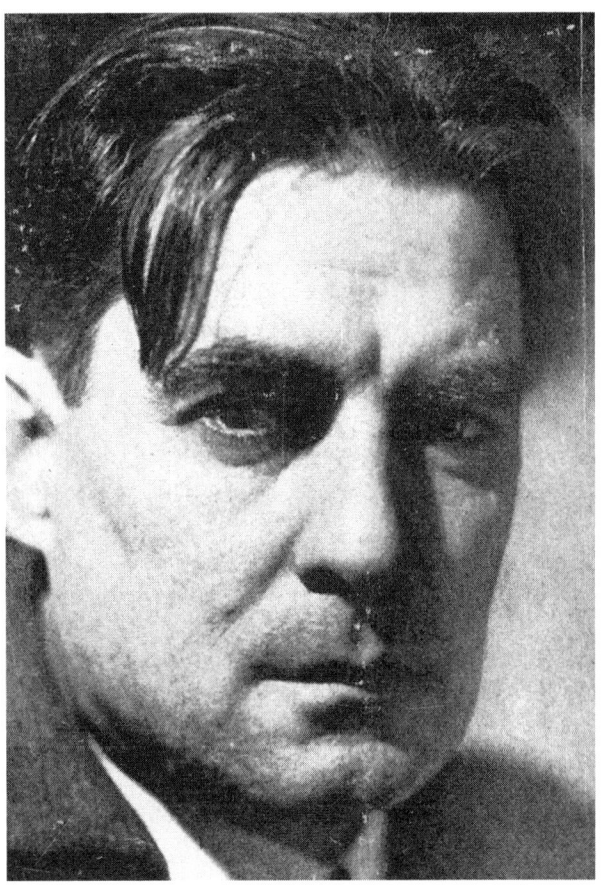

Roberto Arlt, 1942 (from Obra completa, *1981; Thomas Cooper Library, University of South Carolina)*

El desierto entra a la ciudad: Farsa dramática en cuatro actos (Buenos Aires: Futuro, 1952);

Nuevas aguafuertes porteñas (Buenos Aires: Hachette, 1960);

Saverio el cruel; La isla desierta (Buenos Aires: Editorial Universitaria de Buenos Aires, 1965 [i.e., 1964]);

Un viaje terrible (Buenos Aires: Tiempo Contemporáneo, 1968);

Teatro completo, 2 volumes (Buenos Aires: Schapire, 1968);

Cronicón de sí mismo (Buenos Aires: Edicom, 1969);

Entre crotos y sabihondos, aguafuertes porteñas (Buenos Aires: Edicom, 1969);

Las muchachas de Buenos Aires: Aguafuertes porteñas (Buenos Aires: Edicom, 1969);

El traje del fantasma (Buenos Aires: Edicom, 1969);

La isla desierta; Saverio el cruel (Buenos Aires: Kapelusz, 1974);

Nuevas aguafuertes (Buenos Aires: Losada, 1975);

Las aguafuertes porteñas de Roberto Arlt: Publicadas en El Mundo, 1928-1933, edited by Daniel C. Scroggins (Buenos Aires: Ediciones Culturales Argentinas, 1981);

Estoy cargada de muerte y otros borradores (Buenos Aires: Torres Agüero, 1984);

Las fieras y otros cuentos (Montevideo: Ediciones de la Banda Oriental, 1984);

Ester primavera y otros cuentos (Montevideo: Signos, 1993);

Silla en la vereda y otros cuentos (Montevideo: Ediciones de la Banda Oriental, 1993);

El crimen casi perfecto, edited by Omar Borré (Buenos Aires: Clarín/Aguilar, 1994);

Un argentino entre gangsters: Cuentos policiales (Montevideo: Ediciones de la Banda Oriental, 1994);

Noche terrible; Una tarde de domingo (Madrid: Alianza, 1995);

Aguafuertes uruguayas y otras páginas, edited by Borré (Montevideo: Ediciones de la Banda Oriental, 1996);

El resorte secreto y otras páginas, edited by Gastón Gallo (Buenos Aires: Simurg, 1996);

Secretos femeninos: Aguafuertes inéditas (Buenos Aires: La Página, 1996);

Tratado de la delincuencia: Aguafuertes inéditas, edited by Sylvia Saítta (Buenos Aires: La Página, 1996);

Aguafuertes gallegas, edited by Rodolfo Alonso (Sada, A Coruña: Ediciones Do Castro, 1997);

En el país del viento: Viaje a la Patagonia (1934), edited by Saítta (Buenos Aires: Simurg, 1997);

Notas sobre el cinematógrafo, edited by Gallo (Buenos Aires: Simurg, 1997);

Aguafuertes gallegas y asturianas, edited by Saítta (Buenos Aires: Losada, 1999);

Escuela de delincuencia: Aguafuertes, edited by Saítta (Montevideo: Ediciones de la Banda Oriental, 2000);

Aguafuertes madrileñas: Presagios de una guerra civil, edited by Saítta (Buenos Aires: Losada, 2001);

Al margen del cable: Crónicas publicadas en El Nacional, México, 1937-1941, edited by Rose Corral (Buenos Aires: Losada, 2003).

Editions and Collections: *Novelas completas y cuentos,* 3 volumes (Buenos Aires: Compañía General Fabril Editora, 1963);

Antología, edited by Noé Jitrik (Mexico City: Siglo XXI, 1980);

Obra completa (2 volumes, Buenos Aires: Carlos Lohlé, 1981; 3 volumes, Buenos Aires: Planeta/Carlos Lohlé, 1991);

La isla desierta; Saverio el cruel (La Plata, Argentina: Altamira, 1996);

Saverio el cruel; La isla desierta (Buenos Aires: Losada, 1998).

SELECTED PERIODICAL PUBLICATION–UNCOLLECTED: *Separación feroz, El Litoral* (Santa Fe), 1938.

Although Roberto Arlt's plays have significantly influenced the development of Argentine theater, little has been written about this aspect of his work, partly because the general public and literary critics are more familiar with his production in other genres. Another reason is the fact that most of his pieces for the theater were performed within the independent sector, outside the world of commercial theater. Even though Arlt dedicated the last part of his short life to writing dramas, critics still prefer to write about his powerful novels.

During his lifetime he was largely ignored by the critics. On the other hand, several of his fellow left-wing writers were able to perceive the talent he possessed in communicating the inner feelings of solitude and helplessness of the antiheroes in his dramas as well as his novels. These antiheroes are similar to Arlt himself and represent many people who are unable to communicate with each other and who live within the boundaries of an indifferent and often hostile society. For other writers and critics, however, Arlt was no more than an imaginative writer who did not follow the rules of good writing. He had friends in both of the two main groups of Argentine writers of that time: those of Florida Street, which represented sophistication in Buenos Aires, and those of Boedo Street, the street of the proletariat. Both groups considered Arlt as belonging to them, but Arlt always preferred to be independent. He did not conceal his criticism of the most prominent writers of his time, nor did he try to hide his high opinion of his own abilities. He once wrote:

> Estoy muy atraido hacia la belleza. !Cuántas veces quise trabajar una novela conteniendo panorámicos telones de fondo como los de Flaubert! Pero ahora, escuchando los crujidos de la sociedad, no es más posible pensar en hacer bordados. Entonces, debemos crear nuestra propia literatura, en orgullosa soledad,

escribiendo libros que contengan la violencia de un cross a la mandíbula.

(I am greatly attracted by beauty. How often have I wanted to work on a novel containing panoramic backdrops like Flaubert's! But now, hearing the creaking of a crumbling social edifice, it's no longer possible to think of doing embroidery. So we have to create our literature, in proud solitude, by writing books that will contain the violence of a hook to the jaw.)

In his prime Arlt was a popular journalist at the newspaper *El Mundo* (The World), to which, from May 1928 to April 1933, he contributed a few articles each week in a section titled "Aguafuertes porteñas" (Etchings of Buenos Aires; *porteños* is the name given to people living in that city). His commentaries detailing different aspects of everyday life in the big city allowed him to have a more comfortable lifestyle and to be better appreciated by many readers who bought the newspaper with the sole intention of reading his articles. On the days when his commentaries appeared, the newspaper would double its circulation. Because of this large increase in sales the editors decided not to publicize in advance when the articles would appear, thereby forcing readers to buy it every day. Never before or since has anyone else received a similar reaction from the (by that time) powerful Argentine middle class, who felt their lives were mirrored in Arlt's stories.

Roberto Godofredo Christophersen Arlt was born in Buenos Aires on 26 April 1900 in a house on La Piedad Street, number 677. His parents were Karl Arlt, a glassblower and accountant of German origin, and Ekatherine Iobstraibitzer of Trieste, Italy. From childhood he was a friend of another professional writer, Conrado Nalé Roxlo. In 1916 he left his parents' house to live alone, and during the rest of his life he made no reference to his parents again. In 1918 he published his first short story, "Jehová," in the *Revista Popular,* edited by Juan José De Soiza Reilly. He also published work in Félix Propato's magazine, *La Estrella.* In 1920 he published the essay "Las ciencias ocultas en la ciudad de Buenos Aires" (Hidden Sciences in Buenos Aires). His mandatory year of national military service was done in Córdoba, Argentina's second largest city. He also worked as a journalist for the newspaper *Patria,* affiliated with the Liga Patriótica Argentina (Argentine Patriotic League).

In 1922 he married Carmen Antinucci. His daughter, Mirta, was born in Cosquín, Córdoba, the next year. She became his principal critic and the person who held all the legal rights to his work for seventy years after his death. In 1924 he returned to Buenos Aires with his family and began to write in different publications such as *Extrema Izquierda, Izquierda,* and

The People's Theater in Buenos Aires, founded in 1930, where many of Arlt's plays were produced (from Omar Borré, Roberto Arlt: Su vida y su obra, *2000; William T. Young Library, University of Kentucky)*

Ultima Hora. In 1925 the magazine *Proa* published two chapters of his first novel, the title of which was later changed from "La vida puerca" (The Porky Life) to *El juguete rabioso* (The Rabid Plaything; translated as *Mad Toy,* 2002).

The completed *El juguete rabioso,* in which Arlt recalls his difficult childhood, was published in 1926. It is dedicated to his mentor, the renowned author Ricardo Güiraldes, for whom Arlt worked as a private secretary for several years. He continued to write articles for *Don Goyo* and Carlos Muzio's *Mundo Argentino.* Hoping to create a better profile with the general public, he published his autobiography in the popular newspaper *Crítica* in 1927, where he was working as a journalist.

In 1928 he began to write for *El Mundo,* publishing first some short stories and later other articles, particularly on criminal matters. From these experiences came the ideas for his first piece for the theater, *Trescientos millones* (Three Hundred Millions, performed and published in 1932). But his "Aguafuertes porteñas"

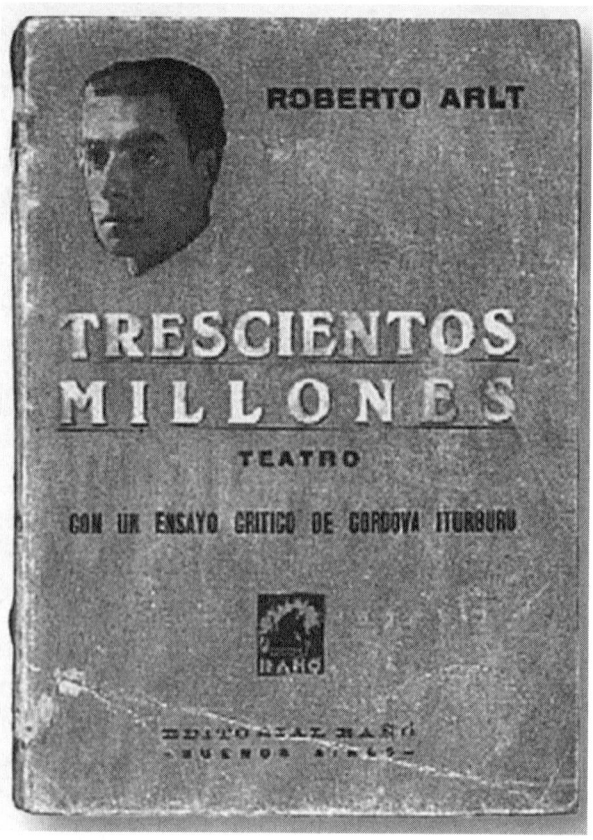

Cover for Arlt's first play, which premiered in 1932 and tells the story of a maid who fantasizes about inheriting three hundred million pesos (from Omar Borré, Roberto Arlt, *2000; William T. Young Library, University of Kentucky)*

were what brought him public recognition. In total he wrote 231 "Aguafuertes." In 1929 "El humillado" (The Humiliated), the first chapter of his novel *Los siete locos* (1929; translated as *The Seven Madmen,* 1984), was published in the anthology *Cuentistas argentinos de hoy* (Contemporary Argentine Short-Story Writers), edited by Álvaro Yunque (pseudonym of Arístides Gandolfi Herrero) and Miranda Klix. A further preview of *Los siete locos* appeared in the magazine *Claridad* (Clarity) under the pseudonym of Naufragio (which means Shipwreck).

Los siete locos is now considered by both the general public and literary critics to be one of the most important Argentine novels of the twentieth century. In this novel a group of seven *locos* (mad people) prepare for a revolution using counterfeit money and the profits from prostitutes working in brothels. Two additional characteristics of *Los siete locos* are that it is written in the language that was in common use in Buenos Aires and that the main characters discuss universal problems relating to the loneliness and indifference that people normally experience in the big city. These elements have the effect of making readers feel that this novel could have been written about the current situation.

In 1930 Arlt wrote six articles about the military overthrow of the civil government of Hipólito Yrigoyen by the general José Félix Uriburu that year. "S.O.S," part of the novel *Los lanzallamas* (1931, The Flamethrowers), appeared in the magazine *Argentina*. He also published "El bloque de oro" (A Block of Gold) in *Claridad*. His novel *Los siete locos* took third place in the competition for the Municipal Prize in Buenos Aires. In 1931 Arlt continued his collaboration in *Bandera Roja* (Red Flag) and also published "Una noche terrible" (A Terrible Night) in *Mundo Argentino* and "Un alma al desnudo" (A Soul for the Nude), part of *Los lanzallamas,* in *Claridad*. His first collection of short stories, *El jorobadito* (1933, The Little Hunchback), was also published.

Arlt's first three novels are all concerned with the general crisis in the world, not only in economic terms but also in relation to the lack of values that people had. In 1932 Arlt wrote *El amor brujo* (The Love Wizard), his last novel before he dedicated himself to writing for the theater. In this work he analyzes the difficulties that men and women have in relating to each other as well as the hypocrisies and falsehoods that are common in many relationships.

In 1930 the Teatro del Pueblo (People's Theater) was created under the direction of Leónidas Barletta. In 1932 Barletta adapted "El humillado" for the theater. In Barletta's adaptation of *El humillado* the principal characters are Erdosain, his wife, and el Capitán (the Captain), her lover. Erdosain is humiliated when he witnesses his wife being seduced by the Captain and when she decides to go and live with him. This chapter of the novel is one of the strongest and the one on which the conclusion of the narrative depends.

The first initiative to create an independent theater in Argentina that placed more importance on artistic considerations rather than economic factors came in 1928 with the establishment of the Teatro Experimental de Arte (Experimental Theater of Art, TEA), a left-wing organization created by people such as Barletta, Yunque, Elías Castelnuovo, and Ricardo Passano. The first work that they performed was Castelnuovo's dramatic piece *En nombre de Cristo* (In the Name of Cristo), which embraced many ideas from the European avant-garde movement.

Trescientos millones, Arlt's first play, premiered on 17 June 1932 in Buenos Aires at the Teatro del Pueblo. In this play, Rocambole, Reina Bizantina, Compadre Vulcano, Hombre Cúbico, Muerte, and Rufián Honrado are romantic characters who live in the imagination of Sofía (based upon a real person), a poor maid from Spain, whose daydreams about inheriting three hundred million pesos help her to cope with her loneliness and the indifference of the people around her. Finally, she decides to kill herself by throwing herself in front of a tram. As a journalist, Arlt was present at the scene after the real person's suicide and was so impressed by her story that he originally decided to write about it in 1927 for the newspaper *Crítica*. Also, in one "Aguafuerte" of 9 July 1929, titled "Usura transatlántica" (Transatlantic Usury), he describes how much money many young women like Sofía paid in order to come to Argentina from Spain, and the loneliness they felt. The piece is concerned with a dreamworld where love is possible. In contrast Arlt describes a more somber reality, where people such as the son of the maid's employer are intent upon forcing her into a physical relationship against her will.

The influence of German expressionism on this play is clear, as is the work of French writer Henri Rene Lenormand, who wrote *El hombre y sus fantasmas* (1924; translated as *Man and His Phantoms*, 1928). Lenormand's plays, like Arlt's, are heavily symbolic, and there is not much difference between dreaming and real life. Another important influence upon Arlt is the Italian dramatist Luigi Pirandello, particularly his masterpiece *Sei personaggi in cerca d'Autore* (1921; translated as *Six Characters in Search of an Author*, 1922), in which the characters strive to be independent of the master who created them, or *Enrico IV* (1921; translated as *Henry IV*, 1929) in which a supposedly insane man imagines that he is a medieval emperor, and in which imagination and reality become strangely confused.

In *Prueba de amor* (Proof of Love), Arlt's next play, which premiered on 20 October 1932 at the Casa del Teatro in Buenos Aires, protagonist Guinter invites his girlfriend, Frida, to his house so he can test whether she really loves him. He invites her to go into the bathroom, where a lot of money has been left in the bath. He tells her he will set fire to all the money as a *prueba de amor*: if she truly loves him, he says, she should not do anything. But if she saves the money, he will think that money is more important to her than her love for him. Frida does nothing, and Guinter explains to her that his act was a hoax, and the money was not real. As usual in Arlt's theater, the effect this action produces is contrary to the one audiences are led to expect: Frida decides to leave Guinter for good, because the game he was playing was far from the ideal of true love. She expects romantic love, the kind that people normally see in movies.

In 1933 the Teatro Proletario (Proletarian Theater) was created with the aim of staging plays for the working classes. The group had many problems with the government because of their political ideas. That same year, Arlt published the short story "La luna roja" (Red Moon) in the magazine *El Hogar* as well as sixty "Aguafuertes porteñas." His short stories "Un hombre sensible" (A Sensible Man) and "La juerga de los polichinelas" (The Clowns' Spree) were published in *La Nación*, the most important journal in Argentina in 1934. "Escenas de un grotesco" (A Grotesque's Scenes), a story that forms the basis of Arlt's 1936 drama *Saverio el cruel* (Saverio the Cruel, published in 1950), was published in *Gaceta de Buenos Aires*. "La muerte del sol" appeared in *Mundo Argentino*. In 1935 Arlt traveled throughout the year in Spain and Morocco in order to write "Aguafuertes españolas" (Spanish Etchings) for *El Mundo*.

On 4 September 1936 Arlt's plays *Saverio el cruel* and *El fabricante de fantasmas* (The Manufacturer of Phantoms) were performed in the Teatro del Pueblo. In *Saverio el cruel* Saverio is a simple seller of butter on whom a group of young people decide to play a trick. They ask him to help them try to cure the mental problems of Susana, who is playing along with their ruse. To do so, Saverio takes on the role of a colonel of an imaginary country and tries to seduce Susana. As normally happens in Arlt's work, the roles change, and Saverio takes his new life as a dictator seriously; he even buys a guillotine to "cortar cabezas" (decapitate people), because a "revolución sin cortar cabezas, no es revolución" (revolution without decapitation is not a revolution). Finally, Saverio decides to tell Susana the truth. But Susana does not believe him because, having played her part so well, she has, in fact, become insane. She kills Saverio, accusing him of being a colonel who has disguised himself as a seller of butter. In this drama it is possible to visualize what could happen to the country in the future, if a real colonel wanted to save the country using such drastic measures. This piece also shows that for Arlt, nothing is absolute, and roles can change easily in society.

In *El fabricante de fantasmas* the protagonist, Pedro, is writing a piece for the theater but is unable to finish it. He is haunted by thoughts of his former wife, whom he killed in a cool and calculated plot. The ghosts of his wife and his lovers often appear and torment him. In a curious "game," Pedro describes in his writing the events that really took place with his wife. He thinks that because he is writing a work of fiction and the time limit for prosecution has passed, he can live without fear. But a former judge at the trial reads the text when it is published. He waits to see if Pedro will confess to his crime, and he visits Pedro at home to talk about the case. Finally, Pedro kills himself. This work is typical of Arlt's theater, in that the situation is crude and strong. In the Argentine theater at this time, it was seldom possible to see plots of this nature, because commercial demands dictated traditional forms and realistic plays, the forms that the impresarios considered would attract the unsophisticated public. One of the most important elements of Arlt's works is the comical aspect, which is

Arlt observing a production of one of his plays (from Omar Borré, Roberto Arlt, *2000; William T. Young Library, University of Kentucky)*

work that does not allow any possibility of escapism. In this play Arlt criticizes a society that is only interested in production and not the human factor.

In 1938 Arlt published the plays *Africa* and *Separación feroz* (Fierce Separation) in the newspaper *El Litoral* (The Coast) of Santa Fe. The idea for *Africa* came to Arlt when he was visiting Morocco, representing his newspaper and writing several articles. The play is divided into six acts. Within Arlt's larger body of work this play is more realistic, an exception to his style. He shows some of the exotic and vivid traditions of the Arabs he met in his journeys. More than fifty characters are needed, which is one of the reasons this work is difficult to perform. It is one of the least popular of his creations. *Separación feroz* is a one-act drama that was never performed in a theater. Little is known about it by the public and the critics, because copies of *El Litoral* from that time are difficult to find.

In 1939 Arlt's short story "Los gorilas" (The Gorillas) appeared in the *Antología de cuentistas rioplatenses* (Anthology of Río Plate Short-Story Writers) edited by Julia Prilusky Farnny. He also wrote pieces for *El Hogar* (Home) and *Mundo Argentino*. His next play, *La fiesta del hierro* (The Iron Party), premiered at the Teatro del Pueblo in Buenos Aires on 18 July 1940. In *La fiesta del hierro* a man calling himself Rey del Hierro (The King of Iron) owns a factory where firearms are manufactured and sold. He organizes a party to celebrate his good fortune in the business. In the living room where his guests will eat, he builds an iron monster that will later be set on fire. Before the party begins, his twelve-year-old son gets inside the iron monster so as to be better able to spy on the guests. When he is inside he finds he cannot move or call for help, and he perishes inside the burning iron monster. There is a strong message in this work: that the technology that creates machines to kill strangers is also capable of killing the innocent child of the industrialist who profits from their manufacture.

In 1939 Arlt married Elizabeth Shine (his first wife had died ten years earlier), and in 1940 he traveled to Chile. In 1941 he wrote for *La Hora* and published short stories. By that time he had published fifty short stories, more than two thousand journalistic notes, and four novels in addition to his dramas. In the same year he collaborated on *Santa Fe de Hoy* and worked on his drama *El desierto entra a la ciudad* (The Desert Comes to Town, performed in 1953, published in 1952). *El desierto entra a la ciudad* is a play that Arlt was unable to finish because of his unexpected death. It is divided in four parts and shows the metaphysical and philosophical problems that César, the main character, must face after a life dedicated only to physical pleasures. César is tormented by a guilty past, mostly by the apparition of a phantom. He decides to leave the city

constantly situated within a framework of innocent argument. At the time Arlt was writing his dramas, the theater—and the country in general—were in crisis, like other parts of the world: suffering high unemployment, military dictatorship, a lack of values, and widespread corruption. The phantoms and the importance of their actions are similar to those represented in *Trescientos millones*.

La isla desierta (The Deserted Island) was performed for the first time at the Teatro del Pueblo in Buenos Aires on 5 January 1938. In this play the action takes place in one of many gray public offices in Buenos Aires, near the port. There, the black Cipriano, a low-ranking employee, begins telling a story to his bored fellow workers. His story is set on an idyllic island. As the tale unfolds, his fellow workers become totally involved through the power of their imaginations, and some people even begin to take off their clothes. But the boss arrives unexpectedly and fires all the employees. There is clear criticism of the unchanging day-to-day world of and stay in the desert. For some he is mad, but others consider him a saint and join the life he leads. They are waiting for him to perform a miracle. Finally, he is killed by an enemy of the city, and his miraculous abilities remain a mystery.

"Pasaje en las nubes" (Journey in the Clouds), Arlt's last article, appeared in *La Nación*. His short story "Los esbirros de Venecia" was published in *Mundo Argentino*. On 26 July 1942 he suffered a fatal heart attack. The following day only a few lines of information about his death appeared in the newspapers. Three Arlt-related plays were produced posthumously: *Erdosain, el humillado* (1955, Erdosain, the Humiliated); *Los siete locos* (1956); and *La cabeza separada del tronco* (1963, The Head Separated from the Trunk). *Erdosain, el humillado* is a sequel to *El humillado*. The play deals with the anguish, desolation, and humiliation that Erdosain suffers when his wife leaves him for her Captain. Because this suffering is largely a mental process, the work fails to show the situation in a convincing way when transferred to the theater. *Los siete locos* (1956) is a three-act drama that was adapted from the novel by the same name and performed at the Teatro de los Independientes. *La cabeza separada del tronco*, performed at the Teatro del Pueblo in Buenos Aires on 15 May 1963, is believed by some critics to be Arlt's work. The plot is quite complicated and appears to be written by Arlt, but it is in fact an outline that remained unfinished at the time of his death. Barletta, the director of the play and the person who always corrected Arlt's works before performance, worked extensively on it, perhaps taking too much control of it. Mirta Arlt and Luis Ordaz, one of the most important critics of Argentine theater, believe that this work was begun by Arlt but should be credited to Barletta, as he was the person who did most of the work on the play.

After Arlt's death, critics did not write about him until the late 1950s. Young writers of the left-wing and revisionist magazine *Contorno*, edited by David Viñas, dedicated one issue in 1954 to a discussion of Arlt's importance. They compared him ideologically to the principal Argentine writer Jorge Luis Borges. The first critic to produce a complete study on Arlt was Raúl Larra (pseudonym of Raúl Larragione), an active member of the Argentine Communist Party. In 1950 he wrote a biography because he considered Arlt's ideas to be left wing, although Arlt never spoke openly about his political views. Several critics, however, consider Arlt's ideas to be more right wing, because in his works he predicted chaos in this country of dictators and the use of force to change society. In this respect he can be considered a truly visionary writer, because of what happened later in Argentina. He was able to combine in his novels both communist theories and an extreme fascist outlook, mixed with a little messianic fanaticism. Suicide, perversion, desperation, and alienation are all themes explored by Arlt in his works.

Elizabeth Shine, Arlt's second wife, in 1937 (from Omar Borré, Roberto Arlt, *2000; William T. Young Library, University of Kentucky)*

One of the main aspects of Roberto Arlt's work is that it is easy to read and understand; his style makes audiences feel that the narrator or the main characters are talking directly to them. His experience as a journalist helped him learn how to sustain the interest of the reader. He often used humor in his descriptions of the daily lives of *porteños,* and he was a master in describing them accurately in their own language. In fact, he was one of the few writers of his time to reflect the real language of the big city, and not the artificial one used by most of his fellow authors.

Bibliographies:

Horacio Jorge Becco, "Microbibliografía de Roberto Arlt," *Macedonio,* 11 (1971): 75–80;

Rita Gnutzmann, "Bibliografía selectiva sobre Roberto Arlt," *Revista Interamericana de Bibliografía,* 39 (1989): 3–20;

Gnutzmann, "Bibliografía de y sobre Roberto Arlt," *Chasqui,* 25, no. 2 (1996): 44–62.

Biographies:

Raúl Larra, *Roberto Arlt, el torturado* (Buenos Aires: Futuro, 1950);

Sylvia Saítta, *El escritor en el bosque de ladrillos: Una biografía de Roberto Arlt* (Buenos Aires: Sudamericana, 2000).

References:

José Amícola, "Arachne's Thread and Distancing (Roberto Arlt, Julio Cortázar, Manuel Puig)," *Revista Iberoamericana,* 66.190 (2000): 163–174;

Mirta Arlt, *Prólogos a la obra de mi padre* (Buenos Aires: Torres Agüero, 1986);

Arlt and Omar Borré, *Para leer a Roberto Arlt* (Buenos Aires: Torres Agüero, 1985);

Leónidas Barletta, *Boedo y Florida: Una versión distinta* (Buenos Aires: Metrópolis, 1967);

Silvia Bonino, *Roberto Arlt: "La isla desierta": Intento de un descubrimiento* (Montevideo: Ediciones del Nuevo Siglo, 1990);

Omar Borré, *Arlt y la crítica (1926–1990)* (Buenos Aires: América Libre, 1996);

Borré, *Roberto Arlt: Su vida y su obra* (Buenos Aires: Planeta, 2000);

José Alberto Bravo de Rueda, "El cuerpo humano: Un nexo entre la narrativa y la dramática de Roberto Arlt," dissertation, 1997;

Raúl Castagnino, *El teatro de Roberto Arlt* (Buenos Aires: Nova, 1970);

Jorge Castro Vega, *Aproximación al teatro de Roberto Arlt: "La isla desierta"* (Montevideo: Túpac Amaru, 1988);

Emilce B. Cersósimo, *Literatura y profecía: Arlt, Sábato, Marechal, Güiraldes* (Buenos Aires: Docencia, 1982);

Glen Close, *La imprenta enterrada: Baroja, Arlt y el imaginario anarquista* (Rosario: Beatriz Viterbo, 2000);

Conducta, special Arlt issue, 21 (July–August 1942);

Contorno, special Arlt issue, 2 (May 1954);

Cayetano Córdova Iturburu, ed., *Roberto Arlt* (Buenos Aires: Privately printed, 1948);

Raúl Crisafio, "El teatro independiente en Argentina: El *caso* Roberto Arlt," *Letterature d'America,* 5, no. 24–25 (1984): 95–106;

Norma Edith Crotti, "¿Literatura/periodismo, una distinción vana? *La isla desierta* y las *Aguafuertes porteñas* de Roberto Arlt," *Celéis,* 5, no. 6–8 (1996): 217–223;

Silvia G. Dapia, "Roberto Arlt: Lo reprimido de la literatura argentina," *Romance Languages,* 6 (1994): 434–438;

Lee Dowling, "Chronology," *Review,* 31 (1982): 26–28;

Elsa Drucaroff, *Arlt: Profeta del miedo* (Buenos Aires: Catálogos, 1998);

Jorge A. Dubatti, "Roberto Arlt en los noventa: Notas sobre la poética teatral de *El pecado que no se puede nombrar* de Ricardo Bartís," *Itinerarios,* 2, no. 2 (1999): 103–113;

Juan Marial Erostarbe, *Roberto Arlt: 300 millones* (San Juan, Argentina: UN de San Juan, 1983);

Nira Etchenique, *Roberto Arlt* (Buenos Aires: La Mandrágora, 1962);

Sinesio Fernández, "La obra dramática de Roberto Arlt," dissertation, 1975;

Fernández, "Roberto Arlt y el teatro hispanoamericano," in *Homenaje a Humberto Piñera: Estudios de literatura, arte e historia,* edited by Wayne H. Finke and Enrique Ledesma (Madrid: Playor, 1979);

Jack M. Flint, "Fantasy, the Absurd and the Gratuitous Act in the Works of Roberto Arlt," *Neophilologus,* 68, no. 1 (1984): 63–71;

Carlos Gazzera, "El organito: Entre Alvear, Arlt, Borges y Armando Discépolo," *Revista de Lengua y Literatura,* 7, no. 17 (1997): 21–31;

Enrique Giordano, *La teatralización de la obra dramática: De Florencio Sánchez a Roberto Arlt* (Mexico City: Premia, 1982);

Giordano, "Los textos dramáticos de Roberto Arlt," in *Doctores y proscritos: La nueva generación de latinoamericanistas chilenos en U. S. A.,* edited by Silverio Muñoz (Minneapolis: Institute for the Study of Ideologies & Literature, 1987);

Jaime Giordano, "Roberto Arlt: Escritura expresionista," *Revista de Estudios Hispánicos,* 19, no. 1 (1992): 55–70;

Rita Gnutzmann, "Homenaje a Arlt, Borges y Onetti de Ricardo Piglia," *Revista Iberoamericana,* 58, no. 159 (1992): 437–448;

Horacio González, *Arlt: Política y locura* (Buenos Aires: Colihue, 1996);

Diana Guerrero, *Roberto Arlt, el habitante solitario* (Buenos Aires: Granica, 1972);

Alberto Gutiérrez de la Solana, "Huellas surrealistas en el teatro de Roberto Arlt," in *Surrealismo/Surrealismos: Latinoamérica y España,* edited by Peter G. Earle and Germán Gullón (Philadelphia: University of Pennsylvania Press, 1977);

Domingo Luis Hernández, *Roberto Arlt: La sombra pronunciada* (Barcelona: Montesinos, 1995);

Eduardo Gonzalez Lanuza, *Roberto Arlt* (Buenos Aires: Amorrotu e Hijos, SA, 1971);

Raúl Larra, "Polémica: Roberto Arlt es nuestro," *Cuadernos de Cultura Democrática y Popular* (1952): 104–219;

Gerardo Luzuriaga, "Las máscaras de la crueldad en el teatro de Roberto Arlt," *Texto Crítico,* 10 (1978): 95–103;

Macedonio, special Arlt issue, 11 (1971);

Oscar Masotta, *Sexo y tradición en Roberto Arlt* (Buenos Aires: Centro Editor de América Latina, 1982);

Beatriz Pastor, *Roberto Arlt y la rebelión alienada* (Gaithersburg, Md.: Hispamérica, 1980);

Osvaldo Pellettieri, ed., *Roberto Arlt: Dramaturgia y teatro Independiente* (Buenos Aires: Galerna, 2000);

Walter Rela, "Argumentos renovadores de Roberto Arlt en el teatro argentino moderno," *Latin American Theatre Review,* 13, no. 2 (1980): 65–71;

Raimundo Rodríguez, *Divagaciones en torno del misterio de un autor: Roberto Arlt y su obra* (Buenos Aires: Nuevo Meridión, 1987);

Eduardo Romano, "Arlt y la vanguardia argentina," *Cuadernos Hispanoamericanos,* 373 (1981): 143–149;

David Russi, "Metatheatre: Roberto Arlt's Vehicle Toward the Public's Awareness of an Art Form," *Latin American Theatre Review,* 24, no. 1 (1990): 65–75;

María Teresa Sanhueza, "La influencia cervantina en *Saverio el cruel* de Roberto Arlt," *Acta Literaria,* 18 (1993): 161–170;

Beatriz Sarlo, "Arlt: Ciudad real, ciudad imaginaria, ciudad reformada," *Punto de Vista,* 15, no. 41 (1992): 15–21;

Laura Rosana Scarano, "Metateatro e identidad en *Saverio el cruel* de Roberto Arlt y *El gesticulador* de Rodolfo Usigli," *Alba de América,* 6, no. 10–11 (1988): 199–207;

James J. Troiano, "Cervantinism in Two Plays by Roberto Arlt," *American Hispanist,* 4, no. 29 (1978): 20–22;

Troiano, "The Grotesque Tradition and the Interplay of Fantasy and Reality in the Plays of Roberto Arlt," *Latin American Literary Review,* 7, no. 8 (1976): 7–14;

Troiano, "Literary Traditions and the Interplay of Illusion and Reality in the Works of Roberto Arlt," dissertation, State University of New York at Buffalo, 1973;

Troiano, "Pirandellism in the Theater of Roberto Arlt," *Latin American Theatre Review,* 8, no. 1 (1974): 37–44;

Troiano, "Social Criticism and the Fantastic in Roberto Arlt's *La fiesta del hierro,*" *Latin American Theatre Review,* 13, no. 1 (1979): 39–45;

Ana María Zubieta, *El discurso narrativo arltiano: Intertextualidad, grotesco y utopía* (Buenos Aires: Hachette, 1987).

Antón Arrufat
(14 August 1935 -)

Laurietz Seda
University of Connecticut

PLAY PRODUCTIONS: *El caso se investiga,* Havana, Teatro Lyceum, 28 June 1957; Cuba, Teatro Tespis, 1963;

El vivo al pollo, Havana, Teatro Prometeo, 1 April 1961;

El último tren, Havana, Teatro Arlequín, January 1963;

La repetición, Havana, Teatro Las Máscaras, 1963;

Todos los domingos, Havana, Teatro Estudio, 1966;

Los siete contra Tebas, Mexico, 1970; translated by Mike Gonzales as *Seven Against Thebes,* Glasgow, Ramshorn Theatre, 2001;

El caso se investiga, Puerto Rico, 1986.

BOOKS: *En claro* (Havana: La Tertulia, 1962);

Mi antagonista, y otras observaciones (Havana: Ediciones R[evolución], 1963);

Teatro (Havana: Unión, 1963)–comprises *El caso se investiga, El vivo al pollo, El último tren, La repetición,* and *La zona cero;*

Repaso final (Havana: Ediciones R[evolución], 1964);

Todos los domingos (Havana: Ediciones R[evolución], 1965);

Escrito en las puertas (Havana: Unión, 1968);

Los siete contra Tebas (Havana: Unión, 1968);

La caja está cerrada (Havana: Letras Cubanas, 1984);

La huella en la arena (Havana: Letras Cubanas, 1986);

La tierra permanente (Havana: Letras Cubanas, 1987);

Las pequeñas cosas (Havana: Unión de Escritores y Artistas de Cuba, 1988); expanded as *De las pequeñas cosas* (Valencia: Pre-Textos, 1997);

¿Qué harás después de mí? (Havana: Letras Cubanas, 1988);

Cámara de amor (Havana, 1994)–comprises *El caso se investiga, El vivo al pollo, El último tren, La repetición, La zona cero,* and *Todos los domingos;*

Virgilio Piñera: Entre él y yo (Havana: Unión, 1994);

La divina Fanny (Havana: Unión, 1995);

Lirios sobre un fondo de espadas (Havana: Letras Cubanas, 1995);

Celare navis y otros poemas (Matanzas, Cuba: Vigía, 1996);

Ejercicios para hacer de la esterilidad virtud (Havana: Unión, 1997);

Antón Arrufat (from the cover for La divina Fanny, *1995; Perkins Library, Duke University)*

El viejo carpintero (piezas de 1998) (Havana: Unión, 1999);

Un examen de medianoche (Matanzas, Cuba: Vigía, 2000);

La noche del Aguafiestas (Havana: Letras Cubanas, 2000);

Antología personal (Barcelona: Mondadori, 2001);

Las tres partes del criollo (Havana: Letras Cubanas, 2003).

OTHER: *Nuevos cuentistas cubanos,* edited by Arrufat and Fausto Masó (Havana: Casa de las Américas, 1961);

Julios Cortázar, *Cuentos,* edited by Arrufat (Havana: Casa de las Américas, 1964);

August Strindberg, *Teatro,* edited by Arrufat (Havana: Editora del Consejo Nacional de Cuba, 1964);

Gertrudis Gómez de Avellaneda y Arteaga, *Espatolino,* foreword by Arrufat (Havana: Letras Cubanas, 1984);

Virgilio Piñera, *La carne de René,* edited by Arrufat (Havana: Unión, 1995);

Piñera, *La isla en peso: Obra poética,* edited by Arrufat (Havana: Unión, 1998);

Gómez de Avellaneda y Arteaga, *La noche de insomnio: Antología poética,* edited by Arrufat (Havana: Letras Cubanas, 2003).

SELECTED PERIODICAL PUBLICATIONS–
UNCOLLECTED: "El teatro bufo," *Unión,* 1, no. 3–4 (September–December 1962): 61–72;
"Examen de medianoche o discurso de aceptación," *Unión,* 42 (January–March 2001): 4–6.

Within the study of Cuban drama, the name of Antón Arrufat is commonly associated with that of José Triana; both are considered outstanding and well-known postrevolutionary playwrights, nationally as well as internationally, and their interest in renovating the Cuban theater scene sets them apart. With the triumph of the Cuban Revolution in 1959, playwrights were confronted with a change in attitude toward the arts, the result of economic support from the government, the appearance of new theaters, and the backing of the public. However, intellectual freedom from restrictions began to wane, and in 1961 the head of government, Fidel Castro, in his famous "Speech to the Intellectuals," exhorted artists to contribute to the interests of the Revolution, obliging them to find ways to do so without sacrificing the artistic content of their works.

Although the majority of Arrufat's plays deal primarily with the existential problems of humanity, he states openly in conversations, talks, and interviews that a writer's artistic freedom is an absolute necessity. Arrufat does not subscribe to writing plays that are simple political pamphlets, and he constantly points out that definitive ideas and closed systems repulse him. One of his major contributions to Cuban theater consists of the fusion of the traditional forms of the *teatro bufo* (buffo theater) with the techniques of the emerging postrevolutionary theater. Arrufat considers *teatro bufo* the most important theatrical legacy of the nineteenth century. In his article "El teatro bufo," published in 1962 in the journal *Unión,* he expounds on the origins and the principal characteristics of this type of theater: humor, parody, the use of elements such as masks and Cuban music, absurd situations and language (the accumulation of words without apparent meaning or with a different meaning), stereotyped characters (whites, blacks, Chinese, Catalans, rich people, poor people, drunks), and a return to order and harmony at the end of the play.

Born in Santiago de Cuba on 14 August 1935, Antón Arrufat Mrad attended primary school in his hometown at the Colegio de Dolores de la Compañía de Jesús. His father, Antonio Arrufat (a salesman) was of Catalan origin, and his mother, Isabel Mrad (a housewife), was of Arab and Muslim origins. In 1947 he moved with his parents and his sister, Virginia, to Havana, where he studied in the Instituto de la Habana (Havana Institute), and later he studied at the University of Havana. After returning to Santiago de Cuba because of his mother's death in 1953, he finished his secondary education in the Sagarra School. His interest in theater emerged when his father took him as a child to see *zarzuela* performances (light Spanish opera) and shows by the Spanish theater companies that visited the capital. The figure who was most influential in his career as a dramatic writer was the Cuban Virgilio Piñera, an author known for his experimental and nonrealistic theater.

In 1957, after the death of his father, Arrufat moved to New York, where he had the opportunity to study both the Spanish classics and contemporary avant-garde theater. With the triumph of the Revolution in 1959 he returned to Cuba, where he worked as an editor of the literary supplement *Lunes de Revolución* (Revolution Monday) until 1961. From there he became editor in chief of the magazine *Casa de las Américas* (House of the Americas), only to be dismissed in 1964 for not proclaiming openly to be in favor of the Cuban Revolution. From 1964 to 1970 he worked for the group Teatro Estudio (Studio Theater). Later on he worked as a librarian for the magazine *Revolución y Cultura* (Revolution and Culture).

His first play, written when he was twenty-two years old, is titled *El caso se investiga* (The Case Is Being Investigated). By selling tickets and collecting the money themselves, the author and his friends were able to stage the play on 28 June 1957 at the Lyceum Theatre. However, the play ran for only three days, poorly received by the audience as well as by the critics. The theater community was not used to the illogical framework introduced by the new Cuban drama of this time. Nevertheless, when *El caso se investiga* was next performed in the Tespis Theatre in 1963, it was received enthusiastically, because the public and the critics were ready for a change. From this date on, the play has had more than thirty productions in Cuba and abroad. Arrufat himself, referring to the later success of the play, points out in his prologue to the book *Cámara de*

Title page for Arrufat's controversial play, performed in Mexico in 1970, in which Arrufat adapts Aeschylus's tragedy about the struggle for control of Thebes as a metaphor for the political situation in Cuba (Wilson Library, University of North Carolina at Chapel Hill)

amor (Love Chamber, 1994) that "Lo que ha cambiado es el público" (What has changed is the audience).

El caso se investiga is a one-act play in which an Inspector arrives at Eulalia's home to investigate the death of Eulalia's husband, Fernando Ramírez (alias The Neat One), a merchant. At the end of the play the Inspector discovers that Eulalia, in complicity with her sister, Amalia, poisoned Ramírez with an overdose of the ulcer medicine he was taking. During the investigation the three women in the play—Eulalia, Amalia, and Eugenia, the maid—try to throw off the Inspector by blaming each other, talking to him about various topics, or playing card games.

The play portrays women who are wrapped up in a world full of miscommunication and incomprehension and who commit murder in an attempt to escape the emptiness and boredom of their daily lives. The characters are driven by obsessions, routines, and fixed schedules. Amalia is deaf from 7:00 to 11:00 in the morning, while Eugenia is a maid from 7:00 to 12:00, sleeps on the ironing board in order to stay slim, and takes pictures repeatedly in order to capture the moment in which they get old. The Inspector constantly asks questions; he even says that there are twenty-eight questionnaires for twenty-eight crime possibilities. *El caso se investiga* combines many of the elements and tendencies that characterize Arrufat's later plays: *teatro bufo,* the Theater of the Absurd, metadrama, illogical themes and structure, humor, and an obsession with time.

Also written in 1957 was *El último tren* (The Last Train), the playwright's second play, which premiered in 1963 in the Arlequín Theatre. Arrufat has said in *Cámara de amor* that the six-year delay in staging was because he did not have the desire or the strength that had motivated him to collect the money for his first play. *El último tren* has been perceived as more logical and realistic than *El caso se investiga*. For the playwright, it was a way to present his intellectual preoccupations regarding time by using the theme of eternal bachelorhood.

El último tren concerns Alicia and Martel, who have been partners for thirty years. Alicia is tired of waiting for Martel to propose. When the play begins she is waiting for him anxiously because she has decided to ask him to marry her. Martel points out that his business is not going well and promises her that they will get married in a year. Alicia, furious, asks him to leave the house because she has been waiting too long for them to get married. Martel leaves angrily but returns in a few minutes to look for his cane that he left behind. Martel asks Marieta, Alicia's sister, to give him his cane because he swore he would never enter the house again. But Marieta, upon seeing that Alicia is serving food as usual, makes a gesture to Martel to sit at the table as he has always done, and he complies. In this way, each returns to his or her routine as if nothing had happened.

Alicia is conscious of the facts that she and Martel have little in common, that the love between them hardly exists anymore, and that he has a lover. But Martel is the only possible escape from her spinsterhood and solitude. However, when Martel refuses to marry her, Alicia resigns herself to missing "the last train" and continuing to follow the routine to which she is accustomed because she no longer has any strength to effect change. Time, as in *El caso se investiga,* imprisons the protagonists in a repetitive circle from which they manage to escape, but only momentarily.

On 1 April 1961 the first three-act play written by Arrufat, *El vivo al pollo* (Long Live Life), premiered at the Prometeo Theatre. In that same year he received honorable mention in the Third Inter-American Literary Competition celebrated in Havana. *El vivo al pollo* is inspired by the Robreño Brothers' *El velorio de Pachencho* (Pachencho's Wake, 1901), one of the most well known and most often staged of the *teatro bufo*. The playwright has said in *Cámaro de amor* that he conceived the first act while residing in New York. Upon his return to Cuba in 1959, this first act was published in *Lunes de Revolución;* as a result, it became widely known, and many of his friends asked him to finish it. One day, the Cuban director Francisco Morín approached Arrufat and indicated to him that he planned to begin rehearsals, so the author committed to finishing it.

In *El vivo al pollo* protagonist Matilde has just lost her husband, Vicente, a lawyer, to a heart attack. She refuses to accept the fact that his death has taken him away from her forever. Against her daughter Rosita's wishes, she has her dead husband embalmed in order to preserve him at her house. When the body arrives, Matilde talks to it and acts as if it were alive. She also protects it from destructive elements such as the sun, water, dust, and flies. Matilde feels that she is finally able to control her husband and be happy with him as she had always wished. At the end of the play, she and the embalmer Ramad decide to start a business–Embalmment, Inc.–for all of the widows who refuse to give up their dead husbands.

The title of the play comes from the proverb "long live life and into the dirt with the dead." *El vivo al pollo* is by nature farcical and full of irony and humor. Once again, the themes of time, death, routine, and old age are treated with audacity. Based on elements of *teatro bufo*–black humor, the use of popular music, class differences, stereotyped characters–this play was praised by some critics and rejected by others.

La repetición (The Repetition), another one-act play that premiered in Las Máscaras Theatre in 1963, consists of only three actors: a man and two women. The stage directions suggest that the stage be divided into two planes: one upper and one lower. The Muchacha's (Girl's) bedroom is on the upper level, while the Vecina's (Neighbor's) and the Esposo's (Husband's) bedroom is part of the lower level, featuring furniture and flowers identical to those of the Muchacha, but older and more faded. At the beginning of the play, the Vecina is talking to her husband and complaining about his difficult situation because he is impoverished and unemployed. Later, she goes to the Muchacha's house to ask her for a piece of fabric in order to sew a costume for her son. When she leaves, the Vendedor (Salesman), played by the same actor as the Esposo, arrives at the Muchacha's house and tries to sell her an iron. At first he is only interested in setting up a commercial transaction with her; however, they end up falling in love. In the last scene of the play, the Muchacha and the Vendedor come down from the upper level and stand facing the audience; the Muchacha then puts on the Vecina's mask, and the Vendedor puts on the Esposo's mask. The Muchacha enters the Vecina's studio, and the Vecina goes up to the Muchacha's studio. The play finishes when the Muchacha (with the Vecina's mask on) begins to say the same words that the Vecina pronounced at the beginning of the play.

The circular structure and the repetition of the Vecina's words at the end prove the impossibility of rising above the economic situation that traps the characters. They are from the poor, lower class: the Muchacha sews for a living, and the Vecina's husband is unemployed. The audience realizes that any hope for the Muchacha through her love for the Vendedor is false. When all is said and done, she will end up in the same situation as the Vecina. Time appears once again in this play as a component that erodes love, as in *El último tren*. The difference resides in the characters' economic situations. It does not matter if the characters are married or friends, rich or poor; time keeps passing, and their situations do not improve or change. Through the use of masks, from the tradition of *teatro bufo*, Arrufat shows how poverty is another element that imprisons and wears down a person.

La zona cero (Zero Zone), Arrufat's fifth play, has been considered by critics to be the strangest, most ambiguous and unsettling of his plays, which explains why it has never been staged. It was published in his 1963 volume *Teatro* (Theater). This play consists of two versions, one from 1959 and the other from 1964, the latter not published until 1994 when it was included in *Cámara de amor*. Daniel Zalacaín (referring to the first version) and George Woodyard (referring to the second) point out that the play corresponds to the style of the Theater of the Absurd. Martha Betancourt Chiarella states that the second version is superior to the first because it clears up certain points and develops several characters more in depth. Betancourt Chiarella explains that this play is "more a parable than a play" and that Arrufat has selected, as the visible form for his parable, the medieval conflict between World and Cloister, earthly life with its passions in opposition to the monastic life, contemplative and silent. According to Betancourt Chiarella, this parable turns out to be ironic, because the memories and desires of living in the world are those that are described as temptations and sins in the play. However, Betancourt Chiarella affirms that *La zona cero* should not be considered as "an attack on the church or any other specific institution."

Arrufat's sixth play, *Todos los domingos* (Every Sunday), was finished in 1964. It premiered in 1966 in Cuba. Frank N. Dauster has stated that this play, along with *El vivo al pollo,* is one of Arrufat's best. Betancourt Chiarella points out that *Todos los domingos* was quite successful with Cuban critics of the time. The play unfolds in the home of Elvira, a financially comfortable spinster in a wheelchair who lives on her memories. For thirty years, every Sunday, she re-creates the happiest day of her life, the day before her fiancé abandoned her forever. In order to do so, she makes her maid, Alejandrina, recruit any young man to play the part of her fiancé. The man she chooses one Sunday asks Elvira to allow him to return next Sunday, which she does. When he returns, he refuses to keep playing the role of the Novio (Boyfriend) and confesses to Elvira that he is in love with her. When he insists that his feelings are real, Alejandrina murders him with a pair of scissors.

Once again the themes of time, memories, ritual, and routine appear. Any change in ritual and routine cannot be tolerated. The death of the Novio is a return to the order and daily life that keeps the two women alive. The play is also a commentary on the type of theater that rejects improvisation: Elvira functions as a director and principal actress; Alejandrina carries out the casting; and the Novio is the main actor. When the Novio violates the contract established beforehand and begins to improvise his role according to his feelings for Elvira, the women retake their authority by eliminating him.

Los siete contra Tebas (Seven Against Thebes, 1968) is Arrufat's work that has caused the most controversy in the Cuban theater community. This play simultaneously conferred fame and ostracism upon him. In 1968 he won the José Antonio Ramos Prize, granted by the Unión de Escritores y Artistas de Cuba (UNEAC, Union of Writers and Artists of Cuba). The voting for this prize was not unanimous. Of the five judges on the panel (Adolfo Gutkin, Ricardo Salvat, Triana, Raquel Revuelta, and Juan Larco) the last two voted against Arrufat's play, considering it far removed from the interests of the Cuban Revolution. Arrufat himself pointed out, in an interview with Jesús J. Barquet, that a personal reason was converted into a "reason of state." Arrufat had denied Vicente Revuelta (the brother of Raquel Revuelta) the rights to stage *Los siete contra Tebas,* causing him to accuse the piece of having ideological problems. Within this controversial atmosphere Arrufat was awarded the prize, but not without being condemned by Larco and Raquel Revuelta in a manifesto included at the beginning of the published play text. As Arrufat explained to Barquet:

El premio nunca me fue entregado. Ni diploma, viaje a Hungría, ni metal. La dirección de la UNEAC estaba en contra de ese Premio, como lo manifiesta en el prólogo que antecede a la edición. Si la obra se editó, nunca se vendió en las librerías del país. Circuló clandestinamente: ejemplares robados de los almacenes, robados por gente desconocida, y ejemplares mimeografiados, también por gente desconocida. Circuló oficialmente sólo en las embajadas cubanas, a las que se remitieron para demostrar que se había editado y por si algún extranjero curioso la procuraba.

(The theater award was never given to me. Not a diploma, a trip to Hungary, or even money. UNEAC's committee director was against this award, and made that known in the prologue that precedes the edition. If the work was published, it was never sold in the country's bookstores. It circulated secretly: copies stolen from the stores, stolen by strangers, and photocopies, also by strangers. It circulated officially only in Cuban embassies, where copies were delivered in order to show that the play had been published and in case some curious foreigner wanted to obtain it.)

Following this controversy Arrufat was excluded from the Cuban cultural scene: "Mi nombre se borró de la historia literaria, de las antologías y hasta de los catálogos de las bibliotecas" (My name was erased from literary history, from anthologies and even library catalogues), he told Barquet. Fourteen years later, during a less dogmatic period, Arrufat was allowed to appear again gradually in the literary field as an essayist, short-story writer, novelist, and poet. Nevertheless, his career as a playwright in Cuba continues to be clouded because of the repercussions against *Los siete contra Tebas.* The play has not been performed in Cuba; however, in 1970, the director Salvador Flores staged it in Mexico. In 2001 the play was translated into English by Mike González and staged in Glasgow, Scotland at the Ramshorn Theatre.

The writing of this play was motivated initially by Cuban director Armando Suárez del Villar, who asked Arrufat to adapt Aeschylus's tragedy. Thus, the playwright developed his version (for which he also uses ideas from Euripides' *Phoenicians*), which suppresses three scenes from the original text as well as the characters of the Messenger, the Town Crier, Antigone, and Ismene. At the same time, he added a second Spy and gave voices to the soldiers. Other changes consist of his modernization of certain names and his omission of Greek cities. Arrufat focuses his text on the conflict between the two brothers (Eteocles and Polyneices) who die at each other's hands in the seventh gate of the city in a fight for power to govern Thebes. Another difference with regard to Aeschylus's text consists of the fact that the burial of Polyneices' body is permitted.

With the deaths of the brothers, Arrufat shows the town's freedom from excessive pride and opens a new path full of hope. The play ends on an optimistic note and not in the pessimistic manner of Aeschylus's version.

Carlos Espinosa Domínguez explains in his article "A Century of Theatre in Cuba: An Introduction to Cuban Theatre" (2004) that "during these years ideology was a battlefront. The United States had increased its hostility against Cuba and the whole country was on a grip of what was called the 'Revolutionary Offensive.'" Anything that was not in favor of the ideology of the Cuban Revolution was deemed against it. The censors interpreted *Los siete contra Tebas* as a play that re-created the imperialist propaganda of the United States, because, they argued, some of the ideas presented in the play were similar to those of John F. Kennedy.

The critics agree that *Los siete contra Tebas* marks a new stage in Arrufat's playwriting. At the same time, they share the analysis that this play represents a metaphor for Cuba's postrevolutionary political reality. Matías Montes Huidobro, in his book *Persona, vida y máscara en el teatro cubano* (Persona, Life and Masks in Cuban Theater, 1973), and Barquet, in his article "Heteroglosia y subversión en *Los siete contra Tebas*" (Heteroglossia and Subversion in *Seven Against Thebes*, 1995), establish the paradigms: Thebes/Cuba, Aeschylus/Fidel Castro, Polyneices/Exiled Cubans, and Commanders and Soldiers/Cuban militia. Abilio Estévez calls the play "the metaphor of a country with sons forced into exile as a consequence of a political reality in which they did not believe or simply could not understand." Since Fidel Castro saw the exiled ones as traitors of the Cuban Revolution, the censors also condemned the idea of exile that was presented in the play.

After Arrufat's obligatory disappearance from the Cuban theater scene because of the censorship of *Los siete contra Tebas,* no dramatic work by Arrufat appeared until *La tierra permanente* (The Solid Earth) in 1987. The text, conceived between 1974 and 1976, written in verse, and divided into two parts, still has not been performed. According to Arrufat, the work presents the classical structure of the *auto sacramental* (a religious work that deals with moral and theological problems) in a modern form. However, instead of theological problems, he expounds on the vicissitudes that the natives, Creoles, whites, Chinese, and slaves face in the land conquered by Spaniards. *La tierra permanente* is the first of Arrufat's works to function as a tribute to Cuba: the land as a country, as fertile atmosphere, as a place of happiness and sadness, as the fruit of life. At the same time, he pays homage to the legacy, culture, and history of Cuba.

Cover for Arrufat's unstaged 1995 play, about Austrian dancer Fanny Elssler's introduction of ballet to Havana in 1841 (Perkins Library, Duke University)

One of the elements that stands out in this play is the technical control of time. The characters continually move from present to past and vice versa. The setting is the festive atmosphere of a sugarcane plantation, and Arrufat uses popular speech as well as a variety of poetic verses and genres: ten-line poems, quatrains, riddles, refrains, hymns, and music. The themes dealt with by the playwright are current: fear, lack of freedom, prejudice, violence, suffering, hunger, and dehumanization. The published version of *La tierra permanente* received the Premio de la Crítica (Critics' Prize).

In 1995 Arrufat published another play, titled *La divina Fanny* (Fanny the Divine). This work, commissioned by the Cuban ballerina Alicia Alonso and written in 1984, has not yet been staged. This drama was originally created as a ballet script based on the famous Austrian ballerina Fanny Elssler and her visit to Cuba in 1841.

Arrufat states in a "Note for Staging" published at the beginning of the text that the play is proposed for a total theater in which the word, the body, and music should be integrated. At the same time, he suggests two distinct ways of staging the play: one in a conventional setting with an elaborate and complicated performance, and the other in any small stage space with a simple performance. In addition, the playwright gives more freedom to the director to cut from the play what he or she deems necessary.

La divina Fanny is much more technically complicated than Arrufat's previous plays. In this work, comments related to theatrical writing are interspersed with the ballerina's biography in such a way that readers are aware the play is a fictionalized, romantic version of Elssler's visit to Cuba. The playwright mixes ballet with rumba, Afro-Cuban religion, and other local customs. The play is written in free verse and depicts how Elssler managed to get a producer and a town interested in performing and watching this new genre of ballet that she introduced in Havana. At the same time, one observes how the foreign ballerina interacts with and learns to understand the Cuban people during her short stay in the country. She decides to use slaves, blacks, and mulattos to compose her ballet *La Sylphide,* which she performs on the island. The playwright takes advantage of this interaction between whites, mulattos, and blacks to criticize the racial and class prejudice still present in Cuba.

In spite of the sanctions and the ostracism suffered by the playwright for almost two decades, Arrufat stayed in Cuba, where he still resides, supporting himself by writing poetry, fiction, essays, and theatrical criticism. He finished a B.A. in philology at the University of Havana. He has never married or had children. With regard to his literary projects, he published in 2003 his latest play, *Las tres partes del criollo* (The Creole's Three Stages), which he started writing in 1983 under the title, "El retrato del criollo Juan" (The Portrait of John Creole). His theatrical works can be divided around *Los siete contra Tebas*. The plays written before *Los siete contra Tebas* deal with the existential problems of humanity and manifest tendencies taken from *teatro bufo* and the Theater of the Absurd. In the plays written after *Los siete contra Tebas,* Arrufat experiments with other theatrical, artistic forms such as ballet, total theater, *autos sacramentales,* and theater in verse. His plays have been translated into Portuguese, Polish, English, and French and have been staged in the United States, Venezuela, Mexico, Puerto Rico, and Poland. In 2000 he received the Premio Nacional de Literatura (National Prize for Literature). The same year, he received the Alejo Carpentier Prize for his novel *La noche del Aguafiestas* (The Spoilsports' Night, 2000).

Los siete contra Tebas has attracted the most attention of Antón Arrufat's plays, nationally and internationally. Both the artistic quality of the text and the subsequent censorship have caused this play to be studied with care and caution. Even though Arrufat's development as a playwright grew rapidly during the first years of the Cuban Revolution, his progress was frustrated by UNEAC's sanction of *Los siete contra Tebas,* which is the reason the writer's dramatic corpus is not extensive. After his exclusion from theater, Arrufat began to explore other literary genres. For Arrufat, theater is intended for the stage. If he is not allowed to stage his plays, he finds no motivation for writing them.

Interviews:

Nancy Christoph, "'El teatro me ha dejado a mí': Una entrevista con Antón Arrufat," *Latin American Theatre Review,* 32 (Spring 1999): 143–149;

Jesús J. Barquet, "Antón Arrufat habla claro sobre *Los siete contra Tebas*," *Encuentro de la Cultura Cubana,* 14 (Autumn 1999): 91–100;

Charo Guerra, "Entrevista a Antón Arrufat: Herramientas del viejo carpintero," *Unión,* 42 (January–March 2001): 2–7.

References:

Consuelo Alvarez and Rosa Iglesias Montiel, "Fidelidad y libertad mitográficas en *Los siete contra Tebas* de Antón Arrufat," *Unión,* 42 (January–March 2001): 17–21;

Leopoldo Avila, "Antón se va a la guerra," *Verde Olivo,* 9, no. 46 (1968): 16–18;

Jesús J. Barquet, "Heteroglosia y subversión en *Los siete contra Tebas* de Antón Arrufat," *Anales Literarios,* 1, no. 1 (1995): 74–87;

Barquet, "Subversión desde el discurso no-verbal y verbal de *Los siete contra Tebas*," *Latin American Theatre Review,* 32 (Spring 1999): 19–31;

Barquet, *Teatro y Revolución Cubana: Subversión y utopía en Los siete contra Tebas de Antón Arrufat / Theater and the Cuban Revolution: Subversion and Utopia in Seven Against Thebes by Antón Arrufat* (Lewiston, N.Y.: Edwin Mellen Press, 2002);

Emilio Bejel, "La dirección del conjuro en *Los siete contra Tebas*," in his *Literatura de Nuestra América. Estudios de literatura cubana e hispanoamericana* (Xalapa: Universidad Veracruzana, 1983), pp. 123–133;

Martha Betancourt Chiarella, "El carácter agónico de los personajes en las obras de Antón Arrufat," dissertation, University of Iowa, 1982;

Frank N. Dauster, "El tiempo amargo: El teatro de Antón Arrufat," in his *Ensayos sobre teatro hispanoamericano* (Mexico: SEP, 1975), pp. 37–59;

Dauster, "The Theater of Antón Arrufat," in *Dramatists in Revolt,* edited by Leon Lyday and George Woodyard (Austin: University of Texas Press, 1976), pp. 3–18;

José A. Escarpanter, "Tres dramaturgos del inicio revolucionario: Abelardo Estorino, Antón Arrufat y José Triana," *Revista Iberoamericana,* 56 (July–December 1990): 1091–1102;

Carlos Espinosa Domínguez, "A Century of Theatre in Cuba: An Introduction to Cuban Theatre," *Repertorio Español* <http://www.repertorio.org/education/index.php?area=sg&id=32>;

Abilio Estévez, "El golpe de dados de Arrufat," in *Teatro cubano contemporáneo,* edited by Carlos Espinosa Domínguez (Madrid: Fondo de Cultura Económica, 1992), pp. 861–867;

Manuel Galich, "Arrufat en el Teatro Experimental," *La Gaceta de Cuba,* 29 (5 November 1963): 15;

Abel González Melo, "Del teatro de Arrufat," *Proscenio,* 125 (2003) <http://www.lajiribilla.cu/2003/n125_09/paraimprimir/proscenio_imp.html>;

Jorge Luis Llopiz, "Otro premio para Antón Arrufat," *Encuentro de la Cultura Cubana,* 20 (Spring 2001): 24–28;

Elina Miranda Cancela, "El homenaje a Esquilo de Antón Arrufat," *Unión,* 42 (January–March 2001): 7–15;

Matías Montes Huidobro, *Persona, vida y máscara en el teatro cubano* (Miami: Universal, 1973), pp. 378–383, 401–412;

Terry Palls, "The Theatre in Revolutionary Cuba: 1959–1969," dissertation, University of Kansas, 1974;

"Premio Nacional de Literatura: Antón Arrufat," *Cuba Literaria* <http://www.cubaliteraria.com/autor/anton_arrufat/paginas/final_home.htm>;

Rodney Karl Reading, "The Renewal of Traditional Myth and Form in the Works of Antón Arrufat," *Revista Interamericana,* 10 (Fall 1980): 357–377;

José Sánchez-Boudy, "El pueblo en la obra de Antón Arrufat: *Los siete contra Tebas,*" in *National Symposium on Hispanic Theatre,* edited by Adolfo M. Franco (Cedar Falls: University of Northern Iowa, 1982), pp. 198–202;

George Woodyard, "The Theatre of the Absurd in Spanish America," *Comparative Drama,* 3, no. 3 (1969): 183–192;

Daniel Zalacaín, "Antón Arrufat," in his *Teatro absurdista hispanoamericano* (Valencia & Chapel Hill, N.C.: Albatros Hispanófila, 1985), pp. 72–76.

Sabina Berman
(21 August 1955 -   )

Francine A'ness
Dartmouth College

PLAY PRODUCTIONS: *El jardín de las delicias,* Mexico City, Universidad Autónoma de México, 1978; revised as *El suplicio del placer,* Mexico City, Camarata del Punta Este, 1986;

Bill, Mexico City, Teatro El Granero, 1980; revised as *Yankee,* Mexico City, El Foro Shakespeare, 1983;

Rompecabezas, Mexico City, 1981; revised as *El rompecabezas,* Coyoacán, Mexico City, Casa Museo León Trotsky, 1996;

La maravillosa historia del chiquito Pingüica, Mexico City, Teatro Independencia, 1983;

Herejía, Mexico City, Teatro Wilberto Cantón, 1984; revised as *En el nombre de Dios,* Mexico City, Teatro Reforma, 20 May 1992;

Aguila o sol, toured Mexico, 1985;

Muerte súbita, Mexico City, Teatro El Granero, October 1988; revised, Mexico City, El Foro Shakespeare, 26 February 1998;

Entre Villa y una mujer desnuda, San Angel, Mexico City, Teatro Hélenico, 28 January 1993;

La grieta, Mexico City, Foro de la Conchita, 1996;

Krisis, Mexico City, Teatro Telón de Asfalto, 1996;

Molière, Mexico City, Teatro Julio Castillo, 16 October 1998;

Feliz nuevo siglo doktor Freud, Mexico City, Teatro Orientación, 16 November 2000.

BOOKS: *Rompecabezas* (Mexico City: Oasis, 1983);

Teatro de Sabina Berman (Mexico City: Mexicanos Unidos, 1985)–comprises *Bill, Rompecabezas, Herejía, Aguila o sol, Esta no es una obra de teatro,* and *Un actor se repara;*

Poemas de agua (Mexico City: Shanik, 1986);

Volar: La tecnología Maharishi del campo unificado, by Berman and José Gordon (Mexico City: Posada, 1987); republished as *Volar: Aprendiendo a actuar desde la forma más simple de la conciencia* (Mexico City: Planeta Mexicana, 1992);

Muerte súbita: Obra de teatro original (Mexico City: Katún, 1988);

Lunas (Mexico City: Katún, 1988);

Sabina Berman (photograph by Rosario Guillermo; from the cover of a 1994 edition of Entre Villa y una mujer desnudo; *James B. Duke Library, Furman University)*

La bobe (Mexico: Planeta Mexicana, 1990); translated by Andrea G. Labinger as *Bubbeh* (Pittsburgh: Latin American Literary Review Press, 1998);

Entre Villa y una mujer desnuda: Obra en cuatro actos (Mexico City: SOGEM, 1992); revised as *Entre Villa y una mujer desnuda* (Mexico City: El Milagro, 1994); translated by Shelley Tepperman as "Between

Pancho Villa and a Naked Woman," *TheaterForum,* 14 (1998): 91–108;

Berman (Mexico City: Gaceta, 1994)—comprises *Entre Villa y una mujer desnuda, Muerte súbita,* and *El suplicio del placer;*

El suplicio del placer (Aguascalientes, Mexico: Instituto Cultural de Aguascalientes, 1994)—comprises *La pistola, La casa chica, Los dientes,* and *El gordo, la pájara y el narco;*

El árbol de humo (Mexico City: ECO, 1994);

Un grano de arroz (Mexico City: Seix Barral México, 1994);

Caracol y colibrí (Mexico City: Instituto Nacional de Antropología e Historia, 1996);

Amante de lo ajeno (Mexico City: Océano, 1997);

Cortometrajes (Mexico City: El Milagro, 1997);

La grieta (Mexico City: Instituto de Seguridad y Servicios Sociales de los Trabajadores del Estado, 1999);

Molière (Mexico City: Plaza y Janés, 2000);

Feliz nuevo siglo doktor Freud (Mexico City: El Milagro, 2001).

Editions in English: "The Mustache," translated by Adam Versényi, *Performing Arts Journal,* 20, no. 2 (1998): 111–118;

The Theatre of Sabina Berman: The Agony of Ecstasy and Other Plays, translated by Versényi (Carbondale: Southern Illinois University Press, 2003)—comprises *The Agony of Ecstasy, Yankee, Puzzle,* and *Heresy.*

PRODUCED SCRIPT: *Entre Villa y una mujer desnuda,* motion picture, Televisa, 1995.

OTHER: *Bill,* in *Más teatro joven,* edited by Emilio Carballido (Mexico City: Editores Mexicanos Unidos, 1982), pp. 123–171;

Bill, in *Avanzada,* edited by Carballido (Mexico City: EDIMUSA, 1984), pp. 113–161;

Pingüica, in *Jardín con animales,* edited by Carballido (Mexico City: Mexicanos Unidos, 1985), pp. 257–296;

"The Form and Nature of Women's Plays," "Women's Voices in Hispanic Theater," and "The Woman Playwright: Identity and Transformation," in *International Women Playwrights: Voices of Identity and Transformation–Proceedings of the First International Women Playwrights Conference, October 18–23, 1988,* edited by Anna Kay France and P. J. Corso (Metuchen, N.J. & London: Scarecrow Press, 1993), pp. 93–95, 213–221, and 238–247;

"Hugo Argüelles: La dramaturgia como el arte de la acción," in *Hugo Argüelles: Estilo y dramaturgia,* edited by Edgar Ceballos (Mexico City: INBA, 1994), pp. 597–616;

Muerte súbita, in *La nueva dramaturgia mexicana,* edited by Vicente Leñero (Mexico City: El Milagro, 1996);

Mujeres y poder, edited by Berman and Denise Maerker (Mexico: Hoja Casa, 2000);

Feliz nuevo siglo doktor Freud, in *Teatro, mujer y país,* edited by Carlos A. Limón (Mexico City: Tablado Iberoamericano, 2000), pp. 59–103;

"La comedia como forma de vida," in *Oficio de dramaturgo,* edited by Silvia Peláez and Hugo Argüelles (Mexico City: Editarte, 2002).

SELECTED PERIODICAL PUBLICATIONS–UNCOLLECTED: "Y alzaron los ojos de la tierra: Teatro campesino maya de X'Ocen," *Latin American Theater Review,* 24, no. 1 (1990): 77–80;

"El principio de la experimentación: Aquí no hay nada," *Tramoya,* 22 (1990): 9–13.

Since the early 1980s, when Sabina Berman first came to critical attention by winning four national playwriting awards, she has written and revised more than fifteen plays. Some of her works, such as *Entre Villa y una mujer desnuda* (Between Pancho Villa and a Naked Woman, performed in 1993), *Molière* (performed in 1998), and *Feliz nuevo siglo doktor Freud* (Happy New Century, Doctor Freud, performed in 2000), in addition to garnering several awards, have enjoyed uncharacteristically long runs in major Mexico City theaters. They have also been produced in important cultural centers abroad, such as Santiago, Cádiz, Montreal, New York City, and Los Angeles. Berman has won both critical and commercial acclaim and has become one of Mexico's most well-known and widely performed professional playwrights.

Berman is often associated with the generation of playwrights known as the Nueva Dramaturgia Mexicana (New Mexican Playwrights). The term, which was first used by Guillermo Serrat, refers to a series of dramatized readings held at the Universidad Autónoma Metropolitana (UAM) in the early 1980s. The "new dramatists" were a heterogeneous group of young, mainly male, writers. All attended workshops with older, more established playwrights and wrote new plays under their guidance. The term *Nueva Dramaturgia* was subsequently used by Serrat as the title for the anthology he published at the close of the series. The term has continued to be used to refer to the group of writers launched by the UAM readings, who went on to become famous in the late 1980s.

Sabina Berman was born in Mexico City in 1955. She was the third of four children born to Enrique and Raquel Berman, both Polish Jews who had immigrated to Mexico in the late 1930s and early 1940s respectively. Once in Mexico, Berman's father, a former communist, became a successful businessman. Berman's mother trained and worked as a psychoanalyst, sparking Berman's own fascination for psychology. Although both parents were multilingual, they were eager to make Mexico their home. Thus, while Berman attended Jewish schools with other children of European immigrants, her parents also made sure that she did not live completely confined to a cultural ghetto. They spoke only Spanish to their children and filled their house with books on Mexican history, literature, and art. Weekends were spent attending the theater or visiting exhibitions of contemporary artists. She recalls that one of her parents' main vocations was to "become Mexican" and to help their children to do the same.

Her parents also socialized with a broad circle of intellectual friends, many of them psychoanalysts like Berman's mother. Berman has admitted that when these gatherings took place at her parents' home, she would often hide behind the sofa and listen to the conversations. She claims that this early encounter with eavesdropping gave her the ear for dialogue that has served her so well in the theater. Another activity that allowed Berman to experience more of Mexico than her neighbors was tennis, which she played competitively at the national level until entering college.

While Berman regularly attended the theater as a child and occasionally performed with a theater group at the local synagogue, her vocation for the stage did not develop until much later. After attending El Colegio Columbia, an elite prep school, she went on to study Mexican literature and psychology at the Universidad Iberoamericana in Mexico City. She admits that her initial calling was not the stage but poetry, through which she not only received her preliminary aesthetic training but also learned the economy of the written word. This training was further enhanced during Berman's second year of college when she received a scholarship from the Instituto de Bellas Artes to attend a poetry workshop at the Capilla Alfonsina, a prominent cultural institution in the heart of Mexico City. Berman admits that she discovered dramatic writing quite by accident during her second year of college. She and a group of friends decided to enter a playwriting competition held by the university, and together they wrote and produced an eleven-minute play called *Mariposa* (Butterfly). To everyone's surprise, they won. The group spent the rest of the year performing, and when they had completed their tour Berman challenged the group to give up their studies and dedicate themselves full-time to the stage. Her friends, she likes to recall, thought she had gone crazy, but Berman was serious; the experience of doing live theater had marked her in a profound way.

Buoyed by this affinity to the stage and attracted by the romantic life it promised, the nineteen-year-old Berman actively set about pursuing her passion more seriously. While still attending university, she signed up to take acting classes at the Centro de Artes Dramáticas de Coyoacán (CADAC), an independent theater school founded and run by the director/playwright Héctor Azar. For more than a year Berman attended evening classes at CADAC, and, under Azar's guidance, she immersed herself in the theatrical process. A confrontation with Azar led to her leaving the school and auditioning to be an actress with Teatro T, another independent stage school established by the avant-garde director Abraham Oceransky. With Teatro T, Berman worked as assistant to the director and started to write short dramatic pieces for the group. Her early one-act play *Esta no es una obra de teatro* (This Is Not a Play, published 1985), which was later renamed *Un actor se repara* (An Actor Prepares, an allusion to Konstantin Stanislavsky's classic acting manual, translated in 1936), became the final exam for graduating students. Also from this period are the three one-act plays *Uno* (One), *Dos* (Two), and *Tres* (Three), which make up *El jardín de las delicias* (The Garden of Delights, 1978), later revised as *El suplicio del placer* (The Agony of Ecstasy).

In *El jardín de las delicias* each play centers on a male-female relationship and explores the dynamic inseparability of love and pain. *Uno* (later renamed *El bigote* [The Mustache]) humorously examines the impact that a key personal accessory has on an androgynous couple and their relationships with members of the other sex. El (He) and Ella (She), it is stressed, are virtually identical. Only the addition of a mustache marks their difference and highlights their respective genders. Berman, however, complicates this idea by making the mustache they share migratory. As it passes back and forth between the lovers, its significance and value change. For example, when El wears the large, black mustache, his masculinity is unmistakable, and both his perceived virility and popularity rise. On the other hand, when Ella assumes the mustache, it confuses the issue. In a heterosexual context the mustache instantly masculinizes her, thus rendering her less attractive to men. Yet, in a homoerotic context the mustache not only gives her the confidence to flirt but also apparently makes her more attractive to women. By using this simple prop, Berman is able to explore the unspoken rules and biases upon which gender is constructed, as well as expose the heterosexist framework in which it normally functions. Although it is one of Berman's earliest plays and a piece she herself now finds naive, *El bigote* continues to be a popular play with critics in the United States who point out how well the piece dramatizes contemporary theories of gender construction.

Dos (later renamed *La pistola* [The Gun]) takes the monotony and lack of communication typical of a married couple to an absurd extreme by showing what happens to their relationship when another prop, this time a gun, is introduced. Like many couples, the Ella and El in this play speak to each other but consistently fail to communicate. Their conversation goes in comic circles as they themselves run from room to room trying to outsmart each other. Ella believes that she has seen her husband enter the house with a gun and becomes increasingly convinced that he is trying to kill her. At first he admits that he possesses a gun but that he purchased it for self-defense. He then changes his story and denies he has a gun at all. Afraid he is going to use it against her, she tries to hide the gun; but as she is doing so, a figure appears at the window. Thinking it is the intruder that her husband spoke of, she takes aim and fires, only to find that she has shot her husband. Mortified, she breaks down. However, just when she thinks her husband is dead, he rises unscathed from the floor and insists she has imagined the whole thing, causing her to doubt her own sanity. The piece, both humorous and ominous, explores the hidden motives behind the most innocent-seeming actions and exposes the potential for violence beneath the power struggles and lies that lovers navigate on a daily basis.

The final play, *Tres* (later renamed *La casa chica* [The Love Nest]), exposes the sociosexual dynamic between a man and his lover. In this piece, unlike the others, the female character does not appear on stage at all. Instead, only her voice is heard as she engages in lighthearted banter with the man who, pacing back and forth, impatiently waits for her to appear on stage. The longer she spends in the bathroom getting ready, the more aggressive her suitor becomes, to the point where he ends up insulting her and comparing her unfavorably with his wife. The irony, however, remains evident: although he may praise his wife, he is still intent upon spending the evening with his lover. Embodying the double standard that marks sexual politics in Mexico, this businessman wants the best of both worlds and sees nothing wrong with trying. Berman has often stressed her admiration for the quick wit and ironic edge of Mexican baroque poet Sor Juana Inés de la Cruz, and she worked hard to hone those skills herself. This play echoes many of the sentiments found in Sor Juana's famous poem that begins "hombres necios" (Oh, stubborn men), which, like *La casa chica*, skillfully exposes the man who blames the women for his own philandering ways.

Not long after their initial meeting, Oceransky and Berman became lovers. She moved in with him

Patricia Bernal as Gloria in the 1988 Teatro El Granero premiere of Berman's play Muerte súbita *(Sudden Death), in which a couple's relationship is tested by an old friend (photograph by José Zepeda; from Vicente Leñero, ed.,* La nueva dramaturgia mexicana, *1996; Jean and Alexander Heard Library, Vanderbilt University)*

and, at his encouragement, started to write full-time for the stage. Berman's early partnership with Oceransky was central to her development as both playwright and theater practitioner. Through Oceransky, a director fully committed to the aesthetics of total theater, Berman came to appreciate the plastic potential of the stage and the importance of spectacle as well as drama. Oceransky also recognized that Berman needed expert guidance if she were to advance as a playwright. For this reason, he recommended that she attend the playwriting workshops of Hugo Argüelles, a dramatist who, like Oceransky, was well connected in the world of professional Mexican theater. At these workshops, which she attended for some four years, Berman perfected her craft and interacted with other promising young writers. Together they became the core figures of the Nueva Dramaturgia Mexicana.

Guided and encouraged by her mentors, over the next four years Berman wrote four prizewinning plays (three of which were directed by Oceransky): *Bill* (performed in 1980), *Rompecabezas* (Jigsaw Puzzle, performed in 1981), *La maravillosa historia del chiquito Pingüica* (The Wonderful Story of Little Pingüica, performed in 1983), and *Anatema* (Anathema, performed as *Herejía* [Heresy] in 1984). She also published a collection of her play texts, was included in various anthologies, and received a commission from the Department of Education to write an historical drama, based on the Conquest, for the national curriculum. This play became a touring production called *Aguila o sol* (Heads or Tails, performed in 1985). This early success and recognition has been described by some as a "heroic feat" since, at the time Berman began writing for the stage, few contemporary Mexican playwrights and almost no new playwrights were being professionally produced in Mexico City.

The first full-length play that Berman wrote and workshopped with Argüelles was *Bill* (later retitled *Yankee*). In 1979 the Instituto Nacional de Bellas Artes (INBA) gave *Bill* the institution's first national playwriting award, and the piece was included in Emilio Carballido's anthology *Más teatro joven* (More New Theater, 1982). It premiered in 1980 under the direction of José Caballero at one of the INBA's smaller theaters, the Granero. The general critical consensus was that Berman, then only twenty-three, not only showed talent but also had the makings of a playwright of stature.

Predominantly naturalistic, *Bill* tells the story of a Mexican couple whose life is transformed by the arrival at their beach house in Veracruz of a mysterious American. Who he is and what he wants is never clarified, but his presence is the catalyst for a drama that begins with curiosity, develops into mutual mistrust, and ends with violence. Only Rosa, the young wife, recent mother, and erstwhile mediator between the two men, escapes the violence by leaving the scene before it erupts. But the play is not, as the second title and synopsis may seem to suggest, a diatribe against neo-imperialism and rampant U.S. intervention. The tension that develops between the two male characters—Alberto, a struggling novelist, and Bill, an apparent Vietnam veteran—stems more from their inability to communicate or understand each other beyond the wider cultural stereotypes they supposedly represent.

In 1983 the text was reperformed under the more ambivalent new title *Yankee*. Oceransky was the director, and the intimate Foro Shakespeare served as the new venue. Yet, while *Bill* was a prizewinning play, many critics have identified it as Berman's weakest. The playwright and anthologist Vicente Leñero, for example, who in 1994 categorized Berman's theater into three types—relationship plays, political plays, and history plays—refers to *Bill* (a relationship play) as a "timid" text. He argues that it possesses neither the characteristic irony nor the irreverence that is such a feature of her subsequent plays, even those that were written just a few years later.

In 1980 Berman was awarded another INBA national playwriting award for *Rompecabezas*, originally called "Un buen trabajador del piolet" (A Man Skilled with the Pickaxe), which was first staged by Oceransky in 1981. The play, a political whodunit set in Mexico City in 1940, revolves around the actual assassination of the Communist intellectual Leon Trotsky and the thwarted investigation that ensued. Audiences know from the history books and from an early reenactment of the crime "who done it" and how. What is not clear, though, is the motive, which is examined over the course of the play. Through constant retellings and reenactments and an almost absurd accumulation of conflicting points of view and opinion, the "truth" about what happened to Trotsky, an "historical" truth that at the outset of the play had seemed so clear and unequivocal, is placed in doubt and ultimately elided.

The action, a combination of caricature and slapstick, analysis and drama, oscillates between three main locations: the house where Trotsky is attacked and where an exaggerated police reenactment occurs; the hospital to which he and his aggressor are removed and where Trotsky eventually dies; and various rooms in the commissary where the assassin is detained and subjected to torture and interrogation. Shorter scenes are interspersed with longer ones, and the number of characters progressively accumulates. However, rather than clarifying the investigation and helping to solve the crime, their function primarily serves to confound it.

Most of the characters involved in the play remain secondary to the two protagonists—Salazar, the officer in charge of the investigation, and his nemesis Jacques Monard, the assassin. Within the main circus of the play an existential drama takes place between these two opposing and contradictory characters. Salazar is an aging Indian and former general. The Mexican Revolution and his abiding belief in what it stood for have served him well. In spite of his indigenous origins, he has a career, a name, a rank, and a position in society. He is a staunch believer in something called the Truth and will go to almost any extreme, including violence, to ascertain or maintain it. Monard, on the other hand, is a professional cynic. He believes in nothing and no one. His origins are never clear, and his name is a constantly changing label. Salazar calls him Señor X, others Frank or Jacques. He is, like Bill in *Yankee,* puzzling and unpeggable. Ultimately, as both the motive for the crime and the identity of the criminal fade into confusion, the likelihood of establishing the truth and closing the case dwindles. Salazar, a man defined by absolute values and beliefs, is unable to continue. His very identity comes into question and becomes unstable. Confused, bitter, and increasingly unsure, he gives up his badge and abandons the investigation.

The play, an unfinished puzzle, raises more questions than it answers, and there is ultimately no resolution. At the close of *Rompecabezas* the audience is left under the watchful eye of a cadet, who brandishes a gun in their direction, daring anyone to speak. It appears that the only way to hold opinion in sway and enforce absolutes is ultimately through violence. With *Rompecabezas* Berman exposes the gulf that lies between historical facts and the events they supposedly represent, a theme to which she returns in subsequent plays. She dramatizes the biases that motivate and lie at the heart of all forms of representation. Through irony and exaggeration, elements that became characteristic of Berman's style, she shows how contradiction and relativity are the norm and places Truth and Absolutes in the realm of fiction. But it is an attractive fiction that is often only enforceable through violence and the repression of dissent. In a country where counterdiscourse was, for a long time, carefully controlled by the State and often punished with force, the allusion is clear.

In 1982 Berman won another INBA award, this time in the category of children's theater, for her play *La maravillosa historia del chiquito Pingüica*. The title was later shortened simply to *Pingüica*. The play, a parable based on the sacred book of the Maya, the Popol Vuh, was written for Oceransky's three-year-old daughter, who played the role of the tortoise in the first production. The veteran Mexican playwright Carballido, whom Berman had recently met on a train journey, asked to include *Pingüica* in a collection of plays for children he was putting together titled *Jardín con animales* (The Animal Garden, 1985). Since *Pingüica,* Berman, who recognizes the importance of nurturing a love of the theater in young audiences, has written three more plays for children. These are *El árbol de humo* (The Tree of Smoke, 1994), *Caracol y colibrí* (The Snail and the Hummingbird, 1996), and *Los ladrones del tiempo* (The Thieves of Time), an adaptation of Michael Ende's 1973 novel *Momo*.

Berman's fourth and final INBA award came in 1983 for her play *Anatema*. The title was later changed to *Marranos* (Swine), then *Herejía,* and in 1992 to *En el nombre de Dios* (In God's Name). Based on archival material and published texts and set in sixteenth-century New Spain, the play presents the story of Don Luis Carvajal y de la Cueva, proud patriarch and governor of New León, who, along with his extended family, settled in the Americas only to be persecuted by the Inquisition for being Jewish. While Don Luis has actually renounced his Judaism and, for pragmatic reasons, has adopted Catholicism, the rest of the family (unbeknownst to him) continue to defend their faith and practice its rituals in secret. Not until the second act, when the death of his brother-in-law causes him to have an existential crisis, does Don Luis discover the truth about his family. The news leaves him torn between denouncing them all, including his heir, Luis Carvajal the Younger, or remaining silent and, at great personal risk, defending the family's honor. He decides to remain silent, only to learn that his right-hand man, Felipe Núñez, has other plans. In a thwarted attempt to protect his master and avenge himself for being repeatedly slighted by the other Carvajals, Felipe Núñez reports the family to the Inquisition, unleashing a power he had failed to anticipate and is unable to contain.

Using the published prison notes of Luis Carvajal the Younger as well as Alfonso Toro's study of the case from the Inquisition archives, Berman re-creates this tale in a series of nonsequential scenes and flashbacks. The action oscillates between the private space of the home, where the family practice their faith far from the prying eyes of the authorities, and the public spheres of inquisitorial and political power. Interspersed between these scenes are flashes of Luis Carvajal the Younger alone in his prison cell, remembering happier times with his family. These moments are presented using the aesthetic of flamenco dance and the haunting sounds of the *cante jondo* (deep song), a transcultural tradition produced by the fusion of Gypsy, Jewish, and Moorish sounds. Berman's use of flamenco song and dance is not, however, merely decorative. Not only does it underline the creativity that occurs when different cultures intersect, but also it alludes to the violence that often occurs when they do. All three groups who contributed to the creation of flamenco in Southern Spain—Gypsies, Jews, and Arabs—were forced to convert, were expelled, or were persecuted by the Inquisition. Forced conversion, expulsion, and persecution are all themes that are central to her play. By using the aesthetic of flamenco dance and *cante jondo,* Berman is able to marry form and content to create meaning as well as to emphasize theatricality.

On the basis of her unprecedented success, Berman, who was still only twenty-eight years old, was commissioned in 1983 to write *Aguila o sol*. The play is, at first glance, almost quintessentially Mexican since the subject is an archetypal and foundational moment in Mexican history—the conquest of the Aztecs by the

Spaniards at Tenochtitlán. The commissioning body was none other than the Secretaría de Educación Pública (SEP), the same ministry that, in the 1920s and 1930s, under the directorship of José Vasconcelos, had promoted cultural *mestizaje* (miscegenation) as an aesthetic ideal and funded investigations into *lo mexicano* (Mexicanness). Nevertheless, even though Berman was commissioned by the State to write the play, she ultimately subverted the authority of the commissioning body by questioning the ideological bias of the texts upon which its authority is founded.

In *Aguila o sol,* Berman does not represent the Conquest the way it had been taught in school or most often told in the history books; instead, she takes aim at official history by pitting an alternative and conflicting version against it. Using Miguel León Portilla's collection of indigenous testimonies of the Conquest, which he gathered in the book *Visión de los vencidos* (The Broken Spears, 1959), she dramatizes the fall of Tenochtitlán from the perspective of the defeated Indians. In a departure from the more traditional version of events, the Indians, represented in the play by Montezuma, Patlahuatzin, and La Malinche, are coherent and speak a Spanish that is intelligible. The audience, therefore, identifies with them and not the Spaniards, who, represented by Hernán Cortés, speak an absurd stream of nonsense and behave in increasingly extravagant ways. Usually, as the Conquest is told from the perspective of the victors, it is the Spaniards who interpret and translate the extravagances and incoherence of the Indians and are thus granted the privilege of representing the other culture. In *Aguila o sol* they, not the Indians, must rely on a translator to be understood. Based on La Malinche's inconsistencies and elaborations each time she mediates between the two cultures, audiences see quite clearly and with humor the arbitrariness of translation and the difficulties in representing or even understanding the Other.

Berman's inversion, like León Portilla's collection, destabilizes the idea of objective truth and static identities. In a country where the official versions of the foundation, independence, revolution, and development of the nation are learned like a sacred catechism in school, Berman takes a risk. Yet, in *Aguila o sol* Berman does not just question and critique the Spaniards and the official institutions their descendants have come to represent, nor does she simply memorialize a long-ago defeated people. Instead, by using contemporary slang, mariachi music, and the type of sketch most commonly associated with *carpas* (popular theater performed in tents) and street theater, she breathes life into the past. She uses the theater as a space not just for critical reflection but also for social satire, slapstick, and amusement. With now-characteristic irreverence, she parodies all those involved in the Conquest, so that Cortés is not the only fool. Montezuma, while coherent, is obsequious and as a leader inept. La Malinche mediates between the two men while arbitrarily and purposefully mistranslating everything they say. The play is satirical and profane, a twentieth-century revision of an historical moment that has, over time, become ritualized and distorted, but one that, nonetheless, is still used to erase the people it most purports to represent—the contemporary indigenous peoples of Mexico.

Berman first began to write for the stage during a time when there was a call from within the theater world for a new national theater. Many veteran members of the theater world, Berman's mentor Argüelles included, believed that Mexican theater could benefit stylistically by returning to its protonational and national roots in indigenous, Hispanic, and local performance traditions. This return meant exploring and modernizing ritual, spectacle, pageant, the three-act *comedia* (cloak-and-dagger renaissance play) and, moreover, the popular and political *carpas,* or circus. With *Aguila o sol* Berman explores the creative fusion of an aesthetic form (the satirical *carpa*) with one of the foundational discourses of the nation (the Conquest). By doing so she responds to all those older members of the field who wished to assert the "national" in the idea of a national theater.

In their unmistakably Mexican themes, tone, and style, all of Berman's early plays answer the call for a new national theater. Both formally and aesthetically, Berman draws on indigenous, Hispanic, and Mexican visual and performance traditions. In *Rompecabezas,* for example, she proposes that the death of Trotsky be presented using traditional Mexican Day of the Dead iconography. Trotsky's burial, therefore, takes the form of a carnivalesque *calavera* (skeleton) parade. Similarly, the lone woman who mourns his death resembles the legendary figure of La Llorona (The Crying Woman), an emblematic figure of the Conquest who also appears, as to be expected, in *Aguila o sol*. Even *Bill,* which is less conspicuous in its presentation of Mexican symbols and mythology, is nonetheless laden with allusions to national identity and foundational fictions.

The SEP, however, did not agree with those who, anticipating the criticism it might receive from official sources, praised the novelty of *Aguila o sol*. The SEP ultimately did not produce the play nor distribute it in schools. Instead, Oceransky pressured the INBA to produce the play. They also refused to take it into the schools, but after some initial reservations, they did agree to fund a tour. In 1985, again under Oceransky's direction, *Aguila o sol* began a one-and-a-half-year tour of the provinces. Berman recalls that the only set piece they used was a plastic bench, which was set up wherever people assembled to watch the show, on the streets and in the plazas of rural Mexico. The experience taught Berman how important it was to genuinely communicate with the audience rather than, as many playwrights tried to do, preach at them from the proscenium. As her popularity has grown, Berman has actively nurtured the relationship with her local audience in Mexico City, acknowledging them directly through the media or addressing them metatheatrically in her later plays such as in *Molière* and *Feliz nuevo siglo doktor Freud*.

In 1984 a rift began to develop between Berman and her mentors. After seeing Oceransky's production of *Herejía* at the Teatro Wilberto Cantón, a production she genuinely disapproved of, Berman started to seriously question the type of theater that she wanted to write. The production was so far removed from her own vision of the play that she felt that Oceransky had used her work as a mere pretext for a production of his own authorship. This tendency was by no means limited to Oceransky; it was a trend among directors in Mexico at the time as many of them, in their attempt to modernize the Mexican stage, were experimenting with new theater theories and stage technologies from abroad. Shortly after the staging of *Herejía* Berman and Oceransky parted ways; and not long afterward, the workshop that she had attended for so long with Argüelles and the other members of the incipient Nueva Dramaturgia Mexicana disbanded.

Between 1985 and 1988, in an attempt to reconnect with her primary passion, Berman turned her attention back to poetry. In three years she produced two volumes, one of which, *Poemas de agua* (Water Poems, 1986), is an erotic, autobiographical account of her new life as a lesbian. In 1986 she also revised the more intimate one-act plays of *El jardín de las delicias* and renamed the collection *El suplicio del placer*. It premiered that same year at the Camarata del Punto Este under the direction of the highly respected Marta Luna.

Berman remembers these years as a period of crisis and change. Not only had she branched out as an artist on her own, leaving behind the security provided by her mentors, but she had also turned thirty, started to live openly as a lesbian, and recommitted herself to writing as both craft and vocation. Nevertheless, from this crisis a more confident and original playwright was born. She now knew that what she wanted to do was write theater that functioned not only at the level of spectacle but at an intellectual and poetic level as well. She felt it important that her theater tell stories, possess a clear narrative structure, and communicate with the audience. *Muerte súbita* (Sudden Death, as the term is used in the sporting world) was Berman's first attempt

Cover for the revised 1994 edition of Berman's 1992 play (Between Pancho Villa and a Naked Woman; performed in 1993), a romantic comedy about an entrepreneur and a professor who is writing a novel about Pancho Villa, his political and sexual role model (Howard-Tilton Memorial Library, Tulane University)

to put theory into practice and write a play from a more intimate, naturalistic, and less epic perspective.

Over the next two years Berman wrote poetry and worked on the text of *Muerte súbita*, writing and rewriting different versions until she was satisfied. She now insists that, while it remains relatively ignored by the critics, it is a play pivotal in her development as a playwright, because writing it was an intentional exercise in dramatic precision and personal honesty. Her aim was to move away from the ludic and spectacular nature of her previous work and closer to a type of realism in which every phrase and gesture inexorably advanced the action. The result is a play that exists in multiple versions and has gained an almost cult status among young Mexican theatergoers.

Muerte súbita, which premiered at the Teatro El Granero in 1988, studies how the staid relationship of a young heterosexual couple is shaken to the core by the arrival of an old male friend, Odiseo. This uninvited and self-appointed mythical figure, who likes to call himself the Angel of Destruction, sets out to overturn the insular little world that Alberto and Gloria have made for themselves in an abandoned old art deco building in the Colonia Condesa. This building, severely damaged in the 1985 earthquake, is where Alberto has escaped in order to write his third novel. As a writer he is in a rut. His second novel was a failure, and his confidence has been sorely tested. Gloria, his partner, is a flighty and fun-loving model who spends her days flitting between photo shoots and visits to her psychotherapist. The arrival of Odiseo puts to the test not only their relationship but also the very foundations of their individual and collective identities.

Before the arrival of Odiseo, Gloria and Alberto's life is marked by routine. The passion and spontaneity they had previously shared has been replaced by a predictable pattern of day-to-day activities. They get up, get dressed, make coffee; Gloria leaves for work; and Alberto sits down at the typewriter to write. They communicate poorly, and when they do, they bicker and spar. Their relationship, like the building they are living in, shows signs of wear, but neither Gloria nor Alberto does anything to change. Alberto refuses to move until he has finished his novel, and Gloria accepts the status quo even though, deep down, it makes her unhappy and she feels ignored. Odiseo's unexpected arrival is the catalyst that causes everything to change.

Once a good friend of Alberto's before the latter met Gloria, Odiseo has spent the last few years in prison on minor drug charges. Now free, he seeks out his old buddy and is horrified by the banality of what he finds. He accuses Alberto of becoming timid, of shielding himself from the pain and ugliness in the world to the detriment of his creative potential. Using the metaphor of a rose, Odiseo declares that he has come to teach Alberto to see the thorns as well as the flowers: "Voy a enseñarte a ver las espinas. A no voltearles la cara. A no tenerles pánico. Y al final vas a caer de rodillas ante la rosa entera, delicada y terrible" (I am going to teach you to not turn away from the thorns; to not be afraid of them. Then you will fall to your knees before the whole rose, that delicate and terrible flower). Afraid of Odiseo's intensity, Alberto resists; but Odiseo presses on with his mission, determined to transform their lives, for better or for worse. He seduces Gloria by giving her the attention she craves and times it so that Alberto will find them in bed together. The discovery forces Alberto to break up with Gloria, who takes off with all of her belongings in tow, including the typewriter. As she leaves she declares that she is planning to "cambiar totalmente de vida" (change my life completely). Once alone with Alberto, Odiseo continues his lesson in the creative art of destruction. With almost sadistic pleasure, he continues to challenge his friend, ultimately goading him into a violent confrontation.

The 1990s were busy years for Berman. In 1991 she saw two more of her plays for children produced and also published a new play, *La grieta,* in the theater magazine *Tramoya*. This work is a longer version of her one-act play *El polvo del tiempo* (The Dust of Time), published three years earlier in *Tramoya*. Both *El polvo del tiempo* and *La grieta* are absurdist in tone and highly critical of the Mexican government's love of red tape and bureaucracy. Using the waiting room as the central conceit of the play, Berman exposes this bureaucracy as not only bloated and ineffectual but also nepotistic, hierarchical, and abusive. The two central characters, El and Ella, have been summoned to a lawyer's office and ordered to wait. Why they are there and how long they will have to stay is never revealed, not even to them, but as the play progresses the situation becomes increasingly absurd.

As representatives of Mexico's educated middle class, El and Ella are, at first, confident that they will be seen shortly and treated with the respect to which they have grown accustomed. Yet, although there is much hustle and bustle around them with employees coming and going, nothing changes, not even when El tries to use his status to demand attention from the Licenciado (lawyer). After a confrontation, the humiliation of being forced to carry out a mindless chore, and a ridiculously detailed lesson in how to use the sofa bed in the waiting room (as if they were to remain there forever), the couple are left to ponder their fate. The Licenciado and his two employees go home, and El and Ella are no closer to knowing why they were summoned in the first place. In the script it is stipulated that the lights go down to mark the end of the play, but when they come up again, El and Ella are still there waiting. This lowering of the lights is repeated several times, yet still they do not leave. In spite of being pushed around, ignored, humiliated, and insulted, they remain in the waiting room simply because they have nowhere else to go.

The audience realizes that El and Ella, like many other middle-class Mexicans, are desperate for work and feel marginalized by a system that functions through corruption, nepotism, and favors. The veneer of confidence, complacency, and class security that had marked the couple at the beginning of the play gradually disappears, leaving them exposed and most uncertain of their future. Talking about the current state of affairs, at one point Ella sobs, "es como un amante al que cualquier día una deja de amar" (it's like a lover who one day you just stop loving). In criticizing the system and the petty bureaucrats who represent it, Berman also satirizes the passivity and latent snobbery of many intellectual, middle-class Mexicans. Until now they, unlike other less fortunate Mexicans, thought they were insulated from economic insecurities and social injustices, and for this reason they largely ignored them.

During the 1990s, in addition to writing three important new plays—*Entre Villa y una mujer desnuda, Krisis* (performed in 1996), and *Molière*—Berman revised several of her earlier plays and gave permission for them to be restaged. Berman has become somewhat infamous for her constant, almost obsessive, rewriting of her plays; many of them, such as *Muerte súbita* and *Herejía,* exist under multiple titles and different versions. In 1992, to coincide with the quincentenary celebrations of the conquest and colonization of the Americas, she wrote a newer, streamlined version of *Herejía* called *En el nombre de Dios.* In the newer version of this play the order of the scenes is rearranged, and a new character, El Padre Jeremías (Father Jeremías), is added along with his two Indian slaves, thus intensifying the criticism of the church in the play. The explicit torture scenes are removed, and the prison sequences are presented entirely using the *cante jondo* and the aesthetics of flamenco, a change that gives more internal coherence to the text. Rosenda Montero, widely known for her work as an actress, directed the play with a new ensemble of dancers and young actors known collectively as El Foro Dramático de México. The production, which opened at the Teatro Reforma on 20 May 1992, was favorably reviewed in spite of the unknown actors and minimalist staging. Many of the critics who reviewed this newer version of the play highlighted how well the themes of intolerance and ethnic tension still resonated within a contemporary Mexican context.

In 1993 Berman had her biggest success to date when she wrote, directed, and produced *Entre Villa y una mujer desnuda.* The play, which opened on 28 January at the Centro Cultural Helénico in the affluent suburb of San Angel, is an irreverent comedy that challenges the hegemony of certain widely accepted social and sexual stereotypes in the Mexican collective consciousness. It especially scrutinizes all cultural norms that elevate the masculine over the feminine or exclusively conflate virility with violence, mobility, and revolutionary politics, and femininity with submission, stasis, political apathy, and domesticity. The action centers on the love affair between Gina, a forty-year-old widow and fledgling entrepreneur, and Adrián, a twice-divorced, middle-aged history professor and journalist who is writing a novel about his revolutionary hero, Pancho Villa. While Gina is financially independent (she and her friend Andrea are taking full advantage of the soon-to-be-ratified North American Free Trade Agreement [NAFTA] by setting up a toy-manufacturing plant in the border town of Ciudad Juárez) she is far from liberated ideologically. In a similar contradiction, while Adrián may still espouse revolutionary social politics, his sexual politics, modeled upon those embodied by Villa, leave a lot to be desired. Both characters are in search of love, yet they have different ideas about what it entails and how their affair should ensue. Gina would like to remarry, develop a secure and stable companionship, and perhaps have another baby. Adrián, on the other hand, prefers intermittent sexual encounters on his own terms and a relationship with no strings attached. Berman, however, complicates this age-old dilemma (and makes it specifically Mexican) by introducing the character of Villa. His hapless and periodic appearances onstage form the central conceit of the play and allow Berman to both highlight and comment upon the social and sexual contradictions embodied in the characters.

Parallel to the surface comedy runs the subtext of the play, which underscores not the sexual but the social inequities that still undergird modern Mexico—inequities that, as the play shows, have changed little in the last eighty years and have been exacerbated by the process of modernization. In 1993 Cuidad Juárez, which was once the site of a customs post and home to Villa, was about to become the site of a transnational economic experiment—NAFTA. *Maquiladoras* (border factories) and free-trade agreements were to "revolutionize" the Mexican border, but only by keeping social and sexual inequities in place. Most of these factories are now owned by high-tech multinationals that enjoy fat profits at the expense of cheap (usually female) labor and looser environmental laws. Gina's toy-manufacturing plant is a sarcastic dig against Mexico's ruling class and the apparent naiveté of those who believe that the soon-to-be-ratified NAFTA will be a liberating economic experience for Mexico. In the same way that Gina is economically liberated but socially oppressed and restricted by her "open" yet lopsided relationship with Adrián, the liberation of Mexico will take more than "open" borders and an economic pact with the United States that is both compromising and unidirectional.

Through complex characterization, an informed use of stereotypes, and strategic humor, Berman begins to dissect some of the contradictions that structure contemporary Mexican society—contradictions created when inherited ideas and traditions clash with the contingencies brought about by modernization. *Entre Villa y una mujer desnuda* ultimately asks tough questions such as what it means to be revolutionary in a time of reactionary politics. Moreover, by using the popular model of the romantic comedy, Berman asks whether there are alternative ways to be male and female, modern

Villa y una mujer desnuda is often referred to as a watershed production in Berman's trajectory as a playwright. Yet, its success, while bringing Berman a considerable amount of publicity, also angered some members of the theater world who accused her of crossing over to the mainstream. The same accusation has followed her with each subsequent box-office success and is a theme she addresses metatheatrically in the later play *Molière*.

In 1994 Berman was invited to publish two collections of her plays. The first, simply titled *Berman*, comprises *Entre Villa y una mujer desnuda*, *Muerte súbita*, and *El suplicio del placer*. The second, titled *El suplicio del placer*, comprises *La pistola*, *La casa chica,* and two new plays: *Los dientes* (Teeth, which was commissioned and ultimately rejected by an international conference of dentists), and *El gordo, la pájara y el narco* (The Fat Guy, the Slut and the Drug Dealer). *El bigote,* the third one-act from *El jardín de las delicias,* was omitted from this collection in spite of the fact that it still appeared in the other and continued to be popular within academic circles. Of particular interest in this collection is *El gordo, la pájara y el narco,* since it was incorporated almost in its entirety into Berman's next full-length play, the controversial *Krisis*.

El gordo, la pájara y el narco is a hyperbolic black comedy that, as Iani Moreno has argued with reference to *Krisis,* uses the aesthetic of pulp fiction to address the pervasive culture of violence associated with Mexico's growing drug trade. Alberto, a large and depressive husband, accidentally kills his cheating wife, Patricia. He and his proselytizing spinster sister, Gabriela, brainstorm ways to dispose of the body and escape punishment. Before they can finish their cover-up, the wife's lover Ramón, a mafioso drug trafficker, appears for a night of passion. While Gabriela proceeds to dismember the body of Patricia in the bathtub, Alberto tries to keep Ramón entertained. Ramón begins to get suspicious, draws a gun, and threatens to shoot Alberto if he does not let him into the bathroom. Alberto is quicker with his gun, and now the siblings have two bodies to dispose of. Knowing that Ramón is involved with drugs and being hunted by a rival from Tampico, they position the bodies in such a way that the crime looks like a vendetta killing. They then take turns shooting the corpses while drinking from a bottle of champagne that was mysteriously left for Patricia. Their staging of the crime becomes progressively more elaborate as they imagine how a drug trafficker might torture and kill a rival. The irony of all their playacting only becomes apparent when they realize that the champagne they have drunk is poisoned and that the brand-new clock that has continued to tick and chime throughout the play is actually a bomb; both were left by the mafioso from Tampico. The play, a clear indictment of the state

Hector Ortega playing the title role in a Teatro Argos production of Berman's 1998 play, Molière *(photograph by José Jorge Carreon; from* Molière, *2000; James Branch Cabell Library, Virginia Commonwealth University)*

and democratic, in a country that, although rapidly changing, is still ruled by atavistic and authoritarian models from the past.

Berman was forced to produce and direct the play herself since, when she initially tried to sell the script, most producers balked, rejecting the play on the grounds that it was either too "light" or too intellectual for their respective audiences. In spite of the initial skepticism, *Entre Villa y una mujer desnuda* became a huge box-office success. It ran for more than a year and a half and only closed after an exceptional run of 460 sellout performances. The media giant Televisa bought the rights to the script, and in 1995 Berman turned *Entre Villa y una mujer desnuda* into a moderately successful movie, co-directed by Berman and her partner, Isabelle Tardán, that represented Mexico at the Oscars. *Entre* of the country, shows how endemic crime has become in Mexico and how violence permeates all sectors of society.

Berman's subsequent plays reflect her growing concern for the state of the country, which had reached crisis levels not seen in decades. If the danger of neoliberal politics was alluded to in *Entre Villa y una mujer desnuda,* for the most part it remained at the level of subtext. However, by 1996 the true neoliberal economic model was in crisis, and Mexico teetered on the brink of economic collapse and social unrest. The guerrilla-led Zapatista uprising in Chiapas in 1994 and rising inflation had forced the Salinas administration to devalue the peso. The ensuing austerity only served to bring massive hardship to a large sector of the Mexican population from the middle classes and to a rapidly growing social underclass as well. Finally, a series of high-profile political assassinations had rocked the country, provoking angry reactions to the perceived conspiracies, abuse of power, and widespread corruption within the upper echelons of the ruling party, the Partido Revolucionario Institucional (Institutional Revolutionary Party, PRI). For Berman the economic and moral crises could not be ignored, and for the next few years she sought different aesthetic forms to represent the decadence of contemporary Mexico. In an interview published in the cultural magazine *Motivos* Berman admitted to becoming an avid spectator of her immediate social reality "con la sensación repentina de que en realidad no estoy escribiendo, sino coordinando información" (with the sudden sensation that I was not inventing stories but simply coordinating information).

Berman's next new play, *Krisis,* is a scathing and only thinly veiled indictment of the PRI, which, through authoritarian measures, cronyism, and violence, had ruled Mexico, ostensibly unopposed, for more than sixty years. The epigraph to the published script is a quotation from James Joyce: "La historia es un sueño pesado . . . y ya quiero despertar" (History is like a bad dream . . . and right now I want to wake up). The play centers on the lives of childhood friends Polo, Pedrero, Jorge, Seijas, and Jesús—the Group of Five—who go on to occupy prominent positions, including the presidency, in the ruling party of an unnamed country. The play opens with a short movie projected onto a giant screen above the stage. It shows the boys as ten-year-olds playing an aggressive game of Monopoly. When the Indian maid interrupts their game and tells one of the boys it is time for bed, he insults her with racist barbs. Later, when she mistakenly brings him a vanilla milkshake instead of chocolate, he calmly takes a gun from the display case on the wall and shoots her in the head. Their game of speculation and the callous violence that ensues foreshadow the manner in which these boys will govern the country later in life, and the play exposes their government in a series of short, almost cinematographic scenes. Bonded by crime and the oath of secrecy that marked them in childhood, they pull each other to the pinnacle of power through contacts and bribes. Once they have achieved success, their fraternal bond begins to show signs of strain, ultimately snapping violently under the pressures of greed, adultery, and the danger of dissent.

The world that is dramatized in *Krisis* is devoid of any moral compass. Its historical referents in the Salinas administration would be clear to any Mexican audience. Perhaps for this reason, Berman found it difficult to get the play produced, and once again she chose to produce and direct it herself. Her production was fast-paced and loud. Once the audience had entered the auditorium at the Telón de Asfalto they were not allowed to leave, adding a sense of claustrophobic immediacy to the event. The scenes amassed with vertiginous speed and absolute fluidity, and the explosions and gunshots of the final scenes were loud enough to hurt. The reception to *Krisis* was divided. While some members of the audience enjoyed the aggressive satire and giddy atmosphere, many others found the production too close for comfort. They felt under attack and argued that the theater should be a space of enjoyment, an escape from the violence and scandals of everyday life. The critics—perhaps fearing censorship, as Jacqueline E. Bixler has argued—largely ignored the production. Even Olga Harmony of *La Jornada,* a theater critic who had supported Berman throughout her career, felt that the play would not endure the test of time. Berman was deeply disappointed with their reaction. She admits that she wrote *Krisis* from a position of moral outrage and wanted the theater to be a forum of dissent and a space for much-needed community.

After the production of *Krisis,* Berman left Mexico for a year and went to the United States to focus on a new project. While she was away, the director Carlos Haro took two of her earlier political plays to the stage. *Rompecabezas* was restaged under the modified title *El rompecabezas.* Its themes of political assassination, internal corruption, and abuse of power resonated well, possibly better than they had in the 1980s. Haro chose to produce *El rompecabezas* on location at the Casa Museo León Trotsky—the house, now a museum, where Trotsky had lived and was actually assassinated. In the manner of environmental theater, the audience did not remain seated but followed the action from the courtyard through different rooms of the house and back again. Questions about the efficacy of this approach divided the critics in their reception.

In 1997 Haro directed another of Berman's plays, *La grieta,* the absurdist piece that criticizes rampant bureaucracy and exposes the dangers of complacency in Mexico's intellectual class. It premiered at Martha Olga Dávila's Foro de la Conchita (a small, independent theater that stages contemporary texts by living authors) and formed part of a series of five contemporary plays written by Mexican authors. Unlike *Krisis* and *El rompecabezas*, *La grieta* was received extremely well by critics and audience alike. This time Harmony praised Berman for writing a "provocative text" that used "exquisite metaphors" to carry out a "feroz crítica" (ferocious criticism) of the system. She also commended Haro for his use of space, which included three doors that opened and closed in a vaudevillian fashion to reveal the different offices within. The play reopened for a second run later in the year.

With the critical distance provided by being abroad, Berman wrote her next full-length play, *Molière*, a metatheatrical piece about power and politics in the competitive world of the arts. *Molière* was commissioned by the INBA for their permanent acting ensemble, the Compañía Nacional de Teatro (CNT), and from the beginning it was designed to be a big-budget affair. It premiered at the Teatro Julio Castillo, one of Mexico City's most important theaters, on 16 October 1998. Directed by Antonio Serrano (known more widely for his directorial work in movies and television), the play was immediately well received by the critics, many of whom felt that the production, one of Berman's best, should travel and represent Mexico abroad. Rene Franco of *El Economista* argued that *Molière* was not only the most important Mexican theater event of the decade but also the first play written by a Mexican that had the potential to become a success on the international stage. Likewise, Martha Bátiz Zuk of *Unomásuno* referred to *Molière* as "un clásico inmediato" (an instant classic) and proposed that it be translated into several languages and produced around the world. As had been the case with *Entre Villa y una mujer desnuda*, the play was popular with Mexico City audiences. By November *Molière* had started to win major awards, and Berman once again received the accolade of best national playwright.

While the critics praised *Molière* for being one of Mexico's best plays and a sign of a healthy national stage, it marks the first time Berman wrote about something other than Mexico and set the action abroad. She pits two French playwrights (icons of the French national stage) and the types of theater they espouse against each other in dramatic opposition. Molière, a firm proponent of Comedy, believes that the aim of the theater is to entertain first and educate second. It is a popular art form designed to delight everyone involved, including the audience. For him, the theater is a space for intimacy and enjoyment, sex and laughter, social satire and critique. For Jean Racine, a proponent of Tragedy, the theater is a noble cause. Its aim is to exalt, educate, and honor, to celebrate those in power. Such service to crown and country, he believes, dignifies the artist and elevates the theater above all other arts. In Serrano's production, although the two protagonists were equally matched as actors and shared the stage as characters, the play, a tragicomedy, ultimately endorses Molière's philosophy and celebrates comedy both as a form of popular entertainment and an ontological outlook on life.

The simple opposition of Tragedy and Comedy forms the focal point of Act 1; but in Act 2 the audience sees that the stake is much higher than the hegemony of Comedy or Tragedy within the art world. Both Racine and Molière are artists who, like most Mexican theater practitioners, rely on the patronage of state institutions (or, increasingly, private corporations) to see their work produced. Within their seventeenth-century world of theater, the dynamic opposition of Comedy and Tragedy necessarily defines their field. Outside that sphere, however, both playwrights and the types of theater they produce are either dominated or co-opted by the fields of power–the Catholic Church and the French Crown. The Court, for example, closes down Molière's theater, and the type of social satire he writes is censored by the Church. Racine, the official historian and new favorite of the king, is also manipulated by the agents of power. By the end, the pompous, powdered, and bewigged Racine recognizes that, by allowing himself to be seduced by power, he has become a mere mouthpiece, prop, and servant of the State.

Ultimately, the play is a poetic treatise on comedy and a magical exploration in metatheatricality. It is also an allegory, a reminder that the "autonomous" nature of the art world is, at least in Mexico, still an illusion, and that the type of patronage offered by the State comes with contingencies and temptations. Berman reminds her audience how the fields of power still seduce, co-opt, censor, and control the artist and intellectual. She also sends an ironic wink to those critics who continued to accuse her of catering to her audience and writing what they deemed to be "light" theater.

One of the major strengths of this first production of *Molière* was Serrano's creative use of space and Gabriel Pascual's spectacular stage. Taking advantage of the imminent closure and controversial proposed full-scale refurbishment of the Teatro Julio Castillo and other local theaters, Serrano and Pascual totally transformed the interior of the building. They not only incorporated the giant auditorium into the acting area of the stage but also seated the audience, much reduced in size, in the area that originally had been set aside for the backstage. Two heavy curtains divided the acting areas. The first curtain divided the auditorium and the smaller stage. When the curtain was open, the larger acting area it revealed symbolized the epic spaces of courtly and religious power. When the curtain was down, it formed the backdrop to the smaller and more intimate space occupied by Molière and his troupe. Throughout the production the action shifted back and forth between these multiple acting areas, effectively revealing the tension between the individual and the State.

Also in 1998 Berman again revised *Muerte súbita*, this time in collaboration with well-known director Francisco Franco for his production at the Foro Shakespeare, the same theater where *Yankee* had been produced fifteen years earlier. With each rewriting of *Muerte súbita* Berman has streamlined the script: a scene is modified, a character deleted, a dialogue pruned. The ambiguities of the earlier versions were clarified so that, for example, the latent homosexuality that had existed between Odiseo and Alberto in the 1988 version becomes explicit in the 1998 production. The new version of the play originally opened on 26 February 1998, only to close shortly afterward when there were problems between the actors and the producers over pay. It reopened on 17 June with a further modified script and a completely new cast. All three actors were well-known television stars, and their presence onstage at the Foro Shakespeare assured a crowd.

Berman has called *Muerte súbita* a portrait of her generation. In the late 1980s when the play first premiered, the characters, who are all in their late twenties or early thirties, would have been born in the mid to late 1950s, which would make them from the same generation as Berman—the generation that experienced the 1960s as children but came of age after its revolutionary phase, after the failed student uprising at Tlatelolco, and during the Vietnam War. Odiseo, interestingly, is thirty-three. That he should be the same age as Christ when he died highlights his messianic nature. By the 1990s *Muerte súbita* had become more realistic and even more representative of a generation of disillusioned and disenchanted youth. In 1998 Gloria, Alberto, and Odiseo are no longer children of the 1950s and 1960s but of the 1970s. Alberto's thirty years would make him born in 1968, the year of the uprising in Tlatelolco. Gloria is twenty-eight. Their birth dates transform them into members of Generation X, that generation of post-revolutionary children brought up on mass media and globalization, spiritually bereft, politically disillusioned, and stagnant.

Berman's next play, *Feliz nuevo siglo doktor Freud*, opened at the Teatro Orientación on 16 November 2000 under the direction of Sandra Félix, one of Mexico's most promising young female directors. It was an

Cover for Berman's play (Happy New Century, Doctor Freud), performed in 2000 and published the next year, which shows how Sigmund Freud's study of a woman's hysteria was influenced by the cultural environment in which he lived (James B. Duke Library, Furman University)

instant box-office success and received several awards and prizes. After finishing its initial run at the tiny Teatro Orientación the play reopened at the larger Teatro Julio Castillo for a new season. Like *Entre Villa y mujer desnuda* and *Molière*, it ran for more than two hundred performances.

Feliz nuevo siglo doktor Freud is, like some of Berman's earlier plays, based closely upon an historical text—this time, on Sigmund Freud's case study of the hysteria of a young woman he calls Dora. Through treating Dora, Freud is able to advance some of his most enduring theories on female subjectivity and sexuality, namely, the ideas of transference, displacement, and penis envy. Such ideas, while hypotheses, have not only influenced the entire field of psychology but have entered into common parlance and understanding as though they were irrefutable truths. By dramatizing the contradictions and biases inherent within the Dora case, Berman challenges audiences to reconsider the origins of Freud's ideas and recognize how contingent they were upon the context in which they were conceived. According to Berman, the guiding metaphor behind *Feliz nuevo siglo doktor Freud* is that of a giant caught in a cage. The cage is the cultural milieu into which Freud was born and educated and from which he was unable to escape. Freud's continual misunderstanding of Dora shows that no matter how radical or revolutionary his ideas concerning subjectivity and sexuality were, they were still informed by the prevailing ideas on sexuality and gender at the end of the twentieth century.

Berman proposes that only four actors play all of the characters, a decision that is apparently more artistic than economic. By having the same actor play multiple roles, the play visually exemplifies Freud's theory of transference, the idea that in every new encounter, an individual confers upon a stranger the identity of someone close to him or her. According to Freud, this "recognition," or transference of identity, predetermines how an individual will behave each time they meet someone new. Therefore, the actor who plays Freud also plays Dora's father and his friend Herr K, whom Dora accuses of sexually molesting her. Likewise, to dramatize Freud's theory of the id, the ego, and the superego, Berman divides the character of Freud and has three different actors play him.

With the exception of *Krisis* and to a lesser degree *El rompecabezas,* which received mixed reviews, all of Sabina Berman's plays written and produced in the 1990s have fared extremely well on Mexico City stages, and many critics now agree that Berman is Mexico's most popular and successful contemporary playwright. *Entre Villa y una mujer desnuda, Molière,* and *Feliz nuevo siglo Doktor Freud* also have enjoyed popular runs abroad both in Spanish and in translation. Adam Versényi's translations of her complete plays into English in 2003 will no doubt continue to expand her audience further.

Interviews:

Lydia M. Gil, "Entre Fronteras: Entrevista con Sabina Berman," *Dactylus,* 13 (1994): 29–36;

Luis Enrique Ramírez, *La Jornada* (Mexico City), 22 February 1995, p. 25; 23 February 1995, p. 27;

Emily Hind, "Entrevista con Sabina Berman," *Latin American Theater Review,* 33, no. 2 (2000): 133–139;

Maricruz Jiménez Flores, "Recrea Sabina Berman el mundo de Racine y Molière," *La Crónica de Hoy* (Mexico City), 16 May 2000;

Héctor González Jordán, "Sabina Berman: Después del teatro autista," *La Crónica de Hoy* (Mexico City), 16 July 2000.

References:

Francine A'ness, "The Production of a National Playwright: Sabina Berman, Her Audience, and the Changing Mexico City Stage," dissertation, University of California, Berkeley, 2001;

Jacqueline E. Bixler, "Entre Berman y una historia desnuda," *Tramoya,* 71 (2002): 107–115;

Bixler, "The Postmodernization of History in the Theater of Sabina Berman," *Latin American Theater Review,* 30, no. 2 (1997): 45–60;

Bixler, "Power Plays and the Mexican Crisis: The Recent Theater of Sabina Berman," in *Performance, pathos, política de los sexos: Teatro postcolonial de autoras latinoamericanas,* edited by Heidrun Adler and Kati Rottger (Frankfurt & Madrid: Vervuert/Iberoamericana, 1999), pp. 83–99;

Bixler, "Re-casting the Past: The Dramatic Debunking of Mexico's 'Official' History," *RHM,* 42 (1989): 163–172;

Ronald Burgess, "Bad Girls and Good Boys in Mexican Theater in the 1990s," in *Perspectives on Contemporary Spanish American Theater,* edited by Frank N. Dauster (Lewisburg, Pa.: Bucknell University Press, 1996), pp. 67–76;

Burgess, "Nuestra realidad múltiple en el drama múltiple de Sabina Berman," *Texto Crítico,* 2, no. 2 (January–June 1996): 21–28;

Burgess, "Sabina Berman's Undone Threads," in *Latin American Women Dramatists: Theater, Texts, and Theories,* edited by Catherine Larson and Margarita Vargas (Bloomington: Indiana University Press, 1998), pp. 145–158;

Burgess, "Sabina's Act of Creative Failure," *Gestos,* 2, no. 3 (1987): 103–113;

Roselyn Costantino, "El discurso del poder en *El suplico del poder* de Sabina Berman," in *De la colonia a la posmodernidad: Teoría teatral y crítica sobre el teatro latinoamericano,* edited by Peter Roster and Mario Rojas (Buenos Aires: Galerna, 1992), pp. 245–252;

Costantino, "Resistant Creativity: Interpretative Strategies and Gender Representation in Contemporary Women's Writing in Mexico," dissertation, Arizona State University, 1992;

Sandra Messinger Cypess, "Dramaturgia femenina y transposición histórica," *Alba de América,* 7, no. 12–13 (1989): 283–304;

Cypess, "Ethnic Identity in the Plays of Sabina Berman," in *Tradition and Innovation: Reflections on Latina American Jewish Writing,* edited by Robert

DiAntonio and Nora Glickman (Albany: State University of New York Press, 1993), pp. 165–177;

Stuart A. Day, "Berman's Pancho Villa versus Neoliberal Desire," *Latin American Theater Review,* 33 (Fall 1999): 5–23;

Lydia M. Gil, "Sabina Berman: Writing the Border," *Postcolonial Perspectives* (1994): 39–55;

Amalia Gladhart, *The Leper in Blue: Coercive Performance and the Contemporary Latin American Theater* (Chapel Hill: University of North Carolina Press, 2000);

Gladhart, "Playing Gender," *Latin American Literary Review,* 24 (January–June 1996): 59–89;

Emily Hind, "Historical Arguments: Carlos Salinas and Mexican Women Writers," *Journal for Theoretical Studies in Media and Culture,* 23 (Spring 2001): 82–101;

Vicente Leñero, ed., *La nueva dramaturgia mexicana* (Mexico: Milagro, 1996);

Sharon Magnarelli, "Masculine Acts / Anxious Encounters: Sabina Berman's *Entre Villa y una mujer desnuda*," *Intertexts,* 1, no. 1 (1997): 40–50;

Magnarelli, "Tea for Two: Performing History and Desire in Sabina Berman's *Entre Villa y una mujer desnuda*," *Latin American Theater Review,* 30, no. 1 (1996): 55–74;

Manuel F. Medina, "La batalla de los sexos: Estrategias de desplazamiento en *Entre Pancho Villa y una mujer desnuda* de Sabina Berman," *Revista Fuentes Humanísticas,* 4, no. 8 (1994): 107–111;

Priscilla Meléndez, "Co(s)mic Conquest in Sabina Berman's *Aguila o sol,*" in *Perspectives on Contemporary Spanish American Theater,* edited by Frank N. Dauster (Lewisburg, Pa.: Bucknell University Press, 1996), pp. 19–36;

Iani Moreno, "La cultura 'Pulp' en dos obras: *Krisis* de Sabina Berman y *Pulp Fiction* de Quentin Tarantino," *Gestos,* 13, no. 26 (1998): 67–82;

Kirsten F. Nigro, "The Theater of Sabina Berman," *TheaterForum,* 14 (Winter/Spring 1999): 88–90;

Nigro, "Theater, Women, and Mexican Society: A Few Exemplary Cases," in *Perspectives on Contemporary Spanish American Theater,* edited by Dauster (Lewisburg, Pa.: Bucknell University Press, 1996), pp. 53–66;

Mario A. Rojas, "*Krisis* de Sabina Berman y el escenario político mexicano," in *Tradición, modernidad y posmodernidad,* edited by Osvaldo Pelletieri (Buenos Aires: Galerna, 1999), pp. 119–134;

Diana Taylor, "*La pistola* de Sabina Berman: ¿Violencia doméstica o envidia del pene?" in *Antología crítica del teatro breve hispanoamericano. 1948–1993,* edited by María Mercedes Jaramillo y Mario Yepes (Antioquia: Editorial Universidad de Antioquia, 1997), pp. 60–65;

Margarita Vargas, "*Entre Villa y una mujer desnuda* de Sabina Berman," *Revista de Literatura Mexicana Contemporánea,* 2, no. 4 (1996): 76–81;

Jennifer A. Zachman, "El placer fugaz y el amor angustiado: Metateatro, género y poder en *El suplicio del placer* de Sabina Berman y *Noches de amor efímero* de Paloma Pedrero," *Gestos,* 31 (2001): 37–50.

Enrique Buenaventura
(23 August 1925 – 31 December 2003)

Beatriz J. Rizk

SELECTED PLAY PRODUCTIONS: *El misterio de la adoración de los Reyes Magos,* Cali, Teatro Escuela de Cali/Teatro Experimental de Cali (TEC), 1957;

The Marriage Proposal, translation of Anton Chekhov's play, Cali, TEC, 1957;

Casamiento a la fuerza, adaptation of Molière's play, Cali, TEC, 1957;

A la diestra de Dios Padre, Cali, TEC, January 1958; revised, Cali, TEC, 1960; revised, Quito, Teatro Sucre, May 1962; revised, Bogotá, Plaza de Bolívar, August 1975; revised, Cali, TEC, December 1984;

Tío Conejo Zapatero, Cali, TEC, 1958;

El monumento, Cali, TEC, 1959;

Blanca Nieves y los siete enanos, Cali, TEC, 1959;

Edipo Rey, adapted from Sophocles' *Oedipus Rex,* Cali, TEC, 1959; revised, Cali, TEC, 1965;

Cenicienta, Cali, TEC, 1960;

La tragedia del Rey Christophe, 1961;

Simbad el marino, Cali, TEC, 1963;

Un réquiem por el Padre de Las Casas, Cali, TEC, 1963;

Panorama desde el puente, translation of Arthur Miller's *A View from the Bridge,* Cali, TEC, 1965;

Ubú rey, adaptation of Alfred Jarry's play, Cali, TEC, 1966;

Macbeth, translation of William Shakespeare's play, Bogotá, Teatro de la Casa de la Cultura, 1967;

Los inocentes, adapted from Emmanuel Roblès's *Monserrat,* Cali, TEC, 1967;

La trampa, Cali, TEC, 1967;

Los papeles del infierno, Bogotá, National Theater Festival, 1968;

Soldados, adapted from Carlos José Reyes's play, Cali, TEC, 1968; revised, Cali, TEC, 1970; revised, Cali, TEC, 1971; revised, Cali: TEC, 1982;

Tirano Banderas, adaptado from Ramón del Valle-Inclán's novel, Manizales, Teatro Estudio de la Universidad Nacional, September 1968;

Canto del Fantoche Lusitano, adapted from Peter Weiss's *Gesang vom Lusitanishen Popanz,* Cali, TEC, 1969;

Enrique Buenaventura (from the cover for Máscaras y ficciones, *1992; Howard-Tilton Memorial Library, Tulane University)*

revised, Cali, TEC, 1974; revised, Cali, TEC, 1976;

Seis horas en la vida de Frank Kulak, Bogotá, Teatro Colón, 1969;

El menú, Nancy, France, International Theater Festival, 1970;

El convertible rojo, Cali, TEC, 1970;

La denuncia, Manizales, Manizales First World Theater Festival, 1973;

Historia de una bala de plata, Cali, TEC, 1979;

Opera bufa, Cali, TEC, 1982;

La gran farsa de las equivocaciones, Cali, TEC, 1984;

El encierro, Cali, TEC, 1987;

Escuela para viajeros, Cali, TEC, May 1988; revised as *La estación,* Cali, TEC, 1989;

Proyecto piloto, Cali, TEC, 1991;

Crónica, San Antonio, Texas, Guadalupe Arts Center, 1992;

El lunar en la frente, Cali, TEC, 1994;

El dragón de los mares, Cali, TEC, 1995;

La isla de todos los santos, Bogotá, Festival Iberoamericano, 2002;

Preguntas inútiles, Cali, TEC, 2002.

BOOKS: *Teatro* (Bogotá: Tercer Mundo, 1963)–comprises *Un réquiem por el Padre de Las Casas, La tragedia del Rey Christophe,* and *A la diestra de Dios Padre;*

Se hizo justicia (Cali: Publicación de la Universidad del Valle, 1977);

Teatro (Bogotá: Instituto Colombiano de Cultura, 1977)–comprises *Los papeles del infierno, El menú, La orgía, Soldados,* and *A la diestra de Dios Padre;*

Qué es la Corporación Colombiana de Teatro (Cali: Comisión de Publicaciones del TEC, 1977);

Historia de una bala de plata: Creación colectiva del Teatro Experimental de Cali (Havana: Casa de las Américas, 1980);

Teatro, edited by Francisco Garzón Céspedes (Havana: Casa de las Américas, 1980)–comprises *A la diestra de Dios Padre, Los papeles del infierno (La maestra, La tortura, La audiencia, La autopsia, La orgía, El menú),* and *Vida y muerte del fantoche lusitano;*

La orgía (Bogotá: Oveja Negra, 1985);

Notas sobre dramaturgia: Tema, mitema y contexto; La dramaturgia del actor; Metáfora y puesta en escena; El enunciado verbal y la puesta en escena (Buenos Aires: Asociación Argentina de Actores/TEC, 1988);

Los papeles del infierno y otros textos (Mexico City: Siglo XXI, 1990)–comprises *La maestra, La tortura, La autopsia, La audiencia, La requisa, La orgía, El menú, Se hizo justicia, Crónica, Un réquiem por el Padre de Las Casas,* and *El ánima sola;*

Máscaras y ficciones, edited by Carlos Vásquez Zawadski (Cali: Universidad del Valle, 1992);

Tirano Banderas: Tres dramaturgos colombianos (Bogotá: Gestus Separata Dramatúrgica, 1996);

Teatro inédito (Bogotá: Presidencia de la República, 1997)–comprises *Cristóbal Colón, La Corista, La encrucijada, El convertible rojo, La denuncia, Opera bufa, El encierro, La estación, Proyecto piloto, El nudo corredizo, El guinnaru, Ubú rey, Vida y muerte del Fantoche Lusitano, San Antoñito, La Guariconga,* and *Sketch de las Finanzas.*

Editions in English: *The Twisted State, Drama Review,* 14, no. 2 (1970): 151–156;

On the Right Hand Side of God the Father, in *Voices of Change in the Spanish American Theater,* edited by William I. Oliver (Austin: University of Texas Press, 1971);

The Orgy, in *Modern One Act Plays from Latin America,* edited by Gerardo Luzuriaga and Robert S. Rudder (Los Angeles: University of California Press, 1974).

OTHER: *A la diestra de Dios Padre,* in *Teatro,* edited by Carlos Solórzano (Mexico City: Fondo de Cultura Económica, 1964), pp. 263–307;

"El arte no es un lujo," in *Teatro y politica,* edited by Emile Copperman (Buenos Aires: Ediciones de la Flor, 1969);

"Esquema general del método de trabajo colectivo del TEC," in *Cuadernos 3 y 4: Teoría y práctica del Teatro* (Cali: Publicaciones del TEC, 1970);

"La interpretación de los sueños y la improvisación teatral," in *Materiales para una historia del teatro en Colombia,* edited by Carlos José Reyes and Maida Watson (Bogotá: Colcultura, 1978), pp. 285–296;

A la diestra de Dios Padre [fifth version], in *Teatro colombiano contemporáneo,* edited by Jorge Manuel Pardo and Carlos Nicolás Hernández (Bogotá: Tres Culturas Editores, 1985);

"Texto verbal y textos no verbales" *and* "Un movimiento con conciencia histórica," in *Escenario de dos mundos: Inventario teatral de Iberoamérica,* edited by Moisés Pérez Coterillo (Madrid: Centro de Documentación Teatral, 1988), pp. 52–55, 305–307;

Un réquiem por el Padre de Las Casas, in *Antología de teatro colombiano contemporáneo,* edited by Fernando González Cajíao (Madrid: Fondo de Cultura Económica, 1992),

SELECTED PERIODICAL PUBLICATIONS–UNCOLLECTED: "De Stanislavski a Brecht," *Mito,* 21 (1958);

El monumento: Farsa en un acto, seis visitas y un desagravio, Mito, 26 (1959);

"Birds-Eye View of the Latin American Theatre," *World Theatre,* 9, no. 3 (1960): 265–271;

"En busca de un método para la enseñanza teatral," *Periódico del Teatro Escuela de Cali, Archivo del TEC* (1962);

"What Is Realism Today?" *World Theatre,* 14 (1965): 132–133;

"Cómo se monta una obra de teatro en el TEC," *Letras Nacionales,* 2, no. 8 (1966): 28–32;

"L'art n'est pas un luxe," *Partisans,* 36 (1967): 80;

El presidente, Letras Nacionales, 15 (1967): 43–55;

"Un cursillo de dirección en Teatro Estudio dado por Enrique Buenaventura," *Conjunto,* 3, no. 10 (1968): 69–71;

El entierro, Razón y fábula, 8 (1968): 111–121;

"Theatre and Culture," *Drama Review,* 14, no. 2 (1972): 151–156;

"In Colombia: An Invisible Theatre," *International Theatre Information* (1972): 18–19;

"Teatro y cultura," *Primer Acto,* 145 (1972);

"Las últimas experiencias del Teatro Experimental de Cali: Nuestro arte será más arte cuanto más revolucionario sea," *Conjunto,* 14 (1972): 94–100;

"El teatro y la historia," *Primer Acto,* 163/164 (1973–1974): 28–35;

"Cómo trabajamos en *La denuncia*," *Conjunto,* 19 (1974): 81–86;

"Teatro y política," *Conjunto,* 22 (1974): 90–96;

"Teatro o taetro: Diálogo entre dos maneras de ver (1)," *Estravagario: El pueblo,* 16 February 1975, pp. 1+;

"Teatro o taetro: Diálogo entre dos maners de ver (2)," *Estravagario: El pueblo,* 23 February 1975, pp. 3+;

"Notas al método del TEC," *Trabajo teatral,* 4 (1975): 42–59;

"The Impact of Two Cultures," *International Theater Information* (1976);

"Por qué otra vez *La diestra*," *Poligramas,* 4 (1977): 128–135;

"Artistas y obreros en el Nuevo Teatro," *Documentos políticos,* 135 (1978): 40–43;

"El movimiento teatral colombiano en 1978," *El pueblo,* 24 December 1978, pp. 1+;

San Antonito, Semanario Cultural (6 May 1979): 11–12;

"El debate del teatro nacional," *Conjunto,* 43 (1980): 14–23;

"Ensayo de dramaturgia colectiva," *Conjunto,* 43 (1980): 18–26;

"La dramaturgia en el Nuevo Teatro," *Conjunto,* 59 (1984): 34–37;

"Actor, creación colectiva y dramaturgia nacional," *Boletín cultural y bibliográfico del Banco de la República,* 22, no. 4 (1985): 42–46;

"Notas sobre kinesis y proxemia," *Actuemos,* 3, no. 17 (1985): 1–4;

"La dramaturgia nacional y práctica social," *Separata* I. *Actuemos,* 3, no. 17 (1985): 12–18;

"Trayectoria y originalidad del teatro colombiano," *Diógenes,* 87 (1988): 57–63;

"Brecht y el Nuevo Teatro colombiano," *International Brecht Society: Communications,* 19, no. 3 (1990): 43–48;

Proyecto piloto, Gestos, 6, no. 11 (1991): 213–236;

"Dos cartas de Enrique Buenaventura," *Gestos,* 9, no. 18 (1994): 153–156;

La huella, Gestos, 19, no. 37 (2004): 91–131;

Colombian playwright, director, theoretician, poet, teacher, and painter Enrique Buenaventura was one of the most influential personalities of twentieth-century Latin American drama. He played a fundamental role in the creation of the New Theater movement that spread throughout the Americas from the 1950s, and he has been recognized as a great innovator. His work method, referred to as the "TEC method" (El método del Teatro Experimental de Cali/Cali Experimental Theater Method), is based on collective creation; it has been copied and imitated often and is still in use in the region at the beginning of the twenty-first century. His dramatic writing includes many versions of the same play as well as translations and adaptations of classical, national, and international plays, short stories, and novels. His legacy has been an inspiration to all subsequent generations of theater artists and practitioners not only in Colombia but also in the rest of the Spanish-speaking world, including the Latino communities in the United States.

Buenaventura was born in the city of Cali, Colombia, on 23 August 1925. His parents were Cornelio Buenaventura and Julia Emma Adler; he was the tenth of twelve siblings. His high-school years were spent at the Santa Librada School in Cali. After that he attended the National University in Bogotá, where he studied philosophy and painting. He started his multifaceted career in 1945 by writing fiction; his first work was "Cuentos de la selva" (Tales from the Jungle), an unpublished collection of short stories based on the Indians and the African descendants on the Colombian Pacific Coast, where he spent some time researching their culture. During his youth, he traveled extensively throughout Latin America. He saw a performance of the circus company Mesa-Nichols and decided to join them; he performed all over Colombia, ending up in Caracas, Venezuela, with the company of Argentine-born Francisco Petrone. He then traveled to Trinidad, where he collected local folktales and stories while working as a sailor.

At the beginning of the 1950s he moved to Recife, Brazil, where he worked with Hermilo Borba Filho's Teatro do Estudiante. His next stop was Buenos Aires, where he had contact with the newly created Teatro Independiente (Independent Theater) movement, specifically with the group Fray Mocho, who included among their members the playwright Osvaldo Dragún. The group's approach to theater, based on the rejection of a "star system" in favor of a collective entity where every member of the ensemble was responsible for the entire spectacle, had a tremendous impact on Buenaventura's formation as a playwright and as a director. He returned to Colombia in 1955 to head the recently established Escuela Departamental de Teatro (State Theater School) in Cali, which became known as Teatro Escuela de Cali (TEC).

Scene from a 1977 Teatro Experimental de Cali production in France of Buenaventura's 1958 play A la diestra de Dios Padre
*(On the Right-Hand Side of God the Father), adapted from Tomás Carrasquilla's short-story version of a legend from the
Spanish Middle Ages (from* Latin American Theatre Review, *volume 12 [Fall 1979];
Thomas Cooper Library, University of South Carolina)*

From its inception, TEC developed two alternative lines of work. On the one hand, the search for a national identity led to the staging of folkloric, popular, and historical theater as well as adaptations of literary pieces from the national repertoire; on the other hand, the group experimented with the "classics" in search of the particular through universal dramas. The first season of TEC (1956–1957) included the works *El misterio de la adoración de los Reyes Magos* (1957, The Mystery Play on the Visitation of the Three Magi), written by Buenaventura; *Las convulsiones* (The Convulsions), a nineteenth-century play written by Colombian poet Luis Vargas Tejada; *The Marriage Proposal*, by Anton Chekhov (circa 1888); and a farce by Molière, all directed by Buenaventura. Another field that Buenaventura and the group explored at this early stage was theater for younger audiences. He wrote a series of short plays based on legends and children's stories such as *Tío Conejo Zapatero* (1958, Uncle Bunny Shoemaker); *El monumento* (1959, The Monument); *Blanca Nieves y los siete enanos* (1959, Snow White and the Seven Dwarfs); *Cenicienta* (1960, Cinderella); and *Simbad el marino* (1963, Sinbad the Sailor). These plays are important because of his use of increasingly ironic dialogues, with which he contrasted the social classes depicted in the stories. This technique became one of the typical traits associated with his playwriting.

Soon Buenaventura was ready to embark on full-length plays that would address pressing social issues with the intention of raising the consciousness level of his audience. His aim was to make people aware of the injustice of the status quo in order to incite changes in society. In the article "En busca de un método para la enseñanza teatral" (1962, In Search of a Method to Teach Theater) he proposed a theater that would serve as an instrument to reflect reality, and as such it had to be nationalistic in scope, didactic in tone, and entertaining in nature. With this rationale in hand, he began to draw on the traditional repertoire of his own culture for inspiration in his work.

Heavily influenced by historical and dialectic materialism as a way of interpreting the economic relations of society—a philosophical approach that was popular at the time in Latin American intellectual circles and was derived from Georg Wilhelm Friedrich Hegel, Karl Marx, and Brazilian educator Paulo Freire—Buenaventura set out to create a past that would reflect the true nature of the collision, during the Conquest, of the three races that compose the Colombian ethnic background: the Spanish, the indigenous, and the African. This theoretical framework is evident in his first plays: *A la diestra de Dios Padre* (1958; translated as *On the Right Hand Side of God the Father,* 1958), one of his signature pieces, which has been revised several times; *La tragedia del Rey Christophe* (1961, The Tragedy of King Christophe); and *Un réquiem por el Padre de Las Casas* (1963, A Requiem for Father de Las Casas).

A la diestra de Dios Padre is an adaptation of a short story written by nineteenth-century regionalist writer Tomás Carrasquilla, who took the plot and characters from a legend derived from the oral tradition of the Spanish Middle Ages. Ridding the language of the original folkloric overtones, Buenaventura concentrated on the central conflict, the ruses employed by a compulsive gambler/peasant whom Jesus Christ has chosen to grant five wishes in one of his sporadic visits to Earth. Buenaventura presents a paradigm about the struggle of the classes and the formation of a proletariat mentality by the main character. The Spanish legacy, which includes the imposition of Catholicism on the native population, is avowed while the sense of justice and impartiality of the Church is being questioned from the point of view of the impoverished masses. In subsequent revisions of the play, Buenaventura often changed his point of view, his objectives, and even the characters according to the needs of the time.

La tragedia del Rey Christophe is an historical piece in which Buenaventura revisits the Haitian independence movement whose leaders were African slaves brought into the country by French colonizers. Awarded the UNESCO Latin American Theater Award in 1960, the play follows one of the revolutionary leaders, Henri Christophe, a free black man, from 1791 to 1820. At the start of the play, he is working as an assistant to the chef in a Cap-François (now Cap-Haitian) restaurant. From there, the audience sees him on the battlegrounds, first as an officer and later as a general. Once independence was achieved, the historical Henri Christophe seized control of the northern province and declared himself king. Among his first projects was the construction of an enormous fortress, known as La Citadel, which cost the lives and the trust of many of his subjects. Plagued by treason and defeated by his own people, he killed himself, apparently with a silver bullet.

Besides pointing out an historical event that has been largely overlooked by historians and interpreters of Latin American and Caribbean cultural studies alike because of its racial implications, Buenaventura deconstructs the essence of a modern hero, possibly the first caudillo of the region. His Henri Christophe is a character in crisis, struggling between idealist projects and materialistic goals set in motion by his desire to achieve supreme power. His downfall is portrayed as an example of the path many power-hungry leaders will follow in the coming centuries. Buenaventura wrote this play in Paris, where he went in 1960 to explore European theater. He stayed in Paris nearly two years; there he met Jacqueline Vidal, his future longtime companion, TEC member, director of many of his plays, and mother of his son, Nicholas, born on 7 August 1962.

Upon his return to Colombia in 1962, Buenaventura appealed to his countrymen to help him in the creation of a truly national theater. His experience in Europe working with French director Jean Vilar's successful Théâtre National Populaire and in Milan with the Piccolo Teatro prompted him to call for a "complete theater" where playwrights, actors, and directors would work together, as a team, writing plays with the broadest scope possible in regard to the topics in order to reach the widest segment of the population. With this idea in mind he set out to write his next play, *Un réquiem por el Padre de Las Casas,* which resulted from the discussions he maintained with his actors during the writing process. It is another historical piece based on the life of a real person, the famous Padre Bartolomé de Las Casas, a controversial figure who, during the Conquest, openly condoned black slavery to protect the almost annihilated Caribbean indigenous population.

Born in Seville in 1474, Las Casas arrived in America in 1502 accompanying Christopher Columbus on one of his last trips. He became the first priest to be ordained in the New World. In 1513 he took part in Diego Velazquez's conquest of Cuba. Once there, he gave up all his material belongings, including the right to own slaves, and embarked on a lifelong struggle to defend the Indians. He made several trips to Spain, where in 1542 he succeeded in influencing the enactment of new laws protecting the native populations of Latin America. He finally settled down in Spain, where he wrote his voluminous *Historia de las Indias* (completed in 1561, published in 1875; History of the Indies).

In the play, Las Casas's odyssey in America is presented in contrast to the native population's doomed destiny. He is at the vortex of the historical event that changed the world: the opening of transatlantic trade, which eventually moved the center of power from the Mediterranean region to the North Atlantic basin. It was the moment when capitalism, with the help of Catholic proselytism, expanded to the newly discovered lands, with catastrophic results to its inhabitants. The approach Buenaventura takes toward the conflict centers on the abortive efforts of the native population to wage war against the intruders, focusing on another real-life character, the indigenous Enriquillo. This young leader rebelled against the Spaniards, formed a small army, and bravely fought the invaders' forces. Las Casas was then asked by the governor to intervene, and he successfully convinced the Indian leader to surrender with the promise that his life would be spared. Once in prison, Enriquillo starved to death as he found out that the governor planned to kill him. Both Enriquillo and Las Casas are pawns in the larger game that is at stake: the end of a feudal world order and the coming of a new materialistically oriented, pragmatic world that cannot be prevented or stopped. Father de Las Casas continued to hold Buenaventura's interest for decades; he went back to *Un réquiem por el Padre de Las Casas* in 1992 with a new version in which he depicts his main character as a man in agony between his faith and his sometimes contradictory mission on this earth.

In 1965 TEC experienced an internal crisis as some of its members opted for more commercially oriented plays, such as a production of Arthur Miller's 1955 play *A View from the Bridge* (which was not a critical success), and others advocated politically oriented works that would address contemporary issues. Half of the TEC members disbanded, and a new group emerged, committed to bringing the political reality of the continent to the stage. Buenaventura's next play, *La trampa* (1967, The Trap), is a transitional piece between his previous historical search and his more militant later work. The play is loosely based on the life and deeds of Guatemalan dictator Jorge Ubico, who was in power from 1931 to 1944. What attracted Buenaventura and the TEC members to the subject at that moment was the opportunity to present Ubico as an example of a typical dictator in progress, in view of all the military-supported regimes that were taking over many countries in Latin America. In the time range of two years, starting from 1964, seven democratically elected governments in the region (Argentina, Peru, Guatemala, Ecuador, Dominican Republic, Honduras, and Brazil) fell under the "reformist" wave brought about with the support of military forces.

Buenaventura's play also marked the moment in which American capital finally displaced English investments in the region. This transition brought with it the introduction of counterinsurgency tactics (the training of military personnel and the donation of equipment) in order to protect that investment, a strategy that was well received by the hegemonic forces in power. In the play Ubico represents this double stance as the military leader in power and a business partner with keen interest in the development of a U.S.–oriented economy. Two other characters complete the military cadre: the Prussian officer Wolfang August Von Grass, brought by Ubico to train the army in counterterrorism strategies, and Sargento Dinamita, an army sergeant turned into a killing machine. The latter character is shaped after the protagonist of Bertolt Brecht's play *A Man Is a Man* (1926). *La trampa* is a conspiracy piece in which everyone is involved in plotting against each other. At the end, Dinamita dies at the hands of his own soldiers, whom he has trained to be merciless, and Ubico is deposed in a coup orchestrated by both military men and civilians, united under the common threat of an imminent invasion by a foreign power.

Besides using the play as a reflection of contemporary events, Buenaventura continues with his ongoing process of putting on the stage the dialectics embedded in totalitarian power. He denounces its contradictions by having them interplayed by characters at both ends of the social scale: the oppressors and the oppressed. With the obvious purpose to illustrate the manipulations of those who enjoy supreme power, his play unmasks the devices employed to instill blind submissiveness in their subjects in order to completely dominate them. In his next play, *El presidente* (1967, The President), which was not produced and reads more like an epilogue to *La trampa,* he exposes the making of power from within the system. In the format of a play-within-a-play, the one-act piece depicts several jail inmates who are trying to stage a play in which the president, his lawyer, and the prime minister are the main characters. The resulting dialogue centers on who is to take the blame for their forthcoming dismissal, as they are on the verge of falling from grace.

In 1967, Buenaventura continued translating and adapting plays for the stage to polish his own craft and to expand his study of dictators. The first one, a translation of William Shakespeare's *Macbeth* (1606), is probably the closest to the original and the least successful. He directed it with the group La Casa de la Cultura of Bogotá in a directorial exchange program that in turn allowed Santiago García, its director, to stage *La trampa* with the TEC members. Then came *Los inocentes* (1967, The Guiltless), an adaptation of French author Emmanuel Roblès's play *Monserrat* (1948). Roblès's play is based on an historical event that happened in Valencia, Venezuela, in 1813, during the terror regime imposed by the Spaniard "pacifist" Domingo Monteverde. Monserrat is a loyalist army officer who, along with six innocent bystanders, is killed by Spanish general Izquierdo for refusing to disclose the whereabouts of revolutionary leader Simón Bolívar. The basic difference between Buenaventura and Roblès lies in the behavior of the hostages. In the French play they resignedly accept their fate; in Buenaventura's play they all rebel at the end, showing their dissent with those in power and their solidarity with the oppressed.

His next adaptation was based on the novel *Tirano Banderas* (1926), written by the early-twentieth-century Spanish writer Ramón del Valle-Inclán. Buenaventura transcends the somewhat grotesque por-

Scene from the 1968 premiere of Buenaventura's play Tirano Banderas, *adapted from Ramón del Valle-Inclán's 1926 novel about a Latin American dictator (from* Latin American Theatre Review, *volume 10 [Spring 1977]; Thomas Cooper Library, University of South Carolina)*

trayal of a Latin American dictator who succumbs in the middle of a revolution by emphasizing the rather antidemocratic character of most popular movements that have toppled dictators in the region. For Valle-Inclán the interruption of history owing to revolutions was a crucial aspect of his narrative; Buenaventura, on the contrary, concentrates on the continuous character of history that seems to be repeating itself because of the reactionary "bourgeois" character of the self-centered revolutions. The Teatro Estudio de la Universidad Nacional performed *Tirano Banderas* in September 1968 as part of the first Latin American University Theater Festival in Manizales; a month later, the play was taken to Mexico as part of the cultural program of the nineteenth Olympic Games, under the direction of Alberto Castilla.

Over the course of his career Buenaventura's approach as a director changed drastically. He directed most of the productions presented by TEC, including the famous 1959 staging of *Edipo Rey,* the adaptation of *Oedipus Rex,* by Sophocles, which was performed in front of a multitude at the steps of the Congress Palace in Bogotá. According to the critics, it was extremely well received because the topic–the conflict between the personal interests of the king and those of the community–reminded the audience of the events two years earlier when the would-be dictator Gustavo Rojas Pinilla was ousted from power. Another well-remembered production that Buenaventura adapted, even though it was directed by TEC member Helios Fernández, was *Ubú rey* (King Ubu) by Alfred Jarry. It played in an open space for an audience of more than thirty thousand people in 1966. This play marked a departure for the group, which was ready to put into practice the process known as "collective creation" in every aspect of its artistic endeavors.

The censure brought upon the group as a result of the obvious political implications of *La trampa* made them lose the official support that they had enjoyed until then. Buenaventura and several members of the group were expelled from the Escuela Departamental de Teatro, where they taught classes. The group then became independent and eventually changed their name to Teatro Experimental de Cali, preserving the same acronym. Some of the TEC actors and directors that were already prominent on the national stages included Luis Fernando Pérez; siblings Helios, Liber, and Aída Fernández; Pedro Martínez; Fanny Mikey;

Gladys Garcés; Nelly Delgado; Diego Vélez; Danilo Tenorio; Guillermo Piedrahita; Jorge Herrera; Hilda Ruiz; Diego Montoya; Jaime Cabal; C. Bernal; and Gabriel Uribe. By this time, the popular theater movement to which they belonged was recognized all over Latin America as "Nuevo Teatro" (New Theater). It broke ties with any previous conventional or traditional theater forms, meaning a "bourgeois" theater or, in its absence (which was the case in Colombia), whatever took its place. A highly politicized era began for the independent theater, headed by Buenaventura and his group and seconded by other important theater groups such as Teatro La Candelaria, Teatro Libre, and Teatro La Mama.

Ideologically, they continued to recognize historical materialism as the best tool to apprehend reality and to approach past and present events in a critical manner. After the exploration of issues pertaining to the region through individual characters–such as Padre de Las Casas, Ubico, and Henri Christophe–Buenaventura and the group now began to focus on national current events, this time placing the community as a whole on the stage. The emphasis was to be put on the historical process, not on the individual; hence, the characters were now generically named: a beggar, a soldier, an old lady, a peasant. On the other hand, the group was not immune to the restless student movements that were shaking the educational, political, and social institutions of the Western world as well as the sometimes violent reactions to the Vietnam War. They participated actively in street demonstrations and contributed with plays to back the international pacifist movement. Despite the charged political agenda of the times, Buenaventura refused to fall into the trap of writing programmatic "political theater," directed to a "determined audience" and with "specific topics" in mind, as he openly discussed in several articles. In this respect, one of his more "problematic" plays, politically speaking, was *El convertible rojo* (The Red Convertible, 1970), based on the lives of three prostitutes in London, which created a big controversy. According to his detractors, the prostitutes were not representatives of the working classes and therefore controversial to the Marxist-oriented artists who accused him of selling out to the bourgeoisie. In the play, Buenaventura reflects on the mistreatment of these women and the vicious cycle of exploitation in which they find themselves. An obvious pre-feminist movement play, it went totally unnoticed by the critics.

The work of Brecht greatly influenced Buenaventura at this time; *El convertible rojo* resembles Brecht's *Threepenny Opera* (1928). Many of the techniques developed by Brecht in his Epic Theater, such as the use of songs to comment on the action, the making of the unfamiliar familiar and vice versa, and the breaking of the "fourth wall" by letting the actors address the audience directly, were implemented by Nuevo Teatro members all over the country. Buenaventura was also impressed by the fact that Brecht customarily embarked on extensive research of the period he was trying to put on the stage, using several disciplines such as anthropology, sociology, history, and political sciences to elaborate multifaceted concepts in his plays. Politically as well as artistically, Buenaventura was influenced by the way Brecht worked dialectically with his audience, making them critically aware of the issues involved in his theater to entice the desire for social change.

In 1968 a collection of Buenaventura's short plays, *Los papeles del infierno* (Documents from Hell), opened to rave reviews, winning the Best Play Award at the National Theater Festival in Bogotá. It consisted of eight one-act plays: *La audiencia* (The Hearing), *La autopsia* (The Autopsy), *El entierro* (The Funeral), *La maestra* (The Teacher), *La requisa* (The Search), *El sueño* (The Dream), *La tortura* (translated as *The Twisted State*, 1970), and *La orgía* (translated as *The Orgy*, 1974). The TEC members never performed the ninth play in the collection, *El menú* (The Menu); it opened in 1970, produced by the group Teatro La Candelaria (formerly Casa de la Cultura) at the International Theater Festival in Nancy. *Los papeles del infierno* was based on the period from 1948 to 1957, known in Colombia as "The Era of Violence," triggered by the assassination of the liberal political leader José Eliézer Gaitán in 1948. As a direct consequence, the ruling political party, the *conservadores* (conservatives), subjected a good portion of the Colombian people to state terrorism. The undeclared civil war between the two parties produced a partial collapse of the state and a level of violence without precedence in the country; it is estimated that more than three hundred thousand Colombians were killed during this period.

Buenaventura mixed elements derived from the Theater of the Absurd and traditional forms of popular theater and pageantry, including the carnival, along with Brechtian techniques, in the structure of these plays. *Los papeles del infierno* closely resembles Brecht's *Fear and Misery of the Third Reich* (performed as *99%*, 1938; published in 1941; translated as *The Private Life of the Master Race*, 1944), in which Brecht depicted through several sketches the emergence of fascism in his native Germany. The emphasis of Buenaventura's play, however, is not placed on the state representatives but on the individuals upon whom repression is being exercised. In the 1972 article "Teatro y cultura" (Theater and Culture) Buenaventura explains his approach: "Hay que dividir el explotado dentro de él mismo mostrándole cómo, a nivel de hábitos, de condicionamientos, de moral, a nivel de compartimento, sigue teniendo adentro el explotador contra el cual lucha" (We have to divide the exploited one within him/herself to show how at the level of the habits, the conditioning, the moral, the sharing, he/she continues to have inside the exploiter against whom he/she is fighting).

La autopsia is one of the best examples of this contradiction. A coronary medical doctor, who works for the establishment, is forced to sign his own son's death certificate as accidental after the young man was tortured and killed by state agents. In *El entierro* the members of a family sharply and irreconcilably divided between the two main ruling parties express their atavistic hatred for each other during the mother's funeral. In the popular *La maestra,* a small-town teacher, already dead at the time the curtain rises, recalls her slow death by starvation after she was raped several times by soldiers who were looking for her father, a community leader from the opposing political party.

Probably the best-known and most often produced play of the collection is *La orgía,* which has been performed all over Latin America. In the play, an old lady who spent the better part of her life as a high-priced call girl lives in a shack with her mute son, whom she steals from, exploits, and denies her affection. At the end of each month, she celebrates an "orgy of art and remembrances" for which she hires, for a ridiculously small amount of money, a group of beggars to impersonate representatives from the different social classes that surrounded her youth. A woman dwarf beggar represents a bishop; a one-legged man plays a military figure; and another male beggar pretends to be a political leader. Dressed with all the symbols that characterize their positions in society, they enact a banquet at which they talk eloquently and eat, supposedly with moderation. Given the ever-increasing time the old lady is taking to consume the promised food, a watery soup, the beggars decide to kill her. She represents the bourgeoisie, and her death means that they can finally consume the food. Hunger and fear are really the main topics of *Los papeles del infierno,* in a background where violence surrounds the everyday life of the characters. *La orgía,* in this respect, is a celebration of victory over fear; it is a satire that combines the grotesque, the carnival inversion of roles, with the ritual.

In *El menú* food is again the main issue, but all the characters are deformed or handicapped (blind, crippled, mute, deaf, missing upper or lower limbs). Supplementing the visual aspect of this peculiar group, the dialogue revolves around their physical shortcomings in the most cruel and inhuman fashion. The action takes place during another "banquet" in which five "Señoritas" are celebrating a local political candidate; but what really takes center stage is violence as it is displayed by the characters against each other, and as it is directed to the audience. In one instance, the candidate is induced to make a speech, and instead he vomits twice. At a time when Colombians were entering one of the most violent periods of their political and civilian life, it seemed appropriate to confront them with the consequences of its development. At the end of the play, only a child dressed in black is left alone on the stage. He sings the "song of the avenger." This angel of death may be representing a future–not a promising one, as some critics have pointed out, but one fulfilled with threats of worse times to come.

During 1968 Buenaventura closed the collection of short plays with a one-act piece titled *Se hizo justicia* (Justice Has Been Served, published in 1977). Two women representing opposing parties (one of their husbands killed the other one for political reasons) join forces as their families are being evacuated by the armed forces from the shantytown they had illegally occupied. The struggle of the classes thus takes priority over any political feud among the poor. Solidarity has to be pursued in order to recognize the real enemy if national reconstruction is going to take place.

Another major influence on Buenaventura's development was the documentary theater of German director Peter Weiss, known for his famous play *Marat/Sade* (1964), staged in Colombia by García (circa 1965) with Casa de la Cultura. Based on the agitprop theater developed by Erwin Piscator in the 1930s, documentary theater was a sort of living newspaper created to disseminate historical material as directly as possible to a politically uneducated audience. In this style of theater, characters lose their individual identification and personify social forces. Plot is disregarded in favor of historical process; anything else is considered escapism. Weiss's *Gesang vom Lusitanishen Popanz* (1967; translated as *Song of the Lusitanian Bogey,* 1970) caught Buenaventura's attention. His first adaptation of it, *Canto del Fantoche Lusitano,* dates from 1969; it is one of the works that he revised several times (more than five versions in a ten-year time span). According to Buenaventura, the play pays homage to the enslaved people from Africa, whether brought by force into the New World or oppressed under totalitarian regimes. The whole process of colonization by a European power is put on the stage: the play depicts the history of the Angolan people from the time the Portuguese conquistador Diego Câo reached the Congo River delta in 1482, looking for a watercourse to the Indies, until the creation of the liberation movements to get rid of the Portuguese in the 1960s. In addition to pursuing Weiss's didactic goal of instilling an ideological attitude in the audience, Buenaventura appeals to the senses by incorporating traditions, myths, and music from the black population

Buenaventura in 1972 (photograph by Paul Lorgus; from Judith Weiss, Latin American Popular Theatre, 1993; Thomas Cooper Library, University of South Carolina)

of the Colombian Pacific Coast. It was obvious to him that the only way this play would succeed was if it created an artistic parallel between the everyday experience of the Angolan people and their Colombian counterpart, as he expressed in a 1981 interview in *Revista Nueva*.

Under the influence of Weiss's documentary theater and to express solidarity with the current anti–Vietnam War movement, Buenaventura wrote his play *Seis horas en la vida de Frank Kulak* (1969, Six Hours in the Life of Frank Kulak) to be performed at the fifth Theater Festival at the Teatro Colón in Bogotá. Based on a newspaper article published in the *Chicago Tribune*, the play depicts the life of an American Vietnam War veteran who receives a Purple Heart for his bravery but ends up putting a bomb in a toy store when he returns home, killing several people. He then dies in an ensuing shootout with the police. Buenaventura adds a second line of events with the life of Van Troi, a South Vietnamese, who during the war tries to mine a bridge that has to be crossed by an American convoy. Contrasting these two dissimilar lives, the author makes a statement about the futility of the war that involved and destroyed both of them. Even though this play was never considered one of his best works, it enjoyed an important place in the methodological development of the group, as it was one of the first instances where the actors improvised on the texts that Buenaventura brought on a daily basis, contributing collectively to the final product.

In the early 1970s the group codified the process that was thereafter referred to all over Latin America as the TEC method. It was a work method based on collective creation. First published in 1970 under the title "Esquema general del método de trabajo colectivo del TEC" (General Outline of the Collective Creation TEC Method), the process had begun to develop a couple of years earlier as the actors were allowed greater participation in the staging part of the theatrical process. The method was created to give a structure, an organic form, to the text while avoiding previous conventional categories such as acts and scenes. The "collective creation" method was divided into five steps: 1) the research and the actual writing of the text; 2) the division of the text according to its critical analysis; 3) the improvisation stage, which is referred to as the "backbone" of the process; 4) the staging of the play; and 5) its presentation in front of an audience, which will always include the possibility of later changes according to the public's reaction and feedback.

During the first step, the group implemented Russian director Konstantin Stanislavsky's and Brecht's approaches to playwriting in the sense that the actors' responses to the text were incorporated in the final edition of every scene. All the subsequent texts were the combined product of the different research "commissions" (such as social, political, cultural, and historical) who were in charge of investigating the background material on each proposed topic and the actors' improvisations of the same. Buenaventura or a playwright commision then would choose the scenes that would be written down, most of the time by him.

Once the text was more or less complete, it was ready for the next step, in which the ensemble would analyze it through the images suggested by its different parts. At this stage of the process, the main theme and a chronological development of the same (even if the play does not follow it) had to be discerned and understood by every member of the group in order to attain a total vision of the conflict proposed by the play. When the general conflict was clear, the actors would analyze each of its parts, such as the protagonist, antagonist, and the motivations behind their behavior. The text would then be divided into "sequences," "situations," and "actions." The actions represented the nuclei of the conflict but were also determined by the motivations. If the latter changed, the actions also had to change. Once the text had been structured accordingly, it was ready for the improvisation stage.

During this step, the actors took each scene of the play and approached it using different improvisational techniques, such as analogical, metaphorical, disassociation, and oppositional, to build upon. Many times the resulting "text" was totally different than the one originally proposed. In this case, new discussions would be carried out to see if the images derived from the scene were worth altering the original material—sometimes a painstaking and lengthy process. Contrary to the previous stage, this one did not entail a critical approach by the actors; it was based on their emotions, their feelings. Buenaventura, in fact, used Sigmund Freud's interpretation of dreams to explain this step, stating that the actors should bring to the surface through the improvisations the latent content of the text instead of the explicit written one.

When the group had already amassed several improvisations to work with, they went back to the text to start the next step, the staging of the play. There are three subsequent phases or "turns" in this stage. The first turn involves matching the improvisations to the original text in terms of the functioning of every action and its causality. During the second turn, the group concentrates on the characters and their relations within the structure of the play. Finally, in the third turn all the rest of the theatrical elements are combined (including lighting designs, makeup, costumes, props, and choreography).

Now, the play is ready to be performed in front of an audience. This final step was a crucial one within the New Theater movement, as almost every play was immediately followed by an open discussion with the public. On many occasions, plays were entirely transformed in successive versions after the suggestions or criticism received in these open sessions.

Equipped with this method, the group and its director embarked on a new period of work that was marked by prolific productions, political militancy, and an ever-growing influence throughout Latin America. By that time, they had already participated in many national and international theater festivals and had been recognized with several important awards, such as the second National Theater Festival of Bogotá Best Play Award for *A la diestra de Dios Padre* in 1958; the third National Theater Festival of Bogotá Best Play Award for Buenaventura's adaptation of *Oedipus Rex* in 1959; and the National Theater Festival Best Group Award for *Los inocentes* in 1967. They had toured extensively throughout the country and had performed in Venezuela, Ecuador, Mexico, France, and the United States.

Following the line of work initiated with *Los papeles del infierno,* Buenaventura and the group continued to explore the major historical events that contributed to the political unrest of the times. Without a doubt, the episode known as the "massacre of the *bananeras*" (banana plantation companies) is one of them. In 1928 a strike was called by the banana workers at one of the largest plantations on the continent, the United Fruit Company, under the auspices of the Partido Social Revolucionario (Revolutionary Social Party). The workers were asking for recognition from the U.S. company directly and not through third-party contractors as stipulated under Colombian law; an increase to minimal wages; and payment of wages in hard currency, not in coupons redeemable at the grocery stores owned by the same company. The company pressured the conservative government of Miguel Abadía Mendes to settle the strike as fast as possible under the threat of an imminent U.S. Navy landing. The president then authorized the governor of the region, Carlos Cortés Vargas, to take care of the strike, which he referred to as a "subversive complot." Cortés Vargas called for a congregation of the strikers in the main square of the town of Ciénaga, where a train was to arrive bringing the governor to start negotiations with them. The train arrived, but instead of the pertinent authorities, it was loaded with soldiers who opened fire on the multitude, killing more than three thousand peasants, including women and children. The train carried the corpses of the victims back to the coast, where they were thrown into the sea. The event was then treated by the authorities as though it had never happened. The massacre has been retold many times by writers of all genres in Colombia. It was one of the main topics in Gabriel García Márquez's famous novel *Cien años de soledad* (1967; translated as *One Hundred Years of Solitude,* 1970) and in Alvaro Cepeda Zamudio's novel *La casa grande* (1962, The Big House). Playwright Carlos José Reyes adapted some of the chapters of the latter novel in his play *Soldados* (Soldiers, 1966), which was the point of departure of Buenaventura's subsequent adaptation under the same name.

Soldados represents one of the theatrical highlights in Buenaventura's and TEC's development; it went through five versions, in 1968, 1970, 1971 (two versions), and 1982. Keeping the original dialogues of Cepeda Zamudio, which revolved around the soldiers who actually carried out the order to open fire upon the crowd, the group incorporated official documents, press releases, and data obtained through extensive research. Reyes, Buenaventura, Vidal, Herrera, Sergio Gómez, Gilberto Ramírez, and Piedrahita signed the final text of the first version collectively. It was the first completely collective creation text in which the actors, the director, and the assistant to the director worked as a team throughout the entire process, even though the text was finally written down by Buenaventura. A suitable example of documentary theater, *Soldados* puts the emphasis on the confrontation of soldier versus worker. The dialectic relationship of these characters, divided between their "duty" to the country and their natural affiliation with the working/peasant classes from which they both came, forms the central conflict of the play. As the same actors represent both sides of the conflict, changing minimal costumes in front of the audience, the dual and contradictory condition of being soldier and peasant at the same time becomes evident.

From the documents accumulated by the group during the research step of the process emerged their next play, *La denuncia* (1973, The Accusation), directed by Helios Fernández. This work, using the collective creation method, took the group two years to finish. Their course of action was widely documented by Buenaventura in several articles that were published in specialized magazines in and outside the country. As Buenaventura points out in these articles, the motivation behind the play was to confront and compare the oral texts–the eyewitness accounts of the strike itself collected in the documentation–and the "historical version" of the event as it was told by the official historians. The historical background, as in *Soldados,* is represented by the banana workers' strike in 1928, but

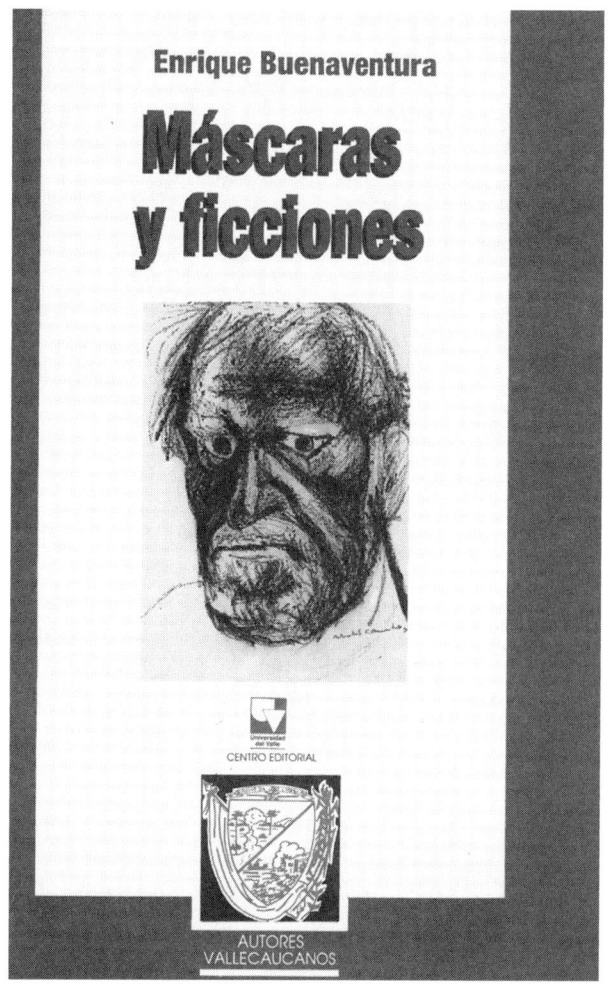

Cover for Buenaventura's 1992 collection (Masks and Fictions) of plays, essays, poems, drawings, and narratives (Howard-Tilton Memorial Library, Tulane University)

this time the context is divided among three simultaneous different levels called "Congress," "Progress," and "the Strike." The first one concentrates on the accusation made by the young representative Jorge Eliézer Gaitán to the National Congress in 1929, which ended with the removal of Cortés Vargas as governor of the region and the reduction of the jail sentences of the convicted leaders of the strike. The second level has to do with the general historical and economic background as U.S. capitalism started to displace English investors from the region. Finally, the strike is represented in its bare context: the early struggle of an incipient working class against a corporate regime that denies it its legal rights.

La denuncia is a period piece that signals the end of a phase and the beginning of the next for the group and its director. It is a play that reflects structurally the major influences of the time, mainly Weiss's documentary theater and Brecht's distancing epic techniques, but also displays an interest in ritual, ceremony, and parody, which have always been present in the productions of Buenaventura and his group. There is a subtle move toward the use of semiotics in the treatment of the actors/characters, which takes an important place in future productions. In the course of his constant search for new sources of expression Buenaventura was drawn to semiotics and began to apply the study of signs and their different components, characteristics, and functions to his theater practice.

Once the group's working method was settled and strengthened by the last two productions, and convinced that a theater practice without a theory to back it up was not a lasting enterprise, Buenaventura, along with other theater directors and practitioners such as García, embarked on a wide-ranging search for theories that would enrich the performing arts. Without disregarding dialectic historicism (in fact, he was in favor of a new Marxist sociology "libre de todo materialismo mecánico" [free of any mechanic materialism]), he found in semiotics, along with communication and linguistics theories, ample ammunition for his writings. Of special importance to his practice was, for example, the use of the concept of intertextuality, as elaborated by Julia Kristeva. For him, as for Kristeva, every text includes within it signs from other texts. In this sense, the text, theatrical or otherwise, is not a unique point of reference but an intersection in which many texts from other times, other authors, and other cultures would cross and interfere with the final product. Another important semiotic principle established by Kristeva and other theorists and put into practice by Buenaventura was the conviction that every theatrical text simultaneously cancels out and asserts another one (destroys and reconstructs), especially in its relationship with the audience, who, in order to decode the text, brings along their own knowledge of the text or any other text related to it.

These theoretical findings were implemented in his Casa de las Américas Award–winning play, *Historia de una bala de plata* (1979, The Story of a Silver Bullet), a loose adaptation of Eugene O'Neill's *Emperor Jones* (1921). Buenaventura and the group embarked on extensive research of texts related to their central topic: the entrance of capitalism in the Caribbean economies. His previous *La tragedia del Rey Christophe*, Alejo Carpentier's novels *El reino de este mundo* (1949; translated as *The Kingdom of This World,* 1957) and *El siglo de las luces* (1962; translated as *Explosion in a Cathedral,* 1963), Miguel Barnet's testimonial narrative *Biografía de un cimarrón* (1966; translated as *The Autobiography of a Runaway Slave,* 1968), and Shakespeare's *The Tempest* (1611) are some of the texts that were used as literary referents in addition to O'Neill's play. A complicated plot revolves around the main character, Cristóbal Jones, an African American who is taken to a French island in the Caribbean to become the "slave liberator" by an unscrupulous white entrepreneur who wants him to become king, obviously for profit. Many of the slaves on the island have run away and formed colonies, openly defying the authorities; other freed slaves and the Creoles are involved in civil strife. The English, who want the French out of the picture, help some of the slaves, and the American marines, whose landing at the end of the play draws the conflict to a close, assist others. Jones, as implied by the title, is killed with a silver bullet, and with his death vanishes the dream of a "black kingdom."

The play was received with apprehension because of its strategy and techniques. In his language, his choice of words, Buenaventura gave preference to connotative terms rather than direct referential ones as in previous productions. The context in the play was no longer expressed only by the conflict, the situation, and the feelings of the characters but also by the use of space, silence, the rhythm of the play, the music, and the lighting. The play was structured in short scenes without clear breaks between them, and it was played without interruption at a fast pace. The rhythm was essential to the denouement of the historical events and added to the effect of the magical and mythical elements that were employed by the author and the group. This play is one of the instances in which magic realism, an aesthetic characteristic of the region, appears in Buenaventura's work and distances the group from their previous, mostly realistic dramaturgy.

In 1980 the group toured throughout Central America and the Caribbean. Their stay in Nicaragua inspired the topic of their next play, *Opera bufa* (1982), based on the Somoza dynasty that ruled the country from 1933 to 1979. Buenaventura and the group thus returned to the theme of the dictator; the idea was to explore the origin of the dictatorships that have propagated throughout the region. As in their previous plays, they set out to examine major works on the topic, such as Buenaventura's *Tirano Banderas* and his translation of *Macbeth;* Carpentier's *El recurso del método* (1974; translated as *Reasons of State,* 1976); Augusto Roa Bastos's *Yo, el supremo* (1974; translated as *I, the Supreme,* 1987); and García Márquez's *El otoño del patriarca* (1975; translated as *The Autumn of the Patriarch,* 1976). Poetic pieces from Rubén Darío, Pablo Neruda, Ernesto Cardenal, and Brecht were also used in the creation of the text. In fact, the poetic language is so prevalent that the play sometimes becomes, as some critics noted, a dramatized reading of poetic texts connected by a common theme.

The central idea was the creation of a dynasty and its legacy.

The function of every character in the play is defined according to the role that person plays in regard to the dictator, either assisting or opposing him. They are also presented in binary positions, which means that every character has a counterpart on the stage, including Death. A symbolic character, Death is split into two entities: the Operatic Death, reserved for the bourgeoisie, and the Criolla (Native) Death for the commoners. Even the dictator is coupled with another power, no less influential in the region: the U.S. ambassador. They are always together; their interests are obviously linked, and they function as subjects of the action. The representatives of the Catholic Church are also present, but this time the bishop represents the traditional side of the church, which has always allied with the hegemonies in power, and the priest is modeled after Camilo Torres, a revolutionary Colombian priest who was one of the foremost advocates of the theology of liberation with its preferential option for the impoverished masses. Two guerrilla fighters are also depicted in the play, representing the still-active liberation movements in Latin America: César Zapata and Joaquin Artola. The former represents the mythical figures of César Augusto Sandino, the leader of the Nicaraguan movement against U.S. intervention during the 1930s, and the Mexican Revolution hero Emiliano Zapata, in whose name several peasant/indigenous movements have emerged, including the Zapatista movement in Chiapas, Mexico. Artola is a member of the Sandinista Liberation Movement that finally ended the Somoza regime in 1979.

The play ended a cycle of works dedicated to the Caribbean, a subject to which Buenaventura returned later but with different perspectives and without the input of the group's methodological approach. The TEC continued to use their method, but in a more relaxed manner, until the end of the decade, when most of the original or long-standing members departed. From then on, the new TEC became a regular theater company, mostly under the supervision of Vidal, losing the sense of a laboratory or research center that it had enjoyed for more than three decades.

During the 1980s Buenaventura systematically returned to his old plays, elaborating new versions of them, or to themes that he felt were left unfinished. In this respect, most of his dramaturgy revolves around a few themes arranged in recurrent cycles. What changes in his various dramatic treatments is the situation and the characters, but the focus remains the same: mainly, the unjust social and political situations in which the majority of the Latin American people live, paired with the contradictions they face in a capitalist world whose leaders are mostly indifferent to their condition. Also, the increase of violence in Colombia with the irruption on the national scene of narcoterrorism and the continuous armed struggle between subversive peasant groups, such as Ejército de Liberación Nacional (ELN, National Liberation Army) or Fuerzas Armadas Revolucionarias de Colombia (FARC, Columbian Revolutionary Armed Forces), and the state made him focus once again on the local situation.

In 1984 he wrote *La gran farsa de las equivocaciones* (The Mishaps Farce), based on his previous one-act plays *El presidente* and *La audiencia;* it addresses the daily bloody occurrences in the midst of institutionalized terrorism on the part of the establishment. *Escuela para viajeros* (1988; School for Travelers), also known in a later version as *La estación* (1989, The Railway Station), is loosely based on the short story "El guardagujas" (1973, The Switchman) by Mexican writer Juan José Arreola. Buenaventura employs the central metaphor—an arbitrary railway company who uses their trains to "remove" and "disappear" passengers, or obliges their customers to disassemble the train and carry it on their backs across a river where the bridge no longer exists, or sells tickets to places where the actual lines have not been installed—to denounce state corporatism, which can operate with total impunity because of the supposed "patriotism" of the clientele. His irreverent sense of humor is evident with the use of ironic dialogue and comical instances, particularly with the characters of the switchman and his assistant, who are reminiscent of a vaudeville duet act. They keep interrupting the action to change the hour on the clock in front of the astonished passengers who are patiently waiting for the previous hourly train.

In addition to his work as a playwright, Buenaventura worked as a teacher and an actor trainer throughout his career. From 1975 until he retired at the beginning of the 1990s, Buenaventura taught in the Department of Languages at the University of Valle, where he helped to create the Department of Drama. He also lectured and gave seminars and workshops throughout the Americas and Europe.

In his next play, *Proyecto piloto* (1991, Lead Project), Buenaventura becomes more critical of the situation of his homeland, denouncing the undeclared war among the different armed groups and the state. The society depicted here is one in which the inhabitants are turning into rats. No one seems to be able to escape his or her destiny. Now, instead of two Deaths, as in *Opera Bufa,* there are four: the "opulent" for the aristocracy; the "white collar" for the executives; the "rat" for the common people, and the "death death" for everyone, as a final social equalizer. Instead of the usual polarization between the bad guys at the top of the hier-

Buenaventura (left) and fellow playwright Santiago García, 2001 (photograph by Francisco Martínez; courtesy of Lucía Garavito)

archical ladder and the good guys at the bottom, Buenaventura directs his criticism at everyone in society. The situation is everyone's fault, either because of active involvement in the struggle or for passively allowing it. Not only is the society going through a degrading process but its members are also becoming totally unmoved by anyone else's pain. The play is reminiscent of those previous literary and theatrical pieces that have used metaphors for the forced indoctrination of an entire population, such as in the novel *La Peste* (1947; translated as *The Plague,* 1948), by Albert Camus, and the play *Rhinocéros* (1959), by Eugène Ionesco, on the emergence of Nazism in Europe.

Besides the tour throughout Central America, Buenaventura and his group continued traveling extensively and participating in many national and international events such as the International Theater Festival of Nancy, France, in 1971, followed by presentations at the Paris Theater Recamier, where they were invited by Jean-Louis Barrault; Joseph Papp's Latino Festival in New York in 1982; the International Theater Festival of Cádiz in 1987, followed by a tour throughout Spain; El Teatro Nacional de Aztlán (TENAZ, The National Theater of Aztlán); the Chicano Theater Festival in San Antonio in 1992; and the Porto Theater Festival in Portugal in 1994. Particularly important was the presentation of Buenaventura's play *Crónica* (1992, Chronicle), in San Antonio; the second version of this play won first prize at the international TENAZ competition on the occasion of the five-hundredth anniversary of the arrival of Columbus in the New World. It opened to great reviews, as the topic—the survival of the Spaniards Jerónimo de Aguilar and Gonzalo Guerrero, whose ship sank near Yucatán at the beginning of the Conquest and who lived for more than a decade with indigenous tribes—scored a point with Chicanos and Latinos living in the United States who were familiar with this episode as part of a common heritage. Buenaventura's rendition of the story comes from the sixteenth-century *Historia verdadera de la Conquista de la Nueva España* (1632, True History of the Conquest of New Spain), by Bernal Díaz del Castillo. De Aguilar went on to become one of the translators for Hernán Cortés, the conqueror of Mexico, when he showed up in 1520 in the region; and Guerrero, already assimilated to Indian life and married to the daughter of a chief, valiantly fought against the Spanish troops and was finally killed during an ambush set by Cortés. In the absence of indigenous testimonies on the Conquest, Guerrero is the closest one can get to the viewpoint of "the other."

After the trip to the United States, Buenaventura returned to the topic of the Caribbean in a series of plays dedicated to exploring different characters associated with local histories. One of them is the woman pirate Mary Read. She inspired two slightly different versions of the same play: *El lunar en la frente* (1994, The Beauty Mark on the Forehead) and *El dragón de los mares* (1995, The Dragon of the Seas), which were joined under the general title of *El nudo corredizo* (1997, The Loophole). The plays follow the life of Read, who from the age of six was dressed as a boy by her mother to replace her dead older brother in the eyes of her grandmother, who supported them with a meager pension. When she was sixteen her grandmother died, and along with her mother she thought that it was more advantageous for her to continue life as a man. She embarked on a series of adventures as a buccaneer roaming the seven seas in the company of other famous pirates such as Francis Drake and John Hawkins. She entered into two ill-fated marriages and finally was taken prisoner by the English and condemned to death. The plays are parables using cross-dressing to underline the social construction of gender roles in society. The Haitian Revolution also continued to haunt Buenaventura in his next play, *La isla de todos los santos* (2002, The Island of All Saints), but this time the characters of Toussaint-Louverture and Napoleon Bonaparte are depicted in their major historical roles in the conflict that ended the French colonization of the island in 1804.

At the beginning of the twenty-first century Buenaventura continued to write, surprising more than a few spectators with his vigor and his keen vision of the troubled society in which he lived. In *La huella* (2001, The Track) he highlights the moments of virtue and lucidity that a serial assassin manifests despite the upturned moral values of the society surrounding him. In *Preguntas inútiles* (2002, Useless Questions), Buenaventura looks at the war victims in Colombia. Forced out of their homes, they arrive in hordes on a daily basis in the big cities looking for safety and a decent way of earning a livelihood. Entire families with children who are doomed to grow up as drug addicts or as gang members settle on the hills encircling the big cities (the so-called *cerros* or *favelas*), fabricating their houses on stilts covered by cardboard boxes and old newspapers. In one of these shantytowns, where water tastes like rusted iron and love "dura diez minutos" (lasts ten minutes), two separate communities battle each other because of the atavistic hatred they inherited from their liberal and conservative ancestors. Through the surviving family characters in the play, Buenaventura reviews the major conflicts the country has endured since the 1950s. It is a process of violence that has fragmented Colombian society and undermined the faith of its people for a peaceful solution. He continues to use Brechtian devices such as intermingling songs in the sometimes sordid dialogues to provide a much needed poetic respite. *Los dientes de la guerra* (2003, The Teeth of War) was his last written play, again on the history of the continuing armed struggle of his country. Buenaventura died on 31 December 2003, in Cali, after three months of intensive care for peritonitis brought on by an undetected stomach ulcer. Vidal has remained at the helm of the group to preserve his legacy and continue staging his plays.

In addition to his dramatic production, Buenaventura wrote several theoretical and historical essays on theater that are by themselves an impressive testimony of his long career in the performing arts. He also was the recipient of many distinctions, including the University of Valle doctor honoris causa degree in 1977; the Calima de Oro Lifetime Achievement Award from the Regional Culture Committee of the Department of Valle in 1985; the Center for the Development of Latin American Theater (CELCIT) Ollantay Award for his theatrical achievements in 1980; and a Lifetime Achievement Award at the International Theater Festival of Miami in 2001. The University of Antioquia Press in Medellín is preparing a major collection of his works, which is still in production and will include his poetry, essays, and short stories.

Enrique Buenaventura's dramatic production is well known and performed all over Latin America. His theories as well as his work method spread across the continent and are still influencing theater practitioners. His is a special voice, the voice of his people, which has not yet been paralleled in the theater production of his homeland and possibly of the region.

Interviews:

Rubén Monasterios, "Entrevista con Enrique Buenaventura," *Primer Acto,* 145 (1972): 22–32;

Carlos Vásquez Zawadski, *Teatro y universidad: Entrevista* (Cali: Folleto, Universidad del Valle, 1977);

Ramón de la Campa, "The New Latin American Stage: An Interview with E. Buenaventura," *Theater,* 12, no. 1 (1980): 19–21;

Luys A. Diez, "Entrevista con Enrique Buenaventura," *Latin American Theatre Review,* 14, no. 2 (1981): 49–57;

"El teatro un fin en sí mismo: Entrevista," *Revista Nueva* (Quito, Ecuador), 77 (1981): 75.

References:

Georgio Antei, "Un paradigma teatral: Notas sobre *Historia de una bala de plata*," *Contexto,* 5 (1979);

Gonzalo Arcila, *Nuevo Teatro en Colombia: Actividad creadora y política cultural* (Bogotá: Ediciones CEIS, 1983);

Raúl H. Castagnino, "Descripción semiótica de un texto dramático hispanoamericano contemporáneo: *En la diestra de Dios Padre* de Enrique Buenaventura," in *Semilogía del teatro,* edited by José M. Díez Borque and Luiciano García Lorenzo (Barcelona: Editorial Planeta, 1975);

Alberto Castillo, "*Tirano Banderas,* versión teatral de Buenaventura," *Latin American Theatre Review,* 10, no. 2 (1977): 65–71;

Nora Eidelberg, "La ritualización de la violencia en cuatro obras teatrales hispanoamericanas," *Latin American Theatre Review,* 13, no. 1 (1979);

Maida Watson Espener, "Enrique Buenaventura's Theory of the Committed Theatre," *Latin American Theatre Review,* 9, no. 2 (1976): 43–47;

Victor Fuentes, "La creación colectiva del Teatro Experimental de Cali," in *Popular Theater for Social Change in Latin America,* edited by Gerardo Luzuriaga (Los Angeles: UCLA Latin American Studies, 1978), pp. 338–349;

Roberto Gacio Suárez, "Historia y realidad social en el teatro de Enrique Buenaventura," *Conjunto,* 45 (1980): 108–109;

Fernando González Cajiao, "Enrique Buenaventura: El maestro," *Letras Nacionales,* 32, no. 33 (1977): 103–106;

Maria Mercedes Jaramillo de Velasco, "La creación colectiva y la colonización cultural en América Latina," *Gestos,* 4, no. 7 (1989): 75–95;

Jaramillo de Velasco, "La proyección teatral de la masacre de las bananeras," *Latin American Theatre Review,* 23, no. 1 (1989): 89–103;

John W. Kronik, "Enrique Buenaventura in the Context of Spanish American Theater," in *Studies in Honor of Myron Lichtblau,* edited by Fernando Burgos (Newark, Del.: Juan de la Cuesta, 2000), pp. 185–194;

Gerardo Luzuriaga, "*En la diestra de Dios Padre* y la contextualización histórica del folclor," in *Narradores Latinoamericanos: 1929–1979* (Caracas: Ediciones del Centro de Estudios Latinoamericanos Rómulo Gallegos, 1980);

Luzuriaga, "Enrique Buenaventura: Un nuevo teatro para un nuevo público," in his *Introducción a las teorías latinoamericanas del teatro* (Mexico City: Universidad Autónoma de Puebla, 1990);

Eduardo Márceles Daconte, "El método de creación colectiva en el teatro colombiano," *Latin American Theatre Review,* 11, no. 1 (1977): 91–97;

Carlos José Reyes, "Una historia del teatro colombiano," *Tramoya,* 15 (1979): 30–44;

Reyes and Maida Watson Espener, eds., *Materiales para una historia del teatro en Colombia* (Bogotá: Colcultura, 1978);

Beatriz J. Rizk, *E. Buenaventura: La dramaturgia de la creación colectiva* (Mexico City: Gaceta, 1991);

Rizk, "Hacia una teoría de la traducción: Adaptaciones, versiones y variaciones de un tema, otra manera de ejercer el oficio de autor en la obra de Enrique Buenaventura," in *Reflexiones sobre teatro latinoamericano del siglo XX* (Buenos Aires: Galerna, 1989), pp. 41–48;

Rizk, "Un maestro que duda: Enrique Buenaventura y el *Réquiem por el Padre de Las Casas,*" in *Antología de teatro colombiano contemporáneo,* edited by Fernando González Cajiao (Madrid: Fondo de Cultura Económica, 1992), pp. 185–190;

Rizk, "El Nuevo Teatro colombiano: Una ruptura que se afianza en la tradición," *Alba de América,* 7, no. 12/13 (1989): 115–117;

José Luis Alonso de Santos, "Enrique Buenaventura y su método de creación colectiva," *Primer Acto,* 183 (1980): 73–82;

Diana Taylor, "Destruir la evidencia: La supresión como historia en *La maestra* de Enrique Buenaventura," *Gestos,* 5, no. 10 (1990): 91–101;

Beatriz Trastoy, "*En la diestra de Dios Padre,* análisis semiólogo de una puesta en escena," *Gestos,* 2, no. 4 (1987): 125–130;

Iván Ulchur Collazos, *Los papeles del infierno de Enrique Buenaventura: Imágenes de la violencia* (Quito: Corporación de Promoción Universitaria, 1989);

Giorgio Ursini Ursic, *Enrique Buenaventura: Le maschere, il teatro. Tesi e testimonianze sul teatro sperimentale colombiano* (Milan: Gaingiacome Feltrinelli, 1979);

Misael Vargas and others, *Teatro colombiano* (Bogotá: Ediciones del Alba, 1985);

Carlos Vásquez Zawadski, "El teatro de Enrique Buenaventura, algunos problemas de lectura," in *Enrique Buenaventura,* edited by Zawodski (Cali: Publicación del Universidad del Valle, 1977);

Penny A. Wallace, "Enrique Buenaventura's *Los papeles del infierno,*" *Latin American Theatre Review,* 9, no. 1 (1975): 37–46;

Judith Weiss, *Latin American Popular Theatre* (Albuquerque: University of New Mexico Press, 1993);

George Woodyard, "Enrique Buenaventura y el teatro colombiano," in *Violencia y literatura en Colombia,* edited by Jonathan Tittler (Madrid: Orígenes, 1989).

José Ignacio Cabrujas
(12 July 1937 – 21 October 1995)

Luis Chesney Lawrence
Central University of Venezuela

PLAY PRODUCTIONS: *Juan Francisco de León,* Caracas, Theatre of the Central University of Venezuela, 1959;

Los insurgentes, Caracas, Theatre of the Central University of Venezuela, 1961;

El extraño viaje de Simón el malo, Caracas, Theatre of the Central University of Venezuela, 1961;

En nombre del rey, Caracas, Theatre of the Central University of Venezuela, 1963;

Tradicional hospitalidad, second part of the play *Triángulo,* by Cabrujas, Román Chalbaud, and Isaac Chocrón, Caracas, Theatre of Art, 1963;

Testimonio, Caracas, Experimental Theatre of the Faculty of Architecture, Central University of Venezuela, 1965;

Fiésole, Caracas, Nuevo Grupo, 1967;

Profundo, Caracas, Nuevo Grupo, 1971;

Acto cultural, Caracas, Nuevo Grupo, 1976;

El día que me quieras, Caracas, Nuevo Grupo, 1979;

Una noche oriental, Caracas, Nuevo Grupo, 1983;

El americano ilustrado, Caracas, Nuevo Grupo, 1986;

Autorretrato de artista con barba y pumpá, Caracas, Grupo Theja, 1990;

La soberia del General Pío Fernández, part of the production *The Seven Capital Sins,* Caracas, Nuevo Grupo, 1994;

Sonny, Caracas, Theatre of the Casa Sindical del Paraíso, 1995.

BOOKS: *Tradicional hospitalidad* (Caracas: Tierra Firme, 1962);

Profundo (Caracas: Tiempo Nuevo, 1972 [i.e., 1971]);

Acto cultural (Caracas: Monte Avila, 1976);

El día que me quieras (Caracas: Monte Avila, 1979); translated by Eduardo Machado as *The Day You'll Love Me, American Theatre,* 6 (September 1989);

Acto cultural; El día que me quieras; La soberia milagrosa del General Pío Fernández (Madrid: Vox/Centro de Documentación Teatral, 1979);

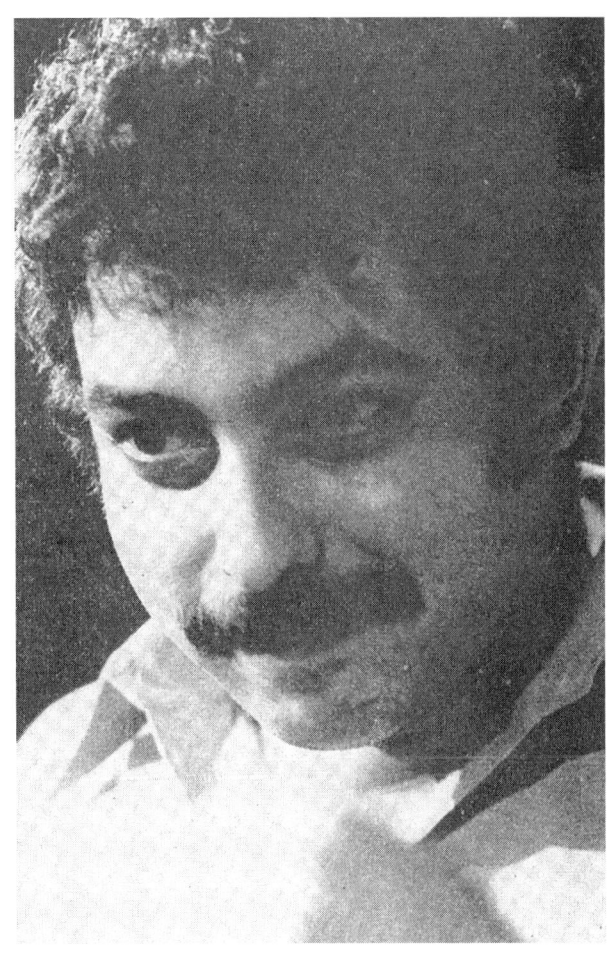

José Ignacio Cabrujas (from Carlos Miguel Suárez Radillo, 13 autores del nuevo teatro venezolano, 1971; Howard-Tilton Memorial Library, Tulane University)

Caracas, text by Cabrujas, photographs by Gorka Dorronsoro (Caracas: Fundación Polar/Oscar Todtmann, 1988);

El día que bajaron los cerros (Caracas: El Nacional/Ateneo de Caracas, 1989);

El pez que fuma, by Cabrujas and Román Chalbaud (Mérida, Venezuela: Letras y Comunicación, 1991);

El teatro de Cabrujas (Caracas: Pomaire/Fuentes, 1991)—comprises *Profundo, Acto cultural, El día que me quieras,* and *El americano ilustrado;*

El país según Cabrujas (Caracas: Monte Avila/El Diario de Caracas, 1992);

Sagrado y obsceno, by Cabrujas and Chalbaud (Caracas & Mérida: Dirección de Cultura de la Universidad Central de Venezuela/Fundación del Nuevo Cine Latinoamericano, 1997);

Y latinoamérica inventó la telenovela, edited by Leonardo Padrón (Caracas: Alfadil, 2002).

PRODUCED SCRIPTS: *Eso era cuando,* radio, Radio Nacional de Venezuela, 1972–1973;

Opera dominical, radio, Radio Nacional de Venezuela, 1972–1973;

Crónica de un subversivo latinoamericano, by Cabrujas and Mauricio Walerstein, motion picture, Alfa Films Internacional, 1975;

Sagrado y obsceno, by Cabrujas and Román Chalbaud, motion picture, 1975;

Doña Bárbara, by Cabrujas, Rómulo Gallegos, and Salvador Garmendia, television, 1975;

La quema de Judas, by Cabrujas and Chalbaud, motion picture, 1976;

La señora de Cárdenas, television, 1976;

El pez que fuma, by Cabrujas and Chalbaud, motion picture, Gente de Cine, 1977;

Silvia Rivas, television, 1977;

Soltera y sin compromiso, television, 1977;

Estefanía, by Cabrujas and Julio César Marmol, television, RCTV, 1 July 1979;

La comadre, by Cabrujas and Chalbaud, television, 1979;

Domingo de Resurección, by Cabrujas and Chalbaud, motion picture, 1980;

Natalia de 8 a 9, television, RCTV, 1980;

Cangrejo I y II, motion picture, 1980, 1982;

Gómez I y II, television, 1980, 1982;

La invasión, by Cabrujas and Marmol, motion picture, 1981;

El asesinato de Delgado Chalbaud, television, 1982;

La Señorita Perdomo, by Cabrujas and Garmendia, television, RCTV, 1982;

La mujer sin rostro, television, 1983;

La dueña, by Cabrujas and Marmol, television, Univisión Network, 1984;

Chao Cristina, television, 1986;

El escándalo, motion picture, 1986;

La dama de rosa, by Cabrujas and Boris Izaguirre, television, 1986;

El día que me quieras, by Cabrujas, Sergio Dow, and Olinta Taverna, motion picture, FOCINE, 1986;

Una noche oriental, by Cabrujas, Miguel Curiel, and Frank Baiz Quevedo, motion picture, 1986;

Señora, by Cabrujas, Ibsen Martínez, Eliseo Morales, and Cristina Policastro, television, Coral Pictures, 1988;

Aventurera, motion picture, 1990;

Emperatriz, by Cabrujas, Carolina Espada, and Carlos González Vega, television, Marte TV, 1990;

Profundo, motion picture, 1990;

Las dos Dianas, television, Marte TV, 1992;

El paseo de la gracia de Dios, television, Marte TV, 1992–1993;

Nada personal, television, 1995;

Amaneció de golpe, motion picture, Blancica, 1998.

OTHER: *Fiésole,* in *13 autores del teatro venezolano,* edited by Carlos Miguel Suárez Radillo (Caracas: Monte Avila, 1971).

José Ignacio Cabrujas is one of the masters of dramatic art in twentieth-century Venezuelan theater. While his technical skill is evident in his work with traditional and innovative forms, the latter constitutes Cabrujas's greatest contributions to the Venezuelan theater. And although he is known primarily as a dramatist, his constant search for innovation and concern for social issues led him to experiment successfully in other genres, including journalism, essays, movie scripts, and television.

The development of Cabrujas's theater can be divided into four periods. The first one comprises his beginnings in the Theatre of the Central University of Venezuela, under the direction of Nicolás Curiel, who had formally introduced Brechtian theater to Venezuela in 1957. During this phase, Cabrujas established both a Brechtian and a social identity, with a marked world vision resembling the works of César Rengifo. These ideas were important in Venezuela at the end of the 1950s and constituted the shift toward modern forms of theatrical drama for the national scene. When he became a playwright seeking to offer solutions to the problems that he observed in the growing Venezuelan democracy, he began to direct most of his own plays. This period was one of transition, marked by the theatrical experimentation in vogue in the 1960s. The third stage followed his deep interest in the main problems of the country during the 1970s until the mid 1980s, when he wrote—with more depth and reflection—what are considered to be his best works. During this period he designed a clear aesthetic that has been called the Cabrujean style. Cabrujas's final period lasted until his death in 1995; while he used popular characters as the leitmotiv of his dramatic creations, this phase was marked most prominently by its great thematic freedom.

Cabrujas was born on 12 July 1937 in Caracas, son of José Ramón Cabrujas, of Catalan origin, and Matilde Lofiego, of Italian origin. He spent most of his youth in one of the oldest and most humble sectors of the capital, called Catia, where he lived for twenty years. At the age of fourteen he read *Les Misérables* (1862) by Victor Hugo, which greatly impressed him. His father also took him to see Giacomo Puccini's opera *Tosca* (1900) at the Municipal Theatre of Caracas. After that his father taught him about the world of the theater and magic. The first time Cabrujas ever acted was when he assisted a magician at a performance. All these experiences inspired his passions for theater, acting and directing, opera, and social concern.

Cabrujas studied in Caracas, first at the San Ignacio Jesuit School, then at the Fermín Toro High School. He studied law at the Central University of Venezuela but abandoned his studies to devote himself to theater. One product of his university readings was his desire to help eliminate social injustice in his country, which led him to become a member of the Party Movement for Socialism. This party of the traditional left first declared itself to be non-Marxist and then part of the social democracy movement. At that point Cabrujas shifted away from the movement to become a politically independent leftist. Cabrujas formed a particular viewpoint and intellectual style that manifested itself in his writing for newspapers, magazines, theater, and television. His writings consisted of a mixture of chronicles, essays, and music, all marked by his acidic sense of humor. Cabrujas's intent was to achieve a direct dialogue with his readers or spectators. He wanted to portray the social and cultural face of Venezuela as he saw it: an illiterate, villainous, and disorderly nation that seemed to write its own history with a mixture of self-censorship and virtuous righteousness.

Beginning in 1945, political conditions made it possible to expand artistic freedom in Venezuela. Some of the most distinguished theater masters from abroad were let into the country, contributing their practical experience to the cultural dynamics; these dramatists included the exiled Spaniard Alberto de Paz y Mateos, the Mexican Jesús Gomez Obregón, the Argentine Juana Sujo, and the Chilean Horacio Peterson. They all contributed to the modernization of the theater in diverse ways and introduced writers such as Federico García Lorca, Eugene O'Neill, and Tennessee Williams to the Venezuelan theater. In 1950 Sujo started the National School of Scenic Art and then opened the Teatro Los Caobos, which helped to put new authors on stage. In 1963, the Theatre of the Athenaeum of Caracas was created. Simultaneously, these same people organized national theater festivals: the first one was undertaken in 1959, the second in 1961, and the third in 1966. These activities stimulated actor training, the emergence of national playwrights, and audiences for the national theater.

Cabrujas started his theatrical career as an actor under the direction of Curiel at the Central University of Venezuela, where he first played the role of Esref in Nazim Hikmet's *Legend of Love* (1948) in 1959. That same year he also played the role of Viola in *Twelfth Night* (circa 1601) by William Shakespeare. At this time he began to write for theater. Cabrujas's first play was *Juan Francisco de León,* written and produced in 1959 at the University Theatre. The play deals with the historical character Juan Francisco de León, who rebelled against Martín Echeverría, head of the Compañía Guipuzcoana in Venezuela and a special representative of the Spanish king. Cabrujas acted the role of Andrés de León, son of the main character. In the program for the production, Curiel introduces the play, stating that the piece is the initial step of modern Venezuelan epic theater.

The play profoundly criticizes the neocolonialist system present in Venezuela from the period of the Spanish Conquest to the present time. It presents the history of the Spanish Compañía Guipuzcoana, in charge of the slave commerce during colonial times, as well as the history of the twentieth-century transnational petroleum companies. The first portion takes place under the colonialist ideology, and the second under advanced capitalism; both are informed by Cabrujas's Marxist viewpoint. In the play Echeverría speaks, addressing the public directly: "¡Eh, Señores! ¿Qué os parece? . . . Hay otras Guipuzcoanas contra las que tenéis que luchar. Por ahora, dejadnos representar nuestra historia" (Hi, Sirs! What do you think about this? . . . There are more Guipuzcoanas to face and fight. For now, leave us to represent our own history).

In 1960 Cabrujas acted in several plays, including Bertolt Brecht's *The Threepenny Opera* (1928). Performing in and studying Brecht's work influenced the artistic style of Cabrujas's early socially oriented plays. During this time he decided to acquaint himself more fully with European theater and went to Milan in 1961 to study at the Italian Piccolo Theatre.

Cabrujas's next play, *Los insurgentes* (The Insurgents), premiered in 1961 at the University Theatre. It is also based on an historic event, the arrival of General Bermudez in Caracas. Bermudez played an important part in the Venezuelan Independence War, and he was well known as an intrepid and aggressive soldier. The conflict occurs when he arrives in Caracas and somebody throws hot water over him from a balcony. He

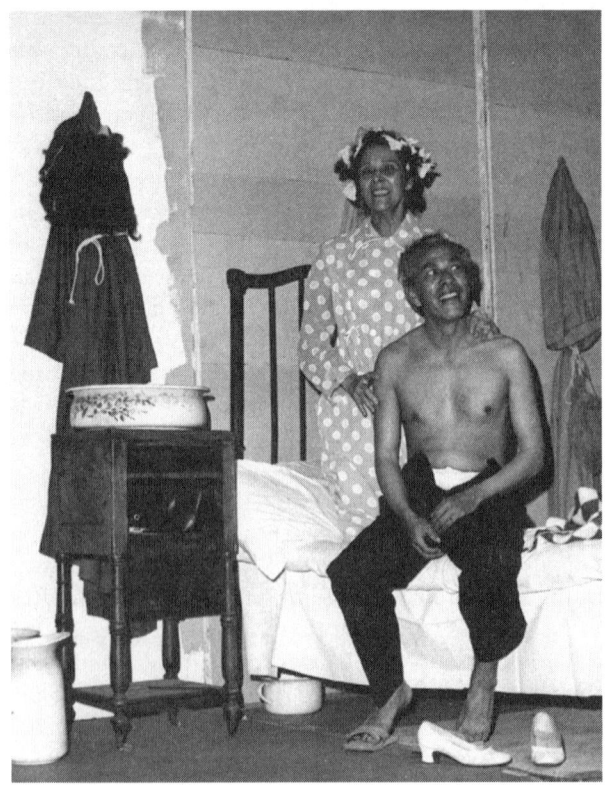

Irene Inaudi and Arturo Calderon in the 1971 Nuevo Grupo premiere of Cabrujas's play Profundo *(Profound), in which a rural family creates a religious cult around a search for buried treasure in their house (photograph by Samuel Dembo; from Dembo,*
El Nuevo Grupo: Un nuevo teatro para
Caracas, *1976; Zimmerman Library
University of New Mexico)*

takes over the house, where a widow lives alone. From this moment on a special relationship is established between them. For some critics the play is psychological, with the submission of one character to the other; for others the play is a Venezuelan version of Shakespeare's *The Taming of the Shrew* (1594).

In both *Los insurgentes* and *Juan Francisco de León* Cabrujas intends to reveal the past as an example or explanation of the present. Both pieces are didactic and, to some extent, politically biased. Many critics feel that these plays lack dramatic strength and were written mostly to express Cabrujas's personal ideas of dissatisfaction and protest concerning the state of the country at a time when the beginning of a new democratic period created more expectations than the regime could fulfill.

His third play was *El extraño viaje de Simón el malo* (The Strange Journey of Simon the Bad), written and produced in 1961 at the University Theatre. With this play Cabrujas acquired national fame and distinction as a playwright. The initial scene is in a circus, where three clowns interpret different roles, resembling the Brechtian narrator, who explains or clearly highlights what is happening during each step of the plot. He announces the sequential scenes with their titles on posters to ensure that the audience receives the emphatic message he gives, creating theater inside theater.

The plot is a journey undertaken by Simon through the obscure path of a corrupt society. He faces seemingly impossible obstacles, including the inefficient bureaucracy and dishonest judges. The main language device is ironic parody, in tune with the circus atmosphere, along with the use of songs, cruel images, and public reflection on the problems of society. The clowns present scenes such as "Pantomimes of Time in Jail," in which Clown III is an old man, Clown II a thief, and Clown I a policeman. The songs are presented in a style similar to musical comedy; in the "Song for Bureaucracy," for example, Clown III sings "Cada una de estas hojas deben pasar / por las sacrosantas manos / del Secretario Organizador" (Each of these papers must pass / through the sacrosanct hands / of the Organization Secretary).

The play *En nombre del rey* (On Behalf of the King) was written and produced in 1963 at the University Theatre. In this work the author once again uses history as the main subject. The protagonist is the Spanish conquistador Gonzalo Jiménez de Quesada, who tried to introduce European culture to Latin America. The theme of the play is the dichotomy between Europe and Latin America. Stylistically the play is a comedy, especially in the nature of the main character.

The unpublished play "Días de poder" (Days of Power) was written in collaboration with Román Chalbaud. The play outlines the life of a rich man who devotes himself to writing his memoirs after he loses his political power. This character resembles Venezuelan dictator Marcos Pérez Jiménez, overthrown in 1958. The play stemmed from Cabrujas's fascination with the early-twentieth-century *costumbrista* theater (local color, focusing on life in a particular region or period), the influence of which can be seen in the characters. As an actor Cabrujas participated in the movie *Los ángeles terribles* (1966, The Terrible Angels) by Chalbaud, for which he was granted the Best Actor Prize for motion pictures by Caracas County. In Curiel's archives is another of Cabrujas's plays from this period: the unpublished "Sopa de piedras" (Stone Soup), written in 1960. It is Cabrujas's version of the children's story that parodies avarice.

This early stage of development was followed by a transitional period during which Cabrujas departed from Brechtian theory and practice to focus more upon historical content and Venezuela's cultural and political problems. This new focus became one of the most important and constant features of his theater. During the 1960s he also continued acting, in productions of Rodolfo Usigli's *El gesticulador* (1947, The Impostor), Friedrich Dürrenmatt's *Romulus der Große* (1949, Romulus the Great), Chalbaud's *La quema de Judas* (1962–1964, The Judas Burning), Isaac Chocrón's *La revolución* (1967, The Revolution), and a 1967 production of Anton Chekhov's *Uncle Vanya* (1898). He won the Foreign Actor Prize from the Association of Critics of New York for his performance in *Uncle Vanya*.

From this point on Cabrujas tried to direct all his dramas himself; he also moved away from the university domain. With Chalbaud, he formed the Group Art Theatre of Caracas in 1962 (where they staged *Triángulo* [Triangle], composed by both of them in collaboration with Chocrón). These three authors joined together to form the theater art group El Nuevo Grupo (The New Group) in 1967. The group produced their own works and combined topics of reality and tradition from Chalbaud, theatrical structures from Chocrón, and analysis and social concern from Cabrujas. El Nuevo Grupo was centered upon the author, a focus they called "art theater." This group was successful not only because they had the real possibility of producing their plays but also because their close contact enriched each individual member's work as well as that of the group. They created a new style for the younger generation growing up in the new regime.

Cabrujas departed from his ethical and didactic focus with the play *Testimonio* (The Statement), a brief monologue acted and directed by himself at the Experimental Theatre of the Faculty of Architecture of the Central University of Venezuela in 1965. Then came the play *Fiésole* (1967), which marks a transition to other forms and contents that become a cornerstone of his playwrighting.

Fiésole is an existential play, rare in Cabrujas's playwriting. The play is based upon a personal experience he had of a one-week imprisonment for political reasons during the democratic period with a friend who was a theater director. He has said that this play marked his encounter with himself. The title is taken from the Italian town of the same name, in Florence. The play depicts three meetings in jail between two characters, One and The Other. The first time, they talk without knowing why they are there. The second time, they prepare imaginary spaghetti while listening to a religious sermon. During the third time, they talk again about Fiésole and why they are in prison. The play ends with a litany invoking the great names of the Renaissance, such as the Medicis, Leonardo da Vinci, and Galileo Galilei.

One could argue that *Fiésole* is more of a literary than a theatrical work. It is written as a sort of lyric aria and should be read like musical notation. In contrast with previous plays, *Fiésole* is a nonlinear drama. The theatrical discourse is complex, similar to the Theater of the Absurd, resembling Samuel Beckett's *Waiting for Godot* (1953) in its dramatic situation of characters waiting for something that will never come. In this case One and The Other wait to be freed, although they have no idea why they have been imprisoned in the first place. The theme of lack of communication replaces Cabrujas's usual political discourse. The most important aspect of the play is the word and the degeneration of symbols and values.

The 1950s were the years of a cruel dictatorship in Venezuela; the events of the 1960s changed that framework, starting a new democracy and at the same time a violent insurgence from the rebel fight of Marxist ideology against the new democracy and in support of the Cuban armed revolution as well. The 1970s were more balanced, a more stable democracy, serene; audiences even began rejecting commercial, frivolous theater and the theater of conventional political discourse, looking for a more authentic drama that reflected human reality in its own present context. Thus, national playwriting turned to a theater of more ideological richness, and at the same time of a new dramatic language, more in tune with these new social conditions. It was more dynamic, more powerful, and more integrated to a universal culture. For these reasons, El Nuevo Grupo was decisive for Cabrujas's dramatic evolution, and with its foundation his dramas acquired greater maturity and quality.

In his third period Cabrujas changed his writing completely, leaving aside philosophical reflections or metaphysical anguish to center on the spontaneous and living human being, close to the national context. Between 1971 and 1986 he wrote five major pieces for the Venezuelan and Hispanic American theater. All of them enjoyed impressive success. Some critics have seen these works as constituting a classical cycle or as a group of works featuring dimensions of history, culture, politics, and national identity.

The first play of this cycle is *Profundo* (Profound), written and premiered in 1971, directed by Cabrujas himself at the Caracas Nuevo Grupo. The play presents a poor, rural family that searches for the buried treasure supposedly hidden in their house by its former occupant, a priest named Father Olegario. In order to carry out their search while showing proper respect for the priest, they create a religious cult centering on the figure of the Sacred Father Olegario. Dressed as the baby Jesus, one family member, Buey, ritualistically digs a hole in the ground each day in search of the treasure, while another, the Franciscana, takes on the role of cult priestess, directing the operations and monitoring the family's behavior.

At the end of the play, flowers grow from Buey's hands, and this miraculous act is taken to mean that they can unearth the treasure. At this moment the rite and the myth collapse; with the failure of their journey, they return to reality. From the hole, they extract a sword, symbol of violence; a flag, symbol of the historical past, always seen in Cabrujas's works; a puppet (fetish); cans and garbage; and finally, as a visual association with Shakespeare, a skull, symbolizing the end of the uncertainty. When the family then discovers that the hole leads to a sewer, the ritual ends without magic or restoration, although hope remains for a fortuitous discovery that will make them millionaires. Having cast aside their religiosity, the family returns to the vacuous and useless rituals of their daily lives. *Profundo* is a dissociated discourse with a deeply ironic tone that creates a distance between the dramatic language, the characters, and the author, echoing the Brechtian style, but without Brecht's ideological, religious, or social undertones.

In 1972 Cabrujas was appointed director of the School of Theatre at the National Institute of Culture and Fine Arts; between 1972 and 1973 he produced, directed, and narrated the radio program *Eso era cuando* (That Was When), and he also wrote and narrated the program *Opera dominical* (Opera on Sunday), both for the National Radio of Venezuela. These activities prefigured his later work as an opera director. From 1974 to 1978 he also wrote humorous articles for weekly publications such as *Punto en domingo* (Sunday Point) and *El sádico ilustrado* (The Enlightened Sadist) under the alias of Sebastian Montes. In 1973 Cabrujas wrote a personal version of *Man is a Man* by Brecht for the University Theatre Group of Maracay. He continued to act as well, appearing in productions of Shakespeare's *Richard III* (circa 1591–1592) and Chocrón's *Alfabeto para analfabetos* (1973, Alphabet for Illiterates) and *La máxima felicidad* (1974, The Maxim Happiness).

In 1976 his play *Acto cultural* (Cultural Act), directed by Cabrujas himself, premiered at the Caracas Nuevo Grupo. From this point on the Cabrujean characters attempt to move away from their rural origins and reach higher social positions in the city. In this case, they are members of "The Louis Pasteur Society for the Promotion of Arts, Science, and Industry" in Saint Rafael of Ejido, a small, poor village in the Andean region of Venezuela, around the year 1929. The society decides to present a drama written by its president, Amadeo Mier. This play within a play is based on Christopher Columbus and the discovery of America. Their play presents an alternate view of history that competes with the historical record and the other daily, minor events that happen to the actors. *Acto cultural* is juxtaposed against the efficacy of history, especially in its aim to be an instrument of social and individual change.

In the society members' play, Columbus is played by Mier; Elizabeth of Castilla is played by Antonieta Parissi, a member of the society; Columbus's wife is played by Herminia Briceño, widow of Petit; Universal History is played by Purificación Chocano, secretary of the society; a Genoa Merchant is played by Cosme Parima, vice president of the society; and the Spanish King Fernando is played by Francisco Xavier, secretary of the society. The audience is the villagers attending the production. The actors try to represent a real history by their own means, including the people of the village in their story. That history is divided into two parts: the real history of the American discovery and that pertaining to the intimate lives of the theatrical society members.

The first portion of *Acto cultural* is devoted to the meeting of the board of the society, where the personal events of each character constitute history, as if to say that "el hombre es un producto de su propia historia" (man is the product of his own history), although degraded. For example, Herminia Briceño joined this society in order to escape the solitude and idleness brought on by the death of her husband. Her personal history is a legacy from her husband, for she always repeats "como decía Petit" (as Petit said). The role of Columbus's wife, to her, equals being the wife of an important man, a maker of history.

The second portion of Cabrujas's play depicts the arrangement of the cultural act: an historic re-creation in the form of a popular sketch about the discovery of America. In the society's version of this event, humor, bad taste, and deformation and exaggeration of historical fact predominate. Mier titled his play *Colón, Cristobal, el Genovés Alucinado* (Columbus, Christopher, the Deluded Genovese). Purificación Chocano provides an example of the humor in the play when she recites, "Como soy la Historia Universal / permítome hablaros en reflexivo / con alguno que otro vocativo / para contaros, con vuestra indulgencia / la verídica historia de Colón, Cristobal / el genovés alucinado y errabundo" (As I am the Universal History / let me talk in reflexive mode / with one and another word / to tell you, with your indulgence / the true history of Columbus, Christopher / the deluded and errant Genovese).

Because the real context of the play is a poor village, Cabrujas's analysis goes from the particular to the general, from local to universal, in order to produce a national theater with universal aims. What emerges in *Acto cultural* is a particular picture of transformational events from the point of view of people living far away from hegemonic centers. He depicts contemporary

Venezuela, where for many people, cultural expression is of an even lower order than that offered by the society. Cabrujas proposes that the past is not simply an evocative cliché. Rather, his parodic play gives audiences the obverse of official culture. *Acto cultural* makes clear that the nation has not escaped its past and that the huge myths of the New World, told by the conquerors, are synthesized in modern Venezuela. Many of these myths have become national obsessions; Mier, playing Columbus's role, says to Isabel,

> Y yo me perdía en aquella vastedad de montañas y cóndores y ñandúes . . . ¡Dios mío, los árboles . . . ! ¡Dios mío, las arañas y los bisontes! ¡Los jaguares, las llamas, los jabalíes, las perlas, las salinas y el oro. . . ! ¡El oro, Isabella. . . ! ¡Ciudades de oro! ¡Un hemisferio de oro! . . . Y todo está aquí en este sextante y en la tradicional astucia náutica de los genoveses.
>
> (And I got lost on that vastness of mountains and condors and rheas . . . my God, the trees. . . ! My God, the spiders and the bison! The jaguars, the llamas, the boars, the pearls, the salt mines and the gold. . . ! The gold, Isabel! Cities of gold! A hemisphere of gold! . . . And everything is here in this sextant, and in the traditional marine cunning of the Genovese).

The play within a play ends when the natives receive Columbus. Cabrujas's play ends with the final speech: "Hombres y mujeres de San Rafael de Ejido! (Grita) ¡Proponemos un minuto de silencio!" (Men and women of San Rafael of Ejido! [He screams] We propose a minute of silence!).

In 1976 Cabrujas began to write dramatic programs for television, an activity he continued for twenty years. During this time he wrote seventeen television soap operas. He took this work quite seriously and was recognized for renovating the soap opera, ennobling the genre by giving it real dramatic force. Cabrujas also taught Latin American and Venezuelan drama in the School of Arts at the Central University of Venezuela from 1978 to 1987.

The next play in his cycle, *El día que me quieras* (translated as *The Day You'll Love Me*, 1989) premiered in 1979, directed by Cabrujas at the Caracas El Nuevo Grupo. Cabrujas was then at the peak of his popularity, owing in part to the soap operas as well as the impact of *Acto cultural*. The success of this new play brought about much discussion concerning its content, particularly by the political left. The end result was a deep division among his critics and followers. The primary bone of contention between the two camps was whether the political or emotional content of the play was more effectively received by its audience. *El día que me quieras* is one of the few plays that really pertains to Venezuelan contemporary theatrical history, and over time it has come to be considered one of the greatest plays of Hispanic American theater.

Where ideological factors contributed to the effectiveness of the treatment of religious hallucinations in *Profundo* and to the cultural confusion in *Acto cultural*, *El día que me quieras* presents a more forceful political analysis. Cabrujas's depiction of the initial steps of democratic transition from a *caudillista* dictatorship, combined with the visit to Caracas in 1935 of the beloved Latin American mythic figure Carlos Gardel, had great emotional impact for various sectors of Venezuelan society. Later, when the play was performed outside of Venezuela, it caused a similar impact. For this reason many critics think that the play has a special universal appeal.

The key to the tremendous success of the play seems to be the opposition of two contemporary Venezuelan myths, represented by Pío Miranda (played by Cabrujas), based on the poet partisan Pío Tamayo, who fought against the dictatorship during the 1930s; and Gardel, the Argentine tango singer who visited the country at that time. Both are simultaneously historically real and part of the country's mythology.

The play is divided into two parts, called times, which correspond with titles of Gardel's songs: "Rubias de Nueva York" (New York Blondes) and "Tut-ankh-amón." The setting is the living room next to the interior yard of the Ancívar family in Caracas. Siblings Elvira, María Luisa, and Plácido Ancívar live next to Matilde, their nephew. María Luisa is in love with Pío Miranda, a Marxist who wants to go and live in the Soviet Union. He tells her he has written to Romain Rolland, a French communist poet, explaining his miseries in Venezuela and asking him to intercede with Joseph Stalin to receive the couple. He believes Rolland's positive response allowing them to leave the country will arrive in only a matter of time. María Luisa firmly believes in everything Pío's letter represents—"vivimos para un día donde habrá justicia social y se repartirá el mundo" (we live for a day when there will be justice and the world will be divided)—and she has decided to stay with him forever. Since he never wrote to Rolland, however, Pío knows that the story of his letter is a lie, and he also knows that his credibility depends on the rhetorical effects that lie will produce.

At this moment, Gardel enters. He is an external factor of the play, an artist visiting Caracas. After his performances the real Gardel indeed used to visit some neighbors in the cities where he stayed. In the play he visits the Ancívar home, where he chats with the family and sings the famous tango "El día que me quieras." He does not confront Pío, but he precipitates the crisis. He is a great artist, a realist, and a pragmatist. Elvira is the one who discovers the lie when she asks Pío for the let-

Rafael Briceño and María Cristina Losada in the 1976 Nuevo Grupo premiere of Cabrujas's play Acto cultural *(Cultural Act), in which the members of a cultural society in a rural village present their version of Christopher Columbus's discovery of America (photograph by Samuel Dembo; from Dembo,* El Nuevo Grupo: Un nuevo teatro para Caracas, *1976; Zimmerman Library, University of New Mexico)*

ter to Rolland. Pío answers that he will not respond, and when Elvira asks how he knows that, Pío replies, "no la envié nunca" (because I did not send it). She finishes the dialogue by saying "Judas." Pío then confesses his entire failure: "¡Mentí! ¡No hay Romain Rolland! ¡Nunca le escribí a Romain Rolland . . . ! ¡Me importa un coño Romain Rolland, y la paz y la amistad de los pueblos . . . !" (I did lie! There is no Romain Rolland! I never wrote a letter to Romain Rolland . . . ! I don't care about Romain Rolland, and peace, and friendship among people . . . !). The play leaves the audience with the impression of a major political falseness.

From the 1980s until the mid 1990s, Cabrujas devoted himself seriously to opera, leading the Taller de Opera de Caracas (Caracas Opera Workshop), where he was the regisseur of six operas up through 1994. He continued his activities as a theater director in productions such as *El pez que fuma* (The Smoking Fish) by Chalbaud, *La casa de Bernarda Alba* (1944, The House of Bernarda Alba) by García Lorca, and his own play *Sonny* (1995). Cabrujas also continued acting, performing in *Prueba de fuego* (1981, Trial by Fire) by Ulive. In 1988 he was awarded the National Theatre Prize. By 1990 he had written fourteen motion-picture scripts.

Una noche oriental (An Oriental Night), the next play in the cycle, premiered in 1983, directed by Enrique Porter at the Caracas El Nuevo Grupo. It was originally titled "Venezuela barata" (Cheap Venezuela). In this play Cabrujas attempts to search for the national context in 1958, following the end of the country's second dictatorship, when democracy was reborn. The plot of the play develops in a cabaret, called Bom-Bom, where the artists are rehearsing for the show "The Oriental Night" on the eve of the fall of the dictatorship (23 January 1958). In this atmosphere of singing and joking, they listen to and comment on the news taking place outside. The owner of the cabaret is a retired soldier, Colonel Vergara. The characters need to rehearse, but at the same time they try to understand what is happening with the government and how it will affect their lives. This transition to democracy is in part cruel, and in part funny: "¡Caballeros! ¡Vamos a inaugurar la democracia en el Bom-Bom. . . ! Y vamos a inaugurarla con un pensamiento profundo . . . ¡El coño de su madre del gobierno! (Grita) ¡Fanfarria!" (Gentleman! Let's open democracy in Bom-Bom. . . ! And let's open it with a profound thought . . . To hell with the government! [Shouting] Fanfare!).

The second act takes place ten years later. The cabaret Bom-Bom now assumes the position of the new regime, the growing democracy, and in this sense the play examines that regime's achievements. As in *El día que me quieras,* Cabrujas makes use of music when the singer María Regina interprets "Vieja luna" (Old Moon), an old popular Caribbean bolero. While the earlier play used the tango, this play uses the bolero, a musical genre much more integrated to the tropical culture than the tango, and still in fashion. *Una noche oriental* was not considered by the critics to be as brilliant as the plays that preceded it, but its thematic view and criticism of democracy seem to be sincere and profound.

Cabrujas's play *El americano ilustrado* (The Enlightened American) premiered in 1986, directed by Armando Gota at the Caracas El Nuevo Grupo. As Cabrujas himself stated, however, this play had been in preparation since 1976, making it earlier in conception than *El día que me quieras* and *Una noche oriental*. Its subject matter is also similar to those plays, making it a part of the cycle. Cabrujas again presents the past by means of the ghosts of Karl Marx and Friedrich Engels, who appear in the prologue of the play speaking and singing in German, as well as the central character of President Antonio Guzmán Blanco. The play takes place in Venezuela toward the end of the nineteenth century. The characters are two brothers, Arístides and Anselmo Lander; the first is a lawyer, and the second one a priest. Arístides is in love with María Eugenia, a lady who comes from a religious family, and in order to marry her he asks his brother to talk to her parents and make the arrangements for the wedding. In so doing Anselmo falls in love with María Eugenia, although he did his job well on behalf of his brother. Cabrujas links governmental acts, official political meetings with the president of the Republic, and the family life of the Lander brothers.

The second act continues ten years later when Arístides is forty years old, married to María Eugenia, and now the protocol secretary of the Foreign Affairs Ministry. He shows his wife a letter he wrote when he was twenty-five years old. In the letter he set himself a deadline of fifteen years to become the supreme chief of the Conservative Party and to modify the National Constitution. In the letter he promises that once this feat is accomplished he will set himself another great goal. If he fails to accomplish it, he will kill himself. Diametrically opposed to the ideals espoused in his youthful letter, Arístides now serves the Liberal Party. Thus, he tells his servant to bring him his father's pistol and, in front of his stupefied wife, points it at his head and pulls the trigger. The weapon, however, is unloaded; Arístides has only made a symbolic gesture.

His brother Anselmo, now an archbishop, comes to visit Arístides and confesses that he is involved as a conspirator against the president. He opposes the government because they want to sell the country to the British. He also offers his brother the post of minister of foreign affairs in the new regime. Arístides refuses to unite in the conspiracy against Guzmán Blanco. Then Anselmo meets María Luisa once more and recalls his love for her after fifteen years, telling her that he plans to leave the church. The coup attempt fails, and the president now offers Arístides the position of minister of foreign affairs. He accepts it and becomes the one to welcome the British mission.

Cabrujas once again employs the theater to ask difficult questions about human nature and attempts to solve political and social problems. The Lander brothers are representatives of the most powerful institutions of the country: state and church. Each one masks his desires and his true personality, which develop through the play, demonstrating the lack of familial relationships, their ill-defined ideologies, and the prevalence of political pragmatism.

El americano ilustrado is considered the most political of Cabrujas's plays. Guzmán Blanco is the only real ruler to actually appear in Cabrujas's works instead of simply being mentioned. Indeed, this president represents a real and particular moment in the history of Venezuela. Guzmán Blanco, "the Enlightened American," presented himself as a model for behavior, a style of government, national identity, and even an aesthetics. The plot of this play encompasses a crucial point in Venezuelan history, when the country's foreign debt to the British Empire led to a loss of territory. Arístides, however, has been only a marginal character in this historical dimension. At forty years of age he discovers that he has not merely put aside the plans he made twenty-five years ago but rather has betrayed them. And when his brother offers him the opportunity to change history, to pass to the central focus of the political scene, his desired opportunity, his answer is marked by frustration and defeat: "afuera está la Historia Universal esperándolo. ¿Qué le digo? –Que tengo gripe" (down there is Universal History looking for you. What do you say? –Tell him I have the flu).

Cabrujas's plays of the 1990s seem to move away from the focus on historical content to emphasize their visual impact. Now the theatrical image becomes more important than the story. The play *Autorretrato de artista de barba y pumpá* (Artist's Self Portrait with Beard and Hut) premiered in 1990, directed by José Simón Escalona at the Grupo Theja theater in Caracas. It tells the story of a well-known Venezuelan painter, Armando Reverón (1889–1954), exploring him both as a man and an artist. In this production the stage is covered by a fine and transparent curtain, creating a nice visual atmosphere. A strong light illuminates the subjects and the paintings themselves. The intention is to establish a sense of what it was like to live with this special character, the painter, and his artistic creation. The production tries to duplicate Reverón's ritualistic approach to painting. He tried to eliminate all noise, rejected rough or hard materials, and exhibited a phobia toward certain metals. Wrapping his brushes in old clothes, he used to paint naked in order to eliminate the interference of his clothes and to remove any colors that would distort the painting. It was important to him to be in direct contact with the ground, because he believed that it transmitted energy to him. He used to paint with a certain violence in his movements, in a nervous, rhythmic, frenetic ritual that he believed enabled him to communicate with his subjects.

In the play Reverón appears along with his psychiatrist in a sanatorium. From this present and sad time he observes how his past evolved, through images and anecdotes about life and art. He is surrounded by his beloved puppets and dolls, and from this stage the actors appear. In this play, contrary to the previous ones, in which Cabrujas placed emphasis on strong characters, he concentrates on images and atmospheres instead. The dramatic structure of this play is developed in two central axes: one is the conversation of the painter with the psychiatrist, who obviously does not understand Reverón or his painting, and the other one consists of flashbacks, images, and paintings that re-create his life and memories. These atmospheres are central to the development of the plot, and they let the public know the context of a great Venezuelan painter.

In 1992 and 1993 Cabrujas taught television scriptwriting at the Institute of Creativity and Communication in Caracas. Starting in 1992 he published a Saturday chronicle about political and cultural topics of national interest in the Caracas newspaper *El Nacional* (The National). In 1995 Cabrujas wrote and premiered *Sonny*, his last play, devoted to telling the story of a popular boxer. The plot takes place in the Caribbean port of La Guayra during the 1950s under the rule of the dictator Pérez Jiménez. Violence appears on all sides, from boxers and military dictatorships. Cabrujas's innovation in this play is the inclusion of opera and tragic dramatic structure; he adapts both Shakespeare's *Othello* (1604) and Giuseppe Verdi's operas for use in the play.

The play has several distinct locations, moving the story from Havana's José Martí Sport Palace to La Guayra's market square, and to Sonny's lover Inmaculada's room. Cabrujas tries to make colloquial language poetic by utilizing a tragic structure with almost mythic characters. The stage setting mirrors the Elizabethan stage, with stairs, levels, and pathways. It includes a great cyclorama and a boxing ring of real dimensions, in which Sonny achieves fame, exercises, is betrayed, and kills his lover and later himself. During the run of *Sonny*, Cabrujas passed away on 21 October 1995.

In the final analysis, what is most relevant in José Ignacio Cabrujas's theater are his everyday characters, the language he uses, the dramatic images he incorporates, and finally the tremendous sense of history and popular culture that emerges from them. He once said that history is the only thing that interested him: "A mi me importa la historia. No me atrevo a hablar de la vida: la vida la he vivido y punto" (I care for history. I don't dare to talk about life: life is for living and full stop). Popular culture is used to capture the Venezuelan character that has gradually become degraded by the influence of external forces.

Cabrujas's final group of plays confirms his status in Venezuelan theater as a major figure and as an innovator of theatrical forms. The subject matter, although borrowed from historical or social sources, is treated freely and imaginatively in all his plays and reveals his preference for topics he had also explored in previous works, such as the question of human dignity in his country and the integrity of history. These themes also show conclusively the existence of a unity of thought in his dramatic production.

References:

Leonardo Azparren Giménez, *Cabrujas en tres actos* (Caracas: El Nuevo Grupo, 1983);

Azparren Giménez, "El americano ilustrado," *Latin American Theatre Review*, 21, no. 2 (1988);

Lubio Cardozo and José Rojas Uzcátegui, *Bibliografía del teatro venezolano* (Mérida, Venezuela: Universidad de Los Andes, 1980);

Susana Castillo, *El desarraigo en el teatro venezolano* (Caracas: Ateneo, 1980);

Isaac Chocrón, ed., *Nueva crítica del teatro venezolano* (Caracas: Fundarte, 1979);

Samuel Dembo, *El Nuevo Grupo: Un nuevo teatro para Caracas* (Caracas: El Grupo, 1976);

Gleider Hernández, *Tres dramaturgos venezolanos de hoy* (Caracas: El Nuevo Grupo, 1979);

Ruben Monasterios, *Un enfoque crítico del teatro venezolano* (Caracas: Monte Avila, 1975);

Francisco Rojas Pozo, *Cabrujerías: Un estudio sobre la dramaturgia de José Ignacio Cabrujas* (Maracay, Venezuela: Universidad Pedagógica Experimental Libertador, 1995);

Carlos Miguel Suárez Radillo, *13 autores del nuevo teatro venezolano* (Caracas: Monte Avila, 1971).

Emilio Carballido
(22 May 1925 -)

Jacqueline E. Bixler
Virginia Tech

PLAY PRODUCTIONS: *El triángulo sutil,* Mexico City, El Teatro de Recámara, 1948;

La triple porfía, Mexico City, Aula José Martí, Universidad Nacional Autónoma de México, 1948;

Rosalba y los Llaveros, Mexico City, Palacio de Bellas Artes, 11 March 1950;

Escribir, por ejemplo, Mexico City, Teatro Caracol, September 1950;

La zona intermedia, Mexico City, Teatro Latino, September 1950;

La sinfonía doméstica, Mexico City, Teatro Ideal, 14 August 1953;

Felicidad, Mexico City, Auditorio Reforma, 10 April 1955;

Las palabras cruzadas, Mexico City, Teatro de la Comedia, June 1955; performed as *La danza que sueña la tortuga,* Xalapa, Veracruz, 1955;

La hebra de oro, Mexico City, Auditorio Reforma, 1956;

Homenaje a Hidalgo, Mexico City, Palacio de Bellas Artes, September 1960;

El relojero de Córdoba, Mexico City, El Teatro del Bosque, 11 November 1960;

Las estatuas de marfil, Mexico City, Teatro Basurto, 14 November 1960;

Teseo, Mexico City, Teatro Xola, 19 October 1962;

El día que se soltaron los leones, Havana, Cuba, Teatro El Sótano, June 1963; Mexico City, Teatro Julio Jiménez Rueda, 1978;

¡Silencio, pollos pelones, ya les van a echar su maíz! Ciudad Juárez, Chihuahua, Teatro del Seguro Social, 28 August 1963; Mexico City, Teatro del Naranjo, September 1963;

Medusa, Ithaca, New York, Cornell University Theater, 14 April 1966; Mexico City, Teatro Jiménez Rueda, 20 September 1968;

Yo también hablo de la rosa, Mexico City, Teatro Jiménez Rueda, 16 April 1966;

Un pequeño día de ira, Havana, 15 August 1966; Pittsburgh, Studio Theater of the University of Pittsburgh, 3 December 1970; Mexico City, Teatro Once de Julio, 22 May 1976;

Emilio Carballido, 2004 (photograph by Jacqueline E. Bixler)

Te juro, Juana, que tengo ganas, Monterrey, 1967; Mexico City, Teatro El Granero, 1967;

Almanaque de Juárez, Mexico City, Teatro del Bosque, April 1969;

Acapulco, los lunes, Mexico City, Teatro Antonio Caso, 30 June 1970;

Un vals sin fin por el planeta, Mexico City, Teatro Orientación, 1970;

Conversation Among the Ruins, translated by Myra Gann, Michigan, Kalamazoo College, 1971; performed as *Coversación entre las ruinas,* Mexico City, Casa de la Paz, 1989;

Las cartas de Mozart, Mexico City, Teatro Jiménez Rueda, 30 October 1975;
Orinoco, Caracas, Venezuela, Teatro Paz y Mateos, 12 September 1982; Mexico City, Teatro Gorostiza, 9 September 1982;
Tiempo de ladrones, Mexico City, Teatro Jiménez Rueda, 1984;
Fotografía en la playa, Mexico City, Casa de la Paz, October 1984;
Nora, Buenos Aires, Teatro Cervantes, 1985;
Ceremonia en el templo del tigre, Mexico City, Teatro Orientación, 5 December 1985;
Rosa de dos aromas, Mexico City, Teatro Coyoacán, 18 July 1986;
Vicente y Ramona, Colima, Teatro Hidalgo, 1986; Mexico City, Teatro de las Artes, 1986;
En-Dor, Monterrey, Teatro de la Ciudad, August 1988;
La caprichosa vida, Mexico City, Teatro Wilberto Cantón, 14 June 1991;
Los esclavos de Estambul, Mexico City, Teatro del Bosque/Julio Castillo, July 1991;
El álbum de María Ignacia, Xalapa, Veracruz, Teatro del Estado, 1991;
Escrito en el cuerpo de la noche, Guadalajara, Mexico, Teatro Juan Ruiz de Alarcón, 1994;
Pasaporte con estrellas, Xalapa, Veracruz, Teatro J. J. Herrera, 21 October 1995;
Engaño colorido con títeres, Santiago, Chile, Escuela Nacional de Teatro, 1995;
El mar y sus misterios, Mexico City, El Teatro del Bosque, 1996;
Mañanas de abril y mayo, Mexico City, Teatro Orientación, April 1997;
Luminaria, Casa de la Paz, Mexico City, 18 June 1998;
Soñar, soñar la noche, Bogota/Santa Marta, Colombia, 1998;
Los zorros chinos, Mexico City, Teatro Villaurrutia, 2001;
Las manchas en la luna, Xalapa, Veracruz, Teatro La Caja, 2001;
La prisionera, Mexico City, Foro Sor Juana Inés de la Cruz, 11 May 2002.

BOOKS: *La zona intermedia: Auto sacramental y "Escribir, por ejemplo"* (Mexico City: Unión Nacional de Autores, 1951);
La veleta oxidada (Mexico City: Los Presentes, 1956);
D.F.: 9 obras en un acto (Mexico City: Helio México, 1957); expanded as *D.F.: 14 obras en un acto* (Xalapa: Universidad Veracruzana, 1962); expanded again as *D.F.: 26 obras en un acto* (Mexico City: Grijalbo, 1978);
La hebra de oro: Auto sacramental en tres jornadas (Mexico City: Imprenta Universitaria, 1957)—includes *El lugar y la hora;*
El norte (Xalapa: Universidad Veracruzana, 1958); translated by Margaret Sayers Peden as *The Norther* (Austin: University of Texas Press, 1968);
Trilogía de obras en un acto (Mexico City: Imprenta Universitaria, 1960)—comprises *Escribir, por ejemplo; La hebra de oro;* and *El lugar y la hora;*
Teatro (Mexico City: Fondo de Cultura Económica, 1960)—comprises *El relojero de Córdoba; Medusa; Rosalba y los Llaveros;* and *El día que se soltaron los leones;*
Las estatuas de marfil (Xalapa: Universidad Veracruzana, 1960);
La caja vacía (Mexico City: Fondo de Cultura Económica, 1962);
Un pequeño día de ira (Havana: Casa de las Américas, 1962);
Las visitaciones del diablo: Folletín romántico en XV partes (Mexico City: Joaquín Mortiz, 1965);
Yo también hablo de la rosa (Mexico City: Instituto Nacional de Bellas Artes, 1966);
Las noticias del día: Coloquio (Mexico City: Colección Teatro de Bolsillo, 1968);
Acapulco, los lunes: Pieza en un acto (Monterrey: Ediciones Sierra Madre, 1969);
El sol (Mexico City: Joaquín Mortiz, 1970);
Te juro, Juana, que tengo ganas; Yo también hablo de la rosa (Mexico City: Novaro, 1970);
Felicidad; Un pequeño día de ira (Mexico City: UNAM, 1972 [i.e., 1971]);
Almanaque de Juárez: Obra en un acto (Monterrey: Ediciones Sierra Madre, 1972);
Medusa: Obra en cinco actos, edited by Jeanine Gaucher-Schultz and Alfredo Morales (Englewood Cliffs, N.J.: Prentice-Hall, 1972);
Tres obras (Mexico City: Extemporáneos, 1978)—comprises *¡Silencio, pollos pelones, ya les van a echar su maíz!; Un pequeño día de ira;* and *Acapulco, los lunes;*
Te juro, Juana, que tengo ganas; Yo también hablo de la rosa; Fotografía en la playa (Mexico City: Editores Mexicanos Unidos, 1979);
Tres comedias (Mexico City: Extemporáneos, 1981)—comprises *Un vals sin fin sobre el planeta; La danza que sueña la tortuga;* and *Felicidad;*
Tiempo de ladrones: La historia de Chucho el Roto (Mexico City: Grijalbo, 1983);
A la epopeya, un gajo: 5 obras dramáticas (Toluca: Universidad Autónoma del Estado de México, 1983)—comprises *Homenaje a Hidalgo; Hoy canta el fénix en nuestro gallinero; Teseo; Almanaque de Juárez;* and *Nahui Ollín;*
Los zapatos de fierro (Mexico City: Grijalbo, 1983);
El pizarrón encantado (Mexico City: Centro de Información y Desarrollo de la Comunicación y la Literatura Infantiles, 1984);

El tren que corría (Mexico City: Fondo de Cultura Popular, 1984);

Orinoco; Las cartas de Mozart; Felicidad (Mexico City: Editores Mexicanos Unidos, 1985); *Orinoco* translated by Peden, *Latin American Literary Review*, 12, no. 23 (1983): 51–83;

¡Silencio, pollos pelones, ya les van a echar su maíz!; Un pequeño día de ira; Acapulco, los lunes (Mexico City: Editores Mexicanos Unidos, 1985);

13 veces el D.F. (Mexico City: Editores Mexicanos Unidos, 1985); republished as *D.F. Nueva serie: 13 obras en un acto* (Mexico City: Grijalbo, 1994);

Ceremonia en el templo del tigre; Rosa de dos aromas; Un pequeño día de ira (Mexico City: Editores Mexicanos Unidos, 1986); *Rosa de dos aromas* translated by Peden as *A Rose, by Any Other Names; Modern International Drama*, 22, no. 1 (1988): 6–29;

El censo (Caracas, Venezuela: CELCIT, 1987);

Teatro 2 (Mexico City: Fondo de Cultura Económica, 1988)–comprises *Un vals sin fin por el planeta; La danza que sueña la tortuga;* and *Las estatuas de marfil;*

La historia de Sputnik y David (Mexico City: Fondo de Cultura Económica, 1991);

La veleta oxidada; El norte; Un error de estilo (Mexico City: Consejo Nacional para la Cultura y las Artes, 1991);

Teatro de Emilio Carballido, 2 volumes (Veracruz: Gobierno del Estado de Veracruz, 1992)–includes *El álbum de María Ignacia;*

Algunos cantos del infierno (Mexico, 1994);

Ceremonia en el templo del tigre: Una ficción profética (Mexico City: Plaza y Valdés, 1994);

Orinoco, Rosa de dos aromas y otras piezas dramáticas (Mexico City: Fondo de Cultura Económica, 1994)–comprises *Orinoco; Rosa de dos aromas; El mar y sus misterios; Escrito en el cuerpo de la noche,* and *Los esclavos de Estambul;*

Flor de abismo (Mexico City: Planeta, 1994);

Loros en emergencias (Mexico City: Fondo de Cultura Económica, 1994);

Querétaro imperial (Querétaro, Mexico: H. Ayuntamiento de Querétaro, 1994);

Fotografía en la playa; Soñar la noche; Las cartas de Mozart (Mexico City: Gaceta, 1994);

La prisionera (Tijuana: Caen, 1995);

Un enorme animal nube (Mexico City: Fondo de Cultura Económica, 1996);

Matrimonio, mortaja y a quien le baja; Las bodas de San Isidro (Xalapa: Universidad Veracruzana, 1996);

Engaño colorido con títeres; Pasaporte con estrellas (Xalapa: Universidad Veracruzana, 1997);

Tres obras para jóvenes (Veracruz: Instituto Veracruzano de Cultura, 1998)–comprises *Mañanas de abril y mayo,* by Carballido and Luisa Josefina Hernández; *La caprichosa vida;* and *Las flores del recuerdo;*

Tejer la ronda: 16 obras en un acto (Mexico City: Grijalbo, 1998);

Vicente y Ramona (Colima: Gobierno del Estado de Colima, 1998);

Felicidad: Obra de teatro en tres actos y un epílogo, edited by Myra S. Gann (Potsdam, N.Y.: Danzón, 1999);

Vicente y Ramona; Algunos cantos del infierno; Las flores del recuerdo (Xalapa: Universidad Veracruzana, 2000);

Luminaria; Zorros chinos; y La prisionera (Xalapa: Universidad Veracruzana, 2000);

El tigre rojo: Drama cinematográfico, by Carballido, Fernando Espejo, and Federico Chao (Mérida: Universidad Autónoma de Yucatán, 2000);

Egeo (Mexico City: Consejo Nacional para la Cultura y las Artes, 2001);

Un error de estilo (Mexico City: Editores Mexicanos Unidos, 2002);

El pabellón del doctor Leñaverde (Mexico City: Santillana, 2002);

Venus-Quetzalcóatl y cinco cuentos (Mexico City: Editores Mexicanos Unidos, 2002);

Dos llaves de una lanza (Mexico City: Editores Mexicanos Unidos, 2002).

Editions in English: *The Golden Thread and Other Plays,* translated by Margaret Sayers Peden (Austin: University of Texas Press, 1970)–comprises *The Mirror; The Time and the Place: Dead Love, The Glacier, The Wine Cellar; The Golden Thread; The Intermediate Zone; The Clockmaker from Cordoba;* and *Theseus;*

I Too Speak of the Rose, translated by William I. Oliver, in *The Modern Stage in Latin America: Six Plays,* edited by George William Woodyard (New York: Dutton, 1971), pp. 289–331;

The Day They Let the Lions Loose, translated by Oliver, in *Voices of Change in the Spanish American Theater: An Anthology,* edited and translated by Oliver (Austin: University of Texas Press, 1971), pp. 1–46.

PRODUCED SCRIPTS: *Macario,* by Carballido and Roberto Gavaldón, adapted from B. Traven's "The Third Guest," motion picture, Clasa Films Mundiales, 1960;

Selaginela, by Carballido and Gerardo Garza Fausti, motion picture, Producciones Cinematográfica Teens, 1967;

Los novios, by Carballido and Gilberto Gazcón, motion picture, Cinematográfica Jalisco S.A., 1971;

La Güera Rodríguez, by Carballido and Julio Alejandro, motion picture, Conacite Uno, 1978;

D.F./Distrito Federal, motion picture, Conacite Uno, 1981;

Escrito en el cuerpo de la noche, by Carballido and Jaime Humberto Hermosillo, motion picture, Instituto Mexicano de Cinematográfica, 2002.

OTHER: *La danza que sueña la tortuga,* in *Teatro mexicano del siglo XX,* volume 3, edited by Celestino Gorostiza (Mexico City: Fondo de Cultura Económica, 1956);

Teatro joven de México, edited by Carballido (Mexico City: Novaro, 1973);

El Arca de Noé: Antología y apostillas de teatro infantil, edited by Carballido (Mexico City: Secretaría de Educación, 1974);

Más teatro joven de México, edited by Carballido (Mexico City: Editores Mexicanos Unidos, 1982);

9 obras jóvenes, edited by Carballido (Mexico City: Editores Mexicanos Unidos, 1985);

Teatro para obreros: Antología, edited by Carballido (Mexico City: Editores Mexicanos Unidos, 1985);

Rosario Castellanos, *El mar y sus pescaditos,* introduction by Carballido (Mexico City: Editores Mexicanos Unidos, 1987);

"Theater and Its Functions," in *Philosophy and Literature in Latin America: A Critical Assessment of the Current Situation,* edited by Jorge E. Gracia and Mireya Camurati (Albany: State University of New York Press, 1989), pp. 140-143;

Lente maravillosa, in *¡Aplauso! Hispanic Children's Theater,* edited by Joe Rosenberg (Houston: Arte Público, 1995);

Taller Colima: Seis obras dramáticas, edited by Carballido (Colima: Gobierno del Estado de Colima, 2002).

SELECTED PERIODICAL PUBLICATIONS—
UNCOLLECTED: "Una cierta rareza," *Latin American Theatre Review,* 26, no. 1 (1992): 99-102;

"La Escuela de Arte Teatral del INBA y sus planes de estudio," *Latin American Theatre Review,* 27, no. 1 (1993): 47-56;

"Para que Xalapa se acuerde," *Tramoya,* 44 (1995): 117-122;

"Publicar teatro," *Latin American Theatre Review,* 29, no. 1 (1995): 93-94.

Emilio Carballido is one of Mexico's most prolific, influential, and commercially successful living playwrights. Since the 1950s he has written more than one hundred works that include both full-length and one-act plays, dramatic adaptations, librettos, movie scripts, children's literature, short stories, and novels. In a country where many plays never get staged, much less published, Carballido has had remarkably good fortune; nearly all of his writings have been published and/or staged, and many of them have also been translated and produced in other languages. His dramatic works frequently appear in anthologies and in university curricula in the United States as well as in Mexico. His one-act pieces, in particular, are commonly used throughout Mexico to train young actors and directors.

Carballido also has made an enormous contribution to Mexican culture through his pedagogical and editorial commitment to the generations of playwrights who have followed in his path. He has taught theater in several Mexican universities, directed many theater workshops, served as director in student productions, and helped many of these aspiring authors to break into the scene by publishing their first as well as subsequent texts in the theater journal *Tramoya* and in his edited collections such as *Teatro joven de México* (Young Mexican Theater, 1973) and *Más teatro joven de México* (More Young Mexican Theater, 1982). Many of the leading members of Mexico's younger generations of playwrights, including Oscar Villegas, Tomas Espinosa, and Hugo Salcedo, owe much of their aesthetic and commercial success to Carballido.

Although he has written theater in many veins, styles, and tones, Carballido is primarily known as a writer of comic theater. This description is, however, deceptively simple, since even the funniest of Carballido's comedies include a darker side that conveys a lasting concern with freedom and personal happiness. The most commonly noted features of his work include: an unusual ability to adapt form to content; the mixture of different planes of reality and dramatic styles within individual works; the sudden insertion of humor and irony in the direst situations; an ear for the dialects spoken in the provinces as well as the slang used by the youth of Mexico City; a sincere interest in female emancipation; a genuine compassion for his characters; the seamless blend of distinctly Mexican characters and language with universal themes; and an uncanny ability to produce a theater that at once seems "light" and at the same time captures the essence of Mexico and conveys his commitment to social justice.

Emilio Carballido Fentanes was born on 22 May 1925 in Córdoba, a small town in the southeastern state of Veracruz, to Francisco Carballido, a railroad worker, and Blanca Rosa Fentanes. When he was seven years old his parents separated, and his mother took him to Mexico City, where he has continued to live for most of his life. (He has a second home in Xalapa, Veracruz, where he enjoys a close relationship with the Universidad Veracruzana and directs *Tramoya.*) At the age of thirteen, Carballido returned to Córdoba to live with his father for a year. This first conscious experience with the sea, the jungle, and provincial life had a profound impact on the adolescent Carballido. Some of his

Scene from Carballido's 1963 farce, ¡Silencio, pollos pelones, ya les van a echar su maíz! *(Be Quiet, You Mangy Chickens, You're Going to Get Your Corn!)*, which makes fun of the inefficiency of Mexican bureaucracy
(photograph by Hector García–Foto Press; from Teatro Mexicano 1963, *1965*;
Thomas Cooper Library, University of South Carolina)

earlier writings, such as *La danza que sueña la tortuga* (The Dance of Which the Turtle Dreams, produced in 1955; published in 1956) and *Un vals sin fin sobre el planeta* (A Never-ending Waltz Around the Earth, produced in 1970; published in 1981), were heavily influenced by that key year. For instance, his father's work with the railroad instilled in Carballido a lifelong fascination with trains, which repeatedly appear in his theater and narrative as a metaphor for movement, adventure, and change.

Carballido was raised in a household of writers and storytellers, where verses were commonly given as birthday gifts. By the age of nine, Carballido was already writing short stories and dialogues. He learned the art of storytelling from his maternal grandmother, Gabriela Ferat, who shared with him stories from the Bible, Greek mythology, and provincial life. She was undoubtedly the model for the many wise and all-seeing elderly women who inhabit his plays. With the support of his family, Carballido continued to write poetry, short stories, and dramas throughout secondary school, where he studied for two years with novelist Agustín Yáñez, whom he later acknowledged as the person who truly taught him how to write.

In 1944 Carballido entered the Universidad Nacional Autónoma de México (UNAM), where he studied alongside novelist, poet, and essayist Rosario Castellanos. Other distinguished members of his literary generation include Sergio Magaña, Jaime Sabines, Sergio Galindo, and Luisa Josefina Hernández. With Hernández, in particular, he has shared a deep, lifelong friendship and professional admiration. He later did graduate work at the same university, specializing in dramatic art and English literature. Julio Torri, Rodolfo Usigli, Fernando Wagner, and Bernardo Ortiz de Montellano were among the teachers who most profoundly influenced the aspiring young writer. Carballido attributes most of his theatrical formation to Wagner, who introduced him to the practical world of the theater by allowing the young playwright to serve as his assistant.

Carballido wrote his first full-length play, "Los dos mundos de Alberta" (The Two Worlds of Alberta), in 1946. Although this three-act drama was never staged or published, its presentation of distinct planes of psychological reality anticipates later plays in which Carballido experiments with the conflict between a fantasy world and daily life. His first published work was

La zona intermedia (produced in 1950; published in 1951; translated as *The Intermediate Zone,* 1970), while his first staged texts were two short pieces titled *El triángulo sutil* (The Subtle Triangle) and *La triple porfía* (The Triple Dispute, published in *México en el arte* [Mexico in Art] in February 1949), which were performed in 1948 in the rooftop bedroom of fellow playwright Sergio Magaña.

La zona intermedia is the most well-known and most developed of Carballido's early short pieces. Common features among these early experiments include: a one-act structure; a dark, mysterious atmosphere; unnamed characters, most of whom are not entirely human; black, sometimes macabre humor; and the discussion of philosophical and metaphysical issues such as death, life, and responsibility. *La zona intermedia* consists of four semihuman characters who meet in limbo as they await their final judgment, which will determine whether they proceed to heaven or hell. The influence of the European existentialists is apparent in the treatment of responsibility and destiny, to which Carballido adds a strong dose of humor. The least human of the characters, the Nahual, is the one who ultimately escapes both heaven and hell, a salvation bestowed upon him after he spares the other characters and humanity in general by devouring the Critic. This play is the first of several in which Carballido pokes fun at his critics.

During the early years, Carballido's theater vacillated between two seemingly opposing styles. The first consisted of what is commonly called *costumbrismo,* a realistic style that is usually comic in tone and focuses on daily life in the provinces. The other vein of those early years is usually labeled "experimental" and displays a strong influence of European vanguardists such as Jean Cocteau, August Strindberg, and Jean Giraudoux.

Carballido was barely twenty-five years old when Novo, director of the Instituto Nacional de Bellas Artes (INBA), recognized his ability and invited him to open the theater season with a comedy. Even though Carballido had not yet written the last act when rehearsals began, *Rosalba y los Llaveros* (Rosalba and the Llaveros, produced in 1950; published in 1960) was a resounding success, lasting a whole year on stage and establishing Carballido as one of Mexico's most talented playwrights. In *Rosalba y los Llaveros,* modern, cosmopolitan, and outspoken Rosalba and her naive and flirtatious mother arrive unexpectedly at their family's provincial home in Otatitlán, Veracruz. Their cigarettes, frank discourse, and Freudian theories create chaos in a household where things are better left unsaid. It does not take Rosalba long to discover that the ghosts in the closet involve her cousin, Lázaro Llavero, and Luz, who initially appears to be a maid but later turns out to be the mother of Lázaro's illegitimate daughter. Most of the humor is provided by the aunt and uncle, who do all they can to keep this fact and other embarrassing family secrets under wraps. Rosalba attempts to settle the problems but creates only more confusion by unwittingly arousing Lázaro's affections, mistakenly believing he is responsible for Luz's latest pregnancy, and scaring away her cousin's suitor. Carballido follows the lines of traditional comedy and allows the complications to multiply before he restores order in the final act. Curiously, however, it is not Rosalba who provides the solutions but rather Luz, who reveals the truth regarding her pregnancy, thus leaving Lázaro free to pursue a future with Rosalba.

Although the characters are more types than fully rounded beings and therefore not completely convincing, Carballido shows an early talent for dialogue and humor. The clash between the cosmopolitan and the rural is best expressed in the dialogue, which pits the aunt and uncle's stiff and formal discourse against Rosalba's scandalous frankness. Carballido shows a willingness to discuss openly topics that remained taboo in 1950–sexual repression, illegitimacy, and racism. While not Carballido's most accomplished drama, *Rosalba y los Llaveros* represents Mexico's first modern comedy with its combination of provincial customs, realism, humor, and irony.

The remarkable success of *Rosalba y los Llaveros* was followed by a grant from the Institute of International Education that provided a three-month stay in New York and launched Carballido's lifelong passion for travel and foreign culture. The playwright's son, Juan de Dios Carballido Olalde, was born in 1950. Nonetheless, the early 1950s were difficult years for the playwright as he struggled with painful and confusing childhood memories and personal conflicts. For three years he wrote almost nothing. After the resounding failure in 1953 of another full-length comedy, *La sinfonía doméstica* (Domestic Symphony), Carballido retreated to Xalapa, Veracruz, where he taught at the Universidad Veracruzana and served as assistant director of the university's School of Theater. This period proved to be a time of recovery and productivity. Carballido wrote several major plays–*Felicidad* (Happiness, produced in 1955; published in 1971); *La hebra de oro* (produced in 1956; published in 1957; translated as *The Golden Thread,* 1970); and *La danza que sueña la tortuga*–all of which won first-place prizes during the years 1955 and 1956. In 1957 he served as public relations adviser for Mexico's National Ballet, a position that allowed him to travel throughout Europe and Asia, where he became more familiar with oriental theater and the European vanguard. In 1957 Carballido also published the first edition of *D.F.* (Federal District, the abbreviation for the

Mexican capital), a collection of nine one-act pieces that has since been revised and expanded several times, growing to fifty-two pieces published in two volumes.

While his one-act plays are not usually mentioned, much less analyzed, in critical studies of Carballido's dramaturgy, they represent nonetheless one of his primary contributions to Mexican theater, having served as the basis for many student productions both in Mexico and abroad. One of these plays, *El censo* (The Census, produced in 1959; published in 1957 in *D.F.*), for example, has been a staple of university classes in acting and dramatic composition. Because of their brevity, these one-act pieces do not offer the technical complexity or the thematic depth of his longer plays, but they do afford a realistic and concise slice of life in the Mexican capital. These short pieces offer a winning combination of humor and social criticism as they explore themes of love, death, adolescence, and urban violence.

During his first decade of playwriting, Carballido also tried his hand at a more traditional, realist style, creating a tetralogy of full-length dramas: *La danza que sueña la tortuga*, *Rosalba y los Llaveros*, *La sinfonía doméstica*, and *Felicidad*. Under the influence of European masters such as Henrik Ibsen and George Bernard Shaw as well as Mexican writers such as Usigli, Carballido created his own brand of realist comedy. His highly developed, three-act dramas portray life in the provinces, where custom prevails and appearances are everything.

Set in his native town of Córdoba, *La danza que sueña la tortuga* offers a humorous yet compassionate portrait of two aging spinsters looking for happiness, love, and freedom in a world dominated by men. While Aminta and Rocío maintain a relative degree of independence by running a small store out of their house, they are nonetheless restrained by their macho brother, Víctor, who treats them more like children than adults. The plot revolves around the clash of young and old, male and female, reality and illusion. Everything seems to follow the usual social order until Rocío, thirty-six years old, single, and fairly deaf, mistakenly thinks that her adored nephew Beto has proposed to her. In a misguided attempt to avoid hurting his aunt, Beto ends up actually proposing marriage to her. Only the violent and melodramatic interference of paternalistic Víctor puts a stop to the illusion. Nonetheless, while Rocío has to acknowledge the end of her dream of happiness, she and Aminta take advantage of Víctor's momentary weakening to demand that he set them up in an apartment in Mexico City. The women's other nephew, Carlos, is the first of a series of male adolescents in Carballido's theater. The facts that Carlos lives in Carballido's native Córdoba, that he studies in Mexico City, and that he is a struggling young writer

Carballido in the early 1960s (photograph by Hector García–Foto Press; from Teatro Mexicano 1963, *1965; Thomas Cooper Library, University of South Carolina)*

suggest that the play draws on the author's own adolescence.

With simplicity, light humor, and satire, Carballido pokes gentle fun at midcentury Mexican values and customs: the unchallenged dominance of the macho; the submissiveness of women; and the infamous double standard that requires the woman to be faithful while allowing her husband to indulge in affairs. The playwright expresses the intensity and complexity of family relationships, a theme that he continues to explore in later plays such as *Fotografía en la playa* (Beach Portrait, produced in 1984; published in 1979) and *Escrito en el cuerpo de la noche* (Written on the Body of the Night, produced and published in 1994) with less realistic detail, a less conventional structure, and less humor.

Although *Felicidad* also belongs to the realist side of Carballido's earliest theater, this bittersweet and somewhat melodramatic portrayal of middle-class mediocrity and hypocrisy lacks the comic tone that prevails in *Rosalba y los Llaveros* and *La danza que sueña la tortuga*. The central character of this three-act dark comedy, Mario, is an aging professor entirely unworthy of compassion. After a lifetime of pinching pennies and in the midst of a midlife crisis, he engages in a blind and egotistic pursuit of happiness, which for him consists of financial security. During most of the play, he battles to collect back pay at the university and to cash in an insurance policy. In the process, he meets a middle-aged office worker named Emma, who falls for the married Mario's lies and surrenders her long-protected virginity. As all the money rolls in, Mario finds himself at his unhappiest moment, revealed to both Emma and his family as an unfaithful husband and a liar. To counter the final bleakness, Carballido offers an optional epilogue in which the characters reconcile and make plans for a happier and more prosperous future. The serious tone, the setting in the capital rather than in the provinces, the focus on the middle class, and the singular lack of compassion that the dramatist displays toward his characters all set *Felicidad* apart from his other early attempts at dramatic realism. Carballido relies heavily on a mixture of realistic detail, symbolism, and derisive irony to ridicule the hypocrisy and mediocrity of Mexico's emerging middle class and to convey the message that happiness cannot be bought.

La hebra de oro represents Carballido's first successful fusion of the realistic portrayal of provincial life and the expressionistic exploration of the unreal and the subconscious. The play is set in a decaying hacienda in rural Ixtla. Two elderly women, Adela and Leonor, have come to the ranch with the hope of finding Silvestre, their long-lost grandson. Their opposing personalities and values provide for comic relief and anticipate later plays in which Carballido sets up two conflicting female personalities. While the grandson himself does not appear, the two women revisit the past through two parallel events: their curing of the infant son of a local woman believed to be a witch, and the periodic appearances of a mysterious man referred to vaguely as the Man in the Kaftan. The latter, in particular, helps them resolve their problems as well as their differences as he leads them back to the past and into their subconsciousness. At the end, this enigmatic young man leaves as suddenly as he first appeared. All the questions have been answered but one: Was he really Silvestre? Ultimately, the Man in the Kaftan is not only a magically real character but also the symbolic golden thread that weaves together distinct levels of time, existence, knowledge, and reality. Technically advanced and highly theatrical, *La hebra de oro* suggests a strong influence of Antonin Artaud and other French Surrealists.

In 1958 Carballido wrote *El relojero de Córdoba* (produced and published in 1960; translated as *The Clockmaker from Cordoba*, 1970), which has its source in the work of seventeenth-century oriental writer Pu-Sung Ling. Carballido started writing the play during extensive travels throughout Europe and the Orient, with the result that it displays a technical influence of European expressionism along with an oriental influence on structure and tone. Its combination of folktale, morality play, and social commentary defies classification. *El relojero de Córdoba* displays an unconventional structure consisting of two *jornadas* (acts that are often fragmented into many short scenes), a structure that allows for more flexibility in place and time. The oriental stories are imbedded in a colonial, provincial setting that involves Martín, a dreamer whose ambition is to build the most incredible clock in the world. His financial straits and sense of insecurity, however, cause him to invent self-aggrandizing stories of robbery and assassination, which land him in jail and in danger of being hung. Only the local magistrate, Don Leandro, with his sagacity and knowledge of Pu-Sung Ling's stories, can save him by inventing yet another story that entraps the true assassin. As the town celebrates Martín's freedom, the clock maker returns to his clocks, a happier and wiser man. *El relojero de Córdoba* displays a complex yet successful blend of metafiction and social concern with colonialism, both past and present. In fact, the play is one of the few Carballido pieces whose subtlety did not escape the watchful eye of Mexico's unofficial censors, who would try to block the streets and ultimately failed to keep these daring critiques off the stage. In addition to its popular ideology, the play displays several characteristics commonly associated with Brechtian theater: imbedded narrative, metafictional role-playing, a concern with justice and human dignity, and the integration of music and song. Although the drama can be understood on one level as the story of Martín's redemption, it can also be read as an indictment of a social system based on marginalization, opportunism, and corruption.

The 1960s were busy years for Carballido. He started the decade in Japan, where he spent half a year under the auspices of the Japanese government, touring the Far East, lecturing and becoming familiar with kabuki and other forms of expressionistic theater. Many of his most innovative and important plays were written and staged during this decade. He also made several trips to Cuba, where, surrounded by the euphoria of the newly born revolution, Carballido became even more committed to the issues of justice, freedom, and human solidarity.

Las estatuas de marfil (The Ivory Statues, produced and published in 1960) stands alongside *Felicidad* and the unpublished *Conversación entre las ruinas* (translated as *Conversation among the Ruins*, produced in 1971) as one of his most serious pieces. Set in Carballido's native state of Veracruz, this work includes autobiographical references to the time he spent in Xalapa during the mid 1950s trying to understand his responsibilities as a writer. This process of self-discovery is reflected in César, a director and playwright who, following a disastrous premiere in the capital similar to that of *La sinfonía doméstica,* has fled to the provinces in order to find himself and regain his confidence. The play focuses on his relationships with several would-be and have-been actors, in particular Sabina, who, in the male-dominated world of the 1950s, is forced to choose her domestic life as a mother and the wife of a vulgar chauvinist over a possible acting career in Mexico City. To amuse themselves, the characters occasionally engage in a game in which they adopt a posture and then freeze, while their rivals try to force them out of their chosen position. This "game" serves as a metaphor of not only their stagnant existence but also their desire to mold themselves into other roles.

Homenaje a Hidalgo (Homage to Hidalgo, produced in 1960; published in 1983) represents Carballido's first experiment with historical drama, a type of theater to which he returned many times throughout his career. Although the published text is more like a short libretto, the staging was a full-blown spectacle that included hundreds of actors as well as a chorus, an orchestra, and dancers. In five sketchy episodes, the play pays homage to priest Miguel Hidalgo and his leadership in Mexico's fight for independence from Spain. Carballido juxtaposes scenes of rebellion with those of repression as the poor join together to fight for independence. *Homenaje a Hidalgo* was one of Carballido's most innovative early pieces and proved that historical drama does not have to be realistic and dry.

Carballido's next full-length play, *El día que se soltaron los leones* (produced in 1963; published in 1960; translated as *The Day They Let the Lions Loose,* 1971), shares with *La hebra de oro* a thematic emphasis on subconscious desires as well as a technical emphasis on visual image and movement, but adds to this formula a madcap pace and an existentialist concern with responsibility and destiny. All of the action in this three-act farce takes place in Chapultepec Park, where Carballido creates an encounter among several people from entirely different walks of life: Ana, a bored and repressed sixty-seven-year-old spinster; the domestically slavish Housewife; the Man, a would-be poet who lives off bribes taken from lovers surprised in the bushes; the Professor; his student cadets; and a group of lions let loose by a rebellious cadet. The characters engage in a frenzied pursuit of happiness, which requires that they gain an awareness of and fight against those structures that oppress them. The magical, almost surreal nature of the park reminds the audience of the fantastic world of *La hebra de oro* and at the same time offers an exciting alternative to the characters' hitherto cloistered existence.

El día que se soltaron los leones is the most complex of Carballido's farces, in terms of both staging and critical interpretation, because of the strangely successful mingling of humor, fantasy, and blatant criticism of Mexico's political, educational, and social institutions. Given the concern in this play with personal freedom and the fact that this freedom occurs only through rebellion, it is hardly surprising that the play was first staged in Cuba, shortly after the revolution, and that six more years had to pass before it could be staged in Mexico.

¡Silencio, pollos pelones, ya les van a echar su maíz! (Be Quiet, You Mangy Chickens, You're Going to Get Your Corn! produced in 1963; published in 1978) stands alongside *El día que se soltaron los leones* as one of Carballido's most successful farces. In both plays Carballido attacks Mexico's social, educational, and political institutions. Nonetheless, *¡Silencio, pollos pelones, ya les van a echar su maíz!* displays less concern with philosophical and ontological issues and therefore comes across as being more blatantly humorous. Furthermore, the work is simpler and more popular in its exposé of everyday bureaucratic bungling. With touches of Brechtian Epic theater, Carballido combines music, narration, vulgar humor, and didacticism to make fun of an illogical and highly ineffective welfare system in which the only response to the death of a poor man is to send a fancy coffin for a body that was never found. The fast pace, exaggerated action, and anti-illusory style of this play all convey the farcical nature of the Mexican bureaucracy. The humor ranges from slapstick to black as Carballido alternates among scenes of bureaucratic absurdity, arbitrary charity, and vulgar songs. In the closing narrative frame, the actors extend the image of the starving chickens of the title to the theater itself, which depends on the governmental "feedbag" for its survival. In this humorous piece, Carballido asserts once again his firm belief that farce is much more effective than overtly political theater in raising social consciousness.

Of all of Carballido's plays, *Yo también hablo de la rosa* (produced and published in 1966; translated as *I, Too, Speak of the Rose,* 1971) has received the most critical attention, particularly from American scholars, because it is highly innovative and thematically dense. Before "postmodern" even became a buzzword for contemporary critics, Carballido produced a play that mocks the master narrative, juxtaposes opposing historical perspectives, fragments history, and makes fun of those who would try to make sense of that history. The play centers on two lower-class adolescents who accidentally, in their innocent quest for amusement, derail a train, an episode that is re-created and reinterpreted several times throughout the play. The author uses a fragmented, Brechtian structure to present the same epi-

The cast of Teatro de la Luna's 1999 Arlington, Virginia, production of Carballido's 1967 play Te juro, Juana, que tengo ganas (I Swear to You, Juana, That I Wanna, published in 1970), his best-known farce (photograph by Daniel Cima; from Latin American Theatre Review, volume 32 [1999]; Thomas Cooper Library, University of South Carolina)

sode from many different points of view and critical perspectives, at the same time poking fun at those, such as Freudian and Marxist professors, who can only see and explain reality from one angle. Carballido relies heavily on the Intermediaria, an enigmatic figure who serves as narrator and unifying image. She also functions as a vehicle for the primary metaphors, the heart and the rose, both of which convey the complexity of interpretation and of human behavior. The phrase "I, too, speak of the rose" has become a cliché among Latin American theater critics, who use it to refer to the impossibility as well as the undesirability of posing just one interpretation.

Un pequeño día de ira (A Small Day of Anger, produced in 1966; published in 1962) is a play to which Carballido has added a strong dose of sociopolitical consciousness. The play is set in a sleepy Caribbean port, where the status quo and oligarchy never change until wealthy Cristina Cifuentes shoots and kills a child stealing fruit from her orchard. This careless act, along with the imprisonment of the town "loco," whose only crime seems to consist of speaking the truth, awakens the town into taking action. The different social groups are united through the narrator, who initially only comments on the action but who eventually joins in the inhabitants' rebellion against repression and corruption. At the end, the narrator warns the audience that although this event is just a short day of anger, it could easily transform into a longer one.

The timing of the play is significant. Written in 1961, just two years after the Cuban Revolution, it was first performed in Havana, where it won the prestigious Casa de las Américas award. Because of its blatant attack on Mexico's socio-economic and political structures, the play had to wait another ten years for its Mexican premiere. While relatively short in length, *Un pequeño día de ira* reflects the influence of Brechtian Epic theater and demonstrates Carballido's commitment to social and political justice.

Te juro, Juana, que tengo ganas (I Swear to You, Juana, That I Wanna, produced in 1967; published in 1970) is Carballido's best-known farce and the work that most clearly fits within the standard parameters of the genre. Although he uses the play to poke fun at Mexico's educational system, the text in general lacks the political objectives of his other farces. All action takes place in a private school run by Diógenes, who believes that "education" should be a strict discipline. Diógenes keeps a tight rein on everyone in the school, including his middle-aged daughter, Juana, whom he forced into marriage with a stammering student and would-be poet, Estánfor, after finding the two in flagrante delicto. The tongue-twisted Estánfor, when nervous, reverses syllables with humorous results. The farcical plot includes several misunderstandings and complications, in particular Juana's love for the school secretary, the latter's persecution at the hands of the libidinous young Lola, and straitlaced Diógenes's own secret trysts with the school librarian. There is a clear contrast between what occurs in the public spaces of the house and what occurs behind closed doors. After a scandal involving his daughter's use of a pseudonym to publish romantic novels, Diógenes is ultimately forced to recognize the reality of the situation, whereupon love prevails and all ends happily.

Carballido's longest work, the five-act *Medusa,* premiered in Ithaca, New York in 1966 and in Mexico in 1968, though it had been completed ten years earlier. It was one of the cultural programs produced in association with the 1968 Olympic Games in Mexico City. *Medusa* and a shorter piece, *Teseo* (produced in 1962; first published in the periodical *La palabra y el hombre,* 1962; translated as *Theseus,* 1970), are the only plays in which Carballido borrows from classical mythology. While both texts follow the basic plotlines of the original myths, they also go far beyond them in their treatment of modern-day concerns and existential dilemmas. This search for inspiration in classical mythology reflects not only Carballido's own desire to break away from provincial realism but also a generational desire for a theater with more universal appeal and transcendence. Nonetheless, Carballido successfully utilizes the myth without losing the sense of Mexican culture. The chorus of Greek tragedy is replaced by gossipy servants, while the Gorgon's palace is converted into a sleazy tourist trap. Through a combination of distinctly Mexican language, black humor, and references to classical mythology Carballido reflects the social and political atmosphere of contemporary Mexico. Although Carballido's Perseo unwittingly ends up fulfilling his mythic destiny, he takes some unexpected detours, the most significant of which is the fact that he falls in love with Medusa. The monster in this play is not Medusa but rather Perseo himself, who not only kills Medusa when he discovers that their love cannot be consummated without causing his own death, but also kills both his mother and her husband to proclaim himself the new ruler. Carballido demythifies and brings contemporary meaning to the ancient tale of Perseus to portray the loss of youthful innocence and the dehumanizing and corruptive influence of power, both of which were about to play out on the broader stage of Mexico.

Teseo complements *Medusa* in the contemporary treatment of ancient myth, but with a bit less humor. Carballido uses the figure of Theseus to explore the passage from adolescence to adulthood and from innocence to responsibility. Theseus assumes his mythic role in a serious but heartless way that conveys the corrosive effect of power on human emotions. More existentialist than mythic, Carballido's Theseus sees himself not as the son of destiny but rather as the product of his own actions and the author of his own future. In both *Medusa* and *Teseo,* Carballido combines classical mythology and contemporary banality in such a way as to make the receiver laugh at these demythified antiheroes and at the same time reflect on eternal questions of love, power, destiny, and responsibility.

After *Homenaje a Hidalgo,* Carballido did not seek inspiration again in Mexican history until *Almanaque de Juárez* (The Juárez Almanac, produced in 1969; published in 1972), written in 1968 to commemorate President Benito Juárez's death in 1868. The play presents in one long act and in chronological order the most important events in the life of the famous Indian president and father of Mexico's greatest reform. While the work displays a marked influence of Brechtian Epic theater in its juxtaposition of past and present, fragmented structure, and use of narrators, Carballido's integration of slides, music, dance, and poetry into the dramatic action is designed not to distance the audience but rather to enrich the theatricality of the history and to underscore his view of history as an alternating series of light and shadows. Carballido presents the former president as a human being who suffered highs and lows and who was capable of making errors of judgment. Furthermore, he uses two contemporary figures—a museum guide and a photographer—not only as narrators but also as links between present and past to convey an endless cycle of progress and repression. These parallels, along with the heavy use of metaphor, permit Juárez to transcend his historical moment and become a symbol of light and hope in the period of darkness after the Tlatelolco massacre of 1968.

During the 1970s Carballido continued to travel extensively, while his plays were translated and staged in the United States, France, and Czechoslovakia. He also served in several different pedagogical and administrative capacities. For example, he was a visiting professor at both the University of Pittsburgh and California State University, Los Angeles, while within Mexico he served as director of the School of Dramatic Art for the INBA. In 1975 he founded *Tramoya,* a trimestral publication of dramatic texts and critical essays that he has continued to direct since its inception. In the late 1970s and early 1980s Carballido became involved in movie projects and also directed plays by many of the young playwrights who later became known as the Nueva Dramaturgia Mexicana (New Mexican Play-

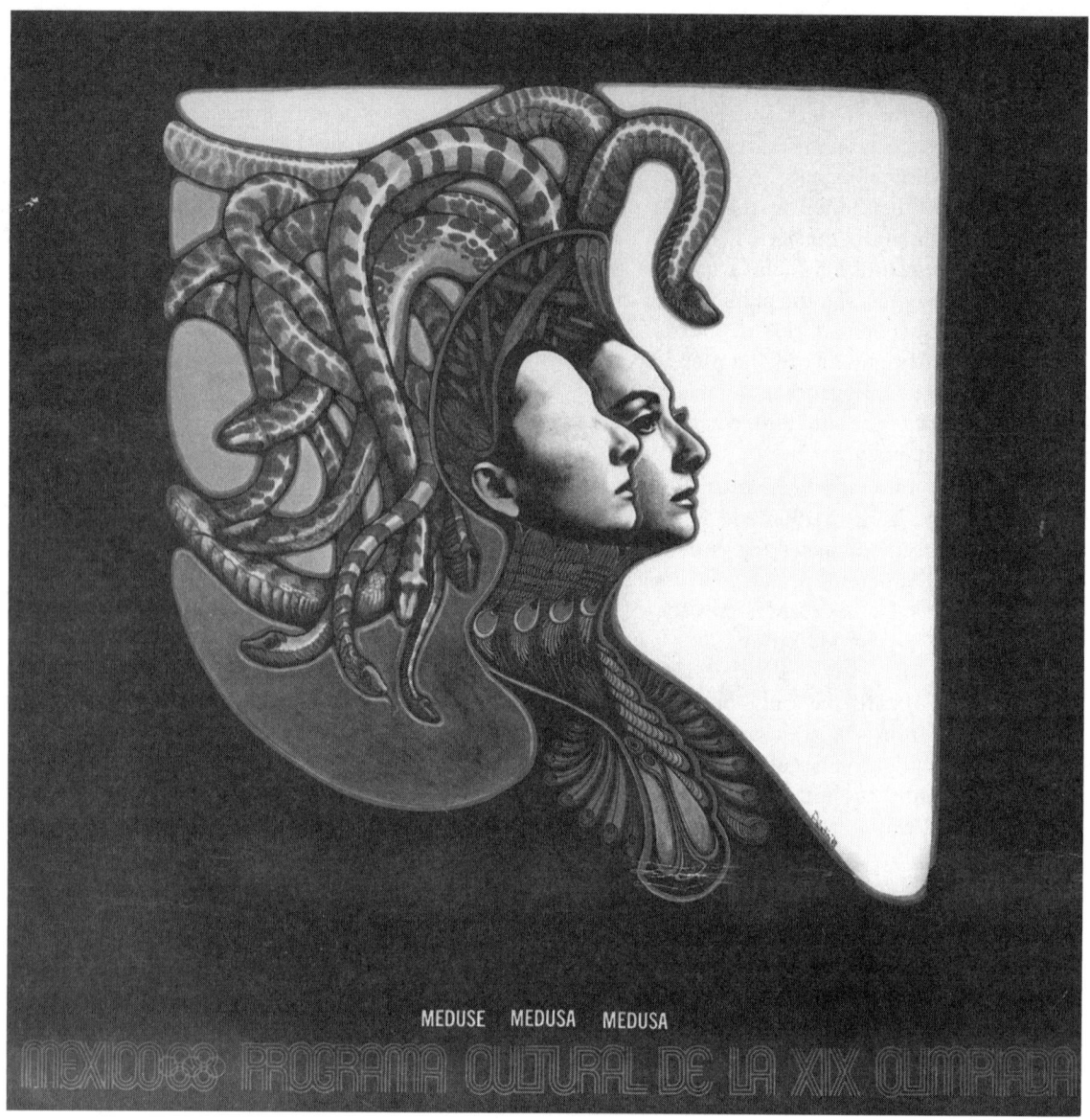

Program for Carballido's version of the Greek tragedy (first produced at Cornell University in 1966), which premiered in Mexico City as part of the cultural program for the 1968 Olympic Games (courtesy of Emilio Carballido)

wrights) and upon whom he had a profound stylistic and thematic influence.

Acapulco, los lunes (Acapulco Mondays, produced in 1970; published in 1969) is one of Carballido's lesser-known pieces. On a superficial level, it portrays the difficulty of surviving in Acapulco's tourist paradise. The enormous cast includes a rock band; a chorus of wealthy, pleasure-seeking tourists; and those who are left to squeeze out a living. These natives are represented by antihero Lucio, who, dispossessed of the family ranch by developers, now survives as a gigolo, thief, and con artist. The hedonism of the tourists is counterbalanced by two American expatriates and a German zoologist, who become Lucio's friends and accomplices as they struggle to find their next meal. As Carballido's spokesperson, German Liuba offers a parody of the carpe diem motif in this dog-eat-dog world. While the play includes all of the normal elements of farce—stock characters, frantic pace, lack of resolution, and unrealistic setting, tone, and action—it also serves as an indictment of the Mexican "miracle" of progress and prosperity that the government was trying to convey to the outside world during the 1960s. What Carballido presents instead is a group of characters bent on obtaining, through theft, prostitution, and chicanery, the little pleasures that life still has to offer.

In content if not in form, *Un vals sin fin sobre el planeta* is a throwback to Carballido's early theater. While it features the same cast of characters as *La danza que sueña la tortuga* and in that sense can be considered a sequel, the later piece actually takes place before the earlier one. In *Un vals sin fin sobre el planeta,* Carballido eschews the traditional three-act structure of his earlier provincial comedies, divides the play into seven scenes, and presents them as if they were chapters in a novel. In fact, two of the scenes are based on short stories from his collection *La caja vacía* (The Empty Box, 1962). Most of the scenes, while concise, follow the same dramatic realism in dialogue and character development as *La danza que sueña la tortuga;* yet, in the last scene Carballido switches to a more expressionistic style when all of the characters crisscross the stage, sleepwalking and expressing their innermost fears. He presents visually the intricate web of interrelationships that exists in the sleeping household, which has been turned upside down by the intrusion of two young and mysterious peddlers. Their physical beauty and nomadic life awaken latent desires for sexual adventure in pubescent Carlos and for personal freedom in spinsters Aminta and Rocío, who live under the paternalistic protection of their brother, Víctor. The play conveys Carballido's view of the world as a web of human relationships in constant flux.

Carballido continues to explore the topic of personal liberty in *Las cartas de Mozart* (The Mozart Letters, produced in 1975; published in 1985). The play combines the staid, repressed atmosphere of nineteenth-century Mexico City, the historical reality of Wolfgang Amadeus Mozart, and a fantasy world shared by young shopkeeper Margarita and her friend, Martín, who just might be Mozart. Several old letters written by Mozart spark Margarita's dreams of escaping her dreary and oppressive world and her mother's plan to marry her to an old lecher. At the side of the young Martín/Mozart—whose true identity, like that of the Man in the Kaftan in *La hebra de oro,* is never clearly resolved—Margarita discovers a new world of music, happiness, and hope. At the end of the play, she leaves with Martín for Vienna, and while their future remains uncertain, she is at least free. *Las cartas de Mozart* requires a talented director who can juggle realistic detail with the poetic quality of the language and the technical need to create an ambiguous, quasi-fantastic setting.

Orinoco (produced in 1982; published in 1985) is one of Carballido's most frequently staged comedies. Inspired by a visit to Venezuela and by a friendship with actress Nelly Garzón, *Orinoco* offers a dramatic situation that is inherently comic and at the same time serves as a metaphor of life itself. While en route to their next engagement along the Orinoco River, would-be showgirls Mina and Fifí suddenly awaken to find themselves adrift and with no one at the helm. The dialogue and scant dramatic action revolve around their attempts to bring both the boat and their own lives under control. The humor arises from the fact that while close friends, Mina and Fifí are absolute opposites. Whereas Mina sees disaster waiting around each bend in the river, Fifí is incurably optimistic. As they float down the river, the two women rehearse, drink, talk, and argue as they present, respectively, the most cynical and most delusional possible explanations and predictions for their predicament. The humor of their verbal give-and-take delights on one level, while on a deeper level, Carballido uses the images of the drifting boat, the unmanned helm, and the winding, ever-flowing river to represent life, with its unexpected curves and inevitable end. Nonetheless, the play ends on a comic and optimistic note when the resolute Fifí exclaims that the best is yet to come.

Tiempo de ladrones: La historia de Chucho el Roto (A Time of Thieves: The History of Chucho el Roto, produced in 1984; published in 1983) is one of Carballido's longest and most ambitious plays. The four-hour stage production was divided into two *tandas,* or sittings, and included nearly one hundred individual characters as well as groups of soldiers, townspeople, and prisoners. *Tiempo de ladrones* is an episodic work in which the scenes can be selected and reordered according to financial exigencies and the director's artistic preferences. All of the scenes revolve around Chucho el Roto, a legendary Mexican version of Robin Hood who terrorized the countryside during the nineteenth century, robbing from the rich to give to the poor. Despite the episodic and unchronological structure, all sixteen scenes are linked by the presence of Chucho and the repetition of the same basic dramatic format: the execution of elaborate schemes whereby the wealthy fall victim to their own ignorance and greed. Carballido acknowledges the use of many sources—dramatic, oral, and historiographical—in his reconstruction of the legend. He resurrects not only a relatively unknown popular hero but also several of Mexico's early theater traditions, including the *tanda,* the *género chico* (small genre, the name used for short, light, comic theater), and the *carpa* (big tent, the term for informal outdoor theater). Rather than attempt to convince the audience of the veracity of the story, Carballido celebrates and strengthens Chucho's mythical status with scene after scene of cunning, courage, and generosity. The obvious parallels between past and present sociopolitical conditions mark this play as one of Carballido's most overtly political pieces.

Fotografía en la playa re-creates a day in the life of a huge multigenerational family who converges at the

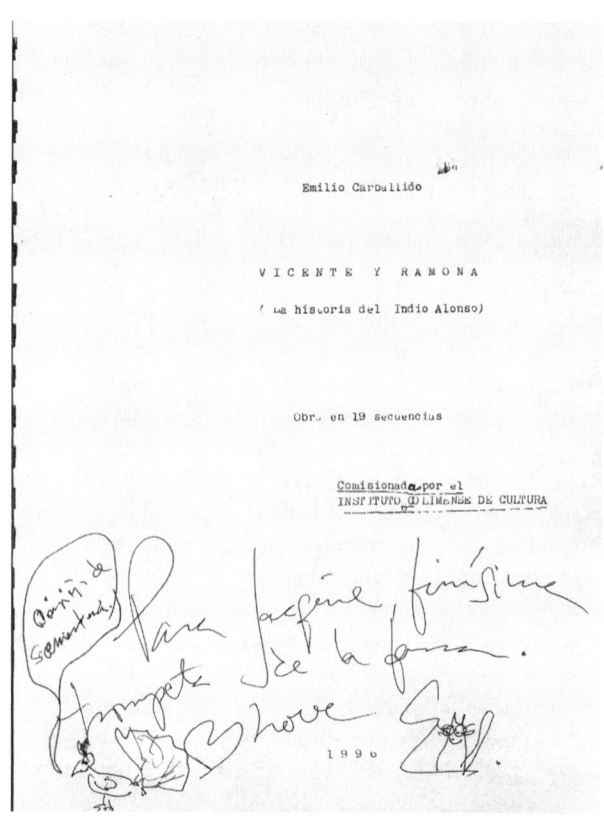

Inscribed title page from a xeroxed typescript of Carballido's 1986 play Vicente y Ramona, *the story of an outlaw brought down by a woman during the Mexican Revolution (Collection of Jacqueline E. Bixler)*

beach for a reunion. While superficially and collectively celebrating their family bonds, individual members struggle to break away from family pressures, obligations, and expectations. *Fotografía en la playa* is one of Carballido's most successful combinations of poetry and realism. The recurrent image of the sea combines with the converging and diverging lines of action to convey the idea that life, while brief, is complex and ambiguous. The only character who comes close to understanding this pattern is the grandmother, who, while regarded as senile by her family, is the only one who truly "sees" the relationships that lie beneath the surface of familial harmony. Her central position as matriarch, her immobility in a house full of constantly shifting alliances, and her role as voyeur all lend a certain amount of unity to an otherwise fragmented and partial view of the family. While the grandmother provides structural unity, Héctor, a liberal professor from the capital, provides the thematic link by conveying the dramatist's views on life, death, and sexuality through his philosophical discourse and his metaphorical descriptions of the ocean. *Fotografía en la playa,* like *Un vals sin fin sobre el planeta,* concludes with a highly expressionistic scene, wherein all the characters come together and pose on the beach for a family portrait. While physically frozen in their smiles and embraces, the characters' facial expressions do not correspond to the secret desires they express to tear away from those same family ties; they then narrate their destinies, which include the deaths of several members. The influence of Anton Chekhov's work is evident in the polylinear structure, the focus on the large family, the uncovering of buried tensions, and the apparent aimlessness of the plot.

Ceremonia en el templo del tigre (Ceremony in the Temple of the Tiger, produced in 1985; published in 1986), although much shorter than *Tiempo de ladrones,* was also inspired by history (the 1983 U.S. invasion of the island of Grenada) and is likewise blatant in exposing the colonialism that still exists in rural Mexico. The play centers around the passage to adulthood of Eugenio, whose liberal education in the capital clashes with the expectation that he will follow in his father's footsteps as landlord of a large hacienda in a state presumed to be Chiapas. The single long, fragmented act allows the young protagonist to witness several scenes that convey the themes of machismo, racism, social injustice, political corruption, and indigenous resentment. The curtain falls as Eugenio stands, pistol raised, between a group of U.S. Marines and a group of mestizo dancers who are re-creating an ancient indigenous dance. No one can be sure in what direction he will fire.

Rosa de dos aromas (translated as *A Rose, by Any Other Names,* produced and published in 1986) is Carballido's most commercially successful play to date. The first Mexico City production had the longest run in his career, lasting more than 3,500 consecutive performances. The work has subsequently been staged in other countries and other parts of Mexico. In this play two women, one an intellectual and the other a vulgar hairdresser, suddenly discover that they share the same man. Although they start out as enemies, Marlene and Gabriela soon discover that as victims of a macho-driven society they have much more in common than just their imprisoned mate, Antonio. After using all of their wits to raise the money necessary to secure his release through bribery, the two women share a drunken catharsis in which they realize that they do not need or even want Antonio and that the money would be better spent on a vacation for themselves in Acapulco. *Rosa de dos aromas* is not only comedy but also the culmination of Carballido's lifelong support for women's emancipation from machismo and other social traditions.

Carballido's recurring interest in historical themes owes not so much to any intent to correct written history but rather to his desire to keep alive some of

Mexico's lesser-known popular heroes. One such personage is Vicente, aka El Indio Alonso, the young leader of a band that terrorized the Mexican countryside during the Mexican Revolution. In *Vicente y Ramona* (produced in 1986; published in 1998), Carballido recreates the story of Vicente and Ramona, the daughter of wealthy landowners, from the time that he kidnaps her to the moment of his death. The structural division of the one act into nineteen sequences suggests a sketchy, fragmented, and unrealistic style of presentation. Rather than fight, Vicente's men devote themselves to theft, rape, and drunken brawls, while Vicente himself inspires fear in the rural population with his reputation as a witch doctor. He is believed to be protected from death—that is, until he meets Ramona, another of Carballido's strong women, and falls not to enemy bullets but rather to love. Ramona finally shoots him in cold blood and thus puts an end to his spell over her as well as his fearful reign over the countryside. It is not clear how much of this story is based on fact, but there is no doubt that Ramona lives in collective memory as one of the first truly liberated women of Mexico. Once again, Carballido underscores the subtle but powerful presence of women in Mexican history. Although usually overlooked in history books, they were often the motive and at times even the catalyst for the action.

In the unpublished text of *En-Dor* (produced in 1988), Carballido mixes not only the tragic and the humorous but also the real and the magical. The play portrays an embittered, wealthy widow who appropriates the powers of vulgar spirits in a willful effort to control her rebellious daughter. Although the play ends on a tragic note, *En-Dor* provides comic relief in the form of a mischievous spirit whose truth-filled obscenities function as the voice of consciousness, allowing Carballido to express social truths that otherwise might have had to remain unsaid.

Soñar, soñar la noche (Dreaming the Night, performed in 1998, published in 1994) was not completed until 1988, although it was begun in 1952, which helps to explain why this play resembles Carballido's earlier dramatic realism and focus on complicated family relationships. The themes are basically the same—frustrated love, mid-century social barriers and hierarchies, and the conflict between the desire for personal freedom and the pull of family obligations. Nonetheless, the play differs from the earlier works in its dramatic structure, which, instead of the traditional three acts, consists of many short scenes that portray several shifting homosexual and heterosexual relationships.

Carballido's pieces written in the 1990s tend to be relatively short, but they continue to display the usual variety of dramatic styles and topics. In 1990 he wrote *Algunos cantos del infierno* (A Few Songs from Hell, published in 1994), in which he combines Dante's *Inferno* (circa 1310–1314), rock-and-roll music, and contemporary drug-related violence to convey a message regarding the drug culture of modern youth and to criticize recent events involving drugs and the clergy. During that same year, Carballido created *Tejer la ronda* (Weaving A/Round; published in 1998), which is admittedly based on Arthur Schnitzler's 1900 comedy *La Ronde*. While Schnitzler's treatment of sex was scandalous in turn-of-the-century Europe, Carballido's treatment is in keeping with the modern atmosphere of sexual liberty. The structure breaks into several short scenes as office workers organize a little party and decide to tell stories about their earliest sexual adventures in order to get to know one another. The play was written for a specific group of students as part of Carballido's lasting agreement with the School of Dramatic Art and inspired by anecdotes related to him by the students themselves.

Another short piece, *La caprichosa vida* (Life on a Whim, produced in 1991; published in 1998) is typical Carballido comedy. When an upper-class couple from the capital goes out for the evening and leaves the children in the hands of their newly hired maid, little do they know that this mild-mannered, deferential woman will break into their liquor cabinet and transform into an obscenity-spewing table-dancer. The humor intensifies as the children become more rambunctious and the maid becomes more inebriated and vulgar. Yet, beneath the surface of this "light" comedy lies a deeper meaning in the portrayal of distinct social classes and the resentment that the have-nots tend to feel toward the well-heeled. Alcohol removes all barriers by allowing for a free flow of social commentary and class resentment.

Los esclavos de Estambul (The Slaves of Istanbul, produced in 1991; published in 1994) represents a return to farce. This time, however, Carballido leaves the sociopolitical criticism behind, replacing it with exotic fantasy and delving into more personal issues such as sexuality, loneliness, love, and loyalty. The plot, complicated and unchronological, takes place in different time zones and continents and involves such diverse elements as lascivious Turkish slaves, Mexican elementary-school teachers, and hashish-laced pastries. With a certain amount of autobiographical reference, the play portrays the visit of teacher/poet Eustasio to Istanbul, from where, against his wishes, he returns to Mexico and to his mother's home with two young Turkish slaves. Like the peddlers of *Un vals sin fin sobre el planeta*, Azael and Amina initially present themselves as brother and sister, but suspicions soon arise as to the exact nature of their relationship. Despite, or perhaps because of his increasing dependence on his slaves, Eustasio ultimately releases them, only to discover that

Advertisement for the premiere of Carballido's one-act play, published in 1995, about the friendship that develops between an imprisoned suffragette and the jailer's wife (courtesy of Emilio Carballido)

he has been deceived from the start. Through this exotic farce, Carballido suggests not only that freedom extends beyond the physical but also that it is a sine qua non for true love.

Returning again to Mexican history, particularly that of the nineteenth century, *El álbum de María Ignacia* (The Album of María Ignacia, produced in 1991; published in 1992) shares with Carballido's previous historical dramas a disregard for historical fact and a penchant for theatricality. In one act composed of seven short scenes, Carballido presents chapters from the life of María Ignacia Rodríguez, the beautiful and cunning criolla commonly known as La Güera (Blondie) Rodríguez. Through the re-creation of her interactions with such notables as Alexander von Humboldt, Simón Bolívar, and Agustín Iturbide, Carballido revives a relatively unknown figure of Mexican history and underscores the subtle yet powerful influence that she had on the most prominent political figures of her time. Mexican historian Artemio de Valle-Arzipe enters the stage and serves as narrator. He provides the historical context and explains that most of that influence was wielded between the sheets of the large bed that remains center stage throughout the play. Structurally similar to Carballido's other historical dramas in its fragmented, episodic, and expressionistic presentation of historical events, *El álbum de María Ignacia* reflects yet again Carballido's predilection for strong female characters, his fascination with the nineteenth century, and his conviction that the past not only parallels but also helps to explain the present.

Escrito en el cuerpo de la noche is somewhat similar to *Soñar, soñar la noche* in its use of a nontraditional structure (eleven sequences) to portray the complexities of a large family. The tone is, however, more comic, despite Carballido's treatment of such contemporary issues as drug abuse, homelessness, and AIDS. In fact, the play is rather like an updated version of *Un vals sin fin sobre el planeta*, which likewise involves the turmoil caused by the sudden appearance of a sensual, mysterious young woman who awakens the sexual desires of the family's adolescent male and unleashes conflicts among the other members.

Pasaporte con estrellas (Passport with Stars, produced in 1995; published in 1997) is an addition to Carballido's long list of monologues, which includes many of his earliest short plays—*Escribir, por ejemplo* (To Write, For Example, 1950); *Hipólito* (Hippolytus, 1967); *Las parásitas* (The Parasites, 1952); *Antes cruzában ríos* (They Used to Cross Rivers, 1967); and *Selaginela* (1951). This short and intensely metaphorical piece is a tour de force for the actor, who must portray the different phases of an entire life span, from conception to death. It also displays Carballido's trademark combination of the serious and the comic.

In 1995 Carballido celebrated his seventieth birthday as well as the twentieth anniversary of *Tramoya* but still showed no signs of slowing down. Although he wrote somewhat less during the 1990s, he traveled throughout the world to witness premieres of his plays in France, Belgium, Argentina, Colombia, the United States, and Spain. Within Mexico, Carballido has had his plays directed by many of the country's leading directors; he has worked most closely with Ricardo Ramírez Carnero. Carballido divides his time between his homes in Mexico City and Xalapa and continues to travel as he is called upon to provide keynote addresses and to serve as a jury member in international theater competitions. He has received several homages within his country, the most important being the one organized by the INBA in 1995.

Carballido is frequently commissioned by cultural and political organizations throughout the country to write plays that celebrate specific historical events. In 1995, on the occasion of the three hundredth anniversary of the death of Mexican poet and muse Sor Juana Inés de la Cruz, Carballido created *Engaño colorido con títeres* (Colorful Deceit with Puppets, produced in 1995; published in 1997). Carballido not only integrates a significant amount of Sor Juana's poetry into the dramatic text but also incorporates a rock band and puppets. Center stage is dominated by a huge baroque altar with flexible, three-dimensional images of important religious and political figures of the time. Throughout the play, these images "speak," summarizing the inner conflicts that Sor Juana experienced as a freethinking, creative woman in an age of social, artistic, and religious repression. Furthermore, the use of life-sized puppets as well as hand puppets serves as a metaphor of the many strings that were being pulled as royalty and clergy alike vied for Sor Juana's affections and loyalty. At times, an actress plays the part of Sor Juana while a large puppet Sor Juana shows how manipulated she was by those around her. Both puppet and human figure produce feminist discourse that supports the common view of Sor Juana as Mexico's first feminist. Victim of seduction, deception, and envy in both the palace and the convent, Sor Juana ultimately welcomes death as the only freedom from torment. *Engaño colorido con títeres* is one of Carballido's most highly metatheatrical pieces.

El mar y sus misterios (The Sea and Its Mysteries, produced in 1996; published in 1994) stands apart from Carballido's other plays in originality and technical exigencies. In terms of the latter, the text requires a huge cast of characters, musicians, and dancers, who represent the sea, waves, rocks, and other natural elements as well as the human beings who happen to pass along the beach. As in *Fotografía en la playa,* the sea serves as a metaphor for the profundity, complexity, and regeneration of life, only in this play it also functions as a character. The collective voice of the sea and the linking voices of the waves establish the elements' sensual and ephemeral nature while underscoring the destructive, insensitive, self-absorbed nature of mankind. The all-encompassing and wise sea is dark, deep, eternal, and scornful of human frivolity. Carballido refers to this highly poetic piece as "theater dance." *El mar y sus misterios* is playful and perhaps even a bit capricious; yet, it speaks volumes about man's general obliviousness to and carelessness with the natural wonders that surround him.

La prisionera (The Prisoner, performed in 2002, published in 1995) parallels *Orinoco* and *Rosa de dos aromas* in its combination of two females from different social and political backgrounds. Based loosely on Venezuelan history, this one-act play concerns the imprisonment of aristocratic suffragette María Antonieta Miranda de la Rosa. Her guardian, a ridiculous colonel named Leonardo Betancur, puts his subservient wife, Catalina, in charge of the prisoner's daily maintenance. The cell is located in a lighthouse, the tower of which serves as a constant visual reminder of a phallocentric order. Resentful of María Antonieta's social status and jealous of her husband's attentions toward his prisoner, Catalina initially scorns her charge. But what begins as hatred slowly turns into camaraderie as the prisoner leads her caretaker to a new consciousness of the latter's position as a female in a male-dominated world. The play also suggests, however, that the elimination of sexual discrimination will not entirely solve the problem for many women, whose difficult economic situation still obviates freedom.

Las flores del recuerdo (The Flowers of Memory, published in 1998) was written expressly for the Laboratorio de Teatro Campesino (Rural Theater Workshop), which helps to explain the lack of technical complexity, the simplicity of the dialogue, and a huge cast of characters that includes most of a small rural population–the dead and living, young and old, lovers and enemies. All come together on the Day of the Dead to follow the ancient indigenous tradition of leaving food and drink for the deceased. In a mixture of grief and vulgar humor, the lives of the many characters intertwine as they share memories and reconcile past disputes and antagonisms. The ritualistic nature of the action and the simple yet poetic quality of the language suggest echoes of Federico García Lorca's rural tragedies.

Luminaria (Luminary, produced in 1998; published in 2000) creates humor as well as tension through the onstage clash between opposing views of reality. These conflicting views belong to the aging, self-proclaimed "princess" Yamilé and the young man, Franz, whom she hires to write her memoirs. In each of the seven scenes, Franz and Yamilé meet and engage in verbal combat as each strips away the other's fictitious mask of importance and well-being. In one of Carballido's most comic dialogues, Franz hammers away at Yamilé's facade of nobility and professional prestige, while she retaliates by exposing his precarious financial situation and his girlfriend's unfaithfulness. Both are ultimately forced to recognize their humble origins and their less-than-successful careers. Unsatisfied with their shabby and sordid realities, Franz and Yamilé ultimately join forces and use the book to write themselves the life that they would have liked to have had. The only person who retains one foot in the real world is Yamilé's homosexual servant, Lupe, who supplies an endless stream of humor, serving as scapegoat, confidant, and referee.

The Palacio de Bellas Artes (Palace of Fine Arts), one of the major theaters in Mexico City, where a new production of Carballido's 1984 play Fotografía en la playa *(Beach Portrait) was staged in 2004 as the theater underwent renovations (photograph by Jacqueline E. Bixler)*

Zorros chinos (Chinese Foxes, produced in 2001; published in 2000) is a short fantasy in which several women of a rural population find sexual fulfillment and personal liberation from their traditional, macho husbands in the form of *zorros chinos,* who, half-human, half-fox, roam the forests and seduce the local women. Although the "victims" eventually return to their homes, they are no longer the same, having experienced true sexual pleasure and exotic love. This play bears echoes of *Las cartas de Mozart* in suggesting that in some cases—particularly for women—fantasy, and in this case death, may provide the only escape from an oppressive reality.

In 2001, Carballido wrote *Las manchas en la luna* (Blotches on the Moon), which premiered in Xalapa that same year. It is a two-part, bittersweet play that deals with aging, time, and eternal love. Toward the end of 2002, he suffered a major stroke. Nonetheless, at the age of nearly eighty and after many months of intense therapy, Caballido is again dictating new plays and traveling nationally and internationally to premieres, conferences, and festivals.

The difficulty of working with Emilio Carballido's theater owes first of all to the sheer volume of it. Nonetheless, a chronological survey of his dramatic production shows an evolution from his earliest experiments with European vanguardist technique, to his vacillation between and then blending of dramatic realism and expressionism, to a succession of full-length plays in which he mixes poetry and realism, humor and social commentary, and a distinctly Mexican setting and language and universal concerns. His most lasting legacies will be his ability to match form to content and to portray, criticize, and at times even attack his country's sociopolitical reality without losing his trademark humor, his compassion for his characters and his countrymen, and his incurable optimism.

Interviews:

Joseph F. Vélez, "Una entrevista con Emilio Carballido," *Latin American Theatre Review,* 7, no. 1 (1973): 17–24;

Teresa B. Rodríguez, "Entrevista con Emilio Carballido," *Hispania,* 67, no. 4 (1984): 655–657;

Rubén Ríos Avila, "Conversando con Carballido," *El Mundo* (San Juan), 28 August 1988, p. 15;

Silvia Peláez, "Emilio Carballido y la capacidad de las imagenes," in *Oficio de dramaturgo* (Mexico City: Editarte, 2002), pp. 87–105.

Bibliographies:

Socorro Merlín, *Catálogo de la obra de Emilio Carballido. Volumen 1 (1946–1967)* (Puebla: Tablado Iberoamericano, 2000);

Merlín, *Catálogo de la obra de Emilio Carballido. Volumen 2 (1968–1989)* (Mexico City: INBA, 2002).

References:

Judith Bissett and Howard Blanning, "Visualizing Carballido's *Orinoco:* The Play in Two Imagined Performances," *Gestos: Teoría y Práctica del Teatro Hispánico,* 5, no. 9 (1990): 65–74;

Jacqueline E. Bixler, *Convention and Transgression: The Theatre of Emilio Carballido* (Lewisburg, Pa.: Bucknell University Press, 1997); translated as *Convención y transgresión: El teatro de Emilio Carballido* (Xalapa: Universidad Veracruzana, 2001);

Becky Boling, "Espacio femenino en dos montajes de *Rosa de dos aromas* de Emilio Carballido," *Literatura Mexicana,* 2, no. 2 (1991): 353–368;

Sandra Messinger Cypess, "I, Too, Speak: 'Female' Discourse in Carballido's Plays," *Latin American Theatre Review,* 18, no. 1 (1984): 45–52;

Frank N. Dauster, "Carballido y el teatro de la liberación," *Alba de América,* 7, no. 12–13 (1989): 205–220;

Dauster, "El teatro de Emilio Carballido," in his *Ensayos sobre teatro hispanoamericano* (Mexico City: SEP, 1975), pp. 143–188;

Roy A. Kerr, "La función de la Intermediaria en *Yo también hablo de la rosa*," *Latin American Theatre Review,* 12, no. 1 (1978): 51–60;

Priscilla Meléndez, "Crítica de la crítica: *Yo también hablo de la rosa* de Emilio Carballido," in her *La dramaturgia hispanoamericana contemporánea: Teatralidad y autoconciencia* (Madrid: Pliegos, 1990), pp. 127–153;

Margaret Sayers Peden, *Emilio Carballido* (Boston: Twayne, 1980);

Peden, "Theory and Practice in Artaud and Carballido," *Modern Drama,* 11, no. 2 (1968): 132–142;

Karen Petersen, "Existential Irony in Three Carballido Plays," *Latin American Theatre Review,* 10, no. 2 (1977): 29–35;

70 años de Carballido: Homenaje nacional (Mexico City: Consejo Nacional para la Cultura y las Artes/ Instituto Nacional de Bellas Artes, 1995);

Diana Taylor, "Theatre and Transculturation: Emilio Carballido," in her *Theatre of Crisis: Drama and Politics in Latin America* (Lexington: University Press of Kentucky, 1991);

Teatro Mexicano 1963 (Madrid: Aguilar, 1965);

Mary Vázquez-Amaral, *El teatro de Emilio Carballido (1950–1965)* (Mexico City: Costa-Amic, 1974).

Roberto Cossa
(30 November 1934 –   )

Melissa A. Fitch
University of Arizona

PLAY PRODUCTIONS: *Nuestro fin de semana,* Buenos Aires, Teatro Rio Bamba, 27 March 1964;

Los días de Julián Bisbal, Buenos Aires, Teatro Regina, 14 January 1966;

La ñata contra el libro, Buenos Aires, Local Nocturno Gotán, 22 August 1966;

La pata de la sota, Buenos Aires, Teatro ABC, 14 April 1967;

El avión negro, by Cossa, Germán Rozenmacher, Carlos Somigliana, and Ricardo Talesnik, Buenos Aires, Teatro Regina, 29 July 1970;

La nona, Buenos Aires, Teatro Lasalle, 1977;

No hay que llorar, Buenos Aires, Auditorio Buenos Aires, 11 May 1979;

El viejo criado, Buenos Aires, Teatro Payró, 26 September 1980;

Tute cabrero, Buenos Aires, Los Teatros de San Telmo, April 1981;

Gris de ausencia, Buenos Aires, Teatro del Picadero, 1981; expanded as *Lejos de aquí,* by Cossa and Mauricio Kartún, Buenos Aires, Teatro Nacional Cervantes, September 1993;

Ya nadie recuerda a Fréderic Chopin, Buenos Aires, Teatro Planeta, 1982;

El tío loco, Buenos Aires, Teatro Margarita Xirgu, 1982;

El viento se los llevó, by Cossa, Francisco Ananía, Eugenio Griffero, and Jacobo Langsner, Buenos Aires, Teatro Margarita Xirgu, 1983;

De pies y manos, Buenos Aires, Teatro Nacional Cervantes, 1984;

Los compadritos, Buenos Aires, Teatro Presidente Alvear, 17 January 1985;

Tartufo, adapted from Molière's play, Buenos Aires, Teatro San Martín, 31 October 1986;

El sur y después, Buenos Aires, Teatro de la Campana, 8 June 1987;

Yepeto, Buenos Aires, Teatro Lorange, 2 October 1987;

Años difíciles, Buenos Aires, Sala Carlos Carella, 1987;

Angelito, Buenos Aires, Teatro de la Campana, 2 June 1991;

Roberto Cossa (from La ñata contra el libro, *1967; Thomas Cooper Library, University of South Carolina)*

Don Pedro dijo que no, Mar de Plata, Centro Cultural Juan Martín de Pueyrredón, 16 January 1993;

Viejos conocidos, Buenos Aires, Teatro General San Martín, 29 September 1994;

Aquellos gauchos judíos, by Cossa and Ricardo Halac, Buenos Aires, Teatro Nacional Cervantes, August 1995;

Pingüinos, Buenos Aires, Teatro Multicentro, May 2001;

Historia de Varieté, Buenos Aires, Teatro de la Gorra, May 2002.

BOOKS: *Nuestro fin de semana* (Buenos Aires: Talía, 1964); translated by Donald A. Yates (New York: Macmillan, 1966);

Los días de Julián Bisbal. Nuestro fin de semana (Buenos Aires: Talía, 1966);

La ñata contra el libro (Buenos Aires: Talía, 1967);

El avión negro, by Cossa, Germán Rozenmacher, Carlos Somigliana, and Ricardo Talesnik, published with *Flores de papel* by Egon Wolff and *La mueca* by Eduardo Pavlovsky, as *Tres obras de teatro* (Havana: Casa de las Américas, 1970); published separately (Buenos Aires: Talía, 1970);

Nuestro fin de semana; Los días de Julián Bisbal; La pata de la sota (Buenos Aires: Talía, 1972);

El viejo criado, published with *Marathon* by Ricardo Monti, as *Cierre de un ciclo*, edited by Luis Ordaz (Buenos Aires: Centro Editor de América Latina, 1981);

Tute Cabrero; No hay que llorar (Rosario, Argentina: Paralelo 32, 1983);

Ya nadie recuerda a Fréderic Chopin (Buenos Aires: Subsecretaría de Cultura, Dirección General de Escuelas y Cultura, 1985);

La pata de la sota; Ya nadie recuerda a Fréderic Chopin, edited by Osvaldo Pellettieri (Buenos Aires: Huemul, 1985);

De pies y manos (Buenos Aires: Cátedra de Literatura Argentina, 1985);

La nona, published with *Stéfano* by Armando Discépolo, as *El grotesco criollo: Discépolo-Cossa*, edited by Irene Pérez (Buenos Aires: Colihue, 1986);

Teatro, 5 volumes (Buenos Aires: Ediciones de la Flor, 1987-1999)—comprises volume 1, *Nuestra fin de semana; Los días de Julián Bisbal; La ñata contra el libro; La pata de la sota; Tute cabrero*; volume 2, *El avión negro; La nona; No hay que llorar*; volume 3, *El viejo criado; Gris de ausencia; Ya nadie recuerda a Fréderic Chopin; El tío loco; De pies y manos; Yepeto; El sur y después*; volume 4, *Angelito; Los compadritos; Tartufo (adaptación)*; and volume 5, *Años difíciles; Viejos conocidos; Don Pedro dijo no; Lejos de aquí*, by Cossa and Mauricio Kartún;

El sur y después (Buenos Aires: Torres Agüero, 1989).

PRODUCED SCRIPTS: *Tute cabrero*, by Cossa and Juan José Jusid, motion picture, Producciones Sur, 1968;

La nona, by Cossa and Héctor Olivera, motion picture, Aries Cinematográfica Argentina, 1979;

El arreglo, by Cossa and Carlos Somigliana, motion picture, Aries Cinematográfica Argentina, 1983;

No habrá más penas ni olvido, by Cossa and Olivera, based on Osvaldo Soriano's novel, motion picture, Aries Cinematográfica Argentina, 1983;

Yepeto, by Cossa and Eduardo Calcagno, motion picture, Calcagno Producciones, 1999.

OTHER: *El tío loco*, in *Teatro abierto 1982*, edited by Nora Mazziotti (Buenos Aires: Puntosur, 1989).

SELECTED PERIODICAL PUBLICATION–UNCOLLECTED: *El Saludador, Teatro XXI*, 9 (1999): 107-117.

Roberto Cossa is considered one of the pillars of contemporary Argentine theater. Critics have labeled him one of the most inventive voices in the country, one who constantly experiments with new ways to present his socially committed vision. In a 1987 interview with Sharon Magnarelli, Cossa said that the three authors who have most influenced his own writing are Arthur Miller, Anton Chekhov, and Florencio Sánchez. Certain themes recur in his theater, among them the expression of frustration on the part of his protagonists, generally members of the middle or lower-middle classes who are disillusioned when faced with the reality of the worsening economic situation in their country. Another common thread is that of debunking the myth of Argentina as a country of abundance.

Roberto Mario Cossa was born on 30 November 1934 in Buenos Aires and was raised in a loving family of Italian origin in which the arts were of primary importance. He began his theatrical career with a brief stint as an actor as part of the Independent Theater movement in San Isidro, Argentina, in 1956; however, the panic he felt on stage prevented him from continuing in that capacity. His formal training was as a journalist; his writing career began with short pieces about theater, and at various times since then he has stopped writing drama to dedicate himself to journalism. His first play, *Nuestro fin de semana* (Our Weekend), was written in 1962 and premiered on 27 March 1964 in the Teatro Rio Bamba of Buenos Aires.

Cossa became associated with what was called the New Realist Generation of Argentine playwrights, also known as the Generation of 1960. The roots of their style may be found in the *sainete criollo*, a short theater form at the turn of the century in which there were many popular character types, easily recognizable for the audience. The Generation of 1960 was known for plays that dealt with the daily hopelessness and frustrations of the Buenos Aires middle class. In *Nuestro fin de semana* and subsequent plays, Cossa moves beyond depictions of Argentine reality and provides an analytical view, one that seeks to promote critical reflection on the part of the audience. He tries to unmask Argentines who are consumed by images of an overly idealized past and their own false expectations for the future.

Scene from the 1964 Teatro Rio Bamba premiere of Nuestro fin de semana *(Our Weekend), Cossa's first play (from* Nuestro fin de semana, *1964; Canaday Library, Bryn Mawr College)*

This view continued with his next play, *Los días de Julián Bisbal* (The Days of Julián Bisbal), which premiered at the Teatro Regina in Buenos Aires on 14 January 1966. Also in 1966 Cossa's *La ñata contra el libro* (The Snout Smashed Against the Book) premiered in the same city at the Local Nocturno Gotán on 22 August. In 1967 his *La pata de la sota* (Knave's Paw or Something's Afoot) premiered in the Teatro ABC on 14 April. All of these plays demonstrate the antihero who lives with dreams that have been vanquished because of the dismal reality of quotidian life.

La ñata contra el libro concerns a young Jewish man, David Belmes, filled with dreams and projects. His ultimate aspiration is to win a tango-writing contest, and he is certain that the prize of one million pesos will enable him to reach the stature he feels he deserves in life. He is so focused on this dream, however, that he is incapable of seeing everything else that surrounds him. The play is performed to live *bandoneón* music, with which the audience follows the tragic and comedic circumstances of the protagonist. The notion of the snout pressed against a book is a reworking of a common refrain, "la ñata contra el vidrio," that originated in the famous tango "Cafetín de Buenos Aires" (1948, Little Tavern of Buenos Aires) by Enrique Santos Discepolo and Mariano Mores. It carries the image of a youth with his face pressed against the glass of a bar in which his elders sit playing cards, drinking, and telling stories. The title thus conveys the notion of wanting to penetrate and be a part of another world.

After these plays there was a period of theatrical inactivity in which Cossa devoted himself to his journalistic pursuits. He returned to drama with *El avión negro* (1970, The Black Plane), written with Germán Rozenmacher, Carlos Somigliana, and Ricardo Talesnik. This play is Cossa's only overtly political play, dealing directly with the myth of political and social unity that surrounded Juan Domingo Perón's then-hoped-for return to Argentina. Perón had been overthrown in 1955 after nine years in power and had spent the majority of his years in exile in Spain. The fantasy of his return to Argentina in a black plane to lead the workers of his country in revenge against the upper class was recurrent. *El avión negro* marks Cossa's departure from realism in order to incorporate other dramatic elements such as the absurd, black humor, the grotesque, the theater of cruelty, and *sainete*. The play is structured as a series of sketches in which, according to Norma Woodward Batchelder, "the social and political fragmentation of Peronism and Argentina are laid bare, and the workers are shown to be undeceived by the Peronist myths and the promise of 'dialogue.'" *El avión negro* was inspired by the many radical and militant groups that emerged in the 1960s, as well as the strikes and acts of terrorism that had become common in the country. As the dramatists predicted, the arrival of Perón's black plane—when it finally did occur in 1973—did not bring about justice but rather provoked more violence.

La nona (1977, The Granny) is probably the playwright's best-known work. It premiered at the Teatro Lasalle during the same year in which it was written and continued for more than a year and a half in Buenos Aires before being made into a motion picture in 1979. In this play Cossa's realist theater takes a decidedly grotesque turn as he depicts the rapidly impoverished world of a lower-middle-class family who serves as a metaphor for the country. The grandmother, La Nona, one hundred years old, has a voracious appetite and is literally consuming everyone and everything around her. The family plans various ways to rid themselves of the old woman, including marrying her off to an elderly gentleman after indicating to him that her demise and a big inheritance would be imminent. There are no redeeming characters in the play; all are in some way pathetic or good-for-nothings. Beyond La Nona, the action focuses on two brothers, Carmello and Chicho. Carmello is trying desperately to work hard in order to live the American Dream (a concept similar in Argentine usage to that of the United States) and remain in the middle class, while the other, Chicho, is a freeloader who calls himself an artist in order to justify his refusal to work. However, because of La Nona's appetite, all the characters are eventually forced to work. The children succeed in marrying La Nona to the elderly Don Francisco; but after six weeks of marriage, during which she has eaten everything in his tiny candy kiosk, Don Francisco has a stroke as he tries to hit her. The two of them are thus forced to return and live with Carmello and his family. Don Francisco is now an invalid, and Carmello and Chicho place him on the street daily in his wheelchair and collect him and whatever change has been thrown into his cap at the end of the day.

La Nona is transformed from a mildly eccentric and irritating woman at the beginning of the play into a monster capable of devouring her own children. Cossa is playing with the traditional image of the Italian grandmother (sacred in Argentine households, as the majority of the population can be traced to Italy), known for her maternal ways, her cooking, and her tenderness. La Nona's clothing is always stuffed with bread and fruit or potato chips, and each time she leaves her room to enter the kitchen, her gait is reminiscent of a rat. She eats constantly and only mutters an occasional word in *cocoliche,* the local argot combination of Italian and Spanish. One by one each family member dies or leaves, until at last Chicho, returning home to find that all have gone except La Nona, decides to commit suicide. The final image is La Nona alone on stage, chewing, with the light fading on her face.

No hay que llorar (No Need to Cry), a play that premiered on 11 May 1979 in Buenos Aires at the Auditorio Buenos Aires, continues in this vein. It is realist but with more significant absurdist and grotesque elements woven into the play. *No hay que llorar* has been considered by some to be the children's revenge following *La nona*. In this play two adult children, Pedro and Osvaldo, have a surprise seventieth birthday party for their mother, who faints from the shock. The conversation revolves around what to do with their mother now that she is unable to care for herself. Another son, Gabriel, finds property deeds in their mother's name. After the discovery, talk turns to how the money from the deeds will be used. As in *La nona,* food becomes the mechanism whereby the grotesque is conveyed as the characters begin to eat voraciously, violently. The party dissolves into a ruckus until their mother, recovered from her fainting spell, rejoins the celebration but begins to cry that it will be her last birthday, whereupon her children taunt her with the words she used on them when they were children: "Sin llorar!" (No crying!). When her sons tell her of the plans they have made to form a business together, the mother suspects that they have found the deeds and refuses to provide financial assistance. Pedro begins to cry, and she scolds him "Sin llorar!" while the other children decide to force-feed their mother, giving her alcohol and food in such abundance that it is bound to kill her. They do so while singing the classic tango "Caminito" (1926, Little Road) by Juan de Dios Filiberto and Gabino Coria Pañaloza. As Jean Graham-Jones points out, the song foreshadows the mother's death and the children's loss but also suggests that they will continue in her footsteps—that is, being as selfish as she was. The children insist that she open her presents and cut the cake, and her cries of "I'm dying" are barely heard above the din of her children singing the birthday song.

Both *No hay que llorar* and *La nona* illustrate not only the failure of so many immigrants to achieve the American Dream but also the petty individualism of the middle class. Each play serves as a metaphor for the atmosphere of the series of military dictatorships that ruled the country from 1976 to 1983 and can be placed squarely within its sociohistorical moment. Graham-Jones demonstrates that in *La nona,* the victims and the victimizers are clearly distinguished from one another as they seemed in 1977 Argentina. But by 1979, the time of *No hay que llorar,* the lines had become blurred as people began to examine their own duplicity in the mechanisms that created the military dictatorships.

Cossa returned to the topic of Perón's rise, fall, and return in *El viejo criado* (The Old Manservant), a play that premiered in the Teatro Payró in Buenos Aires on 26 September 1980 and represents the play-

Cossa in 1964, the year he made his debut as a playwright (from Nuestro fin de semana, *1964; Canaday Library, Bryn Mawr College)*

wright's complete break from realism. The rupture of time and space is total, and there is a preponderance of symbolic images coupled with the almost complete absence of dramatic action, which situates the play squarely within absurdist tendencies. Time is now fluid, with present, past, and future intermingling. The play is another scathing attack on Argentina, albeit one that is presented metaphorically because of the censorship of the time.

The pretext of the play is to debunk the national myths, one by one, that serve to immobilize Argentines. The stage is set to evoke the mythical bars of turn-of-the-century Buenos Aires—magical places where individuals played cards and dice, lamented lost loves, and enjoyed camaraderie. The nostalgia for these bars is often the source of tango lyrics, and in fact the entire play is inundated with tango references, from the names of the characters to the lines spoken by them. Two friends, Alsina and Balmaceda, are sitting at a table engaged in a card game that has apparently been going on for years, judging from the tally of who is in the lead, Balmaceda at 153,204 to Alsina's 67,724. Alsina represents the intellectual poet, spouting off quotations from French thinkers as he lectures on history, while Balmaceda is a former boxer and Alsina's rationalist counterpart. Carlitos and Ivonne, two more characters easily recognizable to Argentine audiences, arrive at the bar. Carlitos enters singing the famous Carlos Gardel tango "Mi Buenos Aires querido" (1934, My Beloved Buenos Aires, lyrics by Alfredo Lepera), and he is clearly imitating Gardel, the most famous tango singer in Argentine history. Ivonne's name is taken from yet another tango, one about a French prostitute in Buenos Aires. The course of the play involves Carlitos's attempts to finish the tango he is writing after a forty-year stay in Paris. He returns to Buenos Aires to try to live the life one would expect of a tango composer, and as such is concerned with finding a manservant. Alsina and Balmaceda become caught up in Carlitos's fantasy. When told that Ivonne slept with Gardel, each character exits the stage to sleep with her as well, going where their idol went.

Andrés Jarque states that the play juxtaposes the stark reality of the present, embodied by Alsina and Balmaceda, with the glorious myth of the past, embodied by Gardel. Graham-Jones argues that Alsina and Balmaceda are also products of Argentine mythmaking who must be unmasked, because they are archetypes, constantly avoiding any real engagement with life by merely talking about it. Neither engages in any action beyond playing cards, in spite of talking about doing things. According to Susana Anaine, "If speaking is making use of language, language consumes these characters: their lines are tango lyrics, [and] the myth-generated fossilization or alienation keeps them from creating."

Although *El viejo criado* takes place in an atemporal realm, there are references to real historical events. Three American presidents are named, and the repeated question "¿Qué pasará que hay tanta gente en la calle?" (What has happened that there are so many people in the streets?) is answered at four separate points in the play, each time by Balmaceda and each time without his even looking out the window. The first response refers to the outpouring of people when Perón was detained in 1945 by military leaders, an event that led to his being swept into power that was held nine years. The second refers to when he left in 1955, and again Argentines took to the streets. The third refers to when he returned in 1973; his arrival at the Ezeiza airport brought half a million people out to greet him, and many were killed when fighting erupted. The last response refers to the tumult when Argentina won the World Cup in 1978, an event that unleashed mass euphoria. As Graham-Jones notes, each occasion demonstrates a "nationalist-based fervor" in which a few individuals served as "puppeteers" to organize the events—mainly the generals of the dictatorship, who sought to mask their own practices by focusing all attention on the World Cup match. In *El viejo criado,* each character is gripped by paralysis and complete nonproductivity.

Cossa was one of the creative forces behind the Teatro Abierto (Open Theater). This cycle of twenty plays performed in 1981 began as an exercise of freedom that is considered the single most important event in Argentine theater history. It was the response of theater practitioners to the brutal dictatorship from 1976 to 1983, the period known as the Dirty War, during which thirty thousand dissidents disappeared; there was severe censorship; and fear permeated the country. *Gris de ausencia* (The Gray of Absence, 1981) was Cossa's first Teatro Abierto play, presented as part of the Buenos Aires festival at the Teatro del Picadero, and it deals with exile and displacement, themes familiar to many Argentines during the Dirty War. This play, short though it is, has become a classic in Argentine theater history, and Cossa considers it one of his best works. Exile is understood in multiple ways, both literal and internal, as the play depicts an Argentine family living in Rome, with their adult children living in Madrid and London, and demonstrates how they seek to connect, communicate with one another, and affirm their Argentine identity in spite of the cultural, linguistic, and geographic factors that separate them.

Teatro Abierto tried to repeat its triumph for a second year, but various factors worked against success, including logistical problems. Cossa's contribution in 1982 was *El tío loco* (The Crazy Uncle), which premiered in the Teatro Margarita Xirgu of Buenos Aires. It is a grotesque play in which insanity and absurdity are combined. *El tío loco* is about a lower-middle-class Argentine family living in their kiosk where they sell candy and gum and trying to keep from falling into a complete state of poverty. In the second half of the play, an uncle returns after thirty years, only to reveal that he has not been abroad, he simply was afraid of crossing the busy intersection of Callao Avenue in downtown Buenos Aires. The family, much like that in *No hay que llorar,* urges him to his eventual death. Also as in *No hay que llorar* and *La nona*, the grotesque consumption of food is highlighted. In what is perhaps the only moderately hopeful element included, the uncle does not die alone, but rather in the arms of his one friend, a German with whom he does not share a language, but with whom he is able to communicate nevertheless. In other words, as Graham-Jones points out, solidarity forms a part of this Cossa story, unlike all previous ones.

In *Ya nadie recuerda a Fréderic Chopin* (Now No One Remembers Fréderic Chopin), which premiered in 1982 in Buenos Aires at the Teatro Planeta, Cossa returned to the theme of the failed intellectual seen earlier in *El viejo criado*. The play deals with an exiled Spaniard living in Argentina as he contemplates his many failures and converses with a young socialist who seeks a better life.

For Teatro Abierto in 1983 Cossa premiered *El viento se los llevó* (They Were Gone With the Wind) in the Teatro Margarita Xirgu in Buenos Aires. This play, written in collaboration with Francisco Ananía, Eugenio Griffero, and Jacobo Langsner, is an exposé of the mechanisms of state terror, control, and internal corruption and violence. Before the play begins, the traditional admonishments to the audience regarding photographs or recordings grow increasingly bizarre as viewers are instructed not to cross their legs or cough. This series of dictates is finished with the German word "Verboten." The play takes place in an apartment built above a movie theater, where movies from the 1940s are shown continuously. The personages from the movies interact with the apartment dwellers. There is a clear connection between the European fascism of the 1930s and 1940s and Argentina in the 1980s, a topic that Cossa also touched upon later in *Los compadritos* (The Buddies, 1985). Spanish and German are used in the play, and three priests from the Inquisition join others associated with Nazi repression, only to be replaced later by three henchmen from Francisco Franco's Spain. Violence permeates the entire production, including sirens, gunshots, and explosions. There is also smoke and tear gas.

In *El viento se los llevó,* there is general confusion regarding victims and victimizers, something common to plays produced immediately following the dictatorship. The work ends with only two people on stage—a wounded man, thought to be dead, and a grandfather. The dead man stands up and reads a letter written to his mother: "Estoy vivo . . . Estoy vivo, mamá" (I'm alive . . . mama, I'm alive). This element shows the need felt by many that the voices of those who disappeared during the dictatorship be brought to life; it is a reminder of how the wave of chaos and violence, the "wind" in the title, swept away so many.

De pies y manos (Hand and Foot) was written during the time in which the dictatorship was ending. The play, which premiered in the Teatro Nacional Cervantes of Buenos Aires in 1984, was conceived as a metaphor for this tumultuous time in Argentine history, focusing on collective memory and justice, but always within the confines of family life as a microcosm of the country. Once again the main subject of Cossa's criticism is the middle class and intellectuals. The play concerns the various ways in which the central character, Miguel, is perceived by those around him. There are four other characters: his friend; his student (although this connection is called into question in the course of the play, and there are allusions to a homosexual rela-

and memory, he is incapable of remembering anything at all. He grows increasingly uncomfortable with the questions of the others, who, in turn, become increasingly violent with him. Miguel attempts to save his "student" Hernán from the pressure to conform to the ideas the others have of him. Hernán, however, elects to join them, leaving Miguel alone. As in other plays, Cossa demonstrates man's incapacity to combine words with deeds. Miguel, like Alsina and Balmaceda, is immobilized. He has erased all memory and is incapable of acting, engaging in the world; he is only able to parrot the ideas of those who have done so in the past.

Cossa is calling attention to the myriad ways of interpreting reality, the malleability of "truth," and the fallibility of perception. During the dictatorship, "truth" was never apparent; there was mass manipulation and distortions in the press. Miguel is perceived to be completely vapid, a chameleon incapable of adhering to any belief at all. The "intellectual" is revealed to be a shallow man, one filled with empty rhetoric, and one who has manipulated words and distorted truths. The first moment he enters, he shouts an empty slogan: "Viva la paz!" (Long live peace!).

De pies y manos demonstrates the complicity of the Argentine in the situation that has befallen the country. An individual capable of articulating resistance, of action, would perhaps not have allowed such an unfortunate fate to occur. Adopting the rhetoric of action affords one the appearance of action without actually involving any. This harsh examination of the nature of truth, history, and memory is meant to leave the audience members uncomfortable.

Los compadritos premiered in the Teatro Presidente Alvear on 17 January 1985 in Buenos Aires. It deals with the sinking of the German commerce raider *Admiral Graf Spee* in 1939 off the Uruguayan coast and the subsequent asylum of one thousand sailors in Argentina, of which two hundred remained in Argentina. The six scenes take place from 1939 to 1945, with a contemporary epilogue. Like many of Cossa's plays, *Los compadritos* is about a man obsessed with succeeding financially but who ultimately fails. In 1987 in Buenos Aires, *El sur y después* (The South and Afterwards) premiered on 8 June at the Teatro de la Campana (Theater of the Bell), and *Yepeto* (Geppetto) premiered at the Teatro Lorange on 2 October. *El sur y después* was done in collaboration with the actors and director of Teatro de la Campana and was created from improvisation and commentaries from these individuals.

Yepeto has become another one of Cossa's canonical plays. It won multiple awards and was presented in Colombia, Uruguay, Spain, and Italy. While Cossa returns to the notion of the failed intellectual hiding behind empty words, the work is also a reflection on

Scene from a 1984 Chilean production of Cossa's 1977 play La nona *(The Granny), one of his best known and most successful works, in which a greedy grandmother devours everything around her (from María Teresa Zegers Nachbauer,* 25 años de teatro en Chile, *1999; W. E. B. Du Bois Library, University of Massachusetts, Amherst)*

tionship); his mother; and his fiancée. Each has a strikingly different view of Miguel that is shared before his arrival in the first third of the play. Each also reflects a different ideological stance taken by Miguel at some moment in his life: he is revealed to have at one time or another adhered to the rhetoric of socialism, nationalism, fascism, and communism. When he finally appears on stage, he voices allegiance only to ecological causes and pacifism.

Through the course of the play, each character attempts to control Miguel and convert him into what they desire to see. Miguel, meanwhile, can only spout the words and theories of others, platitudes empty of all meaning, such as "Tenemos que construir un mundo de amor" (We have to construct a world of love). When Miguel is pressed for information on his own life the nature of love. In it a literature professor and a young athlete, Antonio, are in love with the same woman, Cecilia. Antonio has come to confront the professor over the latter's repeated attempts to seduce the athlete's girlfriend. The intellectual makes constant literary references that escape Antonio. Though the professor is fully clothed, the shallowness of his words serves to reveal his metaphorical nakedness and vulnerability that is juxtaposed with the literal nakedness and sincerity of the young athlete, who is not hiding behind words or anything else. The professor, when faced with Antonio, has a growing sense of the loss of his own youth, creativity, and strength.

Yepeto has as its foundation the story of *Pinocchio* (1881), the famous children's tale by Italian Carlo Collodi about a puppet and his master, Geppetto, the man who created and controls him. Using them as the central metaphor, Cossa questions interpersonal relationships, the need to connect with and love another, the temptation to try to control the other, and finally, the deep-seated fear of aging and losing one's vitality. The professor tries to mold and control Cecilia, and Cecilia is perhaps trying to control the professor. Antonio tries to exert his own control over the professor, demonstrating his physical strength and vitality as contrasted to the professor's intellectual strength. As the men compete for the woman, the question of who is the puppeteer and who is the puppet remains unclear. Meanwhile, the professor is writing a story, one that follows a similar line as his "real" life, about a woman who is attracted intellectually to her professor at the same time she is physically attracted to a young worker. There are multiple other literary references throughout the play, including William Shakespeare's *Othello* (circa 1604) and Victor Hugo's *Les Misérables* (1862). Not until the end of the play does Antonio get the upper hand, by understanding the professor's game and referring to him as "Yepeto." The intellectual moment of enlightenment demonstrates a parallel with Pinocchio, who, when he becomes a real boy, becomes the ultimate threat to his master. Cossa wrote the screenplay for a movie version of *Yepeto,* and the movie was released in 1999, winning several international awards. While Cossa's plays generally are rooted in themes directly relevant to Argentine reality, most often specific to Buenos Aires, *Yepeto* is one play in which the themes have universal appeal, as George Woodyard points out.

Angelito, which premiered on 2 June 1991 at the Teatro de la Campana in Buenos Aires, is the story of a theater group's attempts to tell the life story of the title character, an outstanding socialist. Cossa weaves together several elements in the play, including Brechtian theater, socialist reform, melodrama, and collective creation; yet, each is presented in the most superficial manner possible. The play within a play, in which Angelito has a part, is set in a socialist cabaret. It concerns the role of the socialist artist trying to create new theater for those who are no longer interested in plays that stimulate intellectual awareness. Throughout the collaboration, all of the other personages in the play criticize and undermine the creation involved in telling of Angelito's life and his many loves. His final love is Ella (She), and it is implied that Ella is the coming revolution, the future. At the end all of the actors sing about how there is no finale; the future is yet to come; and the revolution is permanent.

Lejos de aquí (Far from Here), a longer version of *Gris de ausencia* that was written with Mauricio Kartún, appeared in September 1993 at the Teatro Nacional Cervantes. *Viejos conocidos* (Old Acquantances) also appeared in 1994, premiering at the Teatro General San Martín in Buenos Aires on 29 September. *Aquellos gauchos judíos* (Those Jewish Gauchos) premiered in August 1995 in Buenos Aires at the Teatro Nacional Cervantes and was written with Ricardo Halac as a response to the July 1994 bombing of the building in which the Israeli-Argentine Mutualist Association was housed, an event in which nearly one hundred people died. The play deals with a family of Jewish immigrants and is seen as an homage to the richness of the Jewish contribution to Argentina.

El Saludador (The Greeter, published in 1999) has a protagonist without a name, whose sole function becomes reduced merely to greeting others. Unlike prior characters who have been immobilized by their own rhetoric and incapable of serving as a force for social change, Cossa's Saludador has devoted his entire life to traveling the world and engaging in activism. He has worked to save the whales and the rain forest, met both Fidel Castro and Mother Teresa, and engaged in many international events before finally losing a leg in a soccer match with the Taliban, an event that forces him to return to Buenos Aires to reclaim his family—a wife and son, Vicente. Now an adult, Vicente is supporting his mother. El Saludador tries to integrate into the family, but it is impossible. He is perceived as a failure for his lengthy absence. Eventually, his wife allows him to remain as they form a cooperative of three, with her taking care of the home, Vicente supporting the group financially, and El Saludador relegated to greeting the neighbors. Such twisted family dynamics, apparent in almost all of Cossa's plays, are reinforced in his unpublished play *Pingüinos* (Penguins), which premiered in the Teatro Multicentro in Buenos Aires in May 2001. In this play, three siblings flee from the authorities for a crime that is never made clear, although it is insinuated that they killed their parents. The alienation of youth is highlighted with the presence of heavy rock music.

Scene from the 1979 Auditorio Buenos Aires premiere of Cossa's play No hay que llorar *(No Need to Cry), in which adult siblings try to do away with their mother at her birthday party (from* No hay que llorar, *1983; Howard-Tilton Memorial Library, Tulane University)*

When the three are finally sentenced by the court, the ruling is that they must live with their dead parents for eternity. This play is considered by the playwright to be his least successful or fully realized theatrical creation.

Cossa's next play, *Historia de Varieté* (Variety History), like *Pingüinos,* has not been published, though it met with popular success during its run in Buenos Aires. It premiered at Teatro de la Gorra in the spring of 2002 and in the fall of that year was on tour in Spain. In this work Cossa returns to a metatheatrical technique introduced in *Angelito,* that of the vaudeville, or variety show, while he touches upon themes of absence, longing, and vanquished dreams. The play centers around Pepino, an old comic who tours the globe with his two-man comedy show. Cossa was paying homage to eighty-three-year-old Gogo Andreu, one of the most famous Argentine vaudevillian comics, who traveled the world with his songs and comedy routines. Pepino lives his entire life on the road, while his counterpart, Artagnan, in each successive act becomes the son of the previous Artagnan, until in the last act Pepino is with his final partner, Artagnan IV, the great-grandson of his original counterpart.

Pepino's great frustration throughout his life is the desire to present a particular joke, but every time he tries to do so, with each successive Artagnan, he is told it is inappropriate. With each show he is expected and forced by his partner to present the same trademark bit, the one he is most famous for, incomprehensible to the audience but one about which the critics rave. There is a third character with whom Pepino once performed, Nélida, a starlet who emerges from a trunk. She is present, although not visible to the Artagnans. It is clear that she represents Pepino's lost love, who betrayed him when they went on tour by sleeping with various famous men in each city who approached her after seeing the show. She exists in Pepino's imagination, and he summons her and speaks with her until the final act, when he and Artagnan IV go to Buenos Aires. In Buenos Aires at last, the long-delayed joke falls flat, representing Pepino's crushing failure after a lifetime of longing to be back home. The play ends with Nélida returning to the stage, an elderly woman now, and the two old people dancing awkwardly off stage to a romantic melody.

In Cossa's plays there is little hope for salvation or escape from the disenchantment with life, gross materialism, and confusion that enslave everyone. National myths have deformed the individual, immobilized him, and turned him into a grotesque being. Failure or simply fear of change keeps Cossa's characters from ever advancing as they lose themselves in alcohol, television, food, violence, or nostalgia for the past. Words and rhetoric betray individuals, as do their own family members, as does the country.

As Osvaldo Pellettieri points out, younger playwrights of the postmodern aesthetic have attempted to denigrate Cossa by referring to his theater as old-fashioned and reminiscent of the 1960s. They have failed in their attempts to marginalize his continuing contributions to the Argentine stage. He is no longer a dramatist of one decade, but rather one who in some ways may be seen to represent every epoch. Pellettieri also points out that Cossa is the only theater practitioner who is routinely called upon by the national press to offer his views on current events; he is seen as a wise man and an authority on many things, not merely theater. The plays of Roberto Cossa are among the most honored, the most reviewed, the most researched by scholars, and the most widely seen and read Argentine dramas. His plays, dealing with consumer culture, national myths, hollow rhetoric, the disenchantment of the middle class, the ambiguity of truth, the spiritual death of daily life, and the malleability of reality, all demonstrate the greatest themes of Argentine identity and history. Theater, for Cossa, is first and foremost socially committed, a way of better knowing oneself and understanding Argentina.

Interviews:

Jorge Eines, "Metaforizando la realidad," *Primer Acto,* 213 (March–April 1986): 46–47;

Sharon Magnarelli, "Roberto Cossa habla de su teatro," *Latin American Theatre Review,* 20 (1987): 133–139.

References:

Susana Anaine, "El teatro de Roberto Cossa o la puesta en escena de una conciencia histórica," *Espacio de crítica e investigación teatral,* 4, no. 6–7 (1990): 85–89;

Omar Basabe, "*El avión negro:* El discurso político implícito en la parodia a una irrealidad grotesca," *Confluencia: Revista Hispánica de Cultura y Literatura,* 11, no. 1 (1995): 163–172;

Norma Woodward Batchelder, "*El avión negro:* The Political and Structural Context," *Latin American Theatre Review,* 20 (1987): 17–28;

Alberto Ciria, "Variaciones sobre la historia argentina en el teatro de Roberto Cossa," *Revista Canadiense de Estudios Hispánicos,* 18, no. 3 (1994): 445–453;

Miguel Angel Giella, "Entre la justicia poética y las leyes penales: *Años difíciles* de Roberto Cossa," *Indagaciones sobre el fin de siglo: Teatro iberoamericano y argentino,* edited by Osvaldo Pellettieri (Buenos Aires: Galerna, 2000), pp. 185–188;

Giella, "Immigración y exilio: El limbo del lenguaje," *Latin American Theatre Review,* 26, no. 2 (1993): 111–121;

Jean Graham-Jones, *Exorcising History: Argentine Theater Under the Dictatorship* (Lewisburg, Pa.: Bucknell University Press, 2000);

Andrés Francisco Jarque, "El tango como intertexto en la creatividad de *El viejo criado,*" *Revista canadiense de estudios hispánicos,* 15, no. 3 (1991): 465–481;

Claudia Kaiser-Lenior, *El grotesco-criollo: Estilo teatral de una época* (Havana: Casa de las Américas, 1977);

Luis Ordaz, "Tres hitos en la dramaturgia de Roberto Cossa," *Teatro,* 5, no. 20 (1985): 16–18;

Osvaldo Pellettieri, "Roberto Cossa y el teatro dominante, 1985–1999," in *Teatro Argentino del 2000,* edited by Pellettieri (Buenos Aires: Galerna/Fundación Roberto Arlt, 2000), pp. 27–35;

María Silvina Persino, "Teatro en Buenos Aires, julio del 2000," *Latin American Theatre Review,* 34 (2001): 127–138;

Roberto Previdi Froelich, "América deshecha: El neo-grotesco gastronómico y el discurso del facismo en *La nona* de Roberto M. Cossa," in *Teatro argentino durante el Proceso, 1976–1983,* edited by Juana Alcira Arancibia and Zulema Mirkin (Buenos Aires: Vinciguerra, 1992), pp. 38–46;

George Woodyard, "The Theater of Roberto Cossa: A World of Broken Dreams," *Bucknell Review: A Scholarly Journal of Letters, Arts and Sciences,* 40, no. 2 (1996): 94–108;

Woodyard, "Yepeto de Cossa: Arte y Realidad," in *El teatro y sus claves: Estudios sobre teatro argentino e iberoamericano,* edited by Pellettieri (Buenos Aires: Galerna, 1996), pp. 87–92;

Perla Zayas de Lima, "Tres metáforas sobre un país dominado," in *Teatro argentino durante el Proceso, 1976–1983,* edited by Arancibia and Mirkin (Buenos Aires: Vinciguerra, 1992), pp. 68–75;

María Teresa Zegers Nachbauer, *25 años de teatro en Chile* (Santiago: Ministerio de Educación, 1999).

Sor Juana Inés de la Cruz
(12 November 1651 – 17 April 1695)

Julie Greer Johnson
University of Georgia

SELECTED PLAY PRODUCTIONS: *Los empeños de una casa*, Mexico City, 4 October 1683; *Amor es más labyrinto*, Mexico City, 1689.

BOOKS: *Villancicos que se cantaron . . . [a] la Purísma Concepción . . .* (Mexico City, 1676);
Neptuno alegorico, oceano de colores, simulacro politico, que erigio la muy esclarecida, sacra y augusta Iglesia Metropolitana de Mexico en las lucidas alegoricas ideas de Arco triumphal . . . (Mexico City: Juan de Ribera, 1680);
Villancicos que se cantaron en la Santa Iglesia Cathedral de la ciudad de la Puebla de los Angeles, en los maytines solemnes del nacimiento de nuestro Señor Jesucristo . . ., music by Miguel Mateo Dallo y Lana (Puebla: Diego Fernández de León, 1689);
Villancicos que se cantaron en la Santa Iglesia Cathedral de la ciudad de la Puebla de los Angeles, en los maytines solemnes de la Purissima Concepcion de nuestra Señora . . ., music by Dallo y Lana (Puebla: Diego Fernández de León, 1689);
Inundación castálida de la única poetisa, musa décima Soror Juana Inés de la Cruz . . . que en varios metros, idiomas, y estilos fertiliza varios assuntos: Con elegantes, sutiles, claros e ingeniosos, útiles versos . . ., edited by Juan Camacho Gayna (Madrid: Juan García Infanzón, 1689); revised as *Poema de . . . Soror Juana Ines de la Cruz . . . que en varios metros, idiomas, y estilos, fertiliza varios assumptos, con elegantes, sutiles, claros, ingeniosos, utiles versos, para enseñanza, recreo y admiracion . . .* (Madrid: Juan García Infanzón, 1690); revised as *Poemas de la única poetisa americana, musa dezima* (Barcelona: Joseph Llopis, 1691);
Auto sacramental del divino Narciso, por alegorias (Mexico City: Bernardo Calderón, 1690); translated by Patricia A. Peters and Renée Domeier as *The Divine Narcissus* (Albuquerque: University of New Mexico Press, 1998);
Carta athenagórica (Puebla: Diego Fernández de León, 1690);
*Villancicos con que se solemnizaron en la Santa Iglesia Cathedral de la ciudad de la Puebla de los Angeles, los maytines del

Sor Juana Inés de la Cruz (artist unknown; Philadelphia Museum of Art; from Octavio Paz, Sor Juana or, The Traps of Faith, *1988; Thomas Cooper Library, University of South Carolina)*

gloriosissimo patriarcha señor San Joseph . . .*, music by Dallo y Lana (Puebla: Diego Fernández de León, 1690);
Ofrecimientos para el Rosario de quinze misterios que se ha de rezar el dia de los dolores de N. Señora la Virgen Maria: Sacados solo de lo que padeció desde que llegó al Calvario, siguiendo los passos dolorosos de Nuestro Salvador . . . (Mexico City: Francisco Rodríguez Lupercio, 1691);

Los empeños de una casa: Segundo volumen de las obras . . . (Seville, 1692);

Fama y obras postumas . . . (Madrid, 1700);

Amor es más labyrinto, by Sor Juana and Juan de Guevara (Seville: Diego López de Haro, n.d.);

Obras completas, 4 volumes, edited by Alfonso Méndez Plancarte and Alberto G. Salceda (Mexico City: Imprenta Nuevo Mundo, 1955; Mexico City: Fondo de Cultura Económica, 1957);

La segunda Celestina: Una comedia perdida de Sor Juana, by Sor Juana and Agustín de Salazar y Torres, edited by Guillermo Schmidhuber and Olga Martha Peña Doria (Mexico City: Vuelta, 1990).

Editions in English: *A Woman of Genius: The Intellectual Autobiography of Sor Juana Ines de la Cruz,* translated by Margaret Sayers Peden (Salisbury, Conn.: Lime Rock Press, 1982);

A Sor Juana Anthology, translated and edited by Alan S. Trueblood (Cambridge, Mass.: Harvard University Press, 1988);

The Answer/La Respuesta: Including a Selection of Poems, translated by Electa Arenal and Amanda Powell (New York: Feminist Press at the City University of New York, 1994);

The House of Trials, translated by David Pasto (New York: Peter Lang, 1997);

Pawns of a House/Los empeños de una casa, translated by Michael McGaha, edited by Susana Hernández Araico (Tempe, Ariz.: Bilingual Press/Editorial Bilingue, 2002).

Sor Juana Inés de la Cruz was one of the most outstanding playwrights to write in Spain's American colonies. Although she is best known for her poetry, her theatrical works comprise nearly one-third of her literary production, and they demonstrate the brilliance for which she was famous. Writing for both the Catholic Church and the viceregal court of New Spain, she composed *loas,* short dramatic pieces that served as an introduction to a longer play; three-act comedies that were often accompanied by *sainetes,* or brief one-act intermezzos; *autos sacramentales,* one-act plays on the sacrament of the Holy Eucharist; and church carols known as *villancicos.* These works generally followed the dramatic forms of the early modern theater in Spain, a period that corresponds to the Spanish Golden Age. Although Sor Juana was well versed in this theatrical tradition in general, Pedro Calderón de la Barca most consistently provided the models for both her secular and religious plays. In keeping with the elaborate ornamentation that characterized artistic expression in the seventeenth century, her works came to epitomize baroque style in the Indies. While emulating the dramatic forms and technical devices of Spanish playwrights, however, Sor Juana often recontextualized conventional themes to reflect her New World surroundings and, moreover, reinterpreted typical characters to highlight issues of gender. She also reacted against the imposition of peninsular theater on colonial stages to the exclusion of the performance of plays by local dramatists.

Although Sor Juana was a renowned figure among her contemporaries and although her life and works have been scrutinized by scholars of colonial studies ever since, she remains an enigma. The most precise information about her, albeit brief, comes from her own pen in a letter she wrote to the bishop of Puebla in 1691, which served as the principal source for her first biographer, Diego Calleja, whose profile of her prefaced the posthumous volume of her works published in 1700. Her name was known from the villages of New Spain to the elite social circles of Spain and its viceregal capitals, and her works were published on both sides of the Atlantic. From 1676, the earliest date of the publication of one of her *villancicos,* her dramatic poems set to music were staged in churches throughout the viceroyalty; this dissemination continued until their publication ceased some fifteen years later. In 1690 her best religious drama, *El divino Narciso* (The Divine Narcissus), appeared in print in Mexico City, and in 1692 the second volume of her collected works, including her courtly comedy *Los empeños de una casa* (The House of Trials, performed in 1683), was published in Seville. Virtually all of Sor Juana's works were published during her lifetime or shortly after her death, and they have been reprinted in many editions for several centuries. By the advent of the twentieth century, the life of the Mexican nun known as the Tenth Muse had become the set piece for the study of early Spanish American womanhood.

Sor Juana was born Juana Ramírez de Asbaje in San Miguel de Nepantla, in present-day Mexico, the illegitimate daughter of Isabel Ramírez de Santillana of New Spain and the Spaniard Pedro Manuel de Asbaje y Vargas Machuca, who was in the military. The exact date of her birth has been the subject of some controversy, which has never been definitively resolved. In his prefatory essay to the third volume of Sor Juana's works published in 1700, Calleja gives her birth date as 12 November 1651. A baptismal certificate for a child named Inés, whose godparents were siblings of Sor Juana's mother, was found in a neighboring town; if that child was Sor Juana, this record places her birth three years earlier. Some question has been raised about the validity of this discovery, however, as "Inés" appears only in Sor Juana's religious name, taken at the time she entered the convent.

Title page for the first volume of Sor Juana's works, published in 1689 (from Octavio Paz, Sor Juana or, The Traps of Faith, *1988; Thomas Cooper Library, University of South Carolina)*

Few educational opportunities existed for women during the colonial era, but this fact did not deter the young Juana from pursuing her intellectual goals. Before her third birthday, as she herself states in her letter to the bishop of Puebla, she insisted upon attending school with an older sister in order to learn to read and write as soon as possible. At the age of eight she won her first literary prize for her "Loa al Santísimo Sacramento" (Poem to the Holiest Sacrament of Communion). Sor Juana later developed the genre of the *loa* to its fullest extent by adding characters and plot to this basically laudatory, poetic prologue to a dramatic work. Obsessed by the acquisition of knowledge, she often denied herself some of the indulgences of childhood, and in the spirit of maintaining her self-imposed discipline, she vowed to attend the university in Mexico City, a privilege reserved for young men only. Even when she considered wearing pants to class, she did not gain admission to this institution of higher learning but was forced to remain at home in the countryside without the benefit of professorial guidance. However, having honed her talent for self-instruction, she set out to read and study the entire contents of her grandfather's extensive library, an endeavor that won her many accolades.

By the time Don Antonio Sebastián de Toledo Molina y Salazar, the Marqués de Mancera, occupied the viceroyship of New Spain in 1664, Juana's scholarly achievements had become widely known. Impressed with her erudition and taken by her physical beauty, the marqués invited her to his court, a social and cultural center unlike any other in the Americas. There she mingled with its distinguished visitors, whose power and influence promoted and protected her for years. She wrote many poems to honor their notable presence and to commemorate their various official occasions. In deference to her stature as a learned woman, the viceroy assembled a panel of some forty professors from the university, and before this examining board she conclusively proved her mastery of a variety of subjects.

Even though she had won the affection and admiration of the court and had become the vicereine's favorite lady-in-waiting, she became disenchanted by the artificiality of courtly life and longed for the solitude that would give her time to read, reflect, and write. In 1667 she entered the convent of the Discalced Carmelites of Saint Joseph, but the rigorous routine affected her health to such an extent that she was forced to leave the order that same year. Back at court and under the care of the vicereine, Doña Leonor Carreto, she recuperated from her ordeal. The next year, however, she once again took up a religious calling, this time making a lifelong commitment to the convent of the order of Saint Jerome.

In the years that immediately followed her entrance into the convent, Sor Juana actively pursued her gift as a lyric poet. By 1676 she began writing celebratory verses to be sung in church on special occasions, and their presentation often involved a certain degree of theatricality. Although the term *villancico* originally referred to a peasant song, it gradually took on a specific poetic form over the years and was cultivated in Spain by such poets as Lope de Vega and Luis de Góngora y Argote. For fifteen years or more Sor Juana wrote a series of carols that capture aspects of popular culture during the colonial era and document the incorporation of non-Hispanics in Christian religious rites and rituals. Although they are not regarded as dramatic works, Sor Juana was clearly trying out her skills as a dramatist. In these carefully structured works, singers became actors through role-playing, and they engaged in dialogue about fictional situations. African American dialects and rhythms are reflected in Sor Juana's *villancicos*, and she included on occasion a portion of the Aztec dance known as the *tocotín*, which was executed to the beat of a Nahuatl chant. Moors and Basques were also included in the cast of characters.

The 1680s were especially productive for Sor Juana, and during this time she reached the pinnacle of her literary career. Not only did she write her philosophical poem *Primero sueño* (The Dream), which is considered to be her masterpiece, but she wrote all of her full-length dramatic programs. Sor Juana's first comedy, *Los empeños de una casa*, was performed in Mexico City on 4 October 1683 before an aristocratic audience, to celebrate the viceroyship of Don Tomás Antonio de la Cerda, the Marquis de la Laguna, and the arrival of the new archbishop, Francisco de Aguiar y Seijas (who was actually an outspoken opponent of the theater). This entertainment, presented under the auspices of an eminent city official, Don Fernando Deza, included not just the presentation of the comedy but also the staging of an entire dramatic program, or festival. Opening with a *loa*, the extended event included two poems sung in honor of the viceroy's family, two *sainetes*, and a concluding soiree that followed the third act.

Much attention has been given to the similarities between Sor Juana's play and *Los empeños de un acaso* (The Trials of Happenstance) by Calderón de la Barca. Calderonian theater did, indeed, serve as a model, and the presence of love triangles, questions of honor, and instances of mistaken identity in *Los empeños de una casa* confirm this relationship. However, in most cases Sor Juana uses these similarities to call into question the dramatic art form of the typical cloak-and-dagger play that was so popular on the Spanish stage. Her work was additionally separated from Calderón de la Barca's by her characters Doña Leonor and Castaño, who tie Sor Juana's work to the New World and to her own personal situation as an artist and intellectual in a patriarchal colonial society. Throughout her comedy Sor Juana challenged existing roles for women in a male-dominated theater both on stage and off, and she was determined to invalidate the perception of femininity that limits the attractiveness of a woman to her appearance. She achieves this goal by making her female characters strong-willed individuals who seek to control their own destinies and by forcing men to see themselves as women do, as when the cross-dressed buffoon Castaño confronts the family patriarch.

The action of *Los empeños de una casa* takes place in the home of Pedro Arellano and his sister, Ana, in Toledo, Spain. As the curtain goes up, Ana reveals to her maid that her brother plans to kidnap Leonor, with whom he is in love. Pedro has already left the residence with several of his friends, disguised as police, and they intend to take Leonor forcibly just as she is eloping from her father's house with her true love, Carlos. In the confusion of the two suitors' clashing swords, Leonor is spirited away to Pedro's house, where Ana is expecting her, and Carlos and his servant Castaño flee, fearing arrest by the police. When Leonor arrives at the Arellano household, she confesses her plight to Ana, and some of the details of her life, such as her beauty, intelligence, and life at court, correspond to those of Sor Juana. Carlos also arrives at Ana's door, seeking refuge; taken by his good looks, she permits him to enter and hide somewhere in the house. When Pedro finally returns to enjoy his prize, he finds the house in chaos as the characters make their way around in the darkness bumping into each other and mistaking one another for someone else.

The highlight of the comedy occurs when Castaño, who had been carrying Leonor's belongings when he and Carlos were approached by Pedro and his companions, dons one of her gowns in order to escape from the house. However, when Pedro, who had been searching in vain for Leonor, catches a glimpse of her clothing, he immediately detains the elaborately draped comic and starts making amorous overtures. Castaño, who is amazed at Pedro's outrageous behavior, suddenly begins to understand a woman's point of view and openly challenges the patriarch in defense of womanhood. The play concludes when Leonor and Carlos are reunited and married; Ana accepts the proposal of a former suitor; and Castaño and Ana's maid wed. Only Pedro remains single at the end of the third act—a punishment, perhaps, for attempting to destroy Leonor's happiness and for enlisting the help of his sister in another woman's downfall.

During the intermissions of this three-act comedy, Sor Juana staged two *sainetes*. These pieces are related to the principal play but are not essential to an understanding of it. The first one, *Sainete de palacio* (Intermezzo about the Palace), consists of a courtly contest among the abstract characters of Love, Respect, Courtesy, Kindness, and Hope for the unusual prize of the disdain of the ladies of the palace. The *sainete* concludes when the judge of the competition decides that no one is worthy of the prize. The artificiality of the scene is probably indicative of Sor Juana's impression of the atmosphere she encountered at court, the same one referred to by Leonor in the main play.

The most original part of Sor Juana's complete program of *Los empeños de una casa,* and, indeed, one of

Portrait of Sor Juana by Miguel Cabrera (National Historical Museum, Mexico City; from Octavio Paz, Sor Juana or, The Traps of Faith, *1988; Thomas Cooper Library, University of South Carolina)*

the more innovative examples of colonial theater, is the *Sainete segundo* (Second Intermezzo), staged between the second and third acts. In this short enactment two spectators, Arias and Muñiz, offer criticism of the performance they have just witnessed onstage, and in this respect the piece is metatheatrical. Attributing the work to a contemporary male playwright of Sor Juana, Acevedo, they object to the length of the play and complain about its lack of humor, suggesting that it is not as good as the theater written in Spain. The two wonder if they can stop the play by hissing, and this controversy provokes the playwright to come forward. When Acevedo appears onstage, he is overwhelmed by the negative review of his work. Although he vows to stop writing plays, the audience believes that his punishment should be worse and sentences him to copy his play over again. Distraught by the severity of this judgment, he has no alternative but to die of shame in the theater amid a hissing public.

By naming a male playwright in this *sainete* rather than identifying herself, Sor Juana calls attention to the lack of acceptance of women in the theater world and the fact that plays written by men are not sufficiently criticized on their theatrical merits. She also raises the question of the cultural identity of theatergoing colonists whose own dramatists were preempted by those of Spain's national theater. The act of hissing or producing an *s* sound has political ramifications. Residents born in the New World often dropped the *s* when speaking, which would make it impossible in Sor Juana's sketch to express their protest, while those who were Spanish by birth were at complete liberty to respond.

After the third act of the comedy, there was a brief finale for the entire program that reminded spectators of the occasion they were celebrating. In the so-called *Sarao de cuatro naciones* (Soiree of Four Nations), representatives of Spain, Africa, Italy, and New Spain stepped forward to pay their respects to the viceroy. Although this piece is similar to some of her *villancicos,* it is contrived and lacks the artistic vitality and social relevance of her dramatic, religious poetry set to music.

The success of *Los empeños de una casa* prompted the author to collaborate with Juan de Guevara on a similar project; however, *Amor es más labyrinto* (Love Is the Greater Labyrinth), which was staged in 1689, did not receive the praise of its predecessor. Sor Juana may also have written or contributed to a third secular play, titled *La segunda Celestina* (The Second Celestina).

Amor es más labyrinto is based on the legend of Theseus, the son of the king of Athens, who is one of a group of young people sent to Crete as a form of tribute to be sacrificed to the creature that is half man and half bull. In Sor Juana's version, Theseus is brought before the Cretan king Minos, and the tyrant's two daughters, Ariadne and Phaedra, fall desperately in love with him even though they both have suitors. Phaedra is the one to whom he is attracted, but Ariadne vows to win his affection by providing him with a means of escape from the immense labyrinth where the monstrous Minotaur resides. In the second act, the one composed by Guevara, Theseus uses the thread that Ariadne has given him. After entering the maze, he slays the monster and exits the labyrinth. That evening a masked ball takes place in the palace, thrown by the two sisters to entertain their father, who is unaware that Theseus has survived his ordeal. The young hero is secretly expected to attend by both Ariadne and Phaedra, and all exchange tokens to be worn at the event so that each can recognize the other in disguise. Theseus confuses Ariadne with Phaedra in the darkened ballroom, however, and mistakenly expresses his love for her.

In the third act, in which Sor Juana again assumes authorship, further complications ensue. Theseus finds himself in the middle of a dispute between the princesses' suitors. In the mix-up he, thinking he is confronting Prince Bacchus of Thebes, engages in a duel with Lidorus, the Prince of Epirus, and kills him. On shore, the Athenian army arrives to take over King Minos's kingdom in Theseus's name. Order is restored in the final scene, in which the Cretan ruler is pardoned and Phaedra and Ariadne are betrothed to Theseus and Bacchus, respectively.

Amor es más labyrinto did not receive the acclaim accorded *Los empeños de una casa,* probably because of the inconsistencies in the play resulting from the collaboration and the development of a mythological theme into a commonplace drama of intrigues propelled by a series of mistaken identities. Of particular note, however, is Sor Juana's treatment of the Amazons in the speech Theseus makes in the first act when he arrives at the court of King Minos. Recounting his heroic deeds, the young Athenian gives courtly consideration to these female warriors, a surprisingly rare topic among early Spanish American dramatists, even though they are associated with the exploration of the New World.

While Sor Juana was criticized by church officials for her failure to dedicate her time and efforts solely to religious endeavors after entering the convent, her deep spirituality cannot be denied. Proof of her intense Christian belief, as well as her devotion to the Virgin of Guadalupe, may be found in *El divino Narciso*. The *auto sacramental,* a one-act play that has as its theme the Holy Eucharist, was a popular dramatic form customarily presented during the religious holiday of Corpus Christi. Calderón de la Barca was the undisputed master of this theatrical subgenre, and his works clearly inspired the young colonial dramaturge. Works of this type, which were allegorical in nature, were usually performed on carts, which provided the necessary platform and scenery, and song and dance frequently added to the overall spectacle.

The program of *El divino Narciso* opens with a *loa* that introduces the theme of the eucharistic sacrament. In this prefatory piece, the Spanish conqueror Zeal and his female companion, the Spanish lady Religion, engage in a debate with members of Aztecan nobility, Occident and America, over whose god is the real one. The ensuing discussion pits the pagan ritual of Teocualo, in which an idol of blood and seed is consumed by worshipers, against that of Christian communion, in which the faithful symbolically partake of the body of Christ. While Christianity inevitably wins out, the Aztec rite is presented as a prefiguration of the Holy Eucharist. The *auto sacramental,* then, is designed to instruct the audience in the importance of this sacrament as well as to highlight major events in the evolution of Christianity.

The central piece of Sor Juana's program is based upon the myth of Narcissus and Echo, as told in Ovid's *Metamorphoses*. According to this account, the nymph Echo, who was in love with Narcissus, was condemned by Juno for her loquaciousness and her complicity in Jupiter's amorous affairs. The punishment Juno metes out to Echo reduces her utterances to the mere repetition of the expressions of others. Desolate at receiving this sentence and at the rejection of Narcissus, she disappears physically, leaving only the sound of her voice. Narcissus dies when he falls in love with his own image and drowns after seeing it reflected in a pool of water. Only the flower is left as a reminder of his beauty.

Combining classical mythology with Christian theology, Sor Juana endows her allegory with religious significance by interpreting Narcissus as the figure of Christ who is pursued by the shepherdess Echo. Flanked by the characters of Pride and Self-Love, she represents Satan, or angelic nature in a fallen state. To complete the love triangle, Sor Juana casts Human Nature as a rustic maiden, who is also enamored of Narcissus. She, however, is not yet worthy of the handsome youth, as her past has been clouded by original sin. With the help of Grace, nonetheless, she finds redemption in the cleansing waters of the fountain, a pure spring represented by the Virgin Mary in her New World context known as the Indian Virgin of Guadalupe. When Narcissus looks into the water of the fountain, then, he sees his reflection, which is that of Human Nature, and his death for her sake is that of the Crucifixion. The sacrament of the Holy Eucharist, therefore, is what remains of the supreme sacrifice that Christ has made for Human Nature. Echo, on the other hand, who has failed in her mission to separate the two, is so enraged that she becomes only a sound, doomed to repeat what others have already voiced.

By blending mythology with theology, Sor Juana creates a pastoral love story in *El divino Narciso,* which is considered to be the best of her religious theater. In addition to the strong female characters in this *auto sacramental,* Sor Juana highlights the importance of the Virgin Mary in the salvation of humankind. She also demonstrates her knowledge of and appreciation for Amerindian culture in the introductory *loa,* a dramatic piece reminiscent of the sixteenth-century *autos* devised by the first missionaries who participated in the evangelization of indigenous peoples.

The script for *El divino Narciso* was taken to Madrid by Sor Juana's benefactor and New Spain's

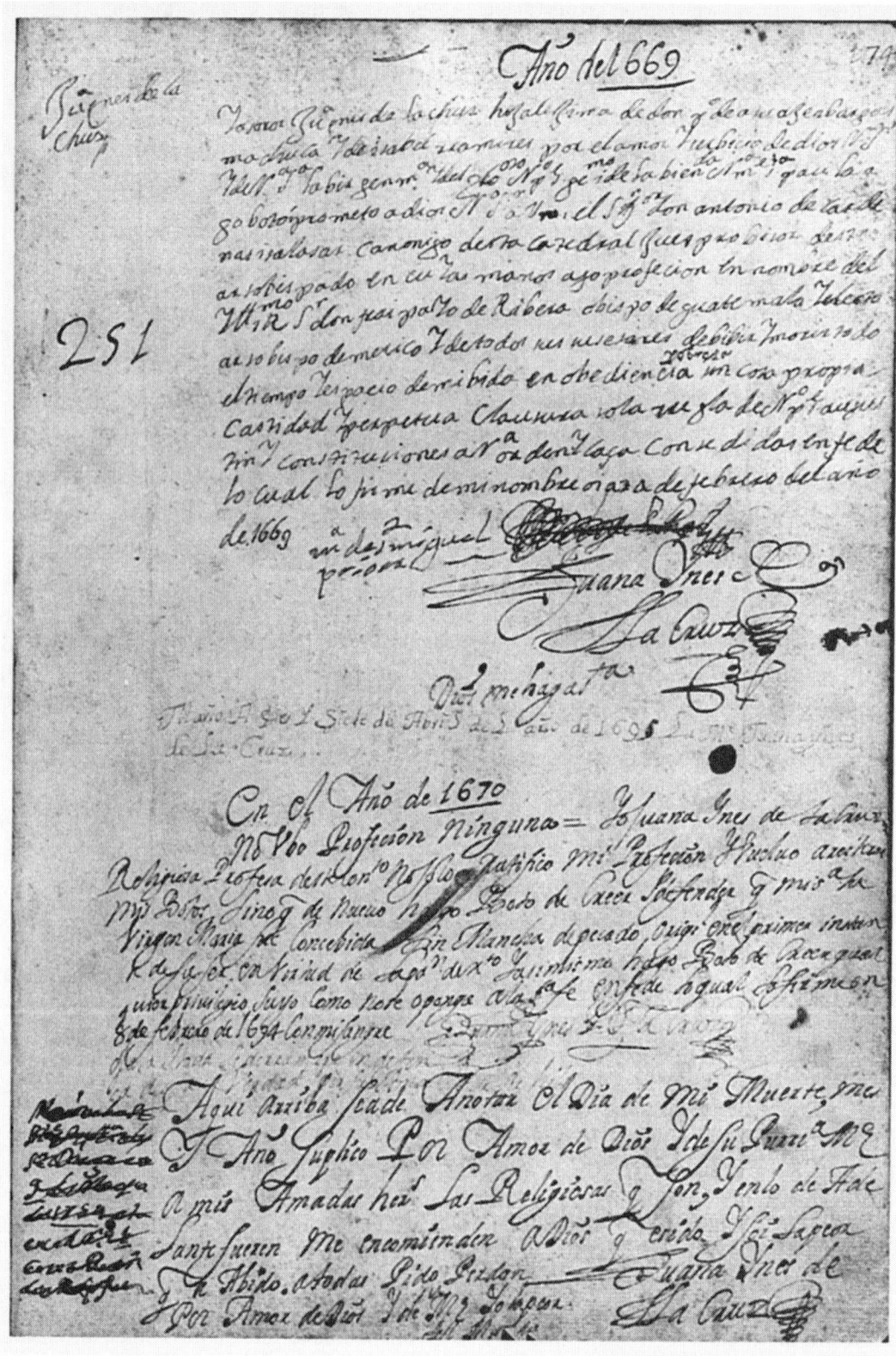

Page from the Book of Professions of the convent of San Jeronimo, in which Sor Juana's death is recorded (University of Texas; from Octavio Paz, Sor Juana or, The Traps of Faith, *1988; Thomas Cooper Library, University of South Carolina)*

vicereine, Doña María Luisa de Laguna, the Countess of Paredes, to be presented at the 1689 Corpus Christi festival. Because of the observance of national mourning for the first wife of Charles II, however, the festivities never took place. Sor Juana wrote two other eucharistic plays, but neither possesses the originality inherent in *El divino Narciso*. The lack of performance dates makes their precise chronology difficult to establish, but all were completed by the end of the 1680s.

El cetro de José (Joseph's Scepter), another of Sor Juana's *autos sacramentales,* is based upon the Bible story of Joseph, who was sold into slavery by his brothers. In this theatrical work Joseph is presented as the prefiguration of Christ, on whom the hope of redemption for all humankind rests. When the play opens, Joseph's brothers are planning their treachery against him. Their sinister plot is followed closely by the appearance of the satanic Lucero and his cohorts Intelligence, Knowledge, Envy, and Conjecture, who sense a greater importance in Joseph's existence but are unable to understand its precise meaning. When the audience first sees Joseph, he has prospered in Egypt along with his master, Potiphar. Prompted by Lucero, however, Potiphar's wife tempts Joseph, and his refusal to accede to her wishes leads to his imprisonment. In prison, he begins to use his visionary powers to interpret dreams, and his gift comes to the attention of the Pharaoh. Joseph predicts seven years of abundance as well as seven of famine, and his extraordinary ability to see into the future and envision man's salvation confounds the efforts of his adversary, Lucero. When Jacob sends his remaining sons to Egypt to get wheat during a time of scarcity in Canaan, the sustenance they seek becomes the Holy Eucharist. Prophecy then announces the significance of Joseph's life as a forerunner of Christ and the promise it holds for all humanity.

Visigothic Spain is the setting for *El mártir del sacramento, San Hermenegildo* (The Martyr of the Sacrament, Saint Hermenegildo), the last of Sor Juana's *autos sacramentales*. More historical than allegorical, it portrays the struggle there between Arianism and Catholicism, which resulted in civil unrest and the martyrdom of a man who would be king. The conflict is played out between the newly converted Catholic Hermenegildo and his father, Leovigildo, the last Arian king of the Visigoths. Torn between loyalty to his father and his belief in Christ, Hermenegildo rebels against his father's wishes. Preferring to die rather than to continue in the traditional faith and refusing to participate in the communion conducted by an Arian bishop, he is put to death by his father for his defiance. By the time Hermenegildo's brother, Recaredo, comes to the throne, however, Catholicism prevails in Spain and establishes religious unity among the Visigoths before the invasion of the Moors.

This play has been criticized for its lack of conformity to the Calderonian model of the *auto sacramental*. Rather than focusing on the Holy Eucharist and important moments in biblical history, it is more a presentation of the life of a saint who demonstrates how much a person must sacrifice to follow the one true religion and a narration of the historical presence of the Visigoths in Spain.

By 1690 the controversy over Sor Juana's production of nonreligious works in conventual seclusion reached a climax with her critical analysis of a 1650 sermon delivered by the Portuguese Jesuit Antonio de Vieyra. The bishop of Puebla, Manuel Fernández de Santa Cruz, was so impressed by this explication that he had it published as the *Carta athenagórica* (Letter Worthy of Minerva, 1690). While praising Sor Juana for this accomplishment, however, he also took the occasion (writing as "Sister Philotea") to reprimand her for not dedicating herself solely to her religious calling. The following year, she answered his criticism of her in the famous *Respuesta a Sor Filotea de la Cruz* (Reply to Sister Philotea of the Cross). This response gave readers the greatest insight into her life and her reasons for conducting it the way she did, but her reply also drew disfavor from church officials. With her backing at court gone and the support of her confessor withdrawn, she found little hope for the continuation of her literary achievements. Denied the right to pursue her inclination to study and write in the manner she desired, she became desolate, which soon affected her health. When an epidemic broke out in Mexico City in 1695, she devotedly remained at the side of her ailing sisters, and having little physical resistance herself, she fell ill and died on 17 April of that year.

Sor Juana Inés de la Cruz recognized the power of the theater to alter the way people view themselves and others and to encourage them to experiment with and accept new roles. Her plays reflect in many ways the time in which she lived, and this historical context is sometimes viewed as an impediment to their production for present-day audiences. But critics have focused on the universality of her literary production, especially her expression of feminism, and the publication of a stellar edition of her complete works by Alfonso Méndez Plancarte and Alberto G. Salceda in 1955 facilitated the investigations of literary critics. Octavio Paz's *Sor Juana Inés de la Cruz, o, Las trampas de la fe* (1982; translated as *Sor Juana or, The Traps of Faith,* 1988), a remarkable account of Sor Juana's life set in the rich context of the colonial period, was subsequently made into the motion picture *Yo, la peor de todas* (I, the Worst of All, 1990), attesting to the continued interest in this talented woman who transcended the centuries with her revolutionary vision for an equitable society.

Biography:

Octavio Paz, *Sor Juana or, The Traps of Faith,* translated by Margaret Sayers Peden (Cambridge, Mass.: Belknap Press of Harvard University Press, 1988).

References:

Raquel Chang-Rodríguez, "Relectura de *Los empeños de una casa,*" *Revista Iberoamericana,* 104–105 (1978): 409–419;

Lee A. Daniels, *The Loa of Sor Juana Inés de la Cruz* (Fredericton, Canada: York, 1994);

Gerald C. Flynn, *Sor Juana Inés de la Cruz* (New York: Twayne, 1971);

Merlin H. Forster, "Theatricality in the *Villancicos* of Sor Juana de la Cruz," in *Engendering the Early Modern Stage: Women Playwrights in the Spanish Empire,* edited by Valerie Hegstrom and Amy Williamsen (New Orleans: University Press of the South, 1999), pp. 271–284;

Edward H. Friedman, "Sor Juana Inés de la Cruz's *Los empeños de una casa:* Sign as Woman," *Romance Notes,* 31 (Spring 1991): 197–203;

Julie Greer Johnson, "Sor Juana and Her *Sainete segundo:* The Creation of a Metatheatrical Encounter on the New World Stage," *Latin American Theatre Review,* 32 (Spring 1999): 5–18;

Johnson, "Sor Juana's Castaño: From *Gracioso* to Comic Hero," *South Atlantic Review,* 66 (Fall 2001): 94–108;

Stephanie Merrim, "*Mores Geometricae:* The 'Womanscript' in the Theater of Sor Juana Inés de la Cruz," in *Feminist Perspectives on Sor Juana Inés de la Cruz,* edited by Merrim (Detroit: Wayne State University Press, 1991), pp. 94–123;

Georgina Sabat de Rivers, "Apología de América y del mundo azteca en tres loas de Sor Juana," *Revista de Estudios Hispánicos* (Universidad de Puerto Rico), 19 (1992): 267–291;

Guillermo Schmidhuber and Olga Martha Peña Doria, *The Three Secular Plays of Sor Juana Inés de la Cruz: A Critical Study,* translated by Shelby Thacker (Lexington: University of Kentucky Press, 2000);

Christopher Brian Weimer, "Sor Juana as Feminist Playwright: The *Gracioso's* Function in *Los empeños de una casa,*" *Latin American Theatre Review,* 26, no. 1 (Fall 1992): 91–98.

Osvaldo Dragún
(7 May 1929 – 14 June 1999)

Amalia Gladhart
University of Oregon

SELECTED PLAY PRODUCTIONS: *La peste viene de Melos,* Buenos Aires, Teatro Independiente Fray Mocho, 1956;

Tupac Amarú, Buenos Aires, Teatro Independiente Fray Mocho, 1957;

Historias para ser contadas, Buenos Aires, Teatro Independiente Fray Mocho, 1957;

Los de las mesa 10, Buenos Aires, Teatro Independiente Fray Mocho, 1958;

Desde el 80, by Dragún and Andrés Lizárraga, Buenos Aires, Teatro Independiente Fray Mocho, 1958;

Historia de mi esquina, Buenos Aires, Teatro Independiente Fray Mocho, 1959;

El jardín del infierno, Buenos Aires, Teatro Universitario de la Plata, 1962;

Y nos dijeron que éramos inmortales, Buenos Aires, Idiche Folks Theater (IFT), 1963;

Amoretta, Mar del Plata, Teatro Buenos Aires, 1964;

Milagro en el Mercado Viejo, Buenos Aires, Nuevo Teatro Bonorino, 1964;

Heroica de Buenos Aires, 1966;

Una mujer por encomienda, Buenos Aires, 1966;

Dos en la ciudad, Mar del Plata, Comedia Marplatense, 1967; revised as *El amasijo,* Buenos Aires, Teatro ABC, 1968;

Juguemos en el bosque, Veracruz, Teatro de la Universidad Veracruzana, 1972;

Historias con cárcel, Buenos Aires, 1972;

Y por casa, ¿cómo andamos? 1979;

Mi obelisco y yo, Buenos Aires, Teatro del Picadero, 1981;

Al vencedor, Buenos Aires, Teatro Odeón, 1982;

Al perdedor, Buenos Aires, Teatro Estudio IFT, 1982;

Al violador, 1983;

Hoy se comen al flaco, Buenos Aires, Teatro Margarita Xirgú, 1983;

Como Pancho por San Telmo, 1986;

¡Arriba Corazón! Buenos Aires, Teatro Municipal General San Martín, 23 April 1987;

Volver a la Habana, 1988;

Los alpinistas, 1989;

Mexican Dream, Mexico, Casa del Teatro, 1995;

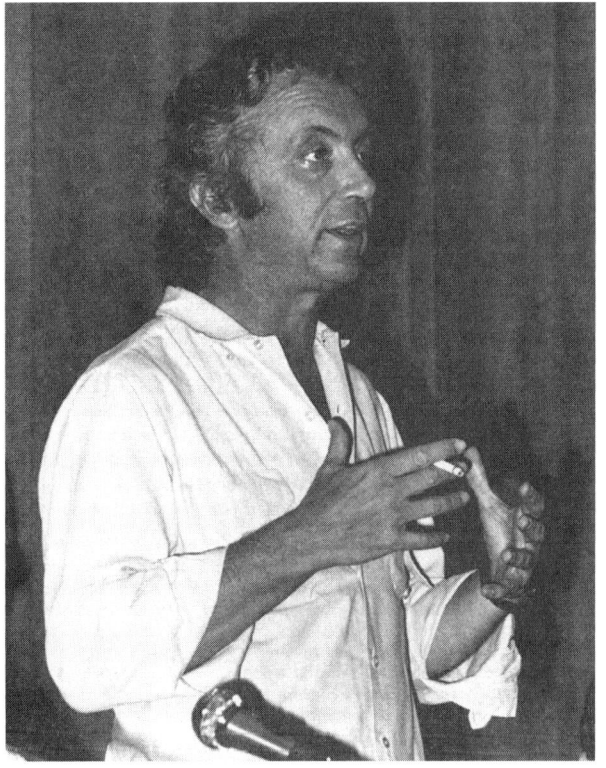

Osvaldo Dragún (from Latin American Theatre Review, *volume 13 [Summer 1980]; Thomas Cooper Library, University of South Carolina)*

El pasajero del barco del sol, Buenos Aires, Teatro Nacional Cervantes, 2000.

BOOKS: *La peste viene de Melos* (Buenos Aires: Ariadna, 1956);

Historias para ser contadas: Cuatro tragicomedias de la vida cotidiana (Buenos Aires: Talía, 1957);

Tupac Amarú (Buenos Aires: Losange, 1957);

Y nos dijeron que éramos inmortales (Xalapa, Mexico: Universidad Veracruzana, 1962); translated by Alden James Green as *And They Told Us We Were Immortal,* in *The Modern Stage in Latin America,* edited by

George W. Woodyard (New York: Dutton, 1971), pp. 119–179;

Milagro en el Mercado Viejo, published with *El atentado* by Jorge Ibargüengoitia (Havana: Casa de las Américas, 1963); published separately (Buenos Aires: Producciones Norte, 1963);

Amoretta (Buenos Aires: Ediciones del Carro de Tespis, 1965);

Teatro (Buenos Aires: G. Davalos/D. C. Hernandez, 1965)–comprises *Historia de mi esquina, Los de la mesa 10,* and *Historias para ser contadas;*

El jardín del infierno, in *Tres jueces para un largo silencio,* by Dragún, Andrés Lizarraga, and Aurelio Ferretti (Buenos Aires: Centro Editor de América Latina, 1966), pp. 71–112;

Heroica de Buenos Aires (Havana: Casa de las Américas, 1966);

¡Un maldito domingo! Y nos dijeron que éramos inmortales; Milagro en el Mercado Viejo, edited by José Monleón (Madrid: Taurus, 1968);

El amasijo (Buenos Aires: Calatayud, 1968);

Los de la mesa 10, published with *La cola de la Sirena* by Conrado Nalé Roxlo and *Temístocles en Salamina* by Román Gómez Masía (Buenos Aires: Centro Editor de América Latina, 1968);

Teatro, edited by Miguel Angel Giella and Peter Roster (Ottawa: Girol, 1981)–includes *Hoy se comen al flaco, Al violador,* "Osvaldo Dragún: Teatro, creación y realidad latinoamericana," and "Osvaldo Dragún: La honesta desnudez";

Historias para ser contadas: Edición completa (Ottawa: Girol, 1982);

Historias para ser contadas: Al perdedor (Rosario, Argentina: Paralelo 32, 1982);

¡Arriba Corazón! (Buenos Aires: Teatro Municipal General San Martín, 1987); translated by Nora Glickman and Gloria F. Waldman as *Onward Corazón!* in *Argentine Jewish Theatre: A Critical Anthology* (Lewisburg, Pa.: Bucknell University Press, 1996), pp. 263–324.

Editions in English: *The Man Who Turned into a Dog,* translated by Francesca Coleccia and Julio Matas, in *Selected Latin American One-Act Plays* (Pittsburgh: University of Pittsburgh Press, 1973), pp. 21–33;

The Story of the Man Who Turned into a Dog and *The Story of Panchito González (Who Felt Responsible for the Outbreak of Bubonic Plague in South Africa),* in *The Orgy: Modern One-Act Plays from Latin America,* edited and translated by Gerardo Luzuriaga and Robert S. Rudder (Los Angeles: UCLA Latin American Center, 1974), pp. 29–51;

Historias para ser contadas, translated by Joe and Graciela Po Rosenberg (Orem, Utah: Encore Performance, 1992).

PRODUCED SCRIPTS: *Los de la mesa 10,* by Dragún and Simón Feldman, motion picture, Siluetas, 1960;

Crónica cubana, by Dragún, Ugo Ulive, and Enrique Pineda Barnet, motion picture, ICAIC, 1963;

La familia Colón, television, TVE, 1968;

Un pacto con los brujos, television, Canal 9, 1969;

¡Robot! television, Canal 9, 1970.

OTHER: *Historias con cárcel,* in *Caminos del teatro latinoamericano* (Havana: Casa de las Américas, 1973), pp. 11–114;

El amasijo, in *Nueve dramaturgos hispanoamericanos: Antología del teatro hispanoamericano del siglo XX,* volume 1, edited by Frank Dauster, Leon Lyday, and George Woodyard (Ottawa: Girol, 1979; revised, 1997), pp. 203–267;

Mi obelisco y yo, in *7 dramaturgos argentinos: Antología del teatro hispanoamericano del siglo XX,* edited by Miguel Angel Giella, Peter Roster, and José Leandro Urbina (Ottawa: Girol, 1983), pp. 29–54.

SELECTED PERIODICAL PUBLICATIONS–UNCOLLECTED: "Nuevos rumbos en el teatro latinoamericano," *Latin American Theatre Review,* 13 (Summer 1980): 11–16;

"Dramaturgia nacional y realidad política," *Conjunto,* 60 (1984): 57–60;

Hijos del terremoto, Gestos, 2 (1986): 157–213;

El pasajero del barco del sol, Conjunto, 118 (July–September 2000): 34–53.

Argentine dramatist Osvaldo Dragún's theater presents an exploration of contemporary society and of the ways in which individuals seek a place for themselves in a dehumanizing and insensitive world. Dragún's plays often reveal a self-conscious theatricality and blur the boundaries between the stage and the audience. Dragún frequently posits storytelling as essential to human existence, a process highlighted by the creation of characters who are at once actors and storytellers. Many critics have noted parallels between Dragún's work and both Brechtian Epic Theater and the Theater of the Absurd. Dragún himself was careful to insist upon a distinction between the absurd and the grotesque, situating his work in the latter category. In an interview with Miguel Angel Giella, included in *Teatro* (1981, Theater), Dragún insisted that the absurd has no hero, because it is senseless, whereas the grotesque presents a senselessness against which one struggles in an attempt to find meaning. Writing in an identifiably Argentine idiom, Dragún addresses dehumanization, alienation, social change, and violence in a theater that is relevant to an international audience.

Dragún was born in San Salvador in the province of Entre Ríos, Argentina, on 7 May 1929. His family was Jewish, although his parents were not religiously observant. Dragún's father initially worked as a horse tamer. Dragún described his paternal grandparents in the preface to ¡Arriba Corazón! (1987; translated as Onward Corazón! 1996) as Russian Jews who fled the pogroms, seeking paradise in the Americas. The theme of the outsider or exile is a recurrent one in Dragún's work. The family moved to Buenos Aires in 1944, and Dragún soon abandoned his university studies in favor of the theater. In 1952 he began acting with amateur troupes. His professional theater career began with the Teatro Independiente Fray Mocho in 1956, part of Argentina's important independent theater movement. Dragún married a woman named Beatriz, but they had no children.

Dragún's first two plays, both premiered by the Teatro Independiente Fray Mocho, are based on historical events. His first play, *La peste viene de Melos* (The Plague Comes from Melos), was first performed in 1956. This historical tragedy uses a simple stage set and clear, unadorned dialogue to represent the siege by Athens against Melos in 416 B.C. *La peste viene de Melos* was also inspired by the U.S.-backed overthrow of Jacobo Arbenz's progressive government in Guatemala in 1954. A small colony, Melos is made the scapegoat of an ambiguous plague. Although Melos is defeated, its resistance serves as an example to other Athenian colonies. The Athenian army is recalled just after the city has been taken; the news arrives too late for Melos, but the message is clear: even the seemingly hopeless battle is worth fighting. The collusion of merchants on both sides is highlighted, as is the betrayal of Melos by its aristocracy, more concerned with its own fortunes than with the good of the whole. The tragic ending, in which the hero is killed just prior to the messenger's arrival, is redeemed slightly by the news that the Melians have inspired rebellion elsewhere.

La peste viene de Melos was followed in 1957 by another historical play, *Tupac Amarú*. The play is based on events of 1780–1781, when the Incan José Gabriel Condorcanqui, Tupac Amarú II, led a rebellion against the repressive Spanish colonial government in Peru. *Tupac Amarú* is a largely realistic play, lacking the playfulness and self-referentiality of Dragún's later work. Despite the title, the play focuses more on the Spanish *visitador general* José Antonio de Areche; the royally appointed official sent to investigate the administration of justice, than on Tupac Amarú. The Incan leader's first entrance occurs relatively late in the play, near the close of the second act. The play stresses Spanish as well as Incan duplicity, as various caciques (hereditary chiefs) sell one another out in pursuit of the title "Inca," which the *visitador* is only too happy to offer to each in turn. With its depiction of criollo as well as Incan self-interest, *Tupac Amarú* is similar in theme to *La peste viene de Melos*. Also central are the themes of decision making and individual responsibility, issues that become a continuing preoccupation in Dragún's work. Tupac Amarú's wife, Micaela Bastidas, underscores the importance of having made decisions on her own when she says that doing so made her feel what it meant to be God.

The *visitador general*'s physical decline parallels the imprisonment and torture of Tupac Amarú, as if to suggest that although the rebel leader has been killed and mutilated, the colonial regime must finally be destroyed as well—indeed, the regime is in the process of bringing about its own destruction. Drums outside the plaza double the thunder and lightning of the storm that rages the day of Tupac Amarú's execution. Just before his own death, Areche repents his actions. He laments that rather than having the Incan leader killed, he should have taken him by the hand that they might walk through the world together. *Tupac Amarú* was Dragún's last distinctly historical play, but the preoccupation with a critical representation of Latin American realities remained evident throughout his career.

Dragún's most successful play was his third, *Historias para ser contadas* (Stories To Be Told), also premiered by Fray Mocho in 1957. The flexibility with which this play combines social commentary with theatrical self-reference provided a model to which Dragún returned throughout his career. *Historias para ser contadas* has been performed throughout Latin America as well as in Europe and the United States and has had a lasting impact on Latin American theater. The several stories that make up the text combine sharp humor and absurd exaggeration with political commentary. A play calling for no more than five actors and a minimal set, *Historias para ser contadas* can be performed on an empty stage or even outside the theater. The loose joining of individual stories has also made possible the inclusion of one segment, "Historia del hombre que se convirtió en perro" (translated as *The Man Who Turned into a Dog*, 1973), in several anthologies. The play originally consisted of three stories and a prologue. Dragún ultimately added a fourth story, not included in earlier versions; the edition of *Historias para ser contadas* published in 1982 opens with "Historia del mono que se convirtió en hombre" (Story of the Monkey Who Turned into a Man).

Historias para ser contadas begins with a prologue in which the actors openly greet the audience. This greeting is central to the structure of the play, which consists of the self-conscious acting out of a series of separate stories by a group of actors always fully aware of their

Cover for Dragún's first play (The Plague Comes from Melos), which premiered in 1956, an historical drama about the siege of Melos by Athens in 416 B.C. (Baylor University)

audience. The plots are simple. In the first story, "Historia de un flemón, una mujer y dos hombres" (Story of an Abcess, a Woman and Two Men), a street vendor relates his predicament: he is plagued by a boil on his gums that prevents him from working. The man's grotesque situation–he ultimately dies of this apparently minor infection–is framed within a highly self-conscious, theatrical mode of representation, as the characters frequently call attention to their existence as actors, producing a distancing effect reminiscent of Bertolt Brecht's Epic Theater.

In the second story, "Historia de cómo nuestro amigo Panchito González se sintió responsable de la epidemia de peste bubónica en Africa del Sur" (translated as *The Story of Panchito González [Who Felt Responsible for the Outbreak of Bubonic Plague in South Africa]*, 1974), Panchito's economic ambitions and family responsibilities lead him to export rat meat to Africa. As the agent of a multinational corporation run by an Italian and an Englishman, he must find ever cheaper sources of meat. As they relate the story to the audience, the actors assume the roles of various characters within Panchito's tale. In this way, they both reenact Panchito's history and comment upon his actions. The Actress, for instance, takes on the role of Panchito's wife, from whose perspective she criticizes Panchito's transformation. Similarly, the actors hum the wedding march at an increasingly funereal pace as Panchito describes his acquisition of the responsibilities that eventually led to his choice of rat meat.

The third story, "Historia del hombre que se convirtió en perro," further explores the plight of the dehumanized worker. In this case, the dehumanization is literal, as the man accepts work as a factory watchdog only to find that the act becomes his identity. This story is the most often anthologized and translated of the *Historias para ser contadas*. The First Actor explains to the audience that everything began in the most ordinary fashion when he went to a factory in search of work; the actor then segues into a representation of the scene with the Third Actor. The man's dehumanization is further reflected in the devaluation of language. The contrast between human speech and the barking required of the man in his job as watchdog could hardly be more stark, and at the end of the story he has entirely lost the ability to speak. At the close of this story, the audience is returned to the initial frame situation. The actors explain that, since they saw the spectators passing by, they thought perhaps this story of their friend might be of interest.

The added fourth story, "Historia del mono que se convirtió en hombre," as Dragún writes in the preface to the 1982 edition of the play, was an attempt to close what he termed "el círculo del grotesco humano" (the circle of the human grotesque). A version of this episode originally appeared as part of the play *Historias con cárcel* (1972, Stories with Jail) before being incorporated into the revision of *Historias para ser contadas*. The structure of this story is somewhat more elaborate than the earlier tales, including a chorus and a Cantor, or singer. Still, the absurdity of human life and the cruelty and indifference of which human beings are capable remain central. The monkey's story stresses its moral or cautionary message more insistently than the original tales, which leave more of the interpretation to the audience. The addition of the monkey story closes the circle of the play in another way as well: the pregnant wife of the man/dog of the final story, terrified that she might give birth to a dog, is prefigured by the female monkey afraid that her baby will be human. This new first story presents the "beginnings" of the civilization that is both attacked and lampooned in subsequent scenes.

Historias para ser contadas addresses both individual and collective human suffering, but the solution to the characters' troubles lies in more than just compassion coupled with decent working conditions. For Dragún's characters, the importance of telling individual histories is clear. Yet, telling those stories is no simple matter, and understanding the means whereby histories are told is equally important. In Dragún's stories, even the trivial or personal tale becomes history, a potential counterpoint to official or public History. Individuals have value not only as the protagonists of their personal dramas but also in the way that each private story becomes part of a collective past.

The significance of *Historias para ser contadas* goes beyond its social commentary. The play is theatrically innovative in its use of a minimal–even nonexistent–set, in the flexibility with which the actors assume multiple roles, and in the insistence with which the audience is addressed and encouraged to participate. *Historias para ser contadas* draws on both national and international dramatic traditions. The prologue situates the play as a direct descendent of the commedia dell'arte. Each story, in turn, can be seen as a compact *grotesco criollo* or Creole grotesque, a style of short theater popular in Argentina in the early twentieth century, often dealing with problems of immigration, economic deprivation, and similar social ills. Dragún's treatment of the audience is also significant, for the spectators are urged not only to empathize with the characters on stage but also to see their own lives as potential stories.

Although initially published with *Historias para ser contadas* under the subtitle *Cuatro tragicomedias de la vida cotidiana* (Four Tragicomedies of Daily Life), *Los de la mesa 10* (1958, The Couple at Table 10), is less improvisational in feel than the *Historias para ser contadas* and offers a more optimistic ending. Like the stories that make up the earlier work, *Los de la mesa 10* opens with an explanation addressed by the actors to the audience of the story they are about to relate. It is the story of two of the actors' friends, José and María (a pair of names that recur often in Dragún's work); the authority of familiarity is called upon, in the manner of the oral storyteller or the casual acquaintance, who reinforces a tale with the implicit corroboration of accessible witnesses. As in *Historias para ser contadas,* the audience is encouraged to see itself in the events portrayed and to respond accordingly outside the theater.

The play tells the story of the romance between María–daughter of prosperous parents, who is studying architecture at her father's behest–and José, a mechanic. José's parents rely on his salary, so that when the two make plans to marry, José takes a second job in order to supplement his income. He is unable to maintain the doubled workday, however, and María's efforts are no more successful. María is willing to leave her studies, but finds she has few marketable skills and fewer opportunities. The two break off their romance. Still, they return repeatedly to "their" table at a local café until they finally encounter one another again and decide that the most important thing is that they be together. The waiter, like a commenting chorus, closes the play with the hope that things will go well for the pair and with an expression of sympathy for young people in difficult times.

Los de la mesa 10 was followed in 1958 by *Desde el 80* (Since 80), an experiment in musical theater written in collaboration with Andrés Lizárraga. *Historia de mi esquina* (Story of My Corner) premiered at the Teatro Independiente Fray Mocho in 1959. While the title immediately connects it to *Historias para ser contadas,* the play offers much more character development in its portrayal of the lives of a group of young people in Buenos Aires. The play is framed by protagonist Aldo introducing to the audience the various characters to be found in his neighborhood. The actors do not move in and out of character, however, nor does music play a major part. Instead, *Historia de mi esquina* presents the limited options confronting Aldo and his friends. The only alternatives to a lifetime of ill-paid drudgery appear to be crime, alcoholism, or an advantageous marriage. Aldo, however, seems blessed with a strong, if unarticulated, sense of right and wrong, and moves almost unconsciously into the role of responsible son and worker.

El jardín del infierno (Garden of Hell) premiered in 1962. The three-act play takes place in a *villa miseria,* one of the slums surrounding Buenos Aires. The set represents a two-room house built of tin and wood. The image of the shantytown is oppressive, inescapable, a world of constant vulnerability. The injustices of the slum are represented at the personal level, in the lives of clearly drawn individual characters. The contradiction inherent in the title is carried through the play in the form of the characters' contradictory lives and stunted possibilities. The action centers on the Bernárdez family, made up of daughters René and Lucy, mother María, son Ricardo–recently returned from military service–and father Pancho. When the play opens, Ricardo has not revealed to his family that he has deserted. There is much talk about the plight of "la hija de los Rosendo" (the Rosendos' daughter), victim of a gang rape and beating, who dies before the end of the play. Although Ricardo participated in the attack on the young woman, the violence occurred offstage, and in his interactions with other characters, in particular with Renata, a young Italian immigrant whom Ricardo seduces and who attempts to defend him, he is a relatively sympathetic character.

Without condoning the act for which Ricardo is arrested at the end, the play suggests that his violence is not so much personal or deliberate as situational, something to which he was driven. Ricardo's destiny is a product of his environment and circumstances; it precludes, or appears to, the realization of his better instincts. The characters' exchanges with one another stress their constant vulnerability. Lucy, the somewhat naive younger sister, is cautioned lest the water jug be stolen or her experiments with lipstick get her into trouble. Ricardo and Renata's tryst occurs while her father sleeps in a drunken stupor in the next room. The play also critiques the unequal systems of justice experienced by rich and poor. Enrique Martín is a police agent whose disdain for the people of the neighborhood, to him little better than animals, is evident. When René was a maid in the police captain's house and was raped by the son, Enrique did nothing to help her. Now, however, he will punish Ricardo along with the rest of those who attacked the Rosendos' daughter. The vulnerability of the immigrant is present as well, as Renata, in the face of Enrique's threats to have her father deported back to Italy, finally admits that Ricardo was not with her the night of the crime.

The action takes place in the context of an ongoing family disagreement about whether to return to Entre Ríos. Life in the slums is transitory, unstable, insecure, constantly under some measure of surveillance, and conditioned by forces beyond the residents' control. María places the fault for Ricardo's actions not with him but on their move to Buenos Aires. The treatment of nostalgia, however, is ambivalent. Ricardo's fascination with trains recalls his days as a boy in Entre Ríos, when he would chase after them, but also his three and a half months in solitary confinement, during which time he constantly heard the passing trains. The play ends on a note of despair. Nothing is resolved, and the longed-for escape remains unattainable.

Y nos dijeron que éramos inmortales (translated as *And They Told Us We Were Immortal*, 1971) premiered in Buenos Aires in 1963 in the Idiche Folks Theater (IFT, Yiddish Folk Theater). The play describes the return of Jorge and Berto after a traumatic military service during which their friend Arón was killed. Jorge's family is eager to welcome him as though nothing had happened; Berto is left alone. Berto subsequently attempts a robbery and is taken into police custody. He calls Jorge for help; but Jorge, dissuaded by his family and caught in a world now separate from Berto's, does not respond.

The development of the action is complicated by Jorge's reveries or flashbacks, in which he sees Arón again, and by musical numbers. The second act opens with a scene in which the fantastic tone contrasts with the more strictly realistic mode of the play and calls into question the easy reality of proper appearances in which Jorge's family struggles to live. In a partial reenactment of the events that led to his death, Arón appears ghost-like to read his poem, from which the title of the play is drawn. Arón later falls as if he had been shot, disappearing from the audience's view. Arón's fall evokes the unavailability of past events to immediate perception along with the instability of performance.

Jorge's disillusionment is also linked to historical events beyond his immediate, personal experiences. While Jorge fires into the audience with an arcade gun, an old man recites important dates in world history, announcing, for example, that in 1789 the French Revolution did away with the aristocracy. Remote from the action of the play, the historical references serve to situate, however precariously, Jorge's experience within a broader context. The old man's list highlights a long history of failed promises and incomplete revolutions: in 1810, the May Revolution did away with the Spanish viceroy; in 1917, the Russian Revolution overthrew the tsar; in 1958, the Cuban Revolution eliminated illiteracy. The scene reinforces Jorge's alienation from those around him. The scene also points to the future: the old man, in the same tone, asserts that in 1990, an eclipse led soldiers to shoot their officers. The seeming hopefulness of this suggestion is undercut by the irony of the promise Jorge and his friends have heard so often, "el futuro es tuyo" (the future is yours), a phrase repeated throughout the play.

Although the play reflects the bitterness of young people who have been asked to make great sacrifices, Jorge's alienation is not simply generational. His experience in the military has been both harsh and life-altering; he is unable to simply reenter his previous environment as though nothing had changed, as if he were the same person who left home some months before. The values of his family and his future in-laws appear hollow, the largely unspoken unhappiness of his siblings evident yet inescapable. The tensions of the play are left unresolved, as the play closes with Jorge's brother Esteban's desperate plea to him to listen.

From 1961 to 1963, Dragún worked in Cuba as the director of the Seminario de Autores Dramáticos de La Habana, a series of playwriting seminars sponsored by the revolutionary government. During this period Dragún also wrote *Milagro en el Mercado Viejo* (Miracle in the Old Market), which won the Casa de las Américas Prize in theater in 1962 and premiered in Buenos Aires in 1964. The market of the title is occupied, at night, by a variety of marginalized individuals, such as the Actor and the Bible Salesman. The play consists largely of a single flashback, introduced with the narrative presentation of Úrsula, a flower seller who identifies the physical setting for the audience and sets the action in motion. On the evening Úrsula's narrative introduces, the group's birthday celebration for the Judge is cut short by the entrance of María and José. Although the Actor is the only character identified as a performer, the other characters assume a variety of roles in the reenactment of José and María's romance and in the staging of their trial for theft.

The demand for a justification of María and José's intrusion occasions the interior drama in which their romance is reenacted. This reenactment is rejected by the Judge, impatient with the sentimental plot. María then announces that, pregnant and lacking money for an abortion, she has stolen 5,000 pesos from Señor Fernández, a wealthy businessman. Deciding to turn her in, the group "rehearses" what they will say, with the Actor playing the role of Fernández. In the process, the Actor gets so carried away that he oversees the beating of his companions by Coya in the role of police officer. To insure that such a transformation will not be repeated, the Judge sentences Fernández to death, and Coya strangles the Actor's dress coat. The play ends with the night watchman's announcement that the real Fernández has died during the night. The miracle of the title refers to the blossoming of Úrsula's exotic Greek flowers but also to the death of Fernández, just in time to save María from having to face the repercussions of her theft.

Milagro en el Mercado Viejo suggests that even an eminently informal theatrical setting can be treacherous, for the performance of possible scenarios may spill over and affect reality. Thus, the Actor explains that, during the reenactment of María and José's meeting, he was acting; in the role of Fernández, however, he was transformed. The Actor's speech, in which he describes his transformation, may be read as a realization of the axiom "power corrupts," but his words also call into question the fictionality of theater. When the roles he had to play were disagreeable to him–a fat hunchback, a woman reeking of alcohol–it was easy to keep his distance, to remain an actor. But when the role began to offer real power, he was seduced and transformed; by playing Fernández, the Actor becomes the businessman to the extent that he shares Fernández's presumed hatred for the occupants of the market. The story the characters are telling each other becomes a self-fulfilling prophecy.

Heroica de Buenos Aires (Epic of Buenos Aires), for which Dragún won the Casa de las Américas Prize in 1966, follows the central character, María, through increasingly humble economic endeavors. The play is divided into two acts or cycles, "El calor" (The Heat) and "El frío" (The Cold). These cycles reflect María's falling fortunes and the growing poverty of those around her. A market woman with a portable stall,

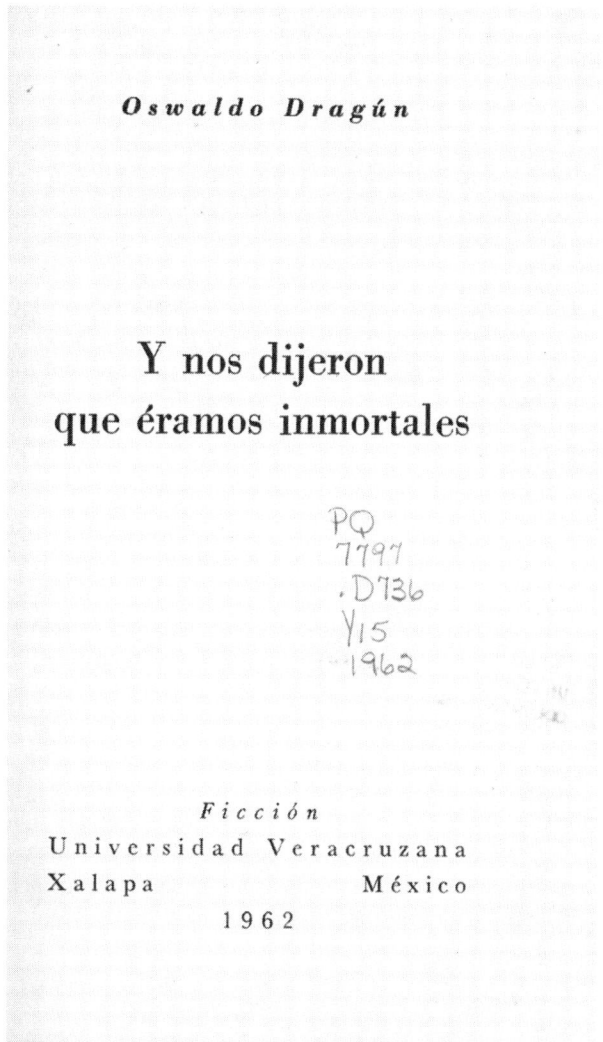

Title page for Dragún's play, which premiered in 1963 and was translated in 1971 as And They Told Us We Were Immortal, *about two young men who are emotionally scarred by their military service (Thomas Cooper Library, University of South Carolina)*

María sees her commercial fortunes sink progressively lower even as those of her children, Carlos and Ada, begin to rise. Despite her humble status, María embraces middle-class values. Yet, when she confirms the rising fortunes of her children, María despairs at how fully they have embraced those values–profit, self-interest–that she herself had tried to instill. The play presents characters oblivious of their overall context or surroundings, unable to think beyond their own immediate circumstances, and unaware of the full implications of their behavior. María pushes her children to better themselves–her dearest wish is that her son become an accountant–yet, once the children are grown, there is no place for her in their lives. Reminiscent of Brecht's *Mother Courage* (1941), with which

Dragún himself in a 1993 interview with John Garganigo compared the play, *Heroica de Buenos Aires* traces María's growing poverty and desperation as her "commerce" is reduced to bartering with the other ragpickers a weak soup in exchange for the odds and ends they have to offer. The military is a constant presence in the play, in the form of soldiers caught up in an absurd and arbitrary war, never certain to which side they belong or what they are fighting about. *Heroica de Buenos Aires* is by far Dragún's longest work, and as such is somewhat repetitive and slow. Although *Heroica de Buenos Aires* has been criticized as heavy-handed in its treatment of sociopolitical issues, which reappear in nearly all of Dragún's plays, Dragún himself ranked it among his favorites.

El amasijo (The Jumble, 1968) was originally performed under the title *Dos en la ciudad* (Two in the City) in 1967 and later adapted by José Monleón and presented in Spain as *¡Un maldito domingo!* (One Damn Sunday!). As in earlier plays, such as *Historias para ser contadas,* Dragún makes use of a minimally furnished stage, and the characters take on a variety of roles, transforming themselves in full view of the spectator and without recourse to elaborate costumes or props. The play centers on José and María, two middle-aged office workers. A third character, Ricardo, appears in a variety of roles. The plot, it might be argued, consists entirely of a succession of possible scenarios for a date between María and José that never takes place. Unable to commit to a course of action or to risk genuine connection to others, José and María essentially tell themselves stories in an attempt to find an acceptable alternative to their present situation or to play out the possible results of a given choice. For María and José, identity is performance, constituted by and limited to a repetitive chain of provisional scenarios. There is nothing outside the performance, only the empty stage of their identical bedrooms.

Each time the characters take their places, they retrace their steps. Their conversations are real, yet distorted, and the audience's suspicions as to the reality of what is being presented on stage are continually aroused. For instance, each character's mother interrupts the action with a refrain-like offstage request for her pills. The audience is left to decide whether the characters have in fact left their apartments and escaped the continual demands of their invalid mothers. The degree of fantasy and reality in the experiences of María and José is never clearly revealed, and the action moves back and forth in time. The disjointed, frequently interrupted conversations between José and María reveal a variety of longings: for a link to the past, for the opportunity to make significant decisions, for human contact. The narrative is not a plot moving unmistakably from one event to the next but instead is an examination of the storytelling process itself. What is most evident throughout the play is the characters' profound loneliness and isolation.

El amasijo elicits the spectator's participation through a paradoxical mix of information and frustration. Through the deliberately disordered and contradictory representation of their lives, Dragún is able to portray the bleakness of José and María's existence while holding the audience distant, continually frustrated in its efforts to understand. Each provisional interpretation the spectator might construct is almost immediately called into question; yet, the continual reformulation of such hypotheses constitutes the spectator's participation in the play. All of the disruptive strategies employed, such as repetition with slight variation or the presence of blanks or gaps in the dialogue, serve to make the familiar unfamiliar and force the audience to participate actively in the interpretation of the play. In many ways José and María are stereotypes—they are largely male and female versions of the same persona—yet viewers see hints of their inner demons. Though it is difficult to follow the narrative line, to determine when or whether a date has taken place, it is possible to sympathize with the protagonists, particularly given their all-too-human tendency to dwell on the potential negative outcomes of their actions. Ultimately, what is highlighted in *El amasijo* is precisely this endless process of making connections, embodied in the hopelessly tentative connection between José and María. *El amasijo* portrays in evocative detail the painful, empty, and frustrated lives of its characters and at the same time explores the nuances of theatrical and narrative representation and interpretation in their full complexity. In its multilayered theatricality, coupled with its ambivalent yet moving representation of José and María, *El amasijo* is one of Dragún's most fully realized plays.

Between 1965 and 1972, Dragún wrote little theater. He wrote for television and movies and spent time working in Spain. Of his work for television, Dragún said in an interview with Juan Raviolo (1972) that he was largely satisfied with his work and that he had been able, for the most part, to do what interested him. However, he also noted a certain mechanical aspect to television work that made the return to writing for the stage more difficult. Because he often wrote for television under a pseudonym to evade government censorship, a full listing of his production is difficult to obtain. His television serial *La familia Colón* (The Columbus Family), presented by Spain's TVE in 1968, was well received. "Pedrito el Grande" (Little Peter the Great), which was never published or performed under this title, was an autobiographical piece relating scenes of childhood and the reunion of schoolmates after many years of separation, was performed in Mexico under Dragún's direction with the title *Juguemos en el bosque* (Let's Play in the Woods) in 1972.

Dragún's next play, *Historias con cárcel,* received an honorable mention in the Casa de las Américas competition of 1973. The play recasts the format of the original *Historias para ser contadas* in a darker vein, as the stories this time deal with torture, detention, and disappearance. Like the earlier work, *Historias con cárcel* opens with a prologue in which the audience is addressed directly and the basic parameters of the play are outlined. A group of six actors take on various roles such as professor, metalworker, soldier, or wife, while one character, Pepe, links the several scenes. The actors move in and out of character, alternately representing the events of their tales and telling the audience what comes next. Pepe, however, retains his identity even as he is drawn into a variety of dangerous or violent situations. His constant refrain, that he does not want any trouble, is that of the onlooker, reluctant to become involved in the lives of those around him. Thus, when asked to escort a young woman from one part of the stage to another, he does so, even in the face of her protests, and then finds that he has hauled her before a judge about to try her on accusations of terrorism. Pepe is also unable to recognize the danger that directly threatens him; in spite of repeated calls from his wife warning of their imminent eviction and begging him to do something, he is confident that he can easily put things right when he is finished at work.

The character of Pepe highlights a theme common to many of Dragún's plays: the right and the obligation of the individual to make decisions, to take a stand. Pepe is a stagehand, ready and able to do anything that will not get him into trouble. His role within the theater suggests a parallel between the theater and the offstage world: he is trapped, in part, because he carries his unquestioning readiness to arrange—to move, to pass, to lift, to bustle—outside the theater and finds himself unwillingly caught up in events. He is abducted along with a lawyer who had defended political prisoners. At the end of the play, Pepe and the lawyer with whom he has been imprisoned die; one of their torturers, in turn, is transformed into the monkey for which his coworker had longed. The play closes with a "Cantata constitucional," in which the cast recites, to music, various articles of the Argentine constitution of 1853 pertaining to individual rights. *Historias con cárcel* is not as economical in its theatricality as the earlier *Historias para ser contadas*. The *historias* of this play are less clearly delineated, less episodic. The play demonstrates again, however, the power and flexibility of the *historias* framework.

Under Argentina's military dictatorship, Dragún found himself subject to increasing political pressure. Between 1976 and 1978, Dragún continued to write for television under pseudonyms, in effect borrowing the name of a less politically threatening writer in order to be able to work. With *Historias con cárcel,* Dragún attempted to revive the Fray Mocho, which had been long inactive, mounting a tour with Oscar Ferrigno, artistic director of that theater. The project was short-lived, however, and Dragún left for Spain to look for work.

In 1981 Dragún was instrumental in the organization of Teatro Abierto (Open Theater), a series of plays presented between 28 July and 12 September 1981 that has been described as the most important theater movement in Argentine history. The cycle of twenty-one one-act plays (twenty of which were performed), conceived by Dragún in conjunction with other Argentine playwrights, was an act of political defiance as well as a significant theatrical event. Most of the participants—playwrights, actors, and directors—had been blacklisted under the military regime; Dragún had been able to work only under pseudonyms for several years. None of the participants were paid, and the performances were scheduled early in the evening in order to allow many of the performers to hold down paying theater jobs as well. Despite the early hour and an unexplained but almost certainly politically motivated fire that destroyed the theater where the festival was originally scheduled, the event played to sold-out audiences. Some twenty-five thousand people attended the performances, and the festival was repeated for the next few years. Dragún continued his involvement with Teatro Abierto until its end in 1985.

Dragún's contribution to the 1981 Teatro Abierto cycle was the one-act play *Mi obelisco y yo* (Me and My Obelisk). The obelisk, at the intersection of the avenues Corrientes and 9 de Julio, was dedicated in 1936 and is a favorite symbol of the city of Buenos Aires. The play presents a simple and somewhat absurd situation. Actor 1 opens the play by introducing the audience to his obelisk, a rather small monument that will grow as the play progresses. The Actor then begins his search for someone to watch over the obelisk and finds a willing subject in a man recently arrived in the city from Paraná. Various characters, representing different moments in Argentine history, enter the plaza and speak to the man about the ever-growing obelisk. When the man dies, he is replaced by the Youth. However, although he is initially compliant and submissive, when the Young Woman arrives, the Youth abandons the obelisk without a backward glance. Though Actor 1 leaves the obelisk with a guardian, he is quick to return at the least suggestion of inattention. The Actor's vigilance reveals the precedence of ideology or tradition (the nationalism and patriotism symbolized by the obelisk) over human compassion or connection. The symbolism of the play is particularly apt for the Teatro Abierto context, embodying as it does a protest against an unquestioning allegiance to an outdated and inhumane ideology.

Dragún wrote *Al vencedor* (To the Victor) for the 1982 Teatro Abierto cycle. *Al vencedor* centers on an army general and the tension between Latin American and European traditions in Argentina. Also in 1982, *Al perdedor* (To the Loser) premiered at the Teatro Estudio IFT. *Al perdedor* revolves around a boxer, Justo, who prefers to give up the privileged role of champion and so escape the political and social pressures that control him while he seems to dominate the ring. Justo is manipulated at every turn by the manager who "discovers" him, by the bombastic and nationalistic president, and by his own mother. Losing is ultimately a victory because it frees him to do as he likes. The play employs a variety of devices, such as a shifting, onstage chorus and individual actors who play multiple roles, to illustrate Justo's lack of control or even, at times, comprehension of his circumstances.

Al violador (To the Rapist/Violator) was written in 1981 and staged in 1983. This one-act play attacks oppressive conformity through the figure of the criminal Aldo, who is more socially acceptable as a murderer than as a rapist. Because of the children possibly engendered through rape, the crime has no end, and the rapist is by far the more threatening criminal. Rape in this play is a social crime, one that goes against society as a whole and also against nature, as evident in the violent storms that accompany Aldo's attacks. *Al violador* presents, in a highly critical light, the need of a society to reproduce itself and to control that reproduction, to be certain of who is born and to whom. The subtler gender issues inherent in the crime of rape go largely unaddressed. The play employs a variety of antirealistic elements, such as two trees that intervene in the action, read aloud the signs posted on their trunks, and tremble at the return of the tempest that accompanies Aldo's rapes. Aldo is ultimately strangled, his body left hanging from the trees.

One of the more troubling elements of the play is the ambivalent representation of the rapist. Aldo is clearly a victim in the play, and the audience will tend to sympathize with him as a violently repressed nonconformist. The play suggests that a search for conformity at all costs is ultimately disastrous. Beyond that, *Al violador* invites a consideration of how crimes are evaluated or ranked. The murderer is seen as more acceptable than the rapist, not because his crime is less violent, but because it is self-contained and finite. The greatest threat or danger is the uncontrolled, the excessive, the unseen future. *Al violador* represents a society fearful of contagion or contamination.

Hoy se comen al flaco (Today They'll Eat the Thin Man) also premiered in 1983 as part of the Teatro Abierto cycle of that year. This play returns to the circus, to the public plaza of the *Historias para ser contadas*. The basic situation is a traditional Argentine *circo criollo*, or Creole circus, this one of such limited means and restricted spectacle that its performers must lure the audience with promises that they–the audience included–will eat the Thin Man as part of the performance. The circus also performs a version of the popular gaucho pantomime *Juan Moreira* (1884), a staple of the circus repertoire in the late nineteenth century, often cited as the beginning of Argentina's national drama. Based on a popular novel of the nineteenth century by Eduardo Gutiérrez, the pantomime presents the adventures of the persecuted gaucho. In *Hoy se comen al flaco*, Juan Moreira becomes part of the full circus spectacle, one that includes acrobats, clowns, animal trainers, and musicians, rather than a freestanding theatrical event. In Dragún's rendering, Juan Moreira enters as an ill-prepared actor. He is missing his horse (the circus having eaten his mount the night before) and ultimately becomes a bronze statue. As befits the protagonist of a pantomime, the statue of Moreira is unable to speak. This statue remains a focal point of the play as the Actress shows up with Moreira's children, begging for a response; when she decides to take them to the city, where they will be safe from the starving wolf who threatens to devour children, one of the threats of the countryside, the statue weeps. Encounters with the statue present the fossilization of the gaucho past and its myths as well as the theatrical conventions of the pantomime.

In common with earlier plays, *Hoy se comen al flaco* presents the dehumanization of the individual, most clearly in the Thin Man kept in a cage by the clowns and left to the mercy of the ravenous crowd, his comrades, who had earlier promised to arrange for his escape. Instead, the clowns who were to protect the Thin Man join the crowd in devouring him. Still hungry, however, the chorus members then devour one another, until only the statue of Moreira is left standing amid the bloody remains. He turns, observes the carnage, then addresses the audience; Moreira's closing speech is a warning in which he, too, confesses hunger. The political charge of the play is aimed at the human capacity for mutual abuse, the degradation of people so hungry and desperate that they are willing to eat one another.

¡Arriba Corazón! described by Dragún in the preface as "una carta a mi mismo" (a letter to myself), traces the efforts of Corazón, a middle-aged architect, to

understand and control his childhood memories. Although Dragún has said that all of his plays are ultimately about his father–the dehumanization and devaluation he experienced in the course of his life–¡Arriba Corazón! is his most openly autobiographical play, featuring references to his childhood in Paraná, to his parents, and to an uncle who died in the Spanish Civil War. Initially published in the periodical Gestos as Hijos del terremoto (Children of the Earthquake) in 1986, ¡Arriba Corazón! was first performed at the Teatro Municipal General San Martín in Buenos Aires in 1987. The play was written during a period of several years, in response to Dragún's return to Argentina after an extended absence in which he traveled to Mexico, Cuba, Spain, and the United States. The role of the title character is divided into three: Hombre (Man), Joven (Youth), and Niño (Child). Corazón Hombre's attempts to construct his own history conflict with the formulaic family story of hard times, a series of shared memories destined to become the personal history Corazón's father wants to transmit. The play includes many flashbacks, which become part of Corazón Hombre's struggle to call up those memories he wishes to retain while turning away from those too painful to view. These flashbacks are frequently complicated by the presence of Corazón Hombre as an observer who also seeks to intervene in the represented action. Corazón Hombre is involved in the situation, yet he remains apart, seemingly unheard by the figures who represent his memories. Early in the play, the mother tries to comb Corazón Niño's hair, at the same time that Corazón Hombre plays at undoing her work. This scene seems to illustrate the role of memory, as the present self is inserted into a remembered situation. The action of rumpling the child's hair reproduces visually the memory processes of ordering and disordering. In a similar manner, in the scene in which Corazón Joven teaches Mara, his uncle Juan's wife, to swim, Corazón Hombre is both part of the scene, answering Mara's questions, and removed, assuring the absent Juan that nothing really happened.

For Corazón, memory is a way of trying to find something outside of himself. Early in the play, Corazón's father informs his friend El Negro, "yo ya estoy en Corazón. Todo yo. Eso le voy a dejar" (I am already in Corazón. All of me. That is what I will leave him). In a literal sense, this statement is already true, for the father is present on stage only as a projection of Corazón's memory. At the same time, the presence of the father within his son is the basis for one of Corazón's greatest difficulties. At the end of the play, when Corazón Hombre returns to Buenos Aires and his ailing father, he insists: "¡Vine a buscar te a vos, papá! ¡No a las partes tuyas que están dentro mío!

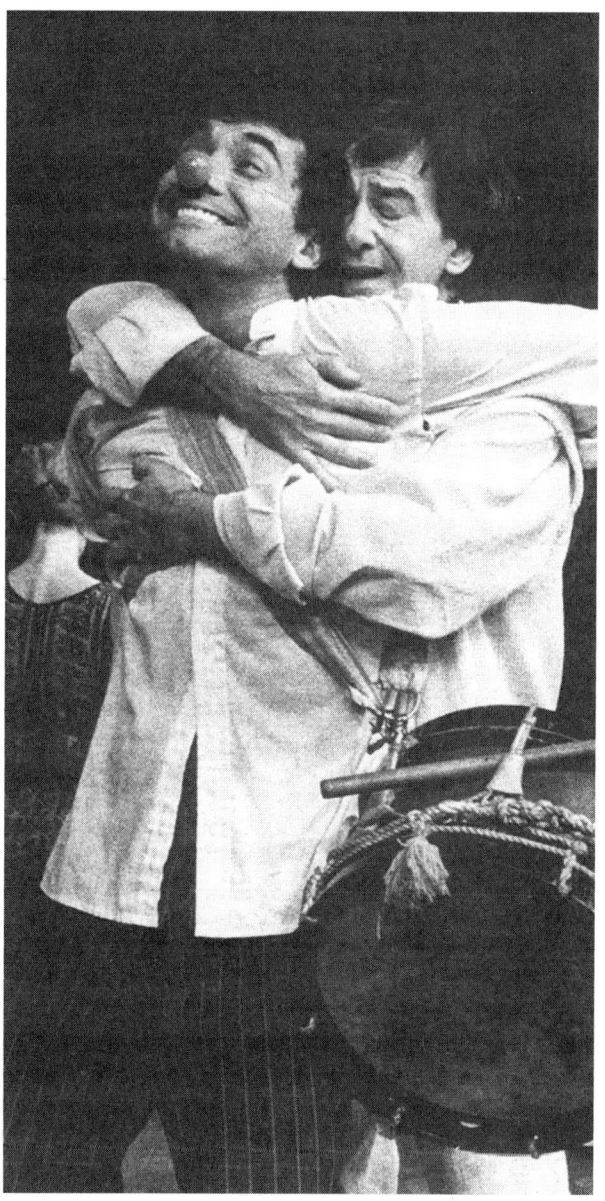

Roberto Ibáñez and Jorge Mayor in the 1987 Teatro Municipal General San Martín premiere of Dragún's autobiographical play ¡Arriba Corazón! (Onward Corazón!), *in which a middle-aged architect tries to understand his childhood memories (from* ¡Arriba Corazón! *1987; Staley Library, Millikin University, Decatur, Illinois)*

¡Debe haber algo tuyo, algo que yo no lleve arrastrando por el mundo" (I came to look for you, Papá! Not the parts of you that are inside me! . . . There must be something of yours, something that I haven't been dragging all over the world). Corazón's personal recollections are also situated within a context of collective memory through the references to the Spanish Civil War and to the locusts that destroyed his father's flax, with its echoes of Old Testament plague and Jewish diaspora. The locust plague is one to which Dragún referred often in interviews, and it recurs in many of his plays. Dragún described his father's attempts to scatter the locusts with smoke, by banging cans, and finally by waving his own clothing. The playwright listed as one of his most vivid memories the image of his father, completely naked, fruitlessly shooing the insects away from the crop he had so carefully tended. *¡Arriba Corazón!* is highly evocative in its treatment of memory, discrimination, and regret. In common with earlier plays, *¡Arriba Corazón!* presents a chronologically disordered sequence of images rather than an elaborated plot. The fragmentation of any narrative line stems from the individual's struggle to make sense of a necessarily disordered series of memories, and also reflects the difficulty all of Dragún's characters face in attempting to come to terms with an often indifferent or unintelligible social world.

In the late 1980s and early 1990s Dragún worked in Cuba and in Mexico. He was founding director of the Escuela Internacional de Teatro de America Latina y el Caribe (EITALC), based in Cuba and founded in 1988. An itinerant theater school, EITALC has conducted workshops throughout Latin America, Europe, and the United States on topics such as the theater of the oppressed, cultural encounters, theater and dance, and the relation between representation and entertainment. In Mexico, Dragún's one-act play *Mexican Dream* (which is in Spanish despite its English title), was performed in 1995 at the small Casa del Teatro as part of the first Teatro Clandestino cycle. Teatro Clandestino aimed for a theater of the present, directly concerned with current events. In 1996 he returned to Buenos Aires as director of the Teatro Nacional Cervantes, a position he held until his death in 1999.

Some of Dragún's plays remain unpublished. His last play, *El pasajero del barco del sol* (The Passenger of the Sun Boat) premiered in April 2000 at the Teatro Nacional Cervantes, nearly a year after Dragún's death, and was subsequently published in the theater journal *Conjunto*. This play takes up threads from the playwright's earlier works, with explicit references, for example, to *Hoy se comen al flaco*. The play is a sort of odyssey, tracing the fragmentary journey of protagonist Ulises. Several circus elements, such as clowns and magicians, are also included, as are music and dance. Problems of memory and isolation, of incomplete communication, are central to this elliptical, poetic script. A collage of recurring imagery of locusts, snails, bread, birds, ashes, and wings recalls Dragún's earlier work while highlighting the themes of noncommunication, distance, memory, and geography. The thematic connections established in the play are tenuous, repeatedly broken or denied; incomplete connections are reflected formally in the fragmentary development of the play. The leitmotiv of ashes points up Ulises's incomplete return, as he is absent at the deaths of both his father and mother. The play closes with a rewriting of Jorge Luis Borges's "Borges y yo" (1960, Borges and I)–an essay in which Borges plays with the public and private personae of the author, questioning who in fact is the creator of the text–and the death of Ulises. *El pasajero del barco del sol* seems unusually appropriate as a last work, presenting as it does a sort of summing up of Dragún's dramatic production. Still, because of its highly allusive, disjointed style, the play demands an audience already familiar with the playwright's earlier work.

In a career spanning more than forty years, Osvaldo Dragún remained active as a dramatist, theater activist, and teacher, directing seminars and workshops and participating in a variety of international theater initiatives. Although Dragún was often criticized for his leftist perspective, he remained committed, throughout his career, to social change and individual freedom, and his work highlights issues of ethics, justice, and morality. He confronted repressive regimes both as an artist and an activist. His work reveals an innovative combination of traditional and modern theater currents. Dragún consistently engaged the audience as part of the spectacle, bearers of stories that are as worthy of representation as those presented on stage, and the necessary interpretative counterpart without whom the play would not exist.

Dragún's reputation as one of Argentina's most important contemporary playwrights rests in large measure on *Historias para ser contadas*. Yet, *Historias para ser contadas* represents not just a single work but a form that Dragún employed in varying ways over the course of his career. Dragún developed a flexible, highly expressive style of theater in which elements of Argentine theater such as the *sainete* (a short, often tragicomic representation of lower-class urban life popular in Argentina from 1890 to 1930) or the distortions of the grotesque are employed alongside music, dance, distancing effects, and defamiliarization to portray the plight of dehumanized or disenfranchised individuals and to stress the importance of individual commitment and responsibility. Dragún's plays call on the audience not only to sympathize with the characters onstage but also to recognize similar situations in the offstage world and work to change them.

Interviews:

Alvaro del Amo and Carlos Rodríguez Sanz, "Conversación con Osvaldo Dragún," *Primer Acto,* 77 (1966): 12–17;

Juan Raviolo, "Dragún vuelve a la lucha," *Teatro 70,* 26–29 (April–May 1972): 35–44;

Ramón V. de la Campa, "Entrevista con el dramaturgo argentino Osvaldo Dragún," *Latin American Theatre Review,* 11, no. 1 (1977): 84–90;

Teresa Naios Najchaus, "Osvaldo Dragún," in her *Conversaciones con el teatro argentino de hoy: No. II (1981–1984)* (Buenos Aires: Agon, 1984), pp. 120–127;

John F. Garganigo, "Entrevistas con Osvaldo Dragún," in *Osvaldo Dragún: Su teatro,* edited by Garganigo (Medellín: Otras Palabras, 1993), pp. 29–95;

Antonio Martorell and Rosa Luisa Márquez, "En el teatro encuentro mi total posibilidad expresiva: Dos entrevistas a Osvaldo Dragún," *Conjunto,* 118 (July–September 2000): 24–33.

References:

Jacqueline Eyring Bixler, "The Game of Reading and the Creation of Meaning in *El amasijo,*" *Revista Canadiense de Estudios Hispánicos,* 12 (1987): 1–16;

Frank N. Dauster, "*Los hijos del terremoto*: Imágenes de un recuerdo," *Latin American Theatre Review,* 22, no. 1 (1988): 5–11;

Amalia Gladhart, "Narrative Foregrounding in the Plays of Osvaldo Dragún," *Latin American Theatre Review,* 26, no. 2 (1993): 93–109;

Jean Graham-Jones, *Exorcising History: Argentine Theater under Dictatorship* (Lewisburg, Pa.: Bucknell University Press, 2000);

Jerónimo López Mozo, "El teatro de Osvaldo Dragún en España," *Cuadernos Hispanoamericanos,* 591 (September 1999): 115–118;

Priscilla Meléndez, *La dramaturgia hispanoamericana contemporánea: Teatralidad y autoconciencia* (Madrid: Pliegos, 1990);

Donald L. Schmidt, "The Theater of Osvaldo Dragún," in *Dramatists in Revolt: The New Latin American Theater,* edited by Leon F. Lyday and George W. Woodyard (Austin: University of Texas Press, 1976), pp. 77–94;

Diana Taylor, "Staging Battles of Gender and Nationness: Teatro Abierto, 1981," in her *Disappearing Acts: Spectacles of Gender and Nationalism in Argentina's "Dirty War"* (Durham, N.C.: Duke University Press, 1997), pp. 223–254.

Cristina Escofet
(8 October 1945 -)

Lola Proaño-Gómez
Pasadena City College

PLAY PRODUCTIONS: *Apuntes sobre la forma,* Buenos Aires, Teatro Margarita Xirgu, 1982;

Brunilda, Buenos Aires, Teatro IFT, 7 July 1983;

Las valijas de Ulises, Buenos Aires, Teatro Nacional Cervantes, 9 June 1984;

Té de tías, Buenos Aires, Teatro de la Fundación de las Artes, 10 October 1985;

Solas en la madriguera, Buenos Aires, Medio Mundo Varieté, 23 May 1988;

Nunca usarás medias de seda, Buenos Aires, Teatro de La Campana, 30 January 1990;

Señoritas en concierto, Buenos Aires, Teatro IFT, coproduced by the Teatro General San Martín, 10 May 1993; Washington, D.C., Catholic University of America, Hartke Theater, 1996; New York, Teatro del Repertorio Español, 1996;

Las que aman hasta morir, Buenos Aires, Sala Bookstore, 18 August 1995;

Ritos del corazón, Buenos Aires, Teatro IFT, 20 October 1997;

Eternity Class/Quedar para siempre, Buenos Aires, Teatro Picadilly, 1999;

Fridas, Buenos Aires, Teatro Picadilly, 9 October 2000; Miami, Monologues Festival, 2001;

Nunca prometí un jardín de rosas, Buenos Aires, El Local de los Apóstoles, 9 January 2002;

Los fantasmas del héroe, Bahía Blanca, Teatro Municipal, 30 July 2004.

BOOKS: *Cyrano de la colina* (Buenos Aires: Plus Ultra, 1981);

Llueve en la ciudad (Buenos Aires: Plus Ultra, 1981);

Primera piel (Buenos Aires: Riesa, 1984);

Mariana (Buenos Aires: Plus Ultra, 1986);

Las valijas de Ulises y otra historia (Buenos Aires: Plus Ultra, 1991);

Teatro completo (Buenos Aires: Torres Agüero, 1994)—comprises *Té de tías; Solas en la madriguera; Nunca usarás medias de seda; Ritos del corazón;* and *Señoritas en concierto;*

Arquetipos, modelos para desarmar (Palabras desde el género) (Buenos Aires: Nueva Generación, 2000);

Tres obras de teatro de Cristina Escofet (Buenos Aires: Nueva Generación, 2001)—comprises *Las que aman hasta morir; Eternity Class;* and *¿Qué pasó con Bette Davis?*

OTHER: "Alicia en el país de las madres," in *Salirse de madre,* edited by Hilda Rais (Buenos Aires: Croquiñol, 1989), pp. 59–81;

"Princesas de las tinieblas: Teatralidad y rito en el espectáculo de la vida y la muerte," in *Peregrinaciones de Shakespeare en la Argentina: Testimonio y lecturas de teatro comparado,* edited by Jorge Dubatti (Buenos Aires: Libros del Rojas, 1996), pp. 101–110;

Los fantasmas del héroe, in *Nueva dramaturgía argentina,* edited by Dubatti (Buenos Aires: Fondo Movilizador, 2000), pp. 291–318;

La doncella de Ámsterdam (El diario de Ana), in *Dramaturgas* (Buenos Aires: Nueva Generación, 2001), pp. 17–75.

Cristina Escofet is a feminist intellectual of Argentine contemporary theater. Her literary production, a profound and singular reflection on gender, gives her a significant place among the women playwrights whose works have been produced in Argentina since 1970. In her work she attacks false cultural constructions in women's lives through a poignant and mercilessly accurate sense of humor, evident in her skillful use of rhythm, language deconstruction, and the ridicule of traditional clichés.

Escofet was born in Caleufú, La Pampa, Argentina, on 8 October 1945. She was the first child born to a cultured middle-class Argentine family. Her mother, Ercolina Angela María Piansone, was a schoolteacher, and her father, Francisco Escofet, was a businessman. Since her parents wanted a boy, she was called "Gustavita," the girl with the big glasses, until the birth of her brother Gustavo. Her other siblings were Horacio, Ana María, and Patricia. Although her family was nonreligious, Escofet was raised by a Catholic Arucarian babysitter and adopted the Catholic Creed at age five.

In 1961, at the age of fifteen, she started a career at La Plata Independent Theatre as an actress and dancer. Her first stage performance was in a production of Thornton Wilder's *The Happy Journey to Trenton and Camden* (1931), followed by a production of Eugène Ionesco's *The Bald Soprano* (1950), both directed by Lisandro Selva in La Plata. Escofet worked with the Independent Theatre movement until she turned twenty years old. At the same time, she took classes on modern dance and theater. Escofet's interest in philosophy, especially that of Jean-Paul Sartre and Simone de Beauvoir, coincided with her interest in Ionesco's work. From Federico García Lorca's poetics she learned how to use language and a wide variety of meters. Franz Kafka, Lewis Carroll, and Bertolt Brecht also provided models. She married Héctor Horacio Ojeda on 21 June 1968.

While studying philosophy at the University of La Plata, Escofet temporarily set aside her activity in the theater, although she continued taking dance classes. Having focused her studies on the works of Georg Wilhelm Friedrich Hegel, she became particularly involved in the investigation of historical dialectical movements. In 1970 Escofet finished her studies and took a position as a teaching assistant in modern philosophy at the University of La Plata until she was dismissed for political reasons in 1974. By this time she was divorced and being persecuted by the "Triple A" (Argentine Anticommunist Association), a paramilitary antiguerrilla group secretly patronized by the government of President Isabel Martínez de Perón. Escofet was forced to flee to Buenos Aires, where she settled with her daughter, Florencia, born in 1973. In an unpublished 3 September 2002 interview, Escofet recalled that during her exile from home she "attempted to survive by selling face creams in the streets, but failed." In those days, her only interesting job was writing entries for the letter "F" for an encyclopedic dictionary; however, her highly philosophical mind caused her to disregard such ordinary words as "fideo" (noodle) or "flan" in favor of more interesting words such as "feedback." She continued to work on improving her writing style, dedicating herself primarily to poetry under the supervision of Mario Goloboff, a poet and novelist who by this time was living in Toulouse, France; the models of Hegel and Immanuel Kant also were replaced by such figures as Stéphane Mallarmé, Pablo Neruda, T. S. Eliot, and Dylan Thomas.

By 1974 her writing was already being influenced by a strong feminist view. She returned to the work of de Beauvoir and met with other Spanish writers such as Rosa Montero and Montserrat Roig, and also became acquainted with the work of the North Americans Lillian Hellman, Marilyn French, and Erica Jong. She began to establish close ties with feminist groups in Argentina and in particular with Leonor Calvera, an Argentine writer whose literature decisively influenced Escofet's work, which from that period has been centered on feminism.

In 1976 Escofet decided to return to theater through dance, completing her training with Patricia Stokoe, a prestigious Argentine dancer and choreographer. Experimenting with nonrealistic and symbolic movement opened the way to signifying meaning in multiple and new ways. In Escofet's opinion, combining physical language with the deconstruction of texts and amalgamating body language with theater codes were features of a newly found freedom. In 1979 she codirected a dance theater group first called Imágenes (Images) and later named Ensayo (Rehearsal or Essay). This group aimed at synthesizing word, movement, and image. The performance *Apuntes sobre la forma* (Notes on the Form), which comprised contributions of twenty-five participants, including Escofet's texts, premiered in 1982 as part of Teatro Abierto (Open Theater), an important movement in the history of Argentine theater, expressing resistance to military dictatorship. In 1982 and 1983 Escofet also participated in Teatro Abierto as an actress.

Escofet's first novel, *Primera piel* (First Skin), was written during the 1970s and published in 1984. It is dedicated to Liliana Galleti and Carlos Veiga. Galleti, a history professor who was Escofet's close friend, disappeared during the Dirty War–the period from 1976 to 1983, during which Argentina was under military dictatorship and thousands of dissidents were kidnapped, tortured, and killed. In an interview with Ricardo Miguelez, Escofet declared that "el propósito principal se explica por el pedido de Liliana" (the main goal of the novel is explained by Liliana's request). Galleti had returned the letters Escofet had sent her since she was thirteen, and asked the author to write about the years of their youth. Their generation had expected to be "la privilegiada, una generación que esperaba echar a los liberals del trono" (a privileged one, a generation that wished to discharge the liberals [conservatives in Argentina] from their throne).

The novel begins in 1945 and ends in 1968. It is a testimonial to a particular time, a generation's twenty-year journey from infancy to adolescence in which the "first skin" is the prime covering that will regenerate when a new "skin" emerges. As Escofet stated in an unpublished 27 August 2002 interview: "the novel was my own testimony after having experienced the disap-

Scene from Cristina Escofet's 1997 play, Ritos del corazón
(Rites of the Heart), *in which a woman in an abandoned
theater converses with the spirits of several female
archetypes and famous figures, including Greta
Garbo (courtesy of Lola Proaño-Gómez)*

pearance and people hunting of all of my generation in Argentina. I think it's a good example of feminine writing since it develops the statement that all individuality is historical, a fact that I became aware of only a long time after." In 1984 *Primera piel* won the Faja de Oro (Golden Sash) granted by the Sociedad Argentina de Escritores (SADE, Argentine Society of Writers).

Also in 1984 Escofet left the stage to start a career as a playwright with Osvaldo Dragún and Eduardo Rovner as her professors. However, her experience as a dancer gives her work a special quality: the integration of text, music, movement, and dance in her scenes is enriched by the use of puns and a generally nonrealistic approach to theater.

In 1986 Escofet published a second novel, *Mariana*. It was her first work about young people and openly chronicled a first adolescent sexual encounter. The novel has a controversial tone that became a per-

manent feature in her later writing. As she said in one interview, "I have always been a rebel. I enjoy the forbidden." In the 27 August 2002 interview Escofet claimed that "el canon de lo prohibido" (the canon of the forbidden) still exists in Argentina.

Té de tías (Aunts' Tea Time), which received the critics award for best drama among those who formed the Teatro Abierto in 1985, was first staged as a part of Teatro Abierto, directed by Eduardo Pavelic. This production was Escofet's first huge success and received unanimous praise from the critics. All the innovative features of Escofet's style were present in *Té de tías* and account for the surprise expressed in the reviews after its premiere. Something different was being seen on stage: a piece with the overwhelming presence of a gender-conscious woman author who looks at history with a clear feminist gaze.

At this point Escofet departed from her teachers Dragún and Rovner to explore different ways of thinking and mostly to depict the imaginary world and social relations from the perspective of women. According to her, this work is based on the destructuring logic of Ionesco's work and her own experience with dance theater. Both of these influences created a conscious determination to break away from realism. Her feminine perspective and her detachment from the realistic tendencies of Argentine theater have characterized the aesthetics of her subsequent production.

In his review for *La Gaceta* (23 April 1985) Julio Audiles Gray called *Té de tías* a "rara avis" and qualified the subject of the play as a "bocanada de poesía" (mouthful of poetry). The dramatic plot is built around a family party attended by its dead members, who come back home after having escaped from pictures and from memories already forgotten; they have escaped from time and the cemetery. For Escofet, the dead live after their physical disappearance. The dramatic tension, as Gray pointed out, emerges from the conflictive relationship between the world of the living and that of the dead. Both worlds, because of a strange magic effect, share the stage.

In June 1988 Escofet received a National Funds for the Arts grant. That same year, *Solas en la madriguera* (Women Alone in the Warren), one of a series of feminist humorous monologues, premiered in Buenos Aires. It was subsequently staged in Mar del Plata, Argentina (1988); Colonia, Uruguay, and Havana, Cuba (1989); and Montevideo, Uruguay (1991).

Nunca usarás medias de seda (You Will Never Wear Silk Stockings, performed in 1990), shows how women have lost their identities. The play denounces the educational system and family institutions as tools that pay service to tradition by helping to maintain the social and cultural feminine roles. The play was directed and staged by Daniel Marcove on 30 January 1990 in El Teatro de la Campana. The rhythm of its language together with the images that it presents allow for the discovery of unforeseen aspects of reality, as a reviewer for *Página* (2 December 1990) commented. Escofet stated that her goal was to "continuar con el tema de los fantasmas que han formado nuestro imaginario" (continue with the topic of those childhood phantoms that have formed our imagination). *Nunca usarás medias de seda* depicts an alienated woman who dreams about her childhood, when she was subject to multiple commandments. A critic for *The Buenos Aires Herald* (10 March 1990) described the play as having plenty of acidic, grotesque humor that reveals the horrors of daily routine as seen from the viewpoint of a woman who is always expected to be a symbol of perfection. This play was awarded the Buenos Aires City Council Honor in 1995.

Escofet's next production was *Señoritas en concierto* (Young Ladies in Concert, performed in 1993), a piece that not only destabilizes the patriarchal system but also deconstructs both the symbolic order and the language supporting this artificial order. In this piece she uncovers "reality" onstage to denounce it as a cultural construct that should be rejected. *Señoritas en concierto*, Escofet's most staged and popular piece, premiered as a coproduction of the Teatro General San Martín and Teatro IFT. The play is divided into thirteen *varieté* (music-hall) scenes that start with a group of women dragging a caravan on stage. The actresses play different roles in sketches that begin in the early twentieth century. Escofet makes use of Brechtian techniques such as a narrator and a chorus, word games, parodies of popular songs, and gaps between words and action.

In the mid 1990s Escofet returned to philosophy and began to define herself as a Jungian feminist. Her subsequent work clearly reflects this new turn. In 1995 *Las que aman hasta morir* (Women Who Love to Death) was staged under the direction of Julio Piquer. The only character in the play is a woman (the stage directions call for an unnamed forty-year-old actress) who is presenting a lecture. Among the people in the audience, she recognizes an old girlfriend of hers who has been a witness to all the sad love episodes in her life. The presence of her friend encourages the character to perform an "interior striptease," as Carlos Llorens wrote in *La Nación* (29 August 1995). Her confessions reveal that her search for love is intrinsically based on the desire and the demands of men. Through the description of different prototypical males, the play demonstrates feminine frustrations in love. As the story develops, the audience discovers that the character's failure to find true love is caused by her insecurity, masochism, narcissism, and mystification—all traits acquired under the severe dominance of a patriarchal society.

In *Ritos del corazón* (Rites of the Heart, performed in 1997) specters of different types of women—including the Romantic, the Medieval, the Grandmother, the Mother, Greta Garbo, and Marilyn Monroe—hold a conversation with Juanita Freijero, a peculiar character who has refused to leave the theater after it was closed down and has remained there forever. The play is about the multiple daily deaths that women suffer throughout their lives. Escofet claims that women should "wake up" from this situation without returning to the past. Laura, the main character, is a playwright who carries the ideology of the play and serves as the mirror figure of Juanita; she wishes to be reborn into the future. *Ritos del corazón* was directed by Pavelic, who "laid the stress on the hallucinatory atmosphere of the text and on the idea of theatre as a privileged space in which to make dreams become alive" (*La Nación*, 5 November 1997).

Eternity Class/Quedar para siempre (performed in 1999) presents a family exhibiting the dangers of technology. In her prologue to *Tres obras de teatro de cristina Escofet* (2001, Three Plays of Cristina Escofet), Escofet describes the plot of the play as "una familia en proceso de volverse de poliuretano y de borrar para siempre los estigmas de la mortalidad. La clase de los que se embalsamarán en vida para no morir" (a family in the process of becoming polyurethane creatures, who try to erase mortality forever. The kind that would rather be embalmed while still alive than die).

In 2000 Escofet published a series of essays, *Arquetipos, modelos para desarmar (Palabras desde el género)* (Archetypes, Patterns to Dismantle [Words through Gender]). This book, in Jorge Dubatti's opinion, is "an unusual text, atypical in many ways, a mixture of feminist manifesto with gender study, historical and autobiographical testimony." He adds, "As a volume of literary criticism and theatrical-poetical writing, Cristina Escofet's book is a real event in the theatre field of Argentina."

Also in 2000, *Fridas,* a poetic depiction of Frida Kahlo reading her experiences from her own paintings, was part of a *teatro semimontado* (spoken theater) series. The characteristics of the *semimontado* consist of a reading of the text with just a few essential movements or actions. The actors generally perform on a bare stage with some occasional lighting or props depending upon the resources of the producers. *Fridas,* codirected by Escofet and Ana María Casó, is a semiconfessional ceremony in which the actress is not hidden behind the character. In Escofet's opinion, in *Fridas* pain is always present and emerges unexpectedly. She commented in the 27 August 2002 interview, "I didn't understand why I turned to such a deep pain, until I was informed that my partner was dying. [Escofet's husband, Danilo Corsaletti, died on 19 July 2001.] I then understood that *Fridas* was teaching me how to live through pain, the same as she herself did."

In 2001 Escofet started composing lyrics for musicals. *Nunca prometí un jardín de rosas* (2002, I Never Promised a Rose Garden) was staged under her direction. In an unpublished 19 February 2002 interview she explained: "The transit to the musical and the poetical together with direction seem to have been decisive for me at the moment. My decision was made mainly because I believe that poetry and music are the best resources with which to confront a reality at war, and also because of a personal need to return to feelings and to prolong my writing through finding a common bond with an audience."

In her introduction to *Teatro completo* (1994, Complete Plays) Escofet summarizes her goals: "To assume our own shadow. To know to what extent we are made of stereotypes. To die in order to be born again." Within the seemingly narrow confines of plays dedicated to the representation of the world of women, Escofet gives extended treatment to a wide variety of concerns. The "feminine theater" tells audiences about women, but also about men and cultural values; it revises official history and calls stereotypes into question.

Interview:

Lola Proaño-Gómez, "De la inmanencia a la trascendencia: Una conversación con Cristina Escofet," *Gestos,* 18 (1994): 215–219.

References:

Magda Castellví de Moor, "Dramaturgia argentina: 'Ritos del corazón' de Cristina Escofet y la escritura del sujeto," in *Homenaje a Carlos Orlando Nállin,* edited by Faviana L. Varela, Magdalena E. De Mállin, and María G. Romano (Mendoza: Universidad Nacional de Cuyo, 1999), pp. 173–186;

Castellví de Moor, "Monólogo dramático y narración: 'Las que aman hasta morir' de Cristina Escofet," in *Tradición, Modernidad y Posmodernidad,* edited by Osvaldo Pellettieri (Buenos Aires: Galerna/Universidad de Buenos Aires, 1999), pp. 273–281;

Daniel Dátola, "Cristina Escofet. Apuntes de una escritora rebelde," *La Razón* (10 December 1986);

Jorge Dubatti, "La lectura de la historia desde el género," *Cuadernos de Historia y Teoría Teatral* (May–July 2000): 4–5;

Lola Proaño-Gómez, "Dramaturgia y feminismo: El teatro de Cristina Escofet," in *El nuevo teatro de Buenos Aires en la postdictadura (1983–2001) Micropoéticas I,* edited by Dubatti (Buenos Aires: Centro Cultural de la Cooperación, 2002), pp. 142–150;

Proaño-Gómez, "El humor feminista de Escofet: Una ironía militante," in *Nuevo Teatro. Nueva Crítica,* edited by Dubatti (Buenos Aires: Atuel, 2000), pp. 161–180;

Osvaldo Quiroga, "Teatro Abierto: Un balance necesario después de cuatro años de funciones," *La Nación,* 4 November 1985, p. 3.

Carlos Felipe
(4 November 1911 - 14 October 1975)

José A. Escarpanter and Charles E. Workman
Auburn University

SELECTED PLAY PRODUCTIONS: *El chino*, Havana, Teatro ADAD, 11 October 1947; Miami, Teatro Avante, 6 June 1989;

Capricho en rojo, Havana, Teatro ADAD, 1950;

El travieso Jimmy, Havana, Teatro Auditorium, 1951;

De película, by Felipe and others, Havana, Teatro Las Máscaras, 1963;

Los compadres, Havana, Teatro Lyceum, 1964;

Réquiem por Yarini, Havana, Teatro Las Máscaras, 1965; New York, Dumé Spanish Theater, 1970;

Tambores [abridged], Havana, Teatro Martí, 1967.

BOOKS: *Teatro* (Santa Clara, Cuba: Universidad Central de Las Villas, 1959)—comprises *El chino, El travieso Jimmy*, and *Ladrillos de plata; El chino* translated by Luis F. González-Cruz and Ann Waggoner Aken as *The Chinaman*, in *Three Masterpieces of Cuban Drama* (Los Angeles: Green Integer, 2000), pp. 89–180;

Capricho en rojo (Havana: Pagrán, 1959);

Teatro (Havana: Unión Nacional de Escritores y Artistas de Cuba, 1967)—comprises *Réquiem por Yarini, El travieso Jimmy, El chino*, and *Los compadres;*

Réquiem por Yarini (Miami: Calesa, 1978);

Teatro, edited by Francisco Garzón Céspedes (Havana: Letras Cubanas, 1979)—comprises *El travieso Jimmy, De película, Réquiem por Yarini*, and *El chino;*

Teatro, edited by José A. Escarpanter and José A. Madrigal (Boulder, Colo.: Society of Spanish and Spanish American Studies, 1988)—comprises *Esta noche en el bosque, Tambores, El chino, Capricho en rojo, El travieso Jimmy, La bruja en el obenque, Ladrillos de plata, Réquiem por Yarini, Ibrahim, De película*, and *Los compadres.*

OTHER: *El travieso Jimmy*, in *Teatro cubano contemporaneo*, edited by Dolores Martí de Cid (Madrid: Aguilar, 1959), pp. 167–249;

Réquiem por Yarini, in *Teatro cubano*, edited by Samuel Feijóo (Santa Clara, Cuba: Universidad Central de Las Villas, 1960), pp. 150–230.

Carlos Felipe (*from Dolores Martí de Cid, ed.*, Teatro cubano contemporáneo, *1959; Ned R. McWherter Library, Memphis State University*)

Among the dramatists who attempted to renovate Cuban theater in the mid twentieth century, Carlos Felipe played a prominent role because of his innovative themes and the importance he placed on stage elements. Felipe introduced to the Cuban theater contributions of Luigi Pirandello and other European dramatists, but he never forgot or excluded the Cuban reality. In his theater appears the world of prostitution, the maritime atmosphere (which is rarely developed in the theater of this island), the Cuban bourgeoisie, and the contrast between the decadent world of the bourgeoisie and the frequent poverty in the cities.

Not much is known about the life of the author because he was a timid and reclusive person. Even his date of birth is uncertain. The majority of the biographical sources indicate the date of his birth as 4 November 1914; however, his sister, Rosa, affirmed in an unpublished interview that the day is correct but contends that it occurred three years earlier, in 1911. The dramatist's surname is also contested. Many critics have stated that the true surname was Fernández and consider Felipe to be a pseudonym, but again his sister contends that she as well as her brother, both of whom were born during their mother's second marriage, were given the name of Fernández, which was the name of their mother's first husband, but later both adopted the surname of her second husband, their true father, Fremión Felipe, native of Medina del Campo in Spain, who died when they were both young. Rosa Felipe has asserted that although the family was extremely poor, Carlos attended the Escuelas Pías (Pious Schools) in the city of Guanabacoa, close to Havana, where he graduated as a mercantile specialist at sixteen.

Felipe worked at various jobs in order to help support the family. He was a waiter in a café, a messenger for a provisions warehouse, and a worker in a tire company up until 1931, when he obtained stable employment with the customs department of Havana. There he spent thirty years of his life. This job paid a meager salary but gave him the leisure to read and study. Although he never pursued upper-level studies in a formal setting, he gained vast knowledge and a degree of culture through his personal reading.

From a young age his artistic preferences compelled him toward theater and music. During his adolescence he began to interpret classical Spanish works and created theatrical groups where he participated as an actor and singer; but because of his shyness, he decided to abandon these activities in order to dedicate himself to writing.

During those early years working in the customs department of Havana, he finished two works set in a maritime environment, a recurrent motif in his theater. This preference can be attributed to his work experience in the Havana ports. These early works are "El divertido viaje de Angelita Cossí" (The Amusing Trip of Angelita Cossí), a short work that won second prize in a radio competition, and "El faro" (The Lighthouse), a two-act play that presents a love triangle. Both works have been lost.

In 1939 he received the National Prize for Theater with *Esta noche en el bosque* (Tonight in the Forest, published in 1988), and four years later he received an honorable mention in the same competition with *Tambores* (Drums, published in 1988). Neither of them had received a theatrical production at that time. *Esta noche en el bosque* has never been produced, and *Tambores* debuted in an extremely summarized version in the Teatro Martí of Havana in 1967.

Esta noche en el bosque has been considered one of Felipe's less important works, but it nevertheless features elements that foreshadow themes and techniques commonly used by the dramatist. In the first act, two friends, Félix and Benito, arrive unexpectedly at the home of a mutual friend and newspaper reporter, Antonio, one Saturday night. Antonio has to finish an article he is working on, but he is constantly interrupted. More people arrive, including Lulú, a young prostitute who has an appointment with Antonio's boss, and later another friend, Andrés, a wealthy lawyer who announces that he is soon to be married. Among all of those present is a feeling of true camaraderie, and one of them suggests taking a trip far away from Havana. Antonio has his reservations but finally accepts the idea, and all of them depart, leaving Antonio's boss without Lulú and without the finished article that Antonio had promised him. The remainder of the play takes place at a beach house and in the forest, where the hidden dreams of the characters are realized. Characters are transformed into moonbeams, become heroes fighting against dictators, or are changed into fairy-tale princesses.

Some critics have perceived *The Blue Bird* (1908) by Maurice Maeterlinck as a direct influence on Felipe's comedy, but this opinion is not sustained by a study of both works. The two share only the idea of a trip to magical places. The piece by Maeterlinck is a reflection about human beings regarding their conduct and aspirations. The central characters are two children. The work by Felipe employs a group as the protagonists and focuses individually on the conflicts of these characters, who take a trip that occurs in the final act, in direct contrast with the work by Maeterlinck, in which the trip is the central theme. Other critics have suggested a similarity to William Shakespeare's *A Midsummer Night's Dream* (circa 1595–1596). In this comedy there are also various protagonists who undergo metamorphoses in one night in a single setting.

Esta noche en el bosque demonstrates many interesting attributes. Another influence is that of the opera *La Bohème* (1896) by Giacomo Puccini in the gathering of friends in the first act, a fact that is pointed out by one of the characters. This allusion marks the beginning of a procedure characteristic of the writer, who often employs expressions and events originating from other genres ranging from opera to melodrama or soap operas. The setting, the technique, and the characters appearing in the first half of the second act reflect the established guidelines for that age of Spanish theater, as presented in one of its then most popular genres: the comedy of manners of Jacinto Benavente y Martínez and the brothers Joaquín and Serafín Álvarez Quintero. In the third act the dramatic structure takes an expressionistic twist. The law of typical causality from the realist technique in the previous acts is abolished, and brief scenes are presented apparently without organization.

Esta noche en el bosque utilizes character types and techniques that are developed further in the later work of the dramatist. Some of the characters suffer from and are dominated by dark premonitions, dreams, and hallucinations, preceding characters in later plays who have no free will. The characters belonging to the upper middle class defend conventional values and are depicted with cartoon-like traits. The open ending is also a precursor to the endings of subsequent plays. The dialogue reveals the author's constant search for language with a poetic quality.

Tambores adds the form of the *sainete* (brief intermezzos, often humorous), which were not always incorporated with success, to the foreign influences already present in Felipe's theater. The work begins with a brief prologue written in an expressionist style, inspired by *The Emperor Jones* (1921) by Eugene O'Neill. It portrays the African slave traders along with the slaves themselves in the middle of the jungle. An allegoric figure, the Soul of the African drum, appears to encourage the unfortunate slaves to survive in the foreign, American lands. The sounds of the drums connect this scene with the first act, which takes place in a house in a neighborhood of Havana in the 1930s. Various characters file onto a communal patio: Concha, a mulatto; Picuita, a clever black character; Melanio, a dirty old man; and Julia and Etelvina. A writer, Oscar, one of the tenants in the neighborhood, is preparing to debut a work with an Indian American setting and is accompanied by Luisa, his girlfriend, and López, his good friend. Pascual, an improvising troubadour (a common personality type among the abundant island population), appears and complains about the political abandonment that the true Cuban people are suffering at that time.

The second act focuses on the conflict of Oscar, who is devastated by the failure of his Indian work. The Soul of the African drum appears to him and provides him with an epiphany: American art should be inspired by the pre-Columbian aborigine. Oscar decides to leave with Luisa and López and to travel around America. The work ends with a general dance, as is common in the Cuban one-act comedies.

In this play two themes intersect: that of the popular *sainete* and that of the problems the author faces in search of his creation. The latter is represented by Oscar, who becomes something like an alter ego of the author. Felipe, through these situations, presents a bitter perspective of the Cuban Democratic Republic shortly after the failure of the revolution of 1933 that removed the dictator Gerardo Machado.

From the ideological point of view, *Tambores* presents some postulates full of youthful enthusiasm but inconsistent because of the confusion and contradictions. Instead of delving into the black races of the Cuban culture—a clear reality—Oscar, following the dictates of the Soul of the African drum, goes around the continent in search of the Indian ancestors, who do not possess the importance on the island that they have in other Hispanic countries.

As in *Esta noche en el bosque,* the play exhibits elements that recur in the future theater of the author. The black motif introduces an element that culminates in *Réquiem por Yarini* (Requiem for Yarini; published in 1960, performed in 1965). The reference to the work of Oscar is an antecedent of the technique of theater inside theater, which is the structure of *El chino* (performed in 1947, published in 1959; translated as *The Chinaman,* 2000). Concha, who inherits the role of the beautiful mulatto of the *sainete,* can be seen as a precursor of the character Jabá in *Réquiem por Yarini*.

Because of his lack of economic resources and little government support, Felipe did not see his prized works brought to the stage. Discouraged, Felipe concentrated his efforts on journalism for several years. He collaborated as a theatrical and movie critic in the journal *Siempre* (Always) and published articles in the magazines *Artes* (Arts), *Redes* (Nets), and *Prometeo* (Prometheus).

In 1947 the theatrical group ADAD held its first competition of theatrical works. *El chino* received first place and a staging of the play, which established the author as the most interesting Cuban dramatist of that time. In this work there is a convergence of the elements present in his two previous works, the renovating intention and the tradition of the popular Cuban theater. Through the title character, Felipe adds an oriental element, which also establishes a magical and mysterious dimension to the work.

The piece consists of three acts. In a parlor in her house, Palma is making preparations for an attempt to reconstruct an event that occurred some years earlier. Her purpose is to motivate Luis, the Chinese owner of a cheap hotel in the Port of Havana, to remember the identity of a sailor known as José the Mexican. Palma wants to find this man, since one night of love with him at the hotel has been the only true one in her agitated life. She has called a meeting of all the witnesses of that night under the direction of Robert, a prestigious theater director. In the elegant parlor, stagehands attempt to re-create the atmosphere of the hotel. When the "representation" is about to begin, a man appears claiming to be José the Mexican. Palma does not recognize the man, and the group decides to continue with the experiment, including the recent arrival, who participates unwillingly. At the end of the "representation" the man keeps asserting that he is José the Mexican, but Palma and the other participants remain unconvinced. So much time has passed that many memories have been lost or distorted. Finally, the man leaves. Palma lies on the sofa, a victim of a strong headache. Although this time the search apparently has been useless, she proposes to continue it.

This text utilizes the technique of a play within a play, but here the purpose is not a representation in itself but rather a psychic reaction, that of Luis, which gives the piece its identity within the psychodrama. In this work, more precisely than in his few statements in articles and interviews, Felipe exposes the concepts that define his idea of theater and are frequently applied in his theatrical presentations. The dramatist rejects the postulates of photographic realism and declares that theater never should be a trustworthy reflection of reality: "La versión taquigráfica de una conversación jamás puede ser un diálogo teatral" (The stenographic version of a conversation could never be a theatrical dialogue). The most important things in theater are the suggestion and the effect produced in the spectator. Felipe maintains that the execution of a dramatic text should correspond to a single author and that the dialogue is a consequence of the dramatic situation and not the opposite: "La situación crea la palabra" (The situation creates the dialogue). Following the modernist school of thought, Felipe states that one should always search for the elegant expression. The author also jokingly and ironically comments about the secular wrongs that plague the theatrical profession, especially vanity. He lashes out at the performers of the old school of acting, who always overacted. These opinions are pertinently articulated in the complex action of the plot.

El chino clearly elaborates on a series of motifs established in earlier works and foreshadows others that appear in later pieces. Since its debut, the play has been the recipient of criticism. When it premiered, critics suggested that the essential merit of the work was purely theatrical. Later, the work was included among the seventeen most important works of Cuban theater in the twentieth century.

In 1948 Felipe once again won the prize in the ADAD competition with *Capricho en rojo* (Fantasy in Red), which debuted in 1950 and was published in 1959. *Capricho en rojo* consists of three acts. The first takes place in the mansion of the count of Soria. At the beginning of the plot the count is speaking with the dressmaker, Laribeau, who for enjoyment has dressed six of his clients in an outfit of the same design, "Capricho en rojo," on the same night, without anyone realizing it. The count comments on the presence of a quiet youth who has remained apart from the party. Finding himself alone, the young man, Pablo, initiates a monologue in which he remembers events that occurred two years ago and have left him profoundly disturbed. A flashback is produced in which a mother appears asking him for help. The action of the play combines Pablo's memories with the women dressed in "Capricho en rojo" and a beautiful girl named Silvia.

The few critics that have examined this piece have focused their interest on an analysis of Pablo's tormented and guilt-ridden mind, suggesting that Silvia's presence at the party is only a hallucination. Nevertheless, if the work is reviewed in light of the rest of the author's work and some suggestive affirmations of Silvia are taken into account, the text supports a different interpretation. When Silvia approaches him it is not a product of his imagination but rather an extraterrestrial appearance. Silvia refuses to be precise when faced with Pablo's questions and alludes to her strange situation in various passages of the dialogue: "No me puedo quedar un minuto más . . . no me pertenezco. Mi presencia aquí es . . . una subversión de la naturaleza" (I cannot stay here a minute longer . . . I do not belong. My presence here is . . . a subversion of nature). Felipe uses preternatural phenomena in several other plays, and in this case Silvia's appearance from the grave seems to provide Pablo with meaning for his disoriented existence. She will patiently await her soul mate "bajo una estrella o cerca de una constelación" (under a star or close to a constellation). In this work the dramatist creates, along with his typical tormented protagonists, an attractive figure who serves as a voice for Felipe to express his concern for helpless humanity and his loyalty to the concept of Neoplatonic love mixed with spiritualist beliefs.

El travieso Jimmy (Mischievous Jimmy), Felipe's next play, won the National Theater Prize in 1949 and debuted two years later. In this work in two acts and six scenes, Felipe once again uses the technique of the flashback. Leonelo, a man at the end of his life, remembers his childhood in New Gerona, capital of the Island of Pinos, a small island to the south of Cuba that in modern times is known as the Island of Youth. In the middle of the night the protagonist remembers characters and events that appear on the stage in the following scenes until the play returns to the present time. The memories are concentrated on the arrival of Jimmy, a blond youth with a friendly appearance who had a decisive influence on the lives of various city inhabitants. One story line deals with the family of a pharmacist, composed of Sixto; his wife, Estefanía; their orphaned niece, Lila; and Dolly, a Jamaican servant. Another story line deals with Raimundo, a timid peasant boy in love with Lila, and Leonelo himself. Raimundo accompanies Lila on her way to take piano lessons, but his timidity prevents him from showing his true feelings to the girl. Leonelo, then a thirteen-year-old boy dependent on the support given to him by some of his neighbors, insists that Dolly tell him about his origin. Leonelo never knew his mother and wants someone to tell him who she was. This desire becomes an obsession that consumes a large part of his life. However, nobody claims to have known her. Throughout the rest of the play, Jimmy earns a friendship with Leonelo and little by little establishes relationships with the other characters; but soon they realize that Jimmy is not the wonderful boy that he seemed. Faced with this situation, Jimmy leaves forever.

Jimmy is a solitary figure, never seen again in Felipe's theater. He is the absolute protagonist of the piece, pulling all the strings in the action. There have been many different opinions about him. He has been interpreted as a little devil or a playful person, like chance, and even as a symbol of the North American political intervention in Cuba. Whatever the interpretation of the character may be, there is a resulting ambiguous element that the author frequently uses in his works. Jimmy acts like a Cupid by creating love and mischief between Lila and Raimundo. However, besides his actions that bring unfortunate consequences, Jimmy contributes to the characters' more youthful experiences and enriches them: the cruel truth for Leonelo, which helps him to mature and to find new horizons in Cuba, and a brief but intense love for Lila and Raimundo.

El travieso Jimmy is one of the author's most balanced works. It presents an environment (the Island of Pinos) that had not been treated by Cuban dramatists. After its debut the play was presented in popular shows in the amphitheater of Havana with enormous success. This work by Felipe, which is particularly Cuban, was the first to reach the general public.

In the 1950s, television developed rapidly in Cuba. Felipe wrote some teleplays, but none was ever produced. Among these scripts is *La bruja en el obenque* (The Witch and the Shroud; published in 1988). This libretto has a theatrical structure, and on more than one occasion the author declared that it could have become

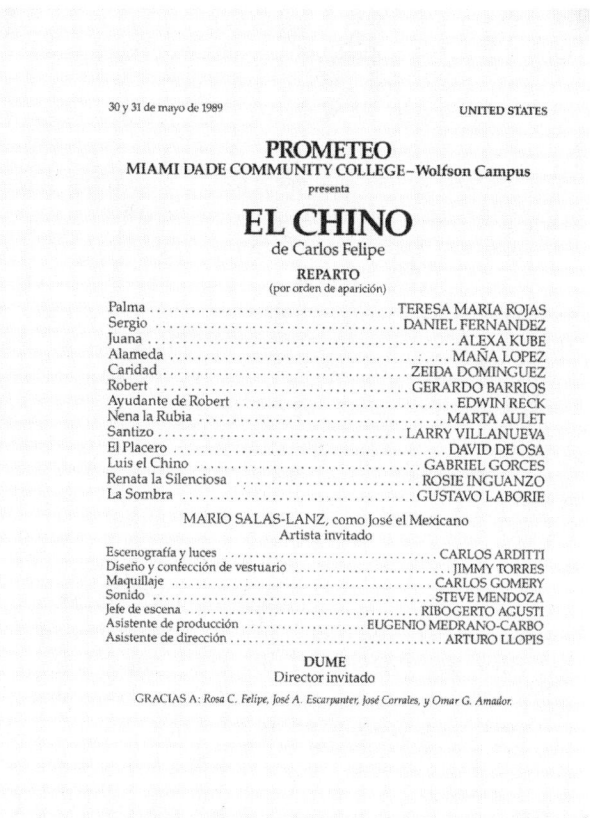

Poster for a United States production of Felipe's first produced play, which premiered in 1947, about a woman seeking the identity of a man with whom she spent one night of true love (courtesy of José A. Escarpanter)

a theatrical production. The text has a single act, and in it Felipe intensifies techniques that he has used before: flashbacks, the ocean theme, characters who are of popular extraction, a realist style of action that ends in the magical world, and the ambiguity that dominates in the ending.

The latter part of the 1950s produced a wave of small theaters in Havana known as *teatros de bolsillo* (pocket theaters), which preferred to produce small pieces with few characters, a single set, and contemporary themes. In 1957 Felipe, motivated by the new trend, wrote *Ladrillos de plata* (Silver Bricks), a work that met these requisites. The National Institute of Culture, created under the dictatorship of Fulgencio Batista, approved the debut of the work in the Palace of Fine Arts, but shortly after the beginning of rehearsals, the piece was canceled because some of the authorities considered the work to be immoral because a lady runs away with a bricklayer. The play was never produced. This frustrated debut was compensated in the following years by the publication of some other works. In 1959 Dolores Martí de Cid included *El travieso Jimmy* in the anthology *Teatro cubano contemporaneo* (Contemporary Cuban Theater), published in Madrid. Also in 1959, the Central University of Las Villas published a volume in which appeared *El chino, El travieso Jimmy,* and *Ladrillos de plata.*

Ladrillos de plata takes place in a country home where Morales, a well-to-do businessman, lives with his two children, Marta and Tonio. Marta is engaged to Gustavo, an architect who has just triumphed with a presentation of new urbanization. In this project a building will be constructed that will contain the new homes of both Morales and the young couple; but Tonio, an adolescent, objects because there has not been a place set aside for his mother, Lisia. Neither Morales nor Marta wants to remember Lisia, who abandoned them years ago and now lives in New York. Tonio, who frequently corresponds with his mother, insists, and the others finally accept his request. This situation is interrupted by the arrival of a bricklayer, Guillo, who has come to construct a brick bar in the salon. Marta supervises Guillo and suffers from his endless chatter. Upon Guillo's departure, Tonio discovers that Lisia is arriving without notice. This news is not well received by the others. Lisia explains that she was compelled by one of the frequent dreams that greatly affect her and felt the need to see her children. The others receive her with hostility, but Lisia finally is lodged in the house.

In spite of the fact that the piece is adapted to the theatrical requirements of the time, its subject matter differs from the comedies that were usually presented then. *Ladrillos de plata* juxtaposes two points of view: one that corresponds to the basic outlines of the upper middle class, governed by reason and good taste, represented by the Morales family and Gustavo; and the individualistic vision of Lisia, who lives in a disorderly, almost chaotic manner, becoming an irresponsible victim of her dreams. Lisia is driven to intense passions that are doomed to fail. However, like the phoenix, she is reborn before a new burst of her emotions. The play carefully describes both universes. In the first one, chance and passion do not fit. Lisia is a threat to this world. She depends on the irrationality of her dreams, in accord with the Freudian theories in vogue during those years. In this instance her irrationality takes the form of passion for a vulgar bricklayer, a character drawn from the popular sentimentalism of the boleros and endowed, at the time, with sexual attraction. When Lisia escapes with Guillo it seems that reason and order have returned to reign in the house, but the ending, as is characteristic of the author, is full of suggestions. Marta, raised according to the traditional guidelines, has observed her mother driven by the passion that she feels for this man, and for the first time she glimpses the fact that reason and order are not the only valid things in life. Using the mechanics of the salon comedy with this ending, Felipe destroys the ideological postulates of this genre.

In 1959 Pagrán published *Capricho en rojo* as part of their Cuban Stage collection. The following year, the Central University of Las Villas included *Réquiem por Yarini* in a volume dedicated to Cuban theater; the play debuted five years later.

Réquiem por Yarini consists of three acts and takes place in Havana on 22 November 1910 on the patio of one of the brothels overseen by Alejandro Yarini. Jabá, the house madam, is visited by the alms collector, Bebo La Reposa, who, in a fortune-telling ceremony following the guidelines of the Afro-Cuban deities, predicts that Yarini is going to be assassinated. Bebo (on a religious level) and Jabá (on a human level) take measures to prevent the crime from occurring. Yarini, a politician and a pimp, has enemies in both areas, especially Luis Lotot, another pimp, who arrives to discuss business. The situation is tense between the rivals, but inside the realm of prostitution is a code of honor that they follow. Lotot has come to offer Yarini some Frenchwomen who have recently arrived in exchange for Santiaguera, one of the women under Yarini's charge, but Yarini at the beginning does not accept the offer. Later he becomes interested in the watch chain carried by Lotot and decides to bet Santiaguera as the prize in a game of Chinese charades. This game consists of figuring out the opponent's riddle with one's eyes blindfolded. Yarini loses, and Lotot leaves with Santiaguera.

In the second act Santiaguera has run away from Lotot. Jabá receives news that the government, which is in crisis, has undertaken an intense campaign of public moralization, and Yarini and all the leaders of the Havana underworld are in danger. Yarini asks Jabá to seek protection for him from the spirit of Macorina, a notorious prostitute whom he has never met. Jabá again searches for Bebo, who brings an answer from the gods on how to prevent the predicted assassination: Yarini should leave the city as quickly as possible and should avoid a specific gesture in the next few hours–namely, looking behind him. Yarini is leaving when he hears voices in the hallway and, driven by a superior force, looks behind him and sees Santiaguera. At this precise moment someone knocks on the door, and when they ask who it is, a woman dressed in white responds: "Me dicen la Macorina" (They call me Macorina).

In the third act Jabá is horrified by this event and suspects that the spirit of Macorina is searching for Yarini in order to take him to the other world. Lotot arrives and challenges Yarini to a knife duel, which if survived would allow him possession of Santiaguera.

Yarini is killed, and Santiaguera, now docile, goes with Lotot.

Felipe, besides presenting the myth of Yarini in accordance with the canons of Greek and neoclassic tragedies, also follows the classic unities of time, action, and place. Yarini responds to the scheme of the tragic hero: one having an ambivalent psychology, with positive and negative qualities. He is arrogant and sure of himself, but he commits a tragic error: as the king of pimps, he falls in love with one of his women and is therefore punished with death. The other characters possess attributes inspired by the Greek tragedies. Santiaguera is reminiscent of Phaedra in Euripides' *Hippolytus:* an instrument of a supernatural being, in this case Macorina, the queen of the prostitutes, who wishes to unite herself with the most famous pimp. Jabá resembles Oedipus as she fights against the divine will, but like him, she ends up conquered, and in her relations with Yarini at times she adopts a tone similar to that of the nannies who advise and suffer through the conflicts of the protagonist. Lotot is the typical antagonist of the tragedy. Bebo has a purpose similar to Tiresias, the fortune-teller in the myth of Oedipus. Macorina is the supernatural force who subjects humans to her will, like Aphrodite in *Hippolytus.* The men and women in Yarini's house of prostitution follow the tradition of the classic chorus. In the third act they accompany a prayer of Jabá to Changó. The fact that the Santería is a polytheistic religion facilitates its identification with that of the Greeks; at the same time, the text gives it an unmistakably Cuban tone. *Réquiem por Yarini* is considered to be the author's masterpiece and is his play that has had the greatest number of productions not only in Cuba but in other Hispanic theaters in New York and Miami.

The Cuban Revolution that began in 1959 unleashed a wave of cultural politics that included the creation of theatrical groups. One of them, the National Dramatic Group, in 1961 hired Felipe for the job of literary consultant. The author, at fifty years of age, for the first time was able to dedicate himself entirely to theater. In 1963 *Unión,* the magazine of the Unión de Escritores y Artistas de Cuba (UNEAC, Union of Writers and Artists of Cuba), published the first scene of *Ibrahim,* a piece that the author did not finish.

In the published fragment, siblings Lena and Daniel are fixing up the old family home where Daniel and his fiancée, Cora, are going to live after the wedding. Lena tries to talk to her brother about some unknown aspects of Cora's life, but Daniel, who met her only fifteen days earlier and is completely in love with her, refuses to talk about them. Cora arrives, and after a friendly reception, the conversation turns to the facts that Lena has been able to compile about the mysterious girl. Cora had been at the point of marrying a distinguished professional, but shortly before the wedding, she became involved in a scandal at a house on the beach, where a man known as Ibrahim tried to kidnap and rape her, but Cora managed to flee.

The elements provided by the fragment suggest that the work would have had a structure similar to *Ladrillos de plata:* a single setting, a bourgeois atmosphere, and few characters. The title character does not appear in the action, according to the stage directions. The text suggests a plot in which intrigue, an infrequent element in Felipe's theater, is important. Daniel and Lena confront the problem of truth and its appearance in relation to the true identity of Cora. It can be hypothesized that Felipe was attempting to construct in *Ibrahim* a suspense play in the style of English and North American drama, with a key character who never intervenes in the action.

In 1963 *De película* (On Film) debuted. Although signed by Felipe, the play was actually the result of a collective undertaking by some members of the National Dramatic Group under the direction of French playwright Pierre Chausat. The participation of Felipe was limited to the writing and arranging of the dialogues and monologues in different scenes from the improvisations of the interpreters and to composing song lyrics. Although not a particularly representative work in Felipe's theater, it was the work that gave him the most fame and popularity through its extraordinary success; it was also well received by the critics.

The libretto offers a brief history of cinema in a tone somewhere between didactic and satirical. In its two parts, movie star Charlie Chaplin appears alongside German expressionist cinema and the genres of the Old West, musical comedies, gangster movies, French intellectual theater, and science fiction. Also included is the phenomenon of the North American star system.

In 1964 Felipe wrote *Los compadres,* which debuted shortly afterward and constituted his last known work. Everything seems to indicate that the piece is the response of the dramatist to the politics of the National Council of Culture, which for some years promoted daily matters among Cuban writers. Nevertheless, it is in certain respects a work of circumstance. It has been perceived as the third part of a trilogy titled "El tren por mi noche criolla" (The Train Through My Creole Night), of which the first two parts are unknown. In an interview Felipe stated: "Le he prestado mucha atención a la ciudad y ahora quiero ir al folklore, al campo, al paisaje, buscando un nuevo vocabulario popular, aunque no populista, incorporando a la escena al negro y su música" (I have paid much attention to the city and now I want to move to the folklore, the country, the landscape, searching for a new common vocabulary,

Poster for a United States production of Felipe's play (published in 1960, premiered in 1965) about the last hours of a brothel owner in 1910 Havana (courtesy of José A. Escarpanter)

although not popular, incorporating on stage the black culture and its music). This statement is surprising in its second part, since black and Cuban folklore elements had already been integrated by Felipe in his theater since *Tambores* but not with the rural and provincial atmosphere. In *Los compadres* the dramatist accomplishes a dissection of the world of provinces, loaded with ironies.

The work is in one act and takes place at a train station in a town in the interior of the island during the chaos of the full-blown Cuban Revolution of the 1960s. A young militiaman arrives at the station with specific instructions to board on the next train two passengers: a lady and a priest, who are leaving the country like many other Cubans. Caela, the lady, appears, but without the priest. A humble peasant named Indio who lives in the mountains arrives with his newborn daughter. He has just lost his wife in childbirth, and his daughter is dying. He is desperately searching for the priest so that the baby can be baptized before her death. Father Servando arrives just as the whistles of the train are heard. At first the priest refuses to baptize the infant because the train will only stop for two minutes, but Indio and Caela insist. The ticket clerk and the militiaman, violating their orders, stop the train so that the baptism can be done. Caela, who never has been able to have children, offers to be the godmother and obliges the militiaman to be the godfather. The baptism is concluded, and as if by a miracle, the child appears to recuperate. Caela decides to cancel the trip and stay behind in order to care for the child. She joins Indio, and both depart with the child toward a humble dwelling in the mountains.

Without the miraculous recovery of the child following the baptism, the piece would be completely orthodox realism. Although melodramatic sentimentalism abounds in the character of Indio, the other main characters, Caela and the militiaman, share a psychology that removes the work from the outlines of the socialist realism that was encouraged in the Cuban art of that time. Both become godparents to the daughter of Indio, through the respect that they feel toward the human being, beyond any ideological conviction. The militiaman, a product of the new political situation, who has lived the humiliation of being disowned by his family, agrees to unite himself with Caela in a religious ceremony in which he apparently does not believe. Caela is not inhumane, as the rich are often portrayed in social realism. Her decision, a consequence of her frustrated maternal instinct and not the result of a dose of political conscience, gives her an intensely human dimension. *Los compadres* does not present the complexities of thought that Felipe's most representative works have, but it conserves the ideal of human fraternity that appears in his first texts.

In 1965 *Réquiem por Yarini* finally debuted, and two years later UNEAC published a volume of plays that included *Los compadres*. The events of those times were quite different from those at the beginning of the revolution. The government enacted strict guidelines for all aesthetic expressions. After Felipe's sister, Rosa, went into exile because she was not pleased with the Cuban Revolution, the dramatist withdrew even more from his family. His health declined; he suffered from emphysema but did not quit smoking. His mother passed away on 8 November 1974. One year later, in the early hours of 14 October 1975, the writer died in a hospital in Havana. Several critics state that Felipe continued writing in his final years, but at his death nothing was found among his scattered papers.

In the field of Cuban literature, Felipe belongs to the generation of the 1940s, which suffered the consequences of the world economic crisis of 1929, the struggles against the dictatorship of Machado, and the frustration with the revolutionary ideals at the hands of another dictator: Batista. These historical conditions caused this generation to exhibit two attitudes: political/social rebellion or avoidance, the need to escape, which is the tendency that was predominant and ended up globally defining these writers. Felipe brings both of these attitudes to his theater.

Felipe, beginning with his first works, explored many themes, characters, and techniques that were elaborated in a quiet and patient manner over some twenty-five years. Even though some critics have insisted that Felipe's most meaningful theme is the recuperation of the past, his principal concern is the incessant search for happiness. Although the characters are compelled to rescue the past, this attempt is not for the past itself but rather to rediscover that single moment in which happiness was achieved, a type of dazzling magic. Happiness in Felipe's theater can be a sentimental erotic culmination, a profound friendship that survives death, or placid filial love. Happiness does not appear as an absolute concept but rather is conditioned by a determined moment, which is modified by the incessant passage of time. Thus, according to Felipe, complete and lasting happiness ends up being unreachable in this life.

Felipe's second important theme is the presence of magic in daily life. Two influences can be noted in this regard: one is intellectual and European in origin, the other is a product of Cuban social reality. The first originates in the European symbolist theater, especially that of Maeterlinck. The second comes from two defining traits of the Cuban culture: spiritualistic beliefs and Afro-Cuban religion, which emerged from the syncretism of African dogmas with Catholic hagiography. These spiritual forces can cause a metamorphosis: a prostitute is changed into a dove in *Tambores*, and nocturnal butterflies become evil beings in *La bruja en el obenque*. The existence of magical places is made possible where the most profound wishes are achieved; superstitions are fulfilled; communication with the dead is natural; and the African divinities can decide the destiny of mortals.

It has been often stated that Carlos Felipe loyally followed the three classical unities of the Renaissance in his dramatic technique. While his texts reveal a certain preference for this schematic, it should be noted that there are many novelties introduced within this canon. For example, there is the use of flashback, open endings, and circular structure. These and other techniques demonstrate that Felipe was one of the most experimental dramatists of his time in Hispanic America.

Interviews:

Reynaldo González, "Diálogo con Carlos Felipe," *Bohemia*, 28 May 1965, p. 32;

Matías Montes Huidobro, "Carlos Felipe. Entrevista a una voz necesaria," in his *El teatro cubano en el vórtice del compromiso, 1959–1961* (Miami: Universal, 2002), pp. 279–283.

References:

Ada Abdo, "Teatro *versus* cine: *De Película* de Carlos Felipe," *La Gaceta de Cuba* (January 1964): 15;

Concepción Alzola, "Lectura de Yarini," in *Festchrift José Cid Pérez*, edited by Helio Alba-Buffill (New York: Senda Nueva de Ediciones, 1981), pp. 111–117;

José Cid Pérez, "Cincuenta años de teatro cubano," *Carteles*, 18 May 1952, pp. 188–189;

Armando Correa, "Carlos Felipe: Encuentro con la imagen," *Tablas* (January–March 1984): 13–21;

Soledad Cruz, "*Teatro* de Carlos Felipe: Un esfuerzo que hay que continuar," *Conjunto*, 42 (1979): 110–111;

Frank N. Dauster, "Cuban Drama Today," *Modern Drama*, 9, no. 2 (1966): 153–164;

Dauster, *Historia del teatro hispanoamericano. Siglos XIX y XX* (Mexico City: De Andrea, 1973), pp. 125–126;

Francisco Beverido Duhalt, "Teatro en el teatro: Dos casos cubanos," *Texto crítico*, 10 (1978): 126–135;

José A. Escarpanter, "El teatro de Carlos Felipe," *Revista Nacional de Teatro*, 1, no. 1 (1961): 26–27;

Natividad González-Freire, "*Réquiem por Yarini* de Carlos Felipe," *Revolución*, 18 May 1965, p. 9;

González-Freire, *Teatro cubano (1927–1961)* (Havana: Ministerio de Relaciones Exteriores, 1961), pp. 114–118;

Rine Leal, *Breve historia del teatro cubano* (Havana: Letras Cubanas, 1980), pp. 139–140;

Leal, *En primera persona (1954–1966)* (Havana: Instituto del Libro, 1976), pp. 189–201;

Leonel López Nussa, "Releyendo a Yarini," *Unión*, 1, no. 3–4 (1982): 86–96;

José Lorenzo Fuentes, "Yarini entra en escena," *El Mundo del Domingo*, 16 May 1965, pp. 6–7;

Bertha Maig, "Figuras de nuestra escena: Carlos Felipe," *Prometeo*, 19 (1949): 9;

Eduardo Manet, "Actitud y obra de Carlos Felipe," *Estudios*, 1 (1950): 46–47;

Manet, "*Tambores* de Carlos Felipe," *Prometeo*, 10 (1948): 20;

Dolores Martí de Cid, ed., *Teatro cubano contemporáneo* (Madrid: Aguilar, 1959), pp. 157–160;

Julio Matas, "Pirandello, Proust and *El chino* by Carlos Felipe," *Hispanic Journal*, 5, no. 1 (1983): 43–47;

Matías Montes Huidobro, *Persona, vida y máscara en el teatro cubano* (Miami: Universal, 1973), pp. 113–131, 254–255, 283–303, 350–351;

Mario Parajón, "Al oído de Carlos Felipe," *El Mundo*, 13 May 1965, p. 4;

José Manuel Valdés Rodríguez, "*Réquiem por Yarini*," *El Mundo*, 9–11 May 1965, p. 6;

Cintio Vitier, "Eros en los infiernos," *Revista de la Biblioteca Nacional José Martí* (1968): 168–175.

Griselda Gambaro
(28 July 1928 -)

Sandra Messinger Cypess
University of Maryland

PLAY PRODUCTIONS: *El desatino,* Buenos Aires, Sala de Experimentación Audiovisual del Instituto Torcuato Di Tella, 27 August 1965;

Matrimonio, Buenos Aires, Teatro 35 de Buenos Aires, 1966; produced again as *Viaje de invierno,* Buenos Aires, Centro Cultural of San Martín Theater, 1985;

Las paredes, Buenos Aires, Agón Theater, 11 April 1966;

Los siameses, Buenos Aires, Sala de Experimentación Audiovisual del Instituto Torcuato Di Tella, 25 August 1967;

El campo, Buenos Aires, SHA [Hebrew Society of Argentina], 11 October 1968;

Cuatro ejercicios para actrices, Rosario, Santa Fé, Teatro la Rivera, 1970;

Nada que ver, Buenos Aires, Teatro Municipal General San Martín, April 1972;

Sólo un aspecto, Buenos Aires, Sala del Departamento de Extensión Universitaria, Universidad de Buenos Aires, 1974;

El viaje a Bahía Blanca, Buenos Aires, Teatro Magnus, 1975;

El nombre, Bueno Aires, Teatro Estrellas, 1976;

Sucede lo que pasa, Buenos Aires, Teatro Popular de la Ciudad de Buenos Aires, 28 April 1976;

Decir sí, Buenos Aires, Teatro Picadero, 28 July 1981;

La malasangre, Buenos Aires, Olimpia Theater, 17 August 1982;

Real envido, Buenos Aires, Teatro Odeón, January 1983;

Del sol naciente, Buenos Aires, Teatro Lorange, September 1984;

Puesta en claro, Buenos Aires, Teatro Payró, July 1986;

Antígona furiosa, Buenos Aires, Goethe Institute, September 1986;

Morgan, Buenos Aires, Teatro Municipal General San Martín, 7 September 1989;

Efectos personales, Madrid, Teatro Alfil, 30 March 1990;

Penas sin importancia, Buenos Aires, Sala Cunil Cabanellas in Teatro San Martín Teatro Municipal, 5 October 1990;

Griselda Gambaro (photograph by Lucas Distéfano; from the dust jacket for Después del día de fiesta, *1994; Thomas Cooper Library, University of South Carolina)*

Putting Two and Two Together, London, Royal Court, 4 July 1991;

La casa sin sosiego, by Gambaro and Gerardo Gandini, Buenos Aires, Teatro Municipal General San Martín, 1992;

Información para extranjeros, Mexico City, El Foro de la Comedia (Colonia Roma), 1993;

Es necesario entender un poco, Buenos Aires, Teatro Municipal General San Martín, 28 June 1995;

Falta de modestia, Buenos Aires, Teatro Municipal General San Martín, 1998;

De profesión maternal, Buenos Aires, Teatro del Pueblo, June 1999;

Dar la vuelta, Buenos Aires, Teatro Municipal General San Martín, 1999;

En la columna, Buenos Aires, El Portón de Sánchez, July 2001;

Lo que va dictando el sueño, Buenos Aires, Teatro Municipal General San Martín, August 2002.

BOOKS: *Cuentos* (Buenos Aires: Américalee, 1953);

Madrigal en ciudad (Buenos Aires: Goyanarte, 1963);

El desatino: Cuentos (Buenos Aires: Emecé, 1965);

El desatino: 2 actos (Buenos Aires: Centro De Experimentación Audiovisual del Instituto Torcuato Di Tella, 1965);

El campo (Buenos Aires: Insurrexit, 1967); translated by William I. Oliver as *The Camp,* in *Voices of Change in the Spanish American Theater* (Austin: University of Texas Press, 1971), pp. 47–103;

Los siameses (Buenos Aires: Insurrexit, 1967);

Una felicidad con menos pena (Buenos Aires: Sudamericana, 1968);

Nada que ver con otra historia (Buenos Aires: Noé, 1972);

La cola mágica (Buenos Aires: Ediciones de la Flor, 1975);

Ganarse la muerte (Buenos Aires: Ediciones de la Flor, 1976);

Conversaciones con chicos: Sobre la sociedad, los padres, los afectos, la cultura (Buenos Aires: Timerman, 1977);

Dios no nos quiere contentos (Barcelona: Lumen, 1979);

Teatro: Las paredes; El desatino; Los siameses (Barcelona: Argonauta, 1979);

Teatro: Nada que ver; Sucede lo que pasa, edited by Miguel Angel Giella, Peter Roster, and Leandro Urbina (Ottawa: Girol, 1983);

Lo impenetrable (Buenos Aires: Torres Agüero, 1984); translated by Evelyn Picon Garfield as *The Impenetrable Madam X* (Detroit: Wayne State Press, 1991);

Teatro 1: Real envido; La malasangre; Del sol naciente (Buenos Aires: Ediciones de la Flor, 1984);

Teatro 2: Dar la vuelta; Información para extranjeros; Puesta en claro; Sucede lo que pasa (Buenos Aires: Ediciones de la Flor, 1987);

Teatro 3: Viaje en invierno; Nosferatu; Cuatro ejercicios para actrices: Un día especial, Si tengo suerte, La que sigue, Oficina; Acuerdo para cambiar la casa; Sólo un aspecto; La gracia; El miedo; El nombre; El viaje a Bahía Blanca; El despojamiento; Decir sí; Antígona furiosa (Buenos Aires: Ediciones de la Flor, 1989);

Teatro 4: Las paredes; El desatino; Los siameses; El campo; Nada que ver (Buenos Aires: Ediciones de la Flor, 1990);

Teatro 5: Efectos personales; Desafiar al destino; Morgan; Penas sin importancia (Buenos Aires: Ediciones de la Flor, 1991);

La casa sin sosiego: Opera de camara sobre un libreto de Griselda Gambaro, by Gambaro and Gerardo Gandini (Buenos Aires: Ricordi, 1992);

Después del día de fiesta (Buenos Aires: Seix Barral, 1994);

Teatro 6: Atando cabos; La casa sin sosiego; Es necesario entender un poco (Buenos Aires: Ediciones de la Flor, 1996);

Lo mejor que se tiene (Buenos Aires: Grupo Editorial Norma, 1998);

Escritos inocentes (Buenos Aires: Grupo Editorial Norma, 1999);

El mar que nos trajo (Buenos Aires: Grupo Editorial Norma, 2001);

Teatro: Falta de modestia; Mi querida; De profesión maternal; Pedir demasiado; Lo que va dictando el sueño (Buenos Aires: Grupo Editorial Norma, 2002);

Gran Nariz y el rey de los seiscientos nombres (Buenos Aires: Alfaguara/Santillana, 2003);

La señora Macbeth: Teatro (Buenos Aires: Grupo Editorial Norma, 2003);

Promesas y desvaríos (Buenos Aires: Grupo Editorial Norma, 2004);

Teatro 7: No hay normales; En la columna; Pisar el palito; Para llevarle a Rosita; Cinco ejercicios para un actor; Almas (Buenos Aires: Ediciones de la Flor, 2004).

Editions in English: *Information for Foreigners: Three Plays,* edited and translated by Marguerite Feitlowitz (Evanston, Ill.: Northwestern University Press, 1992)—comprises *The Walls; Information for Foreigners;* and *Antigona Furiosa;*

Loose Ends, translated by Catherine Boyle, *Travesía: Journal of Latin American Cultural Studies,* 1, no. 1 (1992): 118–144;

Bad Blood, translated by Feitlowitz (Woodstock, Ill.: Dramatic Publishing, 1994);

Saying Yes, translated by Sebastian Doggart, in *Latin American Plays: New Drama from Argentina, Cuba, Mexico and Peru,* edited by Doggart (London: Nick Hern, 1996), pp. 85–100;

Strip, translated by Ana Puga, in *Holy Terrors: Latin American Women Perform,* edited by Diana Taylor and Roselyn Costantino (Durham, N.C.: Duke University Press, 2003).

SELECTED PERIODICAL PUBLICATIONS–UNCOLLECTED:

NONFICTION

"¿Es posible y deseable una dramaturgia específicamente femenina?" *Latin American Theatre Review,* 13 (1980): 17–21;

"Voracidad o canibalismo amoroso," *Quimera: Revista de Literatura,* 24 (1982): 50–51;

"Algunas consideraciones sobre la mujer y la literatura," *Revista Iberoamericana,* 51, no. 132–133 (1985): 471–473;

"Del texto dramático al escenario," by Gambaro, Osvaldo Quiroga, Alejandra Boero, Cecilio Madanes, and Guillermo de la Torre, *La Nación,* Suplemento literario, 8 September 1985, pp. 1–2;

"Los rostros del exilio," *Alba de América: Revista Literaria,* 7, no. 12–13 (1989): 31–35.

The general consensus among critics of Latin American theater is that Griselda Gambaro is one of the most important dramatists of Argentina and Latin America. She is often categorized as the leading Argentine woman playwright, and critics call her the "great matriarch of Argentine Theater," but most agree that she is an outstanding figure in comparison with all writers, and her plays are among those most often produced abroad.

Gambaro was born in La Boca, the section of Buenos Aires that is the port area, on 28 July 1928, to Isabel Russo and José Gambaro. She was the only daughter in a home with four older brothers. Her family has its roots in Italy, and she keeps a reference to her Italian origins by refusing to add a written accent to the spelling of her last name, although she prefers to pronounce the name with the stress on the first syllable. She was raised in a family with limited economic means; her father was first a sailor before becoming a postal worker. Gambaro went to work in the business office of a publishing company right after high school. When she was twenty-five she published *Cuentos* (1953, Tales), a collection of short stories that she prefers not to acknowledge because they do not meet her high standards for her own work; she dates her more acceptable production from *Madrigal en ciudad* (1963, Madrigal in the City), a collection of three novellas. This volume won a prize, El Fondo Nacional de las Artes, in 1963. Because of the prestige of this award, especially for a young woman, she was able to enter the world of theater and see her plays produced from that time onward. She is one of the few dramatists who can earn sufficiently to live off her productions, publications, and translations of her plays and fiction. She is married to the sculptor Juan Carlos Distéfano, with whom she has two children—Andrea, born in 1961, and Lucas, born in 1965.

In the 1960s Gambaro began writing the kind of political plays for which she later became famous on an international scale. Her plays and narratives were consistently awarded prizes in Argentina in those early years. A collection of narrative pieces, *El desatino: Cuentos* (1965, The Blunder: Tales) was awarded the Premio Emecé in 1964; in the same year, a play, *Las paredes* (The Walls; produced in 1966, published in 1979) garnered the Premio de las Asociación de Teatros and El Fondo Nacional de las Artes.

The early plays of the 1960s do not refer to Argentine reality in an obvious way, and the characters do not use the *voseo,* or Argentine manner of speaking Spanish that characterizes the River Plate region. Her first play to be staged, *El desatino* (produced and published in 1965), was adapted from one of the stories in the volume with that title. It caused a sensation among theatergoers in Buenos Aires because of its innovative, nonrealistic approach that echoed aspects of techniques used in the European Theater of the Absurd, as Tamara Holzapfel noted in one of the first essays on Gambaro's plays (1970). *El desatino* was acknowledged as the best national drama of 1965 by the publication *Teatro.* The outline of the plot is a recurring pattern in Gambaro's early plays: an average man is thrust into an inexplicable, frightening situation and is confronted by adversaries who, in this case, turn out to be intimates and members of his own family. *El desatino* reveals Gambaro's skill at creating a deceptively absurdist situation, while her real target is the nature of Argentine political realities.

Protagonist Alfonso awakens one morning to find that an iron block attached to his foot immobilizes him, preventing him from going about his ordinary affairs. He has no idea how this artifact became attached to his foot, and he does not question its presence, much like Gregor Samsa of Franz Kafka's *Metamorphosis* (1915) did not question his transformation into a cockroach. The play shows a series of encounters in which Alfonso is each time further encumbered by the metal piece, yet he receives no help from his mother or his best friend. Rather, they do what they can to restrict his actions even more. His mother complains to Alfonso constantly about her domestic and maternal roles, but she never fulfills those roles in an expected manner. She refuses to comply with any of her son's requests, whether he asks her to bring him the tools that might help him free his foot, or to make a telephone call, or simply to stop wearing the clothes and other items he has bought for his wife, Lily, whose appearance recalls a stereotypical blonde Hollywood sex queen. Lily rarely enters onstage, but when she does, she is as cold to Alfonso as his mother is. The mother blames Alfonso not only for her own problems but for his as well, repeating a paradigmatic behavior of holding the victim responsible for the circumstances that led to his own victimization. Alfonso ends up almost an automaton, unable to act independently, refusing assistance from the one person who might help him—a young man whom critics suggest represents the Argentine working class.

A variation of the early pattern is found in *Las paredes,* the first play she wrote and acknowledges as part of her repertoire. Instead of a young man in his home being mistreated by family, an unnamed youth is waylaid by strangers after returning from an innocuous day in the country. The tone of the opening scene recalls Kafka's *The Trial* (1914): a Young Man is detained against his will for offenses that are not explained to him. The details of his confinement are consistently reinterpreted by the Functionary and the Usher who are his keepers. Although he appears to be in a luxurious room, he discovers that all is not as it seems, for the curtain covers not a window but a brick wall. When he hears agonizing screams emanating from beyond the room he is in, the Usher tells him that the walls had closed in on the other detainees. The Young Man does not believe this matter-of-fact explanation, and gradually he is manipulated by his captors to the extent that he has no sense of reality or deception. Gambaro skillfully dramatizes the transition of the Young Man to the condition of almost mindless automaton. She creates a series of repetitions of events with minor variations so that each slightly changed episode drives the Young Man further down the road to his ultimate degradation as a human being.

The mental collapse of the Young Man is reflected in a parallel degradation of the physical surroundings. The walls are literally closing in on him, a fact that the audience perceives; the initially well-appointed bedroom becomes progressively less comfortable, with fewer furnishings, and always smaller in actual space. Although each encounter with his adversaries, dressed in military uniforms, is a new frustration, the Young Man continues to accept their degrading treatment, hoping that compliance will bring about his freedom. By the time the Young Man is told that the walls will fall on him at midnight, he is already so crushed mentally that he rejects that admission of reality. In the light of the Dirty War (the period of military dictatorship between 1976 and 1983, during which as many as thirty thousand Argentine dissidents were killed or "disappeared") and the many descriptions of real physical and mental torture perpetrated by the military, Gambaro's first produced play seems prophetic; but in a 1971 personal conversation with Sandra Messinger Cypess she also said that she wrote it as a result of events in Córdoba, Argentina, during the early 1960s, at which time there was already political repression in Argentine politics.

Reading as a non-Argentine, the translator and critic Marguerite Feitlowitz (1990) believes that, for an audience with no history of military dictatorship, this play also presents an exploration of a metaphysical question concerning the nature of being. The Young Man represents any human being caught at a time in which he is enjoying his sense of freedom. This freedom is not absolute, since humans have certain obligations and fears that control their free will, and even this limited sense of freedom is shown to be illusory. At any moment one can be seized by inexplicable powers beyond one's control, as represented by the Functionary and the Usher. The question is not whether the end will come, but when. The Young Man's behavior shows one approach to this danger, when he becomes paralyzed into inaction. This nonpoliticized reading is possible, but most critics from 1976 onward more commonly refer to the political interpretations of Gambaro's plays.

In *Los siameses* (The Siamese Twins, produced and published in 1967) the victimizer successfully oppresses the victim, only to fall victim himself at the end. Although Lorenzo suggests that Ignacio is his separated Siamese twin, the stage directions indicate that they do not act or look alike. What their interactions show is that Ignacio allows himself to be the victim of the machinations of Lorenzo, who implicates Ignacio in several offenses against neighbors. Escalating his victimization of Ignacio, Lorenzo falsely accuses Ignacio of malfeasance and brings the police to their home. After the false bills that Lorenzo concealed in Ignacio's suitcase are discovered by the police, Ignacio is imprisoned as a counterfeiter. Lorenzo feels remorse and visits the prison to find out about Ignacio's fate. He discovers that Ignacio died after being tortured, and his body is being readied for burial. In the last action of the play, Lorenzo is curled up in a fetal position in the same cart in which he had brought the body of Ignacio for burial. Although he calls out Ignacio's name and attempts to move, he cannot engage in independent action now that Ignacio is dead. His position is not much different from that of the Young Man or Alfonso, or Ignacio.

In 1968 the play *El campo* (In the Country; published in 1967, produced in 1968; translated as *The Camp,* 1971), was honored with the Premio Municipal de la Ciudad de Buenos Aires. That play, one of Gambaro's most renowned, also received the Premio Revista Talía and prizes from Semanario Teatral del Aire, Radio Municipal de la Ciudad de Buenos Aires, and Argentores, Sociedad General de Autores de la Argentina. Just as the preceding plays do not openly refer to Argentine society, *El campo* also includes no explicit references to a specific time or geographic location. The setting suggests that the characters are in the country, in a place of leisure activity, but soon the menacing acts gradually increase. Irony and counterpoint create an atmosphere of confusion and terror in which the characters and the audience are made to mistrust, then fear, whatever is seen, heard, and done.

Martin, a bookkeeper, is sent to the country on assignment; he is met by Franco, who behaves as if he is in charge of the establishment to which Martin had been sent. Franco's actions reflect the associations of his name with Francisco Franco, the dictator of Spain; he also wears a Gestapo uniform, and the dress of another character, Emma, looks as if she had come from a Nazi concentration camp. Franco manipulates both Emma and Martin, and the audience perceives that Franco's mistreatment of Emma appears to foreshadow Martin's fate. Emma purports to be a concert pianist, but feigns the performance instead of actually giving one. The concert scene at the end of act 1 is a grotesque mockery of a piano recital. Characters in prison garb enter, along with SS troops; although Emma's efforts to play are frustrated, Martin is forced to sit, stand, and move his head like a puppet according to the directives of the soldiers. He becomes an automaton, much like Emma, bullied and beaten. Act 2 begins with the two of them apparently free of their oppressors, and Franco even reappears and tells them to leave the "camp" and return home. Although Martin and Emma do accept the invitation to leave, Franco's henchmen follow them to Martin's home. They enter his space to menace him, questioning him about his identity, playing with him as if he were prey that will be easily captured. The men subdue Martin when they inject him with some potion that renders him helpless, and they are about to use a branding iron on him when the play ends. The final scenes are even more intimidating and threatening than those of the earlier plays. Like Alfonso, Martin is in his own home when his victimization occurs, although the oppressors are not of his own family but rather military men.

In 1967 Gambaro's novel *Una felicidad con menos pena* (1968, A Happiness with Less Pain) received honorable mention in a competition held by Editorial Sudamericana. In 1968 she was invited to the United States on an International Exchange Program, the first of many visits abroad, especially to Spain, France, and Italy. Her first visit to Europe was to Italy in 1969, where she stayed until September 1970, at which time she returned to Argentina.

In *Sólo un aspecto* (Only One Aspect; produced in 1974; first published in the periodical *La palabra y el hombre* in 1973) the audience at first sees only one aspect to the characters, true to the title. The audience soon learns, however, that it is not appropriate to judge someone based on a single perspective, and that one should evaluate all the possible evidence before deciding who might be the adversary, who the ally. The two characters who initiate the action, the married couple Titina and Javier, are waiting for their friend Rolo, and when he arrives at their apartment, they react to him as if he were a feared authoritarian figure. Soon after Rolo arrives, however, the dynamic changes, and Titina and Javier begin to mistreat him, tying him up, then torturing him, burning him with a cigarette, and attacking him in various ways until he dies. Although Titina and Javier act at first like victims, in the end, Rolo is their victim. Their strategy is to denigrate Rolo so he is an acceptable target, a procedure that reflects tactics of the military dictatorship, which first dehumanized the people who became their victims. *Sólo un aspecto* offers a warning to Argentines to beware of those who offer to protect the people from the "enemy," since too often, the very people who were supposed to be protected become that "enemy."

In 1972 Gambaro's novel *Nada que ver con otra historia* (Nothing to Do With Any Other Story) was published, and a stage version titled *Nada que ver* (Nothing To See, published in 1983) was produced at Casacuberta Hall of the Teatro Municipal General San Martín. Gambaro considered this production a breakthrough, since for a while after that she was able to move beyond small experimental theater spaces and open her plays in good theaters of three hundred to four hundred seats. Her access to such venues was curtailed, however, during the time of the military dictatorship, and Gambaro was not able to open her plays because she had been blacklisted. Although the novel and play show some differences in plot and detail, both reflect Gambaro's reworking of the Frankenstein story as it applies to Argentina. Both texts are filled with black humor and parody not only Mary Shelley's original novel but also the Hollywood versions of Frankenstein's monster. While Gambaro has often alternated between the two genres, writing fiction and then transposing its theme into a dramatic form, since 1972 she has dedicated herself more to dramas, although she continues to produce provocative novels that also have political themes.

One of Gambaro's most innovative and daring plays is *Información para extranjeros* (Information for Foreigners; published in 1987, produced in 1993), the subject matter of which reveals both Gambaro's courage and her prophetic disposition. For Feitlowitz the play is a masterpiece in which Gambaro anticipates the emphasis on torture and oppression by the military on the one hand, and the silent conformism of the Argentine populace on the other. Written in the early 1970s, before the excesses of the Dirty War, the play nevertheless incorporates so many concrete details about the nature of military repression—daily violent acts of kidnappings, torture, and murder—that she was not able to publish it until 1987, and it has not been staged in Argentina to date (it premiered instead in Mexico City). Although

Jorge Petraglia as Lorenzo in the 1967 premiere of Gambaro's play Los siameses *(The Siamese Twins) at the Instituto Torcuato Di Tella in Buenos Aires (from* Los siameses, *1967; Thomas Cooper Library, University of South Carolina)*

the title of this play suggests that she is not addressing her countrymen, the content in effect deconstructs that impression and is more akin to the inversions suggested in *Nada que ver,* since the play does have everything to do with Argentine reality, as Feitlowitz observes.

The play is a collage of twenty-one vignettes; the continuity of the action is based on the literal movement of the audience through the rooms of a house. The stage directions specify that the action take place in a real house, if possible, so that the audience members can be divided into small groups and directed by actor guides who lead them through the house along different routes. As the audience members follow their guides, they enter various rooms and view different kinds of activities. In the final scene, the different groups of spectators reassemble, having completed their tour of this "foreign" country. The spectators witness mostly uncomfortable and menacing events: reenactments of kidnappings, murders, beatings, and torture. They come upon a scientific experiment in progress, which is a representation of the Stanley Milgram experiment, in which the scientist from Yale attempted to study the willingness of subjects to inflict torture and punishment on others. In another scene, children play typical Argentine games of childhood; yet, the games end up frightening the children, suggesting the underlying dangers of everyday life. The space through which the audience walks becomes a symbol of the country in which the audience resides. The dividing line between "reality" and "theater" is erased as the spectators are forced to leave the traditional darkness of the theater and their comfortable seats. Whereas at times Gambaro offers a narrow focus on the problem of individual passivity and collusion with oppressors, in *Información para extranjeros* she gives a broader, richly detailed view of what she considers a basic Argentine defect—conformism and the role it plays in permitting tyranny and injustice to flourish.

Sucede lo que pasa (It So Happens That It Happens, or What Happens Is What's Happening; produced in 1976, published in 1983), which received the Premio Argentores in 1976, is a two-act play that signals another change in tone for Gambaro. No clear-cut division between victimizer and victim exists, and the political allegory is attenuated in contrast to the plays of the 1960s. Just as *Información para extranjeros* had included intertextual references to William Shakespeare's *Othello* (circa 1604), Gabriel García Lorca's plays, and Tin Pan Alley songs, the title of this play is a reference to a poem by the Portuguese poet Fernando Pessoa, in which there is a line that says: "Nada es premio, sucede lo que pasa" (Nothing is a prize, what happens is what's happening). The play subverts the idea that the person who apparently has the power has the final say. Gambaro explores power relations among a small group of people who know each other and live on the margins of society.

In this play Teresa is the sister of Tito, a petty thief manqué, and as she interacts with the other three men who show up in her home, she appears to be a flirt, a liar, and a manipulator of their sexual interest in her. As soon as Tito's friend César enters the apartment, Teresa feigns illness and gets him so worried that he runs to bring a doctor to the house. Just as her illness is feigned, so is her interest in both the doctor and César. The only authentic emotion she expresses is her dislike for Zamora, an older man who is the boss in the ring of thieves to which Tito and César belong. Zamora appears to be in love with Teresa, but she always brushes him off. The audience learns in a scene between the two of them that he apparently raped her when she was fifteen. Her manipulation of the other men, then, can be seen as an attempt at revenge against all men, except for her brother. Teresa's emotions come to the fore in her interactions with Tito, who is genuinely ill.

Because they live on the edge of poverty, Tito never gets proper medical attention. The stage directions specify that in each subsequent scene he is to look increasingly unwell, so that it should be apparent by the last act that he will be dying soon. Both Tito and Teresa have kept from each other the secret hurts of their lives. Teresa never said openly that she had been raped by Zamora, but Tito probably would not have reacted, since Zamora is his boss and the little money that he gives them is how they manage to eke out a living. Tito has always complained of feeling ill, but it was not convenient for Teresa to accept his sickness until almost the end. At the conclusion, Tito admits that he does not want to die, and he wishes that Teresa would accept Zamora's invitation to live off of him so they can escape their poverty and he would have an opportunity to get well. Teresa refuses to sell herself, however, even to save Tito, and Tito finally agrees to accept his fate as it is. Teresa acts far more ethically strong than she appeared at the beginning of the play, and Tito, too, seems to have grown morally in spite of his debilitated physical state. Zamora, who expected his money to buy him what he wanted—Teresa as a companion and Tito as an errand boy—discovers that some people will not sell out.

Sucede lo que pasa was staged a month after the military coup bringing General Jorge Rafael Videla to power. Even though Gambaro continued to write during the time of the so-called Proceso de Reorganización Nacional (Process of National Reorganization) or the Dirty War, she soon found herself on a list of prohibited writers when Videla himself placed her novel *Ganarse la muerte* (1976, To Earn One's Death) on a blacklist because he deemed it subversive according to the military junta's values. Nevertheless, in 1976 Gambaro was invited to launch publication of the French version, *Gagner sa mort,* which was a success. The novel tells the horrifying story of a girl, Cledy, who suffers from sexual abuse that continues throughout her life. As Gambaro recounted in an interview with Kathleen Betsko and Rachel Koening (1987), it was forbidden to sell the novel or have it circulate in any way. Unlike many of her own dramatic characters, Gambaro and her family managed to escape from personal danger by going to Barcelona in 1977.

While in Barcelona, she did not write plays but was able to write two novels, *Dios no nos quiere contentos* (1979, God Does Not Want Us Content) and *Lo impenetrable* (1984; translated as *The Impenetrable Madam X,* 1991). While *Dios no nos quiere contentos* is marked by violent sexual actions, especially against María, the central character, *Lo impenetrable* is an atypical work for Gambaro, since it is a parody of a pornographic novel and includes little overt political content. Set in nineteenth-century Spain, *Lo impenetrable* is the story of Madam X and her inability to reach her lover, Jonathan, so that they may consummate their love in a physical manner. Although Jonathan is always inaccessible, other figures in the novel, from the coach driver to her maid, manage to have a physical relationship with Madam X.

Gambaro lived in exile in Barcelona for three years before returning to Buenos Aires in 1980. During that time when she could not return to Argentina, she was invited to many other countries as a special guest. In 1978 she was invited by the government of Canada and the University of Ottawa to attend one of the first Inter-American Conferences on Women Writers. She also returned to France for a symposium on Latin American theater organized by the Sorbonne and the Italo-Latinoamerican Institute of Roma. In 1979 she accepted invitations to the United States, serving as one of the keynote speakers at the Latin American Theatre Symposium held at Florida International University in Miami during April 1979, after which she gave a series of lectures at such universities as Cornell, Yale, Rice, Texas at Austin, and Arizona State. Also during that time several of her plays were adapted for radio in Sweden (where they aired *El campo* in 1978) and in France (where France Culture broadcast an adaptation of *Los siameses* in 1979).

Because of the Dirty War, Gambaro did not stage a play in Argentina until *Decir sí* (first published in the periodical *Hispámerica* in 1978) was produced in Buenos Aires at Teatro Picadero on 28 July 1981. Written in 1974, this brief piece has become identified with Teatro Abierto (Open Theater), a movement that began in

1981 as a series of twenty plays by dramatists who attempted to demonstrate the vitality of Argentine theater despite the military dictatorship's efforts to curtail free speech. Gambaro's piece presents the story of a casual encounter between a client and his barber in a barbershop. As is usual in her dramatic world, however, a familiar, ordinary event is treated in a nonnaturalistic way, so that the final outcome is not the traditional haircut, but the cutting off of the man's head. The client is a victim, but the responsibility for his demise is left open. The barber does commit the atrocious act of actually decapitating his client, but the man's acquiescence to the barber's cruelty is in part the cause of his death, as Gambaro admitted in a 1985 interview with Miguel Angel Giella. In Gambaro's earlier plays, her characters were also victims, but they were passively trapped in circumstances not of their own creation. The man in *Decir sí,* however, keeps on saying "yes" to the wild demands of the barber, never rebelling even when ordered to sweep out the shop or coerced into picking up a corroded knife in order to shave the barber. Whatever demands are made of him, he always appeases the barber and gives in despite any misgivings. As Diana Taylor notes, in this play conformist behavior or indiscriminate assent is exaggerated, but the point becomes clear: Gambaro expresses metaphorically how dangerous it is for anyone to accept passively the evil acts that one witnesses in society.

In 1982 Gambaro was awarded a Guggenheim Fellowship, which enabled her to travel to the United States as well as to Mexico and France. She continued to write plays about the political situation in her country, especially since the military had lost some of its power after 1981. Political repression was still a problem, however, and *Real envido* (Royal Gambit, published in 1984) was produced at the beginning of 1983 and almost closed in a day because of censorship. *Real envido* is a farce that Gambaro wrote to comment on the dictatorship without being obvious, as she admitted in a 2002 interview with Raquel Garzón. *La malasangre* (produced in 1982; published in 1984; translated as *Bad Blood,* 1994) was attacked on two occasions by ultra-right-wing groups, but a small sector of the public remained undeterred and assured its success.

La malasangre and *Del sol naciente* (From the Rising Sun, produced and published in 1984) represent examples of Gambaro's use of displacement strategies: she analyzes the evils of the military dictatorship but places her characters in different temporal and/or geographic locations to avoid censorship issues. In *La malasangre* she reverts to nineteenth-century Argentina and alludes to the time of the dictatorship of Juan Manuel Rosas, who dominated the country from 1829 to 1852. As Sharon Magnarelli notes in a 1994 article, Gambaro presents a dysfunctional family in which the father, the ironically named Don Benigno, is the avatar of Rosas and also a referent to the generals of the current military dictatorship. Benigno's mistreatment of his wife and other characters is reminiscent of the behavior of other dysfunctional characters such as Lorenzo in *Los siameses* and Franco in *El campo*. But if Ignacio, Emma, and Martin were passive, in *La malasangre* Gambaro presents her audience with examples of defiant figures. Rosas's daughter, Dolores, at first behaves according to the pattern of her father; she is disrespectful to her mother, abuses her tutor, and relishes mistreating others. Her tutor, Rafael, is a deformed hunchback; but his ideals are democratic, and his spirit inspires love, not hatred. When Dolores learns from Rafael what had been taking place in her father's dominion, she loses her respect for him. The father resorts to reprehensible means to get rid of Rafael in an attempt to control his daughter.

Despite Rafael's torture and assassination, Dolores is awakened from her passive acceptance of her father's ways and vows to rebel against him. Although the final scene of the play is not optimistic, since Dolores is being carried away by her father's henchmen, nevertheless, she lets out a final scream, which shatters any complacency on the part of the audience: "El silencio grita! Yo me callo, pero el silencio grita!" (Silence screams out! I may be quiet, but silence screams out!). The dictatorship asks for silence, for complicity with its horrific deeds; yet, the very absences they cause, the "disappeared" people they kidnap and torture, are signs of their criminal activity. The death cries of the tortured may have been silenced, but at least some of the Argentine people have been willing to demand an answer to these disappearances. The "bad blood" of the title refers not only to the rebellious, ungrateful daughter, as a colloquial rendering of the title would indicate, but to the blood spilled by the dictatorship. For critics, Dolores offers a paradigm of rebellion where previously so many of the mistreated characters had been passive.

Del sol naciente, with its seven scenes, takes place in feudal Japan at the time of the samurai. The Japanese characters, however, speak with the *voseo* and use Argentine colloquial speech. An Argentine audience would easily see the allusion to the 1982 Malvinas/Falkland Islands War in the wartime setting of the play, especially since Japan and Argentina share a figure of the sun in their national flags. Obán, the Samurai warrior, is a symbol of the military and the control it attempts to exercise over the populace. Suki, the geisha, at first appears to placate Obán, following the paradigm of the complaisant courtesan, but she soon shows that she is not a passive figure accepting her submissive state. She befriends Oscar, an extraordinary figure whom critics identify with all the people who were tortured and assassinated during the Dirty War. Although the military junta wanted the people to ignore or forget the "unfortunate" masses who disappeared, Gambaro reminds her public that they must not forget. Oscar returns from the grave each time he is "finished off" by Obán. The disappeared may be missing, but they are not forgotten, nor will their memory be buried. In the penultimate scene Obán raises his sword against Suki, who had attempted to protect Oscar from being killed by Obán. In admonishing his courtesan, the warrior reminds her that her role is not that of heroine. He brandishes his sword high in the air and shouts his slogan: "Ésta dirá la última palabra!" (This will declare the final word!). But this play has an optimistic perspective: Suki and Oscar act in solidarity with each other and manage to subdue Obán. The warrior does not have the last word, as did Benigno in *La malasangre*.

In *Del sol naciente*, as the title indicates, there is a rising sun, a new day in which the victims of oppression will be vindicated. The last words are pronounced by Oscar, who has returned from his burial place, seemingly resurrected despite all the attempts of Obán to silence him. Suki offers him comfort and support, assuring him that "No te negaré. Ni la tierra ni el fuego los negarán. Ni el futuro los negará" (I won't deny you. Neither the earth nor fire will deny them. Nor will the future deny them). Suki speaks for those who adamantly searched for their missing loved ones, who defied the military dictatorship with their protests. Her unity with Oscar reflects a newfound spirit of commonality among Argentines of different classes, ethnicities, and backgrounds.

The next plays to be staged, in 1986, are also read by critics as commentaries on the military dictatorship, using different techniques. Although *Puesta en claro* (Made Clear, published in 1987) had been written in 1974, it was still relevant when it was finally staged in 1986. Anticipating the strong women characters of *La malasangre* and *Del sol naciente*, Clara begins as a powerless blind woman and ends ready to defend herself with her own stratagems. From a political perspective, it is possible to read Clara and the doctor who manipulates her as metaphors of the Argentine public and the various despots who have ruled that country. Just as Clara at first dares not openly oppose the doctor, so, too, many Argentines refrained from opposing the dictates of their military government. The doctor takes advantage of Clara, exploiting his power over the patient to force her to marry him and provide him with sex. But Clara ends up preparing a meal for the doctor that contains poison and kills him. He becomes a victim of his own abuse: since he has not cured Clara, her blindness leads to her apparent mistake in the kitchen. Gambaro does not make clear, however, whether Clara intentionally chooses the poison or accidentally uses it. In any case, the end result does substantiate the title "puesta en claro": the victimizer has received his "just desserts." For some critics this play has a strong feminist message in addition to its political focus on the abuses of power relations and citizens' rights and responsibilities.

Another of Gambaro's metatheatrical pieces, *Antígona furiosa* (Furious Antigone, produced in 1986; published in 1989), is more openly intertextual with its obvious reference to Sophocles' *Antigone*. Gambaro's reworking of a myth that is well known on the Latin American stage is another way of combining an interest in feminist issues and political problems. Scholars have noted that *Antígona furiosa* works on two levels, for the Sophoclean character reappears in Buenos Aires but also refers to the events in Thebes that form the basis of the Greek tragedy. This myth is relevant to the historical events of Argentina, since it recounts a fratricidal war for power between two sons, similar to the civil war that took place as the military fought against its citizens. Antígona confronts state power and reveals its corruption as she goes about the business of burying her brother Polinices, whose body has been exposed and left unmourned by order of their uncle Creon, the new king. As noted by many critics, Antígona is an appropriate spokesperson for the abused Argentine populace, although in the case of the Argentine people, the need, the burning desire, was to first find the bodies of their loved ones so that they could bury them properly, while Antígona's burden is to bury a body that is there.

Using a play-within-a-play technique, Antígona tells her story to Corifeo and Antinoo, who appear to sympathize with her but then revert to condemning her. Antígona's treatment reminds one of the ways the victims of the Dirty War were treated: denied a fair trial, arbitrarily punished, tortured, and killed. Unlike other victims of Gambaro's dramatic world, however, Antígona kills herself rather than accede to torture when Creon condemns her to death. Her mention of silence, echoing Dolores's words, refers to the silence of the people who did not protest but accepted the state-sponsored violence. Antígona begins the play after she dies and is therefore a revenant like Oscar in *Del sol naciente*. Antígona's words echo the performance that Oscar had enacted: "Siempre querré enterrar a Polinices. Aunque nazca mil veces y él muera mil veces" (I shall always want to bury Polinices. Even if I were to be born a thousand times and he were to die a thousand times). As some critics suggest, her role as dissident, as protector of the dead, is a constant in the play, a reminder of Argentina's still unfinished business related to the disappeared in the Dirty War.

The play that was produced next in her repertory was *Morgan* (produced in 1989; published in 1991), commissioned by the Instituto Torcuato Di Tella in 1989 in honor of the award they bestowed upon her for her entire dramatic canon. The success of *Morgan* was followed by *Penas sin importancia* (Sorrows [or Pains] of No Importance, produced in 1990; published in 1991), which also received special awards: the Premio de Investigadores y Críticos Teatrales de Argentina in 1992, and then in 1996 the Premio Nacional de Teatro por Obras Estrenadas en el Trienio 1990/93. These plays appear to have nothing in common, but they both rely on intertextual devices to multiply their meanings. The title figure of *Morgan* carries the name of an infamous English pirate, and he acts as a metaphor for arbitrary power. This play explores the question of responsibility in one's personal fate, a theme it shares with *Penas sin importancia*.

As Magda Castellví de Moor points out, *Penas sin importancia* is an exploration of love triangles and emotional relationships with many levels of intertextuality. Its six scenes offer a new twist to Gambaro's perennial exploration of power relations and manipulations, dominance and submission. Rita, a young mother-to-be, is almost stereotypical of the long-suffering Latina woman, while her husband, Pepe, is the stereotypical opportunist who takes advantage of his woman and lives off her earnings. He is a liar, a cheat, and a cad. At one point, Rita watches a production of Anton Chekhov's *Uncle Vanya* (1897). She begins to make comments about the characters whose lives she sees being enacted on a "stage" in her own home, on the same level of space, although in a corner of the stage. Rita has advice for the long-suffering characters without ever realizing that their problems reflect her own difficulties. Gambaro reveals her early interest in Luigi Pirandello as well as Chekhov when the characters of the Chekhov play directly address Rita and exchange dialogue with her. As in *Información para extranjeros*, the dividing line between "reality" and "art" is erased. Chekhov's Sonia, in love with Astrov, acts as if she were a faithful dog following him and pleading for his attentions, while Rita lets Pepe treat her like a dog, expecting obedience and submission. Rita shows clarity of thought with regard to Astrov's behavior that she does not express with regard to her life with Pepe. Rita also does not realize that their friend Andrés is in love with her, and she does not know how to interpret his constant gifts for her, just as Astrov does not appreciate all that Sonia has to offer.

While Sonia cannot alter her actions since she is a character in Chekhov's play, in the "real" world Rita can change her destiny so that she does not repeat the pattern of frustrations that Sonia represents. She closes the door to Pepe, locking it so that he cannot enter. Another allusion recognizable to theatergoers is to Henrik Ibsen's *A Doll's House* (1879), when Nora opens the door to her future. Rita may have had to lock a door, but in that way she saves herself from the danger that Pepe represents. According to Castellví de Moor, Gambaro suggests that one must first find the energy and strength from within in order to face the problems and dangers that are present in the external world. Just as Chekhov's work provides Rita with the means of finding a solution to her own predicaments, Gambaro's plays have provided a mirror of action and a site of reflection for the Argentine people.

Atando cabos (Tying Loose Ends, produced in London as *Putting Two and Two Together*, 1991; first published in the periodical *Revista Arte teatral de Valencia* in 1992) is another allegory about the Dirty War but with an emphasis on the need for justice that *Antígona furiosa* had suggested. In this brief one-act play, two characters are faced with possible death because the ship they are on may sink. Various referents suggest that their situation is an allegory for the ship of state, Argentina. Elisa is the mother of a daughter who had been kidnapped during the Dirty War. Martín is a gentleman who expresses romantic interest in Elisa but soon realizes that she carries a burden that she is unwilling to forget. Their current experience, on a sinking ship, reminds Elisa of all those who disappeared: "Y los que caían tampoco se daban cuenta, atontados, un golpecito acá, un golpecito allá, un tranquilizante" (And those who fell, didn't even realize what was happening to them; a little blow here, a little blow there, a tranquilizer). For Argentines in the aftermath of the discoveries of the tactics of the military apparatus, these allusions are clear, since it became known that the military would dump their victims from planes or at sea to hide the growing number of bodies.

Elisa is obsessed with the fate of her daughter and the rest of the victims, but Martín refuses to acknowledge any culpability or collusion with the victimizers. When the two are finally rescued from the lifeboat they had been forced to use to save themselves, Martín wants to forget their dangerous moment and go on with his seduction of Elisa. Martín does not hear the echoes of *Nunca más* (1984, Never Again), the documentary text that records all the testimonials of the victims' families and of those who managed to survive. He refuses to think of himself as a *sobreviviente,* a survivor, since he was on the side of the *vencedores,* those who conquered. In response to his invitation to accompany him to his house (his vision of the country), Elisa rejects his version of events: "¿Es que la historia es esta reconciliación

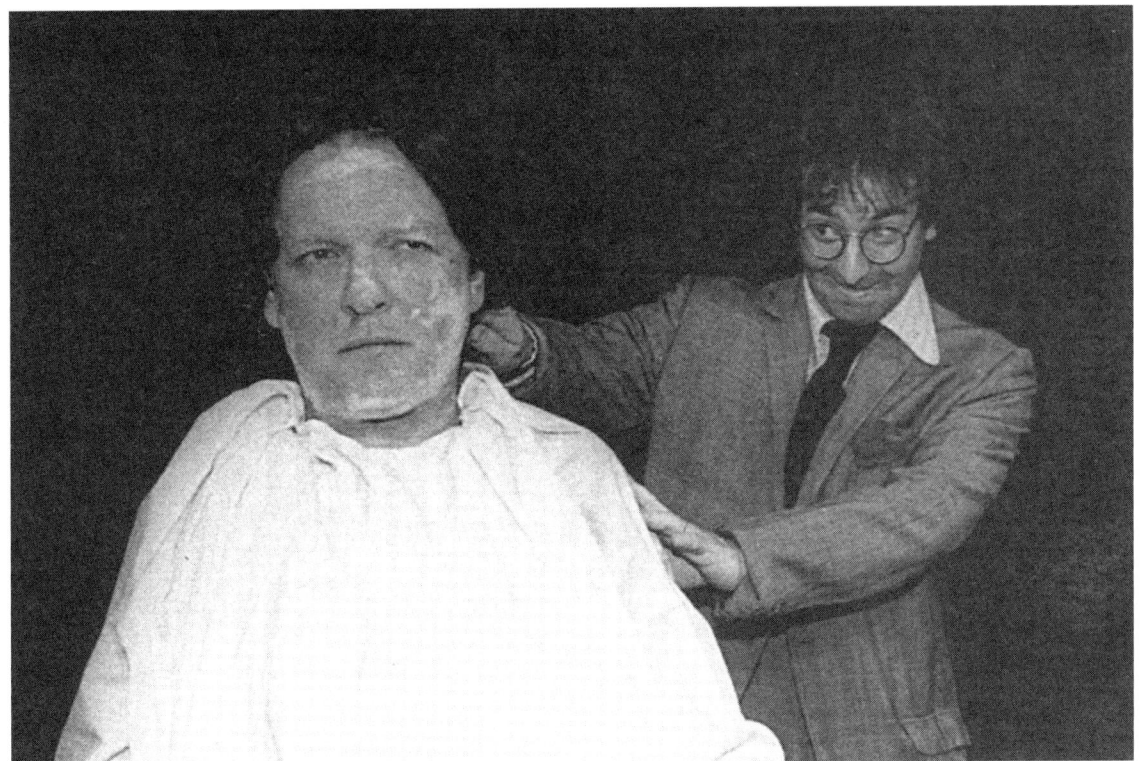

Josh Manheimer and Laurence Davies in a 1987 Dartmouth College production of Gambaro's 1981 play, Decir sí (Say Yes), *in which the danger of passively accepting evil is illustrated by a customer who acquiesces to a sadistic barber who ultimately decapitates him (from Diana Taylor, ed.,* En busca de una imagen: Ensayos críticos sobre Griselda Gambaro y José Triana, *1989; Ekstrom Library, University of Louisville)*

absurda y miserable?" (So the story is this absurd and miserable reconciliation?). The word "reconciliation" is key, since that is the word that President Carlos Menem had used to begin the process of so-called healing. Martín is ready to forget, to proclaim his innocence and his desire to proceed forward, erasing the past by his refusal to acknowledge any wrongdoing. Elisa, on the other hand, is representative of the new woman in Gambaro's dramatic world: fearless, where Emma had been cowed; direct, where Clara had been devious; and talkative, where Dolores had been forced into silence. Elisa faces the Martíns of Argentina and refuses to follow their agenda.

Gambaro uses the setting of this play as a dramatic metaphor to emphasize not only the fate of the disappeared who drowned but also the fate of the oppressors who will be dragged down by documents and testimonies that record their deeds. Now Elisa, as representative of the Asociación Madres de Plaza de Mayo (Mothers of the Plaza de Mayo, a human-rights group who demonstrate weekly in the main plaza of Buenos Aires, demanding to know what happened to their vanished loved ones) and all the other victims, dares to give the orders and set the agenda. Within the context of her intransigence in the face of the war crimes, the military and its supporters will not be able to survive: "No conseguir borrar mi memoria, su naufragio. En esta tierra que transito usted no puede vivir. En estas aguas, usted no sabe nadar" (Your inability to erase my memory is your shipwreck. In this land through which I stride, you cannot live. In these waters, you do not know how to swim). Her threat that Martín will drown proves likely, since in the final words of the play Elisa announces that their ship has once again crashed into something. In this play Gambaro does not provide an easy answer regarding the fate of the Argentine ship of state and its journey to democracy. Unlike Elisa's obstinate refusal to "forgive and forget," the first president after the military dictatorship, Raúl Alfonsín, was pressured (in 1986 and 1987) by the military to extend amnesty to more than one thousand members of the military who faced prosecution, and in 1990, then President Menem pardoned both Generals Roberto Eduardo Viola and Videla, the latter the general who had placed Gambaro on a blacklist in 1977.

Gambaro's focus on the *desaparecidos* (disappeared) as a part of Argentine historical reality that cannot be forgotten was next treated in a novel way for her in *La casa sin sosiego* (The House Not at Peace, produced and published in 1992). This work is a chamber opera with music composed by Gerardo Gandini and was commissioned by the Instituto Torcuato Di Tella. Although the libretto is a departure from her usual work, the opera reflects Gambaro's techniques of displacement, since it is a reworking of the myth of Orpheus and Eurydice as a way of addressing the issue of the disappeared and the social repercussions of the dictatorship. Gambaro presents another side to the legacy of the dictatorship in *Es necesario entender un poco* (It is Necessary to Understand a Little; produced in 1995, published in 1996), consisting of ten short scenes. The story line seems to have nothing to do with Argentina, since it draws its inspiration from an historical occurrence that took place in 1722. A French Jesuit who had resided in Canton, China, had befriended a literate Chinese man, known as John Hu, and returned with him to France. In Gambaro's play, Hue is the name of the Chinese man, but the Jesuit is known only as Padre (Father or Priest). The intertextual references incorporate fragments of poems by the Chinese poet Li Po. Similar to *Del sol naciente,* these geographic and temporal displacements notwithstanding, the play represents aspects of Argentine reality after the Dirty War. Since the text was written well after the end of the military dictatorship, Gambaro did not necessarily have to worry about censorship; yet, the indirectness and non-Argentine setting of the play help to make it a more general message about the damaging effects of dictatorship on the survivors.

This text is an attempt to confront the national myths that sustained the Dirty War and then generated pardons for the perpetrators. By presenting the mistreatment of Hue in the hands of the clergy and the professional class in post-Revolutionary France, Gambaro explores how the military dictatorship justified their imprisonment and torture of so many Argentines by labeling them "strangers" or "foreigners"—that is, as people with alien customs and values, enemies of the state. Gambaro then juxtaposes the plight of the survivors of the torture and imprisonment with the other national myth of the postdictatorship period—that it would be possible to pardon the perpetrators of such injustice. Hue's absence from his home covers seven years, a reminder of the seven years of the military dictatorship (1976 to 1983). Hue's inability to reintegrate easily into daily life and the obvious physical and mental scars remind Argentines how difficult it is to make the transition from dictatorship to democracy, from imprisonment to freedom. Hue serves as a metaphor for all the victims of oppression in any geographical or temporal period.

In 1995 Gambaro was honored with the Premio Nacional de Teatro, and in 1996 she received a special award for her contributions to Latin American theater at the Fourth Annual International Theatre Symposium held in Puebla, México. In the second half of the 1990s Gambaro continued to write and produce plays. *Falta de modestia* (Lack of Modesty; produced in 1998, published in 2002), is a monologue that chronicles the complaints of a mother who feels neglected. *De profesión maternal* (Of the Maternal Profession; produced in 1999, published in 2002) shows a daughter's criticism of the mother who had abandoned her. When the mother wants to establish a relationship with her daughter, the young woman reveals her resentment but finally attempts a reconciliation. Two volumes of fiction that show Gambaro's versatility also appeared—*Lo mejor que se tiene* (1998, The Best That One Has), a collection of short stories, and *El mar que nos trajo* (2001, The Sea That Brought Us), considered an autobiographical novel since it is based freely on her own family's situation of having been Italian immigrants in Argentina.

Gambaro's next play, *Lo que va dictando el sueño* (According to What the Dream Dictates, produced and published in 2002) was staged under the direction of Laura Yusem, who has become closely associated with many of Gambaro's most well known plays from the period of *La malasangre* and *Del sol naciente*. A play in six scenes, with a simple setting in a woman's bedroom, *Lo que va dictando el sueño* alludes to a rich literature in which dreams are important motifs. In Argentine letters, such writers as Jorge Luis Borges have explored the dream phenomenon as one way to change reality. Ana, Gambaro's protagonist, also dreams in order to imagine a better world. For the spectator, it is not clear at first that the initial scene re-creates events in her dreams; and Ana turns out to be not the spoiled sister of a generous and loving brother, the Manuel of her dreams, but rather a maid in a nursing home. Ana searches for love and compassion, but the Director of the home tries to manipulate her for his own interests. Ana tries to cheer up one patient, the Old Man, with little success. Her own family is dysfunctional. Her brother, Manuel, is kind and attentive only in her dreams; in reality, he is cruel and beats his wife, Julia. Yet, for Ana, the imaginary world of her dreams provides her with a way to survive the real world, and she decides to cast her fate with the Old Man, who also realizes that they have to dream—invent—the lives they want to live. Ana and the Old Man find comfort in their solidarity, as once again Gambaro stresses the importance of interconnectedness and mutual interdependence. Despite the poverty and pain that the play suggests is widespread in contemporary Argentina,

Gambaro's final scene reminds her audience to continue to dream.

Although Griselda Gambaro's plays often escalate from unhappiness to scenes of torture and violence, and although her dramatic images are always disquieting and provocative, they nevertheless provide a constructive and satisfying dramatic experience. Her plays are not usually lengthy, yet she manages to build levels of meaning in every phrase. Her dramatic images are memorable and striking in their aptness. Some of her plays have received more attention from the critics than others, but often, the issue is more a question of access to the plays than a reflection of any lack of worth. In several interviews, Gambaro has expressed her belief that the artist should assume a social responsibility, engage with the real world, and oppose abuses of power. Her trust in the possibility of change and the importance of individual responsibility for one's fate, presented with her mordant sense of humor, has enabled her to reach audiences even at the darkest moments of her country's history. While her vision does not provide comfort for the victimizers of this world, she does support those who believe in communal solidarity and in the value of art in everyday life.

Interviews:

Nelly Schnaith, "Imaginar: ¿Juego o compromiso?: Conversación con Griselda Gambaro," *Quimera: Revista de Literatura,* 24 (1982): 47–50;

Ana Seoane, "Entretien avec Griselda Gambaro," *Cahiers du Monde Hispanique et Luso-Bresilien/Caravelle,* 40 (1983): 163–165;

Miguel Angel Giella, "Entrevista: Griselda Gambaro," *Hispamérica,* 14, no. 40 (1985): 35–42;

Sharon Magnarelli, "Griselda Gambaro habla de su obra más reciente y la crítica," *Revista de Estudios Hispánicos,* 20, no. 1 (1986): 123–133;

Kathleen Betsko and Rachel Koening, "Griselda Gambaro," in *Interviews with Contemporary Women Playwrights,* edited by Betsko and Koening (New York: Beech Tree Books, 1987), pp. 184–199;

Teresa Méndez-Faith and Rosa Minc, "Entrevista con Griselda Gambaro," *Alba de América: Revista Literaria,* 7, no. 12–13 (1989): 419–427;

Marina Duranona, "Entrevista con Griselda Gambaro," in *Alba de América: Revista Literaria,* 10, no. 18–19 (1992): 407–418;

Marcela Castro and Silvia Jurovietzky, "Decir no: Entrevista a Griselda Gambaro," *Feminaria Literaria,* 6, no. 11 (1996): 41–45;

María Claudia André, "Entrevista a Griselda Gambaro: Feminismos e influencias en su narrativa," *Confluencia: Revista Hispánica de Cultura y Literatura,* 14, no. 2 (1999): 115–120;

Reina Roffé, "Entrevista a Griselda Gambaro," *Cuadernos Hispanoamericanos,* 588 (1999): 111–124;

Carolina Arenes, "Entrevista con Griselda Gambaro," *La Nación* (Buenos Aires), Suplemento Cultura, 25 March 2001, p. 8;

Roffé, "Libertad condicionada," in *Conversaciones americanas* (Madrid: Páginas de Espuma, 2001);

Raquel Garzón, "Entrevista a la escritora Griselda Gambaro," *Los Andes On Line* (27 April 2002) <http://www.losandes.com.ar/2002/0427/suplementos/cultura/nota70511_1.htm>.

References:

Becky Boling, *Reenacting Politics: The Theater of Griselda Gambaro* (Bloomington: Indiana University Press, 1998);

Magda Castellví de Moor, "Del objeto al sujeto mujer: *Penas sin importancia* de Griselda Gambaro," in *La nueva mujer en la escritura de autoras hispánicas: Ensayos críticos,* edited by Juana Alcira Arancibia and Yolanda Rosas (Westminster, Cal.: Instituto Literario y Cultural Hispánico, 1995), pp. 179–195;

Jason Cortés, "La teatralización de la violencia y la complicidad del espectáculo en *Información para extranjeros* de Griselda Gambaro," *Latin American Theatre Review,* 35, no. 1 (2001): 47–61;

Sandra Messinger Cypess, "Dramatic Strategies Made Clear: The Feminist Politics in 'Puesta en Claro' by Griselda Gambaro," *Studies in Twentieth Century Literature,* 20, no. 1 (1996): 125–145;

Cypess, "Frankenstein's Monster in Argentina: Gambaro's Two Versions," *Revista Canadiense de Estudios Hispánicos,* 14, no. 2 (1990): 349–361;

Cypess, "Physical Imagery in the Works of Griselda Gambaro," *Modern Drama,* 8, no. 4 (1975): 357–364;

Cypess, "The Plays of Griselda Gambaro," in *Dramatists in Revolt,* edited by Leon Lyday and George Woodyard (Austin: University of Texas Press, 1976), pp. 95–109;

Marguerite Feitlowitz, "Crisis, Terror, Disappearance: The Theater of Griselda Gambaro," *Theater,* 21, no. 3 (1990): 34–38;

David William Foster, "The Texture of Dramatic Action in the Plays of Griselda Gambaro," *Hispanic Journal,* 1, no. 2 (1980): 57–66;

Evelyn Picon Garfield, "Una dulce bondad que atempera las crueldades: *El campo* de Griselda Gambaro," *Latin American Theatre Review,* 13 (1980): 95–102;

Miguel Angel Giella, "El victimario como víctima en *Los siameses* de Griselda Gambaro: Notas para el análisis," *Gestos: Teoría y Práctica del Teatro Hispánico,* 2, no. 3 (1987): 77–86;

Amalia Gladhart, "Nothing's Happening: Performance as Coercion in Contemporary Latin American Theatre," *Gestos: Teoría y Práctica del Teatro Hispánico,* 9, no. 18 (1994): 93–112;

Tamara Holzapfel, "Griselda Gambaro's Theatre of the Absurd," *Latin American Theatre Review,* 4, no. 1 (1970): 5–11;

Sharon Magnarelli, "Authoring the Scene, Playing the Role: Mothers and Daughters in Griselda Gambaro's *La malasangre,*" *Latin American Theatre Review,* 27, no. 2 (1994): 5–28;

Nieves Martínez de Olcoz, "Cuerpo y resistencia en el reciente teatro de Griselda Gambaro," *Latin American Theatre Review,* 28, no. 2 (1995): 7–18;

Nora Mazziotti, ed., *Poder, deseo y marginación: Aproximaciones a la obra de Griselda Gambaro* (Buenos Aires: Puntosur Editores, 1989);

Teresa Méndez-Faith, "Sobre el uso y abuso de poder en la producción dramática de Griselda Gambaro," *Revista Iberoamericana,* 51, no. 132–133 (1985): 831–841;

Hortensia R. Morell, "*Penas sin importancia* y *Tío Vania:* Diálogo paródico entre Chejov y Gambaro," *Latin American Theatre Review,* 31, no. 1 (1997): 5–14;

Robert A. Parsons, "Reversals of Illocutionary Logic in Griselda Gambaro's *Las paredes,*" in *Things Done with Words: Speech Acts in Hispanic Drama,* edited by Elias L. Rivers (Newark, Del.: Juan de la Cuesta, 1986), pp. 101–114;

Silvia Pellarolo, "Revisando el canon/la historia oficial: Griselda Gambaro y el heroísmo de Antígona," *Gestos: Teoría y Práctica del Teatro Hispánico,* 7, no. 13 (1992): 79–86;

Jill Scott, "Griselda Gambaro's *Antígona furiosa:* Loco (ex)centrism for jouissan (SA)," *Gestos: Teoría y Práctica del Teatro Hispánico,* 8, no. 15 (1993): 99–110;

Diana Taylor, "Rewriting the Classics: *Antígona furiosa* and the Madres de la Plaza de Mayo," *Bucknell Review,* 40, no. 2 (1996): 77–93;

Taylor, *Theatre of Crisis: Drama and Politics in Latin America* (Lexington: University Press of Kentucky, 1991);

Taylor, ed., *En busca de una imagen: Ensayos críticos sobre Griselda Gambaro y José Triana* (Ottawa: Girol, 1989);

Beatriz Trastoy, "Madres, marginados y otras víctimas: El teatro de Griselda Gambaro en el ocaso del siglo," in *Teatro argentino del 2000,* edited by Osvaldo Pellettieri (Buenos Aires: Galerna, 2000), pp. 37–46.

Santiago García
(20 December 1928 -   )

Lucía Garavito
Kansas State University

PLAY PRODUCTIONS: *Nosotros los comunes,* by García and Teatro La Candelaria, Bogotá, Teatro La Candelaria, 16 March 1972;

La ciudad dorada, by García and Teatro La Candelaria, Bogotá, Teatro La Candelaria, 1973;

Guadalupe/años sin cuenta, by García and Teatro La Candelaria, Bogotá, Teatro La Candelaria, 11 June 1975; New York, 1976;

Los diez días que estremecieron al mundo, by García and Teatro La Candelaria, Bogotá, Teatro La Candelaria, October 1977;

Golpe de suerte, by García and Teatro La Candelaria, Bogotá, Teatro La Candelaria, 1980; New York, 1980;

El diálogo del rebusque, Bogotá, Teatro La Candelaria, 1981; New York, 1984;

Corre, corre, Carigüeta, Bogotá, Teatro La Candelaria, May 1985;

El Paso: Parábola del camino, by García and Teatro La Candelaria, Bogotá, Teatro La Candelaria, 1988; New York, 1989;

Maravilla Estar, Bogotá, Teatro La Candelaria, 1989;

La trifulca, Bogotá, Teatro La Candelaria, 1991;

En la raya, by García and Teatro La Candelaria, Bogotá, Teatro La Candelaria, April 1993;

Manda patibularia, Bogotá, Teatro La Candelaria, 18 June 1996;

El Quijote, Bogotá, Teatro La Candelaria, 1999;

De caos & deca caos, by García and Teatro La Candelaria, Bogotá, Teatro La Candelaria, March 2002.

BOOKS: *Guadalupe/años sin cuenta: Creación colectiva del Grupo La Candelaria* (Bogotá: Teatro La Candelaria, 1975);

Teoría y práctica del teatro (Bogotá: CEIS, 1983; revised and augmented edition, Bogotá: La Candelaria, 1989; revised again, 1994);

5 obras: Creación colectiva, by García and Grupo La Candelaria (Bogotá: Colombia Nueva, 1986)—comprises *Nosotros los comunes (Comuneros 1781); La ciudad dorada; Guadalupe/años sin cuenta; Los diez días que estremecieron al mundo;* and *Golpe de suerte;*

Crisis de valores y políticas culturales (Bogotá: Informática, 1987);

3 obras de teatro: El Paso, Maravilla Estar y La trifulca (Bogotá: Teatro La Candelaria, 1991);

El chiste en el arte de teatro: T'ecnicas, funciones y significado (Santafé de Bogotá: Corporación Colombiana de Teatro/Taller Permanente de Investigacion Teatral/La Taquilla, 1996);

Teoría y práctica del teatro, volumen II (Bogotá: La Candelaria, 2002).

OTHER: *El diálogo del rebusque* and *Corre, corre, Carigüeta,* in *Cuatro obras del Teatro La Candelaria* (Bogotá: Teatro La Candelaria, 1987), pp. 9–115, 259–334;

"Introducción" and *Manda patibularia,* in *6 obras del Teatro La Candelaria* (Santafé de Bogotá: Teatro La Candelaria, 1998), pp. 219–285.

During the 1960s Colombia was one of the Latin American countries where the so-called *Nuevo Teatro* (New Theater) led to unprecedented theatrical activity by fostering the development of a new dramaturgy. Two national figures stood out as the leading forces behind this transformation: Enrique Buenaventura and Santiago García. Although nurtured in world theater tradition and deeply rooted in European theoretical and experimental trends, they looked for a way of their own to explore through theater the complexity and richness of Colombia's and Latin America's cultural identities, past and present. García's multiple roles in this process—actor, director, playwright, set designer, researcher, lecturer, theoretician—have had an unquestionable impact on the direction of theatrical activity both at home and abroad.

García was born in Bogotá on 20 December 1928 to Gabriel García Samudio, who was in the military, and Paulina Pinzón, a homemaker. His family's close-knit structure, centered around the women, was typical

Santiago García at Teatro La Candelaria, 1997 (photograph by Fabio Rojas; courtesy of Lucía Garavito)

of the Santander area. García, his two sisters, Inés and Gloria, and one brother, Arturo, and his parents lived in one section of a large house in the Las Nieves barrio, and the other sections of the house were occupied by the families of five aunts. The house was always full of children engaged in games and various creative forms of entertainment.

García's childhood in Puente Nacional (Santander) in the early 1930s initiated him into the violent political life of the nation. Although the town was overwhelmingly affiliated with the liberal party, the neighboring community of Cite had the opposite, conservative political ideology. The clash resulted in frequent shootings. After García's first few years of school in Puente Nacional, his family moved to Bogotá in search of a better life, including more-favorable educational opportunities. Once in the capital, García entered the Liceo Metropolitano to conclude his primary education. According to an unpublished biography by Fernando Duque Mesa and Jorge Prada, this school was highly unusual: the whole curriculum focused on one subject, the history of Egypt, which was the basis for learning mathematics, geography, astronomy, history, arts and crafts, physics, and all the other required disciplines. There was only one textbook, a history of Egypt, published by Editorial Hachette. As a result of this exposure, García jokingly comments that he was initially more familiar with hieroglyphic writing than with the Latin alphabet. Continuing his education at the Liceo Cervantes, García went through a traumatic transition because of his complete lack of familiarity with Colombian issues, but he quickly caught up with his peers. He subsequently attended the public institutions Camilo Torres and the San Bartolomé Nacional, and finally the private Colegio de los Salesianos, where he earned his high-school diploma.

García showed little initial inclination toward theater. He had attended performances of such works as *The Visit* (1956) by Friedrich Dürrenmatt, *Death of a Salesman* (1949) by Arthur Miller, and some of the plays by Luis Emilio Campos and Luis Enrique Osorio, but his true passions were painting and movies. In school, García's natural talents in painting and building models led him to develop an affinity for the plastic arts. For this reason, he entered the Universidad Nacional in Bogotá in 1948 to study architecture.

When García entered the university, he faced a politically charged atmosphere. Jorge Eliécer Gaitán, a charismatic politician who intended to lead the masses into a new concept of liberalism, was assassinated on 9 April 1948 in downtown Bogotá. The assassination was immediately followed by the *bogotazo*, the violent popular revolt that shook the country and brought much death and destruction to the capital. This time of political turmoil was followed by the repressive presidency of Laureano Gómez (1950–1951) and the dictatorship of General Gustavo Rojas Pinilla (1953–1957). In the first volume of his *Teoría y práctica del teatro* (1983, Theory and Practice of Theater) García evaluates the impact of Gaitán's assassination and the *bogotazo* for middle-class intellectuals in Colombia who were forced to confront the violent reality in which they lived. The resulting cultural awakening led to a shift in focus: instead of looking outward, Colombians started to look at themselves and their circumstances. This new attitude marked the development of a new approach to painting, literature, and theater.

After three years at the Universidad Nacional, García had the opportunity to leave for Europe (France, England, and Italy) in 1951 to pursue studies in organic architecture, made famous by Frank Lloyd Wright. While in Europe, García continued to focus on urbanism and painting, without paying much attention to the theatrical activity of the time. Upon his return to Colombia a few years later, García earned his degree in architecture from the Universidad de los Andes in Bogotá and started his professional life at the Esguerra y Herrera architecture firm. In 1956 he read in a newspaper that National Television of Colombia had hired Seki Sano, a Japanese theater professor, to start a school to train competent actors for its programs. An impulsive and curious García decided to talk with Sano that night, join the new school, and quit his job at the architecture firm.

Sano had been a disciple of Vsevolod Meyerhold, had studied in Moscow, and was familiar with Konstantin Stanislavsky through the teachings of Evgeny Vakhtangov. Although Sano's stay in Colombia was cut short because of the government's fears of his communist views, he had a profound impact on the nation's future development in the area of theater. García considers the introduction of Stanislavsky applied in a nondogmatic way as Sano's greatest legacy to directors and actors in Colombia.

Television, then a new medium with unknown potential, was also extremely attractive to García. The industry not only paid as well or even better than architecture but it also gave him the opportunity to work with people such as Fausto Cabrera (founder of the teleplays of the Spanish national television station), Bernardo Romero Lozano (director of the radioplays at the Spanish national radio station and later the national television station teleplays), and Manuel Drezner (literary and music reviewer and critic for the newspaper *El Espectador* who also directed theater in the early stages of the national television station). García was named director of the Department of Stage Design at National Television and was later appointed director of programming. He had the opportunity to become part of a group of directors in charge of *teleteatros* (teleplays), short pieces that included only a few actors and were produced within a limited budget. García directed about seventy *teleteatros*.

In 1957 García and Cabrera founded the Teatro El Búho (Owl Theater), the first permanent *théâtre de poche* (pocket theater) in Colombia following the European trend of small houses devoted to avant-garde performances. The stage was small, as was the seating area (forty-five to fifty people), and performances were given Thursdays through Sundays. The theater ran on a limited budget that depended on the generosity of friends and colleagues, much personal sacrifice, and occasional contributions from businesses. It incorporated experienced directors and actors, many participants from the Sano school and the Escuela de Teatro del Distrito, and some directors from television such as Marcos Tychbroher, Sergio Bishler, Dina Moscovici, and Arístides Meneghetti. Professors, university students, and writers attended their avant-garde performances, which responded to the tenets endorsed by the literary magazine *Eco* (Echo), the Theater of the Absurd, and contemporary European theatrical trends. The intention of the company was to distance themselves from the traditional, rhetorical, and *costumbrista* Spanish theater focused on depicting the human types and ways of life associated with a given region or period, imbued with local color. They meant to propose a more imaginative and revolutionary dramaturgy, up to date with the latest trends on the world stage, but without a unified approach or even cohesiveness.

The activity of the Teatro El Búho attracted many artists who were working in other disciplines: painters Fernando Botero, Enrique Grau, David Manzur, Omar Rayo, and Eduardo Ramírez Villamizar; sculptor Edgar Negret; photographer Hernán Díaz; and musician Luis Antonio Escobar. This convergence, based on a common interest in the latest artistic tendencies, stimulated collaborative projects while helping to build up a faithful public whose attendance allowed performances to run for a couple of weeks.

García directed his first plays at the Teatro El Búho. Among them were *Conversation-sinfonietta* by Jean Tardieu (1951), *The Lady Aoi* by Yukio Mishima (1956), both of which he directed in 1957, *In Search of Lost Images* by Tardieu, which he directed in 1958, and some plays by American playwrights (Miller, Thornton Wilder, and Tennessee Williams). Teatro El Búho also provided a forum for plays written by Colombian playwrights. Productions of *Montaje HK 111* (Staging HK 111) by Gonzalo Arango, directed by Cabrera with

García in the leading role (Adam Be), and *A la diestra de Dios Padre* (1958; translated as *On the Right Hand Side of God The Father,* 1958) by Buenaventura, directed also by Cabrera and with García playing the role of St. Peter, demonstrate the concern for moving toward a national dramaturgy.

Two years later, when National Television went private in 1959, drastic changes were made in the cultural programming, and there was a strike. García left to go abroad and spent two and a half years pursuing a specialization that combined architecture and theater, "Architectonic Treatment of Space on the Stage." In Prague he studied at the Department of Musical Arts at Karlova Universitat, which included theater. The course of study selected by García involved setting up stagings in different theaters in the city, the most interesting being Tilovo Theater, where *The Seagull* (1896) by Anton Chekhov was being performed under the direction of Otomar Krejca. This stay in Czechoslovakia allowed García to become familiar with the most advanced technology in experimental stage tools available at the time, such as curtains of light, circular stage movement, screen projections on the backdrop, and the *lanterna magica,* a combination of film, theater, and polychrome in which eight to ten projectors showed images on as many screens of different sizes, with live theater scenes taking place simultaneously. The incorporation of these devices by Krejca and set designer Joseph Svoboda encouraged visual and acoustic experimentation among their students. In addition to the technological dimension, García gained key insights in two areas: Brechtian theatrical theory and the process of transforming great nineteenth-century literary works into contemporary works for the stage.

In his second year of study abroad, García chose the Berliner Ensemble in order to closely follow its theater practice, rehearsals, and performances of the works of Bertolt Brecht (under the direction of Helen Weigel) and also of contemporary plays that were a departure from Brecht, such as *Frau Flinz* (1961) by Helmut Baierl. When not involved with these activities, García would go to the Brecht Archive to do research.

When García returned from Europe in 1962, the Teatro El Búho had dissolved, but its impact on the development of Colombian theater was decisive; many participants went on to become prestigious directors and founding members of their own theater groups. García joined the Teatro Estudio de la Universidad Nacional for two different terms, first from 1962 to 1964, and then from 1964 to 1966. Cabrera was directing there at the time. In 1962 Jorge Gaitán Durán asked García to direct his experimental opera *Los hampones* (Thugs), with music by Escobar and the National Symphony Orchestra (directed by Olav Roots) and stage design by Manzur. Renowned Colombian opera singers such as Carmiña Gallo and Marina Tafur also took part in the production. The opera was conceived in the spirit of Brecht's *Threepenny Opera* (1928) and was recognized as the best cultural event of 1962.

After his first two years with the Teatro Estudio de la Universidad Nacional, García went to New York and then to Lyon and Paris, where he joined Buenaventura and Moscovici and finished his theater studies at the Université du Théâtre des Nations. García went to New York by invitation from the Actors Studio to attend their sessions and follow their work for six months. Participation in Lee Strasberg's group discussions and individual exercises was limited to a few privileged individuals who already had experience in movies, television, or theater. García was impressed by the rigorous work involved and the in-depth exploration of the actor's craft. Although the artistic results were extraordinary, he felt that this particular approach was distant from his own theater interests and consequently left the United States to return to France.

In Lyon, García was interested in Roger Planchon's project on popular theater. Planchon's work relied on the support of the French leftist parties and was directed at students, workers, and a wide sector of the population. It was oriented toward reviving the great French classics for the stage and also making young, talented playwrights known. García recognized the quality of the programs led by Planchon but realized that they required great economic support from the state as well as technological sophistication in order to succeed, which meant that it would be impossible to implement them in a country like Colombia; a different, more practical approach was needed.

Upon returning to Colombia, García began his second term at the Teatro Estudio de la Universidad Nacional. During these terms he directed such productions as Brecht's *A Man's a Man* (1926) in 1962, Brecht's *Life of Galileo* (1943) and Chekhov's *The Cherry Orchard* (1904) in 1963, and Edward Albee's *The Zoo Story* (1959) in 1965. In these productions, García attempted to apply the theoretical and practical knowledge he had gained in Europe, such as the special attention given to the use of light in the creation of atmosphere and the suggestive power of the nonverbal dimension of the mise-en-scène. The staging of *Life of Galileo* was significant for many reasons. It was an opportunity to put on the stage García's own understanding and vision of Brecht and to make Brecht's innovative theories more widely known in Colombian theater circles. It also involved an enormous challenge and elaborate teamwork, which García describes in detail in *Teoría y práctica del teatro*.

Although it was a huge success, *Life of Galileo* was performed only four times at the Teatro Colón in Bogotá and three times at the Teatro Municipal in Cali. One of the reasons for such a short season stemmed from an article on physicist Robert Oppenheimer written by García and incorporated into the program. "El caso Oppenheimer (The Oppenheimer Case) denounced the scientists who had collaborated on the construction of the atomic bomb and included images of Hiroshima and Nagasaki. The article had a clear connection with the play, which precisely addressed the scientist's commitment to his time. The directors of the Universidad Nacional, acting as a result of a complaint raised by the United States Embassy, asked García not to include his article with the program, and he agreed to take it out. But the army broke into García's office at the university, confiscated the programs, and destroyed the articles and the pictures. In response, the Student Council mimeographed the censored article and distributed it to the public at the entrance to the Teatro Colón. This situation created the expected friction between the Universidad Nacional and García, who considered it best to resign and give up his dream of creating a School of Theater within this academic setting.

After the incident, García and some of his colleagues and collaborators who had also left the university joined together to found the Casa de la Cultura in 1966. They felt the need to own a place that could be devoted to theater activities all year long and that was not under the jurisdiction of a state institution or organization. The Casa de la Cultura was not limited to theater. It included other arts such as music, painting, and movies, and was open to lectures, exhibits, and other cultural activities.

Many plays were staged at the Casa de la Cultura with García as one of the directors: there were seven plays performed in 1967 and eight in 1969. The plays had an ample thematic range, from the French Revolution to social issues related to the family, the army, the church, and politics, all approached in a new way much influenced by the Theater of the Absurd. The theater at the Casa de la Cultura had a small seating capacity (about 120), and the public included professionals, students, and workers who started to attend because of an agreement between the Casa de la Cultura and the unions. García commented to Duque Mesa and Prada about his role there:

> At the same time that I was directing, I was educating actors, I was educating myself, learning a lot through the staging itself. I was involved in discussing and experimenting how a scene could work out one way or another, working with the light and all the other elements. Of all the problems, the most difficult to face

García in the title role of a 1966 production of Bertolt Brecht's Life of Galileo *(1943) at the Teatro Estudio Universidad Nacional in Bogotá. García helped introduce Brechtian innovations to Colombian theater (courtesy of Lucía Garavito).*

> was the lack of money, since we had some ambitious projects in mind.

The group also introduced the "aesthetics of recycling": material that was to be discarded began to be incorporated into the stage.

In 1968 the theater group of the Casa de la Cultura moved to an old colonial house in the sector of Bogotá known as La Candelaria, turned it into a theater, and changed the group's name to Teatro La Candelaria. A production of *The Good Woman of Setzuan* (1943) by Brecht inaugurated the new location in 1969, and the group has been located there ever since.

In 1970, Teatro La Candelaria under García attended the International Theater Festival at Nancy with productions of *Le cadavre encerclé* (1958, The Corpse Encircled) by Kateb Yacine, *El menú* (The Menu, 1968) by Buenaventura, and *Oresteia* by Aeschylus. They were not overly successful. When they staged Aeschylus in Paris later on, however, the play was enthusiastically received. García subsequently traveled to Holstebro and other cities in Denmark, where the group performed *Oresteia* at the Odin Teatret directed by Eugenio Barba.

If the mise-en-scène of Yacine's and Aeschylus's plays meant for the group a different level of working with the body and experimenting with nonverbal language, Buenaventura's play was significant in the dramaturgical development of Teatro La Candelaria for marking the beginning of their in-depth work in improvisation. They tested the creative potential of improvisation, proposed guidelines to make it functional in front of an audience, and became aware of its limitations. Semiotics and communication science provided a useful theoretical framework for actors to have an analytical perspective on improvisation and to sharpen their capacity to observe reality and human interaction. Although the focus on improvisation initially drove away some members of the group, many of the new people who had participated in seminars and workshops stayed on and eventually came to form the nucleus of the collective.

Improvisation was precisely what catapulted Teatro La Candelaria into the process of *creación colectiva* (collective creation). Actors began to participate in areas that had until then been alien to them, such as dramaturgy, directing, and playwrighting, and the traditional lines between these categories blurred. In addition to improvisation, García identifies two main reference points for the process of collective creation: first, Brecht's proposals concerning the primacy on the stage of the capacity to invent by agreement among the actor, the director, and the playwright; second, psychodrama, in connection with the need to have a better understanding of improvisation. Collaboration with other groups, such as Buenaventura's Teatro Experimental de Cali (TEC), and with some psychoanalysts who were familiar with the theories of Jacob L. Moreno and Rojas Bermúdez in Argentina, was crucial during this phase in which it was difficult to draw the line between theatrical experimentation and psychology.

Nosotros los comunes (1972, We the Commoners) was the group's first play of collective creation. The text was determined by the actors' improvisational skills during each performance, but the range of improvisation was nevertheless subject to certain guidelines set by the group. The play deals with an historical event–the revolt of the commoners in the town of El Socorro and its vicinity (modern-day Santander del Sur) in 1781 against the abuses of Spanish authorities. Teatro La Candelaria made a conscious effort to be faithful to the historical event, consulting the chronicles of the time and working in collaboration with historians. Once the historical event was defined in terms of time and space, the next step for the group was to look for particular, individual incidents that could suggest its possible causes. They then selected characters who embodied the social, economic, and political forces that were shaping the moment.

The fifteen episodes of the play, including a presentation and an epilogue, explore the process of liberation and the relationship between the oppressor and the oppressed within the context of colonial Spanish America. This early play incorporates ideas that are more fully developed in subsequent works by García and Teatro La Candelaria: the collective protagonist, the absence of the hero from the stage (José Antonio Galán, the man who encouraged the people to revolt against the Spaniards and their opresive laws, is never present but only spoken of), the influence of Brecht (episodic structure, introduction of songs and poems to comment on the action, focus on history, emphasis on popular elements), and a key element, the process of insurrection, dialogue, and betrayal, followed by exemplary execution. García points out in Fernando Peñuela's "Pensamiento de la actuación" (Thoughts on Acting), an unpublished 1996 typescript, that this structure repeats itself in Latin American history, as illustrated by the events related to Moctezuma, Atahualpa, Tupac Amaru, and the cacique (Indian chief) Bacata, and it invites the establishment of a correlation between past events and present circumstances.

La ciudad dorada (1973, The Golden City), the second collective creation, was a successful play and a finalist for the Casa de las Américas Award in 1974; it also served as a preamble to the collective's work on drug trafficking some years later. In this play the creative process was different from the one used for *Nosotros los comunes*. The plot was not built from an historical event; rather, the characters came first, and their actions determined the plot. The play focuses on the Pérez family (Gregorio, Dolores, and their three children, Ignacio, Rosalba, and Mario), their critical economic situation, and the many failed attempts to change their circumstances by leaving the countryside and looking for better opportunities in the city. Although the Pérez family members are hardworking and are willing to take risks to improve their life, every risk they take results in a personal or collective loss. The play closes with Dolores looking back at their difficult family history and wondering, "Si alguien escribiera sobre nuestra vida, cómo la pondría?" (If someone were to write about our life, how would it go?).

An innovative element in the staging of the play was the handling of space. García explains in the first volume of *Teoría y práctica del teatro* that the *autos sacramentales* (mystery plays) of the Middle Ages served as inspiration. Horizontal space was broken into different levels, which allowed the group to alternate the presentation of certain episodes or to have them simultaneously, as required by the action. This arrangement also enabled them to act on one level while the other level was being prepared for the following scene.

According to García's comments to Duque Mesa and Prada, the collective's experiences with improvisation in this play gave them insight on some of its unwanted results; for example, the actors found themselves cracking jokes spontaneously as a means of gaining the audience's favor. In order to reflect on this challenge, the collective next chose to stage a text in verse that did not lend itself to improvisation: *Morte e vida Severina* (1956, The Death and Life of a Severino) by João Cabral de Melo Neto, a story of poverty in northeast Brazil told as an *auto sacramental*. The objective was to memorize a text and respect its integrity. Improvisations were still relevant, however, especially in connection with the musical component. The staging of this Brazilian play in 1974 served as a useful exercise for the group in the development of a new actor-text-public relationship that had an impact on subsequent productions.

García explains that *Guadalupe/años sin cuenta* (1975, Guadalupe/Countless Years), the third collective creation, originated in an invitation to participate in a festival in Arauca in the Llanos Orientales. As a result, Teatro La Candelaria developed a particular interest in the music of that region, including the *corridos* and other songs about the liberal uprising and the figure of peasant leader Guadalupe Salcedo in the 1950s. Arturo Alape, who had recorded interviews with former guerrilla fighters, collaborated with the group, as did Umaña Luna, the prosecutor in the trial against the lieutenant who killed Salcedo. In addition, the collective attended a seminar on the agrarian struggles and guerrilla movements of the 1950s, met with historians and sociologists, and consulted newspaper articles and other documents. A chronology of events that could serve as the backbone for a story was the result of this research.

The next step was to construct a plot. Episodes were selected in terms of their theatricality and were submitted to a series of improvisations. The group divided into teams to propose possible structures for the material. After six months, the collective went to Mexico to participate in the Festival Chicano de Teatro (Chicano Theater Festival), an experience that provided the clue for the style of the play in terms of integrating popular music such as *corridos* into the dramatic structure. It became clear that the play would deal with Salcedo's death and also with the betrayal of the liberal peasants by the ruling liberal class. As characters and scenes were discarded or selected, the official and the real versions of the death of Salcedo, framed by the events that accounted for his surrender, became the nucleus of the play, and the act of surrendering became the general theme.

In contrast to previous projects, Teatro La Candelaria now worked with a written text (put together with the collaboration of Alape) before rehearsing. A team went to the Llanos Orientales to gather information about regional music and instruments and to learn how to play them. The actors earned roles through a process of improvisation in which they invented the characters themselves, an approach that seemed to have a direct impact on the quality of the play.

Guadalupe/años sin cuenta is divided into thirteen episodes. The first and last of these episodes confront the official and unofficial versions of Salcedo's death. According to the official version, Salcedo was shot when, instead of surrendering to the waiting authorities, he attempted to open fire against them. The second version gives evidence that the authorities had promised to spare Salcedo's life if he surrendered peacefully, but when he did so, they betrayed and killed him. The obvious manipulation of witnesses and facts by state representatives who are determined to protect their own interests and obstruct justice is presented with highly sarcastic and ironic overtones.

For *Guadalupe/años sin cuenta,* Teatro La Candelaria and García as co-author earned the Casa de las Américas Award for best play in 1976. The play continued to be a part of the group's repertoire for more than fifteen years and was performed more than 1,300 times, until finally it was dropped from the regular season because many of the members of the original cast were no longer with the group. *Guadalupe/años sin cuenta* was presented in twenty-eight cities and towns in Colombia as well as twelve countries of the Americas and Europe, and it has been staged by other theater groups in Mexico, Angola, and the United States.

The fourth collective creation, *Los diez días que estremecieron al mundo* (1977, The Ten Days That Shook the World), represented a new experience for Teatro La Candelaria. This time the point of departure was a nontheatrical literary text, John Reed's 1919 book of the same title, which chronicled the Russian Revolution of 1917. Leaders of the Confederación Sindical de Trabajadores de Colombia (Confederation of Unions of Colombian Workers) approached Teatro La Candelaria to request a play to commemorate the sixtieth anniversary of the revolution. It came to the collective's attention that the Taganka theater group in Moscow under the direction of Yuri Liubimov had already made a collective creation based on Reed's book. Teatro La Candelaria obtained the libretto and staged it, with unsatisfactory results. So they went back to Reed's original chronicle and created a play that responded to the context of Colombia and Latin America. They

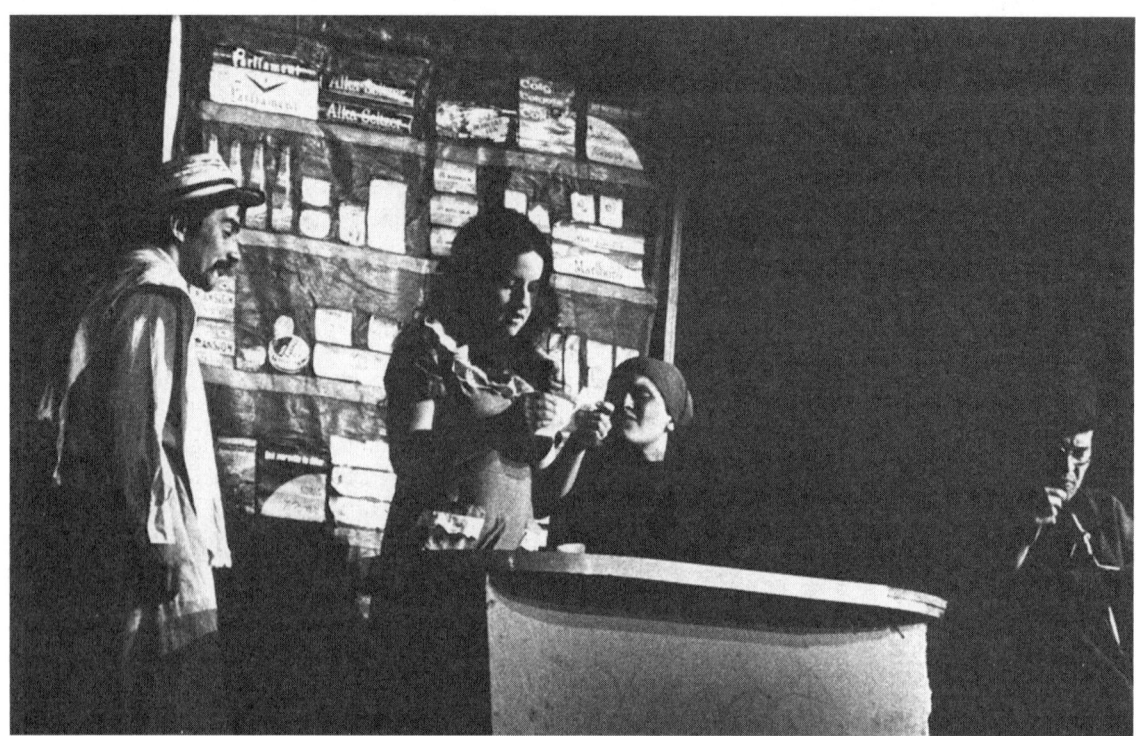

Scene from a 1974 production in Mexico of García and Teatro La Candelaria's 1973 collective play La ciudad dorada
*(City of Gold), about a family struggling to improve their economic situation (photograph by Theodore Shank; from
Gerardo Luzuriaga, ed.,* Popular Theater for Social Change in Latin America, *1978;
Thomas Cooper Library, University of South Carolina)*

researched the subject by attending seminars, working in collaboration with the Center of Social Studies and Research, and meeting with historians and sociologists. The conflicts in the play come from the clashing agendas of the Mensheviks and Bolsheviks during the revolution and of a troupe of actors staging a play about these events. The result is a chaotic presentation of the episodes as the actors in the play-within-a-play deviate from their rehearsed lines, go out of character, omit scenes, and disobey orders. The Trujamán (Director) complains time after time that things are not going as planned because the actors are taking over the performance without consulting him first. The situation gets to such a point that he takes off his costume and says: "¿Esto era lo que buscaban? Esto? Yo quería hacer una obra de arte: arte, un producto artístico. Y ustedes vean, dense cuenta: han reemplazado el arte por la política. *(Al público)*" (Is this what you wanted? This? I wanted to make a work of art: art, an artistic product. And you, look around, see what you have done: you have replaced art with politics. *[To the audience]*). The parallel between the representation of the revolution that is taking place in Russia and the revolt against the Trujamán by the actors on the stage brings out the power struggle inherent in any attempt to change an established structure.

For García, the common link between the Russian Revolution and the situation in Colombia was given by the thematic lines developed throughout the play: bread (the workers, unemployment), land (the peasants, agrarian reform), and peace (the armed forces). By juxtaposing the Russian and Colombian levels, the collective attempted not only to make the public familiar with one of the greatest historical events of the century but also to make it reflect with humor and insight on revolution as a process and on its specific manifestation in Colombia. For their efforts, the collective received their second Casa de las Américas Award in 1978.

By the late 1970s the country was beginning to wake up to the reality of the drug traffic that had started about a decade earlier. Teatro La Candelaria decided to tackle this difficult subject in its fifth collective creation when they were intrigued by the true story of Lucho Barranquilla, which appeared in the national press and tabloids in 1975: Barranquilla was a street vendor who became rich by dealing marijuana and who died as a result of his involvement in a vendetta that took place in the early stages of drug traffic. Because this play was not situated in the past but in events of the real present, the collective had to change their usual methodology and create plotlines that were at least partially fictitious. For the first six months the group did research on Barranquilla in the coastal city of Santa Marta and on the smuggling of marijuana and cocaine to the United States, and they began working on improvisations. After six more months, there was a basic plotline concerning the lives of two friends. Barranquilla's story was left aside, and the group decided to create a happy ending for its protagonist, an ending that would better correspond to everyday life in Colombia than the expected punishment, which would rarely take place.

The resulting play, *Golpe de suerte* (1980, Lucky Strike), was problematic in many ways, as García confessed to Duque Mesa and Prada. First, since the play dealt with the reality of drug trafficking as a situation that was just taking shape in the country, it was difficult for the group to have an epic understanding of its paradigmatic and poetic components. The second large problem was characterization. Teatro La Candelaria had dealt successfully with collective characters before, but this play marked the first time they had focused on an individual protagonist, which made it increasingly difficult to accommodate the creation of such a character within the episodic structure of the play.

The three main characters—Pedro Pablo Palomino; his wife, Marta; and his friend Matamoros—oppose three others: mafia boss Don Felix Bastidas; his lover Poppy; and a multifaced god figure (ambassador, God the Father, gringo, Statue of Liberty, judge, referee). The play focuses on Palomino's inner and outer development as a successful drug lord who happens to be time after time a "lucky man." Palomino's ascent in the world of business goes hand in hand with his moral downfall. He rejects his old world, with its traditional values of honesty, love, loyalty, and respect for family and friends, as he blindly pursues the lifestyle of the *nouveaux riches*. A rivalry soon develops between him and his mentor, with serious consequences for Palomino. His ambition takes him ever higher and leads him to make serious mistakes. Although he has a moment of hesitation and thinks about changing the direction of his life, he succumbs to his inner demons once more. In an apotheosis at the end of the play, Palomino is welcomed again into the world of crime.

Happiness is the dynamic force driving the characters, and two paths are selected to achieve it: Palomino's and Matamoros's. Palomino's illusions make him change from worker (night watchman) to mafioso, to bourgeois, in order to satisfy his personal ambitions. Matamoros's dreams, on the other hand, are those of the honest working class: he wants to have his own workshop in order to become economically independent. While Palomino's reality feels like a dream to him, his dreams (hallucinations) reveal to him the destructive aspects of his supposed success. Matamoros's dreams, on the other hand, focus on reality through his sarcastic songs, in which he opposes and denounces the myths associated with easy money schemes and affirms his ideological commitment to following a respectable path.

According to García, the collective grew, matured, and acquired stability in the 1970s, as did contemporaneous Colombian theater groups such as the TEC, the Teatro Popular de Bogotá, the Teatro Libre de Bogotá, the Teatro Experimental La Mama, and the Teatro El Local. The late 1970s were, then, the appropriate time for García to disseminate the results of more than a decade of theater exploration. Starting in 1971, but mostly after 1977, he published a series of articles and gave lectures in Colombia and abroad on a wide variety of topics. All of these essays were later assembled in the first volume of *Teoría y práctica del teatro*, with editions in 1983, 1989, and 1994 that cover material from 1971 to 1993.

Although in 1981 García resigned his position as director of the Escuela Nacional de Arte Dramático (National School of Dramatic Arts), where he had developed a series of workshops, he went on to found the Taller Permanente de Investigación Teatral (Permanent Workshop for Theatrical Research) in 1983 under the umbrella of the Corporación Nacional de Teatro (National Theater Corporation). The objective of this workshop was to encourage ongoing analysis and research on specific dramaturgical issues, open new paths to creativity, and find current theoretical and practical tools to develop a national dramaturgy.

El diálogo del rebusque (1981, Surviving by Hook or by Crook: A Dialogue) marked a change for García and Teatro La Candelaria from collective creation to individual authorship. He thought it was time to try a new approach to dramaturgy. While so far the whole group had participated in the construction of the text and its staging, in this new approach an individual would bring forward a proposal that they would follow. The staging continued to be a product of collective creation, while now respecting the author's individual seal.

The idea for *El diálogo del rebusque* came from García's childhood in Puente Nacional. His family had a cook who used to delight him and the neighborhood children with stories from the Spanish classical tradition, Francisco de Quevedo in particular. Later on, the version of Quevedo he had encountered in the cook's stories was so completely different from the one he was studying at school that García felt the need to somehow relate the scholarly figure to the popular one. He engaged in a methodical reading of all of Quevedo's works to fully familiarize himself with the characters and the world of the Spanish writer. The result of this reinvestigation belonged to García's imagination and was meant to be not the academic version of Quevedo but a vindication of the Quevedo who belonged to the people.

The text is based on Quevedo's picaresque *Historia de la vida del Buscón llamado Don Pablos* (1626, The Life Story of a Searcher Called Don Pablos) with some additional elements taken from his other works such as *Los sueños* (1627, Dreams), the *Premáticas* (anonymous popular writings on a variety of vulgar or discourteous subjects), and many of his sonnets, poems, *letrillas* (poems written in short lines often having a refrain and usually written on a light or satiric topic), and romances. García aimed in both language and staging to preserve Quevedo's literary style and the satiric tone of his work. The language used sounded like something in between seventeenth-century and contemporary Spanish; as García found out, this language seemed familiar to some uneducated sectors of the present-day population who keep supposedly anachronistic Spanish usages alive. A strong influence from Hieronymus Bosch also was evident in many aspects of the staging (which was done in collaboration with the painter Pedro Alcántara Herrán): masks, costumes taken from street folklore, and a noticeable distortion in the formal elements of the performance.

As the play opens, Don Pablos announces to the audience that the representation of his life is about to take place on the stage as "ejemplo para vuestra meditación, pero también para vuestro regocijo" (an example for your contemplation, but also for your enjoyment). At the moment when Don Pablos is about to begin his account, Quevedo arrives, having just escaped unnoticed from hell thanks to a rebellion that is taking place there. He interrupts Don Pablos to question his true existence (Don Pablos is, after all, one of his characters) and his right to retell a story Quevedo himself regretted telling four hundred years ago. Devils appear and agree to allow Don Pablos to tell his story now because people might learn from it and, consequently, the situation in hell might improve. The staging of Don Pablos's life then proceeds in a fragmented style, depicting the types of incidents that make up the life of a picaro. At the conclusion, the rebellion in hell ends; the devils give Quevedo a new sentence (to have his work published in cheap editions so that it can be read by the masses); and Don Pablos gets a new chance at a new life in today's world to satisfy his desire to know "cuál es su razón y por qué" (what its reason is and why).

As a picaro from Quevedo's time retelling his story in modern times, Don Pablos establishes connections between different spatial and temporal dimensions: the other world (hell) and the reality of the stage, Spain and Latin America, and the past and the present. García states in *Teoría y práctica del teatro* that "Pablos's journey becomes metaphorical in such a way that it is not only the life path of a Pablos in the seventeenth century, but also the life path of the spectator who is attending the performance." The figure of the picaro, his story, and its explicit didactic element continue to be relevant in the contemporary world, especially perhaps in Colombia, given the sociopolitical circumstances of the late twentieth century. Because of the lack of jobs and the concentration of violence in rural areas with the subsequent downturn in agricultural production, a large number of displaced and unemployed populations have come to the cities in an effort to make a living, sometimes through resourceful creativity at the margin of the law. In addition, modern state administrators and politicians are following Don Pablos's footsteps in their skillful corruption schemes. It is not surprising, then, that the adventures of such an antihero could have direct resonance with the Colombian audience.

However, the play was not well received by critics, who either did not know Quevedo well and consequently failed to grasp the implications of García's play, or who knew the Spanish writer quite well and were outraged by García's liberties with the material and irreverence toward the classic. The play did get an enthusiastic reception in Mexico, as evidenced by a letter sent to the media by the ambassador of Colombia in Mexico, who reported this play to be the best in the 1983 Festival Internacional de Teatro.

In order to explore the possibility of individual creation by its members, Teatro La Candelaria set up a contest. Out of the many texts submitted, four were selected to be staged: *La tras-escena* (1984; Behind the Scenes) by Fernando Peñuela, *El viento y la ceniza* (1986; Wind and Ashes) by Patricia Ariza, and *Corre, corre, Carigüeta* (Run, Run, Carigüeta, performed in 1985) and *Maravilla Estar* (performed in 1989), both by García. The first three form a trilogy on the Spanish conquest and the process of acculturation.

García's motivation for writing *Corre, corre, Carigüeta* was an attempt to write a Latin American tragedy without relying on Greek models. He found the answer in *La tragedia del fin de Atau Wallpan* (The Tragedy of the Death of Atahualpa), written in Quechua by an anonymous author around 1555 in Peru. It is a plaza spectacle that recalls the encounter between the last Inca emperor and Francisco Pizarro. García felt the need to reclaim this text for a contemporary audience. He integrated other materials on similar cultural encounters: fragments of the *Chilam Balam* from Chumayel in the seventeenth and eighteenth centuries; testimonies gathered in the sixteenth century by Frey Bernardino de Sahagún among the Tlaxcaltecs on the conquest of Mexico; and sections from the Peruvian Guamán Poma de Ayala's *Crónica de la conquista y del buen gobierno* (1613?

Playbill for García and Teatro La Candelaria's 1975 play (Guadalupe/Countless Years), about the death of peasant leader Guadalupe Salcedo during the liberal uprisings of the 1950s (Bruccoli Clark Layman Archives)

Chronicle of the Conquest and of Good Government). The inclusion of this material transformed the original text and gave a certain unity to its style and images. In addition, García incorporated what he calls *textos puente* (bridge texts) to smooth out the transitions between the original text and the new material.

García's text introduces an original character, Carigüeta, who identifies himself in the opening statements as "el que relata y el que lleva / mensajes. Chasqui soy pero también / canuchi / o sea que relato" (he who tells and carries / messages. / Chasqui am I but also / canuchi / that is to say, I tell). Carigüeta is a link not only between the Inca ruler and his people but also between the past and the present, since he delivers his own vision of the cultural encounter between Pizarro and Atau Wallpan to a modern audience. As narrator-confidant with respect to a contemporary audience, his function is to identify with the public and develop some understanding of the Inca's tragic mistake, an attitude that could be transposed to other heroes in other contexts.

Two story lines develop simultaneously throughout the play. One relates to Atau Wallpan's doubts and fears as he encounters Pizarro. The other follows Carigüeta and provides the perspective of the common people who worked for the Inca and his empire. As the Inca's unrest and fear grow, Carigüeta can sense his inner turmoil and points out the disturbing impact it has had on the people. Carigüeta seems to have much better vision concerning the impending events than the Inca and his advisors, but he fails in his attempts to communicate to them the feelings of the people. At the beginning of the play, Carigüeta drinks as part of a ritual, and then continues drinking throughout the play until he is totally inebriated at the end, connoting the destruction of his cultural values as the Inca empire falls.

The harmonic integration of such elements as masks, music, and ritualistic staging in *Corre, corre, Carigüeta* was a challenging task that many critics considered successful but was difficult for others to accept. There was general consensus, however, that this staging represented a definite break in the style of Teatro La Candelaria and that it contributed to the recovery of Latin America's cultural identity.

The 1980s were a difficult decade for Colombia because of the increasing violence at the national level. In addition to the massacres of peasants, political figures, and union leaders by the various guerrilla fronts, paramilitary groups, and the army (the so-called Dirty War), and the attacks against the homeless, street children, homosexuals, and prostitutes (the so-called *limpieza social,* social cleansing), a new kind of violence developed. This danger was associated with the drug trade and the criminal activities that depended on it directly or indirectly.

El Paso: Parábola del camino (El Paso: A Parable of the Road, performed in 1988) responded to this specific climate. Ariza, a member of Teatro La Candelaria and later director of the Corporación Colombiana de Teatro (Colombian Theater Corporation), comments on the genesis of this play in "Sandino y *El Paso*" (1990). During a trip that the collective took to Nicaragua, they conceived the idea of a play about César Augusto Sandino, the guerilla leader and popular hero for whom the Sandinistas are named. Once they were back in Colombia and began to work on this play, the circumstances of the country's Dirty War were in the foreground: "its dead and disappeared by the hundreds, the massacres, the threats," and a pervasive atmosphere of insecurity and fear. In this context, the improvisations changed: they were quiet, almost silent, as if words were not adequate or relevant to what was taking place.

The plot of *El Paso* puts together two sets of characters in an isolated, rural inn during a storm. A taxi driver, an elegant lady, her lover, a prostitute, and two strangers seek refuge there, comprising the first group. While the first four are waiting and hoping to find a way to get to the city, the two strangers are waiting for a signal or contact of some sort. The locals make up the second group: Don Blanco (a small ranch owner), Chela (the owner of the inn), and her employees: Doris (her daughter), Emiro (Chela's lover), Obdulio (a waiter), and a couple of musicians. The action, if it can be called that, is given in terms of brief, fragmented interactions without any cause-effect connection, defining situation and atmosphere more than character. What these characters share, regardless of social, economic, political, or cultural background, is the outbreak of a violent reality in their ordinary lives.

For García, the image that conveys this sense of a situation that exists in frozen space/time is the eye of the storm. The local characters seem to be at that point of total and even boring tranquility without being aware of the violent country around them until the intrusion of the group formed by the city people. The strangers, their money, the jeep, the helicopter, and finally the boxes with smuggled weapons that are the reason for their mysterious dealings are a terrifying, transforming force.

The collective widened the concept of language to include, in addition to the verbal component, other elements such as sounds, music, movement, and gestures. Stage directions give evidence of the paramount significance of the nonverbal communication. In the written text these directions actually take more space than the characters' speeches, detailing their body language—the way they look at each other, ignore questions, and move around the stage—and the blatant contradiction between what they say and what they do. This kind of nonverbal language weaves a series of disturbing references and allusions to the mysterious criminal dealings in which the strangers are participating and the others are implicated in one way or another.

El Paso was a successful play in Colombia. García acknowledges, however, that performances abroad were not as satisfactory initially, perhaps because the poetic dimension of the mise-en-scène could not be fully appreciated in the absence of a shared cultural background. This situation has changed over the years, however. After thirteen years and more than a thousand successful performances, including a tour of thirteen cities in Germany, this play has become a trademark piece of Teatro La Candelaria's national and international repertoire.

Maravilla Estar, the second play by García to be selected for collective creation by Teatro La Candelaria, was motivated by his reading of Lewis Carroll's *Alice's Adventures in Wonderland* (1865) and *Through the Looking-Glass* (1871). García explains in *Teoría y práctica del teatro* that his intention was neither to illustrate nor to give a theatrical rendition of Carroll's narrative. The English texts were simply a thematic source of inspiration, particularly in connection with the treatment of space and time: "La aventura de Alicia comienza con la pérdida de su espacio. Cae por un agujero y se encuentra, no se 'pierde,' en un dimensión en la que los valores espacio-temporales son manejados por un especie de capricho, de un arbitrariedad entre la voluntad de Alicia y la voluntad del azar" ("Alice's adventure begins with the loss of her space. She falls through a hole and finds herself (does not 'get lost') in a dimension in which spatial-temporal values are handled by a sort of whim, by a certain arbitrariness between Alice's will and the will of chance").

The play opens with Aldo Tarazona Pérez on an empty stage, with a suitcase and a shoulder bag, alone and in the middle of nowhere. Once he verifies that he is in the most absolute solitude, he identifies himself as a new Robinson Crusoe who has left behind his doubts and is ready to enjoy the peace and freedom provided by the open space in front of him. But every one of his perceptions is contradicted through his interaction with three more characters: Bumer, Fritz, and Alicia Maravilla Estar. In a series of situations that cannot be understood in any rational or chronological sequence—a mind-reading game, a physical attack that leaves him unconscious, events that supposedly took place five years ago (such as his fathering a child), a question-and-answer game, a wedding, and a circus act—Aldo explores the workings of his memory without relying on the reference point that chronological time would provide.

The idea of playing is essential for an understanding of *Maravilla Estar*. Basically, Tarazona does not know how to play. Time after time he makes it obvious that he lacks understanding of the rules of the game in which he is forced to participate. Alicia leads him to extreme situations where he is supposed to respond and make a decision, but he consistently fails to do so. Tarazona's need to stop and think, to reexamine his life and give some order and meaning to his experiences, is a common feature to most of García's protagonists.

García invites the audience to play as well by involving them in a complex and at times cryptic game of allusions including Carroll, Quevedo, William Shakespeare, Samuel Beckett, Fernando Arrabal, and even other plays by Teatro La Candelaria. These intertextual references are meant to be polemic elements within their corresponding contexts. To have the spectator participate consciously in this sophisticated game of allusions depends, however, on the spectator's literary and cultural competence. If the intellectual side of the allusion does not find resonance in the audience, it is always possible for the audience to respond instead to the humor of the absurd situation.

The reviews of the play indicate that it was well received. Julio Daniel Chaparro of *El Espectador* praised García's commitment to stage experimentation and acknowledged that the play represents an aesthetic, conceptual, and linguistic break from other productions by the collective. Carlos Gutiérrez of *Nueva Frontera* wrote: "Sólo cuatro actores pisan el escenario. Pero la música, el sonido y las luces prueban que, como generalmente lo hace el Teatro La Candelario, todos los miembros del colectivo están presentes" (Only four actors are on the stage. But the music, the sound, and the lights prove that, as Teatro La Candelaria usually does it, all the collective's members are present).

As García told Duque Mesa and Prada, during the 1980s the dialogue that Teatro La Candelaria had been establishing over the years with the social, economic, and political circumstances of the country became such a source of serious concern for the State that political repression against the group and its theatrical activity was strongly felt. They were accused of hiding weapons and collaborating with the guerrilla movement, and their premises were searched in 1985. The national and international recognition gained by García and the collective in Europe and the United States, however, including the Ollantay Award as Leader in Latin American Theater given to García in 1985, shielded them from more direct State aggression during this challenging period.

In spite of these difficulties, the next individual play by García, *La trifulca* (Squabble, performed in 1991) continued to metaphorically address the violent circumstances in Colombia. The audience, however, seemed to miss the connection, perhaps because it did not have the necessary distance and the play was three or four years ahead of its time. It was also a problematic play because of other factors: some actors left the group, which forced the collective to stop performances, and the music lacked the popular appeal required, a major drawback since it is structurally and thematically a significant component of the play. For all these reasons García calls this play Teatro La Candelaria's "ugly duckling."

The nineteen episodes focus on the deaths and resurrections of Niño Beni, a name that links the character with the Colombian Atlantic coast, where foreign names are common and where adults can be addressed by servants with the title *niño* (child) as a sign of respect. The play deals with various sides of the conflict between him, his group of musicians (the *guacherna*), and his girlfriend (Carlota) on one side, and his mother with her group of weeping women *(las plañideras),* his father, and Dr. Lupus and his followers *(los esbirros),* on the other. The first group represents life as Niño Beni wants to live it; the second, death, understood as the stifling imposition of society.

La trifulca interweaves elements from carnival and popular culture, recent Colombian politics, and life at the *barriadas* (slum areas) in Medellín, where adolescents are lured by drug lords into criminal activity. García used the carnival as a metaphor of the total fragmentation of society, a time of upheaval when there is a reversal of values and when Momus, the Greek deity of mockery and patron of writers and poets, is its leading figure before being sacrificed to Saturn. He is killed only to return again the following year and thus continue the cycle.

According to García, the assassination of a series of political leaders during the 1980s served as inspiration for the play. The assassinations began with members of the Unión Patriótica party such as Jaime Pardo Leal, Carlos Pizarro, and Bernardo Jaramillo Ossa, and continued with political figures of the bourgeoisie such as Luis Antonio Galán, the presidential candidate from the new liberal party, and Alvaro Gómez Hurtado, a prominent leader of the conservative party. During this period, social life in Colombia seemed to revolve around funerals. In the character of Niño Beni, all the fallen men become one. There are political overtones in other characters as well: for example, Dr. Lupus, the force opposing Niño Beni, incarnates right-wing politicians who support state institutions, persecute culture, manipulate power from the sides, and lament the presence of forces that liberate the individual and bring about change to society.

En la raya (1993, On the Edge), the next collective creation by Teatro La Candelaria, had as a point of departure *Crónica de una muerte anunciada* (1981, Chronicle of a Death Foretold) by Gabriel García Márquez. The idea originated in a proposal made by the Ministry of Culture in Spain to dramatize texts by renowned Latin American novelists. Because Teatro La Candelaria could not obtain the rights to García Márquez's novel, instead of staging the novel the group used a metatheatrical strategy, as they had in *Los diez días que estremecieron al mundo*. An inexperienced nonprofessional theater group made up of *ñeros* (short form for *compañero* and used as a slang word for people who live at the margin of society), financed by a European foundation and under a German director, is trying to stage *Crónica de una muerte anunciada* in a room of a building that used to be a gymnasium. They do not make much progress in their rehearsals because of the escalating conflicts among the cast members. Blatant sexual harassment, witchcraft, professional jealousy, incompetence, insubordination, drinking, armed assaults, psychological dysfunctions, and antisocial behavior are some of the problems that plague rehearsals. Rolf, the German director, never shows up to see the group.

Throughout the rehearsals, the actors see threatening presences around the corner and hear increasingly alarming noises coming from the street by the back door. Their fear materializes in the last episode of the play, which is heard but not seen: the back door is broken down by some people on motorcycles who enter the improvised stage to beat up the actors. When the light returns, they appear badly hurt and are trying to escape. Everything is destroyed. Asdrúbal, the actor who was to play Santiago Nasar, has been killed. Emma, one of the actresses, takes him center stage, pours some red liquid on his chest, and sits by him while yellow butterflies fall over his body, an image easily recognized by García Márquez's readers.

Teatro La Candelaria continues its experimentation with verbal and nonverbal languages in this play. The characters use expressions and vocabulary associated with *ñeros,* some of which may not be familiar to an audience with a different social, economic, or cultural background. The published play includes a glossary with the warning that the items included apply to the years 1992 and 1993, when *En la raya* was being staged, since this kind of vocabulary is transitory and is easily discarded by the groups where it originates.

Nonverbal language plays a major role in characterizing this marginal sector of society and reinforces the violence expressed linguistically. The characters' tics, mannerisms, and personal rituals give insight into

García and Ines Ortiz in a scene from Guadalupe/años sin cuenta *(Guadalupe/Countless Years), one of Teatro La Candelaria's most successful plays, performed more than 1,300 times (from the playbill; Bruccoli Clark Layman Archives)*

their psychological vulnerability while also providing effective comic relief. The final scene has as its referent the violent acts of *limpieza social* that cause the homeless, the homosexuals, the prostitutes, and other sectors of the population considered undesirable in Colombia to disappear from the streets.

The ongoing concern for individuals considered outcasts of society is found again in the next play by García. *Manda patibularia* (The Gallows Wish, performed in 1996), his next project to be staged as a collective creation by Teatro La Candelaria, is again based on a literary text, Vladimir Nabokov's *Invitation to a Beheading* (1938). The play, like the novel, deals with a man on death row (Eucario S.) who arrives at a high-security prison to wait for his execution. The personnel there—a warden, his daughter (Sibilia), a guard (Diomedes), a defense lawyer (Severo Tutti), and a librarian (Telémaco Cervantes)—visit the prisoner regularly, supposedly out of concern for his well-being. Eucario's family (mother, wife, and in-laws) comes to see him briefly for the last time. A supposed fellow inmate has been brought in to be his friend, confidant, and game partner. However, the situation is not as it seems. The personnel at the prison set up a series of abusive and oppressive situations for Eucario under the facade of making his stay more comfortable and agreeable. His family is as uncaring as usual toward him, and the prisoner who wants to befriend him is, in fact, his executioner.

Eucario's greatest wish is to know the date and time appointed for his death, because he would like to collect his thoughts and put them down on paper, to find "un punto" (a point) that will help him organize time in such a way that he can establish meaningful connections with himself, other people, his memories, and his dreams. But this opportunity is denied to Eucario until the last minute, and all that is left of him is his pile of white papers scattered on the cell floor.

The conflict between the individual and the State is at the heart of the play. The State—with its laws, documents, regulations, bureaucracy, and system of justice—appropriates, defines, and dehumanizes the individual, who feels powerless to oppose this situation. Eucario's attempts to write his autobiography as a legacy should be understood not only as a means to gain self-awareness but also as a way to affirm himself against the oppressive practices of the State by exercising his right to self-representation.

César Badillo, the actor who played Eucario in the initial production, points out in Fernando

Peñsamiento de la actuación (Thoughts on Acting), an unpublished 1996 typescript, that Manda patibularia "le da mucha importancia al ser humano. Nos hemos acostumbrado a masacres de cuarenta y cincuenta personas. El montaje se centra en la muerte de una sola persona como ser humano y gira alrededor de ese criterio" (gives a lot of importance to the human being. We have become accustomed to massacres of forty, fifty people. The staging centers on the death of a single person as a human being and revolves around this criterion). In a country where violence has become an everyday event, to expose the ways in which the abuse of power by an institution destroys an individual can be a valid strategy toward a national awakening. The reviews noted that the play found a responsive audience who could relate to the dark humor and irony involved in this struggle of the individual against the State and to the question of who really is administering justice in a country where guerrilla groups, paramilitary groups, the army, the drug lords, and the *sicarios* (paid assassins) all claim to have their own (twisted) codes for serving justice.

García acknowledges that his next project, *El Quijote* (performed in 1999), is perhaps the text on which he has worked the most. His intent was to put on the stage the visions and intuitions of his childhood related to the figure of Don Quixote instead of a faithful rendition of Miguel de Cervantes's famous character. One of the features that attracted him to embark on staging this classic was its oral quality. Since literacy was limited in Cervantes's times, oral group readings were common. To go from this recognition of speech act as a social act or event, to theater, was a natural step.

García's guiding criteria in the selection of episodes to be staged included their potential to be performed in a theater setting; the possibility of combining them in such a way that a new plot could be developed with beginning, middle, and end; and finally, the feasibility of presenting them in a period not to exceed two hours. Twelve episodes were chosen. The resulting dramaturgical proposal, primarily based on action, aimed at recovering the festive and ironic spirit of the original text. For Teatro La Candelaria the objective was to question issues related to identity, to explore the roots of Latin American culture and language, and to examine how those roots have been transformed. Cervantes is not seen, then, as a foreigner, but is appropriated as a source of Latin American thinking and of the Spanish language spoken in Latin America.

García received the Medal of Merit from the Colombian Institute of Culture in 1996 and the Medal of Artistic Merit from the Institute of Culture and Tourism of the District (Mayor's Office) in 1997. The Colombian Senate conferred on him the Order of Knighthood in 1998, and he was made Doctor Honoris Causa by the Universidad Nacional the same year. These awards acknowledge his lasting impact as director, playwright, actor, and theoretician.

The publication of the second volume of García's *Teoría y práctica del teatro* in 2002 gives access to material related to his creative endeavors from 1993 to 2001. The volume includes a series of interviews, reflections, critical and production notes, theoretical considerations, lectures, and analytical approaches to the works produced in this period (*El Quijote* in particular). Collective creation and the relationships among history, memory, and theater receive special attention. As Marina Lamus Obregon points out in her introduction to the volume, García's discourse fluctuates between the first-person singular and the first-person plural, revealing his self-awareness as an individual artist while acknowledging the collaborative learning process he shares with the collective.

The next production by Teatro La Candelaria, *De caos & deca caos* (On Chaos & Deca Chaos), first performed in March 2002, represents a tour de force for García as director and the group as a collective. In previous works the emphasis was on characters, situations, and themes associated with the lower strata of society; this time, the oligarchy is in the spotlight. This shift implied the need to explore a new language of representation avoiding the caricatures and clichés associated with the dominant class. The group's extensive research in Lacanian psychoanalysis, chaos theory, fractal theory, and Colombian history, marked by readings of Pierre Bordieu, Benoit Mandelbrot, Ilya Prigogine, Vicente Talanquer, Jean Baudrillard, George Perec, Alfonso López Michelsen, and Ricardo Niño, resulted in more than 120 improvisations. Twenty-five were selected for closer scrutiny, and this set was finally reduced to ten that focused on the broken private lives of the oligarchy.

At this point the task was to find an underlying common ground that could explain the selected improvisations. The concept of *cuplis*, taken from automotive mechanics, became the key structuring principle: the term refers to the gear assembly by which two dynamic systems connect. As applied to the play, *cuplis* serve as a nontraditional bridge between one scene and the next in such a way that the preceding one disintegrates while the actors introduce the new one through a playful and imaginative transition right in front of the spectators. An audience accustomed to the representation of a unified reality on stage now faces a fragmented vision that corresponds to a fractal structure. García acknowledges that movies such as *Magnolia* (1999), *American Beauty* (1999), and *Amores perros* (2000) influenced the composition of this play.

In addition to this structural role in the process of undoing time and space, the *cuplis* also become a vehicle for the actors to create complex characters and situations associated with the dominant class. Issues such as family lineage, the decadence or absence of an authority figure (husband, father, or president), family dissolution, broken relationships between masters and servants, shameful family secrets related to taboo topics (incest, mental retardation, infidelity, loss of fortune), and power abuse are explored to reveal a class whose traditional values and family bonds have been replaced by the violent relationships of a society in crisis.

Over more than four decades, Santiago García has been unwavering in his commitment to make a national dramaturgy a reality. Through improvisation, imagination, contemporary appropriation of classic material, the aesthetics of recycling, rigorous theoretical and acting training, and an integrative but open-minded approach to collective creation, he has succeeded in giving creative answers to the seemingly insurmountable dramaturgical and staging problems of a country with limited resources. The innovative character of García's theatrical proposals has contributed to shifting the cultural focus of the theater community from Europe to Latin America, as evidenced by the steady flow of invitations for lectures, workshops, tours, interviews, and performances received by Teatro La Candelaria and its director.

References:

Patricia Ariza, "Sandino y *El Paso*," *Revista del Teatro La Candelaria: Autor y Personaje*, 5 (1990): 3–7;

Lucía Garavito, "¡Aquí no ha pasado nada!: Narcotráfico, corrupción y violencia en *Golpe de suerte* y *El Paso* de La Candelaria," *Latin American Theatre Review*, 30, no. 2 (1997): 73–88;

Garavito, "*Guadalupe/años sin cuenta*: El lenguaje oral como instrumento ideológico de resistencia," *Latin American Theatre Review*, 20, no. 2 (1987): 5–16;

Garavito, "Representación y justicia en *Manda patibularia* de Santiago García," *Latin American Theatre Review*, 34, no. 2 (2001): 5–19;

Gerardo Luzuriaga, ed., *Popular Theater for Social Change in Latin America* (Los Angeles: UCLA Publications, 1978);

Teatro La Candelaria, 1966–1996, compiled by Fernando Mendoza, Francisco Martínez, Fernando Peñuela, and García (Santafé de Bogotá: Instituto Colombiano de Cultura/Teatro La Candelaria, 1997).

Vicente Leñero
(9 June 1933 –)

Stuart A. Day
University of North Carolina at Chapel Hill

PLAY PRODUCTIONS: *Pueblo rechazado,* Mexico City, Teatro Xola, 25 October 1968;

Los albañiles, Mexico City, Teatro Antonio Caso, 27 June 1969;

Compañero, Mexico City, Teatro Hidalgo, 13 March 1970;

La carpa, Mexico City, Teatro Reforma, 31 March 1971;

El juicio, Mexico City, Teatro de Orientación, 29 October 1971;

Los hijos de Sánchez, Mexico City, Teatro Jorge Negrete, 21 July 1972;

La mudanza, Mexico City, Teatro de la Universidad, 18 May 1979;

Alicia, tal vez, Mexico City, Teatro Jiménez Rueda, 29 August 1980;

Las noches blancas, staged reading, Mexico City, La Casa del Lago, 17 May 1981;

La visita del ángel, Mexico City, Foro Sor Juana Inés de la Cruz, 13 August 1981;

Martirio de Morelos, Mexico City, Centro Universitario de Teatro, 1983;

Jesucristo Gómez, Mexico City, Teatro Juan Ruiz de Alarcón, 10 July 1987;

¿Te acuerdas de Rulfo, Juan José Arreola?: Entrevista en un acto, staged reading, Guadalajara, Feria del Libro, 4 December 1988;

¡Pelearán diez rounds! Bogotá, Teatro Nacional de Bogotá, 10 April 1989;

Hace ya tanto tiempo, Cádiz, Centro Andaluz de Teatro, 1990; Mexico City, Teatro Benito Juárez, 1990;

La noche de Hernán Cortés, Mexico City, 1992;

Todos somos Marcos, Mexico City, Casa del Teatro, March 1995;

Qué pronto se hace tarde, Mexico City, Foro Sor Juana Inés de la Cruz, 26 September 1996;

Los perdedores, selections, Mexico City, Teatro el Galeón, April 1997;

Don Juan en Chapultepec: Carlota, Maximiliano y José Zorrilla, Mexico City, Teatro el Granero, 1997;

Nadie sabe nada, Mexico City, Teatro Galeón, 21 May 1998.

BOOKS: *La polvareda, y otros cuentos* (Mexico City: Jus, 1959);

La voz adolorida (Xalapa: Universidad Veracruzana, 1961); revised as *A fuerza de palabras* (Buenos Aires: Centro Editor de América, 1967);

Los albañiles [novel] (Mexico City: Seix Barral, 1964);

Estudio Q (Mexico City: Joaquín Mortiz, 1965);

El garabato (Mexico City: Joaquín Mortiz, 1967);

Vicente Leñero (Mexico: Empresas Editoriales, 1967);

El derecho de llorar y otros reportajes (Mexico City: Instituto Nacional de la Juventud Mexicana, 1968);

La zona rosa y otros reportajes (Mexico City: Instituto Nacional de la Juventud Mexicana, 1968);

Pueblo rechazado: Obra en cuatro tiempos (Monterrey: Sierra Madre, 1969);

Los albañiles [play] (Mexico City: Joaquín Mortiz, 1970);

El juicio: El jurado de León Toral y la Madre Conchita (Mexico City: Joaquín Mortiz, 1972); republished as *Magnicidio: El juicio a León Toral y a la Madre Conchita por el asesinato del presidente Alvaro Obregón* (Guadalajara: Agata, 1991);

Compañero (Mexico, 1973);

Redil de ovejas (Mexico City: Joaquín Mortiz, 1973);

Viaje a Cuba (Mexico City: Fondo de Cultura Económica, 1974);

El atentado contra Excélsior: Relación de hechos (Puebla: Universidad Autónoma de Puebla, 1976);

Los periodistas (Mexico City: Joaquín Mortiz, 1978);

El evangelio de Lucas Gavilán (Barcelona: Seix Barral, 1979); translated by Robert G. Mowry as *The Gospel of Lucas Gavilán* (Lanham, Md.: University Press of America, 1991);

La mudanza (Mexico City: Joaquín Mortiz, 1980);

Las noches blancas: Obra en cuatro noches (Mexico City: Universidad Nacional Autónoma de México, 1980);

Cajón de sastre (Puebla: Universidad Autónoma de Puebla, 1981);

Vicente Leñero, 2000 (photograph by Stuart A. Day)

La visita del ángel: Obra en dos actos (Mexico City: Universidad Nacional Autónoma de México, 1981);

Martirio de Morelos (Mexico City: Ariel & Seix Barral, 1981);

Teatro documental de Vicente Leñero (Mexico City: INBA, 1981)–compriscs *Pueblo rechazado, Compañero,* and *El juicio;*

Justos por pecadores: Tres guiones cinematográficos: Magnicidio, Los albañiles, Cadena perpetua (Mexico City: Marcha, 1982);

Teatro completo: Tomo I (Mexico City: Universidad Nacional Autónoma de Mexico, 1982)–includes *Compañero; El juicio; El martirio de Morelos;* and *Pueblo rechazado;*

Teatro completo: Tomo II (Mexico City: Universidad Nacional Autónoma de México, 1982)–includes *Los hijos de Sánchez; Alicia, tal vez;* and *La carpa;*

Vivir del teatro (Mexico City: Joaquín Mortiz, 1982);

Talacha periodística (Mexico City: Diana, 1983);

La gota de agua (Mexico City: Plaza y Janés, 1984);

Asesinato: El doble crimen de Flores Muñoz (Mexico City: Plaza y Janés, 1985);

Confrontaciones (Azcapotzalco, Mexico: Universidad Autónoma Metropolitana–Azcapotzalco, 1985);

La mudanza; La visita del ángel; Alicia, tal vez; La carpa (Mexico City: Editores Mexicanos Unidos, 1985);

La ruta crítica de "Martirio de Morelos" (Mexico City: Océano, 1985);

¡Pelearán diez rounds! (Mexico City: Editores Mexicanos Unidos, 1985; revised edition, Guadalajara: Agata, 1990);

Jesucristo Gómez (Mexico City: Océano, 1986);

Juanito Repetido (Mexico City: Edilin, 1986);

Manual de periodismo, by Leñero and Carlos Marín (Mexico City: Grijalbo, 1986);

Puros cuentos (Mexico City: Editores Mexicanos Unidos, 1986);

Vicente Leñero (Mexico City: Universidad Nacional Autónoma de México, 1986);

El hombre equivocado: Novela colectiva, by Leñero and others (Mexico City: Joaquín Mortiz, 1988);

Los hijos de Sánchez (Mexico City: Editores Mexicanos Unidos, 1988);

¿Te acuerdas de Rulfo, Juan José Arreola?: Entrevista en un acto (Guadalajara: Universidad de Guadalajara/Proceso, 1988);

El cordoncito (Mexico City: CIDCLI, 1988);

El infierno: Paráfrasis de "El infierno," primera parte de la Divina Comedia de Dante Alighieri (Mexico City: Universidad Nacional Autónoma de México, 1989);

Tres de teatro: Nadie sabe nada, Jesucristo Gómez, Martirio de Morelos (Mexico City: Cal y Arena, 1989); *Nadie sabe nada* translated by Myra S. Gann as *No One Knows Anything* (Potsdam, N.Y.: Danzón Press, 1995);

Señora (Guadalajara: Agata, 1989);

Los pasos de Jorge (Mexico City: Joaquín Mortiz, 1989);

Vivir del teatro II (Mexico City: Joaquín Mortiz, 1990);

La noche de Hernán Cortés (Madrid: El Público, 1992; Mexico City: El Milagro, 1994);

De cuerpo entero: Escenas de la vida de un escritor (Mexico City: Corunda, 1992);

¡Ay Jalisco! (Guadalajara: Agata, 1993);

El teatro de los insurgentes: 1953–1993, by Leñero and Fernando de Ita (Mexico City: El Milagro, 1993);

Camino de tierra (Mexico City: Plaza y Valdés, 1994);

Hace ya tanto tiempo: Pieza en un acto (Mexico City: Plaza y Valdés, 1994);

¡Pelearán diez rounds!, Los hijos de Sánchez, Nadie sabe nada (Mexico City: Grupo Editorial Gaceta, 1994);

Lotería: Retratos de compinches (Mexico City: Joaquín Mortiz, 1995);

Miroslava (Mexico City: Plaza y Valdés, 1995);

Los perdedores: Siete obras breves de temas deportivos (Mexico City: El Milagro, 1996);

El callejón de los milagros: Basada en la novela homónima de Naguib Mahfouz, Premio Nóbel de Literatura 1988 (Mexico City: El Milagro/Instituto Mexicano de Cinematografía, 1997);

Qué pronto se hace tarde (Mexico City: Universidad Nacional Autónoma de México, 1997);

La vida que se va (Mexico City: Alfaguara, 1999);

Dramaturgia terminal: Cuatro obras (Mexico City: Colibrí, 1999)—comprises *Hace ya tanto tiempo; Avaricia; Todos somos Marcos;* and *Don Juan en Chapultepec;*

La inocencia de este mundo (Mexico City: Universidad Nacional Autónoma de México, 2000);

El padre Amaro (Mexico City: Plaza y Janés, 2003).

PRODUCED SCRIPTS: *El festín de la Loba,* by Leñero and Francisco del Villar, motion picture, Del Villar Films, 1972;

El monasterio de los buitres, by Leñero and del Villar, based on *Pueblo rechazado,* motion picture, Estudio Churubusco Azteca, 1972;

El llanto de la tortuga, by Leñero and del Villar, motion picture, CONACINE, 1974;

Los albañiles, by Leñero, Luis Carrión, and Jorge Fons, motion picture, CONACINE, 1976;

Los de abajo, by Leñero and Servando González, based on the novel by Mariano Azuela, motion picture, CONACINE, 1978;

Las grandes aguas, based on the novel by Luis Spota, motion picture, CONACINE, 1978;

La tía Alejandra, by Leñero and Arturo Ripstein, based on a plot by Delfina Careaga and Sabina Berman, motion picture, CONACINE, 1979;

Cuando tejen las arañas, by Leñero, Fernando Galiana, and del Villar, motion picture, Conacite Dos, 1979;

Cadena perpetua, by Leñero and Ripstein, based on the novel *Lo de antes* by Spota, motion picture, Conaciné Avant, 1979;

Misterio, by Leñero and Marcela Fernández Violante, based on *Estudio Q,* motion picture, Conacite Uno, 1980;

Mariana, Mariana, by Leñero and José Estrada, based on the novel *Las batallas en el desierto* by José Emilio Pacheco, motion picture, Conacite Uno, 1987;

Miroslava, based on the short story by Guadalupe Loaeza, motion picture, Aries Films, 1993;

El callejón de los milagros, based on the novel by Naguib Mahfouz, motion picture, Alameda Films, 1995;

La ley de Herodes, by Leñero, Estrada, Jaime Sampietro, and Fernando Javier León Rodríguez, motion picture, Bandidos Films, 2000;

El crimen del padre Amaro, based on the novel by Eça de Queirós, motion picture, Alameda Films, 2002;

La mudanza, by Leñero and Gabriel Retes, motion picture, Conaculta, 2003.

OTHER: *Cuentos de la fe cristiana,* edited by Leñero (Mexico City: Pepsa, 1975);

El que la hace la paga, edited by Leñero (Mexico City: Pepsa, 1976);

La nueva dramaturgia mexicana, edited by Leñero (Mexico City: El Milagro, 1996);

Letra en escena: Dramaturgia en Guadalajara, edited by Leñero (Guadalajara: Secretaría de Cultura de Jalisco, 1999).

Upon receiving the prestigious Premio Xavier Villaurrutia (Xavier Villaurrutia Prize) in 2000, Vicente Leñero noted that he was pleased to have received the award, but that it had come too late, that it would have been more useful when he was younger and in need of recognition. Leñero's literary career is by no means over; nevertheless, in 1999 he published what he affirmed was his last theater publication, *Dramaturgia terminal* (Terminal Dramaturgy). He writes in the "Advertencia al lector" (Warning to the Reader) of this edition that he has other plays that have not been published or staged, yet he feels that it is time to put a "period" on thirty years of writing for the theater. Leñero's plays have earned him a place as one of the most prolific Mexican writers of the twentieth century, and he is one of Mexico's leading intellectual figures.

In his introduction to *La nueva dramaturgia mexicana* (1996, The New Dramaturgy of Mexico), Leñero recognizes that a new generation of authors, such as Sabina Berman and Víctor Hugo Rascón Banda, has taken over the vanguard of Mexican theater. Yet, he continues to be an integral part of Mexico's theater scene. In the *Diccionario enciclopédico básico de teatro mexicano* (1996, Basic Encyclopedic Dictionary of Mexican Theater), Edgar Ceballos sums up Leñero's position among Mexican writers: "Junto con [Emilio] Carballido y [Hugo] Argüelles forma la Santísima Trinidad del teatro mexicano del fin del milenio" (Along with [Emilio] Carballido and [Hugo] Argüelles he forms the Holy Trinity of Mexican theater of the end of the millennium).

Vicente Leñero was born in Guadalajara, Mexico, on 9 June 1933. Leñero explained in an unpublished July 2001 interview that his parents had always lived in Mexico City, but that at one point they went to Guadalajara so that his father, a businessman, could look for work. His father never found employment there, but Leñero was born before the family went back to Mexico City. Upon their return, the family moved to the house next door to Leñero's current residence, where he still has family. Despite his father's unemployment in Guadalajara, the Leñeros lived a relatively comfortable life. Young Vicente and his brother, Luis, played with puppets and, with the help of other relatives, built a puppet theater. He recalled that, at that time, to him "theater" meant productions of José Zorrilla's play *Don Juan Tenorio* (Don Juan the Rake, 1844), which his family attended yearly.

Leñero studied civil engineering at the Universidad Nacional Autónoma de México in Mexico City. During this period, upon returning home from a play, he decided to become a playwright. He stated that in the 1940s, however, pursuing a career in writing did not seem possible, and so he continued his engineering studies. He earned a degree from the Escuela de Periodismo Carlos Septién García, Mexico's most well-respected school of journalism. He stated in an unpublished interview that he studied journalism in order to learn to write, but that the process turned him into a journalist. Leñero married in 1959, and he credits his wife, Estela, a psychoanalyst, with making it financially possible for him to take up a career as a journalist and fiction writer. Leñero resides in the San Pedro de los Pinos neighborhood of Mexico City. He has four daughters, three of whom are artists; the fourth works with students with learning disabilities.

Luis de Tavira, one of Mexico's most well-known directors, captures the essence of Leñero's work in his introduction to Leñero's play *La noche de Hernán Cortés* (1992, The Night of Hernán Cortés): "Leñero es un autor obsesionado por la verdad: la búsqueda de la verdad es su principal motor dramático; la verdad íntima, la verdad histórica, la verdad política, la verdad social, la verdad dramática" (Leñero is an author obsessed with the truth: the search for truth is the principal dramatic motive; intimate truth, historical truth, political truth, social truth, dramatic truth). Even Leñero's most universal plays are in one way or another grounded in Mexican life. His plays that are less firmly rooted in events specific to Mexico or the rest of Latin America, and thus more universal, have not always been successful abroad. In an interview with Sharon Magnarelli, Leñero explained that, for example, the versions of *Los albañiles* (The Workers, performed in 1969, published in 1970) staged in Spain and Germany did not represent the heart of his play, even though the plight of low-wage construction workers or bricklayers is a "universal" theme.

In addition to writing for radio programs and soap operas, many of which were written under a pseudonym, he has also served as the director of the magazines *Claudia* (1969–1972) and *Revista de Revistas* (1972–1976) and is an owner of the weekly magazine *Proceso,* which he helped found, though he is no longer involved with its daily operations.

His first play, *Pueblo rechazado* (A Rejected People, performed in 1968), was written with the help of a 1967–1968 Guggenheim Fellowship. In 1962 Leñero had gone on a retreat at the Benedictine monastery Santa María de la Resurrección in order to revise the novel version of *Los albañiles* (1964). There he met Prior Gregorio Lemercier, who was in conflict with the Vatican over his advocacy of psychoanalysis and liturgical reform. As Leñero recounts in *Vivir del teatro* (1982, Living from the Theater), one of the first things Lemercier told him was "Psicoanalícese, no lo piense dos veces" (Get psychoanalyzed, don't think twice about it). The prior, and the controversy surrounding his unorthodox religious quest in the 1960s, thus provided the theme for a play based on the politics of religion.

Much of the play takes place in the monastery, which the Prior, who is based on Lemercier, has constructed in order to reach God. As part of this never-ending quest to find God, he invites a psychoanalyst (who sees in the monks the residents of an insane asylum) to the monastery. This invitation, of course, is scandalous in the eyes of the Church. When the Prior is tried by his superiors in act 2, Leñero also puts Mexican society and mob mentality on trial. A Chorus of Catholics points an accusatory finger at the Prior, spelling out for the audience the accusations against him

Enrique Lizalde as the Prior in the 1968 Teatro Xola premiere of Pueblo rechazado *(A Rejected People)*, Leñero's first play *(from a 1971 edition of* Pueblo rechazado, *1969; Thomas Cooper Library, University of South Carolina)*

(Marxist, heretic, blasphemer, insane, rebel, apostate) and defending the conservative views of the Vatican. A Chorus of Reporters, clearly looking for the most scandalous of news, vies for salacious details and gives the audience historical information (albeit exaggerated) about the Lemercier case. There is also a Chorus of Psychoanalysts, from which the spectator might hope to hear the voice of reason; instead, they accuse the Analyst of selling out to the Catholics. In turn, the Chorus of Catholics considers the Analyst to be the emissary of the Devil. The two-act play ends with a still defiant Prior, despite the wrath of the Church, affirming, "Sólo di testimonio público de mi fe y de mi búsqueda" (I only gave testimony of my faith and my search).

In his undated review of *Pueblo rechazado* in *Novedades* (Novelties), Rodolfo Usigli, Mexico's most internationally well-known playwright, gave Leñero's play almost unconditional praise. Usigli wrote that he agreed with Spanish writer Max Aub that *Pueblo rechazado* was the best Mexican play since Usigli's own *El gesticulador* (The Impostor, performed in 1947), which was written thirty years earlier. Usigli emphasized what he saw as the influence of T. S. Eliot, among others, on Leñero, and Leñero affirms in *Vivir del teatro* that Eliot's *Murder in the Cathedral* (1935) was the main influence behind the play. More importantly, Usigli recognized a trait that is common in Leñero's plays, including those that are set in the past: "Leñero basa su obra en un acontecimiento, un documento . . . [que] corresponde a la realidad y la vida inmediata de México" (Leñero bases his plays on an event, a document . . . [that] corresponds to the immediate reality and life of Mexico).

In 1992 Leñero wrote in his autobiography, *De cuerpo entero* (In Full), that he had only read his novel *Los albañiles* two times: once to make corrections, and again before turning the novel into a play. *Los albañiles* is one of Leñero's most moving plays. Based on the 1964 novel by the same name that had established Leñero as a writer in Mexico, *Los albañiles* begins with the discovery, in a building under construction, of a brutally murdered night watchman, Don Jesús. After the initial scene in which Don Jesús's body is found, act 1 introduces the audience to a variety of characters from different social classes, including construction workers and the building engineer, whose son is in charge of the project even though he has not yet learned to deal with the corrupt system. Act 2 presents the systematic interrogations by three investigators. Two of the investigators, who are difficult to distinguish from common criminals, offer to "supply" a quick confession–from any of the various suspects–and thus a quick solution to the case. However, the third, Munguía, actually wants to get to the truth through questioning the many characters, sans beatings or coercion. The different sections of the set allow for scenes from the interrogations to be acted out as flashbacks. The death of Don Jesús, in the end, is shown to be the responsibility of all of the characters, who have ignored–or contributed to–his demise.

Leñero was disappointed that the audiences who read the novel version of *Los albañiles* did not seem to see Don Jesús as a representation of Christ. For the play, he wanted to emphasize this symbolism, although the more overt religious message received mixed reviews. In addition to other, much more laudatory reviews was a scathing assessment of the play by Nancy Cárdenas, from which Leñero quotes in *Vivir del teatro*. In addition to calling the play an uninteresting melodrama not worthy of an author like Leñero, Cárdenas called the plot "infantile." Despite this negative review, *Los albañiles* has endured and is recognized as one of Leñero's best plays.

Leñero wrote *Compañero* (Companion, performed in 1970, published in 1973) after reading *El diario del Che en Bolivia* (1968, The Diary of Che in Bolivia) and other sources about Ernesto "Che" Guevara, the Argentine revolutionary best known for fighting alongside Fidel Castro. The play, which is set in Bolivia and Cuba (there is a different Che for each), was for the most part panned by critics. Some called it reactionary (because one Che, or Comandante, kills the other, which one could argue exculpates the Bolivian military for his execution), and many others called it unoriginal. The reactions to *Compañero* from the Left and the Right indicate the importance of revolutionary figures, including Guevara and Castro, in Mexican politics, given the historically close relationship between Cuba and Mexico.

After the production of *Compañero*, Leñero wrote *La carpa* (The Tent, performed in 1971), which is based on his novel *Estudio Q* (1965, Studio Q). In turn, his screenplay *Misterio* (Mystery, 1980) is based on the novel and play. One of the Ariel Awards the movie version won was actually for best screenplay written "originally" for movies. Leñero claims he turned *Estudio Q* into a play because he was suffering a creative drought. The play is an excellent example of metatheater and is clearly influenced by Luigi Pirandello's play *Sei personaggi in cerca d'autore* (1921, Six Characters in Search of an Author). The main character, Alex, is an actor in a soap opera about his own life. In the published version of the play, Alex and his lover Silvia, who has just committed suicide (against her will, because it was part of her stage directions for the soap opera), escape the confines of their scripted lives by jumping off the stage into the audience, against the objections of the director.

The reviews of *La carpa*, contrary to the take at the box office, were excellent. The title comes from a suggestion that the play be performed outside in a large tent. The name stayed the same, but the outdoor staging did not become a reality because the production was paid for on credit, but the producer did not follow through with his promise of funding. Leñero documents this experience in the first volume of *Vivir del teatro*, and, as in descriptions of other incidents, he does not mince words about his anger. The play was finally produced in the Reforma Theater, which had a reputation for guaranteeing the doom of plays that were staged there. Despite a spiritual cleansing of the theater, which Leñero did not attend, the play was a financial failure.

El juicio (The Trial; performed in 1971, published in 1972), also published as *Magnicidio* (1991, Magnicide), treats the trial of José de León Toral and María Concepción Acevedo de la Llata, called "la Madre Conchita," for the assassination of Alvaro Obregón, the revolutionary general and president of Mexico, in 1928. Leñero wanted, as he had done in the past, to question official history and to confront "el fanatismo religioso de los acusados y el fanatismo político de los acusadores" (the religious fanaticism of the accused and the political fanaticism of the accusers), as he wrote in *Vivir del teatro*. He considered León Toral to be an "admirable martyr" because of his dedication to the cause of Christians in postrevolutionary Mexico. Leñero came across a copy of the published trial transcript while going through the books he inherited from his father, researched the case further, and wrote *El juicio*. This two-act play presents both sides of the jury trial, which ended with guilty verdicts–death for León Toral and twenty years in prison (of which she served twelve) for la Madre Conchita.

After months of problems getting official approval from censors for the staging of the play, Leñero and the director were offered a bribe to put off the opening night and avoid offending people in the government who viewed Obregón as a hero of the revolution. They decided to stage the play anyway, and after having hypnosis performed on the ill leading actor so that he could go on, the play finally made it to the stage. More than six decades after the beginning of the Mexican Revolution, and more than four decades after the assassination of Obregón, the play, while generally reviewed favorably, still brought out emotions on both sides of the controversy. A photo of León Toral after his execution, which shows a pool of blood from his head staining the ground, on the cover of the 1991 edition by Agata of *Magnicidio* emphasizes Leñero's desire to question history–not to mention controversy–on the Mexican stage.

Los hijos de Sánchez (The Children of Sánchez; performed in 1972, published in 1982) is based on Oscar Lewis's 1961 anthropological study by the same name and takes place in a small Mexican village. Over drinks at a hotel in Mexico City's formerly posh *zona rosa* (pink zone), Lewis, who had voted in favor of Leñero's Guggenheim Fellowship, asked Leñero (after being rejected by Carballido and Sergio Magaña and after rejecting a dramatic version by Margarita Urueta) if he would be willing to adapt Lewis's book for the theater. Leñero was slow to write the script, and Lewis died in 1970, before Leñero completed the project. Despite the challenges of creating a play from such a lengthy text, Leñero combines anthropological data about the characters with well-paced action.

In 1975 Leñero and his wife moved temporarily during the remodeling of their home. This change of environment was sufficient to bring Leñero out of a literary dry spell. He wrote the first draft of a new play in one sitting and observed the movers closely as they returned his belongings to his remodeled home. The result of this experience, *La mudanza* (The Move; performed in 1979, published in 1980), takes place in a small, run-down colonial house filled with debris. It is a realistic play that, as the single act progresses, becomes a ghostly commentary on interpersonal relations, not only between the main characters, Jorge and Sara, but also between the middle class and the proletariat. The play begins when Sara and Mari (who is Sara's only friend willing to give up her Sunday to help with the move, but who accepts with pleasure the advances of Sara's husband) enter the dilapidated house. The doors to all rooms except the living room are locked, giving the play, from the beginning, a claustrophobic atmosphere. The first scene of this humorous yet depressing play involves an ongoing argument between Jorge and Sara, both of whom have been unfaithful. Leñero's script for *La mudanza* includes a "Coro de miserables" (Chorus of miserable people) and a "Miserable-parlante" (Miserable-speaker), although for Adam Guevara's production these representatives of the poor were reduced to one. In the written text, the "Miserable-parlante," after begging for water and downing two of Jorge's beers, distributes the couple's lunch among the other poor people. The "miserables," who come out of a trunk in which they could not realistically have fit, stab the couple to death, and Mari returns to see her friends' cadavers and the "miserables," one of whom is playing the violin.

The appearance of the "miserables," while a sharp break from the realism of the first part of the play, fits well with the dialogue between the movers and the couple. Leñero notes in *Vivir del teatro,*

> Quería . . . dar otro paso en mi carrera de dramaturgo: conectar los principios del realismo con otras formas más libres, derivarlo hacia un teatro metafórico, simbólico, tal vez expresionista. . . . En el combate escénico entre dos géneros de literatura dramática se podría ilustrar asimismo, sin hacerla demasiado evidente, la inevitable lucha de clases.

> (I wanted . . . to take another step in my dramatic career: to connect the principles of realism with other forms that were more free, to direct it toward a metaphorical theater, symbolic, perhaps expressionist. . . . In the scenic combat between the two genres of dramatic literature one could also illustrate, without making it too evident, the inevitable class struggle.)

Influenced by the work of such writers as Spanish dramatist Ramón del Valle-Inclán, Leñero's text is convincing, and the audience is left to interpret the message of the play.

After three years of searching for a theater for *La mudanza* Leñero finally found space with the Compañía Nacional de Teatro (National Theater Company) in 1978, until it was determined that the company had more actors than Leñero's play required and that they would use a play by Carballido instead. With this rejection, Leñero took what he calls a "last, desperate act" and approached the theater department of the Universidad Nacional Autónoma de México, about which he writes in *Vivir del teatro:* "desde que tuve conciencia teatral, jamás vi que la Universidad, fueran quienes fueran los jefes de su Departamento de Teatro, pensara en la dramaturgia mexicana" (ever since I had a theatrical consciousness, I never saw the University, no matter whom the directors of the Theater Department were, think about Mexican dramaturgy). Yet, Leñero asked the head of the department about staging the play, and it was finally presented in 1979. Though not all reviewers applauded Leñero's combination of dramatic forms, in his review of the play in *Tiempo* (Time) Carballido noted that in Leñero's play the "acción va rompiendo todo límite y llega al punto promedio: la lucha de clases y la lucha de sexos entremezcladas en un trozo de poesía dramática" (action proceeds, breaking all limits, and arrives at a midpoint: the class struggle and the battle of the sexes are blended in a piece of dramatic poetry).

In writing *Alicia, tal vez* (Alicia, Perhaps; performed in 1980, published in 1982), Leñero hoped to create a strong female protagonist, although he also created somewhat of a scandal. His wife was the first person to object to the fact that at the end of the play, after Alicia leaves her husband to become an independent woman, she ends up rejecting her newfound freedom. At one point, after she has left her husband, her driver suggests that she could work, to which she replies: "¿Romper con todo para terminar convertida en una vulgar secretaria?" (Break with everything to end up a common secretary?). She tells her driver, without irony, that for her such work would be another form of slavery. In the scene where she does apply for a job, she is hired because of her looks, and the first letter her boss dictates is from another typist who will be "resign-

Carlos Barbosa, Sandra Gonzalez, and Santiago Bejarano in the 1989 Teatro Nacional de Bogotá premiere of Leñero's play
¡Pelearán diez rounds! (They Will Fight Ten Rounds!), *about a boxer whose wife wants him to quit the sport
(from* Latin American Theatre Review, *volume 25 [Spring 1992];
Thomas Cooper Library, University of South Carolina)*

ing," although Alicia herself can barely type. The fired typist, Gloria, informs Alicia that no matter how well she does her job, to be successful she will have to sleep not only with the boss and all other managers but also with male coworkers, and that her time will be up when she is no longer a novelty. Marcos, another office worker, creates a "wonderland" for her, including a garden of flowers in which she can recover her lost childhood, but in the end he only does so to seduce her.

For *Alicia, tal vez* Leñero also wanted to revive the "miserables" that had been reduced in *La mudanza*. This time they would be called "Desharrapados" (The Ragged Ones). After another series of encounters with machismo in act 2, Alicia enters one of the three sections of the stage to find the Desharrapados creating makeshift shelters out of trash and the signs feminist protestors had been carrying in the previous scene. The Desharrapados later rape Alicia, who is saved by Marcos and her driver. The next and last scene finds her back in the arms of her husband. At one point Alicia is asked by a group of feminists to speak and she explains, "El problema de las mujeres nunca se ataca de raíz" (The problems of women are never attacked at the roots). The question remains whether Leñero's play gets to the root of the problems women and the poor face in Mexico or simply reinforces the status quo.

Las noches blancas (staged reading in 1981, published in 1980) is based on Fyodor Dostoevsky's *White Nights* (1848), which Leñero read as a child. Leñero's version of *Las noches blancas* takes place over four consecutive nights. The first night, Nástenka, who lives with her cruel Grandmother, meets a stranger on a bridge. The two lonely characters agree to meet again the next night, when she confesses to him that she was waiting to meet someone who had been a tenant in her Grandmother's house. By the fourth night, having heard nothing from the former tenant, the stranger declares his love for Nástenka, and they decide to marry. At this point the former tenant arrives, and Nástenka, who regrets that she cannot love both men at the same time, goes off with him. The play ends as the kind stranger, alone again, watches the couple leave the bridge.

La visita del ángel (The Angel's Visit, performed and published in 1981) treats an elderly couple who are visited by Marú, their granddaughter and the "angel" of the title. The play is characterized by, as much as anything else, a lack of dialogue. Indeed, there are many more stage directions than scripted lines, except during the granddaughter's visit, which exposes a generational gap but not necessarily a lack of understanding. The play, combining both realist and absurdist aspects, again shows Leñero's versatility. In *Vivir del teatro* Leñero explains how his experiment was received by critics:

> A Héctor Mendoza le pareció una obra extraordinaria, a Guillermo Sheridan execrable, a Malkha Rabell interesante. Luisa Josefina Hernández abandonó el teatro al terminar el primer acto, y aunque Esther Seligson y Emilio Carballido elogiaron el experimento, pusieron serias objeciones, como muchos otros espectadores, al remate de la pieza: la muerte del Abuelo.
>
> (To Héctor Mendoza it was an extraordinary play, to Guillermo Sheridan it was execrable, to Malkha Rabell it was interesting. Luisa Josefina Hernández abandoned the theater at the end of the first act, and although Esther Seligson and Emilio Carballido praised the experiment, they had serious objections, as did many other spectators, with the ending: the death of the Grandfather.)

In *Martirio de Morelos* (The Martyrdom of Morelos; published in 1981, performed in 1983) Leñero dramatizes the final days of José María Morelos, a revolutionary fighting for Mexico's independence from Spain in the nineteenth century. The play includes a prologue, during which a Lector (Reader) agrees to help Morelos discover historical information about himself. On a bare stage with a lectern and an enormous book–Mexico's "official" history–the Lector informs Morelos that he is a national hero, that a coin bears his image, that there is a town named after him, and that he is nothing less than a martyr. The play itself takes place in 1815 and employs characters including members of the viceroyalty and insurgents in search of independence. Leñero takes on Mexican history in order to reclaim Morelos not as an idealized national figure molded by postindependence political forces but as a man who, faults and all, fought to liberate Mexico.

After the prologue, the Lector serves as narrator, reading from the massive compilation of Mexican history. Official history and Leñero's presentation of the execution of Morelos collide in scene 7, called "La pena de muerte" (The Death Sentence), when a soldier announces that, even though Morelos has provided specific information that will help the loyalist military squelch the independence movement, he will be put to death. Morelos's body, out of deference to the clergy, will not be mutilated, nor will his head be put on public display. In addition, the soldier notes that Morelos will be given an ecclesiastical burial because he is a priest. The Lector, after hearing Morelos's detailed confession, is at first incredulous and then turns to Morelos, whose head is bowed, as he begins to suspect that something has been left out of his seemingly all-encompassing book of Mexican history. Soon after, Morelos is executed by a firing squad and falls to the ground screaming. It takes a second round of bullets to silence his moans. At this point the Lector again reads from his tome of history and is challenged by the Vice King, who asks why there is no mention of Morelos's statement (to which, he reminds the Lector, there is a reference in the public death sentence that was read) that retracts all of his actions and the quest for independence.

In Leñero's version of this document, Morelos begs forgiveness from the Church, Spain's reinstalled King Fernando VII, the secular and regular clergy, his ecclesiastic and civilian superiors, the villages for which he says he has been a bad example, and even from the Americans and the Europeans for having harmed their "interests" in Mexico. The Lector responds that a footnote in a history text by Lucas Alemán disputes this document. To the Vice King, Alemán is an imbecile; to the Lector he is an impartial historian who in 1851 wrote that Morelos's retraction was not to be believed because the style of the text is different than that of Morelos, and that he would never even have signed such a document. The Vice King replies with the main argument of Leñero's play: it is the Lector's obligation to read Morelos's retraction. That is, Mexican readers should have access to all documents on Morelos so as to judge for themselves the character of this national hero.

José Agustín, in his review in *Excélsior,* wrote that in *Martirio de Morelos* Leñero, in terms of his documentary theater, had reached maturity as a writer: "Leñero ha podido fundir sus extraordinarias capacidades periodísticas con su gran talento narrativo; el resultado, por lo general siempre había sido muy estimulante, pero en esta nueva obra Leñero lleva su género predilecto al máximo brillo" (Leñero has been able to meld his extraordinary journalistic capacity with his great narrative talent; the result had generally been very stimulating, but in this new play Leñero takes his preferred genre to the highest level).

Jesucristo Gómez (Jesus Christ Gómez; published in 1986, performed in 1987) is based on Leñero's 1979 novel *El evangelio de Lucas Gavilán* (1979; translated as *The Gospel of Lucas Gavilán,* 1991). Despite having promised to himself that he would give up writing adaptations, he let himself be convinced to write a version of his text for the theater. In fact, versions of the novel had been adapted and staged by several groups, including by the Chicano group Compañía de Teatro de Albuquerque (Albuquerque Theater Company) in the United States. The play, as the title suggests, paraphrases the Gospel According to Saint Luke in a Mexican context, and Leñero affirms that it was influenced by the ideas of liberation theology. In the author's note, he explains that *Jesucristo Gómez* is meant to be both an "acto de fe" (act of faith) and "una reflexión dramática sobre el país de los humildes" (a dramatic reflection on the country of the humble people).

Leñero judges his plays not by the direct compliments he receives but by what he overhears and observes when he attends a performance. For *Jesucristo Gómez* the reaction was not positive. Yet, instead of blaming the director, Leñero explains in *Vivir del teatro II* (1990) that "yo comprendí que era la obra, mi errado empeño en traer a Jesucristo a nuestro tiempo, lo que no consiguió a convencer" (I understood that it was the play, my erroneous determination to bring Jesus Christ to our time, that was not convincing).

Leñero had held fellowships from the Centro Mexicano de Escritores (Mexican Center for Writers) for 1961–1962 and 1963–1964. Through these fellowships, Leñero came into contact with another of Mexico's most well-known writers, Juan José Arreola, who died in 2001 and who inspired Leñero's 1988 play *¿Te acuerdas de Rulfo, Juan José Arreola?: Entrevista en un acto* (Do you Remember Rulfo, Juan José Arreola?: Interview in One Act). The play is based on an interview with Arreola by Leñero, the mexican writer Federico Campbell, the photographer Juan Mirando, and the journalist Armando Ponce that took place in the house of Arreola's brother shortly after the death of one of Mexico's most well-known writers, Juan Rulfo, in 1986. Formatted like a play and including pictures, a list of "characters," and a description of the set (Antonio Arreola's house), the interview/conversation treats the theme of Arreola and Rulfo's complicated friendship. Leñero wanted to add to the information available in the press regarding the relationship between the two men, which was strong at first but later distant.

This text is also an experiment for Leñero, one in which he highlights the theatricality of the interview genre. *¿Te acuerdas de Rulfo, Juan José Arreola?* was to be performed by Arreola, Leñero, and others at the Guadalajara book fair. However, Leñero was not able to attend because of a family emergency, and Arreola almost missed the performance because he could not find a glass of wine with which to regulate his blood sugar. After he was seen by a doctor, the play went on, although early on it slipped back into the world of "fact" when Arreola discarded the script and began to play the role of himself. In *¿Te acuerdas de Rulfo, Juan José Arreola?*, by framing an interview with the trappings of the theater, Leñero highlights role-playing in everyday life, as well as the not-so-clear line between fact and fiction.

When Leñero was still working at the magazine *Claudia* it was decided that an advice column by the famous actress Dolores del Río (with Leñero as a ghostwriter) would be added in November of 1965; the play

Cover for Leñero's 1990 one-act play (Long Ago Already; published in 1994), about an aging middle-class couple who discover each has a different view of their past (Thomas Cooper Library, University of South Carolina)

Señora (Madam, published in 1989), which was never performed, is based on this venture. Leñero would go to del Río's house with invented questions (the real letters, he notes, were mostly to ask for money or other favors) and his answers, which she approved, even though she was disappointed not to have "real" questions from people who wanted her opinion. In *Vivir del teatro II* Leñero explains his plans for the play: "Todo era cosa de transformar aquella Dolores del Río hosca, asexuada, inapetecible, en una actriz despabilada, muy sexy y ligeramente alcohólica. El galán no sería el reportero de 33 años que era yo en 1966, sino un jovenzuelo veinteañero, verdaderamente galán y con un complejo Edipo" (It was a matter of transforming that sullen, asexual, unappetizing Dolores del Río into a sharp, very sexy and slightly alcoholic actress. The handsome man would not be the thirty-three-year-old reporter I was in 1966, but a twenty-something young man, truly handsome and with an Oedipus complex). Of course, the young reporter does happen to have the same initials as Leñero, not to mention the fact that the name similarity between Dolores del Río (River) and the character Julieta del Mar (Sea) was not missed by many readers.

¡Pelearán diez rounds! (They Will Fight Ten Rounds! published in 1985, performed in 1989) was derived from a 1982 article Leñero read on the boxer Bobby Chacón, whose wife committed suicide that year because he would not give up his career in the ring. Leñero had often contemplated writing a play about a boxer, and reading the article gave him the plot he needed. The protagonist of the play, Bobby Terán, is returning to boxing, against the wishes of his wife, María, who had tried unsuccessfully to take her life two years before. She leaves (or escapes) from a mental hospital in Los Angeles upon hearing that her husband is planning to fight again. Her gift to him is a small pistol, which he can accept if he decides not to fight–if he does, she will use it to commit suicide. In the last scene, having decided to fight, Bobby is knocked out by an opponent who he thought was supposed to throw the fight. Moments before, Bobby sees (or has a vision of) María, who stands up from her seat and shoots herself. The title of the play comes from the fight announcer's jargon, "Pelearáaaaaaaaaan dieeez rooouuuuuunds." This short play is powerful, and the boxing ring becomes a metaphor for human relations. The violence of the ring and domestic violence overlap when Bobby beats María during an argument that takes place in the ring, and the difficult relationship between Bobby and his promoter is reminiscent of similar relationships between young men and father figures in other texts by Leñero.

El infierno (1989) is based on Dante's *Inferno* and takes place in Mexico. Although perhaps impossible to stage, the play takes aim at what Leñero calls "el pequeño infierno que ha conformado la vida pública de nuestro país" (the little hell that has shaped public life in our country). Religion and derision, the subjects of many of Leñero's plays, are the focus in this play. In the introduction to her translation of Leñero's play *Nadie saba nada* (published in 1989, performed in 1998; translated as *No One Knows Anything,* 1995) Myra S. Gann points out that Leñero "is always at the same time profoundly Catholic yet extremely irreverent, a member of the establishment while vehemently critical of it." As one character puts it, many people can be found in the depths of hell, including "Todos los traidores de nuestra historia patria" (All of the traitors of the history of our country).

In *Hace ya tanto tiempo* (So Long Ago Already; performed in 1990, published in 1994), originally published in *Los mayores* (The Elders) in 1984, Leñero takes up a theme that has become more prominent in his work as he has gotten older: relationships among the elderly. In this play, a middle-class couple in their seventies get together after thirty-seven years to discuss their past, which for each has become something different. Memory, lost opportunities, and a sense that seemingly minor decisions can change the course of a lifetime dominate the single act of this moving play.

In *La noche de Hernán Cortés* Leñero treats the conquest of Mexico. The play takes place in four settings (two in Mexico, one in Cuba, and another in Spain) and recedes in time as the play continues, presenting the sixty-two-year-old Cortés in Sevilla, the thirty-something in Mexico, and the twenty-nine-year-old in Cuba, upon his arrival in the Americas. Despite the varied settings, which exist simultaneously, the play is grounded in Mexico: the accents are to be Mexican, and there are indigenous musicians playing prehispanic instruments, in addition to a European who plays the oboe. The Cortés whom Leñero presents as surrounded by the ghosts of his past is by no means the Cortés of the history books. José Luis Martínez, who has written an extensive study on Cortés, writes in his introduction to the 1994 edition of the play that Leñero's character is "nada convencional" (not at all conventional), given that, among many other irregularities, he dies in Cempoala, Mexico. Martínez finds Leñero's version to be less stiff than his own and notes that Leñero's literary license offers a new view of Cortés.

Todos somos Marcos (We Are All Marcos; performed in 1995, published in 1999) demonstrates that Leñero has continued to treat current political events and their effects on society. Set in Mexico City after the 1994 uprising of the revolutionary group knows as the Zapatistas in the Southern state of Chiapas, the play depicts the lives of three people. The text of the play is preceded by a quotation from Subcomandante Marcos, the enigmatic figure who was one of the leaders of the Zapatista National Liberation Army. In a 1994 interview with Leñero, Marcos noted that if he disappears, anyone, as long as they have the black mask he and other Zapatistas wear, can take his place. The title of the play refers to this anonymity as well as to a demonstration in 1995 in Mexico City after the Mexican government revealed the probable identity of Marcos: Rafael Sebastián Guillén Vicente, a former university professor. The people in the city center chanted "we are all Marcos" in support of the Zapatista cause. The play was first performed in 1995 at the Casa del Teatro (House of Theater) as part of Teatro Clandestino (Clandestine Theater), a series of plays that treated current events in Mexico.

Todos somos Marcos takes place in a run-down apartment in Mexico City. The three characters are all in their thirties and face a juncture in their lives. Miguel, who needs to find an affordable place to live, has come to the apartment that Laura and Raúl shared until their recent breakup. As the action unfolds, the audience sees that Raúl and Laura have separated over their conflicting political ideas. They are both self-described leftists. However, they choose different paths: Laura plans to go to the state of Chiapas to join the Zapatista movement, and Raúl decides to leave Mexico City in search of work with an uncle who is well-connected. Although Raúl and his friend Miguel harshly criticize Presidents Carlos Salinas de Gortari (1988–1994) and Ernesto Zedillo Ponce de León (1994–2000), the split within the political Left, as well as gender relations, are the predominant themes in this play.

Los perdedores (The Losers, published in 1996) is a collection of seven vignettes related to baseball, basketball, boxing, soccer, and racewalking. The piece on racewalking, titled "Caminata," is made up of only three words: "Tengo que ganar" (I have to win), which the athlete wearing the number ten repeats over and over as the other racers pass him, until finally he is in last place. Leñero mixes hope and pain in this vignette that, though simple, becomes a powerful message when combined with the other six pieces in the collection. As the title suggests, Leñero focuses on *los de abajo,* the underdogs. Selections from *Los perdedores* were staged at the Teatro el Galeón in April 1997. In his introduction to the play, Juan Villoro captures the common thread: "En las siete caídas de *Los perdedores,* Leñero combina las gestas deportivas con los temores secretos de sus protagonistas. Su triunfo son estas íntimas derrotas" (In the seven losses of *Los perdedores,* Leñero combines sporting exploits with the secret fears of his protagonists. These intimate failures are his triumph).

Qué pronto se hace tarde (How Quickly it Becomes Late; performed in 1996, published in 1997) focuses on two elderly people, presenting the unusual friendship of an aging conservative woman (Malena) and her Marxist neighbor (Genaro), who is assaulted and robbed in

Cover for the 1994 edition of Leñero's 1992 play (The Night of Hernán Cortés), in which he offers an unconventional view of Hernán Cortés's role in the conquest of Mexico, presented in reverse chronological order (Thomas Cooper Library, University of South Carolina)

the hallway of their building. As Malena helps the eighty-year-old Genaro recover, it becomes clear that despite their divergent political views they have much in common, including loneliness. The Marxist's son is a corrupt reporter and an aspiring playwright who is writing a metaplay in which the two elderly characters appear. At one point Genaro asks Malena to tear down the wall that separates them–literally. After asking the question he has a heart attack, and his son runs from his office to the area of the stage where Genaro is, breaking the realistic separation of the previous scenes. The play ends with "El muro de Berlín" (the Berlin Wall) still standing. Malena tells Genaro that she is still married "in the eyes of the Church" and that it is too late to find love. The metaplay becomes more complex when, in the final scene, Genaro tells his son that he is going to write a play–the play that his son could not write.

Leñero (right) and fellow playwright Hugo Argüelles (from Edgar Ceballos, ed., Hugo Argüelles: Estilo y dramaturgia, *1994; John C. Hodges Library, University of Tennessee)*

Perhaps because of the influence of the play *Don Juan Tenorio* in his childhood, Leñero brings one of this character's creators, along with two of Mexico's historical figures, to life in *Don Juan en Chapultepec: Carlota, Maximiliano y José Zorrilla* (Don Juan in Chapultepec: Carlota, Maximilian, and José Zorrilla; performed in 1997, published in 1999). In a dream-like combination of settings in Belgium and Mexico, Carlotta the Empress of Mexico under Napoleon III, appears behind Zorrilla as he writes the first act of *Don Juan Tenorio;* she thinks that he is Don Juan. Zorrilla is later joined by a ghostly Maximiliano, the Emperor of Mexico to whom he confesses his desire to be remembered for plays other than *Don Juan Tenorio*. Indeed, Leñero's play, which ends with Carlotta citing lines from *Don Juan Tenorio* over the body of her dead husband, serves as a creative confessional for all three characters. In his "Advertencia a lectores y espectadores" (Warning to Readers and Spectators), Leñero notes that the play is "pura fantasía" (pure fantasy). While the play is part fantasy, Leñero also bases his characters, as he usually does, on historical documents. The information about Zorrilla, for example, comes in part from Zorrilla's self-criticism of *Don Juan Tenorio*.

Avaricia (Avarice, published in 1999), as Leñero notes, is based on a chapter of Vicente Blasco Ibañez's *El militarismo mejicano* (1920, Mexican Militarism) and takes place in the 1920s. Although the play has not been produced, it is an interesting vignette that brings Blasco Ibañez, Obregón, and León Toral to life. As an orchestra plays typical Mexican music, Obregón tells Blasco Ibañez that the people love him because, having lost one arm in battle, he cannot rob as much as other leaders. After telling another anecdote, in which President Venustiano Carranza steals the watch of the Spanish minister of foreign affairs, Obregón is shot by León Toral; his head falls into his plate; and the last thing the audience hears is the laughter of Obregón's assistants.

In *Vivir del teatro II* Leñero affirms the importance of producing Mexican plays instead of relying too heavily on adaptations of foreign plays. He also states that plays should not be written to conform with the traditional requirements of specific genres if that means they will not be believable to Mexican spectators. His play *Nadie sabe nada* was inspired when Leñero commented to his friend Tavira that Mexico did not have detectives like those portrayed by North American writers such as Dashiell Hammett and Raymond Chandler: "Pero aquí no hay detectives como Spade ni como Marlowe. Ni inspectores que investiguen a fondo. Aquí nomás hay crímenes y crímenes. No hay detectives ni justicia" (But here there are no detectives like [Sam] Spade or [Philip] Marlowe. Nor are there investigators that investigate in depth. Here there are only crimes and more crimes. There are no detectives and there is no justice). This statement led Tavira, who had directed *Martirio de Morelos,* to challenge Leñero to write a detective thriller. The result was *Nadie sabe nada,* which Leñero wrote to highlight the corrupt relationship between the press and the government in Mexico. The play therefore varies from traditional detective stories, which Leñero considered to be unbelievable to a Mexican audience, by avoiding the usual components of a completely honorable protagonist, a clean solution to the crime, and the triumph of good over evil.

This "Thriller en dos actos y catorce escenas" (Thriller in Two Acts and Fourteen Scenes), as the subtitle reads, takes place within a two-week period: three days of one week (act 1) and three of the next (act 2). During the course of the play, the action continues simultaneously in nine scenic spaces, which include a newsroom, governmental offices, a cabaret, a taco stand, and a private club. This technique heightens tension during action scenes and gives the spectator a sense of city life in Mexico, including street vendors, crime, a parade, and many other small details that come together to form a unified whole. Leñero presents the chaotic, behind-the-scenes action that, in the end, results in a sanitized version of political events suitable for public consumption. One could argue that the protagonist of *Nadie sabe nada* is a thin folder containing sensitive documents that have recently crossed the desk of the president of Mexico, and for which the government is willing to pay $80,000. Perhaps the hero of the play is Lorenzo Salcido, who passes the documents—which presumably disclose massive corruption on the part of the Partido Revolucionario Institucional (Institutional Revolutionary Party)—to Pepe Gutiérrez, a journalist for a Mexico City newspaper. Pepe and fellow reporter Juan José Tagle refer to Salcido as their "Deep Throat." They know the elusive documents he offers Pepe (for free) could represent Mexico's Watergate, especially if they were working at a "real newspaper," as Juan José puts it, in the original text and in the translation by Gann:

> JUAN JOSE. Pero qué tan importantes deben ser los papeles para que se arme tanto escándalo, Pepe, ¿no? Yo nunca imaginé.
>
> PEPE. Ni yo tampoco.
>
> JUAN JOSE. Y se arruga el cuero.
>
> PEPE. Sí, se arruga.
>
> JUAN JOSE. Tienes que encontrarlos, pinche Pepe. ¿Te imaginas? A lo mejor resultan pintados para un Watergate. . . . Un Watergate mexicano, no estaría mal, ya es hora. Ya te veo a ti y a mí como esos dos periodistas gringos, ¿te acuerdas?, que le pusieron su cuatro a Nixon. ¿No te gustaría ponerle un cuatro al sistema? . . . Capaz que le damos un susto y en un chico rato la armamos en grande, ¿por qué no? Así empiezan luego las revoluciones.

> (JUAN JOSE: God, those papers must be important for all this to be happening. Pepe, don't you think? I never imagined.
>
> PEPE: Me neither.
>
> JUAN JOSE: It gives me the creeps.
>
> PEPE: Yep.
>
> JUAN JOSE: You've got to find them, Pepe. Just think. They might give us our own Watergate. . . . A Mexican Watergate. Not bad, huh? About time. I can see us now, just like those two gringo journalists, remember? The ones who put the screws to Nixon. Wouldn't you like to put the screws to the whole system? . . . We could just put a scare into them this time and later on we could go for the big time. Why not? That's how revolutions are started.)

Figures from different government agencies pursue Salcido, and later Pepe, to recover the documents in order to please their superiors and further their own usually corrupt careers. By the end of the play, Salcido has been murdered; his mentally ill sister has been raped; and Pepe turns over the documents to a government agent, from whom they are stolen by another government representative and eventually returned to the office of the president. Pepe's motives are, in part, ambiguous. He turns over the documents after Salcido's sister, Dalila, with whom he has had sexual relations, is taken hostage by government agents. As he turns them over, he tries unsuccessfully to claim the reward.

Leñero loosely based some of the characters in *Nadie sabe nada* on public figures. For example, the corrupt Licenciada Magaña, who easily keeps up with her male counterparts in terms of ruthless efficiency, is modeled after Victoria Adato, a high-ranking official in Mexico in the 1980s. Sagrario, the corrupt director of the newspaper where much of the action takes place, is also female. The inclusion of women in powerful governmental and business positions was, according to Leñero, a pragmatic decision based on the number of people in the theater troupe of the Centro de Experimentación Teatral. Regardless of the initial motivation, the decision to create more roles for women resulted in relatively equal access to corruption and other illicit activities as well. The increased role of women in the play mirrors a similar increase in the number of female politicians in Mexico. In the 1990s, for example, Rosario Robles was the mayor of Mexico City.

Leñero's two-volume *Teatro completo* (1982, Complete Theater) presents an excellent overview of his most well-known plays from 1968 to 1981. Bruce Swansey, in the introduction to both volumes, notes that Leñero separates his plays into three categories. The first of these categories, documentary theater, includes *Pueblo rechazado*, *Compañero*, *El juicio*, and *Martirio de Morelos*. Though different in many ways, they are all based on historical documents. The second category of plays, adaptations from works by Leñero and other authors, includes *Los hijos de Sánchez*, *Los albañiles*, and *Las noches blancas*. Leñero's domestic pieces, the third category, include *La mudanza*, *La visita del ángel*, and *Alicia, tal vez*.

These categories provide a useful framework for understanding Leñero's plays. Yet, Leñero affirmed in an unpublished July 2001 interview that his more recent theater cannot necessarily be neatly categorized. *Todos somos Marcos*, for example, is based on historical records but also offers the spectator insight into the relationship of the protagonists, laying bare human emotions while commenting on an historical phenomenon. Perhaps it is this combination of themes, as well as dramatic styles, that has helped Leñero to become one of Mexico's most well-known playwrights.

Interviews:
Kirsten F. Nigro, "Entrevista a Vicente Leñero," *Latin American Theatre Review*, 19 (Spring 1985): 79–82;

Sharon Magnarelli, "Una entrevista con Vicente Leñero," *Gestos: Teoría y Práctica del Teatro Hispánico*, 3 (November 1988): 140–147;

Carlos Paul, "Leñero: Del teatro me retiro con gusto porque ya dije todo," *La Jornada* (Mexico City), 9 March 2000 <http: www.jornada.unam.mx/2000/mar00/000309/cul2.html>.

References:
Danny J. Anderson, *Vicente Leñero: The Novelist as Critic* (New York: Peter Lang, 1989);

Judith I. Bissett, "Constructing the Alternative Version: Vicente Leñero's Documentary and Historical Drama," *Latin American Theatre Review*, 18 (Spring 1985): 71–78;

Jacqueline Eyring Bixler, "Historical (Dis)Authority in Leñero's *Martirio de Morelos*," *Gestos: Teoría y Práctica del Teatro Hispánico*, 2 (November 1986): 87–97;

Adame Domingo, *Vicente Leñero: Ensayos sobre su obra dramática* (Cholula: Universidad de las Américas, 1994);

Homenaje fílmico a Vicente Leñero, edited by Ana Cruz Navarro (Mexico City: Cineteca Nacional/Sociedad General de Escritores de México, 2001);

Sharon Magnarelli, "The Female Other: From the Visible Absence to Recasting the Other in Leñero's *La carpa* and *Señora*," *Gestos: Teoría y Práctica del Teatro Hispánico*, 6 (April 1991): 45–61;

Priscilla Meléndez, "Leñero's *Los albaniles*: Assembling the Stage/Dismantling the Theatre," *Latin American Literary Review*, 21 (June 1993): 39–52;

Meléndez, "On Leñero's *Martirio de Morelos*: Reading the Empty Stage," *Gestos: Teoría y Práctica del Teatro Hispánico*, 7 (April 1992): 51–64;

Kirsten F. Nigro, "De la novela a las tablas: *Los albañiles* de Vicente Leñero," *Alba de América: Revista Literaria*, 7 (July 1989): 233–243;

Nigro, *Lecturas desde afuera: Ensayos sobre la obra de Vicente Leñero* (Mexico City: El Milagro, 1997);

Nigro, "La mudanza de *La mudanza* de Vicente Leñero," *Revista Canadiense de Estudios Hispánicos*, 12 (Autumn 1987): 57–69;

Nigro, "Un revuelto de la historia, la memoria y el genero: Expresiones de la posmodernidad sobre las tablas mexicanas," *Gestos: Teoría y Práctica del Teatro Hispánico*, 9 (April 1994): 29–41;

Howard L. Quackenbush, "El espacio y el tiempo negativos en *Los fantoches* y *Jesucristo Gómez*," *Latin American Theatre Review*, 31 (Spring 1998): 18–31;

Joan Rea, "El conflicto de conciencias en los dramas de Vicente Leñero," *Latin American Theatre Review*, 31 (Spring 1998): 97–105.

Germán Luco Cruchaga
(7 May 1894 – 2 June 1936)

Elsa M. Gilmore
United States Naval Academy

PLAY PRODUCTIONS: *Amo y señor,* Santiago, Teatro Esmeralda, 18 February 1926;
La viuda de Apablaza, Santiago, Teatro La Comedia, 28 August 1928.

BOOKS: *La marsellesa humilde y heroica* (Santiago: Impr. Sociedad Boletín Comercial Salas, 1926);
La viuda de Apablaza (Santiago: Editorial del Nuevo Extremo, 1958);
Teatro (Santiago: Nascimento, 1979)–comprises *Bailabuén, La viuda de Apablaza,* and *Amo y señor.*

Editions: *La viuda de Apablaza. Amo y señor,* edited by Juan Andrés Piña (Santiago: Pehuén, 1990);
La viuda de Apablaza, edited by María de la Luz Hurtado (Santiago: LOM, 1999);
La viuda de Apablaza, digital edition of the Biblioteca Nacional de Chile and the Biblioteca Virtual Miguel de Cervantes <http://www.cervantesvirtual.com/servlet/SirveObras/04705065365736184243379/index.htm>.

Germán Luco Cruchaga's life coincided with a period of momentous transformation in Chilean political, social, and theatrical history. Most literary critics concur that during the Chilean Golden Age between 1917 and 1928, there were three main dramatists who depicted the effects of Chile's socio-economic transformation from the perspective of a particular social class: Antonio Azevedo Hernández gave voice to the marginalized elements of Chilean society; Armando Moock emphasized an aesthetic and content consistent with bourgeois taste and morality; and Luco Cruchaga focused on the portrayal of the traditional upper class and its social values being pushed into historical oblivion by the oncoming tide of modernity and capitalism. Luco Cruchaga's place in Chilean and Latin American literary history is assured primarily by *La viuda de Apablaza* (Apablaza's Widow; performed in 1928, published in 1958). This rural tragedy has become a classic often credited with initiating the history of a national Chilean theater.

Germán Luco Cruchaga (courtesy of Elsa M. Gilmore)

Born in Santiago on 7 May 1894, Luco Cruchaga was the descendant of one of Chile's most distinguished and wealthy families. Since gaining its independence from Spain, Chile had established a republican but undemocratic system of government that maintained class divisions for the benefit of the country's landed oligarchy. Juan Luis Sanfuentes, the last president of this so-called plutocratic republic (1915–1920), was Luco Cruchaga's great-uncle. Nevertheless, in spite of his family's connections, Luco Cruchaga never enjoyed personal wealth. From childhood on, his participation in the social high life was usually as a guest of wealthy relations; for example, he often was invited to spend summers at the Relbuncó estate near Coihueco, Ñuble province. Thus began his exposure to the rural ways of life and the colloquial speech he later depicted in his dramas. By late childhood he also had begun to experience intense emotional states and to manifest the personal insecurities that persisted throughout his adult life.

When Luco Cruchaga was eleven years old, his family decided that he should begin studies at Santiago's Seminario Conciliar. The boy immediately disliked the strict religious rules and rebelled against wearing the obligatory cassock. He left before completing his first year. Soon thereafter, he prevailed upon his elders to allow him to enroll in Santiago's Escuela de Bellas Artes. Unlike the seminary, this institution proved to be well suited to Luco's artistic talents and free-spirited personality. By the age of fifteen or sixteen, he had become an accomplished artist, and his illustrations were beginning to appear in magazines such as *Corre Vuela* and *Sin Sal*. By 1913 he was signing his drawings for *Zig-Zag* with the pseudonym "Whisky." In that same year he began a lifelong career in journalism, publishing interviews and articles under the name "El señor de Phocas." In 1917, at the age of twenty-three, he added *El tanque* magazine in Valparaíso to the list of publications to which he sent his articles, and no longer content with being a mere contributor, he cofounded *La tribuna ilustrada* in Santiago. The following year, *Pacífico* magazine published some of his pieces, and he joined *Sucesos* as a staff illustrator.

As a young man, Luco Cruchaga befriended others who shared his interest in the arts, including the actors Pedro Sienna and Rafael Frontaura, the journalist Jorge Hübner Bezanilla, and the poet Vicente Huidobro. The group was rounded out by Luco Cruchaga's cousins, Juan Guzmán Cruchaga and Miguel Angel Cruchaga Santa María, both of whom were poets who went on to win Chile's Premio Nacional de Literatura (in 1948 and 1962, respectively). Together, they adopted a bohemian lifestyle that involved regular late evenings, long philosophical discussions, and convivial drinking. Such a pattern was common among Santiago theater people, and for Luco Cruchaga it appears to have embodied a rebellious response to the conservative values of his social class. His good looks and the carefree reputation he acquired during his late teens and early twenties persisted throughout much of his life. In a retrospective piece published in *El Mercurio* on 7 December 1941, Januario Espinoza recalled a tall and handsome young man, whose aristocratic manners, artistic interests, and taste for the good life made him irresistible to women.

Luco Cruchaga's particular interest in drama was strongly influenced by the artistic and social fever that gripped his country in the first decades of the twentieth century and that led to the emergence of a truly national theater. European plays, Spanish *zarzuelas,* and even opera, often performed by touring Spanish companies, had been popular in Chile since the nineteenth century. At the conclusion of World War I, as many European troupes disbanded or collapsed, the famous Chilean actors Enrique Báguena and Arturo Bürhle formed the first Chilean theater company with an almost entirely Chilean staff and a repertoire that included many Chilean plays. The Báguena-Bürhle performances were enthusiastically received, and their example was quickly followed by other Chilean actors and entrepreneurs. What emerged was theater written, produced, and performed by Chileans, and featuring national themes, characters, and speech. This metamorphosis had the effect of broadening the appeal of the genre to the emerging Chilean middle class and to the poorer segments of society. By 1919 there were twenty theaters in Santiago, and many Chilean companies were touring the provinces. During what has come to be known as the Golden Age, more than two hundred new Chilean plays were staged. During that same period, stage performers become the first true popular idols of Chilean mass audiences. The popular cult of stars such as Sienna, Bürhle, and Evaristo Lillo was recognized as a new social phenomenon known as *divismo*.

The birth of the national theater mirrored the large-scale evolution of Chilean society from a near-feudal nineteenth-century culture that looked to Europe for social and artistic models into a modern, capitalist society that began to shift its focus toward its own national social concerns and priorities. In the political arena, the 1920 election of president Arturo Alessandri Palma marked the defeat at the polls of Chile's traditional aristocracy and the emergence of the middle class into a new leadership role in the political and cultural life of the nation. Luco Cruchaga's youth coincided with this period of ferment, and most of his active years as a playwright were within the heyday of the Golden Age. This era is generally considered to have ended with the advent of talking motion pictures and the onset of economic crisis in 1928. By the time Luco Cruchaga completed the last of his three well-known plays, *Bailabuén* (published in 1979), in 1931, it had passed.

Sometime during 1921 or 1922 Luco Cruchaga completed his first play, *Amo y señor* (Lord and Master; performed in 1926, published in 1979). He delivered the manuscript to a commercial or *teatro de cartel* company, whose advisory board may have deemed its indictment of an upper-class family's corruption too risky to bring to the stage. The manuscript was shelved until 1926, when Luco Cruchaga gave it to his friend Lillo, who was the founder and star of one of Chile's first and most popular professional theater companies. Lillo appears to have been the ideal interpreter of the character of Don Sepúlveda, and the play enjoyed a successful debut at Santiago's Teatro Esmeralda and a warm reception by critics.

Amo y señor is a metaphor for the passing of nineteenth-century values and the advent of modernity and a capitalist economy. The protagonists, members of the aristocratic Manso-de la Barrera family, have fallen into abject poverty. The military portrait of the deceased family patriarch, Don Dositeo Manso, presides over the chaotic living room and recalls an obsolete heritage. His widow, Doña Adela, proudly traces her family to distinguished origins but is ignored by her children. His ne'er-do-well son, Polito, embodies the worst qualities of an ignoble gentleman: he is unwilling to engage in any work or other productive activity; he mocks his mother's old-fashioned ideas; and he despises those whom he regards as his social inferiors. Elvira, the older of Doña Adela's two daughters, is engaged to Barrenechea, the scion of an equally distinguished but impoverished family. Polito persuades her to instead marry his own coarse but wealthy friend Sepúlveda. The latter's sympathy with the Mansos' fall from social privilege echoes Luco Cruchaga's positivist recognition of the social transformation that provides the background of the play.

At the opening of the second act, two years have elapsed since the marriage of Elvira to Sepúlveda. Financial security has not bought family bliss, however. After failing to find satisfaction in a marriage to a man she regards as her inferior, Elvira has become involved in an affair with Barrenechea, a fact Polito uses to blackmail her in order to guarantee his own security. Sepúlveda's initial goodwill has been poisoned by Elvira's infidelity. Anxious for love and revenge, he seeks both through Elvira's younger sister, Matilde. In the third and final act, the characters have cast aside all pretense of propriety and mutual respect: Matilde has become Sepúlveda's mistress; Polito's moral collapse into gambling and alcoholism is nearly complete; and Doña Adela denies the reality around her. The final confrontation is triggered by Sepúlveda and Matilde's decision to parade their affair by going out to dinner together. Elvira implores Polito to prevent her public humiliation, and a symbolic struggle between the two men follows. Polito is quickly defeated by the lowly butcher Sepúlveda, who

Luco Cruchaga (right) with Armando Moock, another of Chile's leading playwrights during the Golden Age of Chilean theater, from 1917 to 1928 (from Mario Guzman, Historia del teatro chileno, *1974; Thomas Cooper Library, University of South Carolina)*

now affirms his dominance as lord and master of the household, by virtue of the power his money gives him over the entire family.

In *Amo y señor* Luco Cruchaga clearly judges the old socio-economic system as corrupt and views the triumph of capitalist values as complete and irreversible. On the other hand, he does not regard this change as a positive evolution toward more humane personal relationships. Sepúlveda's power is devoid of moral restraints and affirms itself only through violence. Luco Cruchaga's characteristic use of class- and locale-appropriate *chilenismos* is evident in this play, as is his tendency toward the type of ending that moves the audience to personal introspection and a rethinking of their social environment. *Amo y señor* also gives the first indication of Luco Cruchaga's skill in the creation of female characters. Elvira, in particular, is a complex personality who throughout the drama falls prey to conflicting emotions and motivations. Her character is hateful for her ambition and arrogance but at the same time pitiable for her humiliation at the hands of her brother and her husband.

The personal triumph Luco Cruchaga enjoyed with *Amo y señor* was short-lived. In 1926, when the play premiered, he was employed as director of the *La Patria* newspaper in the city of Concepción. He received information about a fraudulent railroad business deal, and under the pseudonym "Arminvs" he wrote and published an indictment of the presumed perpetrator, a local railroad administrator. The owner of *La Patria* thought Luco Cruchaga's article excessively combative and promptly asked for his resignation. Smarting from the dismissal, and in the absence of other job prospects, Luco Cruchaga, who by now had married Marta Vargas, accepted his father-in-law's invitation to manage the latter's estate, or *fundo*, in Quitrahué, a small village located in Villarica province. In this rural isolation Luco Cruchaga failed to develop any interest in the agricultural or management tasks that were set before him. Instead, he wrote assiduously for *El Correo de Valdivia*, signing his articles with a new pseudonym related to the remote location of the *fundo*: "Zacarías Quitratué."

During this period of residence at the Vargas estate, Luco Cruchaga found the inspiration for his best-known drama, *La viuda de Apablaza*. Marta Vargas narrated her recollections of this period to Luis Merino-Reyes, who later reported them in his 1986 article "Aproximaciones a Germán Luco Cruchaga" (Approaches to Germán Luco Cruchaga). Soon after their arrival in Quitrahué, Luco Cruchaga heard about the Widow González, a local semicelebrity who was known less for her trade as a cheese maker than for her masculine and sometimes violent demeanor. Instead of poring over the estate accounts or working with the farmhands, Luco Cruchaga would ride off to the widow's small property in the southernmost Faja Séptima. Vargas was intrigued by her husband's absences and finally asked him why he spent so much time at the widow's. Merino-Reyes quotes her recollection of Luco Cruchaga's reply: "Vas a ver la media obraza que voy a hacer con esta viuda" (You'll see the fine play I'll make with this widow). For the debut of *La viuda de Apablaza,* Luco Cruchaga turned again to Lillo, who by now was associated with Angela Jarques. Their company first performed the play at Santiago's Teatro de La Comedia in 1928, with Lillo playing the role of Ñico and Elsa Alarcón that of the Widow. Luco Cruchaga reveled in success again, as audience and critics gave the performances a warm reception.

Like its predecessor, *La viuda de Apablaza* reflects the cultural transition from traditional values identified with a colonial nineteenth-century heritage to a new capitalist ethos. Unlike *Amo y señor,* however, its action is set in the countryside and features *costumbrista,* or rural, elements that inject irony and comic relief into the plot. In both plays, the decadence of the old values is signified by the older characters who personify them, and the transition to the new era is experienced as a loss. However, *La viuda de Apablaza* also includes the elements of a tragedy. One of the best analyses of this drama is given by María de la Luz Hurtado in her *Teatro chileno y modernidad: Identidad y crisis social* (1997, Chilean Theatre and Modernity: Identity and Social Crisis). She is not the only critic to note the similarities to Euripides' *Hippolytus* (428 B.C.) or Jean Racine's *Phèdre* (1677), but she is the first to identify *La viuda de Apablaza* as one of the two tragedies marking the transition of Chilean rural life into the era of modernity. (The other one is Arturo Orrego Barros's *La marejá,* 1909.) Hurtado points out that the key elements of this tragic drama are desire, incestuous passion, jealousy, abandonment, and the handing over of power, set in a remote and wild Chilean *sur* (southern frontier) in which the rules of culture are often overcome by the laws of nature.

The plot of *La viuda de Apablaza* centers upon a strong-willed and wealthy widow in love with her deceased husband's illegitimate son. The childless and middle-aged Widow took in and raised Ñico, who is now a young man. Through sheer personal will and expert knowledge of her land and of the people who work it with her, she has managed to exercise control of her inheritance. Ten years into this harsh and lonely life, she recognizes her nearly incestuous love for Ñico, and resorting to her authority as a traditional landowner, she demands that he end his relationship with her own niece, Florita, and marry the Widow instead. He is persuaded, as he later admits, because the arrangement conveys to him the title over all of the Widow's earthly possessions. Before the silent but knowing eyes of the farmhands, and with the sympathetic hearing of her confidants, the nearly ruined Spanish merchants Don and Doña Jeldres, the Widow is transformed by her blind passion from a powerful, nearly masculine figure into a scorned wife, reduced to lamenting her helplessness and her unrequited love. Once in control of the estate, Ñico abandons the Widow's matriarchal style of administration and implements new rules meant to maximize profits by minimizing expenses. Key among his economies is the consolidation of the two separate households he has previously maintained for his wife and for Florita, who is now his mistress. In the face of this humiliation, the Widow chooses a final act of dignity and takes her own life on the day Florita is to move into her home. The fact that Ñico belatedly recognizes his love for his "almost mother" and implores Florita to allow him to mourn her underscores the incest theme that propels the tragic outcome. Ñico's reaction to the suicide also reflects the sense that an irrecoverable era has passed into oblivion. The ensuing sense of loss is echoed by Remigio the farmhand. His closing remark confers the ultimate compliment of patriarchal society upon the tragic figure of the Widow, "¡Qu'era más rehombre que todos nosotros!" (Who was more of a man than all of us put together!).

Nearly three decades after *La viuda de Apablaza* was first produced, the Teatro Experimental de la Universidad de Chile included the play in its 1956 season. This revival, directed by the Teatro's celebrated founder Pedro de la Barra, enjoyed an enthusiastic reception in Santiago and was subsequently taken to Chilean stages from Iquique to Puerto Montt during a triumphal national tour. Performances in Buenos Aires and Montevideo followed. In his article "Germán Luco Cruchaga y el teatro chileno moderno" (1981, Germán Luco Cruchaga and the Modern Theater of Chile) Julio Durán Cerda deems this production to have been one of the most decisive events in the history of the Chilean stage. He credits it with the emergence of a new enthusiasm for Chilean drama among young artists and audiences and with the reaffirmation of the theater as an instrument for the portrayal and transformation of society. He suggests that, in this regard, the 1956 production of *La viuda de Apablaza* may have influenced the members of the "Generation of 1950," which included such luminaries as Isidora Aguirre, Fernando Debesa, Jorge Díaz, Luis Alberto Heiremans, María Asunción Requena, Alejandro Sievcking, Sergio Vodanovic, and Egon Wolff. Although Hurtado points out that this group's treatment of female characters is dramatically different from Luco Cruchaga's, there are undeniable points of contact in the identification of politics and gender and the power reversal in Luco Cruchaga's drama. Wolff's *Flores de papel* (1970, Paper Flowers) for example, restates and develops these fundamental relationships within the framework of 1960s Chile. In *Los orígenes del teatro hispanoamericano contemporáneo* (1972, The Origins of Contemporary Latin American Theater) Grínor Rojo agrees that *La viuda de Apablaza* showed the path to combining social commentary with a careful psychological study and may have been a model for such dramatists as Montes López and Zavala Muñiz.

After *La viuda de Apablaza,* Chilean theater began a slow decline related to the onset of worldwide economic crisis and to the growing appeal of the cinema. Luco Cruchaga made a living as director of *La Nación* in Santiago de Chile and as a correspondent for *El Sur.* In 1931 he completed *Bailabuén,* another rural drama. The play features character types, customs, music, and language drawn from the popular milieu; sexual motives are one of the major plot forces; and humor appears in the form of deception, tricks, and abundant verbal innuendo. Ties to other popular or pseudopopular literary forms such as *gauchesca* poetry are emphasized as the protagonists quote verse stanzas originally uttered by other gaucho or *huaso* (Chilean cowboy) literary figures. Among those cited are Estanislao del Campo, Martín Fierro, Anastasio el Pollo, and Juan Moreira. Popular music, particularly the song "La palomita," also has a prominent role. However, *Bailabuén* departs from the model set by nineteenth-century *sainetes* (one-act comedies), and it does not feature the kind of optimistic message that other works of this genre have, such as Carlos Cariola's *Entre gallos y medianoche* (1919), a national favorite enjoying many revivals throughout the years.

The term *bailabuén* is a deformation of *bailahuén* or *vailahuén,* a medicinal Andean herb said to enhance male sexual performance. The title alludes to the central conflict: the vain efforts of the old bandit Don Erasmo to keep the love of the young and beautiful Clarita, who, during one of his many long absences, has taken the virile young Perejil as a lover. Other characters include Don Erasmo's stepmother, Ña Pávez; his partner, the gaucho Tristán Alvarez; and the professional singer La Diuca and her lover El Coipo. The minor characters are Chilean *huasos* and Argentine gauchos who follow Erasmo and Tristán in their common occupation as cattle thieves. The action is set at Erasmo's ranch, in a remote and beautiful location in the Andes from which the town of Lonquimay is visible in the distance. After a prolonged absence, Erasmo returns and reproaches Clarita for her inconstancy. She and Ña Pávez insist that they hired Perejil because they needed help with the animals and the property. Erasmo pretends to be satisfied with this explanation until he learns that Perejil has been stealing his cattle and selling it in Lonquimay. This transgression, Erasmo explains, he cannot overlook, because he has gone to great pains to steal these animals. That same night, during a dance at the ranch, and before Perejil and Clarita can run away together, Erasmo challenges the young man and kills him.

The second act takes place the following morning. A party guest has apparently reported Perejil's murder to the authorities in Lonquimay. In view of their imminent arrival, Erasmo prepares to ride off with Tristán and their followers. Before he departs for a mountain hideout, he breaks with Clarita, orders

Carmen Bunster and Mario Lorca in the 1956 Teatro Experimental revival of Luco Cruchaga's 1928 play, La viuda de Apablaza *(Apablaza's Widow), a production credited with reviving interest in Chilean theater (courtesy of Elsa M. Gilmore)*

her out of the ranch, and threatens to return to kill her if she denounces him to the authorities. He leaves El Coipo and La Diuca in charge of liquidating his cattle and other goods. They and Ña Pávez are to join him later in the sierra. Upon his departure, these three characters and Clarita enter the ranch and vainly attempt to reassure each other while they await the ominous arrival of the authorities. In the final scene, they are cowering in fear as the sounds of horses and the breaking of a door are heard.

Bailabuén was not performed during Luco Cruchaga's lifetime. In 1936, his longtime friend and artistic interpreter Lillo died. A bereaved Luco Cruchaga was asked to deliver the eulogy, which he did with great zeal and emotion. Lillo's death was a heavy personal blow that brought on an emotional crisis for the playwright. Shortly after his friend's funeral, Luco Cruchaga was taken ill, and he died on 2 June 1936. Details of Luco Cruchaga's final days are sketchy, although many of his biographers refer to a dissipated life as the main cause of his premature demise at the age of forty-two.

Luco Cruchaga produced works in other genres besides drama, including the novel *Garabito* (Common Breed) and three short stories published in *Atenea*: "Zarco," "El perfecto funcionario" (A Perfect Government Official), and "Venganza" (Revenge). His many short chronicles and articles appeared in a variety of Chilean publications during his lifetime, often under pseudonyms. However, Luco Cruchaga's reputation today rests upon his three known dramas. His biographers often refer to other plays that may have remained unfinished at the end of his life and whose whereabouts and even survival are uncertain today. According to Durán Cerda's *Repertorio del teatro chileno* (1962, Bibliography of Chilean Theater), as late as 1962 the manuscripts of the plays "Siempre querida" (Always Beloved) and "Camarada" (Comrade) were archived at the Centro de Investigaciones del Teatro Chileno at the Instituto de Teatro de la Universidad de Chile. Durán Cerda, Mario Cánepa Guzmán, and others briefly describe the unpublished "No va más" (No More Bets) as a portrait of upper-class gamblers at the Viña del Mar casino, but they provide no information regarding the whereabouts of this text. Likewise, there are many references to "Miss Rod," another completed play that Luco Cruchaga is said to have delivered to the Flores-Frontaura company but that did not debut. One of the few critics to describe this drama is Lautaro García. In his article "Recuerdo de Germán Luco y de su obra" (Remembrance of Germán Luco Cruchaga and His Work), published in the 27 June 1946 issue of *Zig-Zag*, he describes "Miss Rod" as an urban psychological intrigue lacking the power and spontaneity that characterize Luco Cruchaga's rural dramas. Another play attributed to Luco Cruchaga is "La historia de un marido" (A Husband's Tale), which the same *Zig-Zag* article reports to be based on a short story by Knut Hamsun. Three other undocumented plays are occasionally mentioned: "La montura del patrón" (The Master's Saddle), "Las niñas de sus ojos" (The Apple of His Eyes), and "El Senador Alcornoque" (Senator Corkscrew).

One explanation for the obscurity surrounding most of Luco Cruchaga's works is offered by Juan Andrés Piña in "Sociedad, individualidad y tragedia en la obra de Germán Luco Cruchaga" (Society, the Individual and Tragedy in the Works of Germán Luco Cruchaga), included in his 1990 critical edition of *La viuda de Apablaza* and *Amo y señor*. Piña reports that, according to Luco Cruchaga's contemporaries, the dramatist felt an obsessive need to revise and rewrite his dramas. His perfectionism may have caused him to hold on to texts that might otherwise have been published and/or performed.

Although few in number, Luco Cruchaga's plays give testimony to the positivist thinking and the *costumbrista* style of his time. In her introduction to a 1999 edition of *La viuda de Apablaza*, Hurtado evaluates Luco Cruchaga's own life as an example of unremitting tensions between irreconcilable extremes: poverty and wealth; big-city and country life; religious education and bohemian lifestyle; and the need for gainful employment and the desire to cultivate multiple artistic vocations. Luco Cruchaga's dramas reflect the personal stories of characters who, like their creator, experienced their society's transition from nineteenth-century near feudalism to twentieth-century modernity.

References:

Zlatko Brncic Juricic, *Historia del teatro en Chile* (Santiago: Universitaria, 1963);

Mario Cánepa Guzmán, *El teatro en Chile* (Santiago: Arancibia, 1966);

Julio Durán Cerda, "Germán Luco Cruchaga y el teatro chileno moderno," *Texto crítico,* 7 (July–December 1981): 292–309;

Durán Cerda, *Panorama del teatro chileno 1848–1959* (Santiago: Editorial del Pacífico, 1959);

Teodosio Fernández, *El teatro chileno contemporáneo (1941–1973)* (Madrid: Playor, 1982);

Lautaro García, "Recuerdo de Germán Luco y de su obra," *Zig-Zag* (27 June 1946): 43;

Mario Guzman, *Historia del teatro chileno* (Santiago: Técnica, 1974);

María de la Luz Hurtado, *Teatro chileno y modernidad: Identidad y crisis social* (Irvine, Cal.: Ediciones de Gestos, 1997);

Hurtado, *Teatro Iberoamericano* (Santiago: Escuela de Teatro de la Pontificia Universidad Católica de Chile, 1992);

Mariano Latorre, "Anotaciones sobre el teatro chileno en el siglo XIX," *Atenea,* 26 (September–October 1949): 239–277;

Armando de María y Campos, *Breve historia del teatro en Chile* (Mexico City: Compañía de Ediciones Populares, 1940);

Luis Merino-Reyes, "Aproximaciones a Germán Luco Cruchaga," *Literatura chilena, creación y crítica,* 10 (August–September 1986): 21–22;

Grínor Rojo, *Los orígenes del teatro hispanoamericano contemporáneo* (Valparaíso: Universidad Católica de Valparaíso, 1972).

René Marqués
(4 October 1919 – 22 March 1979)

Lowell Fiet
University of Puerto Rico–Río Piedras

See also the Marqués entry in *DLB 113: Modern Latin-American Fiction Writers, First Series.*

PLAY PRODUCTIONS: *El sol y los MacDonald,* Río Piedras, University of Puerto Rico–Río Piedras, 1950;

La carreta, New York, Nuevo Círculo Dramático, 1953; San Juan, P.R., Ateneo Puertorriqueño, 1953;

Palm Sunday, San Juan, P.R., Teatro Alejandro Tapia y Rivera, 1956;

Los soles truncos, San Juan, P.R., Teatro Alejandro Tapia y Rivera, 1958;

Un niño azul para esa sombra, San Juan, P.R., Teatro Alejandro Tapia y Rivera, 1960;

La casa sin reloj, San Juan, P.R., Ateneo Puertorriqueño, 1961;

Carnaval afuera, carnaval adentro, Havana, Primer Festival de Teatro Latinoamericano, 1962;

El apartamiento, San Juan, P.R., Teatro Alejandro Tapia y Rivera, 1964;

Mariana o el alba, San Juan, P.R., Teatro Alejandro Tapia y Rivera, 1966;

Sacrificio en el Monte Moriah, San Juan, P.R., Teatro Alejandro Tapia y Rivera, 1970;

Vía Crucis del hombre puertorriqueño, San Juan, P.R., presented by the author in front of La Princesa jail during Holy Week 1970;

El hombre y sus sueños, San Juan, P.R., Ateneo Puertorriqueño, May 1971;

La muerte no entrará en palacio, New York, Teatro Rodante Puertorriqueño (Puerto Rican Traveling Theater), 1981–bilingual production, translated by Gregory Rabassa as *Death Shall Not Enter The Palace* for the performances in English;

Los condenados, San Juan, P.R., Festival René Marqués, Ateneo Puertorriqueño, 1982.

BOOKS: *Peregrinación* (Arecibo, P.R.: Privately printed, 1944);

René Marqués (from Ruth S. Lamb, ed., Three Contemporary Latin-American Plays: René Marqués, Egon Wolff, Emilio Carballido, *1971; Thomas Cooper Library, University of South Carolina*)

La carreta (San Juan, P.R.: Casa Baldrich, 1952); translated by Charles Pilditch as *The Oxcart* (New York: Scribners, 1969);

Otro día nuestro (San Juan, P.R.: Imprenta Venezuela, 1955);

Juan Bobo y la Dama de Occidente (Río Piedras, P.R.: Antillana, 1956);

Los derechos del hombre (San Juan, P.R.: Departamento de Instrucción Pública, División de Educación de la Comunidad, 1957);

Cuentos puertorriqueños de hoy, by Marqués and others (Río Piedras, P.R.: Cultural, 1959);

La víspera del hombre (San Juan, P.R.: Club del Libro de Puerto Rico, 1959);

Teatro, 3 volumes: volume 1 (Mexico City: Arrecife, 1959); volumes 2 and 3 (Río Piedras, P.R.: Cultural, 1971)–volume 1 includes *Los soles truncos,* translated by Richard John Wiezell as *The Fanlights,* in *The Modern Stage in Latin America: Six Plays,* edited by George Woodyard (New York: Dutton, 1971), pp. 1–41;

En una ciudad llamada San Juan (Mexico City: Universidad Central de México, 1960);

El puertorriqueño dócil (Buenos Aires: Cuadernos Americanos, 1962);

La casa sin reloj (Xalapa: Universidad Veracruzana, 1962);

Emigración (San Juan, P.R.: Departamento de Instrucción Pública, División de Educación de la Comunidad, 1966);

El apartamiento (Barcelona: Rumbos, 1966);

Ensayos (1953-1966) (Barcelona: Antillana, 1966; revised and enlarged, 1972); revised edition translated by Barbara Bockus Aponte as *The Docile Puerto Rican: Essays* (Philadelphia: Temple University Press, 1976);

Las manos y el ingenio del hombre (San Juan, P.R.: Departamento de Instrucción Pública, División de Educación de la Comunidad, 1966);

La esclavitud (San Juan, P.R.: Departamento de Instrucción Pública, División de Educación de la Comunidad, 1967);

Mariana o el alba (Río Piedras, P.R.: Antillana, 1968);

Liderato (San Juan, P.R.: Departamento de Instrucción Pública, División de Educación de la Comunidad, 1969);

Sacrificio en el Monte Moriah (Río Piedras, P.R.: Antillana, 1969);

La muerte no entrará en palacio (Río Piedras, P.R.: Cultural, 1970);

David y Jonatán; Tito y Berenice: Dos dramas de amor, poder y desamor (Río Piedras, P.R.: Antillana, 1970);

Un niño azul para esa sombra (Río Piedras, P.R.: Cultural, 1970);

El sol y los MacDonald (Río Piedras, P.R.: Antillana, 1971);

Carnaval afuera, carnaval adentro (Río Piedras, P.R.: Antillana, 1971);

El hombre y sus sueños (Río Piedras, P.R.: Antillana, 1971);

Vía Crucis del hombre puertorriqueño (Río Piedras, P.R.: Antillana, 1971);

Ese mosaico fresco sobre aquel mosaico antiguo (Río Piedras, P.R.: Cultural, 1975);

Inmersos en el silencio (Río Piedras, P.R.: Antillana, 1976);

La mirada (Río Piedras, P.R.: Antillana, 1976); translated by Pilditch as *The Look* (New York: Senda Nueva de Ediciones, 1983).

Edition: *El apartamiento,* in *Three Contemporary Latin-American Plays: René Marqués, Egon Wolff, Emilio Carballido,* edited by Ruth S. Lamb (Waltham, Mass.: Xerox College Publishing, 1971).

SELECTED PERIODICAL PUBLICATIONS–
UNCOLLECTED: "Desde España: 'Desromantizada' La Dama de las Camelias," *El Mundo* (San Juan, P.R.), 8 September 1946, p. 2;

"Desde España: Algo sobre teatro puertorriqueño (Recordando un tema olvidado)," *El Mundo* (San Juan, P.R.), 27 October 1946, pp. 2, 14;

"Desde España: La técnica teatral: la escenografía," *El Mundo* (San Juan, P.R.), 3 November 1946, p. 2;

"En el Teatro de la Universidad: *Don Juan Tenorio,*" *El Mundo* (San Juan, P.R.), 1 June 1947, p. 15;

"Teatro Puertorriqueño: *María Soledad,*" *El Mundo* (San Juan, P.R.), 10 August 1947, pp. 10, 17;

Review of *A Streetcar Named Desire,* by Tennessee Williams, *Asomante* (April–June 1948): 73–75;

"Benavente, el hombre, el mito y la obra," *Asomante* (July–September 1948): 58–65;

"José Ferrer, Cyrano maravilloso," *Diario de Puerto Rico,* 11 May 1949, p. 3;

"Observatorio cinematográfico: Cinematografía española," *Diario de Puerto Rico,* 2 June 1949, p. 6;

"Hamlet, el hombre cerebral," *Diario de Puerto Rico,* 14 June 1949, p. 6;

"Vida breve y pasión del teatro puertorriqueño," *Norte* (October 1949): 62–64;

"Después de *El sol y los McDonald,*" *El Mundo* (San Juan, P.R.), 28 September 1950, pp. 6, 13;

"El drama de un río y el esfuerzo de una comunidad," *Educación* (November 1952): 2, 8;

"Apuntes sobre nuestro teatro experimental," *Artes y Letras* (August 1953): 10, 14;

"Teatro puertorriqueño: *El huésped* de Pedro Juan Soto," *El Mundo* (San Juan, P.R.), 6 October 1956, p. 12;

Review of *Breve historia del teatro latinoamericano,* by Willis K. Jones, *Asomante* (January–March 1957): 83–86;

"Luigi Pirandello: El hombre ante su espejo," *Asomante* (October–December 1967): 27–37;

"Memorias mínimas," *Puerto* (October–December 1967): 7–17;

"Noticias literarias," *Claridad* (San Juan, P.R.), 28 February 1971, p. 23;

"Existe un teatro de vanguardia," *La Hora* (San Juan, P.R.), 20 October 1971, p. 20;

"A pesar del fuego, Co-op Arte vivirá," *La Hora* (San Juan, P.R.), 10 January 1972, p. 22;

Review of *Growing Up Puerto Rican,* edited by Paulette Copper, *Sin Nombre* (July–September 1974): 80–84.

René Marqués's plays focus on issues of Puerto Rican national identity and illuminate what he saw as the adverse affects of continued colonial domination by the United States on the island's social, political, and cultural development. His dramatic characters demonstrate the complexity and ambivalence wrought by the control that hegemonic power exerts over virtually every aspect of their daily lives. Continuous experimentation with dramatic form also marks Marqués's dramatic productivity. From realism and poetic drama to surrealism, expressionism, and absurdism, his works reflect a continuous search for new styles and techniques to better communicate his critique of colonialism and the psychological deformation of its subjects. His two most widely recognized plays, *La carreta* (published in 1952, performed in 1953; translated as *The Oxcart,* 1969) and *Los soles truncos* (performed in 1958, published in 1959; translated as *The Fanlights,* 1971), both restaged with regularity, are acknowledged as cornerstones of Puerto Rican national literature and appear as required reading in the curriculum of the Puerto Rican public school system.

Marqués was born on 4 October 1919, in the city of Arecibo, on Puerto Rico's northwestern Atlantic coast. From a landowning family prominent in that community, he grew up in a comfortable upper-middle-class environment and benefited from access to an active cultural life in the urbanized setting of Arecibo that included a variety of locally performed plays and musicals as well as cinema, sporting events, and volumes of classical and contemporary literature in the libraries of relatives. Carnivals and patron saint festivals, the sacred and secular traditions of his Catholic upbringing, as well as the extensive time he spent in the country on his maternal grandparents' farm, also contributed to his eventual career as a writer. Critic Arcadio Díaz Quiñones claims that the rural as opposed to urban values Marqués learned in his early years marked his vision as a mature writer. His choice of university studies was influenced by his family's preferences, and he graduated from the College of Agriculture and Mechanical Arts (now the University of Puerto Rico–Mayagüez) in 1942 as an agronomist.

After graduation, Marqués worked for the Department of Agriculture for two years and then as the manager of a private firm, but his true interests were directed elsewhere. As early as 1941 he founded and directed the Arecibo chapter of the Areyto Dramatic Society. Marqués married Serena Velasco in 1942, and their three children, Raúl Fernando, Brunilda María, and Francisco René, were born during the 1940s. The marriage lasted fifteen years and ended in divorce.

In 1944 Marqués published *Peregrinación* (Pilgrimage), his first book and only published volume of poetry. He also began writing short plays during this time. The bibliography published by Esther Rodríguez Ramos in the journal *Sin Nombre* (Untitled) in 1999 includes the following unpublished play titles: "En la cumbre" (1942, At the Top), "Nuestra noche" (1942 or 1943, Our Night), "Después de la noche" (before 1947, After the Night), "Hombre perdido" (before 1947, Lost Man), "Pueblo agónico" (1947, Agonized People), and "El diablo se divierte" (1947, The Devil Entertains Himself). No production dates are offered. However, she clarifies that she did not have direct access to these materials to verify their condition or availability.

Marqués's first published play, *El hombre y sus sueños* (The Man and His Dreams), which first appeared in the journal *Asomante* (Gazing Out) in 1948 but was not performed until 1971, reveals an admirable simplicity of style that, at the same time, allows the play to function on simultaneously specific or local (Puerto Rican) and abstract or symbolic (universal) levels. The action incorporates the mystical symbolism of Maurice Maeterlinck's *The Intruder* (1891), the indictment of materialistic society made by expressionistic renderings of "Everyman" themes, and contemporary existentialist theory. As the play opens, friends, family, servants, a nurse, a priest, and shadows await the death of a "great man" who sought immortality. Each deathbed visitor wants some part of the power, prestige, or fortune the Man wielded in life and leaves behind in death. Yet, the Man's immortality hangs in the balance as the Red Shadow of his physical life battles the Black Shadow of his religious soul. Neither biological offspring, in the form of his weak and deceitful Son, nor the promises of the Church can guarantee his immortality. Finally, the Blue Shadow intervenes, showing that while eternal life through children and faith prove to be illusions, the Man's acts and deeds guarantee that his life has been worth living.

Marqués visited Spain in 1946 and 1947 and studied literature at the University of Madrid. While there, he wrote many "Desde España" (From Spain) columns for *El Mundo,* then Puerto Rico's most prominent daily newspaper. From that point on, he published articles, play reviews, book reviews, and commentaries in (mainly) Spanish- and English-language Puerto Rican, American, and international newspapers, magazines, and journals throughout the rest of his life.

The play *El sol y los MacDonald* (The Sun and the MacDonalds; performed in 1950, published in 1971) was written at about this time as well. In it Marqués attempted to portray the evolution of the former slaveholding MacDonald family in the American South. The choice of theme was, perhaps, influenced by the premises of leading intellectual Tomas Blanco's *El prejuicio racial en Puerto Rico* (1940, Racial Prejudice in Puerto Rico) or by Marqués's firsthand observation of racism in United States–Puerto Rico relations. The play focuses on the interaction of class, ethnicity, and race in the story of a family sometimes weakened by inbreeding and the Oedipal pull between mothers and sons but also strengthened by genetic mixing with other classes and ethnic groups. The generational culture that preserves family, estate, wealth, and attitudes through the human husbandry of whiteness is best captured thematically in the characters of Gustavo MacDonald, who has no heir and is the end of his family's name, and his nephew, Ramiro García, who assumes the family's attitudes and beliefs as if he were Gustavo's son and not the son of Gustavo's sister, Teodora MacDonald, and her Spanish husband, Enrique García. Another sister, Elisa MacDonald, becomes promiscuous because the family will not permit her to marry the only man she loves because he has a trace of African blood. The relationship between Gustavo and Teodora provokes the suspicion that Ramiro could be a true MacDonald. However, Ramiro finally breaks the incestuous spell of the sexual union of race, class, and culture and leaves to live free of the family that will, according to Gustavo, disappear in smoke and ashes.

Although shorter and more stylized, *El hombre y sus sueños* offers greater artistic promise than *El sol y los MacDonald,* and its publication in 1948 was sufficient to garner the young playwright the Rockefeller Foundation fellowship that took him to Columbia University to study dramaturgy and allowed his participation in Erwin Piscator's Workshop. As important, however, is the characteristic inside/outside duality that surfaces in *El hombre y sus sueños* and in virtually all of Marqués's most accomplished plays, regardless of the degree of specificity of local themes and characters. Throughout his career, he realized that Puerto Rican theater could not evolve in a vacuum, and he remained abreast of international theater movements and developments. His plays engage the dramatic expression of Puerto Rican experience in dynamic dialogue with contemporary international drama, usually without compromising the authenticity of his characters, their language, or the environments they inhabit.

Palm Sunday (performed in 1956) was written in English in 1949 while Marqués studied at Columbia University. The language of the play, while fully competent, controlled, and correct, lacks the complexity, texture, and fluidity that characterizes his more poetic prose dialogue and narrative when writing in Spanish. *Palm Sunday* reads as a fairly one-dimensional exposé of a political event rather than an effective dialogic analysis of the historical and dialectical processes behind the action. Accounts of many of the incidents that mark U.S. intervention in and colonial domination of Puerto Rican life, such as the 1937 Ponce Massacre on which this play is based, are, in truth, one-sided and make history read like heavy-handed melodrama. However, the emotionally charged portrayal of the ethnic, cultural, and ideological conflicts that divide the Winfield family in this play overshadows the importance of the events surrounding the massacre, which left two hundred wounded and twenty dead, including small children, when police opened fire on an otherwise peaceful Nationalist Party demonstration.

The action takes place in Ponce on the day of the massacre. John Winfield, a North American government official of fifty, has lived in Puerto Rico for more than twenty years. His wife, Mercedes, a beautiful Puerto Rican woman of forty, still loves her rigidly pro-American husband but also adores their rebellious twenty-year-old son, Alberto ("Albert" to his father). Alberto's resentment of his father has obvious Oedipal overtones; yet, the division runs deeper because the elder Winfield, in spite of his love for his wife, is deeply prejudiced against Puerto Ricans, whom he sees as morally unable to control their own social and political destiny. The Nationalist Movement, which he sees as a fascist "black-shirt" organization, constitutes part of the evidence supporting his argument. Other issues include his feeling that Spanish nuns at the St. Vincent orphanage should speak English and the notion that the U.S. political administration represents a "civilizing" mission in an otherwise backward society. Alberto counters his father's arguments by relating the ethnic prejudice he encountered as a Puerto Rican when he was sent to the United States to study. He also expresses his pride in the long history of Hispanic culture in the Americas.

Mercedes is caught in the middle of this conflict, as is a family friend, Harry Martin, the good gringo of the play. He is a lawyer who has "adapted" to Puerto Rican life, supports independence, and recognizes the degree of governmental (and Winfield's) collusion in the events that are about to transpire during the Palm Sunday march planned by the Nationalists. He has information, for example, that special police armed with machine guns will be present and that dum-dum bullets have been distributed. Furthermore, he knows that Winfield, a personal friend of the governor, is secretly aware of these circumstances but has said nothing to reveal them. It appears that Alberto is right when he says that his father uses democracy to mask tyranny. However, the events of the dramatic action erupt too quickly through the arguments between the characters. In the street outside, even though the mayor has rescinded the permit, the Nationalist parade proceeds. The audience and characters view it from the rear balcony. Shots are fired, and Alberto runs to the street, where he is among those killed. The family is torn apart, their real contradictions and conflicts no longer masked by the pretense of love and democracy. Although the play was produced in 1956, Marqués seemed to understand the limitations of this text and did not rework the play for publication in English or Spanish. A typescript is available in the Federico de Onis Seminar Collection at the University of Puerto Rico–Río Piedras.

In 1950 Marqués was back in Puerto Rico and working as a writer for the Community Education Division of the Department of Public Instruction; he later headed its editorial division. In that capacity Marqués wrote at least sixteen pamphlets and manuals ranging from textbooks and social counseling guides to historical exposés on emigration, slavery, and workers' rights. He also wrote screenplays for movies made by the division during this same period.

Also in 1950 Marqués formed the group Teatro Nuestro to stage his early plays. With the support of Puerto Rican Athenaeum president Nilita Vientós Gastón, along with such figures as playwright, essayist, and short-story writer Emilio S. Belaval and scene designer and director José M. Lacomba, he also helped found the Athenaeum's Experimental Theater in 1951. *La carreta,* published in three issues of *Asomante* between 1951 and 1952 and also separately in 1952, premiered in New York in 1953 and confirmed for audiences there the initial enthusiastic reactions of readers in Puerto Rico. With the success of this play, Marqués became the most prominent member of a generation of talented Puerto Rican playwrights that included Manuel Méndez Ballester, Francisco Arriví, Gerard Paul Marín, and Piri Fernández de Lewis.

The stage of dramatic apprenticeship and social and political advocacy seen in early plays disappears almost entirely in *La carreta,* Marqués's best-known and, for many, most effective play. There are no scrims, flashbacks, or intellectualizations; the play depends on three hard-edged, realistic settings that confront the more typical nostalgia of *costumbrismo jíbaro* (folkloric peasant customs) with issues of everyday needs and the economic and emotional struggle of a representative Puerto Rican family to survive. It is generally acknowledged as the single most important text of the Puerto Rican national theater.

The three *estampas,* or settings, where the action takes place are *el campo* (the countryside), *el arrabal* (the urban slum "La Perla" in San Juan), and *la metrópolis* (the Bronx in New York). Each *estampa* is separated by a year's time, and even though three of the four major characters continue through all the scenes, each *estampa* is structured nearly as an independent one-act play. These scenes are not new to Puerto Rican drama. Fernando Sierra Berdecía's *Esta noche juega el Jóker* (1937, Tonight the Joker Is Wild), a play similar to the third *estampa* of *La carreta,* dramatizes the difficulties of Puerto Ricans in New York. Ballester's *Tiempo muerto* (1941, The Dead Season), a *jíbaro* (peasant) drama of the life of a sugarcane worker and his family, depends on much the same socio-economic basis as the first *estampa* of the Marqués play. In contrast, however, the cultural radicality of *La carreta* derives from its overextension, the need to catalogue the Puerto Rican experience in such a way that its national character–the racially indeterminate but white *jíbaro*–travels the fullest range possible: from the economically depressed countryside to the urban slum to the South Bronx, hitting almost every national theme in the process.

The first *estampa* shows Doña Gabriela and her family leaving the *finquita* (small farm) that has been the family home for decades but has been sold off piece by piece to larger landholders and mortgaged beyond its worth. Doña Gabriela sees her family's birthright crumble and slip through her fingers. The time period is the years surrounding World War II, a time that begins with Depression-era federal programs and leads to an increased U.S. military presence, war-industry employment, the development of light industry, the formulation of Puerto Rico's commonwealth status, and government-encouraged mass emigration to the U.S. mainland.

Doña Gabriela's adopted son, Luis, who is twenty-four years old as the play begins, responds to that change. Along with his overdeveloped sense of responsibility for Doña Gabriela and her other children–Juanita, who is nineteen, and Chaguito, who is fifteen–Luis considers factory work, wage earning, and eventually emigration to be more dignified than barely scratching out a living on a tiny rural farm. A year later, in the second *estampa,* the crude urban life of "La Perla" has plunged the family into chaos. The police arrest and jail Chaguito for shortchanging a tourist; Juanita has an abortion and attempts suicide; and Luis is forced to borrow money from a married woman with whom he had a brief affair, to move the family to New York. The third setting is a small sixth-floor apartment in the Bronx, the home of Luis and Doña Gabriela. Luis works in a factory, where, with overtime, he makes enough money to support his mother as well as buy a

Anita Hamilton, Irene de Bari, and Lillian Garrett in a 1983 Old Globe Theatre production of Marqués's play Los soles truncos
(Divided Suns, performed in 1958, published in 1959; translated as The Fanlights, *1971), in which two aristocratic sisters cannot cope with the death of their elder sister and the encroachment of the modern world (photograph by Robert Burroughs; from* Latin American Theatre Review, *volume 17 [Spring 1984]; Thomas Cooper Library, University of South Carolina)*

new radio, a fancy wristwatch, and new winter clothes. Juanita also works and earns additional income—what Luis calls "dirty money"—probably as a part-time call girl. One day the Bible-thumping, self-righteous do-gooder Mr. Parkington brings news of an accident at the factory: Luis has been killed. Juanita takes up the wooden model oxcart that she has carried with her from Puerto Rico, and the two women decide to return to Puerto Rico with Luis's body, find Chaguito, and live on the land that Gabriela's brother has offered them.

In spite of his success with *La carreta,* Marqués's next plays encountered resistance because they directly criticized local politicians such as Jaime Benítez, who was a founding member of the ruling Popular Democratic Party, and especially Luis Muñoz Marín, the powerful four-term governor who wrote the Commonwealth or "Free Associated State" Constitution that binds Puerto Rico to the United States. Marqués's plays of this period also allude to the persecuted and imprisoned Pedro Albizu Campos, leader of the Nationalist Party, and to the Nationalist uprising and attempted political assassinations of the early 1950s. Although among his best-crafted and most imaginative works, the plays of this period were often too controversial to produce.

For example, most critical treatments of Marqués's dramaturgy tend to overlook or merely skim the surface of the "pantomime" or dance-drama *Juan Bobo y la Dama de Occidente* (1956, Simple John and the Lady of the West). The plasticity of the theatrical form of this play and the absence of dialogue account, in part, for the critics' avoidance of the text. The language consists of sensuous and textual images instead of spoken words as such, and the choreographic action requires performance by actors who are trained in classical and modern dance as well as character interpretation; when Marqués wrote the play, no dance company or theater group in Puerto Rico possessed the qualifications necessary to stage it.

The most obvious reason for the lack of attempts to stage *Juan Bobo y la Dama de Occidente* is its principal object of satire and ridicule: the character of the Professor is clearly based on the personality, physical appearance, pedagogical practices, and idiosyncrasies of Benítez, at the time the chancellor of the University of Puerto Rico–Río Piedras campus and later resident commissioner in the U.S. House of Representatives in Washington, D.C. The less obvious reason behind the informal censorship of *Juan Bobo y la Dama de Occidente* relates to the political and cultural complexity of issues not always related to Marqués's plays: racial and cultural hybridization, intellectual assimilation versus transculturation, and the local/universal constitution of *puertorriqueñidad* (Puerto Ricanness).

In the play, the folkloric character of Juan Bobo, the village simpleton, becomes John, the common man, still gullible and lacking formal education, but no longer easily tricked or ridiculed. At the outset, popular country or *jíbaro* music and Afro-Puerto Rican *bomba* and *plena* mix freely, as do the dancers of varied ethnic and racial backgrounds. They are interrupted by the arrival of the Professor, accompanied by two Gentlemen in tuxedos, two blonde Wagnerian slaves, two Greco-Roman slaves, and most importantly, the Lady of the West, a statuesque beauty on a pedestal covered by a long blue veil. John, confused and strangely attracted to the Lady, leaves his Girlfriend and Mother and follows the Lady to the capital, where he has disastrously comical social encounters. In the final act, at the university, the Professor is imitated and ridiculed as he anxiously awaits the arrival of new students. Suddenly, John erupts on the scene, dancing to the rhythm of *bomba* with an Afro-Puerto Rican woman, and the scandalized Professor loses control and begins to move to the African beat. John discovers the Lady of the West on a pedestal that he can reach only by passing eight titled panels: *Electra, La Celestina, Macbeth, Death of a Salesman, The Prince, Faust, Nausea,* and *A Streetcar Named Desire*. When John reaches the Lady, her face is masked, expressionless, cold, inert. At that moment, John's Girlfriend enters and pulls the mask off the Lady, who begins to dance ballet "on point" and teaches the Girlfriend to do the same. The eight dancers from the panels of Western literature revive and join them. The musical troupe from the country arrives, as do the Afro-Puerto Rican musicians, and their music synchronizes with tones of a more formal Puerto Rican *danza*. The beautiful Young Woman from the second act dances with John; a Black Dancer cuts in; and John returns to dancing with both his Girlfriend and the Lady of the West.

The resistance to staging the play can no longer be attributed to the lack of groups able to represent the action or to the figure of the Professor, who now reads as a universal representation of academic pretensions and nervousness. The play ridicules the educational hierarchy of the university as a means of Europeanizing and, especially, Americanizing its students in such a way that it numbs or stupefies their responses to universal as well as local intellectual and artistic expression. Yet, the action still creates a sense of discomfort that resides in the close proximity and interweaving of creole, African, and *jíbaro* cultures, as John crosses boundaries of race, culture, and class.

La muerte no entrará en palacio (Death Shall Not Enter the Palace), written in 1956 and published in the 1959 volume of Marqués's *Teatro,* is Marqués's most sophisticated dramatic statement on contemporary Puerto Rican political reality and probes the root issues of the island's colonial relationship to the United States. On one level, it explores how power corrupts and why the Commonwealth or "Free Associated State" of Puerto Rico represents a betrayal of the political ideals of self-determination and independence. However, on a second and more complicated level, the play also exposes the "heart of darkness"—the feelings of inferiority and self-hatred—of Don José, the Saturn-like governor, whose ambitious designs devour his own children. The play has not been produced in Puerto Rico because the portrayal of Don José so closely resembles Governor Muñoz Marín, and the mention of Don Rodrigo and his speeches allude to the imprisoned Nationalist leader Campos. The play premiered in 1981 in New York, directed by Pablo Cabrera, as the inaugural production of the permanent home of Miriam Colón's Teatro Rodante Puertorriqueño (Puerto Rican Traveling Theater).

The play opens with a prologue by blind Teresias, a friend and once a political ally of Don José, reminding the audience that history is not improvised or arbitrary but consists of the acts of men. Don José's daughter is named Casandra, but her function is more like that of Antigone as she moves against the grain of her father's hegemonic decisions. Alberto is Casandra's fiancé and the chief security officer at Don José's mansion. His father, now dead, was another ally of Don José, and together with Teresias, the three formed an ideological triumvirate—poet, philosopher, and politician. Doña Isabel, the governor's wife, who comes from a rural background, tries to counsel Don José on the possible loss of the island's soul as a result of material gain. She also advises her daughter to trust, believe in, and stand by the man she loves. It is a faith that Doña Isabel practices, and Casandra will follow her example as tension grows between Alberto and her father over Don José's plan to make the island a permanent colony, a "protectorate" of the North.

Perhaps the most telling scenes of the play are, first, the confrontation between Don José and Teresias over the lost opportunity or betrayal of independence and the debilitating dependency on the North, and second, the ceremony of the signing of the protectorate treaty. In the first instance, Teresias asserts that the island's independence was within their grasp and required only the "word" from Don José to make it a reality. That word was never spoken because Don José never truly believed in his own people and found them, and himself, to be inferior in light of the power and wealth of the North. In the second instance, the too-casual appearance of the tall, corpulent, blond, good-natured Commissioner of the North contrasts directly with the elegance and formality of the islanders. As the signing ceremony proceeds, the theater audience already knows that Casandra has accidentally killed Alberto with the gun he planned to use to assassinate Don José. Thus the grand celebration over the treaty erasing all vestiges of colonialism and the announcement of Don Rodrigo's release from custody assume even greater irony as Casandra enters in her now blood-stained gown. Casandra kills Don José–perhaps the one questionable gesture in the play. Yet, the most penetrating thought of the action revolves around the hegemonic power–what Doña Isabel sees as a power as absolute as a dictator's–wielded by an elected leader in the context of a supposedly representative democracy.

In 1958 the Institute of Puerto Rican Culture, under the direction of archaeologist Ricardo Alegría, inaugurated the annual Festival of Puerto Rican Theater as a showcase of dramatic arts on the island. The first festival featured plays by Marqués, Belaval, Méndez Ballester, and Arriví. Marqués's contribution, *Los soles truncos,* which explores the complexities of colonial history and cultural identity, reconfirmed his standing as Puerto Rico's preeminent dramatist.

If one believes the aging sisters Inés and Emilia Burkhardt Sandoval in *Los soles truncos,* before the invasion of the "barbarians" and the lowering of the red and gold Spanish flag, Puerto Rican society was an idyllic landscape happily situated within the parameters of their Strasbourg educations and Germanic paternal heritage; their maternal genealogy as non-Moorish, Andalusian Iberians; the benign Burkhardt sugar plantation located west of San Juan in Toa Alta; and the once luxurious house with fanlights or divided suns *(los soles truncos)* on Cristo Street in Old San Juan. They recall elegant dances in the Spanish governor's mansion; their father's horses; the "Nordic god" Burkhardt himself; the jewels of their mother, Eugenia Sandoval de Burkhardt; and the engagement of the Spanish lieutenant to Hortensia, the blonde "Nordic" sister who inherited Burkhardt's genetic profile. However, their memories exclude almost the entire social history of the island: the privileges granted to rich Europeans by royal decrees, the regime of the *libretas de jornal* (workers' passbooks), unscrupulous plantation overseers, the poverty of the peasant and mixed-race classes, high infant mortality rates, general civil censorship and the repression of individual freedoms, the persecution and forced exile of leaders such as Ramón Emeterio Betances and Eugenio María de Hostos, and, of course, slavery. The Burkhardt sisters were born soon after the abolition of slavery (1873) but appear to have lived without any consciousness of the fact that the (now dissipated) wealth, position, and privilege of their family depended on the labor of African slaves and free blacks and mulattoes.

Inés and Emilia prefer to remain enslaved by the illusions of the past that they can only experience through Hortensia and that permit them to be more than ordinary everyday Puerto Ricans and colonial subjects. But as the play opens, Hortensia has died, and she appears onstage only in the memories of her sisters, flashback re-creations of the past. The technique that brings memories into the present is carefully annotated in the text, and the reader understands clearly the relation of Hortensia and the past to the immediate present of Inés and Emilia. Now the sisters face the task of preparing the body for burial: that is the one concrete and definitive action of the play, and Inés and Emilia confront it in different ways.

Inés is practical and utilitarian and has made the necessary arrangements with the local authorities, and the first act ends with the arrival of the coffin. However, Emilia's life for the past fifty years has been one of suspended childhood fantasies, and it is only a partial illusion that the "barbarians" will come to evict them and convert the house into a luxury guesthouse for tourists, bankers, and officers of the U.S. Navy fleet that bombed San Juan more than fifty years earlier. The sisters will, no doubt, be evicted, sent to a home for the aged, or left homeless. Nothing else remains for them, and not even Mamá Eugenia's jeweled diadem or Papá Burkhardt's ring can change that. Chekhovian rhythms, Pirandellian games of illusion and reality, the cinematographic technique of juxtaposing the present and the past, the sense of *esperpento* (distorted vision) of Ramón del Valle-Inclán, and, even more, the grotesque imagery of Jean Genet, blend in this radical play as Marqués explores existentialist issues of "being and not being" and the (im)possibility of a fixed and definable identity inside an always changeable–Puerto Rican and universal–human reality.

Finally, Inés rejects the practical tasks of surrendering the body of Hortensia and leaving the house that represents their only history. Instead, she accepts the fantasies of Emilia, even though she knows it will result more in defeat than a victory: "El triunfo es de ellos" (The triumph is theirs), she says, and later, "Un mundo arriba: el de ellos. Oro mundo abajo: el nuestro" (One world up: theirs. Another world down: ours). She then decides to destroy the isthmus between metaphorically linked worlds: U.S. colonialism and Hispanic Puerto Rico, perhaps, but also between the present and the past, reality and illusion. Inés becomes a resistant Puerto Rican instead of the illusory Germanic-Spaniard that she pretended to be while Hortensia still lived. She decides to burn down the house with herself and Emilia in it rather than face the changes wrought by time.

From 1958 to 1970 Marqués's literary and theatrical output was intense and continuous, and his plays were frequently represented in the annual Festivals of Puerto Rican Theater. Throughout his career, he kept virtually all personal and family concerns distant from his professional life as a writer, director, and literary figure. Yet, the growing fatalism recorded in his works of the late 1950s and early 1960s may also record private resonances such as the end of Marqués's marriage. He returned to anticolonial themes, the political betrayal of the Puerto Rican people by popular leaders, and the crisis of Nationalism in contrast to the forced dependency on U.S. economic and social influences and initiatives. In 1960 he began a period of experimentation in Theater of the Absurd with distorted images of political treachery and torture and stylized parables of cultural and political submission. These themes also characterize his famous essay *El puertorriqueño dócil* (1962, The Docile Puerto Rican).

In *Un niño azul para esa sombra* (A Blue Boy for That Shadow; published in the 1959 *Teatro,* performed in 1960) Marqués represents the impact of collective and individual political convictions and actions inside the domestic as opposed to public sphere. What happens to the young wife and the child of a university professor who spends eight years in jail for his role in a Nationalist uprising? What awaits him, and them, once he is released? The precocious child, Michelín, who is about ten years old, idealizes his father, Michel, and lives with his mother, Mercedes, and their live-in housekeeper and family friend, Cecilia, in a mansion on Ashford Avenue in the exclusive Condado section of San Juan. It is Michelín's birthday, and a party has been planned. But Michelín's imagination leads him to play dangerous games, and he slides into trances during which he communes with his absent father. In another game, he replays his mother's poisoning of a nonbearing male *quenepo* tree. Michelín identifies with the tree and acts its part in his fantasy.

The second act is a flashback to two years earlier. Michel has been released from prison but cannot adjust to a life so changed. Mercedes ends a relationship with a North American friend but can only half-heartedly commit herself to a new life with Michel. She calls her son Mike and not Michelín, and she resents the presence of Cecilia, who is like a sister to Michel. The former professor can no longer withstand the pressures of the charity employment provided for him in a bank owned by Mercedes's family, and he cannot allow his failure to tarnish the heroic stature he has assumed in his son's imagination. He also suspects Mercedes's unfaithfulness and proposes an uncontested divorce.

The success of Michel's plan to reconstruct his self-image flounders when he discovers that Mercedes has destroyed his professional papers and manuscripts. Nothing had prepared this twenty-two-year-old wife of a professor to face the consequences of his revolutionary actions. In his absence, she bent to the pressure of her wealthy, business-class family to reinscribe herself in the politically conservative and pro-American high society. Michelín hears his parents' confrontation but is unable to call his father back. Instead, he vandalizes the just inaugurated miniature Statue of Liberty in the Condado.

As the third act moves forward again, Michelín sleeps on the terrace on his birthday. He awakes to tell his mother of his father's (imaginary) visit earlier in the day and of the news he receives from his father via Cecilia, even though Michel now lives (he believes) in Chile. Shocked, Mercedes tells Michelín the truth: his father died a failure, homeless and forgotten in the streets of New York. As the birthday party begins, Michelín disappears, and when he reappears he carries the blue bottle of poison that was used to kill the tree in act 1. Mercedes calls him to blow out the candles. He replies that God must blow them out, and he dies Christ-like on the fence where the tree once stood.

The play focuses on Mercedes and the negative impact on Michelín of a female-dominated domestic setting in which the father's direct influence is absent. In *El puertorriqueño dócil* Marqués identifies a "patrón matriarchal" (matriarchal pattern), more Anglo-Saxon in nature than Hispanic and similar to the conditions represented in *Un niño azul para esa sombra,* as a factor of increased "docility" in Puerto Rican literature and society since 1940. This view has been challenged, and the issue of misogyny surfaces in various critical approaches to Marqués's work. Marqués's next play, *La casa sin reloj* (The House without a Clock; performed in 1961, published in 1962), pursues a similar theme but in the form of a semi-absurdist parable of love at first sight in the chaotic aftermath—when time seems to stop—of a Nationalist attack on the governor's mansion.

The action of *La casa sin reloj* takes place in the living room of an undistinguished middle-class home in the country. A woman, Micaela, is home alone cleaning, only to be interrupted by strange phone calls followed by the appearances of two detectives—who, without a warrant, search the house—and then a stranger, José, a Nationalist on the run, who also happens to be the brother of Micaela's husband. Micaela and her husband, Pedro, a government employee, live anesthetized suburban lives: her housework, his job, credit, bills, his lover, her affairs, and their son studying business and finance. She claims to have no conscience, to feel no guilt, perhaps because she has never truly loved anything or anyone and thus has never had anything to feel guilty about. José awakens in her a sense of that kind of love. When her husband threatens to turn José over to the police, she forces him, at gunpoint, to go out and buy the plane ticket for José's escape. The movement of time begins again as she realizes that she loves José, that she wants to spend time with him. She asks José to teach her how to shoot the gun she threatened Pedro with so she can defend them against the forces that will come to arrest him. Somewhat astounded that she does not already know how to use the weapon she has been brandishing, José playfully embraces her, is shot, and dies. She calls the police and declares herself guilty, at last.

The dialogue reveals remarkable elasticity as it moves from Ionesco-like phone conversations and existentialist discussions of engagement and living as opposed to just existing, to social commentary ranging from the similar prejudicial treatment of Nationalists, Jews, and African Americans to mindless consumerism and buying on credit, and finally, to the transformative power of love as a radical totality. Instead of acts, the play is divided into "Absurd I" and "Absurd II." Yet, in spite of the obvious influence and textual allusions to Surrealism and absurdism, the play is more a moral accusation of a lack of conscience, of a failed sense of shame and guilt, and of a cheaply purchased political myopia than it is a representation of the absurdity or meaninglessness of existence.

Marqués's next play, *Carnaval afuera, carnaval adentro* (Carnival Outside, Carnival Inside; performed in 1962, published in 1971), rates among his most visually and thematically complex works. Its grotesque carnivalesque form owes much to the *esperpentos* (distorted, funhouse-mirror-like plays) of Spanish playwright Valle-Inclán and the cruelty of Genet's metatheatrical rituals. Once again, the thematic issues revolve around the contract that binds Puerto Rico to the United States. In this case, however, the playwright employs a far greater degree of symbolism. The never-seen, anthropophagic Mack, who operates through his agents, buys a young woman named Rosita, with the consent of her parents—not to sleep with her, as the housekeeper, Felícita, expects, but to consume her. Mack represents a "system" that devours innocent Puerto Ricans, while most of Puerto Rico and the rest of the world masquerade, act, pretend, and accept his cannibalism as normality.

In act 1, Guillermo (alias Willie) and María (alias Mary) act out a comic appraisal process with Mack's Agent to sell their daughter, Rosita (alias Rosie). The Americanized Rosita has no objections. The family's continued prosperity depends on Mack. However, Rosita also meets Angel, a painter, and although she feels she should save herself for Mack, she begins to fall in love. The exchange between Rosita and Angel takes place in a remarkably rich verbal context in which the rhythm, rhyming, repetition, and, at times, cacophonies of sounds take on the character of "dub," "rap," or performance poetry. It is Carnival season, and Angel and Rosita will meet later while Willie, Mary, and Mack's Agent are terrorized by a visit from five *vejigantes,* or carnival devils. Yet, when act 2 begins where the first ended, the threatening *vejigantes* now resemble the guests invited to a cocktail party: the Countess; her nephew, Rasputo; her American agent, George; the former president of an American republic; and the Widow. The cocktail party is a raucous exercise in misdirected dialogue and double-talk in which the guests—political exiles and entrepreneurs—remove their social masks to reveal the dictator behind the former president, the racist behind the liberal, and the counterrevolutionary behind the supposed democrat. The whip-toting Aunt Matilde, who functions as a circus ringmaster, breaks up the party. Then Angel and Rosita meet and climb the stairs to Rosita's room.

In act 3, the luxurious setting of the family's home has been transformed into a tribunal, and the characters now assume new and ornate roles in a more dangerous, inquisitional auto-da-fé. Mack's anthropophagy is not on trial and cannot be questioned. Furthermore, the contract clearly promises that Rosita will be delivered to him a virgin. Since she is not, Angel must pay $90,000,000 in damages or forfeit his life. But Angel does not recognize the authority of Mack or the court. He believes only in love, art, and liberty, and when tortured he refuses to say that he hates Mack. As a system, Mack cannot be loved or hated; "se mantiene, se cambia o se destruye" (it can be maintained, changed, or destroyed). Rosita insists that she substitute for Angel as the sacrificial victim, and she is mortally wounded. The sacrifice is complete, and the masquerade of falseness continues. Angel's struggle for his beliefs will suffer many such defeats, but it continues eternally. *Carnaval afuera, carnaval adentro* won an honorable mention in the 1962 Theater Competition of the Casa de las Américas in Cuba, and it was first produced in that year in Havana during the First Latin American Theater Festival. It was not produced professionally in Puerto Rico until 1983.

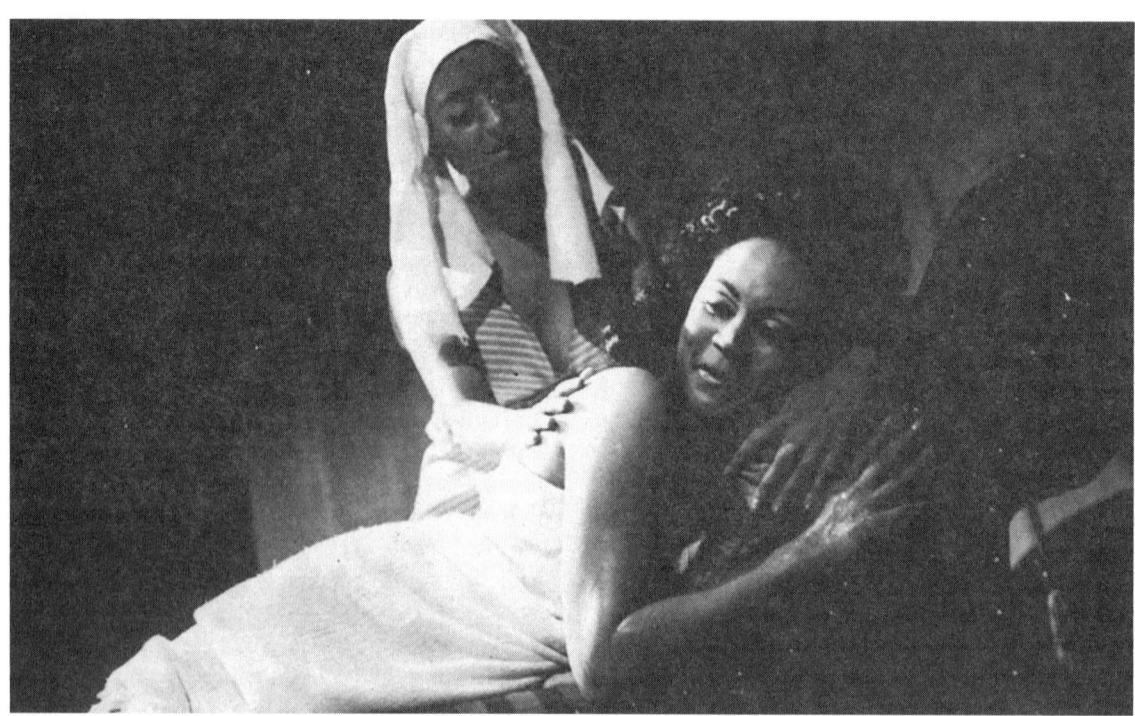

Sharon Riley (left) and Soledad Romero in Sacrificio en el Monte Moriah *(Sacrifice on Mount Moriah, published in 1969, performed in 1970), Marqués's retelling of the biblical story of Abraham, Sarah, and Isaac (from Gloria F. Waldman,* Luis Rafael Sanchez: Pasion teatral, *1988; Robert Muldrow Library, Clemson University)*

Marqués's next play, *El apartamiento* (The Apartment; performed in 1964, published in 1966), represents another experiment in staging a political parable by using the techniques of the Theater of the Absurd. However, *El apartamiento* proves more systematic, consistent, and symmetrical in its representation of what Marqués considered the "absurd" existence against which Puerto Rico and the rest of Latin America have refused to rebel. In a sterile, modernistic, windowless, and artificially illuminated apartment that is coldly furnished with stylized plastic, glass, or synthetic furniture and accessories, Carola, a woman of fifty-eight, measures blue ribbon while Elpidio, a man of sixty, struggles to finish a jigsaw puzzle. Their faces and hands are made up to appear "mortuary white." A door leads to an elevator, and a stairway leads to a second floor, but Carola and Elpidio claim there are no entrances or exits. They do, however, receive packages: gifts of no apparent use, since all their needs are supplied. Two unexpected guests arrive as well: Lucío, a supposed student of Elpidio when the latter was a great composer, and Terra, the supposed secretary of Carola, who was the renowned "poetess of the Americas." Of course, Elpidio and Carola do not remember any of these events, nor do they recognize Lucío and Terra. In fact, they live in fear that these two newcomers, with stories of Elpidio's and Carola's past talents, loves, and accomplishments, will cause them to lose the secure environment of the apartment.

Inspectors arrive to investigate why Carola has incinerated the books that Terra brought to her. Furthermore, Carola and Elpidio have not watched the obligatory television programs in three days, and they are threatened with either disappearing in the Temple of Incineration or being sent to the planet Deserticus, where they would have to create their own civilization. As the inspectors move upstairs, Tlo–an Aztec, Maya, Inca, or a stylized representation of all three–enters dressed in ornate ceremonial costume, and he ascends the stairs with a large knife. But the inspectors are not killed. They capture Tlo and give instructions to Carola and Elpidio that they must kill Tlo and throw his body in the incinerator. Instead, they free Tlo and give him back his knife. Tlo disappears, and as they return to doing their mechanical tasks, the doorbell rings. What awaits them? Death? Or liberty?

The themes of love, liberty, and art are the same as those explored in *La casa sin reloj* and *Carnaval afuera, carnaval adentro*. However, Marqués demonstrates greater precision and control over the elements of dramatic form in *El apartamiento*. The anesthetized characters Carola and Elpidio differ only in degree from Micaela and Pedro in *La casa sin reloj*. The spirit of Tlo and the memory of a past before life in the apartment replace the sense of conscience that the Nationalist José awakens in Micaela. However, the question that ends the play—death or liberty?—contrasts with the ending of *La casa sin reloj*, in which the death of José at Micaela's hand leaves a different kind of unanswered question: accidental, intentional, or both?

Marqués's absurdist experiments were not generally considered either critical or popular successes, and in 1965 he returned to a more optimistic and traditional form to dramatize the role of the legendary patriotic flag-maker, Mariana Bracetti, in the Grito, or Call-to-Arms, against the Spanish colonial regime in Lares, Puerto Rico, in 1868. *Mariana o el alba* (Mariana or The Dawn; performed in 1966, published in 1968) captures in romantic terms the military uprising of plantation owners, farmers, and townsfolk against the oppressive Spanish colonial regime that refused to abolish slavery and was especially known for its oppressive *libretas de jornal*. Mariana Bracetti and her husband, Miguel Rojas, along with his brother Manolo and the entire Rojas plantation, function as the epicenter of the secret planning for the attack on the Spanish garrison in Lares. These plans are carried out under the noses of Spanish merchants and military officers, some of whom are invited to social gatherings—that later turn into strategy meetings—at the Rojas plantation. There is also an antiracist theme as the Rojas' goddaughter, Rosaura, with Mariana and Miguel's blessings, falls in love with Redención, the son of the free-black housekeeper, Nana Monse. Furthermore, strong female characters such as Mariana and her friend Beatriz Serrano de García demonstrate the roles played by women in resisting Spanish oppression.

The action is crafted to include the historical details of the uprising without resorting to overblown rhetoric or too many set patriotic speeches. For example, only once does Mariana say that they must not sell their land because it is their only patrimony. Even her design of the flag is somewhat underplayed. The plans for the uprising are betrayed by another visitor to the Rojas household, Reinaldo Domenech, who sets himself up as a possible suitor to Rosaura and is the Puerto Rican nephew of the Spanish merchant Señor Alonso. After the initial, and too easy, triumph and the declaration of the Republic, the insurrectionists march into a trap, based on information provided by Domenech, set for them by the Spanish commander. Domenech comes to the Rojas plantation to confess his treachery to Mariana. As he departs, he is followed and killed by Redención, who, in turn, is killed by the approaching Spanish forces. Miguel Rojas has, at least temporarily, escaped the Spaniards and will hide in a mountain cave, but Mariana, who leaves the estate in the hands of Rosaura and Nana, is taken to prison by the Spanish commander. Throughout the play, graciousness, presence of mind, commitment to her beliefs, love of family, and shrewd strategical thinking characterize Mariana's actions. She is pregnant with a long-awaited child as she is taken away, and she gives birth the night before she is released. The child is stillborn, and just before dawn she receives the news that Miguel has been captured. Yet, she refuses to let the Spaniard know her suffering, and at daybreak she walks away from the jail with her child in her arms, telling the commander that her son was born in the shadows but will know the sunlight of liberty.

Written to both anticipate and commemorate the centennial of the 1868 Grito, and performed in the historical Teatro Alejandro Tapia y Rivera, *Mariana o el alba* became an extratheatrical event. The extended curtain calls were turned into political rallies as the Lares flag was passed through the auditorium. Furthermore, the production corresponded to a general rebirth of the Puerto Rican Independence Movement during the late 1960s and early 1970s. Yet, after its initial production, the play itself has generated more interest as an historical document than an artistic one.

By 1966, U.S. troops were fighting in Vietnam, and the war and the role of Puerto Ricans in it became an increasing concern for Marqués. In 1968 his oldest son, Raúl, was imprisoned briefly for refusing induction in the U.S. Army. Shortly thereafter, Rafael (Fefel) Varona, a young acquaintance of the writer, was among a group of Latin American students who were killed during a U.S. bombing raid while serving as pacifist observers in Hanoi. Marqués's concerns with the social well-being of Puerto Ricans facing the war, racial and ethnic discrimination in the United States, colonial domination and dependency, and the consumer society, drug abuse, and rising criminality on the island are evident in his participation in protests and in the plays of this period as well. His last plays concentrate on the revision of biblical and classical themes but engage issues of patrimony, warfare, time's corruption of love, and in one play, an overt expression of homosexuality.

After 1969 Marqués taught writing courses in the Hispanic studies department of the University of Puerto Rico–Río Piedras. However, during the 1970s, he increasingly retreated to his country home, designed by his companion, theater director and designer José "Joe" Lacomba, in the mountainous district of Cubuy, Canóvanas, east of San Juan. His last three major plays, written during this period, form a unit that reflects a distinctive change in direction from his political plays of the late 1950s and his more experimental work of the early 1960s. The Old Testament and Roman plots of *Sacrificio en el Monte Moriah* (Sacrifice on Mount Moriah; performed in 1970, published in 1969), *David y Jonatán*

(1970, David and Jonathan), and *Tito y Berenice* (1970, Titus and Berenice) still connect to contemporary themes, but they work those themes out in broader terms and with more personal as opposed to political meanings. The retelling of the biblical tale of Abraham, Sarah, and Isaac in *Sacrificio en el Monte Moriah* relates to issues of patriarchy and the betrayal of principles seen in earlier plays. However, connections to the reality of contemporary Puerto Rican audiences are often difficult to establish. The play is subtitled *Drama en catorce escenas cinematográficas* (Drama in Fourteen Cinematographic Scenes), and the extensive stage directions, the preliminary notes on the legend itself, and the author's justification of his interpretation of Old Testament lore further complicate the text.

Although childless at the beginning of the action, Abrahán epitomizes the materialistic patriarch willing to sacrifice virtually anything—his wife's virtue and body, for example—for material gain and to consolidate wealth and power. Sara understands that Abrahán, the father of his people, the founder of the Hebrew tribe, will beget no children. Resentful of her forced concubinage with the pharaoh and, later, the Philistine king, and of Abrahán's insistence that she worship Yahvé (Jehovah) and not her own god, Nannar, Sara devises the means to make Abrahán believe that Ismael is his son by her servant Agar—in reality, the father is Agar's lover, Efraín. Later, Sara becomes pregnant with Isaac by Ismael, convinces Abrahán that Isaac is his true heir, and forces the banishment of Isaac's older "brother." Each deception complies with the word of Yahvé, and each further convinces Abrahán of the power and righteousness of his own beliefs. When Abrahán takes Isaac off to Mount Moriah to sacrifice him to Yahvé, Sara is forced to follow them and act the role of the Angel of Yahvé to save her son's life. Isaac feels a strong Oedipal pull toward his mother and her god, and he grows to rebel against Abrahán. Finally, the sacrificial lamb is Abrahán. By killing him, Sara saves Canaán from the tyranny of Abrahán and his beliefs.

In *Sacrificio en el Monte Moriah,* Abrahán can easily be identified with Governor Muñoz Marín, and Yahvé represents the colonial domination of the North (the United States), as in *La muerte no entrará en palacio.* The political symbolism of *David y Jonatán* is less evident. In spite of the admonishments of the priest-judge Samuel, the Hebrew people want a human king. Saúl appears before Samuel, is anointed king, and proves himself in battle against the Philistines. Fifteen years pass. Jonatán, Saúl's sixteen-year-old son, and Mikol, Saúl's thirteen-year-old daughter, unaware of the "sin" of incest, are in love and request his permission to marry, which he denies. Samuel introduces the young shepherd and musician David to the court of Saúl, and he immediately becomes Saúl's favorite. After initial friction, Jonatán and David embrace and, along with Mikol, become lovers. Later, Saúl and Jonatán discover that Samuel will anoint David, even against his wishes, and not Jonatán as the new king. Saúl feels disgraced and kills himself on his own sword. Jonatán finds his body and blames David, who has already been anointed king. Jonatán and David struggle, and David mortally wounds his lover. The issues of incest, homosexuality, the anointing of successors, and ambition that kills love do not have precedents in Marqués's earlier works.

Tito y Berenice was published with *David y Jonatán* under the subtitle *Dos dramas de amor, poder y desamor* (Two Dramas of Loving, Power, and Unloving), with the instructions that the plays be staged together. By reworking Jean Racine's 1670 tragedy *Bérénice,* Marqués continues to pursue themes of increasingly private as opposed to public significance. The Roman general Tito loves Berenice, the Hebrew princess, in spite of the fact that she is older (perhaps by a decade or more, although her age is unspecified) than he is. He must leave, he claims, to assume the emperor's throne. He cannot take her with him, because Rome will not yet accept a Hebrew empress, but he promises to return. Time passes, and Tito has enjoyed his libertine reign. When witnessing the eruption of Vesuvius and the destruction of Pompeii shakes him, he decides to reunite with his beloved Berenice and make her his empress. The decision, however, comes too late. Berenice realizes that time had destroyed her beauty and that his love would be a form of pity and not desire. She chooses solitude.

During Holy Week of 1970, at the request of an ecumenical student group, Marqués wrote and read his version of the eleventh *estación* (station) of the cross—Jesus nailed to the cross—as part of a *Vía Crucis del hombre puertorriqueño* (The Way of the Cross of the Puerto Rican Man) staged to protest against the Vietnam War, racism, and poverty; to show the need for schools, housing, and decent living conditions; and to cite the rise in criminality and drug addiction. Marqués read his *estación* in front of the La Princesa jail in Old San Juan, where his son had been jailed for refusing army induction. In the name of Jesus, the text asks God why he is so distant and on the side of the rich and powerful, the exploiters, instead of with the speaker in jail, among the exploited, the oppressed, and the persecuted. It ends with a plea for love, peace, justice, and liberty. This play and the 1971 production of *El hombre y sus sueños* were the last productions during Marqués's lifetime; he died of cancer on 22 March 1979.

Marqués's reputation as a playwright rests principally on what María Teresa Babín calls his plays with "carne y hueso" (flesh and bone) characters who provide "un trozo de la vida de Puerto Rico" (a slice of Puerto Rican life), especially *La carreta* and *Los soles truncos*. However, his controversial political plays such as *Juan Bobo y la Dama de Occidente, La muerte no entrará en palacio,* and *Un niño azul para esa sombra* also explore varied dramatic forms and techniques and deserve more critical attention than they normally receive. At the same time, Marqués's accomplishments as an essayist, reviewer, short-story writer, and novelist cannot be overlooked. Many critics find that his narrative work outpaces what they see as the too-conventional form of even his most acclaimed plays. While the novels *La víspera del hombre* (1959, The Eve of Mankind) and, especially, *La mirada* (1976; translated as *The Look*, 1983) have received ambivalent critical reactions, the stories collected in *Otro día nuestro* (1955, Another Day for Us), *En una ciudad llamada San Juan* (1960, In a City Named San Juan), and *Inmersos en el silencio* (1976, Immersed in Silence) reinforce his reputation as Puerto Rico's most distinguished modern writer. The essays collected in *Ensayos (1953-1966)* (1966; translated as *The Docile Puerto Rican: Essays,* 1976) also continue to be debated in the context of contemporary Puerto Rican political and cultural life.

After Marqués died, the prestigious literary journal *Sin Nombre* devoted its October–December 1979 issue to him as Puerto Rico's leading playwright and most widely acclaimed writer. The journal editor, Vientós Gastón, and the playwright, short-story writer, and novelist Luis Rafael Sánchez wrote moving evocations of the presence and legacy of what Sánchez calls Marqués's "divinas palabras" (divine words). Renowned artist Lorenzo Homar painted the portrait of Marqués that appeared on the cover. Babín, Díaz Quiñones, Margot Arce de Vázquez, and Charles Pilditch were among the prominent scholars who contributed critical essays to the volume. In a similar vein, rehearsals had begun shortly before his death for a revival of Marqués's best-known work, *La carreta*, in an apparent attempt to redress failings cited by Marqués in the 1971 staging of the play. *La carreta* has been more widely staged on the island and abroad than any other Puerto Rican drama; twelve productions are recorded between 1952 and 1979 alone.

Since his death, Marqués has remained the dominant figure in Puerto Rican national drama. Every three to five years, revivals of *La carreta* and *Los soles truncos* play to sold-out houses in the Teatro Alejandro Tapia y Rivera and other theaters throughout the island. During the 1960s and 1970s a new generation of Puerto Rican playwrights emerged who continue to pursue the high standards set by Marqués's work. Sánchez, Myrna Casas, Lydia Milagros González, Abelardo Ceide, and Pedro Santaliz are among the playwrights of that era whose works show his influence. The Puerto Rican theater of the 1980s and 1990s, however, is better represented by the productions of theater ensembles and collectives such as the Taller de Histriones, Teatro del Sesenta, the Teatreros Ambulantes of Cayey, and Agua, Sol y Sereno rather than by dramatic theater as such. Playwrights such as José Luis Ramos Escobar and Roberto Ramos-Perea are among the more notable playwrights of the 1990s, but their work has yet to approach the level of artistry and thematic sophistication demonstrated by the plays of René Marqués.

Bibliography:

Esther Rodríguez Ramos, "Approximación a una bibliografía: René Marqués," *Sin Nombre,* 10 (October–December 1979): 123.

References:

Margot Arce de Vázquez, "*Los soles truncos:* Comedia trágica de René Marqués," *Sin Nombre,* 10 (October–December 1979): 58–70;

Francisco Arriví, *Areyto Mayor* (San Juan, P.R.: Instituto de Cultura Puertorriqueño, 1966);

María Teresa Babín, "*La carreta* en el tiempo," *Sin Nombre,* 10 (October–December 1979): 45–57;

María M. Caballero Wangüemert, *La narrativa de René Marqués* (San Juan, P.R.: Playor, 1986);

Arcadio Díaz Quiñones, "Los desastres de la guerra: Para leer a René Marqués," *Sin Nombre,* 10 (October–December 1979): 15–44;

Lowell Fiet, "*Los soles truncos:* Bárbaros, dioses nórdicos y polvos de arroz," *Conjunto, Revista de teatro latinoamericano,* 124 (January–April 2002): 86–95;

Juan G. Gelpí, *Literatura y paternalismo en Puerto Rico* (Río Piedras, P.R.: University of Puerto Rico Press, 1993), pp. 78–101, 123–125;

José Luis González, *El país de cuatro pisos y otros ensayos* (Río Piedras, P.R.: Huracán, 1980), pp. 35, 45–90;

Angelina Morfi, "Biografía Mínima," *Sin Nombre,* 10 (October–December 1979): 115–118;

Charles Pilditch, *René Marqués: A Study of His Fiction* (New York: Plus Ultra, 1976);

Bonnie Hildebrand Reynolds, *Space, Time and Crisis: The Theatre of René Marqués* (York, S.C.: Spanish Literature Publishing, 1988);

Esther Rodríguez Ramos, *Los cuentos de René Marqués* (Río Piedras, P.R.: University of Puerto Rico Press, 1976);

Luis Rafael Sánchez, "Las divinas palabras de René Marqués," *Sin Nombre,* 10 (October–December 1979): 11–14;

Gloria F. Waldman, *Luis Rafael Sánchez: Pasion teatral* (San Juan, P.R.: Corripio, 1988).

Ricardo Monti
(2 June 1944 -   )

Jean Graham-Jones
City University of New York

PLAY PRODUCTIONS: *Una noche con el Sr. Magnus & hijos,* Neuquén, 2 May 1970; Buenos Aires, Teatro del Centro, 25 June 1970; produced as *Magnus & Hijos, S.A.* by the Venezuelan troupe Rajatabla, Madrid, Barcelona, and Rome, 1975;

Historia tendenciosa de la clase media argentina, de los extraños sucesos en que se vieron envueltos algunos hombres públicos, su completa dilucidación y otras escandalosas revelaciones, Buenos Aires, Teatro Payró, 25 October 1971;

Visita, Buenos Aires, Teatro Payró, 10 March 1977; produced again as *Visit,* Tallahassee, Fla., November 1995;

Marathón, Buenos Aires, Teatros de San Telmo (Teatro Payró), 13 June 1980; Stuttgart, Germany, Theaterhaus, 21 October 1988; operatic version (with music by Pompeyo Camps), Buenos Aires, Teatro Colón, 1990;

La cortina de abalorios, Buenos Aires, Teatro del Picadero, 28 July 1981;

Una pasión sudamericana, Buenos Aires, Teatro Municipal General San Martín, 9 November 1989;

Asunción, Buenos Aires, Teatro Municipal Presidente Alvear, 2 November 1992;

La oscuridad de la razón, Buenos Aires, Teatro Payró, 8 September 1993; operatic version (with music by Camps), Buenos Aires, Teatro Colón, 1995;

Rayuela, adapted from Julio Cortázar's novel, Buenos Aires, Teatro Payró, 18 August 1994;

El visitante del doctor Freud, translation of Eric-Emmanuel Schmitt's *Le visiteur,* Buenos Aires, Bauen Auditorium Theater, 1996;

Finlandia, staged reading, Buenos Aires, Teatro Municipal Presidente Alvear, 2000; full production, Buenos Aires, La Trastienda, 17 January 2002;

No te soltaré hasta que me bendigas (Hotel Columbus), Buenos Aires, Teatro Nacional Cervantes, 22 May 2003;

Apocalipsis mañana, Buenos Aires, Teatro del Pueblo, 19 March 2004.

Ricardo Monti (from Una noche con el Sr. Magnus & hijos, *1971; George A. Smathers Libraries, University of Florida)*

BOOKS: *Una noche con el Sr. Magnus & hijos* (Buenos Aires: Talía, 1971); revised, in *Del parricidio a la utopía: El teatro argentino actual en 4 claves mayores,* edited by Osvaldo Pellettieri (Ottawa: Girol, 1993), pp. 3–54;

Historia tendenciosa de la clase media argentina, de los extraños sucesos en que se vieron envueltos algunos hombres públicos, su completa delucidación y otras escandalosas revelaciones (Buenos Aires: Talía, 1972);

Visita (Buenos Aires: Talía, 1977);

Una pasión sudamericana; Una historia tendenciosa (nueva versión), edited by Pellettieri (Ottawa: Girol, 1993);

Teatro I, edited by Pellettieri (Buenos Aires: Corregidor, 1995)–comprises *Una pasión sudamericana, Asunción,* and *La oscuridad de la razón;*

Teatro II, edited by Pellettieri (Buenos Aires: Corregidor, 2000)–comprises *Una noche con el Sr. Magnus & hijos* (revised), *Una historia tendenciosa* (revised), and *No te soltaré hasta que me bendigas (Hotel Columbus).*

Edition in English: *Reason Obscured: Nine Plays by Ricardo Monti,* edited and translated by Jean Graham-Jones (Lewisburg, Pa.: Bucknell University Press, 2004).

PRODUCED SCRIPTS: *Saverio el cruel,* by Monti and Ricardo Wulicher, based on the play by Roberto Arlt, motion picture, Cañas-Flores Productions/Patagonia Films, 1977;

Borges para millones, by Monti, Wulicher, and Vlady Kociancich, motion picture, Distrifilms, 1978;

El poder de las tinieblas, by Monti and Mario Sábato, based on a fragment ("Informe para ciegos") from the novel *Sobre héroes y tumbas* by Ernesto Sábato, motion picture, Productores Americanos/Producciones del Plata, 1979;

Roberto Arlt en escena, television, *DNI* [National Identity Card], 1994;

Visita, television, Canal 7, 20 December 2001.

OTHER: Susana Torres Molina, *Extraño juguete,* preface by Monti (Buenos Aires: Apex, 1978);

"Las imágenes en la creación literaria," in *Memoración de Sigmund Freud* (Buenos Aires: Trieb, 1979), pp. 43–47;

Marathón, in *El teatro argentino: 16. cierre de un ciclo,* edited by Luis Ordaz (Buenos Aires: Centro Editor de América Latina, 1981), pp. 57–122;

La cortina de abalorios, in *Teatro Abierto, 1981: 21 estrenos argentinos* (Buenos Aires: Sociedad General de Autores de la república Argentina, 1981);

Teatro (plays by Gabriel Díaz, Mauricio Kartun, Eduardo Pogoriles, and Víctor Winer), prologue by Monti (Buenos Aires: Los Autores, 1983);

"Presentación," in *Del parricidio a la utopía: El teatro argentino actual en 4 claves mayores,* edited by Osvaldo Pellettieri (Ottawa: Girol, 1993), pp. 1–2.

SELECTED PERIODICAL PUBLICATIONS–UNCOLLECTED: "Teatro" [theater reviews], *Crisis,* 38 (May–June 1976): 62–63;

"Teatro" [theater review], *Crisis,* 39 (July 1976): 55;

"Teatro" [theater review], *Crisis,* 40 (August 1976): 68;

"El teatro, un espacio literario," *Tiempo Argentino. Cultura,* 17 February 1985, p. 5;

"Teatro y libertad," *Asuntos culturales,* 4 (March 1989): 22–26;

"Una nueva utopía," *Página/12* (28 June 1992): 26.

Although Ricardo Monti has produced fewer plays than many of his compatriot dramatists, he is widely regarded as one of Argentina's most innovative, individual, and influential playwrights. His plays have been staged in Brazil, Uruguay, Venezuela, Puerto Rico, Spain, France, Italy, Portugal, Germany, and the United States. They have represented Argentina at international theater festivals in Latin America and Europe, and many have been translated. Monti's theater has been described as a social spectacle. His plays mix allegory, tragedy, farce, and mystery play; they intermingle religious and mythological motifs, characters, and plots; and they cross and recross multiple historical zones.

Norberto Ricardo Monti was born in Buenos Aires on 2 June 1944 to Ricardo Victorio Monti and María Pujalka, the children of Italian and Polish émigrés. He and his two older sisters, Lilia Mercedes and Matilde Noemí, were raised in Villa Celina, a lower-middle-class neighborhood on the outskirts of Buenos Aires. At that time it was an area surrounded by fields, giving Monti what he described in an unpublished 2001 letter as "una sensación de espacios abiertos y de mucha libertad" (a sensation of open space and great freedom). These fields were gradually covered by low-income apartment buildings.

Monti acknowledges having always thought of himself as a writer, producing his first poem at the age of eight. His initial contact with the theater also came at an early age, when he was taken to the Variedades Theater to see the old-style comic Charmiello perform. More than twenty years later, in a 1979 interview with Charles B. Driskell, Monti recalled the experience: "Recuerdo perfectamente esa función, el decorado, los personajes. Me llamaba mucho la atención la luminosidad extraña del escenario. . . . Y aún veo muy bien al personaje principal con su peluca roja" (I remember the performance perfectly, the set design, the characters. The stage's strange luminosity had a great effect on me. . . . And I still can see the main character in his red wig). Shortly thereafter, at the age of fourteen, Monti began to study acting at two of Buenos Aires's best-known independent theaters, the Nuevo Teatro and the Fray Mocho. He also began attending plays, including the Instituto de Arte Moderno's landmark production of Samuel Beckett's *Waiting for Godot* (1952), which Monti saw two or three times. During this period, too, he made his first attempt at writing for the theater, as he told Driskell: "A los catorce o quince años presenté una pieza en un acto a un concurso y, por supuesto, no sacó nada" (At fourteen or fifteen I entered a one-act play in a contest, and of course it didn't win anything).

Monti initially left the theater behind as he pursued a writing career, focusing on poetry and narrative. He published one poem in a literary journal and produced many short stories, none of which was published. He began several novels, which were never completed. In the mid 1960s he wrote for cultural programs broadcast on municipal and national radio. He studied various languages, becoming fluent in German. Monti then entered the National University of Buenos Aires, where he first studied philosophy but switched to psychology. His university career was interrupted by the premiere of his first play, and when he returned later to study literature, he was able to endure only one class. He explained to Driskell, "me escapé horrorizado, porque no era lo que yo quería y necesitaba. Y ya no volví a intentar ninguna carrera" (I ran away horrified because it wasn't what I wanted or needed. I've never gone back to try any other major).

Monti's first produced play, *Una noche con el Sr. Magnus & hijos* (An Evening with Mr. Magnus & Sons), has its origins in a fragment of one of his incomplete novels. Monti began writing the play in 1966 and finished it three years later at the age of twenty-five. The 1970 premiere of *Una noche con el Sr. Magnus & hijos* not only marked Monti's debut but also, by melding sociopolitical realism with avant-garde experimentation, signaled a change in Buenos Aires theatrical aesthetics at a moment of great sociopolitical upheaval. *Una noche con el Sr. Magnus & hijos* emphasizes not only familial ceremonies but also the power relations between the dominator and the dominated. The internal performances in the play cycle through such forms of theater and ritual as absurdism, naturalism, tragedy, expressionism, farce, mystery play, and even children's games. Among the themes that are developed more fully in the dramatist's later works are: authoritarian paternal figures as impostors; youthful responses to repression; the redemptive power of the feminine; performances within performances and the easily erased boundary between representation and reality; and the hero and villain, equally relativized.

Una noche con el Sr. Magnus & hijos sets up the middle-class family home as a theater for the staging of the struggles between the patriarch and his children, rivals, and lovers. Magnus is a Western capitalist, engaged in the business of selling images and identities. He obtains his power by offering up himself as the center of meaning, a defining mirror whose reflection not only seduces but also beats his subjects into submission: "Mi éxito fue adelantarme a todo. Apenas veía nacer algo, me lo tragaba. Y después lo ofrecía. Fui un espejo toda mi vida. Una superficie pulida y hueca. Hice una fortuna vendiéndoles a los demás sus propias imágenes. Por supuesto, también a ustedes" (My success lay in anticipating everything. As soon as I saw something being born, I swallowed it up. And only later I offered it up as mine. I was a mirror all my life. A polished, empty surface. I made a fortune selling everyone back their own images. Of course, to all of you, too). When Magnus confesses that he has tricked everyone with his illusion-making and that he intends to abdicate his power, his three sons decide to kill him. The play ends in parricide, the sons aided by Magnus's girlfriend and his old rival.

Yet, even as *Una noche con el Sr. Magnus & hijos* depicts authoritarianism and the response to such repression, it critiques that very response. Magnus is the villain, but he is also at times sympathetic, convincing in his assertions, and quite possibly a victim of the very system he defends. The three sons heroically overturn the old order, but they themselves are perverse and frustrated beings, rendered impotent by the privileged order of Magnus's house. Gato, the family intellectual, is Magnus's chief opponent, and the character's name emphasizes his function as the "cat" chasing after the rat–Magnus. Wolfy, the second son, is an artist, like his beloved namesake Wolfgang Amadeus Mozart. The youngest son, Santiago, is a narcissistic sensualist. Both Wolfy and Santiago have floating loyalties: Wolfy runs back and forth between his brothers' collective resistance and the protective shadow of Magnus; and Santiago, often aloof to the family situation, alternates between self-absorbed sexual pleasure and revolutionary solidarity with Gato–who, in turn, is torn between annihilating Magnus and obtaining his recognition. The fifth member of the household is Magnus's former rival, Lou. The old man has been reduced to the status of family dog after having lost to Magnus in business as well as love. Lou belongs to Magnus's world and accepts its rules; he begs his way back into the house, preferring its repressive order to the outside's uncertain freedom.

One night Magnus brings home Julia, a figure as ambiguous as the others; it is never clear whether she is an innocent virgin or an opportunistic prostitute. Julia, who is of the same age as the sons, is the one who introduces the possibility of actively overturning Magnus. Julia also functions as a substitute for their dead mother, Bibí. Magnus seduces Julia, as he does everyone else, by offering her a defining image of herself. In the process, he nearly destroys her, and the resulting disorientation leads her to join the sons in their struggle.

Although not initially well received by Buenos Aires critics and traditional theater audiences (despite a positive out-of-town premiere in southern Argentina and a modest box-office success during the 1970 season), *Una noche con el Sr. Magnus & hijos* forced the critics to reevaluate its revolutionary theatricality when that same year the original cast production opened the first Patagonian National Theater Festival in the southern coastal city of Comodoro Rivadavia. After this performance, thousands of spectators applauded for fifteen minutes as they called Monti to the stage. *Una noche con el Sr. Magnus & hijos* went on to receive two major awards in 1970, and Monti was declared Buenos Aires's great new playwright.

The new aesthetics exemplified in *Una noche con el Sr. Magnus & hijos* defied easy compartmentalization. Yet, the destruction of repressive powers in the play echoed the complex politics of its time, a moment when social protest against General Juan Carlos Onganía's ongoing military dictatorship was becoming increasingly open. Monti has said that he wrote *Una noche con el Sr. Magnus & hijos* to protest the Onganía dictatorship and growing authoritarianism within Argentine society. In 1970 Argentina, Magnus and his old rival Lou stood in for the older generation and the established bourgeoisie's desire to maintain control at any cost. The three sons, together with Julia, epitomized various responses available to the younger generation. In a 1992 *Página/12* article on political theater, titled "Una nueva utopía" (A New Utopia), Monti wrote:

> el primer objeto de reflexión tiene que ser el del intelectual sobre sí mismo . . . porque no podemos seguir mecánicamente como si acá no hubiera pasado nada. Yo creo que tenemos que buscar un teatro con una visión más problematizada. . . . Meternos profundamente a ver qué pasó con esa generación que estuvo tan comprometida y, aunque sea duro, preguntarse si realmente tuvo razón o se equivocó.
>
> (the first object of reflection has to be the intellectual himself . . . because we cannot continue on mechanically as if nothing had ever happened here. I think that we have to look for a theater with a more problematized vision. . . . Go deep into it to see what happened to that generation that was so committed and, although it may be hard, now must ask itself if it truly was right or if it made a mistake.)

One year after the premiere of *Una noche con el Sr. Magnus & hijos*, Monti wrote his most "political" play to date: *Historia tendenciosa de la clase media argentina, de los extraños sucesos en que se vieron envueltos algunos hombres públicos, su completa dilucidación y otras escandalosas revelaciones* (A Biased History of the Argentine Middle Class, of the Strange Events in which Certain Public Figures Found Themselves Involved, The Complete Elucidation of These Events and Other Scandalous Revelations, performed in 1971, published in 1972). This play, later revised as *Una historia tendenciosa* (1993), is the only text the playwright has not wished to have translated into any other language, saying that it is "too Argentine" for the foreign reader or spectator. *Una historia tendenciosa* is further exceptional within Monti's work for its collectively developed text. Building upon his own initial idea as well as a basic text and characters, Monti worked with the actors and director in various phases to create the performed text. Finally and possibly most important, *Una historia tendenciosa* marked Monti's first of many collaborations with the noted Argentine director Jaime Kogan.

The overt politics of *Una historia tendenciosa* constitute a departure from *Una noche con el Sr. Magnus & hijos* and Monti's later play, *Visita* (Visit, performed and published in 1977), which he began writing that same year. It premiered at the height of militant resistance in twentieth-century Argentina, and its lengthy title recalls the contemporary German theater tradition of Brechtian Epic theater and its successor, the documentary theater associated with the dramatist Peter Weiss (and especially Weiss's best-known play, *Die Verfolgung und Ermordung Jean Paul Marats, dargestellt durch die Schauspielgruppe des Hospizes zu Charenton unter Anleitung des Herrn de Sade* [The Persecution and Death of Jean Paul Marat, as Presented by the Inmates of the Charenton Hospital under the Direction of the Marquis de Sade, or *Marat/Sade,* 1964]). In general, Monti's theater shares with postwar German theater the mixing of historical detail with mythic structures, and *Una historia tendenciosa* is his play that most closely resembles European documentary theater.

Nevertheless, the play transcends mere imitation of the documentary model to become an allegorical overview of Argentine history from the nineteenth century through the early 1970s. The text is structured on three levels: allegorical, historical, and personal. The main plot allegorizes Argentine history through multiple characters, representing various socioeconomic sectors of the country. Even the Argentine nation itself is allegorized in the figure of the prostitute Pola. Marcelo Boñi García, a landowner and representative of the Europeanized local oligarchy, enters into a series of agreements, first with the English (depicted by the character Mr. Hawker), then with the Americans (in the character of Mr. Peagg, pronounced "Pig"), and finally with the military forces of the General. Boñi García appears willing to go to any length in order to consolidate his control over the petit bourgeoisie (personified by the lawyer Matías Bonafede), who have in turn aligned themselves with the liberal Radical party and their leader, "el Peludo" (Shaggy, the nickname given to the country's former president, Hipólito Irigoyen). A middle-class family, the Filipeaus, makes an appearance later in the play, and they exemplify the impact on the average Argentine family of this unholy alliance of oligarchs, foreigners, and military: the father is a failed and ultimately eliminated intellectual; the mother, like Bertolt Brecht's Courage, seeks to rise above her class; and the son unwittingly enters into a blood pact with Boñi García and ends up co-opted by the oligarchy. The working classes make intermittent appearances, in the character of the Obrero (Worker), but he is always silenced because, as another character says to him: "Esta obra se refiere a la clase media. Ud. no tiene nada que hacer aquí" (This play is about the middle class. You have nothing to do here).

The first act of *Una historia tendenciosa* traces the last decades of the nineteenth century, the first military coup of the twentieth century and the "infamous" 1930s, and the rise and fall of Juan Perón, ending with the 9 June 1956 execution of twenty-seven Peronist military members. The second act recounts the consolidation of United States power assisted by Argentina (Pola), the League of Pro-Development Ladies (the three "mannequins" Pulcinelle, Dorotée, and Gaby), and the Council of Native Industrialists (the two clowns Anselmo and Nicanor). The victorious do not have the final word, however; rather, the actors, discarding their characters, repeat the command "Escuchen" (listen) as they talk to each other and the audience about the winners' value system, proposing alternatives that are immediately questioned:

-La lucha está adentro de uno.
-Pero también está afuera.
-Estamos divididos en dos partes.
-. . . hay que tomarse las cosas con calma. . . .
-Hay que mirar alrededor.
-Pongamos la comodidad por encima de todo.
-¿Pero cuánto nos cuesta la comodidad?

(-Each one of us carries the fight within us.
-But that's also outside.
-We're split in two.
-. . . we have to take it easy. . . .
-We have to look around.
-We must place comfort above all else.
-But how much will that comfort cost us?)

Throughout this allegorized story, Monti and company interweave two other historical threads: "real" history and "personal" histories. The characters listen to a radio transmitting speeches by Perón and Eva Perón; and historical and fictitious characters intermix. The "personal" makes itself present at the end of the play, when the actors directly address the audience and each other, and at other moments, which in the published text are called "implosiones" (implosions), based on the actors' memories of lived experiences and either written down by Monti or improvised in performance. Thus, in *Una historia tendenciosa,* the actor plays at least three roles—real, historical, and symbolic. The metadramatic effect is accentuated by the omnipresence of the character Teatro (Theater), who plays the role of director, controlling and intervening whenever he deems it necessary.

Monti, like Weiss, sees history as an immediate and subjective confrontation and not some obscure object of study disconnected from the present. By choosing to present his analysis of modern Argentine history through metadramatics, intertextuality, and multiple theatrical levels, Monti moved "political theater" away from the realist-naturalist aesthetics so often associated with the theater of dissent and toward his own obsessions with issues of history, myth, truth, fiction, reality, and representation.

Throughout the 1970s Monti continued to work with Kogan and the Teatro Payró. He directed two plays: *El contratiempo* (1973, The Contretemps), by Argentine playwright Diana Raznovich, and Brecht's *The Days of the Commune* in 1974. He also began leading playwriting workshops, which he continued to do through the 1990s. Monti married in 1970 and had a daughter, Lila (born in 1972), so the workshops provided a needed source of income. They also became the training ground for some of Argentina's better-known playwrights. In these workshops, Monti developed his own image-based system. He refused to impose any precepts on his students, attempting instead to help each one discover his or her own world of imagery, without preconceived models. In the 1985 article "El teatro, un espacio literario" (Theater, a Literary Space), Monti explained his position:

considero a la imagen (aquella que, en el caso del escritor, es previa a su traducción en palabras) el núcleo central del proceso creativo. . . . El dramaturgo, por su parte, debe reelaborar sus imágenes iniciales, espontáneas, y reubicarlas en un espacio artificial—el espacio escénico—que las transformará a su medida, magnificando algunas o expulsando otras. Personajes, ámbitos y acciones perderán así en libertad lo que ganarán en intensidad. Condensación: tal es el término que mejor relfeja la alquimia propia del espacio escénico.

(I consider the image [i.e., that which exists, in the writer's case, prior to its translation into words] the central nucleus of the writing process. . . . The playwright, for his part, has to rework his initial, spontaneous images, relocating them in an artificial space—the scenic space—that will then transform them, magnifying some and expelling others. Characters, environments, and actions will thus lose in freedom what they gain in intensity. Condensation: this is the term that best reflects the alchemy proper to the scenic space.)

Monti's dramatic system of images had the most influence on his own generation of Argentine writers (whom he has termed the "70s" generation), including Mauricio Kartún, Eduardo Rovner, and Hebe Serebrisky.

In its original staging, *Una historia tendenciosa* ends with a handsome young man, "Criatura" (Creature), entering the stage with a machine gun. For Monti, the image meant nothing more than a warning to the old order; but when it was interpreted by many spectators and critics as a prophetic call to armed revolution, Monti excised the final image from the printed edition. Monti's next play, *Visita,* also has two endings: that of the early performances of director Kogan's original staging, included in the first edition of the published text but labeled as "rejected," as well as the ending adopted during the original production run and included in all subsequent editions.

The 1977 production of *Visita* ran for three years, achieved national and international recognition (by being acclaimed Buenos Aires's best drama of the season and receiving Spain's Carlos Arniches prize), and represented Argentina at the 1978 International Festival of Theater of the Nations in Caracas, Venezuela. Such success notwithstanding, it still remains perhaps the least-studied of Monti's major plays and, when discussed, is often regarded as a hermetic reflection on the limits of human existence. Nevertheless, its two endings point to a meditation on the possibility of sociopolitical transformation. Indeed, much of the hermeticism cloaking *Visita* stems from the circumstances of its premiere during the first and darkest years of Argentina's most repressive military dictatorship to date.

Monti's writing of *Visita* was inspired by a newspaper article about a young man who specialized in breaking into the houses of elderly couples and, over the course of the evening, forcing the couples to treat him as if he were their son. The intruder would leave the next morning with whatever he had stolen. In 1979 Monti recalled to Driskell, "cerré el diario y vi la obra" (I closed the newspaper and saw the play). *Visita* takes place in a strangely lit, enclosed space–the run-down apartment of an old, possibly dead couple named Perla and Lali. Three days have passed since an intruder, Equis (Ex), has arrived, and the old couple appears to have been engaged in a cat-and-mouse game with their uninvited guest. It is unclear if Equis is a murderer, a thief, a prodigal son, or a replacement for the fourth character, Gaspar, who is equally ambiguous and could be the elderly couple's adoptive son, servant, slave, or lover.

The action of this two-act play is built upon a series of power struggles among the four characters, and almost every battle ends in the death and resurrection of one of the characters. Conflicts are multiplied during the sections titled "acciones simultáneas" (simultaneous actions), in which paired characters engage in parallel struggles. Alliances are made, broken, and remade. Each character plays, or attempts to play, roles within roles: Perla at times is sweetly maternal and at others a despot; Lali is a helpless old man, a magician, and a seducer; and even the outsider Equis, copying Perla's death performance that ends the first act, pretends to die, but he is tortured back to life by Lali and Gaspar under Perla's supervision. Nevertheless, the stage directions leave it unclear as to whether or not the characters are pretending. Identities remain confused even as the play ends: Are Perla and Lali immortal? Is Equis the prodigal son, the messiah, or a murderous burglar? Is he the next Gaspar, a younger Lali, or an alternative to the old couple's obsolete but still powerful order?

Visita ends with the visitor draped across his hostess's lap. He is apparently sleeping, but his eyes are still open. This Pietà-inspired image contrasts with the original ending, in which Equis murders Perla and Lali, only to assume their reign upon finding that the outside door is locked. When Gaspar, now Equis's manservant, goes to investigate a sound heard outside, he sees that someone is watching from the other side of the door. The houselights then come up to reveal the theatrical spectacle. This earlier, rejected ending is similar to the parricide staged and critiqued in *Una noche con el Sr. Magnus & hijos* and quite likely stems from Monti's having begun writing *Visita* in 1970. Both plays reflect the 1960s generation's self-critical preoccupation with revolution as a means for effecting sociopolitical change. In both plays the son (albeit symbolic in Equis's case) kills the father but is incapable of constructing his own alternative world. By the time of the premiere of *Visita,* Monti had witnessed the state's violent, negative reaction to his generation's "parricidal tendencies." In all, some thirty thousand people "disappeared" during the 1976–1983 military dictatorship (the period known as the "Dirty War"), and most of them were abducted during the first three years of the regime.

The life/death dichotomy present in all of Monti's plays is perhaps most concentrated in *Visita*. Although *Visita* stages the debate as a metaphysical problem in Perla and Lali's closed world, this world is part of the same national struggle that was taking place outside the theater. The original ending is both too neat and too fatalistic. Much like Magnus's sons, Equis acts, but there is no fundamental change to the power structure. In the original ending, Equis assumes Perla and Lali's power (and even makes himself up in their image), and Gaspar continues as a servant. Equis's revolution has failed. In the second ending, the parricidal ceremony remains unfulfilled; the intruder is in an apparent trance, but he remains vigilant with his revolutionary potential intact even under repression.

Visita premiered at the height of the military dictatorship. Although several plays were officially banned and some theaters closed, theater practitioners were more often subjected to primarily anonymous acts of aggression. Such was Monti's experience. In the late 1970s he began writing for motion pictures: with the director Ricardo Wulicher, he adapted Roberto Arlt's play *Saverio el cruel* (1936, Saverio the Cruel) for the screen (1977); he also cowrote (with Wulicher and the novelist Vlady Kociancich) the dramatic scenes for a documentary on Argentine writer Jorge Luis Borges, titled *Borges para millones* (1978, Borges for Millions). Although Monti was never officially censured and during the dictatorship did not see his name on any unofficial blacklist circulating (learning only in the late 1990s that his name had been listed), he was the victim of unofficial, state-sponsored censorship on at least two occasions during the late 1970s. The director Mario Sábato had hired Monti to co-author the screenplay for *El poder de las tinieblas* (1979, The Power of Shadows), based on a portion of the novel *Sobre héroes y tumbas* (1961, On Heroes and Tombs) by the director's father, Ernesto Sábato. Monti co-authored the script, but his name did not appear on the credits, because Sábato had been told that the censors would not approve a movie project with Monti's name attached. The second instance occurred when Monti, following the international success of *Visita*, was invited to the 1979 New York Theater Festival. Well in advance of the travel dates, Monti applied to have his passport renewed; nevertheless, the renewed passport did not arrive until after the festival had ended, thus denying Monti the opportunity to attend. During this dark period, his second child, Matías, was born (in 1978).

Monti's next play premiered under continuing military repression. After four years, the Argentine people were exhibiting signs of a collective anguish; and *Marathón* (Marathon, performed in 1980, published in 1981) tapped into both this ongoing suffering and a growing critical awareness regarding what have been called the guiding fictions that had led the country to such an end. The premiere of *Marathón* was greatly anticipated and was later awarded that year's ARGENTORES (Sociedad General de Autores de la República Argentina [Argentine Association of Writers]) award for best dramatic play. It was Monti's first play in three years as well as the maiden play (once again under Kogan's direction) of Teatro Payró at the new Teatros de San Telmo, in a theater designed especially for the premiere by noted architect and set designer Tito Egurza.

The set design re-created a 1932 suburban Buenos Aires ballroom, in which six couples are participating in a dance contest. Monti took the idea from discussions with Kogan about working with music to adapt Horace McCoy's 1935 novel (later made into a Hollywood movie), *They Shoot Horses, Don't They?* The result is both Argentine and universal. The six couples represent different socio-economic, cultural, and age groups. The dancers are: an aging poet (Homero Estrella) and his aging muse (Elena García); a young couple with the assumed names of Tom Mix and Ana D.; an unemployed office worker and his wife (Héctor and Ema Expósito); a bankrupt industrialist (who uses the initials "NN" to maintain his anonymity) and a prostitute (Pipa) he has hired as his contest partner; and a tubercular bricklayer and his wife (Pedro and Asunción Vespucci). These five couples are later joined by a sixth couple, two wealthy siblings looking to experience "real life" drama. Another pair, the Guardaespaldas (Bouncer) and the Animador (Emcee), oversees the contest. One physically abuses the contestants while the other inflicts psychological punishment; yet, both are revealed by the end of the play to be nothing more than middlemen in the repressive order of the dance-hall regime.

When the play begins, the couples have already been dancing for an undetermined long time. They are "muñecos sin vida, cubiertos de polvo y telarañas" (lifeless dolls, covered in dust and cobwebs). Throughout the play they dance, take short breaks, visit the Animador's platform to endure various abuses, are beaten by the Guardaespaldas, argue among themselves and then reconcile, witness the death of one of their own and the departures of several others, and end the play continuing to dance as the never-ending marathon drags on. The audience plays multiple roles—the Emcee at times speaks to the spectators as if they were the audience in his 1930s ballroom; at other times, he addresses an invisible, imaginary audience. The real spectator is both included and excluded, participant as well as witness.

This doubling mechanism allows the play to avoid censorship even as it forces the audience to take a distanced, more critical stance. As Monti explained in an interview published in 1992, "Para hablar del presente me fui al pasado, a una época equivalente, la desdichada década del 30" (In order to talk about the present, I went back to the past, to an equivalent period, the unhappy decade of the 1930s).

Marathón is divided into twenty-three episodes in which multiple levels of reality are interwoven: the 1932 dance marathon itself, including the contest events and the dancers' private individual dreams, spoken aloud; and five *mitos* (myths), which function as critical transformations of an Argentine collective historical memory–Conquest, Independence, pastoral America, industrial America, and Fascism. With the *mitos,* Monti draws attention to the relation between history and mythmaking. The dance contest participants play the characters in the five mythic episodes, transforming themselves into historical and symbolic, even collage-like figures. In the first myth of the Conquest, the tubercular bricklayer Pedro Vespucci is transformed into the Spanish *conquistador* Pedro de Mendoza and quite possibly Amerigo Vespucci. In the Independence myth, the contestant calling himself Tom Mix (the hero of the Hollywood Western movies) plays a composite character, who is both Argentine Independence hero Mariano Moreno and an anonymous twentieth-century guerrilla. When the wealthy siblings arrive, the dancers transform themselves into a herd of cattle. The image not only points to class distinctions but also alludes to Esteban Echeverría's nineteenth-century allegorical novella, *El matadero* (The Slaughterhouse), in which the slaughtered cattle are identified with the Argentine people oppressed by the mid-nineteenth-century dictator Juan Manuel Rosas. The fourth myth dramatizes the transformation of the bankrupt "NN" into an investor willing to exploit everyone else for his own gain. Finally, in the fifth myth, the Guardaespaldas is transformed into an authoritarian, antidemocratic nationalist who is easily identified with the Animador's glorification of fascism. All five myths portray degrading, negative, transformations and suggest certain universal negative traits present in both individuals and the national culture. There is no single positive, transformative myth.

In a 1992 interview, Monti said that the true hero of the play is the one dance contestant who chooses to stay–Héctor Expósito. As his surname suggests (the Spanish noun *expósito* means "foundling" and, as an adjective, "abandoned"), Héctor, like Equis and Gaspar in *Visita,* is alone, abandoned, and isolated but not necessarily powerless. His "mythic" transformation occurs during the dance contest and does not require its own episode because his countermyth is a parable for daily life: he is the one who stays, who chooses to live with the uncertainties, and who rejects the easy answers offered by mythologization. Unlike Tom Mix (and the revolutionary "parricidal" characters of Monti's earlier plays and rejected endings), Héctor is the only contestant to question the Animador's and the Guardaespalda's actions and to fight their repression. His heroic stance

Cover for Monti's first play (An Evening with Mr. Magnus & Sons), which premiered in 1970, about a powerful capitalist whose sons, lover, and former rival conspire to murder him (George A. Smathers Libraries, University of Florida)

constitutes a call to human solidarity and the final awakening from isolated private dreams and collective mythical nightmares. Such heroism notwithstanding, Héctor is alone at the end of *Marathón;* the younger dancers are gone, and the rest are lost in their dreams. The Animador has the last word: "si no fuera ridículo, esto sería una tragedia. ¡Y sigue el baile, damas y caballeros, sigue el baile!" (If it weren't ridiculous, this would be a tragedy. On with the dance, ladies and gentlemen, on with the dance!).

A final comment must be made about the deliberate misspelling of the Spanish word for marathon, *maratón.* At the time of the 1980 premiere of the play, Monti stated in an interview published in the Buenos Aires daily newspaper *Clarín:* "Se trata de una *Marathon* concreta y, a la vez, de una metáfora. La 'h' que incluye la palabra es una forma de distanciamiento, es una especie de señal porque la cosa no es tan real como parece" (It's about a real marathon and, at the same time, a metaphor. The 'h' included in the title is a form of distancing, it's a kind of signal that the thing is not as real as it appears). Monti's inclusion of the "h" reinforces his use of Brechtian Epic theater conventions by encouraging his spectators to question what is often taken for (historical) fact.

The last play Monti wrote under dictatorship is noteworthy for both its revision of an earlier play and its presence within one of Argentina's most important mass cultural responses to dictatorship–the 1981 Teatro Abierto (Open Theater) festival. Monti was a founding member of Teatro Abierto and edited the group's short-lived journal. His play *La cortina de abalorios* (The Beaded Curtain) was one of three one-act plays that opened the festival on 28 July 1981 in the Teatro del Picadero. In total, twenty plays were staged in this festival of "open theater for a closed country," with three plays presented each afternoon during the seven-day cycle. When on 6 August an "accidental" fire destroyed the Picadero, the festival was moved to the Tabarís, a much larger commercial theater, where it continued its run until the end of September. Approximately twenty-five thousand spectators attended the festival.

Although Teatro Abierto was an important act of cultural resistance, the majority of the plays, notwithstanding their common defiant oppositional stance, replicated a fairly conventional theatrical aesthetic. *La cortina de abalorios* both built upon and transcended dominant naturalist aesthetics. A play that can easily be read as "political," it overtly focuses on Argentina's discourses of power even as it presents the clearly ambiguous and problematical character of a brothel madam. In the 1981 original staging, this character carried an even greater significance, as she was played by the well-known actress Cipe Lincovsky, recently returned from political exile.

La cortina de abalorios was inspired by a scene from Monti's earlier *Una historia tendenciosa*: the conspiratorial meeting between the local landowner, the Englishman, and the prostitute. The action of *La cortina de abalorios* takes place in a "fantasmal y polvoriento prostíbulo de fines de siblo XIX" (ghostly and dusty brothel from the late nineteenth century), the setting for a sinister coming to terms between the Argentine oligarchy and foreign interests. The landowner is named Pezuela and the Englishman, Popham. Both names allude to historical characters from Argentina's colonial past: in 1806, the British admiral Sir Home Popham, acting on his own initiative, invaded and occupied Buenos Aires. Joaquín de la Pezuela was a late-eighteenth-century Spanish general who later became viceroy of Peru. Once again, Monti makes symbolic use of historical names to dramatize a national mythology. The cattleman Pezuela, recently returned to the brothel after "butchering Indians," receives a visit from Popham, from whom he has borrowed money. The Englishman is dragging a trunk, in which he claims there are jewels, feathers, and various stock certificates for "de todo un poco. Minas, ferrocarriles, bancos . . ." (a bit of everything. Mines, trains, banks . . .). They gamble for the debt, and Pezuela loses everything he owns to the Englishman's cheating. The loss triggers a physical fight between the two men, but they finally end in agreement when Pezuela offers up the madam along with millions of others like her, "regimientos de vacas, una costra de vacas sobre mis campos, reproduciéndose lascivamente" (regiments of cows, a layer of them covering my lands, reproducing lasciviously). Popham begins to conduct behavior-modification experiments on a fourth character, the Mozo (Servant), and when the Mozo resists Popham's needle, the madam stabs the servant with a scalpel. The play ends with the three conspirators exhausted from a brief celebratory orgy under the table.

The madam remains unnamed in the text (Pezuela calls her "mamá," and she in turn refers to him as "bebé" [baby]), but she plays a role similar to Pola's in *Una historia tendenciosa*: she is culturally pretentious and willing to prostitute herself to anyone who will help her rise in power. The Mozo's allegorical role, as the masses victimized by the controlling powers, resembles that of the Obrero in *Una historia tendenciosa*. In *La cortina de abalorios,* the Mozo is first knifed by Pezuela; he comes back to life only to be shot by Popham; and once more he brings himself back to life only to be stabbed by the madam. At the end of the play, the Mozo will once again gather himself up and leave the stage as the madam calls for someone to wait on her.

La cortina de abalorios is clearly a critique of turn-of-the-century colonialism. Its indictment of alliances made to keep the populace subjugated as the country is sold off to the highest bidder is also a none-too-veiled reference to the military dictatorship and its neoliberal economic policies. Even so, the allegorical symbolism is less explicit than that of *Una historia tendenciosa,* and perhaps such ambiguity can explain the mixed critical response to the character of the madam. She has been interpreted as representing the history of Argentina, French corruption of local culture, the country itself as commercial goods, or the "tendentious" Argentine middle class.

Monti's plays written during the 1976–1983 military dictatorship shared several concerns: the possibility or impossibility of a truly "revolutionary" act; individual complicity in collective historiography; and the presence of power structures in all political movements, oppressive and resistant. In later plays, he began to move away from specifically Argentine historical referents and toward a more "American" context. His later plays engage in direct dialogue with the great models of the Western cultural canon: tragedies, passion plays, and even divine comedies.

Monti's next play, *Una pasión sudamericana* (A South American Passion Play, performed in 1989, published in 1993), marked his first attempt to look at America as a frontier land. Even though the play takes place in the "salón de un casco de estancia, enclavado en la campaña bonaerense" (the hall of what remains of a ranch, located in the plains outside Buenos Aires), its title has crossed the national border. Monti's expansion of his demythologizing project is also reflected in his theatrical language. In *Una pasión sudamericana,* Monti's theater is even more hybridic, his storylines more fragmented, and his characters more mediated. Monti's critique of Argentina became a revision of the modern Western tradition.

Monti began writing *Una pasión sudamericana* while his country was still under dictatorship, but he did not finish it until the late 1980s. The play premiered in November 1989 in the main hall of Argentina's largest theater complex, Buenos Aires's Teatro Municipal General San Martín (where Monti also served as artistic adviser for a short period). After a falling out with Kogan, Monti took over the staging of his play. While most spectators (and even Monti himself) were dissatisfied with the production, *Una pasión sudamericana* is regarded by many critics as Monti's greatest play to date.

Una pasión sudamericana appears to tell the real-life story of Camila O'Gorman and her lover, the Jesuit priest Ladislao Gutiérrez. This nineteenth-century tragic romance had already been the subject of many Argentine plays, novels, poems, and even movies, and their story has often been revisited as a metaphor for youthful romantic individualism and martyrdom at the hands of a repressive status quo. Camila O'Gorman was the pampered daughter of a prominent Buenos Aires Federalist and the personal friend of the daughter of General Juan Manuel de Rosas, the Federalist dictator of Argentina at the time the events took place. Camila fell in love with her confessor, and the two ran away together to live in the Argentine littoral. They were discovered, imprisoned, and executed in 1848 for this rebellion. Camila was twenty years old and, by popular account, pregnant. Despite the attraction of such an emotionally charged story and unlike most other fictionalized treatments, *Una pasión sudamericana* subverts the romantic tradition entirely by telling the lovers' story from the executioner's point of view. On the eve of a decisive battle with his enemy the Loco (Madman), the Brigadier must decide if he will execute Camila. During the course of the evening, his five fools or "crazies" re-enact Camila and Ladislao's "passion" as an inverted Divine Comedy.

Monti took great pains to distance *Una pasión sudamericana* from its own historical subject. Some of the characters reinforce the nineteenth-century Argentine setting of the play: the Brigadier, assisted by an aged Aide-de-camp, is and is not Rosas; the Loco's letters that are read aloud include fragments of texts from famous Argentine politicians (and opponents of Rosas). Other characters refer to other historical moments: the British minister Canning (best known for his associations with the government preceding Rosas) calls upon the Brigadier, and the biblical criminal Barrabás, now an enormous gaucho, is chained in the Brigadier's quarters. The lead "crazy" goes by the name of Farfarello but says his real name is Pedro de Angelis (the Italian intellectual known best as a Rosas apologist), and two other buffoons bear historical names as well: San Benito (Saint Benedict, whose monastic order has been credited with pulling Western Europe out of the Dark Ages) and the warring Murat, Napoleon Bonaparte's marshal. The final two buffoons are the murderous Biguá and Estanislao the foundling. Once again, Monti creates a collective mythocultural past that fragments, multiplies, and even contradicts simple historical diachrony. Such "contradiction" reaches its height with what has been perhaps the most contested modification in the play—the birth of Camila's son. *Una pasión sudamericana* ends with the newborn swaddled in the Brigadier's poncho.

A brief prologue sets the foreboding, mystically heightened mood with the four wet and muddy crazies circling trance-like around Farfarello as he sings the Neapolitan *Madonna della Grazia*. The five then whirl offstage before the sole act of the play begins. Throughout the course of the play, the Aide-de-camp comes and goes, delivering reports and pleading mercy for Camila. The Brigadier dictates letters to his general, Flores; these letters are recorded by the two Escribientes (scribes) and serve as meditations on the war and the Brigadier's own role in the struggle. As a diversion from the next day's battle, the Brigadier tells the buffoons to create a farcical "theater of dreams," which the crazies transform into the four-part story of Camila and Ladislao. They begin their story in Inferno, where they tell the legend of the young maid who aroused a priest's lust. The Brigadier at first does not want to participate in the buffoons' "madness of love" and halts the performance. Yet, he is already swept up in the story and wants to know what happened: "¿Por qué supone que una joven de buena familia . . . ? Es un misterio, ¿no cree?" (Why would a girl from a good family . . . ? It's a mystery, don't you think?) His questions lead the buffoons into the second station of their passion play, the World, site of the mystery of the flesh. Estanislao plays Camila, wearing a crown of transparent roses whose thorns cause blood to trickle down his face. The buffoons recite a reworked Song of Solomon to stage the awakening of erotic passion in the two lovers. Once again the Brigadier stops the performance, but once more he cannot resist and allows the buffoons to go on.

In the third station, Purgatory, the Mystic Rose and the sexual act fuse together in the buffoons' language; the Brigadier, now horrified, tries to stay the performance but is instead so completely caught up that he becomes an actor. Wearing a crown of red roses, he enters the crazies' dreamworld. Blood trickles down his temples and cheeks. The Brigadier, brought back to his own immediate reality, asks the Aide-de-camp for details about "esos niños" (those children), which the Aide-de-camp, ever hopeful for Camila's pardon, provides. The buffoons then arrive at the final station, the lovers' escape to Paradise and a return to the moment before the fall from grace. Nevertheless, the lovers' future has already been predicted by the fools: "Somos restos de un Génesis deshecho" (We are the remains of an undone Genesis). When their performance has finally ended, the Brigadier is calm: "¡Qué paz! ¡Qué enorme y simple paz! Ahora todo tiene su orden" (What peace! What enormous and simple peace! Now everything has its order). The Aide-de-camp enters once more and, after recommending that they send the priest to jail and Camila home to her parents, listens in horror to the Brigadier's decision: "Que los fusilen.... ¿Cómo piensa que yo no voy a dar una respuesta valiente al tamaño de su valentía?" (Shoot them.... How could you possibly think that I wouldn't give a response worthy of their bravery?). The play ends in temporary stasis: Camila's newly born son holds promise for a utopian future, but the Brigadier has also unchained the criminal Barrabás, who flees into the violent early dawn as the distant firing of rifles and cannons is heard.

By forcing the spectator to witness the symbolic and concrete events that lead the Brigadier to his final decision, Monti introduces his audience into what fellow Argentine playwright Eduardo Pavlovsky has called the collective subconscious of victims and victimizers. *Una pasión sudamericana* initiates Monti's search for an alternate means of representing and interpreting recent, and not so recent, Argentine-American history. Monti so identified with his project that he named his third child, born earlier that year, Camila.

Despite a flawed original production, *Una pasión sudamericana* was critically well received and awarded the 1989 ARGENTORES and Pepino el 88 prizes for best drama; and Monti received that year's María Guerrero Award for outstanding playwright. Four years later, in 1993, Monti was awarded the First National Award for best drama, tragedy, or historical play during the 1988–1991 period.

Even as Monti continued to write new plays, he often revisited and reworked his own texts. In 1990 he adapted his 1980 play *Marathón* for the opera. With music written by Pompeyo Camps, the opera was staged that year in the Teatro Colón by Kogan. In 1990 also, Monti wrote *Una historia tendenciosa,* a new version of the 1971 play that he subtitled "moralidad en un acto" (a one-act morality play). This new version has not yet been staged. The basic story line has been streamlined but not significantly altered (except for the elimination of extraneous characters such as the three mannequins), and the one-act play focuses more on historical events. Several of the more Brechtian elements of the earlier version have been eliminated, most notably the improvised "implosions" and the actors' direct address to the audience that ended the original. The second act has been modified considerably more than the first, to reflect historical events that took place after the earlier play premiered. In *Una historia tendenciosa* the General (who makes only a brief appearance in the first act of the 1971 version) takes over the clown Nicanor's temporary role as national hero. The change is a comment on Argentina's 1976–1983 military dictatorship, which began some five years after the play was first written. The prostitute (before named Pola and known in the later version merely as the Madame) more clearly assumes her role as *madre patria*, the Argentine nation itself.

There are also significant changes in the narrator/director character of Teatro (Theater): the character plays fewer roles outside his own and comments far less on the significance of the staged events. Instead, Teatro consistently brings the other characters back to the idea of their production as theater and not as life. He limits himself to only veiled allusions to any correlation between on- and offstage worlds (a correlation overtly present in the earlier text) until the end of the play, when he addresses the audience in newly added lines:

> ¡Telón, dije! ¿Están dormidos? ¡Me están arruinando el gran final! (*Hace silencio, como si escuchara a alguien en bastidores.*) ¿Qué? ¿Cómo? ¿No terminó? ¿Hay que seguir? (*Pausa.*) ¿Empezar todo de nuevo? (*Pausa. Se dirige al público, perplejo.*) ¿Pero cuántas veces vamos a tener que repetir la misma historia?
>
> (Curtain, I said! Are you asleep? You're ruining my grand finale! [*He's silent, as if he were listening to someone from offstage.*] What? What do you mean? It's not over? We have to keep going? [*Pause.*] Begin all over again? [*Pause. Perplexed, he addresses the audience.*] But how many times are we going to have to repeat the same history?)

As these final lines make clear, *Una historia tendenciosa* is indeed a didactic morality play.

Monti's next new play, *Asunción* (performed in 1992, first published in *Hispamérica* [April–August 1993]), continued his "American" project. The subtitle of this one-act play summarizes the action of what is principally a monologue: "Delirio místico, pasión y muerte de Doña Blanca, manceba de don Pedro de Mendoza, que también sifilítica agoniza en la inmóvil noche paraguaya, mientras a su lado Asunción, niña indígena, pare el primer mestizo de la tierra, en el año del Señor de 1537" (The Mystical Delirium, Passion, and Death of Doña Blanca, Once the Concubine of Don Pedro de Mendoza, Who Now Ill with Syphilis Agonizes in the Still Paraguayan Night, While at Her Side, Asunción, an Indian Girl, Gives Birth to the First Mestizo in the Land, in the Year of Our Lord 1537). Doña Blanca first allied herself with the conquering Pedro de Mendoza only to take up with a lesser conquistador, Domingo de Irala. Mendoza, the great initial "founder" of Buenos Aires, has died of syphilis, a disease he most probably passed on to the now-dying Doña Blanca. Irala, who went on to spend some thirty years in Paraguay, is the supposed father of Asunción's child. Like so many characters in Monti's plays, Doña Blanca is not easily categorized. Clearly a victim of a masculinist society, she has participated in her own victimization. As she sits on her large throne-like chair next to an enormous baroque cross, she tells her life story, stabbing the palms of her hands with a dagger so that her blood will continue to flow and she will continue to live. The image of flowing water dominates this lyrical text, and Doña Blanca's self-created stigmata suggest her martyrdom by her society.

The premiere of *Asunción* on 2 November 1992, as part of a festival of new Latin American one-act plays ("Voces con la misma sangre" [Voices with the Same Blood]), coincided with the sudden, unexpected death of Monti's second wife, Teresita, to whom *Una pasión sudamericana* had been dedicated. Monti was left alone to raise his young daughter Camila.

Under the direction of Kogan, Monti's play *La oscuridad de la razón* (The Obscurity of Reason) premiered on 8 September 1993 in the Teatro Payró. Both the play and production received almost every Buenos Aires award accorded a dramatic play (including a municipal award for outstanding contribution to the theater and Association of Theater Critics awards for best director, music, and dramatic play).

La oscuridad de la razón is an inverted *Oresteia*, in which the Virgin Mary (costumed in the original staging as Eva Perón and referred to in the published text as the Mujer [Woman]) makes appearances together with various "types" from nineteenth-century Argentine history. *La oscuridad de la razón* celebrates the deaths of modern individualism and the preferred dramatic genre of Western modernity, the tragedy. Monti stated, in an unpublished 1992 interview, that Aeschylus's classical tragedy represents "el pasaje del matriarcado al patriarcado y el establecimiento de la razón . . . , que culmina en el positivismo como dominio soberbio sobre la naturaleza" (the passage from a matriarchy to a patriarchy and the establishment of reason . . . , which culminated in Positivism's arrogant domination of Nature). In an interview with Susana Freire published in the Buenos Aires newspaper *La Nación* at the time of the 1993 premiere, Monti explained that the historical moment of the play is roughly 1830, a year he regards as "el nacimiento de la modernidad y donde se produce el giro cultural que da como producto nuestro mundo" (the birth of modernity, where the cultural turn was made that produced our world).

The three-act play begins with a brief, strange prologue. The young Mariano (an Orestes who also bears a resemblance to Hamlet and to the nineteenth-century Argentine independence hero Mariano Moreno) returns from France to his homeland, now lying in ruins. There he meets the Woman, who promises to lead and "enlighten" him about himself. The first act opens with Mariano's sister, Alma, surrounded by a chorus of Weeping Women. Like her classical counterpart, Aeschylus's Electra, Alma mourns her father's death and vows to avenge his murder. Mariano approaches her, but she does not recognize her French-speaking brother. When he finally speaks to her in Spanish, she unexpectedly stabs him with her knife and then fails to acknowledge her own responsibility for this injury, which Mariano keeps bandaged in a bloodstained cloth throughout the rest of the play. Only when the Chorus demands that "reconozca la sangre / a la sangre" (blood recognize blood) does Alma finally recognize her brother. They are soon joined by their mother, María, who, like Shakespeare's Gertrude, has taken up with her husband's younger brother and murderer, Dalmacio, the local caudillo. Dalmacio, accompanied by a male Chorus of his supporters, attempts to ascertain Mariano's motives in returning. The first act ends with the return of the women characters, who crown Mariano as everyone cries,

> Gloria al hermano perdido,
> gloria al hijo hallado,
> al peregrino,
> al extranjero,
> a nuestro héroe,
> gloria.
>
> (Glory be to our lost brother,
> glory be to our found son,
> to our pilgrim,
> our stranger,

> our hero,
> glory.)

The second act dramatizes Mariano's slow awakening from his dream of reason. In the first scene Alma urges Mariano to kill both Dalmacio and their mother. The second scene stages a confrontation between María, lying next to a sleeping Dalmacio, and the ghost of her dead husband. María unrepentantly confesses to having participated in his murder. Dalmacio awakens to profess his innocence, or justification in his desire to bring "freedom" to his land. The act ends with María, Dalmacio, and the Ghost re-enacting his murder for Mariano and Alma. The Ghost hands Mariano Alma's knife, and Mariano fulfills his destiny by killing Dalmacio.

The third and final act takes place in an old abandoned church, ruined by the ongoing civil war. Mariano, alone and overwhelmed by the horror of what he has done, wonders aloud, "¡Padre, / padre! / ¿Por qué me has abandonado?" (Father, father! Why have you forsaken me?). He is joined by Alma, who brings him out of his delirious state (in which he has confused her with Mary Magdalene) as the male Chorus—now pale, ferocious, armed specters resembling Aeschylus's Furies—clamor for revenge. Mariano refuses Alma's knife, saying:

> No,
> no nací para matar.
> . . . .
> No, hermana,
> nací para engendrar,
> para dar vida.
> Ahora lo sé.
> Y si esta noche muero,
> ya no deseo
> arrastrar conmigo
> nuevas sombras.
>
> (No,
> I was not born to kill.
> . . . .
> No, sister,
> I was born to engender,
> to give life.
> Now I understand.
> And if I should die tonight,
> I no longer wish
> new shadows
> to drag along with me.)

Alma insists, and Mariano is about to take the knife when the Woman reappears. She goes to him and removes the bloodied bandage from his hand; the two, free of the cycle of violence, begin to ascend. Nature appears to reign once more over America as the Woman/Virgin Mary returns Mariano/Jesus to the Holy Trinity. The all-male Chorus attempts to stop them by arguing, "Pero así no hay tragedia" (But that way it's not a tragedy). They continue, "Entonces que lo pague, / ese destino" (So let him pay for it, his destiny), to which the Woman responds, "Ahora el destino / es general" (Destiny now belongs to everyone). The final image, echoing the last scene of *Visita,* is a Pietà that leaves no doubt as to Mariano's imminent resurrection, made explicit in the last stage directions: Mariano, "que yacía inerte en el regazo de la Mujer, parece despertar, se incorpora lentamente, sonriendo, y se sumerge, como si danzara, en la luz que no deja de crecer" (resting motionless on the Woman's lap, appears to wake up; he slowly gets up, smiling, and submerges himself, dancing, in the ever-growing light). This image of triumphant immortality does not necessarily foretell a utopian return; Alma is still alive and, electing to sleep in "derrotada oscuridad" (defeated obscurity), completes this American family portrait. She waits, clutching her knife.

In an unpublished 1992 interview Monti made clear his own awareness of his "American" project: "Creo que sí hay un destino común de América. . . . Estamos viviendo una época de transformaciones increíbles, de la disolución de los estados nacionales. No vamos a hablar de un nacionalismo absurdo, romántico y decimonónico en un momento en que evidentemente se están gestando estructuras más amplias" (I believe that there is a common destiny for America . . . . We are living in a period of incredible transformations, of the dissolution of nation-states. Let's not talk about an absurd, romantic, nineteenth-century nationalism at a moment when it's obvious that larger structures are breaking through). In these later plays, Monti questions the relevance of Western modernity itself.

In 1994 Monti and Kogan again joined forces (with their usual set designer Egurza) to work on a stage adaptation of Julio Cortázar's landmark 1963 novel *Rayuela* (Hopscotch). The Teatro Payró project was underwritten by the Argentine Mercantile Bank Foundation, whose president had contacted Kogan with the idea of commemorating the tenth anniversary of Cortázar's death (and the eightieth anniversary of his birth). Although the initial proposal suggested adapting selected short stories by the famous writer, Monti proposed that they adapt Cortázar's challenging novel. The length of the book (more than six hundred pages) was not the only challenge facing Monti; the text is structured in such a way that it requires the reader's participation in its own reconstruction. (One can elect to read the first two-thirds of the novel alone, or interweave the "dispensable" chapters that make up the other third of the text, following the author's suggested order, or even invent a new reading sequence.) Despite such challenges, Monti said that upon rereading *Rayuela* he clearly saw dramatic "nuclei." The dramatic version is almost entirely faithful to the language of the original novel, with the addition of only a couple of phrases.

Monti focused his adaptation on the relationship between Buenos Aires and Paris, the respective earth and heaven present in the hopscotch pattern of the title. Building upon what the playwright called this "speculative" relationship, he dramatized the two romantic triangles in which the protagonist of the novel, Horacio Oliveira, finds himself entangled. Oliveira loses the love of Talita in Buenos Aires but wins the love of la Maga in Paris, and, because of his relationships with the two women, his friendships with two other characters, Ossip Gregorovius and Traveler, are severely tested. Monti furthered the parallels between the two affairs by having the same actor and actress play both the Buenos Aires and Paris characters. True to the spirit of Cortázar's experimental text, Monti's version condensed space and time to capture the lyricism and magic of the novel. The Buenos Aires production was the last time Monti and Kogan collaborated before Kogan's death in 1996.

During the mid 1990s Monti worked on several adaptations. In 1995 the Teatro Colón staged an operatic version of *La oscuridad de la razón,* with music once again composed by Camps. Rubén Szuchmacher (who had played the role of Gaspar in the original production of *Visita*) was the regisseur for Monti's adaptation of his own play. The following year, Monti provided a translated version, from the French, of Eric-Emmanuel Schmitt's 1993 play, *Le visiteur* (The Visitor). Monti's version, titled *El visitante del doctor Freud* (Dr. Freud's Visitor), was directed by Víctor García Peralta and presented in the Auditorium Theater of the Bauen Hotel.

Monti next began work on a series of one-act, two-character plays, provisionally titled "Encuentros ejemplares" (Exemplary Encounters). The first of the series was published in 2000 under the original title of *No te soltaré hasta que me bendigas* (I Will Not Release You Until You Bless Me), with its alternate title, *Hotel Columbus,* in parentheses. In this thriller, a security agent for the president of an unnamed South American country has a strange encounter with a transvestite, who may or may not have come to assassinate the head of state. Over the course of an evening in the presidential suite of the Columbus Hotel, "Roca" and "Sarah" play a cat-and-mouse game during which each threatens to kill the other and him- or herself with Roca's pistol.

The play opens with Roca receiving a humiliating phone call from his superior. Filled with impotent violence, he begins to drink whisky as Sarah mysteriously enters from another room in the suite. At first she perceives Roca to be the president; it is a confusion Roca exploits until nearly the end of the play. When Sarah suddenly takes Roca's gun, he fears she is an assassin. Sarah responds that, on the contrary, she has come to propose a union, "Por nosotros. Arte y poder. Política y teatro" (To us. Art and power. Politics and theater). Sarah appears to be lost in a dream, or the mad delusion, of a previous love affair during which she, as the famous actress Sarah Bernhardt, performed for Roca and his troops. Roca accompanies Sarah in her invented memories, playing the role of his namesake, General Julio Argentino Roca—the nineteenth-century hero of the "Conquest of the Desert," in which the Argentine government displaced or killed thousands of gauchos and indigenous peoples and cleared the way for white settlers and investors.

Their fiction-making takes increasingly serious turns. Roca's actions oscillate between sudden, violent outbursts of anger and absolute exhaustion even as he maintains his fictitious presidential role and makes several attempts to tell Sarah the story of his violent "bodyguard." Sarah prefers to revisit their old love affair and bemoans the absence of romantic artistic glory in the modern world. These games of death and memory continue, interrupted several times by the telephone. When the final call informs Roca that the real president is on his way to the suite, the bodyguard finally drops the presidential fiction. As if he were telling a police officer, he recounts the afternoon he discovered his son in his dead wife's clothing and makeup:

> Lo que más me dolía fue que era idéntico a la madre, Entonces levanté el brazo así, bien alto, y descargué el puño, con toda mi fuerza, en esa cara hermosa, frágil, amada.... Un segundo antes de darme vuelta vi como le saltó la sangre de la nariz y de la boca.... No sé cuánto tiempo pasó, Señor. Después la casa retumbó.... Corrí al cuarto. Mi hijo, Señor, estaba ahí, muerto, tumbado en la cama con la cabecita destrozada. Sangre, sesos, huesos desparramados, salpicando todo.

> (The thing that hurt me the most was that he was identical to his mother. So I lifted my arm, like this, way up, and I hit him as hard as I could with my fist, hit that beautiful, fragile face I loved so much... And a second before I turned away I saw the blood come pouring out of his nose, his mouth.... I don't know how much time went by, Sir. Then it was like thunder hit the house.... I ran to my room. My son, Sir, my son was there, dead, sprawled out on the bed, his beautiful head destroyed. Blood, brains, bones scattered everywhere, spattering everything.)

Sarah takes the gun from Roca just as he is about to demonstrate his son's suicide. She asks him to hold her, and in the middle of the embrace, the gun discharges. Sarah's body slowly falls to the floor. Monti repeats his favored final image of the Pietà as Roca pulls Sarah onto his lap, saying "Mi hijo" (my son [or child]). He kisses her on the lips as the lights fade to black, whereupon the phone begins to ring once again.

Monti's play *Finlandia* (Finland) is as yet unpublished but premiered in 2002. The manuscript reveals a streamlined version of *Una pasión sudamericana*. Although the basic story line remains unchanged, there are no longer any specific references to Argentine history. Rather, the action now takes place in the "helada llanura finlandesa, cubierta por un espeso manto de nieve, a fines de una Edad Media o a comienzos de un Renacimiento convencionales" (frozen plains of Finland, covered by a thick blanket of snow, at the end of the Middle Ages or the beginning of the Renaissance). The cast has been reduced to four characters: the military leader Beltrami, with his Aide, is entertained by the Mezzogiornos, brother and sister twins conjoined genitally and in a state of perpetual orgasm. Transcending the freak-show oddness of their physiological condition, the Mezzogiornos afford Monti the opportunity to explore gender construction. Both *No te soltaré hasta que me bendigas* and *Finlandia* fall squarely within Monti's larger investigation into Western modernity and modernism.

Monti has continued to write for television and motion pictures as well as for the theater, with two plays in development: "Crucigrama" (Crossword Puzzle), another work in the "Encuentros ejemplares" series, involving two elderly sisters living alone in an apartment; and "Genoma Elektra" (Elektra Genome), which the author describes as a mix of classicism, the absurd, and science fiction. A monologue version of "Crucigrama" was performed at Buenos Aires's 2004 International Festival of Performing Arts under the title *Apocalipsis mañana* (Apocalypse Tomorrow). It was directed by Mónica Viñao. Monti's plays have won every major municipal and national award available to an Argentine dramatist. Monti himself has received various awards for his overall achievement in the theater, including the 1994 Diploma of Merit from the Konex Foundation.

In his search to create what he has called "un realismo más amplio" (a broader realism), Ricardo Monti has traced the enduring presence of nineteenth-century myths in twentieth-century Argentina in order to dramatize the perceived failure of Western modernity and its aesthetic counterpart, modernism. Even Monti's earliest plays demonstrate a rejection of totalizing systems of power and an attempt at experimenting with alternative structures. There are other constants in Monti's plays: the mixing of religious and mythological motifs, the fusion of multiple dramatic genres, and the confluence of historical moments and references. Time and again, Monti has revisited classical formulas and images (and even his own earlier texts) in his critical dialogue with Western tradition. This unrelenting impulse to transform (texts, genres, motifs, and histories) has resulted in a body of work rich in dynamic, theatrical tension.

Interviews:

Jorge Adip, "Reportaje a Ricardo Monti," *Fronteras,* 1–2 (February 1979): 19–22;

Charles B. Driskell, "Conversación con Ricardo Monti," *Latin American Theatre Review,* 12 (Spring 1979): 43–53;

R.G., "Con 'Marathón' vuelven Monti y Kogan," *Clarín,* 18 June 1980;

Osvaldo Pellettieri, "Un teatro de reflexión," *La Escena Latinoamericana,* 2 (August 1989): 75–78;

Jorge Conti, "La difícil enseñanza de la libertad," *Crisis,* 75 (December 1989): 38–42;

Peter Roster, "La pasión como enigma: Entrevista a Ricardo Monti," *La Escena Latinoamericana,* 5 (December 1990): 34–40;

Juana A. Arancibia and Zulema Mirkin, "Entrevista," in *Teatro argentino durante el Proceso (1976–1983),* edited by Arancibia and Mirkin (Buenos Aires: Vinciguerra, 1992), pp. 247–252;

Susana Freire, "Ricardo Monti y el sueño de un Orestes moderno," *La Nación,* 8 September 1993;

Miguel Angel Giella, "Una noche con Ricardo Monti e hijos," in his *De dramaturgos: Teatro latinoamericano actual* (Buenos Aires: Corregidor, 1994), pp. 118–126;

Carlos Pacheco, "El valor de la representación," *La Nación,* 11 February 2002.

References:

Heidrum Adler, "Marathón de Ricardo Monti," *La escena latinoamericana,* 1 (April 1989): 26–31;

Olga Cosentino, "Misterio, poesía y tragedia de América Latina," in *Teatro Contemporáneo Argentino (Antología)* (Madrid: Fondo de Cultura Económica, l992), pp. 1015–1021;

Miguel Angel Giella, "*La cortina de abalorios,* de Ricardo Monti," in his *Teatro Abierto 1981: Teatro Argentino bajo vigilancia* (Buenos Aires: Corregidor, 1991), pp. 177–190;

Ana Ruth Giustachini, "El teatro de la resistencia: *Una pasión sudamericana* y *Postales argentinas,*" in *Teatro Argentino Actual,* Cuadernos Getea 1, no. 1 (Ottawa: Girol/Revista Espacio, 1990), pp. 55–72;

Jean Graham-Jones, "*Camila* y *Una pasión sudamericana:* Bemberg, Monti y un paraíso perdido argentino," in *Segundas Jornadas Internacionales de Literatura Argentina-Comparatística, Actas* (Buenos Aires: Universidad de Buenos Aires, 1998), pp. 102–110;

Graham-Jones, "De la euforia al desencanto y al vacío: La crisis nacional en el teatro argentino de los 80 y los 90," in *Memoria colectiva y políticas de olvido. Argentina y Uruguay. 1970-1990,* edited by Adriana J. Bergero and Fernando Reati (Buenos Aires: Beatriz Viterbo, 1997), pp. 253–277;

Graham-Jones, "*Magnus,* a los (casi) 30 años," in *Indagaciones sobre el fin de siglo,* edited by Osvaldo Pellettieri (Buenos Aires: Galerna, 2000), pp. 143–149;

Graham-Jones, "1976-1979: Theater 'Metaphorizes' Reality" and "1980-1982: Myths Unmasked, Unrealities Exposed," in her *Exorcising History: Argentine Theater under Dictatorship* (Lewisburg, Pa.: Bucknell University Press / London: Associated University Presses, 2000), pp. 25–54, 55–88;

Liliana López, "Las máscaras del poder en la dramaturgia de Ricardo Monti," *Arte y poder* (Buenos Aires: Centro Argentino de Investigadores de Artes, 1993), pp. 467–474;

López, "Los paradigmas de la alteridad en *Asunción,* de Ricardo Monti," in *Actas de ACITA* (Buenos Aires: Asociación de Críticos e Investigadores de Teatro Argentino, 1993), pp. 78–82;

López, "Poéticas refuncionalizadas: Mito e historia en *La oscuridad de la razón,* de Ricardo Monti," in *El teatro y los días,* edited by Osvaldo Pellettieri, volume 3 (Buenos Aires: Galerna, 1995), pp. 101–109;

Jorge Monteleone, "El teatro de Ricardo Monti," *Espacio de crítica e investigación teatral,* 2, no. 2 (April 1987): 63–74;

Luis Ordaz, "Ricardo Monti y el juego de los símbolos," in *El teatro argentino,* edited by Ordaz (Buenos Aires: Centro Editor de América Latina, 1981), pp. vii–x;

Osvaldo Pellettieri, "Historia y teatro," *Todo es Historia,* 212 (December 1984): 32–44;

Pellettieri, "Un microcosmos del país," *La escena latinoamericana,* 2 (August 1989): 12–13;

Pellettieri, "Una tragedia sudamericana," *La escena latinoamericana,* 5 (December 1990): 28–34;

Pellettieri, ed., *De Bertolt Brecht a Ricardo Monti: Teatro en lengua alemana y teatro argentino 1900-1994* (Buenos Aires: Galerna, 1995);

Peter L. Podol, "Surrealism and the Grotesque in the Theatre of Ricardo Monti," *Latin American Theatre Review,* 14 (Fall 1980): 65–72;

Roberto Previdi Froelich, "Víctimas y victimarios: Cómplices del discurso del poder en *Una noche con el sr. Magnus e hijos* de Ricardo Monti," *Latin American Theatre Review,* 23 (Fall 1989): 37–48;

Julia Elena Sagaseta, "La dramaturgia de Ricardo Monti: La seducción de la escritura," in *Teatro argentino de los '60–Polémica, continuidad y ruptura,* edited by Pellettieri (Buenos Aires: Corregidor, 1989), pp. 227–241;

Sagaseta, "Los límites del poder: En torno a *Una pasión sudamericana* de Ricardo Monti," *Boletín del Instituto de Artes Combinadas,* 8 (1990): 19–21;

Sagaseta, "El placer del texto," *Teatro 2,* 3 (July 1993): 20–22;

Adriana Scheinin, "Sobre *Una pasión sudamericana,* de Ricardo Monti," *Boletín del Instituto de Artes Combinadas,* 8 (1990): 22–26;

Diana Taylor, "Staging Battles of Gender and Nation-ness: Teatro Abierto 1981," in her *Disappearing Acts: Spectacles of Gender and Nationalism in Argentina's "Dirty War"* (Durham, N.C.: Duke University Press, 1997), pp. 223–254;

Néstor Tirri, "Los parricidas: Monti y Gentile," in his *Realismo y teatro argentino* (Buenos Aires: La Bastilla, 1973), pp. 185–192;

Beatriz Trastoy, "El teatro argentino de los últimos años: Del parricidio al filicidio," *Espacio,* 2 (April 1987): 74–82;

Trastoy, "Teatro político: producción y recepción (notas sobre *La cortina de abalorios* de Ricardo Monti)," in *Teatro argentino de los '60–Polémica, continuidad y ruptura,* edited by Pellettieri (Buenos Aires: Corregidor, 1989), pp. 217–223;

Lilian Tschudi, *Teatro argentino actual* (Buenos Aires: García Cambeiro, 1974), pp. 81–93, 107–114;

Perla Zayas de Lima, "Historia, antihistoria, intrahistoria en *Una pasión sudamericana* de Ricardo Monti," *Boletín del Instituto de Artes Combinadas,* 8 (1990): 16–18;

Zayas de Lima, "El neorrealismo en dos tiempos: De Gorostiza a Monti," in her *Relevamiento del Teatro Argentino (1943-1975)* (Buenos Aires: Rodolfo Alonso, 1983), pp. 109–118.

Eduardo Pavlovsky
(10 December 1933 -)

Gustavo Geirola
Whittier College

SELECTED PLAY PRODUCTIONS: *Somos,* Buenos Aires, Nuevo Teatro, 5 June 1962;

La espera trágica, Buenos Aires, Nuevo Teatro, 10 December 1962;

Un acto rápido, Buenos Aires, Teatro 35, November 1965;

El robot, Buenos Aires, 1966;

La cacería, Buenos Aires, Teatro Agón, 24 July 1969;

Alguien, by Pavlovsky and Juan Carlos Herme, Buenos Aires, Teatro Municipal General San Martín, 1969;

Match, by Pavlovsky and Herme, Buenos Aires, Teatro Municipal General San Martín, 1970;

La mueca, Buenos Aires, Teatro Olimpia, 12 May 1971;

El señor Galíndez, Buenos Aires, Teatro Payró, 15 January 1973; revised, Buenos Aires, Teatro Babilonia, 1995;

Telerañas, Buenos Aires, Teatro Payró, November 1977;

Cámara lenta (Historia de una cara), Buenos Aires, Teatro Olimpia, April 1981; translated and adapted by Paul Verdier as *Slow Motion,* Los Angeles, Stages Theatre Los Angeles, 12 March 1987;

Tercero incluído, Buenos Aires, Teatro del Pueblo, July 1981;

El señor Laforgue, Buenos Aires, Teatro Olimpia/Teatro Payró, 1982;

Potestad, Buenos Aires, Teatro del Viejo Palermo, 1985; revised, Buenos Aires, La Gran Aldea, 1986; translated as *Potestad/Paternity,* Hollywood, Stages Theatre Center, 28 May 1994;

Pablo, Buenos Aires, Teatro El Hangar, 1987; translated and adapted by Verdier, New York, Cherry Lane Theatre, 1988;

Paso de dos, Buenos Aires, Teatro Babilonia, 19 April 1990;

Rojos globos rojos, Buenos Aires, Teatro Babilonia, August 1994;

Poroto, Buenos Aires, Teatro Calibán, 1999;

La muerte de Marguerite Duras, Buenos Aires, Teatro Babilonia, 24 July 2000.

Eduardo Pavlovsky in the 1980s (from Three Plays by Eduardo Pavlovsky, *1994; University Library, Texas Tech University)*

BOOKS: *Teatro de vanguardia* (Buenos Aires: Cuadernos del Siroco, 1966)—comprises *Somos, La espera trágica, Un acto rápido, El robot,* and *Alguien;*

Teatro de vanguardia, II (Buenos Aires: Ediciones de la Luna, 1967)—comprises *Match,* by Pavlovsky and Juan Carlos Herme, and *La cacería;*

Psicoterapia de grupo en niños y adolescentes (Buenos Aires: Centro Editor de América Latina, 1968);

La mueca, in *Tres obras de teatro,* by Pavlovsky, Roberto Cossa, and Egon Wolff (Havana: Casa de las Américas, 1970);

Psicodrama psicoanalítico en grupos, by Pavlovsky, Carlos Martínez Bouquet, and Fidel Moccio (Buenos Aires: Kargieman, 1970);

Ultimo match, by Pavlovsky and Herme (Buenos Aires: Talía, 1970);

Psicodrama: Cuando y por qué dramatizar, by Pavlovsky, Martínez Bouquet, and Moccio (Buenos Aires: Proteo, 1971);

Clínica grupal (Buenos Aires: Búsqueda, 1974);

Reflexiones sobre el proceso creador; El señor Galíndez (Buenos Aires: Proteo, 1976);

Telarañas (Buenos Aires: Búsqueda, 1976);

Adolescencia y mito (Buenos Aires: Búsqueda, 1977);

Las escenas temidas del coordinador del grupo, by Pavlovsky, Hernán Kesselman, and Luis Frydlewsky (Madrid: Fundamentos, 1979);

Cámara lenta: Historia de una cara (Buenos Aires: Búsqueda, 1979);

Espacios y creatividad, by Pavlovsky and Kesselman (Buenos Aires: Búsqueda, 1980);

La mueca; El Señor Galíndez; Telarañas (Madrid: Fundamentos, 1980);

Clínica grupal II, by Pavlovsky, Kesselman, and Frydlewsky (Buenos Aires: Búsqueda, 1980);

Proceso creador: Terapia y existencia (Buenos Aires: Búsqueda, 1982);

El señor Laforgue (Buenos Aires: Búsqueda, 1982);

El señor Galíndez; y, Pablo (Buenos Aires: Búsqueda, 1986);

Potestad (Buenos Aires: Búsqueda, 1987);

La mueca; y, Cerca (Buenos Aires: Búsqueda, 1988);

Lo grupal 6 (Buenos Aires: Búsqueda, 1988);

Cámara lenta; El señor Laforgue; Pablo; Potestad (Madrid: Fundamentos, 1989);

La multiplicación dramática, by Pavlovsky and Kesselman (Buenos Aires: Búsqueda de Ayllu, 1989);

Voces (Buenos Aires: Búsqueda de Ayllu, 1989);

Paso de dos (Buenos Aires: Búsqueda de Ayllu, 1990);

El cardenal, by Pavlovsky, Susana Evans, and Miguel Dao (Buenos Aires: Búsqueda de Ayllu, 1992);

Teatro del 60 (Buenos Aires: Letra Buena, 1992)—comprises *Somos, La espera trágica, Un acto rápido, El robot, Alguien, Match,* and *La cacería;*

Rojos globos rojos (Buenos Aires: Babilonia, 1994);

El Bocón: Obra en un acto (Concepción, Uruguay: Ayllu, 1995);

Escenas multiplicidad (estética y micropolítica), by Pavlovsky, Kesselman, and Juan Carlos de Brasi (Concepción, Uruguay: Búsqueda de Ayllu, 1996);

Poroto: Historia de una táctica (Concepción Uruguay: Búsqueda de Ayllu, 1996);

Teatro Completo I (Buenos Aires: Atuel, 1997)—comprises *Poroto, Rojos globos rojos* (new version), *Paso de dos, El Bocón, Pablo, Potestad,* and *Cámara lenta;*

Dirección contraria (Concepción Uruguay: Búsqueda de Ayllu, 1997);

Teatro Completo II (Buenos Aires: Atuel, 1998)—comprises *El señor Laforgue, Tercero incluído, Cerca, Telarañas,* and *El señor Galíndez;*

Psicodrama y literatura (Entre Ríos, Argentina: Búsqueda de Ayllu, 1998);

Micropolítica de la resistencia, compiled by Jorge Dubatti (Buenos Aires: Editorial Universitaria de Buenos Aires, 1999);

Textos balbuceantes (Buenos Aires: Teatro Vivo, 1999);

Poroto: Nueva versión para teatro (Buenos Aires: Galerna / Concepción Uruguay: Búsqueda de Ayllu, 1999);

Teatro Completo III (Buenos Aires: Atuel, 2000)—comprises *La muerte de Marguerite Duras, Poroto* (new version), *Textos balbucientes, El cardenal, La ley de la vida, Alguna vez,* and *Trabajo rítmico;*

Pequeño detalle (Buenos Aires: Galerna / Entre Ríos: Búsqueda de Ayllu, 2001);

Potestad (Buenos Aires: Galerna / Entre Ríos: Búsqueda de Ayllu, 2001);

Teatro Completo IV (Buenos Aires: Atuel, 2002)—comprises *Volumnia, Pequeño detalle, Diálogo inconcluso II, Grito fuerte, La espera trágica, Somos, Un acto rápido,* and *Apendice: La ética del cuerpo (tres aproximaciones).*

Edition in English: *Three Plays by Eduardo Pavlovsky,* translated and adapted by Paul Verdier (Hollywood: Stages Theater Press, 1994)—comprises *Slow Motion, Paternity,* and *Pablo.*

Eduardo Pavlovsky is one of the most internationally recognized Argentine dramatists and intellectuals of the second half of the twentieth century. In spite of their political and aesthetic differences, Pavlovsky and other writers such as Osvaldo Dragún, Ricardo Halac, Griselda Gambaro, and Roberto Cossa have created an Argentine theater that raises profound political, aesthetic, and cultural questions. Pavlovsky's contributions to theater are not only the written texts of his works; his aesthetic vision is the result of the combination of his activities as an actor, essayist, and psychoanalyst, all of which he brings to bear on his theater.

Eduardo A. "Tato" Pavlovsky was born in Buenos Aires on 10 December 1933 into an upper-middle-class family of Russian origin. His grandfather Sacha Pavlovsky was an exile from czarist Russia and the author of several books, including a theater piece. Although he never met this grandfather, Pavlovsky has emphasized the importance of his grandfather's influence in the development of his own work. Pavlovsky's relatively conservative family was silent on the subject of his grandfather's life; but he read his grandfather's works, both published and unpublished, which focus upon the political and social oppression of the czarist regime. This tradition of rebellion was continued by Pavlovsky's father, Eduardo Pavlovsky, who, during the regime imposed by Juan Domingo Perón and his wife, Eva Perón (1945–1955), was also pursued and imprisoned (1952). From 1953 to 1955 he was in exile in Montevideo and in Paraguay. Pavlovsky underlines the significance of those two figures as forming a romantic tradition that he has joined as a rebel and an exile as well.

The author also acknowledges the influence of his mother, Celina Onetto, an intuitive, vivacious woman with whom he remained close during the more than ninety years of her life. But above all, Pavlovsky acknowledges the model provided by Pedro Onetto, his mother's brother, a medical doctor who impressed Pavlovsky with his storytelling ability and helped form Pavlovsky's approach to creating character. One of this uncle's stories is included in Pavlovsky's play *Pablo* (1987; published in 1989).

Pavlovsky was educated within the Catholic tradition. Coming from a family of medical professionals, he graduated from the University of Buenos Aires medical school in 1957. He was also dedicated to sports: swimming (in which he excelled as an Argentine and South American champion), boxing, water polo, and rugby. During his last year of medical school, Pavlovsky joined an amateur theater group. In *La ética del cuerpo: Nuevas conversaciones con Jorge Dubatti* (2001; The Ethic of the Body: New Conversations with Jorge Dubatti) Pavlovsky says that his first experience on stage was so intense that it marked him for the rest of his life as an actor and a dramatist. While theater began as a hobby, it soon became the environment in which he experienced a type of existential crisis that created a sense of despair resulting from a meaningless world. One of his first works is called *La espera trágica* (The Tragic Wait, 1962; published in 1966). This loss of meaning appears as an existential vacuum that, according to the author, he was unable to fill with either medicine or psychoanalysis.

During the 1960s and 1970s psychoanalysis became a part of daily Argentine life, and Buenos Aires became the capital of psychoanalysis in South America. First Sigmund Freud and later the French psychoanalyst Jacques Lacan—a dissident of the International Psychoanalytic Association (IPA)—had an enormous influence on the cultural and artistic debates in Argentina and also in all those countries where Argentines went into exile during the military dictatorships from the 1960s until 1983. Yet, Pavlovsky emphasizes how difficult it was toward the end of the 1950s to reconcile theater, medicine, and psychoanalysis. Such a combination was seen as socially counterproductive to both art and science. In a way, a great part of Pavlovsky's work, both his theater and his essays, constitutes an effort to overcome this arbitrary division. Psychoanalytical problems progressively made him question the theater and the actor's profession, which, in turn, caused him to re-create psychoanalytical problems in the theater. In this manner Pavlovsky has moved toward psychodrama.

In the middle of his existential crisis toward the end of the 1950s, Pavlovsky, motivated by his wife, Maria Celia Doyhambehere, decided to get in touch with the theater group El Gallo Petirrojo. Celita—as Pavlovsky calls her—comes from the upper industrial bourgeoisie. During their marriage, which lasted from 1958 to 1971, they had three children: Martin, who became a musician; Maria Carolina, who studied psychology and became a dedicated psychodrama ballerina; and Malenka, who focused on sociology. El Gallo Petirrojo, directed by Maria Ester Piombo, had been producing Spanish comedies for a select group of friends, relatives, and people of the social group to which Pavlovsky's wife belonged. While not having any aesthetic influence on Pavlovsky's theater, his association with the group from 1958 to 1959 promoted his desire to begin a more systematic theater formation. As a result, he contacted Pedro Asquini, Alejandra Boero, and Conrado Ramonet, all important figures in Buenos Aires theater, actors and directors linked to politically leftist parties. They directed the Nuevo Teatro, an institution where generations of Argentine actors were formed.

Beyond his immersion in the theater and vanguardist environment, Pavlovsky was profoundly affected by a 1957 production of *Waiting for Godot* (1952), the famous absurdist play by Samuel Beckett, directed by actor and director Jorge Petraglia. Beckett became one of his favorite authors, along with Eugène Ionesco, Harold Pinter, and Arthur Adamov.

Eschewing Nuevo Teatro's Marxist artistic orthodoxy, Pavlovsky was more interested in avant-garde experimentation, activity considered too petit bourgeois by the members of Nuevo Teatro. As a result, Pavlovsky formed his own group, called Yenesí (a term whose meaning is not documented, but it seems to come from an anecdote involving his father). Yenesí was an independent theater group, unrelated to the official and commercial theater. Yet, unlike many of the independent groups that started to flourish at this time, Yenesí did not have its own building. Perhaps another important difference, at least in comparison with Nuevo Teatro, was that Yenesí had a more democratic structure.

In 1954 Julio Tahier, another medical doctor, joined Yenesí and became an important figure not only to the group but also to Argentine theater in general. Pavlovsky and Tahier's friendship was long lasting, although their professional collaboration only lasted until 1966, with the exception of a 1982 production of Ionesco's *Le tableau* (1955, The Painting). Some critics and theater scholars consider Pavlovsky and Tahier precursors of the Argentine avant-garde. Yenesí produced works by Anton Chekhov, Luigi Pirandello, Ionesco, Friedrich Dürrenmatt, and Jean Anouilh, as well as by Ramón del Valle-Inclán, Fernando Arrabal, Gambaro, and Gregorio de Laferrere. In the midst of the theatrical activity of Yenesí, his professional success as a psychoanalyst, and short escapades as a sports journalist on television and in some magazines, Pavlovsky began his career as a dramatist.

Pavlovsky's work can be divided into three periods. The theater of the first period appears to be influenced by authors known as followers of the Theater of the Absurd: Ionesco, Adamov, and Beckett. Yet, Pavlovsky himself, who has always written theoretical and sociopolitical essays alongside his plays, considers the work of this period to be "teatro total" (total theater). In a famous essay written in 1966, "Algunos conceptos sobre el teatro de vanguardia" (Some Concepts of the Avant-garde Theater), the author tries to rename the "theater of the absurd," calling this new aesthetic "teatro exasperado" (exasperated theater). Symbol, fantasy, and reality are consciously combined to create a new kind of theater.

In "The Uncanny," a famous essay written by Sigmund Freud in 1919, the father of psychoanalysis demonstrates the relationship between the familiar and the uncanny, how the uncanny becomes an invisible part of the familiar. Consequently, from Pavlovsky's perspective, the fascism that becomes invisible, that hides inside everyday relationships, becomes a fundamental topic of his theater. Pavlovsky also emphasizes the loneliness of the human being, the lack of communication between intimates, and profound subterfuges. By evoking the bourgeoisie's manners he shows their mechanical gestures in all their absurdity. His early plays explore human alienation, but they also show how suffering has been camouflaged.

In Pavlovsky's first period all the plays are monosituational. The stage space is conceived abstractly, but it is still a recognizable metaphor of the world. The characters interchange phrases or repeat what others say. They steal each other's memories or confound the time sequence and, quite often, have confused sexual identities. All of these elements create interchangeability; no one has a specific and differentiated identity. The language harms itself: sentences

Pavlovsky in the 1960s (from Ultimo match, *1970; Ekstrom Library, University of Louisville)*

break their logic, and meaning becomes questionable. Silence is as important as speech, and movement is no less important or less expressive than stage immobility. Rhythm is constantly emphasized in the stage directions of these early plays. Accelerations and detained movements turn the stage into a real experience of the unconscious, similar to what is presented in dreams. In some plays the author utilizes photos, movie images or previously taped texts. It is not easy for the spectator to make sense of what is happening onstage; these plays require an active and attentive spectator who is seen as an accomplice to the dramatic action.

Yenesí produced Pavlovsky's first play, *Somos* (We Are), on 5 June 1962 at Nuevo Teatro, with the author playing the role of Mr. Zelake. Pavlovsky often acted in his own plays; his career as a playwright cannot be separated from his career as an actor. *Somos* is a short, one-act play dedicated to Pavlovsky's children. There are four characters, three of whom are males (Mr. Ronald, Mr. Casoq, Mr. Zelake) and one that is hard to identify, called El Otro or La Otra (the male or female Other). The stage directions read:

> En la silla de la derecha hay un hombre o una mujer. Difícil definirlo. Tiene cabellos largos, usa pantalones, tiene pintados los labios y la cara. Está con cartera. Sus

zapatos son de hombre. Debe tener aspecto muy masculino y muy femenino. Es un personaje que no va a hablar ni se va a mover en toda la obra. Sólo bostezar y una sola vez.

(On the chair on the right there is a seated man or woman. It is hard to say. Has long hair, wears pants, has lipstick and makeup on. Has a purse. Wears male shoes. Has to have a very masculine and a very feminine aspect. Is a character that will not talk nor move throughout the entire play. Will only yawn and only once.)

This ambiguous figure draws upon the spectators' unconscious notions of masculine versus feminine and confuses the two.

Opening to the strains of Hector Berlioz's *Symphonie fantastique* (1830), the play "ocurre en el mes de octubre de 1961" (takes place during the month of October 1961). The three male characters talk, repeat themselves, and confront each other. They elaborate or rationalize their difficulties as much as they are able. The scenes employ a circular structure: "De improviso todo vuelve al comienzo, al terminar Mr. Ronald su última palabra" (Suddenly everything starts from the beginning, once Mr. Ronald has finished his last word). The conversations treat such subjects as the Bill of Rights and the invading effects of truth. Mr. Ronald happily remembers the way his mother used to tie him up, to leave him without any food and whip him, while she was having sex with her lovers in front of him; Mr. Casoq says "(visiblemente emocionado): Me emociona la ternura con que habla Ud. de su hogar, Mr. Ronald" ([obviously touched] I am touched by the tenderness with which you talk about your native place, Mr. Ronald). In conclusion he says, "Estoy seguro, Mr. Ronald, que de haber existido madres tan buenas como la suya, el mundo no estaría así" (I am sure, Mr. Ronald, that if there were mothers as good as yours, the world wouldn't be like this). This sentiment calls into question the spectator's assumptions and critiques the possibility of idealism in a world full of dictators and maniacs.

The play also blurs the lines between the characters and the audience. When Mr. Casoq asks, "Y Ud. cómo sabe mi nombre?" (And you, how do you know my name?), Mr. Ronald answers: "Lo leí en el programa antes de entrar" (I read it in the program before I entered). Mr. Casoq confesses the same thing. Pavlovsky thus indicates not only that every spectator could be one of the characters, but also that this strange ceremony on stage is as authentic as the spectators' lives. The work seems to draw a connection between the theater representation and the masks that the spectators use on the social stage.

La espera trágica, which premiered on 10 December 1962, involves four characters: two males (He and The Unknown, the latter played by Pavlovsky) and two females (She and La Señora). The action happens during a "reunión burguesa actual" (bourgeoisie reunion in the present) at which there are supposed to be twenty-seven invisible characters, thirteen men and fourteen women. The work requires regulated gesture, verbal rhythm, and precise mimicry in order to make the invisible characters present. Comical examples break the consistency of language as a vehicle of communication: for example, temporal dislocations are grammatically bewildering and also reveal symbolic coercion over the speaker's freedom of speech: "Murió pasado mañana en un accidente" (He died the day after tomorrow in an accident). As in *Somos,* where the characters (and the audience) seem to take part in a completely repetitive and programmed world where they have no control, in *La espera trágica* the verbal mechanization seems to show how the characters are not the ones who speak. Rather, someone invisible and implacable compels them to speak—someone official and perverted who in the end makes them say what the system requires be said.

The play ends when a couple of policemen show up looking for Jorge Ottis, who is supposedly accused of terrorism. Suddenly, everyone's name seems to be Jorge Ottis. Apart from this confusion of identities, the play shows that anyone can be under suspicion, that anyone can be Jorge Ottis, that any male or female can be confused with someone else or be arrested with or without justification. These verbal games seem uncannily prophetic of the Argentine "Dirty War," the period of military dictatorship between 1976 and 1983.

Un acto rápido (A Quick Act), produced by Yenesí in November 1965, has three characters: Franca; her husband, Teddy; and Willie, Teddy's friend and Franca's lover (played by Pavlovsky). *Un acto rápido* explores the difference between what is said and what is thought, the latter shown through images projected on a screen. A large part of the text is listened to on tape. As in previous works there are abundant repetitions, misunderstandings, and contrasts between what is said and what can be seen, between what is seen and what is not seen. Although the couple pretends to love each other, the screen shows how much they despise each other. While the wife plays with her lover behind the sofa, the husband reminisces about his old friendship with his wife's lover, a man—the husband says—so slippery as a child that he had "la rara habilidad de no ser descubierto" (the exceptional ability not to be discovered). The only purpose of women in the play seems to be to humiliate the men with beauty, lack of love, and obvious unavailability. The only way for men to possess them is by means of the perverted pleasure of transgression, rape, wild passion, and, of course, money. As usually happens in Pavlovsky's plays, hypocrisy and social formalities impose their rules on the characters, who become entirely alienated.

El robot was written and performed in 1966. In it Mr. Ronald and Mr. Casoq show up again, and there is another nameless female character, La Señora. The work takes place in a space that could, at the beginning, be perceived as a hotel room but is slowly revealed to be a prison. Mr. Ronald is a lawyer who has raped a girl; Mr. Casoq is a military person who has set a bomb; and La Señora has murdered her children. In comparison with previous works, linguistic games decrease in this play, while the desire and terror of remembering is emphasized. Taped voices and screen presentations create a kind of dizziness that sets the rhythm for the play. Pavlovsky's topics can be seen explicitly in *El robot*. The relationship with the audience becomes, at certain points, direct, cruel, and uncomfortable, questioning the supposed social innocence: "LOS TRES (al frente, al público): Uds. también son culpables! Culpables de nuestros crímenes! Culpables de vuestros crímenes!" (THE THREE OF THEM [in front, to the audience]: You are guilty as well! You are guilty for our crimes! You are guilty for your crimes!). As usual in Pavlovsky's theater, one argument is opposed by another, so after a significant pause, the three characters add: "¡Uds. también son inocentes! INOCENTES DE NUESTROS CRIMENES! INOCENTES DE VUESTROS CRIMENES!" (You are innocent as well! YOU ARE INNOCENT FOR OUR CRIMES! YOU ARE INNOCENT FOR YOUR CRIMES!). Finally, questions that create new questions emerge: "¿Quién es el culpable? ¿Quiénes son los culpables? ¿Pero es que acaso hay culpables?" (Who is guilty? Who are the guilty ones? Is anyone really guilty?). In these questions are the seed of a problem that Pavlovsky treats in later works: civil society as accomplice to torture and totalitarian regimes.

The title of the play refers to the alienation of human beings within the capitalist system, especially under fascism. The irony is that no matter what the robotic state of these beings consists of, all of them are equally victims and evildoers. All of them are subject to the disciplinary strictures of society: repression, incarceration, and confession. As do characters in previous plays, Mr. Ronald reacts to these moments of vertigo and dehumanization by turning back to his childhood. During the Dirty War, this return to childhood became one of the most hopeless images of the nation. Infantilism, alienation, and contradictory and ambivalent surrender to the paternal figure formed the parameters that lay underneath the civil complicity of totalitarian regimes.

Two major events in Pavlovsky's life took place in 1963. One was his gradual separation from Yenesí, and the other was a trip to New York, where he studied with Jacob Moreno, the creator of psychodrama. Pavlovsky had become known as an actor, and several directors (Jaime Jaimes, Luis Mottura, Oscar Fessler, and Alberto Ure) offered him work. As a result of these opportunities Pavlovsky learned new ways to approach directing and acting and got to know several actors, such as Oscar Ferrigno, who became his friends. His commitments to other groups took him away from Yenesí. In a 1968 interview included in *La ética del cuerpo* he stated that "el Yenesí no existe" (Yenesí does not exist).

Pavlovsky's interest in psychodrama developed out of his medical practice. After receiving his medical degree Pavlovsky worked as a physician in the Quilmes Brewery and in the State Treasury. From 1958 to 1965 he worked at the Children's Hospital and from 1965 to 1969 in the Clinics Hospital. His work with children and with group therapy is yet another link between his medical work and his career as a dramatist and as an actor. Pavlovsky realized that children abandoned violence when they spontaneously began to invent stories and dramatize them.

Upon his return to Buenos Aires from New York in 1963, Pavlovsky founded the Argentinean Psychodrama Association with some friends. But in 1969 he renounced his membership in the association for ideological reasons. What did remain as a passion is his interest in groups. His experience with groups and with psychodrama is documented in *Psicoterapia de grupo en niños y adolescentes* (Group Psychotherapy and Adolescents), written in 1968, and other books written with Carlos Martínez Bouquet and Fidel Moccio: *Psicodrama psicoanalítico en grupos* (1970, Psychoanalytical Psychodrama With Groups), and *Psicodrama: Cuando y por qué dramatizar* (1971, Psychodrama: When and Why to Dramatize). These essays were followed by many more. In *La ética del cuerpo* Pavlovsky points out that at that time there were only a few works in Spanish treating groups and psychoanalysis. Yet, he clarifies that as with his dramatic writings, the experience comes first, and only later does he theorize.

His relationship with psychodrama is framed by the politicization at that time of much of Argentine and world culture. Without invalidating the theoretical foundations of psychoanalysis, some French intellectuals formed a dissident group (International Platform) that questioned the formation of the psychoanalyst, especially his role as an intellectual in a time of social conflict. The social role of psychoanalysis and its social

Tony Abatemarco (Dagomar) and Hal Bokar (Amilcar) in the 1987 Stages Theatre premiere of Slow Motion, Paul Verdier's translation of Pavlovsky's 1981 play Cámara lenta (published in 1979), about a physically declining boxer and his manager (photograph by Jeff Jacobson; from Three Plays by Eduardo Pavlovsky, 1994; University Library, Texas Tech University)

ethics were also questioned. Confronting the practice of psychoanalysis as individualistic, expensive, and noninstitutional, Pavlovsky comments in La ética del cuerpo that there was for example "un límite que imponía la clase social del paciente" (a limit imposed by the patient's social class). Thus, Pavlovsky felt that the way psychoanalysis was practiced did not allow him to understand general and public health in a time of social conflicts and cultural transformation. In Buenos Aires some intellectuals, Pavlovsky among them, founded a local version of Platform. Because of its chaotic internal dynamics, the group only lasted for a year. According to Pavlovsky, however, its existence bore fruit: the foundation of Platform was an important cultural event because it produced new perspectives. In 1971, together with other Marxist and revolutionary Peronist psychoanalysts, Pavlovsky separated from the Argentinean Association of Psychoanalysis. Intensely influenced by the Cuban Revolution, he joined the Partido Socialista de los Trabajadores (PST, Trotskyite Socialist Workers Party). In 1973 he stood for Parliament as a candidate for this party.

In the midst of these cultural and political events, Pavlovsky collaborated with his friend the journalist and writer Juan Carlos Herme on Match or Ultimo match (the play has been published with different titles). This dramatic comedy in nineteen scenes won the Theater IFT First Award in 1967 and was produced in 1970 in the Sala Casacuberta of the Teatro Municipal General San Martín in downtown Buenos Aires. Match is Pavlovsky's only play produced by an official theater. The play also won the ARGENTORES (Sociedad General de Autores de la República Argentina [Argentine Association of Writers]) Award in 1971.

Match tells the story of a boxer manipulated by his managers and by the system, and it also focuses on "la problemática de la relación entre el líder y la masa" (the problem of the relationship between the leader and the mob), a topic extensively discussed in Argentina after the Peronist regime. After a couple of shows, Pavlovsky replaced the actor playing the Champion, a character who represented the necessary and artificially created leader. The play has extensive choral scenes with impressive choreographic movements and an almost cinematic rhythm. According to the program of the production, "it is the rhythm–rhythm of a ring, of a combat drama [that] is actually the central character of this lightning match." Although the play features some of

Pavlovsky's typical topics, the author attributes *Match* and *Alguien* (Someone; published in 1966, performed in 1969) to Herme.

La cacería, which premiered on 24 July 1969, is another transitional play, prefiguring the political and aesthetic positions that become apparent in later works. Pavlovsky wrote *La cacería* in 1968, a year of tremendous social disturbances all over the world. In 1969 he won the Talía Award for best national play. *La cacería* has three characters: a bourgeois (played by Pavlovsky), a revolutionary, and a priest. The three of them come from the same social class and were friends throughout childhood and adolescence. The characters meet again after many years, all looking for a treasure that they already know they will not be able to share. In spite of their mutual affection and their shared past, they turn on each other. Though the play has its comical moments, it culminates with a triple assassination. In addition to the miseries of the individual characters, one of the most prominent aspects of the play is its critique of the authoritarianism and orthodoxy of the Marxist Left, a burning topic at the time when *La cacería* was produced.

The characters in *La cacería* are not persons, but voices or speeches. Beginning with this play and continuing throughout his work Pavlovsky does not focus upon political or macropolitical topics but on a micropolitical one, "el pasaje de la política por el cuerpo" (the passage of the politics through the body). He explains in *La ética del cuerpo:*

> una de las grandes críticas que haría a los partidos de izquierda es que tomaron muy poco en cuenta la subjetividad de la gente, los sentimientos, el deseo, lo que el militante podía vivir humanamente.

> (one of the important critiques that I would make regarding the leftist parties is the fact that they did not take into account the subjectivity of the people, their feelings, desire, what the follower could be able to humanly live. All of that had to be hidden for the sake of political ideals.)

He adds, "Se cometieron muchísimos errores por haber fabricado personas sin sentimientos" (Many errors were committed in order to create people without feelings). In a way, the left wing produced machines as disturbing as the loudly speaking capitalist puppets. Every system and institution is, according to the author, something sad. Pavlovsky calls for "una revolución de la alegría" (a revolution of happiness), which means that "El socialismo será alegre o no será" (Socialism will either be happy or it will not be at all).

In 1969 Ferrigno asked Pavlovsky to write a play for him. Pavlovsky started working from an image that, once again, demonstrates the internal orientation of his theater. The image consisted of a group of zealots, an anarchic group of moviemakers, "que invadían la casa de una pareja para filmarlos y hacer un documental sobre la decrepitud de la moral burguesa" (who invaded the house of a [bourgeois] couple in order to videotape them and make a documentary about the decaying morality of the bourgeoisie). *La mueca* (The Grimace) is a two-act play, premiered by Grupo de Actores Profesionales (GAP) in the Teatro Olimpia of Buenos Aires on 12 May 1971, with Pavlovsky playing the part of Carlos, the husband, and Ferrigno playing "el Sueco," the director of the movie. The central focus of the play is the violation of the couple's environment by a group of artists lacking a political agenda. The author asserts, however, that the play is not a prophetic allegory of the human rights violations carried out by the dictatorship that lasted from 1976 to 1983. In this play the artists, he says, only want to document the decadence of the bourgeoisie. They are not professional torturers and oppressors.

The process of working on *La mueca* demonstrated to Pavlovsky how important it is to be concise when writing a play. A couple of days after the play opened, Ferrigno decided to cut approximately ten minutes from it. The running time was reduced to an hour and five minutes, exactly the length that Pavlovsky later settled on as optimum for his plays. Rhythm and intensity became two fundamental aspects of his aesthetics. The successful production of *La mueca* was interrupted when Pavlovsky was invited to the Soviet Union to participate in an international meeting of Russian and Latin American psychiatrists with Marxist and psychoanalytical orientations. The work went on to be staged in Mexico, Sweden, Brazil, the United States, and Puerto Rico.

La mueca came at a difficult period in Pavlovsky's life. His relationship with his wife had been in decline since 1967, and after fourteen years of marriage, it ended in divorce. Following his divorce Pavlovsky had an intense love affair with Mirta Pizarro, the leader of a hippie movement. From 1971 to 1972 they lived together in a large house beyond the prevailing rules of social conduct and in the company of many other marginalized people who shared their views. Their relationship was profoundly marked by affection, politics, and intellectual life. This affair ended when Pavlovsky became involved with dramatist Susana Torres Molina, the author of *Extraño juguete* (1977, Strange Toy), a work in which Pavlovsky acted. Molina became his second wife; their marriage lasted from 1973 to 1980, and they had a child named Federico. In the throes of these relationships, Pavlovsky wrote *El señor Galíndez.*

Probably Pavlovsky's most internationally recognized play, *El señor Galíndez* was produced for the first time in the Teatro Payró in Buenos Aires on 15 January 1973, directed by Jaime Kogan with Pavlovsky as Beto. After playing for a year in Buenos Aires, the Teatro Payró group toured throughout several Argentine provinces. In 1975 the group was selected to represent Argentina at the 10th Festival of Nantes (France). The production then toured Europe and Latin America. The set design for the international tour was a direct result of a terrorist attack on the Teatro Payró in 1974. A bomb destroyed the better part of the theater, and Kogan decided to rehearse in the basement. Pavlovsky recalls in *La ética del cuerpo* that Kogan "fabrica una especie de jaula redonda, donde el espectador ve la acción como si estuviera en un zoológico, a través de las rejas. Resultó tan impactante que fue ésa la version que se llevó en gira" (creates a round cage, where the audience sees the action as if it were in a zoo, through the bars. The result was so impressive that this version was the one that we took on the tour). In 1995 the work was once again produced in Buenos Aires, directed by Norman Brisky with Pavlovsky playing Beto again. While some intellectuals who had seen Kogan's version in 1973 found the play a bit obsolete, the younger generation embraced the new production.

Unlike earlier plays that focus upon the victims, *El señor Galíndez* explores the torturers' point of view, concentrating upon torture as an institution. The oppressor's subjective viewpoint is a topic that the author returned to in later plays. Pavlovsky's raw material for *El señor Galíndez* consisted of the Argentine political context and a couple of books from which he took inspiration. During the 1970s there was an explosion of paramilitary groups in Argentina. Their goal, especially after the military coup d'état in 1976, was to repress leftist political activity and revolutionary movements. The two books that influenced Pavlovsky were *Máxima peligrosidad* (1973; Maximum Danger), written by Hugo Norberto d'Aguila, a doctor who provided medical assistance to the torturers in the Villa Devoto prison, and Pinter's play *The Dumb Waiter* (1960), which had a tremendous impact on Pavlovsky when he saw it in New York in 1963.

When the curtain rises, the audience attending *El señor Galíndez* faces a weird setting that is also familiar, habitable, with a single entrance that also serves as an exit. It turns out to be the apartment where Doña Sara, a cleaning lady, lives. This domestic space is progressively revealed as a place of torture. The audience realizes that terror nests beneath the familiar and the daily routine. The title character, Galíndez, never shows up; he only communicates by phone. He is a voice that affects and directs the development of the action.

Eduardo, who appears at the beginning as an apprentice torturer who has already read Galíndez's texts on the topic, gets to study with Pepe and Beto, acknowledged masters who have never read Galíndez's work. Galíndez sends them a couple of prostitutes so that the torturers may have fun and practice for the time when the real political prisoners will arrive. Pavlovsky demonstrates how these men are simultaneously torturers and victims of the system of which they are a part. The impressive thing about the work is the fact that although the audience tends to reject these characters, spectators can also discover to what extent they are able to experience the humanity of the torturers, what both audience and character share in common. This terrible realization is what creates "en el espectador un sentimiento de trampa, de cierta indignación" (the spectator's feeling of entrapment, of a certain indignation).

The play also shows the difference between the executive torturers like Pepe and Beto who approach their work without any ideological or theoretical foundation, and the intellectual, ideologically motivated torturer like Eduardo. The latter is exactly the type that appeared in Argentina during the Dirty War. Similar to the way the moviemakers in *La cacería* violated the couple's privacy for aesthetic reasons, the sadistic register in *El señor Galíndez* reaches a musical level as well: Pepe tells Eduardo while showing him a sharp spear, "A estos objetos hay que saberlos usar. Tienen que funcionar a su debido tiempo. Es como una sinfonía. Cada uno debe sonar en su momento preciso. Como dice Galíndez, ya se acabó la época de los matones entre nosotros" (One needs to know how to use these objects. They should work at the appropriate time. They are like a symphony. Each of them should sound at the precise moment. As Galíndez says, the time of simple killers among us is over). Musically, torture should resonate throughout society: Beto adds, "Vos tenés que pensar que por cada trabajo bien hecho hay mil tipos paralizados de miedo. Nosotros actuamos por irradiación" (You should think that for each well done job there will be a thousand people paralyzed by fear. We work through irradiation).

This programmed terror receives its paradoxical support from the silent civil complicity of the audience. Beto's conclusion at the end of the play, therefore, recognizes the lethal effects of Galíndez's voice and its similarity to the unconsciousness obedience that operates in everyone: "A veces pienso que todos . . . que todos laburamos para Galíndez" (Sometimes I think that all of us . . . all of us work for Galíndez).

Following *El señor Galíndez,* Pavlovsky staged *Telarañas* (Spider's Webs) in November 1977. Pavlovsky wrote *Telarañas* in the summer of 1975 for the Teatro Payró group with the intention to take it on a

Joe Spano as The Man in Potestad/Paternity, *the 1994 Stages Theatre premiere of the translation of Pavlovsky's 1985 play (published in 1987) about a man who has stolen a girl whose parents disappeared during the military dictatorship (photograph by Dan McCleary; from* Three Plays by Eduardo Pavlovsky, *1994; University Library, Texas Tech University)*

tour throughout Europe together with *El señor Galíndez*. In 1976 he started rehearsing it with the director Ure and the actress Zulema Katz, whose former husband was the poet Paco Urondo. When the military killed Urondo, Katz went into exile in Madrid, and rehearsals were interrupted. In 1977 rehearsals started again, and the play was performed as a new theater experience, while Pavlovsky was simultaneously performing in *Extraño juguete*.

Telarañas had only two performances; because it explores how fascism emerges from the family, the subject was extremely provocative for the authorities. As a result, the play was immediately forbidden by a decree from the Municipality of Buenos Aires. In the context of its premiere and even decades later, the work is explosive and brutal. It is also Pavlovsky's only work to be published before it was put on stage. Usually, his plays evolve over the course of rehearsals, changed by the directors, actors, and even audience contributions.

Pavlovsky sees *Telarañas* as a problematic work. It is not a realistic work like *El señor Galíndez*. It corresponds to what Pavlovsky calls the "theater of states." For him, the "theater of states" refers to intensities, a hidden logic under the uncanny (and dislocated familiar) surface of the plot. This type of theater also affects the construction of characters and the approach to them by the actor during rehearsals. Since the characters are not psychologically realistic, they cannot be rehearsed using methods for realistic acting. Characters in this play, as in many of Pavlovsky's works, are voices; they appear and react to what confronts them.

There are five characters in *Telarañas* (The Father, The Mother, El Pibe [a son], Beto, and Pepe), and as Pavlovsky explains in his prologue to the play, it was written to explore the violence that exists within family relationships. From the beginning, the spectator gets the clue that he is facing a dream-like space, an unconscious space that, as in other works by Pavlovsky, always is more realistic than what is expressed by expositive or reflexive realism. Pavlovsky, in the prologue of *El señor Laforgue* (performed and published in 1982) refers again to this type of realism as exasperated, where violence fits perfectly because it is an obvious, daily occurrence.

As he explains in *La ética del cuerpo,* Pavlovsky based the play on the famous book *Die Massenpsychologie des Faschismus* (1933, The Mass Psychology of Fascism), written by the psychoanalyst Wilhelm Reich; the idea

Pavlovsky got from Reich was that "la familia alemana fue la fábrica desde donde se gestaban los grandes microfascismos" (the German family was the factory where the big microfascisms were conceived), and that "los 'Hitler' cotidianos" (the everyday Hitler) emerged "de las pequeñas familias" (from small families). Pavlovsky thus explores how torture is already embedded in the family. In one scene El Pibe is tortured by two "gasmen," Pepe and Beto (reminiscent of the characters in *El señor Galíndez,* but not the same), who burst into the house and accuse him of not being masculine enough, of being cowardly, and ultimately of being a closeted homosexual. The torture is carried out with the Father's collaboration. As in previous works, characters such as El Pibe exhibit behaviors that suggest different chronological periods, and familiar situations are presented in unusual ways in order to reveal new meanings to the spectator. When El Pibe is tortured by Beto and Pepe (whose orders come by phone as in *El señor Galíndez*), causing his body to fall into the Father's arms, the latter exclaims: "Hace rato que no nos dabamos un abrazo! Tenía que venir uno de afuera para que nos diéramos un abrazo!" (It's been so long since we've hugged! Someone from the outside had to come, so we can hug!). He adds: "¿Ves cómo a los golpes uno se hace hombre?" (See how a beating makes you a man?). Pavlovsky underlines how Ure contributed to the play during rehearsals. According to the author, Ure worked the character of El Pibe in such a way that he appeared as a victim but also as a torturer of his parents.

Structurally, *Telerañas* works by unfolding many fantasies. These fantasies—mostly based on oppression, fanaticism, and repressed homoeroticism—reveal a coherence beneath the characters' inconsistent desires and establish the effect of social oppression on each family member. Each fantasy is presented as an uncontrollable game of violence, euphoria, and aggression.

Like many other leftist artists, Pavlovsky was considered subversive by the military dictatorship and so was persecuted. On 18 March 1978 Pavlovsky was conducting a psychotherapy session when his secretary informed him that two "gasmen" had come to check the meter. During a period when so many people were "disappeared" by military forces, the eccentricity of his secretary's announcement set off warning bells for Pavlovsky. Because he was in a therapy session, Pavlovsky told his secretary to ask the gasmen to wait for him. He then excused himself to his perplexed patients and escaped through a window. Looking down toward his home from the rooftops of the surrounding houses, he saw his wife and children tied up and threatened by some men. At first he did not know what to do, but quickly drawing upon his experience in theatrical improvisation, Pavlovsky decided to go to a police station, where he filed a complaint against the unknown individuals who were invading his home. He then called his brother and, while pretending to talk to Raúl Alfonsín (who was a human-rights activist before becoming president of Argentina), used a secret code to tell his brother to come pick him up. Knowing his life was in danger, unable to do anything to help his wife and children, Pavlovsky hid in the houses of several generous friends. The gasmen destroyed his house, but they did not find his passport. Pavlovsky was able to escape to Montevideo, later on to Rio de Janeiro, and eventually to Spain. He arrived in Madrid in June 1978. A while later, his wife, son Federico, and two of Molina's children from a previous relationship arrived in Madrid.

Pavlovsky remained in Spain until the mid 1980s. Already well known in both Rio de Janeiro and Madrid, he started a psychoanalytic practice but could never fully establish it. He wrote several articles that his friend Nicolás Caparrós published in the magazine *Clínica y análisis grupal* (Clinical and Group Therapy). While in Spain he began to write *Cámara lenta* (also *Camaralenta;* translated as *Slow Motion,* 1987), which he later read to Norma Aleandro, the famous Argentine actress already in exile in Spain. She was the director of the Spanish production of *Extraño juguete;* Pavlovsky played the male character in that production, in which Molina and Katz also participated. In the meantime, his relationship with Molina deteriorated and eventually ended in separation.

While in Spain, Pavlovsky returned to his work on group therapy. Based on experimentation and not on interpretation, group dynamics promote a new perspective in Pavlovsky's drama. He develops the technique of dramatic multiplication, in which each character's story can be opened up to create new stories that exhibit common social and historical dynamics. Subsequently, Pavlovsky expands his idea of dramatic multiplication to the point of transforming it into an aesthetic of multiplicity. This aesthetic occurs when spectators do not know who is speaking on stage: as he explains in *La ética del cuerpo,* "uno nunca sabe cuando Olmedo está diciendo un texto del personaje, o esta inventando o está hablando él mismo" (one never knows when [the Argentine comedian] Olmedo is reciting the script, or, rather, is re-inventing it by himself, or even more, is speaking by himself as a person).

Pavlovsky was never able to adapt himself, personally or professionally, to Spain, and he suffered from homesickness. In 1980, because of the gradual social and political deterioration of the dictatorship, Pavlovsky decided he could go home. Returning from exile to Buenos Aires, he met the director Laura Yusem, and together they started rehearsing *Cámara lenta*. He also founded the book-magazine *Lo Grupal*, which included works by many Argentine intellectuals who, while in exile, had worked both within and outside psychoanalysis. He also endowed the Psychoanalytical Psychodrama Center. In 1981 he divorced Molina and married Susana Evans, whom he had met in Madrid while she was married to Argentine historian and biographer Pacho O'Donnel.

The rehearsals for *Cámara lenta* took many months, and the work was finally staged in April 1981 at the Olimpia Theater in Buenos Aires and ran until the end of October of that same year. *Cámara lenta* returns to the character of the boxer. Dagomar and his friend and manager Amilcar feel an intense love toward each other. The play follows the progressive physical and mental deterioration of Dagomar; the subtitle is *Historia de una cara* (Tale of a Face), alluding to the boxer's abused and scarred physique. At the final moment, Amilcar apparently decides to kill him out of love, so that Dagomar can avoid the humiliation of a life without heroic dignity. Consisting of twenty named scenes, some of them silent as in previous plays, *Cámara lenta* also introduces a feature that Pavlovsky explored in later works: the use of mumbling.

Pavlovsky began using mumbling or babbling in his works to establish a certain kind of tone that is rhythmic, almost musical in nature. Unlike in expositive realism, where a character is defined by what he or she says and does, in Pavlovsky's work the progressive inability to express oneself becomes the means by which one sees the character's relationship to others as well as his or her emotional state. This rupturing of language in *Cámara lenta* is not an artificial game but a means by which the character's desperate attempts to make sense are tortuously revealed. In this play, babbling represents a return to infancy as well as an alienated feeling of emptiness and lack of certainty. Each word in the mumbling, distanced and obviously disconnected to the previous and following ones, determines the character as a rhythm, as a sequence of contrastive identities. This characteristic makes characters in Pavlovsky's plays difficult to perform. For this reason Pavlovsky often points out that his works require experienced actors.

When Dagomar's deterioration does not let him do whatever he wants any more—to "pasar al tiempo. Ponerme delante del tiempo" (pass over the time. Be ahead of time)—Amilcar lovingly helps him. In "Escena El sueño" (Scene The Dream), Dagomar tells Amilcar about a nightmare, where Amilcar took a knife and stabbed Dagomar and then himself; yet, in spite of the blood Dagomar considers the scene comic. And he says: "me pareció que te moriste . . . yo . . . (Pausa) creo (Pausa) que me moría también (Pausa) como que tenía que ser así una fatalidad o algo así" (it seemed that you died . . . I . . . [Pause] think [Pause] I died too [Pause] as if it had to happen that way a fatality or something like this). As Amilcar faces the sad condition of his friend, the stage directions for the "Escena del final" (Final Scene) say: "Amilcar va al cajón de la cocina y saca un cuchillo bruscamente. Dagomar no lo ve. Amilcar queda con el cuchillo en la mano detrás de él" (Amilcar goes to the box in the kitchen and swiftly takes out a knife. Dagomar does not see him. Amilcar stays with the knife in his hand behind him). The ending of the play is inconclusive: Amilcar does not kill Dagomar nor stab himself. The symbiosis between both of them is such that the existence of one of them depends on the existence of the other.

Symbiosis, a characteristic of Pavlovsky's third marriage, obsessed him to the point that it became central in his play *Cerca* (it can be translated into *Near* or *Fence*), subtitled *Melodía inconclusa de una pareja* (The Unconcluded Melody of a Couple), which he wrote in Spain. The characters, He and She, confront each other in small scenes that go from "el FIN DEL COMIENZO" (the END OF THE BEGINNING) at the beginning of the play to "el COMIENZO DEL FIN" (the BEGINNING OF THE END), which finishes it. This circle is built with typical situations faced by a middle-class heterosexual symbiotic couple. They undergo rituals of mutual cheating, the fear of being abandoned and the impossibility to separate, the routine, the aggressions and regressions to childhood, the subtle and hypocritical negotiations that the culture imposes upon the experience called "love." The work is also interesting in its use of language, especially the use of repetition and spectacular games between He and She, progressively bringing them closer to the question of each other's identity.

In 1981 Pavlovsky participated in Teatro Abierto (Open Theater), a formidable cultural event in which dramatists, actors, directors, and technicians met in Buenos Aires in order to express their rejection of the dictatorship and its oppression by writing and producing short plays together over the course of a seven-day festival. The participation of Pavlovsky was, contrary to what might be expected, marginal. Despite his political criticism of fascism and authoritarian regimes in his plays, he was unable to participate in the organization of this cultural event because he was busy with his role in *Cámara lenta* and other professional activities. But for the festival he quickly wrote, in two days, *Tercero incluído* (The Third One Included), a play he considers minor. Teatro Abierto continued in spite of the terrorist acts that it suffered at the hands of the state—such as the setting on fire of the Teatro Picadero, where the series was performed. The festival was a social and political event

Hal Bokar and Tony Maggio in the 1988 Cherry Lane Theatre premiere of the translation of Pavlovsky's 1987 play Pablo *(published in 1986), about the different perspectives of those who left Argentina during the military dictatorship and those who remained (photograph by Grace Zabriskie; from* Three Plays by Eduardo Pavlovsky, *1994; University Library, Texas Tech University)*

that demonstrated that an alternative political resistance existed that did not necessarily include terrorism. Teatro Abierto–claimed Pavlovsky–provided a form of nonviolent resistance as a model for ethical behavior.

In 1982 Pavlovsky wrote *El señor Laforgue,* yet another play with explicit political content. It ran for two months at the Teatro Olimpia in Buenos Aires and for three months at the Teatro Payró. According to the author, this play is a parenthesis in his work; it does not correspond to what he was developing dramaturgically in the previous plays. *El señor Laforgue* is a work that returns to the direction of political theater he had developed during the 1970s as a means to denounce the horrors of the dictatorship.

El señor Laforgue, with the subtitle *La transformación* (The Transformation), takes place in Haiti between 1958 and 1959; it consists of twelve scenes (two of them simultaneous). The play was inspired by Pavlovsky's reading of *Papa Doc y los Tontons Macoutes,* a chronicle of the dictatorship of François Duvalier, written by Bernard Diederich and Al Burt (published in English as *Papa Doc: The Truth about Haiti Today,* 1969). In a prologue to this volume, Graham Greene sees the Haitian sociopolitical situation as a classic tragedy. Pavlovsky makes Haiti an allegory for any other country, including Argentina, that lives under a dictatorship. The author told Jorge Dubatti in *La ética del cuerpo* that the play has its roots in a conversation with a friend. They were having lunch when a person wearing a white uniform passed by. The friend told him that the person was a doctor who during the Argentine dictatorship was in charge of anesthetizing the political prisoners who were thrown from planes into the Rio de la Plata. Pavlovsky immediately felt the emotional dimension that he calls a clot, the existential knot that sets free the visions. To Pavlovsky, the nucleus of *El señor Laforgue* is "la imagen de los cadáveres que llegan flotando a las islas" (the image of the corpses floating to the islands).

The main character, Juan Carlos Open, is an agent of the regime who obeys orders without question. His job is to anesthetize political prisoners who will be thrown into the sea. He believes that this action is justifiable because they are enemies of the state. What Pavlovsky explores with this character is not so much the torturer's psychology but how the assassin is also a victim of state violence. The play begins when Open, who has started to become delirious, undergoes a procedure of brainwashing that leaves him without memory but with all the fears and horrors of the past that actively haunt him. His wife, Pichona, and the Health Institute employee, Sara (the same character from *El señor Galíndez*), together with Calvet, one of the victims who survived being thrown from the plane and is now helping the regime, do their best to ensure that Open does not resist the treatment. This procedure will convert Open into "el señor Laforgue," an effeminate gymnast with a new invented family name, a kind of robot who does his job automatically. Yet, as with any machine, sometimes something stops functioning, and he starts making dangerous confessions that put him and many others in danger.

Progressively, Laforgue begins to realize that he has been a victim of the regime in the same way as the political prisoners thrown from the plane. On his birthday, Laforgue, under the influence of Pink Floyd music, starts hearing the voodoo rhythm, and all his primitive powers are set free. The authorities accelerate the process of sending him to Philadelphia with the changed identity and family name. However, Laforgue escapes and reappears to incite the crowds to go and look for justice. At the same time a storm starts pushing the corpses that he has thrown from the plane toward the beach. At the end, Calvet, like a messenger in classic tragedy, tells a police inspector that the Haitians are burying the corpses and that Laforgue has been converted into a preacher who leads the crowds in insisting for retaliation against the people responsible for those who have disappeared. It is worth noting that in Argentina some commanders who participated in the Dirty War had no trial because there were no corpses. Meanwhile, the Asociación Madres de Plaza de Mayo (Mothers of the Plaza de Mayo), a human-rights group and the only ones who directly confronted the oppressive government during many years, were demanding the return of their missing loved ones. In 2002 many corpses appeared in Tucumán, in a place called Pozo de Vargas, allowing many families and human-rights organizations to open new trials.

After *El señor Laforgue,* Pavlovsky was invited to work as an actor in several movie projects: *Cuarteles de invierno* (1983, Winter Headquarters), *El exilio de Gardel* (1984, Gardel's Exile), *Los chicos de la guerra* (1984, War Children), and *Miss Mary* (1986). He was also offered roles in the commercial theater, such as in *Teresa Batista* by Jorge Amado, directed by Rubens Correa in 1982. His experiences in commercial theater and cinema led him to seriously question the direction of his career as an actor and dramatist. He resolved this dilemma by returning to what had made him passionate about the theater in the first place—group and "off-off" productions.

In 1985 Molina invited Pavlovsky to write a short play, and he had a vision of a kidnapper of the children of the disappeared. This vision was the genesis of *Potestad* (Paternity), one of his most popular plays. This monologue started a new period in Pavlovsky's career as an author. The play went through several transformations. In the beginning the play lasted for thirty-five minutes and included a musician, a dog, a screen, and a glass. After some performances in Brazil, where Evans played Tita, the silent and distant character witness, the play began to expand, and Pavlovsky eliminated all the extraneous elements.

In 1986, following several performances in Buenos Aires, Pavlovsky was invited to bring *Potestad* to the Festival of Iberoamerican Theater in Cadiz, Spain. From there began an international tour to such cities as London, Manizales, Montreal, Los Angeles, New York, Havana, Madrid, and Paris, while both Pavlovsky as actor and the play won many awards. Pavlovsky considers *Potestad* a text that comes from the actor. The original short version, directed by Brisky, was eventually elaborated using improvisations; the text that was actually published corresponds to a performance that was taped by a friend of the author in Montreal.

It is hard to summarize what happens in Pavlovsky's later plays, since they lack narrative (a characteristic of representational theater, according to Pavlovsky), and what narrative appears is fragmented. The power of *Potestad* is the result of the actor's intensity, a characteristic of what Pavlovsky calls the theater of states. His works of this period have minimal stage direction, something that gives a lot of liberty to directors, actors, and technicians. For example, *Potestad* is an extensive monologue lacking stage directions. Starting with multiple memories and continuing with the assumption of different voices by the character of the oppressor, the cruel logic of the raptors of children whose parents have disappeared during the dictatorship is displayed. The main character is trying to explain to Tita how he won Adriana, the girl he stole during the dictatorship, and what he feels now when the new democratic authorities have taken her from him to restore her identity and return her to her family.

Pavlovsky's next play was *Pablo,* which he started writing before *Potestad,* when he first went into exile. The play, staged in 1987 in Buenos Aires under the direction of Yusem, is an attempt to bridge the gap between those who remained in Argentina during the dictatorship and those who went into exile. The text is fragmented, with strong images. Pavlovsky insists that it is not about individual people but about voices from different social spaces. The set design creates a feeling of instability with its elevated, almost aerial spaces: a three-meter-high bed, two trapezes, and a platform that connects a train station to the bed. There are three characters in *Pablo:* L., V., and Irina. L. is the one who has not left the country and does not want to remember. V., on the other hand, comes from outside and remembers everything. V. (and possibly Irina as well) have come to kill L., to carry out an order. Yet, the focus of exploration is more on multiplicity, as is shown when the two male characters look at a scene with different perspectives. One of them sees a story of love, jealousy, and pain between a young woman and an older man, while the other one sees a scene of torture, robbery, and death. The work was also successful at several festivals. Paul Verdier's version, staged at the Cherry Lane Theatre in New York in 1988, cut the female character, giving the play a Beckettian dimension. For Pavlovsky this development proved the importance of performance, of the aesthetic response of different directors and actors to the same written text.

Pavlovsky's next play was *Paso de dos* (Pas de Deux, originally published with the title *Voces* [Voices], 1989). Staged in the Teatro Babilonia in Buenos Aires on 19 April 1990, and directed by Yusem with scenography by Graciela Galán, the play consists of two characters, HE and SHE. There are no stage directions; the play consists of a dialogue in which HE tries to remember a relationship he had with her in the past. HE needs her to name him, to give him a self, but SHE denies him that opportunity: "Me voy a quedar en silencio. Mi silencio es tu prisión. Mi silencio son los gritos en tu cabeza, mi silencio son los pánicos en tu cabeza allí nadie te va a poder soltar" (I'll remain silent. My silence is your prison. My silence is the screams in your head, my silence is the panic in your head where no one will set you free). The relationship can be interpreted from many perspectives: a story of love and abuse with a woman or with a nation. The man's initial monologue is similar in its description of gestures and movements to the beginning of *Potestad*. To some extent, HE is a torturer or an oppressor. The work underwent a complex and well-documented rehearsal process that resulted in the creation of the female character's split personality, played by two different actresses: on stage is the moribund woman–pure intensity, pure body–performed by a nude actress who responds only physically to the man's repeated blows. Sitting in the audience is another actress from whom erupts the vocal response to all of the man's actions. The play was presented at the Festival of Iberoamerican Theatre in Cadiz, Spain, and was also a success at the Festival Theater der Welt in Essen, Germany.

Some critics have debated to what extent Pavlovsky's representation of the torturer (in *El señor Galíndez,* but also in *El señor Laforgue* and mainly in *Potestad*) seems to ambiguously move the audience to identification not only with victims but also, and dangerously, with torturers. "Pavlovsky's Galindez," Diana Taylor writes in *Disappearing Acts: Spectacles of Gender and Nationalism in Argentina's "Dirty War"* (1997) "reproduces–and fails to challenge–a misogynist discourse predicated on the objectification and erasure of women." These critics question Pavlovsky's own complicity with those he tries to condemn in the sense that, as Taylor argues, the dramatic text and its performance seem to replicate "rather than dismantle the military's authoritarian discourse."

In 1987 Pavlovsky wrote a play initially titled "El último poeta" (The Last Poet). It underwent several revisions, resulting in *El cardenal* (The Cardinal). This play was first published by Editorial Búsqueda de Ayllu in 1992 and was a collaboration between Pavlovsky, Evans, and Miguel Dao. Evans suggested working with images by Francis Bacon, especially with the painting of Pope Innocent II. There are three characters in this play: The Cardinal and Dwarves I and II, who were played by women. The Cardinal is a figure of ambiguous sexuality and perverted behavior. The play resembles Jean Genet's work with its circularity, the repeated simulation of crime, and the continual requirement of a perversely careful ritualism. The conflicts explored by Pavlovsky in previous works reappear (the father-son relationship, fascism, and cultural anesthesia or dumbing-down of the country) along with new ones (such as old age, desperation, and routine) that are amplified in subsequent works.

The text of *El cardenal* was revised and transformed into *Rojos globos rojos* (Red Balloons Red), which has two versions. One version was published by Ediciones Babilonia in 1994 and the other one, included in *Teatro Completo I* (1997, Complete Theater I), was the result of rehearsals directed by Javier Margulis and Correa. The play was staged at the Teatro Babilonia in Buenos Aires in August 1994 and ran until December 1996. The text published in *Teatro Completo I* comes from a transcription of a videotape, revised by Pavlovsky.

The character of The Cardinal appears in *Rojos globos rojos* but is no longer a figure who raves about power. The Cardinal reflects some of the great figures of the Argentine theater, such as Luis Arata, Pepe Arias, Gringue Farías, and Alberto Olmedo. These actors are well known as great improvisers and exponents, according to Pavlovsky, of the acting that supports the multiplication of the senses. With their capacity to split into different voices and to multiply their personas by means of improvisation, these actors maintained a constant state of ambiguity in their performances. It was never clear whether it was the actor who was talking (as an individual or as an actor) or the character, nor whether he was speaking to another actor, to another character, or simply to the audience.

The action in *Rojos globos rojos* happens "En Los Globos Rojos, teatrito marginal y precario de un pequeño pueblo de la Provincia de Buenos Aires" (In Los Globos Rojos, a marginal and precarious small theater of a tiny village in the Buenos Aires Province). The Dwarves from *El cardenal* become Pepi and Pipi, two Argentine female ballet dancers in their mature years, possibly prostitutes, who have learned dances in Thailand. After their artistic failure, Pepi and Pipi return to Buenos Aires to look for The Cardinal, who incorporates them into his variety show performed every day with an equal passion. In this play, The Cardinal speaks directly to the audience and confesses his ideas about sex, old age, illness, progressive physical deterioration, death, passion and the exhaustion of passion, illusion and disillusion, and the necessity for utopias and to confront past defeats–all significant topics in 1994 Argentina. Pavlovsky is concerned with the increasing economic deterioration produced by neoliberalism. The Cardinal considers the theater to be the only way to resist the devastation of national culture carried out by the application of neoliberal economic models.

In 1999 *Poroto,* directed by Brisky, was staged at the Teatro Calibán in Buenos Aires. This text also underwent several revisions and transformations before it reached the stage. The first version, with the same title, is a short story included in *Teatro Completo I.* The short story was the basis for improvisations that led to a stage production. Pavlovsky also reworked it into a short novel, Beckettian in nature, titled *Dirección contraria* (Reverse Direction), published in 1997. In an even more accentuated way than in previous works, the dramatic text of *Poroto* consists of voices. Since it lacks indications as to how it should be performed (the stage directions seem to be transcriptions of what was done in Brisky's production and not definitive for any other production), the play depends entirely upon the director and actors' talent and creativity. In this sense, Pavlovsky is consistent with what he calls the aesthetics of multiplicity and to the body ethics based on micropolitics. In both cases, directors and actors explore the multiplicity of the text and get involved in designing their own strategies and methods for performing it.

The play has four male characters: the Parishioner; Leo (the friend who returns from France); Poroto (who has stayed in Buenos Aires); and finally Willy (the young man who is Poroto's split personality in the third person and who functions as a narrator). There is also the voice of She, one of Leo's personalities. Pavlovsky's idea is to free the voices from the body. The play is conceived as a chorale that illuminates a particular social and historical context. The topic of the play is the mixture of love and hate that leads Poroto to kill his mother, who survives as a pure voice. Leo and Poroto are politically militant friends who meet after many years when Leo returns from exile. They have guilty memories of the explosion of a bomb that tore apart the bodies of those who tried to deactivate it. As in *Pablo,* the play treats the topic of who remembers and who does not want to remember. Poroto specializes in perfecting techniques to escape from situations that he considers toxic; he tries to escape as a way of surviving and protecting himself. The play is difficult to stage, because each production must pay attention to the musical rhythm of the text. This rhythmical factor—which can be traced back to the work of Vsevolod Meyerhold, the Russian director much admired by Pavlovsky—becomes an important dimension within Pavlovsky's aesthetics. This music should come only from the body of the actor, by means of his expressive breathing, voice, and movements.

La muerte de Marguerite Duras was first staged on 24 July 2000 at the Teatro Babilonia, directed by Daniel Veronese. It later moved to the Teatro Calibán. The

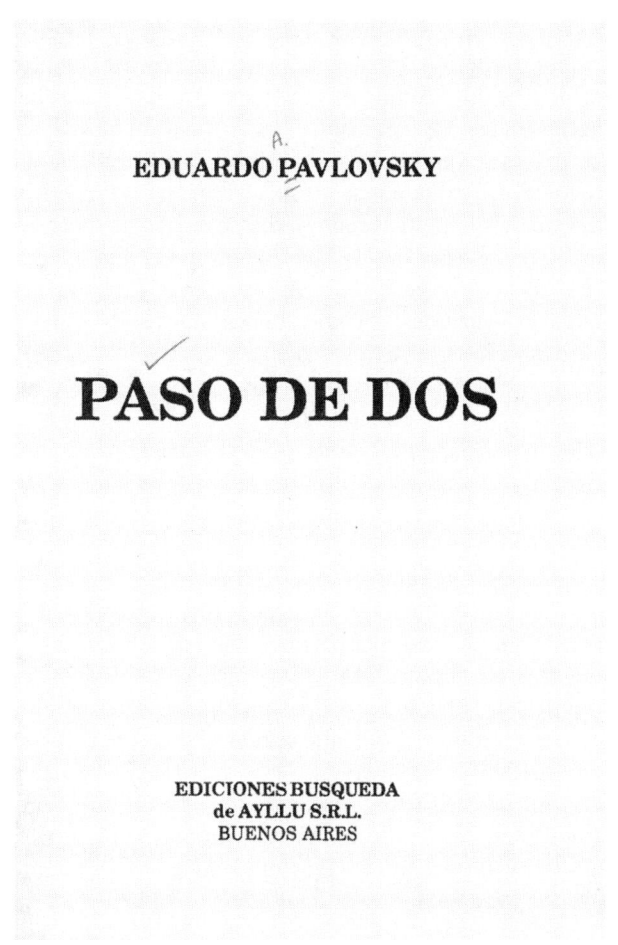

Title page for Pavlovsky's 1990 play (Pas de Deux), a dialogue between two characters, HE and SHE, as they discuss their past relationship (Reinert/Alumni Memorial Library, Creighton University)

work is a monologue performed by Pavlovsky. Rhythm, voices, minimal scenography (only a sofa), just a few impalpable musical sounds, and a passionate direct relationship with the audience define this moment of synthesis of the aesthetics of the author/actor/psychoanalyst. The play is built out of small scenes, fragments of memories unified only by the character's awareness of his old age, loneliness, and death—themes familiar to readers of Duras. Conceived as a final confession in front of an absent woman, the play goes from the contemplation of the lonely death of a fly (which the character calls Marguerite Duras) to the death of the character at the same time in another day. Between both moments, Pavlovsky's preoccupations (or obsessions) appear: fascism, sex, male impotence, the father figure, sport, camouflaged torture, fatigue, and perversion. As in *Poroto* there is a final moment of euphoria when a specific story is told. The story is about a contagious, collective, and dangerous laugh that threatens institutional power. Thus Pavlovsky shows how macropolitics starts with the micropolitics: from the laughter of one person to the general laughter of the whole community. People are not laughing because they are commanded to do so, as in a totalitarian regime, whether socialist or not. This play is about revolutionary happiness. When everyone involved in the story is happily laughing, the police suddenly show up to repress the event. The imposition of this oppressive silence converts them into martyrs. The speaker bitterly concludes: "Hubo demasiado desborde de alegría y eso era peligroso—la alegría cuando se contagia así es peligrosa. La velocidad de la propagación los asustó" (there was too much happiness and that was dangerous—happiness when it is so contagious becomes dangerous. The speed of propagation scared them). In many ways this topic is found throughout Pavlovsky's theater: the idea that any liberation movement ends up creating its own oppressive apparatus.

Eduardo Pavlovsky's theater, his continual reflection on the use and abuse of power and its cultural consequences, creates a space where the senses themselves are multiplied. For this reason, it is a highly liberatory theater, even though his aesthetization of violence and torture has been critically revised and questioned. An active and intellectual artist, Pavlovsky reflects on Argentine culture in particular and Latin America in general, enriching the historical landscape and providing fertile ground for new directors, actors, and audiences.

Interviews:

Eduardo Pavlovsky: Dialoga con Violeta H. De Gainza (Buenos Aires: Lumen, 1997);

La ética del cuerpo: Nuevas conversaciones con Jorge Dubatti (Buenos Aires: Atuel, 2001).

References:

Daniel Altamiranda, "Aspectos del realismo exasperante en Telarañas de Eduardo Pavlovsky," in *Teatro Argentino del Proceso (1976–1983)*, edited by Juana A. Arancibia and Zulema Mirkin (Buenos Aires: Editorial Vinciguerra, 1992), pp. 27–45;

David William Foster, "Ambigüedad verbal y dramática en *El señor Galíndez* de Eduardo Pavlovsky," *Latin American Theater Review*, 13, no. 2 (1980): 103–110;

Gustavo Geirola, "El silencio de la voz: Pavlovsky y la perversión metateatralizada," in his *Teatralidad y experiencia política en América Latina, 1957–77* (Irvine, Cal.: Gestos, 2000), pp. 198–202;

Ana Laura Lusnich, "La dramaturgia de Eduardo Pavlovsky (1999–2000): Nuevas búsquedas a fin de Siglo," in *Teatro Argentino del 2000*, edited by Osvaldo Pellettieri (Buenos Aires: Galerna/Fundación Roberto Arlt, 2000), pp. 55–65;

Osvaldo Pellettieri, "*Paso de dos*, de Eduardo Pavlovsky: Un texto dramático remanente y una puesta eficaz," in his *Teatro Argentino Contemporáneo (1980–1990): Crisis, transición y cambio* (Buenos Aires: Galerna, 1994);

Diana Taylor, *Disappearing Acts: Spectacles of Gender and Nationalism in Argentina's "Dirty War"* (Durham, N.C.: Duke University Press, 1997).

José J. Podestá
(6 October 1858 – 5 March 1937)

Beatriz Seibel

(Translation by Jean Graham-Jones)

PLAY PRODUCTIONS: *Juan Moreira,* adapted from Eduardo Gutiérrez's novel, Chivilcoy, Circo Pabellón Argentino, 10 April 1886; revised, Buenos Aires, Circo San Martín, 13 September 1890; revised, Buenos Aires, Hippodrome Circus, 24 March 1925.

BOOKS: *Canciones de Pepino el 88 para cantar con guitarra* (Buenos Aires: Nacional, 1891);
Canciones inéditas del gran Pepino 88: Para cantar con guitarra (Buenos Aires: N. Tommasi, 1897);
Medio siglo de farándula: Memorias (Río de la Plata: Imprenta Argentina de Córdoba, 1930);
Juan Moreira (1886), edited by Carlos Vega (Buenos Aires: Imprenta de la Universidad, 1935);
Juan Moreira [1891 one-act version], edited by Teodoro Klein (Buenos Aires: Instituto Nacional de Estudios de Teatro, 1986);
Nuevas canciones inéditas del gran Pepino "88" José J. Podestá, 1895–1896, edited by Juan González Urtiaga (Montevideo, Uruguay: Centro de Estudios de Teatro Rioplatense, 1997).
Edition: *Medio siglo de farándula: Memorias,* edited by Osvaldo Pelletieri (Buenos Aires: Galerna, 2003).

José J. Podestá (from Medio siglo de farándula, *2003; Main Library, University of Arizona)*

It is widely considered that Argentina began as a "modern nation" in the 1880s. During this period the country engaged in commerce with Europe, established its governing apparatus, promoted education and granted autonomy to the universities, extended the rail system, and developed midsized industries. As a result of massive immigration, the cities and the middle class developed rapidly, while the urban elites continued to follow European models. In the theater, European companies and plays dominated the Argentine stage as well as most others in Latin America. The premiere of José J. Podestá's *Juan Moreira* in 1886 marked the beginning of an important theatrical change that resulted in a flourishing twentieth-century Argentine theater.

José Juan Podestá was born on 6 October 1858 in Montevideo, Uruguay, the fourth of nine children. His parents, Pedro Podestá and María Teresa Torterolo, were Genoese immigrants and circus performers who arrived in the River Plate region around 1840. Their two eldest children were born in Buenos Aires and the rest in Montevideo, where the family moved in 1851. In the Uruguayan capital, José attended public school, studied music, practiced various circus arts, and in 1875 negotiated his first professional contract, as an acrobat and trapeze artist with the French troupe owned by Félix Hénault. Podestá and his brothers created an equestrian and pantomime troupe, in keeping with the fashion of the times. After performing in Montevideo, in May 1880 the troupe moved to Buenos Aires. There they were contracted out for tours, and in 1881 Podestá made his debut as a white-faced clown under the soon-to-be-famous stage name of Pepino 88. As Pepino 88, Podestá satirized current events and performed songs that quickly became popular.

While on tour in Rosario, Argentina, in 1883, Podestá married Baldomera Arias, an equestrian working in the Raffetto Circus. The couple eventually had eight children. By June 1884 the Podestá family was performing with the Carlo Brothers Circus in Buenos Aires's Teatro Politeama. There, on 2 July, the pantomime *Juan Moreira* premiered, with Podestá in the title role. *Juan Moreira* was adapted by Eduardo Gutiérrez, from his eponymous novel, based on the real case of a famous bandit killed by Buenos Aires provincial police in 1874. First appearing in serial form in the daily newspaper *La Patria Argentina* between 28 November 1879 and 8 January 1880, *Juan Moreira* was later published as a best-selling book. Gutiérrez's Moreira was a victim of the injustice of the social system, and the author exalted the gaucho's courage and nobility.

With only Italian, French, and Spanish companies performing in Buenos Aires at the time the pantomime premiered, Podestá was precisely the criollo artist required to act out the bandit's story. Podestá knew how to use a *facón* (gaucho knife), ride a horse, sing, and play the guitar, and he had experience playing Italian and Spanish bandits in the action-pantomimes that were in vogue.

Gutiérrez's pantomime version of *Juan Moreira* was built on several scenes accompanied by music. The human voice was heard only when the lead performer sang an *estilo* and other actors recited the couplets of the *gato* dance (both the *estilo* and the *gato* being extremely popular musical forms). The original stage space, a ring surrounded by tiers and a platform connected to the ring, resembled the stages in use since the beginnings of the modern circus in 1782. The action took place both on the stage (the interior scenes) and in the ring (the outside action scenes).

The day after the premiere, the daily newspaper *Sud-América* praised Podestá's performance and noted that Gutiérrez had directed the rehearsals. Later, Carlos Olivera, writing under the pseudonym Anacarsis, published an article in the newspaper *El Diario* (10 July 1884) that made clear the polemics accompanying the theme of the persecuted gaucho. Olivera noted:

> la mayoría de los diarios hace el vacío alrededor del suceso. Se ha reído de *Juan Moreira* novela, se continúa riendo de *Juan Moreira* pantomima. Se dice que es "cosa para la plebe," pero la novela hace el éxito de un diario y la pantomima atrae inacabable cadena de espectadores al circo.

(The majority of newspapers have turned a cold shoulder to the event. They laughed at the novel *Juan Moreira*, they'll continue laughing at the pantomime *Juan Moreira*. They say that it's "a trifle for the masses," but the novel brought success to one newspaper and the pantomime is now attracting a never-ending chain of spectators to the circus.)

The original production had thirteen performances, and the pantomime was restaged barely eighteen months later: on 16 January 1886 the Podestá-Scotti company (led by Podestá and Alejandro Scotti) made its debut to clamorous success under the Circo Pabellón Argentino's tent while on tour in the province of Buenos Aires.

Podestá then decided to transform the pantomime into a "spoken play," taking on the task of the new adaptation himself in order to "understand completely the work's plot," as he wrote in his memoirs, *Medio siglo de farándula* (1930, A Half-Century on the Stage). Not unlike what is now known as "dramaturgy of the director" and in keeping with the custom of the day, the lead actor (in this case Podestá) was also in charge of the staging of the play. Podestá created a two-act version of *Juan Moreira,* which premiered in Chivilcoy, Argentina, on 10 April 1886 and once again met with great success. The actors included Podestá in the title role; his wife as Vicenta, Moreira's wife; and other Podestá family members in various roles. Gutiérrez was not involved in the new adaptation, and conflicts over royalties arose; legislation regarding royalties did not yet exist in Argentina.

Podestá's original two-act version of the drama *Juan Moreira* is composed of five scenes in the first act and seven scenes in the second. The stripped-down dialogue, always secondary to the action, is not too removed from late-twentieth-century theater tendencies. Dramatic scenes alternate with festive scenes complete with dances and songs. As in the pantomime, the interior scenes were performed on the platform while the action scenes were presented in the circus ring. The first scene, taking place in a *juzgado de la paz* (rural courtroom), demonstrates the social injustices of the period. Don Francisco, the mayor of the provincial town where Moreira lives, orders that Moreira be placed in the stocks, punished because of a false accusation made by the shopkeeper Sardetti. At the beginning of the second scene, in Sardetti's *pulpería* (tavern/country store), two peasants sing a dueling *milonga* (a form of popular urban dance music); the scene ends with a physical duel in which Moreira kills Sardetti and says, "Ahora, que se cumpla mi destino" (Now, let my destiny be fulfilled). In the third scene Moreira flees his home after saying good-bye to his aging father, Tata Viejo; his wife, Vicenta; and their son, Juancito. Shortly after Moreira leaves, Don Francisco and his soldiers arrive and place everyone else under arrest. In the fourth scene Moreira runs into his friend Julián, who tells him that the soldiers have killed Tata Viejo and that the mayor is now trying to take advantage of Moreira's wife. The first act ends with the deaths of Don Francisco and two soldiers in a saber fight with the gaucho.

In the second act the protagonist displays his nobility as he protects the prestigious politician Marañón from assassination. When Moreira finally returns home, he finds that a friend has betrayed him and has come to live with Vicenta and Juancito. The gaucho then decides to give up and die fighting, but he is unsuccessful. The fifth scene begins with a party at the *pulpería,* where everyone dances a *gato;* Moreira sings an *estilo;* and the black man Agapito provides comic counterpoint to the dramatic Moreira. Suddenly the soldiers arrive, led by the sergeant Navarro, with orders to arrest Moreira. The gaucho wins the ensuing fight but spares the wounded sergeant's life because of his valor; Navarro in turn assures everyone that Moreira is not a bandit. The sixth and seventh scenes are nothing more than stage directions describing the physical actions: gauchos dancing in a brothel where Moreira is found; the arrival of the police; and the death of Moreira.

The play takes place in the countryside of the province of Buenos Aires at a moment of great social transformations brought on by the growth of the railroad, agriculture, industry, and immigration. The gaucho, the mythical free inhabitant of the Argentine pampas, found himself reduced to the status of a ranchhand, a soldier assigned to guard the national border, or a servant of some local political boss. The dramatic text had as its referent the myth of man struggling against injustice. In the theater such mythic themes have produced lasting expressions, and the gaucho's drama has represented, at various moments, the drama of the individual who finds himself oppressed either socially or economically yet who refuses to give in to oppressive authority. The language of *Juan Moreira* is inscribed within the gaucho genre already in existence in the theater of the region since the independence period and the early *sainetes gauchescos* (one-act popular gaucho plays). *Juan Moreira* signals the beginning of the evolution of the gaucho play, developed through many versions of the same protagonist by different dramatists and also through such rebels as Martín Fierro, Juan Cuello, the Hormiga Negra, Pastor Luna, and Santos Vega.

Podestá in the title role of Juan Moreira, *his popular 1886 adaptation of Eduardo Gutiérrez's novel (serialized in 1879-1880) about a notorious Buenos Aires outlaw (from Gutiérrez,* Juan Moreira, *1973; M. D. Anderson Library, University of Houston)*

The Podestás performed *Juan Moreira* before large audiences in many Argentine cities, but the production received little attention in the press, which instead chose to dedicate lengthy reviews to European plays and traveling companies. As the company continued touring, Podestá introduced changes into *Juan Moreira.* At the end of 1889, while performing in a circus-theater in Montevideo, the production premiered the *milonga* "La Estrella," written by Antonio Podestá, and replaced the *gato* dance with a *pericón* (an old rural and highly theatrical dance form). This occasion was the first time that a *milonga* and a *pericón* were performed on the regional stage. The *pericón* enjoyed extraordinary success and spread throughout Argentina after this onstage re-creation; it was performed at various ceremonies as the most important of all traditional Argentine dances.

Likewise, a "dramaturgy of the actor" led to textual changes, through characters created in improvisations, especially for the festive *pulpería* scene. Jorge Garay created the "poor gaucho" surrounded by his dogs; Antonio Podestá was Bentos, a brave yet easily frightened drunkard; Scotti played the Basque character type; Juan Podestá created the gaucho Contreras; Manuel Fernández added a Neapolitan priest; and Celestino Petray created Cocoliche, an Italian immigrant who attempted to pass himself off as a criollo. This comic character went on to have a long history and was performed by many other actors. Cocoliche's costume became popular at carnivals; songs or poems by Cocoliche were published in many leaflets; and his image appeared in advertisements, drawings, and caricatures in newspapers and magazines. Cocoliche's presence became so widespread that his name was soon synonymous for the speech of the "creolized" Italian immigrant. On the Argentine stage the character crossed the boundaries of the criollo drama to appear in such popular local one-act plays as *sainetes* and *grotescos*.

On 13 September 1890 the Podestá family premiered their new dramatic version of *Juan Moreira* in Buenos Aires under the San Martín Circus's tent. Its success grew. The newspapers finally began to pay attention; the daily *Sud-América* (11 November 1890) categorized the production as possessing "originalidades sociales" (social originalities) and noted that "este circo, sitio de reunión hasta ayer de una cierta y determinada clase social, se ve hoy noche a noche invadido por lo más distinguido que tiene Buenos Aires" (this circus, until yesterday a meeting place for a particular and determined social class, sees itself night after night invaded by Buenos Aires's most distinguished inhabitants). The local critic went on to opine that Moreira "no es sino un palidísimo reflejo de la vida heroicamente aventurada de un noble gaucho argentino perseguido por la fatalidad" (is nothing but a very pale reflection of the heroic adventurous life of a noble Argentine gaucho persecuted by his destiny) and made special note of the realism of the country scenes. On 20 December, Podestá produced *Juan Moreira* in the Teatro Politeama. For local circus performers, this theater symbolized the social acceptance needed to expand. That very season, great figures of the European stage had performed on its stage, and it had only been six years since the *Juan Moreira* pantomime premiered there. The performances all sold out, and even the Argentine president, Carlos Pellegrini, was known to have attended several shows. On 29 December a commentary published in *El Diario* newspaper noted that only *Juan Moreira* had managed, "que en esta época de crisis que atravesamos se fije un cartel a la puerta del Politeama diciendo 'No hay más localidades'" (during this moment of crisis we're experiencing, to post on the door of the Politeama a sign saying "Sold Out").

On 31 January 1891 there was a benefit performance for the widow and children of Gutiérrez, who had died in 1889 at the age of thirty-eight. The Podestá-Scotti company gave 142 performances before leaving on tour for Montevideo, where they performed *Juan Moreira* 85 times. On 30 April they returned to Buenos Aires, performing in the Jardín Florida, which had been "convertido en elegante circo ecuestreinto" (converted into an elegant equestrian circus), according to the program, which called *Juan Moreira* a "drama nacional de costumbres criollas" (national criollo costume drama) in two acts and ten scenes. Pellegrini attended the 25 May performance, and the *payador* (improvisational singer) Gabino Ezeiza, a troupe member, created a song in Pellegrini's honor. On 4 June the company moved back to the Teatro Politeama, where they gave 61 performances before once again leaving on tour. On 17 August they debuted in Santa Fe, Argentina, in the Teatro Politeama Gálvez; the 87-person troupe traveled by steamboat. In *Medio siglo de farándula* Podestá recalls a success so extraordinary that the House of Representatives modified their sessions schedule so that congressmen could see the production. The troupe then continued on to Rosario, where they stayed until February 1892.

In the 1891 manuscript version, the play has ten scenes. The first two scenes of the second act—Moreira's rescue of the bandit-besieged Marañón—have been excised. Other modifications appear in the second scene of the first act, in which the characters of Gauchos 1, 2, and 3 are replaced by Agapito, Bentos, and Clinudo, revealing a characterization left undefined in the earlier version. In the eighth scene, the party at the *pulpería*, Bentos has replaced the earlier unnamed peasant. Cocoliche is now called the "Neapolitan Francisco," and, while he has no written lines, there are instructions regarding improvised dialogue. In this scene Francisco takes Agapito's place as the leading comic character. Agapito's relative loss of importance in *Juan Moreira* reflected a social displacement: the darker-skinned *morenos* had become practically invisible, lost in the ethnic mix of the city as their presence was reduced drastically in relation to the European immigrants, who reached nearly a million between 1880 and 1900. The musical modifications also appear in the 1891 version: mention is made of the *pericón* dance, a *milonga,* and the singing of a *décima* (a musical form composed of stanzas of ten octosyllabic lines) by the female partner in the *pericón*. The program shows that this role was played by the "blonde songstress" María Podestá, a popular actress despite the limited presence of women in the criollo theater. The text does not mention any *payadores*, but their performances were commented upon by the local newspapers.

The success of Podestá's *Juan Moreira* continued to grow. An article published in the daily newspaper *La Nación* (26 October 1891) noted that Moreira's image appeared everywhere, even on matchboxes. A month earlier Bartolomé Mitre y Vedia had founded the weekly magazine *Juan Moreira, Semanario político y de caricaturas* (Juan Moreira, Political and Caricature Weekly). The magazine lent support to Mitre's oppositional National Civic Union during the wave of populist sympathy that followed the 1890 revolution. Serialized publications presented many versions of Juan Moreira and other rebel characters, in prose and in gaucho verse. During the 1890s this massively distributed "literatura de cordel" (literary chain) was circulated through nontraditional channels: kiosks, market stalls, train stations, and traveling salesmen. Moreira was a leading character in editorial columns and advertisements. Carnivals underwent a transformation in 1890; gauchos began to appear in abundance, on foot or horseback, carrying the multiplying image of Moreira.

Buenos Aires's recognition of *Juan Moreira* four years after its premiere, and the popular success that accompanied it, inspired most circus troupes to adopt the same repertory, staging *Juan Moreira* in addition to other criollo dramas. At the same time, a new structure was introduced into the circus show that divided the production into two parts: the first half was devoted to such circus acts as acrobatics, displays of skill, and clowning; and the second half presented the theatrical performance. The resulting system, known as the *circo criollo* (Creole circus), was adopted by many of the companies, who enjoyed a broad audience response as they toured the capital and the provinces. *Juan Moreira* was also performed in theaters by professional (even Italian-speaking) companies as well as amateur casts.

The enormous success of *Juan Moreira* in Buenos Aires gave birth to the Golden Age of the *circo criollo,* from 1890 to 1916. The age came to an end when rural traditions were displaced by a new urban popular culture. Popular "creolism" disappeared from center stage, and the circus tents found themselves far from the city center even as their tours introduced thousands and thousands of Argentines to the theater.

Until 1911 the absence of royalty and copyright laws allowed for the text of *Juan Moreira* to be used freely, with or without modifications. One interesting case in point was the Raffetto Circus company's 1893 production of *Juan Moreira* with an all-female cast. The newspaper *El Diario* (22 March 1893) noted: "La gran novedad ha sido la de anoche en el Circo San Carlos. *Juan Moreira* representado por mujeres era lo unico que no faltaba ver" (The big news happened last night at the San Carlos Circus. *Juan Moreira* played by women was the only thing we hadn't seen yet). The acting tradition of gender-crossing was kept alive and resulted in similar versions in other circuses.

Podestá recalled in his memoirs that in Rosario in 1893 the *intendante* (mayor) requested that *Juan Moreira* not be performed, after an oppositional newspaper campaign blamed the criollo plays for an increase in crime. Ernesto Quesada affirms that by 1902, "moreirism" had caused all sort of destruction, and crime reports frequently referred to brawls between *compadritos* (urban ruffians) and vigilantes, during which the former would boast that they were "Moreira." Podestá, for his part, was of the opinion that the reality informing *Juan Moreira* was what provoked the authorities to ban the play by decree because, after any performance, there could not be a single poor gaucho willing to put up with the injustices of the system. But he also pointed out other beneficial influences: the rise of new authors, the increase in the number of amateur dramatic centers, and new business for guitar factories because now the public wanted to play the songs and music made popular by the circus.

In 1900 the Barcelona press praised a criollo dramatic company touring Spain. In July the same troupe staged *Juan Moreira* in Madrid, and Buenos Aires's newspaper *El Diario* (25 July 1900) commented that the exotic gaucho costumes and the strong, wild originality of the production made a noisy impression on the Madrid audience that filled the circus tent. Nevertheless, the local reviewer was of the opinion that such a display of "national art" would surely not contribute to the popularization of Argentine culture, given that what the circus was presenting as examples of present-day Argentine life were really customs of the past. This production marked the first time that an Argentine company had toured Europe.

That same year, the Podestá family decided to leave the circus tent behind, and with it their extensive touring, in order to perform in theater houses. Thus they changed from a *circo criollo* company to a lyrical-dramatic troupe, according to the denomination of the era. A new age had been inaugurated; José Podestá was now the leading actor and director of the only national theater company with a legitimate theater house, at a time when two circus troupes were presenting criollo plays and four Spanish and three Italian companies were announcing their own performances. In March 1901 the Podestá family split, and José Podestá went to the Teatro Apolo, where he stayed for more than seven years. There are different explanations given for the family's separation; it was either because the company had become too large and was no longer economically

Juan Moreira continued to be staged by circus and theater companies in Buenos Aires and the provinces, while polemics regarding the play and its protagonist continued. In a 1910 lecture based on police files, the historian José Ingenieros concluded that Juan Moreira, far from being an anti-authoritarian rebel, was a "congenitally amoral" being. In this case no differentiation was made between historical and dramatic truths. Sánchez maintained that with *Juan Moreira,* a theater of misdeed had been founded, one in which crime as idea and bad taste as form prevailed. He counterposed the success of his own play *M'hijo el dotor* (My Son the Doctor, which had been first performed by Jerónimo Podestá's company in 1903), in which he believed the reflection of lived customs produced a revolution. By ascribing to contemporary European theatrical aesthetics, Sánchez's play went on to be canonized by the hegemonic culture.

In two historical theater studies first published in 1910, Mariano G. Bosch and Vicente Rossi maintain opposing positions. For Rossi, the premiere of *Juan Moreira* marked the true origins of a national theater in the River Plate region; for Bosch, the origins extended back to the colonial period of the region, and thus *Juan Moreira* was an event without any real importance for Argentine theater history. Ricardo Rojas stated in his history of Argentine literature that the "emancipation" of the Argentine theater is owed to the gauchos, because after *Juan Moreira* it did not take long for local authors to see other possibilities for dramatic evolution, resulting in many dramas and comedies, both rural and urban. Those who claim that the founding of the national theater was the premiere of *Juan Moreira* maintain that preceding theatrical events should be regarded as "antecedents." It is more appropriate to call this age the "flowering of Argentine theater," a period inaugurated in 1890 by the *circo criollo* companies and by national companies on Italianate proscenium stages in the early twentieth century.

While Podestá continued working as an actor and director in various theaters and companies, a variety of stagings of *Juan Moreira* were being presented. One such example was Elías Alippi's 1915 production in the Teatro San Martín, with its great display of actors, dancers, singers, guitarists, and the duo of Carlos Gardel (a famous tango singer) and José Razzano.

Podestá returned to the *circo criollo* big top in 1916 during the Buenos Aires summer season; he then went back to touring and continued to work in theater houses. At the end of 1920 he remodeled his La Plata theater and, to honor his father's memory, changed its name from the Olimpo Politeama to the Coliseo Podestá, a name the theater still retains (although it is now the property of the city of La Plata).

Monument to Podestá in Buenos Aires (from Eduardo Gutiérrez, Juan Moreira, *1973; M. D. Anderson Library, University of Houston*)

viable, or because brother Jerónimo Podestá's grown children wanted more independence as a result of artistic differences or other family conflicts. The family's separation led to the multiplication of national companies in theater houses, with a large audience following that encouraged greater production from local playwrights. This first decade of the twentieth century was deemed the Golden Age of the Argentine theater. According to Luis Ordaz, this era began in 1901 with José Podestá's move to the Apolo and ended with playwright Florencio Sánchez's death at the end of 1910.

In 1925 Podestá decided to celebrate his fifty years of artistic activity by restaging *Juan Moreira* in the Hippodrome Circus, a luxurious space in downtown Buenos Aires. He decided to modify the work by adding enough scenes and sketches to make it a full-length (that is, a three-act) play; there is no extant copy of this version of the text. The production debuted on 24 March to great success and sold out every night. In *Medio siglo de farándula* Podestá recalls how no one believed that he, at the age of sixty-seven, would be capable of performing a play such as *Juan Moreira* 127 times onstage, in the ring, and on horseback. On 1 May, the fiftieth anniversary of Podestá's professional debut, a ceremony was held in his honor with the enthusiastic support of audience and press alike. Podestá was the first national artist to receive such a celebration, which was attended by people ranging from the country's president, Marcelo T. de Alvear, to the humblest rural folk in boots and *bombacha* (baggy trousers). On 26 June another event was organized to honor Podestá, this time by an Honoring Committee made up of authorities, noted celebrities, and artists; once again, President Alvear attended.

The playwright Enrique García Velloso, in his 1926 treatise on the actor's art, stated that ever since its premiere, *Juan Moreira* negotiated all change in popular taste and interests, managing to draw not only multiple generations of Argentines but also many different cosmopolitan audiences. García Velloso maintained that both the subject matter of *Juan Moreira* and the principal elements of its action were so human and eternal that even when the play was translated to another language, such as Italian, its scenic vigor remained unharmed. García Velloso pointed out that for thirty years the protective shade of this play had permitted the survival of various companies, out of which sprang Argentina's principal actors. *Juan Moreira* always assured complete success, whether in the circus or the theater.

In 1926 Podestá once again took *Juan Moreira* on tour, this time as his farewell to the Argentine provinces. In December of the following year he gave a farewell run in Buenos Aires's Teatro Apolo, the site of his early successes. In 1930 Podestá published *Medio siglo de farándula*, a valuable contribution to theater history. In 1933 the Argentine Association of Actors named him honorary president and held a special event on 5 August in which actors from all the theaters participated. Podestá himself performed monologues of his character, the clown Pepino 88, and directed the national *pericón*, where he danced next to many performers from his own family.

In 1935 the Institute of Argentine Literature (of the University of Buenos Aires's College of Philosophy and Letters) published for the first time the manuscript of Podestá's original 1886 dramatic version of *Juan Moreira*. On 15 January 1937 in Montevideo, the Compañía de Comedias Musicales, led by Francisco Canaro, announced its "Grandiose Extraordinary Festival in Honor of the Patriarch of River-Plate Theater," Podestá. On 5 March, at the age of seventy-eight, Podestá died in the city of La Plata. He had been living in the Coliseo Podestá (which, in keeping with the customs of the time, had living quarters). That same year a municipal ordinance gave his name to a Buenos Aires street. On 6 October 1958 a sculpture with a bust of Podestá and a bas-relief of a gaucho was placed in a plaza facing the National Cervantes Theater. It carries the inscription: "Artífice del Teatro Argentino–Homenaje del Congreso de la Nación" (Creator of the Argentine Theater–An Homage from the National Congress).

Studies continued to be written about Podestá and *Juan Moreira* throughout the twentieth century. In 1963 Raúl H. Castagnino asserted that, as Podestá took *Juan Moreira* from town to town, a popular phenomenon was produced: an identification involving an absolute community between the audience and the performance, and the loss of any barriers separating fiction and reality. In 1980 Jorge B. Rivera claimed that *Juan Moreira* achieved a type of legitimacy bequeathed by the spectators themselves, who recognized in the hero's social and metaphysical sufferings a version of their own "estar en el mundo" (existence in the world). In 1982 Angel Rama maintained that Buenos Aires's suburban inhabitants were the same gauchos who were displaced from the countryside and beginning to flood into the cities, and thus the big-top performance allowed them to relive the entire cycle of their own lives. Rama noted that what mattered was not the historical Juan Moreira but rather the stage Moreira, who interpreted his audience's feelings.

In 1986, for the centenary of the premiere of *Juan Moreira*, the 1891 manuscript was published, after theater historian Teodoro Klein discovered it in the Archives of the National Institute for Theater Studies. The edition also included a series of analyses of the play and its author.

The various adaptations of *Juan Moreira* by different authors continue and are frequently adapted to the changing times. According to Beatriz Seibel, since 1897 there have been fifty-two known stage versions of *Juan Moreira*, including three versions with female protagonists; since 1892 there have been two operatic versions, one version for television (1969), and five for motion pictures (since 1910). A November 2001 stage version was created by Diego Starosta, a young experimental theater director and actor.

After *Juan Moreira,* José J. Podestá continued to enrich the Argentine stage. He promoted new playwrights, attracted a growing audience, encouraged local actors, spawned the creation of new national companies, provoked debates, and gained historical recognition. In the process Podestá inspired and continues to inspire multiple generations, from different ideologies and aesthetics, but all attracted to the myth of the man who battled injustice.

References:

Mariano G. Bosch, *Historia del teatro en Buenos Aires* (Buenos Aires: Establecimiento Tipográfico El Comercio, 1910), p. 474;

Raúl H. Castagnino, *Sociología del teatro argentino* (Buenos Aires: Nova, 1963), pp. 53–55;

Centenario del Estreno de Juan Moreira (Buenos Aires: Revista del Instituto Nacional de Estudios de Teatro, 1986);

Enrique García Velloso, *El arte del comediante,* volume 2 (Buenos Aires: Ángel Estrada, 1926), p. 171;

Juan Carlos Ghiano, *Teatro gauchesco primitivo* (Buenos Aires: Losange, 1957), p. 15;

Juan González Urtiaga, *José J. Podestá y "Pepino el 88"* (Montevideo, Uruguay: Centro de Estudios de Teatro Rioplatense, 1994);

Eduardo Gutiérrez, *Juan Moreira* (Buenos Aires: Xandu, 1973);

Luis Ordaz, *El teatro en el Río de la Plata* (Buenos Aires: Futuro, 1946), p. 65;

Blanca Podestá, *Algunas recuerdos de mi vida artística* (Buenos Aires: Avellanda, Artes Gráficas Bartolomé U. Chiesino, 1951);

Adolfo Prieto, *El discurso criollista en la formación de la Argentina moderna* (Buenos Aires: Sudamericana, 1988), pp. 116–117;

Ernesto Quesada, *En torno al criollismo: Textos y polémica* (Buenos Aires: Centro Editor de América Latina, 1983), p. 136;

Angel Rama, *Los gauchipolíticos rioplatenses* (Buenos Aires: Centro Editor de América Latina, 1982), pp. 129–146;

Jorge B. Rivera, *El folletín: Eduardo Gutiérrez* (Buenos Aires: Centro Editor de América Latina, 1980), pp. 223–228;

Ricardo Rojas, *Historia de la literatura argentina: Los gauchescos,* volume 2 (Buenos Aires: Losada, 1948), p. 609;

Vicente Rossi, *Teatro nacional rioplatense* (Buenos Aires: Solar, 1969), p. 41;

Florencio Sánchez, *Teatro completo de Florencio Sánchez,* edited by Dardo Cúneo (Buenos Aires: Claridad, 1941), pp. 622–623;

Beatriz Seibel, *Historia del circo* (Buenos Aires: Ediciones del Sol, 1993), pp. 235–238.

Juan Radrigán
(23 January 1937 -   )

Carolyn D. Roark
Baylor University

PLAY PRODUCTIONS: *Testimonio de las muertes de Sabina,* Santiago, Chile, Teatro del Angel, March 1980;

Las brutas, Valparaíso, Chile, Compañía El Farol, 1980;

Cuestión de ubicación, Santiago, Chile, Imagen, 1980;

El loco y la triste, Valdivia, Chile, 1980;

Redoble fúnebre para lobos y corderos (Isabel desterrada en Isabel, Sin motivo aparente, El invitado), Santiago, Chile, El Telón, 1981;

Hechos consumados, Santiago, Chile, El Telón, 1982;

El toro por las astas, Santiago, Chile, El Telón, Sala Camilo Henríquez, September 1982;

Informe para indiferentes, Concepción, Chile, 1983;

Las voces de ira, Santiago, Chile, El Telón, 1984;

Made in Chile, Santiago, Chile, El Telón, 1985;

Pueblo del mal amor, Santiago, Chile, Teatro Universidad Católica, May 1986;

Los borrachos de luna, Santiago, Chile, El Telón, 1986;

La contenida humana, Santiago, Chile, Teatro del Angel, October 1988;

Balada de los condenados a soñar, Santiago, Chile, August 1989;

Como un río de leones, Concepción, Chile, Taller de Teatro del Instituto Chileno Francés de Cultura, 1989;

Piedra de escándalo, Concepción, Chile, 1990;

Islas del porfiado amor, Santiago, Chile, El Telón, November 1994;

El encuentramiento, Santiago, Chile, Discotheque Oz, June 1996;

Perra Celestial, Santiago, Chile, Sala Sergio Aguirre, May 1999;

Medea Mapuche, Santiago, Chile, June 2000;

El exilio de la mujer desnuda, Santiago, Chile, Cía. La Inesperanza, April 2001.

BOOKS: *Los vencidos no creen en Dios* (Santiago, Chile: Entrecerros, 1962);

El vino de la cobardía (Santiago, Chile, 1968);

Juan Radrigán (from María Teresa Zegers Nachbauer, 25 años de teatro en Chile, *1999; W. E. B. Du Bois Library, University of Massachusetts, Amherst)*

Queda estrictamente prohibido, o, La ronda de las manos ajenas, by Radrigán and Divel Mersán (Santiago, Chile: Saotem, 1970);

El día de los muros (Santiago, Chile: Impresora Bio-Bio, 1975);

Hechos consumados (Santiago, Chile: Minga, 1982)—comprises *Hechos consumados, Isabel desterrada en Isabel,* and *El invitado;*

Teatro de Juan Radrigán: 11 Obras (Santiago, Chile & Minneapolis: CENECA/University of Minnesota, 1984)—comprises *Testimonio de las muertes de Sabina, Cuestión de ubicación, Las brutas, El loco y la triste, Redoble fúnebre para lobos y corderos (Isabel desterrada en Isabel, Sin motivo aparente, El invitado), Hechos consumados, El toro por las astas, Informe para indiferentes,* and *La felicidad de los García;* revised as *Hechos consumados: Teatro 11 obras* (Santiago, Chile: LOM, 1993)–comprises *Testimonio de las muertes de Sabina, Cuestión de ubicación, Las brutas, El loco y la triste, Redoble fúnebre para lobos y corderos (Isabel desterrada en Isabel, Sin motivo aparente, El invitado), Hechos consumados, El toro por las astas, Informe para indiferentes,* and *Islas de porfiado amor;*

Tengo aparición de la verdad (Santiago, Chile: Palabra Escrita, 1987);

Pueblo de mal amor; Los borrachos de luna (Santiago, Chile: Ñuke Mapu, 1987);

Nepegñe, peñi, nepegñe / Despierta, hermano, despierta: Poesía Mapuche (Santiago, Chile: Ñuke Mapu, 1987);

La contenida humana (Santiago, Chile: Literatura Alternativa, 1989);

El encuentramiento (Santiago, Chile: SECC, 1995);

Parábolas de la fantasmas borrachos (Santiago, Chile: SECC, 1997).

The military coup of September 1973 created a period of "theatrical blackout" in Chile. Because many productions and artists of the 1960s and early 1970s expressed left-wing, reformist political sentiments, the newly established regime considered the theater as part of the "Marxist cancer" that had to be immediately and radically excised. Many artists went into prison or exile; groups dissolved; venues shut down; and even the university theater programs underwent radical reconstruction. For a time, only light comedy, classical, and imported realist dramas found space on Chilean stages. By 1976, however, several artists emerged to grapple with the aftermath of the coup and the impact of the new authoritarian regime. After purging the more radical activists from the field (through detainment, exile, or death), the government agencies tasked with monitoring dissidence and subversive activity decided that theater was a relatively insignificant means of communication; it then became a fruitful outlet for protest and critical discussion. Of the playwrights that engaged in social discourse during this period, Juan Radrigán stands out because of his ties to the working class. Most playwrights of his generation, including Jorge Díaz, Sergio Vodanovic, and Egon Wolff, had emerged from (and wrote for) Chile's middle class. These artists began their theatrical careers in the 1950s, after attending university, and became influential during the 1960s. Their work featured characters who spoke an educated, bourgeois Spanish, even among the most proletarian groups. Radrigán began his career much later and came out of an entirely different socioeconomic background. He set himself apart by developing a style clearly grounded in the most disadvantaged social sectors of the country and focused on social issues of class, marginalization, political disempowerment, and barriers to economic opportunity.

Galvarino "Juan" Radrigán Rojas was born on 23 January 1937, in the northern desert city of Antofagasta, the child of Samuel Radrigán Lopez, an agricultural mechanic, and Blanca Rojas Liberona, a schoolteacher. His family's difficult financial situation required that the four children enter the labor force at an early age. His father left the family when Radrigán was six years old; his mother then moved the family to the capital city of Santiago. Neither Juan nor his brothers ever attended school; their basic education occurred at home under their mother's tutelage. By age twelve, Radrigán had developed a passion for reading that evolved into a penchant for writing stories and poems, none of which was ever published. As a young adult, he worked in a variety of industries and occupations: textile fabrication, shop assistant, street vendor, and box packer. Through his interests in reading and private study he developed skills that enabled him to assume a leadership position in the labor unions to which he belonged. He regards that experience as the first of two rites of passage prior to his genesis as a playwright. In an interview with Marina Pianca, he stated, "El otro paso sería cuando me casé. No hay nada entre medio más que trabajo, casi todo manual" (The second was when I got married. There is nothing between them other than work, almost all of it manual labor). Radrigán's wife is Josefina Araya Quiroga.

Radrigán's involvement with the theater began well into his adulthood. Prior to his dramatic writing, he published a book of short stories, *Los vencidos no creen en Dios* (1962, The Defeated Don't Believe in God), and two novels, *El vino de la cobardía* (1968, The Wine of Cowardice) and *Queda estrictamente prohibido o, La ronda de las manos ajenas* (1970, It Remains Strictly Prohibited or, Reel for the Empty-Handed) the latter written with poet Divel Mersán, none of which attracted much public attention. At the time of the 1973 coup that began the military regime, he was married and the father of two children. He was working in a textiles factory and serving as the president of his labor union. He lost his job in the aftermath of the coup; because of his long involvement with labor organization, he could not find a job in other industries after the government dismantled the bulk of the textile industry. Shortly thereafter, he began selling books to survive economically, liquidating the large personal library that he had amassed over the years. When director Gustavo Meza came to purchase some books from him, Radrigán offered Meza a play script that he had recently written, his first effort for the theater. Meza produced this first play, *Testimonio de las muertes de Sabina* (1980, Testimony on the Deaths of Sabina), that year in Santiago.

Most of Radrigán's plays require only the most simplistic sets and costuming, giving them a sparse, open feel and making them popular with groups that have few financial resources to spend on production. His use of naturalistic language based on working-class dialect–the very thing that sets Radrigán apart from his middle-class colleagues–can also prove difficult to understand, especially for readers and audience members without much exposure to the Chilean style of Spanish. In the majority of the works only the marginalized and oppressed characters actually appear on stage. Their oppressors–authority figures, government agencies and representatives, and other facets of the power structure–generally exist only in dialogue, in descriptions by the people on stage. Often, these oppressors have no names; the characters refer to a nameless "Him" or "Them" whose actions complicate their lives and steal their dignity.

Testimonio de las muertes de Sabina features an elderly couple, Sabina and Rafael, who sell fruit from a cart on the street. They struggle constantly for economic survival but have always managed to scrape by. A conversation between the two comprises the entire first act. It becomes clear that their life together has been hard, but that they care earnestly for one another in spite of their disappointments. Yet, Sabina still feels isolated because Rafael ignores or makes light of her troubles. As they set out the items for tea, she tries to tell him about a particularly painful dream but cannot hold his attention. At the end of the first act, Sabina tells Rafael that they have received a citation for their cart and must pay a fine. At the end of each act, they hear the sound of approaching footsteps. Each time, the sounds grow louder and more menacing as their situation grows more desperate and Sabina's anxiety increases.

In the second act, the couple has tried to pay the fine but cannot determine why it was assessed. The paper citation has disappeared, misplaced by one of the bureaucrats with whom they consulted. As no one knows which regulation they have broken, they cannot determine why or how much the couple should pay. Back in their apartment, Sabina frets over the possibility of losing the cart if they cannot pay the fine. She expresses her greatest fear: that she will die unnoticed and unremembered. She cries out, "¡Nadie me va'ir o va' hablar de mí; me voy a morir más que toda la gente! ¡Me voy a morir tanto cuando me muera!" (No one will go to see me or talk about me; I'm going to die more than anyone else! I'm going to die so much when I die!)

Sabina finally tells Rafael of her dream, in which she meets herself at a younger age, and both Sabinas grieve over her gradual descent in life. The potential loss of their livelihood brings her closer to death and to complete obliteration. In the third act, they have lost their cart for failing to pay the fine. Sabina feels destroyed, and in the ensuing argument between herself and Rafael, she decides that she cannot trust him to take care of her. Though he insists that they have not yet died and must not lose hope, Sabina indicates that the decision has killed her. The authorities have taken her livelihood, disregarded her humanity, and exposed her to indignity; now she has only to wait for physical death.

In some ways, the play was confusing to critics, who could not easily categorize it. The play offers much more dialogue than action, and though it includes a clear conflict and crisis, it has little dramatic progression. It deals overtly with problematic social issues but offers no solutions. It includes a negative depiction of authority, but the isolation and marginalization of the characters is as much psychological as economic. The concept of marginality as an emotional and ideological as well as economic state weaves throughout Radrigán's plays. *Testimonio de las muertes de Sabina* offered something new to Chilean audiences: a poetic and vernacular narrative of the working class from one of its own members. Its premiere created a fever of interest in the author and his work, enabling him to pursue playwriting more intensely. Over the next four years he wrote plays that were subsequently produced throughout Chile.

Cuestión de ubicación (A Question of Location), *Las brutas* (The Primitive Women), and *El loco y la triste* (The Crazy Man and the Sad Woman) were all performed in 1980. The first was a series of short episodes including a section co-authored with Meza, "¡Viva Somoza!" In it, a girl dies of hunger while her poverty-stricken family obsesses about where to put their new color television, for which they have just used all of their money. *Las brutas,* reminiscent of Anton Chekhov's *Three Sisters* (1901) in a local, proletariat setting, features three women bound together in boredom and misery, unable to escape the house in which they live. Their state of mutual codependence and inability to cope with the outside world ultimately leads them to self-destruct. The economic policies of the government and ruthless capitalist practices serve as the catalyst for their ruin. The sisters live together on a solitary homestead in the mountains, where they raise goats and make cheese for sale. When a trader comes bearing news about an "economic crisis," they discover that even this small livelihood may soon dissipate. Older siblings Justa and Lucia fear change; Luciana, the youngest, worries

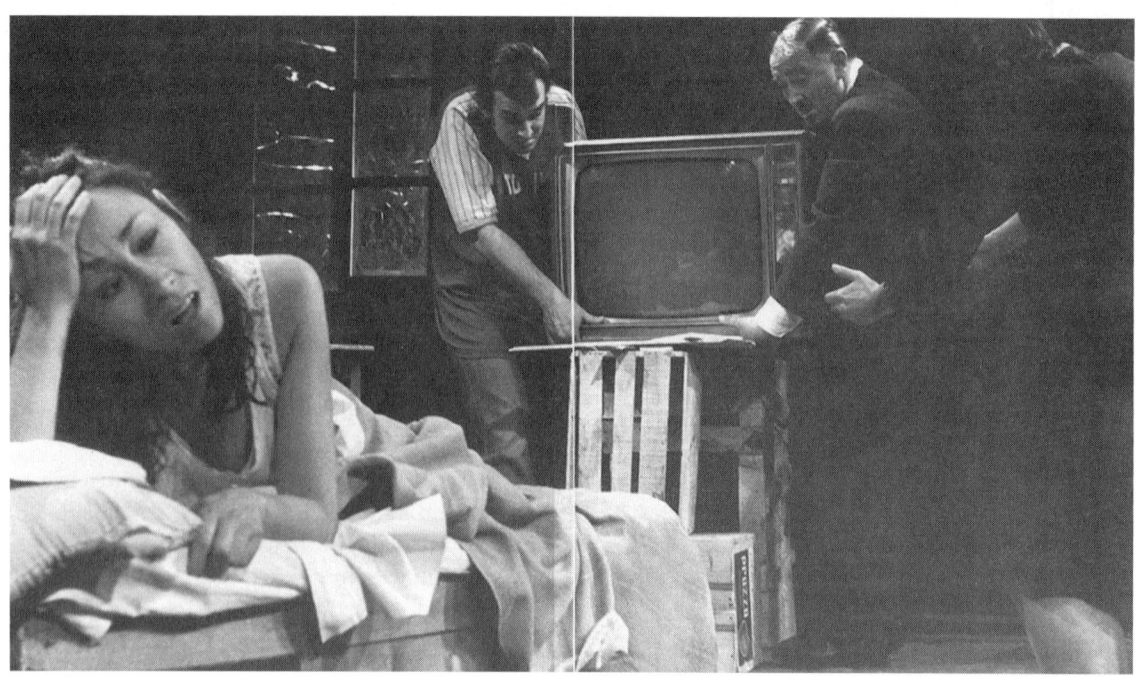

Scene from "¡Viva Somoza!" (Long Live Somoza!), a segment by Radrigán and director Gustavo Meza of Radrigán's play Cuestión de ubicación (1980, A Question of Location), in which a girl dies of hunger while her impoverished family argues over their new television (from María Teresa Zegers Nachbauer, 25 años de teatro en Chile, 1999; W. E. B. Du Bois Library, University of Massachusetts, Amherst)

about dying alone. Radrigán pointedly indicates that social problems and government actions can have far-reaching effects, especially for the poor. On hearing the news that the townspeople who buy their goods have neither money or work, Luciana asks, "¿Y porqué no hay trabajo? Los animales no han muerto, la tierra no ha secao" (And why is there no work? The animals haven't died; the earth hasn't dried up). Javier, the trader, replies, "Son cosas que vienen de la capital: cuando llueé allá los mojamos aquí" (These are things that come from the capital: when it rains there, we get wet here). Even their relationship with Javier depends upon trade rather than any real human contact. He no longer deals in the foodstuffs and supplies they need to survive in the mountains; instead, he brings frilly party clothes and cashmere sweaters that they do not need and cannot afford. When they refuse to buy them, he leaves, denying that he has the power to send other traders who can sell them the goods they need.

In *El loco y la triste,* a prostitute named Eva and a derelict named Huinca share a squalid room in a shantytown and try to build a friendship. Both have been badly mistreated by people and by life. Born with a clubfoot, Eva also struggles with alcoholism and cirrhosis. She remembers having a happy childhood in a stable home and receiving a good education. She knows that she has fallen far in the world. Huinca battles mental illness, suffers from claustrophobia, and fears he will be locked away. Initially they are thrown together in the plaza where Eva seeks clients by a collection of bullies who coerce her into spending the night with him. As they become acquainted, however, a tenderness grows between them. As they finally decide to remain together, construction machines show up to raze the abandoned shanties where they have been sheltering. Afraid to leave the room for fear of being arrested and put away, Huinca determines to stay and fall with the building. He slips into madness. Eva's need to evade loneliness proves stronger than her fear of death, and she chooses to stay with him. The fear of abandonment and obliteration runs through all three of these pieces, and the characters in each evince a strong need to be recognized as human beings. The violation of their rights preoccupies at least one figure in each play.

Also in 1980, Radrigán formed the theater group El Telón (The Curtain) with two actors who felt as he did that the theater was not currently serving certain sectors of the populace. He wrote two monologues, and the group began performing in various low-income neighborhoods. They based the bulk of their activities in the rapidly growing *poblaciones,* or shantytowns, that formed when large groups of laborers lost their employment. The two monologues were *Isabel desterrada en Isabel* (Isabel Exiled in Isabel) and *Sin motivo aparente* (With No Apparent Motive). These pieces, together with a dialogue called *El invitado* (The Guest), became Radrigán's next play, *Redoble fúnebre para lobos y corderos* (Funeral Knell for Wolves and Lambs), which appeared as a complete work in 1981.

In the first scenario of *Redoble fúnebre para lobos y corderos,* Isabel, a solitary woman, drinks and talks to a trash can, lamenting her state of loneliness and the loss of those she loved. A man named Pedro García stands before a large hole in the ground in the second scenario, brought there by an inexplicable compulsion to repeatedly visit a site of trauma. The third scenario features a couple whose home has been invaded by a silent, watching man who has ruined their marriage, their home, and their economic security; they are unable to understand or rid themselves of him. The three episodes relate directly to the emotional and social aftermath of the 1973 coup. Isabel has been abandoned and left begging, "Habla po, ¿qué no soí gente yo tambíen?" (Talk to me. Am I not a person, too?). Pedro García lives in constant terror that "they" will come to get him, or that he will fall into the hole. Sara and her husband, Pedro, ask the audience how they have learned to live with "El Invitado" in their own homes, or if he has ruined their lives, too.

In *Hechos consumados* (Burned Out, performed in 1982), Emilio and Marta camp next to a river on the land of a nameless textiles magnate. He has recently rescued her from drowning, and together they watch a constant stream of tired, disheveled people pass by. She tries to tell him about her past, but he wishes only to know what visions she had while close to death. As they talk, a strange, half-crazy old man passes by; he prophesies that Emilio might be close to his own death. Soon, the watchman Miguel finds them and insists that they move their position so that they are no longer on the textile factory land. The distance is only a few feet; however, feeling that he has already been robbed of too much dignity and independence, Emilio refuses. The two men have much in common: both have been oppressed and bullied by authorities, and both struggle to survive; however, Miguel has capitulated because he fears being without work. He responds to Emilio's stubbornness with a mixture of terror (that he will lose his job) and rage (because yet another person is disrespecting him), and he beats Emilio to death with a stick. His shout of indignation echoes Emilio's reasons for refusing to move: "No soy na basura" (I'm not trash).

Both *Redoble fúnebre para lobos y corderos* and *Hechos consumados* carry thematic parallels to *Testimonio de las muertes de Sabina:* the characters display a need to be remembered, a need to be respected. Marta and Isabel share Sabina's need to be heard and engaged in conversation and to remember the past. Pedro Garciá displays a similar terror of being erased or destroyed by the authorities. Moreover, both plays incorporate elements immediately cogent to the reality of Chile at that moment. *Redoble fúnebre para lobos y corderos* features three situations in which people have been victimized and displaced by recent social events precipitated by a powerful, dictatorial presence. They cannot go back to their former way of life, nor can they bear the current state of things, but they feel powerless to make any changes. *Hechos consumados* is also populated with individuals whose social and economic positions rapidly deteriorate and who face persecution from official channels. Marta ended up in the river because she witnessed two men dumping the body of a murder victim, and they needed to silence her quickly; Emilio dies at the hands of a peer who has internalized the oppressor. At the time when the two plays premiered, many audience members had seen rising homelessness, heard reports of dead bodies left in the street or dumped on the outskirts of the city, and struggled themselves to adjust to the constant military presence of the new government.

The group El Telón premiered *El toro por las astas* (Bull by the Horns) in 1982. The play features five employees of a brothel awaiting the arrival of the Milagrero, a man who can work miracles and change lives. In the first scene, the two prostitutes Jaque and Made hope that the Milagrero can redeem them and get them out of their current situation. The madam, Lucia, longs to see her political dissident son freed from prison; the pimp, Victor, wishes to return to a moment of his childhood when he was denied a chance to share in the meat of a family feast, an incident he claims has left him eternally hungry. They have sent the Milagrero a bribe to entice him to the brothel. Only the doorman, Antonio, who professes to walk through every open door life offers him, has no request for the anticipated visitor. All of them feel fearful and confused because of the violence and uncertainty of their environment. A war has been raging in the country, and they are unsure that it is over. The sounds of battle—gunfire, screaming, and bombs—reach them constantly. Yet, the newspapers declare that peace has been restored and all is well.

When the anticipated Milagrero finally arrives, they initially mistake him for a potential customer. Antonio, the only character who has no interest in his visit, recognizes him. The Milagrero states that he has come only to return the bribe, that he has been "freed" and can no longer perform miracles. Disbelieving, they ask him what has transpired. He explains that he was hired by El Hombrón (The Big Man, God) to perform small miracles and convince the people of the poor neighborhoods and shantytowns to accept their current situation. Before long, he became unable to bear the suffering he witnessed every day and his part in duping those to whom he ministered. He changed his message, exhorting the crowds to learn to see life as it is and fight together to make it better, not to fear physical death but the spiritual death that comes with capitulation. When they refused to listen, he quit the job in order to become a normal man once more. The brothel occupants do not comprehend at first; loath to surrender their dreams, they insist that he must help them, because it is unjust to leave them disillusioned. He insists that he cannot, and returns the money Lucia sent him. As they prepare to drink and dance away their misery, the Milagrero makes one last effort to free them, throwing open the door to the brothel. Though they can hear the noise of a military skirmish outside, he pleads with them to go out in the world. A stray bullet kills him, and Victor, Lucia, Jaque, and Made cower from the open door. Antonio, because he has no dreams or illusions to maintain, takes the opportunity to escape the brothel and go out into the world.

El toro por las astas dealt with many issues plaguing the more disadvantaged sectors of Chilean society: official declarations of peace belied by outbreaks of violence; disappeared and imprisoned activists; and benevolent organizations—both religious and social—that advocated passive acceptance of the current situation. The play touched a chord with audiences and critics. Additionally, it combined Radrigán's usual focus on dialogue with greater physical action, a move that dramatic critic Juan Andrés Piña praised in his October 1982 review for *Mensaje* (Message): "En el momento en que está vía verbal se combine con la acción, estaremos frente a un dramaturgo notable, camino hacia el cual marcha, seguramente, Juan Radrigán" (In the moment when this verbal route combines with action, we will have before us a notable playwright, the road on which Juan Radrigán is certainly traveling). In the same year, the Santiago-based Circle of Arts Critics organization awarded him their 1982 prize for theater, recognizing him as an unexpected force in Chilean theater. The proliferation and quality of his work particularly impressed them in a man with no prior theatrical experience and no formal education.

Informe para indiferentes (Information for the Indifferent, performed in 1983) features Andrés, another subjugated and ill-used man like Miguel of *Hechos consumados*. He is the garage attendant of a large mansion. From his usual seat, he can see the second-story bedroom of his employer through the window, and he lives in constant fear that the man might be watching, waiting for him to make a mistake. In the thirty years of his employment, his terror of losing the job has reduced him to near immobility; all day long he sits on a box and reads from a book of military history. Polo, a locksmith, comes to make an extra key, and the two men begin a conversation. Eventually Andrés reveals that his irrational fear of the boss has cost him his wife and children, his freedom, and his self-respect. Yet, the employer never actually communicates with Andrés in person; when he wants something, he sends a note. Andrés has saved an enormous number of these notes, which he occasionally takes out and reads. During the conversation, Andrés continually loses his thread of concentration, speaking to Polo as if he were someone familiar, oblivious to the visitor's growing pity and contempt. The extent of the man's mental and physical degradation becomes increasingly clear. As a self-defense mechanism, he has learned to forget unpleasant things at will. Throughout the play Andrés insists that he wanted only what everyone deserves: love, family ties, and the right to work. He does not see that he has deprived himself of them by allowing this mysterious employer to dominate his life. When Polo finally leaves him, he has returned to his original seat on the box and is once again reading his book, oblivious to Polo. As with earlier plays, the central character displays a preoccupation with memory and interpersonal relationships, struggles with a loss of dignity and self-respect, and has been damaged and deprived by an unseen oppressor with nearly omnipotent power.

Also in 1983, El Telón received an invitation to participate at the theater festival of Nancy, France. While in Europe, they toured nine countries in total, presenting *Hechos consumados* and *El toro por las astas*. During the nine-month tour, the group members avoided hotels, staying exclusively in the homes of Chilean exiles located in each country. The contact with their displaced countrymen deeply affected Radrigán and the other members of El Telón, and they began considering the possibility of a production that would address the anguish of exile. When they returned to Chile, the group began dividing their time between performing in neighborhoods and in traditional theater venues. All members, including Radrigán, worked solely in theater at this time, as he explained to Pianca in a 1991 interview, "por un lado porque no hay trabajo, y por otro porque este es nuestro trabajo" (on one hand because there is no work, on the other because this is our work).

In 1984 El Telón mounted *Las voces de ira* (The Voices of Rage), inspired by their contact with the Chilean exile community. It features a uniformed dictator as the central character and deals with issues of exile, disappearance, and torture. It was their only production to that date that provoked an official response, and the government acted quickly to crush the show. Authorities refused to allow the group to put up posters or run advertisements in publications. Journalists could not write about the show, nor could critics review it for the newspapers. Because the group had built a set for the production, something they normally avoided, they could not move around and give performances in the neighborhoods or without advance planning. Unable to draw an audience, the show closed quickly.

Made in Chile, Radrigán's first effort at satire, appeared in 1985. (Only the title is in English.) It dealt with social issues of the moment in Chile in a tragicomic style, using elements of *costumbrismo,* folkloric or local flavor. In it, a group of people goes to the complaint department of a Chilean organization, which also houses a "personality development" office, to voice their criticisms. The style is darkly comic and overtly political. A movie version of *Hechos consumados* (with screenplay by Chilean director Luis R. Vera) opened in 1986, but it also received little public notice and soon left the cinemas. Also in 1985, El Telón took *El loco y la triste* to three theater festivals: Festival Latino in New York, Festival Latinoamericano de Teatro in Mexico, and the V Festival de Teatro de Manizales in Colombia.

The theater department of the Universidad Católica produced Radrigán's next play, *Pueblo del mal amor* (The Village of Bad Love), in 1986. Radrigán first proposed the script to directing professor Raúl Osorio in 1984; the school eagerly accepted the invitation. Together, they proceeded to conduct a yearlong workshop in which Radrigán rewrote and expanded the play. Radrigán creates a world parallel to the Old Testament story of Moses and the flight from Egypt, in which the Children of Israel spent forty years wandering the desert as a punishment from God. The central characters are seventeen villagers who have been expelled from their homes by military oppressors. The authorities loaded the group into trucks and promised to take them to a new town; the trucks stopped in a desolate spot, and the authorities announced that they had arrived at their destination. Now, led by Moisés and David (Moses and David), the villagers wander through a desert looking for a new home. As the action progresses, several of the exiles come to believe that all are actually dead, having been massacred prior to the opening scene. Their wandering is a result of having been forgotten by God; their souls have nowhere else to go. One character tries, over the course of the dramatic action, to piece together what happened on the day of their banishment and who they really are. The theme of death and disappearance played an important role in the socially engaged theater of the decade. Radrigán touched on it in *El toro por las astas,* from the perspective of the mother of a *desaparecido,* a disappeared person. In *Pueblo del mal amor* he confronts the issues as the primary victims experience them. The characters question how they will be remembered by the living, if at all, and how they are to define themselves in the middle of limbo. Ultimately, the play offers no answers to these questions, and no hope of finding any. Yet, the characters refuse to stop searching. The production had a successful, well-attended run and gave Radrigán access to a wider audience base than his own group had previously reached. The budget and design capabilities of the university also permitted more elaborate staging with expanded design elements in set, lighting, and costume.

El Telón produced *Los borrachos de luna* (Moondrunk) in 1986. It adhered more closely to Radrigán's established style, heavily emphasizing the dialogue between three characters and requiring only a sparse set and costumes. It builds on the themes of poverty, loneliness, despair, dehumanization, and oppression that have concerned him from the beginning. María and José share a run-down room in a shantytown; they have developed a relationship that is without feeling or intimacy but offers both functionality and stability. She makes a meager living by entertaining men with dancing and drink; he is a repairman and jack-of-all-trades. Both live an existence full of secrets and isolated from other human beings. Because of their fear of punishment, both have emotionally and intellectually disconnected themselves from life. The arrival of a visitor, however, forces them to reexamine their individual situations and attitudes.

Afuerino (Outsider) is a fugitive, running from the authorities that he knows wish to kill him for some unspecified reason. As the evening progresses, an airplane repeatedly flies over the shantytown dropping leaflets that read only "Es estrictamente prohibido" (It is strictly prohibited), a constant reminder of past and present oppression. Afuerino forces María and José to deal with the difficult memories of their own experiences of abuse. Speaking from his own experience of victimization, he encourages the two to awaken from their spiritual torpor and fight against the injustices that have paralyzed them, to take back their lives. After Afuerino leaves them, José and María go outside, braving the danger of the plane and being out after curfew, to admire the moon. At last, they are able to open up and share with one another the horrors of the past. Radrigán uses the character of María to deal directly with the horror of detainment and torture experienced by *desaparecidos.* She describes a scene in which she and her lover meet again for the first time after their detainment. He stands in the doorway to her apartment, and they stare at one another silently, unable to move or speak. María describes being frozen, unable to feel any joy or sorrow at his return: "la injusticia los había puesto lejos de todas las cosas, los había dejao tan destruíos por dentro" (the injustice had pushed us so far from everything, had left us so destroyed inside). The confessions María and José make to one another serve as an exorcism of their fear and paralysis. Sharing the moonlight and their pain does not solve any of their problems but leaves them emotionally ready to try and pick up the pieces of their lives.

In 1987 Radrigán increased his political activity as he participated in public protests against sweeping death threats made to members of the artistic community that year. During 1988, Radrigán and El Telón made their second tour of Europe, traveling for the bulk of that year with their latest play, *La contenida humana* (Human Strife). The show opened in Santiago in October of 1988. It focuses on a playwright named Eladio who has devised a series of games as a means to avoid a difficult and painful responsibility. As a socialist and former left-wing activist, he has faced and continues to experience persecution from the government. His wife is still imprisoned, and he is packing a suitcase of her belongings to deliver to the prison where she is being held. As he prepares the items for a delivery that he has no real intention of making, Eladio engages in a series of dramatic amusements with a dummy, played by a live actor. The puppet is his alter ego who continually tries to remind him of the past and his current obligations. It loses patience with the little diversions that Eladio invents—word plays, sketches, stories—to avoid talking about his trauma or his current guilt for refusing to visit his wife. The dummy takes on different personas to confront the playwright about his faithlessness and his fear of memory. Eventually Eladio stages an "assassination" of the dummy to silence him. As the play ends, he builds a new puppet to begin the series of games again. Yet, he acknowledges the emptiness of his defense mechanisms and his responsibility to be available to his wife and assist her in the midst of her suffering.

Radrigán worked with German director Stephan Stroux in 1989 to produce *Balada de los condenados a soñar* (Ballad of Those Condemned to Dream). The same year, he also participated in a theater workshop sponsored by the Instituto Chileno Francés de Cultura (French-Chilean Institute of Culture) to celebrate the bicentennial of the French Revolution. The event, in which a French director and lighting designer joined Chilean actors, produced *Como un río de leones* (Like a River of Lions) in the city of Concepción. This play relates the story of a French actor who travels to Chile in order to produce Marie-Joseph Chénier's play *Charles IX* (1789) in a fishing village and encounters resistance from the locals.

Radrigán's next play was also produced initially in Concepción. *Piedra de escándalo* (1990, Bone of Contention) addresses AIDS from the perspective of five mentally ill characters. It deals with the unspoken social norm of hiding and ostracizing the sick as well as the marginality that comes with long-term or life-threatening infirmity, experienced even within a person's own family.

Radrigán wrote the play at the request of the Center for Education and Prevention in the Social Health division of the Chilean Ministry of Health.

Islas del porfiado amor (Islands of Stubborn Love, performed in 1994) revisits several themes and dramatic devices of Radrigán's past. Two abandoned souls, Diego and Micaela, wander through a desert populated by ghosts. They wait for a train that never arrives, talking to the spirits that occasionally appear to evoke their more elegant past. The two characters have no established destination or any pattern to their wanderings, only the sense that they are doing penance for something.

The play *El encuentramiento* (The Duel; published in 1995, performed in 1996) was a radical departure from Radrigán's normal style. An opera staged in a discotheque and directed by Willy Semler, the two-act production featured elaborate costumes and scenic elements. The first act takes place in colonial Chile, with an impending duel between the Spaniard Javier de la Rosa and the Mapuche rebel Mulato Taguada, leader of the indigenous insurrection. Both characters have been manipulated into a skirmish by the landowner Tomás de Miranda, who wishes to eliminate both. He wants to seduce the wife of the former and wishes to put down the rebellion of the latter. The second act occurs two hundred years later, in a bar near the same location, where the locals invoke the spirits of the dead contestants to reenact the duel. Unlike any of Radrigán's previous plays, *El encuentramiento* actually places the oppressor on stage with the oppressed, in the guise of the Spaniard. Through de la Rosa, Radrigán examines the possessors of power and their doubts, guilt, and musings on their own practices, and how members of a power-holding class can be marginalized and victimized from within.

During the same period, Radrigán began to expand his role in the Chilean theater, directing some of his own plays and advocating for artistic development and integrity. He has expressed particular concern with the manner in which performances address (or avoid) the issues that face society and how art represents Chile to the rest of the world. In 1998 an annual theater festival that carries his name began; as part of it he gives a playwriting workshop that culminates in production for the works of all the participants. The workshop and festival occur during January and February of each year.

Perra Celestial (Heavenly Bitch, performed in 1999) returned to the two-actor, dialogue-heavy format that Radrigán initially employed, with the added effect of a capella singing. Critic Pedro Labra, writing for *El Mercurio* (7 May 1999), compared this play favorably to Samuel Beckett's *Waiting for Godot* (1952). In addition to themes common to his work, Radrigán also added the marginality of homosexuality and a strong sense of anticlericalism to the play.

Medea Mapuche (performed in 2000) retells the story of the Greek antiheroine within the culture of Chile's indigenous Mapuche people. It premiered in Santiago in June 2000, though an earlier version ran in 1999 in the northern town of Tocopilla. In Radrigán's version of the tale, the central character, Kutral, is a Mapuche woman whose husband has been sent to parley with the Spaniards. They capture him; his family intends to watch the execution, but she refuses. To Kutral, all contact with the Spaniards signifies a betrayal of her people. Evil spirits consult with her, and she decides that parricide will make the best vengeance. Portions of the dialogue occur in the Mapuche language, Mapudungun. For Radrigán, the Medea myth translated well to a Mapuche-centered narrative, as he explained in a 22 May 2000 interview in *La Segunda,* "especialmente en aquel aspecto indomable de amor por la tierra y por la libertad, que les llevaba a sacrificar lo más querido frente a cualquier invasión" (especially in that aspect of untamable love for the earth and for liberty, which made them sacrifice even what they most loved before any invasion). However, Radrigán did not intend the play to create any kind of solidarity with the contemporary Mapuche tribes of Chile, nor did he presume any identification between himself and them.

Comments made by Radrigán stirred some controversy within the Chilean theater community that same year. In a 6 August 2000 *La Tercera* interview with theater critic Leopoldo Pulgar, the playwright indicated that he believes Chilean theater—especially its playwriting—lacks transcendence and international significance. He accused playwrights of seeking public attention and press coverage instead of concentrating on quality of content. Moreover, he insisted that "ninguna obra teatral chilena es parte del repertorio mundial y no son montadas por grupos de otro países como ocurre con *La cantante calva, La muerte del vendedor viajero,* o *La nona*" (No Chilean work of theater is part of the global repertory nor are they produced by groups from other countries in the manner of [Eugène Ionesco's] *The Bald Soprano* [1949], [Arthur Miller's] *Death of a Salesman* [1949], or [Roberto Cossa's] *La nona* [1977]). The root of the problem stems from social attitudes adopted following the coup, he indicated, because people too easily accepted the passive attitude and cultural norms dictated by the military regime. He called the work of younger authors "belleza vacía" (vacuous beauty) and the classics "bien enanos" (stunted).

A second article followed on 8 August, in which Radrigán's theatrical peers—including Marco Antonio de la Parra, Isidora Aguirre, Benjamin Galamiri, and

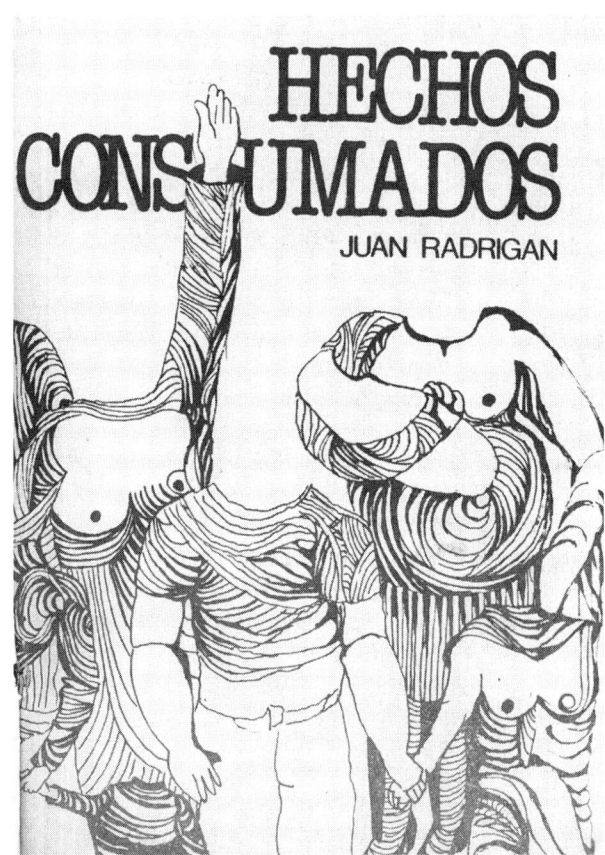

Cover for Radrigán's 1982 play (Burned Out), in which an oppressed watchman beats a homeless man to death for refusing to move off a textile magnate's property (Davis Library, University of North Carolina, Chapel Hill)

Ramón Griffero—responded with strong arguments to the contrary. They particularly stressed that his commentary troubled them because of his contributions, longevity, and stature within the dramatic community. Galamiri described Radrigán as "como un buen padre chileno, es muy severo y autoritario y se le pasó la mano en su crítica" (like a good Chilean father, he is very severe and authoritarian and went a little overboard in his criticism). Nevertheless, Radrigán held fast to his viewpoint, stating in a 22 December interview of the same year, "Aquí la dramaturgia es muy escasa y somos generalmente muy malos, muy mediocres. Hay gente que se enoja mucho cuando digo que no hay ninguna obra chilena capaz de trascender, ninguna que vaya a ser del repertorio universal, pero es la verdad" (Playwriting here is very meager and we are generally very bad, very mediocre. There are people who get very angry when I say that there is no Chilean play capable of transcendence, none that could be part of the universal repertory, but it is the truth). He includes his own work in that category, calling it too "local" to be of interest in the broader arena.

Together with the actors Jorge Larrañaga and Sandra Lema (the 1999 cast of *Perra Celestial*), Radrigán founded a new company in 2001, La Inesperanza (Unhope). In March of the same year, they debuted Radrigán's latest work, *El exilio de la mujer desnuda* (Exile of a Naked Woman), which Radrigán also directed. It tells the story of a woman who feels that her existence only has meaning and validity when she is naked. On her body she bears the scars of lifelong mistreatment. Because she wishes to be naked at all times, including in public, well-meaning people begin to offer her clothing to cover herself. She takes refuge in the house of a writer, a man who has a terrible case of writer's block. Eventually, her nakedness becomes troubling to the authorities, and she receives shipments of clothing from organizations such as the church and the armed forces. In various interviews the playwright has described the woman as symbolic of truth or beauty, which society seeks to suppress, and the play as being about the frustration and futility of language to make an impact on people.

In the middle of the one-act show, the actors drop character, becoming themselves and delivering lines based on autobiographical material. Both use their experiences in the Chilean workforce, she as a food vendor, and he as a real estate agent. "Lo que ellos muestran, finalmente, es el desengaño y la insatisfacción de no poder vivir de su trabajo" (What they show, in the end, is the disillusionment and dissatisfaction of not being able to live [economically] from their work).

Radrigán's identity as a playwright rests largely on his reputation as a voice for the voiceless and as a faithful representative of the working class. He manages to combine writing in their earthy vernacular with lyricism and compelling characters. Moreover, he deals with the problems of marginality from multiple perspectives, looking at social, spiritual, and psychological roots of isolation and victimization. Radrigán became a powerful voice in the Chilean theater because his perspective was as original as his writing was skillful. As he has grown as a playwright, Radrigán has continued to present life on the margins, expanding his viewpoint to include sectors of the populace that have remained largely invisible—including homosexuals, those living with HIV and other chronic illnesses, and indigenous peoples. He has also become an unapologetic critic of his own theater community, arguing for greater reflection and responsibility in play making, and refusing to accept artistic or sociopolitical mediocrity from his colleagues or himself. As he said in a 14 March 2001 interview in *El Mercurio*, "Insisto hasta que descubro que, en realidad, la única posibilidad de rebeldía humana es la negación de todo, incluso de toda posibilidad de reconciliación conmigo y con el mundo" (I persist until I discover that, in reality, the only possibility for human rebellion is the negation of everything, including any possibility of reconciliation with myself and with the world).

Interviews:

Marina Pianca, "Juan Radrigán," in *Testimonios de teatro Latinoamericano* (Buenos Aires: Grupo Editor Latinoamericano, 1991), pp. 183–196;

Javier Ibacache, "Radrigán estrena 'Medea Mapuche' con pasajes en mapudungun," *La Segunda,* 22 May 2000;

Leopoldo Pulgar I., "El teatro chileno no tiene trascendencia," *La Tercera,* 6 August 2000;

Pulgar I., "Dramaturgos responden a críticas de Radrigán," *La Tercera,* 8 August 2000;

Veronica Marinao, "El dramaturgo desnudo," *El Mercurio,* 22 December 2000, pp. 26, 28;

"Radrigán: Las palabras ya no significan mucho," *El Mercurio,* 14 March 2001.

References:

Catherine Boyle, "From Resistance to Revelation: The Contemporary Theatre in Chile," *New Theatre Quarterly,* 4 (August 1998): 209–222;

Enzo Cozzi, "Political Theatre in Present-Day Chile: A Duality of Approaches," *New Theatre Quarterly,* 6 (May 1990): 119–127;

Maria de la Luz Hurtado, *Memorias teatrales: El teatro de la Universidad Católica en su Cincuentenario* (Santiago, Chile: Apuntes, 1993);

Marietta Santi, "Discípulos de Radrigán muestran su trabajo," *Las Ultimas Noticias,* 18 January 2000;

María Teresa Zegers Nachbauer, *25 años de teatro en Chile* (Santiago: Ministerio de Educación, 1999).

Víctor Hugo Rascón Banda
(6 August 1948 -)

José F. Blanco
Florida State University

PLAY PRODUCTIONS: *Nolens Volens,* Mexico City, UNAM College of Law, 1974;

Las fuentes del derecho, Mexico City, UNAM College of Law, 1975;

De lo que aconteció a Litigonio y a su esposa Prudencia con Fraudonio, Mexico City, UNAM College of Law, 1976;

Los ilegales, Mexico City, Teatro Flores Magón, July 1979;

El baile de los montañeses, Mexico City, Teatro Juan Ruíz de Alarcón, 1982;

Armas blancas, Mexico City, UNAM, 1982;

Tina Modotti, Mexico City, Teatro Juan Ruíz de Alarcón, 1983;

Voces en el umbral, Universidad Autónoma de Chihuahua, 1984; performed as *La casa del español,* 1993;

¡Manos arriba! Mexico City, Teatro Independencia, 1984;

La fiera del Ajusco, Mexico City, Teatro Santa Catarina, 1985;

Máscara contra cabellera, Veracruz, Universidad Veracruzana, 1985;

¡Cierren las puertas! Veracruz, Universidad Veracruzana, 1988;

Querido Diego, te abraza quiela, from Elena Poniatowska's book, Mexico City, Casa Estudio Diego Rivera, 1988;

Playa Azul, Mexico City, Teatro Benito Juárez, August 1989;

Elena mil veces, vida y obra de Elena Poniatowska, 1990;

Luces de Therminor, Mexico City, UNAM, 1990;

Contrabando, Mexico City, Teatro Benito Juárez, 1991;

Fugitivos, Mexico City, Teatro Coyoacán, 1992;

Alucinada, Mexico City, Teatro Santa Catalina, 1992;

Días de feria, Banca Cremi, 1992;

El caso Santos, Texas, Teatro Dallas, 1993;

Sabor de engaño, Mexico City, Foro Sor Juana Inés de la Cruz, 1993;

Homicidio calificado, Mexico City, Teatro Julio Castillo, 1994;

Veracruz, Veracruz, Veracruz, Sala Chica de Jalapa, 1995;

Víctor Hugo Rascón Banda (*photograph by Ana Lourdes Herrera; from the cover for* La Malinche, *2000; Thomas Cooper Library, University of South Carolina*)

Por los caminos del sur, Mexico City, UNAM, 1996;

La banca, Mexico City, Teatro Juan Ruíz de Alarcón, 1997;

La Malinche, Veracruz, Teatro Jiménez Rueda, 1998;

La mujer que cayó del cielo, Mexico City, Teatro Museo del Carmen, 1999;

Sazón de mujer, Teatro El Galeón, 2003; translated as *A Taste for Living,* Tucson, Arizona, Borderlands Theater, 18 March 2004.

BOOKS: *Los ilegales* (Mexico City: Universidad Autónoma Metropolitana, 1980);

El baile de los montañeses, as Víctor H. Rascón (Toluca, Mexico: Universidad Autónoma del Estado de México, 1982);

Voces en el umbral (Mexico City: Universidad Autónoma Metropolitana, 1983);

Teatro del delito (Mexico City: Editores Mexicanos Unidos, 1985)–comprises *¡Manos arriba!, La fiera del ajusco,* and *Máscara contra cabellera;*

Tina Modotti y otras obras de teatro (Mexico City: Secretaría de Educación Pública, 1986)–comprises *Tina Modotti, Voces en el umbral,* and *Playa Azul;*

Guerrero negro y ¡Cierren las puertas! (Mexico City: Obra Citada, 1988);

La banca (Mexico City: Obra Citada, 1988);

Las armas blancas (Mexico City: Universidad Autónoma Metropolitana, 1990)–comprises *El machete, La navaja, La daga,* and *El abrecartas;*

De cuerpo entero (Mexico City: UNAM/Corunda, 1990);

Sabor de engaño (Mexico City: Sociedad General de Escritores Mexicanos, 1992);

Días de feria, by Rascón Banda, Luis Mario Schneider, and Alberto Ruy Sánchez (Mexico City: Cremi Grupo Financiero, 1992);

Contrabando [play] (Mexico City: El Milagro, 1993);

Contrabando [novel] (Mexico City: Corunda, 1993);

La banda (Mexico City: Plaza y Valdés, 1994);

¡Manos arriba!; Sabor de engaño; La banca (Mexico City: Grupo Editorial Gaceta, 1994);

Playa Azul [screenplay] (Mexico City: Plaza y Valdés, 1995);

Volver a Santa Rosa (Mexico City: Joaquín Mortiz, 1996);

Escenario del crimen (Mexico City: Instituto de Seguridad y Servicios Sociales de los Trabajadores del Estado, 1999)–comprises *Guerrero negro* and *Fugitivos;*

La Malinche (Mexico City: Plaza y Janés, 2000);

La mujer que cayó del cielo (Mexico City: Escenología, A.C., 2000);

Sazón de mujer; Table Dance (Tijuana: CAEN, 2001);

Los ejecutivos (Mexico City: El Milagro, 2002);

Ahora y en la hora (Mexico City: UNAM, 2003);

Homicidio calificado: El ausente (Mexico City: Editores Mexicanos Unidos, 2003).

Edition in English: *Blue Beach,* translated by Myra S. Gann, in *Azcárate, Rascón, Urtusástegui,* Contemporary Mexican Drama in Translation, 1 (Potsdam, N.Y.: Danzón, 1994), pp. 53–98.

PRODUCED SCRIPTS: *Días difíciles,* by Rascón Banda and Alejandro Pelayo, motion picture, Tabasco Films/IMCINE, 1987;

Morir en el golfo, by Rascón Banda and Pelayo, from Héctor Aguilar Camín's novel, motion picture, Tabasco Films/IMCINE, 1990;

El hijo del Santo en el poder de omnicrón, motion picture, Alfredo Acevedo Bueno, 1991;

Playa Azul, motion picture, IMCINE, 1991.

OTHER: *El nuevo teatro,* 2 volumes, edited by Rascón Banda (Mexico City: El Milagro, 1997, 2000);

La ciudad en el teatro, edited by Rascón Banda (Mexico City: Casa Juan Pablos, 2002).

SELECTED PERIODICAL PUBLICATION–UNCOLLECTED: "El teatro impreso: Recuerdos de Tomás Espinosa," *Tramoya: Cuaderno de Teatro,* 39 (1994): 135–139.

Víctor Hugo Rascón Banda is one of the leading Mexican playwrights of the last quarter of the twentieth century. His theater examines Mexican society and history with seriousness and harshness, exploring major concerns such as political corruption, drug trafficking, migration to the United States of America, flaws in the Mexican legal system, and the life of the disadvantaged classes. Rascón Banda's dramatic styles are as diverse as his topics, partly because of his creative appropriation of different genres of popular culture. In plays such as *Máscara contra cabellera* (Mask Versus Mane, performed in 1985) and *¡Cierren las puertas!* (Shut the Doors! performed in 1988), for example, Rascón Banda uses well-known Mexican traditions such as wrestling and cockfighting to narrate his stories. The final written product has often been achieved through collaboration with established directors and theater groups, making Rascón Banda one of the playwrights most sought after by collaborative-creation teams.

Rascón Banda was born on 6 August 1948 in Uruáchic, a small mining town in the state of Chihuahua. His mother, Rafaela Banda de Rascón, assisted her husband in his duties as agent for the Ministerio Público (a government agency for crime control). Rascón Banda graduated with a degree in language and literature from Escuela Normal Superior José Medrano (José Medrano High School). In 1974 he moved to Mexico City to pursue law studies at the Universidad Nacional Autónoma de México (UNAM). Since his graduation, he has divided his time between his profession as a lawyer and his career as a playwright. Furthermore, he has managed to bring both careers together by writing plays such as *Las fuentes del derecho* (The Source of Law, performed in 1975) and *La fiera del Ajusco* (The Beast from Ajusco, performed in 1985) that address the Mexican legal system.

Rascón Banda's training in theater began in the mid 1970s, when he registered as a participant in Vicente Leñero's playwriting workshop at the Centro de Arte Dramático (CADAC). He also studied playwriting with Hugo Argüelles and pursued directing studies with

Héctor Azar. His early plays are set in an environment resembling his hometown in northern Mexico and are related to the concerns of a young law student. Between 1974 and 1976, he wrote a series of didactic plays in which he explores the Mexican legal system. *Nolens Volens* and *Las fuentes del derecho* are both dramatic versions of *Teoría del proceso* (1974; Process Theory), a law textbook written by Cipriano Gómez Lara. Another of Rascón Banda's early playwriting efforts is *De lo que aconteció a Litigonio y a su esposa Prudencia con Fraudonio* (About What Happened to Litigonio and His Wife Prudencia with Fraudonio), a collection of seven cases from the Roman Law casebook used at UNAM, performed by a group of students at the university in 1976. The names in the title reflect the dispositions of the characters and the roles they play in the story. Fraudonio, a trickster, attempts to involve the other characters in a fraud. Prudencia, the prudent one, warns her husband against Fraudonio. Litigonio uses his knowledge of the law in his defense.

For his next group of plays, Rascón Banda turned to the concerns and stories of the people in the mountain towns of his native Chihuahua. His first major play in this vein, *Los ilegales* (The Illegals), opened at Teatro Ricardo Flores Magón in July 1979 and was directed by Marta Luna. The work is dedicated to the large number of Mexican nationals who risk their lives by illegal immigration to the United States. These people, according to Rascón Banda, do not leave Mexico only in search of a better economic situation but also because they believe in the great promise of a more fulfilling spiritual and moral life.

The episodic plotline follows a group of immigrants from their poverty-stricken Mexican town to the misery they find once they cross the border. The Brechtian structure of the play includes the use of the Informante (Informer) as a narrator who links the stories together, as well as several songs addressed directly to the audience. The original published text uses material and current news from *Revista Proceso,* the *Wall Street Journal,* and *Revista Foro Internacional* in order to introduce and provide a context for each of the episodes. In his introduction the author encourages groups to update these texts to keep the story freshly concerned with current immigration issues. The suggested set background is simply an enormous bridge dividing both countries and a wire fence that separates the actors and the audience, becoming taller as the play progresses.

The first group of scenes is set in Ciudad Juarez, Mexico, and introduces the protagonists: Jesús, José, and Juan. Each of them will leave Mexico for reasons that range from financial to personal concerns. Once the characters cross to the other side (in this case El

Ignacio Retes as Don Matías in the 1989 Teatro Benito Juárez premiere of Rascón Banda's Playa Azul *(Blue Beach, published in 1986), in which a family reunites at their run-down hotel but cannot escape the corruption and secrets that ruin them (photograph by Fernando Moguel; from Vicente Leñero, ed.,* La nueva dramaturgia mexicana, *1996; Jean and Alexander Heard Library, Vanderbilt University)*

Paso, Texas) the author depicts their misfortunes. They are abused both by the "coyotes" (Mexican men who make a living from human trafficking across the border) and the border patrol. The scenes also include conflicts with a boss who uses illegal workers in his fields and then turns them over to the American immigration authorities, and with Protestant preachers who try to change the religion and culture of the recent immigrants. The most poignant depiction of the immigrant's destiny in the new country is a scene in which Jesús is tortured and murdered by members of the Ku Klux Klan. Jesús, with an obviously symbolic name, is the first of many characters in the author's work who become victims of social injustice.

His next text, *La maestra Teresa* (Teresa, The Teacher), was awarded the Premio Nacional de Teatro Ramón López Velarde, offered by the Government of Zacatecas, in 1979. The play was never produced or published; the original manuscript is lost, and a reward has been offered to anyone who finds it. In this play Rascón Banda examines corruption in the educational system. His thesis is that the current educational setting discourages students from thinking independently. For the first time, the author looks at history and utilizes a story from the past to illustrate his discussion of current events. Teresa, a teacher in a small mountain town, faces the possibility of being removed from her post because of her use of "revolutionary and nontraditional" teaching methods that include readings of Santa Teresa's sixteenth-century mystical poetry. In the flashback scenes, the famous Catholic nun and scholar Santa Teresa de Jesús is depicted as a mentor to two of the younger nuns at her convent. The author brings both stories together by establishing several points of connection between the perils and ideas of both Teresas. At the end, however, both stories are truly combined when Teresa, the teacher, fully assumes the personality of the saint and denounces the corrupt procedures of the school administration.

Tina Modotti, produced as a workshop collaboration with the theater group at UNAM, won the Premio Latinoamericano de Teatro in 1983 and was published in 1986. The play is composed of twenty-eight scenes depicting the life of the famous model and photographer-turned-revolutionary. The essential message of the play is not a political one. Rather, the author mainly narrates events and adventures in Modotti's life without addressing details of her communist ideology.

Rascón Banda's first incursion into the potential of rebellion from the popular sectors comes with his next play, a tale of government abuse set once again in a small mountain town in northern Mexico. *El baile de los montañeses* (The Dance of the Mountain Folks), produced at UNAM in 1982, essentially presents a simple tale of good versus evil while advocating community organization to face the challenges of abusive institutions. Government officials known by the townspeople as the *mala hierba* (bad weed) organize a celebration in which the citizens are forced at gunpoint to dance non-stop while following offensive and derogatory instructions. Eventually the abuse reaches unspeakable levels, and the people organize to fight this form of social violence. The author explores a similar concern in a series of four short plays under the title of *Armas blancas* (White Weapons, performed in 1982). In these cases the abuse of power, usually by one of the male characters, generates a tragic murder. Each play bears the name of one of the weapons used to commit a murder: a machete, a knife, a letter opener, and a dagger. The show was first produced under the direction of Julio Castillo at UNAM.

Voces en el umbral (Voices From the Threshold) is one of Rascón Banda's better-known plays. It was first produced in 1984 at the Universidad Autónoma in Chihuahua; in 1993 it was produced under the title *La casa del español* (The House of the Spaniard). The text has been translated into several languages and performed all over the world. The play is usually seen as a metaphor for Mexican history influenced by the Latin American literary tradition of *realismo mágico* (magic realism). The story, set in an abandoned mining town in the mountains of Chihuahua, is based on real events narrated to Rascón Banda as a child. The townspeople would often relate the turn-of-the-century story of two women of different social classes who died together in bed, but whose bodies remained undiscovered for several months. Rascón Banda examines the development of the relationship between the two women and uses it as a framework to expose racial discrimination and the abuse of the working classes in Mexican history. In his play, Valeria is the daughter of a wealthy German miner. Her family and other characters from the upper class symbolize the Porfirian oligarchy in control of Mexico at the time. Her slave, Marciala, is a Tarahumara Indian purchased by Valeria's father as a companion for her.

The play, in addition to having a political message, is a coming-of-age story: Valeria falls in love with one of her father's miners, and with Marciala's assistance, she carries on a forbidden affair with him. When Valeria discovers she is pregnant by this man, who is much below her class, she opts to have an abortion. In a fit of rage, her father confronts and alienates both Valeria and her servant. The last part of the story is set against the backdrop of an uprising by the mine workers. Unable and unwilling to comply with their demands, Valeria's father loses control of the mine, which is eventually blown up and destroyed. All the members of the family die during the conflict except Valeria and Marciala, who tell the story through flashbacks and reflections on their past.

¡Manos arriba! (Hands Up! performed in 1984), labeled by the author as a *juguete cómico* (comic interlude), is Rascón Banda's first incursion in the world of farce. Produced in Mexico City at Teatro Independencia with the famous actors Hector Bonilla and María Rojo, the play was directed by Rafael Sandoval. The story is a domestic drama taking place entirely in a small apartment and portraying the everyday life of Salvador and María, a lower-middle-class couple struggling to make a living in contemporary Mexico. María, who works at home as a typesetter, is obsessed with the

possible repercussions of ignoring chain mail and thus spends an inordinate amount of time typing such letters. She is also distracted by constant visits from her friend Ana Ofelia, a woman infatuated with the self-help literature of Og Mandino, Gail Sheeley, and Robert Conklin. Ana Ofelia also participates in and promotes small-business opportunities, many of which are almost certainly scams. She provides a bridge between the action in the family's apartment and the outside world, since she actively pursues current events and the latest news, often speculating on issues such as drug trafficking and bank-account management. The fourth character is Marcos, a college student who rents a room from the family. A self-declared Marxist, he is also a womanizer and, as María and Salvador discover later, a criminal.

The author weaves a complex set of relationships: Marcos tries to seduce María, and an affair develops between Salvador and Ana Ofelia. The conflict develops once the inherent corruption of each character is revealed. In a series of events, the foursome is exposed as corrupt and violent. They manipulate and lie to each other to obtain financial benefit. In their hypocrisy, they constantly search for ways in which to take advantage of each other.

Salvador mismanages the family's money and reacts defensively and violently when confronted by his wife. María discovers that Salvador has conducted dirty business and stolen from his employer. The husband justifies his actions: "La única solución es ponerse listo para que a uno no se lo madrugen. O robar primero antes de que a uno le roben" (The only solution is to be alert so that no one eats you up. Or to steal before they steal from you). In this philosophy of survival of the fittest, even María plays her part in a corrupt society. Marcos discovers that she extends words and sentences in order to augment the number of typed pages she produces. As the situation worsens, María is forced to become a common thief on the streets. Finally, when Marcos fails to pay several months of rent, the couple expels him from the apartment. In return, he assaults them and leaves them even more impoverished. As Salvador's physical violence toward María increases, she is forced to leave him. The play closes with a scene similar to the opening one, only now Ana Ofelia is living with Salvador and taking over the role of the abused wife.

In his next published play, Rascón Banda returns to drama and once again uses his knowledge of the legal system to inform his writing. *La fiera del Ajusco* is based on the real case of Elvira Cruz, a woman who murdered her four children and attempted to commit suicide in 1982 in a small town in the Ajusco mountains near Mexico City. Originally conceived as a *corrido* (a popular ballad that narrates a story), the play was produced by UNAM and, under the direction of Luna, it closed the Latin American Theater Festival in Mexico City in 1985. Rascón Banda's aim is not to create a piece of documentary drama or testimonial theater but to re-create and explore Elvira's possible motivations. Rather than attempting to justify her actions as a natural result of her social and economic conditions, the drama merely offers a background for the crimes and illustrates the complex tragedy of a human being pushed into extreme situations. The story is told through a series of flashbacks in which Elvira is abused and abandoned by her family, friends, and employers. Misery, desperation, hopelessness, and social violence all conspire to push Elvira to commit her crimes. The playwright, again, presents a dark portrayal of a society that abuses its weakest members repeatedly.

In his next play, Rascón Banda introduces a true popular hero. Apolo García, a professional wrestler, is the main character in *Máscara contra cabellera*. The play was commissioned by theater director Enrique Pineda and a group of actors from the School of Theater at the University of Jalapa. After a successful run in Mexico, the production represented the country at the Latin American Theater Festival in Manizales, Colombia, in 1985. The main character's name establishes a clear reference to classical mythology. Apolo is meant to represent a modern hero in a modern tragedy inspired both by the Spanish *auto sacramental* (play about the Sacrament) and the Greek tragedy. Apolo's mother claims that he is the son of a volcano and was conceived without the intercession of a man. This tale of his supernatural origin provides him with the strength to fight corporate corruption in the "Mount Olympus" of wrestling. Apolo, as the modern popular hero/average Mexican man, struggles with fate, rising from his low upbringing and abused condition to fight for union rights and against the manipulation of wrestlers by owners and managers. Initially, he promotes a peaceful strategy for change; but the directors of the Wrestlers Union insist that he must climb the hierarchy and earn his right to a position on the board before he can have a real influence. As the wrestler becomes an apparent threat, the managers discuss ways to eliminate him.

Rascón Banda also draws clear parallels between Apolo's journey and the public life of Jesus Christ by including several scenes that resemble the latter's agony, death, and resurrection. Apolo's best friend, the Cerebelo, is a Judas figure. He betrays Apolo, "sells" him to the managers, and has a final confrontation with him during their "last supper" together. The mythical and ritual sacrifice of Apolo occurs as he is attacked during one of his fights. The wrestler is taken to the hospital, where he is declared dead. When Apolo's mother, fiancée, and best friend visit the hospital, a young nurse dressed in white explains that Apolo got up and walked out of the hospital by himself. Apolo is raised to the category of myth, perhaps saint. Yet, his battle for justice is not over. His mother proclaims at the end of the play: "Lo van a anunciar otra vez en los programas de lucha. Aparecerá como Apolo II. Vamos a la arena. ¡Apolo Vive!" (They will announce it again in the wrestling programs. He will appear as Apolo II. Let us go to the arena. Apolo Lives!).

Rascón Banda's exploration of the hero's journey leaves Apolo transformed into a figure of hope with an unfinished mission. In *Guerrero negro* (Dark Warrior), his next play, published in 1988 but never performed, the author examines the ordeal of the antihero. His next characters are disposable figures trapped in the corrupt world of drug trafficking. They fight for survival in the deserted environment of a lonely beach in Baja California Sur, but they must also confront the overwhelming feeling that sooner or later their actions will take them to a tragic final destiny. As in Greek tragedy, it is assumed from the beginning that the characters will not avoid fate.

The author creates his characters with compassion and immerses them in a semi-idyllic world, described with poetic details. For example, the sky and sea reflect the inner world of the people at the beach. This magical and even beautiful world creates a harsh contrast for the pathetic lives of the characters. First, an old gypsy woman wanders the beach selling souvenir figures of a dark warrior and desperately waits for the return of her long-lost son. She describes the magical powers of the *guerrero negro* figure and the danger it presents to anyone who mismanages it. Israel el Gato, possibly the gypsy's son, returns to the beach intending to sell a last shipment of drugs and retire from the business to a comfortable life in Los Angeles. Martha, his lover and accomplice, attempts to break away from the relationship to protect her father's reputation while he runs for governor. Her attraction to Israel is, nonetheless, powerful, as evident in an explicit lovemaking scene between the two on the beach. Finally, the author introduces Eloy Bárcena, a mature, sinister man. Formerly a police officer, Bárcena is now an assassin for hire, chasing Israel and hoping to settle down with the gypsy once his job is complete.

Israel's erratic and aggressive behavior is fully manifested when the gypsy tells him she will not assist him any more with his trafficking. He has been using the souvenir figures to smuggle cocaine into the United States; but the gypsy is afraid of the effects the drugs are having on Israel's health and behavior. In a fatal confrontation at the end of the play, Bárcena shoots Israel and is later murdered himself by Martha. The gypsy declares the events to be the result of the *guerrero negro's* curse. After burying Israel, she gives Martha all the money he made by trafficking drugs and embraces her lonely existence at the beach. The final effect of catharsis is accomplished by carefully building the characters so that, though corrupt, they still stimulate pity and fear and can even be perceived as victims of the general corruption of their society.

As *Guerrero negro* resembles classic Greek theater, the playwright's next text emulates Shakespearean tragedy. *¡Cierren las puertas!* (Shut the Doors!) was written in 1988 as a result of a workshop project commissioned by Universidad Veracruzana. The original production was directed by Pineda and represented Mexico at the Latin American Theater Festival in Colombia. The play is meant to be performed in a circular space similar to a *palenque* (the arena where cockfights are usually held). The premise is that all rooster fights have been forbidden by the government, but the group at this *casa gallera* (cockfighting house) defies the law by conducting the fights behind closed doors. The characters, like those in *Máscara contra cabellera,* carry names that indicate their archetypal nature. Examples include Paco La Muerte (Paco The Death) and La Sirena (The Mermaid), a fortune teller who claims early in the play that the death of a single individual has little effect in the flow of life. The central section of the text is structured as a variety show that incorporates not only cockfights but also a series of circus-like performances and a live mariachi band. The entertainment is heralded by the creators as "fun for everyone" regardless of age, gender, and social status.

The play shows overtones of *Hamlet* (circa 1600–1601) in the figure of Rubén Lucero, a young man who returns to the *palenque* after everyone assumed he was dead. It is widely believed that Andrés, the new owner of the *palenque,* is responsible for the mysterious death of Rubén's father. Andrés has now taken over the family business after marrying Olivia, Rubén's mother, claiming that she needed his protection. Rubén's hatred for Andrés and Olivia is fueled by the fact that his sister, Rosa, had an abortion after becoming pregnant by Andrés. The uncomfortable situation is presently ignored by the entire staff of the *palenque,* including Olivia, who does not seem to question Andrés's behavior or culpability. Even Rosa has adapted to the new life and works diligently taking care of the roosters and training them for the fights. In general, Andrés has managed to reorganize the *palenque,* defy the proscription, and turn the endeavor into a successful, yet illegal, business.

Upon his return Rubén confronts Andrés, claiming his right as owner of the *palenque* and chastising him for marrying his mother and abusing his sister. Rubén shares his plans for revenge with his closest friends, generating a drastic division between the characters who support him and those who remain faithful to Andrés. The final confrontation takes place during an illegal show at the *palenque* where Rosa, representing Andrés, and Rubén, defending his own rights and seeking justice for the death of his father, are forced to pit their roosters in a cockfight. The actors must be prepared to play the last scenes and deliver their lines based on the actual outcome of the real cockfight on stage. Regardless of the result of that conflict, the text indicates that at one point Rubén stabs Andrés and, accidentally, his own mother, who dies trying to protect Andrés. The play closes with Rosa urging Rubén to escape. Her brother, reluctant to run away from the law, proclaims his innocence and asserts that his father took possession of him to ensure his own revenge. *¡Cierren las puertas!* is an elaborate spectacle in which, once more, the antiheroes function as agents of the general social decadence.

Another corrupted family is at the center of *Playa Azul* (translated as *Blue Beach*, 1994). The play, written in 1982, was published in 1986 and staged in 1989 under the direction of Raúl Quintanilla at UNAM. Evocative of the style the author explored in *Guerrero negro*, the text is often described as *realismo poético* (poetic realism), mostly because it reflects the emotions and thoughts of the characters through their perception and description of the environment and the symbols of decay around them. Myra S. Gann explains in the introduction to her English translation: "Though realistic in most ways, this play employs the unreal and the surreal to create the atmosphere of putrefaction, of phantasm, and of decadence which makes it so memorable. Ambition and corruption have led to the disintegration of a family and the downfall of its patriarch: the natural world (seagulls, coconuts, breezes) reflects the inner state of the characters."

Set in Playa Azul, Michoacán, the story presents a family struggling with the ghosts from their past and present. After years of separation, the four members of the family return for a reunion in the now virtually ruined hotel they own at the sordid beach, itself a metaphor for social and personal corruption. Gradually, the secrets that plague the family are revealed: the mother's past as a prostitute; the father's corrupt career as a politician; the brother's emotional trauma from a former kidnapping; and the sister's unexpected pregnancy. Completing the family picture are Don Matías, a soothsayer who is also the hotel caretaker, and Teresa, the hotel administrator and mistress of everyone's secrets.

The father has reconvened the family to request their solidarity as he faces what he claims are false accusations. He was once a popular and respected man, but the discovery of his obscure political allegiances and

Liliana Saldaña in the title role of Rascón Banda's 1998 play, La Malinche, *which offers a new perspective on the woman who was mistress and translator to Hernán Cortés and has become a symbol of treason against one's people (photograph by Johann Kresnik; from* La Malinche, *2000; Thomas Cooper Library, University of South Carolina)*

corrupted ways have placed him in a dangerous and unstable political situation that deprives him of support from his peers. The family, however, is unable or disinclined to offer any assistance. All of them struggle with their own issues, trying to find better options for their future and languidly attempting to overcome the insurmountable decadence that surrounds them. Visions of disaster and tragedy are plentiful, and the stink of dead fish increases as more bad news is announced. A warrant has been issued for the father's arrest, and his plans to restore the hotel are dashed when he discovers that a new road will cut right through the property. The bloody dead seagulls at the end of the play are never really explained; they function as a poetic metaphor to indicate the inevitable destruction of the family and demonstrate the overall decadent and morbid imagery of the play. There is nothing salvageable in the corrupt world surrounding them. The explicit violence and death imagery in Rascón Banda's theater offer a reflection of Mexican reality as the author depicts the consequences of corrupt activities and attitudes. The more subtle violence and purposely slow pace of his next major play provide another look at the disruption caused in society by decadent individuals.

Contrabando (Trafficking) was written in 1990 and performed in 1991 by the theater company of the Universidad Veracruzana. It deals, once more, with the drug trade in Chihuahua. Based on true stories collected by the author, the play presents three women waiting in the office of the mayor in a small town in the north of Mexico. The characters–Conrada, Damiana, and Jacinta–share with each other the multiple and sinister ways in which the business of drug trafficking has affected their lives. The corruption and violence of the activity is openly examined, not in the abstract, but by exposing the specific harm it presents to innocent victims and to the women abandoned by the men who devote themselves to the business. The wide-reaching power of the drug lords in the area allows them to manipulate the government and the legal system, generating social unrest and violence. The cruel, destructive, and hated hand of trafficking has left the townspeople unable to determine their own future and often fighting for their own survival without real regard for values and laws.

By providing testimonials from the people most affected by the illegal activity, the author shows how drug trafficking has changed the social and economic structure of the northern region since the 1960s. Through his stories, Rascón Banda also points out that such activity attracts people from the marginal classes because they see in it the only option to overcome poverty and disadvantage. As in *Los ilegales,* people are forced by the unstable economic situation in their country to attempt an escape from their condition; however, as in the case of migration, such options are fraught with violence and tragedy. The clear metaphor for this danger is the powerful ending of *Contrabando,* in which the only important piece of the set, a large window at the mayor's office, is blown to pieces. The destiny of the women who were sitting by it remains unknown.

Sabor de engaño (A Taste of Betrayal) premiered in 1993 at the Centro Universitario de Teatro in Mexico City. With this slice-of-life drama, Rascón Banda turns to the topic of actors and the art of acting. The main characters are Alfonso and Perla, a young couple struggling to remain employed as actors in Mexico City. Alfonso currently works on a soap opera and makes extra money by shooting television commercials. Perla is unemployed, partly because of her firm standards in her choice of material. She explains: "Nos interesa la actuación como una vocación, como un compromiso. No para hacernos millonarios, ni estrellas" (We are interested in acting as a vocation, a commitment. Not because we want to become millionaires or stars).

Perla and Alfonso are true professionals, devoted to their craft. They work hard and constantly help each other learn lines and polish their acting styles. Rascón Banda, however, presents his characters (and actors) with further acting challenges. Rascón Banda indicates that the same actors playing the main characters are also required to play the parts of their visitors, Armando and Paola. It is never clear whether the visitor roles are played by Alfonso and Perla, or by the actors playing Alfonso and Perla. By creating a complex theater game, Rascón Banda explores the intricacies of the craft of acting, not only on the stage but in everyday life.

Armando and Paola have characteristics that are markedly different from those of the main characters. Armando is Alfonso's brother who moves to the capital city in search of a job as an accountant. He believes that all actors are insane alcoholics, drug addicts, and degenerates. In his discussions with Perla, he also argues that television has caused the deterioration of society and that anyone who has acted on it has become an accomplice to that evil mission. Paola, Perla's sister, has moved to the city to pursue a career as an actress. She is a younger and more outspoken version of Perla and flirts openly with Alfonso until she manages to seduce him. A complex web of relationships is developed with only two actors onstage at any given time and occasionally using the actors' recorded voices for conversations on the telephone or through the intercom system. In the closing scenes, Perla and Alfonso must deal with the remains of the storm caused by the interference of their siblings, or perhaps they also confront the real consequences of having become, as actors often do, "the other." Their future as a couple and as struggling actors in Mexico City is uncertain.

In *La banca* (The Bank) Rascón Banda returns to his exploration of crime and social corruption, this time by studying the reactions of a group of women locked in a small room at a bank agency while a robbery is in progress. The play was produced by UNAM in 1997 and directed by Gerard Huillier. Rita, Angeles, and Laura are all employees at the agency. Their male counterparts have been locked in the bathroom and are apparently receiving a harsher treatment from the robbers. Minutes later, María, the janitor, is also brought into the room. As the robbery progresses, so does the tension in the small room, particularly because of the conflict created by the different attitudes the women have toward the burglary. Angeles is cautious and fearful, while María seems fascinated by the opportunity to experience an event she has only seen portrayed on television or movies. Rita attempts to act as a mediator, while Laura maintains a careless attitude by arguing that, since the bank money does not belong to them, the employees are not directly affected by the incident. Issues of class difference also emerge: María, for instance, complains about Angeles's standoffish attitude, which she attributes to the social and educational gap between the two women. When the bank opens at nine in the morning with the robbery still in progress, another woman, an important and distinguished customer, is brought into the room. Even in this extreme situation, Señora Warman de López behaves with extreme arrogance toward the rest of the women, reminds them of her higher status, and insists on giving them orders. The other women react with resentment and promptly point out to her that, because she is a member of the upper class, her life is at a higher risk than anyone else's.

Events turn when the women switch on the radio and realize that the station has been alerted about the robbery and is actually transmitting near the building and providing details about the situation. One of the women manages to call the show and provide information. Tension increases as Laura, at this point, seems to be concerned with the success of the operation. Angeles questions Laura and slowly puts bits of information together to expose Laura as an accomplice to the robbers. Her employment at the bank was just a facade to gather information. The women argue when Laura stoutly rejects the accusation. The robbers, now in a desperate situation, return to the room to claim hostages as they prepare to exit the bank, which is now surrounded by police officers. They eventually select Laura, who willingly goes with the robbers after ordering them to shoot Angeles. The play closes with the rest of the women surrounding Angeles's body while a recorded greeting is heard through the speaker system announcing the agency is "open" for business.

In the controversial *La Malinche*, the author deals with the notorious story of the titular character, a well-known figure in Mexican history. The play was coproduced in 1998 by the Instituto Nacional de Bellas Artes and the Consejo Nacional de Arte y Cultura. La Malinche (called Doña Marina by the Spaniards) was a native woman, an enslaved Aztec who became mistress and translator for the Spanish conquistador Hernán Cortés and thereby gained the hatred of her people. The character has achieved a status of archetype in Mexican culture, usually being considered a symbol of treason, particularly against one's nation. Rascón Banda's version brings the enigmatic woman to present-day Mexico in order to explore several aspects of the story from the vantage point of the twentieth century. His Malinche interacts with a Parliament crowded with loud politicians, a psychotherapist, and an Americanized Cortés, who certainly represents modern imperialism. Her visits to the therapist give her the opportunity to present her perspective and defend herself against the accusations she has carried throughout history.

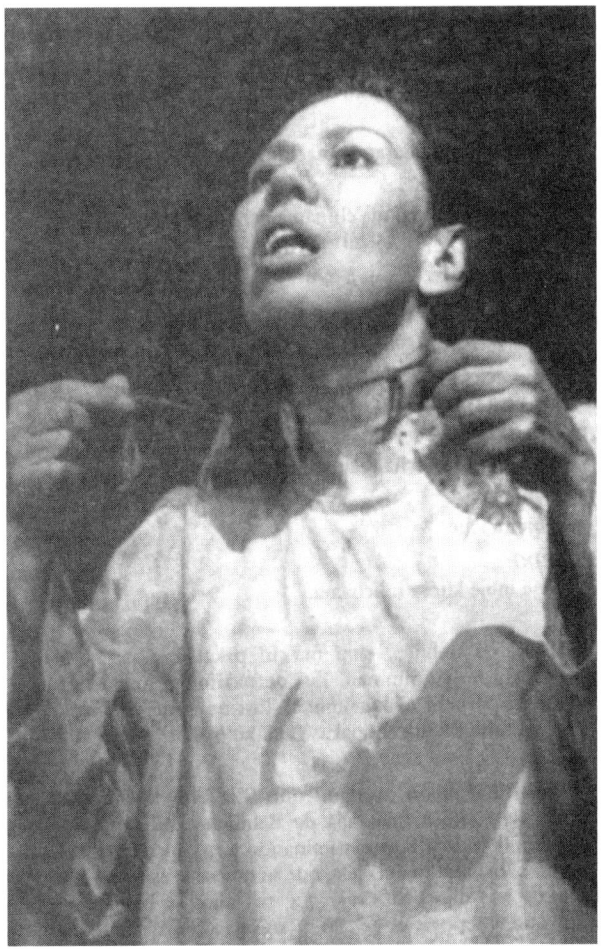

Luisa Huertas as Rita in the 1999 Mexico City premiere of Rascón Banda's play La mujer que cayó del cielo *(The Woman Who Fell from the Sky)*, based on the story of a woman who was institutionalized in Kansas City because no one realized she was able to speak only in her native Rarámuri language (photograph by Fernando Moguel; from La mujer que cayó del cielo, *2000;* Zimmerman Library, New Mexico State University)

The experimental nature of the play allows the author to incorporate several elements of Mexican culture and history in general. Rascón Banda utilizes poetry in original native languages, as well as Catholic imagery such as the venerated Virgin of Guadalupe. Nudity and violence were prominent in the first production of the play, directed by German director Johann Kresnik in 1998 for the Festival International Cervantino, generating mixed reviews. The work can be read as an openly anti-American manifesto, although the author has argued that his harsh criticism is also directed toward many Mexicans who are allowing the country to become permanently linked to the economy of the United States.

One of Rascón Banda's next plays, *La mujer que cayó del cielo* (The Woman Who Fell from the Sky, performed in 1999), narrates the real-life story of Rita Patiño Quintero, a Tarahumara Indian from northern Mexico lost in the United States in 1984. Able to speak only in her native Rarámuri language, Quintero was diagnosed as schizophrenic and mentally retarded, and she was institutionalized in a hospital in Kansas City for twelve years. There she was subjected to "normalizing" treatments and psychotropic medications that eventually caused irreversible mental damage. The woman was discovered and brought back to Mexico by a friend of Rascón Banda's who also appears as one of the characters in the play. *La mujer que cayó del cielo* was first produced by UNAM under the direction of Bruno Bert.

Rascón Banda's reputation as a successful author has extended throughout the world. Many of his plays have been translated and produced in different countries or included in important anthologies. Other titles by Rascón Banda include his 1988 version of the 1987 book *Querido Diego, te abraza quiela* (Dear Diego) by Elena Poniatowska; *Elena mil veces, vida y obra de Elena Poniatowska* (Elena a Thousand Times, The Life and Work of Elena Poniatowska), a play created in 1990 in collaboration with the famous actress Susana Alexander; *Luces de Therminor* (Therminor Lights), performed in 1990 at UNAM; *Fugitivos* (Fugitives) and *Alucinada* (Delusional), both performed in 1992 at UNAM; *Días de feria* (Holidays), presented at Banca Cremi, also in 1992; *El caso Santos* (Santos), commissioned in 1993 by Teatro Dallas, a Hispanic theater company in Texas; *Por los caminos del sur* (On the Roads of the South), directed by José Caballero at UNAM in 1996; *Veracruz, Veracruz,* performed by the theater group at Universidad Veracruzana in 2001 and directed by longtime collaborator Pineda; and *Sazón de mujer* (Taste of a Woman), a group of monologues presented while the actors demonstrate the secrets of northern Mexican cooking, performed in Chihuahua also in 2001.

Rascón Banda has also written several movie scripts, including *Días difíciles* (Difficult Days, 1987) and *Morir en el golfo* (To Die in the Gulf, adapted from Héctor Aguilar Camín's novel, 1989), both with Alejandro Pelayo. His nondramatic works include *De cuerpo entero* (Full Bodied), his autobiography, published in 1990; *Contrabando,* a novel based on his play, for which he won the Juan Rulfo Award in 1991 for a first novel (it was published in 1993); and *Volver a Santa Rosa* (Return to Santa Rosa, 1996), a collection of short stories. Rascón Banda has taught at the Department of Languages and Literature and the School of Law at UNAM. In addition, he has been a member of several organizations including the Consejo Consultivo del Instituto Mexicano de Cinematografía (Advisory Council for the Mexican Film Institute) and the Comisión de Artes y Letras del Consejo Nacional para la Cultura y las Artes (Arts and Literature Committee for the National Council on Arts and Culture). He has also been named president of the Sociedad General de Escritores de México (SOGEM), the Mexican Association of Writers. In 2001 he was awarded the Juan Ruiz de Alarcón Award for his contributions as a playwright and promoter of theater in Mexico.

Víctor Hugo Rascón Banda's theater is filled with antiheroes and common individuals who struggle with disadvantage in a corrupt society. Many of his characters challenge the status quo and successfully rebel against oppressive institutions. Most of them, however, face the consequences of their attempts to disrupt society. The true constant in Rascón Banda's theater is the indication that all of his characters lack better options. Even when their actions are morally wrong and unjustified, the author seems to argue that society is to blame. Regardless of any other political intent or social commentary, Rascón Banda examines society with a critical eye, suggesting that it must be changed before it further corrupts its members, or even worse, before it annihilates them. The playwright's ability to write in different dramatic styles, his willingness to create in collaboration with groups and directors, his prolific nature, and his involvement in several organizations indicate that his already substantial contributions to Mexican literature and Latin American drama will continue.

References:

Ronald D. Burgess, *The New Dramatists of Mexico 1967–1985* (Lexington: University Press of Kentucky, 1991), pp. 97–116;

Myra S. Gann, "El teatro de Víctor Hugo Rascón Banda: Hiperrealismo y destino," *Latin American Theatre Review,* 25, no. 1 (1991): 77–88;

Adriana Berrueco García, *Rascón Banda: La dramaturgia como vehículo de concientización social* (Uruáchic: Fiestas de Aniversario de Uruáchic, 2003);

Vicente Leñero, ed., *La nueva dramaturgia mexicana* (Mexico City: El Milagro, 1996);

César Antonio Sotelo, "La preponderancia del espectáculo en el teatro mexicano: Las armas blancas de Víctor Hugo Rascón Banda," *Revista de Literatura Mexicana Contemporánea,* 1, no. 2 (1996): 102–105.

Carlos José Reyes
(12 March 1941 -)

Christina Marín
Arizona State University

SELECTED PLAY PRODUCTIONS: *Amor de chocolate,* Bogotá, Teatro El Búho, 1960;

Arlequín sobre las piedras negras, Bogotá, Teatro El Búho, for the National Playwrights' Festival, 1960;

Disparate macabro, Bogotá, Independent Theater Group, for the Festival of Colombian Authors, 1961;

El Teatrillo de Aserrín, Bogotá, Independent Theater Group, for the Festival of Colombian Authors, 1961;

Dulcita y el burrito, Bogotá, Teatro de Arte Popular, 1964;

La cabra de Nubia, based on Jesús Zárate Moreno's story, Bogotá, Grupo Escénico de la Universidad de la Incca, 1964;

La piedra de la felicidad, Bogotá, 1965;

Soldados, based on Alvaro Cepeda Samudio's novel *La casa grande,* Bogotá, Casa de la Cultura, 30 June 1966;

Variaciones sobre metamorfosis, adapted from Franz Kafka's *Metamorphosis,* Bogotá, First National Chamber Theater Festival of Colombia, 1966;

Cuentos sobre Macondo, adapted from Gabriel García Márquez's short stories, Bogotá, National University Theater Festival, 1967;

La aventura, Bogotá, 1968;

Los viejos baúles empolvados que nuestros padres nos prohibieron abrir, Bogotá, TEX, 1968;

La fiesta de los muñecos, Bogotá, 1968;

La antesala, Medellín, Grupo de Teatro de la Universidad Bolivariana, 1970;

La verdadera y muy maravillosa historia de María de Santa Fe que vivió en tratos con el diablos durante más de siete años, Bogotá, Liceo Francés de Bogotá, 1971;

Periquillo en el banquillo, Bogotá, El Alacrán, 1971;

El tío conejo zapatero, Bogotá, El Alacrán, 1972;

La muela, Bogotá, El Alacrán, 1973;

Globito manual, Bogotá, El Alacrán, 1974;

El hombre que escondió el sol y la luna, Bogotá, El Alacrán, 1974;

El redentor, 1976;

Reccorido en redondo, 1976;

Carlos José Reyes (from Fernando González Cajiao, Historia del teatro en Colombia, *1986; Thomas Cooper Library, University of South Carolina)*

La mudez, 1989;

La voz, 1990;

Función nocturna, 1991;

El carnaval de la muerte alegre, 1991.

BOOKS: *Soldados,* published with Enrique Buenaventura's *Padre* as *Teatro de Colombia* (Bogotá: Marcha Colombia, 1971);

Teatro para niños (Bogotá: Instituto Colombiano de Cultura, 1972)–comprises *La piedra de la felicidad, La fiesta de los muñecos,* and *Dulcita y el burrito;*

Los viejos baúles empolvados que nuestros padres nos prohibieron abrir (Melodrama y crónica de las desventuras de una familia) (Bogotá: Instituto Colombiano de Cultura, 1973);

Globito manual y El hombre que escondió el sol y la luna (Havana: Casa de las Américas, 1977);

Una década de teatro colombiano, 1981–1991, text by Reyes, photographs by Juan Camilo Segura (Bogotá: Instituto Colombiano de Cultura, 1992);

Dentro y fuera (Medellín: Universidad de Antioquia, 1992);

El carnaval de la muerte alegre: Periplo de Balboa y Pedrarias (Madrid: El Público, 1992; Bogotá: Panamericana, 1996);

Globito manual (Bogotá: Panamericana, 1996);

La piedra de la felicidad (Bogotá: Panamericana, 1997);

El hombre que escondió el sol y la luna: Mito de los indios chamíes (Bogotá: Panamericana, 1998).

PRODUCED SCRIPTS: *Sólo para locos,* adaptation of Hermann Hesse's *Steppenwolf,* television, 1961;

Arlequín sobre las piedras negras, radio, Radiodifusora Nacional de Colombia, 1961;

Bandidos, radio, Radiodifusora Nacional de Colombia, 1961;

Los comuneros, based on Constancio Franco's play, radio, Radiodifusora Nacional de Colombia, 1961;

Juno y el pavo real, based on Sean O'Casey's play *Juno and the Paycock,* television, 1961;

"Lo que pasó realmente," based on Dylan Thomas's story, television, *Pequeño teatro,* Punch Televisión, 1967;

Un día después del Sábado, television, 1968;

Las convulsiones, based on Luis Vargas Tejada's play, television, 1969;

Cóndores no entierran todos los días, based on Gustavo Alvarez Gardeázabal's novel, motion picture, 1975;

Palco de honor, television, RTI Television, 1978;

Una visita inesperada, based on José María Cordovez Moure's book *Reminiscencias de Santafé y Bogotá,* television, 1978;

Así se hizo la historia, television, Cenpro TV, 1979–1981;

Revivamos nuestra historia, Promec TV, 1979–1984;

¡Sálvese quien pueda! television, Cenpro TV, 1982;

Mariana Pineda, based on Federico García Lorca's play, television, 1982;

El Bogotazo, television, 1983;

La libertad de los esclavos, television, Eduardo Lemaitre TV, 1986;

La libertad de prensa, television, Eduardo Lemaitre TV, 1986;

El derecho a la Independencia, television, Eduardo Lemaitre TV, 1986;

El debido proceso, television, Eduardo Lemaitre TV, 1986;

El sufragio universal, television, Eduardo Lemaitre TV, 1986;

La soberanía nacional, television, Eduardo Lemaitre TV, 1986;

Antecedentes de la Constitución de 1886, television, Eduardo Lemaitre TV, 1986.

OTHER: "Metamorphosis: Varaciones en dos partes, sobre un tema original de Franz Kafka," in *Teatro Contemporâneo hispanoamericano,* edited by Carlos Miguel Suárez Radillo and Orlando Rodriguez Sardiñas (Bogotá: Escelicer, 1971);

Materiales para una historia del teatro en Colombia, edited by Reyes and Maida Watson Espener (Bogotá: Instituto Colombiano de Cultura, 1978);

"Cien años de teatro en Colombia," in *Nueva Historia de Colombia, VI,* edited by Jorge Orlando Melo and Jesús Antonio Bejarano (Bogotá: Planeta, 1989), pp. 213–236;

Hitos del teatro colombiano del siglo XX, edited by Reyes (Bogotá: Alcaldía Mayor de Santa Fe de Bogotá, 2000).

SELECTED PERIODICAL PUBLICATIONS–UNCOLLECTED: "La Improvisación: Notas sobre la práctica teatral," *ECO,* 26 (October 1973): 435–448;

"El redentor," *ECO,* 30 (May 1977): 22–34;

"Diversión que da en el clavo: Actualidad de 'La jaula de las locas,'" *Lecturas Dominicales* (11 August 1991): 6–7;

"De los descubrimientos a la invención: La imágen de Colombia," *Senderos,* 5 (August 1993);

"El Poema cómico de Fray Felipe de Jesús," *Senderos,* 5 (December 1993): 718–734;

"Joaquín Pablo Posada: Estampa de un periodista crítico y mordaz," *Senderos,* 7 (December 1994): 954–963;

"La Biblioteca Nacional en el siglo XX: Aspectos principales del desarrollo de la Biblioteca Nacional hasta el presente," *Boletín de Historia y Antiguedades* (Academia Colombiana de Historia), 85, no. 797 (July–September 1995): 677–705;

"Daniel Samper Ortega, un visuario de la cultura (Homenaje en el centenario de su nacimiento)," "Joaquín Pablo Posada (El Alacrán), poeta satírico y periodista comparativo en tiempos de cambio," and "Las edades del libro," *Boletín de Historia y Antiguedades* (Academia Colombiana de Historia), 85, no. 797 (April–June 1997): 63–70, 345–382, 519–542;

"Una farsa prohibida," *Senderos,* 8 (August 1997): 1157–1161.

Carlos José Reyes is an accomplished playwright, director, actor, essayist, critic, and movie and television screenwriter. As an artist, educator, and theater historiographer, Reyes has helped to construct the movement known as El Nuevo Teatro Colombiano (the New Theater of Colombia). The formation of this movement began in the late 1950s. In Colombian history the twentieth century is virtually split in half by the assassination of Liberal Party presidential candidate Jorge Eliécer Gaitán in the capital city on 9 April 1948. At that point the country entered into a period known as "the Violence in Colombia," which lasted until 1953. Close to three hundred thousand deaths were documented during these years, leaving many scars on the population of a country still affected by violence and death on a daily basis. After this period, theater artists all across the country began exploring new methods of representation and expression. Theater was transformed into a reflection of the economic, political, and social unrest in Colombia. Artists such as Enrique Buenaventura, Santiago García, Jairo Aníbal Niño, and Reyes contributed to a theatrical movement that would promote the reevaluation of the official history constructed by the government—a history that tends to ignore the experience of the lower classes. The time had come in the history of the theater in Colombia to express the viewpoint of the masses.

Carlos José Reyes Posada was born on 12 March 1941 in Bogotá. He studied drawing, painting, art history, and theater at the School of Fine Arts in Bogotá from 1959 to 1960. He worked with Bernardo Romero Lozano, Victor Muñoz Valencia, Gonzalo Vera Quintana, and Boris Roth in the Independent Theater Club. Under the tutelage of the Brazilian artist Dina Moscovici, he worked with the Experimental Theater Group of the School of Fine Arts, directing a production of Eugène Ionesco's *The Lesson* (1951) for the Third National Festival of Theater at the Teatro Colón in Bogotá.

Toward the end of 1959 he joined the company Teatro El Búho (The Owl Theater). This company, formed in 1957, is another example of the emergence of theater artists in Colombia dedicated to a serious commentary on the social and economic problems of the country. With actors and directors including García, Fausto Cabrera, Joaquín Casadiego, Paco Barrero, Abraham Zalzman, Mónica Silva, and Celmira Yepes, Reyes worked on productions of several works of Federico García Lorca, Ionesco, and Gabriel Mazaud. In 1960 Teatro El Búho moved its operations to the old Teatro Odeon, a space that later housed the Teatro Popular de Bogotá (TPB).

Another important marker in the development of the Nuevo Teatro Colombiano was the arrival and influence of the Japanese professor and director Seki Sano in 1956. Sano worked with Colombian theater artists, training them in the Method acting techniques of Konstantin Stanislavsky.

In 1960 the premiere of Reyes's first play for children, *Amor de chocolate* (Love of Chocolate), and a production under his direction of El Salvadorian playwright Walter Béneke's play *Funeral Home* (1958), a play set in the United States, were staged by Teatro El Búho. At the end of 1960 his children's theater piece *Arlequín sobre las piedras negras* (Harlequin on the Black Stones) won second prize in the National Authors Competition.

In 1961 Teatro El Búho relocated to the National University in Bogotá, where they mounted a production of *La guarda cuidadosa* (1615, The Vigilant Sentinel), one of the *entreméses* (interludes or short farcical pieces performed during the intermission of a play), written by Miguel de Cervantes. That same year Reyes directed the Italian play *Lo que no sabes* (1946, What You Don't Know), written by Silvio Giovaninetti. In Bogotá, at the Festival of Colombian Authors, he wrote and presented two new works, *Disparate macabro* (Macabre Nonsense) and *El Teatrillo de Aserrín* (The Little Theatre of Asserin).

At that time Reyes also began working in theater for television and radio. He adapted several scenes from Hermann Hesse's *Steppenwolf* (1927), writing a television drama directed by Cabrera titled *Sólo para locos* (Only for the Crazy). In 1961 he also adapted Sean O'Casey's *Juno and the Paycock* (1924) for Barrero to direct for television. For the radio he adapted the work of Constancio Franco, *Los comuneros* (1888, The Commoners), as well as two of his own plays, *Arlequín sobre las piedras negras* and *Bandidos* (Bandits), which were broadcast by Radiodifusora Nacional de Colombia in 1961.

In 1962 Reyes moved to Bucaramanga, Colombia, where he took a position as professor and director of the Teatro Experimental Universitario (TEU) at the Universidad Industrial de Santander. While in residence at the university he directed the works of many international playwrights, including Franz Kafka, Anton Chekhov, Friedrich Dürrenmatt, and Ryūnsuke Akutagawa. He also taught courses in humanities and contributed to the school literary publication *Vanguardia Liberal*.

In 1964 he returned to Bogotá, where he and Carlos Perozzo founded El Teatro de Arte Popular (TAP), along with Jaime Barbini, Carlos Parada, and Margalida Castro. The TAP wanted to create theater to entertain a Colombian audience while addressing and analyzing the social problems that affected the community. With this newly formed company Reyes directed and acted in several productions, including *Amor de chocolate, Dulcita y el burrito* (1964, Dulcita and the Little

Donkey), *Awake and Sing!* (1935) by Clifford Odets, and *Retablo de la avaricia, la lujuria y la muerte* (1927, The Tableau of Avarice, Lust, and Death) by Ramón del Valle-Inclán. While in Bogotá he also joined the faculty of the Universidad Incca as a professor of theater and director of the university theater group, with whom he adapted and directed Jesús Zárate Moreno's story *La cabra de Nubia* (1962, The Goat of Nubia) in 1964.

During 1965 Reyes toured several cities in Colombia with productions of his children's theater plays *Amor de chocolate* and *Dulcita y el burrito*. The latter was awarded several prizes at the Festival of National Authors in Cali, including best play, best cast, best direction (Reyes), and best actress (María Isabel Hernández as Dulcita).

Later that same year, both Teatro El Búho and the Teatro de Arte Popular disbanded. Reyes, like many of the artists from these two companies, became involved in the university theater movement. He joined Teatro Estudio (Studio Theater) at the National University in Bogotá. Starring with Carlos Duplat and Carlos Perozzo, Reyes acted in the role of Pope Urban VIII in Bertolt Brecht's *Life of Galileo* (1943) under the direction of García. Reyes also directed the premiere of another one of his plays for children, *La piedra de la felicidad* (The Stone of Happiness), which was produced with a children's play by the Japanese playwright Akutagawa.

In 1966 the TAP and the Teatro Estudio combined their efforts to create the Casa de la Cultura (House of Culture). On 30 June of that year, the Casa de la Cultura presented Reyes's adaptation of a portion of Alvaro Cepeda Samudio's novel *La casa grande* (1962, The Big House) under the title *Soldados* (Soldiers). The story deals with the events surrounding the strike and subsequent massacre of Colombian workers employed by the United Fruit Company in December 1928. The controversy stems from the fact that the force used to kill the striking workers was the Colombian military; and so the play, like the novel, addresses issues of loyalties, military alienation, and the actual scope of the strike and its consequences. The official version of the massacre diminishes the actual number of victims and has been a subject for many writers and artists. In José Monleón's *América Latina, teatro y revolución* (1978, Latin America: Theater and Revolution), Reyes explains:

> Mi interés por las bananeras es muy concreto, las considero como el epicentro de la cultura colombiana donde del idílico paisaje campesino se pasa un momento dentro del cual se desarrolla la violencia. Esta violencia no hay que verla como algo profundamente negativo, pues dicha violencia removió los cimientos de todo el país. Gaítan usó al máximo el tema de las bananeras lo mismo que Cepeda Samudio y García Márquez. Las bananeras es comparable al 9 de abril que es otra conmocón dentro del país, donde hay una sed de la nueva cultura que trae sangre.

(My interest in the banana workers is very concrete, I consider them to be the epicenter of the Colombian culture where the idyllic country vista passes through a moment in which the violence develops. This violence does not need to be viewed as profoundly negative, said violence turned over all of the foundations of the country. Gaítan used this theme of the banana workers, as did Cepeda Samudio and García Márquez. It is comparable to the 9th of April which is another upheaval in the country, where there is a thirst for the new culture that draws blood.)

Soldados demonstrates the ideological conflicts that plague the Colombian people. Reyes intends that the same actors who play the soldiers should also play the workers; this staging technique illustrates the constant struggle between the different factions of the Colombian population. Buenaventura, one of Reyes's compatriots and fellow playwrights, said in a 1980 article in *Conjunto* (Ensemble) of Reyes's version of *Soldados,* "El mitema de *Soldados* es la contradicción de los soldados, a la vez pueblo e instrumento de repression del pueblo. En cada accióny en todo el discurso verbal de la pieza está ése elemento de contradicción" (The theme of *Soldados* is the contradiction of the soldier, at the same time he represents the people and the instrument of repression against the people. In every action and in the dialogue of this piece exists the element of contradiction).

For the next four years, while Reyes continued to work with the Casa de la Cultura, he also collaborated with the theater group at the Universidad Externado de Colombia known as the TEX (Teatro Externado). In 1966 his play *Variaciones sobre metamorfosis* (Variations on Metamorphosis), based on the work of Kafka, won second place at the Chamber Theater Festival. This play was later published in the Universidad de Los Andes journal *Razón y Fábula* (Reason and Fable) as well as in *Teatro contemporaneo hispanoamericano* (1971, Contemporary Hispanic American Theater), compiled by Carlos Miguel Suárez Radillo and Orlando Rodriguez Sardiñas.

Reyes traveled to Havana, Cuba in 1966 to serve as a judge in the seventh Latin American Theater Festival. He played a direct role in the creation of the journal *Conjunto* and served on the editorial staff of this periodical. In 1967 he traveled throughout Europe, visiting theaters in France, Germany, and Czechoslovakia. He spent time with the Berliner Ensemble, where he attended rehearsals of Brecht's *Saint Joan of the Stockyards* (1932) under the direction of Mamfred Weckwert. He

Scene from the 1971 Teatro Experimental de Cali production at the Festival de Manizales of Reyes's 1966 play Soldados (Soldiers, published in 1971), which depicts the massacre of Colombian banana workers by their own military during a strike at the United Fruit Company in 1928 (from Gerardo Luzuriaga, ed., Popular Theater for Social Change in Latin America, 1978; Thomas Cooper Library, University of South Carolina)

visited other theaters in Berlin as well as in Weimar, Leipzig, and Rostock.

When Reyes returned to Colombia he went into rehearsals with the Casa de la Cultura for a remounting of *Variaciones sobre metamorfosis*. At the end of the year, this production was taken to a theater festival in Caracas, Venezuela. With the TEX he staged an adaptation of several of Colombian writer Gabriel García Márquez's stories for both the National University Theater Festival and the National Theater Festival of Colombia in 1967. The production was titled *Cuentos sobre Macondo* (Stories About Macondo) and included the stories "Rosas artificiales" (Artificial Roses), "Un día de estos" (One of These Days), "Un día despues del Sábado" (One Day after Saturday), "La prodigiosa tarde de Baltasar" (The Marvelous Afternoon of Baltasar), and "Los funerales de la Mamá Grande" (The Funerals of Big Mama). This production won second place at the National University Theater Festival. At the National Theater Festival of Colombia it won best Colombian play, best scene design (designed by Reyes himself), and honorable mention for directing.

In 1968 Reyes directed a production of his new play *Los viejos baúles empolvados que nuestros padres nos prohibieron abrir* (The Dusty Old Trunks that Our Parents Would Not Let Us Open) at the TEX theater company. This production won best play at the National University Theater Festival. That same year the production represented Colombia at the First Latin American University Theater Festival in Manizales, Colombia. This play re-creates the world of a middle-class Colombian family and their difficulty in confronting the realities of their economic downward spiral. They create a facade around their lives, denying the deaths of several family members and inventing intricate lies to hide the harsh truth of their financial ruin. Reyes uses dark humor to reveal how the middle class in Colombia often attempts to ignore the corruption and violence that is so prevalent throughout the country.

During the last few years of the 1960s Reyes worked in both television and theater, adapting several of the works of García Márquez to television screenplays, as well as a one-act by Luis Vargas Tejada, *Las convulsiones* (1828, The Convulsions). This one-act was presented at the 1969 National Theater Festival and won best Colombian play as well as best scene design, again designed by Reyes. That same year, Reyes mounted productions of Seneca's *Medea* with the Casa de la Cultura and Eduardo Manet's *The Nuns* (1969) with the TEX at the Universidad Externado de Colombia, while in Medellín in 1970 his play *La antesala* (The Waiting Room) was directed at the Universidad Bolivariana by Yolanda García.

In the early 1970s Reyes founded a new theater company called El Alacrán (The Scorpion). With this company he mounted many of his plays for young audiences as well as theater for general audiences. In his plays for children, Reyes is recognized for his use of puppets and giant street-theater mannequins. He is also known for his philosophy in regard to young audiences: he believes that children in general, and especially the young people of Colombia, should not be shielded from the harsh realities of life. Through his children's plays he shows a world of conflict and economic hardship that is meant to prepare children for their futures and to motivate their desire to change the world around them.

His plays for young audiences recapture the beauty of the Colombian culture while bringing to life characters who address the social and economic conditions of the country. In a series of plays involving one of his most endearing characters, El Tío Conejo Zapatero (Uncle Bunny Shoemaker), Reyes dramatizes the separation of the city dwellers from the campesinos (people who live in the rural areas of Colombia, usually the poorest sectors of the country). In his play *Dulcita y el burrito* he brings to life the character of a puppeteer who is experiencing the hardships of maintaining a living wage in a country where the suffering economy no longer supports the work of a simple artisan. In his children's plays he demonstrates a sense of responsibility to the children of Colombia by not covering up reality. Using the magic and fantasy of illusion, while sustaining a sense of authenticity, Reyes presents to his young audiences the possibility of hope through their constructive participation in society. His collection *Teatro para niños* (Theater for Children) was published in 1972.

During the early 1970s Reyes traveled throughout Europe, visiting the Theater Festival in Nancy, France, as well as theaters in Madrid and Barcelona, where he delivered several lectures on Colombian theater. From 1973 to 1977 he held the post of director at the Theater School of Bogotá. During this time he also worked as the narrator for the television program *Música para todos* (Music For Everyone) with the Philharmonic Orchestra of Bogotá, presenting such programs as the story of *Peter and the Wolf*.

In 1974 El Alacrán staged two more of Reyes's plays for young audiences, *Globito manual* (Handmade World) and *El hombre que escondió el sol y la luna* (The Man Who Hid the Sun and the Moon). *El hombre que escondió el sol y la luna* is a play based on a myth of the indigenous Chamú tribe of the Pacific coast of Colombia. The following year in Havana, Cuba, these two plays won him the Casa de las Américas Award for children's literature, and they were both published by Casa de las Américas in 1977. In Germany more of his plays for young audiences, *La fiesta de los muñecos* (1968, The Party of the Dolls) and *La piedra de la felicidad,* were translated and performed in Berlin.

From 1975 to 1978 Reyes held the position of professor of Colombian drama at the Universidad Pedagógica Nacional. In 1975 he also wrote the screenplay of *Cóndores no entierran todos los días* (Condors Do Not Inform All of the Days), based on the novel of the same title by Gustavo Alvarez Gardeázabal. This movie, released in 1984, was directed by Francisco Norden and received several awards at international movie festivals.

During the latter half of the 1970s Reyes was invited to participate in the Encounter of Artists of the Third World, the International Theater Festival in Caracas, Venezuela, and the Fourth World Session of Theater of the Nations organized by the International Theater Institute of UNESCO. For the joint Federation of Festivals of Theater of the Americas he gave lectures on the history of scenic space in Venezuela, Costa Rica, and Panama. On a tour through Venezuela he presented various works of puppet theater with El Alacrán at the Children's Theater Festival in Caracas, Mérida, Bolívar City, and Guayana City. In Guayana City he also gave a workshop on creativity and children's theater. Various theater companies in Cuba, Costa Rica, Mexico, Venezuela, Ecuador, and Uruguay performed *Globito manual*. In 1978 he left the Theater School of Bogotá and assumed the directorship of the Center for Children's Arts Education through the Cultural Theater of the National Park of Bogotá. Then, in May of 1979 he participated in the First Encounter of Theater Historians of Latin America, organized by the Latin American Center for the Creation and Investigation of Theater in Caracas, Venezuela. In 1982 the two theaters Teatro Popular de Bogotá and El Alacrán combined to develop a Cultural Center of Audiovisual and Dramatic Arts.

From 1979 to 1984 Reyes wrote and collaborated on the television series *Así se hizo la historia* (That's How History was Made) and *Revivamos nuestra historia* (Let's Relive Our History), documenting various events in the history of Colombia. For these series he wrote accounts of the lives of Simón Bolívar, known as the

Great Liberator; José María Córdova, the hero of Ayacucho; the revolutionary Antonio Nariño; and Rafael Nuñez, president of Colombia during the 1880s. He also wrote a television miniseries that recounts the events surrounding the 1948 assassination of Gaitán, titled *El Bogotazo* (1983). Reyes became a member of the Colombian Academy of History in 1984. At the reception held in his honor he read his essay "El Teatro Colombiano en el Siglo XIX" (Colombian Theater in the Nineteenth Century).

For the centennial celebration of the Colombian Constitution of 1886, Reyes wrote a series of fourteen original television programs. This series centered on seven themes, including the liberation of the slaves, freedom of the press, the right to independence, due process of the law, universal suffrage, national sovereignty, and the precursors to the Constitution.

In 1988 he participated as director of special events and coordinator of the First Playwrights' Encounter at the Premier Festival Iberoamericano of Theater in Bogotá. This festival, directed and produced by Fanny Mikey and Ramiro Osorio, is still held biannually in the capital city of Colombia. At the 1988 festival Reyes directed his new version of a play by Roberto Cossa, *No hay que llorar* (1979, No Need to Cry), with the Teatro Popular de Bogotá. Following the festival this production toured throughout Colombia. That same year, he adapted and directed a play by the Mexican dramatist Emilio Carballido titled *Rosas de dos aromas* (1986, Roses of Two Aromas). This production toured throughout Colombia, presenting at various national festivals, as well as traveling throughout Spain.

In 1989 Reyes traveled to the United States to visit several theaters in Washington, D.C., Kentucky, Illinois, Minnesota, New York, and Michigan. That year he also worked with the Teatro Popular de Bogotá on a production of *Caballito del diablo* (1981, Little Horse of the Devil) by Fermín Cabal. At the Second Festival Iberoamericano of Theater in 1990 he participated as a member of the Board of Directors. As a part of the Special Events Series he moderated several sessions on Brecht and Buenaventura. During the early 1990s he traveled to Venezuela, Spain, and Canada to participate in various playwriting festivals. At the First National Children's Theater Festival in Medellín he directed a workshop on playwriting for young audiences.

In 1992 Reyes was named director of the National Library in Bogotá. During the 1990s he wrote extensively on the development of theater in Colombia for journals, periodicals, and university publications as well as chapters in several books. He has held the position of professor of theater, literature, and film at various schools and universities in Colombia, including Javeriana University, the University of Caldas in Manizales, the University of La Sabana, the National School of Dramatic Arts, and Rosario University. Reyes has also acted as a judge in several playwriting competitions alongside his colleagues García, Gilberto Martínez, Cristóbal Peláez, and Henry Díaz. Throughout the late 1990s he delivered many conference presentations on topics including rare books, art and violence in Colombia, aesthetics and education, theater and the public, and nineteenth-century Colombian theater. In 2001 he received an honorary doctoral degree in scenic arts from the Universidad del Valle in Cali.

As a man of letters, Carlos José Reyes has helped give Colombia the voice of the people, re-creating a history that has traditionally been overshadowed by the official story written by those in power. His plays for young audiences, as well as his works for adults, are important contributions to the emerging canon of Colombian dramatic literature—a canon firmly set in the realities of a struggling country and determined to inspire social change.

References:

Gonzalo R. Arcila, *Nuevo teatro en Colombia: Actividad creadora y política cultural* (Bogotá: Ceis, 1983);

Enrique Buenaventura, "Ensayo de dramaturgia colectiva," *Conjunto,* 43 (1980): 21;

Fernando González Cajiao, *Historia del teatro en Colombia* (Bogotá: Colcultura, 1986);

Maria Mercedes Jaramillo, *Nuevo teatro colombiano: Arte y política* (Medellín: Universidad de Antioquia, 1992);

Jorge Orlando Melo and Jesús Antonio Bejarano, eds., *Nueva historia de Colombia,* volume 6 (Bogotá: Planeta, 1989);

Gerardo Luzuriaga, ed., *Popular Theater for Social Change in Latin America* (Los Angeles: UCLA Publications, 1978);

José Monleón, *América Latina, teatro y revolución* (Caracas: Ateneo de Caracas, 1978).

Hugo Salcedo
(24 September 1964 –   )

Iani del Rosario Moreno
Salve Regina University

SELECTED PLAY PRODUCTIONS: *En la oscuridad del laberinto,* Guadalajara, Teatro Experimental de Jalisco, 5 October 1982;

Misericordia, Guadalajara, Teatro Experimental de Jalisco, May 1986;

El viaje de los cantores, Mexico City, Teatro Jiménez Rueda, 7 September 1990; Chicago, Teatro Vista, 1991;

Sinfonía en una botella, Tijuana, Sala de Espectáculos del Centro Cultural Tijuana, 29 September 1990;

Arde el desierto con los vientos que vienen del sur, Tecate, Teatro Universitario, 1993;

Bárbara Gandiaga: Crimen y condena en la misión de Santo Tomás, Baja California, Teatro de Ensenada, 1994?;

Bulevar, Tijuana, Compañia del Sótano, 5 May 1995;

Cocinar el amor, 1996;

Nigeria esta en otra parte, Baja California, Teatro de Ensenada, 1996;

La Bufadora, Universidad Autonoma de Baja California, Taller de Teatro Universitario de Ensenada, 20 June 1996; Lawrence, Kansas, Organizacion Teatral de la Universidad Veracruzana, 3 April 1997; Xalapa, Teatro Candileja, 2000;

Asesinato en los parques, Guadalajara, Ex Convento del Carmen, 1997;

Selena: La reina del Tex-Mex, Tijuana, Teatro Tijuana del Instituto Mexicano del Seguro Social, 20 November 1998;

Don Tiburcio, el tiburón, Guadalajara, Teatro Univer, 2000;

San Juan de Dios, Guadalajara, Foro do Arte y Cultura, El Tercer Grupo, February 2001;

Una rana croar, Newport, Rhode Island, Mercy Hall Theater, 18 April 2001;

Cumbia (Hasta las tres de la mañana), Guadalajara, Foro do Arte y Cultura, El Tercer Grupo, 21 February 2003;

La ley del ranchero, La Paz, Teatro Benito Juárez, May 2003;

Hugo Salcedo (photograph by Erubiel Ramos; from a 2003 edition of Don Tiburcio, el tiburón, *2000; Collection of Iani del Rosario Moreno)*

El árbol del deseo, Guadalajara, Foro de CEDART, June 2004;

Rasgar la noche, La Paz, Teatro Benito Juárez, August 2004.

BOOKS: *El viaje de los cantores* (Madrid: Ediciones de Cultura Hispánica, 1990);

El viaje de los cantores y otras obras de teatro (Mexico City: Consejo Nacional para la Cultura y las Artes, 1990)–comprises *El viaje de los cantores, Arde el desierto con los vientos que vienen del sur,* and *Sinfonía en una botella;*

Teatro de Hugo Salcedo (Guadalajara: Universidad de Guadalajara, 1990)–comprises *Cumbia (Hasta las tres de la mañana), Vapor,* and *Dos a uno;*

Arde el desierto con los vientos que vienen del sur (Mexicali: Instituto de Cultura de Baja California, 1991);

Vapor: Obra en un acto (Caracas: Centro Latinoamericano de Creación e Investigación Teatral, 1994);

Los endemoniados: En encuentro en Occidente (Mexico: Tablado Iberoamericano, 1996);

10 obras en un acto (Tijuana: CAEN, 1996);

Telón abierto: Ensayos sobre literatura y teatro (Mexicali: Instituto de Cultura de Baja California, 1997);

Hugo Salcedo, Teatro de Frontera, 2 (Durango, Mexico: Espacio Vacío, 1999)—comprises *Bárbara Gandiaga, El árbol del deseo, La estrella del norte, Selena,* and *Asesinato en los parques;*

Selena, la reina del Tex-Mex: Obra en doce cuadros (Monterrey, Mexico: Facultad de Artes Escénicas de la Universidad Autónoma de Nuevo León, 1999);

Don Tiburcio, el tiburón (Guadalajara: Secretaría de Cultura, 2000);

21 obras en un acto (Toluca, Mexico: Consejo Nacional para la Cultura y las Artes, 2002);

El teatro para niños en México (Mexico City: Porrúa, 2002).

Editions: *El viaje de los cantores* (Mexico: CONACULTA, 2002);

Don Tiburcio, el tiburón y otras obras para niños (Mexicali: Instituto de Cultura de Baja California, 2003).

OTHER: *Misericordia,* in *Expresión escénica jalisciense I* (Guadalajara: Departamento de Bellas Artes de Jalisco, 1986), pp. 41–57;

San Juan de Dios, in *Expresión escénica jalisciense II* (Guadalajara: Departamento de Bellas Artes de Jalisco, 1987), pp. 15–44;

Bulevar, Gestos, 20 (November 1995): 107–132;

Vicios privados: Antología, edited by Salcedo (Tijuana: CAEN, 1997);

Los niños mutilados, in *El nuevo teatro: El milagro* (Mexico: CONACULTA, 1997), pp. 325–371;

Teatro del Norte: Antología, edited by Salcedo (Ensenada: Teatro del Norte, 1998);

Teatro del Norte 2: Antología, edited by Salcedo (Tijuana: Teatro del Norte/UABC-FONCA, 2001);

Teatro del Norte 3: Antología, edited by Salcedo (Tijuana: Teatro del Norte/UABC-FONCA, 2002);

Teatro del Norte 4: Antología, edited by Salcedo (Tijuana: Teatro del Norte/UABC-FONCA, 2003);

El otro, in *Exilios,* edited by Susana Gutiérrez Posse (Buenos Aires: Biblos, 2003), pp. 175–180.

Hugo Salcedo is one of the most original voices to appear out of the "New Mexican Dramaturgy" at the end of the twentieth century and is a pioneering force in the recognition and study of border theater of Mexico and the United States. In his plays Salcedo inquires about the problems of the U.S.-Mexico border and presents them in tragic, mythical, and at times absurd ways. Critic Enrique Mijares states that the area discussed in Salcedo's works, the border, is the demarcation point where misery and suicide start and where reality and dreams are the only hope for survival. The preoccupations presented in Salcedo's plays are deeply rooted in the Mexican psyche, though his characters possess qualities that are both individualistic and universal.

Salcedo's dramaturgy demonstrates another important characteristic: it is pessimistic. As he explains in his article "Dramaturgia de la perplejidad" (Dramaturgy of Perplexity), which appears in his collection titled *Telón abierto: Ensayos sobre literatura y teatro* (1997, Open Curtain: Essays on Literature and Theater), existentialist despair, hopelessness, abandonment, conflict, and rupture plague his plays. For Mexican dramatist Emilio Carballido, Salcedo's theater is "difícil el suyo: violento, contrastado, lleno de personajes con recovecos lóbregos" (difficult: it is violent, contradictory, and full of characters with dark secrets). Salcedo's plays are also political. In spite of the hopeless situation in which the characters live, their voices can be heard, pleading for a more just and humane world.

Hugo Octavio Salcedo Larios was born in Ciudad Guzmán, in the state of Jalisco, Mexico, on 24 September 1964. He grew up in a pleasant family environment where he was the eighth of nine children of J. Jesús Salcedo Palomino, a car mechanic specializing in diesel systems, and Matilde Larios Carrillo, a homemaker. His parents would often take the children to the theater as a reward. Young Hugo was an avid learner, and by the age of four he already knew how to read and write. He attended Cedros de Líbano Elementary School and Cristi Martínez de Cossío Secondary School, both located in Guadalajara, Jalisco. When Hugo was young, his sister Martha took him to see a production of a play by Guatemalan playwright Manuel Galich, *El pescado indigesto* (1961, The Fish with an Upset Stomach), done by her high-school theater group. When he found his sister's costume from the play in the laundry room of their house the next day, he was struck by the perception that it had lost its magical powers and metamorphosed into common clothing; this finding inspired his desire to unveil the secret of such transformations.

Three years later Salcedo met with a friend from elementary school who was an actor in the Jalisco Department of Fine Arts Children's Theatre Company. His friend arranged an interview with the demanding director of the company to see if Salcedo could get a part in their next production. He acquired a small role as part of the children's chorus in a production of Carlo

Collodi's *Pinocchio* (1883). He continued developing as an actor and participating in many plays, and in the seventh grade he wrote a children's play that was read in class.

Salcedo did his *preparatoria* (preparatory school) and undergraduate studies at the University of Guadalajara, where he earned a bachelor's degree in Spanish literature in 1989 and wrote his thesis, "Una aproximación a la dramaturgia actual en Jalisco a través del mexicano contemporáneo" (An Approximation of the Current Dramaturgy of Jalisco Seen Through Contemporary Mexican Theater). *En la oscuridad del laberinto* (In the Shadow of the Labyrinth, 1982) was his first staged play, done by Grupo de Teatro El Globo of the University of Guadalajara. His first successful plays were *Misericordia* (Mercy; performed in 1985) and *San Juan de Dios* (Saint John of God; published in 1987, performed in 2001). These two plays, as well as *Dos a uno* (Two to One, performed in 1987) and *Cumbia (Hasta las tres de la mañana)* (Cumbia [Until Three A.M.]; published in 1990, performed in 2003), are considered to be Salcedo's best plays from his early phase. A characteristic of these first works is poignant social and political criticism. All are one-act plays that present human beings living in miserable situations and conditions. In the society presented by Salcedo, no one is concerned with the well-being of the poor and those who suffer. In these plays the author explores how hatred, wickedness, and hunger can destroy families and entire societies.

Misericordia, a play in one act and two scenes, presents two ghosts—a mother and a daughter—having to face eternity recounting the reasons why their family suffered deaths and destruction. *Misericordia* received second place in Expresión Escénica Jalisciense I, a competition run by the Department of Fine Arts of the State of Jalisco in 1985. The scenery presented in the play is mysterious and sad. The two women pretend that they do not know why they are in this old, dark, and damp mansion. Both characters play games; the daughter sings lullabies, and the mother knits. Gradually they reenact the unfortunate events that led them to end their lives in dreadful circumstances. Mother and daughter recall the times when they were happy and alive as well as all the hatred and deceit that brought them to their demise. At the end of the play the mother asks her daughter for mercy and forgiveness, but the daughter tells her that those bonds are now dead. Both women realize that they will have to live in this purgatory forever; at that moment the play restarts, and the cycle repeats itself.

With *San Juan de Dios* Salcedo won first place in the Expresión Escénica Jalisciense II competition in 1986 and also first place in the Punto de Partida Awards given by the Universidad Nacional Autónoma de México (UNAM). There are two temporal spaces in the play. One of them shows the San Juan neighborhood in the city of Guadalajara, Jalisco, in the present as a place of prostitutes, pimps, mariachi bands, violence, sadness, and poverty. The other plane presents the history of St. John of God, a Spanish saint who lived in the sixteenth century, and the many miracles that have been attributed to him all over the world and especially in Mexico. As the play progresses, the historical plane presents the city of Guadalajara during colonial and independence times, and the San Juan neighborhood is contrasted with its present-day ruin and decay.

The main characters of the present-day segments are Maricruz, her mother, and their violent lover, who is also named Juan. All of them live in the San Juan neighborhood, where the two women work as prostitutes. Their relationship is abusive and incestuous; both mother and daughter are in love with Juan and are constantly fighting for his affection and attention. As the historical events escalate in magnitude and the number of miracles attributed to the saint increase, so do the problems at home for the two women. The play ends with violence and despair. This bleakness has led Carballido to conclude that *San Juan de Dios* insinuates an irrational, mechanical, and eternal cause-effect-cause law of the universe: love generates hate, which in turn transforms love to create hate again.

The following year Salcedo won first place in the Punto de Partida Awards for his play *Dos a uno,* which presents the daily life of a low-income Mexican family living in a housing project. The father, Guillermo, does not seem to have interest in anything that has to do with his family. He is a macho womanizer who wants to have his breakfast served and to be left alone watching his Sunday soccer match. Paquita, the mother, does all home chores and never seems to get anyone's attention. Marisela, the daughter, works to support her family. She resents the parental control and lack of freedom. The son, Memo (diminutive for Guillermo), is a younger version of his father. He will probably continue the cycle of machismo and control in the family. Marisela hopes to someday break away from this legacy, and the last scene of the play indicates that it will happen. The change occurs as her father's team is winning by a score of two to one and as her parents are teaming up in a verbal fight against Marisela. The conversations that take place in this household make it obvious that the lines of communication between the members of this family have been broken. The only thing that will make Guillermo stop watching his game will be a terrible accident.

Even though *Dos a uno* is a one-act play, the characters in it are well developed, expressing their dreams and frustrations. The language that they use is colorful, accurately reflecting that of the working-class residents of Mexico City in the later part of the twentieth century. The play sends the message that contemporary Mexicans want to create a new nation and society, one that would preserve the Mexican heritage and culture but would abolish all the social ills that come from machismo and oppression.

In *Cumbia* the deprivation and lack of love that bring all the characters in a family to a tragic end are ignored by Cuca, the protagonist. She explains in her last monologue that dancing, partying, and taking care of herself are the only things she is concerned with in her life. Her personality does not allow her to feel empathy for the problems of others, even if they are her own family:

> Yo no puedo ser una canción romántica de las del radio. Yo soy toda una cumbia, con esas cosas que hablan sólo las cumbias sabrosas y picantes, sin nada de melcocha porque luego te rondan las moscas y no te dejan en paz. Mi vida es eso, un ritmo que entra por los oídos y sale por la punta de los zapatos para bailar y bailar de corrido toda la noche hasta las dos o tres de la mañana.
>
> (I could not be a romantic song like the ones from the radio. I am a *cumbia* song, because I can only talk of hot and juicy things, and I detest sappy endings. This is what my life is, a *cumbia* song, because it has a rhythm that enters through my ears and comes out of the tips of my toes to allow me to dance and dance nonstop until two or three A.M.)

With this play Salcedo won the National Dramaturgy Prize given by the Instituto Nacional de Bellas Artes in 1987.

Salcedo left the city of Guadalajara in 1989 and moved to Tijuana, which offered him new possibilities for work and represented a fresh frontier to explore his art. The geographic distance between the two cities allowed him to find his own voice and to explore new and innovative themes and techniques in his theater. Yet, his first real break came not from an institution in the state of Baja California but from his old alma mater in the state of Jalisco. The University of Guadalajara provided him with a scholarship and the opportunity to continue postgraduate studies in Spain. Salcedo obtained his master's degree in theater in 1992 from the Universidad Autónoma de Barcelona and his doctorate in Spanish literature in 1999 from the Universidad Complutense de Madrid.

Salcedo's early plays and awards established him as a significant figure in what became known as the New Mexican Dramaturgy, but without a doubt *El viaje de los cantores* (The Crossing; performed and published in 1990) has been the play that gave him more international success. With this play Salcedo won the coveted Tirso de Molina Award given by the Spanish organization Instituto de Cooperación Iberoamericana in 1989. In 1990 the same play won the award for best Mexican author of the year from the Association of Mexican Critics and Journalists, and the Punto de Partida Award for the best Mexican play of the year.

El viaje de los cantores is the first play of a trilogy focusing on the U.S.-Mexico border. In this play the border acquires mythical characteristics and proportions that make it become a dark and dangerous place to conquer. The second play, *Arde el desierto con los vientos que vienen del sur* (The Desert is Burning with the Southern Winds; published in 1990, performed in 1993), winner of the Premio Baja California de Teatro given by the Instituto de Cultura de Baja California in 1990, tells the story of how the city of Tijuana was founded. This area is now presented as a place of opportunities. Finally, *Sinfonía en una botella* (Symphony in a Bottle; performed and published in 1990) shows the daily occurrences in the San Ysidro–San Diego international border crossing and focuses on several drivers as they are waiting in their cars to go to the United States. This border crossing is considered to be the point with the most traffic in North America. Salcedo's trilogy presents the border as a geographical, historical, economical, and cultural point of departure.

El viaje de los cantores is a one-act play that is subdivided into ten scenes. The stage directions state that the play can be performed in three different ways: following the linear structure presented in scenes 1 through 10; following the chronological line of events; or randomizing the scenes and each night doing a different combination of them. This last suggestion, Salcedo admits, is reminiscent of Julio Cortázar's novel *Rayuela* (Hopscotch, 1968). With this proposition he hopes to expose the cruelty of events without having to use the Aristotelian model, in which a chronological buildup of a tragic story creates an automatic and sympathetic reaction from an audience toward the characters. Salcedo is interested in making audiences reflect about the incident rather than just show emotions. In the play the different scenes function like fragments of reality, seen and propagated from many individual points of view.

El viaje de los cantores exemplifies all the major themes of Salcedo's dramaturgy. The characters collectively undertake a tragic journey. This play is partially based on an event that made newspaper headlines all over the world when eighteen Mexican men suffocated in a sealed train car while trying to cross the border into the United States; the bodies of the men were found by

Cover for Salcedo's successful collection of one-act plays (10 One-Act Plays, 1996), a volume Salcedo considers one of his favorites (Harold B. Lee Library, Brigham Young University)

the U.S. Border Patrol on 2 July 1987. The play focuses on four characters (Chayo, Timbón, Miqui, and Noé) who start their journey in the small, depressed Mexican town of Ojo Caliente in the state of Zacatecas and end it by dying in Sierra Blanca, Texas. The play also presents two more characters of importance; one is named only El Desconocido (The Stranger). He joins the group about to board the train car to the United States at the last minute. The other is the group's guide whose nickname is El Mosco (The Fly). In the last scene, a priest presides over the burials in Ojo Caliente with a choir of the women left behind by these men. In his sermon he says that these deaths will transcend and acquire greater meaning:

> SACERDOTE. *(Completamente exaltado.)* Señores, este acontecimiento debe ser de reflexión para todos nosotros. Debe de abrigar la justicia y la esperanza que llegará muy pronto y que debemos esperar no con los brazos cruzados, no sentados en actitud contemplativa, sino luchando y defendiendo nuestros derechos.
>
> (PRIEST. *[Completely exalted.]* Ladies and gentlemen, this tragedy ought to make us reflect. It must harbor justice with the hope that it will soon arrive and that we must wait not with our arms crossed, not sitting down in a contemplative way but fighting and defending our own rights.)

He concludes his speech by saying that these undocumented workers have made the greatest sacrifice a person can make for his or her country and therefore are the contemporary heroes that Mexico loses every day. This passionate speech also sends a religious message: the death of El Desconocido is compared to Christ's Crucifixion and his Second Coming.

El viaje de los cantores starts with an epigraph written by Jacques Lacan emphasizing the need for self and societal analysis. The journey the immigrants make is a call for reflection on what it really means for an individual and all Mexicans to cross this border. Traversing the border can have different meanings. Peter Beardsell indicates that the fundamental and universal expressions "to cross" or to "travel to the other side" can be metaphors for the psychological need to know oneself. The poetic and painful language used in the play increases the tragedy and anguish because it explains why so many people make this journey daily. The reasons for their departures vary but may include the search for a new life, a freer environment, and a better future and standards of living for the person and his or her family. In turn the families and loved ones left behind suffer the anguish of losing a family member and the possibility that this person will never return home again.

In *El viaje de los cantores* the border is presented as a geographical space that shows opposing, mysterious, and conflictive qualities. This cryptic space will be the springboard from which these men will cross to another plane and world. From the beginning of the play the characters discuss the dangers and opportunities that this area offers. They all decide that the advantages outweigh the risks, so they leave everything and pay corrupt thugs to guide them in their journey.

The characters in *El viaje de los cantores* show ambiguous qualities. Their personalities have been transformed because of the precarious and dehumanized situation in which they must live. At the beginning of their journey the men are happy and in good spirits. They tell jokes, play cards, and sing while riding in the train car. Finally, when they feel threatened and are dying of asphyxiation, they become a mass of violent animals and end up beating their guide, El Mosco, to death. The description of the body reveals the viciousness: "lo encontraron todo despedazado adentro de un vagón de ferrocarril. Bueno, algunos creemos que es él" (they found him all torn into pieces inside the train car. Well, at least we think that body is his). During El Mosco's death the undocumented men appear to lose their individuality and humanity to become a brutal, animalistic, and perturbing mass. The opposite effect occurs with El Mosco: at the end of the play his grandmother gives information about her grandson, helping recover part of his humanity.

Bárbara Gandiaga: Crimen y condena en la misión de Santo Tomás (Bárbara Gandiaga: Crime and Punishment in the Mission of Santo Tomas; performed in 1994, published in 1999), a two-act play, is a tragedy based on historical information. It re-creates life in the eighteenth and nineteenth centuries in the state of Baja California, in a place ruled by the friars of three different missions: the Jesuits, Franciscans, and Dominicans. The Pai Pai and Kumian Indian nations also inhabited this area. The official historical incident was the violent murder of Eulaldo Surroca, a Dominican friar of the Mission of Santo Tomás de Ensenada in 1803. Surroca's indigenous servant, Bárbara Gandiaga, was accused of his murder; she was later found guilty and sentenced to death. Salcedo wishes to accentuate Bárbara's image as the hero rebelling against the despotic authorities of the time. Her history must be brought out of obscurity so that she can become a symbol of the oppressed people of Mexico. The last monologue of the play exemplifies this point, as an old lady equates Bárbara Gandiaga's fight with the rebellion that Subcomandante Marcos of the Zapatista National Liberation Army was leading in Chiapas, Mexico, in the mid 1990s:

VIEJA. Basta asomarse un poco a las cosas de todos los días y descubrir que hay pueblos sometidos que levantan el fusil para liberarse de la opresión que los encarcela; porque si algo importa de todo esto, es la valentía con que se escucha el grito y que por fortuna sigue formando un eco imparable y expansivo. ¡Y que más da llamarse Bárbara o simplemente Marcos! Aquella mujer fui yo o mi hija o mi hermana o todas juntas a la vez pero siempre alguien que actuaba en el tiempo.

(OLD LADY. And it is enough to take a look at everyday life to discover that some exploited peoples are taking up arms to liberate themselves from the oppression that imprisons them. Because if there is one important point in all of this, it is the courage shown even during their laments and cries that fortunately continues to form an unending and effusive echo. It is not important if a person's name is Bárbara or simply Marcos! That woman could have been me, my daughter, my sister, or any women taking charge of a situation in time.)

Common to Salcedo's works, and specifically in *Bárbara Gandiaga,* is an array of descriptions and perspectives of the protagonist and other characters. Bárbara is alternately described as a demon; a person with strong personality and convictions; a sensual, beautiful woman; and a victim. Salcedo's characters are multidimensional, and seldom is an audience permitted to feel total empathy for any of them. This distancing is also why Bárbara's actual death is not seen at the end of the play. The author is more interested in focusing on her legacy than on her death. The language and scenery of the play help create a mythical, historical, and tragic environment. The language used by the natives is poetic and beautiful, and the one used by the Spaniards is harsh and functional, reflecting the difference between the people of this unspoiled territory, representing the true character of Mexico, and the borrowed culture that they were forced to acquire from the Spanish conquerors.

In addition to the historical and sociopolitical discussion, Salcedo also presents an impossible love affair between Bárbara and her boyfriend Juan Miguel. Bárbara plans with her boyfriend's help to kill Surroca to defend her honor and that of many other indigenous girls. After Surroca's death, there is actually enough evidence to suggest that at least three different individuals are prime suspects: Juan Miguel, a priest named Domingo, and a puppeteer. The evidence presented in the play places all three individuals at the scene of Surroca's brutal killing, symbolically showing how deep the hatred and resentment against Dominican friars were in this time period. Bárbara, however, is the only one who proudly turns herself in to the authorities and confesses to the heinous crime. At the end of the play she accepts the verdict and does not allow anyone else to take the blame for the killing. Bárbara accepts her destiny and hopes to become an example for all peoples unjustly treated.

The one-act play *La Bufadora* (The Bufadora Cliff, 1995) is set in the beautiful maritime environment of Ensenada, Baja California. The story is of a man and a woman meeting in the afterlife in the same place where she had killed her son twenty years earlier. This plot is partially based on real-life events: while living in Spain, Salcedo had read a news article about a woman who had thrown her children off a cliff because of economic difficulties. Mijares says that in this play the two characters are located at a point where time and action are voluntarily turned upside down; they infinitely replay, in the form of a date between a man and a woman, the eternal encounter and evasion of a couple of ghosts.

Unlike Salcedo's other works that denounce social ills, *La Bufadora* is different, because it is more focused upon the complex universe of human feelings and the dialectics of love. The man and woman can finally find spiritual inner peace after meeting at the enigmatic and treacherous Bufadora Cliff. The play equates this ocean precipice to the great mystery of the universe inside them. When the play ends, both characters have a cathartic realization, discovering that true love will keep them together in this marine vortex, La Bufadora, even in the afterlife.

Bulevar (Boulevard; performed and published in 1995) is another play that takes place in the city of Tijuana. It rewrites the popular myth of the origin of the legendary five-and-ten store of downtown Tijuana. In this play the characters–Prometheus, Creon, Hercules, Clytemnestra, Egist, Echo, Narcissus, and Hermes–have similarities to the Greco-Roman characters whose names they bear. Their complicated lives of political intrigues, revenge, and unreciprocated love affairs come together for a brief moment in this Tijuana store. The legend solidifies and explains how this inhospitable area of Mexico was founded and populated.

These characters live separate and sorrowful lives. Creon and Hercules are two politicians and local leaders who refuse to allow Prometheus to protest the corruption and abuse that take place in the *maquiladora* (crossborder assembly plant) factories of the area. As a result of his protests, Prometheus is killed. Clytemnestra dreams of someday being able to kill her long-lost husband, if he ever returns from the North (the United States). She refuses to accept the fact that he died while crossing the border illegally; she keeps on planning the perfect murder so as to become a widow. In another couple's case, Hermes, full of hatred and rage, decides as a form of revenge to cast a spell on his lover Narcissus. In a horrible accident at work, a machine severs both of the young man's hands. At the end of the play, Narcissus's tragedy is not that he lost his two limbs but that he will not be able to communicate with Echo, the deaf-mute girl, with his hands. In *Bulevar* all the characters wish to communicate through languages that are not necessarily oral. They also hope that through myth they can give their day-to-day world, the city of Tijuana, some meaning.

In 1996 Salcedo began working at the Universidad Autónoma de Baja California in the field of Spanish philology. He is engaged in teaching, researching, writing, and theater direction. He was given a leave of absence to finish his doctorate in Spain. In 2003 he was named chairperson of the Spanish Language and Literature Program, which has given him the opportunity to develop graduate and undergraduate courses in his department, organize conferences and symposiums, and invite visiting scholars to campus.

10 obras en un acto (10 One-Act Plays, 1996) is a collection that has been well accepted with student and amateur theater groups all over Mexico and abroad. His themes of love between two people and the impossibility of communication recur in plays such as *Zona neutral* (Neutral Zone), *Endless Love, Descubiertos* (Exposed), and *Vuelve el pájaro a su nido* (The Bird Returns to Its Nest). Social and political criticism is also found in plays such as *Primero de mayo* (May Day) and *Uno de octubre* (October First). There are plays that treat mythical themes, such as *La llorona* (The Weeping Woman), and others that present theatrical innovation, such as *Lear Instamátic*.

In an unpublished 28 January 2002 e-mail to Iani del Rosario Moreno, Salcedo stated that this collection of plays is perhaps the work that has brought him the most satisfaction and recognition. Many groups have preferred to entertain audiences by staging the humorous plays such as *Vuelve el pájaro a su nido*. Other groups have chosen to follow a more tragic and political vein. *Uno de octubre* has been recognized by critics and theater groups alike as one of his best plays. It presents an imaginary but realistic incident that could have taken place the night before the Tlatelolco Massacre in Mexico City in 1968. The character of the Beggar represents the deceit and violence that was attributed to the government forces. The Boy is a symbol of the youthful and naive student movement that was crushed by Mexican security forces on 2 October 1968.

The success of *10 obras en un acto* allowed Salcedo to expand this collection from ten to twenty-one plays. *21 obras en un acto* (21 One-Act Plays) was published in 2002. Most of the plays added to the collection represent the new material that Salcedo wrote between 1996 and 2002. From this new collection some of the plays continue to be poignantly Mexican, either by their language, topics, and geographical location, while others have become globally diverse. Additional plays come from his older body of work already published in magazines and other collections, such as *La Bufadora, Dos a uno,* and *Vapor.*

El árbol del deseo (The Tree of Desire; published in 1999, performed in 2004), a one-act, three-scene play, is a study on how extreme sadness and solitude can lead to incest, punishment, abuse, torture, and death. Bad Boy and the Woman are the only two characters of the piece, and the stage is completely taken over by a luxuriant tree whose branches extend ferociously. Soon the audience perceives that the boy–who is really a man of twenty-some years–has been condemned to live like an animal by his stepmother, who had an affair with him. The Woman lives a life of repentance and is constantly blaming herself for the great sin she has committed. To cleanse herself of this incest, she punishes Bad Boy by keeping him prisoner. When the play starts he is seated on a tree trunk with a long chain tied to his ankle.

The two characters represent the two different sides of this relationship. The boy represents the desire that this mature woman cannot restrain. She does the opposite and tries to stop his advances by mistreating him, calling him names, and punishing him. The play ends tragically. Like many of her compatriots, the Woman decides to make the journey north, to leave once and for all the source of her abnormal desire. The final scene is visual and shocking: Bad Boy hangs dead from the tree. In his last words he says that he knows that in the other life he will be able to break those chains. He adds that even if she goes north, she will not be capable of breaking these bonds of aberrant desire.

There is another category in Salcedo's dramaturgy: theater that portrays heroes of the *Norteño* (Northern Mexico) and Chicano (Mexican American) popular culture. *Selena: La reina del Tex-Mex* (Selena: The Queen of Tex-Mex; performed in 1998, published in 1999) is a one-act, twelve-scene drama that explores the impact on the border communities of the death of famous Tex-Mex singer Selena Quintanilla-Pérez, who was shot by her former fan-club president in 1995. The author used many sources such as the book *El secreto de Selena* (Selena's Secret, 1997) by María Celeste Arrarás, newspapers, magazines, television, poems, and Selena's music. This play marks the first time that Salcedo has a protagonist who is not a Mexican but a Chicana. The play shows how difficult life can be for Chicanos in the United States, as every day they must traverse the "bridge" between their Hispanic and American heritage. Selena, who had great success singing most of her music in Spanish, had been preparing her first English-language album to fulfill her dream of being accepted in the American market. She accomplishes this crossover dream and is hailed by her people, but only after her death.

The play introduces a series of vignettes that present different perspectives of the border condition from both sides of the frontier line. Selena and other characters are continually obligated to cross geographical, political, and cultural borders. Their roles also change. The actress who plays Yolanda Saldívar, Selena's assassin, appears in some scenes as the president of Selena's fan club and Selena's confidante; in other scenes, she plays the role of a poor Mexican American woman who is trying to cross the border with her child and is stopped by a border-patrol officer. The actor who plays American Union, a transvestite who continues Selena's musical legacy, also plays the role of a fan who visits the scene of Selena's death as well as the Mexican American border-patrol officer (Jaime "Jimmy" García Salazar) who stops the woman at the border.

In a symbolic ending to the play, American Union and Selena, the Queen of Mexicans and Immigrants,

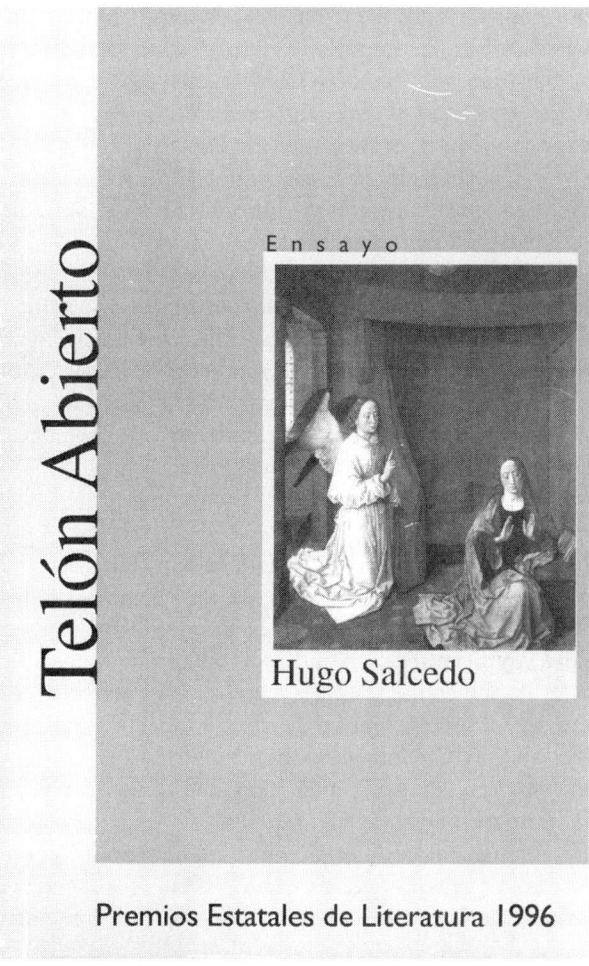

Cover for a 2003 edition of Salcedo's collection of essays about literature and theater (Open Curtain), first published in 1997 (Collection of Iani del Rosario Moreno)

will unite in another dimension to create a new country. As the "new" Selena, American Union will continue performing her music in his show. He says: "Las partes complementarias. Norte y sur y no hay fronteras. Las barreras se borran. Los idiomas se enriquecen. Yo soy la mentira realizable, y entre las dos construimos un puente, un puente entre la gente. ¡Yo soy la Unión Americana!" (The parts will complement themselves. North and South are one. There are no longer any borders. The barriers are erased. Languages are enriched. I am the lie that can become true, and between both of them we can construct a bridge, a bridge amongst the people. I am the American Union!)

La estrella del norte (The Northern Star; published in 1999), subtitled a one-act religious play in nineteen scenes, is a type of contemporary border pastoral play. In it modern Wise Men follow a star that leads them to the city of Tijuana and the northern Mexican border. Life in this town is difficult, and the possibility of going north is the only light that keeps many people motivated to live. Salcedo portrays stylized characters such as the Man with his dogs, the Vulture, and the Commander. In this world two newcomers, José and an expectant María, must survive and succeed.

The characters live in a world of drug traffickers, violence, misery, illnesses, addictions, and illegal traffic of children. The Three Wise Men in the play are presented quite differently than the ones from the gospel. Melchior is a hippie who is a palm and tarot reader. Gaspar is a Native American shaman who cannot read or write and speaks an incomprehensible language of his own. Balthasar is a university student and a homeopathic doctor's assistant. Reminiscent of the biblical story, their search for the Northern Star brings them to the new Herodes (a local police commander).

In this pastoral play, all the characters (José, María, the Three Wise Men, the police chief, and the Vulture) are looking for someone they cannot find. In the last scene María's child is born in a cardboard box far away from the city, and everyone is able to see the Star. At the end of the play there is chant and modern dance. All listen to music interlaced with Beatles melodies and pre-Columbian sounds. In this border juncture the modern, the indigenous, and the foreign unite to indicate the beginning of a new era.

Hugo Salcedo's dramaturgy continues to be at the forefront of Mexican theater in the twenty-first century. The author recognizes that the situation in his country has not been optimal for a long time; in his article "Dramaturgia de la perplejidad" (Dramaturgy of Perplexity), included in *Telón abierto,* he writes: "El ser humano se encuentra en un callejón sin salida, en una carrera desenfrenada hacia la fatalidad" (People are stranded in a blind alley in a reckless race toward misfortune). The ambiguous nature of his characters helps to emphasize the constant conflict of the forces of good and evil that define the essence of human beings and their societies. Even if his plays discuss turbulent mental states, his characters always find a way of reflecting on how to improve their lives. Salcedo heads a new group of dramatists presently showing their compatriots and the world the many faces of Mexico. Their theater has a tendency to be pessimistic and even schizophrenic as a consequence of the economic, social, and ecological chaos they live in, but their most important contribution is the presentation of Mexico in the new millennium.

References:

Peter Beardsell, "Crossing the Border in Three Plays by Hugo Salcedo," *Latin American Theatre Review,* 29 (Spring 1996): 71–84;

Emilio Carballido, "Prólogo," in *Teatro Hugo Salcedo* (Guadalajara: Universidad de Guadalajara, 1990), pp. 5–6;

Enrique Mijares, *Realidad virtual del teatro mexicano* (Mexico City: Casa Juan Pablos, 1999).

Florencio Sánchez
(17 January 1875 – 7 November 1910)

Ricardo Szmetan
University of West Indies–Barbados

SELECTED PLAY PRODUCTIONS: *¡Ladrones!* Montevideo, Centro Internacional de Estudios Sociales, 1897;

Puertas adentro, Montevideo, Centro Internacional de Estudios Sociales, 1897;

Canillita, Rosario, Argentina, Lloret Company, 2 October 1902; Buenos Aires, Teatro de la Cormedia, 4 January 1904;

M'hijo el dotor, Buenos Aires, Teatro de la Cormedia, 13 August 1903;

Cédulas de San Juan, Buenos Aires, Teatro de la Cormedia, August 1904;

La pobre gente, Buenos Aires, Teatro de San Martín, 1904;

La gringa, Buenos Aires, Teatro de San Martín, 21 November 1904;

Barranca abajo, Buenos Aires, Teatro Apolo, 1905;

Mano santa, Buenos Aires, Teatro Apolo, 9 June 1905;

En familia, Buenos Aires, Teatro Apolo, 6 October 1905;

Los muertos, Buenos Aires, Teatro Apolo, 23 October 1905;

El conventillo, Buenos Aires, Teatro Marconi, 22 June 1906;

El desalojo, Buenos Aires, Teatro Apolo, July 1906;

El pasado de una vida, Buenos Aires, Teatro Argentino, 22 October 1906;

Los curdas [revision of *La gente honesta*], Buenos Aires, Teatro Apolo, 2 January 1907;

La tigra, Buenos Aires, Teatro Argentino, 2 January 1907;

Moneda falsa, Buenos Aires, Teatro Nacional, 8 January 1907;

El cacique Pichuelo, Buenos Aires, Teatro Argentino, 9 January 1907;

Nuestros hijos, Buenos Aires, Teatro Nacional, 2 May 1907;

Los derechos de la salud, Montevideo, Uruguay, Teatro Solís, 4 December 1907;

Marta Gruni, Montevideo, Uruguay, Teatro Solis, 7 July 1908;

Un buen negocio, Montevideo, Uruguay, 2 May 1909.

BOOKS: *Los muertos; Nuestros hijos; Barranca abajo; La gringa* (Buenos Aires: Tor, 1900);

Los derechos de la salud (Buenos Aires, 1908);

Nuestros hijos (Montevideo: O. M. Bertani, 1909);

Un buen negocio (Buenos Aires: B. Fueyo, 1910);

Marta Gruni (Buenos Aires: B. Fueyo, 1910);

La gringa; Los derechos de la salud (Buenos Aires: El Teatro Criollo, 1910);

Barranca abajo (Buenos Aires: Libreria "Apollo," Alvarez, ca. 1910–1919?);

Cartas de un flojo; Diálogos de actualidad; Estudio sobre Joao Francisco (Montevideo: Archivos de Psiquiatría y Criminología, 1914);

El caudillaje criminal en Sud-América (Montevideo: Maximino García, 1914);

Canillita (Buenos Aires: Librería Teatro Apolo, 1915);

La pobre gente y Mano santa (Buenos Aires: La Escena, 1918);

El desalojo (Buenos Aires: El Teatro Nacional, 1920);

Los derechos de la salud; En familia; Moneda falsa (Valencia: Cervantes, 1920);

La gente honesta (Buenos Aires: El Teatro Nacional, 1920);

Moneda falsa (Buenos Aires: El Teatro Nacional, 1920);

En familia (Tucumán, 1920);

Canillita y Cédulas de San Juan (Buenos Aires: L. Bernard, 1921);

La gringa (Montevideo: Claudio García, 1927); edited by John Thomas Lister and Ruth Richardson (New York: Knopf, 1927); translated by Alfred Coester as *The Foreign Girl,* in *Plays of the Southern Americas* (Stanford, Cal.: Stanford University Press, 1942);

M'hijo el dotor (Buenos Aires: Araujo, 1939);

La de anoche, En familia (Buenos Aires: Ediciones del Carro de Tespis, 1958);

Cartas de un flojo; El caudillaje criminal en Sud-América; Diálogos de actualidad (Montevideo: Ediciones del Río de la Plata, 1962);

Florencio Sánchez (Biblioteca Nacional, Montevideo; from Jorge Pignataro, Florencio Sánchez, *1979; Paley Library, Temple University)*

Cartas de un flojo (Montevideo: Siglo Ilustrado, 1968).

Editions and Collections: *Barranca abajo; Los muertos* (Buenos Aires: La Cultura Argentina, 1916);

El teatro del uruguayo Florencio Sánchez (Valencia: Cervantes, 1917);

Teatro de Florencio Sánchez, 2 volumes (Buenos Aires: Sopena Argentina, 1939);

Teatro completo de Florencio Sánchez, edited by Dardo Cúneo (Buenos Aires: Claridad, 1941);

Teatro completo, edited by Vicente Martínez Cuitiño (Buenos Aires: El Ateneo, 1951);

Moneda falsa, edited by Ricardo Rojas (Buenos Aires: Quetzal, 1953);

Teatro (Havana: Casa de las Américas, 1963);

Teatro, 2 volumes, edited by Walter Rela (Montevideo: Barreiro y Ramos, 1967);

Obras completas, edited by Jorge Raúl Lafforgue (Buenos Aires: Schapire, 1968).

Edition in English: *Representative Plays,* translated by Willis Knapp Jones, edited by Glenn Barr (Washington, D.C.: Pan American Union, 1961).

OTHER: *¡Ladrones!* in Eva Montoya, *Teatro y folletines libertarios rioplatenses, 1895–1910: Estudio y antología* (Ottawa: Girol, 1996).

Dramatist Florencio Sánchez was born and raised in Uruguay, but most of his plays were produced in Argentina, raising the question of whether he belongs to Argentine or Uruguayan theater. The best way to describe him may be to use the term *rioplatense,* which means that he belongs to both countries. Sánchez created most of his works while living in Argentina and always considered his work to belong to Argentine theater. Sánchez liked to describe the human drama of those people who lived in the large old hotels called *conventillos,* where many families shared sparse rooms and lived under difficult conditions. He also described the inhuman working conditions of the labor force, who were made to work long hours for low wages under the permanent fear of being laid off or even deported from the country.

An additional important aspect of his plays is the clash of values between the new forces of capitalism, with their thrust toward change and their presumed lack of respect for the local traditions, and the basic structures of society. Normally in Sánchez's plays, the idea of progress is represented by young entrepreneurial characters, and the local tradition is represented by ancient gauchos. The latter is not simply an icon, but a complicated and often negative figure, different from the one presented by many of Sánchez's contemporaries. The gaucho in Sánchez is also partially urbanized and the point of union between indigenous and European tendencies.

Before Sánchez staged his first pieces in Buenos Aires, the major center of Argentine theater, the extent of local production amounted to just a few plays written after Argentina gained independence in 1817. Even as late as 1890, European theater was practically the only theater available; groups of actors were coming over from Spain or Italy and staging performances in their own language. Therefore, conditions were not yet right for the formation of a national theater with local writers. This situation changed in the 1890s with the arrival of the Podestás, a large theatrical family whose origins had been in the circus. With their simple presence and presentations, they practically dominated the local performance scene for many years. José J. Podestá, known as Pepino 88, was the most prominent member of the family and probably the best actor among them. His dramatic version of *Juan Moreira* (1886), based on the novel by Eduardo Gutiérrez that had been published in the newspaper *La Patria Argentina* between 1879 and 1880, was a great success; he and his family continued to stage other classical works using popular and mythical gaucho characters such as Martín Fierro, Juan Cuello, and Santos Vega. The gaucho was described in a simple way, and these characteristics were fixed in their representation: love, friendship, loyalty, freedom, and austerity. The gaucho was frequently presented in conflict with authority, but in neither a brutal nor a bloody manner. The frequent use of the gaucho was probably caused by his increasing disappearance from Argentine society.

At the end of the nineteenth century, conditions in Buenos Aires were beginning to reflect the developing local community. The foreign population outnumbered the national population, with most foreigners coming from Spain and Italy. This generation of newcomers, with their mix of different cultures and languages, provided inspiration for the creation of local comic characters. They were also an enthusiastic audience, though perhaps not the most intellectually discriminating. Many of the new theater pieces were often prepared for performance by a new generation of writers whose family names revealed that they were also first-generation immigrants who were using the stage as a way of becoming integrated into their adopted country. Sánchez was perhaps the first writer whose plays described the increasingly contradictory world created by this melting pot of people of different origins, exposing their daily life in the big city and reflecting their personal sufferings.

Sánchez was born in Montevideo, capital of Uruguay, on 17 January 1875. He was the oldest of eleven children born to Olegario Sánchez and Govila Musante. After a few years, the family moved to the parish of "Treinta y Tres" (Thirty-three), where they lived for the next seven years. From 1882 Florencio attended an elementary school for a few years, the only official education that he ever had. He also spent a few years in a private high school in Montevideo but left without completing his education. The young Sánchez read extensively, though not always systematically. In 1889 he moved to the Minas region, where he held a minor position in a government office. He started to experiment with writing, at first producing poetry and articles that were critical of the local political situation. In 1891 he was fired. His writing at this time appeared under the pseudonym of Jack the Ripper and marked the emergence of his anarchist ideas.

In 1893 Sánchez moved to Buenos Aires and took up an appointment in the public office of statistics and anthropometrics, which was headed by Juan Vucetich, the soon-to-be-famous inventor of a system of international dactiloscopy. Sánchez wrote his first literary work, "Un regalo al natural" (A Natural Gift), which was never published. On his return to Montevideo, he began to write articles on daily police investigations for newspapers such as *El Siglo* and *La Razón* under the pseudonym of Ovidio Paredes. He took part as a regular soldier and member of the White Party (one of the two main parties in Uruguay) in the "Revolution of '96," which was instigated by the leader of the White Party, Aparicio Saravia, against the Red Party. Sánchez also joined the anarchist group Centro Internacional de Estudios Sociales (International Center for Social Studies). There he presented and won a prize for his work *¡Ladrones!* (Robbers; produced in 1897, published in 1996), which was never again performed. From this time on he presented his most radical works before such gatherings of working-class people or political societies.

In 1898 Sánchez was asked by the famous Argentine politician Lisandro de la Torre to edit the newspaper *La República*. Sánchez returned to Rosario, the second most important city in Argentina, and remained in that country for the rest of his life. After accomplishing his duties in Rosario, he became part of the bohemian life of Buenos Aires, which was centered on bars and restaurants and cafés such as Los Inmortales, París, and Aue's Keller. In those circles he formed lifelong friendships with many of the better-known Argentine writers of his time. Under the pseudonym of Luciano Stein, he contributed several pieces to the anarchist newspaper *El Sol* about the writer and activist Alberto Ghiraldo, and he wrote articles for *El País* on Carlos

House in Montevideo, Uruguay, where Sánchez was born (from Jorge Cruz, Genio y figura de Florencio Sánchez, *1966; Thomas Cooper Library, University of South Carolina)*

Pellegrini, who later became president. In 1897 he wrote *Puertas adentro* (Doors Within), a scherzo in one act, which was performed at the Centro Internacional de Estudios Sociales in Montevideo. Under his own name he prepared *Cartas de un flojo* (Letters of a Lazy Person), published later in 1914. He also began to collaborate on the most popular satiric magazine of his time, *Caras y Caretas* (Faces and Masks), edited by the famous *costumbrista* (local color) writer Fray Mocho (pseudonym of José Sixto Álvarez).

Emilio O. Schiffner, owner of *La República*, accused Sánchez of being an anarchist and fired him. In retaliation, Sánchez based his model for the satirical character of Chifle in *La gente honesta* (1902, The Honest People) on Schiffner. The play was to have been performed on 26 June 1902 in the new Teatro Politeama, but the municipal authorities prohibited its performance, probably because of transparent satirizations (the petition to cancel came from Schiffner). Although Sánchez published the play in *La Época* the next day, the piece was not performed until 2 January 1907 at the Teatro Apolo in Buenos Aires, under the title *Los curdas* (The Drunks). Sánchez also wrote *Canillita* (1915, Newspaper Vendor), a *sainete* (one-act intermezzo) first performed by the Lloret Company in Rosario on 2 October 1902. The piece is part melodrama, part farce, part tragedy, with an urban or immigrant theme. The dark material about the misery of a family and the limitations of life in a slum is the main factor of the work. *Canillita* is a realistic piece concerning the life of the poor. It is also a discussion of the benefits of a trade union for workers distributing newspapers. Sánchez used his own experiences in Rosario in dealing with poor boys and their families who lived in misery. The play presents a negative picture of its characters but reflects the daily life of many families in the big cities.

Sánchez's friend José Ingenieros, a well-known essayist and doctor, asked him to write a psychological study of Joao Francisco Pereyra de Souza, the Brazilian leader of Coty, Río Grande, for the May 1903 issue of *Archivos de Psiquiatría y Criminología* (Archives of Psychiatry and Criminology), a scientific journal that Ingenieros edited. Sánchez published it under the title *El caudillaje criminal en Sud-América* (1914, The Criminal Popular Leaders in South America) and in 1962 it was edited and published together with *Cartas de un flojo* and *Diálogos de actualidad* (1914; Dialogue of the Present Times). Sánchez also published at this time "La nena y el juez" (The Girl and the Judge), an article protesting against the death penalty; "Pedro y Juan," a satiric work on a public political gathering; "Las veladas en la cocina" (The Days in the Kitchen), a short story; "La señora P. Y. X." (The Lady P.Y.X.), protesting against social conventions; "La justicia en China" (The Justice in China), a short story; "Ciencia política" (Political Science); and "Diálogos de oportunidad" (Dialogue of Opportunity).

M'hijo el dotor (1939, My Son the Doctor), first performed by Jerónimo Podestá's company in Buenos Aires on 13 August 1903, established Sánchez's fame with the general public. *M'hijo el dotor* is a dramatic comedy in three acts. Initially it consisted of four acts and was called "Las dos conciencias" (The Two Consciousnesses). It was Sánchez's first great success and went on to be performed thirty-eight successive times. The action takes place in the countryside and focuses on the conflict between two generations: the gaucho Don Olegario and his son, Julio, an egotistical, educated young man. Julio seduces a woman named Jesusa but refuses to make her his wife, because he is in love with another woman, Sara. Finally, there is reconciliation between Julio and Jesusa. In the father, one sees the traditional gaucho's loyalty to freedom. Everything Julio has learned in the city seems to be a direct insult to the gaucho's personal honor, which Don Olegario is unable to defend as he did when he was a young man. One positive aspect of this play, which recurs in other works by Sánchez, is that gauchos of the old school are portrayed more realistically than by his predecessors. Sánchez's character is devoid of any of the Romantic elements that were often found in many contemporary gaucho novels. The play was warmly received by public and critics alike; never before had a new writer become so famous overnight.

On 25 September 1903 Sánchez married Catalina Raventos, his beloved "Catita," whom he had known for four years. During this period he also collaborated on *La Opinión* with Carlos Rodríguez Larreta and became secretary on the staff at Mariano de Vedia y Mitre's *Tribuna*. Neither of these positions were well paid; in fact, for several months he did not receive any salary at all.

His next new play after a 1904 production of *Canillita* was *Cédulas de San Juan* (The Seals of San Juan), premiering in August 1904 in Buenos Aires, a two-act play that depicts the life of gauchos and their particular language and traditions. The scene is a ranch during the celebration of the saint's day of Don Juan, the owner of the house. The plot centers on the love of Fortunato, Don Juan's son, for Adela, and the opposition of Hilario, another suitor. The piece finishes tragically after a fight between the two men, in which Hilario is killed. Another play, *La pobre gente* (1918, The Poor People), premiered in Buenos Aires in 1904. This naturalistic two-act comedy portrays the life of a tyrannical father and his family in a *conventillo*. It is clearly pessimistic in outlook, but it vividly depicts the problems caused by alcohol and poverty as well as the manner in which workers sell themselves to their bosses in order to survive. Misfortune seems to be the eternal companion of the poor families. In this context people struggle to be honest, but survival becomes paramount. As often happens in Sánchez's pieces, the strongest finally win in a permanent fight against nature and adverse social conditions.

La gringa (1900, The Foreign Girl), which premiered at the Teatro San Martín in Buenos Aires on 21 November 1904, is a four-act drama. Sánchez considered it his best play. The action is once more set in the countryside, portraying the conflict between natives and foreigners. Once again, the playwright places the vision of progress against that of tradition. This play is clearly inspired by the plot of *Sobre las ruinas* (On the Ruins), a drama written by one of the best Argentine writers of this time, Roberto J. Payró, also published in 1904. Don Cantalicio, an older gaucho, is confronted by Don Nicola, an Italian immigrant who is an advocate of modern farming methods, and his two children, Próspero and Victoria (the gringa), who are, as their names indicate, the final victors. Cantalicio is beset by misfortunes, the greatest of which is the loss of his ranch to the neighboring Nicola. Moreover, Cantalicio's honor is in pieces, because as part of the land improvements, Nicola tries to destroy the romantic but useless *ombú* tree on the property. Finally, all four reconcile, and the last words of the piece are: "¡a trabajar!" (go to work!). It was important to Sánchez to depict the animosity between the criollos and the gringos; by the time the play was written, there were more foreigners than nationals in Buenos Aires. In Sánchez's opinion, a combination of these two groups' ideas idealism on the one hand, materialism and progress on the other, the values of the past and the reality of the present–was not only possible but the only way forward.

In 1905 Sánchez produced the play most critics consider his best, *Barranca abajo* (1900, Down the Cliffs), at the Teatro Apolo in Buenos Aires. It continued to be performed after his death and has received the most critical commentary of all of his works. The plot is similar to that of *La gringa*. The action takes place on Don Zoilo's land. As a result of circumstances beyond his control, Zoilo has lost his family estate and his livelihood. Zoilo opposes the changes and modernization that are taking place; he would prefer to kill himself rather than live in a world that he does not understand anymore and in which his ideas are considered outdated. In his youth he might have killed others in order to defend his honor, but now Zoilo is an old man. The scene in which Zoilo commits suicide is so powerfully written that it created a great deal of contro-

Manuscript page from act 1 of Barranca abajo *(Down the Cliffs; published in 1900, performed in 1905), Sánchez's best-known play, about the decline of an aging gaucho who cannot cope with the changing world (Biblioteca Nacional, Montevideo; from Jorge Pignataro,* Florencio Sánchez, *1979; Paley Library, Temple University)*

versy at the time. Even now it is seldom portrayed directly but is shown in a way that only suggests the outcome. When the rope with which he prepares to hang himself becomes entangled in a bird's nest, Zoilo utters his last words, which have become symbolic of the waning freedom of the old criollo, as contrasted with the freedom that he enjoyed in his youth when undoubtedly he was a vigorous gaucho proud of his traditions: "¡Se deshace más fácilmente el nido de un hombre que el nido de un pájaro!" (A man's nest is destroyed so much more easily than a bird's!). The nest itself symbolizes not only freedom but family honor and also the gaucho's own personal sense of honor, his strength and nobility. Sánchez's dramatic treatment is realistically objective and exposes the problems in society.

Later came Sánchez's drama *El conventillo* (The Slum, performed in 1906), a one-act zarzuela, the original manuscript of which has disappeared. He wrote several plays in 1905. *Mano santa* (Holy Hand), which premiered at the Teatro Apolo in Buenos Aires on 9 June, is a *sainete*. This piece is still quite popular because of its simple plot. It ridicules the allegiance that certain people have for magical solutions to the problems of the world. *En familia* (In Family), which premiered at the Teatro Apolo on 6 October 1905, is a tragicomedy. It concerns a middle-class Uruguayan family who face economic problems caused by drinking and gambling, and it shows how they try to avoid revealing to the outside world the extent of their situation. The play can be seen as a Zolaesque study of the consequences for a family living within certain social conditions. The old man, Jorge, regularly disappears for days and returns to the family home penniless or in debt. His son Eduardo does not lift a finger to help, while another young son, Tomasito, is a thief. There are also two daughters in their late teens whose love of finery and cosmetics lends poignant meaning to their vague threats to leave home soon and fend for themselves. The only thing that holds this dissolute father and the four worthless children together is the energy and devotion of Mercedes, the mother. Suddenly hope comes as the oldest son, Damián, who is married, goes into business in another city. He has sold his business for a profit, and when he learns about the miserable existence his family is enduring, he decides to move in and take charge. However, he is defeated at each attempt to improve their lives.

Los muertos (1900, The Dead), premiering at the Teatro Apolo in Buenos Aires on 23 October 1905, is a three-act drama about people who lack willpower. It is one of Sánchez's more popular pieces and the one that gives the protagonist, the Capocómico (Head Comic), many opportunities to display his talents, particularly the comic ones. Clearly naturalistic, the play is centered on the character of Lisandro, a middle-class member of Buenos Aires society and a long-term alcoholic who cannot deal with the daily problems that he faces. Sánchez displays some sympathy for his suffering.

Sánchez was then living in Banfield (a province of Buenos Aires) in a large old house, rented with the 2,000 pesos that the Podestá brothers paid him for *Barranca abajo*. In 1906 he attempted to write a psychological comedy under the title "El pasado" (The Past). Further plays followed: *El desalojo* (The Eviction; produced in 1906, published in 1920), *El pasado de una vida* (1906, The Past of a Life), and *Nuestros hijos* (Our Children; produced in 1907, published in 1900). Although by this time he was seriously ill with tuberculosis, he continued to write and produced *Los derechos de la salud* (The Rights of the Healthy; produced in 1907, published in 1908), *Los curdas, La tigra* (1907, The Tiger) and *Moneda falsa* (False Money; produced in 1907, published in 1920), and in 1908, *Marta Gruni* (published in 1910).

El desalojo, which premiered at the Teatro Marconi in Buenos Aires in July 1906, is a *sainete*. In this play Sánchez is critical of the social conditions of many Argentine families of this time. In order to make the play as realistic as possible, Sánchez injects elements from his own experience as a journalist. He describes the traumatic experiences of a poor family living in a *conventillo* who are in danger of being evicted from their home when they are unable to pay the rent. Indalecía is the mother of five children, and her husband is in the hospital. Before the eviction, *La Nación*, the best-known journal of the time, raises a subscription for Indalecía. Later, a member of the magazine *Caras y Caretas* comes to take a picture of the family.

El pasado de una vida, premiering in La Plata at the Teatro Argentino on 22 October 1906, is a comedy in three acts. The complex plot is about one woman's infidelity. One of her sons understands and accepts the situation while the other does not, and his final acceptance of the situation concludes the work. *Los curdas,* which premiered in Buenos Aires at the Teatro Apolo 2 January 1907, is a *sainete*. The three *cuadros* (scenes) are set in Buenos Aires. The play concerns the doubts of Luisa, a young wife, about her husband's fidelity. This piece is an example of Sánchez's hastily done works that only provide a hint of what might have been accomplished. *La tigra,* premiering in La Plata at the Teatro Argentino 2 January 1907, is a *sainete*. Following in the tradition of Emile Zola, this piece deals with the delicate problem of a prostitute who is also a mother, and the intention of the protagonist, Luis, to try to help her change her life. *El cacique Pichuleo* (performed in 1907) is also a *sainete*. Little is known about this work of Sánchez. *Moneda falsa,* which premiered in Buenos Aires at the Teatro Nacional on 8 January 1907, is a *sainete* about people from the lower classes in Buenos Aires and their private lives.

Nuestros hijos, which also premiered at the Teatro Nacional on 2 May 1907, is a three-act drama. In this work, Sánchez defends a woman's right to decide whether to have children. Mecha is pregnant but unmarried, and she is condemned by a society that fails to understand her intentions. Her father, Señor Díaz, supports her decision to have children without marrying a person she no longer loves.

Los derechos de la salud, premiering in Montevideo at the Teatro Solís on 4 December 1907, has a powerful message: only the strong have the right to live in society. The author's pessimistic vision was apparently influenced by his own illness. The action takes place in an artistic community in Montevideo. Luisa is the wife of a novelist, Roberto. They are a devoted couple with two charming children. However, Luisa becomes ill, and her children are not allowed any contact with her. Her husband runs into debt to pay doctors, and the strain leads him to neglect his work. Renata, Luisa's

Title page for Sánchez's tragicomedy (performed in 1905, published in 1920) about a family trying to hide the financial difficulties caused by their father's drinking and gambling (from Ruth Richardson, Florencio Sánchez and the Argentine Theatre, 1933; Thomas Cooper Library, University of South Carolina)

younger sister, consoles him. She has come to look after the children, and she even sacrifices her own fortune to help the family financially and encourage Roberto to persevere with his writing. Luisa becomes jealous and suspicious of her husband and sister, and the doctor warns that death is imminent. Sánchez's analysis of jealous love aggravated by a haunting sense of death is masterful.

Marta Gruni, premiering in Montevideo at the Teatro Solis on 7 July 1908, is a *sainete*. The action takes place once again in a *conventillo*. This work did not receive any particular attention from the general public or the critics. Also in 1908, however, *Nosotros* (We), the most widely respected Argentine literary journal at this time, dedicated an issue to Sánchez, including commentaries from literary critics and the complete transcription of his play *Los derechos de la salud*.

Statue of Sánchez by Augustín Riganelli, erected in Montevideo in 1927 (from Jorge Cruz, Genio y figura de Florencio Sánchez, 1966; Thomas Cooper Library, University of South Carolina)

Un buen negocio (1909, A Good Business) is Sánchez's final work, completed in a short time. Performed in Montevideo on 2 May 1909, it deals with the tough life of a mother and her four children. That same year, the Uruguayan parliament agreed to pay Sánchez's expenses to allow him to travel to Europe where he hoped to break into European literary circles. He arrived on 13 October 1909 in Genoa, Italy, and traveled throughout Italy and France, settling in Milan in 1910. That fall, Sánchez became ill and had to be admitted to the Fate Bene Fratelli hospital in Milan. Two old friends, Santiago Devic and Fernando Palombo, stayed with him. He died of tuberculosis on 7 November 1910. In 1925 his remains were returned to Uruguay. Four brief dramatic sketches found among Sánchez's manuscripts–*El autor* (The Author), *Los acosados* (The Pursued), *Diálogos de actualidad,* and *Pedro y Juan*–were published posthumously.

In common with the majority of his fellow writers, Sánchez struggled to survive by using his talents as a writer in a capitalist society that had little interest in the well-being of its artistic community. Permanent economic deprivation and a bohemian lifestyle were characteristics that few writers could avoid. Their economic survival depended upon selling their work cheaply to theater owners or to the actor-managers of theater groups. They also contributed regularly to magazines and newspapers. But the pay, if any, did not help them to overcome their financial difficulties. Sánchez always understood the fate of the have-nots in society, perhaps because even with all his success he believed that he still belonged to that group.

Because of the popularity of his plays, Sánchez was paid for his theatrical contributions more generously than was the norm, but the amount was still not enough to dissipate the economic insecurity that was his permanent companion. Nor did it help to alleviate his poor health during his short life. His talents as a creative writer enabled him to change, in only a few years, the local theatrical scene in a way that nobody had done before or has done since. Although in most of his works the pursuit of social change is an evident characteristic, critics in general prefer to remember him as representative of the popular genre of *costumbrismo*, with which he was proud to be associated. He supported a theater of ideas, but he used his comic characters as a way of combining his ideology with the representation of everyday life, the use of colorful popular language, and the particular customs of the people of the street.

The collected works of Sánchez, with nine of his plays, were published by the Editorial Cervantes of Valencia, Spain, in 1917. The first scholarly study of Sánchez's work in book form, *Florencio Sánchez: Su vida y su obra* (Florencio Sánchez: His Life and His Works) was published by the critic Roberto Giusti in Argentina in 1920. For Giusti this work was a precursor of other studies that make him the principal critic on Sánchez. Arturo Vázquez Cey published (in Argentina) a second book about Sánchez in 1929; his work includes personal anecdotes. At that time critics generally agreed that Sánchez was the leading dramatist of Spanish America. It was also agreed that his work could be divided into three distinct dramatic groups: rural, urban, and thesis. Ruth Richardson's 1933 study, published in New York by the well-known Instituto de las Españas en os Estados Unidos and later reprinted in 1975, is important not only because of the quality of the investigation but also because it helped to make Sánchez's name better known in the United States. Karl E. Shedd also published a significant article, "Thirty Years of Criticism of the Works of Florencio Sánchez," in 1955.

Many have questioned whether Florencio Sánchez could be considered a great dramatist. From the point of view of literary form and style, most critics do not consider him one. However, he was able to create many important works in only seven years, and he was admired by the general public and many critics. When forming an opinion about Sánchez's work it is necessary to take into consideration other factors, such as his power of observation, which allowed him to create realistic characters, and his ability to artistically portray social problems. He was the most talented playwright of his generation.

Bibliographies:

Walter Rela, *Repertorio bibliográfico anotado sobre Florencio Sánchez 1891-1971* (Buenos Aires: Facultad de Filosofía y Letras, Universidad de Buenos Aires, 1973);

Centenario de su nacimiento 1875-1975: Bibliografía (Montevideo: Biblioteca Nacional, 1975).

Biography:

María Isabel Martínez Navarrete, *Florencio Sánchez: Biografía cronológica* (Montevideo: Consejo Nacional de Educación, Consejo de Educación Primaria, Biblioteca Pedagógica Central, 1975).

References:

Eduardo Acevedo Díaz, "Los últimos momentos de Florencio Sánchez," *Revista Nacional*, 39, no. 116 (1948): 300-311;

Mariano Bosch, *Historia de los orígenes del teatro nacional argentino: Y la época de Pablo Podestá* (Buenos Aires: Solar-Hachette, 1969);

René A. Campos, "La trayectoria del llamado teatro chico y el aporte a la especie del sainete en las piezas breves de Florencio Sánchez," *Antar*, 2, no. 2 (1975): 7-16;

Arturo Carril, *Nuestro hermano Florencio* (Buenos Aires: Mecenas, 1959);

Homero Castillo, "Procedimientos dramáticos en *La gringa*," *Duquesne Hispanic Review*, 6, no. 1 (1967): 31-36;

Griselda Castro, *Sainetes: Análisis de obras de Florencio Sánchez y Armando Discépolo* (Montevideo: Técnica, 1988);

Jorge Cruz, *Genio y figura de Florencio Sánchez* (Buenos Aires: EUDEBA, 1966);

Cruz, "Rostros de Florencio Sánchez: A propósito de su centenario," *Boletín de la Academia Argentina de Letras*, 40 (1975): 127-137;

Vicente Martínez Cuitiño, *Florencio Sánchez y su obra: Ensayo crítico* (Buenos Aires: Empresa Cultura y Civismo, 1919);

Giuseppe D'Angelo, "Algunos italianismos en el teatro de Florencio Sánchez," *Thesaurus*, 23, no. 3 (1968): 480-514;

René De Costa, "The Dramaturgy of Florencio Sánchez: An Analysis of *Barranca abajo*," *Latin American Theatre Review*, 7, no. 2 (1974): 25-37;

José Alberto Dibarboure, *Proceso del teatro uruguayo (1808-1910): Significación de Florencio Sánchez en la escena rioplatense* (Montevideo: Carlos García, 1940);

Jorge Dubatti, "Los intertextos europeos en el teatro de Florencio Sánchez: *El honor* y *Magda* de Hermann Sudermann," *Latin American Theatre Review*, 29, no. 1 (1995): 7-20;

Diony Durán, "Teatro de Florencio Sánchez," *Conjunto*, 23 (1975): 25-32;

Julio Durán Cerda, "Otra valoración de Florencio Sánchez," *Confluencia*, 1, no. 1 (1985): 43-52;

Juan Pablo Echagüe, "Florencio Sánchez," *Revista Iberoamericana*, 9, no. 17 (1945): 9-24;

María Rosa Elaskar, "La mujer de fines del siglo XIX en el teatro de Florencio Sánchez," in *Érase una vez la mujer: La mujer argentina de los siglos XIX y XX según fuentes históricas y literarias*, edited by Martha Susana Páramo (Mendoza: Universidad Nacional de Cuyo, 1995), pp. 9-28;

Carlos Espinosa Domínguez, "Algo más sobre Florencio Sánchez," *Conjunto*, 65 (1985): 13-24;

José Enrique Etcheverry, "Permanencia de Florencio Sánchez: Análisis de *La gringa*," in his *Temas literarios* (Montevideo: Comisión Nacional de Homenaje del Sesquicentenario de los Hechos Históricos de 1825, 1975);

David William Foster, "Ideological Shift in the Rural Images in Florencio Sánchez's Theater," *Hispanic Journal*, 11, no. 1 (1990): 97-106;

Tabaré José Freire, *Florencio Sánchez artesano del sainete* (Pôrto Alegre: Cebela, 1966);

Manuel Galich, "Florencio: Un viejo amigo mío," *Conjunto*, 23 (1975): 4-13;

Juan Carlos Ghiano, "Cien años de Florencio Sánchez," *La Nación*, 19 January 1975;

Enrique Alberto Giordano, *La teatralización de la obra dramática: De Florencio Sánchez a la generación de 27 en Argentina* (Mexico City: Premia, 1982);

Roberto Giusti, *Florencio Sánchez: Su vida y su obra* (Buenos Aires: Justicia, 1920);

Giusti, "Florencio Sánchez y el teatro rioplatense," *Revista Interamericana de Biblio-grafía,* 12 (1962): 73-88;

Edmundo Guibourg, "Homenaje a Florencio Sánchez," *Revista de Estudios de Teatro,* 2 (1959): 15-19;

Ruth Temple House, "Florencio Sánchez, a Great Uruguayan Dramatist," *Poet Lore,* 34 (1923): 281;

Roberto Ibáñez, "Florencio Sánchez: Aportes y enmiendas a su biografía," *Revista de la Biblioteca Nacional,* 11 (1975): 9-27;

Julio Imbert, *Florencio Sánchez: Vida y creación* (Buenos Aires: Paidós, 1967);

Robert Kemp, "La crítica francesa juzga a Florencio Sánchez," *Nosotros,* 4 (1939): 266-271;

Willis Knapp Jones, "Florencio Sánchez: The *Gringa* Theme in River Plate Drama," in his *Behind Spanish American Footlights* (Austin: University of Texas Press, 1966), pp. 105-125;

Antonio Larreta, "El naturalismo en el teatro de Florencio Sánchez," *Número,* 2, no. 6-8 (1950): 227-235;

Washington Lockhart, *Florencio Sánchez: Todos lo mordieron* (Mercedes: ICIA, 1985);

Miguel Victor Martínez, *Florencio Sánchez: Episodios de su vida* (Montevideo: Renacimiento, 1918);

Nora de Marval McNair, *Los sainetes de Florencio Sánchez: Su originalidad, su trascendencia* (New York: Abra, 1982);

Charlotte E. Miller, "Florencio Sánchez, the South American Eugene O'Neill," dissertation, University of Washington, 1946;

Eva Montoya, "El manuscrito Maestrini de *¡Ladrones!*: La primera obra de Florencio Sánchez; fragmento de la primera escena de la obra," *Caravelle,* 50 (1988): 209-213;

Montoya, "Sobre *¡Ladrones!* (1897) y *Canillita* (1902-1904): Florencio Sánchez y la delegación de poderes," *Gestos,* 3, no. 6 (1988): 87-97;

Vladimiro Muñoz and W. Johnson, eds., *Florencio Sánchez: A Chronology* (New York: Gordon Press, 1979);

Héctor Alberto Murena, "La pugna contra el silencio: Florencio Sánchez," in his *El pecado original de América* (Buenos Aires: Sur, 1954), pp. 133-160;

Nosotros, special Sánchez issue, 2 (1908);

Nicasio Perera San Martín, "El cocoliche en el teatro de Florencio Sánchez: Descripción, elementos de evaluación estilística," *Bulletin Hispanique,* 80, no. 1-2 (1978): 108-122;

Perera San Martín, "Vers une revision critique du theatre de Florencio Sánchez," *Cahiers du Monde Hispanique et Luso Brasilien,* 24 (1975): 47-61;

Jorge Pignataro, *Florencio Sánchez* (Montevideo: Arca, 1979);

José J. Podestá, "Florencio Sánchez y *Barranca abajo,*" in his *Medio siglo de farándula* (Córdoba: Imprenta Argentina, 1930), pp. 172-183;

Manuel D. Ramírez, "Florencio Sánchez and His Social Consciousness of the River Plate Region," *Journal of Latin American Studies,* 8, no. 4 (1966): 585-594;

Mercedes Rein, *Florencio Sánchez: Su vida, su obra* (Montevideo: Casa del Estudiante, 1975);

Walter Rela, *Florencio Sánchez, persona y teatro: "Barranca abajo" y "En familia"* (Montevideo: Ciencias, 1981);

Ruth Richardson, *Florencio Sánchez and the Argentine Theatre* (New York: Instituto de las Españas en los Estados Unidos, 1933; New York: Gordon Press, 1975);

Hugo Riva, *Valoración de Florencio Sánchez en el teatro latinoamericano* (Montevideo: Asociación General de Autores del Uruguay, 1976);

Santiago Rojas, "El criollo viejo en la trilogía rural de Florencio Sánchez: Perspectivas de un ocaso," *Latin American Theatre Review,* 14, no. 1 (1980): 5-13;

Avenir Rosell, "Florencio Sánchez en sus cartas," *Revista de la Biblioteca Nacional,* 11 (1975): 169-207;

Ignacio Rosso, *Anatomía de un genio: Florencio Sánchez* (Montevideo: Casa del Estudiante, 1988);

Miguel Ángel Santagada, *Las ópticas convergentes: En familia de Florencio Sánchez* (Buenos Aires: Universidad Nacional del Centro, 1996);

Karl E. Shedd, "Florencio Sánchez's Debt to Eugène Brieux," *Studies in Philology,* 33, no. 3 (1956): 29-39;

Shedd, "Thirty Years of Criticism of the Works of Florencio Sánchez," *Kentucky Foreign Language Quarterly,* 3, no. 1 (1955): 29-39;

David T. Sisto, "The Gaucho-Criollo Honor Code in the Theatre of Florencio Sánchez," *Hispania,* 38, no. 4 (1955): 451-455;

Juan José de Soiza Reilly, "Cosas inéditas de un gran dramaturgo: Florencio Sánchez," in his *Hombres luminosos* (Buenos Aires: Araujo, 1920), pp. 13-23;

Arturo Vázquez Cey, *Florencio Sánchez y el teatro argentino* (Buenos Aires: Juan Toia, 1929);

David Viñas, "Florencio Sánchez y la revolución de los intelectuales," in his *Literatura argentina y realidad política* (Buenos Aires: Jorge Álvarez, 1964), pp. 309-335;

Bonnie Davis Warren, "A Translation of *Nuestros hijos* and an Index of the Characters in the Plays of Florencio Sánchez," M.A. thesis, University of Texas at Austin, 1948;

David William Wogan and Américo Babino, "Los americanismos de Florencio Sánchez," *Revista Iberoamericana,* 14, no. 27 (1948): 145-197.

Luis Rafael Sánchez
(17 November 1936 -)

Gloria F. Waldman
York College and The Graduate Center, CUNY

See also the Sánchez entry in *DLB 145: Modern Latin-American Fiction Writers, Second Series.*

PLAY PRODUCTIONS: *La espera,* San Juan, Teatro Experimental del Departamento de Drama de la Universidad de Puerto Rico, 23 February 1959;

Cuento de Cucarachita Viudita, San Juan, Academia de Arte Escénico Santo Domingo, 1961;

Farsa del amor compradito, San Juan, Teatro Yukayeke at Teatro Experimental del Ateneo Puertorriqueño, 1961; New York, Puerto Rican Traveling Theatre, 1968;

Los ángeles se han fatigado, San Juan, Teatro Tapia, 1961; Pasadena, California, Pasadena Playhouse, February 1964;

La hiel nuestra de cada día, San Juan, Teatro Tapia, 11 May 1961; New York, Henry Street Settlement Playhouse, 1976;

O casi el alma, San Juan, Teatro Tapia, 23 April 1964; New York, Repertorio Español, October 1974;

La pasión según Antígona Pérez, San Juan, Teatro Tapia, 30 May 1968; New York, Puerto Rican Traveling Theatre at Cathedral of St. John the Divine, 19 May 1972;

Parábola del andarín, San Juan, Tambor Inc. at Teatro Tapia, 5 June 1979;

Quíntuples, San Juan, Compañia Teatro de Puerto Rico at Centro de Bellas Artes, Sala Experimental René Marqués, 3 October 1984; New York, Puerto Rican Traveling Theatre, 1989.

BOOKS: *Los ángeles se han fatigado; Farsa del amor compradito: Teatro* (Hato Rey: Lugar, 1960);

Sol 13, interior (suite de obras en un acto y dos actos respectivamente): La hiel nuestra de cada día; Los ángeles se han fatigado (San Juan: Instituto de Cultura Puertorriqueña, 1962);

O casi el alma (auto de fe en tres actos) (Barcelona: Rumbos, 1966); republished as *Casi el alma: Auto de fe en tres actos* (Río Piedras: Cultural, 1974);

Luis Rafael Sánchez (photograph by Gabriel Suau; from Quíntuples, *fifth edition, 1996; Thomas Cooper Library, University of South Carolina)*

En cuerpo de camisa (San Juan: Lugar, 1966; revised and enlarged edition, Río Piedras: Cultural, 1984);

La pasión según Antígona Pérez (Hato Rey: Lugar, 1968);

Los ángeles se han fatigado (Río Piedras: Cultural, 1976);

Farsa del amor compradito (Río Piedras: Cultural, 1976);

La hiel nuestra de cada día (Río Piedras: Cultural, 1976);

Sol 13, interior: Teatro de Luis Rafael Sánchez (Río Piedras: Cultural, 1976)—comprises *Farsa del amor compradito, La hiel nuestra de cada día,* and *Los ángeles se han fatigado;*

La guaracha del Macho Camacho (Buenos Aires: La Flor, 1976); translated by Gregory Rabassa as *Macho Camacho's Beat* (New York: Pantheon, 1980);

Fabulación e ideología en la cuentística de Emilio S. Belaval (San Juan: Instituto de Cultura Puertorriqueña, 1979);

Quíntuples (Hanover, N.H.: Ediciones del Norte, 1985);

La importancia de llamarse Daniel Santos: Fabulación (Hanover, N.H.: Ediciones del Norte, 1988);

La guagua aérea (Río Piedras: Cultural, 1994);

¿Por qué escribe usted? (San Juan: Fundación Puertorriqueña de las Humanidades, 1996);

No llores por nosotros, Puerto Rico (Hanover, N.H.: Ediciones del Norte, 1997);

El himno de la vida, Conferencia Magistral con motivo del Centenario de la Universidad de Puerto Rico (Río Piedras: Universidad de Puerto Rico, 2004).

SELECTED PERIODICAL PUBLICATIONS–UNCOLLECTED: *La espera, Cuadernos de Artes y Letras,* 37–38 (1960): 15–20; 39 (1960): 11–17;

"Los lujos de la memoria," *Cultura: Revista de la División de Promoción Cultural en los Pueblos* (April 1997): 19–21.

Luis Rafael Sánchez is one of Puerto Rico's most renowned living playwrights. His incursions into not only the theater but also the novel, short story, and essay have made him one of Puerto Rico's most significant links with Latin American literature. His plays present the complexity of the Puerto Rican experience, creating a theater both national and universal. In addition to productions at university centers in the United States, at the Pasadena Playhouse in Los Angeles, in Madrid, Mexico City, São Paulo, the Dominican Republic, Venezuela, and Germany, all of his plays have been presented in New York, some of them by more than one theater group.

Sánchez was born on 17 November 1936 in Humacao, a city on the east coast of Puerto Rico. He is from a working-class background, growing up in the Antonio Roig *caserío,* or housing project. His father, Luis Sánchez Cruz, was a baker, and his mother, Agueda Ortiz Tirado, was a seamstress. He has a younger sister, Elba Ivelisse, and a younger brother, Nestor Manuel. His primary and secondary schooling took place in the public schools of Humacao and San Juan. This situation was because he became a radio actor in the national soap operas and had to attend high schools that either finished at noon or had evening sessions so that he could get to the studio on time, which meant he attended a different high school every year. In a 1972 interview with Artemio Torres he referred to the transient nature of his secondary-school years and its effect on him, lamenting that he felt like a delinquent, always changing schools. He remembers a difficult childhood, tense and sad. As a shy and withdrawn child, disinterested in the athletic activities of his schoolmates, he placed all his enthusiasm in his classes. He became a voracious reader, devouring everything the public library had to offer: from detective stories to the works of Emilio Salgari and Jules Verne. He came to appreciate popular culture–an integral element in his theater–through the radio, a medium that unleashed his imagination, just as it developed his ear for the spoken word, for the well-turned phrase.

When he was twelve years old his family moved to Viejo San Juan, Calle Sol (Old San Juan, Sol Street). He remembers a San Juan not yet devoured by tourism, with cobblestone paths and the old arched gateway leading to the sea. Both these sets of memories are present in his work: the small-town life inspired by Humacao serves as a background for many of his short stories, while the vivid and sensitive portrayal of Viejo San Juan is background in some of his plays. Another memory, which eventually helped to create a political consciousness in the young Sánchez, was the attack in 1953 by the Puerto Rican police on the house of the Puerto Rican nationalist leader Don Pedro Albízu Campos, whom Sánchez had met.

Early experience with the theater brought Sánchez's shyness and withdrawal to an end. As a ninth grader at the Baldorioty School he met Victoria Espinosa, director and faculty member of the drama department at the University of Puerto Rico, who had a great influence on his life. She was the founder of the Commedietta Universitaria, a program that brought theater to the public schools. Inspired by Espinosa, Sánchez founded the Teatro Experimental José Julián Acosta, along with his childhood friends Pedro Juán Hernández and the actor Alberto Rodríguez, in 1953.

Not only was Sánchez becoming involved in theater, he was also part of what has been called the Golden Age of radio, working with the great Puerto Rican actresses Mona Martí and Madeline Willemsen on soap operas for station WNEL from 1953 to 1955. He recalls that when television first came to Puerto Rico in 1954, a group of actors was selected to participate in the early incursion into the medium, but his criollo type did not suit the norm. That discrimination proved to be positive, since it drove him to the university, although he still dreamed of an acting career.

In 1955 he went to Mexico, where he acted in the play *La familia del boticario* (The Pharmacist's Family) by the eighteenth-century Spanish playwright Bretón de los Herreros for the Instituto Nacional de la Juventud Mexicana (National Institute for Mexican Youth). In 1956 he returned to the University of Puerto Rico, where he collaborated on ten plays with the Commedietta Universitaria and played the lead in a 1957 production of Federico García Lorca's play *Títeres de*

Cachiporra (1953, Puppets of Cachiporra), which toured the island every weekend, sponsored by the Traveling Theatre of the University of Puerto Rico. He also became a member of the group Tablado del Coquí (The Coquí Stage, named for the tree frog indigenous to Puerto Rico), directed by Georgina de Uriate.

For Sánchez, the experience of doing theater precipitated the experience of writing literature, although his first literary ventures during his university years were in the short-story genre. Sánchez graduated from the University of Puerto Rico in 1960 with a major in drama and a minor in Spanish literature. Theater held a prominent place at the university in those years; the entire community mobilized when there was a show.

Sánchez's first full-length play was *La espera* (The Wait, produced in 1959), directed by Nilda González. It inaugurated the Teatro Experimental Universitario, a hundred-seat space designed by Rafael Cruz Emeric, and it was the first time in the history of the drama department at the University of Puerto Rico that a student's work was performed. The avant-garde nature of the play was an appropriate choice for a new theater desirous of exhibiting its modernity. The work premiered on 23 February 1959. In 1962 Sánchez, as librettist, adapted *La espera* for presentation by the Ballets of San Juan at the Fifth Festival of Puerto Rican Theatre, with music by Frank Martin, choreography by Juan Anduze, and set design by Lorenzo Homar.

The play is based on a Sánchez short story that was published in the newspaper *El Mundo* in 1957. It is a technically competent play belonging to a type of theater that still had resonance in 1958: an existential theater, laden with symbolic figures playing out the anguish of unrequited love against a backdrop of passing time and inevitable death. He introduces expressionistic techniques through dream-like sequences and characters who represent La Hermana's (The Sister's) guilty conscience about her treatment of her sister, Georgina. Sánchez also incorporates music, ambitious lighting, and the additional elements of El Payaso (The Clown) and La Niña (The Girl), lively figures who lighten the tone and add originality to the play. In this work Sánchez provides a glimpse of what became his strongest assets as a dramatist: his creative use of the stage and its theatrical possibilities; dramatic coherence; a grasp of structure; and rich verbal texture.

The play portrays the internal workings of Georgina's tormented mind, her longing, and her ambivalence about existing in a state of continual waiting for her love, Gabriel, to come. The lighting, costumes, and music all work together as a unit to convey the phantasmagorical nature of the work. The dual concepts of reality and illusion are exposed, with time represented by El Payaso, death represented by La Sombra (The

Madeline Willemsen in the 1961 Festival de Teatro production of Sánchez's 1961 play Los ángeles se han fatigado *(The Angels are Exhausted), in which an aging prostitute retreats from harsh reality into memories and fantasies (from Gloria F. Waldman,* Luis Rafael Sánchez: Pasion teatral, *1988; Robert Muldrow Library, Clemson University)*

Shadow), and Georgina's childhood represented by La Niña. They interact alongside the only live characters: the Policeman, who represents authority and societal order, and La Hermana. The others are phantoms or materializations of the fears and complexes of La Hermana. The integration of children's rhymes and popular folk songs, native Puerto Rican fauna and flora, and Georgina's evocation of the plaza at Humacao, where Sánchez spent his early childhood, all foreshadow Sánchez's creation of a complex mixture of universal and national imagery in his subsequent theater.

The reader is introduced to favorite Sánchez themes: the interplay between reality and illusion and the element of time, the central metaphor that provides artistic unity to this work, as evidenced in the subtitle to the play, *Juego del amor y del tiempo* (A Game of Love and Time). There are other points of contact between *La espera* and a later work, *Los ángeles se han fatigado* (The Angels Are Exhausted; published in 1960, performed in 1961). The themes of abandonment, waiting, disappointment in love, madness, and time as a destructive, inexorable element are developed in *Los ángeles se han fatigado,* although in a less abstract and symbolic way than in *La espera*. Even the portrayal of the wasted prostitute and the drunken sailors that provide the central image for *Los ángeles se han fatigado* is first revealed in *La espera,* in the way that Gabriel, the illusive love interest of both Georgina and her sister, describes the wife of the coal supplier.

In *Cuento de Cucarachita Viudita* (1961, The Story of the Little Widowed Cockroach) and *Farsa del amor compradito* (Farce of Bought Love; published in 1959, produced in 1961), the reader sees another side of Sánchez: a rich humor that draws upon traditional Puerto Rican folklore, and a linguistic playfulness, full of double entendres and puns, accompanied by a willingness to experiment with new forms: in *Cuento de Cucarachita Viudita,* children's theater; in *Farsa del amor compradito,* commedia dell'arte. In 1959 *Cuento de Cucarachita Viudita* received a prize from the Academia de Arte Escénico Santo Domingo (The Santo Domingo Academy of Scenic Arts) as the best children's theater work sent to their Christmas contest that year. Sánchez adapted this play from his own short story, in which he takes certain liberties with the plot, characters, and location of the original folktale, "La Cucarachita Martina," known throughout Latin America, in order to create dramatic conflict and intensity. The original tale recounts the loves, marriage, and widowhood of Cucarachita Martina, who prefers Ratoncito Pérez (Little Perez the Rat) to her other suitors. Sánchez, however, creates a lively battle among her suitors and changes the nature of her relationship with Ratoncito Pérez. Although he is her original suitor, she prefers the attention of the gentler, more modest Lagartijón Primero (Big Lizard the First) and "forgets" her commitment to Ratoncito Pérez. The tension increases and culminates in a fight, with Ratoncito Pérez killing Lagartijón Primero and then marrying Cucarachita Martina. Ratoncito Pérez's immediate desire to eat causes him to fall to his death into a cauldron of food. Also differing from the original folktale are the human attitudes that Sánchez reveals through his characters—for example, the Abuela's (Grandmother's) pride in her "race" when she admonishes Cucarachita not to marry a lizard but rather a cockroach, as her family has done for time immemorial.

In *Farsa del amor compradito* Sánchez incorporates distinctly Puerto Rican elements and humor into the traditionally popular commedia dell'arte genre, while preserving the early-sixteenth-century elements of improvised dialogue, jokes, audience-actor repartee, and the insertion of poems and speeches taken from literary sources. The theme is familiar: an amorous entanglement involving Arlequín, the villain; General Cataplúm, the deceived lover; Colombina, the loved one, who lives in the unexpected setting of a bordello owned by her Aunt Quintana; and Pirulí Pulcinello, director, organizer, and improviser par excellence, who complains to the audience about the rigors to which the other actors, and life, subject him. The author often uses Pirulí as his spokesperson to address the "inhabitants of the Island of Culture a Priori," a play on the Institute of Puerto Rican Culture.

The satire is revealed through dialogue heavy with double meaning and insinuation and recited by classic characters from the commedia dell'arte as well as the original characters added by Sánchez. Critics point to Sánchez's poetic language as essentially Lorquian, recalling Lorca's *Retablillo de don Cristobal* (1938, Don Cristobal's Stage) and *Títeres de Cachiporra*. The fun Sánchez has in the onomatopoeic creation of the characters' names is only one element in the festive mood he creates and sustains in this farce; he also uses singularly Puerto Rican humor, affectionately called "relajo criollo" as well as multiple theatrical devices, plays on words, a fanciful mixture of the vernacular with literary jargon, piquant sexual allusions that enliven the dialogue and folkloric elements, popular music, and children's rhymes. Even the diminutive "compradito" suggests the mocking tone that characterizes the farce. He uses Brechtian devices such as obvious props and signs, direct address to the audience, and the metatheatrical creation of a play within a play—for example, when the drama begins, the audience finds the actors still putting on their makeup, actively discussing the work they are about to perform as well as commenting on its author, allowing Sánchez to indulge in some amusing self-criticism.

Certain consistent elements in Sánchez's theater appear in *Farsa del amor compradito,* such as the elaboration of the theme of time. Different from the seriousness with which he develops the metaphysical and existential overtones in *La espera,* he adopts an amused attitude toward time in *Farsa del amor compradito*. Social criticism is present in all of his work, and no less so when he uses humor to make his point—in this case, against the eternal monotony of the bourgeoisie as well as the literary conventions and hypocrisy of pseudointellectuals. Sánchez pokes fun at the world of tradition as well as the obsession to be modern, as Arlequín desperately fights against a traditional wedding.

In a 1961 production by actress Iris Martínez's Teatro Yukayeke at the Ateneo Puertorriqueño, the cos-

Marta Rivera and Jacobo Morales in the 1964 Teatro Tapia premiere of Sánchez's play O casi el alma
(Almost the Soul, published in 1966), in which a prostitute and a philosopher spend Good Friday together
(from Gloria F. Waldman, Luis Rafael Sánchez: Pasion teatral, 1988;
Robert Muldrow Library, Clemson University)

tumes, consistent with the absurdist vein of the comedy, did not correspond to any definite time period and varied in style from Madame Pompadour to modern sports clothes. Critics praised the original music, written by Puerto Rican composer Amaury Veray, and the effective choice of having the three musicians onstage, interacting with the characters. Sánchez began an association with Miriam Colón's Puerto Rican Traveling Theatre with their production of *Farsa del amor compradito* in 1968; they took the work to playgrounds, schools, parks, and housing projects, where the concept of traditional commedia dell'arte characters addressing Puerto Rican realities intensified the theatrical impact.

As Sánchez said in a November 2002 interview in *La Jornada Semanal* (The Weekly Installment), the 1960s were a particularly productive decade for him: he began to teach at the University of Puerto Rico; he took part in the Actors Studio playwrighting unit in New York in 1962; he completed his master's degree at New York University in Romance Languages in 1963; he took courses for his doctorate; and he wrote three or four plays and narratives. All of that creative and literary activity responded to his need to find his authentic voice, which begins to be heard in his suite, *Sol 13, interior* (Sol Street, Number 13, Courtyard Apartment), comprising *Los ángeles se han fatigado* and *La hiel nuestra de cada día* (Our Daily Bitterness, performed in 1961).

In most criticism written about *La hiel nuestra de cada día* and *Los ángeles se han fatigado* both works are treated separately. They are, however, part of a "Suite de obras en un acto y dos actos respectivamente" (Suite of plays in one act and two acts, respectively), as Sánchez indicates in his subtitle, and they do form an organic whole, providing complementary facets of a picture of despair and lost dreams in a San Juan tenement. The human condition is reflected in the physical setting of both plays: in *La hiel nuestra de cada día,* the couple, Píramo and Tisbe, are as old and broken down as their furniture, the apartment building they live in, and their tarnished hopes and aspirations. In *Los ángeles se han fatigado,* aging prostitute Angela's interior state of mind and the physical setting she inhabits are one; there is a richness of experience, of loving and suffering, in the disorder that is her life. Sánchez resolves the technical aspect of rendering the chaos in Angela's life through the use of flashbacks and juxtaposition of time. The tone of helplessness, depression, death, and insanity that pervades the atmosphere is tempered with unexpected playfulness on the part of the characters, revealing Sánchez's talent for portraying the complex relationship between humor and pain.

Sol 13, interior is not simply a presentation of one couple's or one prostitute's situation but rather a dramatic metaphor for a society's insensitivity toward the nuances of feeling and need in its citizens. *Los ángeles se han fatigado* is also rich in political allegory. Angela can be seen as the embodiment of the themes of destruction and abandonment, essentially the historical trajectory of Puerto Rico: the Spaniards, the French, the English, the Dutch, and the Americans exploited her and moved on to richer conquests. One of Angela's recourses for dealing with her life is to escape into the past. The play moves inexorably through an atmosphere of fatalism and intimations of destruction. The reader may also view her retreat into madness as her ultimate freedom, as she exchanges abusive treatment for the richer world of memories and fantasies. It is ambiguous as to whether or not she killed her pimp and lover Santiago, and in the final scene she is led from her room by police or mental-heath workers, in the manner of Tennessee Williams's Blanche DuBois.

In 1964 Sánchez became a member of the Advisory Board of the Theatre Arts Committee of the Institute of Puerto Rican Culture, the premier government-sponsored cultural entity of the island. That same year, critics agree that in *O casi el alma* (1964, Almost the Soul) Sánchez achieved full artistic maturity, successfully transforming the stage experience into a poetic metaphor. The female protagonist, "Maggie, from Apartment Seven," is a prostitute, friendly and outspoken. The male protagonist, simply called El Hombre (The Man), is a mysterious, somewhat shabby stranger who fascinates her with his harmonica and philosophizing about the meaning of his life and the lives of the people who pass through it. It is Lent, Good Friday, and business is slow. Maggie is planning to go out with her friends, but El Hombre's harmonica recital attracts her attention, and she reluctantly allows him into the dingy room where she has earned her living for the past six years. The readers witness the verbal seduction of Maggie as well as her transformation from a tired prostitute to a modern-day saint and, finally, to a person in possession of a deeper knowledge of herself.

With *La pasión según Antígona Pérez* (1968, The Passion According to Antígona Pérez), Sánchez creates his own motivation for the title character's defiance of the state. In the Greek version by Sophocles, Antigone justifies her behavior by claiming that the dead would be denied eternal rest if her brother's body were not buried; in the 1944 French version by Jean Anouilh, her rebellion is more capricious; in Sánchez's version, the Latina Antígona defies the order of the dictator Creón Molina out of her commitment to the defense of a human and political cause—to overthrow a dictator. This Antígona is an existential one whose refusal to reveal the burial place of her friends' bodies, although a suicidal act, is nevertheless authentic and consistent with her personal and public persona. What ensues is a direct confrontation between Creón's law and Antígona's individual conscience. Using the framework of the Greek myth as a metaphor for the affirmation of human values over static hierarchical values and despotic civil law, Sánchez creates a theatrical experience that allows the audience to participate in Antígona's "passion" as well as in her search for freedom and authenticity.

Sánchez emphasizes the Latin American context of the play in its subtitle, "crónica americana en dos actos" (an American chronicle in two acts). What makes it particularly Latin American is the author's criticism of the major political and social institutions in Latin America (the church, the military, the press, the dictatorship); the mixture of races, as in the mestiza Antígona; the symbolism of her common last name, Pérez, a choice that identifies her with the Latin American everyman; and the technical aspects that situate the play within the mainstream of contemporary Latin American theater, for example, the original use of lighting, music, and Brechtian elements. Sánchez incorporates various epic theater elements into the play: direct address to the audience; characters relating events that have already occurred; abrupt transitions from scene to scene; and a generally stark mise-en-scène.

The 1972 production of *La pasión según Antígona Pérez* in the thousand-seat Cathedral of St. John the Divine in New York City was a spectacular inauguration of the summer tour of the play by the Puerto Rican Traveling Theatre. The impressive setting intensified the theatricality of the play and reinforced its origins in the Greek tragedy. In counterpoint to the sumptuous cathedral setting, the actual staging was appropriately stark, allowing for the emphasis on dialogue and interaction among the characters. The split-level staging was particularly successful in creating the feeling of Antígona's dungeon and its supposed distance from the actual palace on the upper level of the scaffolding where the rest of the action took place.

In the 1970s Sánchez continued to teach at the University of Puerto Rico, to write cultural essays, and to participate in the international literary scene with his first novel, *La guaracha del Macho Camacho* (1976), translated by Gregory Rabassa in 1980 as *Macho Camacho's Beat*. This work is a linguistic tour de force intertwining the lives of characters from every social strata in a scathing critique of contemporary Puerto Rico. The 1970s closed with Sánchez's entry in the Twentieth Festival of Puerto Rican Theatre at the Teatro Tapia, *Parábola del andarín* (Parable of the Itinerant Traveler, performed in 1979). In this play he re-creates a character from Puerto Rican popular culture of the 1940s: the itinerant worker traveling from town to town. Although the play was never published, the production featured strong performances by Luis (Chavito) Marrero, Cordelia González, and Luz Minerva Rodríguez.

Sánchez has often criticized the phenomenon of being a dramatist who writes solely for festivals, alluding to the annual festivals of Puerto Rican theater initiated by the Institute of Puerto Rican Culture in 1958. Like his Latin American compatriots, he laments the lack of an official policy to foster the development of theater on a national scale.

In 1984 Sánchez returned to the theater with *Quíntuples* (Quintuplets, published in 1985), a tour de force for two actors. Originally written for Puerto Rican actors Idalia Pérez Garay and the late Francisco (Paco) Prado, it has been performed on various occasions by Rosalba Rolón, actress and founder of the New York–based Pregones Theatre, as well as by Mary Alice Vergueiro, who produced and starred in a production in São Paulo in the 1990s. Sánchez's deconstruction of the family, with its attendant criticism of the institutions of machismo, the church, the educational system, and pervasive societal hypocrisy, is revealed through the monologues of the Morrison quintuplets and their extravagant father, "El Gran Semental" (The Great Breeder), each one more neurotic and hysterical than the last. The pretext for the revelation of the true nature of their family relations, including incest, homosexuality, bisexuality, and sexual repression, is a Conference on Family Affairs, and the suggestion by sister Dafne that they depart from their usual script and improvise leads to their actively involving the audience in the performance by handing them props and assigning them tasks: someone to light the cigarette of secretly lesbian and overtly neurotic Bianca; to prepare for the imminent birth of the quintuplets of the pregnant Carlota; to respond to the overly confident and seductive Mandrake, or to the insecure and tormented brother, Baby.

The end of the play is a metatheatrical unmasking that also occurs in *Parábola del andarín* and in *Farsa del amor compradito,* as the actors remove their makeup and confront the audience with the risky and illusive nature of theater. This tactic connects the public with the players and further establishes the need to create identities anew at every performance, just as in life. Sánchez's most innovative play to date, *Quíntuples* features the linguistic richness and originality that is also found in his novels.

Until his retirement in the 1980s from the Department of Hispanic Studies at the University of Puerto Rico, Sánchez alternated his creative work with his academic work, making an enormous contribution to

Francisco Prado in the 1984 Centro de Bellas Artes premiere of Sánchez's play Quíntuples *(published in 1985), which Sánchez wrote for Prado and Idalia Peréz Garay; the two actors played all five siblings and their father (photograph by Doel Vasquez; from* Quíntuples, *fifth edition, 1996; Thomas Cooper Library, University of South Carolina)*

Puerto Rican culture not only through his writing but also through his teaching career. His next novel, *La importancia de llamarse Daniel Santos* (The Importance of Being Daniel Santos), a fictional search for the larger-than-life romantic singer and bohemian Daniel Santos in a nonlinear, postmodern blending of genres, appeared in 1988. Sánchez also wrote a column of social commentary, "Escrito en puertorriqueño" (Written in Puerto Rican), for *Claridad* (Clarity), the newspaper of the Puerto Rican Socialist Party.

The 1990s and 2000s brought Sánchez his greatest recognition as a Latin American writer. He published two collections of essays, *La guagua aérea* (1994, The Air Bus) and *No llores por nosotros, Puerto Rico* (1997, Don't Cry for Us, Puerto Rico). He was named Distinguished Professor at the City College of New

York and received many invitations to speak at major North American and international campuses and forums. He became a Rockefeller grant and Guggenheim Fellowship recipient; a visiting professor and guest lecturer at national and international literary conferences, theater festivals, and workshops; and a judge for literary competitions.

Sanchez's creative contribution lies in his ability to artistically transform the Puerto Rican experience into literature and to universalize it. Sánchez shares with Osvaldo Dragún, Enrique Buenaventura, Agustin Cuzzani, and José Triana a concern for social justice, and with Emilio Carballido, Sergio Vodanovic, Luisa Josefina Hernández, Egon Wolff, Alberto Heiremans, Griselda Gambaro, and Jorge Díaz a singular interest in language and a desire for structural innovation, as well as a willingness to experiment. Critics agree that Sánchez's work poetically captures the essence of the Puerto Rican soul, as he criticizes the particular reality of which he is a part. His protagonists are the casualties of the way in which Puerto Rico has embraced the North American ethic of progress and industrialization, as well as moral corruption (the U.S. Marines in *Los ángeles se han fatigado*) and false values (religion as a business in *O casi el alma*). His work reveals sensitivity to the struggle for cultural autonomy that Puerto Rico wages daily.

Critics concur in naming language as the central protagonist in his theater, especially in his most acclaimed play, *Quíntuples*. The baroque nature of his language has been extensively documented, as well as his ability to communicate an unmistakable stamp of *puertorriqueñidad*, which he achieves by capturing the flavor of the idiomatic turns of Puerto Rican Spanish. His style is characterized by the preciseness of his language, the successful integration of popular elements, and a suffusion of the poetic, a legacy of the expressionist movement. The particularly lyrical nature of his language has been described by many critics, as has the inherent musicality of his texts.

Sánchez has created fictional characters who have become part of the Puerto Rican literary canon as well as vital symbols of Puerto Rican life: Antígona, for her strength; Píramo and Tisbe, for their essential Latin warmth; and Dafne, Bianca, Carlota, Mandrake, Baby, and Papa Morrison, for their pure theatricality, exuberance, humor, neuroses, and sexuality. Not necessarily heroes or heroines, nor possessing outstanding talent or ability, they do accomplish an affirmation of their own identities.

The themes he writes about include the need for freedom, for love, for faith, the existence of poverty, loneliness, prostitution, and by analogy, the social system and specific situations that are at their root, all within the context of the Puerto Rican experience. He writes about societal outsiders, the alienated, those who are somehow different, marginal: prostitutes (in *O casi el alma* and *Los ángeles se han fatigado*), the poor (in *La hiel nuestra de cada día*), religious fakers (in *O casi el alma*), the morally resolute and the morally destitute (in *La pasión según Antígona Pérez*), and the ultimate dysfunctional family (in *Quíntuples*).

Woven throughout Luis Rafael Sánchez's work are the dual motifs of hope and despair: for the future of Puerto Rico, for humankind. He asserts that the Puerto Rican artist comes from a colonial context, which, although contaminating, is nevertheless a permanent source of inspiration. His theatrical exploration of seemingly disparate problems—problems of religious faith in the modern world, of time, of reality and illusion, of chance, of the clash in cultural values—nevertheless reveals an affirmation of the human spirit.

Interviews:

Artemio Torres, "Sin prisa, pero sin pausa como las estrellas," *La Hora,* 29 September 1972, pp. 18-20;

Gloria F. Waldman, "Luis Rafael Sánchez: An Interview," *Revista/Review Interamericana,* 60, no. 1 (1979): 9-23;

Julio Cordero Avila, "Wico en la intimidad," *El Nuevo Día,* 23 March 1980, p. 17;

Arcadio Díaz Quiñones, "El oficio y la memoria: Luis Rafael Sánchez," *Sin Nombre,* 12, no. 1 (1981): 27-38;

Gregory Rabassa, "De la guaracha al beat," in *Espejo de escritores: Entrevistas con Borges, Cortázar, Fuentes, Goytisolo, Onetti, Puig, Rama, Rulfo, Sánchez, Vargas Llosa,* edited by Reina Roffe (Hanover, N.H.: Ediciones del Norte, 1985), pp. 173-194;

Julio Ortega, *Reapropiaciones: Cultura y nueva escritura en Puerto Rico* (Río Piedras: Universidad de Puerto Rico, 1991), pp. 237-243;

Alida Millán Ferrer, "En palabras del escritor: Entrevista a Luis Rafael Sánchez," *Claridad,* 20-26 August 1993, pp. 22-23;

Norberto Bogard, "Nueva York es el gran sueño de Bolivar," *El Diario/La Prensa* (New York), 11 November 1994, pp. 6-7;

Carmen Dolores Hernández, "Desde fuera del canon," *La Jornada Semanal* (Mexico), 3 November 2002, pp. 1-6.

Bibliography:

"Luis Rafael Sánchez: Selected Bibliography," in *The Demythologization of Language, Gender, and Culture and the Re-Mapping of Latin American Identity in Luis Rafael Sánchez's Works,* edited by Elba D. Birmingham-Pokorny (Miami, Fla.: Universal, 1999), pp. 125–142.

References:

Efraín Barradas, *Para leer en puertorriqueño: Acercamiento a la obra de Luis Rafael Sánchez* (Río Piedras: Cultural, 1981);

Eliseo R. Colón Zayas, *El teatro de Luis Rafael Sánchez: Códigos, ideología y lenguaje* (Madrid: Playor, 1985);

Lowell A. Fiet, "Luis Rafael Sánchez's *The Passion of Antígona Pérez:* Puerto Rican Drama in North American Performance," *Latin American Theatre Review,* 10, no. 1 (1976): 97–101;

Nélida Hernández Vargas and Daisy Caraballo Abreu, eds., *Luis Rafael Sánchez: Crítica y bibliografía* (Río Piedras: Universidad de Puerto Rico, 1985);

Johanna Emmanuelli Huertas, "Quíntuples: Las máscaras de la representación," in *De la colonia a la postmodernidad: Teoría teatral y crítica sobre teatro latinoamericano,* edited by Peter Roster and Mario Rojas (Buenos Aires: Galerna, 1992), pp. 285–294;

Priscilla Meléndez, "Lo uno y lo múltiple: Farsa e incesto en *Quíntuples* de Sánchez," *Latin American Theatre Review,* 26, no. 1 (1992): 7–22;

Meléndez, "Towards A Characterization of Latin American Farce," *Siglo XX/20th Century,* 11, no. 1–2 (1993): 135–153;

Mayuli Morales Faedo, "Variaciones sobre la relación público-actor/personaje en el teatro de Luis Rafael Sánchez," *Conjunto* (Havana), 80 (1989): 60–68;

Hortensia R. Morell, "*Quíntuples* y el vértigo del teatro autorreflexivo de Luis Rafael Sánchez," *Latin American Theatre Review,* 27, no. 2 (1994): 39–51;

Angelina Morfi, *Historia crítica de un siglo de teatro puertorriqueño* (San Juan: Instituto de Cultura Puertorriqueña, 1981);

John Dimitri Perivolaris, *Puerto Rican Cultural Identity and the Work of Luis Rafael Sánchez* (Chapel Hill: University of North Carolina Press, 2000);

Gloria F. Waldman, "Lo mejor en teatro: El Andarín, Chavito y Cordelia," *El Nuevo Día,* 31 December 1979;

Waldman, "Los personajes femeninos en la obra teatral de Luis Rafael Sánchez," *La Torre, Revista General de la Universidad de Puerto Rico,* 27, nos. 103–104, 105–106 (1979): 212–220;

Waldman, *Luis Rafael Sanchez: Pasión teatral* (San Juan: Instituto de Cultura Puertorriqueña, 1988).

Carlos Solórzano
(1 May 1922 -)

Wilma Feliciano
State University of New York College at New Paltz

SELECTED PLAY PRODUCTIONS: *Doña Beatriz, la sin ventura*, Mexico City, Sala Molière of the University Theater of UNAM, 25 September 1952;

El hechicero, Mexico City, Teatro del Seguro Social, 16 July 1954;

Las manos de Dios, Mexico City, Teatro del Seguro Social, 24 August 1956;

El crucificado; Los fantoches; and *Mea culpa*, Mexico City, Teatro del Seguro Social, 17 October 1958;

El sueño del ángel, Mexico City, University of UNAM, July 1960;

Cruce de vías, Mexico City, Teatro de la Paz, August 1966;

El zapato, Mexico City, University Theater of UNAM, 1970.

BOOKS: *Del sentimiento de lo plástico en la obra de Unamuno* (Mexico City: UNAM, 1944);

Espejo de novelas (Mexico: Stylo, 1945);

Doña Beatriz, la sin ventura (Mexico City: Coleccion Teatro Mexicano, 1954);

El hechicero: Tragedia en tres actos (Mexico City: Cuadernos Americanos, 1955);

Las manos de Dios: Auto en tres actos (Mexico City: B. Costa-Amic, 1957); translated by W. Keith Leonard and Mario T. Soria as *The Hands of God* (Hiram, Ohio: Hiram College, 1968);

El crucificado, published with Carlos Prieto's *El lepero* as *Dos obras* (Mexico City: A. Mijares, 1957); translated by Gerardo Luzuriaga and Robert S. Rudder as *The Crucifixion*, in *The Orgy: Modern One-Act Plays from Latin America*, edited by Luzuriaga and Rudder (Los Angeles: UCLA Latin American Center, 1974), pp. 137–153;

Tres actos (Mexico City: Unicornio, 1959)—comprises *Cruce de vías, El crucificado,* and *Los fantoches;*

Teatro latinoamericano del siglo XX (Buenos Aires: Nueva Visión, 1961); revised and expanded as *Teatro latinoamericano en el siglo XX* (Mexico City: Pormaca, 1964);

Los falsos demonios (Mexico City: Joaquin Mortiz, 1966);

Carlos Solórzano (from Teatro breve, 1977; Thomas Cooper Library, University of South Carolina)

Las celdas (Mexico City: Joaquin Mortiz, 1971);

Teatro (San José, Costa Rica: Universitaria Centroamericana, 1972)—comprises *Los fantoches, El crucificado, Las manos de Dios,* and *El sueño de un ángel;*

Testimonios teatrales de México (Mexico: UNAM, 1973);

Teatro breve (Mexico City: Joaquin Mortiz, 1977)—comprises *El zapato, Cruce de vías, El sueño de un ángel, Mea culpa, El crucificado,* and *Los fantoches;*

Teatro (Mexico: Difusión Cultural/UNAM, 1992)—comprises *Doña Beatriz, El hechicero, Las manos de Dios, El zapato, Cruce de vías, El sueño de un ángel, Mea culpa, El crucificado,* and *Los fantoches;*

Teatro completo (Mexico City: CONACULTA, 2002).

Edition in English: *Crossroads, and Other Plays,* translated and edited by Francesca Colecchia (Rutherford, N.J.: Fairleigh Dickinson University Press, 1993)–comprises *Crossroads, The Crucified, Mea culpa, The Puppets, And Death Brought Forth the Light, The Angel's Forty Winks, The Shoe,* and *Hands of God.*

RECORDINGS: *El sueño del ángel, Teatro,* read by Solórzano, Mexico City, Voz Viva de América Latina VVAL-18 [i.e. 19] 1971;

Carlos Solórzano, voz del autor, selections from *Los falsos demonios* and *Las celdas,* read by Solórzano, Mexico City, Voz Viva de América Latina VVAL-27 1974).

OTHER: *El sueño del ángel,* in *Tercera antología de obras en un acto,* edited by Maruxa Vilalta (Mexico City: Colección Teatro Mexicano, 1960), pp. 41–53;

El teatro hispanoamericano contemporáneo: Antología, 2 volumes, edited by Solórzano (Mexico: Fondo de Cultura Económica, 1962–1964);

"Procesos de creación del autor dramático," in *El autor dramático* (San Juan: Instituto de Cultura Puertorriqueña, 1963), pp. 17–30;

Teatro guatemalteco contemporáneo, edited by Solórzano (Madrid: Aguilar, 1964)–includes *Doña Beatriz, la sin ventura;*

Teatro breve hispanoamericano contemporáneo, edited by Solórzano (Madrid: Aguilar, 1969);

El teatro actual latinoamericano (antología), edited by Solórzano (Mexico: Ediciones de Andrea, 1972);

"Algunos paralelismos entre la novela y el teatro hispanoamericano de este siglo," in *Testimonios teatrales de México* (Mexico City: UNAM, 1973), pp. 191–200;

Cruce de vías, translated by Francesca Colecchia and Julio Matas as *Crossroads,* in *Selected Latin American One-Act Plays,* edited by Colecchia and Matas (Pittsburgh: University Press, 1973), pp. 53–68;

The World Encyclopedia of Contemporary Theatre, volume 2: *The Americas,* edited by Solórzano and Don Rubin (London & New York: Routledge, 2001).

SELECTED PERIODICAL PUBLICATIONS–UNCOLLECTED: "Antonio Caso en las letras," *Revista de Guatemala,* 5, no. 1 (1946): 17–25;

La muerte hizo la luz: Drama en un acto, Revista de Guatemala, 3 (1951): 74–97;

"El teatro de la posguerra en México," *Hispania,* 46 (December 1964): 693–697;

"The Contemporary Latin American Theater," *Prairie Schooner,* 39 (1965): 118–125;

"El visitante," *Cronauta,* 1 (1966): 54–56;

"Primer Festival de Teatro Nuevo de Latinoamerica," *Latin American Theatre Review,* 2 (Spring 1969): 60–68;

"El teatro de la posguerra en México," *Artes de México,* 16, no. 123 (1969): 62–73, 99–100.

When Carlos Solórzano returned to Mexico City from Paris in 1952, Spanish models of realism and regional comedies still ruled the Mexican stage. Thematically, dramatists such as Rodolfo Usigli, Salvador Novo, and Celestino Goroztiza had already begun the transition toward a national theater in content, but realism remained the dominant expression. Influenced by the avant-garde movements of postwar France, Solórzano–along with other playwrights such as Emilio Carballido and Elena Garro–experimented with new visions and techniques while they renovated centuries-old forms. Solórzano's plays, written in the 1950s, combine elements of classic Aristotelian poetics, medieval morality plays, Indo-Hispanic ritualism and popular culture, and the post–World War II aesthetics of expressionism, theater of cruelty, and Theater of the Absurd. An artist of mestizo origins, Solórzano fuses diverse art forms to create a stylized drama of existential despair that is universal in content and Indo-Hispanic in its theatricality.

Born on 1 May 1922 on a plantation in San Marcos, Guatemala, and raised in the capital, Carlos Solórzano Fernández grew up among the landed aristocracy; his great-grandfather, Justo Rufino Barrios, governed the country from 1871 to 1888. As a child Solórzano excelled at the piano and considered becoming a concert performer. His family, however, decided that architecture was a more practical career for a boy with artistic aspirations. His father, José María Solórzano, was an engineer and coffee farmer; he espoused strict morality but took liberties with women. His mother, Elisa Fernández Barrios, was a zealot who dissimulated her puritanical ethics with rhetoric; she divorced her husband and "consecrated" herself to the children (Solórzano was the youngest of six). The rupture traumatized Solórzano and made him feel like a burden on his mother. At the age of ten, he entered a Marist school that insisted on strict religious teachings. Born just after the reign of terror headed by Manuel Estrada Cabrera (1898–1920), Solórzano came of age during the dictatorship of Jorge Ubico (1931–1944). As a result of Solórzano's formative experiences, priests, patriarchs, and tyrants became the antagonists in his plays. His first play, the one-act *La muerte hizo la luz* (published in 1951, performed in 1977; translated as *And Death Brought Forth the Light,* 1993), denounces the betrayals that despots use to attain or stay in power.

The author still resents the incongruities and suffocating narrowness of his "enclaustramiento inicial" (early confinement). In his youth the Guatemalan upper class was composed of about 100 families, some

1,500 people, owners of the land and all of its resources, enclosed in their own circle of foreign literature, Paris fashions, classical concerts, and, in his own case, a German governess. His family spoke German and French at home, while around them, 5 million starving Mayan Indians spoke mainly their own languages. The disjunction between his life and the reality of the country, especially the misery of the peasants, became a focus of his drama.

Solórzano's immersion into theater began with the rituals and pageantry of Catholicism. As an altar boy he became enthralled by the incense, the luxurious vestments, and the gestures that translated the enigmatic language of the Latin Mass. In an interview with Wilma Feliciano, included in her *El teatro mítico de Carlos Solórzano* (The Mythic Theater of Carlos Solórzano, 1995), Solórzano recalled that the spectacle and mystery of the Sacrament transported him to a purer spiritual world. Surprisingly, given the anticlericalism of his future dramaturgy, the teenage acolyte briefly considered the priesthood. In time, theater replaced religion as a means of transcending the sordidness of his world.

After graduating from high school in Guatemala City in 1939, the future dramatist expected to complete his university studies in Germany; but World War II precluded travel to Europe, so he studied in Mexico. By 1946 he had completed degrees in architecture and literature at the Universidad Nacional Autónoma de México (UNAM). Both his master's thesis and doctoral dissertation analyzed the dialectics of reason and religion in the writings of Miguel de Unamuno. The Spanish philosopher's struggle to reconcile the contradictions between logic and faith became Solórzano's as well. In 1946 Solórzano married Beatriz Caso, the daughter of Alfonso Caso, famed for his contributions to Mesoamerican anthropology. Facilitated by his 1949 Rockefeller Award for advanced studies at the Sorbonne, the couple spent three years perfecting their crafts; he became a playwright, she a sculptor.

The cultural ambience of Paris stimulated Solórzano's creative impulses. He assimilated the metaphysical questions of postwar intellectuals in France and added them to those elicited by his studies of Unamuno. The existentialism of Jean-Paul Sartre and Albert Camus, Antonin Artaud's ritualized theater of cruelty, and the folkloric elements of Michel de Ghelderode's dramaturgy influenced Solórzano's artistic development. He singles out Camus and Ghelderode as particularly decisive: Camus for his ideas and characterizations; Ghelderode for his puppetry and the sacred madness of his plays. Solórzano returned to Mexico in 1952 with his script for *Doña Beatriz, la sin ventura* (Doña Beatriz, The Luckless Woman) and became director of the newly created University Theater at UNAM.

Set in colonial Guatemala, *Doña Beatriz, la sin ventura* is an historical drama that recounts the life and death of Beatriz de la Cueva, the second wife of Pedro de Alvarado and the first woman governor of the Americas. Driven by a desire to foster Catholicism and divided by contradictory sexual urges, Doña Beatriz marries Alvarado, her widowed brother-in-law. Guilt, however, taints her marriage; in despair the protagonist clings to her faith. While her disillusion grows as she witnesses the rapacity and carnage of the colonization, Doña Beatriz is not motivated by humanity; the Indians, in fact, disgust her. With growing desperation, she watches her dream of evangelization succumb to the reality of miscegenation; she considers mestizos to be animals and a sin against God. Tormented by her sexuality and her sterility, she alternates between lusting for her husband and, at the suggestion of the Friar, withholding conjugal visits to punish his womanizing. Doña Leonor, her husband's mestiza daughter, becomes the target of her bitterness. Shortly before the climax, Alvarado leaves Guatemala in search of new conquests and dies; Doña Beatriz convinces the municipal authorities to name her governor. The chronicles state that on 9 September 1541 she signed the document of her investiture, "Beatriz de la Cueva, la sin ventura." Then, motivated by a mysterious force, she crossed out her name, leaving only the tag, "the luckless woman." The next day a flood killed thousands of Indians and hundreds of Spaniards, including the principal characters depicted in the play. Only Leonor survives, fulfilling Alvarado's boast that he would live forever through his daughter.

Doña Beatriz, la sin ventura bears the subtitle "auto histórico," or historical allegory. *Auto* refers to the *auto sacramental,* morality plays that dramatize the struggle between good and evil to affirm Christian doctrine. Plays by Pedro Calderón de la Barca represent the culmination of the *auto* form, but while his *autos* confirm the divine order of the universe, the apocalyptic denouement of *Doña Beatriz, la sin ventura* subverts that belief. The play closes in a cacophony of confusion as Blanca, confidante of the protagonist, praises Spain for the honor of founding new worlds, new races, and new cultures. Doña Beatriz, on the other hand, interprets the flood as the wrath of God for the cupidity of the Spaniards and the lasciviousness of the Indians.

Despite its historicity and realism, the symbolism in *Doña Beatriz, la sin ventura* suggests a myth of origins that examines the seeds of mestizo self-degradation implanted by colonialism—a concept known as *malinchismo*. Imitating the haughty protagonist, Leonor wants to act, speak, and dress like Doña Beatriz and disdains her fellow Indians. Ashamed of her bronze color, she hides her hands. Leonor thus embodies the wounds of race, religion, and culture that still infect

Latin America. Significantly, an Indian saves her life during the flood, affirming the redemptive value of natives to the new race.

El hechicero (1954, The Sorcerer), Solórzano's next play, relies on a mythic structure and stock characters. Although the action suggests the Middle Ages, the setting is atemporal and undefined. Motivated by idealism, Merlin attempts to decipher the Philosopher's Stone to re-create the world and distribute its resources more equitably. Casilda and Lisandro, his treacherous wife and brother, murder the alchemist to take control of the formula. The famished peasants spread Merlin's ashes on the barren fields, which turn green with the promise of rebirth. Casilda's evil brings to mind Clytemnestra, while Beatriz, the vengeful daughter, evokes Electra. *El hechicero* received mixed reviews in Mexico but triumphed in Paris in 1955. Emmanuel Roblés and Ghelderode praised it, although subsequent scholars have criticized its melodramatic tone and weak structure. Today even the author dismisses *El hechicero* as too ideological; the hero wants to save the world but cannot save his family. Yet, Merlin voices Solórzano's humanist vision: "Ningún dios puede resolver este enigma, sólo los hombres mismos" (No god can resolve this enigma, only men themselves).

Solórzano's first two plays helped him perfect his craft. *Doña Beatriz, la sin ventura* transforms history into myth to probe the lingering effects of colonialism on mestizo America. *El hechicero* previews the themes of sacrifice and salvation, the portrayal of archetypal characters, and the function of a Greek chorus—elements that acquire distinct cultural immediacy in Solórzano's subsequent plays.

Las manos de Dios (1956; translated as *The Hands of God*, 1968), Solórzano's most celebrated play, subverts the archetypes of redemption to dramatize the conflict between experience and religion with a Mexican artistic sensibility. It is subtitled a "Miracle Play in Three Acts," and the introduction prepares the reader to reinterpret the *auto sacramental* to discover how traditional beliefs shackle contemporary people. Using a church-prison metaphor to symbolize superstition and injustice, the author denounces the feudal structures that determine human choices. The denouement inverts the Christian dogma of good and evil. Instead of affirming divine goodness, *Las manos de Dios* challenges human beings to reclaim the love they have given him and to love themselves more than God. Love, not sacrifice, is the miracle that sustains life.

The action unfolds "today" in a poor Latin American village, but the mood and mores are medieval. Beatriz, a young woman, seeks to free her brother, imprisoned for criticizing the Boss. The Jailer, a lascivious coward in love with the town prostitute, hints that

Scene from Solórzano's historical drama about the first woman governor of the Americas, Doña Beatriz, la sin ventura *(Doña Beatriz, The Luckless Woman), first staged in 1952 (from* Teatro, *1992; Thomas Cooper Library, University of South Carolina)*

Beatriz can buy her brother's freedom with money or sex. Repulsed, she curses the Jailer. The Devil, her alter ego, appears to her but is invisible to all save those who harbor an inner spark of defiance. Prayers, tears, and pleas, he insists, are futile. She needs a pragmatic solution: steal the jewels from a statue in the church to give to the Jailer. Her mission becomes messianic when it grows to embrace the freedom of Mankind. The only truly free character is the Prostitute; she remains indifferent to the judgments of others. The Priest, who justifies poverty as one of God's inscrutable laws, entraps Beatriz and instigates the townspeople to condemn her. The crazed women beat her mercilessly, then whip themselves. Like Antigone, the heroine fails to achieve her goal, but her challenge to God and the Boss symbolizes the moral triumph of the individual over dogma and hypocrisy. When she steals the jewels from the hands of God, Beatriz leaves the wooden image in the church as empty as the values it represents.

As with his first two plays, Solórzano retains the structure of exposition, complication, denouement, and the unity of action and place. Temporal unity, however, is fragmented into chronological and psychic sequences. The action occurs over five days, but the main character evolves by means of stage techniques that supercede time. Lighting effects, mood music, pantomimes, and slow-motion sequences project her conflicting emotions and the eternal suffering of her people. Using flashbacks of her family history, tableau images of the present, and flash-forwards to her brother's execution, the Devil guides Beatriz through the process of self-awareness to strengthen her for the moment when she must forge her own destiny.

Despite its universal themes, the theatricality of the play mixes Mexican plastic arts and traditions with avant-garde symbolism. The original set, designed by Mexican artist Miguel Covarrubias, depicts the reality of peasant life: Church, State, and poverty. A baroque church dominates stage left, the sinister side. Its solidity and sumptuousness contrast sharply with the huts dotting the background: "En medio de las chozas que la rodean, ésta debe tener un aspecto fabuloso" (In the midst of the huts that surround it, the church should have a marvelous appearance, like a legendary palace). Likewise, the well in front of the church increases the funereal landscape of dead trees and yellow fields. A dead tree by the well becomes the site of the heroine's martyrdom. The jail, a dirty building with a twisted sign, sits stage right, the military side; its deformity manifests the sordidness of the civil administration.

The appearance and actions of the characters are as expressionistic as the set design. Dressed in the white costume made famous by José Clemente Orozco in his painting *Zapatistas* (1931), the people outwardly resemble the rebels of the Mexican Revolution. The peasants, however, seem as miserable as the natural world; languid church bells and sad music announce their entrance. They bear their burdens stoically. Their faces fixed like masks, the men carry dry reeds and the women carry children. They allow the Priest to manipulate them, evoking the hierarchies of Mesoamerica, medieval Spain, and colonial Mexico. Always fearful, the silent chorus comments on the action with uniform rhythmic movements fraught with diffidence and confusion.

The people come alive briefly toward the end of act 3 when they react to the arguments of the Priest and the Devil, litigants in the trial to save the heroine's soul. Moved to compassion by the Devil, the chorus responds timidly with Yes/No answers as it oscillates in ballet-like movements between resignation and rebellion. The Priest warns the wavering jury that God punishes defiance. At that moment an icy wind starts to howl, extinguishing their ephemeral identification with the heroine. Incited by the Priest, they wound Beatriz mortally, then beat themselves for the double sin of listening to then rejecting their would-be redeemer. To expiate their guilt, they conduct a "Burning of Judas." This custom, popular during Holy Week, forms the structure of *Los fantoches* (The Puppets, performed in 1958), Solórzano's next play. As the effigy burns and the life of Beatriz seeps away, the Priest heaps guilt on the congregation. The Devil tries to dispel their feelings of worthlessness: "No se flagelen más. No se odien de esa manera. ¡Ámense a sí mismos más que a Dios!" (Don't scourge yourselves anymore. Don't hate yourselves that way. Love yourselves more than God). In contrast, the Priest yells, "¡Fuerte! ¡Más fuerte! ¡Más fuerte!" (Hard! Harder! Harder!) as he shepherds them into the church. The docile movements of the chorus suggest ancient rituals dictated by superior beings, a central idea of Artaud's theater of cruelty.

A heroine in the classic mold, Beatriz struggles with her faith, perceives a new truth, and carries out the decisive action that closes the tragedy. Her triumph, however, is bittersweet. Nothing changes; the social-religious structure remains intact. The jewels go full circle: from the Jailer to the Prostitute, to a friend, to the Boss, who will presumably return them to the church as proof of his piety. Yet, bound to the tree of death, the protagonist begins to feel freer than ever. She recognizes that the Devil inside her is "el verdadero bien" (the true good) and exhorts him to continue to fight the churches and prisons that limit spiritual and personal freedom. The denouement remains essentially open. Solórzano represents these problems to make people confront their own complacency and complicity, but individuals must define their own solutions.

The inversion of good and evil in *Las manos de Dios* provoked scandals. The majority of critics praised its blend of classical and innovative techniques, its penetrating portrayal of the fanaticism and fatalism of popular worship, its defense of self-worth and metaphysical rebellion, and its Mexican features and stagecraft. Conversely, some critics (notably fellow playwright Luis G. Basurto) assailed it as demagogic, anti-Catholic, and anti-Mexican. Occasionally, members of the audience left in mid performance. The controversy intensified when the Mexican congress considered a proposal to deport Solórzano for defiling the common faith. Despite its detractors, the play has been included in several anthologies and translated into various languages. *Las manos de Dios,* along with *Los fantoches, El crucificado* (The Crucified, published in 1957, performed in 1958; translated as *The Crucifixion,* 1974), and *Cruce de vías* (published in 1959, performed in 1966; translated as *Crossroads,* 1973)—his most often published and produced works—established Solórzano's international reputation as a playwright.

After these full-length productions, Solórzano wrote several one-act plays that range from crude realism to poetic allegories. In 1958 he presented a trilogy composed of *Los fantoches, Mea culpa,* and *El crucificado.* Written at different times but premiered together, the three share the themes, characters, and devotions of the Lenten season. *El crucificado* and *Los fantoches* derive from traditions associated with Good Friday and Holy Saturday, respectively. Structured as a double confession, *Mea culpa* compares the sin of Pontius Pilate with those of the Bishop, who represents two thousand years of institutionalized religion. Finally, although the action in all three occurs within one day, each one uses a different form to probe the nature of sin, sacrifice, and salvation. Nevertheless, the trilogy retains the motifs of *Las manos de Dios* of an indifferent God and dogma as prison.

Transposed directly from the "Burning of Judas," *Los fantoches* assimilates the ritual punishment of Judas. During Holy Week, the people fashion and publicly hang huge, brilliantly painted puppets made of bamboo and cardboard wired with explosives, then detonate them on Holy Saturday during raucous street festivals. They heap their sins onto the scapegoat to avenge his betrayal and cleanse themselves for the Resurrection. Over the years the range of puppet characters has grown to include the Devil and social and political personages currently out of favor. Eager to make the gestation of the play accessible to audiences of other countries, Solórzano provided an "Explanation to the Foreign Reader." He foreshadows a grim cosmic vision by explaining that he dramatized the Judas figures of popular culture to suggest "la existencia de un mundo que, tras su brillante colorido aparente, encierra un fondo desgarrado y cruel" (the existence of a world that, behind its apparent brilliant coloring, encloses a wretched, cruel abyss).

Los fantoches, "a Mime-Drama for Marionettes," is the most theatrical and pessimistic work in Solórzano's repertoire. It portrays the Sisyphean absurdity of the human condition with few words and much action, spectacle, and symbolism. A convergence of French existentialism and innovative pantomimes performed by Mexican human puppets, *Los fantoches* captivated audiences in Paris at the Theater of Nations Festival in 1963. It was the first Mexican play performed in an international festival, and artist Rufino Tamayo designed the set. Since then it has been performed in Spanish, English, French, German, and Slovenian. Set in the interval from sunrise to moonlight, the play represents life: from creation, to self-consciousness of one's uniqueness, to a failed insurgency and symbolic fall leading to knowledge, death, and nothingness. Before the fall, the puppets yearn to escape their dreary warehouse; periodically the door opens, and one of them is selected to leave. The others imagine an outer world of liberty and happiness, but they cannot reach to see out the window in the warehouse.

The six marionettes all have a cartridge box on their chests and wires to their extremities like an exposed circulatory system. Their faces painted in the same whimsical fashion as the outfits that designate their tasks, they resume their daily routines in a series of pantomimes. The Young Man works; the Woman loves; the *Cabezón* (a puppet with a big, pumpkin-like head) thinks; the Old Man counts his wealth; the Artist dreams; and Judas suffers silently. They perform their functions faithfully in the hope that the Old Puppet Maker and his daughter, the Girl, will liberate them.

The bearded and robed Puppet Maker is deaf, mute, blind, and clumsy; he limps and leans on his daughter to get around. Dressed in ruffles and lace and skipping like a child, the Girl wears the mask of "la muerte catrina," the stylish image of death made famous by Mexican artist José Guadalupe Posada. The Puppet Maker laughs softly but never responds to the questions of the marionettes; he is a *deus otiosus,* a god indifferent to his creations. The Girl, on the other hand, chides them derisively, spins wildly, and roughly shoves the next puppet she has chosen to "liberate" out the door.

The three major episodes in *Los fantoches* allude to life, love, and death. The first one dramatizes the gamut of human activities and emotions: duty, pleasure, and grief. The second is creative; the sexual coupling of the Young Man and the Woman suggests love, marriage, and parenthood. The final episode is apocalyptic; the puppets scramble to evade the menacing finger of the Girl. Between these episodes, the marionettes struggle to give meaning to their existence. Curious as to why the Puppet Maker would fashion them in his own likeness only to shut them in a world of ignorance and monotony, they begin to learn new words: "traitor, liberty, gunpowder." When Judas is taken away, the *Cabezón* suggests that they stand on each other's shoulders to reach the window. As he describes how the Puppet Maker and his daughter hang Judas and bring a torch to his chest, the resulting explosion causes their pyramid to collapse; they all grip their cartridges in terror. They learn a new word, "death," but cannot define it: "Muerte ¿es eso? . . . ¿Ser nada?" (Death, is that? . . . To be nothing?), asks the Woman in amazement.

The puppets rationalize that Judas dissolved into ashes and nothingness because he was a traitor; but when they hear the approaching steps of the Puppet Maker and his daughter, they attempt to barricade the door with their bodies. The Girl laughs at their feeble rebellion and deliberately chooses as her next victim the Artist, a young man who brings beauty to their drab world. Cynically, the Girl tells them that it is necessary to clean out the warehouse to store the new puppets awaiting creation. Indifferent to their questions and tears, the Puppet Maker sleeps tranquilly. In contrast, dissonant music accompanies the Girl's whirling dance of death. As the dissonance increases, the puppets cower and cry. Suddenly the Girl stops, targets the audience, and the curtain drops. *Los fantoches* thus challenges the audience's spiritual conformity and forces them to confront their own mortality.

Composed essentially of two monologues, *Mea culpa* falls into the same pattern of wordiness and abstraction as *El hechicero*. A dignified old judge identified as "the Man" learns that he has terminal cancer and goes to confession. Always secure in his ability to distinguish right from wrong, he now doubts his conviction of a rabble-rouser called "the Master," the leader of twelve deluded men who attempted to subvert the established order. The Bishop-Confessor fails to communicate with or absolve the Man, laughing softly at first, then loudly as the Man attempts to discharge his guilt. Instead the Bishop forcefully inverts their roles and confesses that his sin is greater; he poisoned believers with resignation and fear.

Mea culpa attacks centuries of institutionalized guilt. When the Bishop emerges from the confessional, his appearance symbolizes the condition of the Church: old, tired, messy hair, tense hands, vestments torn and dirty, his unfocused eyes staring vacantly upward. Deliriously he begs the Man's forgiveness for killing his brethren with despair and condemning them to self-annihilation in preparation for Judgment. He even sentenced the people in Latin—a language as dead as the Church—because the enigmatic words increased their sense of awe. The raging Bishop throws himself face down and begs the Man to whip him until his blood flows so he may redeem all the blood the faithful shed for him.

The Man, who has come to save his soul, ends up self-destructing also. When he first enters the confessional, he observes dust everywhere and feels suffocated. His instinct is to run away, but guilt keeps him kneeling. He even perceives that the Bishop's chuckles underscore the futility of his contrition. He admits that it is laughable to believe that a man's words can save another dying man. Disconcerted by the Bishop's madness and unable to complete the rite of expiation, the Man sits in the confessional and closes the curtain until he is totally invisible.

Despite the verbosity of *Mea culpa*, its stark images are charged with symbolism. The set is almost empty, emblematic of the naked soul in the face of ultimate truth. The lights are dark purple, almost black. At center stage a white column rises from and disappears into the shadows; the axis that unites earth to the ethereal zones. The shadows at either end allude to the obscurity of the doctrine of salvation; it can lead to either torment or bliss. At the foot of the column sits a heavily gilded baroque confessional with a purple curtain, the color of mourning in Christian tradition. The claustrophobic confessional is analogous to Doña Beatriz's prayer room, the puppets' warehouse, and the prison-church of *Las manos de Dios*. The Man's movements are deliberate and dignified despite his anxiety, in contrast to the ramblings of the Bishop. The religious strains that open the somber exchange become the dissonant chords of a twisted ritual at the end. The Man's symbolic entombment decries the absurdity that, at times, one must destroy the body to save the soul, a grotesque ritual that is repeated in *El crucificado*.

El crucificado is Solórzano's most controversial play, despite its derivation from historical precedents. Although it was based on the Passion plays performed yearly, Mexican audiences objected to the depiction of an ignorant, drunken peasant who plays his role so faithfully that he demands to be crucified. Scholars such as Frances Toor have documented, however, that such occurrences did take place. Perhaps anticipating the controversy that the trilogy would arouse, the author added a note to the program stating that the aim of these plays was to illustrate his concern with the emptiness of an ineffective doctrine "que responde a la angustia racional con una invariable y rígida forma de evasión: la fe" (that responds to rational anguish with an unchanging and rigid form of evasion: faith). Searching to resolve their doubts, the characters in each play must confront the decisive moment when their fate turns toward tragedy and comedy at the same time.

Structured as a play within a play, *El crucificado* declines from ritual to carnival to collective madness as the Gospel of Saint Matthew degenerates into a ludicrous game. In addition to the metadramatic doubling of characters and themes, much of the dialectal language parodies the Scriptures. On the outside, the players prepare for their roles in the Passion, while the inner play is a hodgepodge of liquor, ribald religiosity, and arcane biblical statements. Set in a hut with dirt floors and sooty walls, the action begins as the peasants, all with marked Indian features, talk enthusiastically about the performance. Each one stresses his or her own contribution with pride: the purple tunic, the crown of thorns, the cross. Chucho (the Spanish nickname for men named Jesus) enters looking downcast and not yet costumed. The peasants poke fun at his sadness, comment on his likeness to the "real Jesus,"

Scene from the 1958 Mexico City premiere of Solórzano's controversial play El crucificado *(The Crucified), in which the drunken cast of a Passion play get carried away and actually kill the peasant playing Jesus (from* Teatro, *1992; Thomas Cooper Library, University of South Carolina)*

and remember that his grandfather died shortly after playing the role. Chucho fears the Priest's words that only blood and sacrifice can cleanse their sins, especially original sin. The peasants speculate on the significance of original sin. Does it mean that it is sad to be born and have to die, or that birth itself is the original sin? Another peasant rejects that notion; he did not ask to be born, especially in this barren land where the sun turns a man into ashes.

The "Apostles" arrive already drunk, their dirty rural garments visible below their disheveled robes. Aware of Chucho's reticence to assume his role, they kneel before him, then keel over with laughter, question his manhood, fill him with drink, and encourage and ridicule him simultaneously. Matthew warns him not to take the role seriously; he is just a man disguised as the Messiah. Meanwhile Peter assures him that something miraculous will happen, and after death he will have the consolation of the Resurrection. Duped by their words and liquor, the reluctant hero allows two women to dress him. The light becomes "unreal" as the protagonist becomes transfigured. The women, equally deceived by the illusion, kneel in prayer. Assuring Chucho that he is the Savior, Matthew jokingly encourages him to drink more so he will feel like "el hijo de todos los dioses en la tierra" (the son of all the gods of the Earth). And if he prefers, more like a son of God than the rest of them. Beyond blasphemy, the comparison of Christ to telluric deities and the jokes about sacrificing Chucho connote the latent pantheism of native religiosity. It also recalls that in Mesoamerican rituals, the actor who impersonated the god performed his role only once.

This religious dualism increases with the arrival of Mary and Magdalena, played by Chucho's mother and bride-to-be. Like those of the other players, their apostolic costumes contradict the sacredness of the event. Mary looks clumsy, her halo always on the verge of falling off. Magdalena has flowing hair, and her outfit is pressed to her body, revealing her robust sensuality. Despite her seductive appearance, Magdalena loves Chucho; love, she states, "es lo único que importa" (is the only thing that matters). An exchange of dialectal wordplay then juxtaposes everyday language to the

Scriptures. Totally inebriated, Chucho begins to mumble biblical phrases punctuated by the refrain: "It is written." Mary undercuts his pronouncements in a comic parody. When he says he has no mother, only a father, she reminds him that he does not even know who his father was. When he claims to have multiplied the loaves of bread, Mary retorts that she purchased them. Poor people, she scolds him, must earn their daily bread; words and nonsense will not feed them. Hearing the impatient shouts of the revelers outside, Magdalena attempts to entice Chucho with visions of their future. The Priest arrives, and the women beg him to stop the charade. Insisting that Jesus must perform in order for the people to believe, he arranges the ragtag players in a procession. The shouts, fireworks, and catcalls mix with the whining music of a dissonant *pasodoble,* music generally associated with bullfights. The light fades gradually until the stage is totally dark.

The second scene, after Chucho has been crucified, is even more cynical and irreverent than the first. The Apostles discard their disguises and reveal their true characters. More concerned about their own punishment than the death of their friend, they insist that Chucho instigated his own fate. He demanded to be sacrificed, and the drunken crowd complied. The Priest, who might have prevented the tragedy, had already left. Fearful of being blamed for Chucho's death, they hatch a great idea. They will affirm it was a miracle; Jesus was a "sort of Savior," and his death was necessary. Before exiting, they seal their pact and speculate that someday they may attain "algo provechoso" (something profitable) from the crucifixion. This pragmatic "miracle" implies the genesis of the Gospels. It suggests that miracles are another form of deceiving believers.

In contrast to the visceral realism of *El crucificado*, *Cruce de vías* is a poetic allegory about illusion and disillusion in love. A stylized "Sad Vaudeville" about loneliness and lost opportunities, *Cruce de vías* uses the alienating effects of the Theater of the Absurd to examine how the lack of communication locks people into patterns of solitude. The plot is simple. A mature Woman with an elegant, ageless figure writes letters and sends touched-up photographs of herself to young men, then agrees to meet them but never appears. On one occasion she does decide to meet a Man at a railroad crossing, symbolic of their brief encounter and eternal separation. Afraid of rejection, the veiled Woman speaks in double entendres about her friend who writes to and makes dates with young men. In one last pathetic attempt to communicate, she closes the Man's eyes and charms him with mellifluous words as she slowly lifts her veil; but her withered face dispels his rapture. Blind to her illusion and even to the white rose that was to be the clue to their mutual identification, he dismisses her and determines to wait for his idealized woman. Reluctantly the Woman boards the train and leaves in a pantomime of writhing movements as if the train is dragging her off.

The author's stage directions assure that *Cruce de vías* achieves poignancy without falling into melodrama. The characters move mechanically, like those in silent movies. The Man's gestures are impatient and abrupt; the Woman's slow and graceful. Her sensuous tenderness deepens her despair. The third character, the railroad Flagman, is stiff, disinterested in the couple, and moves and speaks like a robot. Three men dressed in gray suits make up the train; each man extends his arm to the shoulder of the one in front and makes a circular motion with the other arm synchronized to the rhythm of the Flagman's monotonous litany about the trains. From the shadowy ceiling hangs a clock set to five o'clock, but the clock does not run, foretelling both the couple's failed encounter and their lifelong solitude. The director, Solórzano states in his author's note, may align the motions to the meaning of the text to achieve a more sentimental effect. If the director prefers to accent the cruelty of the situation, however, the pantomime should contradict the text to reveal how the emotions run counter to the words.

The abyss between words and communication, a technique common to absurdist drama, begins with the rambling conversation between the Flagman and the Man. In fact, the latter comments, "tengo la impresión que no hablamos el mismo idioma" (I have the impression that we aren't speaking the same language). The Flagman speaks only nonsense but carries the lantern of truth and enlightenment. When the Woman arrives, he raises the lantern, blinding the Man. Playing for time, she tears the white flower off her dress and turns away. Despite all the verbal and visual clues the Woman gives him as to her identity, the Man looks wistfully at the photo of the woman he awaits. Some of Solórzano's most poetic dialogue precedes the coup de théâtre, the unmasking of the Woman: her solitude, the unsatisfied longing of her body, the need for love that grows greater with age. As she raises the veil, she pleads: "El tiempo es el peor enemigo de ella. ¿Luchará usted?" (Time is her worst enemy. Will you fight it?). Mesmerized by the voice but repelled by the face, the Man stands brusquely. They allow the moment to pass and then separate to follow their futile quest forever.

El sueño del ángel (performed in 1960; translated as *The Angel's Forty Winks,* 1993), like *Cruce de vías,* reproduces the drama of a mature woman trapped in a loveless life. Nonetheless, it shares a greater similarity of structure and tone with *Mea culpa.* Both evoke the continuing guilt of a youthful transgression; both dramatize rituals of confession and expiation. The old judge erred because of his ambition; the Woman, for love. In a moment of weakness she lulled her guardian angel to sleep and allowed her brother-in-law to make love to her, a sin bordering on incest. Since then the Woman relives the act and vacillates between nostalgia and remorse. Unable to condemn even an illicit love, she struggles with the Angel, her conscience, to rebel against or revel in her self-imposed nightly act of contrition. Solórzano reenacts her psychic battle with stylized pantomimes like those in earlier plays. As in *El hechicero, Mea culpa,* and *El crucificado,* the Woman's punishment requires a bloody lashing. More than inflicting pain, however, the whip becomes an instrument of sublimated sex.

Characteristically Solórzano proposes an expressionistic setting and inverts the moral values embodied in each character. The old, worn furniture and faded flowers give an impression of abandonment, of decrepitude, of disenchantment. Likewise, the fifty-year-old Woman looks shriveled and wasted. She sits under an intense light, dressed in black and surrounded by religious statues, a prayer stand, and a creaking clock. The Angel does not carry the sword of justice, but he resembles a baroque image of Saint Michael, the warrior in the Book of Daniel who fights the hordes of Satan at the "end of time," then stands before the celestial throne to impart the penalty. Despite his beauty, the Angel's bearing appears cruel, with an air of insolent authority. His wings creak with a dead sound, and he remains always in the shadows behind the Woman. She repeats his actions mechanically, giving the impression that they are joined by invisible threads like those of puppets. She represents human frailty, starved for love and terrorized by damnation; he represents the fury of the Almighty. Once her friend and protector, the Angel has become her tormentor. His constant barrage, the contrast of intense light and shadows, and the religious imagery suggest a trial, the Last Judgment.

Every evening the Angel submits the Woman to an interrogation. Steadfastly she denies any remorse; but love and faith divide her soul. The Woman's rebellious side treasures her transgression as an act of love, not evil. Defiantly she calls it a moment of liberation, the only happy time in a long succession of identical days filled with prayer. While the Angel slept, she freed herself from his oppression, experienced love, and steeled herself for the years of torment he would impose on her. God invented evil and nestled it within her body, but she is the one who must pay for it. The price of forgiveness, self-degradation, is too high. The Angel berates her defense; it is her own soul that compels her to repent and redeem herself. Every time she runs to another part of the room, he draws her back, recasting the string-puppet metaphor of *Los fantoches*. Weakened by his harangue, she obeys his commands with pitiful movements but cannot force herself to admit any guilt. The sweet, languid rhythms of dance music carry her back to the day, the kiss on the nape of the neck, on her breasts, and the arms of her brother-in-law, while the Angel condemns her "lascivious dreams." Strengthened by the music, she retorts that even a sinful love is always good.

Yet, her defiance falters as he keeps badgering her. Exhausted and hypnotized, she submits. The rhythm and repetition of their dual chant accent the liturgical cadences of the scene. Paradoxically, sexual allusions saturate the objects of her expiation. Moving like an automaton, the Woman raises the whip, kisses it, and kneels. He chants, she repeats. She admits her guilt; promises never to ask why she is guilty; recognizes that she was created that way; and repents all her sins, especially the sin of having been born. In the respite between her confession and penance, the Woman hears the dance music again and stands up, perhaps to defy the Angel. But the music fades, and the Woman succumbs. Convinced now of her guilt, she and the Angel repeat the chant, and she begins her scourging. Dissonant music rises and then ebbs away while the Angel sinks into a delirium of pleasure, emitting moans similar to those of an orgasm. Still kneeling, the Woman keeps lashing herself with a hallucinatory stare fixed on the body of the Angel.

The convergence of the dramatic and sexual climaxes subverts the ritual. In her delusion, the Woman confuses expiation with ecstasy. As the Angel predicted, she whips herself until she "feels pleasure." The sadomasochistic orgy reveals her mental imbalance and the perversion of Christ's message that love is the greatest virtue. Trapped in the passivity society imposes on women (especially in the provinces, where the drama occurs), unloved and lacking an emotional escape, she fixates on the virility of her guardian angel. Unable to satisfy her sexuality in a healthy relationship, the Woman withdraws from reality and sublimates her desires in sexual fantasies.

Sexual fantasies also drive the action in *El zapato* (performed in 1970; translated as *The Shoe,* 1993). The plot portrays the struggle of an adolescent boy and his father for the affections of the mother, the Oedipus complex. A family portrait painted with life-size images dominates the stage, just as the family dominates the Youth. Accompanied by sad music, the Youth hobbles on stage; his short pants and mustache allude to his liminal state between childhood and manhood, while his difficulty walking recasts the oedipal clubfoot. His disdain for the "damned shoe" seems meaningless until the Father waves it menacingly. The shoe represents the love-hate relationship between them. The Father is tired of supporting the weight of his son; the Youth resents his father's power but caresses the shoe. Angered by the Father's taunting, he rips out the shoe tongue and "castrates" the Father, who screams in pain. Spitefully he calls his son a eunuch because "yo hago lo que tú no puedes hacer" (I do what you cannot do).

Their hostile discourse evolves into pantomimes charged with erotic innuendo. Dance music arises, and the Mother's movements become more provocative; the Youth grabs her waist, and they dance until his father's beating forces him to retreat. With crazed intensity the Youth rips the shoe apart and stomps on it. Between rancor and tears, he gathers the fragments, reconstructs the shoe, and puts it back on. Each button increases his torment; off stage, the Father laughs. Dinnertime ends the torture, for today.

The dramatic tension suggests that the Youth must control his impulses to survive a difficult family dynamic. Beyond the oedipal fantasies, however, resounds a personal tone: the author's words about the severity of his own father and how he felt like a burden on his mother. The playwright translated the resentment of living under a dictatorial father and a manipulative mother into the stage images of *El zapato,* his last play.

The 1973 and 1992 editions of Solórzano's collected plays identify *El zapato* as "A Mime-Drama in One Act." Translator Francesca Colecchia changed the subtitle to "A Mime-Drama for a Ventriloquist" and rewrote it with Solórzano's permission; sections of dialogue are omitted, added, or rearranged. Her only character is the Youth; the Shoe recites the Father's dialogue in ventriloquist form, and the Mother never appears. Colecchia also omits the author's introduction about the family portrait and how each figure is depicted. In her introduction she interprets the play as "the difficult struggle of young people to realize their independence." While it retains the father-son hostility, her revision undermines the extreme cruelty in Solórzano's original drama.

From 1966 to 1971 Solórzano turned to fiction and published *Los falsos demonios* (False Demons, 1966), "El visitante" (The Visitor, 1966), and *Las celdas* (The Cells, 1971), his last piece of creative writing. While these narratives retain the themes of physical and metaphysical prisons, the characterization is psychological, the fear more internalized than on stage. A story about sexual awakening, "El visitante" reflects a counterimage of *El zapato.* The story takes place in bed; until recently, the protagonist's mother had allowed him to sleep with her. Every night since his fifteenth birthday—when he accidentally cut his father and made him bleed—a filthy demon with horns, a tail, and an enormous penis has tormented him. His only defense is to become immobile, blind to the demon's obscene dancing and deaf to his lewd remarks about the boy's mother's legs. Consumed with guilt, he determines to free himself from the demon by remaining paralyzed forever.

Somewhat similar in theme and characterization, *Los falsos demonios* takes the form of a deathbed letter from an exiled father to his son to explain why political terror forced him to abandon his family. The narrative is semi-autobiographical. Born in San Marcos, Guatemala, while Estrada Cabrera still ruled, Canastuj, the protagonist, comes of age during the dictatorship of Ubico, a world of distrust and atrocities. Shriveled by cowardice and the urge for self-preservation, his defense, like the boy's in "El visitante," is solitude and immobility. The soulless antihero keeps a low profile, eschews politics and rebels, accepts fear as the natural order, but self-destructs nonetheless. The capture of a seditious friend convinces Canastuj to flee; exile exacerbates his torments. More than focusing on the history of tyranny in Latin America, the novel underscores the centuries of passivity that allow dictators to thrive. The real demons are in the soul.

Las celdas derives from an historical incident in which the monks of a Benedictine monastery in Cuernavaca underwent psychoanalysis. Mexican playwright Vicente Leñero dramatized this experiment in *Pueblo rechazado* (A Rejected People, 1968). In *Las celdas* Manuel, a Guatemalan novice self-exiled in Mexico, enters the cloister to escape a patriarchal father, a tearful mother, and the dictator of the moment. To achieve wholeness, Manuel must reconcile the ready answers of religion with the painful process of self-discovery, transcend his estrangement, and learn to love. Again, the autobiographical allusions abound. Even the title recalls what Solórzano described as his "early confinement." Don Antonio, the former prior of the monastery, and Antonia, Manuel's Indian *nana,* become Manuel's surrogate parents. The book is dedicated to Solórzano's wife, "A Beatriz: el desvarío y la redención" (To Beatriz: madness and redemption).

Solórzano remained a major force of the Mexican stage for two decades as a playwright, director, professor of dramatic literature (he initiated the bachelor's degree program in dramatic literature at UNAM), theater critic, and historian, and is still honored for his contributions. As director of the University Theater at UNAM from 1952 to 1962, he balanced its repertoire with classical and modern, national and international productions, and also served as director of the Museo Nacional de Teatro from 1964 to 1967. After devoting a decade mainly to creating and directing drama, Solórzano became a scholar. He began to teach at UNAM in 1962 and published major works of Latin American

Scene from a 1969 New York production of Solórzano's play Cruce de vías *(Crossroads; published in 1959, performed in 1966), about the failed meeting between an older woman and the young man with whom she has been corresponding (from* Teatro, *1992; Thomas Cooper Library, University of South Carolina)*

theater history: *Teatro latinoamericano del siglo XX* (Latin American Theater of the Twentieth Century, 1961), which he later expanded into *Teatro latinoamericano en el siglo XX* (Latin American Theater in the Twentieth Century, 1964), and the two-volume anthology *El teatro hispanoamericano contemporáneo* (Contemporary Hispanoamerican Theater, 1962–1964). Subsequently he edited more anthologies and contributed critical essays to journals in Europe, Latin America, and the United States. He was the theater critic for *Siempre* in Mexico and a correspondent for *Rendez-Vous du Théâtre* in Paris and for *Primer Acto* in Madrid. In 1973 he was named a member of the Royal Spanish Academy in Madrid; in the same year, UNAM published his *Testimonios teatrales,* a collection of one hundred of his reviews of plays produced in Mexico City between 1960 and 1970.

In 1974 Solórzano's only child, Diego, died in a hunting accident. Solórzano declined a Fulbright Visiting Artist Award and withdrew from almost all his professional endeavors except teaching. Later the Solórzanos recomposed their family with two daughters, Juana Inés and Beatriz. His drama continues to attract audiences and critical attention; universities invite him to lecture, and honors and prestigious posts recognize his contributions to the diffusion of Latin American culture through theater. In 1984 he was selected to edit the Americas volume of *The World Encyclopedia of Contemporary Theatre* (2001). The next year UNAM named him Professor Emeritus, an honor conferred on only fifty professors among a faculty of ten thousand, then bestowed on him the National Literary Award in 1988. That same year he received the Miguel Angel Asturias National Literary Award in Guatemala, and in 1997 his homeland's University of San Carlos conferred on him an honorary doctorate. He served as president of the Mexican Center of the International Theater Institute of UNESCO (1991–2000), as honorary president of the Association of Theater Researchers of Mexico (1990–1993), and in the same post for the Latin American Association of Theater Researchers (1992–1994). In 2001 the University of Buenos Aires honored him with the Armando Piscépolo Award in recognition of his international stature as a man of the theater.

Carlos Solórzano's drama uses Christian imagery to explore the timeless concerns of the relationships of mortals to God and to other human beings, relying on mestizo forms that are specifically Indo-Hispanic yet accessible to audiences everywhere. Evidence of his enduring ability to reach across cultures is the 16 October 2000 performance of *Los fantoches* (as *Lutke* [Puppets]) at a Slovenian theater festival in Gorica, Italy, sponsored by the Festinvala 2000 of Ljubljana. Ensemble Productions of Minneapolis-St. Paul revived *Los manos de Dios* at the Minnesota Fringe Festival on 4 August 2001. The religious and political anguish suffered by Solórzano's characters seeks to incite the audience to question its own values. Implicit in the symbolism of rebellion and redemption is his conviction that salvation is the work of mortals, not of gods.

Interviews:

Rosa Castro, "Tiempo del teatro: Entrevista con Solórzano," *Mexico en la Cultura,* 261 (March 1954): 3;

Ligia Bernal, "Autor Guatemalteco," *El Imparcial* (Guatemala), 19 June 1954, p. 3;

Juan de Montan, "Entreacto: El Estreno de Hoy," *Novedades,* 24 August 1956, p. 19;

Armando Guerra, "*Las manos de Dios:* Viguroso Drama de Solórzano," *La Hora en México* (16 October 1956): 62–63;

Isabel Cuchi Coli, "En Torno al Primer Seminario de Teatro," *El Mundo* (San Juan), 9 December 1961;

Elena Poniatowska, "Entrevista con Solórzano," *El Día* (Mexico), 1 September 1964, p. 11;

"Carlos Solórzano nos habla de su *Antología del teatro hispanoamericano,*" *La Gaceta,* 126 (February 1965);

J. H. Firman, "Renaissance in Mexican Drama Told by Playwright," *Progress Bulletin* (Pomona, Cal.), 22 January 1966, p. 2;

Poniatowska, "Latinoamérica, el miedo y *Los falsos demonios:* Habla el dramaturgo Solórzano," *Novedades,* 20 June 1966, pp. 1, 7;

Elena Garro, "El presidente de Solórzano," *La cultura en México,* 230 (July 1966): xiii–xiv;

Yolanda Argudín, "Entrevista a Solórzano: Dieciocho países participarán en el Festival Olimpiada Teatral," *Ovaciones* (4 June 1968): 6;

Claude Fell, "Carlos Solórzano ou le desarroi des pantins," *Le Monde* (Paris), 5 April 1969, p. vii;

Graciela Mendoza, "Solórzano habla del teatro en America Latina," *Revista Mexicana de la Cultura,* 29 (August 1969): 4;

Dora Krinsky, "Una encuesta: ¿Para qué sirve la crítica teatral?" *La cultura en México,* 482 (May 1971): xiii–xiv;

M. A. Acosta, "Entrevista con Solórzano," *El Gallo Ilustrado,* 562 (April 1973): 13;

María Sten, "Solórzano: La universidad, único camino para dignificar el teatro en México," *Diorama de la Cultura* (26 August 1973): 14;

Tomás Moharro, "Charla con Solórzano por la muerte de Ghelderode," *El Sol de México en la Cultura,* 71 (August 1976): 5–6;

Magdalena Saldaña, "Entrevista con Solórzano: El disco como instrumento de la cultura," *Diorama de la cultura* (20 April 1977): 14;

Teresa Méndez-Faith, "Dos tardes con Carlos Solórzano," *Latin American Theatre Review,* 18 (Fall 1984): 103–110.

Bibliography:

Pedro de Andrea, "Carlos Solórzano: Bibliografía," in *Comunidad latinoamericana de escritores,* Boletín No. 7 (Mexico: Editorial Libros de Mexico, 1970), pp. 25–59.

References:

Robert K. Anderson, "*Los fantoches,* un drama expresionista de Carlos Solórzano," *Hispanic Journal,* 2, no. 2 (1981): 111–117;

Phillip Raymond Baker, "Carlos Solórzano: The Man and His Creative Works," dissertation, Florida State University, 1973;

Luis G. Basurto, "En Carta a Carlos Solórzano, Basurto hace la defensa de su carrera teatral," *Siempre,* 756 (December 1967): 6–7;

Basurto, "LGB da la absolución a Carlos Solórzano," *Siempre,* 758 (January 1968): 4;

Pedro Bravo-Elizondo, "*Las manos de Dios:* El encadenamiento de Promoteo," in his *Teatro hispanoamericano de crítica social* (Madrid: Playor, 1975), pp. 109–119;

Luis Antonio Calderón, "El miedo: Elementos de contacto existencialista en las obras dramáticas de Albert Camus y Carlos Solórzano," dissertation, University of Georgia, 1988;

Raúl Hector Castagnino, "*Las manos de Dios,*" in his *Semiótica, ideología y teatro hispanoamericano contemporáneo* (Buenos Aires: Nova, 1974), pp. 107–124;

Frank N. Dauster, "Carlos Solórzano: La libertad sin límites," in his *Ensayos sobre teatro hispanoamericano* (Mexico: Sepsetentas, 1975), pp. 127–142;

Dauster, "Carlos Solórzano o la tragedia como subversión," *Hispanic Journal,* 6 (Spring 1985): 27–32;

Dauster, "The Drama of Carlos Solórzano," *Modern Drama,* 7 (May 1964): 89–100;

Dauster, "Hacia el teatro nuevo: Un novel autor dramático," *Hispania,* 41 (May 1958): 170–172;

Dauster, "New Values in Latin American Theater," *Theatre Arts,* 43 (February 1959): 56–59, 72–73;

Wilma Feliciano, "La desmitificación de los dioses en tres dramas de Carlos Solórzano/Archetypal Inversions in Three Dramas by Solórzano," *Teatro, Revista del Centro Mexicano,* 9/11 Instituto Internacional de Teatro UNESCO (October 2000): 3–8;

Feliciano, "La figura de Dios en tres dramas de Carlos Solórzano," *Chasqui,* 21 (November 1992): 27–34;

Feliciano, *El teatro mítico de Carlos Solórzano* (Mexico: UNAM, 1995);

Adrienne P. Hawley, "The Great Round: Cyclical Patterns in the Works of Carlos Solórzano," dissertation, Rutgers University, 1978;

Francisco Javier Higuero, "Incomunicación múltiple en el *Teatro breve* de Carlos Solórzano," *Latin American Theatre Review,* 26 (Fall 1992): 111–121;

Nilda Galang Joven, "The Allegorical Plays of Carlos Solórzano," dissertation, Stanford University, 1970;

Steve Martínez Rivas, *Carlos Solórzano y el teatro mexicano* (Mexico: Anáhuac, 1970);

Margarita Mendoza López, ed., *Teatro Mexicano del Siglo XX: 1900–1986,* volume 1 (Mexico: Instituto Mexicano del Seguro Social, 1987), pp. 256–259;

Anne-Grethe Ostergaard, "Semiología de la destrucción y autodestrucción en el teatro de Carlos Solórzano," *Revista Canadiense de Estudios Hispánicos,* 7 (Autumn 1982): 173–180;

José M. Oviedo, "Notas a una (deprimente) lectura del teatro hispanoamericano," *Revista Iberoamericana,* 37 (July–December 1971): 753–762;

L. Howard Quackenbush, "El anticlericalismo religioso del teatro centroamericano actual," *Chasqui,* 11 (February 1980): 13–22;

Quackenbush, *Devotas irreverencias: El auto en el teatro latinoamericano* (Mexico: University of Tlaxcala / Utah: Brigham Young University, David M. Kennedy for International Studies, 1998), pp. 88–95;

Quackenbush, "El espacio y tiempo negativo en *Los fantoches* y *Jesucristo Gómez,*" *Latin American Theatre Review,* 31 (Spring 1998): 17–31;

Douglas Radcliff-Umstead, "Solórzano's Tormented Puppets," *Latin American Theatre Review,* 4 (Spring 1971): 5–11;

Orlando Rodríguez, "Sobre autores y temas: Carlos Solórzano," *Chasqui,* 1 (1972): 12–19;

John R. Rosenberg, "The Ritual of Solórzano's *Las manos de Dios,*" *Latin American Theatre Review,* 17 (Spring 1984): 39–48;

Agustín del Saz, "La rebeldía contra todo interrogante, *Las manos de Dios,*" in his *Teatro social hispanoamericano* (Barcelona: Nueva Coleccion Labor, 1967), pp. 130–133;

Peter J. Schoenbach, "La libertad en *Las manos de Dios,*" *Latin American Theatre Review,* 3 (Spring 1970): 21–29;

Samuel S. Trifilio, "Mexican Theater Goes to Paris . . . and . . . a Polemic," *Hispania,* 47 (May 1964): 335–337;

María R. Uría-Santos, "El simbolismo de *Doña Beatriz,*" *Revista de Estudios Hispánicos,* 6 (January 1972): 63–70;

George W. Woodyard, "Theater of the Absurd in Spanish-America," *Comparative Drama,* 3 (1969): 183–192.

José Triana
(4 January 1931 -)

Kirsten F. Nigro
University of Texas at El Paso

PLAY PRODUCTIONS: *El mayor general hablará de teogonía,* Havana, Sala Arlequín, 1960;

Medea en el espejo, Havana, Teatro Prometeo, 1960; translated as *Medea in the Mirror,* London, Brixton Shaw Theatre, 1996;

La casa ardiendo, Havana, Teatro Prometeo, 1962;

El parque de la fraternidad, Havana, Teatro Prometeo, 1962;

La muerte del ñeque, Havana, Teatro Prometeo, 1964;

La visita del ángel, Havana, Sala Arlequín, 1964;

La noche de los asesinos, Havana, Teatro Hubert de Blarick, 1966;

Worlds Apart (Palabras comunes), Stratford-upon-Avon, The Other Place, 1986;

Cruzando el puente, Valencia, Spain, Teatro Trapeze, 1991.

BOOKS: *De la madera del sueño* (Madrid, 1953);

El parque de la fraternidad (Havana: Unión de Escritores y Artistas de Cuba, 1962)–comprises *Medea en el espejo, El mayor general hablará de teogonía,* and *El parque de la fraternidad;*

La muerte del ñeque: Obra en tres actos (Havana: Ediciones R[evolución], 1964);

La noche de los asesinos (Havana: Casa de las Américas, 1965); translated by Pablo Armando Fernández and Michael Kustow as *The Criminals,* adapted by Adrian Mitchell, in *The Modern Stage in Latin America: Six Plays,* edited by George W. Woodyard (New York: Dutton, 1971), pp. 237–287;

Aproximaciones (Málaga, Spain: Plaza de la Marina, 1989);

Cuaderno de familia: La Habana, 1945 (Málaga, Spain: DADOR / Madrid: Sociedad Estatal Quinto Centenario, 1990);

Ceremonial de guerra (Honolulu: Persona, 1990);

Medea en el espejo; La noche de los asesinos; Palabras comunes (Madrid: Verbum, 1991);

Oscuro el enigma (Coral Gables, Fla.: La Torre de Papel, 1993);

José Triana (photograph by Luis Mallo; from Kirsten F. Nigro, ed., Palabras más que comunes: Ensayos sobre el teatro de José Triana, *1994; University of South Carolina, Aiken, Library)*

Les cinq femmes, translated by Alexandra Carrasco (Arles: Actes Sud, 1999).

Edition in English: *Medea in the Mirror,* translated by Gwynne Edwards, in *The Methuen Book of Contemporary Latin American Plays,* edited by Edwards (London: Methuen Drama, 2004).

PRODUCED SCRIPTS: *Una pelea cubana contra los demonios,* by Triana, Miguel Barnet, Vicente Revuelta, and Tomás Gutiérrez Alea, motion picture, ICAIC, 1972;

Cuadernos de familia, by Triana and Heidrun Adler, radio, Broadcasting W Deutschland, 1983;

Paroles communes, by Triana and Carlos Semprún, radio, France Culture, 1984;

Worlds Apart, by Triana and Barbara Thompson, radio, BBC, 1987;

La noche de los asesinos, radio, Radio Marti, 1989;

Rosa la china, by Triana and Valeria Sarmiento, motion picture, ICAIC, 2002.

OTHER: *La generación del 98: Unamuno, Valle-Inclán, Baroja, Machado, Azorín,* edited by Triana (Havana: Editorial Nacional de Cuba, 1965);

Teatro español actual, edited by Triana (Havana: Instituto del Libro, 1970);

"Alusiones al delirio," in *En busca de una imagen: Ensayos críticos sobre Griselda Gambaro y José Triana,* edited by Diana Taylor (Ottawa: Girol, 1989), pp. 125–131;

La fiesta, in *Teatro: 5 autores cubanos,* edited by Rine Leal (Jackson Heights, N.Y.: Ollantay, 1995);

José Lezama Lima, *Cartas a Eloísa y otra correspondencia,* edited by Triana (Madrid: Verbum, 1998);

El tiempo en un acto, edited by Triana (Jackson Heights, N.Y.: Ollantay, 1999).

SELECTED PERIODICAL PUBLICATIONS– UNCOLLECTED: "Coloquio de sombras," *Cuadernos hispanoamericanos,* 374 (1981): 317–321;

Cruzando el puente, Latin American Theatre Review, 26, no. 2 (1993): 59–87;

Revolico en el Campo de Marte, Gestos: Teoría y práctica del teatro hispánico, 10, no. 19 (1995): 139–205;

Ahí están los tarahumaras, Puentelibre: Revista de cultura, 3, no. 5–6 (1995): 130–134.

Although José Triana has lived in exile since 1980, his name is still prominent in studies of contemporary Cuban theater, and he continues to be cited as a major influence in the artistic revolution that immediately followed the political one initiated by Fidel Castro in 1959. Triana is the author of a small but significant corpus of plays. One of these is perhaps the most widely produced and critically acclaimed Latin American play since the 1960s: *La noche de los asesinos* (Night of the Assassins; published in 1965, produced in 1966), which won Triana Cuba's prestigious Premio Casa de las Americas for the best Latin American play of 1965.

Triana's childhood background influenced his dramatic imagination and his preoccupation, if not obsession, with themes of freedom and revolution. Born on 4 January 1931 in the small town of Hatuey in the province of Camaguey, José Triana was raised in the provincial town of Bayamo, a key site in the failed 1868 uprising for independence from Spain, for which the town paid by being burned to the ground. Remnants of this heroic and rebellious past were, for the young Triana, a constant reminder of Cuba's long history of colonial rule and repressive politics. His father, a telephone employee, was avid in his liberal leanings, and Triana remembers how the men of the family would gather to talk about the Spanish Civil War and their support of the anti-Franco Republican forces. Among Triana's other fond memories is the grove of trees in the backyard of their antique Bayamo house; the natural surroundings inspired him to weave fantastical tales about dragons and other magical creatures. His sister, Gladys, was born in 1937; she became an artist and lives in New York City. Triana's gift for thinking in images and for seeing dramatic connections between them has been fundamental to his success as a playwright, as have his childhood visits to the theater with his father as well as his mother's nightly readings of much-loved Cuban poems. These pleasant memories notwithstanding, Triana grew up in a provincial Cuba with conservative values and a deeply imbedded racism. This environment was also a major influence in his playwriting, which consistently explores the consequences of reactionary politics and out-of-date social structures.

Triana received his undergraduate degree from the Institute of Manzanillo in 1950 and studied philosophy at the University of Santiago de Cuba from 1952 to 1954. During this period, he met Virgilio Piñera, then the enfant terrible of Cuba's literary world, who invited him to collaborate on the literary magazine *Ciclón* (Cyclone). Triana's contribution was a series of poems; not until 1957 did he begin to experiment with playwriting. That year he wrote a play called "Un incidente cotidiano" (A Quotidian Incident) which he claims to have thrown away, and *El mayor general hablará de teogonía* (The Major General Will Speak of Theogony; performed in 1960, published in 1962), his first published play. At that time, Triana lived in Spain, having been sent there in 1955 by his father, who had been advised that the Batista government was in pursuit of his son for participating in antiregime activities.

While at the university in Madrid, Triana was encouraged to write for the theater, which he did, tentatively, aided by the memory of works by Federico García Lorca, Jean Genet, Jean-Paul Sartre, and Tennessee Williams, which he had seen in Havana. He also was inspired by playwrights such as Eugène Ionesco and Samuel Beckett, whose works were being staged in

Madrid at that time. Triana convinced the people directing these plays to hire him; the only work available was washing floors for rehearsals, but the job allowed him to observe and study stagecraft up close. Increasingly excited about the theater, Triana managed to get various Latin American plays produced in Madrid and gained further experience by acting in them. Many details about his personal life are not known; at some point he met and married his wife, Chantal, who is French.

A youthful experiment that was not well received by critics or audiences, *El mayor general hablará de teogonía* nevertheless anticipates most of the trademarks of Triana's playwriting, among them an experimental style and a preoccupation with the power structures of Cuban institutions, especially the family, which Triana consistently uses as metaphor for society as a whole. The main characters are Petronila; her husband, Higinio; her sister Elisiria; and the Major General, who owns the boardinghouse where they live. The year is 1929, on the night the group gathers to celebrate Petronila and Higinio's twenty-seventh wedding anniversary. Although the Major General does not join them until the end of the play, he is a constant presence, both in the other characters' obsession with him and in his disembodied voice, heard offstage occasionally breaking into song or proclaiming his tenants' damnation.

As with most of the families that populate Triana's plays, this one is made up of utterly common, mediocre, and dysfunctional people who are divided by hatred, recriminations, envy, and above all, guilt. Petronila is haunted by the memory of her daughter, who was stillborn twenty-five years before the action of the play commences. Petronila has preserved the fetus's dried remains in a kind of holy urn, revealing her inability to let go of the past and of her sickly obsessions. She blames herself for the fall that caused the stillbirth; but Higinio and Elisiria confess, first to having tried to kill her, thus occasioning the fall, and then to the illicit love affair that motivated their criminal intent. Concomitant to their private family wars is the characters' fear and loathing of the Major General. Higinio and Elisiria hate him especially, and speak of him as a violent, tyrannical madman who might be planning to kill them all, while Petronila speaks more kindly of their landlord, being grateful for the way that he took them in after she lost her child. Still, she is convinced by the others to help them murder the Major General in some kind of perverse ritual that supposedly will cleanse them of their sins and guilt. But for all their talk of revenge and redemption, when the Major General does finally arrive, they immediately fall to their knees. The object of their worship is a small, shriveled man with a long goatee who is able to reduce them to helplessness with an inscrutable smile and a bellowing voice that demands that they stop their chatter and nonsense. He throws the holy urn onto the floor, smashing the past, and without having said a word about theogony, he exits, leaving them prostrate on the floor, empty-handed and without direction for the future.

Many critics have noted the allusions to Christian liturgy in *El mayor general hablará de teogonía*. References throughout the text to biblical motifs such as deluges, apostles, relics, sacrificial blood, communion, and redemption, as well as scenic effects such as the canticle that is heard as the play closes, all indicate this play is a parody of religious, especially Catholic, rituals. The God figure, for whom the characters wait and whose final appearance does not bring salvation, is certainly reminiscent of Beckett's Godot, the worshiped but absent Pater Nostra. There are also echoes of the Theater of the Absurd in Triana's text, with its sometimes disconnected dialogues, the seeming senselessness of the central situation, and its lack of traditional development. And while Triana has been associated with European absurdism, with which he did have a firsthand acquaintance, there are also strong connections to a specifically Cuban social and political reality in *El mayor general hablará de teogonía*. These connections are usually oblique or metaphorical; one example is the 1929 setting, a time when Cuba was under the iron-fisted rule of the military dictator Gerardo Machado y Morales. That the Major General is a fictive relative of Machado (and the latter a relative of Fulgencio Batista, who was dictator of Cuba when Triana wrote this play) seems a sound argument. By presenting the Major General as aged, prune-like, and physically weak, Triana downsizes him from infallible god to fallible human being. That the other characters do not see this weakness and are incapable of killing him suggests that they are as much to blame for the abuse of power as is the tyrant who abuses it, something that Triana repeatedly suggests in subsequent plays.

In 1959 Triana returned to Cuba, exhilarated, like so many other Cubans, by Fidel Castro's revolution. One of Triana's first important projects upon returning was to help organize the Union Nacional de Escritores y Artistas Cubanos (UNEAC, The National Union of Cuban Writers and Artists), which was instrumental in sponsoring Cuba's post-Batista intellectual and artist community. His reputation as a talented young playwright grew, and *Medea en el espejo* (performed in 1960, published in 1962; translated as *Medea in the Mirror*, 1996) won him increasing critical success. This play polishes some of the techniques and themes of the first one, while introducing two more: the use of Afro-Cuban motifs and the recasting of classical texts to a modern Cuban context. Like much postwar European and North American theater that looked at the present through the lens of Greek tragedy (for example, the plays of Jean Anouilh and Eugene O'Neill), many Latin American dramatists explored ways of telling stories about local, contemporary protagonists by casting them as variations on mythical characters from Attic theater. Perhaps the closest model for Triana was that of his mentor Piñera, whose *Electra Garrigó* (written in 1941) had had four major productions between 1948 and 1961. Piñera's Electra, like Triana's Medea, is lifted from Cuban popular culture. Both are women whose language, dress, and values are born of their lower-class roots, and both inhabit worlds where having a dark skin color leads to tragic consequences.

In *Medea en el espejo,* Triana closely follows the story line of Euripides' play, in which a mother kills her children when her lover abandons her for another woman. The classical Medea becomes María in Triana's text, while Jason is her lover Julián. She is of mixed blood; he is white. María is a passionate woman who loses control when she finds out that Julián, a rather shadowy and self-engrossed character, plans to marry the white daughter of a local political boss, Perico Piedra Fina (Triana's version of Euripides' Creon). Euripides' palimpsest leaves no doubt that this story will end with infanticide and madness.

The real appeal of Triana's *Medea en el espejo* is the new way that he tells old tales. Most notable in this regard is the Cuban frame and the focus on characters who inhabit a reality quite different from that of the white, upper-middle-class theatergoers of pre-Revolutionary Cuba. The tenement life of María and the black servant Erundira, and the underworld of Perico Piedra Fina, combine to mirror back to a new audience a different vision of Cuba, especially of one that finally acknowledges its racial tensions. Like Euripides' heroine, María is an outsider, a social "other," not so much for reasons of the *polis* as because of her race. While Julián's rejection of her is above all self-serving, it is no mere coincidence that he chooses a white woman over a mulatto; indeed, one of the other characters laments how having dark skin is a *desgracia* (misfortune).

Triana's play appeared at a time when the recuperation and valorization of Afro-Cuban culture was high on the list of Cuba's Revolutionary projects. Black Cuba is pivotal not only to the human conflicts and themes in *Medea en el espejo* but also to its internal structure and theatricality. Triana had a model in the movement of Afro-Cuban poetry practiced and championed by poets such as Nicolás Guillén in the 1930s and 1940s. Like them, Triana borrows from the vocabulary, folklore, religion, music, and speech rhythms of Cubans descended of African slaves, not merely as window dressing, but as integral parts of a dramatic whole. Especially notable is the way Triana combines the use of anaphora and rhythmic repetitions typical of this poetry with the recitative of the Greek chorus, the latter composed of types from urban Cuban folklore.

Another important element is the mirror referred to in the title, which is both functional and symbolic. Medea continuously looks at it as a way of confirming her existence and of finding her authentic self. With her gradual descent into uncontrolled anger and madness, this looking into the mirror comes to symbolize her fading identity as a woman, a lover, and a mother; it also reflects her fractured identity as a mulatto in a world of powerful whites. While the motif of the mirror and its reflection has a long history and is almost universal, in this case it also can be traced to various black groups in Cuba for whom looking in the mirror is a way to locate a missing person. Other black Cuban elements in *Medea en el espejo* include the use of instruments such as the bongo and dance rhythms such as the *son,* as well as terms from the Yoruba language. Many of these words come from magical-religious beliefs and rituals that are practiced by some of the characters. All these elements contribute to the theatricality of the play, which is considered by critics of Triana's work to be the hallmark of his experimental style.

In 1962 Triana had two plays produced: *La casa ardiendo* (The Burning House) and *El parque de la fraternidad* (Brotherhood Park; published in 1962). Neither was a great critical success, and Triana destroyed the manuscript of the first one. The park referred to in the second piece was, according to Triana, one of his favorite places in Havana. This setting is where the three characters meet: La Negra (the Negress), El Viejo (the Old Man), and the Muchacho (the Young Man). Not much happens in this one-act play, in which all traditional notions of dramatic action are reduced to the characters' incoherent or undirected blather. Their lack of communication, which belies the ideas of fraternity suggested in the title, is a major theme of the text. Some critics have interpreted these communication problems as signaling the distances between Cuba's social levels: the Afro-Cuban, the intellectual (represented by El Viejo's insistent reading of a book about the search for Truth), and the youth of the island. Other readings of the text underscore its racial allusions, with one black character and two who are white. La Negra and El Viejo seem to represent African and Christian theologies, respectively; she utters words in *lucumbi,* a Yoruba language, while also making references to *la Santísima* (the Holy Mother); he speaks of some vague beginning, of the seventh day, and quotes the sacrificed Christ on the cross when he asks why his mother and father have abandoned him. In this scheme, El Muchacho's willingness to believe that the wildly attired and strange black woman possesses the magical powers attributed to the shamans of Afro-Cuban religion would make him, though white, come to symbolize the hybrid quality of Cuban culture. However, when La Negra asks at the end of the play where the bus stop for Route 76 is, she is asking about a real bus line that went to a nearby insane asylum; so *El parque de la fraternidad* may instead be about the short circuits in communication among the mad. One thing that critics agree on is that these various readings of the text owe more to conceptual weaknesses than to a rich ambiguity.

In *La muerte del ñeque* (The Ñeque's Death; performed and published in 1964) the action again takes place among the lower classes, with an effort on Triana's part to capture their language and lifestyles. Aspects of classical tragedy are present—the rise and fall of a powerful man is witnessed and commented upon by a contemporary Cuban chorus of three men: Juan, *el cojo* (the cripple), who is black; the white man Nico; and Pepe the mulatto. The fallen "hero" is the mulatto Hilario García, a corrupt and violent policeman whose nickname is El Ñeque, which in Yoruba signifies a person who has fallen out of grace. The plot, whose motive forces are pride, lust, and revenge, is organized around three acts that slowly reveal the reasons why some of the characters hate Hilario and conspire to kill him. The most important of these is Juvencio, whose father fell victim to the policeman's brutality. Juvencio seduces Hilario's white mistress, the former prostitute Blanca Estela, which sets the stage for the sexually charged atmosphere of the play. Hilario, who actually does not make an appearance onstage until the third and last act, is described as prideful, puffed up with his own sense of importance and convinced that he will be rewarded for his crimes with a significant promotion. When this advancement does not materialize, he becomes the *ñeque* of the title, defenseless in the face of the chorus of petty criminals who kill him. Save for his daughter, no one mourns Hilario, who has come to represent the incarnation of a corrupt political system. Indeed, Triana has indicated in various interviews that he meant for Hilario to symbolize all that was polluted in the Batista regime.

While the political overtones of *La muerte del ñeque* are much more noticeable than in Triana's previous plays, the work also continues his use of elements from classical drama and Afro-Cuban culture. Hilario can be considered a kind of ironic modern tragic hero, a little man brought down by his blinding pride (hubris), whose awakening *(anagnorisis)* is utterly banal; he is proof of how easily power can slip through one's fingers. The men who pursue and kill him are a variation on the Furies of classical tragedy, but again, they are brought down to human size by being cast as petty criminals and ordinary street thugs. The staccato rhythms of classical recitative and the ritual quality they evoke are duplicated in the rhythms of Afro-Cuban poetry, with their trance-like beats. This aspect is especially notable in the scene when Hilario is pursued and surrounded by his killers, who speak in one-line sentences that function as a kind of perverse chant or deadly game of "ring-around-the-rosy" accompanied by the sounds of the bongo, the *clave*, and the maraca. Indeed, games are prominent in *La muerte del ñeque*, which opens with a crapshoot, and later, when Juvencio seduces Blanca Estela, an erotically charged imaginary game of pool enacted by Juan, Pepe, and Nico. These games, with their combination of skill and chance, are a substitute for the Greek *fatum* (fate) and have an expiatory or cathartic function. Triana again combines the classical with the local, especially in the highly theatrical use of the chants from the Afro-Cuban *Orile,* a ceremony for scaring away bad spirits.

One year after the first staging of *La muerte del ñeque,* Triana finished writing the play that gained him international attention and praise: *La noche de los asesinos*. Staged for the first time in 1966 during the sixth Havana Festival of Latin American Theater, *La noche de los asesinos* has been translated into more than twenty languages and has been performed throughout Europe, the Americas, Africa, and Asia. All of the playwright's prior theater experiments converge to produce an extraordinary piece of dramaturgy, one that is complemented by a compelling theatricality. As before, Triana focuses on the family unit, in this case consisting of the three siblings Lalo, Cuca, and Beba, adults who engage in child-like but perverse games of make-believe murder. The would-be victims are their parents, who do not ever appear physically onstage, yet are always present in their children's role-playing. *La noche de los asesinos* opens with Lalo's demand that a door be closed. He then pounds his chest, falls to his knees, and proclaims himself an assassin. His sister Cuca asks what this fuss is all about, to which Beba answers rather casually that the show has begun. This initial moment sets up the game to be played throughout this complex play. Lalo claims to have murdered his parents, and his two sisters play along with him, a charade in which the siblings are at one moment themselves and then seamlessly morph into other characters. As the play progresses through its two acts, Lalo, Cuca, and Beba will assume the roles of their snoopy and disapproving neighbors Pantaleón and Margarita, of a newspaper vendor who shouts out the headline of the parents' brutal murder, of people on the street who comment on the perpetrators' villainy, of the police who investigate the crime, of the judge and prosecutor at the trial, and of their parents. Their performance is fascinating but often perplexing, because one cannot always be sure just what they are doing. Perhaps more important, their game is always highly dramatic, punctuated with grating, rhythmic sound effects such as when Lalo mimics the noise of knives being sharpened and when Beba pretends to be typing the court transcript. The play closes as dramatically as it opened, with Beba proclaiming that it is now her turn to take the lead, as Lalo and Cuca already have done so in the two preceding acts. However, the audience is left to imagine what Beba's Act III will consist of: more of the same imaginary games, or a breakthrough that culminates in the actual murder of their parents?

The dramatic tension throughout the siblings' play-within-a-play is between those who have power and those who do not: for example, between parents and children, between husband and wife, among the siblings themselves, and between the law and its citizens. Because these conflicts range from private family matters to more public ones, many critics place *La noche de los asesinos* within a tradition of Cuban playwriting that uses the family as metaphor for the history and politics of the country. The problem here is that because the text does not specifically state to which history and to which politics it might refer, *La noche de los asesinos* has been interpreted in many ways, some of which were personally prejudicial to the playwright. Early readers of the text in the United States and Europe made connections with Antonin Artaud's theories on the so-called theater of cruelty as well as with Jean Genet's ritualistic play *The Maids* (1947). Other possible influences cited were Sartre's *No Exit* (1946), which, like Triana's text, has three characters trapped behind closed doors in an isolated, private hell. While making these connections with much-applauded European models produced many articulate and insightful analyses of *La noche de los asesinos*, many of these critics may not have taken into account sufficiently the meaning of the play and its reception within the particular context of Revolutionary Cuba in the mid 1960s. Although there had been considerable artistic freedom on the heels of the political events of 1959, gradually this freedom of expression was whittled away. Fidel Castro's proclamation, "Inside the Revolution, everything. Outside the Revolution, nothing," had not only far-reaching political consequences but also artistic ones, as the parameters of what was considered within and without the revolutionary were considerably narrowed. The official imposition of a Soviet-style measuring stick that disallowed art that was considered experimental or "bourgeois," either in content or form, made plays like *La noche de los asesinos* highly suspect in official eyes.

D. Honde, S. Allrud, and K. Howell in a 1987 Dartmouth College production of Triana's 1966 play, La noche de los asesinos *(Night of the Assassins, published in 1965), in which three siblings repeatedly role-play the murder of their parents (from Diana Taylor, ed.,* En busca de una imagen: Ensayos críticos sobre Griselda Gambaro y José Triana, *1989; Ekstrom Library, University of Louisville)*

Although the play received Cuba's highest artistic award and while there was initial approval of its international success, Triana soon began to feel the pressure of censorship. Because the play is set in the 1950s, Triana's supporters argued that he had the Batista regime in mind when depicting the power struggles and repressive behavior of the characters. In such a reading, the absent third act promises true revolution, the final break with the unjust and overbearing rule of tyranny. Some of Triana's statements at the time tended to support this reading, as he was quoted as saying that he had actually begun writing the text during pre-Castro years. But the official position, even among some of the members of the UNEAC, was to label Triana and his play as counterrevolutionary, for without a clear and celebratory reference to Castro's victory, *La noche de los asesinos* could be (and was) read by some as a critique of the new regime. Perhaps without meaning to contradict himself, years later Triana said that he wrote the play after 1959 and that he meant to expose not the failing of revolution as a process and goal but rather the Cuban Revolution's slide into dictatorship. While it is important to know the history of the play, *La noche de los asesinos* stands on its own artistic merits as one of the best Latin American plays of the twentieth century. It continues to have an active international stage life, playing to audiences whose applause by now is not dictated solely, if at all, by a commitment to a particular political project.

While Triana's situation in Cuba became progressively more difficult, and he was not able to have his work produced, he continued to write, finishing his next play, *Ceremonial de guerra* (War Ceremonial) in 1973 (published in 1990). Set in 1895, during Cuba's wars for independence, with reminiscences of Sophocles' *Philoctetes,* the plot revolves around notions of revolution, betrayal, and truth, exactly the ones that were passionately, if not mortally, being fought over in Castro's Cuba during the 1960s. Triana's supposed position on these notions led to his professional banishment, and in *Ceremonial de guerra* there are echoes of his situation in the main character Aracelio Fonseca, who also has suffered expulsion and abandonment by fellow revolutionaries. A so-called *mambís,* a soldier in the Cuban insurrection against Spain, Aracelio is gravely wounded in the leg during a particularly ferocious battle and is left to die by his fellow soldiers. But days later, when they realize that Aracelio has in his possession a map that is pivotal to accomplishing their mission—the taking of the Spanish fort La Calendaria—they send the young commander Carlos to find Aracelio and dupe him into handing over the map. Carlos pretends to be fleeing Spanish forces and acts surprised at his supposedly chance encounter with the legendary Aracelio. He also claims to be the son of a close friend of Aracelio, a soldier who had worked for the same general who gave Aracelio the map. Much of the play consists of the debate these two characters have about loyalty, forgiveness, and revolutionary ideals. Carlos, by nature honest and forthright, feels so guilty about his charade that he confesses his true purpose, which only hardens Aracelio's refusal to help in any way. However, patriotism and devotion to a free Cuba win him over, and the play closes as Aracelio leads Carlos in the assault on La Calendaria.

While *Ceremonial de guerra* is less experimental in form than Triana's previous plays, there are clear traces of earlier works in the magical, almost poetical character of the street vendor who appears twice, as if out of nowhere. Wearing face paint and dressed only from the waist down with leaves and a cloth made of jute, the street vendor carries his wares in an old wooden suitcase and beats on a small drum with a stick. He comes onstage near the end of the first act, hawking a wide array of goods, the names of which evoke ceremonies for white and black magic. His speech is interspersed with references to wars, munitions, and explosives. He appears once again as the play ends, and as before, he speaks in riddles. But his clearly understood rallying cry for a free Cuba is just the push that Aracelio needed to finally forgive his betrayers and to join forces with Carlos in a public mission that goes well beyond personal animosities. While the notion of ceremony or ritual is not the overriding structural element that it is in *La noche de los asesinos,* it is definitely present in Carlos's little play of deceit, as well as in certain highly theatrical moments; for example, when soldiers sing lullabies while cleaning their rifles. The whole play also can be seen as a ceremony that, unlike the one in *La noche de los asesinos,* leads up to a definite course of action. The possible results of this action, however, are not so clear, given that the Wars of Independence actually led to Cuba's political and economic dependence on the United States, and that Castro's revolution led to a similar situation, only this time with the Soviet Union.

In a 1989 interview with Diana Taylor, Triana said that although *Ceremonial de guerra* was written at a time when the Revolution was beginning to derail, he still believed that a free Cuba was a possibility, but only if it was made by and for freedom fighters like Aracelio Fonseca. However, it eventually became clear to Triana that the Aracelio Fonsecas were being silenced, or worse yet, "disappeared" by the Castro regime. By 1980 Triana's situation as a persona non grata had become so intolerable that he left Cuba for France, where he has resided ever since. He brought with him two play scripts in progress, which he did not finish definitively until the 1990s. Chronologically, the first of these is *Revolico en el Campo de Marte* (A Little Turbulence in Mars Park; published in 1995), which had a preliminary staged reading by students in 1981, while Triana was a visiting professor at Dartmouth College. It is a verse play that harks back in theme and form to the drama of the Spanish Golden Age. Triana began writing *Revolico en el Campo de Marte* at the time when he was most under siege by Cuba's political and by now less tolerant artistic community. According to Priscilla Meléndez (1995), he has said that because of this persecution, writing this text—with its enchanted nights, lovestruck characters, music, and verbal pyrotechnics—was for him life-affirming and life-saving. Borrowing heavily from the Spanish comedy of errors, the three acts of *Revolico en el Campo de Marte* bring together a series of characters who pursue and abandon each other in a game of amorous chess. It is set in 1917, during a particularly prosperous and corrupt period in Cuban history known as "the dance of the millions." The many characters couple and uncouple as if dancing a sexually charged minuet, aided by Rosa, the go-between, and Luis, the tailor who sews their costumes and masks. In the end, the chess pieces rearrange in yet another, quite unexpected way, prompting the character Alicia to ask whether the whole thing has not been just a crazy dream. Triana purposefully never clears this question up for her or for the audience.

While *Revolico en el Campo de Marte* is certainly Triana's most whimsical play, it bears the stamp of previous works, especially in the use of popular culture and of Afro-Cuban motifs. The use of an eight-syllable verse form associated with low or popular poetry in Spanish is the first clue of Triana's intent in this play. The occasional lapse into the eleven-syllable verse typical of high Spanish verse is meant to be a parody of this poetic form in the mouths of characters from the lower classes. But the fact that Triana has them speaking in poetry at all goes beyond his desire to write theater in the style of the Spanish masters; it is also a way of capturing the poetic, florid, and at times bombastic speech patterns of ordinary Cubans, something that the playwright greatly admires. The play of identities through the use of masks and costumes is typical of Cuban carnival, and the go-between Rosa is yet another character with roots in Afro-Cuban rituals and magical religious practices. Other popular types in *Revolico en el Campo de Marte,* especially the ruffians, can be traced back to nineteenth-century Cuban literature, as well as to a theatrical mode called the *bufo* which, like Triana's piece, made ample use of Afro-Cuban rhythms, social practices, and speech patterns, as well as urban characters provoked into violence and confusion over amorous conflicts. The *bufo* was also born of a period of political and economic crisis, and while mostly wanting to entertain, it reflected the unstable social conditions of its time. That Triana means for his play to be something more than a whimsy is hinted at with the word *revolico* in the title–a playful, made-up diminutive form of *revolution*. The characters' frivolous pursuits, in which they confuse lust with love and love with money, is indicative of how they have lost their moral compasses and, in so doing, have made trivial the very notion of a revolutionary chaos out of which could be born significant and exemplary human behavior.

Another project that Triana brought with him into exile was *Diálogo para mujeres* (Dialogue for Women), written in 1979. As with many of his works, Triana reworked this one, and it later became *Palabras comunes* (Common Words; performed in English translation as *Worlds Apart,* 1986, published in 1991). With its 1986 production, Triana became the only Latin American playwright to be twice produced by the prestigious Royal Shakespeare Company. *Palabras comunes* begins in 1894, just before the outbreak of the war depicted in *Ceremonial de guerra,* and ends twenty years later, with the outbreak of World War I and the final collapse of Cuba's dying colonial socio-economic system. Divided into five parts with episodes that do not follow a strictly chronological order, *Palabras comunes* traces the lives of three siblings–Victoria, Alicia, and Gastón–as they negotiate the repressive and corrupt social codes of their extended family and the larger Cuban society of the time. The children of a wealthy and conservative family, they grow up seeing the contradiction in what their elders say–that there must be cleanliness, honor, and order above all–and what they do: cheat, lie, drink, fornicate in excess, and practice dirty politics. The men are hyperbolic machos, while the women are sexually repressed. All of them are racist, and few see what is coming–that is, the end of their way of life.

The key character among many is Victoria, the irony of whose name becomes clear as she grows up to be a frigid woman incapable of consummating her marriage until she has a passionate and illicit affair. By age thirty, she has grown old in spirit, and despite her efforts at rebellion, she is anything but victorious. Her sister, Alicia, marries a man whose gift to her is syphilis; and Gastón must finally abandon Cuba in order to lead a morally healthy life. The only characters who manage to save themselves are Gracielita and Pedro Arturo, the young black married couple who have worked for and known Victoria's family for years. By dint of hard work and a drive for success, they rise above their class roots to enter the ranks of the new middle class, which with time will also end by ruling under the banner of order and cleanliness in the name of progress.

The play ends almost as it began, with children playing as their mothers look on and converse; the difference is that at the beginning the children are Victoria and her siblings, and at the end, the mother is Victoria and the child her daughter Adriana. As in Triana's other plays, there is a circularity, a sense that things in Cuba never change, that they are always in transition but never fully becoming something new and different. As in *La noche de los asesinos,* the family acts as a metaphor for society, although Triana is much more explicit in linking key episodes in the characters' lives, such as Victoria's first passionate sexual encounter, with outside events such as explosive popular uprisings. These public, historical moments also take on a sense of déjà vu when seen in the light, not of the past, but of the future that marked Cuba throughout the twentieth century. These historical cycles end by becoming commonplace, which is one possible explanation of the title. The other is the almost banal conversation that the characters often have, indicating their inability to rise above the ordinary. They also tend to overuse common phrases and sayings as a way of reducing life to the obvious. The English title, on the other hand, underscores the many degrees of separation among the characters and perhaps the fact that the distance between the characters' private world and the one outside is too great for theirs to survive.

During what has been called the second phase of his artistic life, the post-Cuba one, Triana has worked as a translator for UNESCO and has given theater workshops in Europe and the United States. He has continued writing poetry and has renewed the work with movie scripts that had been interrupted by his political situation in Cuba. In 1987 he received a Guggenheim Fellowship. His first play wholly from this period is *Cruzando el puente* (Crossing the Bridge, performed in 1991; published in 1993). The only monologue written by Triana, *Cruzando el puente* takes place at the end of the 1980s and has as its sole character a homeless man named Heriberto who keeps insisting that he is not crazy. A middle-aged mulatto, he wears a threadbare white suit, black-and-white shoes, and a straw hat. Smoking a smelly cigar, he enters onstage pulling a cart piled high with an odd assortment of goods: glass bottles, musical instruments like the *clave* and maracas, feather dusters, hats, various articles of clothing, a candelabra, a broom, and candles. He draws a large chalk circle around himself and then proceeds to build an improvised altar with bits and pieces from the cart, including well-worn effigies of various saints. In the course of the monologue, he will destroy and rebuild the altar.

Despite Heriberto's protestations to the contrary, at first glance he does indeed seem to be crazy. The story he tells is a confusing one that he himself is trying to sort out in the telling of it. He speaks of having been in jail, of having once tried to kill his sister, and of having strangled his lover to death. He remembers having once been admired for his bravado in front of the many women who called him the "Saint." He also recalls that one of them bewitched him. Reminiscent of Perico Piedra Fina in *Medea en el espejo,* Heriberto is a throwback to another time, but he is also caught, or trapped, as the circle would indicate, in an imprisoning present. That this situation is Cuba's present reality is made clear by the many references to repression, to police agents, to food and housing shortages, to long ration lines, to thirty years of being promised paradise and getting hell instead.

As in all his plays, Triana works by indirection and by metaphor. The time frame for *Cruzando el puente*—the end of the decade that started with the mass emigration of the Cuban *Marielitos* (so named because they left from the port of Mariel)—also works as a kind of code. A key sign in its deciphering is the man who Heriberto says appeared to him on various occasions. But this man is not real; only Heriberto sees him, and all indications are that he is the manifestation of Heriberto's guilty conscience. Heriberto first encounters the man while he is passing time drinking at a bar. Wearing drill pants, a straw hat, and two-toned shoes, the man asks Heriberto if his "balls are frozen," if he has lost his courage. The inferred question is why he is not doing something constructive, and the man's attire suggests that he appears to Heriberto at the beginning of the Revolution, when there was the possibility of becoming the "new man" envisaged by Che Guevara. The second time he appears, he carries a gold-handled cane with a winged serpent in one hand, and a handkerchief in the other. The man offers to accompany Heriberto across the bridge, but Heriberto does not understand the reference. By the man's third appearance, however, Heriberto has begun to understand that the bridge is one between sanity and madness, life and death, heaven and hell. Still, he has not understood that the bridge is also an escape from repression into freedom.

Throughout the monologue Heriberto has shown himself to be a coward, unable to assume the responsibility for his own crimes and for his own situation. Everything is always someone else's fault, and Heriberto claims that he was born free and will die free. But he forgets that he too, not just the political system in which he lives, has drawn the circle around himself. The circle is both the island of Cuba under Castro and also the self-made prison that keeps Cubans from fleeing the island. Triana seems to be saying that if Heriberto is indeed crazy, then both these circles explain his madness.

Given that the Cuban presence in Miami has become such a major one, it is not surprising that Triana's next play, *La fiesta* (The Party; published in 1995), should take place in that Florida city. However, this work is not a standard text about exile and its discontents; rather, it is a fanciful play-within-a-play that revolves around the "party to beat all parties" that the character Gerardo, a successful forty-eight-year-old Cuban American, wants to throw at a hotel in Coconut Grove. Combining the characters, song, dance, and dialogue of the *teatro bufo,* the popular vernacular theater in Cuba, *La fiesta* is, in Triana's own words in the introduction to the work in *Teatro: 5 autores cubanos,* a kind of chiaroscuro in which images appear and then fade out, creating a sense of an unreal reality. The use of creative lighting effects, as in *Cruzando el puente,* is fundamental in creating the necessary ambience, with lighting almost becoming another character. The fade-ins and fade-outs during the three acts of *La fiesta* help mark transitions between reality and fantasy, although these divisions are intentionally not always clear. The lighting changes also help outline the sometimes fuzzy edges between the core action of the play and the rehearsal for the show that Gerardo hopes will crown the party events. Wanting to make a big impression, Gerardo has mandated that his family dress as masked and fantastical characters, and that his aged mother appear in a small plane hanging as a centerpiece from the hotel lobby ceiling.

Mandating is the exact term for describing Gerardo's actions, and with this character Triana returns to the dynamics of the Cuban family and one of his favorite metonyms: the family as metaphor for Cuba. While this family functions like many of those in Triana's other plays, a major difference is that the characters live in Miami, and that with their success has come a kind of nouveau riche and tasteless ostentation. For Gerardo, the party is his way of publicly proclaiming his success, and his tyrannical organization of it is a way of maintaining the patriarchal traditions of his homeland in a new country where the family unit is under constant assault. His eighteen-year-old daughter Rosi and her Cuban American boyfriend Johnny are respectful, but in the end become rebellious and disdainful of Gerardo's old-world ways. His wife and mother rebel, and even his father takes him to task for his tyrannical and thoughtless behavior. As Gerardo begs forgiveness, and just when it seems that the party will be no more than a rehearsal, there is a kind of musical deus ex machina, typical of *bufo* theater, with mambo rhythms and guitar music. Sounds of waves on a beach are heard; someone sings a sentimental and nostalgic Cuban song; and the night fills with stars. As this scene then fades into and back to the first one, the text closes with a question mark: was any of what happened real?

Triana said in the introduction that in *La fiesta* he wanted to combine the tragic and comical according to the edicts and stage practices of Spain's masterful Golden Age playwright Lope de Vega. This intent explains the rather archaic feel to the language and tone of this play, making it similar to *Revolico en el Campo de Marte*. Triana's next work, *Ahí están los tarahumaras* (The Tarahumaras Are There, published in 1995) recalls his early absurdist works, with its married couple who engage in seemingly random activities and who never manage to truly communicate despite their constant chatter. The action takes place in the present, in what appears to be the characters' living or dining room. Everywhere there is a mess of broken furniture, junk, and the leftovers from the rag dolls the wife spends all of her time making. Water from an open faucet can be heard running. There is the murmur of voices offstage, mixed with the sound of chains hitting against each other and of violent blows as well as psalms being sung amid the crackle of burning paper or trees. The sounds subside, and the husband (neither character has a name) announces that the Tarahumaras are there, to which she asks what in the world he is talking about.

During the rest of this brief one-act play, the two characters alternate being loving and hateful, and through their talk it becomes clear that he is, if not paranoid, certainly delusional in his belief that he has been called on to impose a new world order. In this quest, he has forced his wife to make dolls, hoping to create the new man of the future. The problem is that she is never able to finish the perfect specimen, and he has been unable to keep the things in his world—such as furniture, chairs, or tables—under control.

Again, Triana uses metaphor and indirection to make a comment about Castro's Cuba, its failed experiment with communism and with the utopia once envisioned by Guevara, in which all human selfishness would be replaced by a "new man," the epitome of human selflessness. References in the dialogue to Dr. Frankenstein, Merlin the Magician, King Midas, and robots are codes for Triana's critique of Castro's efforts to impose on Cubans a new society crafted in his own image. The Tarahumaras (an indigenous tribe in northern Mexico who never allowed themselves to be completely conquered) are the symbol of what Triana sees as the indomitable spirit of anti-Castro Cubans. The final defeat of the two characters and all that they stand for is signaled by the return of all the noises heard at the beginning of the play, and by the image of the couple imprisoned in a fish tank.

Ahí están los tarahumaras is an example of how Triana so often works with a kind of theatrical shorthand. Only five pages long in its published form, the text is dense and complex both dramatically and theatrically, with its effective use of sound and lighting effects, the latter especially notable in the final image of the play. The unpublished one-act "El último día del verano" (The Last Day of Summer, finished in 1994) is similar in its highly symbolic setting—an empty beach on which various characters are at work digging holes, as useless a task as the making of rag dolls in *Ahí estan los tarahumaras*. Another character, Adela, tears up piles of legal documents about absurd laws and regulations meant to control such things as "severe arteriosclerosis in the field of diversionary ideologies." There are many references to someone named Valderrama, a tyrant who in one way or another controls all of the characters. Many of them are full of anger about having made useless sacrifices over thirty or even fifty years. The older characters have trouble remembering when certain things—such as past wars, slave uprisings, and revolutions—happened. This confusion is echoed in the fact that the play does not seem to happen in any specific time frame, but rather in a kind of historical aleph with Valderrama being the key ingredient. Some of the characters are more preoccupied with their inability to remember or make sense of the past; others are more concerned with satisfying their sexual appetites and pass much of the play rolling in the sand, making passionate love. Others recognize their dilemma but refuse to accept any blame for it. One character, however, the young Jorge, is determined to kill the cause of so much suffering. When the play ends with the sound of a gunshot, everyone but Jorge is on stage. The implication is that he has accomplished his mission, although it is never made clear who he has shot. Perhaps it is not just one person but a whole way of life; the cry of a newborn baby, which is also heard at the beginning of the play, suggests that maybe now a new start can be made.

Throughout his playwriting career, José Triana has sought to explore the causes and effects of tyranny, be it in the family or in the larger society. In many of his plays he never mentions Cuba by name, but the island is always there–in the language that Triana uses, with its abundance of Cuban sayings and vocabulary; in the references to historical events; in the many symbolic objects on stage with Cuban referents; and in the representation of Cuba's racial dynamics. Although he has not had another international success to match that of *La noche de los asesinos,* many of Triana's plays continue to be staged professionally. While some of the later ones have not yet seen the stage, they are testimony to Triana's continued development as a playwright, to his keen sense for the theatrical, and to his never-wavering commitment to his homeland.

Interviews:

Diana Taylor, "Entrevista con José Triana," in *En busca de una imagen: Ensayos críticos sobre Griselda Gambaro y José Triana,* edited by Taylor (Ottawa: Girol, 1989), pp. 115–123;

José A. Escarpenter, "Imagen de imagen: Entrevista con José Triana," in *Palabras más que comunes: Ensayos sobre el teatro de José Triana,* edited by Kirsten F. Nigro (Boulder, Colo.: Society of Spanish and Spanish-American Studies, 1994), pp. 1–12.

References:

Severino João Albuquerque, *Violent Acts: A Study of Contemporary Latin American Theatre* (Detroit: Wayne State University Press, 1991);

Frank N. Dauster, "The Game of Chance: The Theatre of José Triana," in *Dramatists in Revolt: The New Latin American Theater,* edited by Leon F. Lyday and George W. Woodyard (Austin: University of Texas Press, 1976), pp. 166–189;

Román de la Campa, *José Triana: Ritualización de la sociedad cubana* (Minneapolis: Institute for the Study of Ideologies and Literature, 1979);

William García, "Tragedy and Marginality in José Triana's *Medea en el espejo,*" in *Perspectives on Contemporary Spanish American Theatre,* edited by Dauster (Lewisburg, Pa.: Bucknell University Press, 1996), pp. 145–157;

Jerry Hoeg, "Coding, Context, and Punctuation in Triana's *La noche de los asesinos,*" *Gestos: Teoría y práctica del teatro hispánico,* 15 (1993): 83–98;

Priscilla Meléndez, "El espacio dramático como signo: La autoconciencia del juego representacional en *La noche de los asesinos* de José Triana," in her *La dramaturgia hispanoamericana contemporánea: Teatralidad y autoconciencia* (Madrid: Pliegos, 1990), pp. 107–125;

Meléndez, "Politicemos el humor y riámonos de la política: *Revolico en el Campo de Marte* de José Triana," *Gestos,* 10, no. 19 (1995): 133–137;

Matías Montes Huidobro, "Máscara familiar: esquizofrenia mágica," in his *Persona, vida y máscara en el teatro cubano* (Miami: Universal, 1973), pp. 413–427;

Anne C. Murch, "Genet-Triana-Kopit: Ritual as 'danse macabre,'" *Drama Review,* 15 (1973): 369–381;

Kirsten F. Nigro, "*La noche de los asesinos:* Playscript and Stage Enactment," *Latin American Theatre Review,* 11, no. 1 (1977): 45–57;

Nigro, ed., *Palabras más que comunes: Ensayos sobre el teatro de José Triana* (Boulder, Colo.: Society of Spanish and Spanish-American Studies, 1994);

Diana Taylor, "Theatre and Revolution: José Triana," in her *Theatre of Crisis: Drama and Politics in Latin America* (Lexington: University Press of Kentucky, 1991), pp. 64–95;

Taylor, ed., *En busca de una imagen: Ensayos críticos sobre Griselda Gambaro y José Triana* (Ottawa: Girol, 1989).

Rodolfo Usigli
(17 November 1905 – 18 June 1979)

Ramón Layera
Miami University, Ohio

SELECTED PLAY PRODUCTIONS: *El apóstol,* Mexico City, private reading, 13 January 1930;
El presidente y el ideal, Mexico City, 1935;
Estado de secreto, Guadalajara, Teatro Degollado, 1936;
La última puerta, Mexico City, 1936;
Medio tono, Mexico City, Palacio de Bellas Artes, 13 November 1937;
Sueño de día, Mexico City, Teatro Radiofónico, Secretaría de Educación Pública, 14 April 1939;
La mujer no hace milagros, Mexico City, Teatro Ideal, October 1939;
Vacaciones I, Mexico City, Teatro Rex, 23 March 1940;
La familia cena en casa, Mexico City, Teatro Ideal, 19 December 1942;
Otra primavera, Mexico City, Teatro Virginia Fábregas, August 1945;
Corona de sombra, Mexico City, Teatro Arbeu, 11 April 1947;
El gesticulador, Mexico City, Palacio de Bellas Artes, 17 May 1947; translated by Edward Landberg as *The Gesturer,* Moylan, Pa., Hedgerow Theater, 1953; translated by Ramón Layera as *The Impostor,* Miami, Ohio, Miami University Theatre, 15 November 1996;
Noche de estío, Mexico City, Teatro Ideal, 6 July 1950;
Los fugitivos, Mexico City, Teatro Arbeu, 22 July 1950;
El niño y la niebla, Mexico City, Teatro del Caracol, 6 April 1951;
Aguas estancadas, Mexico City, Teatro Colón, 18 January 1952;
Jano es una muchacha, Mexico City, Teatro Colón, 20 June 1952;
La función de despedida, Mexico City, Teatro Ideal, 10 April 1953;
Un día de éstos, Mexico City, Teatro Esperanza Iris, 8 January 1954;
Corona de fuego, Mexico City, Teatro Xola, 15 September 1961;
Carta de amor, Mexico City, 1968;
Corona de luz, Mexico City, Teatro Hidalgo, 5 January 1969;

Rodolfo Usigli (from Teatro Mexicano 1963, *1965; Thomas Cooper Library, University of South Carolina)*

El gran circo del mundo, Mexico City, 1969;
Los viejos, Mexico City, 1971;
Las madres, Mexico City, 1972;
Estreno en Broadway, Lawrence, University of Kansas, 29 April 1992.

BOOKS: *México en el teatro* (Mexico City: Imprenta Mundial, 1932); translated by Wilder P. Scott as

Mexico in the Theater (University, Miss.: Romance Monographs, 1975);

El apóstol (Mexico, 1932);

Caminos del teatro en México (Mexico City: Secretaría de Relaciones Exteriores, 1933);

Conversación desesperada (Mexico City: Nandino, 1938);

Medio tono (Mexico: Dialéctica, 1938); translated by Edna Furness as *The Great Middle Class, Poet Lore,* 63 (1966);

Itinerario del autor dramático (Mexico: Casa de España en México, 1940);

La familia cena en casa (Mexico City: Sociedad General Autores de México, 1942);

Corona de sombra (Mexico, 1943); translated by William F. Stirling as *Crown of Shadows* (London: Wingate, 1946);

El gesticulador (Mexico: Letras de México, 1944);

Ensayo de un crimen (Mexico City: América, 1944);

Otra primavera (Mexico City: Sociedad General Autores de México, 1947); translated by Wayne Wolfe as *Another Springtime* (New York: S. French, 1961);

Vacaciones (Mexico, 1948);

Mientras amemos (Mexico: Revista Panoramas, 1948);

La mujer no hace milagros (Mexico: Departamento de Divulgación de la Secretaría de Educación Pública, 1949);

Rodríguez Lozano, by Usigli, José Clemente Orozco, and Manuel Rodríguez Lozano (Mexico: Clardecor, 1949);

Sueño de día (Mexico: América, 1949);

La función de despedida (Mexico, 1951);

El niño y la niebla (Mexico, 1951);

Jano es una muchacha (Mexico, 1952);

Sonetos del tiempo y de la muerte (Mexico City, 1954);

La niña de los cabellos blancos (Atlacomulco, Mexico, 1956);

Un día de éstos (Mexico: Stylo, 1957); translated by Thomas Bledsoe as *One of These Days . . . ,* in *Two Plays: Crown of Light, One of These Days . . .* (Carbondale: Southern Illinois University Press, 1965);

La exposición (Mexico: Cuadernos Americanos, 1960);

Teatro completo, volume 1 (Mexico City: Fondo de Cultura Económica, 1963)–comprises *El apóstol, Falso drama, 4 Chemins 4, Alcestes, Noche de estío, El presidente y el ideal, Estado de secreto, La última puerta, El niño y la niebla, Medio tono, Mientras amemos, Aguas estancadas, Otra primavera, El gesticulador, La mujer no hace milagros,* and *La crítica de "La mujer no hace milagros";*

Corona de luz (Mexico: Fondo de Cultura Económica, 1965); translated by Bledsoe as *Crown of Light,* in *Two Plays: Crown of Light, One of These Days . . .* (Carbondale: Southern Illinois University Press, 1965);

Teatro completo, volume 2 (Mexico City: Fondo de Cultura Económica, 1966)–comprises *Sueño de día, Vacaciones I, Vacaciones II, La familia cena en casa, Corona de sombra, Dios, Batidillo y la mujer, La función de despedida, Los fugitivos, Jano es una muchacha, Un día de éstos, La exposición, Las madres, La diadema, Corona de fuego, Corona de luz;*

Anatomía del teatro (Mexico: Ecuador O O' O", 1966);

Tres comedietas (Mexico: Ecuador O O' O", 1966)–comprises *Un navío cargado de . . . , El testamento y el viudo,* and *El encuentro;*

Voces: Diario de trabajo, 1932-1933 (Mexico: Seminario de Cultura Mexicana, 1967);

Juan Ruiz de Alarcón en el tiempo (Mexico: Secretaría de Educación Pública, 1967);

Los viejos (Mexico: Finisterre, 1971);

Imagen y prisma de México (Mexico: Seminario de Cultura Mexicana, 1972);

¡Buenos días, señor Presidente! (Mexico City: J. Mortiz, 1972);

Obliteración (Madrid, 1972; Mexico: Usigli, 1973);

Presencia de Juárez en el teatro universal (Mexico: Seminario de Cultura Mexicana, 1972);

Corona de sombra, Corona de fuego, Corona de luz (Mexico: Porrúa, 1974);

Conversaciones y encuentros (Mexico: Novaro, 1974);

Anatomía del teatro (Mexico City, 1974);

Las madres (Mexico: Aguilar, 1977);

Teatro completo, volume 3 (Mexico City: Fondo de Cultura Económica, 1979)–comprises *Un navío cargado de. . . . , El testamento y el viudo, El encuentro, Carta de amor, El gran circo del mundo, Los viejos, El caso Flores, ¡Buenos días, señor Presidente!* and *Prólogos, epílogos y otros textos;*

Tiempo y memoria en conversación desesperada: Poesía 1923-1974, edited by José Emilio Pacheco (Mexico: Universidad Nacional Autónoma de México, 1981);

Comedias impolíticas (Mexico City: Gaceta, 1994)–comprises *Estado de secreto, Un día de éstos,* and *Noche de estío;*

Teatro completo, volume 4, edited by Luis de Tavira (Mexico City: Fondo de Cultura Económica, 1996)–comprises *Escritos sobre la historia del teatro en México.*

Collection: *Conversación desesperada: Antología,* edited by Antonio Deltoro (Mexico City: Seix Barral, 2000).

PRODUCED SCRIPTS: *Corona de sombra,* radio, BBC, 15 September 1945;

Susana, motion picture, adapted from Manuel Reachi's novel by Luis Buñuel and Jaime Salvador, additional dialogue by Usigli, Internacional Cinematográfica, 1951;

Ensayo de un crimen, by Usigli, Buñuel, and Eduardo Ugarte, motion picture, Alianza Cinematográfica Española, 1955.

TRANSLATIONS: T. S. Eliot, *El canto de amor de J. Alfred Prufrock* (Mexico, 1938);

Joseph Edward Davies, *Misión en Moscú* (Mexico: Nuevo Mundo, 1942);

Babette Deutsch, *Walt Whitman constructor para América* (Mexico City, 1942);

Dashiell Hammett, *La llave de cristal* (Mexico City, 1942);

John Patrick, *La casa de té de la luna de agosto* (Mexico City, 1957);

Georges Schéhadé, *Historia de Vasco* (Mexico City: Universidad Nacional Autónoma de México, 1959);

Giorgos Theotokas, *Alcibíades* (Mexico City: Universidad Nacional Autónoma de México, 1969);

André Malraux, *La condición humana* (Mexico City, 1971);

Jacques Soustelle, *México, tierra india* (Mexico City: Secretaría de Educación Pública, 1971).

A widely published author, drama historian, and teacher, as well as a successful playwright, Rodolfo Usigli was a powerful and effective force in the creation of a national drama movement in Mexico in the early part of the twentieth century. Because of his multiple talents and stubborn dedication, Usigli is singled out among several important dramatists of his generation as "the Playwright of the Mexican Revolution" or "the apostle" or "redeemer" of Mexican theater. In most general histories of Latin American literature and, more specifically, in histories of Latin American drama, he is listed as one of the founders of modern Mexican drama.

Usigli's overall contribution is multifaceted, as it includes his roles as drama critic and reviewer, pioneering historian of Mexican theater, drama theoretician and teacher, translator of American, French, and English drama and poetry, and author of some of the best-known and most-often-performed drama classics in the history of Mexican (if not Latin American) theater. The author of comedies, farces, tragedies, historical plays, and dramas of ideas as well as novels, literary diaries, books of poetry, monographs and histories of Mexican drama, collections of essays, and a manual of dramatic composition, Usigli was a man of considerable intellectual and artistic accomplishment.

Usigli was born on 17 November 1905 in Mexico City. The facts of his early life are rather atypical for a Mexican, especially because his parents were a recent European émigré couple who had arrived during the years leading up to the violent upheaval of the 1910 revolution. His father was Alberto Usigli, an Italian national who had been born in the North African port city of Alexandria. His mother, Carlota Wainer, a woman of Austro-Hungarian origin, had been born in Poland. Alberto Usigli died when Rodolfo was only a child, leaving his unprepared mother to raise her two daughters and two sons on a meager income derived from cleaning homes, sewing, and managing a small neighborhood grocery store. From multiple references in his writings it can be deduced that Usigli's resourceful mother played a key role in the development of his value system, his ambition and drive, and especially his view of women, as evidenced in their portrayal as strong characters in several of his plays.

Having grown up during the most violent and chaotic period of the Mexican Revolution, Usigli was deprived of a complete formal education; yet, by dint of individual effort he became one of the most complex and learned scholars of his generation. From his intellectually motivated, polyglot mother (in addition to Spanish, she spoke German and French), he learned the value of foreign languages and the importance of literary and intellectual pursuits. Usigli had to overcome both physical and social limitations, as he was a weak and physically challenged child. Legally blind during his early childhood and suffering from a squint, he was the victim of cruel jokes for the rest of his life; some of his unfriendly literary associates gave him the malicious nickname of *El Vizconde* (The Viscount), from the Spanish word *bizco* (cross-eyed) and his penchant for elegant dress. Under his mother's influence he overcame those obstacles and compensated by concentrating on intellectual and artistic pursuits. He developed an early interest in puppets, something he used to entertain himself and his friends.

In 1917 he made his debut on the stage, appearing as a paid child extra in a play at the Teatro Colón. At that same age he had already started working as an errand boy for an American distributor of patent medicine. He also began to study French and English on his own. His command of these two languages proved to be valuable tools in his development as an artist and intellectual and, later, in his career as a diplomat. His ability with English enabled him to secure employment at Sanborn's (a famous drugstore/restaurant/giftshop) and the Wells Fargo Express as an office boy. This work was a mixed blessing, as, on the one hand, he was able to supplement the family budget, while on the other, he was unable to complete the last two years of his secondary education. As a result, he was forced to attend night classes normally reserved for workers and other poor students. But this early employment did not conflict

Scene from the 1947 Palacio de Bellas Artes premiere of Usigli's play El gesticulador *(The Impostor, published in 1944)*, which critics consider the start of modern theater in Mexico *(Rodolfo Usigli Archive, Miami University Libraries, Oxford, Ohio)*

with his informal, self-administered education. During his adolescence and for the rest of his adult life he continued to read regularly; he reports that in addition to many English Elizabethan and Jacobean classics, between 1925 and 1931, he read an average of four plays per day, mostly in French. He also continued to attend theatrical productions and to consider the possibility of a career as a writer, artist, and intellectual.

The 1920s were a propitious time for the early development of Usigli's artistic and intellectual project. The election in November 1920 of President Alvaro Obregón marked the end of the military phase of the revolution and the start of the reconstruction of Mexico along populist, reformist lines. Obregón's presidency also signaled the start of an artistic and intellectual renaissance in postrevolutionary Mexico. The appointment of the essayist José Vasconcelos as secretary of education brought a redefinition of the role of the state and of the artist and intellectual as builders and purveyors of a new vision of Mexican cultural identity. In addition to proclaiming a nationalistic, socially committed mandate, the Vasconcelos administration provided material resources and ideological guidance to both the educational and artistic establishments.

Mexico's nascent modern drama movement also began to take shape during this climate of artistic and intellectual ferment. During the early 1920s, state subsidies and the formation of a dramatists' union forced commercial theaters to start producing plays written by Mexican playwrights. To add to a general climate of artistic experimentation there were also attempts at political and agitprop as well as workers' theater. Toward the end of the decade Usigli had started to define his own artistic inclinations, writing dramatic exercises and frequenting literary circles. His literary diary that covers the period between 1925 and 1933 traces the evolution of his apprenticeship. He reports that in 1924, when he was not quite twenty years of age, he was already writing satirical poems, epigrams, and theater reviews for the magazine *El Sábado* (Saturday) for 10 pesos a week. Meanwhile, intellectual challenges to the old Porfirian order that had started much earlier in 1906 with the Ateneo de la Juventud (Athenaeum of Youth; eventually the activities of this group led to the creation of a national university in 1910) continued more aggressively during the postrevolutionary period. Inspired by new incentives and a more receptive public, various groups attempted to add new life to the artistic and literary scene. While the majority cultivated a new form of cultural nationalism that stressed vernacular themes, others struck a more cosmopolitan pose, openly embracing foreign models and influences. Around this time, Usigli and authors such as Xavier Villaurrutia, Celestino Gorostiza, and Salvador Novo—among the most important dramatists of the formative period of the theater movement—began to experiment with new dramatic forms and to stage and publish their work. Usigli maintained contacts with members of the most active and influential literary circles of the time, such as the Teatro de Ulises (1928–1929) and the Teatro Orientación; however, in keeping with his own idiosyncratic style, he continued to carve out an independent artistic and professional path.

The 1930s brought significant advancement in Usigli's professional career. By this time he had achieved considerable expertise as a theater scholar: he published his history of Mexican drama *México en el teatro* (translated as *Mexico in the Theater,* 1975) in 1932 and a long prologue to Francisco Monterde's *Bibliografía del teatro en México* (Bibliography of the Theater in Mexico) in 1933. His knowledge secured a teaching post for him at the national university (later the Universidad Nacional Autónoma de México, UNAM) and an administrative position at the Ministry of Education, where he directed a radio program that put drama classics on the air. More importantly, he earned a Rockefeller Foundation scholarship to study drama in the United States. After an unsuccessful first application (the prologue that he wrote for Monterde's book was part of the application process) he was awarded the scholarship, and he spent the academic year 1935–1936, together with Villaurrutia, studying drama composition and direction at Yale University. In addition to occasional visits to New York City to attend theatrical productions, Usigli's classes and critical readings strengthened his conviction that he was destined for a successful career in the theater. In the literary supplement of the magazine *Resumen* he published *El apóstol* (The Apostle, performed in 1930), a faintly autobiographical play that includes ill-disguised references to Vasconcelos and his messianic style. In 1932 he also wrote *4 Chemins 4* (4 Ways 4; first published in volume 1 of *Teatro completo* [Complete Plays], 1963), in French, in order to rid himself of the temptation to write comedies in the French style, as was the fashion among some of his contemporaries. The thematic and intellectual range of his plays as well as his scholarly and critical writings began to reflect a comprehensive knowledge of the classics, of the central tenets of dramatic theory, and of the dramatic literature of both Europe and the United States. Upon his return from Yale he went back to teaching at the university, directed the theater section at the Ministry of Education, and, at the end of the decade, served as press secretary for President Lázaro Cárdenas.

Usigli was particularly prolific during the 1930s as he wrote more than a dozen plays, including some of his most successful efforts; several of them, however, remained unpublished and unperformed until much later in his career, in some instances because of their political and satirical nature. The plays that he wrote during this decade can be grouped into those of a political and social nature and those that focus on psychological issues. Under the category of political plays, the best known are three comedies that Usigli called *comedias impolíticas* (impolitical comedies): *Noche de estío* (Summer Night; performed in 1950, published in 1963) about the issue of presidential succession; and *El presidente y el ideal* (The President and the Ideal; performed in 1935, published in 1963) and *Estado de secreto* (State of Secret; performed in 1936, published in 1963), both about the behind-the-scenes machinations of the military and political leader General Plutarco Elías Calles. Also in the category of political plays is *La última puerta* (The Last Door; performed in 1936, published in 1963), a more experimental and farcical attack against the insensitivity and arbitrariness of government bureaucracy. This play stretches the limits of satire to such a degree that it borders on the absurd. Despite Usigli's own protestations against the modern avant-garde currents in vogue in Mexico in the 1960s, *La última puerta* has been singled out as a precursor of Samuel Beckett's *Waiting for Godot* (1952). Among the psychological plays that he wrote in the 1930s, *El niño y la niebla* (The Child and the Mist; performed and published in 1951) was one of his two biggest commercial successes. The other commercial hit was *Jano es una muchacha* (Janus is a Girl; performed and published in 1952), about Mexico's hypocritical attitudes toward sex and prostitution.

Peter R. Beardsell, in his book *A Theatre for Cannibals: Rodolfo Usigli and the Mexican Stage* (1992), accurately defined the overall purpose and intent of Usigli's politically informed dramatic production during this period. Beardsell states that "these works of the 1930s seem designed to compel the audience to think about two types of problem: in the first place, the burning issues of the day; and in the second place, the underlying and persistent problems of Mexico." These subjects define not only the thematic concerns of Usigli's *comedias impolíticas* but also other plays written in the same political and satirical vein. Indeed, this uncompromisingly critical stance became Usigli's trademark and the source of constant polemics with drama critics, the Church, unions, and government bureaucrats. The strong didactic urge that seems to permeate his criticism of contemporary issues reflects both aesthetic and moral concerns, since Usigli viewed the stage as a viable and effective arena for public discussion. His goal was not to admonish and chastise or even preach but rather to engage the audience in a conscious examination of their own plight as members of a civil society. In this approach Usigli is following his intellectual and dramatic model, George Bernard Shaw, whose combative and polemical style Usigli consciously emulated. Usigli not only acknowledged the Shavian tone and inspiration of some of his plays but also understood the function of the theater as a vehicle for moral suasion and intellectual and political debate.

The first of his impolitical comedies, *Noche de estío,* is a good example of his writing in this vein. It is a series of comedic scenes in which members of the political elite find themselves trapped in the home of the minister of finance during a presumed communist takeover of the government. Unexplained electrical failures, the loss of telephone communication, and a sense of being at the mercy of circumstances provoke outbursts of gratuitous sincerity from everyone. Until the situation is finally clarified, they expose their real selves and reveal the truth about their abusive and corrupting ways. The character of the General is an unmistakable reference to Calles, who had been president of Mexico from 1924 until 1928; he chose his successor and still exercised power from behind the scenes until the mid 1930s. The central political issue suggested by the play is the question of his succession. In a long prologue (written in 1935 with a short note added in 1950) to this *comedia shaviana* (Shavian comedy) Usigli provided plenty of referential evidence to demonstrate the accurate and realistic nature of the play. Some critics have suggested that Usigli's insistence on a re-creation of contemporary events and the portrayal of lesser historical figures give his play limited currency in terms of future audiences' familiarity with those dated references. As Beardsell correctly points out, however, one of the strengths of the play is its continued relevance as it deals with intractable issues and problems that Mexicans have continued to endure throughout their modern history. The strongest argument on behalf of this series of political plays continues to be Usigli's ability to engage in humorous, biting, and at times farcical comedy.

During the next two decades Usigli left Mexico twice for extended periods as a member of the diplomatic service. Like many Latin American artists and intellectuals, he found it convenient and rewarding to travel overseas, in order to experience firsthand a reality that he only knew through reading, to have access to other cultural and intellectual centers, and to meet some of the writers he admired. Another possible explanation for his separation from Mexico is the need to recover from the experience of his failed marriage (1940–1944) to Josette Simó (stage name for Josefina Martínez), an actress and the mother of Cordelia, Usigli's first child. (Usigli later maried Argentina Casas, with whom he had three children: Lavinia, Leonardo, and Alejandro.) Some scholars have also suggested that he suffered the kind of "diplomatic exile" that was routinely reserved for controversial and intractable artists and intellectuals. But the most plausible explanation is that his worsening financial situation had prompted him to seek employment in the foreign service. The first time, he served as the second secretary in the Mexican embassy in Paris from 1944 to 1946. The third secretary was his friend Octavio Paz, with whom he shared, as Paz reports in his *Al paso* (1992, In Passing), an "amor a la poesía y al teatro" (love for poetry and theater). Although they later parted ways over their reactions to political events in 1968, Paz still considered Usigli "el mejor dramaturgo de este siglo" (the best [Mexican] playwright in this century). Usigli's second, more extended period in the diplomatic service, this time as ambassador, took him first to Lebanon in 1956 and, finally, to Norway in 1962. In addition to this work, he participated actively in the leadership of the moviemakers' guild, representing it at cinema festivals in France, Italy, Czechoslovakia, and Belgium.

Postwar Europe provided Usigli with an opportunity to seek out the company of the most important writers. Although he met with Jean Cocteau and Henri René Lenormand, the French dramatists were not particularly friendly. T. S. Eliot (whose "The Love Song of J. Alfred Prufrock" [1915] Usigli translated into Spanish in 1938) and Shaw were far more receptive. Shaw had read some of Usigli's dramatic output in English translation and had offered to sign "an Irish certificate of vocation as a dramatic poet" for him. He had even praised Usigli's talent by writing (on a postcard now in the Rodolfo Usigli Archive) "Mexico can starve you; but it cannot deny your genius."

After he returned from France in 1946, Usigli experienced both success and failure as a dramatist. At age thirty-five he had already written about half of his entire dramatic production and had received a moderate degree of recognition. His composition in 1938 of *El gesticulador* (The Impostor; performed in 1947, published in 1944), his most sophisticated political play, was further proof that during the 1930s he had reached the most advanced stage in his development as an artist. But the play had to wait a decade until it was finally put on the stage. In 1947 Usigli saw both *El gesticulador* and *Corona de sombra* (Crown of Shadows, published in 1943) premiere with mixed results. Since their inauspicious beginnings, however, they have become his best-known and most critically acclaimed plays. *El gesticulador* is by now a true Latin American drama classic with a growing body of critical commentary. Initially, the play was praised for its realistic portrayals of a Mexican family and of Mexico's corrupt political establishment, and, especially, for its thematic association with the Mexican Revolution.

The performance history of this play deserves special attention, as critics have established its premiere as the start of Mexico's modern theater. Even before its two-week run starting on 17 May 1947, *El gesticulador* was surrounded by controversy. It had appeared in three installments in the magazine *El hijo pródigo* (The Prodigal Son) in 1943 and in book form the following year. Part of the controversy had originated because of Usigli's own outspoken comments about various social and political topics. Usigli was accused of attacking the ideals of the revolution and, by extension, specific members of the government elite. Still, the play was a resounding box-office success. In several articles collected in volume 3 of *Teatro completo* (1979) Usigli reports that during the opening and subsequent nights the full-capacity crowd of 1,995 spectators at the Instituto Nacional de Bellas Artes (National Institute of Fine Arts) theater came from every sector of Mexican society. Despite this audience approval, the play was discontinued under questionable circumstances. The dispute involved actors, politicians, journalists, labor leaders, and government representatives who felt alluded to and criticized in the play. Usigli was forced to resign from his government post in the foreign service and was even involved in a physical confrontation with Salvador Novo, the fellow dramatist who was in charge of the drama season and was pressured to close the play. The details of the entire incident have become legendary, and, five decades later, they are still debated in critical and literary circles. Despite the tumultuous episode, Usigli felt vindicated by the favorable response from the audience.

His contemporary audiences not only saw the relevance and incisiveness of his criticism of political corruption and deception but also intuitively perceived the structural and presentational complexity of the play. Audiences in other countries around the world also identified with the universality of his message. As many interpreters have pointed out, *El gesticulador* goes well beyond the superficial, mimetic representation of objective Mexican reality. In a subtle interplay between the fictive and the real, both the plot and the identities of the characters go to the very heart of the illusion of dramatic representation.

In the story, César Rubio, a failed history professor, deceives his family and himself into believing that he can usurp the identity of a legendary hero of the revolution who bore the same name. A visiting Harvard University history professor and members of the political establishment jump at the opportunity to believe the impostor. Navarro, the regional political boss—the same man who had murdered the original General Rubio—challenges Rubio and decides to unmask and destroy

Award given to Usigli in 1977 by the Instituto Mexicano del Seguro Social for his 1947 play (published in 1943; translated as Crown of Shadows, *1946), the first in a trilogy centered on significant moments in Mexican history (Rodolfo Usigli Archive, Miami University Libraries, Oxford, Ohio)*

him. But the people become convinced that their hero has returned and hail Rubio as their leader. Rubio is promptly murdered by Navarro's henchmen and enshrined, once again, as a martyr of the revolution. Navarro, the true impostor, proclaims Rubio's memory to a populace that is too willing to believe in a mythological hero. Truth and falsehood, authenticity and imposture, history and myth, and reality and illusion are some of the themes of this highly complex play. Those interested in the realistic representation of Mexican reality find Usigli's portrayal of political institutions accurate and insightful; others find his depiction of Rubio's family dynamics intriguing. In a 1977 article, John W. Kronik observes that "the historical reality of the play is a metaphor for the nature of fiction and the fact of language." In addition to its structural intricacies, some critics have highlighted Usigli's deft use of self-reflexive metatheatrical techniques.

During Usigli's lifetime *El gesticulador* was produced many times in Mexico and in other countries (including the United States and Chile) in versions that he disavowed; he did approve, however, of the versions that were presented in Colombia, Czechoslovakia, and Poland. He was particularly disappointed over the "insufficient" English translation by Edward Landberg that was circulated as *The Gesturer* by his agent in the United States. Usigli remembers that in 1940 Barrett H. Clark and Mordecai Gorelik had spoken favorably of the play. That same year, however, John Gassner, the play reader for the Theatre Guild, had rejected the play, suggesting unsuccessfully that Usigli turn Rubio into a "would-be fascist dictator." In 1953 Usigli traveled to Moylan, Rose Valley, Pennsylvania, to see a production of his play at the Hedgerow Theater. Although he was flattered by the effort, he referred to Landberg's translation as "deficient" and was disappointed by the poor coverage in the papers, in particular by a negative comment from critic Eric Bentley, who accused him of having made "an unfortunate Pirandellian effort." Also in 1953, in New York City, there was a television adaptation by Michael Dyne of the play with the title *Another Caesar*, of which Usigli disapproved. In 1960 the play was made into a successful movie in Mexico, directed by Emilio (El Indio) Fernández, with Pedro Armendáriz in the role of Rubio. The 1996 world premiere at Miami University in Ohio of *The Impostor*, the newest English translation (by Ramón Layera) of *El gesticulador*, drew 1,779 spectators during a successful seven-day run attended by Alejandro Usigli, the playwright's son and literary executor, and Mexican drama specialists Frank N. Dauster, Kirsten F. Nigro, Beardsell, and Sandra Messinger Cypess.

Dissatisfied with the mixed reception of his political plays, Usigli turned in the 1950s to other subjects. He had already explored the possibilities of psychological drama, but he was finally rewarded for his efforts in this decade. In 1951 and 1952 Usigli enjoyed financial success with the commercial productions of *El niño y la niebla* and *Jano es una muchacha*. These two plays further confirmed his reputation as a social critic and a keen observer of middle-class values, an image he had acquired with his earlier plays *Medio tono* (The Great Middle Class; performed in 1937, published in 1938) and *La familia cena en casa* (The Family Dines at Home; performed and published in 1942). *El niño y la niebla* and *Jano es una muchacha* are melodramas that deal with controversial issues, and their treatment of family life in a middle-class setting is far from conventional. *El niño y la niebla* is the story of an unhappy marriage and a love triangle that ends in tragedy. A frustrated upper-middle-class couple suffers from the husband's lack of ambition and the wife's interest in his friend's affection. To complicate matters, they disagree strongly over the upbringing of their teenage son. The boy, who is caught in the middle, acts out their estrangement and in a sleepwalking incident points a gun at his father. The wife confesses to her would-be lover that she had attempted to influence and guide her son's potentially murderous actions. There are hints that pathological and hereditary factors motivate the actions of the mother and of the son. In the end, the son commits suicide while his parents reach an unsatisfactory compromise. The general public reacted with morbid curiosity, if not utter outrage, at such an emotionally charged dramatic conflict; the play became one of Usigli's greatest financial successes.

Jano es una muchacha was also based on a controversial topic and had an equally successful box-office reception. The scandal that accompanied its production was even more pronounced as it involved the vociferous objections of both the Church and the League of Decency. At the heart of the controversy was Usigli's realistic and unambiguous portrayal of sex and prostitution. The use of a seemingly innocent schoolgirl as the symbol of duplicity and the coarse portrayal of a brothel underscored the provocative nature of the moral intent of the play. Following the example of his Shavian model, Usigli introduced a difficult topic in a way that forced audiences to reexamine universally accepted notions about illicit, commercial sex. Equally provocative was Usigli's bold attempt at exposing the hypocritical acceptance of male prerogatives, let alone the unequal and unethical terms of exchange in the Mexican sex trade. In keeping with Usigli's intended artistic goal, the play succeeded in provoking wide debate about a taboo topic.

In the 1960s Usigli became increasingly detached from the local theatrical scene in Mexico. In his second period of diplomatic service, he spent six years in Lebanon and was transferred to Norway until his retirement in 1971. Because younger and more successful playwrights and directors had transformed Mexico's contemporary drama, and because of Usigli's own diminishing creative energies, this stage in his career as a dramatist was one of relative decline. But it was also a time for summation and closure. Distance and job security provided him with the necessary perspective and leisure time to reevaluate his entire creative project. He became the first Mexican living playwright to have his complete works published. Fondo de Cultura Económica, the most important publishing house in the country, started with sixteen of Usigli's early plays in the first volume of his *Teatro completo* in 1963. The third volume, published in 1979, the year of his death, included 565 pages of prologues, notes, and epilogues, a few of which Usigli had updated. The fourth volume appeared much later, in 1996. Another and more significant task in the 1960s was the completion of his *Corona* trilogy: the earlier *Corona de sombra* plus *Corona de fuego* (Crown of Fire; performed in 1961, published in 1966) and *Corona de luz* (published in 1965, performed in 1969; translated as *Crown of Light*, 1965). He also wrote all the plays that appear in the third volume of his *Teatro completo* during this period, but the *Corona* trilogy is certainly his most ambitious and far-reaching artistic effort.

Since the early 1930s Usigli had harbored the hope of completing a select group of plays that would summarize and symbolize the very essence of the social and historical reality of the New World. He called his grandiose project "El gran teatro del Nuevo Mundo" (The Great Theater of the New World). He compared his proposed series of plays, begrudgingly, to Diego Rivera's mural style of painting. In other words, archetypal Mexican characters and themes would decorate a vast and comprehensive imaginary canvas of continental scope on which he would "paint" his artistic interpretation. When told about this idea, both Shaw and Eliot showed little interest, but Usigli persisted. In reality, the *Corona* trilogy is the closest Usigli came to fulfilling his dream of completing part of his "Gran teatro del Nuevo Mundo."

Thematically the *Coronas* have an historical base and can be regarded as standard historical plays, although Usigli subtitled them *piezas antihistóricas* (antihistorical pieces). The term (which he coined) refers to his goal of interpreting the significance of certain historical figures and events rather than adhering strictly to the accuracy of the historical record. The true intent of his "antihistorical" method, in his own explanation in the prologue to *Corona de sombra* (included in volume 3 of *Teatro completo*), is to recover those select foundational myths of origin, "recordar con la ayuda de la imagi-

Usigli in the late 1960s (Rodolfo Usigli Archive, Miami University Libraries, Oxford, Ohio)

nación" (to remember with the help of the imagination), in order to grasp the essence of Mexico's concept of nationhood and cultural identity—or, as Dauster explains, to concentrate not on "la verdad del detalle histórico" (the truth of the historical detail) but rather on "su importancia en el desarrollo del concepto de la nacionalidad" (its importance to the concept of nationality). True to his method and mindful of the specific requirements of drama, Usigli indulged in deliberate anachronisms in order to accomplish such a difficult artistic goal. More than in any of his other plays, in the *Coronas* Usigli combined two seemingly incompatible realms, namely, the disputed facts of historical knowledge and the more free-ranging but probing demands of his own imagination.

Taken chronologically, the *Coronas* are centered on three crucial moments in Mexican history and in the evolution of the country's national cultural identity. These specific historical moments are the basis for what Usigli described as Mexico's "superlative" or essential myths. According to Usigli, the significance of these incidents resides in the fact that at each of those historical crossroads Mexico acquired, respectively, its material, spiritual, and political sovereignty from Europe.

Viewed in chronological sequence, the first moment, in *Corona de fuego,* takes place during the clash between Aztecs and Spaniards at the start of the Conquest. The second moment, in *Corona de luz,* occurs during the miraculous appearance of the Virgin of Guadalupe to an Indian, Juan Diego, on the hill of Tepeyac outside the Mexican capital in 1531. Finally, in *Corona de sombra,* the exceptional moment occurs during the execution of Emperor Maximilian in 1867 at the end of the French occupation. Judging by the critical interest that the three plays have generated as a group, they can be considered an artistic success; further, because of their novel thematic content and interpretive breadth, they have served as both model and challenge for successive generations of Mexican playwrights.

Corona de fuego is based on Mexico's quintessential foundational myth, that of the destruction of the Aztec civilization and of the heroic sacrifice of Cuauhtémoc, the last Aztec emperor. Significantly, Usigli focuses on the conflict between Hernán Cortés and Cuauhtémoc, rather than Moctezuma, the reigning Aztec emperor at the moment of Cortés's arrival in Tenochtitlán, the Aztec capital. By the time Moctezuma had lost everything, including his life, his memory had taken on the connotation of a vacillating, inept leader who gave up the fight too soon. In contrast, according to Mexican history and popular belief, Cuauhtémoc is the brave warrior who took up arms and defended the dying Aztec nation. His story is one of heroism, defeat, and martyrdom, the stuff of epic drama. Accused of treason by the Spaniards, Cuauhtémoc was brutally executed after four years of torture and imprisonment. Symbolically, a light in the shape of a cross shines over the sacred tree from which the bodies of the executed are supposed to hang in the closing scene of the play. The visual juxtaposition of the cross over the sacred tree adds meaning to Cuauhtémoc's martyrdom. In addition to the central rivalry of Cuauhtémoc and Cortés, Usigli includes a subsidiary element in the role of La Malinche (Doña Marina), the Indian woman who served as Cortés's interpreter and lover. As in the historical record and in the popular imagination, La Malinche's ambiguous role in the play is one of both conflict and resolution. She is both the treacherous woman who facilitates the Conquest by serving the Spaniards and the loyal Indian who watches out for the interests of her fellow natives. She bears the conqueror's child, the first mestizo child: she is thus the mother of all Mexicans. Similarly, Cuauhtémoc's death also gives birth to the new nation. In Usigli's general *Corona* framework, both La Malinche's mestizo child and Cuauhtémoc's sacrifice signal Mexico's material sovereignty from Spain.

Corona de luz is also based on a foundational myth from the Conquest period, during the destruction of the native religious institutions and their replacement by the Catholic Church. Abandoned by their own gods, the indigenous population sees little meaning in the evangelization efforts of the Church. How can a church be born out of the ashes of destruction and despair? Can the natives accept an alien god? In his *Corona de luz* Usigli provides a bold and imaginative alternative that conflates both secular and divine intervention. His play is about the miracle of the dark Virgin of Guadalupe and the establishment of an autonomous New World branch of Christendom. In Usigli's version the miraculous appearance of the Virgin to the native Juan Diego goes beyond the pious belief commonly held by the general population. His play includes not only the familiar elements of the legend but also a series of "antihistorical" elements in order to suggest the complicitous role of the Crown and the Church in their efforts to expedite the pacification of the native population. In addition to a series of anachronistic appearances by the Spanish monarchs and a few Franciscan chroniclers and historians, there is a Murcian gardener who is capable of growing roses in an unlikely, rocky site and a dark-complexioned Clarist nun from Seville who is prone to beatific trances. All these elements help Usigli construct a clever and intricate plot that momentarily suggests the perpetration of a deliberate fraud intended to lure the Indians into the Catholic faith. But the unexplained, miraculous appearance of the Virgin in the end cancels the possibility that there may be a hoax. In the concluding scene the Bishop and the other Church leaders bow down to the clamorous outburst of religious fervor by the Indians. The Bishop concludes that the real miracle is the newly found faith of the native population.

The performance history of the *Corona* trilogy shows that audiences have given the greatest preference to *Corona de sombra.* Critical judgment, also, has deemed it the most successful of the three. As in *El gesticulador,* ambiguity marks *Corona de sombra.* On the surface the play appears to be centered on the two protagonists, Carlota and Maximilian, depicting their psychological turmoil and the sentimental details of their love story and tragic end. But Usigli's subtly crafted plot accomplishes a much more transcendent objective, which is to explain the meaning of their fate in the context of the larger historical picture. Using factual material from both European and Mexican history, Usigli explores the multiplicity of private and state motivations that brought the two monarchs to Mexico. There is no lack of contending forces in the historical narrative, and Usigli takes full advantage of them in his design of the dramatic plot. In the 1860s Mexico was in the middle of a civil war between Liberals and Conservatives. The

Poster for the 1996 English-language production of Usigli's play El gesticulador, in which a history professor briefly assumes the identity of a legendary hero of the Mexican Revolution who shares the same name (Rodolfo Usigli Archive, Miami University Libraries, Oxford, Ohio)

Liberal leader, Benito Juárez, defeated the Conservatives, and they, in turn, appealed to their European allies. A large expeditionary French force invaded Mexico and occupied the capital in 1863. Napoleon III, who sought to expand the French presence in the New World and to restore the monarchy where Spain had failed, installed Archduke Maximilian of Austria as emperor of Mexico. The Vatican responded to the supplications of those Mexican Conservatives who hoped to restore the Church's and their own privileges, while Juárez, their Liberal nemesis, desperately fought for the restoration of the republic. Caught in the middle were Carlota and Maximilian, the hapless royal couple whose ill-fated imperial dream ended with Maximilian's execution.

In Usigli's portrayal, Carlota and Maximilian have come to Mexico under the impression that they are wanted and needed, although Carlota's ambition appears to be a stronger motivation. Maximilian's motives, as Usigli depicts them, appear to be purer and more altruistic; he shows signs of sympathy for the Liberal cause and even seems to be a latent democrat who secretly favors Juárez and the republic. Upon his execution the reader and spectator feel sympathy for someone who has literally been martyred to save the republic. In the meantime, Carlota, who has traveled to Paris and Rome to seek support, goes insane. In the play, as in actuality, she outlives her husband by sixty years and dies in Brussels in 1927. Her inordinately long life and the "shadow" of her madness are supposed to help expiate her blind ambition and the death of her husband. Usigli creates the character of Erasmo Ramírez, a Mexican historian who physically resembles Juárez and who visits Carlota in her palace in Brussels, seeing her in a rare, last moment of lucidity right before her death. During their conversation, Carlota understands the reason for her madness, and the historian understands the reason and the purpose of Maximilian's "sacrifice" for Mexico. In Usigli's interpretation, his death signals the end of the monarchy in the New World and the true beginning of Mexican independence.

During the last part of his career Usigli wrote several other plays of uneven quality. He tried his hand less successfully at verse drama in *La exposición* (The Exhibition, published in 1960); at light comedy in *Un navío cargado de . . .* (A Ship Laden with . . . ; published in 1966), *El testamento y el viudo* (The Widower's Last Will; published in 1966), and *El encuentro* (The Encounter; published in 1966); and at political commentary in *El gran circo del mundo* (The World's Great Arena; produced and published in 1969), a play about nuclear disarmament. He also revisited earlier revolutionary themes, albeit with moderate success, in *Las madres* (The Mothers; published in 1966, performed in 1972). *Las madres* includes not only the character of a boy who witnesses the ravages of war during the Mexican Revolution but also a tender and moving portrayal of an embattled, widowed mother who can be strong and dignified but also generous and kind. In addition to its obvious autobiographical dimension, the play offers a series of realistic tableaux depicting neighborhood life in the Mexican capital during the periodic incursions by marauding revolutionary factions. Usigli authorized the staging of this particular play on the occasion of his receiving the National Prize in literature in 1972.

Two plays from this stage in his career have attracted critical attention: *Los viejos* (The Elderly; performed and published in 1971) and *¡Buenos días, señor Presidente!* (Good Morning, Mister President! published in 1972). In both plays Usigli is concerned with issues that refer to the role of youth, aging, and the inexorable passing of time. The latter play deals with the events surrounding the 1968 student unrest that ended in a massacre in Mexico City. Usigli's implicit impatience with the reform movement and his tacit acceptance of the official interpretation of events that was given by the Mexican government put him at odds with practically everyone. This reaction contributed to his isolation and a sense that his time had passed. To his credit, *Los viejos* has been singled out for the experimental nature of its dramatic structure and especially for Usigli's use of cinematic technique. While his creative efforts continued into the early 1970s, critics concur that his best efforts had occurred much earlier. Usigli died of natural causes on 18 June 1979.

Critical assessment of Usigli's work has evolved through the years. Initially, his dramatic works were celebrated because they synthesized Mexico's major historical and cultural themes. He was also credited with providing an accessible and accurate portrayal of its familiar national traits, values, and institutions. He received special credit for offering an unflinchingly critical view of Mexico's middle class, with all its insecurities, pettiness, and unrealistic aspirations. But these characterizations of his artistry were mostly superficial and subjective. In this regard, Dauster was right in pointing out that a common mistake had been to regard Usigli's style as naively realistic. Later and insightful analysis of his work has revealed the existence of a far more subtle and nuanced manipulation of dramatic form than had been traditionally observed. Critical studies of several of his plays have pointed out his artful use of language and metatheatrical technique, his expert use of tragedy, his exploration of the power of language, and in particular, his complex interpretation of history and myth.

Rodolfo Usigli's entire artistic and intellectual project can be summarized into three basic categories: he was a theater practitioner, a drama scholar and teacher, and a playwright. He participated in the foundational period of Mexico's modern drama and played a key role in defining the artistic parameters of a theater movement that began in the latter part of the 1920s and early 1930s. During the 1930s his administrative post in the Ministry of Education enabled him to influence the direction of artistic and theatrical trends. As one of the first professors of dramaturgy at the national university in the 1930s and 1940s, Usigli taught a whole generation of Mexican playwrights, including Luisa Josefina Hernández, Emilio Carballido, Héctor Mendoza, and Rosario Castellanos. Others, such as Jorge Ibarguengoitia, Vicente Leñero, and Guillermo Schmidhuber, who were not his students, nevertheless have acknowledged his influence. His disciples and successors recognize his exemplary role and credit him with their own development of a similar professional dedication to the craft and genuine interest in a wider diversity of thematic, ideological, and aesthetic concerns. In addition to teaching the next generation of playwrights, he was a drama scholar in his own right: he wrote or co-authored the first histories of Mexican drama as well as manuals of dramaturgy and composition. But his greatest contribution came in the form of a corpus of dramatic works that has withstood the test of time. His *El gesticulador* and his *Corona* trilogy are among the best-known and most anthologized and produced plays in Mexican and Latin American drama.

Throughout a remarkable career that began at a difficult time in the history of Mexico, Usigli expressed a passionate commitment and an unswerving dedication to the development of a national theater. In recognition of his contribution to the promotion of the dramatic arts, the Centro de Investigación Teatral Rodolfo Usigli (CITRU), one of Mexico's most important centers for theater scholarship and research, bears his name. In an epigraph to one of his essays, Usigli stated his philosophy: "Un pueblo sin teatro es un pueblo sin verdad" (A people without drama is a people without truth).

Bibliography:

Wilder P. Scott, "Toward an Usigli Bibliography (1931–1971)," *Latin American Theatre Review*, 6, no. 1 (1972): 53–63.

References:

Peter R. Beardsell, "Cinema and Theater in Rodolfo Usigli's *Los viejos*," *Bulletin of Hispanic Studies*, 75 (October 1998): 455–467;

Beardsell, *A Theatre for Cannibals: Rodolfo Usigli and the Mexican Stage* (London & Toronto: Associated University Presses, 1992);

Beardsell, "Usigli's Political Drama in Perspective," *Bulletin of Hispanic Studies*, 66, no. 3 (1989): 251–261;

Vera F. Beck, "La fuerza motriz, en la obra dramática de Rodolfo Usigli," *Revista Iberoamericana*, 18, no. 36 (1953): 369–383;

Pedro Bravo-Elizondo, "El concepto de la revolución de lo mexicano en *El gesticulador*," *Texto Crítico*, 10, no. 29 (May–August 1984): 197–205;

Timothy G. Compton, "'Máscaras mexicanas' in Rodolfo Usigli's *Jano es una muchacha*," *Latin American Theatre Review*, 25, no. 1 (Fall 1991): 63–71;

Carlos Coria-Sanchez, "*El gesticulador*: Contextualización del 'yo' mexicano," *Cuadernos Americanos*, 3 (May–June 1999): 208–214;

Frank N. Dauster, "Rodolfo Usigli," in his *Perfil generacional del teatro hispanoamericano (1894–1924): Chile, México, El Río de la Plata* (Ottawa: Girol, 1993), pp. 152–166;

Denise M. Di Puccio, "Metatheatrical Histories in *Corona de luz*," *Latin American Theatre Review*, 20, no. 1 (1986): 29–36;

Francis Donahue, "Toward a Mexican National Theater," *Revista/Review Interamericana*, 9 (Fall–Winter 1989): 29–40;

Sidney Donnell, "Quixotic Desire and the Avoidance of Closure in Luis Buñuel's 'The Criminal Life of Archibaldo de la Cruz,'" *Modern Language Notes*, 114 (March 1999): 269–296;

Kelly Dunn, "*Noticias del imperio* y *Corona de sombra*: Dos visiones distintas," *Cincinnati Romance Review*, 16 (1997): 74–83;

Mark S. Finch, "Rodolfo Usigli's *Corona de sombra*, *Corona de fuego*, *Corona de luz*: The Mythopoesis of Antihistory," *Romance Notes*, 22, no. 2 (1981): 151–154;

David William Foster, "*El gesticulador*: El Gran Teatro de México," in his *Estudios sobre teatro mexicano contemporáneo: Semiología de la competencia teatral* (New York: Peter Lang, 1984), pp. 13–26;

Myra S. Gann, "*El gesticulador*: Tragedy or Didactic Play?" *Revista de Literatura Hispánica*, 32–33 (Fall 1990–Spring 1991): 148–157;

José García Lorca, "Rodolfo Usigli 'esperó a Godot' dieciséis años antes que Samuel Beckett," *Papeles de son armadans*, 90, no. 269–270 (1978): 129–147;

Eunice G. Gates, "Usigli as Seen in His Prefaces and Epilogues," *Hispania*, 37, no. 4 (1954): 432–439;

Theda M. Herz, "Jorge Ibarguengoitia's Carnival Pageantry: The Mexican Theatre of Power and the Power of the Theatre," *Latin American Theatre Review*, 28, no. 1 (1994): 31–47;

John W. Kronik, "Usigli's *El gesticulador* and the Fiction of Truth," *Latin American Theatre Review*, 11, no. 1 (1977): 5–16;

Andrea G. Labinger, "Age, Alienation and the Artist in Usigli's *Los viejos*," *Latin American Theatre Review*, 14, no. 2 (1981): 41–47;

Catherine Larsen, "No conoces el precio de las palabras: Language and Meaning in Usigli's *El gesticulador*," *Latin American Theatre Review*, 20, no. 1 (1986): 21–28;

Ramón Layera, "*Conversaciones y encuentros*: Prolegómenos para la autobiografía de Rodolfo Usigli," in *De la crónica a la nueva narrativa: Coloquio sobre la literatura mexicana*, edited by Merlin H. Forster and Julio Ortega (Mexico City, 1986), pp. 151–160;

Layera, "Mecanismos de fabulación y mitificación de la historia en las 'comedias impolíticas' y las *Coronas* de Rodolfo Usigli," *Latin American Theatre Review*, 18, no. 2 (1985): 49–55;

Layera, "El monólogo como acto de fe: *Estreno en Broadway* de Rodolfo Usigli," *Latin American Theatre Review*, 28, no. 1 (1994): 81–87;

Layera, *Usigli en el teatro: Testimonios de sus contemporáneos, sucesores y discípulos* (Mexico City: Universidad Nacional Autónoma de México, 1996);

Francisco A. Lomelí, "Los mitos de la mexicanidad en la trilogía de Rodolfo Usigli," *Cuadernos Hispanoamericanos*, 333 (1978): 466–477;

Gerardo Luzuriaga, "Rodolfo Usigli y Estados Unidos," *Gestos: Teoría y Práctica del Teatro Hispánico*, 7, no. 14 (1992): 191–195;

Porfirio Martínez Peñaloza, "Sobre el poeta Rodolfo Usigli," *Abside*, 39, no. 4 (1975): 429–436;

Priscilla Meléndez, "La 'antihistoria' y la metaficción en *Corona de sombra* de Rodolfo Usigli," *La Torre: Revista de la Universidad de Puerto Rico*, 4 (January–March 1990): 29–69;

Marianna Merritt Matteson, "On the Function of the Imposter in the Plays of Rodolfo Usigli," *Selecta*, 2 (1981): 120–123;

Merritt Matteson, "Usigli's *Obliteración*: An Intimate Inferno," *Selecta*, 3 (1982): 127–133;

Daniel Meyrán, *El discurso teatral de Rodolfo Usigli, del signo al discurso* (Mexico City: INBA/CITRU, 1993);

Francisco Monterde, "Juárez, Maximiliano y Carlota en las obras de los dramaturgos mexicanos," *Cuadernos Americanos*, 136, no. 5 (1964): 231–240;

Mabel Moraña, "Historicismo y legitimación del poder en *El gesticulador* de Rodolfo Usigli," *Revista Iberoamericana*, 148–149 (July–December 1989): 1261–1275;

Arthur A. Natella Jr., "Christological Symbolism in Rodolfo Usigli's *El gesticulador*," *Discurso Literario: Revista de Temas Hispánicos*, 5 (Spring 1988): 455–461;

Kirsten F. Nigro, "Light and Darkness in Usigli's *Corona de sombra*," *Chasqui: Revista de Literatura Latinoamericana*, 17 (November 1988): 27–34;

Nigro, "On Reading and Responding to (Latin American) Playtexts," *Gestos: Teoría y Práctica del Teatro Hispánico*, 2 (November 1987): 101–113;

Nigro, "Rhetoric and History in Three Mexican Plays," *Latin American Theatre Review*, 21, no. 1 (1987): 65–73;

Octavio Paz, "Teatro de la memoria," in his *Al paso* (Barcelona: Seix Barral, 1992), pp. 45–54;

Mehl Penrose, "La historia en dos obras de Rodolfo Usigli, o el juego entre la fantasía y la realidad," *Mester*, 27 (1998): 129–140;

Dennis Perri, "The Artistic Unity of *Corona de sombra*," *Latin American Theatre Review*, 15, no. 1 (1981): 13–19;

Gerald W. Petersen, "El mundo circular de Rodolfo Usigli," *Explicación de textos literarios*, 6, no. 1 (1977–1978): 105–108;

Gordon Ragle, "Rodolfo Usigli and His Mexican Scene," *Hispania*, 46, no. 2 (1963): 307–311;

Rodolfo Usigli, ciudadano del teatro: Memorias de los homenajes a Rodolfo Usigli 1990–1991 (Mexico City: INBA, Serie Memorias, 1992);

Roberto R. Rodríguez, "La función de la imaginación en las *Coronas* de Rodolfo Usigli," *Latin American Theatre Review*, 10, no. 2 (1977): 37–44;

Rodríguez, "Vida y teatro de Rodolfo Usigli: Tres Conversaciones," *Tramoya*, 13 (October–December 1978): 45–70;

Asela Rodríguez-Seda, "Las últimas obras de Rodolfo Usigli: Efebocracia o gerontocracia," *Latin American Theatre Review*, 81 (1974): 45–48;

Vance R. Savage, "Rodolfo Usigli's Idea of Mexican Theater," *Latin American Theatre Review*, 4, no. 2 (1971): 13–20;

Rosana Laura Scarano, "Correspondencias estructurales y semánticas entre *El gesticulador* y *Corona de sombra*," *Latin American Theatre Review*, 22, no. 1 (1988): 29–36;

Scarano, "Metateatro e identidad en *Saverio El Cruel* de Roberto Arlt y *El gesticulador* de Rodolfo Usigli," *Alba de América: Revista Literaria*, 6 (July 1988): 199–207;

George O. Schanzer, "Usigli, Calderón and the Revolution," *Kentucky Romance Quarterly*, 26, no. 2 (1979): 189–201;

Wilder P. Scott, "French Literature and the Theater of Rodolfo Usigli," *Romance Notes*, 16, no. 1 (1974): 228–231;

Scott, "Rodolfo Usigli and Contemporary Dramatic Theory," *Romance Notes*, 11, no. 3 (1970): 526–530;

Donald L. Shaw, "Dramatic Technique in Usigli's *El gesticulador*," *Theatre Research International*, 1 (1976): 125–133;

Eduardo Thomas, "Metáforas de la identidad en el teatro hispanoamericano contemporáneo," *Revista Chilena de Literatura*, 50 (April 1997): 39–50;

Solomon H. Tilles, "Rodolfo Usigli's Concept of Dramatic Art," *Latin American Theatre Review*, 3, no. 2 (1970): 31–38;

Fernando Carlos Vevia Romero, *La sociedad mexicana en el teatro de Rodolfo Usigli* (Guadalajara: Universidad de Guadalajara, 1990).

Papers:

The Rodolfo Usigli Archive in the Walter Havighurst Special Collections at the King Library in Miami University in Oxford, Ohio, is the repository for Rodolfo Usigli's most important literary papers. It includes correspondence, manuscripts and typed drafts of original plays and translations of works by other artists, photographs, essays, books, playbills, posters, awards, newspaper and magazine articles, memorabilia, and ephemera. The Centro de Investigación Teatral Rodolfo Usigli (CITRU) in Mexico City also has additional materials.

Egon Wolff
(13 April 1926 -)

José L. Urbina
Catholic University of America

PLAY PRODUCTIONS: *Mansión de lechuzas,* Santiago, Sala Talía, March 1958;

Discípulos del miedo, Santiago, Sala Antonio Varas, August 1958;

Parejas de trapo, Santiago, Sala Antonio Varas, March 1960;

Niñamadre, Concepción, Sala Maccabi, April 1962;

Los invasores, Santiago, Sala Antonio Varas, October 1963;

El signo de Caín, Santiago, Sala Mozart, 1969;

Flores de papel, Santiago, Sala Mozart, November 1970;

Kindergarten, Santiago, Teatro Galpón de Los Leones, November 1977;

Espejismos, Santiago, Teatro Universidad Católica, 1978;

El sobre azul, Santiago, Sala Camilo Henriquez, 1978;

José, Santiago, Teatro de Cámara del Teatro Municipal, 1980;

Alamos en la azotea, Santiago, Teatro Municipal, May 1981;

La balsa de la Medusa, Santiago, Teatro Universidad Católica, April 1984;

Háblame de Laura, Santiago, Teatro Universidad Católica, July 1986;

Invitación a comer, Santiago, Corporación Cultural de Las Condes, May 1993;

Cicatrices, Santiago, Teatro Universidad Católica, June 1994;

Claroscuro, Santiago, Teatro Apoquindo, September 1995;

Encrucijada, Santiago, Teatro Apoquindo, April 2000.

BOOKS: *Niñamadre: Comedia dramática en 3 actos* (Santiago: Instituto Chileno-Norteamericano de Cultura, 1966);

Flores de papel, in *Tres obras de teatro,* by Wolff, Roberto Cossa, and Eduardo Pavlovsky (Havana: Casa de las Américas, 1970); translated by Margaret Sayers Peden as *Paper Flowers: A Play in Six Scenes* (Columbia: University of Missouri Press, 1971);

Los invasores: Obra en dos actos, el primero dividido en dos cuadros (Santiago: Ercilla, 1970);

Egon Wolff (*from Ruth S. Lamb, ed.,* Three Contemporary Latin-American Plays: René Marqués, Egon Wolff, Emilio Carballido, *1971; Thomas Cooper Library, University of South Carolina*)

El signo de Caín; Discípulos del miedo (Santiago: Valores Literarios, 1971);

Teatro (Santiago: Nascimento, 1978)—comprises *Niñamadre, Flores de papel,* and *Kindergarten;*

Parejas de trapo; La balsa de la Medusa (Santiago: Universitaria, 1988);

Los invasores; José (Santiago: Pehuén, 1990);

Teatro completo (Boulder, Colo.: Society of Spanish and Spanish-American Studies, 1990);

Invitación a comer; Cicatrices (Santiago: Universitaria, 1995);

Antología de obras teatrales (Santiago: RiL, 2002)—comprises *Niñamadre, Los invasores, Flores de papel, Kindergarten, Alamos en la azotea, La balsa de la Medusa, Háblame de Laura, Invitación a comer, Cicatrices,* and *Tras una puerta cerrada.*

Edition: *Los invasores,* in *Three Contemporary Latin-American Plays: René Marqués, Egon Wolff, Emilio Carballido,* edited by Ruth S. Lamb (Waltham, Mass.: Xerox College Publishing, 1971).

Editions in English: *The Raft of the Medusa,* translated by Kirsten F. Nigro, *Modern International Drama,* 24 (Fall 1990): 29–70;

Paper Flowers, translated by Gwynne Edwards, in *The Methuen Book of Contemporary Latin American Plays,* edited by Edwards (London: Methuen Drama, 2004).

SELECTED PERIODICAL PUBLICATION–UNCOLLECTED: *Crónicas de un edificio psicótico, Teatrae,* 5 (Summer–Fall 2003): 49–71.

Egon Wolff is one of the most important Chilean playwrights of the 1950s generation. His versatility in matters of theatrical techniques, his capacity to create aesthetic and ethical challenges, and his willingness to explore metaphysical and social themes have earned him respect and admiration within and outside Chile.

Born on 13 April 1926, Egan Raúl Wolff Grobler is the son of Walter Wolff, a German engineer who immigrated to Chile in 1913 to work with Siemens, which was looking into the possibility of building a subway system in Santiago. His mother, Ines Grobler, was a German-Chilean with Swedish and Norwegian maternal ancestors. He has an older sister, Herna. Until the age of seventeen, Wolff spoke German regularly at home. Relatives back in Germany included academics and philologists; still, his father considered it useless to engage in artistic activity in Chile, because great art was not in Chile but in Europe. In any case, all art carried a connotation of indolence that Wolff's father found unacceptable. Wolff had a bout of pneumonia at the age of eight, after which he remained a sickly youth. During his convalescence, he read extensively, especially European literature. He was educated in a German elementary school, Lota Schule, and then in Deutsche Schule. In 1941 he entered military school, but he became sick. The next year he entered the National Institute, where he finished high school. Between 1944 and 1949 he studied chemical engineering at the Catholic University in Santiago de Chile, following the typical pattern for upper-middle-class Chileans. The path to success for this social group was through science and the technical professions, and they evinced contempt for the humanities. This formula is clearly motivated by the economic advantages and ensuing social prestige of the technical professions. Moreover, a degree from the Catholic University, a private institution, was a ticket to the elite.

This backdrop is crucial to understanding the significance of Wolff's decision to exercise his scientific profession, with a certain dissatisfaction, but to devote his energies and intelligence to the theater. This act can undoubtedly be interpreted as a rebellious gesture against paternal authority and the social strictures that, in the authoritarian and conservative Chilean society of the time, placed reproduction of the class above individual wishes. In a 1976 interview with Rafael Otano, Wolff declared: "Mas para mis padres la literatura era una perversión y nunca permitieron que yo siguiese mi inclinación. Pero yo escribía ocultamente y a veces publicaba con seudónimo" (My parents thought literature was a perversion and would never allow me to follow my inclinations. But I wrote in secret and sometimes published under a pseudonym).

Continuing to play his role as one of the captains of industry, Wolff pursued his goal of becoming a playwright, despite its questionable economic reward in an underdeveloped society and the fact that artists in Chile were generally regarded with indifference and silence. Overcoming his family's opposition with the support of his wife, Carmen Peña, whom he married in 1953, Wolff began to write during the 1950s. In an unpublished interview he remembered: "A pesar de que eramos una pareja joven ella nunca demostró preocupación por el hecho de que yo escribiera en vez de dedicarme a actividades más remunerativas" (Although we were a young couple, she never demonstrated any worries about the fact that I was dedicated to writing instead of to more lucrative activities). But his friendship with director and actor Eugenio Guzmán Ovalle—whom he met while in the Quilpue sanitorium after a bout of tuberculosis in 1948, when Guzmán visited a cousin also afflicted with lung disease—opened up a whole new horizon of theater. Up to that point, Wolff had written only narrative and poetry.

In 1954 Guzmán invited Wolff to attend a production of Arthur Miller's *Death of a Salesman* (1949) in which he was acting. Wolff took Miller's play as a challenge to try his own hand at drama. He saw the production five or six times and obtained an English edition of the text. It captivated him, opening up the possibilities of writing for the theater. He then spent 1955 and 1956 writing dialogues. Guzmán and the playwright Isidora Aguirre were his two readers and supported him

Barbara McColl, Denis Comey, and John Adams in a 1981 Kitsilano Company production of Wolff's 1977 comedy, Kindergarten (published in 1978), in which the mutual dependency of two brothers is threatened by the arrival of their sister (from Latin American Theatre Review, volume 15 [Spring 1982]; Thomas Cooper Library, University of South Carolina)

through this learning period. Guzmán later directed several of his plays.

Within an environment of mediocre commercial theater and actors who eked out a living between the stage and radio, university theater had evolved in the 1940s as a place of experimentation and a school for new directors, actors, playwrights, and scene designers. Among them were the Experimental Theater at the University of Chile, the Experimental Theater at Catholic University, the Concepción University Theater, and Teknos at the State Technical University Theater. These groups carried out a remarkable process of renewal that culminated in the early 1960s. Several independent groups emerged about the same time, rounding out the Chilean stage through the following decades—groups such as Ictus, who staged and sponsored a large number of plays by Chilean authors. Wolff's generation—including Luis Alberto Heiremans, Alejandro Sieveking, Sergio Vodanovic, and Jorge Diaz—developed in this dynamic environment.

Although Wolff recognized the talent of Chileans such as Acevedo Hernández, he took foreign playwrights as his models. In addition to Miller, William Shakespeare, Samuel Beckett, and Bertolt Brecht, Wolff admired Anton Chekhov, "quien puede decir tanto con tan poco" (who can say so much with so little), as he commented in an unpublished interview. He and the Russian share two characteristics: a central concern with ethics, and an acute awareness of language. For Wolff, it is impossible to conceive of a play without an ethical core, a play that does not produce some kind of illumination or at least insinuate the possibility of human betterment. Because he focuses more on the writing process rather than involvement in the staging, he considers himself more a writer for theater than a practical man of theater.

In 1957 Wolff delivered his first dialogue, "Maní para la novia" (Peanuts for the Bride), to Guzmán. This dialogue, after being reworked and rewritten, became his first play, *Discípulos del miedo* (Disciples of Fear; performed in 1958, published in 1971), and was awarded an honorable mention in a competition sponsored by the Institute of Theater of the University of Chile.

That same year, he wrote *Mansión de lechuzas* (The House of Owls, performed in 1958), and after it won a second honorable mention for Wolff in the Catholic University Experimental Theater Competition, both plays were staged. At this point Wolff began to explore a theme that became a central motif in all his work: the state of terror and paranoia produced in the Chilean bourgeoisie by the possibility of poverty and loss of power. This generational motif can also be seen in the works of Vodanovic and José Donoso. It provides an interesting counterpoint to the colonial literature that emerged on other continents around the same time. In this dramatic world the Chilean bourgeoisie considers anyone outside of its own race and class as simply rabble. This axiom gives rise to two related motifs: confinement, or a kind of hunkering down, in response to feeling exposed and besieged; and invasion.

Mansión de lechuzas was staged first. It was produced in Santiago by the Sociedad de Autores Teatrales (SATCH) at the Sala Talía in March 1958. Marta, a young widow, wants to keep her sons Andrés and Felipe in a state of permanent childhood to protect them from the outside world. She does so by repeating and promoting rituals, games, and subsistence strategies in a crumbling house, selling off her property bit by bit to maintain a semiaristocratic lifestyle, of which only an old servant is left who carries some of the family secrets. The play chronicles the rebellion of Andrés, the oldest son, who tries to escape the asphyxiating fate imposed upon him by Marta, and the invasion of the others, vulgar foreigners, Italian immigrants who come from outside to break up the family's fragile order and bring a fresh breeze of brute, seductive humanity. This intrusion coincides with the boys' sexual awakening, which to a large extent provokes the crisis.

Relations between social classes are an integral part of life outside the closed world of the house, and much as the family tries to avoid it, those relations come knocking on the door in the form of Mottola, whom Wolff describes as "un hombretón rozagante y macizo" (a splendid specimen of a man). In the outside world can also be found, in the possession of their Aunt Laura, the secret Marta fears and that will liberate the boys, tearing them from the claustrophobic space created by their mother. The revelation that their father was a violent, abusive man obsessed with sexual purity, and not the ideal image Marta created for her children of an "afectuoso y fino" (affectionate and fine) man, breaks the routine of the family farce and creates an opportunity to renew the relations between its members and the world. Andrés recognizes this point: "Hemos vivido en un error, mamacita. Toda nuestra vida dedicada en mantener una ilusión . . . , la más destructiva de las ilusiones: creer que podíamos desafiar la realidad, ¡y tú ves! . . . No pudiste detenerla. Se cuela por todos los huecos" (We have been living a lie, Mommy. Our whole lives to maintain an illusion . . . the most destructive of all illusions: to believe that we could defy reality, and you see? We couldn't stop it. It's coming in through all the cracks).

Although some critics considered this play somewhat lacking, it did attract interest. In *Mansión de lechuzas,* Wolff begins to articulate his symbolic universe and explore the techniques of psychological realism–or more properly, psychosocial realism, to account for not only its modes of representation but also the combination of individual and social forces unleashed upon the stage.

In *Discípulos del miedo,* staged in Santiago by Teatro Experimental de la Universidad de Chile (TEUCH) at Sala Antonio Varas in August 1958, Wolff moved in a new direction. Matilde, head of a lower-class household, feels so besieged by the specter of poverty that she pushes the entire family into her plans for social betterment. The solution, and her chimera, is to buy a sweater factory. Without knowing much about business, obtaining bank loans secured by a small store that has been their livelihood for years, she prepares to take this brave step that will change their lives. Jorge, the eldest son, wants like his mother to be important and rich, but his methods are petty fraud and showing off. His brother, Ricardo, is an unambitious, conformist mechanic who likes to work but does not want to join the rat race; he would rather be poor but happy. Their sister, the youngest, looks for true love but is forced by her mother to leave the man she loves and become engaged to a wealthier boy.

The family enters a crisis when Jorge comes home with the young daughter of a rich family and says he wants to marry her. This announcement coincides with the need to complete the factory purchase and the discovery that Juan, the father, has lost their savings in an "investment" in a mining company. In trying to realize his wife's ambitions, he has been cheated and ruined. Excusing himself, he says about the man he lent money to: "Parecía honrado, mujer" (He seemed honorable, dear). The family breaks apart. Juan dies, and Matilde goes to live with Ricardo, whom she scorns. In this play the problems of the lower classes–money, the desire for social ascension, and the ethical dilemmas involved in the options of social mobility—are joined by contact with the other, from a wealthier class.

As the culmination in a series of experiments combining similar elements, *Parejas de trapo* (Rag Couples), which won first prize in the Instituto de Teatro de la Universidad de Chile (ITUCH) Competition of 1959 and premiered in Santiago at Sala Antonio Varas in March 1960, goes one step further and shows the consequences of a marriage between Jaime, a social-climbing middle-class employee turned entrepreneur, and Cristina, the "rebellious" daughter of a landowner, whom he needs to support in a lifestyle that exceeds his possibilities. His management of a marketing office that appears to have no precise objective is reduced to a series of gesticulations designed, according to his partner Charlie, "Para tirarte facha delante de la familia de tu mujer.... El día que inauguramos este palacio trajiste la caravana de parientes a admirar lo bien que te iba yendo" (To show off in front of your wife's family.... The day we inaugurated this palace you brought a whole procession of relatives to see how successful you were). The gradual dilapidation of the workplace and the deteriorating relationships among the characters as a result of Jaime's manipulation of his colleagues lead to economic and moral ruin. To solve his perennial financial crisis he goes to Tolín, the naive partner who loves and admires him most, and ends up stealing from him. He seduces Charlie's girlfriend to compensate for his insecurities and to feel lord and owner of the world they share.

Into this context enters a European, a Czechoslovakian war refugee who is seen as a salvation, prey for Jaime and his unwilling partners to swindle out of some easy money. The mores and work ethic shown by Jan Balik, the glass manufacturer, contrast with the values of the local "businessmen." Balik trusts fully in his technical abilities and his art. He plans to reach his goal of economic comfort by the long route of dedicated hard work. At the moment of crisis he says to Cristina: "Todavía tengo mis manos... Es lo único que no perdí en seis años de guerra y diez años sin patria" (I still have my hands... It's the only thing I didn't lose in six years of war and ten years without a homeland). Jaime and his partners, on the other hand, live off the chimera of making the most possible money with the least possible effort, without possessing any ostensible skill to do so. This grotesque and vain illusion has its origins in the social incompatibility of Jaime and his wife, and above all in the underlying competition with her father, Don Jorge, and her brother, members of a family of landowners and part of the old rich, accustomed to controlling the destiny of others.

Don Jorge's tone of contempt in all his offers to "help" makes them impossible to accept. Jaime, whose honor and virility are threatened by his father-in-law, considers every maneuver to solve his money problems as an act of humiliating subjugation. This conflict arises in the framework of a culture of suppliers and beautiful idle women who fulfill a reproductive role and adorn the home.

In Wolff's first three plays the pressures of money and material conditions, expressed in the anxiety to preserve or acquire a certain lifestyle, ultimately define a notion of happiness for the characters in terms of security and economic well-being and uphold a social order that—though claustrophobic—assures class reproduction. Being unable to acquire the right values and social position leads to failure or disaster. But simply adhering to the ideologies of social triumph, reflected in money, to the detriment of love and human solidarity, leads to loneliness, disaffection, and anguish.

A different dynamic is apparent in *Niñamadre* (A Touch of Blue), which premiered in Concepción, Sala Maccabi, in April 1962 and was given the critics' prize for the best play of the year. Polla, the female protagonist, is an ingenue stigmatized by a series of past relationships with men who took advantage of her fears. Redeemed by love, however, she does not consider the past an impediment to happiness; but Pablo, her current partner, does. Polla is expecting a child that he does not want. He does not wish to marry her or take responsibility for the baby. The son of a prostitute from whom he escaped at the age of twelve, Pablo projects his own fears and insecurities onto his lover: "La Polla no es para madre... La recogí de la calle" (Polla is not the mother type... I picked her up off the street), he says to Paulina, their landlady, toward the end of the play. Paulina, acting as a kind of psychoanalyst, obliges Pablo to confess that his resentment and obsession with Polla's past are attributable to his relationship with his own mother. When this fact becomes apparent, she says to him: "Siento gran piedad por Ud. joven... Ha estado viviendo cuatro años con una mujer llena de ternura... un hermoso ser humano... y no ha podido ver en ella más que a una cualquiera... ¡Qué pérdida de tiempo!" (I feel great pity for you, young man... For four years you have been living with a woman who is full of tenderness... a beautiful human being... and all you can see is a slut... What a waste of time!).

The conflict between Polla, who has a last opportunity to give life, and her lover, who is fighting his own childhood ghosts, takes place in a dilapidated boardinghouse. Once "una buena propiedad de un promisorio barrio de arrabal residencial" (a good property in an up-and-coming suburban neighborhood), it is now "sólo un rincón de adobe y polvo que resiste difícilmente el abandono de la civilización" (just a corner of adobe and dust trying to hold out against the

Scene from a 1982 Teatro Universidad Católica production of Wolff's 1960 play, Parejas de trapo (Rag Couples; published in 1988), about the unhappy marriage of a social-climbing entrepreneur and his wealthy wife (from María Teresa Zegers Nachbauer, 25 años de teatro en Chile, 1999; W. E. B. Du Bois Library, University of Massachusetts, Amherst)

abandonment of civilization). Eight characters move about this stage, five of them having ended up living there as a result of their own personal dramas. Three come from the outside: Hans Potte is a weekly visitor, a habitué; the shady Victor, the youngest character, comes once to visit his Aunt Ana, who supports him and pays for his tuition at a university that he is not actually attending; and Rufo is a neighbor and friend of Pablo. Again, a foreign character appears and, like Mottola and Jan Balik, acts as a foil for the locals. The German Potte, a small farmer, unsubtly but sincerely offers his love to Paulina. His efforts unfold in an atmosphere of petty intrigue, suspicion, and manipulation by the characters, who fear abandonment and poverty as well as commitment. The play has a happy ending, with everyone making an effort to reconcile and restore order to the extent that it is possible in these circumstances.

Niñamadre was followed in October 1963 by the first staging of *Los invasores* (The Invaders) by the Theater Institute at the University of Chile. This work is the most acclaimed of Wolff's plays and the one that best embodies his poetics. Attacked by conservative critics as superficial and dramatically defective, the play nevertheless became a springboard to international recognition for Wolff. A staging in Lima, Peru, in 1965 was followed by productions throughout Latin America, the United States, and Europe. The subject of dozens of studies and publications, *Los invasores* touches the ethical and political nerve of social conflict in Chile and Latin America. From an aesthetic point of view, it represents a break with psychological realism and the clearest demonstration of what can be done with political theater with imagination and using representational media that may be considered at odds with the subject matter. The use of Surrealistic techniques that imbue the atmosphere and frame the story, as well as techniques of characterization taken from popular forms such as the circus, gives the whole a meaningful density.

Los invasores is the story of Lucas Meyer; his wife, Pietá; and their children, Bobby and Marcela. A factory owner, Meyer has given his family the material comforts represented in the "Meyer Mansion" as well as social status. The play begins as the parents are returning from a party. Pietá is in an exuberant mood. As soon as she enters the stage she exclaims: "Oh, Lucas, es maravilloso . . . es maravilloso! ¡La vida es un sueño . . . un sueño!" (Oh Lucas, it's wonderful . . . wonderful! Life is a dream . . . a dream!). Following a conversation in which she speaks of her fears about the future and a feeling of insecurity—a conversation that points up the couple's guilty conscience about the social situation of the poor people, the "ragged people from the garbage dumps"—they go to bed. A little while later, Meyer is awakened by a noise. Going downstairs, he realizes that someone has entered the house. Moments later he discovers China, a poor wretch who has broken a window and now stands before Meyer with a revolver, asking for bread. The invasion begins: Toletole, Ali Baba, and The Gimp come in. They are the advance guard of the poor people who come from the other side of the river to invade rich neighborhoods. Without encountering any real resistance, they destroy furniture and decorations, free servants, and force everyone else to work.

Meyer thinks that China and his people are taking vengeance for the death of a man called Mirelis, a partner or worker in the factory, whom Meyer has pushed to suicide with a false accusation of theft. He even calls China "Mirelis" and persists in seeing the invasion as a punishment. Finally Meyer breaks down and confesses his crime, and his wife wakes him up and tells him he is having a nightmare. Meyer, relieved, recovers his composure and walks around the house, hugging his children. But as he recounts part of the dream to his son, Bobby interrupts him to say that it is true, that the episode he is referring to actually happened the day before at his university. At that moment a window breaks, and a hand appears to open the bolt. Meyer's nightmare has ended, but the story has not.

Many have ascribed prophetic qualities to this play. During the ten years following its first staging, Chile underwent major reforms and political and social convulsions, beginning with the government of Eduardo Frei Montalva (1964–1970) and continuing with the government of Salvador Allende (1970–1973), which culminated with the coup d'état by General Augusto Pinochet and a military dictatorship that would check the hunger of new expectations by the masses. Social phenomena develop slowly, and a progressive intensification of social conflict was already apparent during the gestation of the play. Critics such as Hernán Vidal consider *Los invasores* a response by Wolff as a Catholic artist to the tensions of his time: a call to awareness for a bourgeoisie that has become more and more predatory and threatening to the social equilibrium. He quotes Wolff as saying:

> Dos tercios de los hombres de hoy viven sumergidos, y esos dos tercios no pueden esperar más. No se trata ya de condenar el problema a la ignorancia, envolviéndolo en banderas de un color u otro. Ese es un cómodo artificio para postergar la hora en que a la violencia de un lado del río, responderá la violencia del otro, si no actuamos inteligentemente, y hacemos un mundo mejor para todos, a la manera humana, con el espíritu, la razón y la ternura.

(Two thirds of today's people live submerged, and those two thirds have nothing to hope for. It's no longer a question of condemning ignorance and wrapping it in flags of one color or another. That is a convenient artifice that only puts off the time when violence on one side of the river will be met by violence on the other side of the river, unless we act intelligently and create a better world for all, as humans, with spirit, reason, and tenderness.)

Although *Los invasores* appears to attack Chile's problems in the early 1960s and exploits the potential of the theater to dramatize collective situations, the resonance of the play goes much further. It is written in a dense literary language, with techniques that open up many nuances, where language encounters history. In the context of what several critics have said, a purely psychological approach to this play is insufficient. Wolff seeks to put the bourgeois unconscious onstage as a class that expresses itself in enigmatic speeches charged with allusions. But it is also possible to look at the play from the point of view of postcolonial criticism. The people on the other side of the river are not only the poor, working-class, disadvantaged masses but represent a complex ethnic otherness exploited by the group of European descent such as Lucas Meyer. The rabble have only nicknames: China, Toletole, Ali Baba, The Gimp, The Marshal. They are referred to as "las obreras feas" (ugly working-class women), a "sucia recua de hombres" (dirty pack of men), "la manada maloliente" (stinking rabble), "crápulas" (drunks), "criminales" (criminals), "reptiles" (reptiles), and "pobre diablos" (poor devils). These designations dehumanize the group, converting them into a mass of monstrous delinquents who can be exploited and mistreated, like Caliban from *The Tempest*, who never attains dignity as a man.

A six-year silence followed *Los invasores*, during which Wolff dedicated himself to his profession as an engineer and to assimilating the unforeseen triumph of his play. Having by this time become one of the most respected playwrights in Latin America, Wolff wrote *El signo de Caín* (The Mark of Cain), first staged in Santiago, Teatro del Callejón de la Sala Mozart, in 1969. It received the Theater Critics Award the same year. Although it can be considered a lesser work, it is of interest when read as part of the corpus of plays written by Wolff during the 1960s and 1970s. Divided into four scenes that take place in "una habitación pobre y estrecha en el tercer piso de una casa antigua de clase media modesta" (a poor, narrow room on the third floor of an old, modest middle-class house), the play has only four characters: two couples brought together by a long-standing friendship between the two men, Portus and Joaquín, now thirty-five years old. The play examines the situation of one who refuses to live the life that is expected of him by his social class and merit.

At the beginning of the play, Joaquín comes to look for his admired Portus, now a lone wolf who survives in an attic with his lover Charito, a lower-class woman who looks after him. Why Portus chooses to live in marginality, drinking tea, smoking, and doing translations for an old friend, and why he has chosen to set up a household with a lower-class woman and his illegitimate son, is the mystery of the play. Gradually it becomes clear that the reason is a political disappointment. Portus was betrayed by his union brothers and since then has found no justification to continue functioning within a social structure that he cannot change. He uses several Friedrich Nietzsche–inspired intellectual arguments to explain his decision. Joaquín and his wife, Leonor, come to find him and take him back to the world where he belongs. They want him to realize his potential, and they offer him economic incentives. At the same time as he refuses to be tempted, he feels that this couple has come to disturb his order, his life choices, and that they have wounded his lover, who is in a weaker position, since his return to his class would mean her leaving his world. There is no room for a Charito in the place to which Portus would return. A series of confrontations ensues, and he continues to refuse. But Leonor has begun to seduce Charito with promises of help for her son and a better situation. Only once the final revelations have occurred, creating a truer image of the characters, can there be a return to the order that was upset by these presences from the past.

These revelations, unknown to the public, are in fact known to the characters. What they are arguing about is not what it seems at first. Leonor is fighting the ghost of a young Portus, who wields an influence on her husband through a love that she cannot overcome. Joaquín seeks to divest himself of the precepts he learned from Portus, which do not allow him to live in ignorance of the world's conflicts.

The theme of Cain in *Los invasores* continues in this play as a leitmotiv. In the relationship between Cain and Abel, Portus sees what constitutes human relations in a violent bourgeois society. This figure also defines Portus's behavior. Joaquín reproaches him:

> Quiero llevar una vida normal . . . Realizarme plenamente; sin escrúpulos, sin dudas . . . ¿Qué no puedes dejarme en paz? Todas esas historias que me contabas de Caín y Abel. Abel, el sacrificio inocente de su pasión de bondad, y Caín, el santo perverso, el conocedor risueño de las debilidades del hombre, el jugador divertido con su propia capacidad de maldad . . . todas esas locuras . . . me han estado persiguiendo todos estos años.

(I want to lead a normal life . . . To feel fulfilled; without scruples, without doubts . . . You can't leave me alone? All these stories you told me about Cain and Abel. Abel, the innocent victim of his passion for goodness, and Cain, the perverse saint, smiling connoisseur of human weaknesses, the player entertained by his own capacity for evil . . . all those things . . . have been pursuing me all these years.)

But Portus will not allow the conflict to be resolved, and each character returns to his own path. Even while recognizing his own lies about his motives for dropping out of his job and social circle, Portus does not feel redeemed, nor does he redeem the world from which he comes.

Another Wolff character who does not seek redemption is El Merluza. On the contrary, this central character of *Flores de papel* (Paper Flowers, performed and published in 1970), another of Wolff's masterpieces, seeks to redeem himself in his own way. This play won the prestigious Casa de las Américas Prize in Havana, Cuba, in 1970 and the Critics' Prize for best foreign play in Argentina. It premiered in Santiago at Sala Mozart in November 1970. The play once again explores the theme of invasion and relations between the middle class and the poor. The setting is the "living de pequeño departamento suburbano, arreglado con esmero, con mano femenina, confortable, íntimo" (living room of a small suburban apartment, nicely decorated with a feminine touch, comfortable and intimate). Into this little nest enter Eva, described as "40, bien vestida, con medida elegancia" (40, well dressed, with an elegant demeanor) and El Merluza (The Hake), who is "30, zarrapastroso, sucio, despeinado, flaco, pálido" (30, a dirty, skinny, pallid tramp with messy hair). He has helped Eva bring home her bags from the supermarket, and when she hands him a bill as a tip, he asks first for a cup of tea and then for asylum from two acquaintances who are waiting outside to finish him off. As they talk, Eva becomes curious about this character and decides to let him stay for the night. But El Merluza stays longer, and she allows herself to be seduced without his making any actual effort.

As Eva's desire grows, El Merluza begins to alter her living space drastically. He replaces the decorations with flowers made out of newspaper, gets rid of the canary and its cage, and destroys the furniture and "remakes" it to his taste without finishing it. As this process evolves, Eva's identity breaks down. He responds to her love with evasion, to her propositions with discreet rejection. She implores him for tenderness, and when in desperation she tries to throw him out, it is too late. He puts off his departure until she is completely at his mercy. The final step is to dress Eva as a bride, destroy her dress, and remake it with pieces of curtain, paper, and upholstery. Once the confident, elegant lady seen at the beginning of the play has become a grotesque figure, he takes her back to his world across the river.

Like Portus, El Merluza wants nothing to do with Eva's world. He is not there to keep her apartment, to become the gigolo of a mature woman who paints flowers at the Botanical Gardens and is prepared to do anything for love. El Merluza wants to transform Eva, remake her in his own image, force her to "Renunciar a su propia identidad en beneficio de la identidad del prójimo, hasta que la identidad propia y la identidad del otro y la propia identidad . . . Propia . . . Identidad . . . Del prójimo . . . Identidad . . . Propia . . . ¿no cree?" (Renounce your own identity for others' identity, until your identity and others' own identity and your identity . . . own . . . identity . . . others . . . own . . . don't you think?). Once the process is complete he takes her from her middle-class paradise to the hell of garbage dumps, to the river where "en las noches de plenilunio, cuando el río viene cuajado de muebles rotos, mucha gente al caer, se ha roto el espinazo" (under the full moon, when the river is clotted with broken furniture, many people have fallen and broken their backs).

Although he takes Eva with him, he does not seem to be much interested in affection, passion, or sex, at least not as she has proposed it. One never sees what El Merluza really wants; as his name indicates, he is as slippery as a fish. He does not seem to have a fixed identity. His mother nicknamed him Beto, and Eva wants him to use that name instead of El Merluza. She is always asking him "¿Quién es usted, Beto? ¿De dónde sacó eso? ¡Usted es múltiple! ¡Realmente multiplc!" (Who arc you, Beto? Where did you get that from? You have many faces. Really!). Later she says, "Yo sé que no eres lo que pareces o lo que pretendes parecer" (I know you are not what you seem or what you pretend to seem), and asks, "Si fueras sólo el pobre vagabundo que aparentas ser, no podríamos siquiera entablar esta conversación, ¿no te parece?" (If you were only the poor vagabond you pretend to be, we would not even be having this conversation, don't you think?). Eva needs to discover that the frog is actually a prince, as in a fairy tale; but her desire to give herself to romance collides with El Merluza's merciless logic, with a kind of demented and cruel rationality that is always putting up more obstacles and putting off the moment of consummation of the relationship Eva wants to believe is possible.

Technically, there is an appearance of stylized realism, but both the dramatic conflict and the language evolve in such a way that they exceed more conventional structures, in terms of character and believability of the plot. In this sense *Flores de papel* has a Brechtian

Ana Carballosa in a 1988 Miami-Dade Community College production of Wolff's 1963 play, Los invasores *(The Invaders, published in 1970), in which a group of poor people from the garbage dumps break into the home of a factory owner (photograph by Marceles-Daconte; from* Latin American Theatre Review, *volume 22 [Fall 1988]; Thomas Cooper Library, University of South Carolina)*

thrust. *Flores de papel* triumphed at the most intense moment of Chile's social and political conflict. Seven years passed, four after the violent coup of 1973, before Wolff reappeared on the Chilean stage with the play *Kindergarten,* which he calls a comedy, in 1977. The use of asphyxiating places reappears: the setting is "Una salita de estar, en la trastienda de un negocio de venta de paraguas" (A living room in the shopkeeper's quarters behind an umbrella shop), where two sixty-odd brothers, Toño and Mico, live together in a symbiotic relationship that combines protection, adversion, and play in a neurotic pattern. The relationship is interrupted by Meche, a sister they have not seen in ten years, and whom Toño does not wish to receive because he senses the threat to their permanence. In her presence a revision of the past takes place through small reenacted fragments from childhood and bits of history told as complaints, which are immediately held up to ridicule by the others and not taken seriously as a source of suffering.

Meche brings the past with her, and at first the brothers have difficulty accepting this intrusion of memory. They live in a permanent present, obsessed with the problem of survival and the scarce resources available to them. Originally a solvent family, they are left with nothing but their pride in the name Sánchez-Uriarte, their threadbare bathrobes, and old slippers.

The oldest brother, Toño, is a man with an aristocratic mentality who appears to have been the wealthiest but now depends entirely on Mico, owner of the umbrella shop, for whom Toño has nothing but contempt but who pays for the housing and living expenses. As the play progresses, these fragments of memory that appear veiled in games, sour jokes, and reciprocal derision gradually sketch out a story that the audience needs to complete. The boundaries between dramatic truth and comedic lies are not quite clear. What spectators can establish are the ties of dependency and the struggle to assimilate new situations in such a way that they do not upset the fragile balance of relations between the brothers.

A comedy of reconciliation, encounter, and mutual acceptance, *Kindergarten* was followed by *El sobre azul* (The Pink Slip, performed in 1978), a "farsa en dos actos inútiles, sobre el inútil acto de escribir farsa" (farce in two useless acts on the useless act of writing farce). Moving completely away from his earlier plays of psychological introspection and following the requirements of his chosen genre, Wolff comments on "las maravillas de la libre empresa" (the wonders of free enterprise). In response to a drop in productivity at an unspecified factory, the manager and his deputy Cereceda come up with possible ways to make people work as if "possessed," in a work force that they consider undisciplined and hedonistic, a product of "current laws" that "wrap the employees in a sybaritic sense of security." Cereceda says, "Y si lo duda, vaya a las poblaciones obreras, a ver a los hombres sentados frente a las puertas de sus casas. El rebalse del empleo pleno permite que dediquen las mejores horas al cuidado de su salud, tomando un sol que los reconforta" (And if you doubt it, go to the workers' developments, look at the men sitting on their front stoops. The trickle-down effect of full employment allows them to spend the best times of their lives looking after their health, taking sun for their well-being). Together the manager and Cereceda decide to use a pink-slip tactic as a threat to raise productivity.

To experiment with its effects, their first test is with Recereda, the other deputy manager, a kind of clone of the first, but he is too smart to fall for it and turns the situation around, using the pink slip to fire the manager. The manager, confused by the twisted arguments of Cereceda and Recereda, submits to the game, though not without some anxiety. To resolve the situation Cereceda, the author of the termination, is appointed manager, but since he is not actually a manager, the termination becomes ineffective. The manager doubts whether Cereceda will want to remain in the position, and to protect himself, writes out a pink slip for him. Recereda, now in charge of both pink slips, tries to eliminate Cereceda but does not succeed. The manager takes charge of the situation and writes out a pink slip for Recereda. The game of ritual expulsions continues, with rhetorical solutions and ever more aggressive exchanges with the factory workers until—in the absence of any solution—they decide to start working.

Although *El sobre azul* is a slight work, the pink-slip motif exhibits in a quasi-Brechtian style the inner workings of the neoliberal system instituted in Chile and elsewhere. The economic problems of poor countries are solved with discourse, using new names for old problems. Unemployment becomes "the trickle-down effect of full employment."

Also in 1978 Wolff produced *Espejismos* (Mirages), a four-character play that takes place in the "living-comedor de un departamento moderno en un barrio de clase media. Decorado funcionalmente, devota cierto mal gusto" (living-dining room of a modern apartment in a middle-class neighborhood. It is decorated in a functional style in somewhat bad taste). It is the home of Martin and his wife, Maite. He is a fifty-year-old businessman, and she is forty-eight. With them lives Ines, seventeen, who is Maite's niece. The girl has neither friends nor boyfriend. She writes poetry, is considered strange by her aunt, and admires her uncle boundlessly. As for the couple, they live a routine life with no children, share few activities, and have a limited sex life. The situation moves rather obviously toward the typical crisis of a mature man attracted by a girl who adores him. A portrait of an irresponsible girl who is incapable of understanding the consequences of her words and gestures, who enters with an innocent ease the world of a dissatisfied man, *Espejismos* is a minor work that does not explore in any depth the disturbing daydreams of intergenerational contact and is resolved in a facile ending.

In *José* (performed in 1980, published in 1990) Wolff examines the situation of a twenty-eight-year-old man who returns to Chile after spending seven years in various parts of the United States. He finds a family full of tensions, and reintegration is not easy because the values governing the family have been redefined according to foreign models that have nothing to do with the tradition of solidarity and generosity that he was used to. But José has already seen the consequences of this lifestyle and can see where his family, and new Chilean society, is headed. When his grandfather is expelled from the house for bothering Raul, José's brother-in-law and head of the household, it seems to José to break a fundamental rule of human cohabitation. Raul is a nouveau-riche owner of a shampoo factory, married to José's sister Estela. He is a typical Wolffian businessman, a mix of pragmatism and arrogance, with a certain capacity for self-examination and an enormous capacity for rationalization. From the outset he feels an instinctive antipathy toward José because of his style of dressing and acting, which Raul sees as hippie or communist. Isabel, the mother, and José's younger sister, Trini, are the most receptive, but they cannot understand what has happened to the brother who departed with so much optimism on his northern adventure and has returned a defeated and wounded saint with goals and values they now find foreign.

When José questions their values and makes decisions that interfere with the order Raul has imposed and enforced with fear, the conflict is unleashed. José brings his grandfather back from the hospice and puts him in his room. Then he confronts his sisters and his mother, questioning the life they lead, focused on money and status and devoid of love and generosity. He starts visiting the workers in his brother-in-law's factory, helping them with their problems. He looks after a dying friend of Estela who was known for being easy. José's behavior is seen as a provocation to the head of the household and the house rules. Emerging at the same time are the conflicts of Estela, who has not been able to have children and has to accept that her husband has a lover; and Trini, who is going to marry a man she does not love in order to ensure her survival. The mother's loyalties are divided, and she does not want any conflict. The play ends with José and the grandfather being thrown out of the house and going out to find a new place in the world. Raul remains in charge of his territory.

Although the play touches upon the problems of exile and return, José does not appear to have a political past. Still, the play demonstrates the conflicts that arose within families when groups of exiles from the Pinochet regime began to return in the early 1980s and confronted—with their experiences in the mythical world of North America and Europe—those who had stayed and assimilated the new rules of the game.

Wolff's next play is *Alamos en la azotea* (Poplars on the Roof, performed in 1981). In this play, conceived as a comedy, Wolff returns to a marginal scene: "Una habitación en la mansarda de una casa de pension, en un barrio residencial venido a menos, en la periferia cercana al centro de la capital" (A room in the attic of a boardinghouse, in a residential neighborhood in decline, on the periphery of the capital city's downtown core). There are four characters: Moncho, Angela, Roberto, and Wanda. Moncho, sixty-five, is the owner of the room. He lives in it and earns subsistence wages cutting paper napkins. The room reflects the disorder of a man who lives alone and cares little about his surroundings. Moncho was once married to Wanda, with whom he owned a hair salon. He was known then as Valentino, a hairdresser in the old style in terms of appearance and methods. He has been separated for thirteen years and has not worked as a hairdresser for ten years. The separation came about when Wanda received an inheritance that, according to Moncho, gave her an edge that placed him in a humiliating position. Since then he has lived on business deals that go bad and grand talk of impossible ventures, while he suffers worsening poverty and declining health. All he has left is an obstinate pride and resentment toward his former wife that he tries to hide behind jokes and irony.

Moncho's son, Roberto, and daughter-in-law, Angela, intervene with a proposal for reconciliation. They believe that Wanda is still interested in patching things up and wants to have Moncho back in her life. At first Moncho rejects the proposal roundly; then, as they soften him up, begins to place conditions on it that are impossible to meet. He wants to go back to the hair salon and reestablish his Valentino persona. He even proposes a haircutting trial with his daughter-in-law that fails miserably. His penchant for offending Wanda and feeling offended by her appears not to have diminished over time. With the experiment on the verge of failure, only Wanda's generosity and understanding that Moncho is a deeply wounded man can save the situation. For his part, Moncho must recognize that the world has changed. Wanda manages a successful business because she is up on the latest styles and techniques. Moncho, however, sticks to the old formulas his father taught him and has lost his touch. At the end, despite all the obstacles, affection triumphs with an arrangement that allows both of them to maintain their dignity.

As in the previous play, Wolff explores the crisis of maturity with the desires, sense of loss, and fears of men who thought they were controlling their destiny and suddenly find themselves marginalized by progress and the emergence of new generations that claim a leading role. Martin's sudden physical attraction for his niece, and Moncho's "joking" erotic insinuations toward his daughter-in-law, mark a line of insecurity and fear at the eclipse of the sexually attractive male. These men lose their small allotments of social and economic power to emerging new forces such as women in the labor force who were once, under more traditional values, subjected to men's designs and relegated to acting upon a private stage.

In 1984 Wolff premiered *La balsa de la Medusa* (The Raft of the Medusa), which some critics consider part of a trilogy with *Los invasores* and *Flores de papel*. This three-act, seventeen-character play takes place within a mansion; but the characters turn the large space into a claustrophobic one as time passes and they are obliged to remain inside. Leonardo, a strange character, invites a group of upper-middle-class guests to a social gathering at his house. The visitors are announced by a group of wretches who live in the ravine near the property and by a pack of dogs that bark furiously at the mere hint of a human presence. When the guests arrive, the host disappears into his rooms and leaves Conrado, the butler, in charge. Conrado excuses his employer's absence by telling the guests that he had to look after "an urgent matter." The group feels rather disoriented but takes over the house and has Conrado wait on them. Wolff gives the guests "foreign" names (Sergetti, Goldberg) combined with Spanish or Catalonian ones (Garcia, Serrano-Soler), while the group of beggars are called simply Him, Her, The Cop, The Gimp. The wretches reappear on stage from time to time and are thrown out by the butler. Added to the strange initial situation and the dream-like atmosphere in the room is the fact that when the guests wish to return home, a series of threatening signs from the outside prevent them from leaving: in the half-light, someone begins shooting and killing women and children, while someone bombs the bridge that would have taken the guests back to the city. Outside is the misery, the vicious dogs, and the uncontrollable violence of the others.

As these unexpected events unfold and inconveniences arise, differences and vulnerabilities emerge. The personality of each guest is revealed, and conflicts break out not only between couples (petty resentment, contempt, lack of affection) but also between members of the group (anti-Semitism, homophobia). Leonardo observes all, briefly appearing when his guests are sleeping to exchange views with Conrado as to how the situation is evolving. His is the gaze of God's intermediary, depressed and alone, who cannot understand these beings in his own house. At the beginning of the second act he says to Conrado: "Es extraño que su sueño pueda ser tan . . . candoroso, y la vida en que se afirma tan . . . violenta . . . Como si fuesen dos humanidades diferentes" (How strange that their dream can be so . . . straightforward, and their lives so . . . violent . . . As if there were two different humanities).

As tensions mount, the ties of solidarity and standards of behavior begin to loosen. Faced with an apocalyptic image brandished by Goldberg in this environment falling apart, Garcia, the small businessman, turns threatening and shouts: "Cállate, judío!" (Shut up, you Jew!). They pursue him: "Muerte al judío!" (Death to the Jew!). They fall to their knees and begin to pray in Latin. As the prayer ends, a violent light enters the room, and Leonardo comes in as "un majestuoso y espléndido hombre de mundo" (a majestic and splendid man of the world). He holds a joking exchange with his irritated and amazed guests, trying to have them believe that they have hallucinated the episode as a result of their guilty consciences, and that the time they have spent in his house has been a matter of minutes, not days. A hurried and reproachful exodus ensues. While Conrado picks up the mess, Leonardo announces the arrival of the next group, as in a never-ending story: "Sí, ordena un poco, que ya llegarán los próximos" (Yes, do tidy up a bit, the next lot is on its way).

Social differences are presented only tangentially in this play. The poor, the violent world of poverty and repression, are outside, an element in absentia. What is played out inside the house is the moral and emotional exhaustion of a group of people who because of their social status feel that they are entitled to all kinds of privileges and services, from vested interests to instant gratification. When pleasure is deferred or they feel unsure of their status, their aggression comes out.

Wolff's next play, *Háblame de Laura* (Tell Me About Laura, performed in 1986), is a deeply disquieting play along the lines of *Flores de papel*. The dramatic intensity it achieves in the interaction of Cata and Alberto, the two characters, is attributable to the use of language and dramatic strategies deployed in a way that keeps the spectator in complete uncertainty about what is unfolding. It is impossible to distinguish between truth and fiction, literalness and metaphor, in the characters' exchanges.

The story is a simple one. In a poor, dilapidated apartment, "puesto de cualquier manera, desordenada, desganadamente" (cluttered and decorated any which way), lives Alberto, "cuarentón, algo gordo, blando, desaliñado" (fortyish, somewhat overweight and flabby, dull), and his mother, Cata, "sesentona, viste bata desaliñada y pantuflas" (sixtyish, wearing an undistinguished dressing gown and slippers). Alberto works in a shoe store. With his salesman's salary, he maintains his mother, but their economic situation is disastrous, and a sense of insecurity permeates both their lives. Still, the two have invented a recipe for survival: they are constantly playing jokes on each other, acting out episodes from life, and inventing imaginary characters. As the play opens, Alberto is tired and eating cookies sleepily in front of the television. His mother comes in, bringing him a cup of hot chocolate that turns out to be undrinkable saltwater. This prank marks the beginning of a kind of combat in which the two provoke each other, fighting verbally with cruel, offensive comments or threats, until they are exhausted. Then they either watch television as a means of distraction while they prepare for the next encounter, or Alberto becomes tender and makes ambiguous declarations of love to his mother. He often treats her as if she were his wife, opening up an inevitable suspicion of incest. At other times, to make her jealous, he tells stories about other women, stories of improbable rapes that show how Alberto has difficulty relating to sex and affection.

One of these love stories is about Laura, "una tímida y fea niña" (a shy and unattractive girl) who thinks she is "inservible" (useless) and shares his passion for graveyards. They develop a relationship there: "A la niña Laura le gusta ver las tumbas; al niño Alberto también. Encontramos de inmediato un gusto en común" (Laura likes graves, and so does Alberto. We discovered immediately that we had this in common). At various times Alberto elaborates on Laura, developing her character until one day he announces that they are to be married. Cata throws him out of the house in a fit of jealousy, only to be reconciled a moment later and console him for the suffering she senses within him. The other focus of narrative attention is Lozada, the shoe store owner. It is never clear whether toward the end of the play Lozada fires Alberto, even though Cata touts him as the best salesman, but Alberto does show aggression toward his boss, recounting a story about raping Lozada's daughter. Then, when Cata contrasts Alberto's attitude with his father's and remembers the amorous passion she felt for him, Alberto replies: "¡Entonces, déjame contarte de cómo me violé, hoy, a la hija del cobrador de gas!" (So, let me tell you the story about how I raped the meterman's daughter today!).

Paradoxically, despite these constant exchanges, the monologues and excessive playfulness make it clear that there is no real communication between these two people, that they never truly open up to each other, and that they live in the perpetual solitude of everyday ritual. Language turns into raving and exasperation, and the characters never manage to say what they are trying to communicate. *Háblame de Laura* is one of Wolff's most theatrical plays in terms of its postulates about reality, awareness of the fictional quality of existence, elements of metatheatricality, and the way it conveys the hidden desperation behind trivial exchanges and attempts at evasion with which people respond to the sense of failure that emerges from the loss of authentic personal and social goals.

Seven years later, after a period of working in his business activities, Wolff reappeared on the Chilean theater scene with *Invitación a comer* (Invitation to Dinner) in May 1993. He directed the play himself. Wolff has expressed his disappointment with the staging of his plays, either because of interpretation or production values in an environment with budget restrictions.

With *Invitación a comer,* Wolff goes back to a more realistic canon, a decision dictated by the subject mat-

Wolff in the 1990s (from María Teresa Zegers Nachbauer, 25 años de teatro en Chile, 1999; W. E. B. Du Bois Library, University of Massachusetts, Amherst)

ter. The play is a direct ethical pronouncement on corruption in the business environment. Public sector, private sector, middlemen, all manage their commercial activities in a venial manner. Power plays, hierarchies, patronage, invitations, and indirect humiliations all form part of the unwritten rules of a culture that presents an honorable face of integrity and reacts with indignation to any suggestion of impropriety.

In this play Wolff depicts three couples who dine together because the husbands are planning a business deal. This deal is secretly destined to fail from the beginning because it has already been sealed with someone else. Moreover, alcohol unleashes tongues and desires during the dinner. Frustrations emerge, and the initial proposal moves into unexpected areas of privacy that the characters cannot control without conflict. The behavior observable in the handling of a potential business deal does not obey only the standards governing economic transactions, but is contaminated by personal actions and emotional relationships. After the ethical crisis has broken out, Wolff attempts to salvage the value of friendship and love as compensations in a world ruled by the predators of the wealthy classes, and the play ends almost happily.

One year later, in June 1994, Wolff premiered the play *Cicatrices* (Scars). Written for a bare stage, *Cicatrices* is an experimental work based explicitly on Johann Wolfgang von Goethe's novel *Elective Affinities* (1809). The characters are Ernesto and Olivia, a mature couple; their friend Germán; and Beatriz, Olivia's young niece. Germán, a fiftyish architect who has been rereading Goethe's novel, suggests to his friends that their situation is similar to the one described by Goethe. Says Ernesto: "El hecho es que Germán, dice que se reproducen las mismas condiciones de la novela . . . Pero eso no es todo, porque dice que en ella, un tipo invita a su casa a un amigo, como experto para aconsejarles a él y a su mujer, respecto a unos cambios que quieren hacer en la casa, y que ese amigo y su mujer, terminan acostándose" (The thing is that Germán says the same conditions in the novel are replicated . . . But that's not all. He says that in the novel, a guy invites a friend to his place as an expert to advise him and his wife on some renovations they want to make, and that the friend and his wife end up sleeping together). Germán laughingly replies, "Bueno, no dije 'acostándose,' porque no lo hacen" (Well, I didn't say 'sleeping together,' because they don't). A little later, Ernesto adds: "Y que solo falta, aquí, la tonta sobrina de la mujer, para que se cierre el círculo" (The only thing missing here is the wife's dumb niece, to close the circle). Naturally, Beatriz, "the dumb niece," arrives "unexpectedly." Ernesto becomes worried; Germán is entertained and tempts his friend to continue the game: "Probemos . . . ¿Total, que podemos perder? (Riendo) En la infinita perfección de nuestra corruptibilidad, en las infinitas gamas de nuestra imaginación pervertible, probemos. No nos corrompemos más ¿no?" (Let's try . . . What do we have to lose? [Laughing] In the infinite perfection of our corruptibility, in the infinite range of our pervertible imagination, let's try. We can't get any more corrupt, right?).

Although *Cicatrices* is a well-crafted play, it is clearly a rereading and conscious experimentation with forms of presentation that seek to attract a distant audience more interested in the intimate world than in a play with a social focus. The direct confrontation between the problems of love and the amoral nature of certain desires speaks more to a young audience, although three of the characters are mature and caught between guilt and fear of the unknown. In the struggle, Beatriz perishes, having lost the desire to live and succumbed to melancholy.

In 1995, following the premiere of Wolff's play *Claroscuro* (Chiaroscuro), Carmen Peña, his wife for more than forty years, died in a car accident. For three years following her death, Wolff suffered a complete writer's block; it seemed to him "grotesque" and "obscene" to write after this loss. He told interviewer Rodrigo Miranda in 2000, "No perdí interés en vivir, pero sí desapareció el estímulo que me impulsaba a crear. Me preguntaba: ¿para qué escribir? ¿Por qué mi presencia en la tierra?" (I didn't lose interest in living, but I did lose the drive to create. Why write? I asked myself. Why am I here on earth?).

Wolff's ensuing silence remained unbroken until 2000, when he reappeared with the play *Encrucijada* (Crossroads), written in 1998. He explained to Miranda, "No había estrenado otras piezas por un trauma que tuve por la muerte de mi mujer. Soy monógamo. Quizá porque me tocó una mujer que no me invitaba a otra cosa y se fue. Me hizo una jugada fea y ahí me dejó" (I had not come out with any more plays because of the trauma my wife's death caused me. I'm a monogamous man. Perhaps because I ended up with a woman who didn't invite me to be anything else, and then went away. She dealt me a bad hand and left me there). Although Wolff's theater has always been autobiographical, this play plumbs the depths of the emotions and terrors present in recent events of his life even more vigorously, as noted by Miranda.

Encrucijada received the José Nuez Martin literature award for theater. The plot is simple. The meeting between Sofia and Renato, a mature couple, opens up life options that neither had considered. Eight scenes tell the story of this meeting between a man and a woman that is to transform the lives of other characters. Sofia is rescued from a monotonous, limited existence as the relationship with Renato revitalizes her, while Renato rediscovers the possibilities of love with change and the potential for happiness. Love acts as a savior, and age is unimportant.

Wolff lives in a small town called Calera de Tango, south of Santiago. For Wolff, it is a place with both public historical importance, as the site of the earliest Jesuit churches, and personal significance, since it was where he lived with his first wife. Some years after she died he initiated a relationship with his sister-in-law, who had been left a widow, and whom he married in 1998. He continues to write and oversee new productions and revivals of his plays. In 2002 RiL published an anthology with ten of his plays, among them an unpublished work written in 2000 that has not yet been staged, called *Tras una puerta cerrada* (Behind a Closed Door). A monologue, titled *Cronicas de un edificio psicótico* (Chronicles of a Psychotic Building), also came out in 2001 in a university publication in Santiago.

In an interview with Pauline Salman in August 1993, Wolff was asked how much longer he intended to write, and he answered: "Me voy a morir con una pluma en la mano. Casi literal: Funciono con lápiz pasta, a mano. Necesito sentir el papel. Y después paso a máquina" (I will die with a pen in my hand. Literally: I write by hand, with a pencil. I need to feel the paper.

And then I type it up). When Salman asked what kind of life he would choose if he could live it over, he replied, "Una más dedicada a la literatura. Me metería también a otros géneros, el periodístico, por ejemplo. No estudiaría ingeniería, porque no soy un buen ingeniero químico, sino uno común y corriente" (A life more devoted to literature. I would explore other genres, for example journalism. I would not study engineering, because I'm not a good chemical engineer, just a regular one).

Egon Wolff has long been considered one of the most important writers for theater in Chile and Latin America. In the 1960s and 1970s, when many playwrights were involved in sometimes dubious experiments, Wolff remained a solid author who made language his core contribution to drama. He admits he never participated fully in the production side of his plays; at the same time, however, he has been highly sensitive to formal innovation. His evolution from psychological realism to poetic drama and his ability to mix social and political concerns with intimate insights have had a major impact on audiences, and his plays are continuously revived and admired by new generations of theatergoers.

Interviews:

Rafael Otano, "Egon Wolff: Un dramaturgo entre el nacimiento y el suicidio," *Mensaje*, no. 252 (September 1976): 443–445;

Pauline Salman, "Entrevista," *YA* (August 1993): 11;

Rodrigo Miranda, "Egon Wolff: El retorno del lobo," *Qué Pasa* (3 April 2000) <http://www.quepasa.cl/rcvista/2000/04/03/t-03.04.soc.LOBO.html>.

References:

Jacqueline Eyring Bixler, "Los juegos crueles de Egon Wolff: ¿Quién juega?" *Alba de América: Revista literaria*, 7 (July 1989): 245–261;

Bixler, "Language in/as Action in Egon Wolff's *Háblame de Laura*," *Latin American Theatre Review*, 23 (Fall 1989): 49–62;

Jennifer Boyd, "*Flores de Papel* as Criticism: The Artist and the Tradition," *Latin American Theatre Review*, 23 (Spring 1990): 7–12;

Catherine M. Boyle, "Egon Wolff's *La balsa de la Medusa*: Is the Bourgeoisie Waving or Drowning?" *Latin American Theatre Review*, 21 (Fall 1987): 43–52;

Pedro Bravo Elizondo, "Reflexiones de Egon Wolff en torno al estreno de José," *Latin American Theatre Review*, 14 (Spring 1981): 65–70;

Iván Carrasco, "*Flores de Papel* de Egon Wolff: La crisis de la identidad," *Revista Chilena de Literatura*, 20 (November 1982): 113–132;

Frank N. Dauster, "Concierto para tres: *Kindergarten* y el teatro ritual," *Caravelle-Cahiers du Monde Hispanique et Luso-Bresilien*, 40 (1983): 9–15;

Myra S. Gann, "Meaning and Metaphor in *Flores de Papel*," *Latin American Theatre Review*, 22 (Spring 1989): 31–36;

Norma Helsper, "The Ideology of Happy Endings: Wolff's *Mansión de Lechuzas*," *Latin American Theatre Review*, 26 (Spring 1993): 123–130;

Francisco Javier Higuero, "Metateatralidad y significado en la obra dramática de Egon Wolff," *Hispanic Journal*, 14 (Fall 1993): 131–143;

Esther P. Mocega-González, "El concepto de la revolución social en dos dramas de Egon Wolff," *Explicación de Textos Literarios*, 14 (1985–1986): 3–13;

Ronald C. Newton, "*Kindergarten* in Vancouver," *Latin American Theatre Review*, 15 (Spring 1982): 83–85;

Juan Andrés Piña, "El retorno de Egon Wolff," *Latin American Theatre Review*, 14 (Spring 1981): 61–64;

Diana Taylor, "Art and Anti-Art in Egon Wolff's *Flores de Papel*," *Latin American Theatre Review*, 18 (Fall 1984): 65–68;

Eduardo Thomas, "*Flores de Papel* de Egon Wolff: La sombra de la burguesía," *Revista Chilena de Literatura*, 30 (November 1987): 55–73;

José R. Varela, "Origen y función de la ambigüedad en *Flores de Papel* de Egon Wolff," *Gestos: Teoría y Práctica del Teatro Hispánico*, 2 (April 1987): 87–101;

Alvaro Vergara-Mery, "El miedo en *Los invasores* de Egon Wolff," *Hispanófila*, 127 (September 1999): 67–79;

Hernán Vidal, "Los invasores: Egon Wolff y la responsibilidad social del artista católico," in *La dramaturgia de Egon Wolff*, edited by Pedro Bravo Elizondo (Santiago: Nascimento, 1985), pp. 59–77;

María Teresa Zegers Nachbauer, *25 años de teatro en Chile* (Santiago: Ministerio de Educación, 1999).

Books for Further Reading

Acercamientos al teatro actual (1970–1995): Historia, teoría, práctica. Madrid: Iberoamericana / Frankfurt am Main: Vervuert, 1998.

Adler, Heidrun and Kati Röttger, eds. *Performance, pathos, política de los sexos.* Madrid: Iberoamericana / Frankfurt am Main: Vervuert, 1999.

Albuquerque, Severino. *Violent Acts: A Study of Contemporary Latin American Theatre.* Detroit: Wayne State University Press, 1991.

Andrade, Elba and Hilde F. Cramsie, eds. *Dramaturgas latinoamericanas contemporáneas: antología crítica.* Madrid: Verbum, 1991.

Arancibia, Juana A. and Zulema Mirkin, eds. *Teatro argentino durante el proceso (1976–1983).* Buenos Aires: Vinciguerra, 1992.

Arrom, José Juan. *El teatro de hispanoamérica en la época colonial.* Havana: Anuario Bibliográfico Cubano, 1956.

Arrom. *Historia de la literatura dramática cubana.* New Haven: Yale University Press, 1944.

Azor Hernandez, Ileana. *Teatro latinoamericano: siglo XX.* Havana: Pueblo y Educación, 1989.

Balderston, Daniel and Donna J. Guy, eds. *Sex and Sexuality in Latin America.* New York: New York University Press, 1997.

Bergmann, Emilie, ed. *Women, Culture, and Politics in Latin America.* Berkeley: University of California Press, 1990.

Boal, Augusto. *Theatre of the Oppressed,* translated by Charles A. McBride and Maria-Odilia Leal McBride. New York: Theatre Communications Group, 1985.

Bonilla, María and Stoyan Vladich. *El teatro latinoamericano en busca de su identidad cultural.* San José, Costa Rica: Cultur Art, 1988.

Bose, Christine E. and Edna Acosta-Belén, eds. *Women in the Latin American Development Process.* Philadelphia: Temple University Press, 1995.

Bravo-Elizondo, Pedro. *Teatro hispanoamericano de crítica social.* Madrid: Playor, 1975.

Brugal, Yana Elsa and Beatriz J. Rizk, eds. *Rito y representación: Los sistemas mágico-religiosos en la cultura cubana contemporáneo.* Madrid: Iberoamericana, 2003.

Castillo, Debra. *Talking Back: Toward a Latin American Feminist Criticism.* Ithaca, N.Y.: Cornell University Press, 1992.

Castillo, Susana, ed. *Las risas de nuestros medusas: teatro venezolano escrito por mujeres.* Caracas, Venezuela: Fundarte, 1992.

Books for Further Reading

Castro-Klarén, Sara, Sylvia Molloy, and Beatriz Sarlo, eds. *Women's Writing in Latin America.* Boulder, Colo.: Westview Press, 1991.

Cid Perez, José and Dolores Martí de Cid. *Teatro indoamericano colonial.* Madrid: Aguilar, 1973.

Cypess, Sandra Messinger. *La Malinche in Mexican Literature from History to Myth.* Austin: University of Texas Press, 1991.

Dauster, Frank. *Historia del teatro hispanoamericano: Siglos XIX y XX.* Mexico: Ediciones de Andrea, 1973.

Dauster, ed. *Perspectives on Contemporary Spanish American Theatre.* Lewisburg, Pa.: Bucknell University Press, 1996.

De la colonia a la postmodernidad: teoría teatral y crítica sobre teatro latinoamericano. Buenos Aires: Galerna, 1992.

Doménech, Fernando, ed. *Teatro breve de mujeres, siglos 17–20.* Madrid: Asociación de Directores de Escena, 1996.

Dubatti, Jorge A., ed. *Otro teatro después de Teatro Abierto.* Buenos Aires: Libros del Quirquincho, 1990.

Eidelberg, Nora and María Mercedes Jaramillo, eds. *Voces en escena: antología de dramaturgas latinoamericanas.* Medellín, Colombia: Editorial Universidad de Antioquia, 1991.

Epskamp, Kees P. *Theatre in Search of Social Change.* The Hague: CESO, 1989.

Escenarios de dos mundos: inventario teatral de Iberoamérica. Madrid: Centro de Documentación Teatral, 1988.

Espener, Maida Watson and Carlos José Reyes, eds. *Materiales para una historia del teatro en Colombia.* Bogotá: Instituto Colombiano de Cultura, 1978.

Fajardo, Ramón. *Rita Montaner: testimonio de una época.* Havana: Fondo Editorial Casa de las Américas, 1997.

Flores, Yolanda. *The Drama of Gender: Feminist Theater by Women of the Americas.* New York: Peter Lang, 2000.

Franco, Jean. *The Modern Culture of Latin America; Society and the Artist.* New York: Praeger, 1967.

Franco. *Plotting Women: Gender and Representation in Mexico.* New York: Columbia University Press, 1989.

Freire, Paulo. *Pedagogy of the Oppressed.* New York: Seabury, 1970.

Geirola, Gustavo. *Teatralidad y experiencias política en América Latina.* Irvine, Cal.: GESTOS, 2000.

Gladhart, Amalia. *The Leper in Blue: Coercive Performance and the Contemporary Latin American Theater.* Chapel Hill: University of North Carolina Press, 2000.

Guido, Beatriz. *Una madre.* Buenos Aires: Emecé, 1973.

Hurtado, María de la Luz. *Teatro chileno y modernidad: identidad y crisis social.* Irvine, Cal.: GESTOS, 1997.

Hurtado, Carlos Ochsenius, and Hernán Vidal, eds. *Teatro chileno de la crisis institucional: 1973–1980.* Santiago: CENECA, 1982.

Inclán, Gabriela and Felipe Galván, eds. *Teatro, mujer y Latinoamérica.* Puebla, Mexico: Tablado Iberoamericano, 2000.

Jones, Willis Knapp. *Behind Spanish American Footlights.* Austin: University of Texas Press, 1966.

Klein, Teodoro. *El actor en el Río de la Plata: de la colonia a la independencia nacional*. Buenos Aires: Asociación Argentina de Actores, 1984.

Klein. *Una historia de luchas: la Asociación Argentina de Actores*. Buenos Aires: La Asociación, 1988.

Larson, Catherine and Margarita Vargas, eds. *Latin American Women Dramatists: Theater, Texts, and Theories*. Bloomington: Indiana University Press, 1998.

Leal, Rine. *Breve historia del teatro cubano*. Havana: Letras Cubanas, 1980.

Leal. *La selva oscura: De los bufos a la neocolonial (Historia del teatro cubano de 1868 a 1902)*. Havana: Arte y Literatura, 1982.

Leal. *La selva oscura: Historia del teatro cubano desde sus orígenes hasta 1868*. Havana: Arte y Literatura, 1975.

Lindstrom, Naomi. *The Social Conscience of Latin American Writing*. Austin: University of Texas Press, 1998.

Lyday, Leon F. and George W. Woodyard, eds. *Dramatists in Revolt: the New Latin American Theatre*. Austin: University of Texas Press, 1976.

Márquez, Carlos. *Juana Sujo: impulsora del teatro contemporáneo venezolano*. Caracas: FUNDARTE, 1996.

Masiello, Francine. *Between Civilization & Barbarism: Women, Nation, and Literary Culture in Modern Argentina*. Lincoln: University of Nebraska Press, 1992.

Mercedes Jaramillo, María and Mario Yepes, eds. *Antología crítica del teatro breve hispanoamericano. 1948–1993*. Medellín, Colombia: Editorial Universidad de Antioquia, 1997.

Miller, Yvette E. and Charles M. Tatum, eds. *Latin American Women Writers: Yesterday and Today*. Pittsburgh: The Review, 1977.

Monleón, José. *América Latina, teatro y revolución*. Caracas: Ateneo de Caracas, 1978.

Montes, Consuelo Morel. *Identidad femenina en el teatro chileno*. Santiago, Chile: Apuntes, 1996.

Montilla, Lorena Pino. *La dramaturgia femenina venezolana*. Caracas: Centro Latinoamericano de Creación e Investigación Teatral, 1994.

Muguercia, Magaly. *Teatro y utopía*. Havana: Unión, 1997.

Ochsenius, Carlos and others. *Práctica teatral y expresión popular en América Latina: Chile, Perú, Uruguay*. Florida, Buenos Aires: Paulinas, 1988.

Ordaz, Luis. *Aproximación a la trayectoria de la dramática argentina*. Ottawa: Giroly, 1992.

Ordaz, ed. *Historia del teatro argentino*. Buenos Aires: Centro Editor de América Latina, 1982.

Pellettieri, Osvaldo and Eduardo Rovner, eds. *La Puesta en escena en Latinoamerica: Teoría y práctica teatral*. Buenos Aires: Galerna, 1995.

Pianca, Marina. *El teatro de nuestro américa: Un próyecto continental, 1959–1989*. Minneapolis: Institute for the Study of Ideologies and Literatures, 1990.

Ramos-Garcia, Luis and Ruth Escudero, eds. *Voces del Interior: Nueva dramaturgia peruana.* Lima: Instituto Nacional de Cultura, 2001.

Rizk, Beatriz J. *El nuevo teatro latinoamericano: una lectura histórica.* Minneapolis: Prisma Institute, 1987.

Rizk. *Posmodernismo y teatro en América Latina: Teórias y practicas en el umbral del siglo XXI.* Madrid: Iberoamericana, 2001.

Rojo, Grinor. *Los origenes del teatro hispanoamericano contemporáneo: La generación de dramaturgos de 1927, dos direcciones.* Santiago, Chile: Ediciones Universitarios de Valparaíso, 1972.

Salas, Teresa Cajiao and Margarita Vargas, eds. and trans. *Women Writing Women: An Anthology of Spanish American Theater of the 1980s.* Albany: State University of New York Press, 1997.

Schutte, Ofelia. *Cultural Identity and Social Liberation in Latin American Thought.* Albany: State University of New York Press, 1993.

Seibel, Beatriz. *De ninfas a capitanas.* Buenos Aires: Legasa, 1990.

Solórzano, Carlos, ed. *El teatro hispanoamericano contemporáneo.* Mexico: Fondo de Cultura Económica, 1964.

Sommer, Doris. *Foundational Fictions: The National Romances of Latin America.* Berkeley: University of California Press, 1991.

Sten, María, Óscar Armando García, and Alejandro Ortiz Bullé-Goyri, eds. *El teatro Franciscano en la Nueva España: Fuentes y ensayos para el estudio del teatro de evangelización en el siglo XVI.* Mexico: UNAM y CONACULTA, 2000.

Stevens, Camilla. *Family and Identity in Contemporary Cuban and Puerto Rican Drama.* Gainesville: University Press of Florida, 2004.

Taylor, Diana. *Disappearing Acts: Spectacles of Gender and Nationalism in Argentina's "Dirty War."* Durham, N.C.: Duke University Press, 1997.

Taylor. *Theatre of Crisis: Drama and Politics in Latin America.* Lexington: University of Kentucky Press, 1991.

Taylor and Juan Villegas, eds. *Negotiating Performance: Gender, Sexuality, and Theatricality in Latino America.* Durham, N.C.: Duke University Press, 1994.

Versényi, Adam. *Theatre in Latin America: Religion, Politics, and Culture from Cortés to the 1980s.* Cambridge: Cambridge University Press, 1993.

Weiss, Judith A., Leslie Demasceno, and others. *Latin American Popular Theatre: The First Five Centuries.* Albuquerque: University of New Mexico Press, 1993.

Contributors

Francine A'ness . . . . *Dartmouth College*
Jacqueline E. Bixler . . . . *Virginia Tech*
José F. Blanco . . . . *Florida State University*
Sandra Messinger Cypess . . . . *University of Maryland*
Stuart A. Day . . . . *University of North Carolina at Chapel Hill*
Alicia del Campo . . . . *California State University, Long Beach*
José A. Escarpanter . . . . *Auburn University*
Wilma Feliciano . . . . *State University of New York College at New Paltz*
Fabiola Fernández Salek . . . . *Chicago State University*
Lowell Fiet . . . . *University of Puerto Rico–Río Piedras*
Melissa A. Fitch . . . . *University of Arizona*
Lucía Garavito . . . . *Kansas State University*
Gustavo Geirola . . . . *Whittier College*
Elsa M. Gilmore . . . . *United States Naval Academy*
Amalia Gladhart . . . . *University of Oregon*
Jean Graham-Jones . . . . *City University of New York*
Julie Greer Johnson . . . . *University of Georgia*
Luis Chesney Lawrence . . . . *Central University of Venezuela*
Ramón Layera . . . . *Miami University, Ohio*
Christina Marín . . . . *Arizona State University*
Iani del Rosario Moreno . . . . *Salve Regina University*
Kirsten F. Nigro . . . . *University of Texas at El Paso*
Lola Proaño-Gómez . . . . *Pasadena City College*
Beatriz J. Rizk . . . . *Key Biscayne, Florida*
Carolyn D. Roark . . . . *Baylor University*
Laurietz Seda . . . . *University of Connecticut*
Beatriz Seibel . . . . *Buenos Aires, Argentina*
Ricardo Szmetan . . . . *University of West Indies–Barbados*
José L. Urbina . . . . *Catholic University of America*
Gloria F. Waldman . . . . *York College and The Graduate Center, CUNY*
Charles E. Workman . . . . *Auburn University*

Cumulative Index

Dictionary of Literary Biography, Volumes 1-305
Dictionary of Literary Biography Yearbook, 1980-2002
Dictionary of Literary Biography Documentary Series, Volumes 1-19
Concise Dictionary of American Literary Biography, Volumes 1-7
Concise Dictionary of British Literary Biography, Volumes 1-8
Concise Dictionary of World Literary Biography, Volumes 1-4

Cumulative Index

DLB before number: *Dictionary of Literary Biography,* Volumes 1-305
Y before number: *Dictionary of Literary Biography Yearbook,* 1980-2002
DS before number: *Dictionary of Literary Biography Documentary Series,* Volumes 1-19
CDALB before number: *Concise Dictionary of American Literary Biography,* Volumes 1-7
CDBLB before number: *Concise Dictionary of British Literary Biography,* Volumes 1-8
CDWLB before number: *Concise Dictionary of World Literary Biography,* Volumes 1-4

A

Aakjær, Jeppe 1866-1930 ....DLB-214
Aarestrup, Emil 1800-1856 ....DLB-300
Abbey, Edward 1927-1989 .... DLB-256, 275
Abbey, Edwin Austin 1852-1911 ....DLB-188
Abbey, Maj. J. R. 1894-1969 ....DLB-201
Abbey Press DLB-49
The Abbey Theatre and Irish Drama,
  1900-1945 ....DLB-10
Abbot, Willis J. 1863-1934.............DLB-29
Abbott, Edwin A. 1838-1926 .... DLB-178
Abbott, Jacob 1803-1879 ....DLB-1, 42, 243
Abbott, Lee K. 1947- DLB-130
Abbott, Lyman 1835-1922..............DLB-79
Abbott, Robert S. 1868-1940 ....DLB-29, 91
Abe Kōbō 1924-1993.................DLB-182
Abelaira, Augusto 1926- DLB-287
Abelard, Peter circa 1079-1142?.....DLB-115, 208
Abelard-Schuman....................DLB-46
Abell, Arunah S. 1806-1888.............DLB-43
Abell, Kjeld 1901-1961................DLB-214
Abercrombie, Lascelles 1881-1938........DLB-19
  The Friends of the Dymock
    Poets........................ Y-00
Aberdeen University Press Limited......DLB-106
Abish, Walter 1931- DLB-130, 227
Ablesimov, Aleksandr Onisimovich
  1742-1783.....................DLB-150
Abraham à Sancta Clara 1644-1709......DLB-168
Abrahams, Peter
  1919- DLB-117, 225; CDWLB-3
Abramov, Fedor Aleksandrovich
  1920-1983.....................DLB-302
Abrams, M. H. 1912- DLB-67
Abramson, Jesse 1904-1979 ....DLB-241
Abrogans circa 790-800 ....DLB-148
Abschatz, Hans Aßmann von
  1646-1699 ....DLB-168
Abse, Dannie 1923- DLB-27, 245
Abutsu-ni 1221-1283 ....DLB-203
Academy Chicago Publishers DLB-46

Accius circa 170 B.C.-circa 80 B.C. DLB-211
Accrocca, Elio Filippo 1923-1996.........DLB-128
Ace Books DLB-46
Achebe, Chinua 1930- DLB-117; CDWLB-3
Achtenberg, Herbert 1938- DLB-124
Ackerman, Diane 1948- DLB-120
Ackroyd, Peter 1949- DLB-155, 231
Acorn, Milton 1923-1986................DLB-53
Acosta, Oscar Zeta 1935?-1974? DLB-82
Acosta Torres, José 1925- DLB-209
Actors Theatre of Louisville DLB-7
Adair, Gilbert 1944- DLB-194
Adair, James 1709?-1783?...............DLB-30
Aðalsteinn Kristmundsson (see Steinn Steinarr)
Adam, Graeme Mercer 1839-1912 ....DLB-99
Adam, Robert Borthwick, II
  1863-1940 ....DLB-187
Adame, Leonard 1947- DLB-82
Adameșteanu, Gabriel 1942- DLB-232
Adamic, Louis 1898-1951 ....DLB-9
Adams, Abigail 1744-1818 ....DLB-183, 200
Adams, Alice 1926-1999 .... DLB-234, Y-86
Adams, Bertha Leith (Mrs. Leith Adams,
  Mrs. R. S. de Courcy Laffan)
  1837?-1912 ....DLB-240
Adams, Brooks 1848-1927..............DLB-47
Adams, Charles Francis, Jr. 1835-1915 ....DLB-47
Adams, Douglas 1952-2001........DLB-261; Y-83
Adams, Franklin P. 1881-1960...........DLB-29
Adams, Hannah 1755-1832 ....DLB-200
Adams, Henry 1838-1918 ...... DLB-12, 47, 189
Adams, Herbert Baxter 1850-1901 ....DLB-47
Adams, James Truslow
  1878-1949 .... DLB-17; DS-17
Adams, John 1735-1826............DLB-31, 183
Adams, John Quincy 1767-1848..........DLB-37
Adams, Léonie 1899-1988..............DLB-48
Adams, Levi 1802-1832................DLB-99
Adams, Richard 1920- DLB-261
Adams, Samuel 1722-1803..........DLB-31, 43
Adams, Sarah Fuller Flower
  1805-1848 ....DLB-199

Adams, Thomas 1582/1583-1652 ....DLB-151
Adams, William Taylor 1822-1897 ....DLB-42
J. S. and C. Adams [publishing house].....DLB-49
Adamson, Harold 1906-1980...........DLB-265
Adamson, Sir John 1867-1950 ....DLB-98
Adamson, Robert 1943- DLB-289
Adcock, Arthur St. John 1864-1930......DLB-135
Adcock, Betty 1938- DLB-105
  "Certain Gifts" DLB-105
  Tribute to James Dickey Y-97
Adcock, Fleur 1934- DLB-40
Addams, Jane 1860-1935 ....DLB-303
Addison, Joseph
  1672-1719 ....DLB-101; CDBLB-2
Ade, George 1866-1944...............DLB-11, 25
Adeler, Max (see Clark, Charles Heber)
Adlard, Mark 1932- DLB-261
Adler, Richard 1921- DLB-265
Adonias Filho 1915-1990..............DLB-145
Adorno, Theodor W. 1903-1969........DLB-242
Adoum, Jorge Enrique 1926- DLB-283
Advance Publishing Company DLB-49
Ady, Endre 1877-1919 ...... DLB-215; CDWLB-4
AE 1867-1935 ....DLB-19; CDBLB-5
Ælfric circa 955-circa 1010.............DLB-146
Aeschines circa 390 B.C.-circa 320 B.C..... DLB-176
Aeschylus 525-524 B.C.-456-455 B.C.
  .... DLB-176; CDWLB-1
Aesthetic Papers......................DLB-1
Aesthetics
  Eighteenth-Century Aesthetic
    Theories.....................DLB-31
African Literature
  Letter from Khartoum Y-90
African American
  Afro-American Literary Critics:
    An Introduction DLB-33
  The Black Aesthetic: Background DS-8
  The Black Arts Movement,
    by Larry Neal.................DLB-38
  Black Theaters and Theater Organizations
    in America, 1961-1982:
    A Research List DLB-38
  Black Theatre: A Forum [excerpts] DLB-38

379

Callaloo [journal] Y-87

Community and Commentators:
Black Theatre and Its Critics DLB-38

The Emergence of Black
Women Writers DS-8

The Hatch-Billops Collection DLB-76

A Look at the Contemporary Black
Theatre Movement DLB-38

The Moorland-Spingarn Research
Center DLB-76

"The Negro as a Writer," by
G. M. McClellan DLB-50

"Negro Poets and Their Poetry," by
Wallace Thurman DLB-50

Olaudah Equiano and Unfinished Journeys:
The Slave-Narrative Tradition and
Twentieth-Century Continuities, by
Paul Edwards and Pauline T.
Wangman DLB-117

PHYLON (Fourth Quarter, 1950),
The Negro in Literature:
The Current Scene DLB-76

The Schomburg Center for Research
in Black Culture DLB-76

Three Documents [poets], by John
Edward Bruce DLB-50

After Dinner Opera Company Y-92

Agassiz, Elizabeth Cary 1822-1907 . . . . . . DLB-189

Agassiz, Louis 1807-1873 . . . . DLB-1, 235

Agee, James
1909-1955 . . . . DLB-2, 26, 152; CDALB-1

The Agee Legacy: A Conference at
the University of Tennessee
at Knoxville Y-89

Aguilera Malta, Demetrio 1909-1981 . . . . DLB-145

Aguirre, Isidora 1919- DLB-305

Agustini, Delmira 1886-1914 . . . . DLB-290

Ahlin, Lars 1915-1997 . . . . DLB-257

Ai 1947- DLB-120

Aichinger, Ilse 1921- DLB-85, 299

Aickman, Robert 1914-1981 . . . . DLB-261

Aidoo, Ama Ata 1942- DLB-117; CDWLB-3

Aiken, Conrad
1889-1973 . . . . DLB-9, 45, 102; CDALB-5

Aiken, Joan 1924- DLB-161

Aikin, Lucy 1781-1864 . . . . DLB-144, 163

Ainsworth, William Harrison
1805-1882 . . . . DLB-21

Aistis, Jonas 1904-1973 . . . . . DLB-220; CDWLB-4

Aitken, George A. 1860-1917 . . . . DLB-149

Robert Aitken [publishing house] DLB-49

Aitmatov, Chingiz 1928- DLB-302

Akenside, Mark 1721-1770 . . . . DLB-109

Akhmatova, Anna Andreevna
1889-1966 . . . . DLB-295

Akins, Zoë 1886-1958 . . . . DLB-26

Aksakov, Ivan Sergeevich 1823-1826 . . . . DLB-277

Aksakov, Sergei Timofeevich
1791-1859 . . . . DLB-198

Aksyonov, Vassily 1932- DLB-302

Akunin, Boris (Grigorii Shalvovich
Chkhartishvili) 1956- DLB-285

Akutagawa Ryūnsuke 1892-1927 . . . . DLB-180

Alabaster, William 1568-1640 . . . . DLB-132

Alain de Lille circa 1116-1202/1203 . . . . DLB-208

Alain-Fournier 1886-1914 . . . . DLB-65

Alanus de Insulis (see Alain de Lille)

Alarcón, Francisco X. 1954- DLB-122

Alarcón, Justo S. 1930- DLB-209

Alba, Nanina 1915-1968 . . . . DLB-41

Albee, Edward 1928- DLB-7, 266; CDALB-1

Albert, Octavia 1853-ca. 1889 . . . . DLB-221

Albert the Great circa 1200-1280 . . . . . . DLB-115

Alberti, Rafael 1902-1999 . . . . DLB-108

Albertinus, Aegidius circa 1560-1620 . . . . DLB-164

Alcaeus born circa 620 B.C. DLB-176

Alcoforado, Mariana, the Portuguese Nun
1640-1723 . . . . DLB-287

Alcott, Amos Bronson
1799-1888 . . . . DLB-1, 223; DS-5

Alcott, Louisa May 1832-1888
. . . DLB-1, 42, 79, 223, 239; DS-14; CDALB-3

Alcott, William Andrus 1798-1859 . . . . DLB-1, 243

Alcuin circa 732-804 . . . . DLB-148

Alden, Henry Mills 1836-1919 . . . . DLB-79

Alden, Isabella 1841-1930 . . . . DLB-42

John B. Alden [publishing house] DLB-49

Alden, Beardsley, and Company DLB-49

Aldington, Richard
1892-1962 . . . . DLB-20, 36, 100, 149

Aldis, Dorothy 1896-1966 . . . . DLB-22

Aldis, H. G. 1863-1919 . . . . DLB-184

Aldiss, Brian W. 1925- DLB-14, 261, 271

Aldrich, Thomas Bailey
1836-1907 . . . . DLB-42, 71, 74, 79

Alegría, Ciro 1909-1967 . . . . DLB-113

Alegría, Claribel 1924- DLB-145, 283

Aleixandre, Vicente 1898-1984 . . . . DLB-108

Aleksandravičius, Jonas (see Aistis, Jonas)

Aleksandrov, Aleksandr Andreevich
(see Durova, Nadezhda Andreevna)

Alekseeva, Marina Anatol'evna
(see Marinina, Aleksandra)

Aleramo, Sibilla (Rena Pierangeli Faccio)
1876-1960 . . . . DLB-114, 264

Aleshkovsky, Petr Markovich 1957- . . . DLB-285

Alexander, Cecil Frances 1818-1895 . . . . . DLB-199

Alexander, Charles 1868-1923 . . . . DLB-91

Charles Wesley Alexander
[publishing house] DLB-49

Alexander, James 1691-1756 . . . . DLB-24

Alexander, Lloyd 1924- DLB-52

Alexander, Sir William, Earl of Stirling
1577?-1640 . . . . DLB-121

Alexie, Sherman 1966- DLB-175, 206, 278

Alexis, Willibald 1798-1871 . . . . DLB-133

Alfred, King 849-899 . . . . DLB-146

Alger, Horatio, Jr. 1832-1899 . . . . DLB-42

Algonquin Books of Chapel Hill DLB-46

Algren, Nelson
1909-1981 . . . . . . DLB-9; Y-81, 82; CDALB-1

Nelson Algren: An International
Symposium Y-00

Aljamiado Literature DLB-286

Allan, Andrew 1907-1974 . . . . DLB-88

Allan, Ted 1916-1995 . . . . DLB-68

Allbeury, Ted 1917- DLB-87

Alldritt, Keith 1935- DLB-14

Allen, Dick 1939- DLB-282

Allen, Ethan 1738-1789 . . . . DLB-31

Allen, Frederick Lewis 1890-1954 . . . . . . DLB-137

Allen, Gay Wilson 1903-1995 . . . . . DLB-103; Y-95

Allen, George 1808-1876 . . . . DLB-59

Allen, Grant 1848-1899 . . . . DLB-70, 92, 178

Allen, Henry W. 1912-1991 . . . . Y-85

Allen, Hervey 1889-1949 . . . . DLB-9, 45

Allen, James 1739-1808 . . . . DLB-31

Allen, James Lane 1849-1925 . . . . DLB-71

Allen, Jay Presson 1922- DLB-26

John Allen and Company DLB-49

Allen, Paula Gunn 1939- DLB-175

Allen, Samuel W. 1917- DLB-41

Allen, Woody 1935- DLB-44

George Allen [publishing house] DLB-106

George Allen and Unwin Limited DLB-112

Allende, Isabel 1942- DLB-145; CDWLB-3

Alline, Henry 1748-1784 . . . . DLB-99

Allingham, Margery 1904-1966 . . . . DLB-77

The Margery Allingham Society Y-98

Allingham, William 1824-1889 . . . . DLB-35

W. L. Allison [publishing house] DLB-49

The *Alliterative Morte Arthure and the Stanzaic
Morte Arthur* circa 1350-1400 . . . . . . DLB-146

Allott, Kenneth 1912-1973 . . . . DLB-20

Allston, Washington 1779-1843 . . . . . . DLB-1, 235

John Almon [publishing house] DLB-154

Alonzo, Dámaso 1898-1990 . . . . DLB-108

Alsop, George 1636-post 1673 . . . . DLB-24

Alsop, Richard 1761-1815 . . . . DLB-37

Henry Altemus and Company DLB-49

Altenberg, Peter 1885-1919 . . . . DLB-81

Althusser, Louis 1918-1990 . . . . DLB-242

Altolaguirre, Manuel 1905-1959 . . . . DLB-108

Aluko, T. M. 1918- DLB-117

Alurista 1947- DLB-82

Alvarez, A. 1929- DLB-14, 40

Alvarez, Julia 1950- DLB-282

Alvaro, Corrado 1895-1956 . . . . DLB-264

Alver, Betti 1906-1989 . . . . . . DLB-220; CDWLB-4

Amadi, Elechi 1934- DLB-117

Amado, Jorge 1912-2001 . . . . DLB-113

Amalrik, Andrei
1938-1980 . . . . DLB-302

Ambler, Eric 1909-1998................DLB-77
The Library of America................DLB-46
The Library of America: An Assessment
    After Two Decades.............Y-02
America: or, A Poem on the Settlement
    of the British Colonies, by Timothy
    Dwight......................DLB-37
American Bible Society
    Department of Library, Archives, and
        Institutional Research..........Y-97
American Conservatory
    Theatre......................DLB-7
American Culture
    American Proletarian Culture:
        The Twenties and Thirties.......DS-11
Studies in American Jewish Literature......Y-02
The American Library in Paris..........Y-93
American Literature
    The Literary Scene and Situation and...
        (Who Besides Oprah) Really Runs
        American Literature?...........Y-99
    Who Owns American Literature, by
        Henry Taylor..................Y-94
    Who Runs American Literature?.......Y-94
American News Company..............DLB-49
A Century of Poetry, a Lifetime of Collecting:
    J. M. Edelstein's Collection of Twentieth-
    Century American Poetry............Y-02
The American Poets' Corner: The First
    Three Years (1983-1986)............Y-86
American Publishing Company..........DLB-49
American Spectator
    [Editorial] *Rationale From the Initial
    Issue of the American Spectator
    (November 1932)*...............DLB-137
American Stationers' Company..........DLB-49
The American Studies Association
    of Norway.......................Y-00
American Sunday-School Union.........DLB-49
American Temperance Union...........DLB-49
American Tract Society..............DLB-49
The American Trust for the British Library..Y-96
American Writers' Congress
    25-27 April 1935...............DLB-303
American Writers Congress
    The American Writers Congress
        (9-12 October 1981)............Y-81
    The American Writers Congress: A Report
        on Continuing Business.........Y-81
Ames, Fisher 1758-1808..............DLB-37
Ames, Mary Clemmer 1831-1884........DLB-23
Ames, William 1576-1633.............DLB-281
Amiel, Henri-Frédéric 1821-1881........DLB-217
Amini, Johari M. 1935-...............DLB-41
Amis, Kingsley 1922-1995
    ......DLB-15, 27, 100, 139, Y-96; CDBLB-7
Amis, Martin 1949-................DLB-14, 194
Ammianus Marcellinus
    circa A.D. 330-A.D. 395..........DLB-211
Ammons, A. R. 1926-2001............DLB-5, 165
Amory, Thomas 1691?-1788............DLB-39
Anania, Michael 1939-...............DLB-193

Anaya, Rudolfo A. 1937-......DLB-82, 206, 278
Ancrene Riwle circa 1200-1225..........DLB-146
Andersch, Alfred 1914-1980............DLB-69
Andersen, Benny 1929-...............DLB-214
Andersen, Hans Christian 1805-1875....DLB-300
Anderson, Alexander 1775-1870........DLB-188
Anderson, David 1929-...............DLB-241
Anderson, Frederick Irving 1877-1947....DLB-202
Anderson, Margaret 1886-1973.........DLB-4, 91
Anderson, Maxwell 1888-1959........DLB-7, 228
Anderson, Patrick 1915-1979...........DLB-68
Anderson, Paul Y. 1893-1938...........DLB-29
Anderson, Poul 1926-2001..............DLB-8
    Tribute to Isaac Asimov.............Y-92
Anderson, Robert 1750-1830...........DLB-142
Anderson, Robert 1917-................DLB-7
Anderson, Sherwood
    1876-1941......DLB-4, 9, 86; DS-1; CDALB-4
Andreae, Johann Valentin 1586-1654....DLB-164
Andreas Capellanus
    flourished circa 1185..............DLB-208
Andreas-Salomé, Lou 1861-1937.........DLB-66
Andreev, Leonid Nikolaevich
    1871-1919......................DLB-295
Andres, Stefan 1906-1970..............DLB-69
Andresen, Sophia de Mello Breyner
    1919-..........................DLB-287
Andreu, Blanca 1959-.................DLB-134
Andrewes, Lancelot 1555-1626......DLB-151, 172
Andrews, Charles M. 1863-1943.........DLB-17
Andrews, Miles Peter ?-1814............DLB-89
Andrews, Stephen Pearl 1812-1886......DLB-250
Andrian, Leopold von 1875-1951........DLB-81
Andrić, Ivo 1892-1975.........DLB-147; CDWLB-4
Andrieux, Louis (see Aragon, Louis)
Andrus, Silas, and Son...............DLB-49
Andrzejewski, Jerzy 1909-1983.........DLB-215
Angell, James Burrill 1829-1916.........DLB-64
Angell, Roger 1920-..............DLB-171, 185
Angelou, Maya 1928-.........DLB-38; CDALB-7
    Tribute to Julian Mayfield............Y-84
Anger, Jane flourished 1589...........DLB-136
Angers, Félicité (see Conan, Laure)
The Anglo-Saxon Chronicle
    circa 890-1154..................DLB-146
Angus and Robertson (UK) Limited.....DLB-112
Anhalt, Edward 1914-2000.............DLB-26
Anissimov, Myriam 1943-.............DLB-299
Anker, Nini Roll 1873-1942............DLB-297
Annenkov, Pavel Vasil'evich
    1813?-1887.....................DLB-277
Annensky, Innokentii Fedorovich
    1855-1909......................DLB-295
Henry F. Anners [publishing house]......DLB-49
Annolied between 1077 and 1081........DLB-148
Anscombe, G. E. M. 1919-2001..........DLB-262

Anselm of Canterbury 1033-1109.......DLB-115
Anstey, F. 1856-1934..............DLB-141, 178
Anthologizing New Formalism..........DLB-282
Anthony, Michael 1932-...............DLB-125
Anthony, Piers 1934-..................DLB-8
Anthony, Susanna 1726-1791...........DLB-200
Antin, David 1932-..................DLB-169
Antin, Mary 1881-1949..........DLB-221; Y-84
Anton Ulrich, Duke of Brunswick-Lüneburg
    1633-1714.....................DLB-168
Antschel, Paul (see Celan, Paul)
Antunes, António Lobo 1942-..........DLB-287
Anyidoho, Kofi 1947-................DLB-157
Anzaldúa, Gloria 1942-...............DLB-122
Anzengruber, Ludwig 1839-1889........DLB-129
Apess, William 1798-1839.........DLB-175, 243
Apodaca, Rudy S. 1939-...............DLB-82
Apollinaire, Guillaume 1880-1918.......DLB-258
Apollonius Rhodius third century B.C....DLB-176
Apple, Max 1941-..................DLB-130
Appelfeld, Aharon 1932-..............DLB-299
D. Appleton and Company.............DLB-49
Appleton-Century-Crofts..............DLB-46
Applewhite, James 1935-..............DLB-105
    Tribute to James Dickey..............Y-97
Apple-wood Books..................DLB-46
April, Jean-Pierre 1948-...............DLB-251
Apukhtin, Aleksei Nikolaevich
    1840-1893......................DLB-277
Apuleius circa A.D. 125-post A.D. 164
    ....DLB-211; CDWLB-1
Aquin, Hubert 1929-1977..............DLB-53
Aquinas, Thomas 1224/1225-1274......DLB-115
Aragon, Louis 1897-1982..........DLB-72, 258
Aragon, Vernacular Translations in the
    Crowns of Castile and 1352-1515....DLB-286
Aralica, Ivan 1930-..................DLB-181
Aratus of Soli
    circa 315 B.C.-circa 239 B.C........DLB-176
Arbasino, Alberto 1930-..............DLB-196
Arbor House Publishing Company.......DLB-46
Arbuthnot, John 1667-1735............DLB-101
Arcadia House.....................DLB-46
Arce, Julio G. (see Ulica, Jorge)
Archer, William 1856-1924.............DLB-10
Archilochhus
    mid seventh century B.C.E.........DLB-176
The Archpoet circa 1130?-?............DLB-148
Archpriest Avvakum (Petrovich)
    1620?-1682.....................DLB-150
Arden, John 1930-................DLB-13, 245
Arden of Faversham................DLB-62
Ardis Publishers.....................Y-89
Ardizzone, Edward 1900-1979..........DLB-160
Arellano, Juan Estevan 1947-..........DLB-122
The Arena Publishing Company.........DLB-49

Arena Stage	DLB-7
Arenas, Reinaldo 1943-1990	DLB-145
Arendt, Hannah 1906-1975	DLB-242
Arensberg, Ann 1937-	Y-82
Arghezi, Tudor 1880-1967	DLB-220; CDWLB-4
Arguedas, José María 1911-1969	DLB-113
Argüelles, Hugo 1932-2003	DLB-305
Argueta, Manlio 1936-	DLB-145
Arias, Ron 1941-	DLB-82
Arishima Takeo 1878-1923	DLB-180
Aristophanes circa 446 B.C.-circa 386 B.C.	DLB-176; CDWLB-1
Aristotle 384 B.C.-322 B.C.	DLB-176; CDWLB-1
Ariyoshi Sawako 1931-1984	DLB-182
Arland, Marcel 1899-1986	DLB-72
Arlen, Michael 1895-1956	DLB-36, 77, 162
Arlt, Roberto 1900-1942	DLB-305
Armah, Ayi Kwei 1939-	DLB-117; CDWLB-3
Armantrout, Rae 1947-	DLB-193
Der arme Hartmann ?-after 1150	DLB-148
Armed Services Editions	DLB-46
Armitage, G. E. (Robert Edric) 1956-	DLB-267
Armstrong, Martin Donisthorpe 1882-1974	DLB-197
Armstrong, Richard 1903-	DLB-160
Armstrong, Terence Ian Fytton (see Gawsworth, John)	
Arnauld, Antoine 1612-1694	DLB-268
Arndt, Ernst Moritz 1769-1860	DLB-90
Arnim, Achim von 1781-1831	DLB-90
Arnim, Bettina von 1785-1859	DLB-90
Arnim, Elizabeth von (Countess Mary Annette Beauchamp Russell) 1866-1941	DLB-197
Arno Press	DLB-46
Arnold, Edwin 1832-1904	DLB-35
Arnold, Edwin L. 1857-1935	DLB-178
Arnold, Matthew 1822-1888	DLB-32, 57; CDBLB-4
Preface to *Poems* (1853)	DLB-32
Arnold, Thomas 1795-1842	DLB-55
Edward Arnold [publishing house]	DLB-112
Arnott, Peter 1962-	DLB-233
Arnow, Harriette Simpson 1908-1986	DLB-6
Arp, Bill (see Smith, Charles Henry)	
Arpino, Giovanni 1927-1987	DLB-177
Arrebo, Anders 1587-1637	DLB-300
Arreola, Juan José 1918-2001	DLB-113
Arrian circa 89-circa 155	DLB-176
J. W. Arrowsmith [publishing house]	DLB-106
Arrufat, Antón 1935-	DLB-305
Art	
John Dos Passos: Artist	Y-99
The First Post-Impressionist Exhibition	DS-5
The Omega Workshops	DS-10
The Second Post-Impressionist Exhibition	DS-5
Artaud, Antonin 1896-1948	DLB-258
Artel, Jorge 1909-1994	DLB-283
Arthur, Timothy Shay 1809-1885	DLB-3, 42, 79, 250; DS-13
Artmann, H. C. 1921-2000	DLB-85
Artsybashev, Mikhail Petrovich 1878-1927	DLB-295
Arvin, Newton 1900-1963	DLB-103
Asch, Nathan 1902-1964	DLB-4, 28
Nathan Asch Remembers Ford Madox Ford, Sam Roth, and Hart Crane	Y-02
Ascham, Roger 1515/1516-1568	DLB-236
Aseev, Nikolai Nikolaevich 1889-1963	DLB-295
Ash, John 1948-	DLB-40
Ashbery, John 1927-	DLB-5, 165; Y-81
Ashbridge, Elizabeth 1713-1755	DLB-200
Ashburnham, Bertram Lord 1797-1878	DLB-184
Ashendene Press	DLB-112
Asher, Sandy 1942-	Y-83
Ashton, Winifred (see Dane, Clemence)	
Asimov, Isaac 1920-1992	DLB-8; Y-92
Tribute to John Ciardi	Y-86
Askew, Anne circa 1521-1546	DLB-136
Aspazija 1865-1943	DLB-220; CDWLB-4
Asselin, Olivar 1874-1937	DLB-92
The Association of American Publishers	Y-99
The Association for Documentary Editing	Y-00
The Association for the Study of Literature and Environment (ASLE)	Y-99
Astell, Mary 1666-1731	DLB-252
Astley, Thea 1925-	DLB-289
Astley, William (see Warung, Price)	
Asturias, Miguel Ángel 1899-1974	DLB-113, 290; CDWLB-3
Atava, S. (see Terpigorev, Sergei Nikolaevich)	
Atheneum Publishers	DLB-46
Atherton, Gertrude 1857-1948	DLB-9, 78, 186
Athlone Press	DLB-112
Atkins, Josiah circa 1755-1781	DLB-31
Atkins, Russell 1926-	DLB-41
Atkinson, Kate 1951-	DLB-267
Atkinson, Louisa 1834-1872	DLB-230
The Atlantic Monthly Press	DLB-46
Attaway, William 1911-1986	DLB-76
Atwood, Margaret 1939-	DLB-53, 251
Aubert, Alvin 1930-	DLB-41
Aubert de Gaspé, Phillipe-Ignace-François 1814-1841	DLB-99
Aubert de Gaspé, Phillipe-Joseph 1786-1871	DLB-99
Aubin, Napoléon 1812-1890	DLB-99
Aubin, Penelope 1685-circa 1731	DLB-39
Preface to *The Life of Charlotta du Pont* (1723)	DLB-39
Aubrey-Fletcher, Henry Lancelot (see Wade, Henry)	
Auchincloss, Louis 1917-	DLB-2, 244; Y-80
Auden, W. H. 1907-1973	DLB-10, 20; CDBLB-6
Audio Art in America: A Personal Memoir	Y-85
Audubon, John James 1785-1851	DLB-248
Audubon, John Woodhouse 1812-1862	DLB-183
Auerbach, Berthold 1812-1882	DLB-133
Auernheimer, Raoul 1876-1948	DLB-81
Augier, Emile 1820-1889	DLB-192
Augustine 354-430	DLB-115
Aulnoy, Marie-Catherine Le Jumel de Barneville, comtesse d' 1650/1651-1705	DLB-268
Aulus Gellius circa A.D. 125-circa A.D. 180?	DLB-211
Austen, Jane 1775-1817	DLB-116; CDBLB-3
Auster, Paul 1947-	DLB-227
Austin, Alfred 1835-1913	DLB-35
Austin, J. L. 1911-1960	DLB-262
Austin, Jane Goodwin 1831-1894	DLB-202
Austin, John 1790-1859	DLB-262
Austin, Mary Hunter 1868-1934	DLB-9, 78, 206, 221, 275
Austin, William 1778-1841	DLB-74
Australie (Emily Manning) 1845-1890	DLB-230
Authors and Newspapers Association	DLB-46
Authors' Publishing Company	DLB-49
Avallone, Michael 1924-1999	Y-99
Tribute to John D. MacDonald	Y-86
Tribute to Kenneth Millar	Y-83
Tribute to Raymond Chandler	Y-88
Avalon Books	DLB-46
Avancini, Nicolaus 1611-1686	DLB-164
Avendaño, Fausto 1941-	DLB-82
Averroës 1126-1198	DLB-115
Avery, Gillian 1926-	DLB-161
Avicenna 980-1037	DLB-115
Ávila Jiménez, Antonio 1898-1965	DLB-283
Avison, Margaret 1918-1987	DLB-53
Avon Books	DLB-46
Avyžius, Jonas 1922-1999	DLB-220
Awdry, Wilbert Vere 1911-1997	DLB-160
Awoonor, Kofi 1935-	DLB-117
Ayckbourn, Alan 1939-	DLB-13, 245
Ayer, A. J. 1910-1989	DLB-262
Aymé, Marcel 1902-1967	DLB-72
Aytoun, Sir Robert 1570-1638	DLB-121
Aytoun, William Edmondstoune 1813-1865	DLB-32, 159

B

B.V. (see Thomson, James)	
Babbitt, Irving 1865-1933	DLB-63
Babbitt, Natalie 1932-	DLB-52
John Babcock [publishing house]	DLB-49

Babel, Isaak Emmanuilovich 1894-1940 ... DLB-272

Babits, Mihály 1883-1941 ... DLB-215; CDWLB-4

Babrius circa 150-200 ... DLB-176

Babson, Marian 1929- ... DLB-276

Baca, Jimmy Santiago 1952- ... DLB-122

Bacchelli, Riccardo 1891-1985 ... DLB-264

Bache, Benjamin Franklin 1769-1798 ... DLB-43

Bachelard, Gaston 1884-1962 ... DLB-296

Bacheller, Irving 1859-1950 ... DLB-202

Bachmann, Ingeborg 1926-1973 ... DLB-85

Bačinskaitė-Bučienė, Salomėja (see Nėris, Salomėja)

Bacon, Delia 1811-1859 ... DLB-1, 243

Bacon, Francis 1561-1626 ... DLB-151, 236, 252; CDBLB-1

Bacon, Sir Nicholas circa 1510-1579 ... DLB-132

Bacon, Roger circa 1214/1220-1292 ... DLB-115

Bacon, Thomas circa 1700-1768 ... DLB-31

Bacovia, George 1881-1957 ... DLB-220; CDWLB-4

Richard G. Badger and Company ... DLB-49

Bagaduce Music Lending Library ... Y-00

Bage, Robert 1728-1801 ... DLB-39

Bagehot, Walter 1826-1877 ... DLB-55

Baggesen, Jens 1764-1826 ... DLB-300

Bagley, Desmond 1923-1983 ... DLB-87

Bagley, Sarah G. 1806-1848? ... DLB-239

Bagnold, Enid 1889-1981 ... DLB-13, 160, 191, 245

Bagryana, Elisaveta 1893-1991 ... DLB-147; CDWLB-4

Bahr, Hermann 1863-1934 ... DLB-81, 118

Bailey, Abigail Abbot 1746-1815 ... DLB-200

Bailey, Alfred Goldsworthy 1905- ... DLB-68

Bailey, H. C. 1878-1961 ... DLB-77

Bailey, Jacob 1731-1808 ... DLB-99

Bailey, Paul 1937- ... DLB-14, 271

Bailey, Philip James 1816-1902 ... DLB-32

Francis Bailey [publishing house] ... DLB-49

Baillargeon, Pierre 1916-1967 ... DLB-88

Baillie, Hugh 1890-1966 ... DLB-29

Baillie, Joanna 1762-1851 ... DLB-93

Bailyn, Bernard 1922- ... DLB-17

Bain, Alexander
English Composition and Rhetoric (1866) [excerpt] ... DLB-57

Bainbridge, Beryl 1933- ... DLB-14, 231

Baird, Irene 1901-1981 ... DLB-68

Baker, Augustine 1575-1641 ... DLB-151

Baker, Carlos 1909-1987 ... DLB-103

Baker, David 1954- ... DLB-120

Baker, George Pierce 1866-1935 ... DLB-266

Baker, Herschel C. 1914-1990 ... DLB-111

Baker, Houston A., Jr. 1943- ... DLB-67

Baker, Howard
Tribute to Caroline Gordon ... Y-81
Tribute to Katherine Anne Porter ... Y-80

Baker, Nicholson 1957- ... DLB-227; Y-00
Review of Nicholson Baker's *Double Fold: Libraries and the Assault on Paper* ... Y-00

Baker, Samuel White 1821-1893 ... DLB-166

Baker, Thomas 1656-1740 ... DLB-213

Walter H. Baker Company ("Baker's Plays") ... DLB-49

The Baker and Taylor Company ... DLB-49

Bakhtin, Mikhail Mikhailovich 1895-1975 ... DLB-242

Bakunin, Mikhail Aleksandrovich 1814-1876 ... DLB-277

Balaban, John 1943- ... DLB-120

Bald, Wambly 1902- ... DLB-4

Balde, Jacob 1604-1668 ... DLB-164

Balderston, John 1889-1954 ... DLB-26

Baldwin, James 1924-1987 ... DLB-2, 7, 33, 249, 278; Y-87; CDALB-1

Baldwin, Joseph Glover 1815-1864 ... DLB-3, 11, 248

Baldwin, Louisa (Mrs. Alfred Baldwin) 1845-1925 ... DLB-240

Baldwin, William circa 1515-1563 ... DLB-132

Richard and Anne Baldwin [publishing house] ... DLB-170

Bale, John 1495-1563 ... DLB-132

Balestrini, Nanni 1935- ... DLB-128, 196

Balfour, Sir Andrew 1630-1694 ... DLB-213

Balfour, Arthur James 1848-1930 ... DLB-190

Balfour, Sir James 1600-1657 ... DLB-213

Ballantine Books ... DLB-46

Ballantyne, R. M. 1825-1894 ... DLB-163

Ballard, J. G. 1930- ... DLB-14, 207, 261

Ballard, Martha Moore 1735-1812 ... DLB-200

Ballerini, Luigi 1940- ... DLB-128

Ballou, Maturin Murray (Lieutenant Murray) 1820-1895 ... DLB-79, 189

Robert O. Ballou [publishing house] ... DLB-46

Bal'mont, Konstantin Dmitrievich 1867-1942 ... DLB-295

Balzac, Guez de 1597?-1654 ... DLB-268

Balzac, Honoré de 1799-1855 ... DLB-119

Bambara, Toni Cade 1939-1995 ... DLB-38, 218; CDALB-7

Bamford, Samuel 1788-1872 ... DLB-190

A. L. Bancroft and Company ... DLB-49

Bancroft, George 1800-1891 ... DLB-1, 30, 59, 243

Bancroft, Hubert Howe 1832-1918 ... DLB-47, 140

Bandelier, Adolph F. 1840-1914 ... DLB-186

Bang, Herman 1857-1912 ... DLB-300

Bangs, John Kendrick 1862-1922 ... DLB-11, 79

Banim, John 1798-1842 ... DLB-116, 158, 159

Banim, Michael 1796-1874 ... DLB-158, 159

Banks, Iain (M.) 1954- ... DLB-194, 261

Banks, John circa 1653-1706 ... DLB-80

Banks, Russell 1940- ... DLB-130, 278

Bannerman, Helen 1862-1946 ... DLB-141

Bantam Books ... DLB-46

Banti, Anna 1895-1985 ... DLB-177

Banville, John 1945- ... DLB-14, 271

Banville, Théodore de 1823-1891 ... DLB-217

Baraka, Amiri 1934- ... DLB-5, 7, 16, 38; DS-8; CDALB-1

Barańczak, Stanisław 1946- ... DLB-232

Baranskaia, Natal'ia Vladimirovna 1908- ... DLB-302

Baratynsky, Evgenii Abramovich 1800-1844 ... DLB-205

Barba-Jacob, Porfirio 1883-1942 ... DLB-283

Barbauld, Anna Laetitia 1743-1825 ... DLB-107, 109, 142, 158

Barbeau, Marius 1883-1969 ... DLB-92

Barber, John Warner 1798-1885 ... DLB-30

Bàrberi Squarotti, Giorgio 1929- ... DLB-128

Barbey d'Aurevilly, Jules-Amédée 1808-1889 ... DLB-119

Barbier, Auguste 1805-1882 ... DLB-217

Barbilian, Dan (see Barbu, Ion)

Barbour, John circa 1316-1395 ... DLB-146

Barbour, Ralph Henry 1870-1944 ... DLB-22

Barbu, Ion 1895-1961 ... DLB-220; CDWLB-4

Barbusse, Henri 1873-1935 ... DLB-65

Barclay, Alexander circa 1475-1552 ... DLB-132

E. E. Barclay and Company ... DLB-49

C. W. Bardeen [publishing house] ... DLB-49

Barham, Richard Harris 1788-1845 ... DLB-159

Barich, Bill 1943- ... DLB-185

Baring, Maurice 1874-1945 ... DLB-34

Baring-Gould, Sabine 1834-1924 ... DLB-156, 190

Barker, A. L. 1918- ... DLB-14, 139

Barker, Clive 1952- ... DLB-261

Barker, Dudley (see Black, Lionel)

Barker, George 1913-1991 ... DLB-20

Barker, Harley Granville 1877-1946 ... DLB-10

Barker, Howard 1946- ... DLB-13, 233

Barker, James Nelson 1784-1858 ... DLB-37

Barker, Jane 1652-1727 ... DLB-39, 131

Barker, Lady Mary Anne 1831-1911 ... DLB-166

Barker, Pat 1943- ... DLB-271

Barker, William circa 1520-after 1576 ... DLB-132

Arthur Barker Limited ... DLB-112

Barkov, Ivan Semenovich 1732-1768 ... DLB-150

Barks, Coleman 1937- ... DLB-5

Barlach, Ernst 1870-1938 ... DLB-56, 118

Barlow, Joel 1754-1812 ... DLB-37
The Prospect of Peace (1778) ... DLB-37

Barnard, John 1681-1770 ... DLB-24

Barnard, Marjorie (M. Barnard Eldershaw) 1897-1987 ... DLB-260

Barnard, Robert 1936- ... DLB-276

Barne, Kitty (Mary Catherine Barne) 1883-1957 ... DLB-160

Barnes, Barnabe 1571-1609 ... DLB-132

Barnes, Djuna 1892-1982 ... DLB-4, 9, 45; DS-15

Barnes, Jim 1933-	DLB-175
Barnes, Julian 1946-	DLB-194; Y-93
Notes for a Checklist of Publications	Y-01
Barnes, Margaret Ayer 1886-1967	DLB-9
Barnes, Peter 1931-	DLB-13, 233
Barnes, William 1801-1886	DLB-32
A. S. Barnes and Company	DLB-49
Barnes and Noble Books	DLB-46
Barnet, Miguel 1940-	DLB-145
Barney, Natalie 1876-1972	DLB-4; DS-15
Barnfield, Richard 1574-1627	DLB-172
Richard W. Baron [publishing house]	DLB-46
Barr, Amelia Edith Huddleston 1831-1919	DLB-202, 221
Barr, Robert 1850-1912	DLB-70, 92
Barral, Carlos 1928-1989	DLB-134
Barrax, Gerald William 1933-	DLB-41, 120
Barrès, Maurice 1862-1923	DLB-123
Barreno, Maria Isabel (see The Three Marias: A Landmark Case in Portuguese Literary History)	
Barrett, Eaton Stannard 1786-1820	DLB-116
Barrie, J. M. 1860-1937	DLB-10, 141, 156; CDBLB-5
Barrie and Jenkins	DLB-112
Barrio, Raymond 1921-	DLB-82
Barrios, Gregg 1945-	DLB-122
Barry, Philip 1896-1949	DLB-7, 228
Barry, Robertine (see Françoise)	
Barry, Sebastian 1955-	DLB-245
Barse and Hopkins	DLB-46
Barstow, Stan 1928-	DLB-14, 139, 207
Tribute to John Braine	Y-86
Barth, John 1930-	DLB-2, 227
Barthelme, Donald 1931-1989	DLB-2, 234; Y-80, 89
Barthelme, Frederick 1943-	DLB-244; Y-85
Barthes, Roland 1915-1980	DLB-296
Bartholomew, Frank 1898-1985	DLB-127
Bartlett, John 1820-1905	DLB-1, 235
Bartol, Cyrus Augustus 1813-1900	DLB-1, 235
Barton, Bernard 1784-1849	DLB-96
Barton, John ca. 1610-1675	DLB-236
Barton, Thomas Pennant 1803-1869	DLB-140
Bartram, John 1699-1777	DLB-31
Bartram, William 1739-1823	DLB-37
Barykova, Anna Pavlovna 1839-1893	DLB-277
Basic Books	DLB-46
Basille, Theodore (see Becon, Thomas)	
Bass, Rick 1958-	DLB-212, 275
Bass, T. J. 1932-	Y-81
Bassani, Giorgio 1916-2000	DLB-128, 177, 299
Basse, William circa 1583-1653	DLB-121
Bassett, John Spencer 1867-1928	DLB-17
Bassler, Thomas Joseph (see Bass, T. J.)	
Bate, Walter Jackson 1918-1999	DLB-67, 103
Bateman, Stephen circa 1510-1584	DLB-136
Christopher Bateman [publishing house]	DLB-170
Bates, H. E. 1905-1974	DLB-162, 191
Bates, Katharine Lee 1859-1929	DLB-71
Batiushkov, Konstantin Nikolaevich 1787-1855	DLB-205
B. T. Batsford [publishing house]	DLB-106
Battiscombe, Georgina 1905-	DLB-155
The Battle of Maldon circa 1000	DLB-146
Baudelaire, Charles 1821-1867	DLB-217
Baudrillard, Jean 1929-	DLB-296
Bauer, Bruno 1809-1882	DLB-133
Bauer, Wolfgang 1941-	DLB-124
Baum, L. Frank 1856-1919	DLB-22
Baum, Vicki 1888-1960	DLB-85
Baumbach, Jonathan 1933-	Y-80
Bausch, Richard 1945-	DLB-130
Tribute to James Dickey	Y-97
Tribute to Peter Taylor	Y-94
Bausch, Robert 1945-	DLB-218
Bawden, Nina 1925-	DLB-14, 161, 207
Bax, Clifford 1886-1962	DLB-10, 100
Baxter, Charles 1947-	DLB-130
Bayer, Eleanor (see Perry, Eleanor)	
Bayer, Konrad 1932-1964	DLB-85
Bayle, Pierre 1647-1706	DLB-268
Bayley, Barrington J. 1937-	DLB-261
Baynes, Pauline 1922-	DLB-160
Baynton, Barbara 1857-1929	DLB-230
Bazin, Hervé (Jean Pierre Marie Hervé-Bazin) 1911-1996	DLB-83
The BBC Four Samuel Johnson Prize for Non-fiction	Y-02
Beach, Sylvia 1887-1962	DLB-4; DS-15
Beacon Press	DLB-49
Beadle and Adams	DLB-49
Beagle, Peter S. 1939-	Y-80
Beal, M. F. 1937-	Y-81
Beale, Howard K. 1899-1959	DLB-17
Beard, Charles A. 1874-1948	DLB-17
Beat Generation (Beats)	
As I See It, by Carolyn Cassady	DLB-16
A Beat Chronology: The First Twenty-five Years, 1944-1969	DLB-16
The Commercialization of the Image of Revolt, by Kenneth Rexroth	DLB-16
Four Essays on the Beat Generation	DLB-16
in New York City	DLB-237
in the West	DLB-237
Outlaw Days	DLB-16
Periodicals of	DLB-16
Beattie, Ann 1947-	DLB-218, 278; Y-82
Beattie, James 1735-1803	DLB-109
Beatty, Chester 1875-1968	DLB-201
Beauchemin, Nérée 1850-1931	DLB-92
Beauchemin, Yves 1941-	DLB-60
Beaugrand, Honoré 1848-1906	DLB-99
Beaulieu, Victor-Lévy 1945-	DLB-53
Beaumont, Francis circa 1584-1616 and Fletcher, John 1579-1625	DLB-58; CDBLB-1
Beaumont, Sir John 1583?-1627	DLB-121
Beaumont, Joseph 1616-1699	DLB-126
Beauvoir, Simone de 1908-1986	DLB-72; Y-86
Personal Tribute to Simone de Beauvoir	Y-86
Beaver, Bruce 1928-	DLB-289
Becher, Ulrich 1910-1990	DLB-69
Becker, Carl 1873-1945	DLB-17
Becker, Jurek 1937-1997	DLB-75, 299
Becker, Jurgen 1932-	DLB-75
Beckett, Samuel 1906-1989	DLB-13, 15, 233; Y-90; CDBLB-7
Beckford, William 1760-1844	DLB-39, 213
Beckham, Barry 1944-	DLB-33
Bećković, Matija 1939-	DLB-181
Becon, Thomas circa 1512-1567	DLB-136
Becque, Henry 1837-1899	DLB-192
Beddoes, Thomas 1760-1808	DLB-158
Beddoes, Thomas Lovell 1803-1849	DLB-96
Bede circa 673-735	DLB-146
Bedford-Jones, H. 1887-1949	DLB-251
Bedregal, Yolanda 1913-1999	DLB-283
Beebe, William 1877-1962	DLB-275
Beecher, Catharine Esther 1800-1878	DLB-1, 243
Beecher, Henry Ward 1813-1887	DLB-3, 43, 250
Beer, George L. 1872-1920	DLB-47
Beer, Johann 1655-1700	DLB-168
Beer, Patricia 1919-1999	DLB-40
Beerbohm, Max 1872-1956	DLB-34, 100
Beer-Hofmann, Richard 1866-1945	DLB-81
Beers, Henry A. 1847-1926	DLB-71
S. O. Beeton [publishing house]	DLB-106
Begley, Louis 1933-	DLB-299
Bégon, Elisabeth 1696-1755	DLB-99
Behan, Brendan 1923-1964	DLB-13, 233; CDBLB-7
Behn, Aphra 1640?-1689	DLB-39, 80, 131
Behn, Harry 1898-1973	DLB-61
Behrman, S. N. 1893-1973	DLB-7, 44
Beklemishev, Iurii Solomonvich (see Krymov, Iurii Solomonovich)	
Belaney, Archibald Stansfeld (see Grey Owl)	
Belasco, David 1853-1931	DLB-7
Clarke Belford and Company	DLB-49
Belgian Luxembourg American Studies Association	Y-01
Belinsky, Vissarion Grigor'evich 1811-1848	DLB-198
Belitt, Ben 1911-	DLB-5
Belknap, Jeremy 1744-1798	DLB-30, 37

Bell, Adrian 1901-1980 ....DLB-191
Bell, Clive 1881-1964................. DS-10
Bell, Daniel 1919- DLB-246
Bell, Gertrude Margaret Lowthian
    1868-1926 ....DLB-174
Bell, James Madison 1826-1902..........DLB-50
Bell, Madison Smartt 1957- DLB-218, 278
    Tribute to Andrew Nelson Lytle........ Y-95
    Tribute to Peter Taylor............... Y-94
Bell, Marvin 1937- DLB-5
Bell, Millicent 1919- DLB-111
Bell, Quentin 1910-1996 ....DLB-155
Bell, Vanessa 1879-1961................ DS-10
George Bell and Sons..................DLB-106
Robert Bell [publishing house]..........DLB-49
Bellamy, Edward 1850-1898 ....DLB-12
Bellamy, Joseph 1719-1790..............DLB-31
John Bellamy [publishing house] DLB-170
La Belle Assemblée 1806-1837 ....DLB-110
Bellezza, Dario 1944-1996 ....DLB-128
Belli, Carlos Germán 1927- DLB-290
Belli, Gioconda 1948- DLB-290
Belloc, Hilaire 1870-1953 .... DLB-19, 100, 141, 174
Belloc, Madame (see Parkes, Bessie Rayner)
Bellonci, Maria 1902-1986..............DLB-196
Bellow, Saul 1915- DLB-2, 28, 299; Y-82;
                                       DS-3; CDALB-1
    Tribute to Isaac Bashevis Singer Y-91
Belmont Productions DLB-46
Belov, Vasilii Ivanovich 1932- DLB-302
Bels, Alberts 1938- DLB-232
Belševica, Vizma 1931- DLB-232; CDWLB-4
Bely, Andrei 1880-1934................DLB-295
Bemelmans, Ludwig 1898-1962..........DLB-22
Bemis, Samuel Flagg 1891-1973.........DLB-17
William Bemrose [publishing house] DLB-106
Ben no Naishi 1228?-1271? DLB-203
Benchley, Robert 1889-1945 ....DLB-11
Bencúr, Matej (see Kukučin, Martin)
Benedetti, Mario 1920- DLB-113
Benedict, Pinckney 1964- DLB-244
Benedict, Ruth 1887-1948 ....DLB-246
Benedictus, David 1938- DLB-14
Benedikt Gröndal 1826-1907..........DLB-293
Benedikt, Michael 1935- DLB-5
Benediktov, Vladimir Grigor'evich
    1807-1873......................DLB-205
Benét, Stephen Vincent
    1898-1943 ....DLB-4, 48, 102, 249
    Stephen Vincent Benét Centenary Y-97
Benét, William Rose 1886-1950.........DLB-45
Benford, Gregory 1941- Y-82
Benítez, Sandra 1941- DLB-292
Benjamin, Park 1809-1864..... DLB-3, 59, 73, 250
Benjamin, Peter (see Cunningham, Peter)

Benjamin, S. G. W. 1837-1914..........DLB-189
Benjamin, Walter 1892-1940 ....DLB-242
Benlowes, Edward 1602-1676 ....DLB-126
Benn, Gottfried 1886-1956 ....DLB-56
Benn Brothers Limited..................DLB-106
Bennett, Arnold
    1867-1931 ....DLB-10, 34, 98, 135; CDBLB-5
    The Arnold Bennett Society Y-98
Bennett, Charles 1899-1995.............DLB-44
Bennett, Emerson 1822-1905...........DLB-202
Bennett, Gwendolyn 1902-1981 ....DLB-51
Bennett, Hal 1930- DLB-33
Bennett, James Gordon 1795-1872........DLB-43
Bennett, James Gordon, Jr. 1841-1918.....DLB-23
Bennett, John 1865-1956 ....DLB-42
Bennett, Louise 1919- DLB-117; CDWLB-3
Benni, Stefano 1947- DLB-196
Benoit, Jacques 1941- DLB-60
Benson, A. C. 1862-1925................DLB-98
Benson, E. F. 1867-1940............ DLB-135, 153
    The E. F. Benson Society Y-98
    The Tilling Society Y-98
Benson, Jackson J. 1930- DLB-111
Benson, Robert Hugh 1871-1914........DLB-153
Benson, Stella 1892-1933..........DLB-36, 162
Bent, James Theodore 1852-1897 ....DLB-174
Bent, Mabel Virginia Anna ?-? DLB-174
Bentham, Jeremy 1748-1832 ... DLB-107, 158, 252
Bentley, E. C. 1875-1956 ....DLB-70
Bentley, Phyllis 1894-1977.............DLB-191
Bentley, Richard 1662-1742 ....DLB-252
Richard Bentley [publishing house] DLB-106
Benton, Robert 1932- and
    Newman, David 1937- DLB-44
Benziger Brothers......................DLB-49
Beowulf circa 900-1000 or 790-825
    ....DLB-146; CDBLB-1
Berent, Wacław 1873-1940 ....DLB-215
Beresford, Anne 1929- DLB-40
Beresford, John Davys
    1873-1947 .... DLB-162, 178, 197
    "Experiment in the Novel" (1929)
    [excerpt] DLB-36
Beresford-Howe, Constance 1922- DLB-88
R. G. Berford Company DLB-49
Berg, Elizabeth 1948- DLB-292
Berg, Stephen 1934- DLB-5
Bergengruen, Werner 1892-1964 ....DLB-56
Berger, John 1926- DLB-14, 207
Berger, Meyer 1898-1959 ....DLB-29
Berger, Thomas 1924- DLB-2; Y-80
    A Statement by Thomas Berger Y-80
Bergman, Hjalmar 1883-1931..........DLB-259
Bergman, Ingmar 1918- DLB-257
Berkeley, Anthony 1893-1971...........DLB-77
Berkeley, George 1685-1753 .... DLB-31, 101, 252

The Berkley Publishing Corporation......DLB-46
Berkman, Alexander 1870-1936........DLB-303
Berlin, Irving 1888-1989 ....DLB-265
Berlin, Lucia 1936- DLB-130
Berman, Marshall 1940- DLB-246
Berman, Sabina 1955- DLB-305
Bernal, Vicente J. 1888-1915 ....DLB-82
Bernanos, Georges 1888-1948...........DLB-72
Bernard, Catherine 1663?-1712 ....DLB-268
Bernard, Harry 1898-1979...............DLB-92
Bernard, John 1756-1828................DLB-37
Bernard of Chartres circa 1060-1124?....DLB-115
Bernard of Clairvaux 1090-1153........DLB-208
Bernard, Richard 1568-1641/1642.......DLB-281
Bernard Silvestris
    flourished circa 1130-1160 ....DLB-208
Bernari, Carlo 1909-1992 ....DLB-177
Bernhard, Thomas
    1931-1989 .... DLB-85, 124; CDWLB-2
Berniéres, Louis de 1954- DLB-271
Bernstein, Charles 1950- DLB-169
Berriault, Gina 1926-1999 ....DLB-130
Berrigan, Daniel 1921- DLB-5
Berrigan, Ted 1934-1983.............DLB-5, 169
Berry, Wendell 1934- DLB-5, 6, 234, 275
Berryman, John 1914-1972 ....DLB-48; CDALB-1
Bersianik, Louky 1930- DLB-60
Thomas Berthelet [publishing house] DLB-170
Berto, Giuseppe 1914-1978 ....DLB-177
Bertocci, Peter Anthony 1910-1989......DLB-279
Bertolucci, Attilio 1911-2000 ....DLB-128
Berton, Pierre 1920- DLB-68
Bertrand, Louis "Aloysius" 1807-1841....DLB-217
Besant, Sir Walter 1836-1901 ...... DLB-135, 190
Bessa-Luís, Agustina 1922- DLB-287
Bessette, Gerard 1920- DLB-53
Bessie, Alvah 1904-1985 ....DLB-26
Bester, Alfred 1913-1987 ....DLB-8
Besterman, Theodore 1904-1976........DLB-201
Beston, Henry (Henry Beston Sheahan)
    1888-1968 ....DLB-275
Best-Seller Lists
    An Assessment Y-84
    What's Really Wrong With
        Bestseller Lists Y-84
Bestuzhev, Aleksandr Aleksandrovich
    (Marlinsky) 1797-1837.............DLB-198
Bestuzhev, Nikolai Aleksandrovich
    1791-1855......................DLB-198
Betham-Edwards, Matilda Barbara
    (see Edwards, Matilda Barbara Betham-)
Betjeman, John
    1906-1984 .... DLB-20; Y-84; CDBLB-7
Betocchi, Carlo 1899-1986.............DLB-128
Bettarini, Mariella 1942- DLB-128
Betts, Doris 1932- DLB-218; Y-82
Beveridge, Albert J. 1862-1927 ....DLB-17

Beverley, Robert circa 1673-1722 ..... DLB-24, 30

Bevilacqua, Alberto 1934- DLB-196

Bevington, Louisa Sarah 1845-1895 ..... DLB-199

Beyle, Marie-Henri (see Stendhal)

Białoszewski, Miron 1922-1983 .... DLB-232

Bianco, Margery Williams 1881-1944 ... DLB-160

Bibaud, Adèle 1854-1941 .... DLB-92

Bibaud, Michel 1782-1857............. DLB-99

Bibliography
   Bibliographical and Textual Scholarship Since World War II Y-89

   Center for Bibliographical Studies and Research at the University of California, Riverside Y-91

   The Great Bibliographers Series Y-93

   Primary Bibliography: A Retrospective ... Y-95

Bichsel, Peter 1935- DLB-75

Bickerstaff, Isaac John 1733-circa 1808.... DLB-89

Drexel Biddle [publishing house] DLB-49

Bidermann, Jacob 1577 or 1578-1639 .... DLB-164

Bidwell, Walter Hilliard 1798-1881 ...... DLB-79

Biehl, Charlotta Dorothea 1731-1788 .... DLB-300

Bienek, Horst 1930-1990 .... DLB-75

Bierbaum, Otto Julius 1865-1910 ...... DLB-66

Bierce, Ambrose 1842-1914?
...... DLB-11, 12, 23, 71, 74, 186; CDALB-3

Bigelow, William F. 1879-1966 .... DLB-91

Biggle, Lloyd, Jr. 1923- DLB-8

Bigiaretti, Libero 1905-1993 .... DLB-177

Bigland, Eileen 1898-1970............. DLB-195

Biglow, Hosea (see Lowell, James Russell)

Bigongiari, Piero 1914-1997 .... DLB-128

Bilenchi, Romano 1909-1989 .... DLB-264

Billinger, Richard 1890-1965 .... DLB-124

Billings, Hammatt 1818-1874 .... DLB-188

Billings, John Shaw 1898-1975 .... DLB-137

Billings, Josh (see Shaw, Henry Wheeler)

Binding, Rudolf G. 1867-1938 .... DLB-66

Bingay, Malcolm 1884-1953 .... DLB-241

Bingham, Caleb 1757-1817 .... DLB-42

Bingham, George Barry 1906-1988 ..... DLB-127

Bingham, Sallie 1937- DLB-234

William Bingley [publishing house] DLB-154

Binyon, Laurence 1869-1943 .... DLB-19

Biographia Brittanica DLB-142

Biography
   Biographical Documents Y-84, 85

   A Celebration of Literary Biography Y-98

   Conference on Modern Biography Y-85

   The Cult of Biography
     Excerpts from the Second Folio Debate: "Biographies are generally a disease of English Literature" Y-86

   New Approaches to Biography: Challenges from Critical Theory, USC Conference on Literary Studies, 1990 .... Y-90

   "The New Biography," by Virginia Woolf, *New York Herald Tribune*, 30 October 1927 .... DLB-149

   "The Practice of Biography," in *The English Sense of Humour and Other Essays*, by Harold Nicolson DLB-149

   "Principles of Biography," in *Elizabethan and Other Essays*, by Sidney Lee .. DLB-149

   Remarks at the Opening of "The Biographical Part of Literature" Exhibition, by William R. Cagle.................. Y-98

   Survey of Literary Biographies Y-00

   A Transit of Poets and Others: American Biography in 1982................. Y-82

   The Year in Literary Biography Y-83–01

Biography, The Practice of:
   An Interview with B. L. Reid......... Y-83

   An Interview with David Herbert Donald .. Y-87

   An Interview with Humphrey Carpenter..... Y-84

   An Interview with Joan Mellen Y-94

   An Interview with John Caldwell Guilds Y-92

   An Interview with William Manchester... Y-85

John Bioren [publishing house].......... DLB-49

Bioy Casares, Adolfo 1914-1999 ...... DLB-113

Bird, Isabella Lucy 1831-1904 .... DLB-166

Bird, Robert Montgomery 1806-1854 ... DLB-202

Bird, William 1888-1963 .... DLB-4; DS-15

   The Cost of the *Cantos*: William Bird to Ezra Pound Y-01

Birken, Sigmund von 1626-1681 .... DLB-164

Birney, Earle 1904-1995............... DLB-88

Birrell, Augustine 1850-1933 .... DLB-98

Bisher, Furman 1918- DLB-171

Bishop, Elizabeth 1911-1979........... DLB-5, 169; CDALB-6

   The Elizabeth Bishop Society........... Y-01

Bishop, John Peale 1892-1944 ...... DLB-4, 9, 45

Bismarck, Otto von 1815-1898......... DLB-129

Bisset, Robert 1759-1805 .... DLB-142

Bissett, Bill 1939- DLB-53

Bitov, Andrei Georgievich 1937- DLB-302

Bitzius, Albert (see Gotthelf, Jeremias)

Bjørnboe, Jens 1920-1976 .... DLB-297

Bjørnvig, Thorkild 1918- DLB-214

Black, David (D. M.) 1941- DLB-40

Black, Gavin (Oswald Morris Wynd) 1913-1998 ....DLB-276

Black, Lionel (Dudley Barker) 1910-1980 ....DLB-276

Black, Winifred 1863-1936............. DLB-25

Walter J. Black [publishing house] DLB-46

Blackamore, Arthur 1679-? DLB-24, 39

Blackburn, Alexander L. 1929- Y-85

Blackburn, John 1923-1993 .... DLB-261

Blackburn, Paul 1926-1971 ....DLB-16; Y-81

Blackburn, Thomas 1916-1977 .... DLB-27

Blacker, Terence 1948- DLB-271

Blackmore, R. D. 1825-1900 .... DLB-18

Blackmore, Sir Richard 1654-1729 ...... DLB-131

Blackmur, R. P. 1904-1965 .... DLB-63

Blackwell, Alice Stone 1857-1950 .... DLB-303

Basil Blackwell, Publisher............ DLB-106

Blackwood, Algernon Henry 1869-1951 .... DLB-153, 156, 178

Blackwood, Caroline 1931-1996 .....DLB-14, 207

William Blackwood and Sons, Ltd. DLB-154

Blackwood's Edinburgh Magazine 1817-1980..................... DLB-110

Blades, William 1824-1890............ DLB-184

Blaga, Lucian 1895-1961 .... DLB-220

Blagden, Isabella 1817?-1873 .... DLB-199

Blair, Eric Arthur (see Orwell, George)

Blair, Francis Preston 1791-1876......... DLB-43

Blair, Hugh
   Lectures on Rhetoric and Belles Lettres (1783), [excerpts]................. DLB-31

Blair, James circa 1655-1743 .... DLB-24

Blair, John Durburrow 1759-1823 .... DLB-37

Blais, Marie-Claire 1939- DLB-53

Blaise, Clark 1940- DLB-53

Blake, George 1893-1961 .... DLB-191

Blake, Lillie Devereux 1833-1913.... DLB-202, 221

Blake, Nicholas (C. Day Lewis) 1904-1972 .... DLB-77

Blake, William 1757-1827 .... DLB-93, 154, 163; CDBLB-3

The Blakiston Company DLB-49

Blanchard, Stephen 1950- DLB-267

Blanchot, Maurice 1907-2003 ...... DLB-72, 296

Blanckenburg, Christian Friedrich von 1744-1796 .... DLB-94

Blandiana, Ana 1942- DLB-232; CDWLB-4

Blanshard, Brand 1892-1987 ....DLB-279

Blaser, Robin 1925- DLB-165

Blaumanis, Rudolfs 1863-1908......... DLB-220

Bleasdale, Alan 1946- DLB-245

Bledsoe, Albert Taylor 1809-1877....................DLB-3, 79, 248

Bleecker, Ann Eliza 1752-1783 .... DLB-200

Blelock and Company DLB-49

Blennerhassett, Margaret Agnew 1773-1842 .... DLB-99

Geoffrey Bles [publishing house] DLB-112

Blessington, Marguerite, Countess of 1789-1849 .... DLB-166

Blew, Mary Clearman 1939- DLB-256

Blicher, Steen Steensen 1782-1848 ...... DLB-300

The Blickling Homilies circa 971 .... DLB-146

Blind, Mathilde 1841-1896 .... DLB-199

Blish, James 1921-1975 .... DLB-8

E. Bliss and E. White [publishing house] DLB-49

Bliven, Bruce 1889-1977 ....DLB-137

Blixen, Karen 1885-1962 .... DLB-214

Bloch, Ernst 1885-1977 .... DLB-296

Bloch, Robert 1917-1994................ DLB-44

Tribute to John D. MacDonald........ Y-86

Block, Lawrence 1938- DLB-226

Block, Rudolph (see Lessing, Bruno)

Blok, Aleksandr Aleksandrovich
1880-1921.....................DLB-295

Blondal, Patricia 1926-1959........DLB-88

Bloom, Harold 1930- DLB-67

Bloomer, Amelia 1818-1894 ....DLB-79

Bloomfield, Robert 1766-1823 ......DLB-93

Bloomsbury Group DS-10

    The *Dreannought* Hoax............. DS-10

Bloor, Ella Reeve 1862-1951.........DLB-303

Blotner, Joseph 1923- DLB-111

Blount, Thomas 1618?-1679 ....DLB-236

Bloy, Léon 1846-1917 ....DLB-123

Blume, Judy 1938-...................DLB-52

    Tribute to Theodor Seuss Geisel......... Y-91

Blunck, Hans Friedrich 1888-1961 ....DLB-66

Blunden, Edmund 1896-1974 ... DLB-20, 100, 155

Blundeville, Thomas 1522?-1606 ....DLB-236

Blunt, Lady Anne Isabella Noel
1837-1917.....................DLB-174

Blunt, Wilfrid Scawen 1840-1922 .... DLB-19, 174

Bly, Nellie (see Cochrane, Elizabeth)

Bly, Robert 1926- DLB-5

Blyton, Enid 1897-1968 ....DLB-160

Boaden, James 1762-1839 ....DLB-89

Boas, Frederick S. 1862-1957..........DLB-149

The Bobbs-Merrill Company........DLB-46, 291

    The Bobbs-Merrill Archive at the
Lilly Library, Indiana University Y-90

Boborykin, Petr Dmitrievich 1836-1921 ..DLB-238

Bobrov, Semen Sergeevich 1763?-1810 ...DLB-150

Bobrowski, Johannes 1917-1965.........DLB-75

Bocage, Manuel Maria Barbosa du
1765-1805 ....DLB-287

Bodenheim, Maxwell 1892-1954........DLB-9, 45

Bodenstedt, Friedrich von 1819-1892 ....DLB-129

Bodini, Vittorio 1914-1970............DLB-128

Bodkin, M. McDonnell 1850-1933 ....DLB-70

Bodley, Sir Thomas 1545-1613 ....DLB-213

Bodley Head DLB-112

Bodmer, Johann Jakob 1698-1783 ......DLB-97

Bodmershof, Imma von 1895-1982......DLB-85

Bodsworth, Fred 1918- DLB-68

Böðvar Guðmundsson 1939- DLB-293

Boehm, Sydney 1908- DLB-44

Boer, Charles 1939- DLB-5

Boethius circa 480-circa 524 ....DLB-115

Boethius of Dacia circa 1240-? DLB-115

Bogan, Louise 1897-1970 ....DLB-45, 169

Bogarde, Dirk 1921-1999..............DLB-14

Bogdanov, Aleksandr Aleksandrovich
1873-1928 ....DLB-295

Bogdanovich, Ippolit Fedorovich
circa 1743-1803 ....DLB-150

David Bogue [publishing house] DLB-106

Bohjalian, Chris 1960- DLB-292

Böhme, Jakob 1575-1624..............DLB-164

H. G. Bohn [publishing house] DLB-106

Bohse, August 1661-1742..............DLB-168

Boie, Heinrich Christian 1744-1806......DLB-94

Boileau-Despréaux, Nicolas 1636-1711 ....DLB-268

Bok, Edward W. 1863-1930 ......DLB-91; DS-16

Boland, Eavan 1944- DLB-40

Boldrewood, Rolf (Thomas Alexander Browne)
1826?-1915 ....DLB-230

Bolingbroke, Henry St. John, Viscount
1678-1751 ....DLB-101

Böll, Heinrich
1917-1985 .... DLB-69; Y-85; CDWLB-2

Bolling, Robert 1738-1775 ....DLB-31

Bolotov, Andrei Timofeevich
1738-1833 ....DLB-150

Bolt, Carol 1941- DLB-60

Bolt, Robert 1924-1995 ....DLB-13, 233

Bolton, Herbert E. 1870-1953 ....DLB-17

Bonaventura DLB-90

Bonaventure circa 1217-1274 ....DLB-115

Bonaviri, Giuseppe 1924- DLB-177

Bond, Edward 1934- DLB-13

Bond, Michael 1926- DLB-161

Bondarev, Iurii Vasil'evich 1924- DLB-302

Albert and Charles Boni
[publishing house]..................DLB-46

Boni and Liveright....................DLB-46

Bonnefoy, Yves 1923- DLB-258

Bonner, Marita 1899-1971 ....DLB-228

Bonner, Paul Hyde 1893-1968........... DS-17

Bonner, Sherwood (see McDowell, Katharine
Sherwood Bonner)

Robert Bonner's Sons DLB-49

Bonnin, Gertrude Simmons (see Zitkala-Ša)

Bonsanti, Alessandro 1904-1984 ....DLB-177

Bontempelli, Massimo 1878-1960 ....DLB-264

Bontemps, Arna 1902-1973 ....DLB-48, 51

The Book Buyer (1867-1880, 1884-1918,
1935-1938 .... DS-13

The Book League of America DLB-46

Book Reviewing

    The American Book Review: A Sketch... Y-92

    Book Reviewing and the
Literary Scene.................Y-96, 97

    Book Reviewing in America Y-87–94

    Book Reviewing in America and the
Literary Scene.................... Y-95

    Book Reviewing in Texas............. Y-94

    Book Reviews in Glossy Magazines Y-95

    Do They or Don't They?
Writers Reading Book Reviews Y-01

    The Most Powerful Book Review
in America [*New York Times
Book Review*].................... Y-82

    Some Surprises and Universal Truths.... Y-92

    The Year in Book Reviewing and the
Literary Situation Y-98

Book Supply Company DLB-49

The Book Trade History Group Y-93

The Booker Prize..................... Y-96–98

    Address by Anthony Thwaite,
Chairman of the Booker Prize Judges
Comments from Former Booker
Prize Winners.................... Y-86

Boorde, Andrew circa 1490-1549 ....DLB-136

Boorstin, Daniel J. 1914- DLB-17

    Tribute to Archibald MacLeish......... Y-82

    Tribute to Charles Scribner Jr......... Y-95

Booth, Franklin 1874-1948.............DLB-188

Booth, Mary L. 1831-1889 ....DLB-79

Booth, Philip 1925- Y-82

Booth, Wayne C. 1921- DLB-67

Booth, William 1829-1912.............DLB-190

Bor, Josef 1906-1979 ....DLB-299

Borchardt, Rudolf 1877-1945...........DLB-66

Borchert, Wolfgang 1921-1947 ....DLB-69, 124

Bording, Anders 1619-1677............DLB-300

Borel, Pétrus 1809-1859................DLB-119

Borgen, Johan 1902-1979..............DLB-297

Borges, Jorge Luis
1899-1986 ... DLB-113, 283; Y-86; CDWLB-3

    The Poetry of Jorge Luis Borges........ Y-86

    A Personal Tribute Y-86

Borgese, Giuseppe Antonio 1882-1952 ...DLB-264

Börne, Ludwig 1786-1837 ....DLB-90

Bornstein, Miriam 1950- DLB-209

Borowski, Tadeusz
1922-1951 .... DLB-215; CDWLB-4

Borrow, George 1803-1881 ...... DLB-21, 55, 166

Bosanquet, Bernard 1848-1923 ....DLB-262

Bosch, Juan 1909-2001 ....DLB-145

Bosco, Henri 1888-1976................DLB-72

Bosco, Monique 1927- DLB-53

Bosman, Herman Charles 1905-1951 ....DLB-225

Bossuet, Jacques-Bénigne 1627-1704 ....DLB-268

Bostic, Joe 1908-1988.................DLB-241

Boston, Lucy M. 1892-1990 ....DLB-161

Boston Quarterly Review................DLB-1

Boston University

    Editorial Institute at Boston University... Y-00

    Special Collections at Boston University.. Y-99

Boswell, James
1740-1795 ....DLB-104, 142; CDBLB-2

Boswell, Robert 1953- DLB-234

Bosworth, David Y-82

    Excerpt from "Excerpts from a Report
of the Commission," in *The Death
of Descartes*..................... Y-82

Bote, Hermann circa 1460-circa 1520....DLB-179

Botev, Khristo 1847-1876..............DLB-147

Botkin, Vasilii Petrovich 1811-1869 .....DLB-277

Botta, Anne C. Lynch 1815-1891 .....DLB-3, 250

Botto, Ján (see Krasko, Ivan)

Bottome, Phyllis 1882-1963 . . . . DLB-197

Bottomley, Gordon 1874-1948 . . . . DLB-10

Bottoms, David 1949- DLB-120; Y-83

    Tribute to James Dickey Y-97

Bottrall, Ronald 1906- DLB-20

Bouchardy, Joseph 1810-1870 . . . . DLB-192

Boucher, Anthony 1911-1968 . . . . DLB-8

Boucher, Jonathan 1738-1804 . . . . DLB-31

Boucher de Boucherville, Georges
    1814-1894 . . . . DLB-99

Boudreau, Daniel (see Coste, Donat)

Bouhours, Dominique 1628-1702 . . . . DLB-268

Bourassa, Napoléon 1827-1916 . . . . DLB-99

Bourget, Paul 1852-1935 . . . . DLB-123

Bourinot, John George 1837-1902 . . . . DLB-99

Bourjaily, Vance 1922- DLB-2, 143

Bourne, Edward Gaylord 1860-1908 . . . . . DLB-47

Bourne, Randolph 1886-1918 . . . . DLB-63

Bousoño, Carlos 1923- DLB-108

Bousquet, Joë 1897-1950 . . . . DLB-72

Bova, Ben 1932- Y-81

Bovard, Oliver K. 1872-1945 . . . . DLB-25

Bove, Emmanuel 1898-1945 . . . . DLB-72

Bowen, Elizabeth
    1899-1973 . . . . DLB-15, 162; CDBLB-7

Bowen, Francis 1811-1890 . . . . DLB-1, 59, 235

Bowen, John 1924- DLB-13

Bowen, Marjorie 1886-1952 . . . . DLB-153

Bowen-Merrill Company DLB-49

Bowering, George 1935- DLB-53

Bowers, Bathsheba 1671-1718 . . . . DLB-200

Bowers, Claude G. 1878-1958 . . . . DLB-17

Bowers, Edgar 1924-2000 . . . . DLB-5

Bowers, Fredson Thayer
    1905-1991 . . . . DLB-140; Y-91

    The Editorial Style of Fredson Bowers . . . Y-91

    Fredson Bowers and
        Studies in Bibliography Y-91

    Fredson Bowers and the Cambridge
        Beaumont and Fletcher Y-91

    Fredson Bowers as Critic of Renaissance
        Dramatic Literature Y-91

    Fredson Bowers as Music Critic Y-91

    Fredson Bowers, Master Teacher Y-91

    An Interview [on Nabokov] Y-80

    Working with Fredson Bowers Y-91

Bowles, Paul 1910-1999 . . . . . . DLB-5, 6, 218; Y-99

Bowles, Samuel, III 1826-1878 . . . . DLB-43

Bowles, William Lisle 1762-1850 . . . . DLB-93

Bowman, Louise Morey 1882-1944 . . . . . . DLB-68

Bowne, Borden Parker 1847-1919 . . . . DLB-270

Boyd, James 1888-1944 . . . . DLB-9; DS-16

Boyd, John 1919- DLB-8

Boyd, Martin 1893-1972 . . . . DLB-260

Boyd, Thomas 1898-1935 . . . . DLB-9; DS-16

Boyd, William 1952- DLB-231

Boye, Karin 1900-1941 . . . . DLB-259

Boyesen, Hjalmar Hjorth
    1848-1895 . . . . DLB-12, 71; DS-13

Boylan, Clare 1948- DLB-267

Boyle, Kay 1902-1992   DLB-4, 9, 48, 86; DS-15;
    . . . . Y-93

Boyle, Roger, Earl of Orrery 1621-1679 . . . DLB-80

Boyle, T. Coraghessan
    1948- DLB-218, 278; Y-86

Božić, Mirko 1919- DLB-181

Brackenbury, Alison 1953- DLB-40

Brackenridge, Hugh Henry
    1748-1816 . . . . DLB-11, 37

    The Rising Glory of America DLB-37

Brackett, Charles 1892-1969 . . . . DLB-26

Brackett, Leigh 1915-1978 . . . . DLB-8, 26

John Bradburn [publishing house] DLB-49

Bradbury, Malcolm 1932-2000 . . . . . . DLB-14, 207

Bradbury, Ray 1920- DLB-2, 8; CDALB-6

Bradbury and Evans DLB-106

Braddon, Mary Elizabeth
    1835-1915 . . . . DLB-18, 70, 156

Bradford, Andrew 1686-1742 . . . . DLB-43, 73

Bradford, Gamaliel 1863-1932 . . . . DLB-17

Bradford, John 1749-1830 . . . . DLB-43

Bradford, Roark 1896-1948 . . . . DLB-86

Bradford, William 1590-1657 . . . . DLB-24, 30

Bradford, William, III 1719-1791 . . . . . DLB-43, 73

Bradlaugh, Charles 1833-1891 . . . . DLB-57

Bradley, David 1950- DLB-33

Bradley, F. H. 1846-1924 . . . . DLB-262

Bradley, Katherine Harris (see Field, Michael)

Bradley, Marion Zimmer 1930-1999 . . . . . DLB-8

Bradley, William Aspenwall 1878-1939 . . . DLB-4

Ira Bradley and Company DLB-49

J. W. Bradley and Company DLB-49

Bradshaw, Henry 1831-1886 . . . . DLB-184

Bradstreet, Anne
    1612 or 1613-1672 . . . . DLB-24; CDALB-2

Bradūnas, Kazys 1917- DLB-220

Bradwardine, Thomas circa 1295-1349 . . . DLB-115

Brady, Frank 1924-1986 . . . . DLB-111

Frederic A. Brady [publishing house] DLB-49

Bragg, Melvyn 1939- DLB-14, 271

Brahe, Tycho 1546-1601 . . . . DLB-300

Charles H. Brainard [publishing house] . . . DLB-49

Braine, John 1922-1986 . . DLB-15; Y-86; CDBLB-7

Braithwait, Richard 1588-1673 . . . . DLB-151

Braithwaite, William Stanley
    1878-1962 . . . . DLB-50, 54

Bräker, Ulrich 1735-1798 . . . . DLB-94

Bramah, Ernest 1868-1942 . . . . DLB-70

Branagan, Thomas 1774-1843 . . . . DLB-37

Brancati, Vitaliano 1907-1954 . . . . DLB-264

Branch, William Blackwell 1927- DLB-76

Brand, Christianna 1907-1988 . . . . DLB-276

Brand, Max (see Faust, Frederick Schiller)

Brandão, Raul 1867-1930 . . . . DLB-287

Branden Press DLB-46

Brandes, Georg 1842-1927 . . . . DLB-300

Branner, H.C. 1903-1966 . . . . DLB-214

Brant, Sebastian 1457-1521 . . . . DLB-179

Brassey, Lady Annie (Allnutt)
    1839-1887 . . . . DLB-166

Brathwaite, Edward Kamau
    1930- DLB-125; CDWLB-3

Brault, Jacques 1933- DLB-53

Braun, Matt 1932- DLB-212

Braun, Volker 1939- DLB-75, 124

Brautigan, Richard
    1935-1984 . . . . DLB-2, 5, 206; Y-80, 84

Braxton, Joanne M. 1950- DLB-41

Bray, Anne Eliza 1790-1883 . . . . DLB-116

Bray, Thomas 1656-1730 . . . . DLB-24

Brazdžionis, Bernardas 1907- DLB-220

George Braziller [publishing house] DLB-46

The Bread Loaf Writers' Conference 1983 . . . Y-84

Breasted, James Henry 1865-1935 . . . . . . DLB-47

Brecht, Bertolt
    1898-1956 . . . . DLB-56, 124; CDWLB-2

Bredel, Willi 1901-1964 . . . . DLB-56

Bregendahl, Marie 1867-1940 . . . . DLB-214

Breitinger, Johann Jakob 1701-1776 . . . . . DLB-97

Brekke, Paal 1923-1993 . . . . DLB-297

Bremser, Bonnie 1939- DLB-16

Bremser, Ray 1934-1998 . . . . DLB-16

Brennan, Christopher 1870-1932 . . . . DLB-230

Brentano, Bernard von 1901-1964 . . . . . . DLB-56

Brentano, Clemens 1778-1842 . . . . DLB-90

Brentano, Franz 1838-1917 . . . . DLB-296

Brentano's DLB-49

Brenton, Howard 1942- DLB-13

Breslin, Jimmy 1929-1996 . . . . DLB-185

Breton, André 1896-1966 . . . . DLB-65, 258

Breton, Nicholas circa 1555-circa 1626 . . . DLB-136

The Breton Lays
    1300-early fifteenth century DLB-146

Brett, Simon 1945- DLB-276

Brewer, Luther A. 1858-1933 . . . . DLB-187

Brewer, Warren and Putnam DLB-46

Brewster, Elizabeth 1922- DLB-60

Breytenbach, Breyten 1939- DLB-225

Bridge, Ann (Lady Mary Dolling Sanders
    O'Malley) 1889-1974 . . . . DLB-191

Bridge, Horatio 1806-1893 . . . . DLB-183

Bridgers, Sue Ellen 1942- DLB-52

Bridges, Robert
    1844-1930 . . . . DLB-19, 98; CDBLB-5

The Bridgewater Library DLB-213

Bridie, James 1888-1951 . . . . DLB-10

Brieux, Eugene 1858-1932 . . . . DLB-192

Brigadere, Anna
   1861-1933 . . . . DLB-220; CDWLB-4

Briggs, Charles Frederick
   1804-1877 . . . . DLB-3, 250

Brighouse, Harold 1882-1958 . . . . DLB-10

Bright, Mary Chavelita Dunne
   (see Egerton, George)

Brightman, Edgar Sheffield 1884-1953 . . . DLB-270

B. J. Brimmer Company DLB-46

Brines, Francisco 1932- DLB-134

Brink, André 1935- DLB-225

Brinley, George, Jr. 1817-1875 . . . . DLB-140

Brinnin, John Malcolm 1916-1998 . . . . DLB-48

Brisbane, Albert 1809-1890 . . . . DLB-3, 250

Brisbane, Arthur 1864-1936 . . . . DLB-25

British Academy DLB-112

The British Critic 1793-1843 . . . . DLB-110

British Library
   The American Trust for the
      British Library Y-96

   The British Library and the Regular
      Readers' Group Y-91

   Building the New British Library
      at St Pancras Y-94

British Literary Prizes DLB-207; Y-98

British Literature
   The "Angry Young Men" DLB-15

   Author-Printers, 1476-1599 . . . . DLB-167

   The Comic Tradition Continued DLB-15

   Documents on Sixteenth-Century
      Literature DLB-167, 172

   Eikon Basilike 1649 . . . . DLB-151

   Letter from London Y-96

   A Mirror for Magistrates DLB-167

   "Modern English Prose" (1876),
      by George Saintsbury DLB-57

   Sex, Class, Politics, and Religion [in the
      British Novel, 1930-1959] DLB-15

   Victorians on Rhetoric and Prose
      Style DLB-57

   The Year in British Fiction Y-99–01

   "You've Never Had It So Good," Gusted
      by "Winds of Change": British
      Fiction in the 1950s, 1960s,
      and After DLB-14

British Literature, Old and Middle English
   Anglo-Norman Literature in the
      Development of Middle English
      Literature DLB-146

   The *Alliterative Morte Arthure and the
      Stanzaic Morte Arthur*
      circa 1350-1400 . . . . DLB-146

   Ancrene Riwle circa 1200-1225 . . . . DLB-146

   The *Anglo-Saxon Chronicle* circa
      890-1154 . . . . DLB-146

   The Battle of Maldon circa 1000 . . . . DLB-146

   Beowulf circa 900-1000 or
      790-825 . . . . DLB-146; CDBLB-1

   The Blickling Homilies circa 971 . . . . . DLB-146

   The Breton Lays
      1300-early fifteenth century DLB-146

   The Castle of Perseverance
      circa 1400-1425 . . . . DLB-146

   The Celtic Background to Medieval
      English Literature DLB-146

   The Chester Plays circa 1505-1532;
      revisions until 1575 . . . . DLB-146

   Cursor Mundi circa 1300 . . . . DLB-146

   The English Language: 410
      to 1500 . . . . DLB-146

   The Germanic Epic and Old English
      Heroic Poetry: *Widsith, Waldere,*
      and *The Fight at Finnsburg* DLB-146

   Judith circa 930 . . . . DLB-146

   The Matter of England 1240-1400 . . . DLB-146

   The Matter of Rome early twelfth to
      late fifteenth centuries DLB-146

   Middle English Literature:
      An Introduction DLB-146

   The Middle English Lyric DLB-146

   Morality Plays: *Mankind* circa 1450-1500
      and *Everyman* circa 1500 . . . . DLB-146

   N-Town Plays circa 1468 to early
      sixteenth century DLB-146

   Old English Literature:
      An Introduction DLB-146

   Old English Riddles
      eighth to tenth centuries DLB-146

   The Owl and the Nightingale
      circa 1189-1199 . . . . DLB-146

   The Paston Letters 1422-1509 . . . . DLB-146

   The Seafarer circa 970 . . . . DLB-146

   The *South English Legendary* circa
      thirteenth to fifteenth centuries DLB-146

*The British Review and London Critical
Journal* 1811-1825 . . . . DLB-110

Brito, Aristeo 1942- DLB-122

Brittain, Vera 1893-1970 . . . . DLB-191

Briusov, Valerii Iakovlevich 1873-1924 . . . DLB-295

Brizeux, Auguste 1803-1858 . . . . DLB-217

Broadway Publishing Company DLB-46

Broch, Hermann
   1886-1951 . . . . DLB-85, 124; CDWLB-2

Brochu, André 1942- DLB-53

Brock, Edwin 1927-1997 . . . . DLB-40

Brockes, Barthold Heinrich 1680-1747 . . . DLB-168

Brod, Max 1884-1968 . . . . DLB-81

Brodber, Erna 1940- DLB-157

Brodhead, John R. 1814-1873 . . . . DLB-30

Brodkey, Harold 1930-1996 . . . . DLB-130

Brodsky, Joseph (Iosif Aleksandrovich
   Brodsky) 1940-1996 . . . . DLB-285; Y-87

   Nobel Lecture 1987 . . . . Y-87

Brodsky, Michael 1948- DLB-244

Broeg, Bob 1918- DLB-171

Brøgger, Suzanne 1944- DLB-214

Brome, Richard circa 1590-1652 . . . . DLB-58

Brome, Vincent 1910- DLB-155

Bromfield, Louis 1896-1956 . . . . DLB-4, 9, 86

Bromige, David 1933- DLB-193

Broner, E. M. 1930- DLB-28

Tribute to Bernard Malamud Y-86

Bronk, William 1918-1999 . . . . DLB-165

Bronnen, Arnolt 1895-1959 . . . . DLB-124

Brontë, Anne 1820-1849 . . . . DLB-21, 199

Brontë, Charlotte
   1816-1855 . . . . . . DLB-21, 159, 199; CDBLB-4

Brontë, Emily
   1818-1848 . . . . . . DLB-21, 32, 199; CDBLB-4

The Brontë Society Y-98

Brook, Stephen 1947- DLB-204

Brook Farm 1841-1847 . . . . DLB-1; 223; DS-5

Brooke, Frances 1724-1789 . . . . DLB-39, 99

Brooke, Henry 1703?-1783 . . . . DLB-39

Brooke, L. Leslie 1862-1940 . . . . DLB-141

Brooke, Margaret, Ranee of Sarawak
   1849-1936 . . . . DLB-174

Brooke, Rupert
   1887-1915 . . . . DLB-19, 216; CDBLB-6

   The Friends of the Dymock Poets Y-00

Brooker, Bertram 1888-1955 . . . . DLB-88

Brooke-Rose, Christine 1923- DLB-14, 231

Brookner, Anita 1928- DLB-194; Y-87

Brooks, Charles Timothy 1813-1883 . . DLB-1, 243

Brooks, Cleanth 1906-1994 . . . . DLB-63; Y-94

   Tribute to Katherine Anne Porter Y-80

   Tribute to Walker Percy Y-90

Brooks, Gwendolyn
   1917-2000 . . . . DLB-5, 76, 165; CDALB-1

   Tribute to Julian Mayfield Y-84

Brooks, Jeremy 1926- DLB-14

Brooks, Mel 1926- DLB-26

Brooks, Noah 1830-1903 . . . . DLB-42; DS-13

Brooks, Richard 1912-1992 . . . . DLB-44

Brooks, Van Wyck 1886-1963 . . . DLB-45, 63, 103

Brophy, Brigid 1929-1995 . . . . DLB-14, 70, 271

Brophy, John 1899-1965 . . . . DLB-191

Brorson, Hans Adolph 1694-1764 . . . . DLB-300

Brossard, Chandler 1922-1993 . . . . DLB-16

Brossard, Nicole 1943- DLB-53

Broster, Dorothy Kathleen 1877-1950 . . . . DLB-160

Brother Antoninus (see Everson, William)

Brotherton, Lord 1856-1930 . . . . DLB-184

Brougham, John 1810-1880 . . . . DLB-11

Brougham and Vaux, Henry Peter
   Brougham, Baron 1778-1868 . . . . DLB-110, 158

Broughton, James 1913-1999 . . . . DLB-5

Broughton, Rhoda 1840-1920 . . . . DLB-18

Broun, Heywood 1888-1939 . . . . DLB-29, 171

Browder, Earl 1891-1973 . . . . DLB-303

Brown, Alice 1856-1948 . . . . DLB-78

Brown, Bob 1886-1959 . . . . DLB-4, 45; DS-15

Brown, Cecil 1943- DLB-33

Brown, Charles Brockden
   1771-1810 . . . . DLB-37, 59, 73; CDALB-2

Brown, Christy 1932-1981 . . . . DLB-14

Brown, Dee 1908-2002 . . . . Y-80

Brown, Frank London 1927-1962 . . . . DLB-76

Brown, Fredric 1906-1972 . . . . DLB-8

Brown, George Mackay
1921-1996 . . . . DLB-14, 27, 139, 271

Brown, Harry 1917-1986 . . . . DLB-26

Brown, Larry 1951- DLB-234, 292

Brown, Lew 1893-1958 . . . . DLB-265

Brown, Marcia 1918- DLB-61

Brown, Margaret Wise 1910-1952 . . . . DLB-22

Brown, Morna Doris (see Ferrars, Elizabeth)

Brown, Oliver Madox 1855-1874 . . . . DLB-21

Brown, Sterling 1901-1989 . . . . . . DLB-48, 51, 63

Brown, T. E. 1830-1897 . . . . DLB-35

Brown, Thomas Alexander (see Boldrewood, Rolf)

Brown, Warren 1894-1978 . . . . DLB-241

Brown, William Hill 1765-1793 . . . . DLB-37

Brown, William Wells
1815-1884. . . . . DLB-3, 50, 183, 248

Brown University
The Festival of Vanguard Narrative Y-93

Browne, Charles Farrar 1834-1867 . . . . DLB-11

Browne, Frances 1816-1879 . . . . DLB-199

Browne, Francis Fisher 1843-1913 . . . . DLB-79

Browne, Howard 1908-1999 . . . . DLB-226

Browne, J. Ross 1821-1875 . . . . DLB-202

Browne, Michael Dennis 1940- DLB-40

Browne, Sir Thomas 1605-1682 . . . . DLB-151

Browne, William, of Tavistock
1590-1645 . . . . DLB-121

Browne, Wynyard 1911-1964 . . . . . . DLB-13, 233

Browne and Nolan DLB-106

Brownell, W. C. 1851-1928 . . . . DLB-71

Browning, Elizabeth Barrett
1806-1861 . . . . DLB-32, 199; CDBLB-4

Browning, Robert
1812-1889 . . . . DLB-32, 163; CDBLB-4

Essay on Chatterton DLB-32

Introductory Essay: *Letters of Percy Bysshe Shelley* (1852) DLB-32

"The Novel in [Robert Browning's] 'The Ring and the Book'" (1912),
by Henry James DLB-32

Brownjohn, Allan 1931- DLB-40

Tribute to John Betjeman Y-84

Brownson, Orestes Augustus
1803-1876 . . . . DLB-1, 59, 73, 243; DS-5

Bruccoli, Matthew J. 1931- DLB-103

Joseph [Heller] and George [V. Higgins] . . . Y-99

Response [to Busch on Fitzgerald] Y-96

Tribute to Albert Erskine Y-93

Tribute to Charles E. Feinberg Y-88

Working with Fredson Bowers Y-91

Bruce, Charles 1906-1971 . . . . DLB-68

Bruce, John Edward 1856-1924
Three Documents [African American poets] DLB-50

Bruce, Leo 1903-1979 . . . . DLB-77

Bruce, Mary Grant 1878-1958 . . . . DLB-230

Bruce, Philip Alexander 1856-1933 . . . . . . DLB-47

Bruce-Novoa, Juan 1944- DLB-82

Bruckman, Clyde 1894-1955 . . . . DLB-26

Bruckner, Ferdinand 1891-1958 . . . . DLB-118

Brundage, John Herbert (see Herbert, John)

Brunner, John 1934-1995 . . . . DLB-261

Tribute to Theodore Sturgeon Y-85

Brutus, Dennis
1924- DLB-117, 225; CDWLB-3

Bryan, C. D. B. 1936- DLB-185

Bryan, William Jennings 1860-1925 . . . . . DLB-303

Bryant, Arthur 1899-1985 . . . . DLB-149

Bryant, William Cullen 1794-1878
. . . . DLB-3, 43, 59, 189, 250; CDALB-2

Bryce, James 1838-1922 . . . . DLB-166, 190

Bryce Echenique, Alfredo
1939- DLB-145; CDWLB-3

Bryden, Bill 1942- DLB-233

Brydges, Sir Samuel Egerton
1762-1837 . . . . DLB-107, 142

Bryskett, Lodowick 1546?-1612 . . . . DLB-167

Buchan, John 1875-1940 . . . . DLB-34, 70, 156

Buchanan, George 1506-1582 . . . . DLB-132

Buchanan, Robert 1841-1901 . . . . DLB-18, 35

"The Fleshly School of Poetry and
Other Phenomena of the Day"
(1872) DLB-35

"The Fleshly School of Poetry:
Mr. D. G. Rossetti" (1871),
by Thomas Maitland DLB-35

Buchler, Justus 1914-1991 . . . . DLB-279

Buchman, Sidney 1902-1975 . . . . DLB-26

Buchner, Augustus 1591-1661 . . . . DLB-164

Büchner, Georg
1813-1837 . . . . DLB-133; CDWLB-2

Bucholtz, Andreas Heinrich 1607-1671 . . . DLB-168

Buck, Pearl S. 1892-1973 . . DLB-9, 102; CDALB-7

Bucke, Charles 1781-1846 . . . . DLB-110

Bucke, Richard Maurice 1837-1902 . . . . . DLB-99

Buckingham, Edwin 1810-1833 . . . . DLB-73

Buckingham, Joseph Tinker 1779-1861 . . . DLB-73

Buckler, Ernest 1908-1984 . . . . DLB-68

Buckley, Vincent 1925-1988 . . . . DLB-289

Buckley, William F., Jr. 1925- DLB-137; Y-80

Publisher's Statement From the
Initial Issue of *National Review*
(19 November 1955) DLB-137

Buckminster, Joseph Stevens
1784-1812 . . . . DLB-37

Buckner, Robert 1906- DLB-26

Budd, Thomas ?-1698 . . . . DLB-24

Budrys, A. J. 1931- DLB-8

Buechner, Frederick 1926- Y-80

Buell, John 1927- DLB-53

Buenaventura, Enrique 1925-2003 . . . . . . DLB-305

Bufalino, Gesualdo 1920-1996 . . . . DLB-196

Job Buffum [publishing house] DLB-49

Bugnet, Georges 1879-1981 . . . . DLB-92

Buies, Arthur 1840-1901 . . . . DLB-99

Bukiet, Melvin Jules 1953- DLB-299

Bukowski, Charles 1920-1994 . . . . DLB-5, 130, 169

Bulatović, Miodrag
1930-1991 . . . . DLB-181; CDWLB-4

Bulgakov, Mikhail Afanas'evich
1891-1940 . . . . DLB-272

Bulgarin, Faddei Venediktovich
1789-1859 . . . . DLB-198

Bulger, Bozeman 1877-1932 . . . . DLB-171

Bull, Olaf 1883-1933 . . . . DLB-297

Bullein, William
between 1520 and 1530-1576 . . . . DLB-167

Bullins, Ed 1935- DLB-7, 38, 249

Bulwer, John 1606-1656 . . . . DLB-236

Bulwer-Lytton, Edward (also Edward
Bulwer) 1803-1873 . . . . DLB-21

"On Art in Fiction" (1838) DLB-21

Bumpus, Jerry 1937- Y-81

Bunce and Brother DLB-49

Bunner, H. C. 1855-1896 . . . . DLB-78, 79

Bunting, Basil 1900-1985 . . . . DLB-20

Buntline, Ned (Edward Zane Carroll
Judson) 1821-1886 . . . . DLB-186

Bunyan, John 1628-1688 . . . . . DLB-39; CDBLB-2

The Author's Apology for
His Book DLB-39

Burch, Robert 1925- DLB-52

Burciaga, José Antonio 1940- DLB-82

Burdekin, Katharine (Murray Constantine)
1896-1963 . . . . DLB-255

Bürger, Gottfried August 1747-1794 . . . . . DLB-94

Burgess, Anthony (John Anthony Burgess Wilson)
1917-1993 . . . . . . DLB-14, 194, 261; CDBLB-8

The Anthony Burgess Archive at
the Harry Ransom Humanities
Research Center Y-98

Anthony Burgess's *99 Novels*:
An Opinion Poll Y-84

Burgess, Gelett 1866-1951 . . . . DLB-11

Burgess, John W. 1844-1931 . . . . DLB-47

Burgess, Thornton W. 1874-1965 . . . . DLB-22

Burgess, Stringer and Company DLB-49

Burgos, Julia de 1914-1953 . . . . DLB-290

Burick, Si 1909-1986 . . . . DLB-171

Burk, John Daly circa 1772-1808 . . . . DLB-37

Burk, Ronnie 1955- DLB-209

Burke, Edmund 1729?-1797 . . . . DLB-104, 252

Burke, James Lee 1936- DLB-226

Burke, Johnny 1908-1964 . . . . DLB-265

Burke, Kenneth 1897-1993 . . . . DLB-45, 63

Burke, Thomas 1886-1945 . . . . DLB-197

Burley, Dan 1907-1962 . . . . DLB-241

Burley, W. J. 1914- DLB-276

Burlingame, Edward Livermore
1848-1922 . . . . DLB-79

Burman, Carina 1960- DLB-257

Burnet, Gilbert 1643-1715 . . . . DLB-101

Burnett, Frances Hodgson 1849-1924 . . . . DLB-42, 141; DS-13, 14

Burnett, W. R. 1899-1982 . . . . DLB-9, 226

Burnett, Whit 1899-1973 . . . . DLB-137

Burney, Fanny 1752-1840 . . . . DLB-39

    Dedication, *The Wanderer* (1814) DLB-39

    Preface to *Evelina* (1778) DLB-39

Burns, Alan 1929- DLB-14, 194

Burns, Joanne 1945- DLB-289

Burns, John Horne 1916-1953 . . . . Y-85

Burns, Robert 1759-1796 . . . . . DLB-109; CDBLB-3

Burns and Oates DLB-106

Burnshaw, Stanley 1906- DLB-48; Y-97

    James Dickey and Stanley Burnshaw Correspondence Y-02

    Review of Stanley Burnshaw: The Collected Poems and Selected Prose Y-02

    Tribute to Robert Penn Warren Y-89

Burr, C. Chauncey 1815?-1883 . . . . DLB-79

Burr, Esther Edwards 1732-1758 . . . . DLB-200

Burroughs, Edgar Rice 1875-1950 . . . . DLB-8

    The Burroughs Bibliophiles Y-98

Burroughs, John 1837-1921 . . . . DLB-64, 275

Burroughs, Margaret T. G. 1917- DLB-41

Burroughs, William S., Jr. 1947-1981 . . . . . DLB-16

Burroughs, William Seward 1914-1997
. . . . DLB-2, 8, 16, 152, 237; Y-81, 97

Burroway, Janet 1936- DLB-6

Burt, Maxwell Struthers
1882-1954 . . . . DLB-86; DS-16

A. L. Burt and Company DLB-49

Burton, Hester 1913- DLB-161

Burton, Isabel Arundell 1831-1896 . . . . . . DLB-166

Burton, Miles (see Rhode, John)

Burton, Richard Francis
1821-1890 . . . . DLB-55, 166, 184

Burton, Robert 1577-1640 . . . . DLB-151

Burton, Virginia Lee 1909-1968 . . . . DLB-22

Burton, William Evans 1804-1860 . . . . DLB-73

Burwell, Adam Hood 1790-1849 . . . . DLB-99

Bury, Lady Charlotte 1775-1861 . . . . DLB-116

Busch, Frederick 1941- DLB-6, 218

    Excerpts from Frederick Busch's USC Remarks [on F. Scott Fitzgerald] Y-96

    Tribute to James Laughlin Y-97

    Tribute to Raymond Carver Y-88

Busch, Niven 1903-1991 . . . . DLB-44

Bushnell, Horace 1802-1876 . . . . DS-13

Business & Literature
    The Claims of Business and Literature: An Undergraduate Essay by Maxwell Perkins Y-01

Bussières, Arthur de 1877-1913 . . . . DLB-92

Butler, Charles circa 1560-1647 . . . . DLB-236

Butler, Guy 1918- DLB-225

Butler, Joseph 1692-1752 . . . . DLB-252

Butler, Josephine Elizabeth
1828-1906 . . . . DLB-190

Butler, Juan 1942-1981 . . . . DLB-53

Butler, Judith 1956- DLB-246

Butler, Octavia E. 1947- DLB-33

Butler, Pierce 1884-1953 . . . . DLB-187

Butler, Robert Olen 1945- DLB-173

Butler, Samuel 1613-1680 . . . . DLB-101, 126

Butler, Samuel
1835-1902 . . . . DLB-18, 57, 174; CDBLB-5

Butler, William Francis 1838-1910 . . . . . . DLB-166

E. H. Butler and Company DLB-49

Butor, Michel 1926- DLB-83

Nathaniel Butter [publishing house] DLB-170

Butterworth, Hezekiah 1839-1905 . . . . DLB-42

Buttitta, Ignazio 1899-1997 . . . . DLB-114

Butts, Mary 1890-1937 . . . . DLB-240

Buzo, Alex 1944- DLB-289

Buzzati, Dino 1906-1972 . . . . DLB-177

Byars, Betsy 1928- DLB-52

Byatt, A. S. 1936- DLB-14, 194

Byles, Mather 1707-1788 . . . . DLB-24

Henry Bynneman [publishing house] DLB-170

Bynner, Witter 1881-1968 . . . . DLB-54

Byrd, William circa 1543-1623 . . . . DLB-172

Byrd, William, II 1674-1744 . . . . DLB-24, 140

Byrne, John Keyes (see Leonard, Hugh)

Byron, George Gordon, Lord
1788-1824 . . . . DLB-96, 110; CDBLB-3

    The Byron Society of America Y-00

Byron, Robert 1905-1941 . . . . DLB-195

C

Caballero Bonald, José Manuel
1926- DLB-108

Cabañero, Eladio 1930- DLB-134

Cabell, James Branch 1879-1958 . . . . DLB-9, 78

Cabeza de Baca, Manuel 1853-1915 . . . . . DLB-122

Cabeza de Baca Gilbert, Fabiola
1898- DLB-122

Cable, George Washington
1844-1925 . . . . DLB-12, 74; DS-13

Cable, Mildred 1878-1952 . . . . DLB-195

Cabral, Manuel del 1907-1999 . . . . DLB-283

Cabrera, Lydia 1900-1991 . . . . DLB-145

Cabrera Infante, Guillermo
1929- DLB-113; CDWLB-3

Cabrujas, José Ignacio 1937-1995 . . . . DLB-305

Cadell [publishing house] DLB-154

Cady, Edwin H. 1917- DLB-103

Caedmon flourished 658-680 . . . . DLB-146

Caedmon School circa 660-899 . . . . DLB-146

Caesar, Irving 1895-1996 . . . . DLB-265

Cafés, Brasseries, and Bistros DS-15

Cage, John 1912-1992 . . . . DLB-193

Cahan, Abraham 1860-1951 . . . . DLB-9, 25, 28

Cahn, Sammy 1913-1993 . . . . DLB-265

Cain, George 1943- DLB-33

Cain, James M. 1892-1977 . . . . DLB-226

Caird, Edward 1835-1908 . . . . DLB-262

Caird, Mona 1854-1932 . . . . DLB-197

Čaks, Aleksandrs
1901-1950 . . . . DLB-220; CDWLB-4

Caldecott, Randolph 1846-1886 . . . . DLB-163

John Calder Limited
[Publishing house] DLB-112

Calderón de la Barca, Fanny
1804-1882 . . . . DLB-183

Caldwell, Ben 1937- DLB-38

Caldwell, Erskine 1903-1987 . . . . DLB-9, 86

H. M. Caldwell Company DLB-49

Caldwell, Taylor 1900-1985 . . . . DS-17

Calhoun, John C. 1782-1850 . . . . DLB-3, 248

Călinescu, George 1899-1965 . . . . DLB-220

Calisher, Hortense 1911- DLB-2, 218

Calkins, Mary Whiton 1863-1930 . . . . DLB-270

Callaghan, Mary Rose 1944- DLB-207

Callaghan, Morley 1903-1990 . . . . . DLB-68; DS-15

Callahan, S. Alice 1868-1894 . . . . DLB-175, 221

Callaloo [journal] Y-87

Callimachus circa 305 B.C.-240 B.C. DLB-176

Calmer, Edgar 1907- DLB-4

Calverley, C. S. 1831-1884 . . . . DLB-35

Calvert, George Henry
1803-1889 . . . . DLB-1, 64, 248

Calverton, V. F. (George Goetz)
1900-1940 . . . . DLB-303

Calvino, Italo 1923-1985 . . . . DLB-196

Cambridge, Ada 1844-1926 . . . . DLB-230

Cambridge Press DLB-49

Cambridge Songs (Carmina Cantabrigensia)
circa 1050 . . . . DLB-148

Cambridge University
    Cambridge and the Apostles DS-5

Cambridge University Press DLB-170

Camden, William 1551-1623 . . . . DLB-172

Camden House: An Interview with
James Hardin Y-92

Cameron, Eleanor 1912-2000 . . . . DLB-52

Cameron, George Frederick
1854-1885 . . . . DLB-99

Cameron, Lucy Lyttelton 1781-1858 . . . . . DLB-163

Cameron, Peter 1959- DLB-234

Cameron, William Bleasdell 1862-1951 . . . DLB-99

Camm, John 1718-1778 . . . . DLB-31

Camões, Luís de 1524-1580 . . . . DLB-287

Camon, Ferdinando 1935- DLB-196

Camp, Walter 1859-1925 . . . . DLB-241

Campana, Dino 1885-1932 . . . . DLB-114

Campbell, Bebe Moore 1950- DLB-227

Campbell, David 1915-1979 . . . . DLB-260

Campbell, Gabrielle Margaret Vere
(see Shearing, Joseph, and Bowen, Marjorie)

Campbell, James Dykes 1838-1895 ..... DLB-144
Campbell, James Edwin 1867-1896 .... DLB-50
Campbell, John 1653-1728 .... DLB-43
Campbell, John W., Jr. 1910-1971 .... DLB-8
Campbell, Ramsey 1946- DLB-261
Campbell, Roy 1901-1957 .... DLB-20, 225
Campbell, Thomas 1777-1844 ...... DLB-93, 144
Campbell, William Edward (see March, William)
Campbell, William Wilfred 1858-1918.... DLB-92
Campion, Edmund 1539-1581 .... DLB-167
Campion, Thomas
  1567-1620 .... DLB-58, 172; CDBLB-1
Campo, Rafael 1964- DLB-282
Campton, David 1924- DLB-245
Camus, Albert 1913-1960 .... DLB-72
Camus, Jean-Pierre 1584-1652 .... DLB-268
The Canadian Publishers' Records Database .. Y-96
Canby, Henry Seidel 1878-1961 .... DLB-91
Cancioneros DLB-286
Candelaria, Cordelia 1943- DLB-82
Candelaria, Nash 1928- DLB-82
Canetti, Elias
  1905-1994 .... DLB-85, 124; CDWLB-2
Canham, Erwin Dain 1904-1982 .... DLB-127
Canitz, Friedrich Rudolph Ludwig von
  1654-1699 .... DLB-168
Cankar, Ivan 1876-1918 ..... DLB-147; CDWLB-4
Cannan, Gilbert 1884-1955 .... DLB-10, 197
Cannan, Joanna 1896-1961 .... DLB-191
Cannell, Kathleen 1891-1974 .... DLB-4
Cannell, Skipwith 1887-1957 .... DLB-45
Canning, George 1770-1827 .... DLB-158
Cannon, Jimmy 1910-1973 .... DLB-171
Cano, Daniel 1947- DLB-209
Old Dogs / New Tricks? New
  Technologies, the Canon, and the
  Structure of the Profession Y-02
Cantú, Norma Elia 1947- DLB-209
Cantwell, Robert 1908-1978 .... DLB-9
Jonathan Cape and Harrison Smith
  [publishing house] DLB-46
Jonathan Cape Limited DLB-112
Čapek, Karel 1890-1938 .... DLB-215; CDWLB-4
Capen, Joseph 1658-1725 .... DLB-24
Capes, Bernard 1854-1918 .... DLB-156
Capote, Truman 1924-1984
  .... DLB-2, 185, 227; Y-80, 84; CDALB-1
Capps, Benjamin 1922- DLB-256
Caproni, Giorgio 1912-1990 .... DLB-128
Caragiale, Mateiu Ioan 1885-1936 ...... DLB-220
Carballido, Emilio 1925- DLB-305
Cardarelli, Vincenzo 1887-1959 .... DLB-114
Cardenal, Ernesto 1925- DLB-290
Cárdenas, Reyes 1948- DLB-122
Cardinal, Marie 1929-2001 .... DLB-83
Cardoza y Aragón, Luis 1901-1992 ..... DLB-290

Carew, Jan 1920- DLB-157
Carew, Thomas 1594 or 1595-1640 ... DLB-126
Carey, Henry circa 1687-1689-1743 ..... DLB-84
Carey, Mathew 1760-1839 .... DLB-37, 73
M. Carey and Company DLB-49
Carey, Peter 1943- DLB-289
Carey and Hart DLB-49
Carell, Lodowick 1602-1675 .... DLB-58
Carleton, William 1794-1869 .... DLB-159
G. W. Carleton [publishing house] DLB-49
Carlile, Richard 1790-1843 .... DLB-110, 158
Carlson, Ron 1947- DLB-244
Carlyle, Jane Welsh 1801-1866 .... DLB-55
Carlyle, Thomas
  1795-1881 .... DLB-55, 144; CDBLB-3
  "The Hero as Man of Letters:
    Johnson, Rousseau, Burns"
    (1841) [excerpt] DLB-57
  The Hero as Poet. Dante; Shakspeare
    (1841) DLB-32
Carman, Bliss 1861-1929 .... DLB-92
Carmina Burana circa 1230 .... DLB-138
Carnap, Rudolf 1891-1970 .... DLB-270
Carnero, Guillermo 1947- DLB-108
Carossa, Hans 1878-1956 .... DLB-66
Carpenter, Humphrey
  1946- DLB-155; Y-84, 99
Carpenter, Stephen Cullen ?-1820? DLB-73
Carpentier, Alejo
  1904-1980 .... DLB-113; CDWLB-3
Carr, Emily (1871-1945) DLB-68
Carr, Marina 1964- DLB-245
Carr, Virginia Spencer 1929- DLB-111; Y-00
Carrera Andrade, Jorge 1903-1978 ...... DLB-283
Carrier, Roch 1937- DLB-53
Carrillo, Adolfo 1855-1926 .... DLB-122
Carroll, Gladys Hasty 1904- DLB-9
Carroll, John 1735-1815 .... DLB-37
Carroll, John 1809-1884 .... DLB-99
Carroll, Lewis
  1832-1898 ...... DLB-18, 163, 178; CDBLB-4
  The Lewis Carroll Centenary Y-98
  The Lewis Carroll Society
    of North America Y-00
Carroll, Paul 1927- DLB-16
Carroll, Paul Vincent 1900-1968 .... DLB-10
Carroll and Graf Publishers DLB-46
Carruth, Hayden 1921- DLB-5, 165
  Tribute to James Dickey Y-97
  Tribute to Raymond Carver Y-88
Carryl, Charles E. 1841-1920 .... DLB-42
Carson, Anne 1950- DLB-193
Carson, Rachel 1907-1964 .... DLB-275
Carswell, Catherine 1879-1946 .... DLB-36
Cartagena, Alfonso de ca. 1384-1456 .... DLB-286
Cartagena, Teresa de 1425?-? DLB-286
Cărtărescu, Mirea 1956- DLB-232

Carter, Angela 1940-1992 ...... DLB-14, 207, 261
Carter, Elizabeth 1717-1806 .... DLB-109
Carter, Henry (see Leslie, Frank)
Carter, Hodding, Jr. 1907-1972 .... DLB-127
Carter, Jared 1939- DLB-282
Carter, John 1905-1975 .... DLB-201
Carter, Landon 1710-1778 .... DLB-31
Carter, Lin 1930-1988 .... Y-81
Carter, Martin 1927-1997 .... DLB-117; CDWLB-3
Carter, Robert, and Brothers DLB-49
Carter and Hendee DLB-49
Cartwright, Jim 1958- DLB-245
Cartwright, John 1740-1824 .... DLB-158
Cartwright, William circa 1611-1643 .... DLB-126
Caruthers, William Alexander
  1802-1846 .... DLB-3, 248
Carver, Jonathan 1710-1780 .... DLB-31
Carver, Raymond 1938-1988 ... DLB-130; Y-83, 88
  First Strauss "Livings" Awarded to Cynthia
    Ozick and Raymond Carver
    An Interview with Raymond Carver Y-83
Carvic, Heron 1917?-1980 .... DLB-276
Cary, Alice 1820-1871 .... DLB-202
Cary, Joyce 1888-1957 ... DLB-15, 100; CDBLB-6
Cary, Patrick 1623?-1657 .... DLB-131
Casal, Julián del 1863-1893 .... DLB-283
Case, John 1540-1600 .... DLB-281
Casey, Gavin 1907-1964 .... DLB-260
Casey, Juanita 1925- DLB-14
Casey, Michael 1947- DLB-5
Cassady, Carolyn 1923- DLB-16
  "As I See It" DLB-16
Cassady, Neal 1926-1968 .... DLB-16, 237
Cassell and Company DLB-106
Cassell Publishing Company DLB-49
Cassill, R. V. 1919- DLB-6, 218; Y-02
  Tribute to James Dickey Y-97
Cassity, Turner 1929- DLB-105; Y-02
Cassius Dio circa 155/164-post 229 ...... DLB-176
Cassola, Carlo 1917-1987 .... DLB-177
Castellano, Olivia 1944- DLB-122
Castellanos, Rosario
  1925-1974 .... DLB-113, 290; CDWLB-3
Castelo Branco, Camilo 1825-1890 ..... DLB-287
Castile, Protest Poetry in DLB-286
Castile and Aragon, Vernacular Translations
  in Crowns of 1352-1515 .... DLB-286
Castillo, Ana 1953- DLB-122, 227
Castillo, Rafael C. 1950- DLB-209
The Castle of Perseverance
  circa 1400-1425 .... DLB-146
Castlemon, Harry (see Fosdick, Charles Austin)
Čašule, Kole 1921- DLB-181
Caswall, Edward 1814-1878 .... DLB-32
Catacalos, Rosemary 1944- DLB-122

Cather, Willa 1873-1947
........DLB-9, 54, 78, 256; DS-1; CDALB-3
    The Willa Cather Pioneer Memorial
        and Education Foundation Y-00
Catherine II (Ekaterina Alekseevna), "The Great,"
    Empress of Russia 1729-1796 ....DLB-150
Catherwood, Mary Hartwell 1847-1902 ...DLB-78
Catledge, Turner 1901-1983 ....DLB-127
Catlin, George 1796-1872.........DLB-186, 189
Cato the Elder 234 B.C.-149 B.C........DLB-211
Cattafi, Bartolo 1922-1979 ....DLB-128
Catton, Bruce 1899-1978 ....DLB-17
Catullus circa 84 B.C.-54 B.C.
    ....DLB-211; CDWLB-1
Causley, Charles 1917- DLB-27
Caute, David 1936- DLB-14, 231
Cavendish, Duchess of Newcastle,
    Margaret Lucas
    1623?-1673 ....DLB-131, 252, 281
Cawein, Madison 1865-1914............DLB-54
William Caxton [publishing house] DLB-170
The Caxton Printers, Limited DLB-46
Caylor, O. P. 1849-1897 ....DLB-241
Cayrol, Jean 1911- DLB-83
Cecil, Lord David 1902-1986 ....DLB-155
Cela, Camilo José 1916-2002..............Y-89
    Nobel Lecture 1989..................Y-89
Celan, Paul 1920-1970 ....DLB-69; CDWLB-2
Celati, Gianni 1937- DLB-196
Celaya, Gabriel 1911-1991 ....DLB-108
Céline, Louis-Ferdinand 1894-1961.......DLB-72
Celtis, Conrad 1459-1508 ....DLB-179
Cendrars, Blaise 1887-1961 ....DLB-258
The Steinbeck Centennial Y-02
Censorship
    The Island Trees Case: A Symposium on
        School Library Censorship......... Y-82
Center for Bibliographical Studies and
    Research at the University of
    California, Riverside................. Y-91
Center for Book Research Y-84
The Center for the Book in the Library
    of Congress Y-93
    A New Voice: The Center for the
        Book's First Five Years Y-83
Centlivre, Susanna 1669?-1723 ....DLB-84
The Centre for Writing, Publishing and
    Printing History at the University
    of Reading......................... Y-00
The Century Company..................DLB-49
A Century of Poetry, a Lifetime of Collecting:
    J. M. Edelstein's Collection of
    Twentieth-Century American Poetry Y-02
Cernuda, Luis 1902-1963 ....DLB-134
Cerruto, Oscar 1912-1981 ....DLB-283
Cervantes, Lorna Dee 1954- DLB-82
de Céspedes, Alba 1911-1997 ....DLB-264
Ch., T. (see Marchenko, Anastasiia Iakovlevna)
Chaadaev, Petr Iakovlevich
    1794-1856 ....DLB-198

Chabon, Michael 1963- DLB-278
Chacel, Rosa 1898-1994 ....DLB-134
Chacón, Eusebio 1869-1948 ....DLB-82
Chacón, Felipe Maximiliano 1873-?.......DLB-82
Chadwick, Henry 1824-1908...........DLB-241
Chadwyck-Healey's Full-Text Literary Databases:
    Editing Commercial Databases of
    Primary Literary Texts Y-95
Challans, Eileen Mary (see Renault, Mary)
Chalmers, George 1742-1825.............DLB-30
Chaloner, Sir Thomas 1520-1565 ....DLB-167
Chamberlain, Samuel S. 1851-1916.......DLB-25
Chamberland, Paul 1939- DLB-60
Chamberlin, William Henry 1897-1969....DLB-29
Chambers, Charles Haddon 1860-1921 ...DLB-10
Chambers, María Cristina (see Mena, María Cristina)
Chambers, Robert W. 1865-1933 ....DLB-202
W. and R. Chambers
    [publishing house]................DLB-106
Chambers, Whittaker 1901-1961 ....DLB-303
Chamisso, Adelbert von 1781-1838.......DLB-90
Champfleury 1821-1889 ....DLB-119
Chandler, Harry 1864-1944 ....DLB-29
Chandler, Norman 1899-1973 ....DLB-127
Chandler, Otis 1927- DLB-127
Chandler, Raymond
    1888-1959 ....DLB-226, 253; DS-6; CDALB-5
    Raymond Chandler Centenary......... Y-88
Channing, Edward 1856-1931...........DLB-17
Channing, Edward Tyrrell
    1790-1856 ....DLB-1, 59, 235
Channing, William Ellery
    1780-1842 ....DLB-1, 59, 235
Channing, William Ellery, II
    1817-1901 ....DLB-1, 223
Channing, William Henry
    1810-1884 ....DLB-1, 59, 243
Chapelain, Jean 1595-1674.............DLB-268
Chaplin, Charlie 1889-1977 ....DLB-44
Chapman, George
    1559 or 1560-1634 ....DLB-62, 121
Chapman, Olive Murray 1892-1977 .....DLB-195
Chapman, R. W. 1881-1960 ....DLB-201
Chapman, William 1850-1917 ....DLB-99
John Chapman [publishing house].......DLB-106
Chapman and Hall [publishing house] ...DLB-106
Chappell, Fred 1936- DLB-6, 105
    "A Detail in a Poem"................DLB-105
    Tribute to Peter Taylor................ Y-94
Chappell, William 1582-1649 ....DLB-236
Char, René 1907-1988 ....DLB-258
Charbonneau, Jean 1875-1960 ....DLB-92
Charbonneau, Robert 1911-1967........DLB-68
Charles, Gerda 1914- DLB-14
William Charles [publishing house].......DLB-49
Charles d'Orléans 1394-1465 ....DLB-208
Charley (see Mann, Charles)

Charskaia, Lidiia 1875-1937............DLB-295
Charteris, Leslie 1907-1993 ....DLB-77
Chartier, Alain circa 1385-1430.........DLB-208
Charyn, Jerome 1937- Y-83
Chase, Borden 1900-1971 ....DLB-26
Chase, Edna Woolman 1877-1957........DLB-91
Chase, James Hadley (René Raymond)
    1906-1985 ....DLB-276
Chase, Mary Coyle 1907-1981 ....DLB-228
Chase-Riboud, Barbara 1936- DLB-33
Chateaubriand, François-René de
    1768-1848 ....DLB-119
Chatterton, Thomas 1752-1770 ....DLB-109
    Essay on Chatterton (1842), by
        Robert Browning DLB-32
Chatto and Windus...................DLB-106
Chatwin, Bruce 1940-1989 ....DLB-194, 204
Chaucer, Geoffrey
    1340?-1400 ....DLB-146; CDBLB-1
    New Chaucer Society Y-00
Chaudhuri, Amit 1962- DLB-267
Chauncy, Charles 1705-1787 ....DLB-24
Chauveau, Pierre-Joseph-Olivier
    1820-1890 ....DLB-99
Chávez, Denise 1948- DLB-122
Chávez, Fray Angélico 1910-1996........DLB-82
Chayefsky, Paddy 1923-1981 .... DLB-7, 44; Y-81
Cheesman, Evelyn 1881-1969 ....DLB-195
Cheever, Ezekiel 1615-1708 ....DLB-24
Cheever, George Barrell 1807-1890.......DLB-59
Cheever, John 1912-1982
    .... DLB-2, 102, 227; Y-80, 82; CDALB-1
Cheever, Susan 1943- Y-82
Cheke, Sir John 1514-1557 ....DLB-132
Chekhov, Anton Pavlovich 1860-1904 ...DLB-277
Chelsea House......................DLB-46
Chênedollé, Charles de 1769-1833 ......DLB-217
Cheney, Brainard
    Tribute to Caroline Gordon Y-81
Cheney, Ednah Dow 1824-1904 ......DLB-1, 223
Cheney, Harriet Vaughan 1796-1889 .....DLB-99
Chénier, Marie-Joseph 1764-1811 ....DLB-192
Chernyshevsky, Nikolai Gavrilovich
    1828-1889 ....DLB-238
Cherry, Kelly 1940 .... Y-83
Cherryh, C. J. 1942- Y-80
Chesebro', Caroline 1825-1873 ....DLB-202
Chesney, Sir George Tomkyns
    1830-1895 ....DLB-190
Chesnut, Mary Boykin 1823-1886 ......DLB-239
Chesnutt, Charles Waddell
    1858-1932 .... DLB-12, 50, 78
Chesson, Mrs. Nora (see Hopper, Nora)
Chester, Alfred 1928-1971 ....DLB-130
Chester, George Randolph 1869-1924 ....DLB-78
The Chester Plays circa 1505-1532;
    revisions until 1575 ....DLB-146

Chesterfield, Philip Dormer Stanhope,
    Fourth Earl of 1694-1773 .... DLB-104
Chesterton, G. K. 1874-1936
    ...DLB-10, 19, 34, 70, 98, 149, 178; CDBLB-6
    "The Ethics of Elfland" (1908)....... .DLB-178
Chettle, Henry
    circa 1560-circa 1607 .... DLB-136
Cheuse, Alan 1940- DLB-244
Chew, Ada Nield 1870-1945........... DLB-135
Cheyney, Edward P. 1861-1947........ DLB-47
Chiara, Piero 1913-1986............... .DLB-177
Chicanos
    Chicano History.................. DLB-82
    Chicano Language................ DLB-82
    Chicano Literature: A Bibliography ...DLB-209
    A Contemporary Flourescence of Chicano
        Literature..................... Y-84
    Literatura Chicanesca: The View From
        Without..................... DLB-82
Child, Francis James 1825-1896 ... DLB-1, 64, 235
Child, Lydia Maria 1802-1880..... DLB-1, 74, 243
Child, Philip 1898-1978 .... DLB-68
Childers, Erskine 1870-1922............ DLB-70
Children's Literature
    Afterword: Propaganda, Namby-Pamby,
        and Some Books of Distinction ... DLB-52
    Children's Book Awards and Prizes... DLB-61
    Children's Book Illustration in the
        Twentieth Century DLB-61
    Children's Illustrators, 1800-1880 ... DLB-163
    The Harry Potter Phenomenon......... Y-99
    Pony Stories, Omnibus
        Essay on DLB-160
    The Reality of One Woman's Dream:
        The de Grummond Children's
        Literature Collection Y-99
    School Stories, 1914-1960 .... DLB-160
    The Year in Children's
        Books................. Y-92–96, 98–01
    The Year in Children's Literature Y-97
Childress, Alice 1916-1994 ....DLB-7, 38, 249
Childress, Mark 1957- DLB-292
Childs, George W. 1829-1894 .... DLB-23
Chilton Book Company............. DLB-46
Chin, Frank 1940- DLB-206
Chinweizu 1943- DLB-157
Chitham, Edward 1932- DLB-155
Chittenden, Hiram Martin 1858-1917 .... DLB-47
Chivers, Thomas Holley 1809-1858... DLB-3, 248
Chkhartishvili, Grigorii Shalvovich
    (see Akunin, Boris)
Chocano, José Santos 1875-1934 .... DLB-290
Cholmondeley, Mary 1859-1925 .... DLB-197
Chomsky, Noam 1928- DLB-246
Chopin, Kate 1850-1904... DLB-12, 78; CDALB-3
Chopin, René 1885-1953 .... DLB-92
Choquette, Adrienne 1915-1973 .... DLB-68
Choquette, Robert 1905-1991 .... DLB-68
Choyce, Lesley 1951- DLB-251

Chrétien de Troyes
    circa 1140-circa 1190 .... DLB-208
Christensen, Inger 1935- DLB-214
Christensen, Lars Saabye 1953- DLB-297
The Christian Examiner DLB-1
The Christian Publishing Company...... DLB-49
Christie, Agatha
    1890-1976........DLB-13, 77, 245; CDBLB-6
Christine de Pizan
    circa 1365-circa 1431 .... DLB-208
Christopher, John (Sam Youd) 1922- .. DLB-255
Christus und die Samariterin circa 950...... DLB-148
Christy, Howard Chandler 1873-1952... DLB-188
Chukovskaia, Lidiia 1907-1996 .... DLB-302
Chulkov, Mikhail Dmitrievich
    1743?-1792 .... DLB-150
Church, Benjamin 1734-1778 .... DLB-31
Church, Francis Pharcellus 1839-1906.... DLB-79
Church, Peggy Pond 1903-1986........ DLB-212
Church, Richard 1893-1972 .... DLB-191
Church, William Conant 1836-1917 .... DLB-79
Churchill, Caryl 1938- DLB-13
Churchill, Charles 1731-1764 .... DLB-109
Churchill, Winston 1871-1947 .... DLB-202
Churchill, Sir Winston
    1874-1965....... DLB-100; DS-16; CDBLB-5
Churchyard, Thomas 1520?-1604 ...... DLB-132
E. Churton and Company DLB-106
Chute, Marchette 1909-1994 .... DLB-103
Ciardi, John 1916-1986................DLB-5; Y-86
Cibber, Colley 1671-1757 .... DLB-84
Cicero 106 B.C.-43 B.C......DLB-211, CDWLB-1
Cima, Annalisa 1941- DLB-128
Čingo, Živko 1935-1987 .... DLB-181
Cioran, E. M. 1911-1995 .... DLB-220
Čipkus, Alfonsas (see Nyka-Niliūnas, Alfonsas)
Cirese, Eugenio 1884-1955............ DLB-114
Cīrulis, Jānis (see Bels, Alberts)
Cisneros, Antonio 1942- DLB-290
Cisneros, Sandra 1954- DLB-122, 152
City Lights Books.................. DLB-46
Civil War (1861–1865)
    Battles and Leaders of the Civil War ...DLB-47
    Official Records of the Rebellion DLB-47
    Recording the Civil War DLB-47
Cixous, Hélène 1937- DLB-83, 242
Clampitt, Amy 1920-1994 .... DLB-105
    Tribute to Alfred A. Knopf Y-84
Clancy, Tom 1947- DLB-227
Clapper, Raymond 1892-1944 .... DLB-29
Clare, John 1793-1864 .... DLB-55, 96
Clarendon, Edward Hyde, Earl of
    1609-1674...................... DLB-101
Clark, Alfred Alexander Gordon
    (see Hare, Cyril)
Clark, Ann Nolan 1896- DLB-52
Clark, C. E. Frazer, Jr. 1925-2001 ..DLB-187; Y-01

C. E. Frazer Clark Jr. and
    Hawthorne Bibliography....... DLB-269
The Publications of C. E. Frazer
    Clark Jr................... DLB-269
Clark, Catherine Anthony 1892-1977 .... DLB-68
Clark, Charles Heber 1841-1915 .... DLB-11
Clark, Davis Wasgatt 1812-1871 .... DLB-79
Clark, Douglas 1919-1993 .... .DLB-276
Clark, Eleanor 1913- DLB-6
Clark, J. P. 1935- DLB-117; CDWLB-3
Clark, Lewis Gaylord
    1808-1873................DLB-3, 64, 73, 250
Clark, Walter Van Tilburg
    1909-1971................... DLB-9, 206
Clark, William 1770-1838......... DLB-183, 186
Clark, William Andrews, Jr.
    1877-1934..................... .DLB-187
C. M. Clark Publishing Company DLB-46
Clarke, Sir Arthur C. 1917- DLB-261
    Tribute to Theodore Sturgeon......... Y-85
Clarke, Austin 1896-1974........... DLB-10, 20
Clarke, Austin C. 1934- DLB-53, 125
Clarke, Gillian 1937- DLB-40
Clarke, James Freeman
    1810-1888 .... DLB-1, 59, 235; DS-5
Clarke, John circa 1596-1658.......... DLB-281
Clarke, Lindsay 1939- DLB-231
Clarke, Marcus 1846-1881 .... DLB-230
Clarke, Pauline 1921- DLB-161
Clarke, Rebecca Sophia 1833-1906 .... DLB-42
Clarke, Samuel 1675-1729 .... DLB-252
Robert Clarke and Company........... DLB-49
Clarkson, Thomas 1760-1846.......... DLB-158
Claudel, Paul 1868-1955 .... DLB-192, 258
Claudius, Matthias 1740-1815 .... DLB-97
Clausen, Andy 1943- DLB-16
Claussen, Sophus 1865-1931 .... DLB-300
Clawson, John L. 1865-1933 .... .DLB-187
Claxton, Remsen and Haffelfinger....... DLB-49
Clay, Cassius Marcellus 1810-1903 ..... DLB-43
Clayton, Richard (see Haggard, William)
Cleage, Pearl 1948- DLB-228
Cleary, Beverly 1916- DLB-52
Cleary, Kate McPhelim 1863-1905...... DLB-221
Cleaver, Vera 1919-1992 and
    Cleaver, Bill 1920-1981 .... DLB-52
Cleeve, Brian 1921- DLB-276
Cleland, John 1710-1789............... DLB-39
Clemens, Samuel Langhorne (Mark Twain)
    1835-1910 .... DLB-11, 12, 23, 64, 74,
                        186, 189; CDALB-3
    Comments From Authors and Scholars on
        their First Reading of *Huck Finn* Y-85
    Huck at 100: How Old Is
        Huckleberry Finn? Y-85
    Mark Twain on Perpetual Copyright Y-92
    A New Edition of *Huck Finn*........... Y-85
Clement, Hal 1922- DLB-8

Clemo, Jack 1916- DLB-27
Clephane, Elizabeth Cecilia 1830-1869 ...DLB-199
Cleveland, John 1613-1658 ....DLB-126
Cliff, Michelle 1946- DLB-157; CDWLB-3
Clifford, Lady Anne 1590-1676.........DLB-151
Clifford, James L. 1901-1978 ....DLB-103
Clifford, Lucy 1853?-1929.....DLB-135, 141, 197
Clift, Charmian 1923-1969 ....DLB-260
Clifton, Lucille 1936- DLB-5, 41
Clines, Francis X. 1938- DLB-185
Clive, Caroline (V) 1801-1873..........DLB-199
Edward J. Clode [publishing house].......DLB-46
Clough, Arthur Hugh 1819-1861 ....DLB-32
Cloutier, Cécile 1930- DLB-60
Clouts, Sidney 1926-1982 ....DLB-225
Clutton-Brock, Arthur 1868-1924 ....DLB-98
Coates, Robert M.
 1897-1973.............DLB-4, 9, 102; DS-15
Coatsworth, Elizabeth 1893-1986 ....DLB-22
Cobb, Charles E., Jr. 1943- DLB-41
Cobb, Frank I. 1869-1923 ....DLB-25
Cobb, Irvin S. 1876-1944.........DLB-11, 25, 86
Cobbe, Frances Power 1822-1904 ....DLB-190
Cobbett, William 1763-1835 ....DLB-43, 107, 158
Cobbledick, Gordon 1898-1969 ....DLB-171
Cochran, Thomas C. 1902- DLB-17
Cochrane, Elizabeth 1867-1922 ......DLB-25, 189
Cockerell, Sir Sydney 1867-1962 ....DLB-201
Cockerill, John A. 1845-1896............DLB-23
Cocteau, Jean 1889-1963 ....DLB-65, 258
Coderre, Emile (see Jean Narrache)
Cody, Liza 1944- DLB-276
Coe, Jonathan 1961- DLB-231
Coetzee, J. M. 1940- DLB-225
Coffee, Lenore J. 1900?-1984...........DLB-44
Coffin, Robert P. Tristram 1892-1955.....DLB-45
Coghill, Mrs. Harry (see Walker, Anna Louisa)
Cogswell, Fred 1917- DLB-60
Cogswell, Mason Fitch 1761-1830 ....DLB-37
Cohan, George M. 1878-1942 ....DLB-249
Cohen, Arthur A. 1928-1986............DLB-28
Cohen, Leonard 1934- DLB-53
Cohen, Matt 1942- DLB-53
Cohen, Morris Raphael 1880-1947 ......DLB-270
Colbeck, Norman 1903-1987..........DLB-201
Colden, Cadwallader
 1688-1776 ....DLB-24, 30, 270
Colden, Jane 1724-1766 ....DLB-200
Cole, Barry 1936- DLB-14
Cole, George Watson 1850-1939.........DLB-140
Colegate, Isabel 1931- DLB-14, 231
Coleman, Emily Holmes 1899-1974 ....DLB-4
Coleman, Wanda 1946- DLB-130
Coleridge, Hartley 1796-1849 ....DLB-96
Coleridge, Mary 1861-1907.........DLB-19, 98

Coleridge, Samuel Taylor
 1772-1834 ....DLB-93, 107; CDBLB-3
Coleridge, Sara 1802-1852............DLB-199
Colet, John 1467-1519 ....DLB-132
Colette 1873-1954 ....DLB-65
Colette, Sidonie Gabrielle (see Colette)
Colinas, Antonio 1946- DLB-134
Coll, Joseph Clement 1881-1921 ....DLB-188
A Century of Poetry, a Lifetime of Collecting:
 J. M. Edelstein's Collection of
 Twentieth-Century American Poetry Y-02
Collier, John 1901-1980........... DLB-77, 255
Collier, John Payne 1789-1883..........DLB-184
Collier, Mary 1690-1762 ....DLB-95
Collier, Robert J. 1876-1918 ....DLB-91
P. F. Collier [publishing house] DLB-49
Collin and Small DLB-49
Collingwood, R. G. 1889-1943 ....DLB-262
Collingwood, W. G. 1854-1932..........DLB-149
Collins, An floruit circa 1653...........DLB-131
Collins, Anthony 1676-1729............DLB-252
Collins, Merle 1950- DLB-157
Collins, Michael 1964- DLB-267
 Tribute to John D. MacDonald..........Y-86
 Tribute to Kenneth Millar.............Y-83
 Why I Write Mysteries: Night and Day ..Y-85
Collins, Mortimer 1827-1876 ....DLB-21, 35
Collins, Tom (see Furphy, Joseph)
Collins, Wilkie
 1824-1889 ....DLB-18, 70, 159; CDBLB-4
 "The Unknown Public" (1858)
  [excerpt] DLB-57
 The Wilkie Collins Society Y-98
Collins, William 1721-1759 ....DLB-109
Isaac Collins [publishing house]..........DLB-49
William Collins, Sons and Company DLB-154
Collis, Maurice 1889-1973.............DLB-195
Collyer, Mary 1716?-1763? DLB-39
Colman, Benjamin 1673-1747 ....DLB-24
Colman, George, the Elder 1732-1794.....DLB-89
Colman, George, the Younger
 1762-1836 ....DLB-89
S. Colman [publishing house] DLB-49
Colombo, John Robert 1936- DLB-53
Colquhoun, Patrick 1745-1820 ....DLB-158
Colter, Cyrus 1910-2002...............DLB-33
Colum, Padraic 1881-1972.............DLB-19
The Columbia History of the American Novel
 A Symposium on....................Y-92
Columella fl. first century A.D..........DLB-211
Colvin, Sir Sidney 1845-1927 ....DLB-149
Colwin, Laurie 1944-1992........ DLB-218; Y-80
Comden, Betty 1915- and
 Green, Adolph 1918- DLB-44, 265
Comi, Girolamo 1890-1968 ....DLB-114
Comisso, Giovanni 1895-1969 ....DLB-264
Commager, Henry Steele 1902-1998......DLB-17

Commynes, Philippe de
 circa 1447-1511 ....DLB-208
Compton, D. G. 1930- DLB-261
Compton-Burnett, Ivy 1884?-1969 ....DLB-36
Conan, Laure (Félicité Angers)
 1845-1924 ....DLB-99
Concord, Massachusetts
 Concord History and Life..........DLB-223
 Concord: Literary History
  of a Town....................DLB-223
 The Old Manse, by Hawthorne DLB-223
 The Thoreauvian Pilgrimage: The
  Structure of an American Cult ...DLB-223
Conde, Carmen 1901-1996............DLB-108
Congreve, William
 1670-1729 ....DLB-39, 84; CDBLB-2
 Preface to Incognita (1692) DLB-39
W. B. Conkey Company...............DLB-49
Conn, Stewart 1936- DLB-233
Connell, Evan S., Jr. 1924- DLB-2; Y-81
Connelly, Marc 1890-1980 .... DLB-7; Y-80
Connolly, Cyril 1903-1974 ....DLB-98
Connolly, James B. 1868-1957..........DLB-78
Connor, Ralph (Charles William Gordon)
 1860-1937 ....DLB-92
Connor, Tony 1930- DLB-40
Conquest, Robert 1917- DLB-27
Conrad, Joseph
 1857-1924 ....DLB-10, 34, 98, 156; CDBLB-5
John Conrad and Company DLB-49
Conroy, Jack 1899-1990 ....Y-81
 A Tribute [to Nelson Algren] Y-81
Conroy, Pat 1945- DLB-6
Considine, Bob 1906-1975............DLB-241
Consolo, Vincenzo 1933- DLB-196
Constable, Henry 1562-1613...........DLB-136
Archibald Constable and Company DLB-154
Constable and Company Limited DLB-112
Constant, Benjamin 1767-1830..........DLB-119
Constant de Rebecque, Henri-Benjamin de
 (see Constant, Benjamin)
Constantine, David 1944- DLB-40
Constantine, Murray (see Burdekin, Katharine)
Constantin-Weyer, Maurice 1881-1964....DLB-92
Contempo (magazine)
 Contempo Caravan:
  Kites in a Windstorm.............Y-85
The Continental Publishing Company DLB-49
A Conversation between William Riggan
 and Janette Turner Hospital Y-02
Conversations with Editors Y-95
Conway, Anne 1631-1679.............DLB-252
Conway, Moncure Daniel
 1832-1907 ....DLB-1, 223
Cook, Ebenezer circa 1667-circa 1732 .....DLB-24
Cook, Edward Tyas 1857-1919 ....DLB-149
Cook, Eliza 1818-1889................DLB-199
Cook, George Cram 1873-1924.........DLB-266

Cumulative Index   DLB 305

Cook, Michael 1933-1994 .... DLB-53
David C. Cook Publishing Company..... DLB-49
Cooke, George Willis 1848-1923 .... DLB-71
Cooke, John Esten 1830-1886 .... DLB-3, 248
Cooke, Philip Pendleton
   1816-1850.................. DLB-3, 59, 248
Cooke, Rose Terry 1827-1892 .... DLB-12, 74
Increase Cooke and Company DLB-49
Cook-Lynn, Elizabeth 1930- DLB-175
Coolbrith, Ina 1841-1928 .... DLB-54, 186
Cooley, Peter 1940- DLB-105
   "Into the Mirror" DLB-105
Coolidge, Clark 1939- DLB-193
Coolidge, Susan
   (see Woolsey, Sarah Chauncy)
George Coolidge [publishing house]..... DLB-49
Cooper, Anna Julia 1858-1964 .... DLB-221
Cooper, Edith Emma 1862-1913 ...... DLB-240
Cooper, Giles 1918-1966 .... DLB-13
Cooper, J. California 19??- DLB-212
Cooper, James Fenimore
   1789-1851....... DLB-3, 183, 250; CDALB-2
   The Bicentennial of James Fenimore Cooper:
      An International Celebration........ Y-89
   The James Fenimore Cooper Society..... Y-01
Cooper, Kent 1880-1965 .... DLB-29
Cooper, Susan 1935- DLB-161, 261
Cooper, Susan Fenimore 1813-1894..... DLB-239
William Cooper [publishing house] DLB-170
J. Coote [publishing house]............. DLB-154
Coover, Robert 1932- DLB-2, 227; Y-81
   Tribute to Donald Barthelme........... Y-89
   Tribute to Theodor Seuss Geisel Y-91
Copeland and Day DLB-49
Ćopić, Branko 1915-1984............. DLB-181
Copland, Robert 1470?-1548 .... DLB-136
Coppard, A. E. 1878-1957 .... DLB-162
Coppée, François 1842-1908 .... DLB-217
Coppel, Alfred 1921- Y-83
   Tribute to Jessamyn West Y-84
Coppola, Francis Ford 1939- DLB-44
Copway, George (Kah-ge-ga-gah-bowh)
   1818-1869..................DLB-175, 183
Copyright
   The Development of the Author's
      Copyright in Britain DLB-154
   The Digital Millennium Copyright Act:
      Expanding Copyright Protection in
      Cyberspace and Beyond Y-98
   Editorial: The Extension of Copyright ... Y-02
   Mark Twain on Perpetual Copyright Y-92
   Public Domain and the Violation
      of Texts........................ Y-97
   The Question of American Copyright
      in the Nineteenth Century
      Preface, by George Haven Putnam
      The Evolution of Copyright, by
         Brander Matthews
      Summary of Copyright Legislation in

      the United States, by R. R. Bowker
      Analysis of the Provisions of the
         Copyright Law of 1891, by
         George Haven Putnam
      The Contest for International Copyright,
         by George Haven Putnam
      Cheap Books and Good Books,
         by Brander Matthews DLB-49
   Writers and Their Copyright Holders:
      the WATCH Project............ Y-94
Corazzini, Sergio 1886-1907 .... DLB-114
Corbett, Richard 1582-1635........... DLB-121
Corbière, Tristan 1845-1875........... DLB-217
Corcoran, Barbara 1911- DLB-52
Cordelli, Franco 1943- DLB-196
Corelli, Marie 1855-1924 .... DLB-34, 156
Corle, Edwin 1906-1956................ Y-85
Corman, Cid 1924- DLB-5, 193
Cormier, Robert 1925-2000 ... DLB-52; CDALB-6
   Tribute to Theodor Seuss Geisel Y-91
Corn, Alfred 1943- DLB-120, 282; Y-80
Corneille, Pierre 1606-1684............DLB-268
Cornford, Frances 1886-1960.......... DLB-240
Cornish, Sam 1935- DLB-41
Cornish, William
   circa 1465-circa 1524 .... DLB-132
Cornwall, Barry (see Procter, Bryan Waller)
Cornwallis, Sir William, the Younger
   circa 1579-1614 .... DLB-151
Cornwell, David John Moore (see le Carré, John)
Coronel Urtecho, José 1906-1994 ...... DLB-290
Corpi, Lucha 1945- DLB-82
Corrington, John William
   1932-1988 .... DLB-6, 244
Corriveau, Monique 1927-1976 .... DLB-251
Corrothers, James D. 1869-1917......... DLB-50
Corso, Gregory 1930-2001 ....DLB-5, 16, 237
Cortázar, Julio 1914-1984....DLB-113; CDWLB-3
Cortéz, Carlos 1923- DLB-209
Cortez, Jayne 1936- DLB-41
Corvinus, Gottlieb Siegmund
   1677-1746 .... DLB-168
Corvo, Baron (see Rolfe, Frederick William)
Cory, Annie Sophie (see Cross, Victoria)
Cory, Desmond (Shaun Lloyd McCarthy)
   1928- DLB-276
Cory, William Johnson 1823-1892....... DLB-35
Coryate, Thomas 1577?-1617.......DLB-151, 172
Ćosić, Dobrica 1921- DLB-181; CDWLB-4
Cosin, John 1595-1672 .... DLB-151, 213
Cosmopolitan Book Corporation DLB-46
Cossa, Roberto 1934- DLB-305
Costa, Maria Velho da (see The Three Marias:
   A Landmark Case in Portuguese
   Literary History)
Costain, Thomas B. 1885-1965 .... DLB-9
Coste, Donat (Daniel Boudreau)
   1912-1957..................... DLB-88
Costello, Louisa Stuart 1799-1870........ DLB-166

Cota-Cárdenas, Margarita 1941- DLB-122
Côté, Denis 1954- DLB-251
Cotten, Bruce 1873-1954 ....DLB-187
Cotter, Joseph Seamon, Jr. 1895-1919 .... DLB-50
Cotter, Joseph Seamon, Sr. 1861-1949 .... DLB-50
Joseph Cottle [publishing house] DLB-154
Cotton, Charles 1630-1687............ DLB-131
Cotton, John 1584-1652 .... DLB-24
Cotton, Sir Robert Bruce 1571-1631..... DLB-213
Coulter, John 1888-1980 .... DLB-68
Cournos, John 1881-1966.............. DLB-54
Courteline, Georges 1858-1929 .... DLB-192
Cousins, Margaret 1905-1996 ....DLB-137
Cousins, Norman 1915-1990 ....DLB-137
Couvreur, Jessie (see Tasma)
Coventry, Francis 1725-1754 .... DLB-39
   Dedication, *The History of Pompey
      the Little* (1751) DLB-39
Coverdale, Miles 1487 or 1488-1569 .... DLB-167
N. Coverly [publishing house] DLB-49
Covici-Friede DLB-46
Cowan, Peter 1914-2002 .... DLB-260
Coward, Noel
   1899-1973......... DLB-10, 245; CDBLB-6
Coward, McCann and Geoghegan....... DLB-46
Cowles, Gardner 1861-1946.......... DLB-29
Cowles, Gardner "Mike", Jr.
   1903-1985 ....DLB-127, 137
Cowley, Abraham 1618-1667...... DLB-131, 151
Cowley, Hannah 1743-1809............ DLB-89
Cowley, Malcolm
   1898-1989 ....DLB-4, 48; DS-15; Y-81, 89
Cowper, Richard (John Middleton Murry Jr.)
   1926-2002 .... DLB-261
Cowper, William 1731-1800........DLB-104, 109
Cox, A. B. (see Berkeley, Anthony)
Cox, James McMahon 1903-1974 ....DLB-127
Cox, James Middleton 1870-1957........DLB-127
Cox, Leonard circa 1495-circa 1550..... DLB-281
Cox, Palmer 1840-1924 .... DLB-42
Coxe, Louis 1918-1993 .... DLB-5
Coxe, Tench 1755-1824 .... DLB-37
Cozzens, Frederick S. 1818-1869 .... DLB-202
Cozzens, James Gould 1903-1978.............
   .... DLB-9, 294; Y-84; DS-2; CDALB-1
   Cozzens's *Michael Scarlett* Y-97
   Ernest Hemingway's Reaction to
      James Gould Cozzens Y-98
   James Gould Cozzens–A View
      from Afar...................... Y-97
   James Gould Cozzens: How to
      Read Him Y-97
   James Gould Cozzens Symposium and
      Exhibition at the University of
      South Carolina, Columbia Y-00
   Mens Rea (or Something) Y-97
   Novels for Grown-Ups Y-97
Crabbe, George 1754-1832............. DLB-93

Crace, Jim 1946- DLB-231

Crackanthorpe, Hubert 1870-1896 ......DLB-135

Craddock, Charles Egbert (see Murfree, Mary N.)

Cradock, Thomas 1718-1770 ....DLB-31

Craig, Daniel H. 1811-1895............DLB-43

Craik, Dinah Maria 1826-1887 ......DLB-35, 163

Cramer, Richard Ben 1950- DLB-185

Cranch, Christopher Pearse
    1813-1892 ....DLB-1, 42, 243; DS-5

Crane, Hart 1899-1932 .....DLB-4, 48; CDALB-4

    Nathan Asch Remembers Ford Madox
    Ford, Sam Roth, and Hart Crane Y-02

Crane, R. S. 1886-1967 ....DLB-63

Crane, Stephen
    1871-1900 ....DLB-12, 54, 78; CDALB-3

    Stephen Crane: A Revaluation, Virginia
    Tech Conference, 1989 .... Y-89

    The Stephen Crane Society......... Y-98, 01

Crane, Walter 1845-1915 ....DLB-163

Cranmer, Thomas 1489-1556 ......DLB-132, 213

Crapsey, Adelaide 1878-1914............DLB-54

Crashaw, Richard 1612/1613-1649 ......DLB-126

Craven, Avery 1885-1980 ....DLB-17

Crawford, Charles 1752-circa 1815 ......DLB-31

Crawford, F. Marion 1854-1909 ....DLB-71

Crawford, Isabel Valancy 1850-1887......DLB-92

Crawley, Alan 1887-1975 ....DLB-68

Crayon, Geoffrey (see Irving, Washington)

Crayon, Porte (see Strother, David Hunter)

Creamer, Robert W. 1922- DLB-171

Creasey, John 1908-1973 ....DLB-77

Creative Age Press.....................DLB-46

Creative Nonfiction Y-02

William Creech [publishing house] DLB-154

Thomas Creede [publishing house] DLB-170

Creel, George 1876-1953 ....DLB-25

Creeley, Robert 1926-
    ....DLB-5, 16, 169; DS-17

Creelman, James
    1859-1915 ....DLB-23

Cregan, David 1931- DLB-13

Creighton, Donald 1902-1979 ....DLB-88

Crémazie, Octave 1827-1879 ....DLB-99

Crémer, Victoriano 1909?- DLB-108

Crescas, Hasdai circa 1340-1412? DLB-115

Crespo, Angel 1926-1995 ....DLB-134

Cresset Press DLB-112

Cresswell, Helen 1934- DLB-161

Crèvecoeur, Michel Guillaume Jean de
    1735-1813 ....DLB-37

Crewe, Candida 1964- DLB-207

Crews, Harry 1935- DLB-6, 143, 185

Crichton, Michael (John Lange, Jeffrey Hudson,
    Michael Douglas) 1942- DLB-292; Y-81

Crispin, Edmund (Robert Bruce Montgomery)
    1921-1978 ....DLB-87

Cristofer, Michael 1946- DLB-7

Criticism
    Afro-American Literary Critics:
    An Introduction DLB-33

    The Consolidation of Opinion: Critical
    Responses to the Modernists DLB-36

    "Criticism in Relation to Novels"
    (1863), by G. H. Lewes DLB-21

    The Limits of Pluralism DLB-67

    Modern Critical Terms, Schools, and
    Movements...................DLB-67

    "Panic Among the Philistines":
    A Postscript, An Interview
    with Bryan Griffin Y-81

    The Recovery of Literature: Criticism
    in the 1990s: A Symposium Y-91

    The Stealthy School of Criticism (1871),
    by Dante Gabriel Rossetti........DLB-35

Crnjanski, Miloš
    1893-1977 ....DLB-147; CDWLB-4

Crocker, Hannah Mather 1752-1829.....DLB-200

Crockett, David (Davy)
    1786-1836 ....DLB-3, 11, 183, 248

Croft-Cooke, Rupert (see Bruce, Leo)

Crofts, Freeman Wills 1879-1957.........DLB-77

Croker, John Wilson 1780-1857 ....DLB-110

Croly, George 1780-1860...............DLB-159

Croly, Herbert 1869-1930 ....DLB-91

Croly, Jane Cunningham 1829-1901......DLB-23

Crompton, Richmal 1890-1969 ....DLB-160

Cronin, A. J. 1896-1981...............DLB-191

Cros, Charles 1842-1888 ....DLB-217

Crosby, Caresse 1892-1970 and
    Crosby, Harry 1898-1929 and ...DLB-4; DS-15

Crosby, Harry 1898-1929 ....DLB-48

Crosland, Camilla Toulmin (Mrs. Newton
    Crosland) 1812-1895................DLB-240

Cross, Gillian 1945- DLB-161

Cross, Victoria 1868-1952 ....DLB-135, 197

Crossley-Holland, Kevin 1941- DLB-40, 161

Crothers, Rachel 1870-1958..........DLB-7, 266

Thomas Y. Crowell Company DLB-49

Crowley, John 1942- Y-82

Crowley, Mart 1935- DLB-7, 266

Crown Publishers DLB-46

Crowne, John 1641-1712 ....DLB-80

Crowninshield, Edward Augustus
    1817-1859 ....DLB-140

Crowninshield, Frank 1872-1947.........DLB-91

Croy, Homer 1883-1965 ....DLB-4

Crumley, James 1939- DLB-226; Y-84

Cruse, Mary Anne 1825?-1910 ....DLB-239

Cruz, Migdalia 1958- DLB-249

Cruz, Sor Juana Inés de la 1651-1695 ....DLB-305

Cruz, Victor Hernández 1949- DLB-41

Csokor, Franz Theodor 1885-1969 ....DLB-81

Csoóri, Sándor 1930- DLB-232; CDWLB-4

Cuadra, Pablo Antonio 1912-2002 ....DLB-290

Cuala Press DLB-112

Cudworth, Ralph 1617-1688 ....DLB-252

Cugoano, Quobna Ottabah 1797-?.......... Y-02

Cullen, Countee
    1903-1946 ....DLB-4, 48, 51; CDALB-4

Culler, Jonathan D. 1944- DLB-67, 246

Cullinan, Elizabeth 1933- DLB-234

Culverwel, Nathaniel 1619?-1651? DLB-252

Cumberland, Richard 1732-1811.........DLB-89

Cummings, Constance Gordon
    1837-1924 ....DLB-174

Cummings, E. E.
    1894-1962 ....DLB-4, 48; CDALB-5

    The E. E. Cummings Society Y-01

Cummings, Ray 1887-1957 ....DLB-8

Cummings and Hilliard................DLB-49

Cummins, Maria Susanna 1827-1866 .....DLB-42

Cumpián, Carlos 1953- DLB-209

Cunard, Nancy 1896-1965 ....DLB-240

Joseph Cundall [publishing house].......DLB-106

Cuney, Waring 1906-1976...............DLB-51

Cuney-Hare, Maude 1874-1936.........DLB-52

Cunningham, Allan
    1784-1842 ....DLB-116, 144

Cunningham, J. V. 1911-1985............DLB-5

Cunningham, Michael 1952- DLB-292

Cunningham, Peter (Peter Lauder, Peter
    Benjamin) 1947- DLB-267

Peter F. Cunningham
    [publishing house]................DLB-49

Cunquiero, Alvaro 1911-1981..........DLB-134

Cuomo, George 1929- Y-80

Cupples, Upham and Company DLB-49

Cupples and Leon DLB-46

Cuppy, Will 1884-1949................DLB-11

Curiel, Barbara Brinson 1956- DLB-209

Edmund Curll [publishing house] DLB-154

Currie, James 1756-1805 ....DLB-142

Currie, Mary Montgomerie Lamb Singleton,
    Lady Currie (see Fane, Violet)

Cursor Mundi circa 1300 ....DLB-146

Curti, Merle E. 1897-1996..............DLB-17

Curtis, Anthony 1926- DLB-155

Curtis, Cyrus H. K. 1850-1933 ....DLB-91

Curtis, George William
    1824-1892 ....DLB-1, 43, 223

Curzon, Robert 1810-1873.............DLB-166

Curzon, Sarah Anne 1833-1898 ....DLB-99

Cusack, Dymphna 1902-1981 ....DLB-260

Cushing, Eliza Lanesford
    1794-1886 ....DLB-99

Cushing, Harvey 1869-1939 ....DLB-187

Custance, Olive (Lady Alfred Douglas)
    1874-1944 ....DLB-240

Cynewulf circa 770-840 ....DLB-146

Cyrano de Bergerac, Savinien de
    1619-1655 ....DLB-268

Czepko, Daniel 1605-1660.............DLB-164

Czerniawski, Adam 1934- DLB-232

D

Dabit, Eugène 1898-1936 .... DLB-65

Daborne, Robert circa 1580-1628 .... DLB-58

Dąbrowska, Maria
 1889-1965 .... DLB-215; CDWLB-4

Dacey, Philip 1939- DLB-105

 "Eyes Across Centuries:
  Contemporary Poetry and 'That
  Vision Thing,'" DLB-105

Dach, Simon 1605-1659 .... DLB-164

Dagerman, Stig 1923-1954 .... DLB-259

Daggett, Rollin M. 1831-1901 .... DLB-79

D'Aguiar, Fred 1960- DLB-157

Dahl, Roald 1916-1990 .... DLB-139, 255

 Tribute to Alfred A. Knopf Y-84

Dahlberg, Edward 1900-1977 .... DLB-48

Dahn, Felix 1834-1912 .... DLB-129

The Daily Worker DLB-303

Dal', Vladimir Ivanovich (Kazak Vladimir
 Lugansky) 1801-1872 .... DLB-198

Dale, Peter 1938- DLB-40

Daley, Arthur 1904-1974 .... DLB-171

Dall, Caroline Healey 1822-1912 ..... DLB-1, 235

Dallas, E. S. 1828-1879 .... DLB-55

 The Gay Science [excerpt](1866) DLB-21

The Dallas Theater Center............. DLB-7

D'Alton, Louis 1900-1951 .... DLB-10

Dalton, Roque 1935-1975 .... DLB-283

Daly, Carroll John 1889-1958 .... DLB-226

Daly, T. A. 1871-1948 .... DLB-11

Damon, S. Foster 1893-1971 .... DLB-45

William S. Damrell [publishing house].... DLB-49

Dana, Charles A. 1819-1897 .... DLB-3, 23, 250

Dana, Richard Henry, Jr.
 1815-1882................. DLB-1, 183, 235

Dandridge, Ray Garfield DLB-51

Dane, Clemence 1887-1965 .... DLB-10, 197

Danforth, John 1660-1730 .... DLB-24

Danforth, Samuel, I 1626-1674 .... DLB-24

Danforth, Samuel, II 1666-1727 .... DLB-24

Daniel, John M. 1825-1865 .... DLB-43

Daniel, Samuel 1562 or 1563-1619....... DLB-62

Daniel Press DLB-106

Daniel', Iulii 1925-1988 .... DLB-302

Daniells, Roy 1902-1979 .... DLB-68

Daniels, Jim 1956- DLB-120

Daniels, Jonathan 1902-1981 .... DLB-127

Daniels, Josephus 1862-1948 .... DLB-29

Daniels, Sarah 1957- DLB-245

Danilevsky, Grigorii Petrovich
 1829-1890 .... DLB-238

Dannay, Frederic 1905-1982 .... DLB-137

Danner, Margaret Esse 1915- DLB-41

John Danter [publishing house] DLB-170

Dantin, Louis (Eugene Seers)
 1865-1945 .... DLB-92

Danto, Arthur C. 1924- DLB-279

Danzig, Allison 1898-1987 ....DLB-171

D'Arcy, Ella circa 1857-1937 .... DLB-135

Darío, Rubén 1867-1916.............. DLB-290

Dark, Eleanor 1901-1985 .... DLB-260

Darke, Nick 1948- DLB-233

Darley, Felix Octavious Carr
 1822-1888 .... DLB-188

Darley, George 1795-1846 .... DLB-96

Darmesteter, Madame James
 (see Robinson, A. Mary F.)

Darrow, Clarence 1857-1938 .... DLB-303

Darwin, Charles 1809-1882 ....DLB-57, 166

Darwin, Erasmus 1731-1802............ DLB-93

Daryush, Elizabeth 1887-1977........ DLB-20

Dashkova, Ekaterina Romanovna
 (née Vorontsova) 1743-1810 .... DLB-150

Dashwood, Edmée Elizabeth Monica de la Pasture
 (see Delafield, E. M.)

Daudet, Alphonse 1840-1897 .... DLB-123

d'Aulaire, Edgar Parin 1898- and
 d'Aulaire, Ingri 1904- DLB-22

Davenant, Sir William 1606-1668 ... DLB-58, 126

Davenport, Guy 1927- DLB-130

 Tribute to John Gardner Y-82

Davenport, Marcia 1903-1996 .... DS-17

Davenport, Robert ?-? DLB-58

Daves, Delmer 1904-1977 .... DLB-26

Davey, Frank 1940- DLB-53

Davidson, Avram 1923-1993 .... DLB-8

Davidson, Donald 1893-1968........... DLB-45

Davidson, Donald 1917- DLB-279

Davidson, John 1857-1909 .... DLB-19

Davidson, Lionel 1922- DLB-14, 276

Davidson, Robyn 1950- DLB-204

Davidson, Sara 1943- DLB-185

Davið Stefánsson frá Fagraskógi
 1895-1964 .... DLB-293

Davie, Donald 1922- DLB-27

Davie, Elspeth 1919-1995............. DLB-139

Davies, Sir John 1569-1626 ....DLB-172

Davies, John, of Hereford 1565?-1618 ... DLB-121

Davies, Rhys 1901-1978 .... DLB-139, 191

Davies, Robertson 1913-1995........... DLB-68

Davies, Samuel 1723-1761 .... DLB-31

Davies, Thomas 1712?-1785 .... DLB-142, 154

Davies, W. H. 1871-1940 ....DLB-19, 174

Peter Davies Limited DLB-112

Davin, Nicholas Flood 1840?-1901....... DLB-99

Daviot, Gordon 1896?-1952 .... DLB-10
 (see also Tey, Josephine)

Davis, Arthur Hoey (see Rudd, Steele)

Davis, Benjamin J. 1903-1964........ DLB-303

Davis, Charles A. (Major J. Downing)
 1795-1867..................... DLB-11

Davis, Clyde Brion 1894-1962.......... DLB-9

Davis, Dick 1945- DLB-40, 282

Davis, Frank Marshall 1905-1987........ DLB-51

Davis, H. L. 1894-1960 .... DLB-9, 206

Davis, John 1774-1854 .... DLB-37

Davis, Lydia 1947- DLB-130

Davis, Margaret Thomson 1926- DLB-14

Davis, Ossie 1917- DLB-7, 38, 249

Davis, Owen 1874-1956 ....DLB-249

Davis, Paxton 1925-1994 ....Y-89

Davis, Rebecca Harding
 1831-1910 ....DLB-74, 239

Davis, Richard Harding 1864-1916
 .... DLB-12, 23, 78, 79, 189; DS-13

Davis, Samuel Cole 1764-1809.......... DLB-37

Davis, Samuel Post 1850-1918 .... DLB-202

Davison, Frank Dalby 1893-1970....... DLB-260

Davison, Peter 1928- DLB-5

Davydov, Denis Vasil'evich
 1784-1839................... DLB-205

Davys, Mary 1674-1732 .... DLB-39

 Preface to *The Works of Mrs. Davys*
  (1725) DLB-39

DAW Books....................... DLB-46

Dawe, Bruce 1930- DLB-289

Dawson, Ernest 1882-1947.........DLB-140; Y-02

Dawson, Fielding 1930- DLB-130

Dawson, Sarah Morgan 1842-1909 ..... DLB-239

Dawson, William 1704-1752............ DLB-31

Day, Angel flourished 1583-1599....DLB-167, 236

Day, Benjamin Henry 1810-1889........ DLB-43

Day, Clarence 1874-1935 .... DLB-11

Day, Dorothy 1897-1980 .... DLB-29

Day, Frank Parker 1881-1950 .... DLB-92

Day, John circa 1574-circa 1640......... DLB-62

Day, Thomas 1748-1789................ DLB-39

John Day [publishing house]...........DLB-170

The John Day Company DLB-46

Mahlon Day [publishing house] DLB-49

Day Lewis, C. (see Blake, Nicholas)

Dazai Osamu 1909-1948 .... DLB-182

Deacon, William Arthur 1890-1977...... DLB-68

Deal, Borden 1922-1985................ DLB-6

de Angeli, Marguerite 1889-1987 .... DLB-22

De Angelis, Milo 1951- DLB-128

Debord, Guy 1931-1994 .... DLB-296

De Bow, J. D. B. 1820-1867 ....DLB-3, 79, 248

Debs, Eugene V. 1855-1926 .... DLB-303

de Bruyn, Günter 1926- DLB-75

de Camp, L. Sprague 1907-2000......... DLB-8

De Carlo, Andrea 1952- DLB-196

De Casas, Celso A. 1944- DLB-209

Dechert, Robert 1895-1975............DLB-187

Dedications, Inscriptions, and
 Annotations Y-01–02

Dee, John 1527-1608 or 1609 ...... DLB-136, 213

Deeping, George Warwick 1877-1950 . . . . DLB-153
Defoe, Daniel
   1660-1731 . . . . DLB-39, 95, 101; CDBLB-2
   Preface to *Colonel Jack* (1722) DLB-39
   Preface to *The Farther Adventures of
      Robinson Crusoe* (1719) DLB-39
   Preface to *Moll Flanders* (1722) DLB-39
   Preface to *Robinson Crusoe* (1719) DLB-39
   Preface to *Roxana* (1724) DLB-39
de Fontaine, Felix Gregory 1834-1896 . . . . . DLB-43
De Forest, John William
   1826-1906 . . . . DLB-12, 189
DeFrees, Madeline 1919- DLB-105
   "The Poet's Kaleidoscope: The
      Element of Surprise in the
      Making of the Poem" DLB-105
DeGolyer, Everette Lee 1886-1956 . . . . . . DLB-187
de Graff, Robert 1895-1981 . . . . Y-81
de Graft, Joe 1924-1978 . . . . DLB-117
De Heinrico circa 980? DLB-148
Deighton, Len 1929- DLB-87; CDBLB-8
DeJong, Meindert 1906-1991 . . . . DLB-52
Dekker, Thomas
   circa 1572-1632 . . . . . . DLB-62, 172; CDBLB-1
Delacorte, George T., Jr. 1894-1991 . . . . . . DLB-91
Delafield, E. M. 1890-1943 . . . . DLB-34
Delahaye, Guy (Guillaume Lahaise)
   1888-1969 . . . . DLB-92
de la Mare, Walter 1873-1956
   . . . . DLB-19, 153, 162, 255; CDBLB-6
Deland, Margaret 1857-1945 . . . . DLB-78
Delaney, Shelagh 1939- DLB-13; CDBLB-8
Delano, Amasa 1763-1823 . . . . DLB-183
Delany, Martin Robinson 1812-1885 . . . . . . DLB-50
Delany, Samuel R. 1942- DLB-8, 33
de la Roche, Mazo 1879-1961 . . . . DLB-68
Delavigne, Jean François Casimir
   1793-1843 . . . . DLB-192
Delbanco, Nicholas 1942- DLB-6, 234
Delblanc, Sven 1931-1992 . . . . DLB-257
Del Castillo, Ramón 1949- DLB-209
Deledda, Grazia 1871-1936 . . . . DLB-264
De León, Nephtalí 1945- DLB-82
Deleuze, Gilles 1925-1995 . . . . DLB-296
Delfini, Antonio 1907-1963 . . . . DLB-264
Delgado, Abelardo Barrientos 1931- DLB-82
Del Giudice, Daniele 1949- DLB-196
De Libero, Libero 1906-1981 . . . . DLB-114
DeLillo, Don 1936- DLB-6, 173
de Lint, Charles 1951- DLB-251
de Lisser H. G. 1878-1944 . . . . DLB-117
Dell, Floyd 1887-1969 . . . . .DLB-9
Dell Publishing Company DLB-46
delle Grazie, Marie Eugene 1864-1931 . . . . DLB-81
Deloney, Thomas died 1600 . . . . DLB-167
Deloria, Ella C. 1889-1971 . . . . DLB-175
Deloria, Vine, Jr. 1933- DLB-175

del Rey, Lester 1915-1993 . . . . DLB-8
Del Vecchio, John M. 1947- DS-9
Del'vig, Anton Antonovich 1798-1831 . . . . DLB-205
de Man, Paul 1919-1983 . . . . DLB-67
DeMarinis, Rick 1934- DLB-218
Demby, William 1922- DLB-33
De Mille, James 1833-1880 . . . . DLB-99, 251
de Mille, William 1878-1955 . . . . DLB-266
Deming, Philander 1829-1915 . . . . DLB-74
Deml, Jakub 1878-1961 . . . . DLB-215
Demorest, William Jennings 1822-1895 . . . DLB-79
De Morgan, William 1839-1917 . . . . DLB-153
Demosthenes 384 B.C.-322 B.C. DLB-176
Henry Denham [publishing house] DLB-170
Denham, Sir John 1615-1669 . . . . . . DLB-58, 126
Denison, Merrill 1893-1975 . . . . DLB-92
T. S. Denison and Company DLB-49
Dennery, Adolphe Philippe 1811-1899 . . . DLB-192
Dennie, Joseph 1768-1812 . . . . . DLB-37, 43, 59, 73
Dennis, C. J. 1876-1938 . . . . DLB-260
Dennis, John 1658-1734 . . . . DLB-101
Dennis, Nigel 1912-1989 . . . . DLB-13, 15, 233
Denslow, W. W. 1856-1915 . . . . DLB-188
Dent, J. M., and Sons DLB-112
Dent, Tom 1932-1998 . . . . DLB-38
Denton, Daniel circa 1626-1703 . . . . DLB-24
DePaola, Tomie 1934- DLB-61
De Quille, Dan 1829-1898 . . . . DLB-186
De Quincey, Thomas
   1785-1859 . . . . DLB-110, 144; CDBLB-3
   "Rhetoric" (1828; revised, 1859)
      [excerpt] DLB-57
   "Style" (1840; revised, 1859)
      [excerpt] DLB-57
Derby, George Horatio 1823-1861 . . . . DLB-11
J. C. Derby and Company DLB-49
Derby and Miller DLB-49
De Ricci, Seymour 1881-1942 . . . . DLB-201
Derleth, August 1909-1971 . . . . DLB-9; DS-17
Derrida, Jacques 1930- DLB-242
The Derrydale Press DLB-46
Derzhavin, Gavriil Romanovich
   1743-1816 . . . . DLB-150
Desai, Anita 1937- DLB-271
Desaulniers, Gonzalve 1863-1934 . . . . DLB-92
Desbordes-Valmore, Marceline
   1786-1859 . . . . DLB-217
Descartes, René 1596-1650 . . . . DLB-268
Deschamps, Emile 1791-1871 . . . . DLB-217
Deschamps, Eustache 1340?-1404 . . . . DLB-208
Desbiens, Jean-Paul 1927- DLB-53
des Forêts, Louis-Rene 1918-2001 . . . . DLB-83
Desiato, Luca 1941- DLB-196
Desjardins, Marie-Catherine
   (see Villedieu, Madame de)
Desnica, Vladan 1905-1967 . . . . DLB-181

Desnos, Robert 1900-1945 . . . . DLB-258
DesRochers, Alfred 1901-1978 . . . . DLB-68
Desrosiers, Léo-Paul 1896-1967 . . . . DLB-68
Dessaulles, Louis-Antoine 1819-1895 . . . . . DLB-99
Dessì, Giuseppe 1909-1977 . . . . DLB-177
Destouches, Louis-Ferdinand
   (see Céline, Louis-Ferdinand)
DeSylva, Buddy 1895-1950 . . . . DLB-265
De Tabley, Lord 1835-1895 . . . . DLB-35
Deutsch, Babette 1895-1982 . . . . DLB-45
Deutsch, Niklaus Manuel (see Manuel, Niklaus)
André Deutsch Limited DLB-112
Devanny, Jean 1894-1962 . . . . DLB-260
Deveaux, Alexis 1948- DLB-38
De Vere, Aubrey 1814-1902 . . . . DLB-35
Devereux, second Earl of Essex, Robert
   1565-1601 . . . . DLB-136
The Devin-Adair Company DLB-46
De Vinne, Theodore Low
   1828-1914 . . . . DLB-187
Devlin, Anne 1951- DLB-245
DeVoto, Bernard 1897-1955 . . . . DLB-9, 256
De Vries, Peter 1910-1993 . . . . DLB-6; Y-82
   Tribute to Albert Erskine Y-93
Dewart, Edward Hartley 1828-1903 . . . . . . DLB-99
Dewdney, Christopher 1951- DLB-60
Dewdney, Selwyn 1909-1979 . . . . DLB-68
Dewey, John 1859-1952 . . . . DLB-246, 270
Dewey, Orville 1794-1882 . . . . DLB-243
Dewey, Thomas B. 1915-1981 . . . . DLB-226
DeWitt, Robert M., Publisher DLB-49
DeWolfe, Fiske and Company DLB-49
Dexter, Colin 1930- DLB-87
de Young, M. H. 1849-1925 . . . . DLB-25
Dhlomo, H. I. E. 1903-1956 . . . . DLB-157, 225
Dhuoda circa 803-after 843 . . . . DLB-148
The Dial 1840-1844 . . . . DLB-223
The Dial Press DLB-46
Diamond, I. A. L. 1920-1988 . . . . DLB-26
Dibble, L. Grace 1902-1998 . . . . DLB-204
Dibdin, Thomas Frognall
   1776-1847 . . . . DLB-184
Di Cicco, Pier Giorgio 1949- DLB-60
Dick, Philip K. 1928-1982 . . . . DLB-8
Dick and Fitzgerald DLB-49
Dickens, Charles 1812-1870
   . . . . DLB-21, 55, 70, 159,
         166; DS-5; CDBLB-4
Dickey, Eric Jerome 1961- DLB-292
Dickey, James 1923-1997 . . . . DLB-5, 193;
   Y-82, 93, 96, 97; DS-7, 19; CDALB-6
   James Dickey and Stanley Burnshaw
      Correspondence Y-02
   James Dickey at Seventy–A Tribute Y-93
   James Dickey, American Poet Y-96
   The James Dickey Society Y-99

The Life of James Dickey: A Lecture to
   the Friends of the Emory Libraries,
   by Henry Hart................Y-98

Tribute to Archibald MacLeish........Y-82

Tribute to Malcolm Cowley..........Y-89

Tribute to Truman Capote...........Y-84

Tributes [to Dickey]................Y-97

Dickey, William 1928-1994.............DLB-5

Dickinson, Emily
   1830-1886..........DLB-1, 243; CDALB-3

Dickinson, John 1732-1808..............DLB-31

Dickinson, Jonathan 1688-1747..........DLB-24

Dickinson, Patric 1914-................DLB-27

Dickinson, Peter 1927-........DLB-87, 161, 276

John Dicks [publishing house]..........DLB-106

Dickson, Gordon R. 1923-2001...........DLB-8

Dictionary of Literary Biography
   Annual Awards for *Dictionary of*
   Literary Biography Editors and
   Contributors...................Y-98–02

Dictionary of Literary Biography
   Yearbook Awards........Y-92–93, 97–02

The Dictionary of National Biography.......DLB-144

Didion, Joan 1934-
   ....DLB-2, 173, 185; Y-81, 86; CDALB-6

Di Donato, Pietro 1911-................DLB-9

Die Fürstliche Bibliothek Corvey...........Y-96

Diego, Gerardo 1896-1987..............DLB-134

Dietz, Howard 1896-1983...............DLB-265

Digby, Everard 1550?-1605..............DLB-281

Digges, Thomas circa 1546-1595........DLB-136

The Digital Millennium Copyright Act:
   Expanding Copyright Protection in
   Cyberspace and Beyond...............Y-98

Diktonius, Elmer 1896-1961............DLB-259

Dillard, Annie 1945-........DLB-275, 278; Y-80

Dillard, R. H. W. 1937-.............DLB-5, 244

Charles T. Dillingham Company........DLB-49

G. W. Dillingham Company.............DLB-49

Edward and Charles Dilly
   [publishing house]................DLB-154

Dilthey, Wilhelm 1833-1911.............DLB-129

Dimitrova, Blaga 1922-....DLB-181; CDWLB-4

Dimov, Dimitr 1909-1966...............DLB-181

Dimsdale, Thomas J. 1831?-1866........DLB-186

Dinescu, Mircea 1950-..................DLB-232

Dinesen, Isak (see Blixen, Karen)

Dingelstedt, Franz von 1814-1881........DLB-133

Dinis, Júlio (Joaquim Guilherme
   Gomes Coelho) 1839-1871........DLB-287

Dintenfass, Mark 1941-..................Y-84

Diogenes, Jr. (see Brougham, John)

Diogenes Laertius circa 200............DLB-176

DiPrima, Diane 1934-..............DLB-5, 16

Disch, Thomas M. 1940-...........DLB-8, 282

Diski, Jenny 1947-....................DLB-271

Disney, Walt 1901-1966................DLB-22

Disraeli, Benjamin 1804-1881........DLB-21, 55

D'Israeli, Isaac 1766-1848..............DLB-107

DLB Award for Distinguished
   Literary Criticism..................Y-02

Ditlevsen, Tove 1917-1976.............DLB-214

Ditzen, Rudolf (see Fallada, Hans)

Dix, Dorothea Lynde 1802-1887.....DLB-1, 235

Dix, Dorothy (see Gilmer, Elizabeth Meriwether)

Dix, Edwards and Company............DLB-49

Dix, Gertrude circa 1874-?.............DLB-197

Dixie, Florence Douglas 1857-1905......DLB-174

Dixon, Ella Hepworth
   1855 or 1857-1932................DLB-197

Dixon, Paige (see Corcoran, Barbara)

Dixon, Richard Watson 1833-1900......DLB-19

Dixon, Stephen 1936-..................DLB-130

DLB Award for Distinguished
   Literary Criticism..................Y-02

Dmitriev, Andrei Viktorovich 1956-....DLB-285

Dmitriev, Ivan Ivanovich 1760-1837.....DLB-150

Dobell, Bertram 1842-1914.............DLB-184

Dobell, Sydney 1824-1874..............DLB-32

Dobie, J. Frank 1888-1964..............DLB-212

Dobles Yzaguirre, Julieta 1943-..........DLB-283

Döblin, Alfred 1878-1957....DLB-66; CDWLB-2

Dobroliubov, Nikolai Aleksandrovich
   1836-1861.......................DLB-277

Dobson, Austin 1840-1921..........DLB-35, 144

Dobson, Rosemary 1920-..............DLB-260

Doctorow, E. L.
   1931-.......DLB-2, 28, 173; Y-80; CDALB-6

Dodd, Susan M. 1946-.................DLB-244

Dodd, William E. 1869-1940............DLB-17

Anne Dodd [publishing house].........DLB-154

Dodd, Mead and Company............DLB-49

Doderer, Heimito von 1896-1966........DLB-85

B. W. Dodge and Company............DLB-46

Dodge, Mary Abigail 1833-1896........DLB-221

Dodge, Mary Mapes
   1831?-1905.................DLB-42, 79; DS-13

Dodge Publishing Company............DLB-49

Dodgson, Charles Lutwidge (see Carroll, Lewis)

Dodsley, Robert 1703-1764..............DLB-95

R. Dodsley [publishing house]..........DLB-154

Dodson, Owen 1914-1983...............DLB-76

Dodwell, Christina 1951-...............DLB-204

Doesticks, Q. K. Philander, P. B.
   (see Thomson, Mortimer)

Doheny, Carrie Estelle 1875-1958......DLB-140

Doherty, John 1798?-1854..............DLB-190

Doig, Ivan 1939-......................DLB-206

Doinaş, Ştefan Augustin 1922-..........DLB-232

Domínguez, Sylvia Maida 1935-.........DLB-122

Donaghy, Michael 1954-...............DLB-282

Patrick Donahoe [publishing house]....DLB-49

Donald, David H. 1920-............DLB-17; Y-87

Donaldson, Scott 1928-.................DLB-111

Doni, Rodolfo 1919-...................DLB-177

Donleavy, J. P. 1926-...............DLB-6, 173

Donnadieu, Marguerite (see Duras, Marguerite)

Donne, John
   1572-1631..........DLB-121, 151; CDBLB-1

Donnelly, Ignatius 1831-1901............DLB-12

R. R. Donnelley and Sons Company.....DLB-49

Donoghue, Emma 1969-...............DLB-267

Donohue and Henneberry..............DLB-49

Donoso, José 1924-1996.....DLB-113; CDWLB-3

M. Doolady [publishing house]..........DLB-49

Dooley, Ebon (see Ebon)

Doolittle, Hilda 1886-1961......DLB-4, 45; DS-15

Doplicher, Fabio 1938-.................DLB-128

Dor, Milo 1923-.......................DLB-85

George H. Doran Company............DLB-46

Dorgelès, Roland 1886-1973.............DLB-65

Dorn, Edward 1929-1999................DLB-5

Dorr, Rheta Childe 1866-1948............DLB-25

Dorris, Michael 1945-1997..............DLB-175

Dorset and Middlesex, Charles Sackville,
   Lord Buckhurst, Earl of 1643-1706...DLB-131

Dorsey, Candas Jane 1952-.............DLB-251

Dorst, Tankred 1925-..............DLB-75, 124

Dos Passos, John 1896-1970
   ....DLB-4, 9; DS-1, 15; CDALB-5

John Dos Passos: A Centennial
   Commemoration.................Y-96

John Dos Passos: Artist...............Y-99

John Dos Passos Newsletter...........Y-00

U.S.A. (Documentary)................DLB-274

Dostoevsky, Fyodor 1821-1881..........DLB-238

Doubleday and Company..............DLB-49

Doubrovsky, Serge 1928-................DLB-299

Dougall, Lily 1858-1923.................DLB-92

Doughty, Charles M.
   1843-1926....................DLB-19, 57, 174

Douglas, Lady Alfred (see Custance, Olive)

Douglas, Ellen (Josephine Ayres Haxton)
   1921-...........................DLB-292

Douglas, Gavin 1476-1522..............DLB-132

Douglas, Keith 1920-1944...............DLB-27

Douglas, Norman 1868-1952........DLB-34, 195

Douglass, Frederick 1817-1895
   ....DLB-1, 43, 50, 79, 243; CDALB-2

Frederick Douglass Creative Arts Center Y-01

Douglass, William circa 1691-1752......DLB-24

Dourado, Autran 1926-................DLB-145

Dove, Arthur G. 1880-1946.............DLB-188

Dove, Rita 1952-..........DLB-120; CDALB-7

Dover Publications....................DLB-46

Doves Press.........................DLB-112

Dovlatov, Sergei Donatovich
   1941-1990.......................DLB-285

Dowden, Edward 1843-1913........DLB-35, 149

Dowell, Coleman 1925-1985............DLB-130

Dowland, John 1563-1626..............DLB-172

Downes, Gwladys 1915- DLB-88

Downing, J., Major (see Davis, Charles A.)

Downing, Major Jack (see Smith, Seba)

Dowriche, Anne
   before 1560-after 1613.............DLB-172

Dowson, Ernest 1867-1900 ....DLB-19, 135

William Doxey [publishing house]........DLB-49

Doyle, Sir Arthur Conan
   1859-1930 ... DLB-18, 70, 156, 178; CDBLB-5

   The Priory Scholars of New York........Y-99

Doyle, Kirby 1932- DLB-16

Doyle, Roddy 1958- DLB-194

Drabble, Margaret
   1939- DLB-14, 155, 231; CDBLB-8

   Tribute to Graham Greene............Y-91

Drach, Albert 1902-1995.............DLB-85

Drachmann, Holger 1846-1908........DLB-300

Dragojević, Danijel 1934- DLB-181

Dragún, Osvaldo 1929-1999...........DLB-305

Drake, Samuel Gardner 1798-1875......DLB-187

Drama (*See* Theater)

The Dramatic Publishing Company......DLB-49

Dramatists Play Service...............DLB-46

Drant, Thomas
   early 1540s?-1578..................DLB-167

Draper, John W. 1811-1882.............DLB-30

Draper, Lyman C. 1815-1891...........DLB-30

Drayton, Michael 1563-1631...........DLB-121

Dreiser, Theodore 1871-1945
   ....DLB-9, 12, 102, 137; DS-1; CDALB-3

   The International Theodore Dreiser
   Society Y-01

   Notes from the Underground
   of *Sister Carrie* Y-01

Dresser, Davis 1904-1977............DLB-226

Drew, Elizabeth A.
   "A Note on Technique" [excerpt]
   (1926) DLB-36

Drewitz, Ingeborg 1923-1986.........DLB-75

Drieu La Rochelle, Pierre 1893-1945......DLB-72

Drinker, Elizabeth 1735-1807.........DLB-200

Drinkwater, John 1882-1937 .....DLB-10, 19, 149

   The Friends of the Dymock Poets.......Y-00

Droste-Hülshoff, Annette von
   1797-1848................DLB-133; CDWLB-2

The Drue Heinz Literature Prize
   Excerpt from "Excerpts from a Report
   of the Commission," in David
   Bosworth's *The Death of Descartes*
   An Interview with David Bosworth.....Y-82

Drummond, William, of Hawthornden
   1585-1649..................DLB-121, 213

Drummond, William Henry 1854-1907...DLB-92

Druzhinin, Aleksandr Vasil'evich
   1824-1864......................DLB-238

Dryden, Charles 1860?-1931...........DLB-171

Dryden, John
   1631-1700 .....DLB-80, 101, 131; CDBLB-2

Držić, Marin
   circa 1508-1567........DLB-147; CDWLB-4

Duane, William 1760-1835.............DLB-43

Dubé, Marcel 1930- DLB-53

Dubé, Rodolphe (see Hertel, François)

Dubie, Norman 1945- DLB-120

Dubin, Al 1891-1945................DLB-265

Dubois, Silvia 1788 or 1789?-1889.......DLB-239

Du Bois, W. E. B.
   1868-1963 ....DLB-47, 50, 91, 246; CDALB-3

Du Bois, William Pène 1916-1993........DLB-61

Dubrovina, Ekaterina Oskarovna
   1846-1913......................DLB-238

Dubus, Andre 1936-1999..............DLB-130

   Tribute to Michael M. Rea............Y-97

Dubus, Andre, III 1959- DLB-292

Ducange, Victor 1783-1833............DLB-192

Du Chaillu, Paul Belloni 1831?-1903.....DLB-189

Ducharme, Réjean 1941- DLB-60

Dučić, Jovan 1871-1943 .....DLB-147; CDWLB-4

Duck, Stephen 1705?-1756..............DLB-95

Gerald Duckworth and Company
   Limited DLB-112

Duclaux, Madame Mary (see Robinson, A. Mary F.)

Dudek, Louis 1918-2001 ....DLB-88

Dudintsev, Vladimir Dmitrievich
   1918-1998......................DLB-302

Dudley-Smith, Trevor (see Hall, Adam)

Duell, Sloan and Pearce................DLB-46

Duerer, Albrecht 1471-1528.............DLB-179

Duff Gordon, Lucie 1821-1869 ....DLB-166

Dufferin, Helen Lady, Countess of Gifford
   1807-1867......................DLB-199

Duffield and Green DLB-46

Duffy, Maureen 1933- DLB-14

Dufief, Nicholas Gouin 1776-1834......DLB-187

Dufresne, John 1948- DLB-292

Dugan, Alan 1923- DLB-5

Dugard, William 1606-1662 ....DLB-170, 281

William Dugard [publishing house].......DLB-170

Dugas, Marcel 1883-1947 ....DLB-92

William Dugdale [publishing house] DLB-106

Duhamel, Georges 1884-1966............DLB-65

Dujardin, Edouard 1861-1949............DLB-123

Dukes, Ashley 1885-1959 ....DLB-10

Dumas, Alexandre *fils* 1824-1895........DLB-192

Dumas, Alexandre *père* 1802-1870.....DLB-119, 192

Dumas, Henry 1934-1968................DLB-41

du Maurier, Daphne 1907-1989..........DLB-191

Du Maurier, George 1834-1896 ....DLB-153, 178

Dummett, Michael 1925- DLB-262

Dunbar, Paul Laurence
   1872-1906........DLB-50, 54, 78; CDALB-3

   Introduction to *Lyrics of Lowly Life* (1896),
   by William Dean Howells DLB-50

Dunbar, William
   circa 1460-circa 1522........DLB-132, 146

Duncan, Dave 1933- DLB-251

Duncan, David James 1952- DLB-256

Duncan, Norman 1871-1916 ....DLB-92

Duncan, Quince 1940- DLB-145

Duncan, Robert 1919-1988.......DLB-5, 16, 193

Duncan, Ronald 1914-1982.............DLB-13

Duncan, Sara Jeannette 1861-1922.......DLB-92

Dunigan, Edward, and Brother..........DLB-49

Dunlap, John 1747-1812................DLB-43

Dunlap, William 1766-1839....... DLB-30, 37, 59

Dunlop, William "Tiger" 1792-1848 ......DLB-99

Dunmore, Helen 1952- DLB-267

Dunn, Douglas 1942- DLB-40

Dunn, Harvey Thomas 1884-1952......DLB-188

Dunn, Stephen 1939- DLB-105

   "The Good, The Not So Good" DLB-105

Dunne, Finley Peter 1867-1936 ....DLB-11, 23

Dunne, John Gregory 1932- Y-80

Dunne, Philip 1908-1992..............DLB-26

Dunning, Ralph Cheever 1878-1930.......DLB-4

Dunning, William A. 1857-1922 ....DLB-17

Duns Scotus, John circa 1266-1308......DLB-115

Dunsany, Lord (Edward John Moreton
   Drax Plunkett, Baron Dunsany)
   1878-1957 ....DLB-10, 77, 153, 156, 255

Dunton, W. Herbert 1878-1936.........DLB-188

John Dunton [publishing house] DLB-170

Dupin, Amantine-Aurore-Lucile (see Sand, George)

Dupuy, Eliza Ann 1814-1880 ....DLB-248

Durack, Mary 1913-1994 ....DLB-260

Durand, Lucile (see Bersianik, Louky)

Duranti, Francesca 1935- DLB-196

Duranty, Walter 1884-1957.............DLB-29

Duras, Marguerite (Marguerite Donnadieu)
   1914-1996......................DLB-83

Durfey, Thomas 1653-1723.............DLB-80

Durova, Nadezhda Andreevna
   (Aleksandr Andreevich Aleksandrov)
   1783-1866......................DLB-198

Durrell, Lawrence 1912-1990
   ....DLB-15, 27, 204; Y-90; CDBLB-7

William Durrell [publishing house] DLB-49

Dürrenmatt, Friedrich
   1921-1990.........DLB-69, 124; CDWLB-2

Duston, Hannah 1657-1737 ....DLB-200

Dutt, Toru 1856-1877 ....DLB-240

E. P. Dutton and Company............DLB-49

Duun, Olav 1876-1939 ....DLB-297

Duvoisin, Roger 1904-1980.............DLB-61

Duyckinck, Evert Augustus
   1816-1878.................DLB-3, 64, 250

Duyckinck, George L.
   1823-1863....................DLB-3, 250

Duyckinck and Company DLB-49

Dwight, John Sullivan 1813-1893 .....DLB-1, 235

Dwight, Timothy 1752-1817 ....DLB-37

   America: or, A Poem on the Settlement
   of the British Colonies, by
   Timothy Dwight................DLB-37

Dybek, Stuart 1942- DLB-130

Tribute to Michael M. Rea Y-97
Dyer, Charles 1928- DLB-13
Dyer, Sir Edward 1543-1607 . . . . DLB-136
Dyer, George 1755-1841. . . . . DLB-93
Dyer, John 1699-1757 . . . . DLB-95
Dyk, Viktor 1877-1931 . . . . DLB-215
Dylan, Bob 1941- DLB-16

E

Eager, Edward 1911-1964 . . . . DLB-22
Eagleton, Terry 1943- DLB-242
Eames, Wilberforce
   1855-1937. . . . . DLB-140
Earle, Alice Morse
   1853-1911. . . . . DLB-221
Earle, John 1600 or 1601-1665 . . . . DLB-151
James H. Earle and Company DLB-49
East Europe
   Independence and Destruction,
     1918-1941 . . . . DLB-220
   Social Theory and Ethnography:
     Languageand Ethnicity in
     Western versus Eastern Man . . . DLB-220
Eastlake, William 1917-1997 . . . . DLB-6, 206
Eastman, Carol ?- DLB-44
Eastman, Charles A. (Ohiyesa)
   1858-1939 . . . . DLB-175
Eastman, Max 1883-1969 . . . . DLB-91
Eaton, Daniel Isaac 1753-1814 . . . . DLB-158
Eaton, Edith Maude 1865-1914 . . . . DLB-221
Eaton, Winnifred 1875-1954 . . . . DLB-221
Eberhart, Richard 1904- DLB-48; CDALB-1
   Tribute to Robert Penn Warren Y-89
Ebner, Jeannie 1918- DLB-85
Ebner-Eschenbach, Marie von
   1830-1916. . . . . DLB-81
Ebon 1942- DLB-41
E-Books' Second Act in Libraries Y-02
Ecbasis Captivi circa 1045 . . . . DLB-148
Ecco Press DLB-46
Eckhart, Meister circa 1260-circa 1328 . . . DLB-115
The Eclectic Review 1805-1868 . . . . DLB-110
Eco, Umberto 1932- DLB-196, 242
Eddison, E. R. 1882-1945 . . . . DLB-255
Edel, Leon 1907-1997 . . . . DLB-103
Edelfeldt, Inger 1956- DLB-257
A Century of Poetry, a Lifetime of Collecting:
   J. M. Edelstein's Collection of Twentieth-
   Century American Poetry Y-02
Edes, Benjamin 1732-1803 . . . . DLB-43
Edgar, David 1948- DLB-13, 233
   Viewpoint: Politics and
     Performance DLB-13
Edgerton, Clyde 1944- DLB-278
Edgeworth, Maria
   1768-1849 . . . . DLB-116, 159, 163
The Edinburgh Review 1802-1929 . . . . DLB-110
Edinburgh University Press DLB-112

Editing
   Conversations with Editors Y-95
   Editorial Statements DLB-137
   The Editorial Style of Fredson Bowers . . . Y-91
   Editorial: The Extension of Copyright . . . Y-02
   We See the Editor at Work Y-97
   Whose *Ulysses*? The Function of Editing . . Y-97
The Editor Publishing Company DLB-49
Editorial Institute at Boston University Y-00
Edmonds, Helen Woods Ferguson
   (see Kavan, Anna)
Edmonds, Randolph 1900-1983 . . . . DLB-51
Edmonds, Walter D. 1903-1998. . . . . DLB-9
Edric, Robert (see Armitage, G. E.)
Edschmid, Kasimir 1890-1966 . . . . DLB-56
Edson, Margaret 1961- DLB-266
Edson, Russell 1935- DLB-244
Edwards, Amelia Anne Blandford
   1831-1892 . . . . DLB-174
Edwards, Dic 1953- DLB-245
Edwards, Edward 1812-1886 . . . . DLB-184
Edwards, Jonathan 1703-1758. . . . . DLB-24, 270
Edwards, Jonathan, Jr. 1745-1801 . . . . DLB-37
Edwards, Junius 1929- DLB-33
Edwards, Matilda Barbara Betham
   1836-1919 . . . . DLB-174
Edwards, Richard 1524-1566 . . . . DLB-62
Edwards, Sarah Pierpont 1710-1758 . . . . . DLB-200
James Edwards [publishing house] DLB-154
Effinger, George Alec 1947- DLB-8
Egerton, George 1859-1945 . . . . DLB-135
Eggleston, Edward 1837-1902 . . . . DLB-12
Eggleston, Wilfred 1901-1986 . . . . DLB-92
Eglītis, Anšlavs 1906-1993 . . . . DLB-220
Eguren, José María 1874-1942 . . . . DLB-290
Ehrenreich, Barbara 1941- DLB-246
Ehrenstein, Albert 1886-1950 . . . . DLB-81
Ehrhart, W. D. 1948- DS-9
Ehrlich, Gretel 1946- DLB-212, 275
Eich, Günter 1907-1972. . . . . DLB-69, 124
Eichendorff, Joseph Freiherr von
   1788-1857 . . . . DLB-90
Eifukumon'in 1271-1342 . . . . DLB-203
Eigner, Larry 1926-1996 . . . . DLB-5, 193
Eikon Basilike 1649 . . . . DLB-151
Eilhart von Oberge
   circa 1140-circa 1195 . . . . DLB-148
Einar Benediktsson 1864-1940 . . . . DLB-293
Einar Kárason 1955- DLB-293
Einar Már Guðmundsson 1954- DLB-293
Einhard circa 770-840 . . . . DLB-148
Eiseley, Loren 1907-1977 . . . . DLB-275, DS-17
Eisenberg, Deborah 1945- DLB-244
Eisenreich, Herbert 1925-1986 . . . . DLB-85
Eisner, Kurt 1867-1919 . . . . DLB-66
Ekelöf, Gunnar 1907-1968 . . . . DLB-259

Eklund, Gordon 1945- Y-83
Ekman, Kerstin 1933- DLB-257
Ekwensi, Cyprian 1921- . . . DLB-117; CDWLB-3
Elaw, Zilpha circa 1790-? DLB-239
George Eld [publishing house] DLB-170
Elder, Lonne, III 1931- DLB-7, 38, 44
Paul Elder and Company DLB-49
Eldershaw, Flora (M. Barnard Eldershaw)
   1897-1956 . . . . DLB-260
Eldershaw, M. Barnard (see Barnard, Marjorie and
   Eldershaw, Flora)
The Electronic Text Center and the Electronic
   Archive of Early American Fiction at the
   University of Virginia Library Y-98
Eliade, Mircea 1907-1986 . . . DLB-220; CDWLB-4
Elie, Robert 1915-1973 . . . . DLB-88
Elin Pelin 1877-1949 . . . . DLB-147; CDWLB-4
Eliot, George
   1819-1880 . . . . . . DLB-21, 35, 55; CDBLB-4
   The George Eliot Fellowship Y-99
Eliot, John 1604-1690. . . . . DLB-24
Eliot, T. S. 1888-1965
   . . . . DLB-7, 10, 45, 63, 245; CDALB-5
   T. S. Eliot Centennial: The Return
     of the Old Possum. Y-88
   The T. S. Eliot Society: Celebration and
     Scholarship, 1980-1999 . . . . Y-99
Eliot's Court Press DLB-170
Elizabeth I 1533-1603 . . . . DLB-136
Elizabeth von Nassau-Saarbrücken
   after 1393-1456 . . . . DLB-179
Elizondo, Salvador 1932- DLB-145
Elizondo, Sergio 1930- DLB-82
Elkin, Stanley
   1930-1995 . . . . DLB-2, 28, 218, 278; Y-80
Elles, Dora Amy (see Wentworth, Patricia)
Ellet, Elizabeth F. 1818?-1877 . . . . DLB-30
Elliot, Ebenezer 1781-1849 . . . . DLB-96, 190
Elliot, Frances Minto (Dickinson)
   1820-1898 . . . . DLB-166
Elliott, Charlotte 1789-1871 . . . . DLB-199
Elliott, George 1923- DLB-68
Elliott, George P. 1918-1980 . . . . DLB-244
Elliott, Janice 1931-1995 . . . . DLB-14
Elliott, Sarah Barnwell 1848-1928 . . . . . . DLB-221
Elliott, Sumner Locke 1917-1991 . . . . DLB-289
Elliott, Thomes and Talbot DLB-49
Elliott, William, III 1788-1863 . . . . DLB-3, 248
Ellis, Alice Thomas (Anna Margaret Haycraft)
   1932- DLB-194
Ellis, Bret Easton 1964- DLB-292
Ellis, Edward S. 1840-1916 . . . . DLB-42
Ellis, George E.
   "The New Controversy Concerning
     Miracles DS-5
Ellis, Havelock 1859-1939 . . . . DLB-190
Frederick Staridge Ellis
   [publishing house] DLB-106
The George H. Ellis Company DLB-49

Ellison, Harlan 1934- DLB-8
   Tribute to Isaac Asimov Y-92
Ellison, Ralph
   1914-1994 ... DLB-2, 76, 227; Y-94; CDALB-1
Ellmann, Richard 1918-1987 ...... DLB-103; Y-87
Ellroy, James 1948- DLB-226; Y-91
   Tribute to John D. MacDonald........ Y-86
   Tribute to Raymond Chandler Y-88
Eluard, Paul 1895-1952 ....DLB-258
Elyot, Thomas 1490?-1546 ....DLB-136
Emanuel, James Andrew 1921- DLB-41
Emecheta, Buchi 1944- DLB-117; CDWLB-3
Emerson, Ralph Waldo
   1803-1882 ...... DLB-1, 59, 73, 183, 223, 270;
                        DS-5; CDALB-2
   Ralph Waldo Emerson in 1982......... Y-82
   The Ralph Waldo Emerson Society Y-99
Emerson, William 1769-1811............DLB-37
Emerson, William R. 1923-1997 .... Y-97
Emin, Fedor Aleksandrovich
   circa 1735-1770 ....DLB-150
Emmanuel, Pierre 1916-1984............DLB-258
Empedocles fifth century B.C.......... DLB-176
Empson, William 1906-1984..............DLB-20
Enchi Fumiko 1905-1986................DLB-182
Ende, Michael 1929-1995 ....DLB-75
Endō Shūsaku 1923-1996 ....DLB-182
Engel, Marian 1933-1985................DLB-53
Engel'gardt, Sof'ia Vladimirovna
   1828-1894 ....DLB-277
Engels, Friedrich 1820-1895...........DLB-129
Engle, Paul 1908- DLB-48
   Tribute to Robert Penn Warren Y-89
English, Thomas Dunn 1819-1902 ....DLB-202
Ennius 239 B.C.-169 B.C. DLB-211
Enquist, Per Olov 1934- DLB-257
Enright, Anne 1962- DLB-267
Enright, D. J. 1920- DLB-27
Enright, Elizabeth 1909-1968............DLB-22
Epictetus circa 55-circa 125-130........DLB-176
Epicurus 342/341 B.C.-271/270 B.C. DLB-176
Epps, Bernard 1936- DLB-53
Epshtein, Mikhail Naumovich 1950- ...DLB-285
Epstein, Julius 1909-2000 and
   Epstein, Philip 1909-1952 ....DLB-26
Epstein, Leslie 1938- DLB-299
Editors, Conversations with................ Y-95
Equiano, Olaudah
   circa 1745-1797 ...... DLB-37, 50; CDWLB-3
   Olaudah Equiano and Unfinished
     Journeys: The Slave-Narrative
     Tradition and Twentieth-Century
     Continuities DLB-117
Eragny Press DLB-112
Erasmus, Desiderius 1467-1536 ....DLB-136
Erba, Luciano 1922- DLB-128
Erdman, Nikolai Robertovich
   1900-1970 ....DLB-272

Erdrich, Louise
   1954- DLB-152, 175, 206; CDALB-7
Erenburg, Il'ia Grigor'evich 1891-1967 ... DLB-272
Erichsen-Brown, Gwethalyn Graham
   (see Graham, Gwethalyn)
Eriugena, John Scottus circa 810-877 ..... DLB-115
Ernst, Paul 1866-1933 .... DLB-66, 118
Erofeev, Venedikt Vasil'evich
   1938-1990 ....DLB-285
Erofeev, Viktor Vladimirovich 1947- ...DLB-285
Ershov, Petr Pavlovich 1815-1869.......DLB-205
Erskine, Albert 1911-1993 .... Y-93
   At Home with Albert Erskine Y-00
Erskine, John 1879-1951 ....DLB-9, 102
Erskine, Mrs. Steuart ?-1948 ....DLB-195
Ertel', Aleksandr Ivanovich
   1855-1908 ....DLB-238
Ervine, St. John Greer 1883-1971 ....DLB-10
Eschenburg, Johann Joachim
   1743-1820 ....DLB-97
Escofet, Cristina 1945- DLB-305
Escoto, Julio 1944- DLB-145
Esdaile, Arundell 1880-1956 ....DLB-201
Esenin, Sergei Aleksandrovich
   1895-1925 ....DLB-295
Eshleman, Clayton 1935- DLB-5
Espaillat, Rhina P. 1932- DLB-282
Espanca, Florbela 1894-1930 ....DLB-287
Espriu, Salvador 1913-1985.............DLB-134
Ess Ess Publishing Company............DLB-49
Essex House Press......................DLB-112
Esson, Louis 1878-1943 ....DLB-260
Essop, Ahmed 1931- DLB-225
Estes, Eleanor 1906-1988................DLB-22
Estes and Lauriat......................DLB-49
Estleman, Loren D. 1952 ....DLB-226
Eszterhas, Joe 1944- DLB-185
Etherege, George 1636-circa 1692.......DLB-80
Ethridge, Mark, Sr. 1896-1981..........DLB-127
Ets, Marie Hall 1893-1984..............DLB-22
Etter, David 1928- DLB-105
Ettner, Johann Christoph
   1654-1724 ....DLB-168
Eudora Welty Remembered in
   Two Exhibits.......................... Y-02
Eugene Gant's Projected Works Y-01
Eupolemius flourished circa 1095 ....DLB-148
Euripides circa 484 B.C.-407/406 B.C.
                    DLB-176; CDWLB-1
Evans, Augusta Jane 1835-1909.........DLB-239
Evans, Caradoc 1878-1945..............DLB-162
Evans, Charles 1850-1935 ....DLB-187
Evans, Donald 1884-1921 ....DLB-54
Evans, George Henry 1805-1856........DLB-43
Evans, Hubert 1892-1986 ....DLB-92
Evans, Mari 1923- DLB-41

Evans, Mary Ann (see Eliot, George)
Evans, Nathaniel 1742-1767 ....DLB-31
Evans, Sebastian 1830-1909..............DLB-35
Evans, Ray 1915- DLB-265
M. Evans and Company DLB-46
Evaristi, Marcella 1953- DLB-233
Everett, Alexander Hill 1790-1847.......DLB-59
Everett, Edward 1794-1865 ...... DLB-1, 59, 235
Everson, R. G. 1903- DLB-88
Everson, William 1912-1994 ...... DLB-5, 16, 212
Ewald, Johannes 1743-1781 ....DLB-300
Ewart, Gavin 1916-1995 ....DLB-40
Ewing, Juliana Horatia
   1841-1885 ....DLB-21, 163
The Examiner 1808-1881 ....DLB-110
Exley, Frederick 1929-1992 .... DLB-143; Y-81
Editorial: The Extension of Copyright Y-02
von Eyb, Albrecht 1420-1475............DLB-179
Eyre and Spottiswoode DLB-106
Ezera, Regīna 1930- DLB-232
Ezzo ?-after 1065 ....DLB-148

F

Faber, Frederick William 1814-1863 ......DLB-32
Faber and Faber Limited DLB-112
Faccio, Rena (see Aleramo, Sibilla)
Facsimiles
   The Uses of Facsimile: A Symposium.... Y-90
Fadeev, Aleksandr Aleksandrovich
   1901-1956 ....DLB-272
Fagundo, Ana María 1938- DLB-134
Fainzil'berg, Il'ia Arnol'dovich
   (see Il'f, Il'ia and Petrov, Evgenii)
Fair, Ronald L. 1932- DLB-33
Fairfax, Beatrice (see Manning, Marie)
Fairlie, Gerard 1899-1983 ....DLB-77
Faldbakken, Knut 1941- DLB-297
Falkberget, Johan (Johan Petter Lillebakken)
   1879-1967 ....DLB-297
Fallada, Hans 1893-1947 ....DLB-56
Fancher, Betsy 1928- Y-83
Fane, Violet 1843-1905 ....DLB-35
Fanfrolico Press DLB-112
Fanning, Katherine 1927- DLB-127
Fanon, Frantz 1925-1961 ....DLB-296
Fanshawe, Sir Richard 1608-1666 ....DLB-126
Fantasy Press Publishers DLB-46
Fante, John 1909-1983........... DLB-130; Y-83
Al-Farabi circa 870-950................DLB-115
Farabough, Laura 1949- DLB-228
Farah, Nuruddin 1945- ... DLB-125; CDWLB-3
Farber, Norma 1909-1984 ....DLB-61
Fargue, Léon-Paul 1876-1947...........DLB-258
Farigoule, Louis (see Romains, Jules)
Farjeon, Eleanor 1881-1965............DLB-160
Farley, Harriet 1812-1907 ....DLB-239

Farley, Walter 1920-1989 .... DLB-22
Farmborough, Florence 1887-1978 ...... DLB-204
Farmer, Penelope 1939- DLB-161
Farmer, Philip José 1918- DLB-8
Farnaby, Thomas 1575?-1647 .... DLB-236
Farningham, Marianne (see Hearn, Mary Anne)
Farquhar, George circa 1677-1707 .... DLB-84
Farquharson, Martha (see Finley, Martha)
Farrar, Frederic William 1831-1903 ..... DLB-163
Farrar, Straus and Giroux............... DLB-46
Farrar and Rinehart DLB-46
Farrell, J. G. 1935-1979 .... DLB-14, 271
Farrell, James T. 1904-1979 ... DLB-4, 9, 86; DS-2
Fast, Howard 1914- DLB-9
Faulkner, William 1897-1962
....DLB-9, 11, 44, 102; DS-2; Y-86; CDALB-5
    Faulkner and Yoknapatawpha
      Conference, Oxford, Mississippi...... Y-97
    Faulkner Centennial Addresses Y-97
    "Faulkner 100–Celebrating the Work,"
      University of South Carolina,
      Columbia...................... Y-97
    Impressions of William Faulkner Y-97
    William Faulkner and the People-to-People
      Program...................... Y-86
    William Faulkner Centenary
      Celebrations Y-97
    The William Faulkner Society Y-99
George Faulkner [publishing house] DLB-154
Faulks, Sebastian 1953- DLB-207
Fauset, Jessie Redmon 1882-1961......... DLB-51
Faust, Frederick Schiller (Max Brand)
  1892-1944 .... DLB-256
Faust, Irvin
  1924- DLB-2, 28, 218, 278; Y-80, 00
    I Wake Up Screaming [Response to
      Ken Auletta] Y-97
    Tribute to Bernard Malamud........... Y-86
    Tribute to Isaac Bashevis Singer Y-91
    Tribute to Meyer Levin................ Y-81
Fawcett, Edgar 1847-1904............. DLB-202
Fawcett, Millicent Garrett 1847-1929 .... DLB-190
Fawcett Books...................... DLB-46
Fay, Theodore Sedgwick 1807-1898..... DLB-202
Fearing, Kenneth 1902-1961............. DLB-9
Federal Writers' Project DLB-46
Federman, Raymond 1928- Y-80
Fedin, Konstantin Aleksandrovich
  1892-1977...................... DLB-272
Fedorov, Innokentii Vasil'evich
  (see Omulevsky, Innokentii Vasil'evich)
Feiffer, Jules 1929- DLB-7, 44
Feinberg, Charles E. 1899-1988 ....DLB-187; Y-88
Feind, Barthold 1678-1721 .... DLB-168
Feinstein, Elaine 1930- DLB-14, 40
Feirstein, Frederick 1940- DLB-282
Feiss, Paul Louis 1875-1952 .... DLB-187
Feldman, Irving 1928- DLB-169

Felipe, Carlos 1911-1975............... DLB-305
Felipe, Léon 1884-1968................ DLB-108
Fell, Frederick, Publishers............. DLB-46
Fellowship of Southern Writers Y-98
Felltham, Owen 1602?-1668........ DLB-126, 151
Felman, Shoshana 1942- DLB-246
Fels, Ludwig 1946- DLB-75
Felton, Cornelius Conway
  1807-1862...................... DLB-1, 235
Mothe-Fénelon, François de Salignac de la
  1651-1715 ....DLB-268
Fenn, Harry 1837-1911................ DLB-188
Fennario, David 1947- DLB-60
Fenner, Dudley 1558?-1587? DLB-236
Fenno, Jenny 1765?-1803 .... DLB-200
Fenno, John 1751-1798 .... DLB-43
R. F. Fenno and Company DLB-49
Fenoglio, Beppe 1922-1963.............DLB-177
Fenton, Geoffrey 1539?-1608 .... DLB-136
Fenton, James 1949- DLB-40
    The Hemingway/Fenton
      Correspondence Y-02
Ferber, Edna 1885-1968 ...... DLB-9, 28, 86, 266
Ferdinand, Vallery, III (see Salaam, Kalamu ya)
Ferguson, Sir Samuel 1810-1886......... DLB-32
Ferguson, William Scott 1875-1954 ..... DLB-47
Fergusson, Robert 1750-1774 .... DLB-109
Ferland, Albert 1872-1943.............. DLB-92
Ferlinghetti, Lawrence
  1919- DLB-5, 16; CDALB-1
    Tribute to Kenneth Rexroth Y-82
Fermor, Patrick Leigh 1915- DLB-204
Fern, Fanny (see Parton, Sara Payson Willis)
Ferrars, Elizabeth (Morna Doris Brown)
  1907-1995...................... DLB-87
Ferré, Rosario 1942- DLB-145
Ferreira, Vergílio 1916-1996............ DLB-287
E. Ferret and Company DLB-49
Ferrier, Susan 1782-1854.............. DLB-116
Ferril, Thomas Hornsby 1896-1988..... DLB-206
Ferrini, Vincent 1913- DLB-48
Ferron, Jacques 1921-1985 .... DLB-60
Ferron, Madeleine 1922- DLB-53
Ferrucci, Franco 1936- DLB-196
Fet, Afanasii Afanas'evich
  1820?-1892......................DLB-277
Fetridge and Company................. DLB-49
Feuchtersleben, Ernst Freiherr von
  1806-1849 .... DLB-133
Feuchtwanger, Lion 1884-1958 .... DLB-66
Feuerbach, Ludwig 1804-1872 .... DLB-133
Feuillet, Octave 1821-1890 .... DLB-192
Feydeau, Georges 1862-1921 .... DLB-192
Fibiger, Mathilde 1830-1872........... DLB-300
Fichte, Johann Gottlieb 1762-1814 ...... DLB-90
Ficke, Arthur Davison 1883-1945........ DLB-54

Fiction
    American Fiction and the 1930s........ DLB-9
    Fiction Best-Sellers, 1910-1945......... DLB-9
    Postmodern Holocaust Fiction...... DLB-299
    The Year in Fiction Y-84, 86, 89, 94–99
    The Year in Fiction: A Biased View Y-83
    The Year in U.S. Fiction Y-00, 01
    The Year's Work in Fiction: A Survey ... Y-82
Fiedler, Leslie A. 1917- DLB-28, 67
    Tribute to Bernard Malamud Y-86
    Tribute to James Dickey Y-97
Field, Barron 1789-1846 .... DLB-230
Field, Edward 1924- DLB-105
Field, Eugene 1850-1895 ..DLB-23, 42, 140; DS-13
Field, John 1545?-1588................ DLB-167
Field, Joseph M. 1810-1856 .... DLB-248
Field, Marshall, III 1893-1956 ....DLB-127
Field, Marshall, IV 1916-1965 ....DLB-127
Field, Marshall, V 1941- DLB-127
Field, Michael (Katherine Harris Bradley)
  1846-1914 .... DLB-240
    "The Poetry File"................. DLB-105
Field, Nathan 1587-1619 or 1620 .... DLB-58
Field, Rachel 1894-1942 .... DLB-9, 22
Fielding, Helen 1958- DLB-231
Fielding, Henry
  1707-1754 .... DLB-39, 84, 101; CDBLB-2
    "Defense of *Amelia*" (1752) DLB-39
    The History of the Adventures of Joseph Andrews
      [excerpt] (1742) DLB-39
    Letter to [Samuel] Richardson on *Clarissa*
      (1748)..................... DLB-39
    Preface to *Joseph Andrews* (1742) DLB-39
    Preface to Sarah Fielding's *Familiar
      Letters* (1747) [excerpt] DLB-39
    Preface to Sarah Fielding's *The
      Adventures of David Simple* (1744)... DLB-39
    Review of *Clarissa* (1748)........... DLB-39
    Tom Jones (1749) [excerpt] DLB-39
Fielding, Sarah 1710-1768 .... DLB-39
    Preface to *The Cry* (1754) DLB-39
Fields, Annie Adams 1834-1915 .... DLB-221
Fields, Dorothy 1905-1974 .... DLB-265
Fields, James T. 1817-1881 .... DLB-1, 235
Fields, Julia 1938- DLB-41
Fields, Osgood and Company DLB-49
Fields, W. C. 1880-1946............... DLB-44
Fierstein, Harvey 1954- DLB-266
Figes, Eva 1932- DLB-14, 271
Figuera, Angela 1902-1984............. DLB-108
Filmer, Sir Robert 1586-1653 .... DLB-151
Filson, John circa 1753-1788 .... DLB-37
Finch, Anne, Countess of Winchilsea
  1661-1720...................... DLB-95
Finch, Annie 1956- DLB-282
Finch, Robert 1900- DLB-88
Findley, Timothy 1930-2002 .... DLB-53

Finlay, Ian Hamilton 1925- DLB-40
Finley, Martha 1828-1909 ....DLB-42
Finn, Elizabeth Anne (McCaul)
    1825-1921 ....DLB-166
Finnegan, Seamus 1949- DLB-245
Finney, Jack 1911-1995 ....DLB-8
Finney, Walter Braden (see Finney, Jack)
Firbank, Ronald 1886-1926 ....DLB-36
Firmin, Giles 1615-1697 ....DLB-24
First Edition Library/Collectors'
    Reprints, Inc. Y-91
Fischart, Johann
    1546 or 1547-1590 or 1591 ....DLB-179
Fischer, Karoline Auguste Fernandine
    1764-1842 ....DLB-94
Fischer, Tibor 1959- DLB-231
Fish, Stanley 1938- DLB-67
Fishacre, Richard 1205-1248 ....DLB-115
Fisher, Clay (see Allen, Henry W.)
Fisher, Dorothy Canfield 1879-1958 ...DLB-9, 102
Fisher, Leonard Everett 1924- DLB-61
Fisher, Roy 1930- DLB-40
Fisher, Rudolph 1897-1934 ....DLB-51, 102
Fisher, Steve 1913-1980 ....DLB-226
Fisher, Sydney George 1856-1927 ....DLB-47
Fisher, Vardis 1895-1968 ....DLB-9, 206
Fiske, John 1608-1677 ....DLB-24
Fiske, John 1842-1901 ....DLB-47, 64
Fitch, Thomas circa 1700-1774 ......DLB-31
Fitch, William Clyde 1865-1909 .....DLB-7
FitzGerald, Edward 1809-1883 ....DLB-32
Fitzgerald, F. Scott 1896-1940
    ....DLB-4, 9, 86; Y-81, 92;
    DS-1, 15, 16; CDALB-4
    F. Scott Fitzgerald: A Descriptive
        Bibliography, Supplement (2001) Y-01
    F. Scott Fitzgerald Centenary
        Celebrations Y-96
    F. Scott Fitzgerald Inducted into the
        American Poets' Corner at St. John
        the Divine; Ezra Pound Banned Y-99
    "F. Scott Fitzgerald: St. Paul's Native Son
        and Distinguished American Writer":
        University of Minnesota Conference,
        29-31 October 1982 ....Y-82
    First International F. Scott Fitzgerald
        Conference Y-92
    The Great Gatsby (Documentary) DLB-219
    Tender Is the Night (Documentary) DLB-273
Fitzgerald, Penelope 1916- DLB-14, 194
Fitzgerald, Robert 1910-1985 ....Y-80
FitzGerald, Robert D. 1902-1987 ....DLB-260
Fitzgerald, Thomas 1819-1891 ......DLB-23
Fitzgerald, Zelda Sayre 1900-1948 ....Y-84
Fitzhugh, Louise 1928-1974 ....DLB-52
Fitzhugh, William circa 1651-1701 ...DLB-24
Flagg, James Montgomery 1877-1960 ..DLB-188
Flanagan, Thomas 1923-2002 ....Y-80
Flanner, Hildegarde 1899-1987 ......DLB-48

Flanner, Janet 1892-1978 ....DLB-4; DS-15
Flannery, Peter 1951- DLB-233
Flaubert, Gustave 1821-1880 ....DLB-119, 301
Flavin, Martin 1883-1967 ....DLB-9
Fleck, Konrad (flourished circa 1220) ...DLB-138
Flecker, James Elroy 1884-1915 .....DLB-10, 19
Fleeson, Doris 1901-1970 ....DLB-29
Fleißer, Marieluise 1901-1974 ......DLB-56, 124
Fleischer, Nat 1887-1972 ....DLB-241
Fleming, Abraham 1552?-1607 ....DLB-236
Fleming, Ian 1908-1964 ...DLB-87, 201; CDBLB-7
Fleming, Joan 1908-1980 ....DLB-276
Fleming, May Agnes 1840-1880 ......DLB-99
Fleming, Paul 1609-1640 ....DLB-164
Fleming, Peter 1907-1971 ....DLB-195
Fletcher, Giles, the Elder 1546-1611 ...DLB-136
Fletcher, Giles, the Younger
    1585 or 1586-1623 ....DLB-121
Fletcher, J. S. 1863-1935 ....DLB-70
Fletcher, John 1579-1625 ....DLB-58
Fletcher, John Gould 1886-1950 .....DLB-4, 45
Fletcher, Phineas 1582-1650 ....DLB-121
Flieg, Helmut (see Heym, Stefan)
Flint, F. S. 1885-1960 ....DLB-19
Flint, Timothy 1780-1840 ....DLB-73, 186
Fløgstad, Kjartan 1944- DLB-297
Florensky, Pavel Aleksandrovich
    1882-1937 ....DLB-295
Flores, Juan de fl. 1470-1500 ....DLB-286
Flores-Williams, Jason 1969- DLB-209
Florio, John 1553?-1625 ....DLB-172
Fludd, Robert 1574-1637 ....DLB-281
Flynn, Elizabeth Gurley 1890-1964 ....DLB-303
Fo, Dario 1926- Y-97
    Nobel Lecture 1997: Contra Jogulatores
        Obloquentes Y-97
Foden, Giles 1967- DLB-267
Fofanov, Konstantin Mikhailovich
    1862-1911 ....DLB-277
Foix, J. V. 1893-1987 ....DLB-134
Foley, Martha 1897-1977 ....DLB-137
Folger, Henry Clay 1857-1930 ....DLB-140
Folio Society DLB-112
Follain, Jean 1903-1971 ....DLB-258
Follen, Charles 1796-1840 ....DLB-235
Follen, Eliza Lee (Cabot) 1787-1860 ...DLB-1, 235
Follett, Ken 1949- DLB-87; Y-81
Follett Publishing Company DLB-46
John West Folsom [publishing house] DLB-49
Folz, Hans
    between 1435 and 1440-1513 ....DLB-179
Fonseca, Manuel da 1911-1993 ....DLB-287
Fontane, Theodor
    1819-1898 ....DLB-129; CDWLB-2
Fontenelle, Bernard Le Bovier de
    1657-1757 ....DLB-268

Fontes, Montserrat 1940- DLB-209
Fonvisin, Denis Ivanovich
    1744 or 1745-1792 ....DLB-150
Foote, Horton 1916- DLB-26, 266
Foote, Mary Hallock
    1847-1938 ....DLB-186, 188, 202, 221
Foote, Samuel 1721-1777 ....DLB-89
Foote, Shelby 1916- DLB-2, 17
Forbes, Calvin 1945- DLB-41
Forbes, Ester 1891-1967 ....DLB-22
Forbes, Rosita 1893?-1967 ....DLB-195
Forbes and Company DLB-49
Force, Peter 1790-1868 ....DLB-30
Forché, Carolyn 1950- DLB-5, 193
Ford, Charles Henri 1913-2002 .....DLB-4, 48
Ford, Corey 1902-1969 ....DLB-11
Ford, Ford Madox
    1873-1939 ....DLB-34, 98, 162; CDBLB-6
    Nathan Asch Remembers Ford Madox
        Ford, Sam Roth, and Hart Crane....Y-02
J. B. Ford and Company DLB-49
Ford, Jesse Hill 1928-1996 ....DLB-6
Ford, John 1586-? DLB-58; CDBLB-1
Ford, R. A. D. 1915- DLB-88
Ford, Richard 1944- DLB-227
Ford, Worthington C. 1858-1941 ....DLB-47
Fords, Howard, and Hulbert DLB-49
Foreman, Carl 1914-1984 ....DLB-26
Forester, C. S. 1899-1966 ....DLB-191
    The C. S. Forester Society Y-00
Forester, Frank (see Herbert, Henry William)
Anthologizing New Formalism DLB-282
The Little Magazines of the
    New Formalism DLB-282
The New Narrative Poetry DLB-282
Presses of the New Formalism and
    the New Narrative DLB-282
The Prosody of the New Formalism DLB-282
Younger Women Poets of the
    New Formalism DLB-282
Forman, Harry Buxton 1842-1917 ....DLB-184
Fornés, María Irene 1930- DLB-7
Forrest, Leon 1937-1997 ....DLB-33
Forsh, Ol'ga Dmitrievna 1873-1961 ...DLB-272
Forster, E. M.
    1879-1970 ....DLB-34, 98, 162, 178, 195;
    DS-10; CDBLB-6
    "Fantasy," from *Aspects of the Novel*
        (1927) DLB-178
Forster, Georg 1754-1794 ....DLB-94
Forster, John 1812-1876 ....DLB-144
Forster, Margaret 1938- DLB-155, 271
Forsyth, Frederick 1938- DLB-87
Forsyth, William
    "Literary Style" (1857) [excerpt] DLB-57
Forten, Charlotte L. 1837-1914 .....DLB-50, 239
    Pages from Her Diary DLB-50
Fortini, Franco 1917-1994 ....DLB-128

Fortune, Mary ca. 1833-ca. 1910 .... DLB-230
Fortune, T. Thomas 1856-1928 .... DLB-23
Fosdick, Charles Austin 1842-1915 .... DLB-42
Fosse, Jon 1959- DLB-297
Foster, David 1944- DLB-289
Foster, Genevieve 1893-1979 .... DLB-61
Foster, Hannah Webster
 1758-1840 .... DLB-37, 200
Foster, John 1648-1681 .... DLB-24
Foster, Michael 1904-1956 .... DLB-9
Foster, Myles Birket 1825-1899 .... DLB-184
Foster, William Z. 1881-1961 .... DLB-303
Foucault, Michel 1926-1984 .... DLB-242
Robert and Andrew Foulis
 [publishing house] DLB-154
Fouqué, Caroline de la Motte 1774-1831 .... DLB-90
Fouqué, Friedrich de la Motte
 1777-1843 .... DLB-90
Four Seas Company DLB-46
Four Winds Press DLB-46
Fournier, Henri Alban (see Alain-Fournier)
Fowler, Christopher 1953- DLB-267
Fowler, Connie May 1958- DLB-292
Fowler and Wells Company DLB-49
Fowles, John
 1926- DLB-14, 139, 207; CDBLB-8
Fox, John 1939- DLB-245
Fox, John, Jr. 1862 or 1863-1919 ... DLB-9; DS-13
Fox, Paula 1923- DLB-52
Fox, Richard Kyle 1846-1922 .... DLB-79
Fox, William Price 1926- DLB-2; Y-81
 Remembering Joe Heller Y-99
Richard K. Fox [publishing house] DLB-49
Foxe, John 1517-1587 .... DLB-132
Fraenkel, Michael 1896-1957 .... DLB-4
France, Anatole 1844-1924 .... DLB-123
France, Richard 1938- DLB-7
Francis, Convers 1795-1863 .... DLB-1, 235
Francis, Dick 1920- DLB-87; CDBLB-8
Francis, Sir Frank 1901-1988 .... DLB-201
Francis, Jeffrey, Lord 1773-1850 .... DLB-107
C. S. Francis [publishing house] DLB-49
Franck, Sebastian 1499-1542 .... DLB-179
Francke, Kuno 1855-1930 .... DLB-71
Françoise (Robertine Barry) 1863-1910 ... DLB-92
François, Louise von 1817-1893 .... DLB-129
Frank, Bruno 1887-1945 .... DLB-118
Frank, Leonhard 1882-1961 .... DLB-56, 118
Frank, Melvin 1913-1988 .... DLB-26
Frank, Waldo 1889-1967 .... DLB-9, 63
Franken, Rose 1895?-1988 ..... DLB-228, Y-84
Franklin, Benjamin
 1706-1790 .... DLB-24, 43, 73, 183; CDALB-2
Franklin, James 1697-1735 .... DLB-43
Franklin, John 1786-1847 .... DLB-99
Franklin, Miles 1879-1954 .... DLB-230

Franklin Library DLB-46
Frantz, Ralph Jules 1902-1979 .... DLB-4
Franzos, Karl Emil 1848-1904 .... DLB-129
Fraser, Antonia 1932- DLB-276
Fraser, G. S. 1915-1980 .... DLB-27
Fraser, Kathleen 1935- DLB-169
Frattini, Alberto 1922- DLB-128
Frau Ava ?-1127 .... DLB-148
Fraunce, Abraham 1558?-1592 or 1593 .. DLB-236
Frayn, Michael 1933- DLB-13, 14, 194, 245
Frazier, Charles 1950- DLB-292
Fréchette, Louis-Honoré 1839-1908 ..... DLB-99
Frederic, Harold 1856-1898 ... DLB-12, 23; DS-13
Freed, Arthur 1894-1973 .... DLB-265
Freeling, Nicolas 1927- DLB-87
 Tribute to Georges Simenon Y-89
Freeman, Douglas Southall
 1886-1953 .... DLB-17; DS-17
Freeman, Joseph 1897-1965 .... DLB-303
Freeman, Judith 1946- DLB-256
Freeman, Legh Richmond 1842-1915 ..... DLB-23
Freeman, Mary E. Wilkins
 1852-1930 .... DLB-12, 78, 221
Freeman, R. Austin 1862-1943 .... DLB-70
Freidank circa 1170-circa 1233 .... DLB-138
Freiligrath, Ferdinand 1810-1876 ...... DLB-133
Fremlin, Celia 1914- DLB-276
Frémont, Jessie Benton 1834-1902 ..... DLB-183
Frémont, John Charles
 1813-1890 .... DLB-183, 186
French, Alice 1850-1934 .... DLB-74; DS-13
French, David 1939- DLB-53
French, Evangeline 1869-1960 .... DLB-195
French, Francesca 1871-1960 .... DLB-195
James French [publishing house] DLB-49
Samuel French [publishing house] DLB-49
Samuel French, Limited DLB-106
French Literature
 Epic and Beast Epic DLB-208
 French Arthurian Literature DLB-208
 Lyric Poetry DLB-268
 Other Poets DLB-217
 Poetry in Nineteenth-Century France:
  Cultural Background and Critical
  Commentary DLB-217
 Roman de la Rose: Guillaume de Lorris
  1200 to 1205-circa 1230, Jean de
  Meun 1235/1240-circa 1305 .... DLB-208
 Saints' Lives DLB-208
 Troubadours, Trobairitz, and
  Trouvères DLB-208
French Theater
 Medieval French Drama DLB-208
 Parisian Theater, Fall 1984: Toward
  a New Baroque Y-85
Freneau, Philip 1752-1832 .... DLB-37, 43
 The Rising Glory of America DLB-37
Freni, Melo 1934- DLB-128

Freshfield, Douglas W. 1845-1934 ...... DLB-174
Freud, Sigmund 1856-1939 .... DLB-296
Freytag, Gustav 1816-1895 .... DLB-129
Frída Á. Sigurðardóttir 1940- DLB-293
Fridegård, Jan 1897-1968 .... DLB-259
Fried, Erich 1921-1988 .... DLB-85
Friedan, Betty 1921- DLB-246
Friedman, Bruce Jay 1930- DLB-2, 28, 244
Friedman, Carl 1952- DLB-299
Friedman, Kinky 1944- DLB-292
Friedrich von Hausen circa 1171-1190 ... DLB-138
Friel, Brian 1929- DLB-13
Friend, Krebs 1895?-1967? DLB-4
Fries, Fritz Rudolf 1935- DLB-75
Frisch, Max
 1911-1991 .... DLB-69, 124; CDWLB-2
Frischlin, Nicodemus 1547-1590 .... DLB-179
Frischmuth, Barbara 1941- DLB-85
Fritz, Jean 1915- DLB-52
Froissart, Jean circa 1337-circa 1404 .... DLB-208
Fromm, Erich 1900-1980 .... DLB-296
Fromentin, Eugene 1820-1876 .... DLB-123
Frontinus circa A.D. 35-A.D. 103/104 ... DLB-211
Frost, A. B. 1851-1928 .... DLB-188; DS-13
Frost, Robert
 1874-1963 .... DLB-54; DS-7; CDALB-4
 The Friends of the Dymock Poets Y-00
Frostenson, Katarina 1953- DLB-257
Frothingham, Octavius Brooks
 1822-1895 .... DLB-1, 243
Froude, James Anthony
 1818-1894 .... DLB-18, 57, 144
Fruitlands 1843-1844 .... DLB-1, 223; DS-5
Fry, Christopher 1907- DLB-13
 Tribute to John Betjeman Y-84
Fry, Roger 1866-1934 .... DS-10
Fry, Stephen 1957- DLB-207
Frye, Northrop 1912-1991 ..... DLB-67, 68, 246
Fuchs, Daniel 1909-1993 ..... DLB-9, 26, 28; Y-93
 Tribute to Isaac Bashevis Singer Y-91
Fuentes, Carlos 1928- DLB-113; CDWLB-3
Fuertes, Gloria 1918-1998 .... DLB-108
Fugard, Athol 1932- DLB-225
The Fugitives and the Agrarians:
 The First Exhibition Y-85
Fujiwara no Shunzei 1114-1204 .... DLB-203
Fujiwara no Tameaki 1230s?-1290s? DLB-203
Fujiwara no Tameie 1198-1275 .... DLB-203
Fujiwara no Teika 1162-1241 .... DLB-203
Fuks, Ladislav 1923-1994 .... DLB-299
Fulbecke, William 1560-1603? DLB-172
Fuller, Charles 1939- DLB-38, 266
Fuller, Henry Blake 1857-1929 .... DLB-12
Fuller, John 1937- DLB-40
Fuller, Margaret (see Fuller, Sarah)
Fuller, Roy 1912-1991 .... DLB-15, 20

Tribute to Christopher Isherwood Y-86
Fuller, Samuel 1912-1997 .... DLB-26
Fuller, Sarah 1810-1850 .... DLB-1, 59, 73, 183, 223, 239; DS-5; CDALB-2
Fuller, Thomas 1608-1661 .... DLB-151
Fullerton, Hugh 1873-1945 .... DLB-171
Fullwood, William flourished 1568 ..... DLB-236
Fulton, Alice 1952- DLB-193
Fulton, Len 1934- Y-86
Fulton, Robin 1937- DLB-40
Furbank, P. N. 1920- DLB-155
Furetière, Antoine 1619-1688 .... DLB-268
Furman, Laura 1945- Y-86
Furmanov, Dmitrii Andreevich 1891-1926 .... DLB-272
Furness, Horace Howard 1833-1912 ..... DLB-64
Furness, William Henry 1802-1896 .... DLB-1, 235
Furnivall, Frederick James 1825-1910 .... DLB-184
Furphy, Joseph (Tom Collins) 1843-1912 .... DLB-230
Furthman, Jules 1888-1966 .... DLB-26
  Shakespeare and Montaigne: A Symposium by Jules Furthman Y-02
Furui Yoshikichi 1937- DLB-182
Fushimi, Emperor 1265-1317 .... DLB-203
Futabatei Shimei (Hasegawa Tatsunosuke) 1864-1909 .... DLB-180
Fyleman, Rose 1877-1957 .... DLB-160

G

Gaarder, Jostein 1952- DLB-297
Gadallah, Leslie 1939- DLB-251
Gadamer, Hans-Georg 1900-2002 .... DLB-296
Gadda, Carlo Emilio 1893-1973 .... DLB-177
Gaddis, William 1922-1998 .... DLB-2, 278
  William Gaddis: A Tribute Y-99
Gág, Wanda 1893-1946 .... DLB-22
Gagarin, Ivan Sergeevich 1814-1882 .... DLB-198
Gagnon, Madeleine 1938- DLB-60
Gaiman, Neil 1960- DLB-261
Gaine, Hugh 1726-1807 .... DLB-43
Hugh Gaine [publishing house] DLB-49
Gaines, Ernest J. 1933- DLB-2, 33, 152; Y-80; CDALB-6
Gaiser, Gerd 1908-1976 .... DLB-69
Gaitskill, Mary 1954- DLB-244
Galarza, Ernesto 1905-1984 .... DLB-122
Galaxy Science Fiction Novels DLB-46
Galbraith, Robert (or Caubraith) circa 1483-1544 .... DLB-281
Gale, Zona 1874-1938 .... DLB-9, 228, 78
Galen of Pergamon 129-after 210 .... DLB-176
Gales, Winifred Marshall 1761-1839 .... DLB-200
Medieval Galician-Portuguese Poetry DLB-287
Gall, Louise von 1815-1855 .... DLB-133
Gallagher, Tess 1943- DLB-120, 212, 244

Gallagher, Wes 1911- DLB-127
Gallagher, William Davis 1808-1894 ..... DLB-73
Gallant, Mavis 1922- DLB-53
Gallegos, María Magdalena 1935- DLB-209
Gallico, Paul 1897-1976 .... DLB-9, 171
Gallop, Jane 1952- DLB-246
Galloway, Grace Growden 1727-1782 .... DLB-200
Gallup, Donald 1913-2000 .... DLB-187
Galsworthy, John 1867-1933 ...... DLB-10, 34, 98, 162; DS-16; CDBLB-5
Galt, John 1779-1839 .... DLB-99, 116, 159
Galton, Sir Francis 1822-1911 .... DLB-166
Galvin, Brendan 1938- DLB-5
Gambaro, Griselda 1928- DLB-305
Gambit DLB-46
Gamboa, Reymundo 1948- DLB-122
Gammer Gurton's Needle DLB-62
Gan, Elena Andreevna (Zeneida R-va) 1814-1842 .... DLB-198
Gandlevsky, Sergei Markovich 1952- .. DLB-285
Gannett, Frank E. 1876-1957 .... DLB-29
Gao Xingjian 1940- Y-00
  Nobel Lecture 2000: "The Case for Literature" Y-00
Gaos, Vicente 1919-1980 .... DLB-134
García, Andrew 1854?-1943 .... DLB-209
García, Cristina 1958- DLB-292
García, Lionel G. 1935- DLB-82
García, Richard 1941- DLB-209
García, Santiago 1928- DLB-305
García Márquez, Gabriel 1928- DLB-113; Y-82; CDWLB-3
  The Magical World of Macondo Y-82
  Nobel Lecture 1982: The Solitude of Latin America Y-82
  A Tribute to Gabriel García Márquez Y-82
García Marruz, Fina 1923- DLB-283
García-Camarillo, Cecilio 1943- DLB-209
Gardam, Jane 1928- DLB-14, 161, 231
Gardell, Jonas 1963- DLB-257
Garden, Alexander circa 1685-1756 .... DLB-31
Gardiner, John Rolfe 1936- DLB-244
Gardiner, Margaret Power Farmer (see Blessington, Marguerite, Countess of)
Gardner, John 1933-1982 .... DLB-2; Y-82; CDALB-7
Garfield, Leon 1921-1996 .... DLB-161
Garis, Howard R. 1873-1962 .... DLB-22
Garland, Hamlin 1860-1940 .. DLB-12, 71, 78, 186
  The Hamlin Garland Society Y-01
Garneau, François-Xavier 1809-1866 ..... DLB-99
Garneau, Hector de Saint-Denys 1912-1943 .... DLB-88
Garneau, Michel 1939- DLB-53
Garner, Alan 1934- DLB-161, 261
Garner, Hugh 1913-1979 .... DLB-68
Garnett, David 1892-1981 .... DLB-34

Garnett, Eve 1900-1991 .... DLB-160
Garnett, Richard 1835-1906 .... DLB-184
Garrard, Lewis H. 1829-1887 .... DLB-186
Garraty, John A. 1920- DLB-17
Garrett, Almeida (João Baptista da Silva Leitão de Almeida Garrett) 1799-1854 .... DLB-287
Garrett, George 1929- DLB-2, 5, 130, 152; Y-83
  Literary Prizes Y-00
  My Summer Reading Orgy: Reading for Fun and Games: One Reader's Report on the Summer of 2001 ..... Y-01
  A Summing Up at Century's End Y-99
  Tribute to James Dickey Y-97
  Tribute to Michael M. Rea Y-97
  Tribute to Paxton Davis Y-94
  Tribute to Peter Taylor Y-94
  Tribute to William Goyen Y-83
  A Writer Talking: A Collage Y-00
Garrett, John Work 1872-1942 .... DLB-187
Garrick, David 1717-1779 .... DLB-84, 213
Garrison, William Lloyd 1805-1879 .... DLB-1, 43, 235; CDALB-2
Garro, Elena 1920-1998 .... DLB-145
Garshin, Vsevolod Mikhailovich 1855-1888 .... DLB-277
Garth, Samuel 1661-1719 .... DLB-95
Garve, Andrew 1908-2001 .... DLB-87
Gary, Romain 1914-1980 .... DLB-83, 299
Gascoigne, George 1539?-1577 .... DLB-136
Gascoyne, David 1916-2001 .... DLB-20
Gash, Jonathan (John Grant) 1933- DLB-276
Gaskell, Elizabeth Cleghorn 1810-1865 .... DLB-21, 144, 159; CDBLB-4
  The Gaskell Society Y-98
Gaskell, Jane 1941- DLB-261
Gaspey, Thomas 1788-1871 .... DLB-116
Gass, William H. 1924- DLB-2, 227
Gates, Doris 1901-1987 .... DLB-22
Gates, Henry Louis, Jr. 1950- DLB-67
Gates, Lewis E. 1860-1924 .... DLB-71
Gatto, Alfonso 1909-1976 .... DLB-114
Gault, William Campbell 1910-1995 .... DLB-226
  Tribute to Kenneth Millar Y-83
Gaunt, Mary 1861-1942 .... DLB-174, 230
Gautier, Théophile 1811-1872 .... DLB-119
Gautreaux, Tim 1947- DLB-292
Gauvreau, Claude 1925-1971 .... DLB-88
The *Gawain*-Poet flourished circa 1350-1400 .... DLB-146
Gawsworth, John (Terence Ian Fytton Armstrong) 1912-1970 .... DLB-255
Gay, Ebenezer 1696-1787 .... DLB-24
Gay, John 1685-1732 .... DLB-84, 95
Gayarré, Charles E. A. 1805-1895 ..... DLB-30
Charles Gaylord [publishing house] DLB-49

Gaylord, Edward King 1873-1974 ...... DLB-127
Gaylord, Edward Lewis 1919- DLB-127
Gébler, Carlo 1954- DLB-271
Geda, Sigitas 1943- DLB-232
Geddes, Gary 1940- DLB-60
Geddes, Virgil 1897- DLB-4
Gedeon (Georgii Andreevich Krinovsky)
 circa 1730-1763 .... DLB-150
Gee, Maggie 1948- DLB-207
Gee, Shirley 1932- DLB-245
Geibel, Emanuel 1815-1884 .... DLB-129
Geiogamah, Hanay 1945- DLB-175
Geis, Bernard, Associates DLB-46
Geisel, Theodor Seuss 1904-1991... DLB-61; Y-91
Gelb, Arthur 1924- DLB-103
Gelb, Barbara 1926- DLB-103
Gelber, Jack 1932- DLB-7, 228
Gélinas, Gratien 1909-1999 .... DLB-88
Gellert, Christian Füerchtegott
 1715-1769 .... DLB-97
Gellhorn, Martha 1908-1998 .... Y-82, 98
Gems, Pam 1925- DLB-13
Genet, Jean 1910-1986 .... DLB-72; Y-86
Genette, Gérard 1930- DLB-242
Genevoix, Maurice 1890-1980 .... DLB-65
Genis, Aleksandr Aleksandrovich
 1953- DLB-285
Genovese, Eugene D. 1930- DLB-17
Gent, Peter 1942- Y-82
Geoffrey of Monmouth
 circa 1100-1155 .... DLB-146
George, Henry 1839-1897 .... DLB-23
George, Jean Craighead 1919- DLB-52
George, W. L. 1882-1926 .... DLB-197
George III, King of Great Britain
 and Ireland 1738-1820 .... DLB-213
Georgslied 896? DLB-148
Gerber, Merrill Joan 1938- DLB-218
Gerhardie, William 1895-1977 ...... DLB-36
Gerhardt, Paul 1607-1676 .... DLB-164
Gérin, Winifred 1901-1981 .... DLB-155
Gérin-Lajoie, Antoine 1824-1882 ... DLB-99
German Literature
 A Call to Letters and an Invitation
  to the Electric Chair DLB-75
 The Conversion of an Unpolitical
  Man DLB-66
 The German Radio Play DLB-124
 The German Transformation from the
  Baroque to the Enlightenment.... DLB-97
 Germanophilism DLB-66
 A Letter from a New Germany ... Y-90
 The Making of a People DLB-66
 The Novel of Impressionism DLB-66
 Pattern and Paradigm: History as
  Design DLB-75
 Premisses DLB-66

 The 'Twenties and Berlin DLB-66
 Wolfram von Eschenbach's *Parzival*:
  Prologue and Book 3 .... DLB-138
 Writers and Politics: 1871-1918 .. DLB-66
German Literature, Middle Ages
 Abrogans circa 790-800 .... DLB-148
 Annolied between 1077 and 1081 .. DLB-148
 The Arthurian Tradition and
  Its European Context DLB-138
 Cambridge Songs (Carmina Cantabrigensia)
  circa 1050 .... DLB-148
 Christus und die Samariterin circa 950 .. DLB-148
 De Heinrico circa 980? DLB-148
 Ecbasis Captivi circa 1045 .... DLB-148
 Georgslied 896? DLB-148
 German Literature and Culture from
  Charlemagne to the Early Courtly
  Period DLB-148; CDWLB-2
 The Germanic Epic and Old English
  Heroic Poetry: *Widsith, Waldere,*
  and *The Fight at Finnsburg* DLB-146
 Graf Rudolf between circa
  1170 and circa 1185 .... DLB-148
 Heliand circa 850 .... DLB-148
 Das *Hildebrandslied*
  circa 820 .... DLB-148; CDWLB-2
 Kaiserchronik circa 1147 .... DLB-148
 The Legends of the Saints and a
  Medieval Christian
  Worldview DLB-148
 Ludus de Antichristo circa 1160 ... DLB-148
 Ludwigslied 881 or 882 .... DLB-148
 Muspilli circa 790-circa 850 ...... DLB-148
 Old German Genesis and *Old German
  Exodus* circa 1050-circa 1130 .... DLB-148
 Old High German Charms
  and Blessings DLB-148; CDWLB-2
 The *Old High German Isidor*
  circa 790-800 .... DLB-148
 Petruslied circa 854? DLB-148
 Physiologus circa 1070-circa 1150 .. DLB-148
 Ruodlieb circa 1050-1075 .... DLB-148
 "Spielmannsepen" (circa 1152
  circa 1500) DLB-148
 The Strasbourg Oaths 842 .... DLB-148
 Tatian circa 830 .... DLB-148
 Waltharius circa 825 .... DLB-148
 Wessobrunner Gebet circa 787-815 .. DLB-148
German Theater
 German Drama 800-1280 .... DLB-138
 German Drama from Naturalism
  to Fascism: 1889-1933 .... DLB-118
Gernsback, Hugo 1884-1967 .... DLB-8, 137
Gerould, Katharine Fullerton
 1879-1944 .... DLB-78
Samuel Gerrish [publishing house] ... DLB-49
Gerrold, David 1944- DLB-8
Gersão, Teolinda 1940- DLB-287
Gershon, Karen 1923-1993 .... DLB-299
Gershwin, Ira 1896-1983 .... DLB-265

 The Ira Gershwin Centenary Y-96
Gerson, Jean 1363-1429 .... DLB-208
Gersonides 1288-1344 .... DLB-115
Gerstäcker, Friedrich 1816-1872 ..... DLB-129
Gertsen, Aleksandr Ivanovich
 (see Herzen, Alexander)
Gerstenberg, Heinrich Wilhelm von
 1737-1823 .... DLB-97
Gervinus, Georg Gottfried
 1805-1871 .... DLB-133
Gery, John 1953- DLB-282
Geßner, Solomon 1730-1788 .... DLB-97
Geston, Mark S. 1946- DLB-8
Al-Ghazali 1058-1111 .... DLB-115
Gibbings, Robert 1889-1958 .... DLB-195
Gibbon, Edward 1737-1794 .... DLB-104
Gibbon, John Murray 1875-1952 ... DLB-92
Gibbon, Lewis Grassic (see Mitchell, James Leslie)
Gibbons, Floyd 1887-1939 .... DLB-25
Gibbons, Kaye 1960- DLB-292
Gibbons, Reginald 1947- DLB-120
Gibbons, William ?-? DLB-73
Gibson, Charles Dana
 1867-1944 .... DLB-188; DS-13
Gibson, Graeme 1934- DLB-53
Gibson, Margaret 1944- DLB-120
Gibson, Margaret Dunlop 1843-1920....DLB-174
Gibson, Wilfrid 1878-1962 .... DLB-19
 The Friends of the Dymock Poets Y-00
Gibson, William 1914- DLB-7
Gibson, William 1948- DLB-251
Gide, André 1869-1951 .... DLB-65
Giguère, Diane 1937- DLB-53
Giguère, Roland 1929- DLB-60
Gil de Biedma, Jaime 1929-1990 ... DLB-108
Gil-Albert, Juan 1906-1994 .... DLB-134
Gilbert, Anthony 1899-1973 .... DLB-77
Gilbert, Elizabeth 1969- DLB-292
Gilbert, Sir Humphrey 1537-1583 ... DLB-136
Gilbert, Michael 1912- DLB-87
Gilbert, Sandra M. 1936- DLB-120, 246
Gilchrist, Alexander 1828-1861 ..... DLB-144
Gilchrist, Ellen 1935- DLB-130
Gilder, Jeannette L. 1849-1916 ..... DLB-79
Gilder, Richard Watson 1844-1909 ....DLB-64, 79
Gildersleeve, Basil 1831-1924 .... DLB-71
Giles, Henry 1809-1882 .... DLB-64
Giles of Rome circa 1243-1316 ..... DLB-115
Gilfillan, George 1813-1878 .... DLB-144
Gill, Eric 1882-1940 .... DLB-98
Gill, Sarah Prince 1728-1771 .... DLB-200
William F. Gill Company DLB-49
Gillespie, A. Lincoln, Jr. 1895-1950 ... DLB-4
Gillespie, Haven 1883-1975 .... DLB-265
Gilliam, Florence ?-? DLB-4

Gilliatt, Penelope 1932-1993 .... DLB-14

Gillott, Jacky 1939-1980 .... DLB-14

Gilman, Caroline H. 1794-1888 .... DLB-3, 73

Gilman, Charlotte Perkins 1860-1935 .... DLB-221

    The Charlotte Perkins Gilman Society ... Y-99

W. and J. Gilman [publishing house] DLB-49

Gilmer, Elizabeth Meriwether
    1861-1951 .... DLB-29

Gilmer, Francis Walker 1790-1826 .... DLB-37

Gilmore, Mary 1865-1962 .... DLB-260

Gilroy, Frank D. 1925- DLB-7

Gimferrer, Pere (Pedro) 1945- DLB-134

Gingrich, Arnold 1903-1976 .... DLB-137

    Prospectus From the Initial Issue of
      Esquire (Autumn 1933) DLB-137

    "With the Editorial Ken," Prospectus
      From the Initial Issue of *Ken*
      (7 April 1938) DLB-137

Ginsberg, Allen
    1926-1997 .... DLB-5, 16, 169, 237; CDALB-1

Ginzburg, Evgeniia
    1904-1977 .... DLB-302

Ginzburg, Lidiia Iakovlevna
    1902-1990 .... DLB-302

Ginzburg, Natalia 1916-1991 .... DLB-177

Ginzkey, Franz Karl 1871-1963 .... DLB-81

Gioia, Dana 1950- DLB-120, 282

Giono, Jean 1895-1970 .... DLB-72

Giotti, Virgilio 1885-1957 .... DLB-114

Giovanni, Nikki 1943- DLB-5, 41; CDALB-7

Giovannitti, Arturo 1884-1959 .... DLB-303

Gipson, Lawrence Henry 1880-1971 ..... DLB-17

Girard, Rodolphe 1879-1956 .... DLB-92

Giraudoux, Jean 1882-1944 .... DLB-65

Girondo, Oliverio 1891-1967 .... DLB-283

Gissing, George 1857-1903 ...... DLB-18, 135, 184

    The Place of Realism in Fiction (1895) ... DLB-18

Giudici, Giovanni 1924- DLB-128

Giuliani, Alfredo 1924- DLB-128

Gjellerup, Karl 1857-1919 .... DLB-300

Glackens, William J. 1870-1938 .... DLB-188

Gladilin, Anatolii Tikhonovich
    1935- DLB-302

Gladkov, Fedor Vasil'evich 1883-1958 ... DLB-272

Gladstone, William Ewart
    1809-1898 .... DLB-57, 184

Glaeser, Ernst 1902-1963 .... DLB-69

Glancy, Diane 1941- DLB-175

Glanvill, Joseph 1636-1680 .... DLB-252

Glanville, Brian 1931- DLB-15, 139

Glapthorne, Henry 1610-1643? DLB-58

Glasgow, Ellen 1873-1945 .... DLB-9, 12

    The Ellen Glasgow Society Y-01

Glasier, Katharine Bruce 1867-1950 .... DLB-190

Glaspell, Susan 1876-1948 ...... DLB-7, 9, 78, 228

Glass, Montague 1877-1934 .... DLB-11

Glassco, John 1909-1981 .... DLB-68

Glauser, Friedrich 1896-1938 .... DLB-56

F. Gleason's Publishing Hall DLB-49

Gleim, Johann Wilhelm Ludwig
    1719-1803 .... DLB-97

Glendinning, Victoria 1937- DLB-155

Glidden, Frederick Dilley (Luke Short)
    1908-1975 .... DLB-256

Glinka, Fedor Nikolaevich 1786-1880 ... DLB-205

Glover, Keith 1966- DLB-249

Glover, Richard 1712-1785 .... DLB-95

Glück, Louise 1943- DLB-5

Glyn, Elinor 1864-1943 .... DLB-153

Gnedich, Nikolai Ivanovich 1784-1833 ... DLB-205

Gobineau, Joseph-Arthur de
    1816-1882 .... DLB-123

Godber, John 1956- DLB-233

Godbout, Jacques 1933- DLB-53

Goddard, Morrill 1865-1937 .... DLB-25

Goddard, William 1740-1817 .... DLB-43

Godden, Rumer 1907-1998 .... DLB-161

Godey, Louis A. 1804-1878 .... DLB-73

Godey and McMichael DLB-49

Godfrey, Dave 1938- DLB-60

Godfrey, Thomas 1736-1763 .... DLB-31

Godine, David R., Publisher DLB-46

Godkin, E. L. 1831-1902 .... DLB-79

Godolphin, Sidney 1610-1643 .... DLB-126

Godwin, Gail 1937- DLB-6, 234

M. J. Godwin and Company DLB-154

Godwin, Mary Jane Clairmont
    1766-1841 .... DLB-163

Godwin, Parke 1816-1904 ..... DLB-3, 64, 250

Godwin, William 1756-1836 ...... DLB-39, 104,
    142, 158, 163, 262; CDBLB-3

    Preface to *St. Leon* (1799) DLB-39

Goering, Reinhard 1887-1936 .... DLB-118

Goes, Albrecht 1908- DLB-69

Goethe, Johann Wolfgang von
    1749-1832 .... DLB-94; CDWLB-2

Goetz, Curt 1888-1960 .... DLB-124

Goffe, Thomas circa 1592-1629 .... DLB-58

Goffstein, M. B. 1940- DLB-61

Gogarty, Oliver St. John 1878-1957 .... DLB-15, 19

Gogol, Nikolai Vasil'evich 1809-1852 .... DLB-198

Goines, Donald 1937-1974 .... DLB-33

Gold, Herbert 1924- DLB-2; Y-81

    Tribute to William Saroyan Y-81

Gold, Michael 1893-1967 .... DLB-9, 28

Goldbarth, Albert 1948- DLB-120

Goldberg, Dick 1947- DLB-7

Golden Cockerel Press DLB-112

Golding, Arthur 1536-1606 .... DLB-136

Golding, Louis 1895-1958 .... DLB-195

Golding, William 1911-1993
    .... DLB-15, 100, 255; Y-83; CDBLB-7

    Nobel Lecture 1993 .... Y-83

    The Stature of William Golding Y-83

Goldman, Emma 1869-1940 .... DLB-221

Goldman, William 1931- DLB-44

Goldring, Douglas 1887-1960 .... DLB-197

Goldschmidt, Meir Aron 1819-1887 .... DLB-300

Goldsmith, Oliver 1730?-1774
    .... DLB-39, 89, 104, 109, 142; CDBLB-2

Goldsmith, Oliver 1794-1861 .... DLB-99

Goldsmith Publishing Company DLB-46

Goldstein, Richard 1944- DLB-185

Gollancz, Sir Israel 1864-1930 .... DLB-201

Victor Gollancz Limited DLB-112

Gomberville, Marin Le Roy, sieur de
    1600?-1674 .... DLB-268

Gombrowicz, Witold
    1904-1969 .... DLB-215; CDWLB-4

Gómez-Quiñones, Juan 1942- DLB-122

Laurence James Gomme
    [publishing house] DLB-46

Gompers, Samuel 1850-1924 .... DLB-303

Goncharov, Ivan Aleksandrovich
    1812-1891 .... DLB-238

Goncourt, Edmond de 1822-1896 ...... DLB-123

Goncourt, Jules de 1830-1870 .... DLB-123

Gonzales, Rodolfo "Corky" 1928- DLB-122

Gonzales-Berry, Erlinda 1942- DLB-209

    "Chicano Language" DLB-82

González, Angel 1925- DLB-108

Gonzalez, Genaro 1949- DLB-122

González, Otto-Raúl 1921- DLB-290

Gonzalez, Ray 1952- DLB-122

González de Mireles, Jovita
    1899-1983 .... DLB-122

González Martínez, Enrique 1871-1952 ... DLB-290

González-T., César A. 1931- DLB-82

Goodis, David 1917-1967 .... DLB-226

Goodison, Lorna 1947- DLB-157

Goodman, Allegra 1967- DLB-244

Goodman, Nelson 1906-1998 .... DLB-279

Goodman, Paul 1911-1972 .... DLB-130, 246

The Goodman Theatre DLB-7

Goodrich, Frances 1891-1984 and
    Hackett, Albert 1900-1995 .... DLB-26

Goodrich, Samuel Griswold
    1793-1860 .... DLB-1, 42, 73, 243

S. G. Goodrich [publishing house] DLB-49

C. E. Goodspeed and Company DLB-49

Goodwin, Stephen 1943- Y-82

Googe, Barnabe 1540-1594 .... DLB-132

Gookin, Daniel 1612-1687 .... DLB-24

Goran, Lester 1928- DLB-244

Gordimer, Nadine 1923- DLB-225; Y-91

    Nobel Lecture 1991 .... Y-91

Gordon, Adam Lindsay 1833-1870 ..... DLB-230

Gordon, Caroline
    1895-1981 .... DLB-4, 9, 102; DS-17; Y-81

Gordon, Charles F. (see OyamO)

Gordon, Charles William (see Connor, Ralph)

Gordon, Giles 1940- DLB-14, 139, 207

Gordon, Helen Cameron, Lady Russell 1867-1949................. DLB-195

Gordon, Lyndall 1941- DLB-155

Gordon, Mack 1904-1959 .... DLB-265

Gordon, Mary 1949- DLB-6; Y-81

Gordone, Charles 1925-1995 .... DLB-7

Gore, Catherine 1800-1861 .... DLB-116

Gore-Booth, Eva 1870-1926 .... DLB-240

Gores, Joe 1931- DLB-226; Y-02

Tribute to Kenneth Millar Y-83

Tribute to Raymond Chandler Y-88

Gorey, Edward 1925-2000 .... DLB-61

Gorgias of Leontini circa 485 B.C.-376 B.C. ...DLB-176

Gor'ky, Maksim 1868-1936 .... DLB-295

Gorodetsky, Sergei Mitrofanovich 1884-1967................. DLB-295

Gorostiza, José 1901-1979............. DLB-290

Görres, Joseph 1776-1848 .... DLB-90

Gosse, Edmund 1849-1928..... DLB-57, 144, 184

Gosson, Stephen 1554-1624 ....DLB-172

The Schoole of Abuse (1579) DLB-172

Gotanda, Philip Kan 1951- DLB-266

Gotlieb, Phyllis 1926- DLB-88, 251

Go-Toba 1180-1239 .... DLB-203

Gottfried von Straßburg died before 1230 ...... DLB-138; CDWLB-2

Gotthelf, Jeremias 1797-1854........... DLB-133

Gottschalk circa 804/808-869 .... DLB-148

Gottsched, Johann Christoph 1700-1766................. DLB-97

Götz, Johann Nikolaus 1721-1781......... DLB-97

Goudge, Elizabeth 1900-1984 .... DLB-191

Gough, John B. 1817-1886 .... DLB-243

Gould, Wallace 1882-1940 .... DLB-54

Govoni, Corrado 1884-1965 .... DLB-114

Govrin, Michal 1950- DLB-299

Gower, John circa 1330-1408 .... DLB-146

Goyen, William 1915-1983......DLB-2, 218; Y-83

Goytisolo, José Augustín 1928- DLB-134

Gozzano, Guido 1883-1916 .... DLB-114

Grabbe, Christian Dietrich 1801-1836 ... DLB-133

Gracq, Julien (Louis Poirier) 1910- DLB-83

Grady, Henry W. 1850-1889 .... DLB-23

Graf, Oskar Maria 1894-1967........... DLB-56

Graf Rudolf between circa 1170 and circa 1185................. DLB-148

Graff, Gerald 1937- DLB-246

Richard Grafton [publishing house] DLB-170

Grafton, Sue 1940- DLB-226

Graham, Frank 1893-1965 .... DLB-241

Graham, George Rex 1813-1894 .... DLB-73

Graham, Gwethalyn (Gwethalyn Graham Erichsen-Brown) 1913-1965......... DLB-88

Graham, Jorie 1951- DLB-120

Graham, Katharine 1917-2001 .... DLB-127

Graham, Lorenz 1902-1989 .... DLB-76

Graham, Philip 1915-1963 .... DLB-127

Graham, R. B. Cunninghame 1852-1936 ....DLB-98, 135, 174

Graham, Shirley 1896-1977 .... DLB-76

Graham, Stephen 1884-1975........... DLB-195

Graham, W. S. 1918-1986 .... DLB-20

William H. Graham [publishing house] ... DLB-49

Graham, Winston 1910- DLB-77

Grahame, Kenneth 1859-1932 ...DLB-34, 141, 178

Grainger, Martin Allerdale 1874-1941 .... DLB-92

Gramatky, Hardie 1907-1979 .... DLB-22

Gramcko, Ida 1924-1994 .... DLB-290

Gramsci, Antonio 1891-1937 .... DLB-296

Grand, Sarah 1854-1943..........DLB-135, 197

Grandbois, Alain 1900-1975 .... DLB-92

Grandson, Oton de circa 1345-1397..... DLB-208

Grange, John circa 1556-? DLB-136

Granger, Thomas 1578-1627 .... DLB-281

Granich, Irwin (see Gold, Michael)

Granin, Daniil 1918- DLB-302

Granovsky, Timofei Nikolaevich 1813-1855................. DLB-198

Grant, Anne MacVicar 1755-1838 .... DLB-200

Grant, Duncan 1885-1978 ....DS-10

Grant, George 1918-1988 .... DLB-88

Grant, George Monro 1835-1902......... DLB-99

Grant, Harry J. 1881-1963 .... DLB-29

Grant, James Edward 1905-1966 .... DLB-26

Grant, John (see Gash, Jonathan)

War of the Words (and Pictures): The Creation of a Graphic Novel................. Y-02

Grass, Günter 1927- ...DLB-75, 124; CDWLB-2

Nobel Lecture 1999: "To Be Continued..." Y-99

Tribute to Helen Wolff Y-94

Grasty, Charles H. 1863-1924 .... DLB-25

Grau, Shirley Ann 1929- DLB-2, 218

Graves, John 1920- Y-83

Graves, Richard 1715-1804............. DLB-39

Graves, Robert 1895-1985 ....DLB-20, 100, 191; DS-18; Y-85; CDBLB-6

The St. John's College Robert Graves Trust............. Y-96

Gray, Alasdair 1934- DLB-194, 261

Gray, Asa 1810-1888 .... DLB-1, 235

Gray, David 1838-1861 .... DLB-32

Gray, Simon 1936- DLB-13

Gray, Thomas 1716-1771 .... DLB-109; CDBLB-2

Grayson, Richard 1951- DLB-234

Grayson, William J. 1788-1863.... DLB-3, 64, 248

The Great Bibliographers Series............. Y-93

The Great Gatsby (Documentary) DLB-219

"The Greatness of Southern Literature": League of the South Institute for the Study of Southern Culture and History Y-02

Grech, Nikolai Ivanovich 1787-1867..... DLB-198

Greeley, Horace 1811-1872 ...DLB-3, 43, 189, 250

Green, Adolph 1915-2002 .... DLB-44, 265

Green, Anna Katharine 1846-1935 .... DLB-202, 221

Green, Duff 1791-1875? DLB-43

Green, Elizabeth Shippen 1871-1954 .... DLB-188

Green, Gerald 1922- DLB-28

Green, Henry 1905-1973 .... DLB-15

Green, Jonas 1712-1767............. DLB-31

Green, Joseph 1706-1780............. DLB-31

Green, Julien 1900-1998 .... DLB-4, 72

Green, Paul 1894-1981........ DLB-7, 9, 249; Y-81

Green, T. H. 1836-1882 .... DLB-190, 262

Green, Terence M. 1947- DLB-251

T. and S. Green [publishing house] DLB-49

Green Tiger Press................. DLB-46

Timothy Green [publishing house]....... DLB-49

Greenaway, Kate 1846-1901 .... DLB-141

Greenberg: Publisher DLB-46

Greene, Asa 1789-1838 .... DLB-11

Greene, Belle da Costa 1883-1950 ....DLB-187

Greene, Graham 1904-1991 ....DLB-13, 15, 77, 100, 162, 201, 204; Y-85, 91; CDBLB-7

Tribute to Christopher Isherwood........ Y-86

Greene, Robert 1558-1592 ....DLB-62, 167

Greene, Robert Bernard (Bob), Jr. 1947- DLB-185

Benjamin H Greene [publishing house] ... DLB-49

Greenfield, George 1917-2000 .... Y-91, 00

Derek Robinson's Review of George Greenfield's *Rich Dust* Y-02

Greenhow, Robert 1800-1854 .... DLB-30

Greenlee, William B. 1872-1953.........DLB-187

Greenough, Horatio 1805-1852 .... DLB-1, 235

Greenwell, Dora 1821-1882 .... DLB-35, 199

Greenwillow Books DLB-46

Greenwood, Grace (see Lippincott, Sara Jane Clarke)

Greenwood, Walter 1903-1974.......DLB-10, 191

Greer, Ben 1948- DLB-6

Greflinger, Georg 1620?-1677 .... DLB-164

Greg, W. R. 1809-1881 .... DLB-55

Greg, W. W. 1875-1959 .... DLB-201

Gregg, Josiah 1806-1850............. DLB-183, 186

Gregg Press................. DLB-46

Gregory, Horace 1898-1982............. DLB-48

Gregory, Isabella Augusta Persse, Lady 1852-1932................. DLB-10

Gregory of Rimini circa 1300-1358 ..... DLB-115

Gregynog Press DLB-112

Greiff, León de 1895-1976 .... DLB-283

Greiffenberg, Catharina Regina von 1633-1694 ....DLB-168

Greig, Noël 1944- DLB-245

Grekova, Irina (Elena Sergeevna Venttsel') 1907- DLB-302

Grenfell, Wilfred Thomason 1865-1940.....................DLB-92

Gress, Elsa 1919-1988 ....DLB-214

Greve, Felix Paul (see Grove, Frederick Philip)

Greville, Fulke, First Lord Brooke 1554-1628 ....DLB-62, 172

Grey, Sir George, K.C.B. 1812-1898.....DLB-184

Grey, Lady Jane 1537-1554 ....DLB-132

Grey, Zane 1872-1939 ....DLB-9, 212

Zane Grey's West Society............ Y-00

Grey Owl (Archibald Stansfeld Belaney) 1888-1938 ....DLB-92; DS-17

Grey Walls Press DLB-112

Griboedov, Aleksandr Sergeevich 1795?-1829 ....DLB-205

Grice, Paul 1913-1988 ....DLB-279

Grier, Eldon 1917- DLB-88

Grieve, C. M. (see MacDiarmid, Hugh)

Griffin, Bartholomew flourished 1596....DLB-172

Griffin, Bryan

"Panic Among the Philistines": A Postscript, An Interview with Bryan Griffin Y-81

Griffin, Gerald 1803-1840 ....DLB-159

The Griffin Poetry Prize Y-00

Griffith, Elizabeth 1727?-1793 ....DLB-39, 89

Preface to *The Delicate Distress* (1769) ...DLB-39

Griffith, George 1857-1906 ....DLB-178

Ralph Griffiths [publishing house].......DLB-154

Griffiths, Trevor 1935- DLB-13, 245

S. C. Griggs and Company DLB-49

Griggs, Sutton Elbert 1872-1930 ....DLB-50

Grignon, Claude-Henri 1894-1976........DLB-68

Grigor'ev, Apollon Aleksandrovich 1822-1864 ....DLB-277

Grigorovich, Dmitrii Vasil'evich 1822-1899 ....DLB-238

Grigson, Geoffrey 1905-1985 ....DLB-27

Grillparzer, Franz 1791-1872 ....DLB-133; CDWLB-2

Grimald, Nicholas circa 1519-circa 1562.................DLB-136

Grimké, Angelina Weld 1880-1958....DLB-50, 54

Grimké, Sarah Moore 1792-1873 ....DLB-239

Grimm, Hans 1875-1959 ....DLB-66

Grimm, Jacob 1785-1863 ....DLB-90

Grimm, Wilhelm 1786-1859 ....DLB-90; CDWLB-2

Grimmelshausen, Johann Jacob Christoffel von 1621 or 1622-1676......DLB-168; CDWLB-2

Grimshaw, Beatrice Ethel 1871-1953....DLB-174

Grímur Thomsen 1820-1896............DLB-293

Grin, Aleksandr Stepanovich 1880-1932 ....DLB-272

Grindal, Edmund 1519 or 1520-1583 ....DLB-132

Gripe, Maria (Kristina) 1923- DLB-257

Griswold, Rufus Wilmot 1815-1857 ....DLB-3, 59, 250

Gronlund, Laurence 1846-1899.........DLB-303

Grosart, Alexander Balloch 1827-1899 ...DLB-184

Grosholz, Emily 1950- DLB-282

Gross, Milt 1895-1953.................DLB-11

Grosset and Dunlap...................DLB-49

Grosseteste, Robert circa 1160-1253 .....DLB-115

Grossman, Allen 1932- DLB-193

Grossman, David 1954- DLB-299

Grossman, Vasilii Semenovich 1905-1964 ....DLB-272

Grossman Publishers...................DLB-46

Grosvenor, Gilbert H. 1875-1966 ....DLB-91

Groth, Klaus 1819-1899................DLB-129

Groulx, Lionel 1878-1967 ....DLB-68

Grove, Frederick Philip (Felix Paul Greve) 1879-1948 ....DLB-92

Grove Press........................DLB-46

Groys, Boris Efimovich 1947- DLB-285

Grubb, Davis 1919-1980 ....DLB-6

Gruelle, Johnny 1880-1938 ....DLB-22

von Grumbach, Argula 1492-after 1563?..................DLB-179

Grundtvig, N. F. S. 1783-1872 ....DLB-300

Grymeston, Elizabeth before 1563-before 1604 ....DLB-136

Grynberg, Henryk 1936- DLB-299

Gryphius, Andreas 1616-1664 ....DLB-164; CDWLB-2

Gryphius, Christian 1649-1706 ....DLB-168

Guare, John 1938- DLB-7, 249

Guberman, Igor Mironovich 1936- DLB-285

Guðbergur Bergsson 1932 ....DLB-293

Guðmundur Böðvarsson 1904-1974 .....DLB-293

Guðmundur Gíslason Hagalín 1898-1985 ....DLB-293

Guðmundur Magnússon (see Jón Trausti)

Guerra, Tonino 1920- DLB-128

Guest, Barbara 1920- DLB-5, 193

Guèvremont, Germaine 1893-1968......DLB-68

Guglielminetti, Amalia 1881-1941 ....DLB-264

Guidacci, Margherita 1921-1992 ....DLB-128

Guillén, Jorge 1893-1984 ....DLB-108

Guillén, Nicolás 1902-1989 ....DLB-283

Guilloux, Louis 1899-1980 ....DLB-72

Guilpin, Everard circa 1572-after 1608?...............DLB-136

Guiney, Louise Imogen 1861-1920 ....DLB-54

Guiterman, Arthur 1871-1943 ....DLB-11

Gumilev, Nikolai Stepanovich 1886-1921 ....DLB-295

Günderrode, Caroline von 1780-1806 ....DLB-90

Gundulić, Ivan 1589-1638 ...DLB-147; CDWLB-4

Gunesekera, Romesh 1954- DLB-267

Gunn, Bill 1934-1989..................DLB-38

Gunn, James E. 1923- DLB-8

Gunn, Neil M. 1891-1973 ....DLB-15

Gunn, Thom 1929- DLB-27; CDBLB-8

Gunnar Gunnarsson 1889-1975.........DLB-293

Gunnars, Kristjana 1948- DLB-60

Günther, Johann Christian 1695-1723....DLB-168

Gurik, Robert 1932- DLB-60

Gurney, A. R. 1930- DLB-266

Gurney, Ivor 1890-1937 .... Y-02

The Ivor Gurney Society............. Y-98

Guro, Elena Genrikhovna 1877-1913.....DLB-295

Gustafson, Ralph 1909-1995 ....DLB-88

Gustafsson, Lars 1936- DLB-257

Gütersloh, Albert Paris 1887-1973 ....DLB-81

Guterson, David 1956- DLB-292

Guthrie, A. B., Jr. 1901-1991 ....DLB-6, 212

Guthrie, Ramon 1896-1973 ....DLB-4

Guthrie, Thomas Anstey (see Anstey, FC)

Guthrie, Woody 1912-1967..............DLB-303

The Guthrie Theater DLB-7

Gutiérrez Nájera, Manuel 1859-1895 ....DLB-290

Guttormur J. Guttormsson 1878-1966....DLB-293

Gutzkow, Karl 1811-1878 ....DLB-133

Guy, Ray 1939- DLB-60

Guy, Rosa 1925- DLB-33

Guyot, Arnold 1807-1884 .... DS-13

Gwynn, R. S. 1948- DLB-282

Gwynne, Erskine 1898-1948 ....DLB-4

Gyles, John 1680-1755.................DLB-99

Gyllembourg, Thomasine 1773-1856.....DLB-300

Gyllensten, Lars 1921- DLB-257

Gyrðir Elíasson 1961- DLB-293

Gysin, Brion 1916-1986.................DLB-16

H

H.D. (see Doolittle, Hilda)

Habermas, Jürgen 1929- DLB-242

Habington, William 1605-1654.........DLB-126

Hacker, Marilyn 1942- DLB-120, 282

Hackett, Albert 1900-1995..............DLB-26

Hacks, Peter 1928- DLB-124

Hadas, Rachel 1948- DLB-120, 282

Hadden, Briton 1898-1929 ....DLB-91

Hagedorn, Friedrich von 1708-1754......DLB-168

Hagelstange, Rudolf 1912-1984..........DLB-69

Hagerup, Inger 1905-1985..............DLB-297

Haggard, H. Rider 1856-1925 ....DLB-70, 156, 174, 178

Haggard, William (Richard Clayton) 1907-1993 ....DLB-276; Y-93

Hagy, Alyson 1960- DLB-244

Hahn-Hahn, Ida Gräfin von 1805-1880 ..DLB-133

Haig-Brown, Roderick 1908-1976 ....DLB-88

Cumulative Index

Haight, Gordon S. 1901-1985.......... DLB-103
Hailey, Arthur 1920- DLB-88; Y-82
Haines, John 1924- DLB-5, 212
Hake, Edward flourished 1566-1604 .... DLB-136
Hake, Thomas Gordon 1809-1895....... DLB-32
Hakluyt, Richard 1552?-1616.......... DLB-136
Halas, František 1901-1949 .... DLB-215
Halbe, Max 1865-1944................ DLB-118
Halberstam, David 1934- DLB-241
Haldane, Charlotte 1894-1969 .... DLB-191
Haldane, J. B. S. 1892-1964 .... DLB-160
Haldeman, Joe 1943- DLB-8
Haldeman-Julius Company............. DLB-46
Hale, E. J., and Son.................. DLB-49
Hale, Edward Everett
 1822-1909 ....DLB-1, 42, 74, 235
Hale, Janet Campbell 1946- DLB-175
Hale, Kathleen 1898-2000 .... DLB-160
Hale, Leo Thomas (see Ebon)
Hale, Lucretia Peabody 1820-1900....... DLB-42
Hale, Nancy
 1908-1988 ....DLB-86; DS-17; Y-80, 88
Hale, Sarah Josepha (Buell)
 1788-1879 .... DLB-1, 42, 73, 243
Hale, Susan 1833-1910 .... DLB-221
Hales, John 1584-1656 .... DLB-151
Halévy, Ludovic 1834-1908 .... DLB-192
Haley, Alex 1921-1992 .... DLB-38; CDALB-7
Haliburton, Thomas Chandler
 1796-1865.................... DLB-11, 99
Hall, Adam (Trevor Dudley-Smith)
 1920-1995 ....DLB-276
Hall, Anna Maria 1800-1881 .... DLB-159
Hall, Donald 1928- DLB-5
Hall, Edward 1497-1547 .... DLB-132
Hall, Halsey 1898-1977................ DLB-241
Hall, James 1793-1868 ....DLB-73, 74
Hall, Joseph 1574-1656 .... DLB-121, 151
Hall, Radclyffe 1880-1943 .... DLB-191
Hall, Rodney 1935- DLB-289
Hall, Sarah Ewing 1761-1830 .... DLB-200
Hall, Stuart 1932- DLB-242
Samuel Hall [publishing house] DLB-49
Hallam, Arthur Henry 1811-1833 .... DLB-32
 On Some of the Characteristics of
  Modern Poetry and On the
  Lyrical Poems of Alfred
  Tennyson (1831)............... DLB-32
Halldór Laxness (Halldór Guðjónsson)
 1902-1998 .... DLB-293
Halleck, Fitz-Greene 1790-1867 ...... DLB-3, 250
Haller, Albrecht von 1708-1777......... DLB-168
Halliday, Brett (see Dresser, Davis)
Halliwell-Phillipps, James Orchard
 1820-1889 .... DLB-184
Hallmann, Johann Christian
 1640-1704 or 1716? DLB-168
Hallmark Editions DLB-46

Halper, Albert 1904-1984............... DLB-9
Halperin, John William 1941- DLB-111
Halstead, Murat 1829-1908 .... DLB-23
Hamann, Johann Georg 1730-1788....... DLB-97
Hamburger, Michael 1924- DLB-27
Hamilton, Alexander 1712-1756 .... DLB-31
Hamilton, Alexander 1755?-1804 .... DLB-37
Hamilton, Cicely 1872-1952 ....DLB-10, 197
Hamilton, Edmond 1904-1977 .... DLB-8
Hamilton, Elizabeth 1758-1816..... DLB-116, 158
Hamilton, Gail (see Corcoran, Barbara)
Hamilton, Gail (see Dodge, Mary Abigail)
Hamish Hamilton Limited DLB-112
Hamilton, Hugo 1953- DLB-267
Hamilton, Ian 1938-2001 .... DLB-40, 155
Hamilton, Janet 1795-1873 .... DLB-199
Hamilton, Mary Agnes 1884-1962...... DLB-197
Hamilton, Patrick 1904-1962 .... DLB-10, 191
Hamilton, Virginia 1936-2002 ...DLB-33, 52; Y-01
Hamilton, Sir William 1788-1856....... DLB-262
Hamilton-Paterson, James 1941- DLB-267
Hammerstein, Oscar, 2nd 1895-1960.... DLB-265
Hammett, Dashiell
 1894-1961 ... DLB-226, 280; DS-6; CDALB-5
 An Appeal in *TAC*................. Y-91
 The Glass Key and Other Dashiell
  Hammett Mysteries................ Y-96
 Knopf to Hammett: The Editoral
  Correspondence Y-00
Hammon, Jupiter 1711-died between
 1790 and 1806 .... DLB-31, 50
Hammond, John ?-1663 .... DLB-24
Hamner, Earl 1923- DLB-6
Hampson, John 1901-1955............ DLB-191
Hampton, Christopher 1946- DLB-13
Hamsun, Knut 1859-1952 .... DLB-297
Handel-Mazzetti, Enrica von 1871-1955... DLB-81
Handke, Peter 1942- DLB-85, 124
Handlin, Oscar 1915- DLB-17
Hankin, St. John 1869-1909 .... DLB-10
Hanley, Clifford 1922- DLB-14
Hanley, James 1901-1985............. DLB-191
Hannah, Barry 1942- DLB-6, 234
Hannay, James 1827-1873............. DLB-21
Hannes Hafstein 1861-1922 .... DLB-293
Hano, Arnold 1922- DLB-241
Hanrahan, Barbara 1939-1991 .... DLB-289
Hansberry, Lorraine
 1930-1965 .... DLB-7, 38; CDALB-1
Hansen, Martin A. 1909-1955 .... DLB-214
Hansen, Thorkild 1927-1989 .... DLB-214
Hanson, Elizabeth 1684-1737 .... DLB-200
Hapgood, Norman 1868-1937 .... DLB-91
Happel, Eberhard Werner 1647-1690.... DLB-168
Harbach, Otto 1873-1963 .... DLB-265
The Harbinger 1845-1849 .... DLB-1, 223

Harburg, E. Y. "Yip" 1896-1981 .... DLB-265
Harcourt Brace Jovanovich DLB-46
Hardenberg, Friedrich von (see Novalis)
Harding, Walter 1917- DLB-111
Hardwick, Elizabeth 1916- DLB-6
Hardy, Alexandre 1572?-1632...........DLB-268
Hardy, Frank 1917-1994............... DLB-260
Hardy, Thomas
 1840-1928 ...... DLB-18, 19, 135; CDBLB-5
 "Candour in English Fiction" (1890)... DLB-18
Hare, Cyril 1900-1958 .... DLB-77
Hare, David 1947- DLB-13
Hare, R. M. 1919-2002................ DLB-262
Hargrove, Marion 1919- DLB-11
Häring, Georg Wilhelm Heinrich
 (see Alexis, Willibald)
Harington, Donald 1935- DLB-152
Harington, Sir John 1560-1612......... DLB-136
Harjo, Joy 1951- DLB-120, 175
Harkness, Margaret (John Law)
 1854-1923 ....DLB-197
Harley, Edward, second Earl of Oxford
 1689-1741..................... DLB-213
Harley, Robert, first Earl of Oxford
 1661-1724..................... DLB-213
Harlow, Robert 1923- DLB-60
Harman, Thomas flourished 1566-1573... DLB-136
Harness, Charles L. 1915- DLB-8
Harnett, Cynthia 1893-1981........... DLB-161
Harnick, Sheldon 1924- DLB-265
 Tribute to Ira Gershwin................ Y-96
 Tribute to Lorenz Hart............... Y-95
Harper, Edith Alice Mary (see Wickham, Anna)
Harper, Fletcher 1806-1877 .... DLB-79
Harper, Frances Ellen Watkins
 1825-1911 .... DLB-50, 221
Harper, Michael S. 1938- DLB-41
Harper and Brothers DLB-49
Harpur, Charles 1813-1868 .... DLB-230
Harraden, Beatrice 1864-1943 .... DLB-153
George G. Harrap and Company
 Limited..................... DLB-112
Harriot, Thomas 1560-1621........... DLB-136
Harris, Alexander 1805-1874 .... DLB-230
Harris, Benjamin ?-circa 1720....... DLB-42, 43
Harris, Christie 1907-2002 .... DLB-88
Harris, Errol E. 1908- DLB-279
Harris, Frank 1856-1931 ....DLB-156, 197
Harris, George Washington
 1814-1869 ....DLB-3, 11, 248
Harris, Joanne 1964- DLB-271
Harris, Joel Chandler
 1848-1908 ....DLB-11, 23, 42, 78, 91
 The Joel Chandler Harris Association.... Y-99
Harris, Mark 1922- DLB-2; Y-80
 Tribute to Frederick A. Pottle Y-87
Harris, William Torrey 1835-1909 ......DLB-270

Harris, Wilson 1921- DLB-117; CDWLB-3

Harrison, Mrs. Burton
  (see Harrison, Constance Cary)

Harrison, Charles Yale 1898-1954. ...... DLB-68

Harrison, Constance Cary 1843-1920 .... DLB-221

Harrison, Frederic 1831-1923 .... DLB-57, 190

  "On Style in English Prose" (1898). ... DLB-57

Harrison, Harry 1925- DLB-8

James P. Harrison Company DLB-49

Harrison, Jim 1937- Y-82

Harrison, M. John 1945- DLB-261

Harrison, Mary St. Leger Kingsley
  (see Malet, Lucas)

Harrison, Paul Carter 1936- DLB-38

Harrison, Susan Frances 1859-1935 ..... DLB-99

Harrison, Tony 1937- DLB-40, 245

Harrison, William 1535-1593 .... DLB-136

Harrison, William 1933- DLB-234

Harrisse, Henry 1829-1910 .... DLB-47

The Harry Ransom Humanities Research Center
  at the University of Texas at Austin Y-00

Harryman, Carla 1952- DLB-193

Harsdörffer, Georg Philipp 1607-1658 ... DLB-164

Harsent, David 1942- DLB-40

Hart, Albert Bushnell 1854-1943 .... DLB-17

Hart, Anne 1768-1834 .... DLB-200

Hart, Elizabeth 1771-1833 .... DLB-200

Hart, Julia Catherine 1796-1867 ...... DLB-99

Hart, Lorenz 1895-1943 .... DLB-265

  Larry Hart: Still an Influence Y-95

  Lorenz Hart: An American Lyricist Y-95

  The Lorenz Hart Centenary Y-95

Hart, Moss 1904-1961 .... DLB-7, 266

Hart, Oliver 1723-1795 .... DLB-31

Rupert Hart-Davis Limited DLB-112

Harte, Bret 1836-1902
  .... DLB-12, 64, 74, 79, 186; CDALB-3

Harte, Edward Holmead 1922- DLB-127

Harte, Houston Harriman 1927- DLB-127

Hartlaub, Felix 1913-1945 .... DLB-56

Hartleben, Otto Erich 1864-1905 ...... DLB-118

Hartley, David 1705-1757 .... DLB-252

Hartley, L. P. 1895-1972 .... DLB-15, 139

Hartley, Marsden 1877-1943 .... DLB-54

Hartling, Peter 1933- DLB-75

Hartman, Geoffrey H. 1929- DLB-67

Hartmann, Sadakichi 1867-1944 .... DLB-54

Hartmann von Aue
  circa 1160-circa 1205 .... DLB-138; CDWLB-2

Hartshorne, Charles 1897-2000 .... DLB-270

Haruf, Kent 1943- DLB-292

Harvey, Gabriel 1550?-1631 ... DLB-167, 213, 281

Harvey, Jack (see Rankin, Ian)

Harvey, Jean-Charles 1891-1967 ...... DLB-88

Harvill Press Limited DLB-112

Harwood, Gwen 1920-1995 .... DLB-289

Harwood, Lee 1939- DLB-40

Harwood, Ronald 1934- DLB-13

Hašek, Jaroslav 1883-1923 ... DLB-215; CDWLB-4

Haskins, Charles Homer 1870-1937 ..... DLB-47

Haslam, Gerald 1937- DLB-212

Hass, Robert 1941- DLB-105, 206

Hasselstrom, Linda M. 1943- DLB-256

Hastings, Michael 1938- DLB-233

Hatar, Győző 1914- DLB-215

The Hatch-Billops Collection DLB-76

Hathaway, William 1944- DLB-120

Hatherly, Ana 1929- DLB-287

Hauch, Carsten 1790-1872 .... DLB-300

Hauff, Wilhelm 1802-1827 .... DLB-90

Hauge, Olav H. 1908-1994 .... DLB-297

Haugen, Paal-Helge 1945- DLB-297

Haugwitz, August Adolph von
  1647-1706 .... DLB-168

Hauptmann, Carl 1858-1921 .... DLB-66, 118

Hauptmann, Gerhart
  1862-1946 .... DLB-66, 118; CDWLB-2

Hauser, Marianne 1910- Y-83

Havel, Václav 1936- DLB-232; CDWLB-4

Haven, Alice B. Neal 1827-1863 .... DLB-250

Havergal, Frances Ridley 1836-1879 ..... DLB-199

Hawes, Stephen 1475?-before 1529 ..... DLB-132

Hawker, Robert Stephen 1803-1875 ..... DLB-32

Hawkes, John
  1925-1998 .... DLB-2, 7, 227; Y-80, Y-98

  John Hawkes: A Tribute Y-98

  Tribute to Donald Barthelme Y-89

Hawkesworth, John 1720-1773 .... DLB-142

Hawkins, Sir Anthony Hope (see Hope, Anthony)

Hawkins, Sir John 1719-1789 ...... DLB-104, 142

Hawkins, Walter Everette 1883-? DLB-50

Hawthorne, Nathaniel 1804-1864
  ... DLB-1, 74, 183, 223, 269; DS-5; CDALB-2

  The Nathaniel Hawthorne Society Y-00

  The Old Manse DLB-223

Hawthorne, Sophia Peabody
  1809-1871 .... DLB-183, 239

Hay, John 1835-1905 .... DLB-12, 47, 189

Hay, John 1915- DLB-275

Hayashi Fumiko 1903-1951 .... DLB-180

Haycox, Ernest 1899-1950 .... DLB-206

Haycraft, Anna Margaret (see Ellis, Alice Thomas)

Hayden, Robert
  1913-1980 .... DLB-5, 76; CDALB-1

Haydon, Benjamin Robert 1786-1846 .... DLB-110

Hayes, John Michael 1919- DLB-26

Hayley, William 1745-1820 .... DLB-93, 142

Haym, Rudolf 1821-1901 .... DLB-129

Hayman, Robert 1575-1629 .... DLB-99

Hayman, Ronald 1932- DLB-155

Hayne, Paul Hamilton
  1830-1886 .... DLB-3, 64, 79, 248

Hays, Mary 1760-1843 .... DLB-142, 158

Hayward, John 1905-1965 .... DLB-201

Haywood, Eliza 1693?-1756 .... DLB-39

  Dedication of *Lasselia* [excerpt]
    (1723) DLB-39

  Preface to *The Disguis'd Prince*
    [excerpt] (1723) DLB-39

  The Tea-Table [excerpt] DLB-39

Haywood, William D. 1869-1928 .... DLB-303

Willis P. Hazard [publishing house] DLB-49

Hazlitt, William 1778-1830 ...... DLB-110, 158

Hazzard, Shirley 1931- DLB-289; Y-82

Head, Bessie
  1937-1986 .... DLB-117, 225; CDWLB-3

Headley, Joel T. 1813-1897 ... DLB-30, 183; DS-13

Heaney, Seamus 1939- ... DLB-40; Y-95; CDBLB-8

  Nobel Lecture 1994: Crediting Poetry ... Y-95

Heard, Nathan C. 1936- DLB-33

Hearn, Lafcadio 1850-1904 ...... DLB-12, 78, 189

Hearn, Mary Anne (Marianne Farningham,
  Eva Hope) 1834-1909 .... DLB-240

Hearne, John 1926- DLB-117

Hearne, Samuel 1745-1792 .... DLB-99

Hearne, Thomas 1678?-1735 .... DLB-213

Hearst, William Randolph 1863-1951 ..... DLB-25

Hearst, William Randolph, Jr.
  1908-1993 .... DLB-127

Heartman, Charles Frederick
  1883-1953 .... DLB-187

Heath, Catherine 1924- DLB-14

Heath, James Ewell 1792-1862 .... DLB-248

Heath, Roy A. K. 1926- DLB-117

Heath-Stubbs, John 1918- DLB-27

Heavysege, Charles 1816-1876 .... DLB-99

Hebbel, Friedrich
  1813-1863 .... DLB-129; CDWLB-2

Hebel, Johann Peter 1760-1826 .... DLB-90

Heber, Richard 1774-1833 .... DLB-184

Hébert, Anne 1916-2000 .... DLB-68

Hébert, Jacques 1923- DLB-53

Hecht, Anthony 1923- DLB-5, 169

Hecht, Ben 1894-1964 .... DLB-7, 9, 25, 26, 28, 86

Hecker, Isaac Thomas 1819-1888 ..... DLB-1, 243

Hedge, Frederic Henry
  1805-1890 .... DLB-1, 59, 243; DS-5

Hefner, Hugh M. 1926- DLB-137

Hegel, Georg Wilhelm Friedrich
  1770-1831 .... DLB-90

Heiberg, Johan Ludvig 1791-1860 ...... DLB-300

Heiberg, Johanne Luise 1812-1890 ..... DLB-300

Heide, Robert 1939- DLB-249

Heidegger, Martin 1889-1976 .... DLB-296

Heidish, Marcy 1947- Y-82

Heißenbüttel, Helmut 1921-1996 ...... DLB-75

Heike monogatari DLB-203

Hein, Christoph 1944- DLB-124; CDWLB-2

Hein, Piet 1905-1996 .... DLB-214

Cumulative Index

Heine, Heinrich 1797-1856 ... DLB-90; CDWLB-2

Heinemann, Larry 1944- DS-9

William Heinemann Limited DLB-112

Heinesen, William 1900-1991.......... DLB-214

Heinlein, Robert A. 1907-1988 .... DLB-8

Heinrich, Willi 1920- DLB-75

Heinrich Julius of Brunswick
1564-1613.................... DLB-164

Heinrich von dem Türlîn
flourished circa 1230 .... DLB-138

Heinrich von Melk
flourished after 1160 .... DLB-148

Heinrich von Veldeke
circa 1145-circa 1190 .... DLB-138

Heinse, Wilhelm 1746-1803 .... DLB-94

Heinz, W. C. 1915- DLB-171

Heiskell, John 1872-1972........... DLB-127

Hejinian, Lyn 1941- DLB-165

Helder, Heberto 1930- DLB-287

Heliand circa 850.................. DLB-148

Heller, Joseph
1923-1999 ......DLB-2, 28, 227; Y-80, 99, 02

  Excerpts from Joseph Heller's
  USC Address, "The Literature
  of Despair" Y-96

  Remembering Joe Heller, by William
  Price Fox Y-99

  A Tribute to Joseph Heller............. Y-99

Heller, Michael 1937- DLB-165

Hellman, Lillian 1906-1984 ..... DLB-7, 228; Y-84

Hellwig, Johann 1609-1674........... DLB-164

Helprin, Mark 1947- Y-85; CDALB-7

Helwig, David 1938- DLB-60

Hemans, Felicia 1793-1835 .... DLB-96

Hemenway, Abby Maria 1828-1890..... DLB-243

Hemingway, Ernest 1899-1961
.... DLB-4, 9, 102, 210; Y-81, 87, 99;
DS-1, 15, 16; CDALB-4

  A Centennial Celebration Y-99

  Come to Papa Y-99

  The Ernest Hemingway Collection at
  the John F. Kennedy Library........ Y-99

  Ernest Hemingway Declines to
  Introduce *War and Peace*............ Y-01

  Ernest Hemingway's Reaction to
  James Gould Cozzens Y-98

  Ernest Hemingway's Toronto Journalism
  Revisited: With Three Previously
  Unrecorded Stories Y-92

  Falsifying Hemingway Y-96

  Hemingway Centenary Celebration
  at the JFK Library................Y-99

  The Hemingway/Fenton
  Correspondence Y-02

  Hemingway in the *JFK* Y-99

  The Hemingway Letters Project
  Finds an Editor Y-02

  Hemingway Salesmen's Dummies....... Y-00

  Hemingway: Twenty-Five Years Later ... Y-85

A Literary Archaeologist Digs On:
A Brief Interview with Michael
Reynolds..................... Y-99

Not Immediately Discernible...but
Eventually Quite Clear: The *First
Light* and *Final Years* of
Hemingway's Centenary........... Y-99

Packaging Papa: *The Garden of Eden*..... Y-86

Second International Hemingway
Colloquium: Cuba Y-98

Hémon, Louis 1880-1913............... DLB-92

Hempel, Amy 1951- DLB-218

Hempel, Carl G. 1905-1997 ....DLB-279

Hemphill, Paul 1936- Y-87

Hénault, Gilles 1920-1996 .... DLB-88

Henchman, Daniel 1689-1761 .... DLB-24

Henderson, Alice Corbin 1881-1949 ..... DLB-54

Henderson, Archibald 1877-1963 .... DLB-103

Henderson, David 1942- DLB-41

Henderson, George Wylie 1904-1965 .... DLB-51

Henderson, Zenna 1917-1983........... DLB-8

Henighan, Tom 1934- DLB-251

Henisch, Peter 1943- DLB-85

Henley, Beth 1952- Y-86

Henley, William Ernest 1849-1903 .... DLB-19

Henniker, Florence 1855-1923 .... DLB-135

Henning, Rachel 1826-1914 .... DLB-230

Henningsen, Agnes 1868-1962......... DLB-214

Henry, Alexander 1739-1824 .... DLB-99

Henry, Buck 1930- DLB-26

Henry, Marguerite 1902-1997 .... DLB-22

Henry, O. (see Porter, William Sydney)

Henry, Robert Selph 1889-1970 .... DLB-17

Henry, Will (see Allen, Henry W.)

Henry VIII of England 1491-1547...... DLB-132

Henry of Ghent
circa 1217-1229 - 1293 .... DLB-115

Henryson, Robert
1420s or 1430s-circa 1505 .... DLB-146

Henschke, Alfred (see Klabund)

Hensher, Philip 1965- DLB-267

Hensley, Sophie Almon 1866-1946 ...... DLB-99

Henson, Lance 1944- DLB-175

Henty, G. A. 1832-1902 .... DLB-18, 141

  The Henty Society.................Y-98

Hentz, Caroline Lee 1800-1856 ...... DLB-3, 248

Heraclitus
flourished circa 500 B.C. DLB-176

Herbert, Agnes circa 1880-1960 ....DLB-174

Herbert, Alan Patrick 1890-1971 .... DLB-10, 191

Herbert, Edward, Lord, of Cherbury
1582-1648 .... DLB-121, 151, 252

Herbert, Frank 1920-1986 ..... DLB-8; CDALB-7

Herbert, George 1593-1633 .. DLB-126; CDBLB-1

Herbert, Henry William 1807-1858 .... DLB-3, 73

Herbert, John 1926- DLB-53

Herbert, Mary Sidney, Countess of Pembroke
(see Sidney, Mary)

Herbert, Xavier 1901-1984 .... DLB-260

Herbert, Zbigniew
1924-1998 .... DLB-232; CDWLB-4

Herbst, Josephine 1892-1969 .... DLB-9

Herburger, Gunter 1932- DLB-75, 124

Herculano, Alexandre 1810-1877 .... DLB-287

Hercules, Frank E. M. 1917-1996........ DLB-33

Herder, Johann Gottfried 1744-1803 ..... DLB-97

B. Herder Book Company DLB-49

Heredia, José-María de 1842-1905 ....DLB-217

Herford, Charles Harold 1853-1931 .... DLB-149

Hergesheimer, Joseph 1880-1954..... DLB-9, 102

Heritage Press................... DLB-46

Hermann the Lame 1013-1054.......... DLB-148

Hermes, Johann Timotheu 1738-1821 .... DLB-97

Hermlin, Stephan 1915-1997 .... DLB-69

Hernández, Alfonso C. 1938- DLB-122

Hernández, Inés 1947- DLB-122

Hernández, Miguel 1910-1942 .... DLB-134

Hernton, Calvin C. 1932- DLB-38

Herodotus circa 484 B.C.-circa 420 B.C.
.....................DLB-176; CDWLB-1

Heron, Robert 1764-1807 .... DLB-142

Herr, Michael 1940- DLB-185

Herrera, Darío 1870-1914............. DLB-290

Herrera, Juan Felipe 1948- DLB-122

E. R. Herrick and Company DLB-49

Herrick, Robert 1591-1674 .... DLB-126

Herrick, Robert 1868-1938..........DLB-9, 12, 78

Herrick, William 1915- Y-83

Herrmann, John 1900-1959 .... DLB-4

Hersey, John
1914-1993 ...DLB-6, 185, 278, 299; CDALB-7

Hertel, François 1905-1985............ DLB-68

Hervé-Bazin, Jean Pierre Marie (see Bazin, Hervé)

Hervey, John, Lord 1696-1743 .... DLB-101

Herwig, Georg 1817-1875 .... DLB-133

Herzen, Alexander (Aleksandr Ivanovich
Gersten) 1812-1870 ....DLB-277

Herzog, Emile Salomon Wilhelm
(see Maurois, André)

Hesiod eighth century B.C. DLB-176

Hesse, Hermann
1877-1962............ DLB-66; CDWLB-2

Hessus, Eobanus 1488-1540............DLB-179

Heureka! (see Kertész, Imre and Nobel Prize
in Literature: 2002) Y-02

Hewat, Alexander circa 1743-circa 1824... DLB-30

Hewett, Dorothy 1923-2002.......... DLB-289

Hewitt, John 1907-1987............. DLB-27

Hewlett, Maurice 1861-1923 ...... DLB-34, 156

Heyen, William 1940- DLB-5

Heyer, Georgette 1902-1974 ....DLB-77, 191

Heym, Stefan 1913-2001 .... DLB-69

Heyse, Paul 1830-1914................DLB-129

Heytesbury, William
circa 1310-1372 or 1373 .... DLB-115

Heyward, Dorothy 1890-1961........DLB-7, 249

Heyward, DuBose 1885-1940...DLB-7, 9, 45, 249

Heywood, John 1497?-1580?...........DLB-136

Heywood, Thomas 1573 or 1574-1641....DLB-62

Hiaasen, Carl 1953-...............DLB-292

Hibberd, Jack 1940-...............DLB-289

Hibbs, Ben 1901-1975..............DLB-137

"The Saturday Evening Post reaffirms
a policy," Ben Hibb's Statement
in *The Saturday Evening Post*
(16 May 1942).................DLB-137

Hichens, Robert S. 1864-1950..........DLB-153

Hickey, Emily 1845-1924..............DLB-199

Hickman, William Albert 1877-1957.....DLB-92

Hicks, Granville 1901-1982............DLB-246

Hidalgo, José Luis 1919-1947..........DLB-108

Hiebert, Paul 1892-1987...............DLB-68

Hieng, Andrej 1925-..................DLB-181

Hierro, José 1922-2002................DLB-108

Higgins, Aidan 1927-..................DLB-14

Higgins, Colin 1941-1988..............DLB-26

Higgins, George V.
1939-1999...........DLB-2; Y-81, 98-99

Afterword [in response to Cozzen's
Mens Rea (or Something)]..........Y-97

At End of Day: The Last George V.
Higgins Novel....................Y-99

The Books of George V. Higgins:
A Checklist of Editions
and Printings....................Y-00

George V. Higgins in Class............Y-02

Tribute to Alfred A. Knopf...........Y-84

Tributes to George V. Higgins........Y-99

"What You Lose on the Swings You Make
Up on the Merry-Go-Round"...Y-99

Higginson, Thomas Wentworth
1823-1911.................DLB-1, 64, 243

Highwater, Jamake 1942?-.......DLB-52; Y-85

Hijuelos, Oscar 1951-................DLB-145

Hildegard von Bingen 1098-1179........DLB-148

Das Hildesbrandslied
circa 820..............DLB-148; CDWLB-2

Hildesheimer, Wolfgang 1916-1991..DLB-69, 124

Hildreth, Richard 1807-1865...DLB-1, 30, 59, 235

Hill, Aaron 1685-1750.................DLB-84

Hill, Geoffrey 1932-.........DLB-40; CDBLB-8

George M. Hill Company...............DLB-49

Hill, "Sir" John 1714?-1775............DLB-39

Lawrence Hill and Company,
Publishers......................DLB-46

Hill, Joe 1879-1915..................DLB-303

Hill, Leslie 1880-1960................DLB-51

Hill, Reginald 1936-.................DLB-276

Hill, Susan 1942-................DLB-14, 139

Hill, Walter 1942-...................DLB-44

Hill and Wang.......................DLB-46

Hillberry, Conrad 1928-..............DLB-120

Hillerman, Tony 1925-................DLB-206

Hilliard, Gray and Company............DLB-49

Hills, Lee 1906-2000.................DLB-127

Hillyer, Robert 1895-1961.............DLB-54

Hilsenrath, Edgar 1926-..............DLB-299

Hilton, James 1900-1954............DLB-34, 77

Hilton, Walter died 1396.............DLB-146

Hilton and Company...................DLB-49

Himes, Chester 1909-1984...DLB-2, 76, 143, 226

Joseph Hindmarsh [publishing house]....DLB-170

Hine, Daryl 1936-....................DLB-60

Hingley, Ronald 1920-................DLB-155

Hinojosa-Smith, Rolando 1929-.........DLB-82

Hinton, S. E. 1948-.................CDALB-7

Hippel, Theodor Gottlieb von
1741-1796........................DLB-97

Hippius, Zinaida Nikolaevna
1869-1945.......................DLB-295

Hippocrates of Cos flourished circa
425 B.C.............DLB-176; CDWLB-1

Hirabayashi Taiko 1905-1972..........DLB-180

Hirsch, E. D., Jr. 1928-..............DLB-67

Hirsch, Edward 1950-................DLB-120

"Historical Novel," The Holocaust.....DLB-299

Hoagland, Edward 1932-................DLB-6

Hoagland, Everett H., III 1942-.......DLB-41

Hoban, Russell 1925-............DLB-52; Y-90

Hobbes, Thomas 1588-1679...DLB-151, 252, 281

Hobby, Oveta 1905-1995...............DLB-127

Hobby, William 1878-1964.............DLB-127

Hobsbaum, Philip 1932-................DLB-40

Hobsbawn, Eric (Francis Newton)
1917-...........................DLB-296

Hobson, Laura Z. 1900-................DLB-28

Hobson, Sarah 1947-.................DLB-204

Hoby, Thomas 1530-1566..............DLB-132

Hoccleve, Thomas
circa 1368-circa 1437..............DLB-146

Hochhuth, Rolf 1931-................DLB-124

Hochman, Sandra 1936-.................DLB-5

Hocken, Thomas Morland 1836-1910....DLB-184

Hocking, William Ernest 1873-1966.....DLB-270

Hodder and Stoughton, Limited........DLB-106

Hodgins, Jack 1938-..................DLB-60

Hodgman, Helen 1945-.................DLB-14

Hodgskin, Thomas 1787-1869...........DLB-158

Hodgson, Ralph 1871-1962..............DLB-19

Hodgson, William Hope
1877-1918..............DLB-70, 153, 156, 178

Hoe, Robert, III 1839-1909............DLB-187

Hoeg, Peter 1957-...................DLB-214

Hoel, Sigurd 1890-1960...............DLB-297

Hoem, Edvard 1949-..................DLB-297

Hoffenstein, Samuel 1890-1947.........DLB-11

Hoffman, Alice 1952-.................DLB-292

Hoffman, Charles Fenno 1806-1884...DLB-3, 250

Hoffman, Daniel 1923-.................DLB-5

Tribute to Robert Graves..............Y-85

Hoffmann, E. T. A.
1776-1822.............DLB-90; CDWLB-2

Hoffman, Frank B. 1888-1958..........DLB-188

Hoffman, William 1925-...............DLB-234

Tribute to Paxton Davis...............Y-94

Hoffmanswaldau, Christian Hoffman von
1616-1679.......................DLB-168

Hofmann, Michael 1957-................DLB-40

Hofmannsthal, Hugo von
1874-1929..........DLB-81, 118; CDWLB-2

Hofmo, Gunvor 1921-1995.............DLB-297

Hofstadter, Richard 1916-1970.....DLB-17, 246

Hogan, Desmond 1950-.................DLB-14

Hogan, Linda 1947-..................DLB-175

Hogan and Thompson...................DLB-49

Hogarth Press....................DLB-112; DS-10

Hogg, James 1770-1835.......DLB-93, 116, 159

Hohberg, Wolfgang Helmhard Freiherr von
1612-1688......................DLB-168

von Hohenheim, Philippus Aureolus
Theophrastus Bombastus (see Paracelsus)

Hohl, Ludwig 1904-1980...............DLB-56

Højholt, Per 1928-..................DLB-214

Holan, Vladimir 1905-1980............DLB-215

Holberg, Ludvig 1684-1754............DLB-300

Holbrook, David 1923-............DLB-14, 40

Holcroft, Thomas 1745-1809....DLB-39, 89, 158

Preface to *Alwyn* (1780)............DLB-39

Holden, Jonathan 1941-...............DLB-105

"Contemporary Verse Story-telling"...DLB-105

Holden, Molly 1927-1981...............DLB-40

Hölderlin, Friedrich
1770-1843.............DLB-90; CDWLB-2

Holdstock, Robert 1948-..............DLB-261

Holiday House.......................DLB-46

Holinshed, Raphael died 1580..........DLB-167

Holland, J. G. 1819-1881..............DS-13

Holland, Norman N. 1927-..............DLB-67

Hollander, John 1929-..................DLB-5

Holley, Marietta 1836-1926............DLB-11

Hollinghurst, Alan 1954-.............DLB-207

Hollingsworth, Margaret 1940-.........DLB-60

Hollo, Anselm 1934-..................DLB-40

Holloway, Emory 1885-1977............DLB-103

Holloway, John 1920-.................DLB-27

Holloway House Publishing Company....DLB-46

Holme, Constance 1880-1955............DLB-34

Holmes, Abraham S. 1821?-1908.........DLB-99

Holmes, John Clellon 1926-1988....DLB-16, 237

"Four Essays on the Beat
Generation".....................DLB-16

Holmes, Mary Jane 1825-1907.....DLB-202, 221

Holmes, Oliver Wendell
1809-1894.......DLB-1, 189, 235; CDALB-2

Holmes, Richard 1945-...............DLB-155

Holmes, Thomas James 1874-1959......DLB-187

415

The Holocaust "Historical Novel" DLB-299
Holocaust Fiction, Postmodern......... DLB-299
Holocaust Novel, The "Second-Generation"
.... DLB-299
Holroyd, Michael 1935- DLB-155; Y-99
Holst, Hermann E. von 1841-1904....... DLB-47
Holt, John 1721-1784 .... DLB-43
Henry Holt and Company DLB-49, 284
Holt, Rinehart and Winston............ DLB-46
Holtby, Winifred 1898-1935 .... DLB-191
Holthusen, Hans Egon 1913-1997 .... DLB-69
Hölty, Ludwig Christoph Heinrich
1748-1776 .... DLB-94
Holub, Miroslav
1923-1998 .... DLB-232; CDWLB-4
Holz, Arno 1863-1929 .... DLB-118
Home, Henry, Lord Kames
(see Kames, Henry Home, Lord)
Home, John 1722-1808................. DLB-84
Home, William Douglas 1912- DLB-13
Home Publishing Company DLB-49
Homer circa eighth-seventh centuries B.C.
.... DLB-176; CDWLB-1
Homer, Winslow 1836-1910 .... DLB-188
Homes, Geoffrey (see Mainwaring, Daniel)
Honan, Park 1928- DLB-111
Hone, William 1780-1842......... DLB-110, 158
Hongo, Garrett Kaoru 1951- DLB-120
Honig, Edwin 1919- DLB-5
Hood, Hugh 1928-2000 .... DLB-53
Hood, Mary 1946- DLB-234
Hood, Thomas 1799-1845 .... DLB-96
Hook, Sidney 1902-1989 ....DLB-279
Hook, Theodore 1788-1841 .... DLB-116
Hooker, Jeremy 1941- DLB-40
Hooker, Richard 1554-1600 .... DLB-132
Hooker, Thomas 1586-1647 .... DLB-24
hooks, bell 1952- DLB-246
Hooper, Johnson Jones
1815-1862................. DLB-3, 11, 248
Hope, A. D. 1907-2000 .... DLB-289
Hope, Anthony 1863-1933........ DLB-153, 156
Hope, Christopher 1944- DLB-225
Hope, Eva (see Hearn, Mary Anne)
Hope, Laurence (Adela Florence
Cory Nicolson) 1865-1904......... DLB-240
Hopkins, Ellice 1836-1904 .... DLB-190
Hopkins, Gerard Manley
1844-1889 .... DLB-35, 57; CDBLB-5
Hopkins, John ?-1570 .... DLB-132
Hopkins, John H., and Son............ DLB-46
Hopkins, Lemuel 1750-1801............ DLB-37
Hopkins, Pauline Elizabeth 1859-1930.... DLB-50
Hopkins, Samuel 1721-1803............ DLB-31
Hopkinson, Francis 1737-1791......... DLB-31
Hopkinson, Nalo 1960- DLB-251

Hopper, Nora (Mrs. Nora Chesson)
1871-1906..................... DLB-240
Hoppin, Augustus 1828-1896.......... DLB-188
Hora, Josef 1891-1945 ..... DLB-215; CDWLB-4
Horace 65 B.C.-8 B.C. DLB-211; CDWLB-1
Horgan, Paul 1903-1995......DLB-102, 212; Y-85
Tribute to Alfred A. Knopf Y-84
Horizon Press........................ DLB-46
Horkheimer, Max 1895-1973 .... DLB-296
Hornby, C. H. St. John 1867-1946 ..... DLB-201
Hornby, Nick 1957- DLB-207
Horne, Frank 1899-1974............... DLB-51
Horne, Richard Henry (Hengist)
1802 or 1803-1884................. DLB-32
Horne, Thomas 1608-1654 .... DLB-281
Horney, Karen 1885-1952 .... DLB-246
Hornung, E. W. 1866-1921 .... DLB-70
Horovitz, Israel 1939- DLB-7
Horta, Maria Teresa (see The Three Marias:
A Landmark Case in Portuguese
Literary History)
Horton, George Moses 1797?-1883?...... DLB-50
George Moses Horton Society......... Y-99
Horváth, Ödön von 1901-1938 ..... DLB-85, 124
Horwood, Harold 1923- DLB-60
E. and E. Hosford [publishing house]..... DLB-49
Hoskens, Jane Fenn 1693-1770? DLB-200
Hoskyns, John circa 1566-1638 .... DLB-121, 281
Hosokawa Yūsai 1535-1610 .... DLB-203
Hospers, John 1918- DLB-279
Hostovský, Egon 1908-1973 .... DLB-215
Hotchkiss and Company DLB-49
Hough, Emerson 1857-1923 .... DLB-9, 212
Houghton, Stanley 1881-1913 .... DLB-10
Houghton Mifflin Company............ DLB-49
Hours at Home DS-13
Household, Geoffrey 1900-1988......... DLB-87
Housman, A. E. 1859-1936 ... DLB-19; CDBLB-5
Housman, Laurence 1865-1959 .... DLB-10
Houston, Pam 1962- DLB-244
Houwald, Ernst von 1778-1845 .... DLB-90
Hovey, Richard 1864-1900............. DLB-54
Howard, Donald R. 1927-1987......... DLB-111
Howard, Maureen 1930- Y-83
Howard, Richard 1929- DLB-5
Howard, Roy W. 1883-1964 .... DLB-29
Howard, Sidney 1891-1939 ....DLB-7, 26, 249
Howard, Thomas, second Earl of Arundel
1585-1646 .... DLB-213
Howe, E. W. 1853-1937 .... DLB-12, 25
Howe, Henry 1816-1893 .... DLB-30
Howe, Irving 1920-1993............... DLB-67
Howe, Joseph 1804-1873 .... DLB-99
Howe, Julia Ward 1819-1910 .... DLB-1, 189, 235
Howe, Percival Presland 1886-1944 ..... DLB-149
Howe, Susan 1937- DLB-120

Howell, Clark, Sr. 1863-1936........... DLB-25
Howell, Evan P. 1839-1905 .... DLB-23
Howell, James 1594?-1666 .... DLB-151
Howell, Soskin and Company DLB-46
Howell, Warren Richardson
1912-1984 .... DLB-140
Howells, William Dean 1837-1920
.........DLB-12, 64, 74, 79, 189; CDALB-3
Introduction to Paul Laurence
Dunbar's *Lyrics of Lowly Life*
(1896) DLB-50
The William Dean Howells Society....... Y-01
Howitt, Mary 1799-1888 ....DLB-110, 199
Howitt, William 1792-1879 .... DLB-110
Hoyem, Andrew 1935- DLB-5
Hoyers, Anna Ovena 1584-1655 .... DLB-164
Hoyle, Fred 1915-2001............... DLB-261
Hoyos, Angela de 1940- DLB-82
Henry Hoyt [publishing house] DLB-49
Hoyt, Palmer 1897-1979 ....DLB-127
Hrabal, Bohumil 1914-1997 .... DLB-232
Hrabanus Maurus 776?-856 .... DLB-148
Hronský, Josef Cíger 1896-1960........ DLB-215
Hrotsvit of Gandersheim
circa 935-circa 1000 .... DLB-148
Hubbard, Elbert 1856-1915 .... DLB-91
Hubbard, Kin 1868-1930 .... DLB-11
Hubbard, William circa 1621-1704....... DLB-24
Huber, Therese 1764-1829 .... DLB-90
Huch, Friedrich 1873-1913 .... DLB-66
Huch, Ricarda 1864-1947.............. DLB-66
Huddle, David 1942- DLB-130
Hudgins, Andrew 1951- DLB-120, 282
Hudson, Henry Norman 1814-1886 ..... DLB-64
Hudson, Stephen 1868?-1944..........DLB-197
Hudson, W. H. 1841-1922......DLB-98, 153, 174
Hudson and Goodwin DLB-49
Huebsch, B. W., oral history Y-99
B. W. Huebsch [publishing house]....... DLB-46
Hueffer, Oliver Madox 1876-1931 .....DLB-197
Huet, Pierre Daniel
Preface to *The History of Romances*
(1715)......................... DLB-39
Hugh of St. Victor circa 1096-1141 ..... DLB-208
Hughes, David 1930- DLB-14
Hughes, Dusty 1947- DLB-233
Hughes, Hatcher 1881-1945............ DLB-249
Hughes, John 1677-1720 .... DLB-84
Hughes, Langston 1902-1967........ DLB-4, 7, 48,
51, 86, 228; ; DS-15; CDALB-5
Hughes, Richard 1900-1976 .... DLB-15, 161
Hughes, Ted 1930-1998 .... DLB-40, 161
Hughes, Thomas 1822-1896 .... DLB-18, 163
Hugo, Richard 1923-1982 .... DLB-5, 206
Hugo, Victor 1802-1885.......DLB-119, 192, 217
Hugo Awards and Nebula Awards........ DLB-8
Huidobro, Vicente 1893-1948 .... DLB-283

Hull, Richard 1896-1973 . . . . .DLB-77

Hulda (Unnur Benediktsdóttir Bjarklind)
    1881-1946 . . . . .DLB-293

Hulme, T. E. 1883-1917 . . . . .DLB-19

Hulton, Anne ?-1779? DLB-200

Humboldt, Alexander von 1769-1859 . . . . .DLB-90

Humboldt, Wilhelm von 1767-1835 . . . . . . .DLB-90

Hume, David 1711-1776 . . . . .DLB-104, 252

Hume, Fergus 1859-1932 . . . . .DLB-70

Hume, Sophia 1702-1774 . . . . .DLB-200

Hume-Rothery, Mary Catherine
    1824-1885 . . . . .DLB-240

Humishuma
    (see Mourning Dove)

Hummer, T. R. 1950- DLB-120

Humor

    American Humor: A Historical
        Survey DLB-11

    American Humor Studies Association Y-99

    The Comic Tradition Continued
        [in the British Novel] DLB-15

    Humorous Book Illustration DLB-11

    International Society for Humor Studies . . Y-99

    Newspaper Syndication of American
        Humor DLB-11

    Selected Humorous Magazines
        (1820-1950) DLB-11

Bruce Humphries [publishing house] DLB-46

Humphrey, Duke of Gloucester
    1391-1447 . . . . .DLB-213

Humphrey, William
    1924-1997 . . . . .DLB-6, 212, 234, 278

Humphreys, David 1752-1818 . . . . .DLB-37

Humphreys, Emyr 1919- DLB-15

Humphreys, Josephine 1945- DLB-292

Huncke, Herbert 1915-1996 . . . . .DLB-16

Huncker, James Gibbons 1857-1921 . . . . . .DLB-71

Hunold, Christian Friedrich 1681-1721 . . .DLB-168

Hunt, Irene 1907- DLB-52

Hunt, Leigh 1784-1859 . . . . . . .DLB-96, 110, 144

Hunt, Violet 1862-1942 . . . . .DLB-162, 197

Hunt, William Gibbes 1791-1833 . . . . .DLB-73

Hunter, Evan 1926- Y-82

    Tribute to John D. MacDonald Y-86

Hunter, Jim 1939- DLB-14

Hunter, Kristin 1931- DLB-33

    Tribute to Julian Mayfield Y-84

Hunter, Mollie 1922- DLB-161

Hunter, N. C. 1908-1971 . . . . .DLB-10

Hunter-Duvar, John 1821-1899 . . . . .DLB-99

Huntington, Henry E. 1850-1927 . . . . .DLB-140

    The Henry E. Huntington Library Y-92

Huntington, Susan Mansfield
    1791-1823 . . . . .DLB-200

Hurd and Houghton DLB-49

Hurst, Fannie 1889-1968 . . . . .DLB-86

Hurst and Blackett DLB-106

Hurst and Company DLB-49

Hurston, Zora Neale
    1901?-1960 . . . . .DLB-51, 86; CDALB-7

Husserl, Edmund 1859-1938 . . . . .DLB-296

Husson, Jules-François-Félix (see Champfleury)

Huston, John 1906-1987 . . . . .DLB-26

Hutcheson, Francis 1694-1746 . . . . . . .DLB-31, 252

Hutchinson, Ron 1947- DLB-245

Hutchinson, R. C. 1907-1975 . . . . .DLB-191

Hutchinson, Thomas 1711-1780 . . . . . .DLB-30, 31

Hutchinson and Company
    (Publishers) Limited DLB-112

Huth, Angela 1938- DLB-271

Hutton, Richard Holt 1826-1897 . . . . .DLB-57

von Hutten, Ulrich 1488-1523 . . . . .DLB-179

Huxley, Aldous 1894-1963
    . . . . . .DLB-36, 100, 162, 195, 255; CDBLB-6

Huxley, Elspeth Josceline
    1907-1997 . . . . DLB-77, 204

Huxley, T. H. 1825-1895 . . . . .DLB-57

Huyghue, Douglas Smith 1816-1891 . . . . . .DLB-99

Huysmans, Joris-Karl 1848-1907 . . . . .DLB-123

Hwang, David Henry 1957- DLB-212, 228

Hyde, Donald 1909-1966 . . . . .DLB-187

Hyde, Mary 1912- DLB-187

Hyman, Trina Schart 1939- DLB-61

I

Iavorsky, Stefan 1658-1722 . . . . .DLB-150

Iazykov, Nikolai Mikhailovich
    1803-1846 . . . . .DLB-205

Ibáñez, Armando P. 1949- DLB-209

Ibáñez, Sara de 1909-1971 . . . . .DLB-290

Ibarbourou, Juana de 1892-1979 . . . . .DLB-290

Ibn Bajja circa 1077-1138 . . . . .DLB-115

Ibn Gabirol, Solomon
    circa 1021-circa 1058 . . . . .DLB-115

Ibuse Masuji 1898-1993 . . . . .DLB-180

Ichijō Kanera
    (see Ichijō Kaneyoshi)

Ichijō Kaneyoshi (Ichijō Kanera)
    1402-1481 . . . . .DLB-203

Iffland, August Wilhelm
    1759-1814 . . . . .DLB-94

Iggulden, John 1917- DLB-289

Ignatieff, Michael 1947- DLB-267

Ignatow, David 1914-1997 . . . . .DLB-5

Ike, Chukwuemeka 1931- DLB-157

Ikkyū Sōjun 1394-1481 . . . . .DLB-203

Iles, Francis (see Berkeley, Anthony)

Il'f, Il'ia (Il'ia Arnol'dovich Fainzil'berg)
    1897-1937 . . . . .DLB-272

Illich, Ivan 1926-2002 . . . . .DLB-242

Illustration
    Children's Book Illustration in the
        Twentieth Century DLB-61

    Children's Illustrators, 1800-1880 . . . .DLB-163

    Early American Book Illustration DLB-49

The Iconography of Science-Fiction
    Art DLB-8

The Illustration of Early German
    Literary Manuscripts, circa
    1150-circa 1300 . . . . .DLB-148

    Minor Illustrators, 1880-1914 . . . . . . .DLB-141

Illyés, Gyula 1902-1983 . . . . . DLB-215; CDWLB-4

Imbs, Bravig 1904-1946 . . . . .DLB-4; DS-15

Imbuga, Francis D. 1947- DLB-157

Immermann, Karl 1796-1840 . . . . .DLB-133

Inchbald, Elizabeth 1753-1821 . . . . . . .DLB-39, 89

Indiana University Press Y-02

Ingamells, Rex 1913-1955 . . . . .DLB-260

Inge, William 1913-1973 . . . DLB-7, 249; CDALB-1

Ingelow, Jean 1820-1897 . . . . .DLB-35, 163

Ingemann, B. S. 1789-1862 . . . . .DLB-300

Ingersoll, Ralph 1900-1985 . . . . .DLB-127

The Ingersoll Prizes Y-84

Ingoldsby, Thomas (see Barham, Richard Harris)

Ingraham, Joseph Holt 1809-1860 . . . . .DLB-3, 248

Inman, John 1805-1850 . . . . .DLB-73

Innerhofer, Franz 1944- DLB-85

Innes, Michael (J. I. M. Stewart)
    1906-1994 . . . . .DLB-276

Innis, Harold Adams 1894-1952 . . . . .DLB-88

Innis, Mary Quayle 1899-1972 . . . . .DLB-88

Inō Sōgi 1421-1502 . . . . .DLB-203

Inoue Yasushi 1907-1991 . . . . .DLB-182

"The Greatness of Southern Literature":
    League of the South Institute for the
    Study of Southern Culture and History
    . . . . Y-02

International Publishers Company DLB-46

Internet (publishing and commerce)
    Author Websites Y-97

    The Book Trade and the Internet Y-00

    E-Books Turn the Corner Y-98

    The E-Researcher: Possibilities
        and Pitfalls Y-00

    Interviews on E-publishing Y-00

    John Updike on the Internet Y-97

    LitCheck Website Y-01

    Virtual Books and Enemies of Books Y-00

Interviews
    Adoff, Arnold Y-01

    Aldridge, John W. Y-91

    Anastas, Benjamin Y-98

    Baker, Nicholson Y-00

    Bank, Melissa Y-98

    Bass, T. J. Y-80

    Bernstein, Harriet Y-82

    Betts, Doris Y-82

    Bosworth, David Y-82

    Bottoms, David Y-83

    Bowers, Fredson Y-80

    Burnshaw, Stanley Y-97

    Carpenter, Humphrey Y-84, 99

Carr, Virginia Spencer Y-00	Mooneyham, Lamarr. Y-82	Iskander, Fazil' Abdulevich 1929- DLB-302
Carver, Raymond Y-83	Murray, Les. Y-01	The Island Trees Case: A Symposium on
Cherry, Kelly Y-83	Nosworth, David Y-82	School Library Censorship
Conroy, Jack Y-81	O'Connor, Patrick Y-84, 99	An Interview with Judith Krug
Coppel, Alfred Y-83	Ozick, Cynthia Y-83	An Interview with Phyllis Schlafly An Interview with Edward B. Jenkinson
Cowley, Malcolm Y-81	Penner, Jonathan Y-83	An Interview with Lamarr Mooneyham
Davis, Paxton Y-89	Pennington, Lee Y-82	An Interview with Harriet Bernstein Y-82
Devito, Carlo Y-94	Penzler, Otto Y-96	Islas, Arturo
De Vries, Peter. Y-82	Plimpton, George. Y-99	1938-1991 . . . . DLB-122
Dickey, James. Y-82	Potok, Chaim. Y-84	Issit, Debbie 1966- DLB-233
Donald, David Herbert Y-87	Powell, Padgett. Y-01	Ivanišević, Drago 1907-1981. . . . . DLB-181
Editors, Conversations with. Y-95	Prescott, Peter S. Y-86	Ivanov, Viacheslav Ivanovich 1866-1949 . . . . DLB-295
Ellroy, James Y-91	Rabe, David Y-91	Ivanov, Vsevolod Viacheslavovich
Fancher, Betsy Y-83	Rechy, John Y-82	1895-1963 .DLB-272
Faust, Irvin. Y-00	Reid, B. L. Y-83	Ivaska, Astrīde 1926- DLB-232
Fulton, Len. Y-86	Reynolds, Michael Y-95, 99	M. J. Ivers and Company DLB-49
Furst, Alan Y-01	Robinson, Derek Y-02	Iwaniuk, Wacław 1915- DLB-215
Garrett, George Y-83	Rollyson, Carl Y-97	Iwano Hōmei 1873-1920. . . . . DLB-180
Gelfman, Jane. Y-93	Rosset, Barney Y-02	Iwaszkiewicz, Jarosław 1894-1980. . . . . . DLB-215
Goldwater, Walter Y-93	Schlafly, Phyllis Y-82	Iyayi, Festus 1947- DLB-157
Gores, Joe Y-02	Schroeder, Patricia Y-99	Izumi Kyōka 1873-1939 . . . . DLB-180
Greenfield, George. Y-91	Schulberg, Budd. Y-81, 01	
Griffin, Bryan. Y-81	Scribner, Charles, III Y-94	# J
Groom, Winston Y-01	Sipper, Ralph Y-94	Jackmon, Marvin E. (see Marvin X)
Guilds, John Caldwell Y-92	Smith, Cork Y-95	Jacks, L. P. 1860-1955 . . . . DLB-135
Hamilton, Virginia. Y-01	Staley, Thomas F. Y-00	Jackson, Angela 1951- DLB-41
Hardin, James Y-92	Styron, William Y-80	Jackson, Charles 1903-1968 . . . . DLB-234
Harris, Mark Y-80	Talese, Nan Y-94	Jackson, Helen Hunt 1830-1885 . . . . .DLB-42, 47, 186, 189
Harrison, Jim Y-82	Thornton, John Y-94	Jackson, Holbrook 1874-1948. . . . . DLB-98
Hazzard, Shirley. Y-82	Toth, Susan Allen Y-86	Jackson, Laura Riding 1901-1991. . . . . . . DLB-48
Herrick, William Y-01	Tyler, Anne Y-82	Jackson, Shirley 1916-1965 . . . . DLB-6, 234; CDALB-1
Higgins, George V. Y-98	Vaughan, Samuel. Y-97	Jacob, Max 1876-1944 . . . . DLB-258
Hoban, Russell. Y-90	Von Ogtrop, Kristin. Y-92	Jacob, Naomi 1884?-1964. . . . . DLB-191
Holroyd, Michael. Y-99	Wallenstein, Barry Y-92	Jacob, Piers Anthony Dillingham
Horowitz, Glen Y-90	Weintraub, Stanley Y-82	(see Anthony, Piers)
Iggulden, John Y-01	Williams, J. Chamberlain. Y-84	Jacob, Violet 1863-1946 . . . . DLB-240
Jakes, John Y-83	Into the Past: William Jovanovich's Reflections in Publishing Y-02	Jacobi, Friedrich Heinrich 1743-1819 . . . . . DLB-94
Jenkinson, Edward B. Y-82	Ireland, David 1927- DLB-289	Jacobi, Johann Georg 1740-1841. . . . . DLB-97
Jenks, Tom. Y-86	The National Library of Ireland's	George W. Jacobs and Company DLB-49
Kaplan, Justin. Y-86	New James Joyce Manuscripts Y-02	Jacobs, Harriet 1813-1897. . . . . DLB-239
King, Florence Y-85	Irigaray, Luce 1930- DLB-296	Jacobs, Joseph 1854-1916 . . . . DLB-141
Klopfer, Donald S. Y-97	Irving, John 1942- DLB-6, 278; Y-82	Jacobs, W. W. 1863-1943. . . . . DLB-135
Krug, Judith Y-82	Irving, Washington 1783-1859 . . . . DLB-3, 11, 30, 59, 73, 74, 183, 186, 250; CDALB-2	The W. W. Jacobs Appreciation Society . . Y-98
Lamm, Donald Y-95		Jacobsen, J. P. 1847-1885 . . . . DLB-300
Laughlin, James Y-96		Jacobsen, Jørgen-Frantz 1900-1938. . . . . DLB-214
Lawrence, Starling Y-95	Irwin, Grace 1907- DLB-68	Jacobsen, Josephine 1908- DLB-244
Lindsay, Jack Y-84	Irwin, Will 1873-1948. . . . . DLB-25	Jacobsen, Rolf 1907-1994 . . . . DLB-297
Mailer, Norman Y-97	Isaksson, Ulla 1916-2000 . . . . DLB-257	Jacobson, Dan 1929- DLB-14, 207, 225
Manchester, William Y-85	Iser, Wolfgang 1926- DLB-242	Jacobson, Howard 1942- DLB-207
Max, D. T. Y-94	Isherwood, Christopher 1904-1986 . . . . .DLB-15, 195; Y-86	Jacques de Vitry circa 1160/1170-1240 . . . DLB-208
McCormack, Thomas Y-98		Jæger, Frank 1926-1977. . . . . DLB-214
McNamara, Katherine Y-97	The Christopher Isherwood Archive, The Huntington Library Y-99	William Jaggard [publishing house] DLB-170
Mellen, Joan. Y-94	Ishiguro, Kazuo 1954- DLB-194	Jahier, Piero 1884-1966 . . . . DLB-114, 264
Menaker, Daniel Y-97	Ishikawa Jun 1899-1987 . . . . DLB-182	Jahnn, Hans Henny 1894-1959 . . . . . DLB-56, 124

Jaimes, Freyre, Ricardo 1866?-1933......DLB-283
Jakes, John 1932- DLB-278; Y-83
    Tribute to John Gardner.............. Y-82
    Tribute to John D. MacDonald......... Y-86
Jakobína Johnson (Jakobína Sigurbjarnardóttir)
    1883-1977 ....DLB-293
Jakobson, Roman 1896-1982..........DLB-242
James, Alice 1848-1892 ....DLB-221
James, C. L. R. 1901-1989..............DLB-125
James, George P. R. 1801-1860..........DLB-116
James, Henry 1843-1916
    ......DLB-12, 71, 74, 189; DS-13; CDALB-3
    "The Future of the Novel" (1899).....DLB-18
    "The Novel in [Robert Browning's]
      'The Ring and the Book'"
      (1912) DLB-32
James, John circa 1633-1729...............DLB-24
James, M. R. 1862-1936..........DLB-156, 201
James, Naomi 1949- DLB-204
James, P. D. (Phyllis Dorothy James White)
    1920- DLB-87, 276; DS-17; CDBLB-8
    Tribute to Charles Scribner Jr. Y-95
James, Thomas 1572?-1629 ....DLB-213
U. P. James [publishing house] DLB-49
James, Will 1892-1942................ DS-16
James, William 1842-1910............DLB-270
James VI of Scotland, I of England
    1566-1625 .... DLB-151, 172
    *Ane Schort Treatise Conteining Some Reulis
    and Cautelis to Be Obseruit and
    Eschewit in Scottis Poesi* (1584) DLB-172
Jameson, Anna 1794-1860 ....DLB-99, 166
Jameson, Fredric 1934- DLB-67
Jameson, J. Franklin 1859-1937 ....DLB-17
Jameson, Storm 1891-1986 ....DLB-36
Jančar, Drago 1948- DLB-181
Janés, Clara 1940- DLB-134
Janevski, Slavko 1920- DLB-181; CDWLB-4
Janowitz, Tama 1957- DLB-292
Jansson, Tove 1914-2001................DLB-257
Janvier, Thomas 1849-1913............DLB-202
Japan
    "The Development of Meiji Japan"...DLB-180
    "Encounter with the West"..........DLB-180
Japanese Literature
    Letter from Japan Y-94, 98
    Medieval Travel Diaries DLB-203
    Surveys: 1987-1995 ....DLB-182
Jaramillo, Cleofas M. 1878-1956 ....DLB-122
Jaramillo Levi, Enrique 1944- DLB-290
Jarman, Mark 1952- DLB-120, 282
Jarrell, Randall
    1914-1965 ....DLB-48, 52; CDALB-1
Jarrold and Sons....................DLB-106
Jarry, Alfred 1873-1907 ....DLB-192, 258
Jarves, James Jackson 1818-1888 ....DLB-189
Jasmin, Claude 1930- DLB-60
Jaunsudrabiņš, Jānis 1877-1962 ....DLB-220

Jay, John 1745-1829 ....DLB-31
Jean de Garlande (see John of Garland)
Jefferies, Richard 1848-1887 ....DLB-98, 141
    The Richard Jefferies Society Y-98
Jeffers, Lance 1919-1985 ....DLB-41
Jeffers, Robinson
    1887-1962 ....DLB-45, 212; CDALB-4
Jefferson, Thomas
    1743-1826 ....DLB-31, 183; CDALB-2
Jégé 1866-1940.....................DLB-215
Jelinek, Elfriede 1946- DLB-85
Jellicoe, Ann 1927- DLB-13, 233
Jemison, Mary circa 1742-1833 ....DLB-239
Jenkins, Dan 1929- DLB-241
Jenkins, Elizabeth 1905- DLB-155
Jenkins, Robin 1912- DLB-14, 271
Jenkins, William Fitzgerald (see Leinster, Murray)
Herbert Jenkins Limited DLB-112
Jennings, Elizabeth 1926- DLB-27
Jens, Walter 1923- DLB-69
Jensen, Axel 1932-2003 ....DLB-297
Jensen, Johannes V. 1873-1950 ....DLB-214
Jensen, Merrill 1905-1980 ....DLB-17
Jensen, Thit 1876-1957.................DLB-214
Jephson, Robert 1736-1803 ....DLB-89
Jerome, Jerome K. 1859-1927 .... DLB-10, 34, 135
    The Jerome K. Jerome Society Y-98
Jerome, Judson 1927-1991 ....DLB-105
    "Reflections: After a Tornado" DLB-105
Jerrold, Douglas 1803-1857 ....DLB-158, 159
Jersild, Per Christian 1935- DLB-257
Jesse, F. Tennyson 1888-1958 ....DLB-77
Jewel, John 1522-1571 ....DLB-236
John P. Jewett and Company............DLB-49
Jewett, Sarah Orne 1849-1909 .... DLB-12, 74, 221
The Jewish Publication Society DLB-49
    Studies in American Jewish Literature Y-02
Jewitt, John Rodgers 1783-1821 ....DLB-99
Jewsbury, Geraldine 1812-1880 ....DLB-21
Jewsbury, Maria Jane 1800-1833 ....DLB-199
Jhabvala, Ruth Prawer 1927- DLB-139, 194
Jiménez, Juan Ramón 1881-1958........DLB-134
Jin, Ha 1956- DLB-244, 292
Joans, Ted 1928- DLB-16, 41
Jōha 1525-1602 ....DLB-203
Jóhann Sigurjónsson 1880-1919 ....DLB-293
Jóhannes úr Kötlum 1899-1972 ....DLB-293
Johannis de Garlandia (see John of Garland)
John, Errol 1924-1988 ....DLB-233
John, Eugenie (see Marlitt, E.)
John of Dumbleton
    circa 1310-circa 1349..............DLB-115
John of Garland (Jean de Garlande,
    Johannis de Garlandia)
    circa 1195-circa 1272 ....DLB-208
The John Reed Clubs DLB-303

Johns, Captain W. E. 1893-1968........DLB-160
Johnson, Mrs. A. E. ca. 1858-1922 ....DLB-221
Johnson, Amelia (see Johnson, Mrs. A. E.)
Johnson, B. S. 1933-1973 ....DLB-14, 40
Johnson, Charles 1679-1748.............DLB-84
Johnson, Charles 1948- DLB-33, 278
Johnson, Charles S. 1893-1956 ......DLB-51, 91
Johnson, Colin (Mudrooroo) 1938- DLB-289
Johnson, Denis 1949- DLB-120
Johnson, Diane 1934- Y-80
Johnson, Dorothy M. 1905–1984 ....DLB-206
Johnson, E. Pauline (Tekahionwake)
    1861-1913 ....DLB-175
Johnson, Edgar 1901-1995..............DLB-103
Johnson, Edward 1598-1672 ....DLB-24
Johnson, Eyvind 1900-1976 ....DLB-259
Johnson, Fenton 1888-1958 ....DLB-45, 50
Johnson, Georgia Douglas
    1877?-1966 ....DLB-51, 249
Johnson, Gerald W. 1890-1980 ....DLB-29
Johnson, Greg 1953- DLB-234
Johnson, Helene 1907-1995 ....DLB-51
Jacob Johnson and Company DLB-49
Johnson, James Weldon
    1871-1938 ....DLB-51; CDALB-4
Johnson, John H. 1918- DLB-137
    "Backstage," Statement From the
    Initial Issue of *Ebony*
    (November 1945..............DLB-137
Johnson, Joseph [publishing house] DLB-154
Johnson, Linton Kwesi 1952- DLB-157
Johnson, Lionel 1867-1902..............DLB-19
Johnson, Nunnally 1897-1977 ....DLB-26
Johnson, Owen 1878-1952...............Y-87
Johnson, Pamela Hansford 1912-1981.....DLB-15
Johnson, Pauline 1861-1913 ....DLB-92
Johnson, Ronald 1935-1998.............DLB-169
Johnson, Samuel 1696-1772 ....DLB-24; CDBLB-2
Johnson, Samuel
    1709-1784 ....DLB-39, 95, 104, 142, 213
    Rambler, no. 4 (1750) [excerpt]........DLB-39
The BBC Four Samuel Johnson Prize
    for Non-fiction..................... Y-02
Johnson, Samuel 1822-1882..........DLB-1, 243
Johnson, Susanna 1730-1810 ....DLB-200
Johnson, Terry 1955- DLB-233
Johnson, Uwe 1934-1984..... DLB-75; CDWLB-2
Benjamin Johnson [publishing house] DLB-49
Benjamin, Jacob, and Robert Johnson
    [publishing house]................DLB-49
Johnston, Annie Fellows 1863-1931.......DLB-42
Johnston, Basil H. 1929- DLB-60
Johnston, David Claypole 1798?-1865.....DLB-188
Johnston, Denis 1901-1984 ....DLB-10
Johnston, Ellen 1835-1873 ....DLB-199
Johnston, George 1912-1970 ....DLB-260
Johnston, George 1913- DLB-88

Johnston, Sir Harry 1858-1927 . . . . DLB-174	Michael Joseph Limited DLB-112	Junqueiro, Abílio Manuel Guerra 1850-1923 . . . . DLB-287
Johnston, Jennifer 1930- DLB-14	Josephson, Matthew 1899-1978 . . . . DLB-4	Justice, Donald 1925- Y-83
Johnston, Mary 1870-1936 . . . . DLB-9	Josephus, Flavius 37-100 . . . . DLB-176	Juvenal circa A.D. 60-circa A.D. 130 . . . . DLB-211; CDWLB-1
Johnston, Richard Malcolm 1822-1898 . . . DLB-74	Josephy, Alvin M., Jr. Tribute to Alfred A. Knopf Y-84	The Juvenile Library (see M. J. Godwin and Company)
Johnstone, Charles 1719?-1800? DLB-39	Josiah Allen's Wife (see Holley, Marietta)	
Johst, Hanns 1890-1978 . . . . DLB-124	Josipovici, Gabriel 1940- DLB-14	**K**
Jökull Jakobsson 1933-1978 . . . . DLB-293	Josselyn, John ?-1675 . . . . DLB-24	
Jolas, Eugene 1894-1952 . . . . DLB-4, 45	Joudry, Patricia 1921-2000 . . . . DLB-88	Kacew, Romain (see Gary, Romain)
Jón Stefán Sveinsson or Svensson (see Nonni)	Jouve, Pierre Jean 1887-1976 . . . . DLB-258	Kafka, Franz 1883-1924 . . . . . DLB-81; CDWLB-2
Jón Trausti (Guðmundur Magnússon) 1873-1918 . . . . DLB-293	Jovanovich, William 1920-2001 . . . . Y-01	Kahn, Gus 1886-1941 . . . . DLB-265
Jón úr Vör (Jón Jónsson) 1917-2000 . . . . . DLB-293	Into the Past: William Jovanovich's Reflections on Publishing Y-02	Kahn, Roger 1927- DLB-171
Jónas Hallgrímsson 1807-1845 . . . . DLB-293	[Response to Ken Auletta] Y-97	Kaikō Takeshi 1939-1989 . . . . DLB-182
Jones, Alice C. 1853-1933 . . . . DLB-92	*The Temper of the West:* William Jovanovich Y-02	Káinn (Kristján Níels Jónsson/Kristjan Niels Julius) 1860-1936 . . . . DLB-293
Jones, Charles C., Jr. 1831-1893 . . . . DLB-30	Tribute to Charles Scribner Jr. Y-95	Kaiser, Georg 1878-1945 . . . . DLB-124; CDWLB-2
Jones, D. G. 1929- DLB-53	Jovine, Francesco 1902-1950 . . . . DLB-264	*Kaiserchronik* circa 1147 . . . . DLB-148
Jones, David 1895-1974 . . . . DLB-20, 100; CDBLB-7	Jovine, Giuseppe 1922- DLB-128	Kaleb, Vjekoslav 1905- DLB-181
Jones, Diana Wynne 1934- DLB-161	Joyaux, Philippe (see Sollers, Philippe)	Kalechofsky, Roberta 1931- DLB-28
Jones, Ebenezer 1820-1860 . . . . DLB-32	Joyce, Adrien (see Eastman, Carol)	Kaler, James Otis 1848-1912 . . . . DLB-12, 42
Jones, Ernest 1819-1868 . . . . DLB-32	Joyce, James 1882-1941 . . . . DLB-10, 19, 36, 162, 247; CDBLB-6	Kalmar, Bert 1884-1947 . . . . DLB-265
Jones, Gayl 1949- DLB-33, 278	Danis Rose and the Rendering of *Ulysses* . . . Y-97	Kamensky, Vasilii Vasil'evich 1884-1961 . . . . DLB-295
Jones, George 1800-1870 . . . . DLB-183	James Joyce Centenary: Dublin, 1982 . . . . Y-82	Kames, Henry Home, Lord 1696-1782 . . . . DLB-31, 104
Jones, Glyn 1905-1995 . . . . DLB-15	James Joyce Conference Y-85	Kamo no Chōmei (Kamo no Nagaakira) 1153 or 1155-1216 . . . . DLB-203
Jones, Gwyn 1907- DLB-15, 139	A Joyce (Con)Text: Danis Rose and the Remaking of *Ulysses* Y-97	Kamo no Nagaakira (see Kamo no Chōmei)
Jones, Henry Arthur 1851-1929 . . . . DLB-10	The National Library of Ireland's New James Joyce Manuscripts Y-02	Kampmann, Christian 1939-1988 . . . . . . DLB-214
Jones, Hugh circa 1692-1760 . . . . DLB-24	The New *Ulysses* Y-84	Kandel, Lenore 1932- DLB-16
Jones, James 1921-1977 . . . . DLB-2, 143; DS-17	Public Domain and the Violation of Texts Y-97	Kanin, Garson 1912-1999 . . . . DLB-7
James Jones Papers in the Handy Writers' Colony Collection at the University of Illinois at Springfield Y-98	The Quinn Draft of James Joyce's Circe Manuscript Y-00	A Tribute (to Marc Connelly) Y-80
		Kaniuk, Yoram 1930- DLB-299
The James Jones Society Y-92	Stephen Joyce's Letter to the Editor of *The Irish Times* Y-97	Kant, Hermann 1926- DLB-75
Jones, Jenkin Lloyd 1911- DLB-127	*Ulysses,* Reader's Edition: First Reactions . . Y-97	Kant, Immanuel 1724-1804 . . . . DLB-94
Jones, John Beauchamp 1810-1866 . . . . . DLB-202	We See the Editor at Work Y-97	Kantemir, Antiokh Dmitrievich 1708-1744 . . . . DLB-150
Jones, Joseph, Major (see Thompson, William Tappan)	Whose *Ulysses?* The Function of Editing . . Y-97	Kantor, MacKinlay 1904-1977 . . . . DLB-9, 102
Jones, LeRoi (see Baraka, Amiri)	Jozsef, Attila 1905-1937 . . . . . DLB-215; CDWLB-4	Kanze Kōjirō Nobumitsu 1435-1516 . . . DLB-203
Jones, Lewis 1897-1939 . . . . DLB-15	Juarroz, Roberto 1925-1995 . . . . DLB-283	Kanze Motokiyo (see Zeimi)
Jones, Madison 1925- DLB-152	Orange Judd Publishing Company DLB-49	Kaplan, Fred 1937- DLB-111
Jones, Marie 1951- DLB-233	Judd, Sylvester 1813-1853 . . . . DLB-1, 243	Kaplan, Johanna 1942- DLB-28
Jones, Preston 1936-1979 . . . . DLB-7	*Judith* circa 930 . . . . DLB-146	Kaplan, Justin 1925- DLB-111; Y-86
Jones, Rodney 1950- DLB-120	Juel-Hansen, Erna 1845-1922 . . . . DLB-300	Kaplinski, Jaan 1941- DLB-232
Jones, Thom 1945- DLB-244	Julian of Norwich 1342-circa 1420 . . . . . DLB-1146	Kapnist, Vasilii Vasilevich 1758?-1823 . . . DLB-150
Jones, Sir William 1746-1794 . . . . DLB-109	Julius Caesar 100 B.C.-44 B.C. DLB-211; CDWLB-1	Karadžić, Vuk Stefanović 1787-1864 . . . . DLB-147; CDWLB-4
Jones, William Alfred 1817-1900 . . . . DLB-59		
Jones's Publishing House DLB-49	June, Jennie (see Croly, Jane Cunningham)	Karamzin, Nikolai Mikhailovich 1766-1826 . . . . DLB-150
Jong, Erica 1942- DLB-2, 5, 28, 152	Jung, Carl Gustav 1875-1961 . . . . DLB-296	Karinthy, Frigyes 1887-1938 . . . . DLB-215
Jonke, Gert F. 1946- DLB-85	Jung, Franz 1888-1963 . . . . DLB-118	Karmel, Ilona 1925-2000 . . . . DLB-299
Jonson, Ben 1572?-1637 . . . . DLB-62, 121; CDBLB-1	Jünger, Ernst 1895- DLB-56; CDWLB-2	Karsch, Anna Louisa 1722-1791 . . . . DLB-97
Johsson, Tor 1916-1951 . . . . DLB-297	*Der jüngere Titurel* circa 1275 . . . . DLB-138	Kasack, Hermann 1896-1966 . . . . DLB-69
Jordan, June 1936- DLB-38	Jung-Stilling, Johann Heinrich 1740-1817 . . . . DLB-94	Kasai Zenzō 1887-1927 . . . . DLB-180
Jorgensen, Johannes 1866-1956 . . . . DLB-300		Kaschnitz, Marie Luise 1901-1974 . . . . . . DLB-69
Joseph, Jenny 1932- DLB-40		
Joseph and George Y-99		Kassák, Lajos 1887-1967 . . . . DLB-215

Kaštelan, Jure 1919-1990 . . . . DLB-147	Kelly, Hugh 1739-1777. . . . . .DLB-89	The Jack Kerouac Revival Y-95
Kästner, Erich 1899-1974. . . . . DLB-56	Kelly, Piet and Company. DLB-49	"Re-meeting of Old Friends": The Jack Kerouac Conference Y-82
Kataev, Evgenii Petrovich (see Il'f, Il'ia and Petrov, Evgenii)	Kelly, Robert 1935- DLB-5, 130, 165	Statement of Correction to "The Jack Kerouac Revival" Y-96
Kataev, Valentin Petrovich 1897-1986. . . . DLB-272	Kelman, James 1946- DLB-194	Kerouac, Jan 1952-1996. . . . . DLB-16
Katenin, Pavel Aleksandrovich 1792-1853 . . . . .DLB-205	Kelmscott Press DLB-112	Charles H. Kerr and Company DLB-49
Kattan, Naïm 1928- DLB-53	Kelton, Elmer 1926- DLB-256	Kerr, Orpheus C. (see Newell, Robert Henry)
Katz, Steve 1935- Y-83	Kemble, E. W. 1861-1933 . . . . DLB-188	Kersh, Gerald 1911-1968. . . . . DLB-255
Ka-Tzetnik 135633 (Yehiel Dinur) 1909-2001 . . . . DLB-299	Kemble, Fanny 1809-1893. . . . . DLB-32	Kertész, Imre DLB-299; Y-02
Kauffman, Janet 1945- DLB-218; Y-86	Kemelman, Harry 1908-1996 . . . . DLB-28	Kesey, Ken 1935-2001 . . . . .DLB-2, 16, 206; CDALB-6
Kauffmann, Samuel 1898-1971 . . . . DLB-127	Kempe, Margery circa 1373-1438 . . . . . . .DLB-146	Kessel, Joseph 1898-1979 . . . . DLB-72
Kaufman, Bob 1925-1986 . . . . DLB-16, 41	Kempner, Friederike 1836-1904 . . . . .DLB-129	Kessel, Martin 1901-1990 . . . . DLB-56
Kaufman, George S. 1889-1961. . . . . .DLB-7	Kempowski, Walter 1929- DLB-75	Kesten, Hermann 1900-1996 . . . . DLB-56
Kaufmann, Walter 1921-1980 . . . . DLB-279	Kenan, Randall 1963- DLB-292	Keun, Irmgard 1905-1982 . . . . DLB-69
Kavan, Anna (Helen Woods Ferguson Edmonds) 1901-1968 . . . . DLB-255	Claude Kendall [publishing company]. DLB-46	Key, Ellen 1849-1926 . . . . .DLB-259
Kavanagh, P. J. 1931- DLB-40	Kendall, Henry 1839-1882 . . . . DLB-230	Key and Biddle DLB-49
Kavanagh, Patrick 1904-1967 . . . . DLB-15, 20	Kendall, May 1861-1943 . . . . DLB-240	Keneally, Thomas 1935- DLB-289, 299	Keynes, Sir Geoffrey 1887-1982. . . . . .DLB-201
Kaverin, Veniamin Aleksandrovich (Veniamin Aleksandrovich Zil'ber) 1902-1989 . . . . .DLB-272	Kendell, George 1809-1867 . . . . DLB-43	Keynes, John Maynard 1883-1946 . . . . . . DS-10
	Keneally, Thomas 1935- DLB-289, 299	Keyserling, Eduard von 1855-1918 . . . . . . .DLB-66
Kawabata Yasunari 1899-1972. . . . . DLB-180	Kenedy, P. J., and Sons DLB-49	Khan, Ismith 1925-2002 . . . . .DLB-125
Kay, Guy Gavriel 1954- DLB-251	Kenkō circa 1283-circa 1352 . . . . DLB-203	Kharitonov, Evgenii Vladimirovich 1941-1981 . . . . .DLB-285
Kaye-Smith, Sheila 1887-1956 . . . . DLB-36	Kenna, Peter 1930-1987. . . . . DLB-289	
Kazakov, Iurii Pavlovich 1927-1982. . . . . . DLB-302	Kennan, George 1845-1924. . . . . .DLB-189	Kharitonov, Mark Sergeevich 1937- DLB-285
Kazin, Alfred 1915-1998 . . . . DLB-67	Kennedy, A. L. 1965- DLB-271	Khaytov, Nikolay 1919- DLB-181
Keane, John B. 1928- DLB-13	Kennedy, Adrienne 1931- DLB-38	Khemnitser, Ivan Ivanovich 1745-1784 . . . . DLB-150
Keary, Annie 1825-1879 . . . . DLB-163	Kennedy, John Pendleton 1795-1870 . . . DLB-3, 248	
Keary, Eliza 1827-1918. . . . . DLB-240	Kennedy, Leo 1907-2000 . . . . DLB-88	Kheraskov, Mikhail Matveevich 1733-1807 . . . . DLB-150
Keating, H. R. F. 1926- DLB-87	Kennedy, Margaret 1896-1967 . . . . DLB-36	
Keatley, Charlotte 1960- DLB-245	Kennedy, Patrick 1801-1873 . . . . DLB-159	Khlebnikov, Velimir 1885-1922 . . . . DLB-295
Keats, Ezra Jack 1916-1983 . . . . DLB-61	Kennedy, Richard S. 1920- DLB-111; Y-02	Khomiakov, Aleksei Stepanovich 1804-1860 . . . . DLB-205
Keats, John 1795-1821 . . . .DLB-96, 110; CDBLB-3	Kennedy, William 1928- DLB-143; Y-85	
Keble, John 1792-1866. . . . . .DLB-32, 55	Kennedy, X. J. 1929- DLB-5	Khristov, Boris 1945- DLB-181
Keckley, Elizabeth 1818?-1907. . . . . DLB-239	Tribute to John Ciardi Y-86	Khvoshchinskaia, Nadezhda Dmitrievna 1824-1889 . . . . DLB-238
Keeble, John 1944- Y-83	Kennelly, Brendan 1936- DLB-40	
Keeffe, Barrie 1945- DLB-13, 245	Kenner, Hugh 1923- DLB-67	Khvostov, Dmitrii Ivanovich 1757-1835. . . . . DLB-150
Keeley, James 1867-1934 . . . . DLB-25	Tribute to Cleanth Brooks Y-80	
W. B. Keen, Cooke and Company DLB-49	Mitchell Kennerley [publishing house]. DLB-46	Kibirov, Timur Iur'evich (Timur Iur'evich Zapoev) 1955- DLB-285
The Mystery of Carolyn Keene. Y-02	Kenny, Maurice 1929- DLB-175	
Kefala, Antigone 1935- DLB-289	Kent, Frank R. 1877-1958 . . . . DLB-29	Kidd, Adam 1802?-1831 . . . . DLB-99
Keillor, Garrison 1942- Y-87	Kenyon, Jane 1947-1995 . . . . DLB-120	William Kidd [publishing house]. DLB-106
Keith, Marian (Mary Esther MacGregor) 1874?-1961 . . . . DLB-92	Kenzheev, Bakhyt Shkurullaevich 1950- DLB-285	Kidde, Harald 1878-1918. . . . . .DLB-300
		Kidder, Tracy 1945- DLB-185
Keller, Gary D. 1943- DLB-82	Keough, Hugh Edmund 1864-1912. . . . . . DLB-171	Kiely, Benedict 1919- DLB-15
Keller, Gottfried 1819-1890 . . . . DLB-129; CDWLB-2	Keppler and Schwartzmann. DLB-49	Kieran, John 1892-1981. . . . . DLB-171
	Ker, John, third Duke of Roxburghe 1740-1804 . . . . DLB-213	Kierkegaard, Søren 1813-1855. . . . . .DLB-300
Keller, Helen 1880-1968 . . . . DLB-303		Kies, Marietta 1853-1899. . . . . DLB-270
Kelley, Edith Summers 1884-1956. . . . . .DLB-9	Ker, N. R. 1908-1982. . . . . DLB-201	Kiggins and Kellogg. DLB-49
Kelley, Emma Dunham ?-? DLB-221	Kerlan, Irvin 1912-1963. . . . . DLB-187	Kiley, Jed 1889-1962 .DLB-4
Kelley, Florence 1859-1932 . . . . .DLB-303	Kermode, Frank 1919- DLB-242	Kilgore, Bernard 1908-1967. . . . . DLB-127
Kelley, William Melvin 1937- DLB-33	Kern, Jerome 1885-1945 . . . . DLB-187	Kilian, Crawford 1941- DLB-251
Kellogg, Ansel Nash 1832-1886 . . . . DLB-23	Kernaghan, Eileen 1939- DLB-251	Killens, John Oliver 1916-1987 . . . . DLB-33
Kellogg, Steven 1941- DLB-61	Kerner, Justinus 1786-1862 . . . . DLB-90	Tribute to Julian Mayfield. Y-84
Kelly, George E. 1887-1974 . . . . DLB-7, 249	Kerouac, Jack 1922-1969 . . . DLB-2, 16, 237; DS-3; CDALB-1	Killigrew, Anne 1660-1685 . . . . .DLB-131
		Killigrew, Thomas 1612-1683 . . . . DLB-58
	Auction of Jack Kerouac's *On the Road* Scroll Y-01	Kilmer, Joyce 1886-1918 . . . . DLB-45

Kilroy, Thomas 1934- DLB-233
Kilwardby, Robert circa 1215-1279 ..... DLB-115
Kilworth, Garry 1941- DLB-261
Kim, Anatolii Andreevich 1939- DLB-285
Kimball, Richard Burleigh 1816-1892 ... DLB-202
Kincaid, Jamaica 1949-
.... DLB-157, 227; CDALB-7; CDWLB-3
Kinck, Hans Ernst 1865-1926.......... DLB-297
King, Charles 1844-1933 .... DLB-186
King, Clarence 1842-1901 .... DLB-12
King, Florence 1936- Y-85
King, Francis 1923- DLB-15, 139
King, Grace 1852-1932.......... DLB-12, 78
King, Harriet Hamilton 1840-1920...... DLB-199
King, Henry 1592-1669 .... DLB-126
Solomon King [publishing house]........ DLB-49
King, Stephen 1947- DLB-143; Y-80
King, Susan Petigru 1824-1875......... DLB-239
King, Thomas 1943- DLB-175
King, Woodie, Jr. 1937- DLB-38
Kinglake, Alexander William
  1809-1891 .... DLB-55, 166
Kingo, Thomas 1634-1703 .... DLB-300
Kingsbury, Donald 1929- DLB-251
Kingsley, Charles
  1819-1875........DLB-21, 32, 163, 178, 190
Kingsley, Henry 1830-1876 .... DLB-21, 230
Kingsley, Mary Henrietta 1862-1900 .....DLB-174
Kingsley, Sidney 1906-1995 .... DLB-7
Kingsmill, Hugh 1889-1949 .... DLB-149
Kingsolver, Barbara
  1955- DLB-206; CDALB-7
Kingston, Maxine Hong
  1940- DLB-173, 212; Y-80; CDALB-7
Kingston, William Henry Giles
  1814-1880 .... DLB-163
Kinnan, Mary Lewis 1763-1848 .... DLB-200
Kinnell, Galway 1927- DLB-5; Y-87
Kinsella, Thomas 1928- DLB-27
Kipling, Rudyard 1865-1936
  .... DLB-19, 34, 141, 156; CDBLB-5
Kipphardt, Heinar 1922-1982.......... DLB-124
Kirby, William 1817-1906............. DLB-99
Kircher, Athanasius 1602-1680........ DLB-164
Kireevsky, Ivan Vasil'evich 1806-1856... DLB-198
Kireevsky, Petr Vasil'evich 1808-1856... DLB-205
Kirk, Hans 1898-1962 .... DLB-214
Kirk, John Foster 1824-1904........... DLB-79
Kirkconnell, Watson 1895-1977 .... DLB-68
Kirkland, Caroline M.
  1801-1864 ....DLB-3, 73, 74, 250; DS-13
Kirkland, Joseph 1830-1893 .... DLB-12
Francis Kirkman [publishing house]......DLB-170
Kirkpatrick, Clayton 1915- DLB-127
Kirkup, James 1918- DLB-27
Kirouac, Conrad (see Marie-Victorin, Frère)
Kirsch, Sarah 1935- DLB-75

Kirst, Hans Hellmut 1914-1989 .... DLB-69
Kiš, Danilo 1935-1989 ..... DLB-181; CDWLB-4
Kita Morio 1927- DLB-182
Kitcat, Mabel Greenhow 1859-1922..... DLB-135
Kitchin, C. H. B. 1895-1967........... DLB-77
Kittredge, William 1932- DLB-212, 244
Kiukhel'beker, Vil'gel'm Karlovich
  1797-1846 .... DLB-205
Kizer, Carolyn 1925- DLB-5, 169
Kjaerstad, Jan 1953- DLB-297
Klabund 1890-1928 .... DLB-66
Klaj, Johann 1616-1656 .... DLB-164
Klappert, Peter 1942- DLB-5
Klass, Philip (see Tenn, William)
Klein, A. M. 1909-1972............. DLB-68
Kleist, Ewald von 1715-1759............ DLB-97
Kleist, Heinrich von
  1777-1811 .... DLB-90; CDWLB-2
Klíma, Ivan 1931- DLB-232; CDWLB-4
Klimentev, Andrei Platonovic
  (see Platonov, Andrei Platonovich)
Klinger, Friedrich Maximilian
  1752-1831 .... DLB-94
Kliuev, Nikolai Alekseevich 1884-1937 .. DLB-295
Kliushnikov, Viktor Petrovich
  1841-1892 .... DLB-238
Klopfer, Donald S.
  Impressions of William Faulkner........ Y-97
  Oral History Interview with Donald
    S. Klopfer Y-97
  Tribute to Alfred A. Knopf Y-84
Klopstock, Friedrich Gottlieb
  1724-1803 .... DLB-97
Klopstock, Meta 1728-1758............ DLB-97
Kluge, Alexander 1932- DLB-75
Kluge, P. F. 1942- Y-02
Knapp, Joseph Palmer 1864-1951........ DLB-91
Knapp, Samuel Lorenzo 1783-1838 ..... DLB-59
J. J. and P. Knapton [publishing house] .. DLB-154
Kniazhnin, Iakov Borisovich
  1740-1791 .... DLB-150
Knickerbocker, Diedrich (see Irving, Washington)
Knigge, Adolph Franz Friedrich Ludwig,
  Freiherr von 1752-1796 .... DLB-94
Charles Knight and Company DLB-106
Knight, Damon 1922-2002............. DLB-8
Knight, Etheridge 1931-1992 .... DLB-41
Knight, John S. 1894-1981 .... DLB-29
Knight, Sarah Kemble 1666-1727 .... DLB-24, 200
Knight-Bruce, G. W. H. 1852-1896 .....DLB-174
Knister, Raymond 1899-1932.......... DLB-68
Knoblock, Edward 1874-1945 .... DLB-10
Knopf, Alfred A. 1892-1984.............. Y-84
  Knopf to Hammett: The Editoral
    Correspondence Y-00
Alfred A. Knopf [publishing house] DLB-46
Knorr von Rosenroth, Christian
  1636-1689 .... DLB-168

Knowles, John 1926- DLB-6; CDALB-6
Knox, Frank 1874-1944 .... DLB-29
Knox, John circa 1514-1572 .... DLB-132
Knox, John Armoy 1850-1906.......... DLB-23
Knox, Lucy 1845-1884................ DLB-240
Knox, Ronald Arbuthnott 1888-1957..... DLB-77
Knox, Thomas Wallace 1835-1896 ..... DLB-189
Knudsen, Jakob 1858-1917............ DLB-300
Kobayashi Takiji 1903-1933........... DLB-180
Kober, Arthur 1900-1975 .... DLB-11
Kobiakova, Aleksandra Petrovna
  1823-1892 .... DLB-238
Kocbek, Edvard 1904-1981 .. DLB-147; CDWLB-4
Koch, C. J. 1932- DLB-289
Koch, Howard 1902-1995 .... DLB-26
Koch, Kenneth 1925-2002 .... DLB-5
Kōda Rohan 1867-1947 .... DLB-180
Koehler, Ted 1894-1973............. DLB-265
Koenigsberg, Moses 1879-1945 .... DLB-25
Koeppen, Wolfgang 1906-1996 .... DLB-69
Koertge, Ronald 1940- DLB-105
Koestler, Arthur 1905-1983 ...... Y-83; CDBLB-7
Kohn, John S. Van E. 1906-1976 ....DLB-187
Kokhanovskaia
  (see Sokhanskaia, Nadezhda Stepanova)
Kokoschka, Oskar 1886-1980 .... DLB-124
Kolb, Annette 1870-1967 .... DLB-66
Kolbenheyer, Erwin Guido
  1878-1962................... DLB-66, 124
Kolleritsch, Alfred 1931- DLB-85
Kolodny, Annette 1941- DLB-67
Kol'tsov, Aleksei Vasil'evich
  1809-1842 .... DLB-205
Komarov, Matvei circa 1730-1812 ...... DLB-150
Komroff, Manuel 1890-1974........... DLB-4
Komunyakaa, Yusef 1947- DLB-120
Kondoleon, Harry 1955-1994 .... DLB-266
Koneski, Blaže 1921-1993....DLB-181; CDWLB-4
Konigsburg, E. L. 1930- DLB-52
Konparu Zenchiku 1405-1468? DLB-203
Konrád, György 1933- DLB-232; CDWLB-4
Konrad von Würzburg
  circa 1230-1287 .... DLB-138
Konstantinov, Aleko 1863-1897........DLB-147
Konwicki, Tadeusz 1926- DLB-232
Koontz, Dean 1945- DLB-292
Kooser, Ted 1939- DLB-105
Kopit, Arthur 1937- DLB-7
Kops, Bernard 1926?- DLB-13
Kornbluth, C. M. 1923-1958 .... DLB-8
Körner, Theodor 1791-1813............ DLB-90
Kornfeld, Paul 1889-1942 .... DLB-118
Korolenko, Vladimir Galaktionovich
  1853-1921 ....DLB-277
Kosinski, Jerzy 1933-1991 ......DLB-2, 299; Y-82
Kosmač, Ciril 1910-1980 .... DLB-181

Kosovel, Srečko 1904-1926 . . . . DLB-147
Kostrov, Ermil Ivanovich 1755-1796 . . . . . DLB-150
Kotzebue, August von 1761-1819 . . . . DLB-94
Kotzwinkle, William 1938- DLB-173
Kovačić, Ante 1854-1889 . . . . DLB-147
Kovalevskaia, Sof'ia Vasil'evna
   1850-1891 . . . . DLB-277
Kovič, Kajetan 1931- DLB-181
Kozlov, Ivan Ivanovich 1779-1840 . . . . . . DLB-205
Kracauer, Siegfried 1889-1966 . . . . DLB-296
Kraf, Elaine 1946- Y-81
Kramer, Jane 1938- DLB-185
Kramer, Larry 1935- DLB-249
Kramer, Mark 1944- DLB-185
Kranjčević, Silvije Strahimir 1865-1908 . . . DLB-147
Krasko, Ivan 1876-1958 . . . . DLB-215
Krasna, Norman 1909-1984 . . . . DLB-26
Kraus, Hans Peter 1907-1988 . . . . DLB-187
Kraus, Karl 1874-1936 . . . . DLB-118
Krause, Herbert 1905-1976 . . . . DLB-256
Krauss, Ruth 1911-1993 . . . . DLB-52
Kreisel, Henry 1922-1991 . . . . DLB-88
Krestovsky V.
   (see Khvoshchinskaia, Nadezhda Dmitrievna)
Krestovsky, Vsevolod Vladimirovich
   1839-1895 . . . . DLB-238
Kreuder, Ernst 1903-1972 . . . . DLB-69
Krėvė-Mickevičius, Vincas 1882-1954 . . . . DLB-220
Kreymborg, Alfred 1883-1966 . . . . DLB-4, 54
Krieger, Murray 1923- DLB-67
Krim, Seymour 1922-1989 . . . . DLB-16
Kripke, Saul 1940- DLB-279
Kristensen, Tom 1893-1974 . . . . DLB-214
Kristeva, Julia 1941- DLB-242
Kristján Níels Jónsson/Kristjan Niels Julius
   (see Káinn)
Kritzer, Hyman W. 1918-2002 . . . . Y-02
Krivulin, Viktor Borisovich 1944-2001 . . . DLB-285
Krleža, Miroslav
   1893-1981 . . . . DLB-147; CDWLB-4
Krock, Arthur 1886-1974 . . . . DLB-29
Kroetsch, Robert 1927- DLB-53
Kropotkin, Petr Alekseevich 1842-1921 . . . DLB-277
Kross, Jaan 1920- DLB-232
Kruchenykh, Aleksei Eliseevich
   1886-1968 . . . . DLB-295
Krúdy, Gyula 1878-1933 . . . . DLB-215
Krutch, Joseph Wood
   1893-1970 . . . . DLB-63, 206, 275
Krylov, Ivan Andreevich 1769-1844 . . . . . DLB-150
Krymov, Iurii Solomonovich
   (Iurii Solomonovich Beklemishev)
   1908-1941 . . . . DLB-272
Kubin, Alfred 1877-1959 . . . . DLB-81
Kubrick, Stanley 1928-1999 . . . . DLB-26
Kudrun circa 1230-1240 . . . . DLB-138
Kuffstein, Hans Ludwig von 1582-1656 . . DLB-164

Kuhlmann, Quirinus 1651-1689 . . . . DLB-168
Kuhn, Thomas S. 1922-1996 . . . . DLB-279
Kuhnau, Johann 1660-1722 . . . . DLB-168
Kukol'nik, Nestor Vasil'evich
   1809-1868 . . . . DLB-205
Kukučín, Martin
   1860-1928 . . . . DLB-215; CDWLB-4
Kumin, Maxine 1925- DLB-5
Kuncewicz, Maria 1895-1989 . . . . DLB-215
Kundera, Milan 1929- DLB-232; CDWLB-4
Kunene, Mazisi 1930- DLB-117
Kunikida Doppo 1869-1908 . . . . DLB-180
Kunitz, Stanley 1905- DLB-48
Kunjufu, Johari M. (see Amini, Johari M.)
Kunnert, Gunter 1929- DLB-75
Kunze, Reiner 1933- DLB-75
Kupferberg, Tuli 1923- DLB-16
Kuprin, Aleksandr Ivanovich
   1870-1938 . . . . DLB-295
Kuraev, Mikhail Nikolaevich 1939- DLB-285
Kurahashi Yumiko 1935- DLB-182
Kureishi, Hanif 1954- DLB-194, 245
Kürnberger, Ferdinand 1821-1879 . . . . . . DLB-129
Kurz, Isolde 1853-1944 . . . . DLB-66
Kusenberg, Kurt 1904-1983 . . . . DLB-69
Kushchevsky, Ivan Afanas'evich
   1847-1876 . . . . DLB-238
Kushner, Tony 1956- DLB-228
Kuttner, Henry 1915-1958 . . . . DLB-8
Kuzmin, Mikhail Alekseevich
   1872-1936 . . . . DLB-295
Kuznetsov, Anatoli
   1929-1979 . . . . DLB-299, 302
Kyd, Thomas 1558-1594 . . . . DLB-62
Kyffin, Maurice circa 1560?-1598 . . . . . . DLB-136
Kyger, Joanne 1934- DLB-16
Kyne, Peter B. 1880-1957 . . . . DLB-78
Kyōgoku Tamekane 1254-1332 . . . . DLB-203
Kyrklund, Willy 1921- DLB-257

L

L. E. L. (see Landon, Letitia Elizabeth)
Laberge, Albert 1871-1960 . . . . DLB-68
Laberge, Marie 1950- DLB-60
Labiche, Eugène 1815-1888 . . . . DLB-192
Labrunie, Gerard (see Nerval, Gerard de)
La Bruyère, Jean de 1645-1696 . . . . DLB-268
La Calprenède 1609?-1663 . . . . DLB-268
Lacan, Jacques 1901-1981 . . . . DLB-296
La Capria, Raffaele 1922- DLB-196
Lacombe, Patrice
   (see Trullier-Lacombe, Joseph Patrice)
Lacretelle, Jacques de 1888-1985 . . . . DLB-65
Lacy, Ed 1911-1968 . . . . DLB-226
Lacy, Sam 1903- DLB-171
Ladd, Joseph Brown 1764-1786 . . . . DLB-37

La Farge, Oliver 1901-1963 . . . . DLB-9
Lafayette, Marie-Madeleine, comtesse de
   1634-1693 . . . . DLB-268
Laffan, Mrs. R. S. de Courcy
   (see Adams, Bertha Leith)
Lafferty, R. A. 1914-2002 . . . . DLB-8
La Flesche, Francis 1857-1932 . . . . DLB-175
La Fontaine, Jean de 1621-1695 . . . . DLB-268
Laforge, Jules 1860-1887 . . . . DLB-217
Lagerkvist, Pär 1891-1974 . . . . DLB-259
Lagerlöf, Selma
   1858-1940 . . . . DLB-259
Lagorio, Gina 1922- DLB-196
La Guma, Alex
   1925-1985 . . . . DLB-117, 225; CDWLB-3
Lahaise, Guillaume (see Delahaye, Guy)
Lahontan, Louis-Armand de Lom d'Arce,
   Baron de 1666-1715? DLB-99
Laing, Kojo 1946- DLB-157
Laird, Carobeth 1895-1983 . . . . Y-82
Laird and Lee DLB-49
Lake, Paul 1951- DLB-282
Lalić, Ivan V. 1931-1996 . . . . DLB-181
Lalić, Mihailo 1914-1992 . . . . DLB-181
Lalonde, Michèle 1937- DLB-60
Lamantia, Philip 1927- DLB-16
Lamartine, Alphonse de
   1790-1869 . . . . DLB-217
Lamb, Lady Caroline
   1785-1828 . . . . DLB-116
Lamb, Charles
   1775-1834 . . . . . . DLB-93, 107, 163; CDBLB-3
Lamb, Mary 1764-1874 . . . . DLB-163
Lambert, Angela 1940- DLB-271
Lambert, Betty 1933-1983 . . . . DLB-60
Lamm, Donald
   Goodbye, Gutenberg? A Lecture at
   the New York Public Library,
   18 April 1995 . . . . Y-95
Lamming, George
   1927- DLB-125; CDWLB-3
La Mothe Le Vayer, François de
   1588-1672 . . . . DLB-268
L'Amour, Louis 1908-1988 . . . . DLB-206; Y-80
Lampman, Archibald 1861-1899 . . . . DLB-92
Lamson, Wolffe and Company DLB-49
Lancer Books DLB-46
Lanchester, John 1962- DLB-267
Lander, Peter (see Cunningham, Peter)
Landesman, Jay 1919- and
   Landesman, Fran 1927- DLB-16
Landolfi, Tommaso 1908-1979 . . . . DLB-177
Landon, Letitia Elizabeth 1802-1838 . . . . . . DLB-96
Landor, Walter Savage 1775-1864 . . . . DLB-93, 107
Landry, Napoléon-P. 1884-1956 . . . . DLB-92
Landvik, Lorna 1954- DLB-292
Lane, Charles 1800-1870 . . . . DLB-1, 223; DS-5
Lane, F. C. 1885-1984 . . . . DLB-241
Lane, Laurence W. 1890-1967 . . . . DLB-91

Lane, M. Travis 1934- DLB-60
Lane, Patrick 1939- DLB-53
Lane, Pinkie Gordon 1923- DLB-41
John Lane Company DLB-49
Laney, Al 1896-1988 .... DLB-4, 171
Lang, Andrew 1844-1912 ..... DLB-98, 141, 184
Langer, Susanne K. 1895-1985 .... DLB-270
Langevin, André 1927- DLB-60
Langford, David 1953- DLB-261
Langgässer, Elisabeth 1899-1950 .... DLB-69
Langhorne, John 1735-1779 .... DLB-109
Langland, William circa 1330-circa 1400 . DLB-146
Langton, Anna 1804-1893 .... DLB-99
Lanham, Edwin 1904-1979 .... DLB-4
Lanier, Sidney 1842-1881 .... DLB-64; DS-13
Lanyer, Aemilia 1569-1645 .... DLB-121
Lapointe, Gatien 1931-1983 .... DLB-88
Lapointe, Paul-Marie 1929- DLB-88
Larcom, Lucy 1824-1893 .... DLB-221, 243
Lardner, John 1912-1960 .... DLB-171
Lardner, Ring 1885-1933
  .... DLB-11, 25, 86, 171; DS-16; CDALB-4
  Lardner 100: Ring Lardner
    Centennial Symposium Y-85
Lardner, Ring, Jr. 1915-2000 .... DLB-26, Y-00
Larkin, Philip 1922-1985 ..... DLB-27; CDBLB-8
  The Philip Larkin Society Y-99
La Roche, Sophie von 1730-1807 .... DLB-94
La Rochefoucauld, François duc de
    1613-1680 .... DLB-268
La Rocque, Gilbert 1943-1984 .... DLB-60
Laroque de Roquebrune, Robert
    (see Roquebrune, Robert de)
Larrick, Nancy 1910- DLB-61
Lars, Claudia 1899-1974 .... DLB-283
Larsen, Nella 1893-1964 .... DLB-51
Larsen, Thøger 1875-1928 .... DLB-300
Larson, Clinton F. 1919-1994 .... DLB-256
La Sale, Antoine de
    circa 1386-1460/1467 .... DLB-208
Lasch, Christopher 1932-1994 .... DLB-246
Lasker-Schüler, Else 1869-1945 ..... DLB-66, 124
Lasnier, Rina 1915-1997 .... DLB-88
Lassalle, Ferdinand 1825-1864 .... DLB-129
Late-Medieval Castilian Theater DLB-286
Latham, Robert 1912-1995 .... DLB-201
Lathrop, Dorothy P. 1891-1980 .... DLB-22
Lathrop, George Parsons 1851-1898 ..... DLB-71
Lathrop, John, Jr. 1772-1820 .... DLB-37
Latimer, Hugh 1492?-1555 .... DLB-136
Latimore, Jewel Christine McLawler
    (see Amini, Johari M.)
Latin Literature, The Uniqueness of DLB-211
La Tour du Pin, Patrice de 1911-1975 ... DLB-258
Latymer, William 1498-1583 .... DLB-132
Laube, Heinrich 1806-1884 .... DLB-133

Laud, William 1573-1645 .... DLB-213
Laughlin, James 1914-1997 ...... DLB-48; Y-96, 97
  A Tribute [to Henry Miller] Y-80
  Tribute to Albert Erskine Y-93
  Tribute to Kenneth Rexroth Y-82
  Tribute to Malcolm Cowley Y-89
Laumer, Keith 1925-1993 .... DLB-8
Lauremberg, Johann 1590-1658 .... DLB-164
Laurence, Margaret 1926-1987 .... DLB-53
Laurentius von Schnüffis 1633-1702 .... DLB-168
Laurents, Arthur 1918- DLB-26
Laurie, Annie (see Black, Winifred)
Laut, Agnes Christiana 1871-1936 ...... DLB-92
Lauterbach, Ann 1942- DLB-193
Lautréamont, Isidore Lucien Ducasse,
    Comte de 1846-1870 .... DLB-217
Lavater, Johann Kaspar 1741-1801 ...... DLB-97
Lavin, Mary 1912-1996 .... DLB-15
Law, John (see Harkness, Margaret)
Lawes, Henry 1596-1662 .... DLB-126
Lawler, Ray 1921- DLB-289
Lawless, Anthony (see MacDonald, Philip)
Lawless, Emily (The Hon. Emily Lawless)
    1845-1913 .... DLB-240
Lawrence, D. H. 1885-1930
    ..... DLB-10, 19, 36, 98, 162, 195; CDBLB-6
  The D. H. Lawrence Society of
    North America Y-00
Lawrence, David 1888-1973 .... DLB-29
Lawrence, Jerome 1915- DLB-228
Lawrence, Seymour 1926-1994 .... Y-94
  Tribute to Richard Yates Y-92
Lawrence, T. E. 1888-1935 .... DLB-195
  The T. E. Lawrence Society Y-98
Lawson, George 1598-1678 .... DLB-213
Lawson, Henry 1867-1922 .... DLB-230
Lawson, John ?-1711 .... DLB-24
Lawson, John Howard 1894-1977 ...... DLB-228
Lawson, Louisa Albury 1848-1920 ...... DLB-230
Lawson, Robert 1892-1957 .... DLB-22
Lawson, Victor F. 1850-1925 .... DLB-25
Layard, Austen Henry 1817-1894 .... DLB-166
Layton, Irving 1912- DLB-88
LaZamon flourished circa 1200 .... DLB-146
Lazarević, Laza K. 1851-1890 .... DLB-147
Lazarus, George 1904-1997 .... DLB-201
Lazhechnikov, Ivan Ivanovich
    1792-1869 .... DLB-198
Lea, Henry Charles 1825-1909 .... DLB-47
Lea, Sydney 1942- DLB-120, 282
Lea, Tom 1907-2001 .... DLB-6
Leacock, John 1729-1802 .... DLB-31
Leacock, Stephen 1869-1944 .... DLB-92
Lead, Jane Ward 1623-1704 .... DLB-131
Leadenhall Press DLB-106

"The Greatness of Southern Literature":
  League of the South Institute for the
  Study of Southern Culture and History
    .... Y-02
Leakey, Caroline Woolmer 1827-1881 ... DLB-230
Leapor, Mary 1722-1746 .... DLB-109
Lear, Edward 1812-1888 ...... DLB-32, 163, 166
Leary, Timothy 1920-1996 .... DLB-16
W. A. Leary and Company DLB-49
Léautaud, Paul 1872-1956 .... DLB-65
Leavis, F. R. 1895-1978 .... DLB-242
Leavitt, David 1961- DLB-130
Leavitt and Allen DLB-49
Le Blond, Mrs. Aubrey 1861-1934 ...... DLB-174
le Carré, John (David John Moore Cornwell)
    1931- DLB-87; CDBLB-8
  Tribute to Graham Greene Y-91
  Tribute to George Greenfield Y-00
Lécavelé, Roland (see Dorgeles, Roland)
Lechlitner, Ruth 1901- DLB-48
Leclerc, Félix 1914-1988 .... DLB-60
Le Clézio, J. M. G. 1940- DLB-83
Leder, Rudolf (see Hermlin, Stephan)
Lederer, Charles 1910-1976 .... DLB-26
Ledwidge, Francis 1887-1917 .... DLB-20
Lee, Dennis 1939- DLB-53
Lee, Don L. (see Madhubuti, Haki R.)
Lee, George W. 1894-1976 .... DLB-51
Lee, Harper 1926- DLB-6; CDALB-1
Lee, Harriet 1757-1851 and
    Lee, Sophia 1750-1824 .... DLB-39
Lee, Laurie 1914-1997 .... DLB-27
Lee, Leslie 1935- DLB-266
Lee, Li-Young 1957- DLB-165
Lee, Manfred B. 1905-1971 .... DLB-137
Lee, Nathaniel circa 1645-1692 .... DLB-80
Lee, Robert E. 1918-1994 .... DLB-228
Lee, Sir Sidney 1859-1926 .... DLB-149, 184
  "Principles of Biography," in
    Elizabethan and Other Essays DLB-149
Lee, Tanith 1947- DLB-261
Lee, Vernon
    1856-1935 .... DLB-57, 153, 156, 174, 178
Lee and Shepard DLB-49
Le Fanu, Joseph Sheridan
    1814-1873 .... DLB-21, 70, 159, 178
Leffland, Ella 1931- Y-84
le Fort, Gertrud von 1876-1971 .... DLB-66
Le Gallienne, Richard 1866-1947 .... DLB-4
Legaré, Hugh Swinton
    1797-1843 .... DLB-3, 59, 73, 248
Legaré, James Mathewes 1823-1859 .... DLB-3, 248
Léger, Antoine-J. 1880-1950 .... DLB-88
Leggett, William 1801-1839 .... DLB-250
Le Guin, Ursula K.
    1929- DLB-8, 52, 256, 275; CDALB-6
Lehman, Ernest 1920- DLB-44

Lehmann, John 1907-1989 . . . . DLB-27, 100

John Lehmann Limited DLB-112

Lehmann, Rosamond 1901-1990 . . . . DLB-15

Lehmann, Wilhelm 1882-1968 . . . . DLB-56

Leiber, Fritz 1910-1992 . . . . DLB-8

Leibniz, Gottfried Wilhelm 1646-1716 . . . . DLB-168

Leicester University Press DLB-112

Leigh, Carolyn 1926-1983 . . . . DLB-265

Leigh, W. R. 1866-1955 . . . . DLB-188

Leinster, Murray 1896-1975 . . . . DLB-8

Leiser, Bill 1898-1965 . . . . DLB-241

Leisewitz, Johann Anton 1752-1806 . . . . . . DLB-94

Leitch, Maurice 1933- DLB-14

Leithauser, Brad 1943- DLB-120, 282

Leland, Charles G. 1824-1903 . . . . DLB-11

Leland, John 1503?-1552 . . . . DLB-136

Lemay, Pamphile 1837-1918 . . . . DLB-99

Lemelin, Roger 1919-1992 . . . . DLB-88

Lemercier, Louis-Jean-Népomucène 1771-1840 . . . . DLB-192

Le Moine, James MacPherson 1825-1912 . . DLB-99

Lemon, Mark 1809-1870 . . . . DLB-163

Le Moyne, Jean 1913-1996 . . . . DLB-88

Lemperly, Paul 1858-1939 . . . . DLB-187

Leñero, Vicente 1933- DLB-305

L'Engle, Madeleine 1918- DLB-52

Lennart, Isobel 1915-1971 . . . . DLB-44

Lennox, Charlotte 1729 or 1730-1804 . . . . DLB-39

Lenox, James 1800-1880 . . . . DLB-140

Lenski, Lois 1893-1974 . . . . DLB-22

Lentricchia, Frank 1940- DLB-246

Lenz, Hermann 1913-1998 . . . . DLB-69

Lenz, J. M. R. 1751-1792 . . . . DLB-94

Lenz, Siegfried 1926- DLB-75

Leonard, Elmore 1925- DLB-173, 226

Leonard, Hugh 1926- DLB-13

Leonard, William Ellery 1876-1944 . . . . . . DLB-54

Leonov, Leonid Maksimovich 1899-1994 . . . . DLB-272

Leonowens, Anna 1834-1914 . . . . . . DLB-99, 166

Leont'ev, Konstantin Nikolaevich 1831-1891 . . . . DLB-277

Leopold, Aldo 1887-1948 . . . . DLB-275

LePan, Douglas 1914-1998 . . . . DLB-88

Lepik, Kalju 1920-1999 . . . . DLB-232

Leprohon, Rosanna Eleanor 1829-1879 . . . DLB-99

Le Queux, William 1864-1927 . . . . DLB-70

Lermontov, Mikhail Iur'evich 1814-1841 . . . . DLB-205

Lerner, Alan Jay 1918-1986 . . . . DLB-265

Lerner, Max 1902-1992 . . . . DLB-29

Lernet-Holenia, Alexander 1897-1976 . . . . DLB-85

Le Rossignol, James 1866-1969 . . . . DLB-92

Lescarbot, Marc circa 1570-1642 . . . . DLB-99

LeSeur, William Dawson 1840-1917 . . . . . DLB-92

LeSieg, Theo. (see Geisel, Theodor Seuss)

Leskov, Nikolai Semenovich 1831-1895 . . . . DLB-238

Leslie, Doris before 1902-1982 . . . . DLB-191

Leslie, Eliza 1787-1858 . . . . DLB-202

Leslie, Frank (Henry Carter) 1821-1880 . . . . DLB-43, 79

Frank Leslie [publishing house] DLB-49

Leśmian, Bolesław 1878-1937 . . . . DLB-215

Lesperance, John 1835?-1891 . . . . DLB-99

Lessing, Bruno 1870-1940 . . . . DLB-28

Lessing, Doris 1919- DLB-15, 139; Y-85; CDBLB-8

Lessing, Gotthold Ephraim 1729-1781 . . . . DLB-97; CDWLB-2

The Lessing Society Y-00

Le Sueur, Meridel 1900-1996 . . . . DLB-303

Lettau, Reinhard 1929-1996 . . . . DLB-75

The Hemingway Letters Project Finds an Editor Y-02

Lever, Charles 1806-1872 . . . . DLB-21

Lever, Ralph ca. 1527-1585 . . . . DLB-236

Leverson, Ada 1862-1933 . . . . DLB-153

Levertov, Denise 1923-1997 . . . . DLB-5, 165; CDALB-7

Levi, Peter 1931-2000 . . . . DLB-40

Levi, Primo 1919-1987 . . . . DLB-177, 299

Levien, Sonya 1888-1960 . . . . DLB-44

Levin, Meyer 1905-1981 . . . . DLB-9, 28; Y-81

Levin, Phillis 1954- DLB-282

Lévinas, Emmanuel 1906-1995 . . . . DLB-296

Levine, Norman 1923- DLB-88

Levine, Philip 1928- DLB-5

Levis, Larry 1946- DLB-120

Lévi-Strauss, Claude 1908- DLB-242

Levitov, Aleksandr Ivanovich 1835?-1877 . . . . DLB-277

Levy, Amy 1861-1889 . . . . DLB-156, 240

Levy, Benn Wolfe 1900-1973 . . . . . . DLB-13; Y-81

Lewald, Fanny 1811-1889 . . . . DLB-129

Lewes, George Henry 1817-1878 . . . . . DLB-55, 144

"Criticism in Relation to Novels" (1863) DLB-21

The Principles of Success in Literature (1865) [excerpt] DLB-57

Lewis, Agnes Smith 1843-1926 . . . . DLB-174

Lewis, Alfred H. 1857-1914 . . . . DLB-25, 186

Lewis, Alun 1915-1944 . . . . DLB-20, 162

Lewis, C. Day (see Day Lewis, C.)

Lewis, C. I. 1883-1964 . . . . DLB-270

Lewis, C. S. 1898-1963 . . . . DLB-15, 100, 160, 255; CDBLB-7

The New York C. S. Lewis Society Y-99

Lewis, Charles B. 1842-1924 . . . . DLB-11

Lewis, David 1941-2001 . . . . DLB-279

Lewis, Henry Clay 1825-1850 . . . . DLB-3, 248

Lewis, Janet 1899-1999 . . . . Y-87

Tribute to Katherine Anne Porter Y-80

Lewis, Matthew Gregory 1775-1818 . . . . DLB-39, 158, 178

Lewis, Meriwether 1774-1809 . . . . . . DLB-183, 186

Lewis, Norman 1908- DLB-204

Lewis, R. W. B. 1917- DLB-111

Lewis, Richard circa 1700-1734 . . . . DLB-24

Lewis, Sinclair 1885-1951 . . . . . . DLB-9, 102; DS-1; CDALB-4

Sinclair Lewis Centennial Conference . . . Y-85

The Sinclair Lewis Society Y-99

Lewis, Wilmarth Sheldon 1895-1979 . . . . . DLB-140

Lewis, Wyndham 1882-1957 . . . . DLB-15

Time and Western Man [excerpt] (1927) DLB-36

Lewisohn, Ludwig 1882-1955 . . . DLB-4, 9, 28, 102

Leyendecker, J. C. 1874-1951 . . . . DLB-188

Leyner, Mark 1956- DLB-292

Lezama Lima, José 1910-1976 . . . . . . DLB-113, 283

L'Heureux, John 1934- DLB-244

Libbey, Laura Jean 1862-1924 . . . . DLB-221

Libedinsky, Iurii Nikolaevich 1898-1959 . . . . DLB-272

The Liberator DLB-303

Library History Group Y-01

E-Books' Second Act in Libraries Y-02

The Library of America DLB-46

The Library of America: An Assessment After Two Decades Y-02

Licensing Act of 1737 . . . . DLB-84

Leonard Lichfield I [publishing house] . . . DLB-170

Lichtenberg, Georg Christoph 1742-1799 . . . . DLB-94

The Liddle Collection Y-97

Lidman, Sara 1923- DLB-257

Lieb, Fred 1888-1980 . . . . DLB-171

Liebling, A. J. 1904-1963 . . . . DLB-4, 171

Lieutenant Murray (see Ballou, Maturin Murray)

Lighthall, William Douw 1857-1954 . . . . . . DLB-92

Lihn, Enrique 1929-1988 . . . . DLB-283

Lilar, Françoise (see Mallet-Joris, Françoise)

Lili'uokalani, Queen 1838-1917 . . . . DLB-221

Lillo, George 1691-1739 . . . . DLB-84

Lilly, J. K., Jr. 1893-1966 . . . . DLB-140

Lilly, Wait and Company DLB-49

Lily, William circa 1468-1522 . . . . DLB-132

Limited Editions Club DLB-46

Limón, Graciela 1938- DLB-209

Lincoln and Edmands DLB-49

Lind, Jakov 1927- DLB-299

Linda Vilhjálmsdóttir 1958- DLB-293

Lindesay, Ethel Forence (see Richardson, Henry Handel)

Lindgren, Astrid 1907-2002 . . . . DLB-257

Lindgren, Torgny 1938- DLB-257

Lindsay, Alexander William, Twenty-fifth Earl of Crawford 1812-1880 . . . . DLB-184

Cumulative Index

Lindsay, Sir David circa 1485-1555 ..... DLB-132
Lindsay, David 1878-1945 .... DLB-255
Lindsay, Jack 1900-1990 .... Y-84
Lindsay, Lady (Caroline Blanche
  Elizabeth Fitzroy Lindsay)
  1844-1912 .... DLB-199
Lindsay, Norman 1879-1969 .... DLB-260
Lindsay, Vachel
  1879-1931 .... DLB-54; CDALB-3
Linebarger, Paul Myron Anthony
  (see Smith, Cordwainer)
Link, Arthur S. 1920-1998 .... DLB-17
Linn, Ed 1922-2000 .... DLB-241
Linn, John Blair 1777-1804 .... DLB-37
Lins, Osman 1924-1978 .... DLB-145
Linton, Eliza Lynn 1822-1898 .... DLB-18
Linton, William James 1812-1897 ..... DLB-32
Barnaby Bernard Lintot
  [publishing house] DLB-170
Lion Books DLB-46
Lionni, Leo 1910-1999 .... DLB-61
Lippard, George 1822-1854 .... DLB-202
Lippincott, Sara Jane Clarke
  1823-1904 .... DLB-43
J. B. Lippincott Company DLB-49
Lippmann, Walter 1889-1974 .... DLB-29
Lipton, Lawrence 1898-1975 .... DLB-16
Lisboa, Irene 1892-1958 .... DLB-287
Liscow, Christian Ludwig 1701-1760 ... DLB-97
Lish, Gordon 1934- DLB-130
  Tribute to Donald Barthelme Y-89
  Tribute to James Dickey Y-97
Lisle, Charles-Marie-René Leconte de
  1818-1894 .... DLB-217
Lispector, Clarice
  1925-1977 .... DLB-113; CDWLB-3
LitCheck Website Y-01
Literary Awards and Honors Y-81-02
  Booker Prize Y-86, 96-98
  The Drue Heinz Literature Prize Y-82
  The Elmer Holmes Bobst Awards
    in Arts and Letters Y-87
  The Griffin Poetry Prize Y-00
  Literary Prizes [British] DLB-15, 207
  National Book Critics Circle
    Awards Y-00-01
  The National Jewish Book Awards Y-85
  Nobel Prize Y-80-02
  Winning an Edgar Y-98
The Literary Chronicle and Weekly Review
  1819-1828 .... DLB-110
Literary Periodicals:
  Callaloo Y-87
  Expatriates in Paris DS-15
  New Literary Periodicals:
    A Report for 1987 .... Y-87
    A Report for 1988 .... Y-88
    A Report for 1989 .... Y-89

A Report for 1990 .... Y-90
A Report for 1991 .... Y-91
A Report for 1992 .... Y-92
A Report for 1993 .... Y-93
Literary Research Archives
  The Anthony Burgess Archive at
    the Harry Ransom Humanities
    Research Center Y-98
  Archives of Charles Scribner's Sons DS-17
  Berg Collection of English and
    American Literature of the
    New York Public Library Y-83
  The Bobbs-Merrill Archive at the
    Lilly Library, Indiana University Y-90
  Die Fürstliche Bibliothek Corvey Y-96
  Guide to the Archives of Publishers,
    Journals, and Literary Agents in
    North American Libraries Y-93
  The Henry E. Huntington Library Y-92
  The Humanities Research Center,
    University of Texas Y-82
  The John Carter Brown Library Y-85
  Kent State Special Collections Y-86
  The Lilly Library Y-84
  The Modern Literary Manuscripts
    Collection in the Special
    Collections of the Washington
    University Libraries Y-87
  A Publisher's Archives: G. P. Putnam Y-92
  Special Collections at Boston
    University Y-99
  The University of Virginia Libraries Y-91
  The William Charvat American Fiction
    Collection at the Ohio State
    University Libraries Y-92
Literary Societies Y-98-02
  The Margery Allingham Society Y-98
  The American Studies Association
    of Norway Y-00
  The Arnold Bennett Society Y-98
  The Association for the Study of
    Literature and Environment
    (ASLE) Y-99
  Belgian Luxembourg American Studies
    Association Y-01
  The E. F. Benson Society Y-98
  The Elizabeth Bishop Society Y-01
  The [Edgar Rice] Burroughs
    Bibliophiles Y-98
  The Byron Society of America Y-00
  The Lewis Carroll Society
    of North America Y-00
  The Willa Cather Pioneer Memorial
    and Education Foundation Y-00
  New Chaucer Society Y-00
  The Wilkie Collins Society Y-98
  The James Fenimore Cooper Society Y-01
  The Stephen Crane Society Y-98, 01
  The E. E. Cummings Society Y-01
  The James Dickey Society Y-99
  John Dos Passos Newsletter Y-00

The Priory Scholars [Sir Arthur Conan
  Doyle] of New York Y-99
The International Theodore Dreiser
  Society Y-01
The Friends of the Dymock Poets Y-00
The George Eliot Fellowship Y-99
The T. S. Eliot Society: Celebration and
  Scholarship, 1980-1999 .... Y-99
The Ralph Waldo Emerson Society Y-99
The William Faulkner Society Y-99
The C. S. Forester Society Y-00
The Hamlin Garland Society Y-01
The [Elizabeth] Gaskell Society Y-98
The Charlotte Perkins Gilman Society ... Y-99
The Ellen Glasgow Society Y-01
Zane Grey's West Society Y-00
The Ivor Gurney Society Y-98
The Joel Chandler Harris Association Y-99
The Nathaniel Hawthorne Society Y-00
The [George Alfred] Henty Society Y-98
George Moses Horton Society Y-99
The William Dean Howells Society Y-01
WW2 HMSO Paperbacks Society Y-98
American Humor Studies Association Y-99
International Society for Humor Studies ... Y-99
The W. W. Jacobs Appreciation Society ... Y-98
The Richard Jefferies Society Y-98
The Jerome K. Jerome Society Y-98
The D. H. Lawrence Society of
  North America Y-00
The T. E. Lawrence Society Y-98
The [Gotthold] Lessing Society Y-00
The New York C. S. Lewis Society Y-99
The Sinclair Lewis Society Y-99
The Jack London Research Center Y-00
The Jack London Society Y-99
The Cormac McCarthy Society Y-99
The Melville Society Y-01
The Arthur Miller Society Y-01
The Milton Society of America Y-00
International Marianne Moore Society ... Y-98
International Nabokov Society Y-99
The Vladimir Nabokov Society Y-01
The Flannery O'Connor Society Y-99
The Wilfred Owen Association Y-98
Penguin Collectors' Society Y-98
The [E. A.] Poe Studies Association Y-99
The Katherine Anne Porter Society Y-01
The Beatrix Potter Society Y-98
The Ezra Pound Society Y-01
The Powys Society Y-98
Proust Society of America Y-00
The Dorothy L. Sayers Society Y-98
The Bernard Shaw Society Y-99
The Society for the Study of
  Southern Literature Y-00

The Wallace Stevens Society........... Y-99
The Harriet Beecher Stowe Center...... Y-00
The R. S. Surtees Society............. Y-98
The Thoreau Society................. Y-99
The Tilling [E. F. Benson] Society....... Y-98
The Trollope Societies............... Y-00
H. G. Wells Society.................. Y-98
The Western Literature Association..... Y-99
The William Carlos Williams Society.... Y-99
The Henry Williamson Society......... Y-98
The [Nero] Wolfe Pack............... Y-99
The Thomas Wolfe Society Y-99
Worldwide Wodehouse Societies Y-98
The W. B. Yeats Society of N.Y......... Y-99
The Charlotte M. Yonge Fellowship..... Y-98
Literary Theory
    The Year in Literary Theory Y-92–Y-93
Literature at Nurse, or Circulating Morals (1885),
    by George Moore DLB-18
Litt, Toby 1968- DLB-267
Littell, Eliakim 1797-1870.............. DLB-79
Littell, Robert S. 1831-1896............ DLB-79
Little, Brown and Company DLB-49
Little Magazines and Newspapers DS-15
    Selected English-Language Little
    Magazines and Newspapers
    [France, 1920-1939] DLB-4
The Little Magazines of the
    New Formalism................... DLB-282
The Little Review 1914-1929 .... DS-15
Littlewood, Joan 1914-2002............ DLB-13
Lively, Penelope 1933- DLB-14, 161, 207
Liverpool University Press DLB-112
The Lives of the Poets (1753) DLB-142
Livesay, Dorothy 1909-1996............ DLB-68
Livesay, Florence Randal 1874-1953...... DLB-92
Livings, Henry 1929-1998.............. DLB-13
Livingston, Anne Howe 1763-1841 ... DLB-37, 200
Livingston, Jay 1915-2001 .... DLB-265
Livingston, Myra Cohn 1926-1996....... DLB-61
Livingston, William 1723-1790......... DLB-31
Livingstone, David 1813-1873.......... DLB-166
Livingstone, Douglas 1932-1996........ DLB-225
Livshits, Benedikt Konstantinovich
    1886-1938 or 1939 .... DLB-295
Livy 59 B.C.-A.D. 17....... DLB-211; CDWLB-1
Liyong, Taban lo (see Taban lo Liyong)
Lizárraga, Sylvia S. 1925- DLB-82
Llewellyn, Richard 1906-1983........... DLB-15
Lloréns Torres, Luis 1876-1944......... DLB-290
Edward Lloyd [publishing house] DLB-106
Lobel, Arnold 1933- DLB-61
Lochridge, Betsy Hopkins (see Fancher, Betsy)
Locke, Alain 1886-1954................ DLB-51
Locke, David Ross 1833-1888........ DLB-11, 23
Locke, John 1632-1704..... DLB-31, 101, 213, 252

Locke, Richard Adams 1800-1871........ DLB-43
Locker-Lampson, Frederick
    1821-1895 .... DLB-35, 184
Lockhart, John Gibson
    1794-1854 .... DLB-110, 116 144
Lockridge, Ross, Jr. 1914-1948 .... DLB-143; Y-80
Locrine and Selimus.................... DLB-62
Lodge, David 1935- DLB-14, 194
Lodge, George Cabot 1873-1909......... DLB-54
Lodge, Henry Cabot 1850-1924 .... DLB-47
Lodge, Thomas 1558-1625 .... DLB-172
    Defence of Poetry (1579) [excerpt] DLB-172
Loeb, Harold 1891-1974 .... DLB-4; DS-15
Loeb, William 1905-1981 .... DLB-127
Loesser, Frank 1910-1969 .... DLB-265
Lofting, Hugh 1886-1947................ DLB-160
Logan, Deborah Norris 1761-1839 ...... DLB-200
Logan, James 1674-1751............. DLB-24, 140
Logan, John 1923-1987 .... DLB-5
Logan, Martha Daniell 1704?-1779 ..... DLB-200
Logan, William 1950- DLB-120
Logau, Friedrich von 1605-1655 .... DLB-164
Logue, Christopher 1926- DLB-27
Lohenstein, Daniel Casper von
    1635-1683 .... DLB-168
Lo-Johansson, Ivar 1901-1990.......... DLB-259
Lokert, George (or Lockhart)
    circa 1485-1547 .... DLB-281
Lomonosov, Mikhail Vasil'evich
    1711-1765..................... DLB-150
London, Jack
    1876-1916 ..... DLB-8, 12, 78, 212; CDALB-3
    The Jack London Research Center...... Y-00
    The Jack London Society Y-99
The London Magazine 1820-1829 .... DLB-110
Long, David 1948- DLB-244
Long, H., and Brother................. DLB-49
Long, Haniel 1888-1956 .... DLB-45
Long, Ray 1878-1935.................. DLB-137
Longfellow, Henry Wadsworth
    1807-1882 .... DLB-1, 59, 235; CDALB-2
Longfellow, Samuel 1819-1892 .... DLB-1
Longford, Elizabeth 1906-2002 .... DLB-155
    Tribute to Alfred A. Knopf............ Y-84
Longinus circa first century DLB-176
Longley, Michael 1939- DLB-40
T. Longman [publishing house]......... DLB-154
Longmans, Green and Company DLB-49
Longmore, George 1793?-1867 .... DLB-99
Longstreet, Augustus Baldwin
    1790-1870 .... DLB-3, 11, 74, 248
D. Longworth [publishing house] DLB-49
Lønn, Øystein 1936- DLB-297
Lonsdale, Frederick 1881-1954 .... DLB-10
Loos, Anita 1893-1981..... DLB-11, 26, 228; Y-81
Lopate, Phillip 1943- Y-80
Lopes, Fernão 1380/1390?-1460?........ DLB-287

Lopez, Barry 1945- DLB-256, 275
López, Diana (see Isabella, Ríos)
López, Josefina 1969- DLB-209
López de Mendoza, Íñigo
    (see Santillana, Marqués de)
López Velarde, Ramón 1888-1921 ...... DLB-290
Loranger, Jean-Aubert 1896-1942 .... DLB-92
Lorca, Federico García 1898-1936....... DLB-108
Lord, John Keast 1818-1872 .... DLB-99
Lorde, Audre 1934-1992................ DLB-41
Lorimer, George Horace 1867-1937...... DLB-91
A. K. Loring [publishing house]......... DLB-49
Loring and Mussey DLB-46
Lorris, Guillaume de (see *Roman de la Rose*)
Lossing, Benson J. 1813-1891 .... DLB-30
Lothar, Ernst 1890-1974 .... DLB-81
D. Lothrop and Company............... DLB-49
Lothrop, Harriet M. 1844-1924.......... DLB-42
Loti, Pierre 1850-1923................. DLB-123
Lotichius Secundus, Petrus 1528-1560 ... DLB-179
Lott, Emmeline ?-?.................... DLB-166
Louisiana State University Press Y-97
Lounsbury, Thomas R. 1838-1915 .... DLB-71
Louÿs, Pierre 1870-1925 .... DLB-123
Løveid, Cecile 1951- DLB-297
Lovejoy, Arthur O. 1873-1962 .... DLB-270
Lovelace, Earl 1935- DLB-125; CDWLB-3
Lovelace, Richard 1618-1657............ DLB-131
John W. Lovell Company DLB-49
Lovell, Coryell and Company........... DLB-49
Lover, Samuel 1797-1868............ DLB-159, 190
Lovesey, Peter 1936- DLB-87
    Tribute to Georges Simenon........... Y-89
Lovinescu, Eugen
    1881-1943 .... DLB-220; CDWLB-4
Lovingood, Sut
    (see Harris, George Washington)
Low, Samuel 1765-? DLB-37
Lowell, Amy 1874-1925............. DLB-54, 140
Lowell, James Russell 1819-1891
    ...... DLB-1, 11, 64, 79, 189, 235; CDALB-2
Lowell, Robert
    1917-1977............. DLB-5, 169; CDALB-7
Lowenfels, Walter 1897-1976............. DLB-4
Lowndes, Marie Belloc 1868-1947........ DLB-70
Lowndes, William Thomas 1798-1843 ... DLB-184
Humphrey Lownes [publishing house] ... DLB-170
Lowry, Lois 1937- DLB-52
Lowry, Malcolm 1909-1957..... DLB-15; CDBLB-7
Lowther, Pat 1935-1975................. DLB-53
Loy, Mina 1882-1966 .... DLB-4, 54
Loynaz, Dulce María 1902-1997 .... DLB-283
Lozeau, Albert 1878-1924 .... DLB-92
Lubbock, Percy 1879-1965 .... DLB-149
Lucan A.D. 39-A.D. 65 .... DLB-211
Lucas, E. V. 1868-1938 .... DLB-98, 149, 153

Fielding Lucas Jr. [publishing house] DLB-49
Luce, Clare Booth 1903-1987 .... DLB-228
Luce, Henry R. 1898-1967 .... DLB-91
John W. Luce and Company DLB-46
Lucena, Juan de ca. 1430-1501 .... DLB-286
Lucian circa 120-180................. DLB-176
Lucie-Smith, Edward 1933- DLB-40
Lucilius circa 180 B.C.-102/101 B.C. DLB-211
Lucini, Gian Pietro 1867-1914 .... DLB-114
Luco Cruchaga, Germán 1894-1936 .... DLB-305
Lucretius circa 94 B.C.-circa 49 B.C.
.... DLB-211; CDWLB-1
Luder, Peter circa 1415-1472 .... DLB-179
Ludlam, Charles 1943-1987 .... DLB-266
Ludlum, Robert 1927-2001................ Y-82
Ludus de Antichristo circa 1160 .... DLB-148
Ludvigson, Susan 1942- DLB-120
Ludwig, Jack 1922- DLB-60
Ludwig, Otto 1813-1865............ DLB-129
Ludwigslied 881 or 882............. DLB-148
Luera, Yolanda 1953- DLB-122
Luft, Lya 1938- DLB-145
Lugansky, Kazak Vladimir
(see Dal', Vladimir Ivanovich)
Lugn, Kristina 1948- DLB-257
Lugones, Leopoldo 1874-1938 .... DLB-283
Luhan, Mabel Dodge 1879-1962 .... DLB-303
Lukács, Georg (see Lukács, György)
Lukács, György
1885-1971........ DLB-215, 242; CDWLB-4
Luke, Peter 1919- DLB-13
Lummis, Charles F. 1859-1928......... DLB-186
Lundkvist, Artur 1906-1991........... DLB-259
Lunts, Lev Natanovich 1901-1924 ...... DLB-272
F. M. Lupton Company DLB-49
Lupus of Ferrières circa 805-circa 862 ... DLB-148
Lurie, Alison 1926- DLB-2
Lussu, Emilio 1890-1975............. DLB-264
Lustig, Arnošt 1926- DLB-232, 299
Luther, Martin
1483-1546 ....DLB-179; CDWLB-2
Luzi, Mario 1914- DLB-128
L'vov, Nikolai Aleksandrovich
1751-1803 .... DLB-150
Lyall, Gavin 1932- DLB-87
Lydgate, John circa 1370-1450 .... DLB-146
Lyly, John circa 1554-1606......... DLB-62, 167
Lynch, Patricia 1898-1972 .... DLB-160
Lynch, Richard flourished 1596-1601 ....DLB-172
Lynd, Robert 1879-1949............. DLB-98
Lyon, Matthew 1749-1822 .... DLB-43
Lyotard, Jean-François 1924-1998 ...... DLB-242
Lyricists
Additional Lyricists: 1920-1960 ..... DLB-265
Lysias circa 459 B.C.-circa 380 B.C...... DLB-176
Lytle, Andrew 1902-1995.......... DLB-6; Y-95

Tribute to Caroline Gordon Y-81
Tribute to Katherine Anne Porter Y-80
Lytton, Edward
(see Bulwer-Lytton, Edward)
Lytton, Edward Robert Bulwer
1831-1891 .... DLB-32

M

Maass, Joachim 1901-1972 .... DLB-69
Mabie, Hamilton Wright 1845-1916 ..... DLB-71
Mac A'Ghobhainn, Iain (see Smith, Iain Crichton)
MacArthur, Charles 1895-1956 ..... DLB-7, 25, 44
Macaulay, Catherine 1731-1791 .... DLB-104
Macaulay, David 1945- DLB-61
Macaulay, Rose 1881-1958............. DLB-36
Macaulay, Thomas Babington
1800-1859 .... DLB-32, 55; CDBLB-4
Macaulay Company.................. DLB-46
MacBeth, George 1932-1992 .... DLB-40
Macbeth, Madge 1880-1965 .... DLB-92
MacCaig, Norman 1910-1996 .... DLB-27
MacDiarmid, Hugh
1892-1978 .... DLB-20; CDBLB-7
MacDonald, Cynthia 1928- DLB-105
MacDonald, George 1824-1905.... DLB-18, 163, 178
MacDonald, John D. 1916-1986...... DLB-8; Y-86
MacDonald, Philip 1899?-1980 .... DLB-77
Macdonald, Ross (see Millar, Kenneth)
Macdonald, Sharman 1951- DLB-245
MacDonald, Wilson 1880-1967 .... DLB-92
Macdonald and Company (Publishers) .. DLB-112
MacEwen, Gwendolyn 1941-1987 ... DLB-53, 251
Macfadden, Bernarr 1868-1955 ..... DLB-25, 91
MacGregor, John 1825-1892 .... DLB-166
MacGregor, Mary Esther (see Keith, Marian)
Macherey, Pierre 1938- DLB-296
Machado, Antonio 1875-1939......... DLB-108
Machado, Manuel 1874-1947 .... DLB-108
Machar, Agnes Maule 1837-1927 ...... DLB-92
Machaut, Guillaume de
circa 1300-1377 .... DLB-208
Machen, Arthur Llewelyn Jones
1863-1947................DLB-36, 156, 178
MacIlmaine, Roland fl. 1574............ DLB-281
MacInnes, Colin 1914-1976 .... DLB-14
MacInnes, Helen 1907-1985 .... DLB-87
Mac Intyre, Tom 1931- DLB-245
Mačiulis, Jonas (see Maironis, Jonas)
Mack, Maynard 1909- DLB-111
Mackall, Leonard L. 1879-1937 ..... DLB-140
MacKay, Isabel Ecclestone 1875-1928 .... DLB-92
MacKaye, Percy 1875-1956 .... DLB-54
Macken, Walter 1915-1967 .... DLB-13
Mackenzie, Alexander 1763-1820 .... DLB-99
Mackenzie, Alexander Slidell
1803-1848 .... DLB-183

Mackenzie, Compton 1883-1972 ..... DLB-34, 100
Mackenzie, Henry 1745-1831.......... DLB-39
The Lounger, no. 20 (1785) DLB-39
Mackenzie, Kenneth (Seaforth Mackenzie)
1913-1955 .... DLB-260
Mackenzie, William 1758-1828......... DLB-187
Mackey, Nathaniel 1947- DLB-169
Mackey, Shena 1944- DLB-231
Mackey, William Wellington 1937- DLB-38
Mackintosh, Elizabeth (see Tey, Josephine)
Mackintosh, Sir James 1765-1832....... DLB-158
Macklin, Charles 1699-1797 .... DLB-89
Maclaren, Ian (see Watson, John)
MacLaverty, Bernard 1942- DLB-267
MacLean, Alistair 1922-1987 .... DLB-276
MacLean, Katherine Anne 1925- DLB-8
Maclean, Norman 1902-1990 .... DLB-206
MacLeish, Archibald 1892-1982
........DLB-4, 7, 45; Y-82; DS-15; CDALB-7
MacLennan, Hugh 1907-1990 .... DLB-68
MacLeod, Alistair 1936- DLB-60
Macleod, Fiona (see Sharp, William)
Macleod, Norman 1906-1985........... DLB-4
Mac Low, Jackson 1922- DLB-193
Macmillan and Company............. DLB-106
The Macmillan Company DLB-49
Macmillan's English Men of Letters,
First Series (1878-1892) DLB-144
MacNamara, Brinsley 1890-1963........ DLB-10
MacNeice, Louis 1907-1963 .... DLB-10, 20
Macphail, Andrew 1864-1938 .... DLB-92
Macpherson, James 1736-1796 .... DLB-109
Macpherson, Jay 1931- DLB-53
Macpherson, Jeanie 1884-1946......... DLB-44
Macrae Smith Company.............. DLB-46
MacRaye, Lucy Betty (see Webling, Lucy)
John Macrone [publishing house]....... DLB-106
MacShane, Frank 1927-1999........... DLB-111
Macy-Masius DLB-46
Madden, David 1933- DLB-6
Madden, Sir Frederic 1801-1873........ DLB-184
Maddow, Ben 1909-1992 .... DLB-44
Maddux, Rachel 1912-1983 ....DLB-234; Y-93
Madgett, Naomi Long 1923- DLB-76
Madhubuti, Haki R. 1942- DLB-5, 41; DS-8
Madison, James 1751-1836............. DLB-37
Madsen, Svend Åge 1939- DLB-214
Madrigal, Alfonso Fernández de (El Tostado)
ca. 1405-1455 .... DLB-286
Maeterlinck, Maurice 1862-1949 .... DLB-192
Mafūz, Najīb 1911- Y-88
Nobel Lecture 1988 .... Y-88
The Little Magazines of the
New Formalism DLB-282
Magee, David 1905-1977 .... DLB-187
Maginn, William 1794-1842 ....DLB-110, 159

Magoffin, Susan Shelby 1827-1855 ......DLB-239

Mahan, Alfred Thayer 1840-1914........DLB-47

Maheux-Forcier, Louise 1929- DLB-60

Mahin, John Lee 1902-1984............DLB-44

Mahon, Derek 1941- DLB-40

Maiakovsky, Vladimir Vladimirovich
  1893-1930....................DLB-295

Maikov, Apollon Nikolaevich
  1821-1897....................DLB-277

Maikov, Vasilii Ivanovich 1728-1778.....DLB-150

Mailer, Norman 1923-
  ....DLB-2, 16, 28, 185, 278; Y-80, 83, 97;
                              DS-3; CDALB-6

  Tribute to Isaac Bashevis Singer Y-91

  Tribute to Meyer Levin Y-81

Maillart, Ella 1903-1997..............DLB-195

Maillet, Adrienne 1885-1963...........DLB-68

Maillet, Antonine 1929- DLB-60

Maillu, David G. 1939- DLB-157

Maimonides, Moses 1138-1204 ....DLB-115

Main Selections of the Book-of-the-Month
  Club, 1926-1945 ....DLB-9

Mainwaring, Daniel 1902-1977 ....DLB-44

Mair, Charles 1838-1927 ....DLB-99

Mair, John circa 1467-1550 ....DLB-281

Maironis, Jonas 1862-1932 ..DLB-220; CDWLB-4

Mais, Roger 1905-1955 .....DLB-125; CDWLB-3

Maitland, Sara 1950- DLB-271

Major, Andre 1942- DLB-60

Major, Charles 1856-1913 ....DLB-202

Major, Clarence 1936- DLB-33

Major, Kevin 1949- DLB-60

Major Books DLB-46

Makanin, Vladimir Semenovich
  1937- DLB-285

Makarenko, Anton Semenovich
  1888-1939....................DLB-272

Makemie, Francis circa 1658-1708........DLB-24

The Making of Americans Contract Y-98

Maksimov, Vladimir Emel'ianovich
  1930-1995....................DLB-302

Maksimović, Desanka
  1898-1993..........DLB-147; CDWLB-4

Malamud, Bernard 1914-1986
  ....DLB-2, 28, 152; Y-80, 86; CDALB-1

  Bernard Malamud Archive at the
    Harry Ransom Humanities
    Research Center................Y-00

Mălăncioiu, Ileana 1940- DLB-232

Malaparte, Curzio
  (Kurt Erich Suckert) 1898-1957......DLB-264

Malerba, Luigi 1927- DLB-196

Malet, Lucas 1852-1931...............DLB-153

Mallarmé, Stéphane 1842-1898 ....DLB-217

Malleson, Lucy Beatrice (see Gilbert, Anthony)

Mallet-Joris, Françoise (Françoise Lilar)
  1930- DLB-83

Mallock, W. H. 1849-1923 ....DLB-18, 57

"Every Man His Own Poet; or,
  The Inspired Singer's Recipe
  Book" (1877)..................DLB-35

"Le Style c'est l'homme" (1892) DLB-57

Memoirs of Life and Literature (1920),
  [excerpt] DLB-57

Malone, Dumas 1892-1986 ....DLB-17

Malone, Edmond 1741-1812 ....DLB-142

Malory, Sir Thomas
  circa 1400-1410 - 1471....DLB-146; CDBLB-1

Malouf, David 1934- DLB-289

Malpede, Karen 1945- DLB-249

Malraux, André 1901-1976 ....DLB-72

Malthus, Thomas Robert
  1766-1834 ....DLB-107, 158

Maltz, Albert 1908-1985 ....DLB-102

Malzberg, Barry N. 1939- DLB-8

Mamet, David 1947- DLB-7

Mamin, Dmitrii Narkisovich
  1852-1912....................DLB-238

Manaka, Matsemela 1956- DLB-157

Manchester University Press..........DLB-112

Mandel, Eli 1922-1992...............DLB-53

Mandel'shtam, Nadezhda Iakovlevna
  1899-1980....................DLB-302

Mandel'shtam, Osip Emil'evich
  1891-1938....................DLB-295

Mandeville, Bernard 1670-1733 ....DLB-101

Mandeville, Sir John
  mid fourteenth century DLB-146

Mandiargues, André Pieyre de
  1909-1991....................DLB-83

Manea, Norman 1936- DLB-232

Manfred, Frederick 1912-1994....DLB-6, 212, 227

Manfredi, Gianfranco 1948- DLB-196

Mangan, Sherry 1904-1961 ....DLB-4

Manganelli, Giorgio 1922-1990 ....DLB-196

Manilius fl. first century A.D. DLB-211

Mankiewicz, Herman 1897-1953 ....DLB-26

Mankiewicz, Joseph L. 1909-1993 ......DLB-44

Mankowitz, Wolf 1924-1998 ....DLB-15

Manley, Delariviére 1672?-1724.....DLB-39, 80

  Preface to *The Secret History, of Queen
    Zarah, and the Zarazians* (1705).....DLB-39

Mann, Abby 1927- DLB-44

Mann, Charles 1929-1998 ....Y-98

Mann, Emily 1952- DLB-266

Mann, Heinrich 1871-1950 ....DLB-66, 118

Mann, Horace 1796-1859 ....DLB-1, 235

Mann, Klaus 1906-1949..............DLB-56

Mann, Mary Peabody 1806-1887 ....DLB-239

Mann, Thomas 1875-1955....DLB-66; CDWLB-2

Mann, William D'Alton 1839-1920......DLB-137

Mannin, Ethel 1900-1984 ....DLB-191, 195

Manning, Emily (see Australie)

Manning, Frederic 1882-1935 ....DLB-260

Manning, Laurence 1899-1972 ....DLB-251

Manning, Marie 1873?-1945 ....DLB-29

Manning and Loring DLB-49

Mannyng, Robert flourished
  1303-1338....................DLB-146

Mano, D. Keith 1942- DLB-6

Manor Books.......................DLB-46

Manrique, Gómez 1412?-1490.........DLB-286

Manrique, Jorge ca. 1440-1479 ....DLB-286

Mansfield, Katherine 1888-1923 ....DLB-162

Mantel, Hilary 1952- DLB-271

Manuel, Niklaus circa 1484-1530 ....DLB-179

Manzini, Gianna 1896-1974............DLB-177

Mapanje, Jack 1944- DLB-157

Maraini, Dacia 1936- DLB-196

Maramzin, Vladimir Rafailovich
  1934- DLB-302

March, William (William Edward Campbell)
  1893-1954....................DLB-9, 86

Marchand, Leslie A. 1900-1999........DLB-103

Marchant, Bessie 1862-1941 ....DLB-160

Marchant, Tony 1959- DLB-245

Marchenko, Anastasiia Iakovlevna
  1830-1880....................DLB-238

Marchessault, Jovette 1938- DLB-60

Marcinkevičius, Justinas 1930- DLB-232

Marcus, Frank 1928- DLB-13

Marcuse, Herbert 1898-1979 ....DLB-242

Marden, Orison Swett 1850-1924 ....DLB-137

Marechera, Dambudzo 1952-1987.......DLB-157

Marek, Richard, Books DLB-46

Mares, E. A. 1938- DLB-122

Margulies, Donald 1954- DLB-228

Mariani, Paul 1940- DLB-111

Marie de France flourished 1160-1178....DLB-208

Marie-Victorin, Frère (Conrad Kirouac)
  1885-1944....................DLB-92

Marin, Biagio 1891-1985 ....DLB-128

Marinetti, Filippo Tommaso
  1876-1944..................DLB-114, 264

Marinina, Aleksandra (Marina Anatol'evna
  Alekseeva) 1957- DLB-285

Marinković, Ranko
  1913- DLB-147; CDWLB-4

Marion, Frances 1886-1973 ....DLB-44

Marius, Richard C. 1933-1999 ....Y-85

Markevich, Boleslav Mikhailovich
  1822-1884....................DLB-238

Markfield, Wallace 1926-2002.........DLB-2, 28

Markham, Edwin 1852-1940 ....DLB-54, 186

Markle, Fletcher 1921-1991........DLB-68; Y-91

Marlatt, Daphne 1942- DLB-60

Marlitt, E. 1825-1887 ....DLB-129

Marlowe, Christopher
  1564-1593.............DLB-62; CDBLB-1

Marlyn, John 1912- DLB-88

Marmion, Shakerley 1603-1639.........DLB-58

Der Marner before 1230-circa 1287......DLB-138

Marnham, Patrick 1943- DLB-204

The *Marprelate Tracts* 1588-1589 .... DLB-132
Marquand, John P. 1893-1960 ...... DLB-9, 102
Marques, Helena 1935- DLB-287
Marqués, René 1919-1979 .... DLB-113, 305
Marquis, Don 1878-1937 .... DLB-11, 25
Marriott, Anne 1913-1997 .... DLB-68
Marryat, Frederick 1792-1848 ..... DLB-21, 163
Marsh, Capen, Lyon and Webb......... DLB-49
Marsh, George Perkins
   1801-1882 .... DLB-1, 64, 243
Marsh, James 1794-1842............ DLB-1, 59
Marsh, Narcissus 1638-1713.......... DLB-213
Marsh, Ngaio 1899-1982 .... DLB-77
Marshall, Alan 1902-1984............ DLB-260
Marshall, Edison 1894-1967 .... DLB-102
Marshall, Edward 1932- DLB-16
Marshall, Emma 1828-1899 .... DLB-163
Marshall, James 1942-1992 .... DLB-61
Marshall, Joyce 1913- DLB-88
Marshall, Paule 1929- DLB-33, 157, 227
Marshall, Tom 1938-1993 .... DLB-60
Marsilius of Padua
   circa 1275-circa 1342 .... DLB-115
Mars-Jones, Adam 1954- DLB-207
Marson, Una 1905-1965............. DLB-157
Marston, John 1576-1634 ....DLB-58, 172
Marston, Philip Bourke 1850-1887....... DLB-35
Martens, Kurt 1870-1945 .... DLB-66
Martí, José 1853-1895................ DLB-290
Martial circa A.D. 40-circa A.D. 103
   .... DLB-211; CDWLB-1
William S. Martien [publishing house] DLB-49
Martin, Abe (see Hubbard, Kin)
Martin, Catherine ca. 1847-1937........ DLB-230
Martin, Charles 1942- DLB-120, 282
Martin, Claire 1914- DLB-60
Martin, David 1915-1997 .... DLB-260
Martin, Jay 1935- DLB-111
Martin, Johann (see Laurentius von Schnüffis)
Martin, Thomas 1696-1771........... DLB-213
Martin, Violet Florence (see Ross, Martin)
Martin du Gard, Roger 1881-1958....... DLB-65
Martineau, Harriet
   1802-1876.....DLB-21, 55, 159, 163, 166, 190
Martínez, Demetria 1960- DLB-209
Martínez de Toledo, Alfonso
   1398?-1468................. DLB-286
Martínez, Eliud 1935- DLB-122
Martínez, Max 1943- DLB-82
Martínez, Rubén 1962- DLB-209
Martinson, Harry 1904-1978 .... DLB-259
Martinson, Moa 1890-1964 .... DLB-259
Martone, Michael 1955- DLB-218
Martyn, Edward 1859-1923 .... DLB-10
Marvell, Andrew
   1621-1678............ DLB-131; CDBLB-2

Marvin X 1944- DLB-38
Marx, Karl 1818-1883 .... DLB-129
Marzials, Theo 1850-1920 .... DLB-35
Masefield, John 1878-1967
   .... DLB-10, 19, 153, 160; CDBLB-5
Masham, Damaris Cudworth, Lady
   1659-1708................ DLB-252
Masino, Paola 1908-1989 .... DLB-264
Mason, A. E. W. 1865-1948........... DLB-70
Mason, Bobbie Ann
   1940- DLB-173; Y-87; CDALB-7
Mason, William 1725-1797 .... DLB-142
Mason Brothers DLB-49
The Massachusetts Quarterly Review
   1847-1850...................... DLB-1
The Masses........................ DLB-303
Massey, Gerald 1828-1907 .... DLB-32
Massey, Linton R. 1900-1974 .... DLB-187
Massie, Allan 1938- DLB-271
Massinger, Philip 1583-1640 .... DLB-58
Masson, David 1822-1907 .... DLB-144
Masters, Edgar Lee
   1868-1950 .... DLB-54; CDALB-3
Masters, Hilary 1928- DLB-244
Mastronardi, Lucio 1930-1979 ....DLB-177
Matevski, Mateja 1929- ... DLB-181; CDWLB-4
Mather, Cotton
   1663-1728....... DLB-24, 30, 140; CDALB-2
Mather, Increase 1639-1723 .... DLB-24
Mather, Richard 1596-1669 .... DLB-24
Matheson, Annie 1853-1924........... DLB-240
Matheson, Richard 1926- DLB-8, 44
Matheus, John F. 1887- DLB-51
Mathews, Cornelius 1817?-1889... DLB-3, 64, 250
Elkin Mathews [publishing house] DLB-112
Mathews, John Joseph 1894-1979........DLB-175
Mathias, Roland 1915- DLB-27
Mathis, June 1892-1927 .... DLB-44
Mathis, Sharon Bell 1937- DLB-33
Matković, Marijan 1915-1985 .... DLB-181
Matoš, Antun Gustav 1873-1914 .... DLB-147
Matos Paoli, Francisco 1915-2000 ...... DLB-290
Matsumoto Seichō 1909-1992 .... DLB-182
The Matter of England 1240-1400...... DLB-146
The Matter of Rome early twelfth to late
   fifteenth century................ DLB-146
Matthew of Vendôme
   circa 1130-circa 1200 .... DLB-208
Matthews, Brander 1852-1929 ..DLB-71, 78; DS-13
Matthews, Jack 1925- DLB-6
Matthews, Victoria Earle 1861-1907 .... DLB-221
Matthews, William 1942-1997 .... DLB-5
Matthías Jochumsson 1835-1920 .... DLB-293
Matthías Johannessen 1930- DLB-293
Matthiessen, F. O. 1902-1950 .... DLB-63
Matthiessen, Peter 1927- DLB-6, 173, 275
Maturin, Charles Robert 1780-1824......DLB-178

Maugham, W. Somerset 1874-1965
   ..... DLB-10, 36, 77, 100, 162, 195; CDBLB-6
Maupassant, Guy de 1850-1893........ DLB-123
Maupin, Armistead 1944- DLB-278
Mauriac, Claude 1914-1996............ DLB-83
Mauriac, François 1885-1970 .... DLB-65
Maurice, Frederick Denison 1805-1872 ... DLB-55
Maurois, André 1885-1967............. DLB-65
Maury, James 1718-1769............... DLB-31
Mavor, Elizabeth 1927- DLB-14
Mavor, Osborne Henry (see Bridie, James)
Maxwell, Gavin 1914-1969 .... DLB-204
Maxwell, William
   1908-2000 ....DLB-218, 278; Y-80
   Tribute to Nancy Hale................ Y-88
H. Maxwell [publishing house].......... DLB-49
John Maxwell [publishing house] DLB-106
May, Elaine 1932- DLB-44
May, Karl 1842-1912 .... DLB-129
May, Thomas 1595/1596-1650 .... DLB-58
Mayer, Bernadette 1945- DLB-165
Mayer, Mercer 1943- DLB-61
Mayer, O. B. 1818-1891 .... DLB-3, 248
Mayes, Herbert R. 1900-1987 ....DLB-137
Mayes, Wendell 1919-1992 .... DLB-26
Mayfield, Julian 1928-1984..........DLB-33; Y-84
Mayhew, Henry 1812-1887 ......DLB-18, 55, 190
Mayhew, Jonathan 1720-1766........... DLB-31
Mayne, Ethel Colburn 1865-1941 ....DLB-197
Mayne, Jasper 1604-1672 .... DLB-126
Mayne, Seymour 1944- DLB-60
Mayor, Flora Macdonald 1872-1932 ..... DLB-36
Mayröcker, Friederike 1924- DLB-85
Mazrui, Ali A. 1933- DLB-125
Mažuranić, Ivan 1814-1890 ....DLB-147
Mazursky, Paul 1930- DLB-44
McAlmon, Robert 1896-1956... DLB-4, 45; DS-15
   "A Night at Bricktop's" Y-01
McArthur, Peter 1866-1924 .... DLB-92
McAuley, James 1917-1976 .... DLB-260
Robert M. McBride and Company DLB-46
McCabe, Patrick 1955- DLB-194
McCaffrey, Anne 1926- DLB-8
McCann, Colum 1965- DLB-267
McCarthy, Cormac 1933- DLB-6, 143, 256
   The Cormac McCarthy Society......... Y-99
McCarthy, Mary 1912-1989.........DLB-2; Y-81
McCarthy, Shaun Lloyd (see Cory, Desmond)
McCay, Winsor 1871-1934 .... DLB-22
McClane, Albert Jules 1922-1991........DLB-171
McClatchy, C. K. 1858-1936 .... DLB-25
McClellan, George Marion 1860-1934.... DLB-50
   "The Negro as a Writer" DLB-50
McCloskey, Robert 1914- DLB-22
McClung, Nellie Letitia 1873-1951....... DLB-92

McClure, James 1939- DLB-276
McClure, Joanna 1930- DLB-16
McClure, Michael 1932- DLB-16
McClure, Phillips and Company DLB-46
McClure, S. S. 1857-1949..............DLB-91
A. C. McClurg and Company............DLB-49
McCluskey, John A., Jr. 1944- DLB-33
McCollum, Michael A. 1946- Y-87
McConnell, William C. 1917- DLB-88
McCord, David 1897-1997...............DLB-61
McCord, Louisa S. 1810-1879 ....DLB-248
McCorkle, Jill 1958- DLB-234; Y-87
McCorkle, Samuel Eusebius 1746-1811....DLB-37
McCormick, Anne O'Hare 1880-1954 ....DLB-29
McCormick, Kenneth Dale 1906-1997 ......Y-97
McCormick, Robert R. 1880-1955 ....DLB-29
McCourt, Edward 1907-1972.............DLB-88
McCoy, Horace 1897-1955 ....DLB-9
McCrae, Hugh 1876-1958 ....DLB-260
McCrae, John 1872-1918 ....DLB-92
McCullagh, Joseph B. 1842-1896........DLB-23
McCullers, Carson
  1917-1967 ..... DLB-2, 7, 173, 228; CDALB-1
McCulloch, Thomas 1776-1843..........DLB-99
McDermott, Alice 1953- DLB-292
McDonald, Forrest 1927- DLB-17
McDonald, Walter 1934- DLB-105, DS-9
  "Getting Started: Accepting the
  Regions You Own–or Which
  Own You" DLB-105
Tribute to James Dickey Y-97
McDougall, Colin 1917-1984............DLB-68
McDowell, Katharine Sherwood Bonner
  1849-1883 ....DLB-202, 239
Obolensky McDowell
  [publishing house]................DLB-46
McEwan, Ian 1948- DLB-14, 194
McFadden, David 1940- DLB-60
McFall, Frances Elizabeth Clarke
  (see Grand, Sarah)
McFarland, Ron 1942- DLB-256
McFarlane, Leslie 1902-1977 ....DLB-88
McFee, William 1881-1966 ....DLB-153
McGahern, John 1934- DLB-14, 231
McGee, Thomas D'Arcy 1825-1868 ......DLB-99
McGeehan, W. O. 1879-1933 ....DLB-25, 171
McGill, Ralph 1898-1969...............DLB-29
McGinley, Phyllis 1905-1978 ....DLB-11, 48
McGinniss, Joe 1942- DLB-185
McGirt, James E. 1874-1930 ....DLB-50
McGlashan and Gill...................DLB-106
McGough, Roger 1937- DLB-40
McGrath, John 1935- DLB-233
McGrath, Patrick 1950- DLB-231
McGraw-Hill..........................DLB-46
McGuane, Thomas 1939- DLB-2, 212; Y-80

Tribute to Seymour Lawrence Y-94
McGuckian, Medbh 1950- DLB-40
McGuffey, William Holmes 1800-1873....DLB-42
McGuinness, Frank 1953- DLB-245
McHenry, James 1785-1845............DLB-202
McIlvanney, William 1936- DLB-14, 207
McIlwraith, Jean Newton 1859-1938......DLB-92
McInerney, Jay 1955- DLB-292
McIntosh, Maria Jane 1803-1878....DLB-239, 248
McIntyre, James 1827-1906 ....DLB-99
McIntyre, O. O. 1884-1938............DLB-25
McKay, Claude 1889-1948 .... DLB-4, 45, 51, 117
The David McKay Company DLB-49
McKean, William V. 1820-1903 ....DLB-23
McKenna, Stephen 1888-1967..........DLB-197
The McKenzie Trust....................Y-96
McKerrow, R. B. 1872-1940 ....DLB-201
McKinley, Robin 1952- DLB-52
McKnight, Reginald 1956- DLB-234
McLachlan, Alexander 1818-1896........DLB-99
McLaren, Floris Clark 1904-1978 ......DLB-68
McLaverty, Michael 1907- DLB-15
McLean, Duncan 1964- DLB-267
McLean, John R. 1848-1916 ....DLB-23
McLean, William L. 1852-1931.........DLB-25
McLennan, William 1856-1904..........DLB-92
McLoughlin Brothers..................DLB-49
McLuhan, Marshall 1911-1980 ....DLB-88
McMaster, John Bach 1852-1932........DLB-47
McMillan, Terri 1951- DLB-292
McMurtry, Larry 1936-
  ...... DLB-2, 143, 256; Y-80, 87; CDALB-6
McNally, Terrence 1939- DLB-7, 249
McNeil, Florence 1937- DLB-60
McNeile, Herman Cyril 1888-1937 ......DLB-77
McNickle, D'Arcy 1904-1977.......DLB-175, 212
McPhee, John 1931- DLB-185, 275
McPherson, James Alan 1943- DLB-38, 244
McPherson, Sandra 1943- Y-86
McTaggart, J. M. E. 1866-1925 ....DLB-262
McWhirter, George 1939- DLB-60
McWilliam, Candia 1955- DLB-267
McWilliams, Carey 1905-1980 ....DLB-137
  "The Nation's Future," Carey
  McWilliams's Editorial Policy
  in Nation DLB-137
Mda, Zakes 1948- DLB-225
Mead, George Herbert 1863-1931......DLB-270
Mead, L. T. 1844-1914 ....DLB-141
Mead, Matthew 1924- DLB-40
Mead, Taylor ?- DLB-16
Meany, Tom 1903-1964 ....DLB-171
Mechthild von Magdeburg
  circa 1207-circa 1282..............DLB-138
Medieval Galician-Portuguese Poetry DLB-287

Medill, Joseph 1823-1899 ....DLB-43
Medoff, Mark 1940- DLB-7
Meek, Alexander Beaufort
  1814-1865 ....DLB-3, 248
Meeke, Mary ?-1816? DLB-116
Mei, Lev Aleksandrovich 1822-1862.....DLB-277
Meinke, Peter 1932- DLB-5
Mejia Vallejo, Manuel 1923- DLB-113
Melanchthon, Philipp 1497-1560 ......DLB-179
Melançon, Robert 1947- DLB-60
Mell, Max 1882-1971...........DLB-81, 124
Mellow, James R. 1926-1997 ....DLB-111
Mel'nikov, Pavel Ivanovich 1818-1883 ...DLB-238
Meltzer, David 1937- DLB-16
Meltzer, Milton 1915- DLB-61
Melville, Elizabeth, Lady Culross
  circa 1585-1640.................DLB-172
Melville, Herman
  1819-1891........DLB-3, 74, 250; CDALB-2
  The Melville Society Y-01
Melville, James
  (Roy Peter Martin) 1931- DLB-276
Mena, Juan de 1411-1456 ....DLB-286
Mena, María Cristina 1893-1965....DLB-209, 221
Menander 342-341 B.C.-circa 292-291 B.C.
  .... DLB-176; CDWLB-1
Menantes (see Hunold, Christian Friedrich)
Mencke, Johann Burckhard 1674-1732 ...DLB-168
Mencken, H. L. 1880-1956
  .... DLB-11, 29, 63, 137, 222; CDALB-4
  "Berlin, February, 1917" Y-00
  From the Initial Issue of American Mercury
  (January 1924)................DLB-137
  Mencken and Nietzsche: An
  Unpublished Excerpt from H. L.
  Mencken's My Life as Author and
  Editor.........................Y-93
Mendelssohn, Moses 1729-1786..........DLB-97
Mendes, Catulle 1841-1909............DLB-217
Méndez M., Miguel 1930- DLB-82
The Mercantile Library of New York Y-96
Mercer, Cecil William (see Yates, Dornford)
Mercer, David 1928-1980 ....DLB-13
Mercer, John 1704-1768 ....DLB-31
Mercer, Johnny 1909-1976.............DLB-265
Meredith, George
  1828-1909 .... DLB-18, 35, 57, 159; CDBLB-4
Meredith, Louisa Anne 1812-1895 ..DLB-166, 230
Meredith, Owen
  (see Lytton, Edward Robert Bulwer)
Meredith, William 1919- DLB-5
Meres, Francis
  Palladis Tamia, Wits Treasurie (1598)
  [excerpt] DLB-172
Merezhkovsky, Dmitrii Sergeevich
  1865-1941.....................DLB-295
Mergerle, Johann Ulrich
  (see Abraham à Sancta Clara)
Mérimée, Prosper 1803-1870........DLB-119, 192

Merivale, John Herman 1779-1844 ... DLB-96
Meriwether, Louise 1923- ... DLB-33
Merleau-Ponty, Maurice 1908-1961 ... DLB-296
Merlin Press ... DLB-112
Merriam, Eve 1916-1992 ... DLB-61
The Merriam Company ... DLB-49
Merril, Judith 1923-1997 ... DLB-251
    Tribute to Theodore Sturgeon ... Y-85
Merrill, James 1926-1995 ... DLB-5, 165; Y-85
Merrill and Baker ... DLB-49
The Mershon Company ... DLB-49
Merton, Thomas 1915-1968 ... DLB-48; Y-81
Merwin, W. S. 1927- ... DLB-5, 169
Julian Messner [publishing house] ... DLB-46
Mészöly, Miklós 1921- ... DLB-232
J. Metcalf [publishing house] ... DLB-49
Metcalf, John 1938- ... DLB-60
The Methodist Book Concern ... DLB-49
Methuen and Company ... DLB-112
Meun, Jean de (see *Roman de la Rose*)
Mew, Charlotte 1869-1928 ... DLB-19, 135
Mewshaw, Michael 1943- ... Y-80
    Tribute to Albert Erskine ... Y-93
Meyer, Conrad Ferdinand 1825-1898 ... DLB-129
Meyer, E. Y. 1946- ... DLB-75
Meyer, Eugene 1875-1959 ... DLB-29
Meyer, Michael 1921-2000 ... DLB-155
Meyers, Jeffrey 1939- ... DLB-111
Meynell, Alice 1847-1922 ... DLB-19, 98
Meynell, Viola 1885-1956 ... DLB-153
Meyrink, Gustav 1868-1932 ... DLB-81
Mézières, Philipe de circa 1327-1405 ... DLB-208
Michael, Ib 1945- ... DLB-214
Michael, Livi 1960- ... DLB-267
Michaëlis, Karen 1872-1950 ... DLB-214
Michaels, Anne 1958- ... DLB-299
Michaels, Leonard 1933- ... DLB-130
Michaux, Henri 1899-1984 ... DLB-258
Micheaux, Oscar 1884-1951 ... DLB-50
Michel of Northgate, Dan circa 1265-circa 1340 ... DLB-146
Micheline, Jack 1929-1998 ... DLB-16
Michener, James A. 1907?-1997 ... DLB-6
Micklejohn, George circa 1717-1818 ... DLB-31
Middle Hill Press ... DLB-106
Middleton, Christopher 1926- ... DLB-40
Middleton, Richard 1882-1911 ... DLB-156
Middleton, Stanley 1919- ... DLB-14
Middleton, Thomas 1580-1627 ... DLB-58
Miegel, Agnes 1879-1964 ... DLB-56
Miežalaitis, Eduardas 1919-1997 ... DLB-220
Miguéis, José Rodrigues 1901-1980 ... DLB-287
Mihailović, Dragoslav 1930- ... DLB-181
Mihalić, Slavko 1928- ... DLB-181

Mikhailov, A. (see Sheller, Aleksandr Konstantinovich)
Mikhailov, Mikhail Larionovich 1829-1865 ... DLB-238
Mikhailovsky, Nikolai Konstantinovich 1842-1904 ... DLB-277
Miles, Josephine 1911-1985 ... DLB-48
Miles, Susan (Ursula Wyllie Roberts) 1888-1975 ... DLB-240
Miliković, Branko 1934-1961 ... DLB-181
Milius, John 1944- ... DLB-44
Mill, James 1773-1836 ... DLB-107, 158, 262
Mill, John Stuart 1806-1873 ... DLB-55, 190, 262; CDBLB-4
    Thoughts on Poetry and Its Varieties (1833) ... DLB-32
Andrew Millar [publishing house] ... DLB-154
Millar, Kenneth 1915-1983 ... DLB-2, 226; Y-83; DS-6
Millay, Edna St. Vincent 1892-1950 ... DLB-45, 249; CDALB-4
Millen, Sarah Gertrude 1888-1968 ... DLB-225
Miller, Andrew 1960- ... DLB-267
Miller, Arthur 1915- ... DLB-7, 266; CDALB-1
    The Arthur Miller Society ... Y-01
Miller, Caroline 1903-1992 ... DLB-9
Miller, Eugene Ethelbert 1950- ... DLB-41
    Tribute to Julian Mayfield ... Y-84
Miller, Heather Ross 1939- ... DLB-120
Miller, Henry 1891-1980 ... DLB-4, 9; Y-80; CDALB-5
Miller, Hugh 1802-1856 ... DLB-190
Miller, J. Hillis 1928- ... DLB-67
Miller, Jason 1939- ... DLB-7
Miller, Joaquin 1839-1913 ... DLB-186
Miller, May 1899-1995 ... DLB-41
Miller, Paul 1906-1991 ... DLB-127
Miller, Perry 1905-1963 ... DLB-17, 63
Miller, Sue 1943- ... DLB-143
Miller, Vassar 1924-1998 ... DLB-105
Miller, Walter M., Jr. 1923-1996 ... DLB-8
Miller, Webb 1892-1940 ... DLB-29
James Miller [publishing house] ... DLB-49
Millett, Kate 1934- ... DLB-246
Millhauser, Steven 1943- ... DLB-2
Millican, Arthenia J. Bates 1920- ... DLB-38
Milligan, Alice 1866-1953 ... DLB-240
Mills, Magnus 1954- ... DLB-267
Mills and Boon ... DLB-112
Milman, Henry Hart 1796-1868 ... DLB-96
Milne, A. A. 1882-1956 ... DLB-10, 77, 100, 160
Milner, Ron 1938- ... DLB-38
William Milner [publishing house] ... DLB-106
Milnes, Richard Monckton (Lord Houghton) 1809-1885 ... DLB-32, 184
Milton, John 1608-1674 ... DLB-131, 151, 281; CDBLB-2
    The Milton Society of America ... Y-00

Miłosz, Czesław 1911- ... DLB-215; CDWLB-4
Minakami Tsutomu 1919- ... DLB-182
Minamoto no Sanetomo 1192-1219 ... DLB-203
Minco, Marga 1920- ... DLB-299
The Minerva Press ... DLB-154
Minnesang circa 1150-1280 ... DLB-138
    The Music of *Minnesang* ... DLB-138
Minns, Susan 1839-1938 ... DLB-140
Minton, Balch and Company ... DLB-46
Mirbeau, Octave 1848-1917 ... DLB-123, 192
Mirk, John died after 1414? ... DLB-146
Miró, Ricardo 1883-1940 ... DLB-290
Miron, Gaston 1928-1996 ... DLB-60
A Mirror for Magistrates ... DLB-167
Mishima Yukio 1925-1970 ... DLB-182
Mistral, Gabriela 1889-1957 ... DLB-283
Mitchel, Jonathan 1624-1668 ... DLB-24
Mitchell, Adrian 1932- ... DLB-40
Mitchell, Donald Grant 1822-1908 ... DLB-1, 243; DS-13
Mitchell, Gladys 1901-1983 ... DLB-77
Mitchell, James Leslie 1901-1935 ... DLB-15
Mitchell, John (see Slater, Patrick)
Mitchell, John Ames 1845-1918 ... DLB-79
Mitchell, Joseph 1908-1996 ... DLB-185; Y-96
Mitchell, Julian 1935- ... DLB-14
Mitchell, Ken 1940- ... DLB-60
Mitchell, Langdon 1862-1935 ... DLB-7
Mitchell, Loften 1919- ... DLB-38
Mitchell, Margaret 1900-1949 ... DLB-9; CDALB-7
Mitchell, S. Weir 1829-1914 ... DLB-202
Mitchell, W. J. T. 1942- ... DLB-246
Mitchell, W. O. 1914-1998 ... DLB-88
Mitchison, Naomi Margaret (Haldane) 1897-1999 ... DLB-160, 191, 255
Mitford, Mary Russell 1787-1855 ... DLB-110, 116
Mitford, Nancy 1904-1973 ... DLB-191
Mittelholzer, Edgar 1909-1965 ... DLB-117; CDWLB-3
Mitterer, Erika 1906- ... DLB-85
Mitterer, Felix 1948- ... DLB-124
Mitternacht, Johann Sebastian 1613-1679 ... DLB-168
Miyamoto Yuriko 1899-1951 ... DLB-180
Mizener, Arthur 1907-1988 ... DLB-103
Mo, Timothy 1950- ... DLB-194
Moberg, Vilhelm 1898-1973 ... DLB-259
Modern Age Books ... DLB-46
Modern Language Association of America
    The Modern Language Association of America Celebrates Its Centennial ... Y-84
The Modern Library ... DLB-46
Modiano, Patrick 1945- ... DLB-83, 299
Moffat, Yard and Company ... DLB-46
Moffet, Thomas 1553-1604 ... DLB-136
Mofolo, Thomas 1876-1948 ... DLB-225

Mohr, Nicholasa 1938- DLB-145

Moix, Ana María 1947- DLB-134

Molesworth, Louisa 1839-1921 ....DLB-135

Molière (Jean-Baptiste Poquelin)
1622-1673 ....DLB-268

Møller, Poul Martin 1794-1838 ....DLB-300

Möllhausen, Balduin 1825-1905 ....DLB-129

Molnár, Ferenc 1878-1952 ...DLB-215; CDWLB-4

Molnár, Miklós (see Mészöly, Miklós)

Momaday, N. Scott
1934- DLB-143, 175, 256; CDALB-7

Monkhouse, Allan 1858-1936 ....DLB-10

Monro, Harold 1879-1932 ....DLB-19

Monroe, Harriet 1860-1936 ....DLB-54, 91

Monsarrat, Nicholas 1910-1979 ....DLB-15

Montagu, Lady Mary Wortley
1689-1762 ....DLB-95, 101

Montague, C. E. 1867-1928 ....DLB-197

Montague, John 1929- DLB-40

Montale, Eugenio 1896-1981..........DLB-114

Montalvo, Garci Rodríguez de
ca. 1450?-before 1505 ....DLB-286

Montalvo, José 1946-1994 ....DLB-209

Monterroso, Augusto 1921-2003 ....DLB-145

Montesquiou, Robert de 1855-1921 ....DLB-217

Montgomerie, Alexander
circa 1550?-1598 ....DLB-167

Montgomery, James 1771-1854 ......DLB-93, 158

Montgomery, John 1919- DLB-16

Montgomery, Lucy Maud
1874-1942 ....DLB-92; DS-14

Montgomery, Marion 1925- DLB-6

Montgomery, Robert Bruce (see Crispin, Edmund)

Montherlant, Henry de 1896-1972 ....DLB-72

The Monthly Review 1749-1844.........DLB-110

Monti, Ricardo 1944- DLB-305

Montigny, Louvigny de 1876-1955 ......DLB-92

Montoya, José 1932- DLB-122

Moodie, John Wedderburn Dunbar
1797-1869 ....DLB-99

Moodie, Susanna 1803-1885 ....DLB-99

Moody, Joshua circa 1633-1697.........DLB-24

Moody, William Vaughn 1869-1910....DLB-7, 54

Moorcock, Michael 1939- DLB-14, 231, 261

Moore, Alan 1953- DLB-261

Moore, Brian 1921-1999 ....DLB-251

Moore, Catherine L. 1911-1987...........DLB-8

Moore, Clement Clarke 1779-1863 ....DLB-42

Moore, Dora Mavor 1888-1979..........DLB-92

Moore, G. E. 1873-1958 ....DLB-262

Moore, George 1852-1933....DLB-10, 18, 57, 135

Literature at Nurse, or Circulating Morals
(1885) DLB-18

Moore, Lorrie 1957- DLB-234

Moore, Marianne
1887-1972.........DLB-45; DS-7; CDALB-5

International Marianne Moore Society ...Y-98

Moore, Mavor 1919- DLB-88

Moore, Richard 1927- DLB-105

"The No Self, the Little Self, and
the Poets" DLB-105

Moore, T. Sturge 1870-1944 ....DLB-19

Moore, Thomas 1779-1852 ....DLB-96, 144

Moore, Ward 1903-1978 ....DLB-8

Moore, Wilstach, Keys and Company DLB-49

Moorehead, Alan 1901-1983 ....DLB-204

Moorhouse, Frank 1938- DLB-289

Moorhouse, Geoffrey 1931- DLB-204

The Moorland-Spingarn Research
Center DLB-76

Moorman, Mary C. 1905-1994 ....DLB-155

Mora, Pat 1942- DLB-209

Moraga, Cherríe 1952- DLB-82, 249

Morales, Alejandro 1944- DLB-82

Morales, Mario Roberto 1947- DLB-145

Morales, Rafael 1919- DLB-108

Morality Plays: *Mankind* circa 1450-1500
and *Everyman* circa 1500 ....DLB-146

Morand, Paul (1888-1976) DLB-65

Morante, Elsa 1912-1985..............DLB-177

Morata, Olympia Fulvia 1526-1555......DLB-179

Moravia, Alberto 1907-1990 ....DLB-177

Mordaunt, Elinor 1872-1942 ....DLB-174

Mordovtsev, Daniil Lukich 1830-1905 ...DLB-238

More, Hannah
1745-1833 ....DLB-107, 109, 116, 158

More, Henry 1614-1687 ....DLB-126, 252

More, Sir Thomas
1477/1478-1535 ....DLB-136, 281

Morejón, Nancy 1944- DLB-283

Morency, Pierre 1942- DLB-60

Moreno, Dorinda 1939- DLB-122

Moretti, Marino 1885-1979 ....DLB-114, 264

Morgan, Berry 1919- DLB-6

Morgan, Charles 1894-1958 ....DLB-34, 100

Morgan, Edmund S. 1916- DLB-17

Morgan, Edwin 1920- DLB-27

Morgan, John Pierpont 1837-1913 ......DLB-140

Morgan, John Pierpont, Jr. 1867-1943 ....DLB-140

Morgan, Robert 1944- DLB-120, 292

Morgan, Sydney Owenson, Lady
1776?-1859 ....DLB-116, 158

Morgner, Irmtraud 1933-1990..........DLB-75

Morhof, Daniel Georg 1639-1691 ....DLB-164

Mori Ōgai 1862-1922 ....DLB-180

Móricz, Zsigmond 1879-1942 ....DLB-215

Morier, James Justinian
1782 or 1783?-1849 ....DLB-116

Mörike, Eduard 1804-1875 ....DLB-133

Morin, Paul 1889-1963 ....DLB-92

Morison, Richard 1514?-1556 ....DLB-136

Morison, Samuel Eliot 1887-1976.........DLB-17

Morison, Stanley 1889-1967 ....DLB-201

Moritz, Karl Philipp 1756-1793 ....DLB-94

Moriz von Craûn circa 1220-1230.........DLB-138

Morley, Christopher 1890-1957 ....DLB-9

Morley, John 1838-1923 ....DLB-57, 144, 190

Moro, César 1903-1956................DLB-290

Morris, George Pope 1802-1864 ....DLB-73

Morris, James Humphrey (see Morris, Jan)

Morris, Jan 1926- DLB-204

Morris, Lewis 1833-1907..............DLB-35

Morris, Margaret 1737-1816............DLB-200

Morris, Mary McGarry 1943- DLB-292

Morris, Richard B. 1904-1989..........DLB-17

Morris, William 1834-1896
.....DLB-18, 35, 57, 156, 178, 184; CDBLB-4

Morris, Willie 1934-1999................Y-80

Tribute to Irwin Shaw................Y-84

Tribute to James Dickey Y-97

Morris, Wright
1910-1998 ....DLB-2, 206, 218; Y-81

Morrison, Arthur 1863-1945....DLB-70, 135, 197

Morrison, Charles Clayton 1874-1966 ....DLB-91

Morrison, John 1904-1998..............DLB-260

Morrison, Toni 1931-
........DLB-6, 33, 143; Y-81, 93; CDALB-6

Nobel Lecture 1993....................Y-93

Morrissy, Mary 1957- DLB-267

William Morrow and Company DLB-46

Morse, James Herbert 1841-1923 ....DLB-71

Morse, Jedidiah 1761-1826..............DLB-37

Morse, John T., Jr. 1840-1937 ....DLB-47

Morselli, Guido 1912-1973 ....DLB-177

Morte Arthure, the *Alliterative* and the
Stanzaic circa 1350-1400..........DLB-146

Mortimer, Favell Lee 1802-1878 ....DLB-163

Mortimer, John
1923- DLB-13, 245, 271; CDBLB-8

Morton, Carlos 1942- DLB-122

Morton, H. V. 1892-1979 ....DLB-195

John P. Morton and Company DLB-49

Morton, Nathaniel 1613-1685 ....DLB-24

Morton, Sarah Wentworth 1759-1846.....DLB-37

Morton, Thomas circa 1579-circa 1647 ....DLB-24

Moscherosch, Johann Michael
1601-1669 ....DLB-164

Humphrey Moseley
[publishing house]................DLB-170

Möser, Justus 1720-1794 ....DLB-97

Mosley, Nicholas 1923- DLB-14, 207

Moss, Arthur 1889-1969 ....DLB-4

Moss, Howard 1922-1987 ....DLB-5

Moss, Thylias 1954- DLB-120

Motion, Andrew 1952- DLB-40

Motley, John Lothrop
1814-1877 ....DLB-1, 30, 59, 235

Motley, Willard 1909-1965 ....DLB-76, 143

Mott, Lucretia 1793-1880................DLB-239

Benjamin Motte Jr. [publishing house] DLB-154

Motteux, Peter Anthony 1663-1718 ...... DLB-80

Mottram, R. H. 1883-1971 .... DLB-36

Mount, Ferdinand 1939- DLB-231

Mouré, Erin 1955- DLB-60

Mourning Dove (Humishuma) between 1882 and 1888?-1936 .... DLB-175, 221

Movies
Fiction into Film, 1928-1975: A List of Movies Based on the Works of Authors in British Novelists, 1930-1959 .... DLB-15

Movies from Books, 1920-1974 .... DLB-9

Mowat, Farley 1921- DLB-68

A. R. Mowbray and Company, Limited DLB-106

Mowrer, Edgar Ansel 1892-1977 .... DLB-29

Mowrer, Paul Scott 1887-1971 .... DLB-29

Edward Moxon [publishing house] DLB-106

Joseph Moxon [publishing house] DLB-170

Moyes, Patricia 1923-2000 .... DLB-276

Mphahlele, Es'kia (Ezekiel) 1919- DLB-125, 225; CDWLB-3

Mrożek, Sławomir 1930- .. DLB-232; CDWLB-4

Mtshali, Oswald Mbuyiseni 1940- DLB-125, 225

Mucedorus DLB-62

Mudford, William 1782-1848 .... DLB-159

Mudrooroo (see Johnson, Colin)

Mueller, Lisel 1924- DLB-105

Muhajir, El (see Marvin X)

Muhajir, Nazzam Al Fitnah (see Marvin X)

Mühlbach, Luise 1814-1873 .... DLB-133

Muir, Edwin 1887-1959 .... DLB-20, 100, 191

Muir, Helen 1937- DLB-14

Muir, John 1838-1914 .... DLB-186, 275

Muir, Percy 1894-1979 .... DLB-201

Mujū Ichien 1226-1312 .... DLB-203

Mukherjee, Bharati 1940- DLB-60, 218

Mulcaster, Richard 1531 or 1532-1611 .. DLB-167

Muldoon, Paul 1951- DLB-40

Mulisch, Harry 1927- DLB-299

Müller, Friedrich (see Müller, Maler)

Müller, Heiner 1929-1995 .... DLB-124

Müller, Maler 1749-1825 .... DLB-94

Muller, Marcia 1944- DLB-226

Müller, Wilhelm 1794-1827 .... DLB-90

Mumford, Lewis 1895-1990 .... DLB-63

Munby, A. N. L. 1913-1974 .... DLB-201

Munby, Arthur Joseph 1828-1910 ...... DLB-35

Munday, Anthony 1560-1633 ...... DLB-62, 172

Mundt, Clara (see Mühlbach, Luise)

Mundt, Theodore 1808-1861 .... DLB-133

Munford, Robert circa 1737-1783 ...... DLB-31

Mungoshi, Charles 1947- DLB-157

Munk, Kaj 1898-1944 .... DLB-214

Munonye, John 1929- DLB-117

Munro, Alice 1931- DLB-53

George Munro [publishing house] DLB-49

Munro, H. H. 1870-1916 .... DLB-34, 162; CDBLB-5

Munro, Neil 1864-1930 .... DLB-156

Norman L. Munro [publishing house] DLB-49

Munroe, Kirk 1850-1930 .... DLB-42

Munroe and Francis DLB-49

James Munroe and Company DLB-49

Joel Munsell [publishing house] DLB-49

Munsey, Frank A. 1854-1925 .... DLB-25, 91

Frank A. Munsey and Company DLB-49

Murakami Haruki 1949- DLB-182

Murav'ev, Mikhail Nikitich 1757-1807 ... DLB-150

Murdoch, Iris 1919-1999 .... DLB-14, 194, 233; CDBLB-8

Murdock, James
From *Sketches of Modern Philosophy* DS-5

Murdoch, Rupert 1931- DLB-127

Murfree, Mary N. 1850-1922 .... DLB-12, 74

Murger, Henry 1822-1861 .... DLB-119

Murger, Louis-Henri (see Murger, Henry)

Murnane, Gerald 1939- DLB-289

Murner, Thomas 1475-1537 .... DLB-179

Muro, Amado 1915-1971 .... DLB-82

Murphy, Arthur 1727-1805 .... DLB-89, 142

Murphy, Beatrice M. 1908-1992 ...... DLB-76

Murphy, Dervla 1931- DLB-204

Murphy, Emily 1868-1933 .... DLB-99

Murphy, Jack 1923-1980 .... DLB-241

Murphy, John H., III 1916- DLB-127

Murphy, Richard 1927-1993 .... DLB-40

John Murphy and Company DLB-49

Murray, Albert L. 1916- DLB-38

Murray, Gilbert 1866-1957 .... DLB-10

Murray, Jim 1919-1998 .... DLB-241

John Murray [publishing house] DLB-154

Murray, Judith Sargent 1751-1820 .... DLB-37, 200

Murray, Les 1938- DLB-289

Murray, Pauli 1910-1985 .... DLB-41

Murry, John Middleton 1889-1957 ..... DLB-149

"The Break-Up of the Novel" (1922) DLB-36

Murry, John Middleton, Jr. (see Cowper, Richard)

Musäus, Johann Karl August 1735-1787 ... DLB-97

Muschg, Adolf 1934- DLB-75

Musil, Robert 1880-1942 .... DLB-81, 124; CDWLB-2

Muspilli circa 790-circa 850 .... DLB-148

Musset, Alfred de 1810-1857 .... DLB-192, 217

Benjamin B. Mussey and Company DLB-49

Muste, A. J. 1885-1967 .... DLB-303

Mutafchieva, Vera 1929- DLB-181

Mutis, Alvaro 1923- DLB-283

Mwangi, Meja 1948- DLB-125

Myers, Frederic W. H. 1843-1901 ...... DLB-190

Myers, Gustavus 1872-1942 .... DLB-47

Myers, L. H. 1881-1944 .... DLB-15

Myers, Walter Dean 1937- DLB-33

Myerson, Julie 1960- DLB-267

Mykle, Agnar 1915-1994 .... DLB-297

Mykolaitis-Putinas, Vincas 1893-1967 .... DLB-220

Myles, Eileen 1949- DLB-193

Myrdal, Jan 1927- DLB-257

Mystery
1985: The Year of the Mystery: A Symposium Y-85

Comments from Other Writers Y-85

The Second Annual New York Festival of Mystery Y-00

Why I Read Mysteries Y-85

Why I Write Mysteries: Night and Day, by Michael Collins Y-85

N

Na Prous Boneta circa 1296-1328 ...... DLB-208

Nabl, Franz 1883-1974 .... DLB-81

Nabokov, Véra 1902-1991 .... Y-91

Nabokov, Vladimir 1899-1977 .. DLB-2, 244, 278; Y-80, 91; DS-3; CDALB-1

International Nabokov Society Y-99

An Interview [On Nabokov], by Fredson Bowers Y-80

Nabokov Festival at Cornell Y-83

The Vladimir Nabokov Archive in the Berg Collection of the New York Public Library: An Overview Y-91

The Vladimir Nabokov Society Y-01

Nádaši, Ladislav (see Jégé)

Naden, Constance 1858-1889 .... DLB-199

Nadezhdin, Nikolai Ivanovich 1804-1856 .... DLB-198

Nadson, Semen Iakovlevich 1862-1887 ... DLB-277

Naevius circa 265 B.C.-201 B.C. DLB-211

Nafis and Cornish DLB-49

Nagai Kafū 1879-1959 .... DLB-180

Nagel, Ernest 1901-1985 .... DLB-279

Nagibin, Iurii Markovich 1920-1994 .... DLB-302

Nagrodskaia, Evdokiia Apollonovna 1866-1930 .... DLB-295

Naipaul, Shiva 1945-1985 .... DLB-157; Y-85

Naipaul, V. S. 1932- DLB-125, 204, 207; Y-85, Y-01; CDBLB-8; CDWLB-3

Nobel Lecture 2001: "Two Worlds" Y-01

Nakagami Kenji 1946-1992 .... DLB-182

Nakano-in Masatada no Musume (see Nijō, Lady)

Nałkowska, Zofia 1884-1954 .... DLB-215

Namora, Fernando 1919-1989 .... DLB-287

Joseph Nancrede [publishing house] DLB-49

Naranjo, Carmen 1930- DLB-145

Narbikova, Valeriia Spartakovna 1958- DLB-285

Narezhny, Vasilii Trofimovich 1780-1825 ....DLB-198

Narrache, Jean (Emile Coderre) 1893-1970 ....DLB-92

Nasby, Petroleum Vesuvius (see Locke, David Ross)

Eveleigh Nash [publishing house] DLB-112

Nash, Ogden 1902-1971.................DLB-11

Nashe, Thomas 1567-1601?..........DLB-167

Nason, Jerry 1910-1986.................DLB-241

Nasr, Seyyed Hossein 1933- DLB-279

Nast, Condé 1873-1942.................DLB-91

Nast, Thomas 1840-1902.................DLB-188

Nastasijević, Momčilo 1894-1938 ....DLB-147

Nathan, George Jean 1882-1958 ....DLB-137

Nathan, Robert 1894-1985 ....DLB-9

Nation, Carry A. 1846-1911 ....DLB-303

National Book Critics Circle Awards.....Y-00–01

The National Jewish Book Awards Y-85

Natsume Sōseki 1867-1916...........DLB-180

Naughton, Bill 1910-1992 ....DLB-13

Navarro, Joe 1953- DLB-209

Naylor, Gloria 1950- DLB-173

Nazor, Vladimir 1876-1949 ....DLB-147

Ndebele, Njabulo 1948- DLB-157, 225

Neagoe, Peter 1881-1960.................DLB-4

Neal, John 1793-1876.................DLB-1, 59, 243

Neal, Joseph C. 1807-1847 ....DLB-11

Neal, Larry 1937-1981.................DLB-38

The Neale Publishing Company DLB-49

Nearing, Scott 1883-1983.................DLB-303

Nebel, Frederick 1903-1967.................DLB-226

Nebrija, Antonio de 1442 or 1444-1522 ...DLB-286

Nedreaas, Torborg 1906-1987 ....DLB-297

F. Tennyson Neely [publishing house].....DLB-49

Negoițescu, Ion 1921-1993 ....DLB-220

Negri, Ada 1870-1945 ....DLB-114

Neihardt, John G. 1881-1973......DLB-9, 54, 256

Neidhart von Reuental circa 1185-circa 1240.................DLB-138

Neilson, John Shaw 1872-1942.......DLB-230

Nekrasov, Nikolai Alekseevich 1821-1877 ....DLB-277

Nekrasov, Viktor Platonovich 1911-1987 ....DLB-302

Neledinsky-Meletsky, Iurii Aleksandrovich 1752-1828 ....DLB-150

Nelligan, Emile 1879-1941 ....DLB-92

Nelson, Alice Moore Dunbar 1875-1935 ...DLB-50

Nelson, Antonya 1961- DLB-244

Nelson, Kent 1943- DLB-234

Nelson, Richard K. 1941- DLB-275

Nelson, Thomas, and Sons [U.K.].......DLB-106

Nelson, Thomas, and Sons [U.S.].......DLB-49

Nelson, William 1908-1978 ....DLB-103

Nelson, William Rockhill 1841-1915......DLB-23

Nemerov, Howard 1920-1991 .....DLB-5, 6; Y-83

Németh, László 1901-1975.................DLB-215

Nepos circa 100 B.C.-post 27 B.C.........DLB-211

Nėris, Salomėja 1904-1945 ..DLB-220; CDWLB-4

Neruda, Pablo 1904-1973.................DLB-283

Nerval, Gérard de 1808-1855 ....DLB-217

Nervo, Amado 1870-1919 ....DLB-290

Nesbit, E. 1858-1924 ....DLB-141, 153, 178

Ness, Evaline 1911-1986 ....DLB-61

Nestroy, Johann 1801-1862.................DLB-133

Nettleship, R. L. 1846-1892.................DLB-262

Neugeboren, Jay 1938- DLB-28

Neukirch, Benjamin 1655-1729 ....DLB-168

Neumann, Alfred 1895-1952 ....DLB-56

Neumann, Ferenc (see Molnár, Ferenc)

Neumark, Georg 1621-1681 ....DLB-164

Neumeister, Erdmann 1671-1756.......DLB-168

Nevins, Allan 1890-1971 .... DLB-17; DS-17

Nevinson, Henry Woodd 1856-1941 ....DLB-135

The New American Library DLB-46

New Directions Publishing Corporation ...DLB-46

The New Monthly Magazine 1814-1884.....DLB-110

New York Times Book Review Y-82

John Newbery [publishing house].......DLB-154

Newbolt, Henry 1862-1938.................DLB-19

Newbound, Bernard Slade (see Slade, Bernard)

Newby, Eric 1919- DLB-204

Newby, P. H. 1918- DLB-15

Thomas Cautley Newby [publishing house].................DLB-106

Newcomb, Charles King 1820-1894 ...DLB-1, 223

Newell, Peter 1862-1924 ....DLB-42

Newell, Robert Henry 1836-1901 ....DLB-11

Newhouse, Samuel I. 1895-1979 ....DLB-127

Newman, Cecil Earl 1903-1976 ....DLB-127

Newman, David 1937- DLB-44

Newman, Frances 1883-1928.................Y-80

Newman, Francis William 1805-1897 ....DLB-190

Newman, John Henry 1801-1890.................DLB-18, 32, 55

Mark Newman [publishing house].........DLB-49

Newmarch, Rosa Harriet 1857-1940 .....DLB-240

George Newnes Limited DLB-112

Newsome, Effie Lee 1885-1979 ....DLB-76

Newton, A. Edward 1864-1940 ....DLB-140

Newton, Sir Isaac 1642-1727 ....DLB-252

Nexø, Martin Andersen 1869-1954 ....DLB-214

Nezval, Vítěslav 1900-1958 ....DLB-215; CDWLB-4

Ngugi wa Thiong'o 1938- DLB-125; CDWLB-3

Niatum, Duane 1938- DLB-175

The Nibelungenlied and the Klage circa 1200 ....DLB-138

Nichol, B. P. 1944-1988.................DLB-53

Nicholas of Cusa 1401-1464 ....DLB-115

Nichols, Ann 1891?-1966 ....DLB-249

Nichols, Beverly 1898-1983.................DLB-191

Nichols, Dudley 1895-1960 ....DLB-26

Nichols, Grace 1950- DLB-157

Nichols, John 1940- Y-82

Nichols, Mary Sargeant (Neal) Gove 1810-1884 ....DLB-1, 243

Nichols, Peter 1927- DLB-13, 245

Nichols, Roy F. 1896-1973.................DLB-17

Nichols, Ruth 1948- DLB-60

Nicholson, Edward Williams Byron 1849-1912 ....DLB-184

Nicholson, Geoff 1953- DLB-271

Nicholson, Norman 1914- DLB-27

Nicholson, William 1872-1949.................DLB-141

Ní Chuilleanáin, Eiléan 1942- DLB-40

Nicol, Eric 1919- DLB-68

Nicolai, Friedrich 1733-1811 ....DLB-97

Nicolas de Clamanges circa 1363-1437 ...DLB-208

Nicolay, John G. 1832-1901 and Hay, John 1838-1905 ....DLB-47

Nicole, Pierre 1625-1695 ....DLB-268

Nicolson, Adela Florence Cory (see Hope, Laurence)

Nicolson, Harold 1886-1968 ...... DLB-100, 149

"The Practice of Biography," in The English Sense of Humour and Other Essays DLB-149

Nicolson, Nigel 1917- DLB-155

Niebuhr, Reinhold 1892-1971 ..... DLB-17; DS-17

Niedecker, Lorine 1903-1970.................DLB-48

Nieman, Lucius W. 1857-1935 ....DLB-25

Nietzsche, Friedrich 1844-1900 ....DLB-129; CDWLB-2

Mencken and Nietzsche: An Unpublished Excerpt from H. L. Mencken's *My Life as Author and Editor* Y-93

Nievo, Stanislao 1928- DLB-196

Niggli, Josefina 1910-1983 ....Y-80

Nightingale, Florence 1820-1910 ....DLB-166

Nijō, Lady (Nakano-in Masatada no Musume) 1258-after 1306.................DLB-203

Nijō Yoshimoto 1320-1388 ....DLB-203

Nikitin, Ivan Savvich 1824-1861 ....DLB-277

Nikitin, Nikolai Nikolaevich 1895-1963 ..DLB-272

Nikolev, Nikolai Petrovich 1758-1815....DLB-150

Niles, Hezekiah 1777-1839 ....DLB-43

Nims, John Frederick 1913-1999 ....DLB-5

Tribute to Nancy Hale Y-88

Nin, Anaïs 1903-1977.................DLB-2, 4, 152

Nína Björk Árnadóttir 1941-2000 ....DLB-293

Niño, Raúl 1961- DLB-209

Nissenson, Hugh 1933- DLB-28

Niven, Frederick John 1878-1944.......DLB-92

Niven, Larry 1938- DLB-8

Nixon, Howard M. 1909-1983 ....DLB-201

Nizan, Paul 1905-1940.................DLB-72

435

Njegoš, Petar II Petrović
   1813-1851............DLB-147; CDWLB-4
Nkosi, Lewis 1936- DLB-157, 225
Noah, Mordecai M. 1785-1851........DLB-250
Noailles, Anna de 1876-1933 ....DLB-258
Nobel Peace Prize
   The Nobel Prize and Literary Politics....Y-88
   Elie Wiesel..................Y-86
Nobel Prize in Literature
   Joseph Brodsky................Y-87
   Camilo José Cela................Y-89
   Dario Fo...................Y-97
   Gabriel García Márquez.............Y-82
   William Golding................Y-83
   Nadine Gordimer................Y-91
   Günter Grass..................Y-99
   Seamus Heaney................Y-95
   Imre Kertész.................Y-02
   Najīb Mahfūz.................Y-88
   Toni Morrison.................Y-93
   V. S. Naipaul.................Y-01
   Kenzaburō Ōe................Y-94
   Octavio Paz..................Y-90
   José Saramago................Y-98
   Jaroslav Seifert................Y-84
   Claude Simon.................Y-85
   Wole Soyinka.................Y-86
   Wisława Szymborska..............Y-96
   Derek Walcott................Y-92
   Gao Xingjian..................Y-00
Nobre, António 1867-1900 ....DLB-287
Nodier, Charles 1780-1844............DLB-119
Noël, Marie (Marie Mélanie Rouget)
   1883-1967.....................DLB-258
Noel, Roden 1834-1894 ....DLB-35
Nogami Yaeko 1885-1985 ....DLB-180
Nogo, Rajko Petrov 1945- DLB-181
Nolan, William F. 1928- DLB-8
   Tribute to Raymond Chandler Y-88
Noland, C. F. M. 1810?-1858 ....DLB-11
Noma Hiroshi 1915-1991 ....DLB-182
Nonesuch Press DLB-112
Creative Nonfiction Y-02
Nonni (Jón Stefán Sveinsson or Svensson)
   1857-1944.....................DLB-293
Noon, Jeff 1957- DLB-267
Noonan, Robert Phillipe (see Tressell, Robert)
Noonday Press DLB-46
Noone, John 1936- DLB-14
Nora, Eugenio de 1923- DLB-134
Nordan, Lewis 1939- DLB-234
Nordbrandt, Henrik 1945- DLB-214
Nordhoff, Charles 1887-1947 ....DLB-9
Norén, Lars 1944- DLB-257
Norfolk, Lawrence 1963- DLB-267
Norman, Charles 1904-1996 ....DLB-111

Norman, Marsha 1947- DLB-266; Y-84
Norris, Charles G. 1881-1945 ....DLB-9
Norris, Frank
   1870-1902.......DLB-12, 71, 186; CDALB-3
Norris, Helen 1916- DLB-292
Norris, John 1657-1712 ....DLB-252
Norris, Leslie 1921- DLB-27, 256
Norse, Harold 1916- DLB-16
Norte, Marisela 1955- DLB-209
North, Marianne 1830-1890...........DLB-174
North Point Press DLB-46
Nortje, Arthur 1942-1970 ....DLB-125, 225
Norton, Alice Mary (see Norton, Andre)
Norton, Andre 1912- DLB-8, 52
Norton, Andrews 1786-1853.... DLB-1, 235; DS-5
Norton, Caroline 1808-1877 ...DLB-21, 159, 199
Norton, Charles Eliot
   1827-1908................DLB-1, 64, 235
Norton, John 1606-1663..............DLB-24
Norton, Mary 1903-1992 ....DLB-160
Norton, Thomas 1532-1584............DLB-62
W. W. Norton and Company DLB-46
Norwood, Robert 1874-1932 ....DLB-92
Nosaka Akiyuki 1930- DLB-182
Nossack, Hans Erich 1901-1977 ....DLB-69
Notker Balbulus circa 840-912 ....DLB-148
Notker III of Saint Gall
   circa 950-1022 ....DLB-148
Notker von Zweifalten ?-1095 ....DLB-148
Nourse, Alan E. 1928- DLB-8
Novak, Slobodan 1924- DLB-181
Novak, Vjenceslav 1859-1905 ....DLB-147
Novakovich, Josip 1956- DLB-244
Novalis 1772-1801 ....DLB-90; CDWLB-2
Novaro, Mario 1868-1944 ....DLB-114
Novás Calvo, Lino 1903-1983 ....DLB-145
Novelists
   Library Journal Statements and
     Questionnaires from First Novelists....Y-87
Novels
   The Columbia History of the American Novel
     A Symposium on................Y-92
   The Great Modern Library Scam Y-98
   Novels for Grown-Ups...............Y-97
   The Proletarian Novel DLB-9
   Novel, The "Second-Generation" Holocaust
     ....DLB-299
   The Year in the Novel......Y-87–88, Y-90–93
Novels, British
   "The Break-Up of the Novel" (1922),
     by John Middleton Murry.......DLB-36
   The Consolidation of Opinion: Critical
     Responses to the Modernists.....DLB-36
   "Criticism in Relation to Novels"
     (1863), by G. H. Lewes.........DLB-21
   "Experiment in the Novel" (1929)
     [excerpt], by John D. Beresford...DLB-36
   "The Future of the Novel" (1899), by
     Henry James.................DLB-18

   The Gay Science (1866), by E. S. Dallas
     [excerpt].....................DLB-21
   A Haughty and Proud Generation
     (1922), by Ford Madox Hueffer ..DLB-36
   Literary Effects of World War II.....DLB-15
   "Modern Novelists –Great and Small"
     (1855), by Margaret Oliphant....DLB-21
   The Modernists (1932),
     by Joseph Warren Beach........DLB-36
   A Note on Technique (1926), by
     Elizabeth A. Drew [excerpts].....DLB-36
   Novel-Reading: *The Works of Charles
     Dickens; The Works of W. Makepeace
     Thackeray* (1879),
     by Anthony Trollope DLB-21
   Novels with a Purpose (1864), by
     Justin M'Carthy...............DLB-21
   "On Art in Fiction" (1838),
     by Edward Bulwer DLB-21
   The Present State of the English Novel
     (1892), by George Saintsbury DLB-18
   Representative Men and Women:
     A Historical Perspective on
     the British Novel, 1930-1960.....DLB-15
   "The Revolt" (1937), by Mary Colum
     [excerpts]....................DLB-36
   "Sensation Novels" (1863), by
     H. L. Manse DLB-21
   Sex, Class, Politics, and Religion [in
     the British Novel, 1930-1959]....DLB-15
   Time and Western Man (1927),
     by Wyndham Lewis [excerpts]...DLB-36
Noventa, Giacomo 1898-1960 ....DLB-114
Novikov, Nikolai Ivanovich
   1744-1818.....................DLB-150
Novomeský, Laco 1904-1976.........DLB-215
Nowlan, Alden 1933-1983 ....DLB-53
Noyes, Alfred 1880-1958 ....DLB-20
Noyes, Crosby S. 1825-1908 ....DLB-23
Noyes, Nicholas 1647-1717 ....DLB-24
Noyes, Theodore W. 1858-1946 ....DLB-29
Nozick, Robert 1938-2002 ....DLB-279
N-Town Plays circa 1468 to early
   sixteenth century................DLB-146
Nugent, Frank 1908-1965.............DLB-44
Nušić, Branislav 1864-1938 ..DLB-147; CDWLB-4
David Nutt [publishing house] DLB-106
Nwapa, Flora 1931-1993 ....DLB-125; CDWLB-3
Nye, Edgar Wilson (Bill)
   1850-1896...............DLB-11, 23, 186
Nye, Naomi Shihab 1952- DLB-120
Nye, Robert 1939- DLB-14, 271
Nyka-Niliūnas, Alfonsas 1919- DLB-220

O

Oakes, Urian circa 1631-1681 ....DLB-24
Oakes Smith, Elizabeth
   1806-1893 ....DLB-1, 239, 243
Oakley, Violet 1874-1961..............DLB-188
Oates, Joyce Carol 1938-
   ....DLB-2, 5, 130; Y-81; CDALB-6

Tribute to Michael M. Rea Y-97

Ōba Minako 1930- DLB-182

Ober, Frederick Albion 1849-1913 ......DLB-189

Ober, William 1920-1993 .... Y-93

Oberholtzer, Ellis Paxson 1868-1936......DLB-47

The Obituary as Literary Form Y-02

Obradović, Dositej 1740?-1811 ....DLB-147

O'Brien, Charlotte Grace 1845-1909.....DLB-240

O'Brien, Edna 1932- ...DLB-14, 231; CDBLB-8

O'Brien, Fitz-James 1828-1862...........DLB-74

O'Brien, Flann (see O'Nolan, Brian)

O'Brien, Kate 1897-1974 ....DLB-15

O'Brien, Tim
1946- DLB-152; Y-80; DS-9; CDALB-7

O'Casey, Sean 1880-1964 .....DLB-10; CDBLB-6

Occom, Samson 1723-1792 ....DLB-175

Occomy, Marita Bonner 1899-1971.......DLB-51

Ochs, Adolph S. 1858-1935.............DLB-25

Ochs-Oakes, George Washington
1861-1931 ....DLB-137

O'Connor, Flannery 1925-1964
........DLB-2, 152; Y-80; DS-12; CDALB-1

The Flannery O'Connor Society........ Y-99

O'Connor, Frank 1903-1966 ....DLB-162

O'Connor, Joseph 1963- DLB-267

Octopus Publishing Group DLB-112

Oda Sakunosuke 1913-1947 ....DLB-182

Odell, Jonathan 1737-1818 ....DLB-31, 99

O'Dell, Scott 1903-1989................DLB-52

Odets, Clifford 1906-1963 ....DLB-7, 26

Odhams Press Limited................DLB-112

Odio, Eunice 1922-1974................DLB-283

Odoevsky, Aleksandr Ivanovich
1802-1839 ....DLB-205

Odoevsky, Vladimir Fedorovich
1804 or 1803-1869 ....DLB-198

O'Donnell, Peter 1920- DLB-87

O'Donovan, Michael (see O'Connor, Frank)

O'Dowd, Bernard 1866-1953 ....DLB-230

Ōe, Kenzaburō 1935- DLB-182; Y-94

Nobel Lecture 1994: Japan, the
Ambiguous, and Myself Y-94

Oehlenschläger, Adam 1779-1850 ....DLB-300

O'Faolain, Julia 1932- DLB-14, 231

O'Faolain, Sean 1900-1991 ....DLB-15, 162

Off-Loop Theatres......................DLB-7

Offord, Carl Ruthven 1910- DLB-76

O'Flaherty, Liam 1896-1984 ... DLB-36, 162; Y-84

Ogarev, Nikolai Platonovich 1813-1877 ..DLB-277

J. S. Ogilvie and Company DLB-49

Ogilvy, Eliza 1822-1912................DLB-199

Ogot, Grace 1930- DLB-125

O'Grady, Desmond 1935- DLB-40

Ogunyemi, Wale 1939- DLB-157

O'Hagan, Howard 1902-1982...........DLB-68

O'Hara, Frank 1926-1966 .... DLB-5, 16, 193

O'Hara, John
1905-1970 ....DLB-9, 86; DS-2; CDALB-5

John O'Hara's Pottsville Journalism Y-88

O'Hare, Kate Richards 1876-1948.......DLB-303

O'Hegarty, P. S. 1879-1955 ....DLB-201

Ohio State University
The William Charvat American Fiction
Collection at the Ohio State
University Libraries Y-92

Okara, Gabriel 1921- DLB-125; CDWLB-3

O'Keeffe, John 1747-1833................DLB-89

Nicholas Okes [publishing house] DLB-170

Okigbo, Christopher
1930-1967 ....DLB-125; CDWLB-3

Okot p'Bitek 1931-1982.....DLB-125; CDWLB-3

Okpewho, Isidore 1941- DLB-157

Okri, Ben 1959- DLB-157, 231

Ólafur Jóhann Sigurðsson 1918-1988 ....DLB-293

Old Dogs / New Tricks? New Technologies,
the Canon, and the Structure of
the Profession Y-02

Old Franklin Publishing House DLB-49

Old German Genesis and Old German Exodus
circa 1050-circa 1130...............DLB-148

The Old High German Isidor
circa 790-800 ....DLB-148

Older, Fremont 1856-1935 ....DLB-25

Oldham, John 1653-1683................DLB-131

Oldman, C. B. 1894-1969 ....DLB-201

Olds, Sharon 1942- DLB-120

Olearius, Adam 1599-1671 ....DLB-164

O'Leary, Ellen 1831-1889 ....DLB-240

O'Leary, Juan E. 1879-1969............DLB-290

Olesha, Iurii Karlovich 1899-1960......DLB-272

Oliphant, Laurence 1829?-1888......DLB-18, 166

Oliphant, Margaret 1828-1897...DLB-18, 159, 190

"Modern Novelists–Great and Small"
(1855) DLB-21

Oliveira, Carlos de 1921-1981..........DLB-287

Oliver, Chad 1928-1993 ....DLB-8

Oliver, Mary 1935- DLB-5, 193

Ollier, Claude 1922- DLB-83

Olsen, Tillie 1912/1913-
.............DLB-28, 206; Y-80; CDALB-7

Olson, Charles 1910-1970 .... DLB-5, 16, 193

Olson, Elder 1909- DLB-48, 63

Olson, Sigurd F. 1899-1982 ....DLB-275

The Omega Workshops DS-10

Omotoso, Kole 1943- DLB-125

Omulevsky, Innokentii Vasil'evich
1836 [or 1837]-1883 ....DLB-238

Ondaatje, Michael 1943- DLB-60

O'Neill, Eugene 1888-1953 .....DLB-7; CDALB-5

Eugene O'Neill Memorial Theater
Center..........................DLB-7

Eugene O'Neill's Letters: A Review Y-88

Onetti, Juan Carlos
1909-1994 ....DLB-113; CDWLB-3

Onions, George Oliver 1872-1961.......DLB-153

Onofri, Arturo 1885-1928 ....DLB-114

O'Nolan, Brian 1911-1966.............DLB-231

Oodgeroo of the Tribe Noonuccal
(Kath Walker) 1920-1993 ....DLB-289

Opie, Amelia 1769-1853..........DLB-116, 159

Opitz, Martin 1597-1639 ....DLB-164

Oppen, George 1908-1984...........DLB-5, 165

Oppenheim, E. Phillips 1866-1946 ....DLB-70

Oppenheim, James 1882-1932...........DLB-28

Oppenheimer, Joel 1930-1988 ....DLB-5, 193

Optic, Oliver (see Adams, William Taylor)

Orczy, Emma, Baroness 1865-1947.......DLB-70

Oregon Shakespeare Festival Y-00

Origo, Iris 1902-1988..................DLB-155

O'Riordan, Kate 1960- DLB-267

Orlovitz, Gil 1918-1973 ....DLB-2, 5

Orlovsky, Peter 1933- DLB-16

Ormond, John 1923- DLB-27

Ornitz, Samuel 1890-1957 ....DLB-28, 44

O'Rourke, P. J. 1947- DLB-185

Orozco, Olga 1920-1999 ....DLB-283

Orten, Jiří 1919-1941..................DLB-215

Ortese, Anna Maria 1914- DLB-177

Ortiz, Simon J. 1941- DLB-120, 175, 256

Ortnit and Wolfdietrich circa 1225-1250 ....DLB-138

Orton, Joe 1933-1967.........DLB-13; CDBLB-8

Orwell, George (Eric Arthur Blair)
1903-1950 ...DLB-15, 98, 195, 255; CDBLB-7

The Orwell Year..................... Y-84

(Re-)Publishing Orwell Y-86

Ory, Carlos Edmundo de 1923- DLB-134

Osbey, Brenda Marie 1957- DLB-120

Osbon, B. S. 1827-1912 ....DLB-43

Osborn, Sarah 1714-1796 ....DLB-200

Osborne, John 1929-1994 .....DLB-13; CDBLB-7

Osgood, Frances Sargent 1811-1850 .....DLB-250

Osgood, Herbert L. 1855-1918 ....DLB-47

James R. Osgood and Company DLB-49

Osgood, McIlvaine and Company DLB-112

O'Shaughnessy, Arthur 1844-1881 ....DLB-35

Patrick O'Shea [publishing house] DLB-49

Osipov, Nikolai Petrovich 1751-1799.....DLB-150

Oskison, John Milton 1879-1947 ....DLB-175

Osler, Sir William 1849-1919 ....DLB-184

Osofisan, Femi 1946- DLB-125; CDWLB-3

Ostenso, Martha 1900-1963 ....DLB-92

Ostrauskas, Kostas 1926- DLB-232

Ostriker, Alicia 1937- DLB-120

Ostrovsky, Aleksandr Nikolaevich
1823-1886 ....DLB-277

Ostrovsky, Nikolai Alekseevich
1904-1936 ....DLB-272

Osundare, Niyi 1947- DLB-157; CDWLB-3

Oswald, Eleazer 1755-1795 ....DLB-43

Oswald von Wolkenstein
1376 or 1377-1445 ....DLB-179

Otero, Blas de 1916-1979 . . . . DLB-134
Otero, Miguel Antonio 1859-1944 . . . . DLB-82
Otero, Nina 1881-1965. . . . . DLB-209
Otero Silva, Miguel 1908-1985. . . . . DLB-145
Otfried von Weißenburg
 circa 800-circa 875? DLB-148
Otis, Broaders and Company. DLB-49
Otis, James (see Kaler, James Otis)
Otis, James, Jr. 1725-1783 . . . . DLB-31
Ottaway, James 1911-2000 . . . . DLB-127
Ottendorfer, Oswald 1826-1900. . . . . DLB-23
Ottieri, Ottiero 1924- DLB-177
Otto-Peters, Louise 1819-1895 . . . . DLB-129
Otway, Thomas 1652-1685 . . . . DLB-80
Ouellette, Fernand 1930- DLB-60
Ouida 1839-1908 . . . . DLB-18, 156
Outing Publishing Company DLB-46
Overbury, Sir Thomas
 circa 1581-1613 . . . . DLB-151
The Overlook Press DLB-46
Ovid 43 B.C.-A.D. 17 . . . . . . DLB-211; CDWLB-1
Owen, Guy 1925- DLB-5
Owen, John 1564-1622. . . . . DLB-121
John Owen [publishing house] DLB-49
Peter Owen Limited DLB-112
Owen, Robert 1771-1858 . . . . .DLB-107, 158
Owen, Wilfred
 1893-1918. . . . . DLB-20; DS-18; CDBLB-6
 A Centenary Celebration. Y-93
 The Wilfred Owen Association Y-98
The Owl and the Nightingale
 circa 1189-1199 . . . . DLB-146
Owsley, Frank L. 1890-1956 . . . . DLB-17
Oxford, Seventeenth Earl of, Edward
 de Vere 1550-1604. . . . . .DLB-172
OyamO (Charles F. Gordon)
 1943- DLB-266
Ozerov, Vladislav Aleksandrovich
 1769-1816. . . . . DLB-150
Ozick, Cynthia 1928- . . .DLB-28, 152, 299; Y-82
 First Strauss "Livings" Awarded
  to Cynthia Ozick and
  Raymond Carver
   An Interview with Cynthia Ozick Y-83
 Tribute to Michael M. Rea Y-97

P

Pace, Richard 1482?-1536 . . . . DLB-167
Pacey, Desmond 1917-1975. . . . . DLB-88
Pacheco, José Emilio 1939- DLB-290
Pack, Robert 1929- DLB-5
Padell Publishing Company DLB-46
Padgett, Ron 1942- DLB-5
Padilla, Ernesto Chávez 1944- DLB-122
L. C. Page and Company. DLB-49
Page, Louise 1955- DLB-233
Page, P. K. 1916- DLB-68

Page, Thomas Nelson
 1853-1922 . . . . .DLB-12, 78; DS-13
Page, Walter Hines 1855-1918. . . . . DLB-71, 91
Paget, Francis Edward 1806-1882 . . . . . . DLB-163
Paget, Violet (see Lee, Vernon)
Pagliarani, Elio 1927- DLB-128
Pain, Barry 1864-1928 . . . . .DLB-135, 197
Pain, Philip ?-circa 1666 . . . . DLB-24
Paine, Robert Treat, Jr. 1773-1811 . . . . DLB-37
Paine, Thomas
 1737-1809 . . . . DLB-31, 43, 73, 158; CDALB-2
Painter, George D. 1914- DLB-155
Painter, William 1540?-1594 . . . . DLB-136
Palazzeschi, Aldo 1885-1974 . . . . DLB-114, 264
Palei, Marina Anatol'evna 1955- DLB-285
Palencia, Alfonso de 1424-1492 . . . . DLB-286
Palés Matos, Luis 1898-1959 . . . . DLB-290
Paley, Grace 1922- DLB-28, 218
Paley, William 1743-1805 . . . . DLB-252
Palfrey, John Gorham
 1796-1881. . . . . DLB-1, 30, 235
Palgrave, Francis Turner 1824-1897. . . . . DLB-35
Palmer, Joe H. 1904-1952. . . . . .DLB-171
Palmer, Michael 1943- DLB-169
Palmer, Nettie 1885-1964 . . . . DLB-260
Palmer, Vance 1885-1959 . . . . DLB-260
Paltock, Robert 1697-1767. . . . . DLB-39
Paludan, Jacob 1896-1975 . . . . DLB-214
Paludin-Müller, Frederik 1809-1876 . . . . DLB-300
Pan Books Limited DLB-112
Panaev, Ivan Ivanovich 1812-1862. . . . . . DLB-198
Panaeva, Avdot'ia Iakovlevna
 1820-1893 . . . . DLB-238
Panama, Norman 1914- and
 Frank, Melvin 1913-1988. . . . . DLB-26
Pancake, Breece D'J 1952-1979 . . . . DLB-130
Panduro, Leif 1923-1977. . . . . DLB-214
Panero, Leopoldo 1909-1962 . . . . DLB-108
Pangborn, Edgar 1909-1976 . . . . DLB-8
Panizzi, Sir Anthony 1797-1879 . . . . DLB-184
Panneton, Philippe (see Ringuet)
Panova, Vera Fedorovna 1905-1973. . . . . DLB-302
Panshin, Alexei 1940- DLB-8
Pansy (see Alden, Isabella)
Pantheon Books DLB-46
Papadat-Bengescu, Hortensia
 1876-1955. . . . . DLB-220
Papantonio, Michael 1907-1976 . . . . DLB-187
Paperback Library DLB-46
Paperback Science Fiction. DLB-8
Papini, Giovanni 1881-1956 . . . . DLB-264
Paquet, Alfons 1881-1944. . . . . DLB-66
Paracelsus 1493-1541 . . . . .DLB-179
Paradis, Suzanne 1936- DLB-53
Páral, Vladimír, 1932- DLB-232
Pardoe, Julia 1804-1862 . . . . DLB-166

Paredes, Américo 1915-1999 . . . . DLB-209
Pareja Diezcanseco, Alfredo 1908-1993 . . DLB-145
Parents' Magazine Press DLB-46
Parfit, Derek 1942- DLB-262
Parise, Goffredo 1929-1986 . . . . .DLB-177
Parish, Mitchell 1900-1993 . . . . DLB-265
Parizeau, Alice 1930-1990. . . . . DLB-60
Park, Ruth 1923?- DLB-260
Parke, John 1754-1789 . . . . DLB-31
Parker, Dan 1893-1967. . . . . DLB-241
Parker, Dorothy 1893-1967 . . . . . . DLB-11, 45, 86
Parker, Gilbert 1860-1932 . . . . DLB-99
Parker, James 1714-1770 . . . . DLB-43
Parker, John [publishing house] DLB-106
Parker, Matthew 1504-1575 . . . . DLB-213
Parker, Stewart 1941-1988 . . . . DLB-245
Parker, Theodore 1810-1860 . . . DLB-1, 235; DS-5
Parker, William Riley 1906-1968 . . . . DLB-103
J. H. Parker [publishing house] DLB-106
Parkes, Bessie Rayner (Madame Belloc)
 1829-1925 . . . . DLB-240
Parkman, Francis
 1823-1893 . . . . .DLB-1, 30, 183, 186, 235
Parks, Gordon 1912- DLB-33
Parks, Tim 1954- DLB-231
Parks, William 1698-1750. . . . . DLB-43
William Parks [publishing house] DLB-49
Parley, Peter (see Goodrich, Samuel Griswold)
Parmenides late sixth-fifth century B.C. DLB-176
Parnell, Thomas 1679-1718 . . . . DLB-95
Parnicki, Teodor 1908-1988 . . . . DLB-215
Parnok, Sofiia Iakovlevna (Parnokh)
 1885-1933 . . . . DLB-295
Parr, Catherine 1513?-1548 . . . . DLB-136
Parra, Nicanor 1914- DLB-283
Parrington, Vernon L. 1871-1929 . . . . . .DLB-17, 63
Parrish, Maxfield 1870-1966. . . . . DLB-188
Parronchi, Alessandro 1914- DLB-128
Parshchikov, Aleksei Maksimovich
 (Raiderman) 1954- DLB-285
Partisan Review DLB-303
Parton, James 1822-1891 . . . . DLB-30
Parton, Sara Payson Willis
 1811-1872. . . . . .DLB-43, 74, 239
S. W. Partridge and Company DLB-106
Parun, Vesna 1922- DLB-181; CDWLB-4
Pascal, Blaise 1623-1662 . . . . .DLB-268
Pasinetti, Pier Maria 1913- DLB-177
 Tribute to Albert Erskine. Y-93
Pasolini, Pier Paolo 1922-1975 . . . . . .DLB-128, 177
Pastan, Linda 1932- DLB-5
Pasternak, Boris
 1890-1960 . . . . DLB-302
Paston, George (Emily Morse Symonds)
 1860-1936 . . . . .DLB-149, 197
The Paston Letters 1422-1509 . . . . DLB-146

Pastorius, Francis Daniel 1651-circa 1720 . . . . DLB-24

Patchen, Kenneth 1911-1972 . . . . DLB-16, 48

Pater, Walter 1839-1894 . . DLB-57, 156; CDBLB-4

    Aesthetic Poetry (1873) DLB-35

    "Style" (1888) [excerpt] DLB-57

Paterson, A. B. "Banjo" 1864-1941 . . . . . DLB-230

Paterson, Katherine 1932- DLB-52

Patmore, Coventry 1823-1896 . . . . DLB-35, 98

Paton, Alan 1903-1988 . . . . DLB-225; DS-17

Paton, Joseph Noel 1821-1901 . . . . DLB-35

Paton Walsh, Jill 1937- DLB-161

Patrick, Edwin Hill ("Ted") 1901-1964 . . . DLB-137

Patrick, John 1906-1995 . . . . DLB-7

Pattee, Fred Lewis 1863-1950 . . . . DLB-71

Patterson, Alicia 1906-1963 . . . . DLB-127

Patterson, Eleanor Medill 1881-1948 . . . . . DLB-29

Patterson, Eugene 1923- DLB-127

Patterson, Joseph Medill 1879-1946 . . . . . . DLB-29

Pattillo, Henry 1726-1801 . . . . DLB-37

Paul, Elliot 1891-1958 . . . . DLB-4; DS-15

Paul, Jean (see Richter, Johann Paul Friedrich)

Paul, Kegan, Trench, Trubner and Company Limited DLB-106

Peter Paul Book Company DLB-49

Stanley Paul and Company Limited DLB-112

Paulding, James Kirke 1778-1860 . . . . DLB-3, 59, 74, 250

Paulin, Tom 1949- DLB-40

Pauper, Peter, Press DLB-46

Paustovsky, Konstantin Georgievich 1892-1968 . . . . DLB-272

Pavese, Cesare 1908-1950 . . . . DLB-128, 177

Pavić, Milorad 1929- DLB-181; CDWLB-4

Pavlov, Konstantin 1933- DLB-181

Pavlov, Nikolai Filippovich 1803-1864 . . . . DLB-198

Pavlova, Karolina Karlovna 1807-1893 . . . . DLB-205

Pavlović, Miodrag 1928- DLB-181; CDWLB-4

Pavlovsky, Eduardo 1933- DLB-305

Paxton, John 1911-1985 . . . . DLB-44

Payn, James 1830-1898 . . . . DLB-18

Payne, John 1842-1916 . . . . DLB-35

Payne, John Howard 1791-1852 . . . . DLB-37

Payson and Clarke DLB-46

Paz, Octavio 1914-1998 . . . . . . DLB-290; Y-90, 98

    Nobel Lecture 1990 . . . . Y-90

Pazzi, Roberto 1946- DLB-196

Pea, Enrico 1881-1958 . . . . DLB-264

Peabody, Elizabeth Palmer 1804-1894 . . . . DLB-1, 223

    Preface to *Record of a School: Exemplifying the General Principles of Spiritual Culture* DS-5

Elizabeth Palmer Peabody [publishing house] DLB-49

Peabody, Josephine Preston 1874-1922 . . . DLB-249

Peabody, Oliver William Bourn 1799-1848 . . . . DLB-59

Peace, Roger 1899-1968 . . . . DLB-127

Peacham, Henry 1578-1644? DLB-151

Peacham, Henry, the Elder 1547-1634 . . . . DLB-172, 236

Peachtree Publishers, Limited DLB-46

Peacock, Molly 1947- DLB-120

Peacock, Thomas Love 1785-1866 . . . DLB-96, 116

Pead, Deuel ?-1727 . . . . DLB-24

Peake, Mervyn 1911-1968 . . . . . DLB-15, 160, 255

Peale, Rembrandt 1778-1860 . . . . DLB-183

Pear Tree Press DLB-112

Pearce, Philippa 1920- DLB-161

H. B. Pearson [publishing house] DLB-49

Pearson, Hesketh 1887-1964 . . . . DLB-149

Peattie, Donald Culross 1898-1964 . . . . . . DLB-275

Pechersky, Andrei (see Mel'nikov, Pavel Ivanovich)

Peck, George W. 1840-1916 . . . . DLB-23, 42

H. C. Peck and Theo. Bliss [publishing house] DLB-49

Peck, Harry Thurston 1856-1914 . . . . . DLB-71, 91

Peden, William 1913-1999 . . . . DLB-234

    Tribute to William Goyen Y-83

Peele, George 1556-1596 . . . . DLB-62, 167

Pegler, Westbrook 1894-1969 . . . . DLB-171

Péguy, Charles 1873-1914 . . . . DLB-258

Peirce, Charles Sanders 1839-1914 . . . . . . DLB-270

Pekić, Borislav 1930-1992 . . . DLB-181; CDWLB-4

Pelevin, Viktor Olegovich 1962- DLB-285

Pellegrini and Cudahy DLB-46

Pelletier, Aimé (see Vac, Bertrand)

Pelletier, Francine 1959- DLB-251

Pellicer, Carlos 1897?-1977 . . . . DLB-290

Pemberton, Sir Max 1863-1950 . . . . DLB-70

de la Peña, Terri 1947- DLB-209

Penfield, Edward 1866-1925 . . . . DLB-188

Penguin Books [U.K.] DLB-112

    Fifty Penguin Years Y-85

    Penguin Collectors' Society Y-98

Penguin Books [U.S.] DLB-46

Penn, William 1644-1718 . . . . DLB-24

Penn Publishing Company DLB-49

Penna, Sandro 1906-1977 . . . . DLB-114

Pennell, Joseph 1857-1926 . . . . DLB-188

Penner, Jonathan 1940- Y-83

Pennington, Lee 1939- Y-82

Penton, Brian 1904-1951 . . . . DLB-260

Pepper, Stephen C. 1891-1972 . . . . DLB-270

Pepys, Samuel 1633-1703 . . . . DLB-101, 213; CDBLB-2

Percy, Thomas 1729-1811 . . . . DLB-104

Percy, Walker 1916-1990 . . . . . . DLB-2; Y-80, 90

    Tribute to Caroline Gordon Y-81

Percy, William 1575-1648 . . . . DLB-172

Perec, Georges 1936-1982 . . . . DLB-83, 299

Perelman, Bob 1947- DLB-193

Perelman, S. J. 1904-1979 . . . . DLB-11, 44

Pérez de Guzmán, Fernán ca. 1377-ca. 1460 . . . . DLB-286

Perez, Raymundo "Tigre" 1946- DLB-122

Peri Rossi, Cristina 1941- DLB-145, 290

Perkins, Eugene 1932- DLB-41

Perkins, Maxwell

    The Claims of Business and Literature: An Undergraduate Essay Y-01

Perkins, William 1558-1602 . . . . DLB-281

Perkoff, Stuart Z. 1930-1974 . . . . DLB-16

Perley, Moses Henry 1804-1862 . . . . DLB-99

Permabooks DLB-46

Perovsky, Aleksei Alekseevich (Antonii Pogorel'sky) 1787-1836 . . . . . DLB-198

Perrault, Charles 1628-1703 . . . . DLB-268

Perri, Henry 1561-1617 . . . . DLB-236

Perrin, Alice 1867-1934 . . . . DLB-156

Perry, Anne 1938- DLB-276

Perry, Bliss 1860-1954 . . . . DLB-71

Perry, Eleanor 1915-1981 . . . . DLB-44

Perry, Henry (see Perri, Henry)

Perry, Matthew 1794-1858 . . . . DLB-183

Perry, Sampson 1747-1823 . . . . DLB-158

Perse, Saint-John 1887-1975 . . . . DLB-258

Persius A.D. 34-A.D. 62 . . . . DLB-211

Perutz, Leo 1882-1957 . . . . DLB-81

Pesetsky, Bette 1932- DLB-130

Pessanha, Camilo 1867-1926 . . . . DLB-287

Pessoa, Fernando 1888-1935 . . . . DLB-287

Pestalozzi, Johann Heinrich 1746-1827 . . . . DLB-94

Peter, Laurence J. 1919-1990 . . . . DLB-53

Peter of Spain circa 1205-1277 . . . . DLB-115

Peterkin, Julia 1880-1961 . . . . DLB-9

Peters, Ellis (Edith Pargeter) 1913-1995 . . . . DLB-276

Peters, Lenrie 1932- DLB-117

Peters, Robert 1924- DLB-105

    "Foreword to *Ludwig of Baviria*" DLB-105

Petersham, Maud 1889-1971 and Petersham, Miska 1888-1960 . . . . DLB-22

Peterson, Charles Jacobs 1819-1887 . . . . . DLB-79

Peterson, Len 1917- DLB-88

Peterson, Levi S. 1933- DLB-206

Peterson, Louis 1922-1998 . . . . DLB-76

Peterson, T. B., and Brothers DLB-49

Petitclair, Pierre 1813-1860 . . . . DLB-99

Petrescu, Camil 1894-1957 . . . . DLB-220

Petronius circa A.D. 20-A.D. 66 . . . . DLB-211; CDWLB-1

Petrov, Aleksandar 1938- DLB-181

Petrov, Evgenii (Evgenii Petrovich Kataev) 1903-1942 . . . . DLB-272

Petrov, Gavriil 1730-1801 . . . . DLB-150

Petrov, Valeri 1920- DLB-181

Petrov, Vasilii Petrovich 1736-1799 ..... DLB-150

Petrović, Rastko 1898-1949 .... DLB-147; CDWLB-4

Petrushevskaia, Liudmila Stefanovna 1938- DLB-285

Petruslied circa 854? DLB-148

Petry, Ann 1908-1997 .... DLB-76

Pettie, George circa 1548-1589 .... DLB-136

Pétur Gunnarsson 1947- DLB-293

Peyton, K. M. 1929- DLB-161

Pfaffe Konrad flourished circa 1172 ..... DLB-148

Pfaffe Lamprecht flourished circa 1150 .. DLB-148

Pfeiffer, Emily 1827-1890 .... DLB-199

Pforzheimer, Carl H. 1879-1957 .... DLB-140

Phaedrus circa 18 B.C.-circa A.D. 50 .... DLB-211

Phaer, Thomas 1510?-1560 .... DLB-167

Phaidon Press Limited DLB-112

Pharr, Robert Deane 1916-1992 .... DLB-33

Phelps, Elizabeth Stuart 1815-1852 ..... DLB-202

Phelps, Elizabeth Stuart 1844-1911 ... DLB-74, 221

Philander von der Linde (see Mencke, Johann Burckhard)

Philby, H. St. John B. 1885-1960 .... DLB-195

Philip, Marlene Nourbese 1947- DLB-157

Philippe, Charles-Louis 1874-1909 ...... DLB-65

Philips, John 1676-1708 .... DLB-95

Philips, Katherine 1632-1664 .... DLB-131

Phillipps, Sir Thomas 1792-1872 .... DLB-184

Phillips, Caryl 1958- DLB-157

Phillips, David Graham 1867-1911 .... DLB-9, 12, 303

Phillips, Jayne Anne 1952- DLB-292; Y-80

 Tribute to Seymour Lawrence Y-94

Phillips, Robert 1938- DLB-105

 "Finding, Losing, Reclaiming: A Note on My Poems" DLB-105

 Tribute to William Goyen Y-83

Phillips, Stephen 1864-1915 .... DLB-10

Phillips, Ulrich B. 1877-1934 .... DLB-17

Phillips, Wendell 1811-1884 .... DLB-235

Phillips, Willard 1784-1873 .... DLB-59

Phillips, William 1907-2002 .... DLB-137

Phillips, Sampson and Company DLB-49

Phillpotts, Adelaide Eden (Adelaide Ross) 1896-1993 .... DLB-191

Phillpotts, Eden 1862-1960 ... DLB-10, 70, 135, 153

Philo circa 20-15 B.C.-circa A.D. 50 ..... DLB-176

Philosophical Library DLB-46

Philosophy
 Eighteenth-Century Philosophical Background DLB-31

 Philosophic Thought in Boston DLB-235

 Translators of the Twelfth Century: Literary Issues Raised and Impact Created DLB-115

Elihu Phinney [publishing house] DLB-49

Phoenix, John (see Derby, George Horatio)

PHYLON (Fourth Quarter, 1950), The Negro in Literature: The Current Scene DLB-76

Physiologus circa 1070-circa 1150 .... DLB-148

Piccolo, Lucio 1903-1969 .... DLB-114

Pickard, Tom 1946- DLB-40

William Pickering [publishing house] DLB-106

Pickthall, Marjorie 1883-1922 .... DLB-92

Picoult, Jodi 1966- DLB-292

Pictorial Printing Company DLB-49

Piel, Gerard 1915- DLB-137

 "An Announcement to Our Readers," Gerard Piel's Statement in *Scientific American* (April 1948) DLB-137

Pielmeier, John 1949- DLB-266

Piercy, Marge 1936- DLB-120, 227

Pierro, Albino 1916-1995 .... DLB-128

Pignotti, Lamberto 1926- DLB-128

Pike, Albert 1809-1891 .... DLB-74

Pike, Zebulon Montgomery 1779-1813 ... DLB-183

Pillat, Ion 1891-1945 .... DLB-220

Pil'niak, Boris Andreevich (Boris Andreevich Vogau) 1894-1938 .... DLB-272

Pilon, Jean-Guy 1930- DLB-60

Pinar, Florencia fl. ca. late fifteenth century DLB-286

Pinckney, Eliza Lucas 1722-1793 .... DLB-200

Pinckney, Josephine 1895-1957 .... DLB-6

Pindar circa 518 B.C.-circa 438 B.C. DLB-176; CDWLB-1

Pindar, Peter (see Wolcot, John)

Pineda, Cecile 1942- DLB-209

Pinero, Arthur Wing 1855-1934 .... DLB-10

Piñero, Miguel 1946-1988 .... DLB-266

Pinget, Robert 1919-1997 .... DLB-83

Pinkney, Edward Coote 1802-1828 ..... DLB-248

Pinnacle Books DLB-46

Piñon, Nélida 1935- DLB-145

Pinsky, Robert 1940- Y-82

 Reappointed Poet Laureate Y-98

Pinter, Harold 1930- DLB-13; CDBLB-8

 Writing for the Theatre DLB-13

Pinto, Fernão Mendes 1509/1511?-1583 .. DLB-287

Piontek, Heinz 1925- DLB-75

Piozzi, Hester Lynch [Thrale] 1741-1821 .... DLB-104, 142

Piper, H. Beam 1904-1964 .... DLB-8

Piper, Watty DLB-22

Pirandello, Luigi 1867-1936 .... DLB-264

Pirckheimer, Caritas 1467-1532 .... DLB-179

Pirckheimer, Willibald 1470-1530 ...... DLB-179

Pires, José Cardoso 1925-1998 .... DLB-287

Pisar, Samuel 1929- Y-83

Pisarev, Dmitrii Ivanovich 1840-1868 ... DLB-277

Pisemsky, Aleksei Feofilaktovich 1821-1881 .... DLB-238

Pitkin, Timothy 1766-1847 .... DLB-30

Pitter, Ruth 1897- DLB-20

Pix, Mary 1666-1709 .... DLB-80

Pixerécourt, René Charles Guilbert de 1773-1844 .... DLB-192

Pizarnik, Alejandra 1936-1972 .... DLB-283

Plá, Josefina 1909-1999 .... DLB-290

Plaatje, Sol T. 1876-1932 .... DLB-125, 225

Plante, David 1940- Y-83

Platen, August von 1796-1835 .... DLB-90

Plantinga, Alvin 1932- DLB-279

Plath, Sylvia 1932-1963 .... DLB-5, 6, 152; CDALB-1

Plato circa 428 B.C.-348-347 B.C. DLB-176; CDWLB-1

Plato, Ann 1824?-? DLB-239

Platon 1737-1812 .... DLB-150

Platonov, Andrei Platonovich (Andrei Platonovich Klimentev) 1899-1951 ... DLB-272

Platt, Charles 1945- DLB-261

Platt and Munk Company DLB-46

Plautus circa 254 B.C.-184 B.C. DLB-211; CDWLB-1

Playboy Press DLB-46

John Playford [publishing house] DLB-170

Der Pleier flourished circa 1250 .... DLB-138

Pleijel, Agneta 1940- DLB-257

Plenzdorf, Ulrich 1934- DLB-75

Pleshcheev, Aleksei Nikolaevich 1825?-1893 .... DLB-277

Plessen, Elizabeth 1944- DLB-75

Pletnev, Petr Aleksandrovich 1792-1865 .... DLB-205

Pliekšāne, Elza Rozenberga (see Aspazija)

Pliekšāns, Jānis (see Rainis, Jānis)

Plievier, Theodor 1892-1955 .... DLB-69

Plimpton, George 1927-2003 .. DLB-185, 241; Y-99

Pliny the Elder A.D. 23/24-A.D. 79 ..... DLB-211

Pliny the Younger circa A.D. 61-A.D. 112 .... DLB-211

Plomer, William 1903-1973 .... DLB-20, 162, 191, 225

Plotinus 204-270 .... DLB-176; CDWLB-1

Plowright, Teresa 1952- DLB-251

Plume, Thomas 1630-1704 .... DLB-213

Plumly, Stanley 1939- DLB-5, 193

Plumpp, Sterling D. 1940- DLB-41

Plunkett, James 1920- DLB-14

Plutarch circa 46-circa 120 .... DLB-176; CDWLB-1

Plymell, Charles 1935- DLB-16

Pocket Books DLB-46

Podestá, José J. 1858-1937 .... DLB-305

Poe, Edgar Allan 1809-1849 .... DLB-3, 59, 73, 74, 248; CDALB-2

 The Poe Studies Association Y-99

Poe, James 1921-1980 .... DLB-44

The Poet Laureate of the United States Y-86

Statements from Former Consultants
in Poetry Y-86

Poetry

Aesthetic Poetry (1873) DLB-35

A Century of Poetry, a Lifetime of
Collecting: J. M. Edelstein's
Collection of Twentieth-
Century American Poetry Y-02

"Certain Gifts," by Betty Adcock DLB-105

Contempo Caravan: Kites in a
Windstorm Y-85

"Contemporary Verse Story-telling,"
by Jonathan Holden DLB-105

"A Detail in a Poem," by Fred
Chappell DLB-105

"The English Renaissance of Art"
(1908), by Oscar Wilde DLB-35

"Every Man His Own Poet; or,
The Inspired Singer's Recipe
Book" (1877), by
H. W. Mallock DLB-35

"Eyes Across Centuries: Contemporary
Poetry and 'That Vision Thing,'"
by Philip Dacey DLB-105

A Field Guide to Recent Schools
of American Poetry Y-86

"Finding, Losing, Reclaiming:
A Note on My Poems,
by Robert Phillips" DLB-105

"The Fleshly School of Poetry and Other
Phenomena of the Day" (1872) DLB-35

"The Fleshly School of Poetry:
Mr. D. G. Rossetti" (1871) DLB-35

The G. Ross Roy Scottish Poetry Collection
at the University of South Carolina . . Y-89

"Getting Started: Accepting the Regions
You Own—or Which Own You,"
by Walter McDonald DLB-105

"The Good, The Not So Good," by
Stephen Dunn DLB-105

The Griffin Poetry Prize Y-00

The Hero as Poet. Dante; Shakspeare
(1841), by Thomas Carlyle DLB-32

"Images and 'Images,'" by Charles
Simic DLB-105

"Into the Mirror," by Peter Cooley . . . DLB-105

"Knots into Webs: Some Autobiographical
Sources," by Dabney Stuart DLB-105

"L'Envoi" (1882), by Oscar Wilde DLB-35

"Living in Ruin," by Gerald Stern . . . DLB-105

Looking for the Golden Mountain:
Poetry Reviewing Y-89

Lyric Poetry (French) DLB-268

Medieval Galician-Portuguese
Poetry DLB-287

"The No Self, the Little Self, and the
Poets," by Richard Moore DLB-105

On Some of the Characteristics of Modern
Poetry and On the Lyrical Poems of
Alfred Tennyson (1831) DLB-32

The Pitt Poetry Series: Poetry Publishing
Today Y-85

"The Poetry File," by Edward
Field DLB-105

Poetry in Nineteenth-Century France:
Cultural Background and Critical
Commentary DLB-217

The Poetry of Jorge Luis Borges Y-86

"The Poet's Kaleidoscope: The Element
of Surprise in the Making of the
Poem" by Madeline DeFrees DLB-105

The Pre-Raphaelite Controversy DLB-35

Protest Poetry in Castile DLB-286

"Reflections: After a Tornado,"
by Judson Jerome DLB-105

Statements from Former Consultants
in Poetry Y-86

Statements on the Art of Poetry DLB-54

The Study of Poetry (1880), by
Matthew Arnold DLB-35

A Survey of Poetry Anthologies,
1879-1960 . . . . DLB-54

Thoughts on Poetry and Its Varieties
(1833), by John Stuart Mill DLB-32

Under the Microscope (1872), by
A. C. Swinburne DLB-35

The Unterberg Poetry Center of the
92nd Street Y Y-98

Victorian Poetry: Five Critical
Views DLBV-35

Year in Poetry Y-83–92, 94–01

Year's Work in American Poetry Y-82

Poets

The Lives of the Poets (1753) DLB-142

Minor Poets of the Earlier
Seventeenth Century DLB-121

Other British Poets Who Fell
in the Great War DLB-216

Other Poets [French] DLB-217

Second-Generation Minor Poets of
the Seventeenth Century DLB-126

Third-Generation Minor Poets of
the Seventeenth Century DLB-131

Pogodin, Mikhail Petrovich 1800-1875 . . . DLB-198

Pogorel'sky, Antonii
(see Perovsky, Aleksei Alekseevich)

Pohl, Frederik 1919- DLB-8

Tribute to Isaac Asimov Y-92

Tribute to Theodore Sturgeon Y-85

Poirier, Louis (see Gracq, Julien)

Poláček, Karel 1892-1945 . . . DLB-215; CDWLB-4

Polanyi, Michael 1891-1976 . . . . DLB-100

Pole, Reginald 1500-1558 . . . . DLB-132

Polevoi, Nikolai Alekseevich 1796-1846 . . DLB-198

Polezhaev, Aleksandr Ivanovich
1804-1838 . . . . DLB-205

Poliakoff, Stephen 1952- DLB-13

Polidori, John William 1795-1821 . . . . . DLB-116

Polite, Carlene Hatcher 1932- DLB-33

Pollard, Alfred W. 1859-1944 . . . . DLB-201

Pollard, Edward A. 1832-1872 . . . . DLB-30

Pollard, Graham 1903-1976 . . . . DLB-201

Pollard, Percival 1869-1911 . . . . DLB-71

Pollard and Moss DLB-49

Pollock, Sharon 1936- DLB-60

Polonsky, Abraham 1910-1999 . . . . DLB-26

Polonsky, Iakov Petrovich 1819-1898 . . . . DLB-277

Polotsky, Simeon 1629-1680 . . . . DLB-150

Polybius circa 200 B.C.-118 B.C. DLB-176

Pomialovsky, Nikolai Gerasimovich
1835-1863 . . . . DLB-238

Pomilio, Mario 1921-1990 . . . . DLB-177

Ponce, Mary Helen 1938- DLB-122

Ponce-Montoya, Juanita 1949- DLB-122

Ponet, John 1516?-1556 . . . . DLB-132

Ponge, Francis 1899-1988 . . . . DLB-258; Y-02

Poniatowska, Elena
1933- DLB-113; CDWLB-3

Ponsard, François 1814-1867 . . . . DLB-192

William Ponsonby [publishing house] DLB-170

Pontiggia, Giuseppe 1934- DLB-196

Pontoppidan, Henrik 1857-1943 . . . . . . DLB-300

Pony Stories, Omnibus Essay on DLB-160

Poole, Ernest 1880-1950 . . . . DLB-9

Poole, Sophia 1804-1891 . . . . DLB-166

Poore, Benjamin Perley 1820-1887 . . . . . DLB-23

Popa, Vasko 1922-1991 . . . . DLB-181; CDWLB-4

Pope, Abbie Hanscom 1858-1894 . . . . . DLB-140

Pope, Alexander
1688-1744 . . . . . . DLB-95, 101, 213; CDBLB-2

Popov, Aleksandr Serafimovich
(see Serafimovich, Aleksandr Serafimovich)

Popov, Evgenii Anatol'evich 1946- DLB-285

Popov, Mikhail Ivanovich
1742-circa 1790 . . . . DLB-150

Popović, Aleksandar 1929-1996 . . . . DLB-181

Popper, Karl 1902-1994 . . . . DLB-262

Popular Culture Association/
American Culture Association Y-99

Popular Library DLB-46

Poquelin, Jean-Baptiste (see Molière)

Porete, Marguerite ?-1310 . . . . DLB-208

Porlock, Martin (see MacDonald, Philip)

Porpoise Press DLB-112

Porta, Antonio 1935-1989 . . . . DLB-128

Porter, Anna Maria 1780-1832 . . . . . DLB-116, 159

Porter, Cole 1891-1964 . . . . DLB-265

Porter, David 1780-1843 . . . . DLB-183

Porter, Eleanor H. 1868-1920 . . . . DLB-9

Porter, Gene Stratton (see Stratton-Porter, Gene)

Porter, Hal 1911-1984 . . . . DLB-260

Porter, Henry ?-? DLB-62

Porter, Jane 1776-1850 . . . . DLB-116, 159

Porter, Katherine Anne 1890-1980
. . . . . . DLB-4, 9, 102; Y-80; DS-12; CDALB-7

The Katherine Anne Porter Society Y-01

Porter, Peter 1929- DLB-40, 289

Porter, William Sydney (O. Henry)
1862-1910 . . . . . . DLB-12, 78, 79; CDALB-3

Porter, William T. 1809-1858 . . . . . DLB-3, 43, 250

Porter and Coates DLB-49

Portillo Trambley, Estela 1927-1998 . . . . . DLB-209	Préfontaine, Yves 1937- DLB-53	Protagoras circa 490 B.C.-420 B.C. DLB-176
Portis, Charles 1933- DLB-6	Prelutsky, Jack 1940- DLB-61	Protest Poetry in Castile ca. 1445-ca. 1506 . . . . DLB-286
Medieval Galician-Portuguese Poetry DLB-287	Prentice, George D. 1802-1870 . . . . DLB-43	Proud, Robert 1728-1813 . . . . DLB-30
Posey, Alexander 1873-1908 . . . . DLB-175	Prentice-Hall DLB-46	Proust, Marcel 1871-1922 . . . . DLB-65
Postans, Marianne circa 1810-1865 . . . . . DLB-166	Prescott, Orville 1906-1996 . . . . Y-96	Marcel Proust at 129 and the Proust Society of America. Y-00
Postgate, Raymond 1896-1971 . . . . DLB-276	Prescott, William Hickling 1796-1859 . . . . DLB-1, 30, 59, 235	
Postl, Carl (see Sealsfield, Carl)	Prešeren, Francè 1800-1849 . . . . DLB-147; CDWLB-4	Marcel Proust's *Remembrance of Things Past*: The Rediscovered Galley Proofs Y-00
Postmodern Holocaust Fiction DLB-299		Prutkov, Koz'ma Petrovich 1803-1863 . . . . DLB-277
Poston, Ted 1906-1974 . . . . DLB-51	Presses (*See also* Publishing) Small Presses in Great Britain and Ireland, 1960-1985 . . . . DLB-40	Prynne, J. H. 1936- DLB-40
Potekhin, Aleksei Antipovich 1829-1908 . . . . DLB-238		Przybyszewski, Stanislaw 1868-1927 . . . . . DLB-66
Potok, Chaim 1929-2002 . . . . DLB-28, 152	Small Presses I: Jargon Society Y-84	Pseudo-Dionysius the Areopagite floruit circa 500 . . . . DLB-115
A Conversation with Chaim Potok Y-84	Small Presses II: The Spirit That Moves Us Press Y-85	Public Lending Right in America PLR and the Meaning of Literary Property Y-83
Tribute to Bernard Malamud Y-86		
Potter, Beatrix 1866-1943 . . . . DLB-141	Small Presses III: Pushcart Press Y-87	
The Beatrix Potter Society Y-98	Preston, Margaret Junkin 1820-1897 . . . . DLB-239, 248	Statement by Sen. Charles McC. Mathias, Jr. PLR Y-83
Potter, David M. 1910-1971 . . . . DLB-17	Preston, May Wilson 1873-1949 . . . . DLB-188	Statements on PLR by American Writers . . . Y-83
Potter, Dennis 1935-1994 . . . . DLB-233	Preston, Thomas 1537-1598 . . . . DLB-62	Public Lending Right in the United Kingdom The First Year in the United Kingdom . . . Y-83
John E. Potter and Company DLB-49	Prévert, Jacques 1900-1977 . . . . DLB-258	
Pottle, Frederick A. 1897-1987 . . . . . DLB-103; Y-87	Price, Anthony 1928- DLB-276	Publishers [listed by individual names] Publishers, Conversations with: An Interview with Charles Scribner III . . . Y-94
Poulin, Jacques 1937- DLB-60	Price, Reynolds 1933- DLB-2, 218, 278	
Pound, Ezra 1885-1972 . . . . DLB-4, 45, 63; DS-15; CDALB-4	Price, Richard 1723-1791 . . . . DLB-158	An Interview with Donald Lamm Y-95
	Price, Richard 1949- Y-81	An Interview with James Laughlin Y-96
The Cost of the *Cantos*: William Bird to Ezra Pound Y-01	Prichard, Katharine Susannah 1883-1969 . . . . DLB-260	An Interview with Patrick O'Connor Y-84
The Ezra Pound Society Y-01		Publishing The Art and Mystery of Publishing: Interviews Y-97
Poverman, C. E. 1944- DLB-234	Prideaux, John 1578-1650 . . . . DLB-236	
Povich, Shirley 1905-1998 . . . . DLB-171	Priest, Christopher 1943- DLB-14, 207, 261	
Powell, Anthony 1905-2000 . . . DLB-15; CDBLB-7	Priestley, J. B. 1894-1984 . . . . DLB-10, 34, 77, 100, 139; Y-84; CDBLB-6	Book Publishing Accounting: Some Basic Concepts Y-98
The Anthony Powell Society: Powell and the First Biennial Conference Y-01		1873 Publishers' Catalogues DLB-49
	Priestley, Joseph 1733-1804 . . . . DLB-252	The Literary Scene 2002: Publishing, Book Reviewing, and Literary Journalism . . Y-02
Powell, Dawn 1897-1965 Dawn Powell, Where Have You Been All Our Lives? Y-97	Prigov, Dmitrii Aleksandrovich 1940- . . DLB-285	
	Prime, Benjamin Young 1733-1791 . . . . . . DLB-31	Main Trends in Twentieth-Century Book Clubs DLB-46
Powell, John Wesley 1834-1902 . . . . DLB-186	Primrose, Diana floruit circa 1630 . . . . . . DLB-126	
Powell, Padgett 1952- DLB-234	Prince, F. T. 1912- DLB-20	Overview of U.S. Book Publishing, 1910-1945 . . . . DLB-9
Powers, J. F. 1917-1999 . . . . DLB-130	Prince, Nancy Gardner 1799-? DLB-239	
Powers, Jimmy 1903-1995 . . . . DLB-241	Prince, Thomas 1687-1758 . . . . DLB-24, 140	The Pitt Poetry Series: Poetry Publishing Today Y-85
Pownall, David 1938- DLB-14	Pringle, Thomas 1789-1834 . . . . DLB-225	
Powys, John Cowper 1872-1963 . . . . . DLB-15, 255	Printz, Wolfgang Casper 1641-1717 . . . . . DLB-168	Publishing Fiction at LSU Press Y-87
Powys, Llewelyn 1884-1939 . . . . DLB-98	Prior, Matthew 1664-1721 . . . . DLB-95	The Publishing Industry in 1998: *Sturm-und-drang.com* Y-98
Powys, T. F. 1875-1953 . . . . DLB-36, 162	Prisco, Michele 1920- DLB-177	
The Powys Society Y-98	Prishvin, Mikhail Mikhailovich 1873-1954 . . . . DLB-272	The Publishing Industry in 1999 . . . . Y-99
Poynter, Nelson 1903-1978 . . . . DLB-127		Publishers and Agents: The Columbia Connection Y-87
Prado, Pedro 1886-1952 . . . . DLB-283	Pritchard, William H. 1932- DLB-111	
Prados, Emilio 1899-1962 . . . . DLB-134	Pritchett, V. S. 1900-1997 . . . . DLB-15, 139	Responses to Ken Auletta Y-97
Praed, Mrs. Caroline (see Praed, Rosa)	Probyn, May 1856 or 1857-1909 . . . . DLB-199	Southern Writers Between the Wars . . . DLB-9
Praed, Rosa (Mrs. Caroline Praed) 1851-1935 . . . . DLB-230	Procter, Adelaide Anne 1825-1864 . . . . DLB-32, 199	The State of Publishing Y-97
	Procter, Bryan Waller 1787-1874 . . . . DLB-96, 144	Trends in Twentieth-Century Mass Market Publishing DLB-46
Praed, Winthrop Mackworth 1802-1839 . . DLB-96	Proctor, Robert 1868-1903 . . . . DLB-184	
Praeger Publishers DLB-46	Prokopovich, Feofan 1681?-1736 . . . . DLB-150	The Year in Book Publishing Y-86
Praetorius, Johannes 1630-1680 . . . . DLB-168	Prokosch, Frederic 1906-1989 . . . . DLB-48	Pückler-Muskau, Hermann von 1785-1871 . . . . DLB-133
Pratolini, Vasco 1913-1991 . . . . DLB-177	Pronzini, Bill 1943- DLB-226	
Pratt, E. J. 1882-1964 . . . . DLB-92	Propertius circa 50 B.C.-post 16 B.C. DLB-211; CDWLB-1	Pufendorf, Samuel von 1632-1694 . . . . . . DLB-168
Pratt, Samuel Jackson 1749-1814 . . . . DLB-39		Pugh, Edwin William 1874-1930 . . . . DLB-135
Preciado Martin, Patricia 1939- DLB-209	Propper, Dan 1937- DLB-16	Pugin, A. Welby 1812-1852 . . . . DLB-55
	Prose, Francine 1947- DLB-234	Puig, Manuel 1932-1990 . . . . . DLB-113; CDWLB-3

Pulgar, Hernando del (Fernando del Pulgar)
ca. 1436-ca. 1492..................DLB-286

Pulitzer, Joseph 1847-1911 ....DLB-23

Pulitzer, Joseph, Jr. 1885-1955..........DLB-29

Pulitzer Prizes for the Novel, 1917-1945 ....DLB-9

Pulliam, Eugene 1889-1975 ....DLB-127

Purcell, Deirdre 1945- DLB-267

Purchas, Samuel 1577?-1626 ....DLB-151

Purdy, Al 1918-2000 ....DLB-88

Purdy, James 1923- DLB-2, 218

Purdy, Ken W. 1913-1972...............DLB-137

Pusey, Edward Bouverie 1800-1882 ......DLB-55

Pushkin, Aleksandr Sergeevich
1799-1837 ....DLB-205

Pushkin, Vasilii L'vovich
1766-1830 ....DLB-205

Putnam, George Palmer
1814-1872 ....DLB-3, 79, 250, 254

G. P. Putnam [publishing house].......DLB-254

G. P. Putnam's Sons [U.K.]............DLB-106

G. P. Putnam's Sons [U.S.] DLB-49

A Publisher's Archives: G. P. Putnam....Y-92

Putnam, Hilary 1926- DLB-279

Putnam, Samuel 1892-1950........DLB-4; DS-15

Puttenham, George 1529?-1590.........DLB-281

Puzo, Mario 1920-1999 ....DLB-6

Pyle, Ernie 1900-1945 ....DLB-29

Pyle, Howard
1853-1911 ....DLB-42, 188; DS-13

Pyle, Robert Michael 1947- DLB-275

Pym, Barbara 1913-1980 .....DLB-14, 207; Y-87

Pynchon, Thomas 1937- DLB-2, 173

Pyramid Books DLB-46

Pyrnelle, Louise-Clarke 1850-1907 ....DLB-42

Pythagoras circa 570 B.C.-? DLB-176

Q

Quad, M. (see Lewis, Charles B.)

Quaritch, Bernard 1819-1899 ....DLB-184

Quarles, Francis 1592-1644 ....DLB-126

The Quarterly Review 1809-1967...........DLB-110

Quasimodo, Salvatore 1901-1968 ....DLB-114

Queen, Ellery (see Dannay, Frederic, and
Manfred B. Lee)

Queen, Frank 1822-1882................DLB-241

The Queen City Publishing House DLB-49

Queirós, Eça de 1845-1900 ....DLB-287

Queneau, Raymond 1903-1976......DLB-72, 258

Quennell, Peter 1905-1993 ....DLB-155, 195

Quental, Antero de 1842-1891..........DLB-287

Quesada, José Luis 1948- DLB-290

Quesnel, Joseph 1746-1809 ....DLB-99

Quiller-Couch, Sir Arthur Thomas
1863-1944 ....DLB-135, 153, 190

Quin, Ann 1936-1973 ....DLB-14, 231

Quinault, Philippe 1635-1688 ....DLB-268

Quincy, Samuel, of Georgia ?-? DLB-31

Quincy, Samuel, of Massachusetts
1734-1789 ....DLB-31

Quindlen, Anna 1952- DLB-292

Quine, W. V. 1908-2000...............DLB-279

Quinn, Anthony 1915-2001..............DLB-122

Quinn, John 1870-1924 ....DLB-187

Quiñónez, Naomi 1951- DLB-209

Quintana, Leroy V. 1944- DLB-82

Quintana, Miguel de 1671-1748
A Forerunner of Chicano
Literature DLB-122

Quintilian
circa A.D. 40-circa A.D. 96.........DLB-211

Quintus Curtius Rufus
fl. A.D. 35 ....DLB-211

Harlin Quist Books DLB-46

Quoirez, Françoise (see Sagan, Françoise)

R

Raabe, Wilhelm 1831-1910 ....DLB-129

Raban, Jonathan 1942- DLB-204

Rabe, David 1940- DLB-7, 228; Y-91

Raboni, Giovanni 1932- DLB-128

Rachilde 1860-1953................DLB-123, 192

Racin, Kočo 1908-1943 ....DLB-147

Racine, Jean 1639-1699 ....DLB-268

Rackham, Arthur 1867-1939 ....DLB-141

Raczymow, Henri 1948- DLB-299

Radauskas, Henrikas
1910-1970 ....DLB-220; CDWLB-4

Radcliffe, Ann 1764-1823............DLB-39, 178

Raddall, Thomas 1903-1994 ....DLB-68

Radford, Dollie 1858-1920 ....DLB-240

Radichkov, Yordan 1929- DLB-181

Radiguet, Raymond 1903-1923........DLB-65

Radishchev, Aleksandr Nikolaevich
1749-1802 ....DLB-150

Radnóti, Miklós
1909-1944 ....DLB-215; CDWLB-4

Radrigán, Juan 1937- DLB-305

Radványi, Netty Reiling (see Seghers, Anna)

Rahv, Philip 1908-1973 ....DLB-137

Raich, Semen Egorovich 1792-1855......DLB-205

Raičković, Stevan 1928- DLB-181

Raiderman (see Parshchikov, Aleksei Maksimovich)

Raimund, Ferdinand Jakob 1790-1836.....DLB-90

Raine, Craig 1944- DLB-40

Raine, Kathleen 1908- DLB-20

Rainis, Jānis 1865-1929 .....DLB-220; CDWLB-4

Rainolde, Richard
circa 1530-1606...............DLB-136, 236

Rainolds, John 1549-1607 ....DLB-281

Rakić, Milan 1876-1938.....DLB-147; CDWLB-4

Rakosi, Carl 1903- DLB-193

Ralegh, Sir Walter
1554?-1618 ....DLB-172; CDBLB-1

Raleigh, Walter
Style (1897) [excerpt] DLB-57

Ralin, Radoy 1923- DLB-181

Ralph, Julian 1853-1903 ....DLB-23

Ramat, Silvio 1939-..................DLB-128

Ramée, Marie Louise de la (see Ouida)

Ramírez, Sergío 1942- DLB-145

Ramke, Bin 1947- DLB-120

Ramler, Karl Wilhelm 1725-1798 ....DLB-97

Ramon Ribeyro, Julio 1929-1994 ....DLB-145

Ramos, Manuel 1948- DLB-209

Ramos Sucre, José Antonio 1890-1930 ...DLB-290

Ramous, Mario 1924- DLB-128

Rampersad, Arnold 1941- DLB-111

Ramsay, Allan 1684 or 1685-1758........DLB-95

Ramsay, David 1749-1815..............DLB-30

Ramsay, Martha Laurens 1759-1811.....DLB-200

Ramsey, Frank P. 1903-1930............DLB-262

Ranch, Hieronimus Justesen
1539-1607 ....DLB-300

Ranck, Katherine Quintana 1942- DLB-122

Rand, Avery and Company.............DLB-49

Rand, Ayn 1905-1982 ...DLB-227, 279; CDALB-7

Rand McNally and Company DLB-49

Randall, David Anton 1905-1975 ....DLB-140

Randall, Dudley 1914- DLB-41

Randall, Henry S. 1811-1876............DLB-30

Randall, James G. 1881-1953............DLB-17

The Randall Jarrell Symposium: A Small
Collection of Randall Jarrells Y-86

Excerpts From Papers Delivered at the
Randall Jarrel Symposium Y-86

Randall, John Herman, Jr. 1899-1980 ....DLB-279

Randolph, A. Philip 1889-1979 ....DLB-91

Anson D. F. Randolph
[publishing house]................DLB-49

Randolph, Thomas 1605-1635 ......DLB-58, 126

Random House DLB-46

Rankin, Ian (Jack Harvey) 1960- DLB-267

Henry Ranlet [publishing house] DLB-49

Ransom, Harry 1908-1976..............DLB-187

Ransom, John Crowe
1888-1974 ....DLB-45, 63; CDALB-7

Ransome, Arthur 1884-1967 ....DLB-160

Raphael, Frederic 1931- DLB-14

Raphaelson, Samson 1896-1983 ....DLB-44

Rare Book Dealers
Bertram Rota and His Bookshop Y-91

An Interview with Glenn Horowitz Y-90

An Interview with Otto Penzler Y-96

An Interview with Ralph Sipper Y-94

New York City Bookshops in the
1930s and 1940s: The Recollections
of Walter Goldwater Y-93

Rare Books
Research in the American Antiquarian
Book Trade Y-97

Two Hundred Years of Rare Books and
  Literary Collections at the
  University of South Carolina Y-00
Rascón Banda, Víctor Hugo 1948- DLB-305
Rashi circa 1040-1105................. DLB-208
Raskin, Ellen 1928-1984............... DLB-52
Rasputin, Valentin Grigor'evich
  1937- DLB-302
Rastell, John 1475?-1536............DLB-136, 170
Rattigan, Terence
  1911-1977............... DLB-13; CDBLB-7
Raven, Simon 1927-2001 ....DLB-271
Ravnkilde, Adda 1862-1883............. DLB-300
Rawicz, Piotr 1919-1982............... DLB-299
Rawlings, Marjorie Kinnan 1896-1953
  .... DLB-9, 22, 102; DS-17; CDALB-7
Rawlinson, Richard 1690-1755........ DLB-213
Rawlinson, Thomas 1681-1725 .... DLB-213
Rawls, John 1921-2002.................DLB-279
Raworth, Tom 1938- DLB-40
Ray, David 1932- DLB-5
Ray, Gordon Norton 1915-1986 ... DLB-103, 140
Ray, Henrietta Cordelia 1849-1916 ...... DLB-50
Raymond, Ernest 1888-1974........... DLB-191
Raymond, Henry J. 1820-1869....... DLB-43, 79
Raymond, René (see Chase, James Hadley)
Razaf, Andy 1895-1973................ DLB-265
Rea, Michael 1927-1996 .... Y-97
  Michael M. Rea and the Rea Award for
    the Short Story Y-97
Reach, Angus 1821-1856 .... DLB-70
Read, Herbert 1893-1968......... DLB-20, 149
Read, Martha Meredith DLB-200
Read, Opie 1852-1939 .... DLB-23
Read, Piers Paul 1941- DLB-14
Reade, Charles 1814-1884 .... DLB-21
Reader's Digest Condensed Books....... DLB-46
Readers Ulysses Symposium Y-97
Reading, Peter 1946- DLB-40
Reading Series in New York City........... Y-96
Reaney, James 1926- DLB-68
Rebhun, Paul 1500?-1546..............DLB-179
Rèbora, Clemente 1885-1957 .... DLB-114
Rebreanu, Liviu 1885-1944 .... DLB-220
Rechy, John 1931- DLB-122, 278; Y-82
Redding, J. Saunders 1906-1988...... DLB-63, 76
J. S. Redfield [publishing house] DLB-49
Redgrove, Peter 1932- DLB-40
Redmon, Anne 1943- Y-86
Redmond, Eugene B. 1937- DLB-41
Redol, Alves 1911-1969 .... DLB-287
James Redpath [publishing house] DLB-49
Reed, Henry 1808-1854 .... DLB-59
Reed, Henry 1914-1986 .... DLB-27
Reed, Ishmael
  1938- DLB-2, 5, 33, 169, 227; DS-8

Reed, Rex 1938- DLB-185
Reed, Sampson 1800-1880 .... DLB-1, 235
Reed, Talbot Baines 1852-1893 .... DLB-141
Reedy, William Marion 1862-1920 ...... DLB-91
Reese, Lizette Woodworth 1856-1935 .... DLB-54
Reese, Thomas 1742-1796 .... DLB-37
Reeve, Clara 1729-1807 .... DLB-39
  Preface to The Old English Baron
    (1778)........................ DLB-39
  The Progress of Romance (1785)
    [excerpt].................... DLB-39
Reeves, James 1909-1978 .... DLB-161
Reeves, John 1926- DLB-88
Reeves-Stevens, Garfield 1953- DLB-251
Régio, José (José Maria dos Reis Pereira)
  1901-1969 .... DLB-287
Henry Regnery Company DLB-46
Rehberg, Hans 1901-1963 .... DLB-124
Rehfisch, Hans José 1891-1960 .... DLB-124
Reich, Ebbe Kløvedal 1940- DLB-214
Reid, Alastair 1926- DLB-27
Reid, B. L. 1918-1990................ DLB-111
Reid, Christopher 1949- DLB-40
Reid, Forrest 1875-1947 .... DLB-153
Reid, Helen Rogers 1882-1970 .... DLB-29
Reid, James ?-? DLB-31
Reid, Mayne 1818-1883 .... DLB-21, 163
Reid, Thomas 1710-1796 .... DLB-31, 252
Reid, V. S. (Vic) 1913-1987 .... DLB-125
Reid, Whitelaw 1837-1912 .... DLB-23
Reilly and Lee Publishing Company DLB-46
Reimann, Brigitte 1933-1973 .... DLB-75
Reinmar der Alte circa 1165-circa 1205 .. DLB-138
Reinmar von Zweter
  circa 1200-circa 1250 .... DLB-138
Reisch, Walter 1903-1983 .... DLB-44
Reizei Family DLB-203
Religion
  A Crisis of Culture: The Changing
    Role of Religion in the
    New Republic DLB-37
Remarque, Erich Maria
  1898-1970............. DLB-56; CDWLB-2
Remington, Frederic
  1861-1909 ....DLB-12, 186, 188
Remizov, Aleksei Mikhailovich
  1877-1957 .... DLB-295
Renaud, Jacques 1943- DLB-60
Renault, Mary 1905-1983................. Y-83
Rendell, Ruth (Barbara Vine)
  1930- DLB-87, 276
Rensselaer, Maria van Cortlandt van
  1645-1689 .... DLB-200
Repplier, Agnes 1855-1950 .... DLB-221
Reshetnikov, Fedor Mikhailovich
  1841-1871...................... DLB-238
Rettenbacher, Simon 1634-1706 .... DLB-168
Retz, Jean-François-Paul de Gondi,
  cardinal de 1613-1679 ....DLB-268

Reuchlin, Johannes 1455-1522..........DLB-179
Reuter, Christian 1665-after 1712....... DLB-168
Fleming H. Revell Company DLB-49
Reverdy, Pierre 1889-1960............ DLB-258
Reuter, Fritz 1810-1874................ DLB-129
Reuter, Gabriele 1859-1941 .... DLB-66
Reventlow, Franziska Gräfin zu
  1871-1918..................... DLB-66
Review of Reviews Office............. DLB-112
Rexroth, Kenneth 1905-1982
  .... DLB-16, 48, 165, 212; Y-82; CDALB-1
  The Commercialization of the Image
    of Revolt DLB-16
Rey, H. A. 1898-1977................. DLB-22
Reyes, Carlos José 1941- DLB-305
Reynal and Hitchcock DLB-46
Reynolds, G. W. M. 1814-1879 .... DLB-21
Reynolds, John Hamilton 1794-1852 ..... DLB-96
Reynolds, Sir Joshua 1723-1792 .... DLB-104
Reynolds, Mack 1917-1983.............. DLB-8
Reznikoff, Charles 1894-1976........ DLB-28, 45
Rhetoric
  Continental European Rhetoricians,
    1400-1600, and Their Influence
    in Reaissance England DLB-236
  A Finding Guide to Key Works on
    Microfilm................ DLB-236
  Glossary of Terms and Definitions of
    Rhetoic and Logic DLB-236
Rhett, Robert Barnwell 1800-1876 .... DLB-43
Rhode, John 1884-1964 .... DLB-77
Rhodes, Eugene Manlove 1869-1934.... DLB-256
Rhodes, James Ford 1848-1927 .... DLB-47
Rhodes, Richard 1937- DLB-185
Rhys, Jean 1890-1979
  .....DLB-36, 117, 162; CDBLB-7; CDWLB-3
Ribeiro, Bernadim
  fl. ca. 1475/1482-1526/1544 .... DLB-287
Ricardo, David 1772-1823 .... DLB-107, 158
Ricardou, Jean 1932- DLB-83
Rice, Anne (A. N. Roquelare, Anne Rampling)
  1941- DLB-292
Rice, Christopher 1978- DLB-292
Rice, Elmer 1892-1967 .... DLB-4, 7
Rice, Grantland 1880-1954..........DLB-29, 171
Rich, Adrienne 1929- DLB-5, 67; CDALB-7
Richard, Mark 1955- DLB-234
Richard de Fournival
  1201-1259 or 1260................ DLB-208
Richards, David Adams 1950- DLB-53
Richards, George circa 1760-1814 ...... DLB-37
Richards, I. A. 1893-1979............. DLB-27
Richards, Laura E. 1850-1943 .... DLB-42
Richards, William Carey 1818-1892 ..... DLB-73
Grant Richards [publishing house] DLB-112
Richardson, Charles F. 1851-1913 .... DLB-71
Richardson, Dorothy M. 1873-1957...... DLB-36

The Novels of Dorothy Richardson
 (1918), by May Sinclair DLB-36

Richardson, Henry Handel
 (Ethel Florence Lindesay Robertson)
 1870-1946 .... DLB-197, 230

Richardson, Jack 1935- DLB-7

Richardson, John 1796-1852 ....DLB-99

Richardson, Samuel
 1689-1761 ....DLB-39, 154; CDBLB-2

 Introductory Letters from the Second
  Edition of *Pamela* (1741) DLB-39

 Postscript to [the Third Edition of]
  Clarissa (1751) DLB-39

 Preface to the First Edition of
  Pamela (1740)...................DLB-39

 Preface to the Third Edition of
  Clarissa (1751) [excerpt]..........DLB-39

 Preface to Volume 1 of *Clarissa*
  (1747) DLB-39

 Preface to Volume 3 of *Clarissa*
  (1748) DLB-39

Richardson, Willis 1889-1977 ....DLB-51

Riche, Barnabe 1542-1617 ....DLB-136

Richepin, Jean 1849-1926 ....DLB-192

Richler, Mordecai 1931-2001...........DLB-53

Richter, Conrad 1890-1968..........DLB-9, 212

Richter, Hans Werner 1908-1993 ....DLB-69

Richter, Johann Paul Friedrich
 1763-1825 ....DLB-94; CDWLB-2

Joseph Rickerby [publishing house]......DLB-106

Rickword, Edgell 1898-1982 ....DLB-20

Riddell, Charlotte 1832-1906...........DLB-156

Riddell, John (see Ford, Corey)

Ridge, John Rollin 1827-1867...........DLB-175

Ridge, Lola 1873-1941................DLB-54

Ridge, William Pett 1859-1930 ....DLB-135

Riding, Laura (see Jackson, Laura Riding)

Ridler, Anne 1912- DLB-27

Ridruego, Dionisio 1912-1975 ....DLB-108

Riel, Louis 1844-1885 ....DLB-99

Riemer, Johannes 1648-1714 ....DLB-168

Rifbjerg, Klaus 1931- DLB-214

Riffaterre, Michael 1924- DLB-67

A Conversation between William Riggan
 and Janette Turner Hospital Y-02

Riggs, Lynn 1899-1954 ....DLB-175

Riis, Jacob 1849-1914................DLB-23

John C. Riker [publishing house].........DLB-49

Riley, James 1777-1840..............DLB-183

Riley, John 1938-1978 ....DLB-40

Rilke, Rainer Maria
 1875-1926 ....DLB-81; CDWLB-2

Rimanelli, Giose 1926- DLB-177

Rimbaud, Jean-Nicolas-Arthur
 1854-1891 ....DLB-217

Rinehart and Company...............DLB-46

Ringuet 1895-1960..................DLB-68

Ringwood, Gwen Pharis 1910-1984........DLB-88

Rinser, Luise 1911- DLB-69

Ríos, Alberto 1952- DLB-122

Ríos, Isabella 1948- DLB-82

Ripley, Arthur 1895-1961 ....DLB-44

Ripley, George 1802-1880 .....DLB-1, 64, 73, 235

The Rising Glory of America:
 Three Poems....................DLB-37

The Rising Glory of America: Written in 1771
 (1786), by Hugh Henry Brackenridge
 and Philip Freneau DLB-37

Riskin, Robert 1897-1955..............DLB-26

Risse, Heinz 1898- DLB-69

Rist, Johann 1607-1667 ....DLB-164

Ristikivi, Karl 1912-1977 ....DLB-220

Ritchie, Anna Mowatt 1819-1870 .....DLB-3, 250

Ritchie, Anne Thackeray 1837-1919 ......DLB-18

Ritchie, Thomas 1778-1854 ....DLB-43

The Ritz Paris Hemingway Award Y-85

 Mario Varga Llosa's Acceptance Speech.. Y-85

Rivard, Adjutor 1868-1945 ....DLB-92

Rive, Richard 1931-1989..........DLB-125, 225

Rivera, José 1955- DLB-249

Rivera, Marina 1942- DLB-122

Rivera, Tomás 1935-1984 ....DLB-82

Rivers, Conrad Kent 1933-1968 ....DLB-41

Riverside Press....................DLB-49

Rivington, James circa 1724-1802 ....DLB-43

Charles Rivington [publishing house] DLB-154

Rivkin, Allen 1903-1990 ....DLB-26

Roa Bastos, Augusto 1917- DLB-113

Robbe-Grillet, Alain 1922- DLB-83

Robbins, Tom 1936- Y-80

Roberts, Charles G. D. 1860-1943.........DLB-92

Roberts, Dorothy 1906-1993 ....DLB-88

Roberts, Elizabeth Madox
 1881-1941 ....DLB-9, 54, 102

Roberts, John (see Swynnerton, Thomas)

Roberts, Keith 1935-2000 ....DLB-261

Roberts, Kenneth 1885-1957 ....DLB-9

Roberts, Michèle 1949- DLB-231

Roberts, Theodore Goodridge
 1877-1953 ....DLB-92

Roberts, Ursula Wyllie (see Miles, Susan)

Roberts, William 1767-1849............DLB-142

James Roberts [publishing house] DLB-154

Roberts Brothers DLB-49

A. M. Robertson and Company DLB-49

Robertson, Ethel Florence Lindesay
 (see Richardson, Henry Handel)

Robertson, William 1721-1793..........DLB-104

Robin, Leo 1895-1984 ....DLB-265

Robins, Elizabeth 1862-1952 ....DLB-197

Robinson, A. Mary F. (Madame James
 Darmesteter, Madame Mary
 Duclaux) 1857-1944 ....DLB-240

Robinson, Casey 1903-1979............DLB-44

Robinson, Derek Y-02

Robinson, Edwin Arlington
 1869-1935 ....DLB-54; CDALB-3

 Review by Derek Robinson of George
  Greenfield's *Rich Dust* Y-02

Robinson, Henry Crabb 1775-1867......DLB-107

Robinson, James Harvey 1863-1936 ......DLB-47

Robinson, Lennox 1886-1958 ....DLB-10

Robinson, Mabel Louise 1874-1962.......DLB-22

Robinson, Marilynne 1943- DLB-206

Robinson, Mary 1758-1800 ....DLB-158

Robinson, Richard circa 1545-1607......DLB-167

Robinson, Therese 1797-1870........DLB-59, 133

Robison, Mary 1949- DLB-130

Roblès, Emmanuel 1914-1995 ....DLB-83

Roccatagliata Ceccardi, Ceccardo
 1871-1919 ....DLB-114

Rocha, Adolfo Correira da (see Torga, Miguel)

Roche, Billy 1949- DLB-233

Rochester, John Wilmot, Earl of
 1647-1680 ....DLB-131

Rochon, Esther 1948- DLB-251

Rock, Howard 1911-1976 ....DLB-127

Rockwell, Norman Perceval 1894-1978...DLB-188

Rodgers, Carolyn M. 1945- DLB-41

Rodgers, W. R. 1909-1969 ....DLB-20

Rodney, Lester 1911- DLB-241

Rodríguez, Claudio 1934-1999 ....DLB-134

Rodríguez, Joe D. 1943- DLB-209

Rodríguez, Luis J. 1954- DLB-209

Rodriguez, Richard 1944- DLB-82, 256

Rodríguez Julia, Edgardo 1946- DLB-145

Roe, E. P. 1838-1888................DLB-202

Roethke, Theodore
 1908-1963 ....DLB-5, 206; CDALB-1

Rogers, Jane 1952- DLB-194

Rogers, Pattiann 1940- DLB-105

Rogers, Samuel 1763-1855.............DLB-93

Rogers, Will 1879-1935 ....DLB-11

Rohmer, Sax 1883-1959 ....DLB-70

Roiphe, Anne 1935- Y-80

Rojas, Arnold R. 1896-1988 ....DLB-82

Rojas, Fernando de ca. 1475-1541 ....DLB-286

Rolfe, Edwin (Solomon Fishman)
 1909-1954.....................DLB-303

Rolfe, Frederick William
 1860-1913 ....DLB-34, 156

Rolland, Romain 1866-1944 ....DLB-65

Rolle, Richard circa 1290-1300 - 1340....DLB-146

Rölvaag, O. E. 1876-1931 ....DLB-9, 212

Romains, Jules 1885-1972 ....DLB-65

A. Roman and Company DLB-49

Roman de la Rose: Guillaume de Lorris
 1200/1205-circa 1230, Jean de
 Meun 1235-1240-circa 1305 ....DLB-208

Romano, Lalla 1906-2001 ....DLB-177

Romano, Octavio 1923- DLB-122

Rome, Harold 1908-1993 ....DLB-265

Romero, Leo 1950- DLB-122
Romero, Lin 1947- DLB-122
Romero, Orlando 1945- DLB-82
Rook, Clarence 1863-1915 .... DLB-135
Roosevelt, Theodore
  1858-1919 .... DLB-47, 186, 275
Root, Waverley 1903-1982 .... DLB-4
Root, William Pitt 1941- DLB-120
Roquebrune, Robert de 1889-1978 .... DLB-68
Rorty, Richard 1931- DLB-246, 279
Rosa, João Guimarães 1908-1967 .... DLB-113
Rosales, Luis 1910-1992 .... DLB-134
Roscoe, William 1753-1831 .... DLB-163
Rose, Reginald 1920-2002 .... DLB-26
Rose, Wendy 1948- DLB-175
Rosegger, Peter 1843-1918 .... DLB-129
Rosei, Peter 1946- DLB-85
Rosen, Norma 1925- DLB-28
Rosenbach, A. S. W. 1876-1952 ... DLB-140
Rosenbaum, Ron 1946- DLB-185
Rosenbaum, Thane 1960- DLB-299
Rosenberg, Isaac 1890-1918 .... DLB-20, 216
Rosenfeld, Isaac 1918-1956 .... DLB-28
Rosenthal, Harold 1914-1999 ..... DLB-241

  Jimmy, Red, and Others: Harold
    Rosenthal Remembers the Stars of
    the Press Box Y-01

Rosenthal, M. L. 1917-1996 .... DLB-5
Rosenwald, Lessing J. 1891-1979 .... DLB-187
Ross, Alexander 1591-1654 .... DLB-151
Ross, Harold 1892-1951 .... DLB-137
Ross, Jerry 1926-1955 .... DLB-265
Ross, Leonard Q. (see Rosten, Leo)
Ross, Lillian 1927- DLB-185
Ross, Martin 1862-1915 .... DLB-135
Ross, Sinclair 1908-1996 .... DLB-88
Ross, W. W. E. 1894-1966 .... DLB-88
Rosselli, Amelia 1930-1996 ...... DLB-128
Rossen, Robert 1908-1966 .... DLB-26
Rosset, Barney Y-02
Rossetti, Christina 1830-1894 ... DLB-35, 163, 240
Rossetti, Dante Gabriel
  1828-1882 .... DLB-35; CDBLB-4
  The Stealthy School of
    Criticism (1871) DLB-35
Rossner, Judith 1935- DLB-6
Rostand, Edmond 1868-1918 .... DLB-192
Rosten, Leo 1908-1997 .... DLB-11
Rostenberg, Leona 1908- DLB-140
Rostopchina, Evdokiia Petrovna
  1811-1858 .... DLB-205
Rostovsky, Dimitrii 1651-1709 .... DLB-150
Rota, Bertram 1903-1966 .... DLB-201
  Bertram Rota and His Bookshop Y-91
Roth, Gerhard 1942- DLB-85, 124
Roth, Henry 1906?-1995 .... DLB-28

Roth, Joseph 1894-1939 .... DLB-85
Roth, Philip
  1933- DLB-2, 28, 173; Y-82; CDALB-6
Rothenberg, Jerome 1931- DLB-5, 193
Rothschild Family DLB-184
Rotimi, Ola 1938- DLB-125
Rotrou, Jean 1609-1650 .... DLB-268
Routhier, Adolphe-Basile 1839-1920 .... DLB-99
Routier, Simone 1901-1987 .... DLB-88
George Routledge and Sons DLB-106
Roversi, Roberto 1923- DLB-128
Rowe, Elizabeth Singer 1674-1737 .... DLB-39, 95
Rowe, Nicholas 1674-1718 .... DLB-84
Rowlands, Samuel circa 1570-1630 .... DLB-121
Rowlandson, Mary
  circa 1637-circa 1711 .... DLB-24, 200
Rowley, William circa 1585-1626 ... DLB-58
Rowling, J. K.
  The Harry Potter Phenomenon Y-99
Rowse, A. L. 1903-1997 .... DLB-155
Rowson, Susanna Haswell
  circa 1762-1824 .... DLB-37, 200
Roy, Camille 1870-1943 .... DLB-92
The G. Ross Roy Scottish Poetry Collection
  at the University of South Carolina Y-89
Roy, Gabrielle 1909-1983 .... DLB-68
Roy, Jules 1907-2000 .... DLB-83
The Royal Court Theatre and the English
  Stage Company DLB-13
The Royal Court Theatre and the New
  Drama DLB-10
The Royal Shakespeare Company
  at the Swan Y-88
Royall, Anne Newport 1769-1854 ... DLB-43, 248
Royce, Josiah 1855-1916 .... DLB-270
The Roycroft Printing Shop DLB-49
Royde-Smith, Naomi 1875-1964 .... DLB-191
Royster, Vermont 1914-1996 ...... DLB-127
Richard Royston [publishing house] DLB-170
Rozanov, Vasilii Vasil'evich
  1856-1919 .... DLB-295
Różewicz, Tadeusz 1921- DLB-232
Ruark, Gibbons 1941- DLB-120
Ruban, Vasilii Grigorevich 1742-1795 .... DLB-150
Rubens, Bernice 1928- DLB-14, 207
Rubina, Dina Il'inichna 1953- DLB-285
Rubinshtein, Lev Semenovich 1947- DLB-285
Rudd and Carleton DLB-49
Rudd, Steele (Arthur Hoey Davis) DLB-230
Rudkin, David 1936- DLB-13
Rudnick, Paul 1957- DLB-266
Rudnicki, Adolf 1909-1990 .... DLB-299
Rudolf von Ems circa 1200-circa 1254 ... DLB-138
Ruffin, Josephine St. Pierre 1842-1924 .... DLB-79
Ruganda, John 1941- DLB-157
Ruggles, Henry Joseph 1813-1906 ..... DLB-64

Ruiz de Burton, María Amparo
  1832-1895 .... DLB-209, 221
Rukeyser, Muriel 1913-1980 .... DLB-48
Rule, Jane 1931- DLB-60
Rulfo, Juan 1918-1986 ...... DLB-113; CDWLB-3
Rumaker, Michael 1932- DLB-16
Rumens, Carol 1944- DLB-40
Rummo, Paul-Eerik 1942- DLB-232
Runyon, Damon
  1880-1946 .... DLB-11, 86, 171
Ruodlieb circa 1050-1075 .... DLB-148
Rush, Benjamin 1746-1813 .... DLB-37
Rush, Rebecca 1779-? DLB-200
Rushdie, Salman 1947- DLB-194
Rusk, Ralph L. 1888-1962 .... DLB-103
Ruskin, John
  1819-1900 ..... DLB-55, 163, 190; CDBLB-4
Russ, Joanna 1937- DLB-8
Russell, Benjamin 1761-1845 ...... DLB-43
Russell, Bertrand 1872-1970 ..... DLB-100, 262
Russell, Charles Edward 1860-1941 .... DLB-25
Russell, Charles M. 1864-1926 .... DLB-188
Russell, Eric Frank 1905-1978 .... DLB-255
Russell, Fred 1906-2003 .... DLB-241
Russell, George William (see AE)
Russell, Countess Mary Annette Beauchamp
  (see Arnim, Elizabeth von)
Russell, Willy 1947- DLB-233
B. B. Russell and Company DLB-49
R. H. Russell and Son DLB-49
Rutebeuf flourished 1249-1277 .... DLB-208
Rutherford, Mark 1831-1913 .... DLB-18
Ruxton, George Frederick
  1821-1848 .... DLB-186
R-va, Zeneida (see Gan, Elena Andreevna)
Ryan, James 1952- DLB-267
Ryan, Michael 1946- Y-82
Ryan, Oscar 1904- DLB-68
Rybakov, Anatolii Naumovich
  1911-1994 .... DLB-302
Ryder, Jack 1871-1936 .... DLB-241
Ryga, George 1932-1987 .... DLB-60
Rylands, Enriqueta Augustina Tennant
  1843-1908 .... DLB-184
Rylands, John 1801-1888 .... DLB-184
Ryle, Gilbert 1900-1976 .... DLB-262
Ryleev, Kondratii Fedorovich
  1795-1826 .... DLB-205
Rymer, Thomas 1643?-1713 .... DLB-101
Ryskind, Morrie 1895-1985 .... DLB-26
Rzhevsky, Aleksei Andreevich
  1737-1804 .... DLB-150

S

The Saalfield Publishing Company DLB-46
Saba, Umberto 1883-1957 .... DLB-114
Sábato, Ernesto 1911- DLB-145; CDWLB-3

Saberhagen, Fred 1930- DLB-8
Sabin, Joseph 1821-1881 ....DLB-187
Sacer, Gottfried Wilhelm 1635-1699 .....DLB-168
Sachs, Hans 1494-1576 ..... DLB-179; CDWLB-2
Sá-Carneiro, Mário de 1890-1916 ....DLB-287
Sack, John 1930- DLB-185
Sackler, Howard 1929-1982.............DLB-7
Sackville, Lady Margaret 1881-1963 .....DLB-240
Sackville, Thomas 1536-1608 and
 Norton, Thomas 1532-1584 ....DLB-62
Sackville, Thomas 1536-1608 ....DLB-132
Sackville-West, Edward 1901-1965 ......DLB-191
Sackville-West, V. 1892-1962 ....DLB-34, 195
Sá de Miranda, Francisco de
 1481-1588? DLB-287
Sadlier, Mary Anne 1820-1903 ....DLB-99
D. and J. Sadlier and Company DLB-49
Sadoff, Ira 1945- DLB-120
Sadoveanu, Mihail 1880-1961 ....DLB-220
Sadur, Nina Nikolaevna 1950- DLB-285
Sáenz, Benjamin Alire 1954- DLB-209
Saenz, Jaime 1921-1986 ....DLB-145, 283
Saffin, John circa 1626-1710 ....DLB-24
Sagan, Françoise 1935- DLB-83
Sage, Robert 1899-1962.................DLB-4
Sagel, Jim 1947- DLB-82
Sagendorph, Robb Hansell 1900-1970 ....DLB-137
Sahagún, Carlos 1938- DLB-108
Sahkomaapii, Piitai (see Highwater, Jamake)
Sahl, Hans 1902-1993 ....DLB-69
Said, Edward W. 1935- DLB-67
Saigyō 1118-1190......................DLB-203
Saiko, George 1892-1962...............DLB-85
Sainte-Beuve, Charles-Augustin
 1804-1869 ....DLB-217
Saint-Exupéry, Antoine de 1900-1944 ....DLB-72
St. John, J. Allen 1872-1957 ....DLB-188
St John, Madeleine 1942- DLB-267
St. Johns, Adela Rogers 1894-1988 ......DLB-29
St. Omer, Garth 1931- DLB-117
Saint Pierre, Michel de 1916-1987 ....DLB-83
St. Dominic's Press DLB-112
The St. John's College Robert Graves Trust .. Y-96
St. Martin's Press.....................DLB-46
St. Nicholas 1873-1881 .... DS-13
Saintsbury, George 1845-1933 .... DLB-57, 149
 "Modern English Prose" (1876) DLB-57
 The Present State of the English
 Novel (1892), ...DLB-18
Saiokuken Sōchō 1448-1532 ....DLB-203
Saki (see Munro, H. H.)
Salaam, Kalamu ya 1947- DLB-38
Šalamun, Tomaž 1941- ...DLB-181; CDWLB-4
Salas, Floyd 1931- DLB-82
Sálaz-Marquez, Rubén 1935- DLB-122

Salcedo, Hugo 1964- DLB-305
Salemson, Harold J. 1910-1988 ....DLB-4
Salesbury, William 1520?-1584? DLB-281
Salinas, Luis Omar 1937- DLB-82
Salinas, Pedro 1891-1951...............DLB-134
Salinger, J. D.
 1919- DLB-2, 102, 173; CDALB-1
Salkey, Andrew 1928- DLB-125
Sallust circa 86 B.C.-35 B.C.
 .... DLB-211; CDWLB-1
Salt, Waldo 1914-1987.................DLB-44
Salter, James 1925- DLB-130
Salter, Mary Jo 1954- DLB-120
Saltus, Edgar 1855-1921 ....DLB-202
Saltykov, Mikhail Evgrafovich
 1826-1889 ....DLB-238
Salustri, Carlo Alberto (see Trilussa)
Salverson, Laura Goodman 1890-1970 ....DLB-92
Samain, Albert 1858-1900 ....DLB-217
Sampson, Richard Henry (see Hull, Richard)
Samuels, Ernest 1903-1996 ....DLB-111
Sanborn, Franklin Benjamin
 1831-1917 ....DLB-1, 223
Sánchez, Luis Rafael 1936- DLB-145, 305
Sánchez, Philomeno "Phil" 1917- DLB-122
Sánchez, Ricardo 1941-1995 ....DLB-82
Sánchez, Saúl 1943- DLB-209
Sanchez, Sonia 1934- DLB-41; DS-8
Sánchez de Arévalo, Rodrigo
 1404-1470 ....DLB-286
Sánchez, Florencio 1875-1910 ....DLB-305
Sand, George 1804-1876 ....DLB-119, 192
Sandburg, Carl
 1878-1967 .... DLB-17, 54; CDALB-3
Sandel, Cora (Sara Fabricius)
 1880-1974 ....DLB-297
Sandemose, Aksel 1899-1965. ....DLB-297
Sanders, Edward 1939- DLB-16, 244
Sanderson, Robert 1587-1663 ....DLB-281
Sandoz, Mari 1896-1966 ....DLB-9, 212
Sandwell, B. K. 1876-1954..............DLB-92
Sandy, Stephen 1934- DLB-165
Sandys, George 1578-1644.........DLB-24, 121
Sangster, Charles 1822-1893 ....DLB-99
Sanguineti, Edoardo 1930- DLB-128
Sanjōnishi Sanetaka 1455-1537 ....DLB-203
San Pedro, Diego de fl. ca. 1492 ....DLB-286
Sansay, Leonora ?-after 1823............DLB-200
Sansom, William 1912-1976.............DLB-139
Santayana, George
 1863-1952 ...... DLB-54, 71, 246, 270; DS-13
Santiago, Danny 1911-1988............DLB-122
Santillana, Marqués de (Íñigo López de Mendoza)
 1398-1458 ....DLB-286
Santmyer, Helen Hooven 1895-1986........ Y-84
Sanvitale, Francesca 1928- DLB-196
Sapidus, Joannes 1490-1561............DLB-179

Sapir, Edward 1884-1939 ....DLB-92
Sapper (see McNeile, Herman Cyril)
Sappho circa 620 B.C.-circa 550 B.C.
 .... DLB-176; CDWLB-1
Saramago, José 1922- DLB-287; Y-98
 Nobel Lecture 1998: How Characters
 Became the Masters and the Author
 Their Apprentice Y-98
Sarban (John W. Wall) 1910-1989 ......DLB-255
Sardou, Victorien 1831-1908...........DLB-192
Sarduy, Severo 1937-1993 ....DLB-113
Sargent, Pamela 1948- DLB-8
Saro-Wiwa, Ken 1941- DLB-157
Saroyan, Aram
 Rites of Passage [on William Saroyan] ... Y-83
Saroyan, William
 1908-1981..... DLB-7, 9, 86; Y-81; CDALB-7
Sarraute, Nathalie 1900-1999...........DLB-83
Sarrazin, Albertine 1937-1967 ....DLB-83
Sarris, Greg 1952- DLB-175
Sarton, May 1912-1995 ....DLB-48; Y-81
Sartre, Jean-Paul 1905-1980.........DLB-72, 296
Sassoon, Siegfried
 1886-1967 ....DLB-20, 191; DS-18
 A Centenary Essay Y-86
 Tributes from Vivien F. Clarke and
 Michael Thorpe Y-86
Sata Ineko 1904- DLB-180
Saturday Review Press DLB-46
Saunders, James 1925- DLB-13
Saunders, John Monk 1897-1940.........DLB-26
Saunders, Margaret Marshall
 1861-1947 ....DLB-92
Saunders and Otley DLB-106
Saussure, Ferdinand de 1857-1913.......DLB-242
Savage, James 1784-1873 ....DLB-30
Savage, Marmion W. 1803?-1872 ....DLB-21
Savage, Richard 1697?-1743 ....DLB-95
Savard, Félix-Antoine 1896-1982.........DLB-68
Savery, Henry 1791-1842 ....DLB-230
Saville, (Leonard) Malcolm 1901-1982 ...DLB-160
Savinio, Alberto 1891-1952 ....DLB-264
Sawyer, Robert J. 1960- DLB-251
Sawyer, Ruth 1880-1970 ....DLB-22
Sayers, Dorothy L.
 1893-1957 .... DLB-10, 36, 77, 100; CDBLB-6
 The Dorothy L. Sayers Society......... Y-98
Sayle, Charles Edward 1864-1924.......DLB-184
Sayles, John Thomas 1950- DLB-44
Sbarbaro, Camillo 1888-1967 ....DLB-114
Scalapino, Leslie 1947- DLB-193
Scannell, Vernon 1922- DLB-27
Scarry, Richard 1919-1994 ....DLB-61
Schack, Hans Egede 1820-1859..........DLB-300
Schaefer, Jack 1907-1991...............DLB-212
Schaeffer, Albrecht 1885-1950...........DLB-66
Schaeffer, Susan Fromberg 1941- ...DLB-28, 299

Schaff, Philip 1819-1893 . . . . DS-13

Schaper, Edzard 1908-1984 . . . . DLB-69

Scharf, J. Thomas 1843-1898 . . . . DLB-47

Schede, Paul Melissus 1539-1602 . . . . DLB-179

Scheffel, Joseph Viktor von 1826-1886 . . . DLB-129

Scheffler, Johann 1624-1677 . . . . DLB-164

Schelling, Friedrich Wilhelm Joseph von 1775-1854 . . . . DLB-90

Scherer, Wilhelm 1841-1886 . . . . DLB-129

Scherfig, Hans 1905-1979 . . . . DLB-214

Schickele, René 1883-1940 . . . . DLB-66

Schiff, Dorothy 1903-1989 . . . . DLB-127

Schiller, Friedrich 1759-1805 . . . . DLB-94; CDWLB-2

Schirmer, David 1623-1687 . . . . DLB-164

Schlaf, Johannes 1862-1941 . . . . DLB-118

Schlegel, August Wilhelm 1767-1845 . . . . . DLB-94

Schlegel, Dorothea 1763-1839 . . . . DLB-90

Schlegel, Friedrich 1772-1829 . . . . DLB-90

Schleiermacher, Friedrich 1768-1834 . . . . . DLB-90

Schlesinger, Arthur M., Jr. 1917- DLB-17

Schlumberger, Jean 1877-1968 . . . . DLB-65

Schmid, Eduard Hermann Wilhelm (see Edschmid, Kasimir)

Schmidt, Arno 1914-1979 . . . . DLB-69

Schmidt, Johann Kaspar (see Stirner, Max)

Schmidt, Michael 1947- DLB-40

Schmidtbonn, Wilhelm August 1876-1952 . . . . DLB-118

Schmitz, Aron Hector (see Svevo, Italo)

Schmitz, James H. 1911-1981 . . . . DLB-8

Schnabel, Johann Gottfried 1692-1760 . . . DLB-168

Schnackenberg, Gjertrud 1953- DLB-120

Schnitzler, Arthur 1862-1931 . . . . DLB-81, 118; CDWLB-2

Schnurre, Wolfdietrich 1920-1989 . . . . DLB-69

Schocken Books DLB-46

Scholartis Press DLB-112

Scholderer, Victor 1880-1971 . . . . DLB-201

The Schomburg Center for Research in Black Culture DLB-76

Schönbeck, Virgilio (see Giotti, Virgilio)

Schönherr, Karl 1867-1943 . . . . DLB-118

Schoolcraft, Jane Johnston 1800-1841 . . . . . DLB-175

School Stories, 1914-1960 . . . . DLB-160

Schopenhauer, Arthur 1788-1860 . . . . DLB-90

Schopenhauer, Johanna 1766-1838 . . . . . . DLB-90

Schorer, Mark 1908-1977 . . . . DLB-103

Schottelius, Justus Georg 1612-1676 . . . . . DLB-164

Schouler, James 1839-1920 . . . . DLB-47

Schoultz, Solveig von 1907-1996 . . . . DLB-259

Schrader, Paul 1946- DLB-44

Schreiner, Olive 1855-1920 . . . . DLB-18, 156, 190, 225

Schroeder, Andreas 1946- DLB-53

Schubart, Christian Friedrich Daniel 1739-1791 . . . . DLB-97

Schubert, Gotthilf Heinrich 1780-1860 . . . . DLB-90

Schücking, Levin 1814-1883 . . . . DLB-133

Schulberg, Budd 1914- DLB-6, 26, 28; Y-81

Excerpts from USC Presentation [on F. Scott Fitzgerald] Y-96

F. J. Schulte and Company DLB-49

Schulz, Bruno 1892-1942 . . . DLB-215; CDWLB-4

Schulze, Hans (see Praetorius, Johannes)

Schupp, Johann Balthasar 1610-1661 . . . . DLB-164

Schurz, Carl 1829-1906 . . . . DLB-23

Schuyler, George S. 1895-1977 . . . . DLB-29, 51

Schuyler, James 1923-1991 . . . . DLB-5, 169

Schwartz, Delmore 1913-1966 . . . . DLB-28, 48

Schwartz, Jonathan 1938- Y-82

Schwartz, Lynne Sharon 1939- DLB-218

Schwarz, Sibylle 1621-1638 . . . . DLB-164

Schwarz-Bart, Andre 1928- DLB-299

Schwerner, Armand 1927-1999 . . . . DLB-165

Schwob, Marcel 1867-1905 . . . . DLB-123

Sciascia, Leonardo 1921-1989 . . . . DLB-177

Science Fiction and Fantasy Documents in British Fantasy and Science Fiction DLB-178

Hugo Awards and Nebula Awards DLB-8

The Iconography of Science-Fiction Art DLB-8

The New Wave DLB-8

Paperback Science Fiction DLB-8

Science Fantasy DLB-8

Science-Fiction Fandom and Conventions DLB-8

Science-Fiction Fanzines: The Time Binders DLB-8

Science-Fiction Films DLB-8

Science Fiction Writers of America and the Nebula Award DLB-8

Selected Science-Fiction Magazines and Anthologies DLB-8

A World Chronology of Important Science Fiction Works (1818-1979) DLB-8

The Year in Science Fiction and Fantasy Y-00, 01

Scot, Reginald circa 1538-1599 . . . . DLB-136

Scotellaro, Rocco 1923-1953 . . . . DLB-128

Scott, Alicia Anne (Lady John Scott) 1810-1900 . . . . DLB-240

Scott, Catharine Amy Dawson 1865-1934 . . . . DLB-240

Scott, Dennis 1939-1991 . . . . DLB-125

Scott, Dixon 1881-1915 . . . . DLB-98

Scott, Duncan Campbell 1862-1947 . . . . . . DLB-92

Scott, Evelyn 1893-1963 . . . . DLB-9, 48

Scott, F. R. 1899-1985 . . . . DLB-88

Scott, Frederick George 1861-1944 . . . . . . DLB-92

Scott, Geoffrey 1884-1929 . . . . DLB-149

Scott, Harvey W. 1838-1910 . . . . DLB-23

Scott, Lady Jane (see Scott, Alicia Anne)

Scott, Paul 1920-1978 . . . . DLB-14, 207

Scott, Sarah 1723-1795 . . . . DLB-39

Scott, Tom 1918- DLB-27

Scott, Sir Walter 1771-1832 . . . . DLB-93, 107, 116, 144, 159; CDBLB-3

Scott, William Bell 1811-1890 . . . . DLB-32

Walter Scott Publishing Company Limited DLB-112

William R. Scott [publishing house] DLB-46

Scott-Heron, Gil 1949- DLB-41

Scribe, Eugene 1791-1861 . . . . DLB-192

Scribner, Arthur Hawley 1859-1932 . . . . DS-13, 16

Scribner, Charles 1854-1930 . . . . DS-13, 16

Scribner, Charles, Jr. 1921-1995 . . . . Y-95

Reminiscences DS-17

Charles Scribner's Sons DLB-49; DS-13, 16, 17

Archives of Charles Scribner's Sons DS-17

Scribner's Magazine DS-13

Scribner's Monthly DS-13

Scripps, E. W. 1854-1926 . . . . DLB-25

Scudder, Horace Elisha 1838-1902 . . . . DLB-42, 71

Scudder, Vida Dutton 1861-1954 . . . . DLB-71

Scudéry, Madeleine de 1607-1701 . . . . DLB-268

Scupham, Peter 1933- DLB-40

Seabrook, William 1886-1945 . . . . DLB-4

Seabury, Samuel 1729-1796 . . . . DLB-31

Seacole, Mary Jane Grant 1805-1881 . . . . DLB-166

The Seafarer circa 970 . . . . DLB-146

Sealsfield, Charles (Carl Postl) 1793-1864 . . . . DLB-133, 186

Searle, John R. 1932- DLB-279

Sears, Edward I. 1819?-1876 . . . . DLB-79

Sears Publishing Company DLB-46

Seaton, George 1911-1979 . . . . DLB-44

Seaton, William Winston 1785-1866 . . . . . DLB-43

Martin Secker [publishing house] DLB-112

Martin Secker, and Warburg Limited . . . DLB-112

The "Second Generation" Holocaust Novel DLB-299

Sedgwick, Arthur George 1844-1915 . . . . . DLB-64

Sedgwick, Catharine Maria 1789-1867 . . . . DLB-1, 74, 183, 239, 243

Sedgwick, Ellery 1872-1960 . . . . DLB-91

Sedgwick, Eve Kosofsky 1950- DLB-246

Sedley, Sir Charles 1639-1701 . . . . DLB-131

Seeberg, Peter 1925-1999 . . . . DLB-214

Seeger, Alan 1888-1916 . . . . DLB-45

Seers, Eugene (see Dantin, Louis)

Segal, Erich 1937- Y-86

Segal, Lore 1928- DLB-299

Šegedin, Petar 1909- DLB-181

Seghers, Anna 1900-1983 . . . . DLB-69; CDWLB-2

Seid, Ruth (see Sinclair, Jo)

Seidel, Frederick Lewis 1936- Y-84

Seidel, Ina 1885-1974 . . . . DLB-56

Seifert, Jaroslav 1901-1986 . . . . . . DLB-215; Y-84; CDWLB-4

Jaroslav Seifert Through the Eyes of the English-Speaking Reader Y-84
Three Poems by Jaroslav Seifert Y-84
Seifullina, Lidiia Nikolaevna 1889-1954 ..DLB-272
Seigenthaler, John 1927- DLB-127
Seizin Press DLB-112
Séjour, Victor 1817-1874 ....DLB-50
Séjour Marcou et Ferrand, Juan Victor (see Séjour, Victor)
Sekowski, Józef-Julian, Baron Brambeus (see Senkovsky, Osip Ivanovich)
Selby, Bettina 1934- DLB-204
Selby, Hubert, Jr. 1928- DLB-2, 227
Selden, George 1929-1989..............DLB-52
Selden, John 1584-1654................DLB-213
Selenić, Slobodan 1933-1995...........DLB-181
Self, Edwin F. 1920- DLB-137
Self, Will 1961- DLB-207
Seligman, Edwin R. A. 1861-1939........DLB-47
Selimović, Meša 1910-1982............DLB-181; CDWLB-4
Sellars, Wilfrid 1912-1989 ....DLB-279
Sellings, Arthur (Arthur Gordon Ley) 1911-1968...........................DLB-261
Selous, Frederick Courteney 1851-1917...DLB-174
Seltzer, Chester E. (see Muro, Amado)
Thomas Seltzer [publishing house] DLB-46
Selvon, Sam 1923-1994 .....DLB-125; CDWLB-3
Semel, Nava 1954- DLB-299
Semmes, Raphael 1809-1877 ....DLB-189
Senancour, Etienne de 1770-1846 ....DLB-119
Sena, Jorge de 1919-1978...............DLB-287
Sendak, Maurice 1928-..................DLB-61
Seneca the Elder circa 54 B.C.-circa A.D. 40 ....DLB-211
Seneca the Younger circa 1 B.C.-A.D. 65 .....DLB-211; CDWLB-1
Senécal, Éva 1905- DLB-92
Sengstacke, John 1912-1997 ....DLB-127
Senior, Olive 1941- DLB-157
Senkovsky, Osip Ivanovich (Józef-Julian Sekowski, Baron Brambeus) 1800-1858 ....DLB-198
Šenoa, August 1838-1881.... DLB-147; CDWLB-4
Sepamla, Sipho 1932- DLB-157, 225
Serafimovich, Aleksandr Serafimovich (Aleksandr Serafimovich Popov) 1863-1949 ....DLB-272
Serao, Matilde 1856-1927 ....DLB-264
Seredy, Kate 1899-1975 ....DLB-22
Sereni, Vittorio 1913-1983..............DLB-128
William Seres [publishing house]........DLB-170
Sergeev-Tsensky, Sergei Nikolaevich (Sergei Nikolaevich Sergeev) 1875-1958......DLB-272
Serling, Rod 1924-1975 ....DLB-26
Sernine, Daniel 1955- DLB-251
Serote, Mongane Wally 1944- DLB-125, 225
Serraillier, Ian 1912-1994................DLB-161

Serrano, Nina 1934- DLB-122
Service, Robert 1874-1958 ....DLB-92
Sessler, Charles 1854-1935 ....DLB-187
Seth, Vikram 1952- DLB-120, 271
Seton, Elizabeth Ann 1774-1821.........DLB-200
Seton, Ernest Thompson 1860-1942..................DLB-92; DS-13
Seton, John circa 1509-1567...........DLB-281
Setouchi Harumi 1922- DLB-182
Settle, Mary Lee 1918- DLB-6
Seume, Johann Gottfried 1763-1810.......DLB-94
Seuse, Heinrich 1295?-1366..........DLB-179
Seuss, Dr. (see Geisel, Theodor Seuss)
Severianin, Igor' 1887-1941 ....DLB-295
Severin, Timothy 1940- DLB-204
Sévigné, Marie de Rabutin Chantal, Madame de 1626-1696 ....DLB-268
Sewall, Joseph 1688-1769...............DLB-24
Sewall, Richard B. 1908- DLB-111
Sewall, Samuel 1652-1730 ....DLB-24
Sewell, Anna 1820-1878................DLB-163
Sexton, Anne 1928-1974 ...DLB-5, 169; CDALB-1
Seymour-Smith, Martin 1928-1998 ......DLB-155
Sgorlon, Carlo 1930- DLB-196
Shaara, Michael 1929-1988 .... Y-83
Shabel'skaia, Aleksandra Stanislavovna 1845-1921 ....DLB-238
Shadwell, Thomas 1641?-1692 ....DLB-80
Shaffer, Anthony 1926- DLB-13
Shaffer, Peter 1926- DLB-13, 233; CDBLB-8
Shaftesbury, Anthony Ashley Cooper, Third Earl of 1671-1713 ....DLB-101
Shaginian, Marietta Sergeevna 1888-1982......................DLB-272
Shairp, Mordaunt 1887-1939 ....DLB-10
Shakespeare, Nicholas 1957- DLB-231
Shakespeare, William 1564-1616 ......DLB-62, 172, 263; CDBLB-1
The New Variorum Shakespeare Y-85
Shakespeare and Montaigne: A Symposium by Jules Furthman Y-02
$6,166,000 for a *Book!* Observations on *The Shakespeare First Folio: The History of the Book* Y-01
Taylor-Made Shakespeare? Or Is "Shall I Die?" the Long-Lost Text of Bottom's Dream? Y-85
The Shakespeare Globe Trust Y-93
Shakespeare Head Press DLB-112
Shakhova, Elisaveta Nikitichna 1822-1899 ....DLB-277
Shakhovskoi, Aleksandr Aleksandrovich 1777-1846........................DLB-150
Shalamov, Varlam Tikhonovich 1907-1982 ....DLB-302
Shange, Ntozake 1948- DLB-38, 249
Shapcott, Thomas W. 1935- DLB-289
Shapir, Ol'ga Andreevna 1850-1916 .....DLB-295
Shapiro, Karl 1913-2000 ....DLB-48

Sharon Publications...................DLB-46
Sharov, Vladimir Aleksandrovich 1952- DLB-285
Sharp, Margery 1905-1991 ....DLB-161
Sharp, William 1855-1905.............DLB-156
Sharpe, Tom 1928- DLB-14, 231
Shaw, Albert 1857-1947 ....DLB-91
Shaw, George Bernard 1856-1950 .... DLB-10, 57, 190, CDBLB-6
The Bernard Shaw Society Y-99
"Stage Censorship: The Rejected Statement" (1911) [excerpts] DLB-10
Shaw, Henry Wheeler 1818-1885 ....DLB-11
Shaw, Irwin 1913-1984 ...... DLB-6, 102; Y-84; CDALB-1
Shaw, Joseph T. 1874-1952 ....DLB-137
"As I Was Saying," Joseph T. Shaw's Editorial Rationale in *Black Mask* (January 1927) DLB-137
Shaw, Mary 1854-1929 ....DLB-228
Shaw, Robert 1927-1978...........DLB-13, 14
Shaw, Robert B. 1947- DLB-120
Shawn, Wallace 1943- DLB-266
Shawn, William 1907-1992 ....DLB-137
Frank Shay [publishing house]..........DLB-46
Shchedrin, N. (see Saltykov, Mikhail Evgrafovich)
Shcherbakova, Galina Nikolaevna 1932- DLB-285
Shcherbina, Nikolai Fedorovich 1821-1869.....................DLB-277
Shea, John Gilmary 1824-1892 ....DLB-30
Sheaffer, Louis 1912-1993 ....DLB-103
Sheahan, Henry Beston (see Beston, Henry)
Shearing, Joseph 1886-1952.............DLB-70
Shebbeare, John 1709-1788 ....DLB-39
Sheckley, Robert 1928- DLB-8
Shedd, William G. T. 1820-1894.........DLB-64
Sheed, Wilfrid 1930- DLB-6
Sheed and Ward [U.S.] DLB-46
Sheed and Ward Limited [U.K.] DLB-112
Sheldon, Alice B. (see Tiptree, James, Jr.)
Sheldon, Edward 1886-1946 ....DLB-7
Sheldon and Company DLB-49
Sheller, Aleksandr Konstantinovich 1838-1900 ....DLB-238
Shelley, Mary Wollstonecraft 1797-1851 .... DLB-110, 116, 159, 178; CDBLB-3
Preface to *Frankenstein; or, The Modern Prometheus* (1818) DLB-178
Shelley, Percy Bysshe 1792-1822 .....DLB-96, 110, 158; CDBLB-3
Shelnutt, Eve 1941- DLB-130
Shenshin (see Fet, Afanasii Afanas'evich)
Shenstone, William 1714-1763..........DLB-95
Shepard, Clark and Brown DLB-49
Shepard, Ernest Howard 1879-1976......DLB-160
Shepard, Sam 1943- DLB-7, 212
Shepard, Thomas I, 1604 or 1605-1649 ...DLB-24

449

Shepard, Thomas, II, 1635-1677 .... DLB-24
Shepherd, Luke flourished 1547-1554.... DLB-136
Sherburne, Edward 1616-1702 .... DLB-131
Sheridan, Frances 1724-1766 .... DLB-39, 84
Sheridan, Richard Brinsley
    1751-1816.............. DLB-89; CDBLB-2
Sherman, Francis 1871-1926........... DLB-92
Sherman, Martin 1938- DLB-228
Sherriff, R. C. 1896-1975 ...... DLB-10, 191, 233
Sherrod, Blackie 1919- DLB-241
Sherry, Norman 1935- DLB-155
    Tribute to Graham Greene Y-91
Sherry, Richard 1506-1551 or 1555 ..... DLB-236
Sherwood, Mary Martha 1775-1851 ..... DLB-163
Sherwood, Robert E. 1896-1955....DLB-7, 26, 249
Shevyrev, Stepan Petrovich
    1806-1864 .... DLB-205
Shiel, M. P. 1865-1947 .... DLB-153
Shiels, George 1886-1949 .... DLB-10
Shiga Naoya 1883-1971 .... DLB-180
Shiina Rinzō 1911-1973 .... DLB-182
Shikishi Naishinnō 1153?-1201........ DLB-203
Shillaber, Benjamin Penhallow
    1814-1890................ DLB-1, 11, 235
Shimao Toshio 1917-1986............. DLB-182
Shimazaki Tōson 1872-1943.......... DLB-180
Shimose, Pedro 1940- DLB-283
Shine, Ted 1931- DLB-38
Shinkei 1406-1475................... DLB-203
Ship, Reuben 1915-1975 .... DLB-88
Shirer, William L. 1904-1993 .... DLB-4
Shirinsky-Shikhmatov, Sergii Aleksandrovich
    1783-1837..................... DLB-150
Shirley, James 1596-1666 .... DLB-58
Shishkov, Aleksandr Semenovich
    1753-1841..................... DLB-150
Shockley, Ann Allen 1927- DLB-33
Sholokhov, Mikhail Aleksandrovich
    1905-1984 .... DLB-272
Shōno Junzō 1921- DLB-182
Shore, Arabella 1820?-1901 .... DLB-199
Shore, Louisa 1824-1895 .... DLB-199
Short, Luke (see Glidden, Frederick Dilley)
Peter Short [publishing house] DLB-170
Shorter, Dora Sigerson 1866-1918 ...... DLB-240
Shorthouse, Joseph Henry 1834-1903 .... DLB-18
Short Stories
    Michael M. Rea and the Rea Award
        for the Short Story................ Y-97
    The Year in Short Stories............. Y-87
    The Year in the Short Story...... Y-88, 90–93
Shōtetsu 1381-1459.................. DLB-203
Showalter, Elaine 1941- DLB-67
Shreve, Anita 1946- DLB-292
Shukshin, Vasilii Makarovich
    1929-1974.................... DLB-302
Shulevitz, Uri 1935- DLB-61

Shulman, Max 1919-1988.............. DLB-11
Shute, Henry A. 1856-1943 .... DLB-9
Shute, Nevil (Nevil Shute Norway)
    1899-1960 .... DLB-255
Shuttle, Penelope 1947- DLB-14, 40
Shvarts, Evgenii L'vovich 1896-1958......DLB-272
Sibbes, Richard 1577-1635 .... DLB-151
Sibiriak, D. (see Mamin, Dmitrii Narkisovich)
Siddal, Elizabeth Eleanor 1829-1862 .... DLB-199
Sidgwick, Ethel 1877-1970............ DLB-197
Sidgwick, Henry 1838-1900 .... DLB-262
Sidgwick and Jackson Limited DLB-112
Sidney, Margaret (see Lothrop, Harriet M.)
Sidney, Mary 1561-1621 .... DLB-167
Sidney, Sir Philip
    1554-1586 .... DLB-167; CDBLB-1
    An Apologie for Poetrie (the Olney edition,
        1595, of *Defence of Poesie*) DLB-167
Sidney's Press..................... DLB-49
Sierra, Rubén 1946- DLB-122
Sierra Club Books.................. DLB-49
Siger of Brabant circa 1240-circa 1284 ... DLB-115
Sigourney, Lydia Huntley
    1791-1865.......DLB-1, 42, 73, 183, 239, 243
Silkin, Jon 1930-1997 .... DLB-27
Silko, Leslie Marmon
    1948- DLB-143, 175, 256, 275
Silliman, Benjamin 1779-1864.......... DLB-183
Silliman, Ron 1946- DLB-169
Silliphant, Stirling 1918-1996 .... DLB-26
Sillitoe, Alan 1928- DLB-14, 139; CDBLB-8
    Tribute to J. B. Priestly Y-84
Silman, Roberta 1934- DLB-28
Silone, Ignazio (Secondino Tranquilli)
    1900-1978..................... DLB-264
Silva, Beverly 1930- DLB-122
Silva, Clara 1905-1976 .... DLB-290
Silva, José Asunció 1865-1896 .... DLB-283
Silverberg, Robert 1935- DLB-8
Silverman, Kaja 1947- DLB-246
Silverman, Kenneth 1936- DLB-111
Simak, Clifford D. 1904-1988........... DLB-8
Simcoe, Elizabeth 1762-1850........... DLB-99
Simcox, Edith Jemima 1844-1901 ...... DLB-190
Simcox, George Augustus 1841-1905..... DLB-35
Sime, Jessie Georgina 1868-1958 .... DLB-92
Simenon, Georges 1903-1989........DLB-72; Y-89
Simic, Charles 1938- DLB-105
    "Images and 'Images'" DLB-105
Simionescu, Mircea Horia 1928- DLB-232
Simmel, Georg 1858-1918 .... DLB-296
Simmel, Johannes Mario 1924- DLB-69
Valentine Simmes [publishing house] DLB-170
Simmons, Ernest J. 1903-1972 .... DLB-103
Simmons, Herbert Alfred 1930- DLB-33
Simmons, James 1933- DLB-40

Simms, William Gilmore
    1806-1870............DLB-3, 30, 59, 73, 248
Simms and M'Intyre................ DLB-106
Simon, Claude 1913- DLB-83; Y-85
    Nobel Lecture Y-85
Simon, Neil 1927- DLB-7, 266
Simon and Schuster DLB-46
Simonov, Konstantin Mikhailovich
    1915-1979..................... DLB-302
Simons, Katherine Drayton Mayrant
    1890-1969 .... Y-83
Simović, Ljubomir 1935- DLB-181
Simpkin and Marshall
    [publishing house] DLB-154
Simpson, Helen 1897-1940 .... DLB-77
Simpson, Louis 1923- DLB-5
Simpson, N. F. 1919- DLB-13
Sims, George 1923- DLB-87; Y-99
Sims, George Robert 1847-1922 ...DLB-35, 70, 135
Sinán, Rogelio 1902-1994......... DLB-145, 290
Sinclair, Andrew 1935- DLB-14
Sinclair, Bertrand William 1881-1972..... DLB-92
Sinclair, Catherine 1800-1864 .... DLB-163
Sinclair, Jo 1913-1995................ DLB-28
Sinclair, Lister 1921- DLB-88
Sinclair, May 1863-1946........... DLB-36, 135
    The Novels of Dorothy Richardson
        (1918) DLB-36
Sinclair, Upton 1878-1968 ..... DLB-9; CDALB-5
Upton Sinclair [publishing house]........ DLB-46
Singer, Isaac Bashevis 1904-1991
    ....DLB-6, 28, 52, 278; Y-91; CDALB-1
Singer, Mark 1950- DLB-185
Singmaster, Elsie 1879-1958 .... DLB-9
Siniavsky, Andrei (Abram Tertz)
    1925-1997..................... DLB-302
Sinisgalli, Leonardo 1908-1981.......... DLB-114
Siodmak, Curt 1902-2000.............. DLB-44
Sîrbu, Ion D. 1919-1989.............. DLB-232
Siringo, Charles A. 1855-1928 .... DLB-186
Sissman, L. E. 1928-1976 .... DLB-5
Sisson, C. H. 1914- DLB-27
Sitwell, Edith 1887-1964 ...... DLB-20; CDBLB-7
Sitwell, Osbert 1892-1969.........DLB-100, 195
Skácel, Jan 1922-1989 .... DLB-232
Skalbe, Kārlis 1879-1945.............. DLB-220
Skármeta, Antonio
    1940- DLB-145; CDWLB-3
Skavronsky, A. (see Danilevsky, Grigorii Petrovich)
Skeat, Walter W. 1835-1912 .... DLB-184
William Skeffington [publishing house] .. DLB-106
Skelton, John 1463-1529............... DLB-136
Skelton, Robin 1925-1997..........DLB-27, 53
Škėma, Antanas 1910-1961 .... DLB-220
Skinner, Constance Lindsay
    1877-1939..................... DLB-92
Skinner, John Stuart 1788-1851 .... DLB-73

Skipsey, Joseph 1832-1903 . . . . DLB-35

Skou-Hansen, Tage 1925- DLB-214

Skrzynecki, Peter 1945- DLB-289

Škvorecký, Josef 1924- DLB-232; CDWLB-4

Slade, Bernard 1930- DLB-53

Slamnig, Ivan 1930- DLB-181

Slančeková, Božena (see Timrava)

Slataper, Scipio 1888-1915 . . . . DLB-264

Slater, Patrick 1880-1951 . . . . DLB-68

Slaveykov, Pencho 1866-1912 . . . . DLB-147

Slaviček, Milivoj 1929- DLB-181

Slavitt, David 1935- DLB-5, 6

Sleigh, Burrows Willcocks Arthur
  1821-1869 . . . . DLB-99

Sleptsov, Vasilii Alekseevich 1836-1878 . . . DLB-277

Slesinger, Tess 1905-1945 . . . . DLB-102

Slessor, Kenneth 1901-1971 . . . . DLB-260

Slick, Sam (see Haliburton, Thomas Chandler)

Sloan, John 1871-1951 . . . . DLB-188

Sloane, William, Associates DLB-46

Slonimsky, Mikhail Leonidovich
  1897-1972 . . . . DLB-272

Sluchevsky, Konstantin Konstantinovich
  1837-1904 . . . . DLB-277

Small, Maynard and Company DLB-49

Smart, Christopher 1722-1771 . . . . DLB-109

Smart, David A. 1892-1957 . . . . DLB-137

Smart, Elizabeth 1913-1986 . . . . DLB-88

Smart, J. J. C. 1920- DLB-262

Smedley, Menella Bute 1820?-1877 . . . . . . DLB-199

William Smellie [publishing house] DLB-154

Smiles, Samuel 1812-1904 . . . . DLB-55

Smiley, Jane 1949- DLB-227, 234

Smith, A. J. M. 1902-1980 . . . . DLB-88

Smith, Adam 1723-1790 . . . . DLB-104, 252

Smith, Adam (George Jerome Waldo
  Goodman) 1930- DLB-185

Smith, Alexander 1829-1867 . . . . DLB-32, 55

  "On the Writing of Essays" (1862) DLB-57

Smith, Amanda 1837-1915 . . . . DLB-221

Smith, Betty 1896-1972 . . . . Y-82

Smith, Carol Sturm 1938- Y-81

Smith, Charles Henry 1826-1903 . . . . DLB-11

Smith, Charlotte 1749-1806 . . . . DLB-39, 109

Smith, Chet 1899-1973 . . . . DLB-171

Smith, Cordwainer 1913-1966 . . . . DLB-8

Smith, Dave 1942- DLB-5

  Tribute to James Dickey Y-97

  Tribute to John Gardner Y-82

Smith, Dodie 1896- DLB-10

Smith, Doris Buchanan 1934- DLB-52

Smith, E. E. 1890-1965 . . . . DLB-8

Smith, Elihu Hubbard 1771-1798 . . . . DLB-37

Smith, Elizabeth Oakes (Prince)
  (see Oakes Smith, Elizabeth)

Smith, Eunice 1757-1823 . . . . DLB-200

Smith, F. Hopkinson 1838-1915 . . . . DS-13

Smith, George D. 1870-1920 . . . . DLB-140

Smith, George O. 1911-1981 . . . . DLB-8

Smith, Goldwin 1823-1910 . . . . DLB-99

Smith, H. Allen 1907-1976 . . . . DLB-11, 29

Smith, Harry B. 1860-1936 . . . . DLB-187

Smith, Hazel Brannon 1914-1994 . . . . DLB-127

Smith, Henry circa 1560-circa 1591 . . . . . DLB-136

Smith, Horatio (Horace)
  1779-1849 . . . . DLB-96, 116

Smith, Iain Crichton 1928-1998 . . . . . . DLB-40, 139

Smith, J. Allen 1860-1924 . . . . DLB-47

Smith, James 1775-1839 . . . . DLB-96

Smith, Jessie Willcox 1863-1935 . . . . DLB-188

Smith, John 1580-1631 . . . . DLB-24, 30

Smith, John 1618-1652 . . . . DLB-252

Smith, Josiah 1704-1781 . . . . DLB-24

Smith, Ken 1938- DLB-40

Smith, Lee 1944- DLB-143; Y-83

Smith, Logan Pearsall 1865-1946 . . . . DLB-98

Smith, Margaret Bayard 1778-1844 . . . . . DLB-248

Smith, Mark 1935- Y-82

Smith, Michael 1698-circa 1771 . . . . DLB-31

Smith, Pauline 1882-1959 . . . . DLB-225

Smith, Red 1905-1982 . . . . DLB-29, 171

Smith, Roswell 1829-1892 . . . . DLB-79

Smith, Samuel Harrison 1772-1845 . . . . . . DLB-43

Smith, Samuel Stanhope 1751-1819 . . . . . . DLB-37

Smith, Sarah (see Stretton, Hesba)

Smith, Sarah Pogson 1774-1870 . . . . DLB-200

Smith, Seba 1792-1868 . . . . DLB-1, 11, 243

Smith, Stevie 1902-1971 . . . . DLB-20

Smith, Sydney 1771-1845 . . . . DLB-107

Smith, Sydney Goodsir 1915-1975 . . . . DLB-27

Smith, Sir Thomas 1513-1577 . . . . DLB-132

Smith, Wendell 1914-1972 . . . . DLB-171

Smith, William flourished 1595-1597 . . . . DLB-136

Smith, William 1727-1803 . . . . DLB-31

  A General Idea of the College of Mirania
    (1753) [excerpts] DLB-31

Smith, William 1728-1793 . . . . DLB-30

Smith, William Gardner 1927-1974 . . . . . . DLB-76

Smith, William Henry 1808-1872 . . . . DLB-159

Smith, William Jay 1918- DLB-5

Smith, Elder and Company DLB-154

Harrison Smith and Robert Haas
  [publishing house] DLB-46

J. Stilman Smith and Company DLB-49

W. B. Smith and Company DLB-49

W. H. Smith and Son DLB-106

Leonard Smithers [publishing house] DLB-112

Smollett, Tobias
  1721-1771 . . . . DLB-39, 104; CDBLB-2

  Dedication to *Ferdinand Count Fathom*
    (1753) DLB-39

Preface to *Ferdinand Count Fathom*
  (1753) DLB-39

Preface to *Roderick Random* (1748) DLB-39

Smythe, Francis Sydney 1900-1949 . . . . . DLB-195

Snelling, William Joseph 1804-1848 . . . . . DLB-202

Snellings, Rolland (see Touré, Askia Muhammad)

Snodgrass, W. D. 1926- DLB-5

Snorri Hjartarson 1906-1986 . . . . DLB-293

Snow, C. P.
  1905-1980 . . . . . DLB-15, 77; DS-17; CDBLB-7

Snyder, Gary
  1930- DLB-5, 16, 165, 212, 237, 275

Sobiloff, Hy 1912-1970 . . . . DLB-48

The Society for Textual Scholarship and
  TEXT Y-87

The Society for the History of Authorship,
  Reading and Publishing Y-92

Söderberg, Hjalmar 1869-1941 . . . . DLB-259

Södergran, Edith 1892-1923 . . . . DLB-259

Soffici, Ardengo 1879-1964 . . . . DLB-114, 264

Sofola, 'Zulu 1938- DLB-157

Sokhanskaia, Nadezhda Stepanovna
  (Kokhanovskaia) 1823?-1884 . . . . DLB-277

Sokolov, Sasha (Aleksandr Vsevolodovich
  Sokolov) 1943- DLB-285

Solano, Solita 1888-1975 . . . . DLB-4

Soldati, Mario 1906-1999 . . . . DLB-177

Soledad (see Zamudio, Adela)

Šoljan, Antun 1932-1993 . . . . DLB-181

Sollers, Philippe (Philippe Joyaux)
  1936- DLB-83

Sollogub, Vladimir Aleksandrovich
  1813-1882 . . . . DLB-198

Sollors, Werner 1943- DBL-246

Solmi, Sergio 1899-1981 . . . . DLB-114

Sologub, Fedor 1863-1927 . . . . DLB-295

Solomon, Carl 1928- DLB-16

Solórzano, Carlos 1922- DLB-305

Soloukhin, Vladimir Alekseevich
  1924-1997 . . . . DLB-302

Solov'ev, Sergei Mikhailovich
  1885-1942 . . . . DLB-295

Solov'ev, Vladimir Sergeevich
  1853-1900 . . . . DLB-295

Solstad, Dag 1941- DLB-297

Solway, David 1941- DLB-53

Solzhenitsyn, Aleksandr
  1918- DLB-302
  Solzhenitsyn and America Y-85

Some Basic Notes on Three Modern Genres:
  Interview, Blurb, and Obituary Y-02

Somerville, Edith Œnone 1858-1949 . . . . . DLB-135

Somov, Orest Mikhailovich 1793-1833 . . . DLB-198

Sønderby, Knud 1909-1966 . . . . DLB-214

Song, Cathy 1955- DLB-169

Sonnevi, Göran 1939- DLB-257

Sono Ayako 1931- DLB-182

Sontag, Susan 1933- DLB-2, 67

Sophocles 497/496 B.C.-406/405 B.C. DLB-176; CDWLB-1

Šopov, Aco 1923-1982 . . . . DLB-181

Sorel, Charles ca.1600-1674. . . . . DLB-268

Sørensen, Villy 1929- DLB-214

Sorensen, Virginia 1912-1991. . . . . DLB-206

Sorge, Reinhard Johannes 1892-1916. . . . DLB-118

Sorokin, Vladimir Georgievich 1955- DLB-285

Sorrentino, Gilbert 1929- DLB-5, 173; Y-80

Sosa, Roberto 1930- DLB-290

Sotheby, James 1682-1742 . . . . DLB-213

Sotheby, John 1740-1807. . . . . DLB-213

Sotheby, Samuel 1771-1842 . . . . DLB-213

Sotheby, Samuel Leigh 1805-1861 . . . . . . DLB-213

Sotheby, William 1757-1833 . . . . DLB-93, 213

Soto, Gary 1952- DLB-82

Soueif, Ahdaf 1950- DLB-267

Souster, Raymond 1921- DLB-88

The *South English Legendary* circa thirteenth-fifteenth centuries. DLB-146

Southerland, Ellease 1943- DLB-33

Southern, Terry 1924-1995 . . . . DLB-2

Southern Illinois University Press Y-95

Southern Literature
Fellowship of Southern Writers Y-98

The Fugitives and the Agrarians: The First Exhibition Y-85

"The Greatness of Southern Literature": League of the South Institute for the Study of Southern Culture and History Y-02

The Society for the Study of Southern Literature Y-00

Southern Writers Between the Wars . . . DLB-9

Southerne, Thomas 1659-1746 . . . . DLB-80

Southey, Caroline Anne Bowles 1786-1854. . . . . DLB-116

Southey, Robert 1774-1843. . . . . . DLB-93, 107, 142

Southwell, Robert 1561?-1595 . . . . DLB-167

Southworth, E. D. E. N. 1819-1899 . . . . . DLB-239

Sowande, Bode 1948- DLB-157

Tace Sowle [publishing house] DLB-170

Soyfer, Jura 1912-1939 . . . . DLB-124

Soyinka, Wole 1934- DLB-125; Y-86, Y-87; CDWLB-3

Nobel Lecture 1986: This Past Must Address Its Present Y-86

Spacks, Barry 1931- DLB-105

Spalding, Frances 1950- DLB-155

Spanish Travel Writers of the Late Middle Ages. DLB-286

Spark, Muriel 1918- . . . DLB-15, 139; CDBLB-7

Michael Sparke [publishing house] DLB-170

Sparks, Jared 1789-1866 . . . . DLB-1, 30, 235

Sparshott, Francis 1926- DLB-60

Späth, Gerold 1939- DLB-75

Spatola, Adriano 1941-1988 . . . . DLB-128

Spaziani, Maria Luisa 1924- DLB-128

Specimens of Foreign Standard Literature 1838-1842 . . . . DLB-1

The Spectator 1828- DLB-110

Spedding, James 1808-1881 . . . . DLB-144

Spee von Langenfeld, Friedrich 1591-1635 . . . . DLB-164

Speght, Rachel 1597-after 1630. . . . . DLB-126

Speke, John Hanning 1827-1864. . . . . . . DLB-166

Spellman, A. B. 1935- DLB-41

Spence, Catherine Helen 1825-1910. . . . DLB-230

Spence, Thomas 1750-1814 . . . . DLB-158

Spencer, Anne 1882-1975 . . . . DLB-51, 54

Spencer, Charles, third Earl of Sunderland 1674-1722. . . . . DLB-213

Spencer, Elizabeth 1921- DLB-6, 218

Spencer, George John, Second Earl Spencer 1758-1834. . . . . DLB-184

Spencer, Herbert 1820-1903 . . . . DLB-57, 262

"The Philosophy of Style" (1852) DLB-57

Spencer, Scott 1945- Y-86

Spender, J. A. 1862-1942 . . . . DLB-98

Spender, Stephen 1909-1995 . . DLB-20; CDBLB-7

Spener, Philipp Jakob 1635-1705 . . . . DLB-164

Spenser, Edmund circa 1552-1599 . . . . DLB-167; CDBLB-1

Envoy from *The Shepheardes Calender*. . . . DLB-167

"The Generall Argument of the Whole Booke," from *The Shepheardes Calender* DLB-167

"A Letter of the Authors Expounding His Whole Intention in the Course of this Worke: Which for that It Giueth Great Light to the Reader, for the Better Vnderstanding Is Hereunto Annexed," from *The Faerie Qveene* (1590) DLB-167

"To His Booke," from *The Shepheardes Calender* (1579) . . . DLB-167

"To the Most Excellent and Learned Both Orator and Poete, Mayster Gabriell Haruey, His Verie Special and Singular Good Frend E. K. Commendeth the Good Lyking of This His Labour, and the Patronage of the New Poete," from *The Shepheardes Calender* DLB-167

Sperr, Martin 1944- DLB-124

Spewack, Bella Cowen 1899-1990 . . . . . . DLB-266

Spewack, Samuel 1899-1971 . . . . DLB-266

Spicer, Jack 1925-1965 . . . . DLB-5, 16, 193

Spiegelman, Art 1948- DLB-299

Spielberg, Peter 1929- Y-81

Spielhagen, Friedrich 1829-1911. . . . . . . DLB-129

"*Spielmannsepen*" (circa 1152-circa 1500) . . DLB-148

Spier, Peter 1927- DLB-61

Spillane, Mickey 1918- DLB-226

Spink, J. G. Taylor 1888-1962 . . . . DLB-241

Spinrad, Norman 1940- DLB-8

Tribute to Isaac Asimov. Y-92

Spires, Elizabeth 1952- DLB-120

Spitteler, Carl 1845-1924 . . . . DLB-129

Spivak, Lawrence E. 1900- DLB-137

Spofford, Harriet Prescott 1835-1921 . . . . DLB-74, 221

Sports
Jimmy, Red, and Others: Harold Rosenthal Remembers the Stars of the Press Box. Y-01

The Literature of Boxing in England through Arthur Conan Doyle Y-01

Notable Twentieth-Century Books about Sports DLB-241

Sprigge, Timothy L. S. 1932- DLB-262

Spring, Howard 1889-1965 . . . . DLB-191

Squibob (see Derby, George Horatio)

Squier, E. G. 1821-1888 . . . . DLB-189

Stableford, Brian 1948- DLB-261

Stacpoole, H. de Vere 1863-1951 . . . . . . DLB-153

Staël, Germaine de 1766-1817. . . . . . . DLB-119, 192

Staël-Holstein, Anne-Louise Germaine de (see Staël, Germaine de)

Staffeldt, Schack 1769-1826 . . . . DLB-300

Stafford, Jean 1915-1979. . . . . DLB-2, 173

Stafford, William 1914-1993. . . . . DLB-5, 206

Stallings, Laurence 1894-1968 . . . . DLB-7, 44

Stallworthy, Jon 1935- DLB-40

Stampp, Kenneth M. 1912- DLB-17

Stănescu, Nichita 1933-1983 . . . . DLB-232

Stanev, Emiliyan 1907-1979 . . . . DLB-181

Stanford, Ann 1916- DLB-5

Stangerup, Henrik 1937-1998 . . . . DLB-214

Stanihurst, Richard 1547-1618 . . . . DLB-281

Stanitsky, N. (see Panaeva, Avdot'ia Iakovlevna)

Stankevich, Nikolai Vladimirovich 1813-1840 . . . . DLB-198

Stanković, Borisav ("Bora") 1876-1927. . . . . DLB-147; CDWLB-4

Stanley, Henry M. 1841-1904 . . . DLB-189; DS-13

Stanley, Thomas 1625-1678 . . . . DLB-131

Stannard, Martin 1947- DLB-155

William Stansby [publishing house] DLB-170

Stanton, Elizabeth Cady 1815-1902 . . . . . DLB-79

Stanton, Frank L. 1857-1927 . . . . DLB-25

Stanton, Maura 1946- DLB-120

Stapledon, Olaf 1886-1950 . . . . DLB-15, 255

Star Spangled Banner Office DLB-49

Stark, Freya 1893-1993. . . . . DLB-195

Starkey, Thomas circa 1499-1538 . . . . . . DLB-132

Starkie, Walter 1894-1976 . . . . DLB-195

Starkweather, David 1935- DLB-7

Starrett, Vincent 1886-1974 . . . . DLB-187

Stationers' Company of London, The DLB-170

Statius circa A.D. 45-A.D. 96 . . . . DLB-211

Stead, Christina 1902-1983. . . . . DLB-260

Stead, Robert J. C. 1880-1959 . . . . DLB-92

Steadman, Mark 1930- DLB-6

Stearns, Harold E. 1891-1943. . . . . . DLB-4; DS-15

Stebnitsky, M. (see Leskov, Nikolai Semenovich)

Stedman, Edmund Clarence 1833-1908 ...DLB-64

Steegmuller, Francis 1906-1994 ....DLB-111

Steel, Flora Annie 1847-1929 ....DLB-153, 156

Steele, Max 1922- Y-80

Steele, Richard 1672-1729 ....DLB-84, 101; CDBLB-2

Steele, Timothy 1948- DLB-120

Steele, Wilbur Daniel 1886-1970 ....DLB-86

Wallace Markfield's "Steeplechase"......... Y-02

Steere, Richard circa 1643-1721.........DLB-24

Stefán frá Hvítadal (Stefán Sigurðsson) 1887-1933 ....DLB-293

Stefán Guðmundsson (see Stephan G. Stephansson)

Stefán Hörður Grímsson 1919 or 1920-2002 ....DLB-293

Steffens, Lincoln 1866-1936...........DLB-303

Stefanovski, Goran 1952- DLB-181

Stegner, Wallace 1909-1993 .... DLB-9, 206, 275; Y-93

Stehr, Hermann 1864-1940 ....DLB-66

Steig, William 1907- DLB-61

Stein, Gertrude 1874-1946 ......DLB-4, 54, 86, 228; DS-15; CDALB-4

Stein, Leo 1872-1947 ....DLB-4

Stein and Day Publishers..............DLB-46

Steinbeck, John 1902-1968 .... DLB-7, 9, 212, 275; DS-2; CDALB-5

John Steinbeck Research Center, San Jose State University Y-85

The Steinbeck Centennial............ Y-02

Steinem, Gloria 1934- DLB-246

Steiner, George 1929- DLB-67, 299

Steinhoewel, Heinrich 1411/1412-1479 ... DLB-179

Steinn Steinarr (Aðalsteinn Kristmundsson) 1908-1958 ....DLB-293

Steinunn Sigurðardóttir 1950- DLB-293

Steloff, Ida Frances 1887-1989 ....DLB-187

Stendhal 1783-1842 ....DLB-119

Stephan G. Stephansson (Stefán Guðmundsson) 1853-1927 ....DLB-293

Stephen, Leslie 1832-1904 ...... DLB-57, 144, 190

Stephen Family (Bloomsbury Group) DS-10

Stephens, A. G. 1865-1933.............DLB-230

Stephens, Alexander H. 1812-1883 ....DLB-47

Stephens, Alice Barber 1858-1932 ....DLB-188

Stephens, Ann 1810-1886 .... DLB-3, 73, 250

Stephens, Charles Asbury 1844?-1931.....DLB-42

Stephens, James 1882?-1950 .... DLB-19, 153, 162

Stephens, John Lloyd 1805-1852 .... DLB-183, 250

Stephens, Michael 1946- DLB-234

Stephensen, P. R. 1901-1965 ....DLB-260

Sterling, George 1869-1926 ....DLB-54

Sterling, James 1701-1763 ....DLB-24

Sterling, John 1806-1844 ....DLB-116

Stern, Gerald 1925- DLB-105

"Living in Ruin" DLB-105

Stern, Gladys B. 1890-1973 ....DLB-197

Stern, Madeleine B. 1912- DLB-111, 140

Stern, Richard 1928- DLB-218; Y-87

Stern, Stewart 1922- DLB-26

Sterne, Laurence 1713-1768 ... DLB-39; CDBLB-2

Sternheim, Carl 1878-1942 ....DLB-56, 118

Sternhold, Thomas ?-1549............DLB-132

Steuart, David 1747-1824..............DLB-213

Stevens, Henry 1819-1886..............DLB-140

Stevens, Wallace 1879-1955....DLB-54; CDALB-5

The Wallace Stevens Society Y-99

Stevenson, Anne 1933- DLB-40

Stevenson, D. E. 1892-1973 ....DLB-191

Stevenson, Lionel 1902-1973 ....DLB-155

Stevenson, Robert Louis 1850-1894 .... DLB-18, 57, 141, 156, 174; DS-13; CDBLB-5

"On Style in Literature: Its Technical Elements" (1885) ...DLB-57

Stewart, Donald Ogden 1894-1980 ....DLB-4, 11, 26; DS-15

Stewart, Douglas 1913-1985 ....DLB-260

Stewart, Dugald 1753-1828 ....DLB-31

Stewart, George, Jr. 1848-1906 ....DLB-99

Stewart, George R. 1895-1980 ....DLB-8

Stewart, Harold 1916-1995 ....DLB-260

Stewart, J. I. M. (see Innes, Michael)

Stewart, Maria W. 1803?-1879 ....DLB-239

Stewart, Randall 1896-1964............DLB-103

Stewart, Sean 1965- DLB-251

Stewart and Kidd Company DLB-46

Sthen, Hans Christensen 1544-1610 .....DLB-300

Stickney, Trumbull 1874-1904..........DLB-54

Stieler, Caspar 1632-1707..............DLB-164

Stifter, Adalbert 1805-1868 ....DLB-133; CDWLB-2

Stiles, Ezra 1727-1795 ....DLB-31

Still, James 1906-2001 .... DLB-9; Y-01

Stirling, S. M. 1953- DLB-251

Stirner, Max 1806-1856...............DLB-129

Stith, William 1707-1755................DLB-31

Stivens, Dal 1911-1997...............DLB-260

Elliot Stock [publishing house].........DLB-106

Stockton, Annis Boudinot 1736-1801.....DLB-200

Stockton, Frank R. 1834-1902 ....DLB-42, 74; DS-13

Stockton, J. Roy 1892-1972 ....DLB-241

Ashbel Stoddard [publishing house].......DLB-49

Stoddard, Charles Warren 1843-1909....DLB-186

Stoddard, Elizabeth 1823-1902 ....DLB-202

Stoddard, Richard Henry 1825-1903 .... DLB-3, 64, 250; DS-13

Stoddard, Solomon 1643-1729 ....DLB-24

Stoker, Bram 1847-1912 .... DLB-36, 70, 178; CDBLB-5

On Writing *Dracula*, from the Introduction to *Dracula* (1897) ...DLB-178

Dracula (A Documentary Volume) ...DLB-304

Frederick A. Stokes Company..........DLB-49

Stokes, Thomas L. 1898-1958 ....DLB-29

Stokesbury, Leon 1945- DLB-120

Stolberg, Christian Graf zu 1748-1821.....DLB-94

Stolberg, Friedrich Leopold Graf zu 1750-1819 ....DLB-94

Stone, Lucy 1818-1893 .... DLB-79, 239

Stone, Melville 1848-1929 ....DLB-25

Stone, Robert 1937- DLB-152

Stone, Ruth 1915- DLB-105

Stone, Samuel 1602-1663..............DLB-24

Stone, William Leete 1792-1844 ....DLB-202

Herbert S. Stone and Company..........DLB-49

Stone and Kimball....................DLB-49

Stoppard, Tom 1937- DLB-13, 233; Y-85; CDBLB-8

Playwrights and Professors..........DLB-13

Storey, Anthony 1928- DLB-14

Storey, David 1933- DLB-13, 14, 207, 245

Storm, Theodor 1817-1888 .... DLB-129; CDWLB-2

Storni, Alfonsina 1892-1938 ....DLB-283

Story, Thomas circa 1670-1742 ....DLB-31

Story, William Wetmore 1819-1895 ...DLB-1, 235

Storytelling: A Contemporary Renaissance... Y-84

Stoughton, William 1631-1701 ....DLB-24

Stow, John 1525-1605 ....DLB-132

Stow, Randolph 1935- DLB-260

Stowe, Harriet Beecher 1811-1896 ...... DLB-1,12, 42, 74, 189, 239, 243; CDALB-3

The Harriet Beecher Stowe Center...... Y-00

Stowe, Leland 1899-1994..............DLB-29

Stoyanov, Dimitr Ivanov (see Elin Pelin)

Strabo 64/63 B.C.-circa A.D. 25 ....DLB-176

Strachey, Lytton 1880-1932...... DLB-149; DS-10

Preface to *Eminent Victorians* DLB-149

William Strahan [publishing house]......DLB-154

Strahan and Company.................DLB-106

Strand, Mark 1934- DLB-5

The Strasbourg Oaths 842.............DLB-148

Stratemeyer, Edward 1862-1930 ....DLB-42

Strati, Saverio 1924- DLB-177

Stratton and Barnard..................DLB-49

Stratton-Porter, Gene 1863-1924 .... DLB-221; DS-14

Straub, Peter 1943- Y-84

Strauß, Botho 1944- DLB-124

Strauß, David Friedrich 1808-1874 ......DLB-133

The Strawberry Hill Press.............DLB-154

Strawson, P. F. 1919- DLB-262

Streatfeild, Noel 1895-1986 ....DLB-160

Street, Cecil John Charles (see Rhode, John)

Street, G. S. 1867-1936...............DLB-135

Street and Smith....................DLB-49

Streeter, Edward 1891-1976............DLB-11

Streeter, Thomas Winthrop 1883-1965 .. DLB-140
Stretton, Hesba 1832-1911 .... DLB-163, 190
Stribling, T. S. 1881-1965................ DLB-9
Der Stricker circa 1190-circa 1250 ...... DLB-138
Strickland, Samuel 1804-1867........... DLB-99
Strindberg, August 1849-1912 .... DLB-259
Stringer, Arthur 1874-1950............. DLB-92
Stringer and Townsend DLB-49
Strittmatter, Erwin 1912-1994 .... DLB-69
Strniša, Gregor 1930-1987 .... DLB-181
Strode, William 1630-1645............. DLB-126
Strong, L. A. G. 1896-1958............. DLB-191
Strother, David Hunter (Porte Crayon)
  1816-1888.................. DLB-3, 248
Strouse, Jean 1945- DLB-111
Strugatsky, Arkadii Natanovich
  1925- DLB-302
Strugatsky, Boris Natanovich 1933- ... DLB-302
Stuart, Dabney 1937- DLB-105
  "Knots into Webs: Some
    Autobiographical Sources" DLB-105
Stuart, Jesse 1906-1984......DLB-9, 48, 102; Y-84
Lyle Stuart [publishing house] DLB-46
Stuart, Ruth McEnery 1849?-1917 ..... DLB-202
Stub, Ambrosius 1705-1758............. DLB-300
Stubbs, Harry Clement (see Clement, Hal)
Stubenberg, Johann Wilhelm von
  1619-1663........................ DLB-164
Stuckenberg, Viggo 1763-1905 .... DLB-300
Studebaker, William V. 1947- DLB-256
Studies in American Jewish Literature Y-02
Studio DLB-112
Stump, Al 1916-1995 .... DLB-241
Sturgeon, Theodore
  1918-1985.................. DLB-8; Y-85
Sturges, Preston 1898-1959 .... DLB-26
Styron, William
  1925- ... DLB-2, 143, 299; Y-80; CDALB-6
  Tribute to James Dickey Y-97
Suárez, Clementina 1902-1991 .... DLB-290
Suárez, Mario 1925- DLB-82
Such, Peter 1939- DLB-60
Suckling, Sir John 1609-1641? DLB-58, 126
Suckow, Ruth 1892-1960 .... DLB-9, 102
Sudermann, Hermann 1857-1928....... DLB-118
Sue, Eugène 1804-1857................ DLB-119
Sue, Marie-Joseph (see Sue, Eugène)
Suetonius circa A.D. 69-post A.D. 122 ... DLB-211
Suggs, Simon (see Hooper, Johnson Jones)
Sui Sin Far (see Eaton, Edith Maude)
Suits, Gustav 1883-1956.... DLB-220; CDWLB-4
Sukenick, Ronald 1932- DLB-173; Y-81
  An Author's Response Y-82
Sukhovo-Kobylin, Aleksandr Vasil'evich
  1817-1903........................DLB-277
Suknaski, Andrew 1942- DLB-53

Sullivan, Alan 1868-1947 .... DLB-92
Sullivan, C. Gardner 1886-1965......... DLB-26
Sullivan, Frank 1892-1976 .... DLB-11
Sulte, Benjamin 1841-1923............. DLB-99
Sulzberger, Arthur Hays 1891-1968..... DLB-127
Sulzberger, Arthur Ochs 1926- DLB-127
Sulzer, Johann Georg 1720-1779 .... DLB-97
Sumarokov, Aleksandr Petrovich
  1717-1777....................... DLB-150
Summers, Hollis 1916- DLB-6
Sumner, Charles 1811-1874 .... DLB-235
Sumner, William Graham 1840-1910.....DLB-270
Henry A. Sumner
  [publishing house] DLB-49
Sundman, Per Olof 1922-1992 .... DLB-257
Supervielle, Jules 1884-1960 .... DLB-258
Surtees, Robert Smith 1803-1864 .... DLB-21
  The R. S. Surtees Society............. Y-98
Sutcliffe, Matthew 1550?-1629 .... DLB-281
Sutcliffe, William 1971- DLB-271
Sutherland, Efua Theodora
  1924-1996 ....DLB-117
Sutherland, John 1919-1956 .... DLB-68
Sutro, Alfred 1863-1933 .... DLB-10
Svava Jakobsdóttir 1930- DLB-293
Svendsen, Hanne Marie 1933- DLB-214
Svevo, Italo (Ettore Schmitz)
  1861-1928 .... DLB-264
Swados, Harvey 1920-1972 .... DLB-2
Swain, Charles 1801-1874.............. DLB-32
Swallow Press....................... DLB-46
Swan Sonnenschein Limited........... DLB-106
Swanberg, W. A. 1907-1992 .... DLB-103
Swedish Literature
  The Literature of the Modern
    Breakthrough DLB-259
Swenson, May 1919-1989.............. DLB-5
Swerling, Jo 1897- DLB-44
Swift, Graham 1949- DLB-194
Swift, Jonathan
  1667-1745 ...... DLB-39, 95, 101; CDBLB-2
Swinburne, A. C.
  1837-1909.......... DLB-35, 57; CDBLB-4
  Under the Microscope (1872) DLB-35
Swineshead, Richard floruit circa 1350 .. DLB-115
Swinnerton, Frank 1884-1982 .... DLB-34
Swisshelm, Jane Grey 1815-1884 .... DLB-43
Swope, Herbert Bayard 1882-1958...... DLB-25
Swords, James ?-1844................. DLB-73
Swords, Thomas 1763-1843 .... DLB-73
T. and J. Swords and Company......... DLB-49
Swynnerton, Thomas (John Roberts)
  circa 1500-1554 .... DLB-281
Sykes, Ella C. ?-1939 ....DLB-174
Sylvester, Josuah 1562 or 1563-1618 .... DLB-121
Symonds, Emily Morse (see Paston, George)

Symonds, John Addington
  1840-1893 ....DLB-57, 144
  "Personal Style" (1890) DLB-57
Symons, A. J. A. 1900-1941 .... DLB-149
Symons, Arthur 1865-1945 ...... DLB-19, 57, 149
Symons, Julian 1912-1994 ..... DLB-87, 155; Y-92
  Julian Symons at Eighty.............. Y-92
Symons, Scott 1933- DLB-53
Synge, John Millington
  1871-1909.......... DLB-10, 19; CDBLB-5
  Synge Summer School: J. M. Synge
    and the Irish Theater, Rathdrum,
    County Wiclow, Ireland Y-93
Syrett, Netta 1865-1943 ....DLB-135, 197
Szabó, Lőrinc 1900-1957 .... DLB-215
Szabó, Magda 1917- DLB-215
Szymborska, Wisława
  1923- DLB-232, Y-96; CDWLB-4
  Nobel Lecture 1996:
    The Poet and the World........... Y-96

T

Taban lo Liyong 1939?- DLB-125
Tablada, José Juan 1871-1945.......... DLB-290
Tabori, George 1914- DLB-245
Tabucchi, Antonio 1943- DLB-196
Taché, Joseph-Charles 1820-1894 .... DLB-99
Tachihara Masaaki 1926-1980......... DLB-182
Tacitus circa A.D. 55-circa A.D. 117
  ....DLB-211; CDWLB-1
Tadijanović, Dragutin 1905- DLB-181
Tafdrup, Pia 1952- DLB-214
Tafolla, Carmen 1951- DLB-82
Taggard, Genevieve 1894-1948 .... DLB-45
Taggart, John 1942- DLB-193
Tagger, Theodor (see Bruckner, Ferdinand)
Taiheiki late fourteenth century DLB-203
Tait, J. Selwin, and Sons.............. DLB-49
Tait's Edinburgh Magazine 1832-1861 ..... DLB-110
The Takarazaka Revue Company Y-91
Talander (see Bohse, August)
Talese, Gay 1932- DLB-185
  Tribute to Irwin Shaw Y-84
Talev, Dimitr 1898-1966 .... DLB-181
Taliaferro, H. E. 1811-1875 .... DLB-202
Tallent, Elizabeth 1954- DLB-130
TallMountain, Mary 1918-1994........ DLB-193
Talvj 1797-1870.................. DLB-59, 133
Tamási, Áron 1897-1966 .... DLB-215
Tammsaare, A. H.
  1878-1940............ DLB-220; CDWLB-4
Tan, Amy 1952- DLB-173; CDALB-7
Tandori, Dezső 1938- DLB-232
Tanner, Thomas 1673/1674-1735...... DLB-213
Tanizaki Jun'ichirō 1886-1965......... DLB-180
Tapahonso, Luci 1953- DLB-175
The Mark Taper Forum................ DLB-7

Taradash, Daniel 1913- DLB-44

Tarasov-Rodionov, Aleksandr Ignat'evich
 1885-1938 ....DLB-272

Tarbell, Ida M. 1857-1944 ....DLB-47

Tardivel, Jules-Paul 1851-1905 ....DLB-99

Targan, Barry 1932- DLB-130

 Tribute to John Gardner............. Y-82

Tarkington, Booth 1869-1946 ....DLB-9, 102

Tashlin, Frank 1913-1972 ....DLB-44

Tasma (Jessie Couvreur) 1848-1897.....DLB-230

Tate, Allen 1899-1979 ..... DLB-4, 45, 63; DS-17

Tate, James 1943- DLB-5, 169

Tate, Nahum circa 1652-1715 ....DLB-80

Tatian circa 830 ....DLB-148

Taufer, Veno 1933- DLB-181

Tauler, Johannes circa 1300-1361 .....DLB-179

Tavares, Salette 1922-1994 ....DLB-287

Tavčar, Ivan 1851-1923...............DLB-147

Taverner, Richard ca. 1505-1575........DLB-236

Taylor, Ann 1782-1866 ....DLB-163

Taylor, Bayard 1825-1878 .... DLB-3, 189, 250

Taylor, Bert Leston 1866-1921 ....DLB-25

Taylor, Charles H. 1846-1921..........DLB-25

Taylor, Edward circa 1642-1729 ....DLB-24

Taylor, Elizabeth 1912-1975 ....DLB-139

Taylor, Sir Henry 1800-1886...........DLB-32

Taylor, Henry 1942- DLB-5

 Who Owns American Literature........ Y-94

Taylor, Jane 1783-1824 ....DLB-163

Taylor, Jeremy circa 1613-1667.........DLB-151

Taylor, John 1577 or 1578 - 1653 ....DLB-121

Taylor, Mildred D. 1943- DLB-52

Taylor, Peter 1917-1994... DLB-218, 278; Y-81, 94

Taylor, Susie King 1848-1912 ....DLB-221

Taylor, William Howland 1901-1966....DLB-241

William Taylor and Company DLB-49

Teale, Edwin Way 1899-1980 ....DLB-275

Teasdale, Sara 1884-1933 ....DLB-45

Teillier, Jorge 1935-1996 ....DLB-283

Telles, Lygia Fagundes 1924- DLB-113

The Temper of the West: William Jovanovich ... Y-02

Temple, Sir William 1555?-1627 ....DLB-281

Temple, Sir William 1628-1699.........DLB-101

Temple, William F. 1914-1989 ....DLB-255

Temrizov, A. (see Marchenko, Anastasia Iakovlevna)

Tench, Watkin ca. 1758-1833 ....DLB-230

Tender Is the Night (Documentary) DLB-273

Tendriakov, Vladimir Fedorovich
 1923-1984....................DLB-302

Tenn, William 1919- DLB-8

Tennant, Emma 1937- DLB-14

Tenney, Tabitha Gilman 1762-1837 .. DLB-37, 200

Tennyson, Alfred 1809-1892.. DLB-32; CDBLB-4

 On Some of the Characteristics of
 Modern Poetry and On the Lyrical
 Poems of Alfred Tennyson
 (1831) DLB-32

Tennyson, Frederick 1807-1898.........DLB-32

Tenorio, Arthur 1924- DLB-209

Tepl, Johannes von
 circa 1350-1414/1415 ....DLB-179

Tepliakov, Viktor Grigor'evich
 1804-1842 ....DLB-205

Terence circa 184 B.C.-159 B.C. or after
 .... DLB-211; CDWLB-1

Terhune, Albert Payson 1872-1942........DLB-9

Terhune, Mary Virginia 1830-1922 .... DS-13

Terpigorev, Sergei Nikolaevich (S. Atava)
 1841-1895 ....DLB-277

Terry, Megan 1932- DLB-7, 249

Terson, Peter 1932- DLB-13

Tesich, Steve 1943-1996 .... Y-83

Tessa, Delio 1886-1939 ....DLB-114

Testori, Giovanni 1923-1993 .... DLB-128, 177

Texas
 The Year in Texas Literature Y-98

Tey, Josephine 1896?-1952 ....DLB-77

Thacher, James 1754-1844.............DLB-37

Thacher, John Boyd 1847-1909 ....DLB-187

Thackeray, William Makepeace
 1811-1863 ...DLB-21, 55, 159, 163; CDBLB-4

Thames and Hudson Limited DLB-112

Thanet, Octave (see French, Alice)

Thaxter, Celia Laighton
 1835-1894....................DLB-239

Thayer, Caroline Matilda Warren
 1785-1844 ....DLB-200

Thayer, Douglas H. 1929- DLB-256

Theater
 Black Theatre: A Forum [excerpts] DLB-38

 Community and Commentators:
 Black Theatre and Its Critics DLB-38

 German Drama from Naturalism
 to Fascism: 1889-1933 ....DLB-118

 A Look at the Contemporary Black
 Theatre Movement..............DLB-38

 The Lord Chamberlain's Office and
 Stage Censorship in England DLB-10

 New Forces at Work in the American
 Theatre: 1915-1925 ....DLB-7

 Off Broadway and Off-Off Broadway ..DLB-7

 Oregon Shakespeare Festival.......... Y-00

 Plays, Playwrights, and Playgoers.....DLB-84

 Playwrights on the Theater..........DLB-80

 Playwrights and Professors DLB-13

 Producing *Dear Bunny, Dear Volodya:*
 The Friendship and the Feud Y-97

 Viewpoint: Politics and Performance,
 by David Edgar DLB-13

 Writing for the Theatre,
 by Harold Pinter..............DLB-13

 The Year in Drama..........Y-82-85, 87–98

 The Year in U.S. Drama............. Y-00

Theater, English and Irish
 Anti-Theatrical Tracts.............DLB-263

 The Chester Plays circa 1505-1532;
 revisions until 1575............DLB-146

 Dangerous Years: London Theater,
 1939-1945....................DLB-10

 A Defense of Actors DLB-263

 The Development of Lighting in the
 Staging of Drama, 1900-1945 ....DLB-10

 Education DLB-263

 The End of English Stage Censorship,
 1945-1968....................DLB-13

 Epigrams and Satires..............DLB-263

 Eyewitnesses and Historians........DLB-263

 Fringe and Alternative Theater in
 Great Britain..................DLB-13

 The Great War and the Theater,
 1914-1918 [Great Britain]........DLB-10

 Licensing Act of 1737 ....DLB-84

 Morality Plays: *Mankind* circa 1450-1500
 and *Everyman* circa 1500 ....DLB-146

 The New Variorum Shakespeare Y-85

 N-Town Plays circa 1468 to early
 sixteenth century.............DLB-146

 Politics and the Theater DLB-263

 Practical Matters DLB-263

 Prologues, Epilogues, Epistles to
 Readers, and Excerpts from
 Plays.......................DLB-263

 The Publication of English
 Renaissance Plays..............DLB-62

 Regulations for the Theater DLB-263

 Sources for the Study of Tudor and
 Stuart Drama DLB-62

 Stage Censorship: "The Rejected
 Statement" (1911), by Bernard
 Shaw [excerpts]................DLB-10

 Synge Summer School: J. M. Synge and
 the Irish Theater, Rathdrum,
 County Wiclow, Ireland........... Y-93

 The Theater in Shakespeare's Time ...DLB-62

 The Theatre Guild DLB-7

 The Townely Plays fifteenth and
 sixteenth centuries DLB-146

 The Year in British Drama Y-99–01

 The Year in Drama: London Y-90

 The Year in London Theatre Y-92

 A Yorkshire Tragedy................DLB-58

Theaters
 The Abbey Theatre and Irish Drama,
 1900-1945....................DLB-10

 Actors Theatre of Louisville DLB-7

 American Conservatory Theatre DLB-7

 Arena Stage.....................DLB-7

 Black Theaters and Theater
 Organizations in America,
 1961-1982: A Research List DLB-38

 The Dallas Theater Center...........DLB-7

 Eugene O'Neill Memorial Theater
 Center......................DLB-7

 The Goodman Theatre..............DLB-7

 The Guthrie Theater DLB-7

 The Mark Taper Forum DLB-7

The National Theatre and the Royal
  Shakespeare Company: The
  National Companies DLB-13

Off-Loop Theatres DLB-7

The Royal Court Theatre and the
  English Stage Company DLB-13

The Royal Court Theatre and the
  New Drama DLB-10

The Takarazaka Revue Company Y-91

Thegan and the Astronomer
  flourished circa 850 . . . . DLB-148

Thelwall, John 1764-1834 . . . . DLB-93, 158

Theocritus circa 300 B.C.-260 B.C. DLB-176

Theodorescu, Ion N. (see Arghezi, Tudor)

Theodulf circa 760-circa 821 . . . . DLB-148

Theophrastus circa 371 B.C.-287 B.C. DLB-176

Thériault, Yves 1915-1983 . . . . DLB-88

Thério, Adrien 1925- DLB-53

Theroux, Paul 1941- DLB-2, 218; CDALB-7

Thesiger, Wilfred 1910- DLB-204

They All Came to Paris DS-15

Thibaudeau, Colleen 1925- DLB-88

Thiele, Colin 1920- DLB-289

Thielen, Benedict 1903-1965 . . . . DLB-102

Thiong'o Ngugi wa (see Ngugi wa Thiong'o)

This Quarter 1925-1927, 1929-1932 . . . . DS-15

Thoma, Ludwig 1867-1921 . . . . DLB-66

Thoma, Richard 1902- DLB-4

Thomas, Audrey 1935- DLB-60

Thomas, D. M.
  1935- . . . DLB-40, 207, 299; Y-82; CDBLB-8

  The Plagiarism Controversy Y-82

Thomas, Dylan
  1914-1953 . . . . . . DLB-13, 20, 139; CDBLB-7

  The Dylan Thomas Celebration Y-99

Thomas, Edward
  1878-1917 . . . . DLB-19, 98, 156, 216

  The Friends of the Dymock Poets Y-00

Thomas, Frederick William 1806-1866 . . DLB-202

Thomas, Gwyn 1913-1981 . . . . DLB-15, 245

Thomas, Isaiah 1750-1831 . . . . . . DLB-43, 73, 187

Thomas, Johann 1624-1679 . . . . DLB-168

Thomas, John 1900-1932 . . . . DLB-4

Thomas, Joyce Carol 1938- DLB-33

Thomas, Lewis 1913-1993 . . . . DLB-275

Thomas, Lorenzo 1944- DLB-41

Thomas, Norman 1884-1968 . . . . DLB-303

Thomas, R. S. 1915-2000 . . . . . DLB-27; CDBLB-8

Isaiah Thomas [publishing house] DLB-49

Thomasîn von Zerclære
  circa 1186-circa 1259 . . . . DLB-138

Thomason, George 1602?-1666 . . . . DLB-213

Thomasius, Christian 1655-1728 . . . . DLB-168

Thompson, Daniel Pierce 1795-1868 . . . . DLB-202

Thompson, David 1770-1857 . . . . DLB-99

Thompson, Dorothy 1893-1961 . . . . DLB-29

Thompson, E. P. 1924-1993 . . . . DLB-242

Thompson, Flora 1876-1947 . . . . DLB-240

Thompson, Francis
  1859-1907 . . . . DLB-19; CDBLB-5

Thompson, George Selden (see Selden, George)

Thompson, Henry Yates 1838-1928 . . . . DLB-184

Thompson, Hunter S. 1939- DLB-185

Thompson, Jim 1906-1977 . . . . DLB-226

Thompson, John 1938-1976 . . . . DLB-60

Thompson, John R. 1823-1873 . . . . DLB-3, 73, 248

Thompson, Lawrance 1906-1973 . . . . . . DLB-103

Thompson, Maurice 1844-1901 . . . . DLB-71, 74

Thompson, Ruth Plumly 1891-1976 . . . . . DLB-22

Thompson, Thomas Phillips 1843-1933 . . . DLB-99

Thompson, William 1775-1833 . . . . DLB-158

Thompson, William Tappan
  1812-1882 . . . . DLB-3, 11, 248

Thomson, Cockburn
  "Modern Style" (1857) [excerpt] DLB-57

Thomson, Edward William 1849-1924 . . . DLB-92

Thomson, James 1700-1748 . . . . DLB-95

Thomson, James 1834-1882 . . . . DLB-35

Thomson, Joseph 1858-1895 . . . . DLB-174

Thomson, Mortimer 1831-1875 . . . . DLB-11

Thomson, Rupert 1955- DLB-267

Thon, Melanie Rae 1957- DLB-244

Thor Vilhjálmsson 1925- DLB-293

Þórarinn Eldjárn 1949- DLB-293

Þórbergur Þórðarson 1888-1974 . . . . DLB-293

Thoreau, Henry David 1817-1862 . . . . DLB-1, 183,
  223, 270, 298; DS-5; CDALB-2

  The Thoreau Society Y-99

  The Thoreauvian Pilgrimage: The
    Structure of an American Cult . . DLB-223

Thorne, William 1568?-1630 . . . . DLB-281

Thornton, John F.
  [Repsonse to Ken Auletta] Y-97

Thorpe, Adam 1956- DLB-231

Thorpe, Thomas Bangs
  1815-1878 . . . . DLB-3, 11, 248

Thorup, Kirsten 1942- DLB-214

Thotl, Birgitte 1610-1662 . . . . DLB-300

Thrale, Hester Lynch
  (see Piozzi, Hester Lynch [Thrale])

The Three Marias: A Landmark Case in
  Portuguese Literary History
  (Maria Isabel Barreno, 1939- ;
  Maria Teresa Horta, 1937- ;
  Maria Velho da Costa, 1938-) DLB-287

Thubron, Colin 1939- DLB-204, 231

Thucydides
  circa 455 B.C.-circa 395 B.C. DLB-176

Thulstrup, Thure de 1848-1930 . . . . DLB-188

Thümmel, Moritz August von
  1738-1817 . . . . DLB-97

Thurber, James
  1894-1961 . . . . DLB-4, 11, 22, 102; CDALB-5

Thurman, Wallace 1902-1934 . . . . DLB-51

  "Negro Poets and Their Poetry" DLB-50

Thwaite, Anthony 1930- DLB-40

The Booker Prize, Address Y-86

Thwaites, Reuben Gold 1853-1913 . . . . . . DLB-47

Tibullus circa 54 B.C.-circa 19 B.C. DLB-211

Ticknor, George 1791-1871 . . . . DLB-1, 59, 140, 235

Ticknor and Fields DLB-49

Ticknor and Fields (revived) DLB-46

Tieck, Ludwig 1773-1853 . . . . DLB-90; CDWLB-2

Tietjens, Eunice 1884-1944 . . . . DLB-54

Tikkanen, Märta 1935- DLB-257

Tilghman, Christopher circa 1948 . . . . . . DLB-244

Tilney, Edmund circa 1536-1610 . . . . DLB-136

Charles Tilt [publishing house] DLB-106

J. E. Tilton and Company DLB-49

Time-Life Books DLB-46

Times Books DLB-46

Timothy, Peter circa 1725-1782 . . . . DLB-43

Timrava 1867-1951 . . . . DLB-215

Timrod, Henry 1828-1867 . . . . DLB-3, 248

Tindal, Henrietta 1818?-1879 . . . . DLB-199

Tinker, Chauncey Brewster 1876-1963 . . . DLB-140

Tinsley Brothers DLB-106

Tiptree, James, Jr. 1915-1987 . . . . DLB-8

Tišma, Aleksandar 1924- DLB-181

Titus, Edward William
  1870-1952 . . . . DLB-4; DS-15

Tiutchev, Fedor Ivanovich 1803-1873 . . . DLB-205

Tlali, Miriam 1933- DLB-157, 225

Todd, Barbara Euphan 1890-1976 . . . . . DLB-160

Todorov, Tzvetan 1939- DLB-242

Tofte, Robert
  1561 or 1562-1619 or 1620 . . . . DLB-172

Tóibín, Colm 1955- DLB-271

Toklas, Alice B. 1877-1967 . . . . DLB-4; DS-15

Tokuda Shūsei 1872-1943 . . . . DLB-180

Toland, John 1670-1722 . . . . DLB-252

Tolkien, J. R. R.
  1892-1973 . . . . . . DLB-15, 160, 255; CDBLB-6

Toller, Ernst 1893-1939 . . . . DLB-124

Tollet, Elizabeth 1694-1754 . . . . DLB-95

Tolson, Melvin B. 1898-1966 . . . . DLB-48, 76

Tolstaya, Tatyana 1951- DLB-285

Tolstoy, Aleksei Konstantinovich
  1817-1875 . . . . DLB-238

Tolstoy, Aleksei Nikolaevich 1883-1945 . . DLB-272

Tolstoy, Leo 1828-1910 . . . . DLB-238

Tomalin, Claire 1933- DLB-155

Tómas Guðmundsson 1901-1983 . . . . . . DLB-293

Tomasi di Lampedusa, Giuseppe
  1896-1957 . . . . DLB-177

Tomlinson, Charles 1927- DLB-40

Tomlinson, H. M. 1873-1958 . . . . DLB-36, 100, 195

Abel Tompkins [publishing house] DLB-49

Tompson, Benjamin 1642-1714 . . . . DLB-24

Tomson, Graham R.
  (see Watson, Rosamund Marriott)

Ton'a 1289-1372 . . . . DLB-203

Tondelli, Pier Vittorio 1955-1991 . . . . . . .DLB-196

Tonks, Rosemary 1932- DLB-14, 207

Tonna, Charlotte Elizabeth 1790-1846 . . .DLB-163

Jacob Tonson the Elder
[publishing house] DLB-170

Toole, John Kennedy 1937-1969 . . . . Y-81

Toomer, Jean
1894-1967 . . . . .DLB-45, 51; CDALB-4

Topsoe, Vilhelm 1840-1881. . . . . .DLB-300

Tor Books DLB-46

Torberg, Friedrich 1908-1979 . . . . .DLB-85

Torga, Miguel (Adolfo Correira da Rocha)
1907-1995 . . . . .DLB-287

Torrence, Ridgely 1874-1950. . . . . . .DLB-54, 249

Torres-Metzger, Joseph V. 1933- DLB-122

El Tostado (see Madrigal, Alfonso Fernández de)

Toth, Susan Allen 1940- Y-86

Richard Tottell [publishing house]. DLB-170

"The Printer to the Reader,"
(1557) DLB-167

Tough-Guy Literature DLB-9

Touré, Askia Muhammad 1938- DLB-41

Tourgée, Albion W. 1838-1905. . . . . .DLB-79

Tournemir, Elizaveta Sailhas de (see Tur, Evgeniia)

Tourneur, Cyril circa 1580-1626. . . . . . . .DLB-58

Tournier, Michel 1924- DLB-83

Frank Tousey [publishing house]. DLB-49

Tower Publications DLB-46

Towne, Benjamin circa 1740-1793 . . . . . .DLB-43

Towne, Robert 1936- DLB-44

The Townely Plays fifteenth and sixteenth
centuries DLB-146

Townsend, Sue 1946- DLB-271

Townshend, Aurelian
by 1583-circa 1651 . . . . .DLB-121

Toy, Barbara 1908-2001 . . . . .DLB-204

Tozzi, Federigo 1883-1920. . . . . DLB 264

Tracy, Honor 1913-1989. . . . . .DLB-15

Traherne, Thomas 1637?-1674 . . . . .DLB-131

Traill, Catharine Parr 1802-1899. . . . . . . .DLB-99

Train, Arthur 1875-1945 . . . . . . .DLB-86; DS-16

Tranquilli, Secondino (see Silone, Ignazio)

The Transatlantic Publishing Company . . .DLB-49

The Transatlantic Review 1924-1925 . . . . DS-15

The Transcendental Club
1836-1840 . . . . .DLB-1; DLB-223

Transcendentalism. DLB-1; DLB-223; DS-5

"A Response from America," by
John A. Heraud DS-5

Publications and Social Movements DLB-1

The Rise of Transcendentalism,
1815-1860. . . . . DS-5

Transcendentalists, American DS-5

"What Is Transcendentalism? By a
Thinking Man," by James
Kinnard Jr. DS-5

transition 1927-1938. . . . . DS-15

Translations (Vernacular) in the Crowns of
Castile and Aragon 1352-1515 . . . . . .DLB-286

Tranströmer, Tomas 1931- DLB-257

Tranter, John 1943- DLB-289

Travel Writing
American Travel Writing, 1776-1864
(checklist) DLB-183

British Travel Writing, 1940-1997
(checklist) DLB-204

Travel Writers of the Late
Middle Ages DLB-286

(1876-1909. . . . . DLB-174

(1837-1875 . . . . DLB-166

(1910-1939 . . . . DLB-195

Traven, B. 1882?/1890?-1969? DLB-9, 56

Travers, Ben 1886-1980 . . . . .DLB-10, 233

Travers, P. L. (Pamela Lyndon)
1899-1996 .DLB-160

Trediakovsky, Vasilii Kirillovich
1703-1769 .DLB-150

Treece, Henry 1911-1966 . . . . .DLB-160

Treitel, Jonathan 1959- DLB-267

Trejo, Ernesto 1950-1991 . . . . .DLB-122

Trelawny, Edward John
1792-1881 . . . . DLB-110, 116, 144

Tremain, Rose 1943- DLB-14, 271

Tremblay, Michel 1942- DLB-60

Trent, William P. 1862-1939. . . . . . .DLB-47, 71

Trescot, William Henry 1822-1898. . . . . .DLB-30

Tressell, Robert (Robert Phillipe Noonan)
1870-1911 .DLB-197

Trevelyan, Sir George Otto
1838-1928 .DLB-144

Trevisa, John circa 1342-circa 1402. . . . . .DLB-146

Trevor, William 1928- DLB-14, 139

Triana, José 1931- DLB-305

Trierer Floyris circa 1170-1180 . . . . .DLB-138

Trifonov, Iurii Valentinovich
1925-1981 . . . . DLB 302

Trillin, Calvin 1935- DLB-185

Trilling, Lionel 1905-1975 . . . . .DLB-28, 63

Trilussa 1871-1950. . . . . .DLB-114

Trimmer, Sarah 1741-1810 . . . . .DLB-158

Triolet, Elsa 1896-1970 . . . . .DLB-72

Tripp, John 1927- DLB-40

Trocchi, Alexander 1925-1984 . . . . .DLB-15

Troisi, Dante 1920-1989 . . . . .DLB-196

Trollope, Anthony
1815-1882 . . . . . . .DLB-21, 57, 159; CDBLB-4

Novel-Reading: *The Works of Charles
Dickens; The Works of W. Makepeace
Thackeray* (1879) DLB-21

The Trollope Societies Y-00

Trollope, Frances 1779-1863 . . . . . . .DLB-21, 166

Trollope, Joanna 1943- DLB-207

Troop, Elizabeth 1931- DLB-14

Trotter, Catharine 1679-1749. . . . . .DLB-84, 252

Trotti, Lamar 1898-1952. . . . . .DLB-44

Trottier, Pierre 1925- DLB-60

Trotzig, Birgitta 1929- DLB-257

Troupe, Quincy Thomas, Jr. 1943- DLB-41

John F. Trow and Company DLB-49

Trowbridge, John Townsend 1827-1916 . .DLB-202

Trudel, Jean-Louis 1967- DLB-251

Truillier-Lacombe, Joseph-Patrice
1807-1863 . . . . .DLB-99

Trumbo, Dalton 1905-1976 . . . . .DLB-26

Trumbull, Benjamin 1735-1820 . . . . .DLB-30

Trumbull, John 1750-1831. . . . . .DLB-31

Trumbull, John 1756-1843. . . . . .DLB-183

Truth, Sojourner 1797?-1883. . . . . .DLB-239

Tscherning, Andreas 1611-1659 . . . . . . .DLB-164

Tsubouchi Shōyō 1859-1935. . . . . .DLB-180

Tsvetaeva, Marina Ivanovna 1892-1941. . .DLB-295

Tuchman, Barbara W.
Tribute to Alfred A. Knopf Y-84

Tucholsky, Kurt 1890-1935. . . . . .DLB-56

Tucker, Charlotte Maria
1821-1893 . . . . .DLB-163, 190

Tucker, George 1775-1861. . . . . .DLB-3, 30, 248

Tucker, James 1808?-1866?. DLB-230

Tucker, Nathaniel Beverley
1784-1851 . . . . .DLB-3, 248

Tucker, St. George 1752-1827 . . . . .DLB-37

Tuckerman, Frederick Goddard
1821-1873 .DLB-243

Tuckerman, Henry Theodore 1813-1871 . . . .DLB-64

Tumas, Juozas (see Vaizgantas)

Tunis, John R. 1889-1975 . . . . .DLB-22, 171

Tunstall, Cuthbert 1474-1559 . . . . .DLB-132

Tunström, Göran 1937-2000 . . . . .DLB-257

Tuohy, Frank 1925- DLB-14, 139

Tupper, Martin F. 1810-1889 . . . . .DLB-32

Tur, Evgeniia 1815-1892 . . . . .DLB-238

Turbyfill, Mark 1896-1991 . . . . .DLB-45

Turco, Lewis 1934- Y-84

Tribute to John Ciardi Y-86

Turgenev, Aleksandr Ivanovich
1784-1845 .DLB-198

Turgenev, Ivan Sergeevich 1818-1883. . . .DLB-238

Turnbull, Alexander H. 1868-1918. . . . . .DLB-184

Turnbull, Andrew 1921-1970 . . . . .DLB-103

Turnbull, Gael 1928- DLB-40

Turner, Arlin 1909-1980 . . . . .DLB-103

Turner, Charles (Tennyson) 1808-1879 . . .DLB-32

Turner, Ethel 1872-1958 . . . . .DLB-230

Turner, Frederick 1943- DLB-40

Turner, Frederick Jackson
1861-1932 . . . . DLB-17, 186

A Conversation between William Riggan
and Janette Turner Hospital Y-02

Turner, Joseph Addison 1826-1868. . . . . .DLB-79

Turpin, Waters Edward 1910-1968. . . . . .DLB-51

Turrini, Peter 1944- DLB-124

Tutuola, Amos 1920-1997 . . .DLB-125; CDWLB-3

Twain, Mark (see Clemens, Samuel Langhorne)

Tweedie, Ethel Brilliana
circa 1860-1940 ....DLB-174

A Century of Poetry, a Lifetime of
Collecting: J. M. Edelstein's
Collection of Twentieth-
Century American Poetry YB-02

Twombly, Wells 1935-1977 .... DLB-241

Twysden, Sir Roger 1597-1672........ DLB-213

Tyler, Anne
1941- DLB-6, 143; Y-82; CDALB-7

Tyler, Mary Palmer 1775-1866........ DLB-200

Tyler, Moses Coit 1835-1900.........DLB-47, 64

Tyler, Royall 1757-1826 .... DLB-37

Tylor, Edward Burnett 1832-1917....... DLB-57

Tynan, Katharine 1861-1931 ...... DLB-153, 240

Tyndale, William circa 1494-1536 ...... DLB-132

Tyree, Omar 1969- DLB-292

U

Uchida, Yoshika 1921-1992 ....CDALB-7

Udall, Nicholas 1504-1556............. DLB-62

Ugrešić, Dubravka 1949- DLB-181

Uhland, Ludwig 1787-1862............. DLB-90

Uhse, Bodo 1904-1963................ DLB-69

Ujević, Augustin "Tin"
1891-1955 .... DLB-147

Ulenhart, Niclas flourished circa 1600 ... DLB-164

Ulfeldt, Leonora Christina 1621-1698 ... DLB-300

Ulibarrí, Sabine R. 1919- DLB-82

Ulica, Jorge 1870-1926 .... DLB-82

Ulitskaya, Liudmila Evgen'evna
1943- DLB-285

Ulivi, Ferruccio 1912- DLB-196

Ulizio, B. George 1889-1969 .... DLB-140

Ulrich von Liechtenstein
circa 1200-circa 1275 .... DLB-138

Ulrich von Zatzikhoven
before 1194-after 1214 .... DLB-138

Unaipon, David 1872-1967 ....DLB-230

Unamuno, Miguel de 1864-1936 .... DLB-108

Under, Marie 1883-1980 ... DLB-220; CDWLB-4

Underhill, Evelyn 1875-1941 .... DLB-240

Undset, Sigrid 1882-1949 .... DLB-297

Ungaretti, Giuseppe 1888-1970......... DLB-114

Unger, Friederike Helene 1741-1813 ..... DLB-94

United States Book Company DLB-49

Universal Publishing and Distributing
Corporation.................... DLB-46

University of Colorado
Special Collections at the University of
Colorado at Boulder Y-98

Indiana University Press................... Y-02

The University of Iowa
Writers' Workshop Golden Jubilee Y-86

University of Missouri Press............... Y-01

University of South Carolina
The G. Ross Roy Scottish
Poetry Collection................ Y-89

Two Hundred Years of Rare Books and
Literary Collections at the
University of South Carolina Y-00

The University of South Carolina Press...... Y-94

University of Virginia
The Book Arts Press at the University
of Virginia..................... Y-96

The Electronic Text Center and the
Electronic Archive of Early American
Fiction at the University of Virginia
Library Y-98

University of Virginia Libraries......... Y-91

University of Wales Press DLB-112

University Press of Florida................ Y-00

University Press of Kansas................ Y-98

University Press of Mississippi............. Y-99

Unnur Benediktsdóttir Bjarklind (see Hulda)

Uno Chiyo 1897-1996 .... DLB-180

Unruh, Fritz von 1885-1970 .... DLB-56, 118

Unsworth, Barry 1930- DLB-194

Unt, Mati 1944- DLB-232

The Unterberg Poetry Center of the
92nd Street Y..................... Y-98

Untermeyer, Louis 1885-1977 .... DLB-303

T. Fisher Unwin [publishing house]..... DLB-106

Upchurch, Boyd B. (see Boyd, John)

Updike, John 1932- DLB-2, 5, 143, 218, 227;
Y-80, 82; DS-3; CDALB-6

John Updike on the Internet Y-97

Tribute to Alfred A. Knopf Y-84

Tribute to John Ciardi................ Y-86

Upīts, Andrejs 1877-1970 .... DLB-220

Uppdal, Kristofer 1878-1961 .... DLB-297

Upton, Bertha 1849-1912............. DLB-141

Upton, Charles 1948- DLB-16

Upton, Florence K. 1873-1922 .... DLB-141

Upward, Allen 1863-1926 .... DLB-36

Urban, Milo 1904-1982 .... DLB-215

Ureña de Henríquez, Salomé
1850-1897..................... DLB-283

Urfé, Honoré d' 1567-1625 ....DLB-268

Urista, Alberto Baltazar (see Alurista)

Urquhart, Fred 1912-1995 .... DLB-139

Urrea, Luis Alberto 1955- DLB-209

Urzidil, Johannes 1896-1970........... DLB-85

Usigli, Rodolfo 1905-1979 .... DLB-305

Usk, Thomas died 1388............... DLB-146

Uslar Pietri, Arturo 1906-2001......... DLB-113

Uspensky, Gleb Ivanovich 1843-1902 ....DLB-277

Ussher, James 1581-1656 .... DLB-213

Ustinov, Peter 1921- DLB-13

Uttley, Alison 1884-1976 .... DLB-160

Uz, Johann Peter 1720-1796 .... DLB-97

V

Vadianus, Joachim 1484-1551 ....DLB-179

Vac, Bertrand (Aimé Pelletier) 1914- ... DLB-88

Vācietis, Ojārs 1933-1983............ DLB-232

Vaculík, Ludvík 1926- DLB-232

Vaičiulaitis, Antanas 1906-1992........ DLB-220

Vaičiūnaite, Judita 1937- DLB-232

Vail, Laurence 1891-1968 .... DLB-4

Vail, Petr L'vovich 1949- DLB-285

Vailland, Roger 1907-1965 .... DLB-83

Vaižgantas 1869-1933 .... DLB-220

Vajda, Ernest 1887-1954.............. DLB-44

Valdés, Gina 1943- DLB-122

Valdez, Luis Miguel 1940- DLB-122

Valduga, Patrizia 1953- DLB-128

Vale Press..................... DLB-112

Valente, José Angel 1929-2000.......... DLB-108

Valenzuela, Luisa 1938- DLB-113; CDWLB-3

Valera, Diego de 1412-1488........... DLB-286

Valeri, Diego 1887-1976 .... DLB-128

Valerius Flaccus fl. circa A.D. 92 .... DLB-211

Valerius Maximus fl. circa A.D. 31 ..... DLB-211

Valéry, Paul 1871-1945 .... DLB-258

Valesio, Paolo 1939- DLB-196

Valgardson, W. D. 1939- DLB-60

Valle, Luz 1899-1971 .... DLB-290

Valle, Víctor Manuel 1950- DLB-122

Valle-Inclán, Ramón del 1866-1936..... DLB-134

Vallejo, Armando 1949- DLB-122

Vallejo, César Abraham 1892-1938..... DLB-290

Vallès, Jules 1832-1885............... DLB-123

Vallette, Marguerite Eymery (see Rachilde)

Valverde, José María 1926-1996 .... DLB-108

Vampilov, Aleksandr Valentinovich (A. Sanin)
1937-1972..................... DLB-302

Van Allsburg, Chris 1949- DLB-61

Van Anda, Carr 1864-1945 .... DLB-25

Vanbrugh, Sir John 1664-1726 .... DLB-80

Vance, Jack 1916?- DLB-8

Vančura, Vladislav
1891-1942 ....DLB-215; CDWLB-4

van der Post, Laurens 1906-1996....... DLB-204

Van Dine, S. S. (see Wright, Williard Huntington)

Van Doren, Mark 1894-1972 .... DLB-45

van Druten, John 1901-1957 .... DLB-10

Van Duyn, Mona 1921- DLB-5

Tribute to James Dickey Y-97

Van Dyke, Henry 1852-1933......DLB-71; DS-13

Van Dyke, Henry 1928- DLB-33

Van Dyke, John C. 1856-1932.......... DLB-186

Vane, Sutton 1888-1963................ DLB-10

Vanguard Press DLB-46

van Gulik, Robert Hans 1910-1967 .... DS-17

van Itallie, Jean-Claude 1936- DLB-7

Van Loan, Charles E. 1876-1919 ....DLB-171

Vann, Robert L. 1879-1940 .... DLB-29

Van Rensselaer, Mariana Griswold
1851-1934 .... DLB-47

Van Rensselaer, Mrs. Schuyler
  (see Van Rensselaer, Mariana Griswold)
Van Vechten, Carl 1880-1964 . . . . DLB-4, 9, 51
van Vogt, A. E. 1912-2000 . . . . DLB-8, 251
Varela, Blanca 1926- DLB-290
Vargas Llosa, Mario
  1936- DLB-145; CDWLB-3
  Acceptance Speech for the Ritz Paris
    Hemingway Award Y-85
Varley, John 1947- Y-81
Varnhagen von Ense, Karl August
  1785-1858 . . . . DLB-90
Varnhagen von Ense, Rahel
  1771-1833 . . . . DLB-90
Varro 116 B.C.-27 B.C. DLB-211
Vasilenko, Svetlana Vladimirovna
  1956- DLB-285
Vasiliu, George (see Bacovia, George)
Vásquez, Richard 1928- DLB-209
Vásquez Montalbán, Manuel 1939- DLB-134
Vassa, Gustavus (see Equiano, Olaudah)
Vassalli, Sebastiano 1941- DLB-128, 196
Vaugelas, Claude Favre de 1585-1650 . . . . DLB-268
Vaughan, Henry 1621-1695 . . . . DLB-131
Vaughan, Thomas 1621-1666 . . . . DLB-131
Vaughn, Robert 1592?-1667 . . . . DLB-213
Vaux, Thomas, Lord 1509-1556 . . . . DLB-132
Vazov, Ivan 1850-1921 . . . . . DLB-147; CDWLB-4
Véa, Alfredo, Jr. 1950- DLB-209
Veblen, Thorstein 1857-1929 . . . . DLB-246
Vedel, Anders Sørensen 1542-1616 . . . . . . DLB-300
Vega, Janine Pommy 1942- DLB-16
Veiller, Anthony 1903-1965 . . . . DLB-44
Velásquez-Trevino, Gloria 1949- DLB-122
Veley, Margaret 1843-1887 . . . . DLB-199
Velleius Paterculus
  circa 20 B.C.-circa A.D. 30 . . . . DLB-211
Veloz Maggiolo, Marcio 1936- DLB-145
Vel'tman, Aleksandr Fomich
  1800-1870 . . . . DLB-198
Venegas, Daniel ?-? DLB-82
Venevitinov, Dmitrii Vladimirovich
  1805-1827 . . . . DLB-205
Verbitskaia, Anastasiia Alekseevna
  1861-1928 . . . . DLB-295
Verde, Cesário 1855-1886 . . . . DLB-287
Vergil, Polydore circa 1470-1555 . . . . DLB-132
Veríssimo, Erico 1905-1975 . . . . DLB-145
Verlaine, Paul 1844-1896 . . . . DLB-217
Vernacular Translations in the Crowns of
  Castile and Aragon 1352-1515 . . . . . DLB-286
Verne, Jules 1828-1905 . . . . DLB-123
Verplanck, Gulian C. 1786-1870 . . . . DLB-59
Very, Jones 1813-1880 . . . . DLB-1, 243; DS-5
Vesaas, Halldis Moren 1907-1995 . . . . . . DLB-297
Vesaas, Tarjei 1897-1970 . . . . DLB-297
Vian, Boris 1920-1959 . . . . DLB-72

Viazemsky, Petr Andreevich
  1792-1878 . . . . DLB-205
Vicars, Thomas 1591-1638 . . . . DLB-236
Vicente, Gil 1465-1536/1540? DLB-287
Vickers, Roy 1888?-1965 . . . . DLB-77
Vickery, Sukey 1779-1821 . . . . DLB-200
Victoria 1819-1901 . . . . DLB-55
Victoria Press DLB-106
Vidal, Gore 1925- DLB-6, 152; CDALB-7
Vidal, Mary Theresa 1815-1873 . . . . DLB-230
Vidmer, Richards 1898-1978 . . . . DLB-241
Viebig, Clara 1860-1952 . . . . DLB-66
Viereck, George Sylvester 1884-1962 . . . . . DLB-54
Viereck, Peter 1916- DLB-5
Vietnam War (ended 1975)
  Resources for the Study of Vietnam War
    Literature DLB-9
Viets, Roger 1738-1811 . . . . DLB-99
Vigil-Piñon, Evangelina 1949- DLB-122
Vigneault, Gilles 1928- DLB-60
Vigny, Alfred de 1797-1863 . . . . DLB-119, 192, 217
Vigolo, Giorgio 1894-1983 . . . . DLB-114
Vik, Bjorg 1935- DLB-297
The Viking Press DLB-46
Vilde, Eduard 1865-1933 . . . . DLB-220
Vilinskaia, Mariia Aleksandrovna
  (see Vovchok, Marko)
Villanueva, Alma Luz 1944- DLB-122
Villanueva, Tino 1941- DLB-82
Villard, Henry 1835-1900 . . . . DLB-23
Villard, Oswald Garrison 1872-1949 . . . DLB-25, 91
Villarreal, Edit 1944- DLB-209
Villarreal, José Antonio 1924- DLB-82
Villaseñor, Victor 1940- DLB-209
Villedieu, Madame de (Marie-Catherine
  Desjardins) 1640?-1683 . . . . DLB-268
Villegas de Magnón, Leonor
  1876-1955 . . . . DLB-122
Villehardouin, Geoffroi de
  circa 1150-1215 . . . . DLB-208
Villemaire, Yolande 1949- DLB-60
Villena, Enrique de
  ca. 1382/84-1432 . . . . DLB-286
Villena, Luis Antonio de 1951- DLB-134
Villiers, George, Second Duke
  of Buckingham 1628-1687 . . . . DLB-80
Villiers de l'Isle-Adam, Jean-Marie
  Mathias Philippe-Auguste,
  Comte de 1838-1889 . . . . DLB-123, 192
Villon, François 1431-circa 1463? DLB-208
Vine Press DLB-112
Viorst, Judith ?- DLB-52
Vipont, Elfrida (Elfrida Vipont Foulds,
  Charles Vipont) 1902-1992 . . . . DLB-160
Viramontes, Helena María 1954- DLB-122
Virgil 70 B.C.-19 B.C. DLB-211; CDWLB-1
Vischer, Friedrich Theodor
  1807-1887 . . . . DLB-133

Vitier, Cintio 1921- DLB-283
Vitruvius circa 85 B.C.-circa 15 B.C. DLB-211
Vitry, Philippe de 1291-1361 . . . . DLB-208
Vittorini, Elio 1908-1966 . . . . DLB-264
Vivanco, Luis Felipe 1907-1975 . . . . DLB-108
Vivian, E. Charles (Charles Henry Cannell,
  Charles Henry Vivian, Jack Mann,
  Barry Lynd) 1882-1947 . . . . DLB-255
Viviani, Cesare 1947- DLB-128
Vivien, Renée 1877-1909 . . . . DLB-217
Vizenor, Gerald 1934- DLB-175, 227
Vizetelly and Company DLB-106
Vladimov, Georgii
  1931-2003 . . . . DLB-302
Voaden, Herman 1903-1991 . . . . DLB-88
Voß, Johann Heinrich 1751-1826 . . . . . . DLB-90
Vogau, Boris Andreevich
  (see Pil'niak, Boris Andreevich)
Voigt, Ellen Bryant 1943- DLB-120
Voinovich, Vladimir Nikolaevich
  1932- DLB-302
Vojnović, Ivo 1857-1929 . . . . . DLB-147; CDWLB-4
Vold, Jan Erik 1939- DLB-297
Volkoff, Vladimir 1932- DLB-83
P. F. Volland Company DLB-46
Vollbehr, Otto H. F.
  1872?-1945 or 1946 . . . . DLB-187
Vologdin (see Zasodimsky, Pavel Vladimirovich)
Voloshin, Maksimilian Aleksandrovich
  1877-1932 . . . . DLB-295
Volponi, Paolo 1924-1994 . . . . DLB-177
Vonarburg, Élisabeth 1947- DLB-251
von der Grün, Max 1926- DLB-75
Vonnegut, Kurt 1922- DLB-2, 8, 152;
  Y-80; DS-3; CDALB-6
  Tribute to Isaac Asimov Y-92
  Tribute to Richard Brautigan Y-84
Voranc, Prežihov 1893-1950 . . . . DLB-147
Voronsky, Aleksandr Konstantinovich
  1884-1937 . . . . DLB-272
Vorse, Mary Heaton 1874-1966 . . . . DLB-303
Vovchok, Marko 1833-1907 . . . . DLB-238
Voynich, E. L. 1864-1960 . . . . DLB-197
Vroman, Mary Elizabeth
  circa 1924-1967 . . . . DLB-33

W

Wace, Robert ("Maistre")
  circa 1100-circa 1175 . . . . DLB-146
Wackenroder, Wilhelm Heinrich
  1773-1798 . . . . DLB-90
Wackernagel, Wilhelm 1806-1869 . . . . . . DLB-133
Waddell, Helen 1889-1965 . . . . DLB-240
Waddington, Miriam 1917- DLB-68
Wade, Henry 1887-1969 . . . . DLB-77
Wagenknecht, Edward 1900- DLB-103
Wägner, Elin 1882-1949 . . . . DLB-259
Wagner, Heinrich Leopold 1747-1779 . . . . DLB-94

Wagner, Henry R. 1862-1957 .... DLB-140
Wagner, Richard 1813-1883........... DLB-129
Wagoner, David 1926- DLB-5, 256
Wah, Fred 1939- DLB-60
Waiblinger, Wilhelm 1804-1830 .... DLB-90
Wain, John
   1925-1994 ...DLB-15, 27, 139, 155; CDBLB-8
   Tribute to J. B. Priestly Y-84
Wainwright, Jeffrey 1944- DLB-40
Waite, Peirce and Company........... DLB-49
Wakeman, Stephen H. 1859-1924 ...... DLB-187
Wakoski, Diane 1937- DLB-5
Walahfrid Strabo circa 808-849 .... DLB-148
Henry Z. Walck [publishing house] DLB-46
Walcott, Derek
   1930-.........DLB-117; Y-81, 92; CDWLB-3
   Nobel Lecture 1992: The Antilles:
    Fragments of Epic Memory......... Y-92
Robert Waldegrave [publishing house]....DLB-170
Waldis, Burkhard circa 1490-1556?......DLB-178
Waldman, Anne 1945- DLB-16
Waldrop, Rosmarie 1935- DLB-169
Walker, Alice 1900-1982 .... DLB-201
Walker, Alice
   1944- DLB-6, 33, 143; CDALB-6
Walker, Annie Louisa (Mrs. Harry Coghill)
   circa 1836-1907 .... DLB-240
Walker, George F. 1947- DLB-60
Walker, John Brisben 1847-1931 ...... DLB-79
Walker, Joseph A. 1935- DLB-38
Walker, Kath (see Oodgeroo of the Tribe Noonuccal)
Walker, Margaret 1915-1998 .... DLB-76, 152
Walker, Obadiah 1616-1699 .... DLB-281
Walker, Ted 1934- DLB-40
Walker, Evans and Cogswell Company... DLB-49
Wall, John F. (see Sarban)
Wallace, Alfred Russel 1823-1913 .... DLB-190
Wallace, Dewitt 1889-1981............ DLB-137
Wallace, Edgar 1875-1932 .... DLB-70
Wallace, Lew 1827-1905............. DLB-202
Wallace, Lila Acheson 1889-1984....... DLB-137
   "A Word of Thanks," From the Initial
   Issue of *Reader's Digest*
   (February 1922).............. DLB-137
Wallace, Naomi 1960- DLB-249
Wallace Markfield's "Steeplechase" Y-02
Wallace-Crabbe, Chris 1934- DLB-289
Wallant, Edward Lewis
   1926-1962 .... DLB-2, 28, 143, 299
Waller, Edmund 1606-1687 .... DLB-126
Walpole, Horace 1717-1797..... DLB-39, 104, 213
   Preface to the First Edition of
   The Castle of Otranto (1764) DLB-39, 178
   Preface to the Second Edition of
   The Castle of Otranto (1765) DLB-39, 178
Walpole, Hugh 1884-1941 .... DLB-34
Walrond, Eric 1898-1966 .... DLB-51
Walser, Martin 1927- DLB-75, 124

Walser, Robert 1878-1956 .... DLB-66
Walsh, Ernest 1895-1926 .... DLB-4, 45
Walsh, Robert 1784-1859.............. DLB-59
Walters, Henry 1848-1931............ DLB-140
Waltharius circa 825.................. DLB-148
Walther von der Vogelweide
   circa 1170-circa 1230 .... DLB-138
Walton, Izaak
   1593-1683 .... DLB-151, 213; CDBLB-1
Wambaugh, Joseph 1937- DLB-6; Y-83
Wand, Alfred Rudolph 1828-1891...... DLB-188
Waniek, Marilyn Nelson 1946- DLB-120
Wanley, Humphrey 1672-1726....... DLB-213
War of the Words (and Pictures):
   The Creation of a Graphic Novel Y-02
Warburton, William 1698-1779 .... DLB-104
Ward, Aileen 1919- DLB-111
Ward, Artemus (see Browne, Charles Farrar)
Ward, Arthur Henry Sarsfield (see Rohmer, Sax)
Ward, Douglas Turner 1930- DLB-7, 38
Ward, Mrs. Humphry 1851-1920 ..... DLB-18
Ward, James 1843-1925 .... DLB-262
Ward, Lynd 1905-1985 .... DLB-22
Ward, Lock and Company DLB-106
Ward, Nathaniel circa 1578-1652 .... DLB-24
Ward, Theodore 1902-1983........... DLB-76
Wardle, Ralph 1909-1988 .... DLB-103
Ware, Henry, Jr. 1794-1843 .... DLB-235
Ware, William 1797-1852 .... DLB-1, 235
Warfield, Catherine Ann 1816-1877 .... DLB-248
Waring, Anna Letitia 1823-1910 .... DLB-240
Frederick Warne and Company [U.K.] ... DLB-106
Frederick Warne and Company [U.S.] DLB-49
Warner, Anne 1869-1913 .... DLB-202
Warner, Charles Dudley 1829-1900 ..... DLB-64
Warner, Marina 1946- DLB-194
Warner, Rex 1905-1986............ DLB-15
Warner, Susan 1819-1885 ... DLB-3, 42, 239, 250
Warner, Sylvia Townsend
   1893-1978................ DLB-34, 139
Warner, William 1558-1609............DLB-172
Warner Books DLB-46
Warr, Bertram 1917-1943............. DLB-88
Warren, John Byrne Leicester (see De Tabley, Lord)
Warren, Lella 1899-1982 .... Y-83
Warren, Mercy Otis 1728-1814 ..... DLB-31, 200
Warren, Robert Penn 1905-1989 .....DLB-2, 48,
   152; Y-80, 89; CDALB-6
   Tribute to Katherine Anne Porter Y-80
Warren, Samuel 1807-1877............ DLB-190
Die Wartburgkrieg circa 1230-circa 1280... DLB-138
Warton, Joseph 1722-1800 ....DLB-104, 109
Warton, Thomas 1728-1790 ....DLB-104, 109
Warung, Price (William Astley)
   1855-1911 .... DLB-230
Washington, George 1732-1799 .... DLB-31

Washington, Ned 1901-1976 .... DLB-265
Wassermann, Jakob 1873-1934 .... DLB-66
Wasserstein, Wendy 1950- DLB-228
Wassmo, Herbjorg 1942- DLB-297
Wasson, David Atwood 1823-1887 ... DLB-1, 223
Watanna, Onoto (see Eaton, Winnifred)
Waten, Judah 1911?-1985 .... DLB-289
Waterhouse, Keith 1929- DLB-13, 15
Waterman, Andrew 1940- DLB-40
Waters, Frank 1902-1995.........DLB-212; Y-86
Waters, Michael 1949- DLB-120
Watkins, Tobias 1780-1855 .... DLB-73
Watkins, Vernon 1906-1967 .... DLB-20
Watmough, David 1926- DLB-53
Watson, Colin 1920-1983 ....DLB-276
Watson, Ian 1943- DLB-261
Watson, James Wreford (see Wreford, James)
Watson, John 1850-1907 .... DLB-156
Watson, Rosamund Marriott
   (Graham R. Tomson) 1860-1911.... DLB-240
Watson, Sheila 1909-1998 .... DLB-60
Watson, Thomas 1545?-1592 .... DLB-132
Watson, Wilfred 1911- DLB-60
W. J. Watt and Company DLB-46
Watten, Barrett 1948- DLB-193
Watterson, Henry 1840-1921........... DLB-25
Watts, Alan 1915-1973 .... DLB-16
Watts, Isaac 1674-1748 .... DLB-95
Franklin Watts [publishing house] DLB-46
Waugh, Alec 1898-1981.............. DLB-191
Waugh, Auberon 1939-2000 ...DLB-14, 194; Y-00
Waugh, Evelyn 1903-1966..... DLB-15, 162, 195;
   CDBLB-6
Way and Williams DLB-49
Wayman, Tom 1945- DLB-53
Weatherly, Tom 1942- DLB-41
Weaver, Gordon 1937- DLB-130
Weaver, Robert 1921- DLB-88
Webb, Beatrice 1858-1943 .... DLB-190
Webb, Francis 1925-1973 .... DLB-260
Webb, Frank J. ?-? DLB-50
Webb, James Watson 1802-1884 .... DLB-43
Webb, Mary 1881-1927 .... DLB-34
Webb, Phyllis 1927- DLB-53
Webb, Sidney 1859-1947 .... DLB-190
Webb, Walter Prescott 1888-1963........DLB-17
Webbe, William ?-1591 .... DLB-132
Webber, Charles Wilkins 1819-1856? ... DLB-202
Weber, Max 1864-1920 .... DLB-296
Webling, Lucy (Lucy Betty MacRaye)
   1877-1952..................... DLB-240
Webling, Peggy (Arthur Weston)
   1871-1949..................... DLB-240
Webster, Augusta 1837-1894 .... DLB-35, 240
Webster, John
   1579 or 1580-1634? DLB-58; CDBLB-1

The Melbourne Manuscript Y-86
Webster, Noah
  1758-1843 . . . . DLB-1, 37, 42, 43, 73, 243
Webster, Paul Francis 1907-1984 . . . . DLB-265
Charles L. Webster and Company DLB-49
Weckherlin, Georg Rodolf 1584-1653 . . . . DLB-164
Wedekind, Frank
  1864-1918 . . . . DLB-118; CDWLB-2
Weeks, Edward Augustus, Jr.
  1898-1989 . . . . DLB-137
Weeks, Stephen B. 1865-1918 . . . . DLB-187
Weems, Mason Locke 1759-1825 . . DLB-30, 37, 42
Weerth, Georg 1822-1856 . . . . DLB-129
Weidenfeld and Nicolson DLB-112
Weidman, Jerome 1913-1998 . . . . DLB-28
Weigl, Bruce 1949- DLB-120
Weil, Jiří 1900-1959 . . . . DLB-299
Weinbaum, Stanley Grauman
  1902-1935 . . . . DLB-8
Weiner, Andrew 1949- DLB-251
Weintraub, Stanley 1929- DLB-111; Y82
Weise, Christian 1642-1708 . . . . DLB-168
Weisenborn, Gunther 1902-1969 . . . . DLB-69, 124
Weiss, John 1818-1879 . . . . DLB-1, 243
Weiss, Paul 1901-2002 . . . . DLB-279
Weiss, Peter 1916-1982 . . . . DLB-69, 124
Weiss, Theodore 1916- DLB-5
Weiß, Ernst 1882-1940 . . . . DLB-81
Weiße, Christian Felix 1726-1804 . . . . DLB-97
Weitling, Wilhelm 1808-1871 . . . . DLB-129
Welch, James 1940- DLB-175, 256
Welch, Lew 1926-1971? DLB-16
Weldon, Fay 1931- DLB-14, 194; CDBLB-8
Wellek, René 1903-1995 . . . . DLB-63
Wells, Carolyn 1862-1942 . . . . DLB-11
Wells, Charles Jeremiah
  circa 1800-1879 . . . . DLB-32
Wells, Gabriel 1862-1946 . . . . DLB-140
Wells, H. G. 1866-1946
  . . . . DLB-34, 70, 156, 178; CDBLB-6
  H. G. Wells Society Y-98
  Preface to *The Scientific Romances of
  H. G. Wells* (1933) DLB-178
Wells, Helena 1758?-1824 . . . . DLB-200
Wells, Rebecca 1952- DLB-292
Wells, Robert 1947- DLB-40
Wells-Barnett, Ida B. 1862-1931 . . . . . DLB-23, 221
Welsh, Irvine 1958- DLB-271
Welty, Eudora 1909-2001 . . . . . . DLB-2, 102, 143;
  Y-87, 01; DS-12; CDALB-1
  Eudora Welty: Eye of the Storyteller Y-87
  Eudora Welty Newsletter Y-99
  Eudora Welty's Funeral Y-01
  Eudora Welty's Ninetieth Birthday Y-99
  Eudora Welty Remembered in
  Two Exhibits Y-02
Wendell, Barrett 1855-1921 . . . . DLB-71

Wentworth, Patricia 1878-1961 . . . . DLB-77
Wentworth, William Charles
  1790-1872 . . . . DLB-230
Werder, Diederich von dem 1584-1657 . . DLB-164
Werfel, Franz 1890-1945 . . . . DLB-81, 124
Werner, Zacharias 1768-1823 . . . . DLB-94
The Werner Company DLB-49
Wersba, Barbara 1932- DLB-52
Wescott, Glenway
  1901-1987 . . . . DLB-4, 9, 102; DS-15
Wesker, Arnold 1932- DLB-13; CDBLB-8
Wesley, Charles 1707-1788 . . . . DLB-95
Wesley, John 1703-1791 . . . . DLB-104
Wesley, Mary 1912-2002 . . . . DLB-231
Wesley, Richard 1945- DLB-38
Wessel, Johan Herman 1742-1785 . . . . . . DLB-300
A. Wessels and Company DLB-46
Wessobrunner Gebet circa 787-815 . . . . . . DLB-148
West, Anthony 1914-1988 . . . . DLB-15
  Tribute to Liam O'Flaherty Y-84
West, Cheryl L. 1957- DLB-266
West, Cornel 1953- DLB-246
West, Dorothy 1907-1998 . . . . DLB-76
West, Jessamyn 1902-1984 . . . . DLB-6; Y-84
West, Mae 1892-1980 . . . . DLB-44
West, Michael Lee 1953- DLB-292
West, Michelle Sagara 1963- DLB-251
West, Morris 1916-1999 . . . . DLB-289
West, Nathanael
  1903-1940 . . . . DLB-4, 9, 28; CDALB-5
West, Paul 1930- DLB-14
West, Rebecca 1892-1983 . . . . DLB-36; Y-83
West, Richard 1941- DLB-185
West and Johnson DLB-49
Westcott, Edward Noyes 1846-1898 . . . . . DLB-202
The Western Literature Association Y-99
The Western Messenger
  1835-1841 . . . . DLB-1; DLB-223
Western Publishing Company DLB-46
Western Writers of America Y-99
The Westminster Review 1824-1914 . . . . . . DLB-110
Weston, Arthur (see Webling, Peggy)
Weston, Elizabeth Jane circa 1582-1612 . . DLB-172
Wetherald, Agnes Ethelwyn 1857-1940 . . . DLB-99
Wetherell, Elizabeth (see Warner, Susan)
Wetherell, W. D. 1948- DLB-234
Wetzel, Friedrich Gottlob 1779-1819 . . . . . DLB-90
Weyman, Stanley J. 1855-1928 . . . . . DLB-141, 156
Wezel, Johann Karl 1747-1819 . . . . DLB-94
Whalen, Philip 1923-2002 . . . . DLB-16
Whalley, George 1915-1983 . . . . DLB-88
Wharton, Edith 1862-1937 . . . . . . DLB-4, 9, 12,
  78, 189; DS-13; CDALB-3
Wharton, William 1920s?- Y-80
Whately, Mary Louisa 1824-1889 . . . . DLB-166
Whately, Richard 1787-1863 . . . . DLB-190

Elements of Rhetoric (1828;
  revised, 1846) [excerpt] DLB-57
Wheatley, Dennis 1897-1977 . . . . DLB-77, 255
Wheatley, Phillis
  circa 1754-1784 . . . . DLB-31, 50; CDALB-2
Wheeler, Anna Doyle 1785-1848? DLB-158
Wheeler, Charles Stearns 1816-1843 . . . DLB-1, 223
Wheeler, Monroe 1900-1988 . . . . DLB-4
Wheelock, John Hall 1886-1978 . . . . DLB-45
  From John Hall Wheelock's
  Oral Memoir Y-01
Wheelwright, J. B. 1897-1940 . . . . DLB-45
Wheelwright, John circa 1592-1679 . . . . . . DLB-24
Whetstone, George 1550-1587 . . . . DLB-136
Whetstone, Colonel Pete (see Noland, C. F. M.)
Whewell, William 1794-1866 . . . . DLB-262
Whichcote, Benjamin 1609?-1683 . . . . . . DLB-252
Whicher, Stephen E. 1915-1961 . . . . DLB-111
Whipple, Edwin Percy 1819-1886 . . . . . . DLB-1, 64
Whitaker, Alexander 1585-1617 . . . . DLB-24
Whitaker, Daniel K. 1801-1881 . . . . DLB-73
Whitcher, Frances Miriam
  1812-1852 . . . . DLB-11, 202
White, Andrew 1579-1656 . . . . DLB-24
White, Andrew Dickson 1832-1918 . . . . . . DLB-47
White, E. B. 1899-1985 . . . . DLB-11, 22; CDALB-7
White, Edgar B. 1947- DLB-38
White, Edmund 1940- DLB-227
White, Ethel Lina 1887-1944 . . . . DLB-77
White, Hayden V. 1928- DLB-246
White, Henry Kirke 1785-1806 . . . . DLB-96
White, Horace 1834-1916 . . . . DLB-23
White, James 1928-1999 . . . . DLB-261
White, Patrick 1912-1990 . . . . DLB-260
White, Phyllis Dorothy James (see James, P. D.)
White, Richard Grant 1821-1885 . . . . DLB-64
White, T. H. 1906-1964 . . . . DLB-160, 255
White, Walter 1893-1955 . . . . DLB-51
Wilcox, James 1949- DLB-292
William White and Company DLB-49
White, William Allen 1868-1944 . . . . . . DLB-9, 25
White, William Anthony Parker
  (see Boucher, Anthony)
White, William Hale (see Rutherford, Mark)
Whitechurch, Victor L. 1868-1933 . . . . . . DLB-70
Whitehead, Alfred North
  1861-1947 . . . . DLB-100, 262
Whitehead, James 1936- Y-81
Whitehead, William 1715-1785 . . . . . . DLB-84, 109
Whitfield, James Monroe 1822-1871 . . . . . DLB-50
Whitfield, Raoul 1898-1945 . . . . DLB-226
Whitgift, John circa 1533-1604 . . . . DLB-132
Whiting, John 1917-1963 . . . . DLB-13
Whiting, Samuel 1597-1679 . . . . DLB-24
Whitlock, Brand 1869-1934 . . . . DLB-12
Whitman, Albery Allson 1851-1901 . . . . . . DLB-50

Whitman, Alden 1913-1990 . . . . Y-91

Whitman, Sarah Helen (Power) 1803-1878 . . . . DLB-1, 243

Whitman, Walt 1819-1892 . . . . DLB-3, 64, 224, 250; CDALB-2

Albert Whitman and Company DLB-46

Whitman Publishing Company DLB-46

Whitney, Geoffrey 1548 or 1552?-1601 . . . . DLB-136

Whitney, Isabella flourished 1566-1573 . . DLB-136

Whitney, John Hay 1904-1982 . . . . DLB-127

Whittemore, Reed 1919-1995 . . . . DLB-5

Whittier, John Greenleaf 1807-1892 . . . . DLB-1, 243; CDALB-2

Whittlesey House DLB-46

Wickham, Anna (Edith Alice Mary Harper) 1884-1947 . . . . DLB-240

Wickram, Georg circa 1505-circa 1561 . . . DLB-179

Wicomb, Zoë 1948- DLB-225

Wideman, John Edgar 1941- DLB-33, 143

Widener, Harry Elkins 1885-1912 . . . . . . DLB-140

Wiebe, Rudy 1934- DLB-60

Wiechert, Ernst 1887-1950 . . . . DLB-56

Wied, Gustav 1858-1914 . . . . DLB-300

Wied, Martina 1882-1957 . . . . DLB-85

Wiehe, Evelyn May Clowes (see Mordaunt, Elinor)

Wieland, Christoph Martin 1733-1813 . . . . DLB-97

Wienbarg, Ludolf 1802-1872 . . . . DLB-133

Wieners, John 1934- DLB-16

Wier, Ester 1910- DLB-52

Wiesel, Elie 1928- DLB-83, 299; Y-86, 87; CDALB-7

Nobel Lecture 1986: Hope, Despair and Memory Y-86

Wiggin, Kate Douglas 1856-1923 . . . . DLB-42

Wigglesworth, Michael 1631-1705 . . . . DLB-24

Wilberforce, William 1759-1833 . . . . DLB-158

Wilbrandt, Adolf 1837-1911 . . . . DLB-129

Wilbur, Richard 1921- . . DLB-5, 169; CDALB-7

Tribute to Robert Penn Warren Y-89

Wilcox, James 1949- DLB-292

Wild, Peter 1940- DLB-5

Wilde, Lady Jane Francesca Elgee 1821?-1896 . . . . DLB-199

Wilde, Oscar 1854-1900 . . DLB-10, 19, 34, 57, 141, 156, 190; CDBLB-5
"The Critic as Artist" (1891) DLB-57
"The Decay of Lying" (1889) DLB-18
"The English Renaissance of Art" (1908) DLB-35
"L'Envoi" (1882) DLB-35

Oscar Wilde Conference at Hofstra University Y-00

Wilde, Richard Henry 1789-1847 . . . . DLB-3, 59

W. A. Wilde Company DLB-49

Wilder, Billy 1906- DLB-26

Wilder, Laura Ingalls 1867-1957 . . . . . DLB-22, 256

Wilder, Thornton 1897-1975 . . . . DLB-4, 7, 9, 228; CDALB-7

Thornton Wilder Centenary at Yale Y-97

Wildgans, Anton 1881-1932 . . . . DLB-118

Wiley, Bell Irvin 1906-1980 . . . . DLB-17

John Wiley and Sons DLB-49

Wilhelm, Kate 1928- DLB-8

Wilkes, Charles 1798-1877 . . . . DLB-183

Wilkes, George 1817-1885 . . . . DLB-79

Wilkins, John 1614-1672 . . . . DLB-236

Wilkinson, Anne 1910-1961 . . . . DLB-88

Wilkinson, Eliza Yonge 1757-circa 1813 . . . . DLB-200

Wilkinson, Sylvia 1940- Y-86

Wilkinson, William Cleaver 1833-1920 . . . DLB-71

Willard, Barbara 1909-1994 . . . . DLB-161

Willard, Emma 1787-1870 . . . . DLB-239

Willard, Frances E. 1839-1898 . . . . DLB-221

Willard, Nancy 1936- DLB-5, 52

Willard, Samuel 1640-1707 . . . . DLB-24

L. Willard [publishing house] DLB-49

Willeford, Charles 1919-1988 . . . . DLB-226

William of Auvergne 1190-1249 . . . . DLB-115

William of Conches circa 1090-circa 1154 . . . . DLB-115

William of Ockham circa 1285-1347 . . . . DLB-115

William of Sherwood 1200/1205-1266/1271 . . . . DLB-115

The William Charvat American Fiction Collection at the Ohio State University Libraries Y-92

Williams, Ben Ames 1889-1953 . . . . DLB-102

Williams, C. K. 1936- DLB-5

Williams, Chancellor 1905-1992 . . . . DLB-76

Williams, Charles 1886-1945 . . . DLB-100, 153, 255

Williams, Denis 1923-1998 . . . . DLB-117

Williams, Emlyn 1905-1987 . . . . DLB-10, 77

Williams, Garth 1912-1996 . . . . DLB-22

Williams, George Washington 1849-1891 . . . . DLB-47

Williams, Heathcote 1941- DLB-13

Williams, Helen Maria 1761-1827 . . . . . . DLB-158

Williams, Hugo 1942- DLB-40

Williams, Isaac 1802-1865 . . . . DLB-32

Williams, Joan 1928- DLB-6

Williams, Joe 1889-1972 . . . . DLB-241

Williams, John A. 1925- DLB-2, 33

Williams, John E. 1922-1994 . . . . DLB-6

Williams, Jonathan 1929- DLB-5

Williams, Miller 1930- DLB-105

Williams, Nigel 1948- DLB-231

Williams, Raymond 1921-1988 . . . . DLB-14, 231, 242

Williams, Roger circa 1603-1683 . . . . DLB-24

Williams, Rowland 1817-1870 . . . . DLB-184

Williams, Samm-Art 1946- DLB-38

Williams, Sherley Anne 1944-1999 . . . . . . DLB-41

Williams, T. Harry 1909-1979 . . . . DLB-17

Williams, Tennessee 1911-1983 . . . . DLB-7; Y-83; DS-4; CDALB-1

Williams, Terry Tempest 1955- . . . DLB-206, 275

Williams, Ursula Moray 1911- DLB-160

Williams, Valentine 1883-1946 . . . . DLB-77

Williams, William Appleman 1921- DLB-17

Williams, William Carlos 1883-1963 . . . . . DLB-4, 16, 54, 86; CDALB-4

The William Carlos Williams Society Y-99

Williams, Wirt 1921- DLB-6

A. Williams and Company DLB-49

Williams Brothers DLB-49

Wililiamson, David 1942- DLB-289

Williamson, Henry 1895-1977 . . . . DLB-191

The Henry Williamson Society Y-98

Williamson, Jack 1908- DLB-8

Willingham, Calder Baynard, Jr. 1922-1995 . . . . DLB-2, 44

Williram of Ebersberg circa 1020-1085 . . DLB-148

Willis, John circa 1572-1625 . . . . DLB-281

Willis, Nathaniel Parker 1806-1867 . . . DLB-3, 59, 73, 74, 183, 250; DS-13

Willkomm, Ernst 1810-1886 . . . . DLB-133

Wills, Garry 1934- DLB-246

Tribute to Kenneth Dale McCormick Y-97

Willson, Meredith 1902-1984 . . . . DLB-265

Willumsen, Dorrit 1940- DLB-214

Wilmer, Clive 1945- DLB-40

Wilson, A. N. 1950- DLB-14, 155, 194

Wilson, Angus 1913-1991 . . . . . . DLB-15, 139, 155

Wilson, Arthur 1595-1652 . . . . DLB-58

Wilson, August 1945- DLB-228

Wilson, Augusta Jane Evans 1835-1909 . . . DLB-42

Wilson, Colin 1931- DLB-14, 194

Tribute to J. B. Priestly Y-84

Wilson, Edmund 1895-1972 . . . . DLB-63

Wilson, Ethel 1888-1980 . . . . DLB-68

Wilson, F. P. 1889-1963 . . . . DLB-201

Wilson, Harriet E. 1827/1828?-1863? DLB-50, 239, 243

Wilson, Harry Leon 1867-1939 . . . . DLB-9

Wilson, John 1588-1667 . . . . DLB-24

Wilson, John 1785-1854 . . . . DLB-110

Wilson, John Anthony Burgess (see Burgess, Anthony)

Wilson, John Dover 1881-1969 . . . . DLB-201

Wilson, Lanford 1937- DLB-7

Wilson, Margaret 1882-1973 . . . . DLB-9

Wilson, Michael 1914-1978 . . . . DLB-44

Wilson, Mona 1872-1954 . . . . DLB-149

Wilson, Robert Charles 1953- DLB-251

Wilson, Robert McLiam 1964- DLB-267

Wilson, Robley 1930- DLB-218

Wilson, Romer 1891-1930 . . . . DLB-191

Wilson, Thomas 1524-1581 . . . . DLB-132, 236

Wilson, Woodrow 1856-1924 . . . . .DLB-47
Effingham Wilson [publishing house] DLB-154
Wimpfeling, Jakob 1450-1528 . . . . .DLB-179
Wimsatt, William K., Jr. 1907-1975 . . . . . . .DLB-63
Winchell, Walter 1897-1972. . . . . .DLB-29
J. Winchester [publishing house] DLB-49
Winckelmann, Johann Joachim
   1717-1768 . . . . .DLB-97
Winckler, Paul 1630-1686 . . . . .DLB-164
Wind, Herbert Warren 1916- DLB-171
John Windet [publishing house]. DLB-170
Windham, Donald 1920- DLB-6
Wing, Donald Goddard 1904-1972 . . . . . .DLB-187
Wing, John M. 1844-1917 . . . . .DLB-187
Allan Wingate [publishing house] DLB-112
Winnemucca, Sarah 1844-1921 . . . . .DLB-175
Winnifrith, Tom 1938- DLB-155
Winsloe, Christa 1888-1944 . . . . .DLB-124
Winslow, Anna Green 1759-1780 . . . . . . .DLB-200
Winsor, Justin 1831-1897. . . . . .DLB-47
John C. Winston Company DLB-49
Winters, Yvor 1900-1968 . . . . .DLB-48
Winterson, Jeanette 1959- DLB-207, 261
Winther, Christian 1796-1876 . . . . .DLB-300
Winthrop, John 1588-1649 . . . . .DLB-24, 30
Winthrop, John, Jr. 1606-1676 . . . . .DLB-24
Winthrop, Margaret Tyndal 1591-1647 . .DLB-200
Winthrop, Theodore 1828-1861 . . . . . . .DLB-202
Wirt, William 1772-1834 . . . . .DLB-37
Wise, John 1652-1725 . . . . .DLB-24
Wise, Thomas James 1859-1937 . . . . .DLB-184
Wiseman, Adele 1928-1992. . . . . .DLB-88
Wishart and Company DLB-112
Wisner, George 1812-1849 . . . . .DLB-43
Wister, Owen 1860-1938. . . . . DLB-9, 78, 186
Wister, Sarah 1761-1804 . . . . .DLB-200
Wither, George 1588-1667 . . . . .DLB-121
Witherspoon, John 1723-1794 . . . . .DLB-31
   The Works of the Rev. John Witherspoon
   (1800-1801) [excerpts]. DLB-31
Withrow, William Henry 1839-1908. . . . . .DLB-99
Witkacy (see Witkiewicz, Stanisław Ignacy)
Witkiewicz, Stanisław Ignacy
   1885-1939 . . . . DLB-215; CDWLB-4
Wittenwiler, Heinrich before 1387-
   circa 1414?. DLB-179
Wittgenstein, Ludwig 1889-1951. . . . . . . .DLB-262
Wittig, Monique 1935- DLB-83
Wodehouse, P. G.
   1881-1975 . . . . .DLB-34, 162; CDBLB-6
   Worldwide Wodehouse Societies Y-98
Wohmann, Gabriele 1932- DLB-75
Woiwode, Larry 1941- DLB-6
   Tribute to John Gardner Y-82
Wolcot, John 1738-1819. . . . . .DLB-109
Wolcott, Roger 1679-1767 . . . . .DLB-24

Wolf, Christa 1929- DLB-75; CDWLB-2
Wolf, Friedrich 1888-1953. . . . . .DLB-124
Wolfe, Gene 1931- DLB-8
Wolfe, Thomas 1900-1938 . . . .
   DLB-9, 102, 229; Y-85; DS-2, DS-16; CDALB-5
   "All the Faults of Youth and Inexperience":
   A Reader's Report on
   Thomas Wolfe's *O Lost*. Y-01
   Emendations for *Look Homeward, Angel* . . . Y-00
   Eugene Gant's Projected Works Y-01
   Fire at the Old Kentucky Home
   [Thomas Wolfe Memorial] Y-98
   Thomas Wolfe Centennial
   Celebration in Asheville Y-00
   The Thomas Wolfe Collection at
   the University of North Carolina
   at Chapel Hill Y-97
   The Thomas Wolfe Society Y-97, 99
Wolfe, Tom 1931- DLB-152, 185
John Wolfe [publishing house]. DLB-170
Reyner (Reginald) Wolfe
   [publishing house] DLB-170
Wolfenstein, Martha 1869-1906 . . . . .DLB-221
Wolff, David (see Maddow, Ben)
Wolff, Egon 1926- DLB-305
Wolff, Helen 1906-1994 . . . . Y-94
Wolff, Tobias 1945- DLB-130
   Tribute to Michael M. Rea Y-97
   Tribute to Raymond Carver Y-88
Wolfram von Eschenbach
   circa 1170-after 1220 . . . . DLB-138; CDWLB-2
   Wolfram von Eschenbach's *Parzival*:
   Prologue and Book 3 . . . . .DLB-138
Wolker, Jiří 1900-1924 . . . . .DLB-215
Wollstonecraft, Mary 1759-1797
   . . . . DLB-39, 104, 158, 252; CDBLB-3
Women
   Women's Work, Women's Sphere:
   Selected Comments from Women
   Writers DLB-200
Wondratschek, Wolf 1943- DLB-75
Wong, Elizabeth 1958- DLB-266
Wood, Anthony à 1632-1695 . . . . .DLB-213
Wood, Benjamin 1820-1900 . . . . .DLB-23
Wood, Charles 1932-1980. . . . . .DLB-13
   The Charles Wood Affair:
   A Playwright Revived Y-83
Wood, Mrs. Henry 1814-1887 . . . . .DLB-18
Wood, Joanna E. 1867-1927 . . . . .DLB-92
Wood, Sally Sayward Barrell Keating
   1759-1855 .DLB-200
Wood, William ?-? DLB-24
Samuel Wood [publishing house] DLB-49
Woodberry, George Edward
   1855-1930 . . . . DLB-71, 103
Woodbridge, Benjamin 1622-1684 . . . . . . .DLB-24
Woodbridge, Frederick J. E. 1867-1940 . . .DLB-270
Woodcock, George 1912-1995 . . . . .DLB-88
Woodhull, Victoria C. 1838-1927 . . . . .DLB-79
Woodmason, Charles circa 1720-? DLB-31

Woodress, James Leslie, Jr. 1916- DLB-111
Woods, Margaret L. 1855-1945 . . . . . . .DLB-240
Woodson, Carter G. 1875-1950. . . . . .DLB-17
Woodward, C. Vann 1908-1999 . . . . .DLB-17
Woodward, Stanley 1895-1965 . . . . .DLB-171
Woodworth, Samuel 1785-1842 . . . . .DLB-250
Wooler, Thomas 1785 or 1786-1853 . . . . .DLB-158
Woolf, David (see Maddow, Ben)
Woolf, Douglas 1922-1992 . . . . .DLB-244
Woolf, Leonard 1880-1969 . . . . . . DLB-100; DS-10
Woolf, Virginia 1882-1941
   . . . . DLB-36, 100, 162; DS-10; CDBLB-6
   "The New Biography," *New York Herald*
   Tribune, 30 October 1927 . . . . . . .DLB-149
Woollcott, Alexander 1887-1943 . . . . .DLB-29
Woolman, John 1720-1772. . . . . .DLB-31
Woolner, Thomas 1825-1892 . . . . .DLB-35
Woolrich, Cornell 1903-1968 . . . . .DLB-226
Woolsey, Sarah Chauncy 1835-1905 . . . . .DLB-42
Woolson, Constance Fenimore
   1840-1894 . . . . DLB-12, 74, 189, 221
Worcester, Joseph Emerson
   1784-1865 . . . . DLB-1, 235
Wynkyn de Worde [publishing house] . . . DLB-170
Wordsworth, Christopher 1807-1885 . . . .DLB-166
Wordsworth, Dorothy 1771-1855 . . . . . . .DLB-107
Wordsworth, Elizabeth 1840-1932 . . . . . . .DLB-98
Wordsworth, William
   1770-1850 . . . . .DLB-93, 107; CDBLB-3
Workman, Fanny Bullock
   1859-1925 .DLB-189
World Literature Today: A Journal for the
   New Millennium Y-01
World Publishing Company DLB-46
World War I (1914-1918) DS-18
   The Great War Exhibit and Symposium
   at the University of South Carolina . . . Y-97
   The Liddle Collection and First World
   War Research Y-97
   Other British Poets Who Fell
   in the Great War DLB-216
   The Seventy-Fifth Anniversary of
   the Armistice: The Wilfred Owen
   Centenary and the Great War Exhibit
   at the University of Virginia. Y-93
World War II (1939–1945)
   Literary Effects of World War II DLB-15
   World War II Writers Symposium
   at the University of South Carolina,
   12–14 April 1995 . . . . Y-95
   WW2 HMSO Paperbacks Society Y-98
R. Worthington and Company DLB-49
Wotton, Sir Henry 1568-1639 . . . . .DLB-121
Wouk, Herman 1915- Y-82; CDALB-7
   Tribute to James Dickey Y-97
Wreford, James 1915- DLB-88
Wren, Sir Christopher 1632-1723 . . . . . . .DLB-213
Wren, Percival Christopher 1885-1941 . . .DLB-153
Wrenn, John Henry 1841-1911 . . . . .DLB-140
Wright, C. D. 1949- DLB-120
Wright, Charles 1935- DLB-165; Y-82

Wright, Charles Stevenson 1932- DLB-33
Wright, Chauncey 1830-1875 .... DLB-270
Wright, Frances 1795-1852 .... DLB-73
Wright, Harold Bell 1872-1944 .... DLB-9
Wright, James 1927-1980
.... DLB-5, 169; CDALB-7
Wright, Jay 1935- DLB-41
Wright, Judith 1915-2000 .... DLB-260
Wright, Louis B. 1899-1984 .... DLB-17
Wright, Richard 1908-1960 .... DLB-76, 102; DS-2; CDALB-5
Wright, Richard B. 1937- DLB-53
Wright, S. Fowler 1874-1965 .... DLB-255
Wright, Sarah Elizabeth 1928- DLB-33
Wright, T. H. "Style" (1877) [excerpt] DLB-57
Wright, Willard Huntington
    (S. S. Van Dine) 1888-1939 .... DS-16
Wrightson, Patricia 1921- DLB-289
Wrigley, Robert 1951- DLB-256
Writers' Forum Y-85
Writing
    A Writing Life Y-02
    On Learning to Write Y-88
    The Profession of Authorship:
        Scribblers for Bread Y-89
    A Writer Talking: A Collage Y-00
Wroth, Lawrence C. 1884-1970 .... DLB-187
Wroth, Lady Mary 1587-1653 .... DLB-121
Wurlitzer, Rudolph 1937- DLB-173
Wyatt, Sir Thomas circa 1503-1542 .... DLB-132
Wycherley, William
    1641-1715 .... DLB-80; CDBLB-2
Wyclif, John circa 1335-1384 .... DLB-146
Wyeth, N. C. 1882-1945 .... DLB-188; DS-16
Wyle, Niklas von circa 1415-1479 ...... DLB-179
Wylie, Elinor 1885-1928 .... DLB-9, 45
Wylie, Philip 1902-1971 .... DLB-9
Wyllie, John Cook 1908-1968 .... DLB-140
Wyman, Lillie Buffum Chace
    1847-1929 .... DLB-202
Wymark, Olwen 1934- DLB-233
Wynd, Oswald Morris (see Black, Gavin)
Wyndham, John (John Wyndham Parkes
    Lucas Beynon Harris) 1903-1969 ... DLB-255
Wynne-Tyson, Esmé 1898-1972 .... DLB-191

X

Xenophon circa 430 B.C.-circa 356 B.C. ... DLB-176

Y

Yasuoka Shōtarō 1920- DLB-182
Yates, Dornford 1885-1960 .... DLB-77, 153
Yates, J. Michael 1938- DLB-60
Yates, Richard 1926-1992 .... DLB-2, 234; Y-81, 92
Yau, John 1950- DLB-234
Yavorov, Peyo 1878-1914 .... DLB-147

Yearsley, Ann 1753-1806 .... DLB-109
Yeats, William Butler
    1865-1939 ... DLB-10, 19, 98, 156; CDBLB-5
    The W. B. Yeats Society of N.Y. Y-99
Yellen, Jack 1892-1991 .... DLB-265
Yep, Laurence 1948- DLB-52
Yerby, Frank 1916-1991 .... DLB-76
Yezierska, Anzia 1880-1970 .... DLB-28, 221
Yolen, Jane 1939- DLB-52
Yonge, Charlotte Mary 1823-1901 ... DLB-18, 163
    The Charlotte M. Yonge Fellowship Y-98
The York Cycle circa 1376-circa 1569 ... DLB-146
A Yorkshire Tragedy DLB-58
Thomas Yoseloff [publishing house] DLB-46
Youd, Sam (see Christopher, John)
Young, A. S. "Doc" 1919-1996 .... DLB-241
Young, Al 1939- DLB-33
Young, Arthur 1741-1820 .... DLB-158
Young, Dick 1917 or 1918-1987 .... DLB-171
Young, Edward 1683-1765 .... DLB-95
Young, Frank A. "Fay" 1884-1957 ..... DLB-241
Young, Francis Brett 1884-1954 ...... DLB-191
Young, Gavin 1928- DLB-204
Young, Stark 1881-1963 ..... DLB-9, 102; DS-16
Young, Waldeman 1880-1938 .... DLB-26
William Young [publishing house] DLB-49
Young Bear, Ray A. 1950- DLB-175
Yourcenar, Marguerite 1903-1987 ... DLB-72; Y-88
Yovkov, Yordan 1880-1937 ... DLB-147; CDWLB-4

Z

Zachariä, Friedrich Wilhelm 1726-1777 ... DLB-97
Zagajewski, Adam 1945- DLB-232
Zagoskin, Mikhail Nikolaevich
    1789-1852 .... DLB-198
Zajc, Dane 1929- DLB-181
Zālīte, Māra 1952- DLB-232
Zalygin, Sergei Pavlovich
    1913-2000 .... DLB-302
Zamiatin, Evgenii Ivanovich 1884-1937 ... DLB-272
Zamora, Bernice 1938- DLB-82
Zamudio, Adela (Soledad) 1854-1928 ... DLB-283
Zand, Herbert 1923-1970 .... DLB-85
Zangwill, Israel 1864-1926 ...... DLB-10, 135, 197
Zanzotto, Andrea 1921- DLB-128
Zapata Olivella, Manuel 1920- DLB-113
Zapoev, Timur Iur'evich
    (see Kibirov, Timur Iur'evich)
Zasodimsky, Pavel Vladimirovich
    1843-1912 .... DLB-238
Zebra Books DLB-46
Zebrowski, George 1945- DLB-8
Zech, Paul 1881-1946 .... DLB-56
Zeidner, Lisa 1955- DLB-120
Zeidonis, Imants 1933- DLB-232

Zeimi (Kanze Motokiyo) 1363-1443 ..... DLB-203
Zelazny, Roger 1937-1995 .... DLB-8
Zenger, John Peter 1697-1746 .... DLB-24, 43
Zepheria DLB-172
Zesen, Philipp von 1619-1689 .... DLB-164
Zhadovskaia, Iuliia Valerianovna
    1824-1883 .... DLB-277
Zhukova, Mar'ia Semenovna
    1805-1855 .... DLB-277
Zhukovsky, Vasilii Andreevich
    1783-1852 .... DLB-205
Zhvanetsky, Mikhail Mikhailovich
    1934- DLB-285
G. B. Zieber and Company DLB-49
Ziedonis, Imants 1933- CDWLB-4
Zieroth, Dale 1946- DLB-60
Zigler und Kliphausen, Heinrich
    Anshelm von 1663-1697 .... DLB-168
Zil'ber, Veniamin Aleksandrovich
    (see Kaverin, Veniamin Aleksandrovich)
Zimmer, Paul 1934- DLB-5
Zinberg, Len (see Lacy, Ed)
Zincgref, Julius Wilhelm 1591-1635 .... DLB-164
Zindel, Paul 1936- DLB-7, 52; CDALB-7
Zinnes, Harriet 1919- DLB-193
Zinov'ev, Aleksandr Aleksandrovich
    1922- DLB-302
Zinov'eva-Annibal, Lidiia Dmitrievna
    1865 or 1866-1907 .... DLB-295
Zinzendorf, Nikolaus Ludwig von
    1700-1760 .... DLB-168
Zitkala-Ša 1876-1938 .... DLB-175
Ziverts, Mārtiņš 1903-1990 .... DLB-220
Zlatovratsky, Nikolai Nikolaevich
    1845-1911 .... DLB-238
Zola, Emile 1840-1902 .... DLB-123
Zolla, Elémire 1926- DLB-196
Zolotow, Charlotte 1915- DLB-52
Zoshchenko, Mikhail Mikhailovich
    1895-1958 .... DLB-272
Zschokke, Heinrich 1771-1848 .... DLB-94
Zubly, John Joachim 1724-1781 .... DLB-31
Zu-Bolton, Ahmos, II 1936- DLB-41
Zuckmayer, Carl 1896-1977 .... DLB-56, 124
Zukofsky, Louis 1904-1978 .... DLB-5, 165
Zupan, Vitomil 1914-1987 .... DLB-181
Župančič, Oton 1878-1949 ... DLB-147; CDWLB-4
zur Mühlen, Hermynia 1883-1951 ...... DLB-56
Zweig, Arnold 1887-1968 .... DLB-66
Zweig, Stefan 1881-1942 .... DLB-81, 118
Zwinger, Ann 1925- DLB-275
Zwingli, Huldrych 1484-1531 .... DLB-179

Ø

Øverland, Arnulf 1889-1968 .... DLB-297

ISBN 0-7876-6842-7

90000

PQ
7082
.D7
L373

2005